Lecture Notes in Computer Science 2525

Edited by G. Goos, J. Hartmanis, and J. van Leeuwen

Springer
Berlin
Heidelberg
New York
Hong Kong
London
Milan
Paris
Tokyo

Heinrich H. Bülthoff Seong-Whan Lee
Tomaso A. Poggio Christian Wallraven (Eds.)

Biologically Motivated Computer Vision

Second International Workshop, BMCV 2002
Tübingen, Germany, November 22-24, 2002
Proceedings

Springer

Series Editors

Gerhard Goos, Karlsruhe University, Germany
Juris Hartmanis, Cornell University, NY, USA
Jan van Leeuwen, Utrecht University, The Netherlands

Volume Editors

Heinrich H. Bülthoff
Christian Wallraven
Max Planck Institute for Biological Cybernetics
Spemannstraße 38, 72076 Tübingen, Germany
E-mail: {heinrich.buelthoff,christian.wallraven}@tuebingen.mpg.de

Seong-Whan Lee
Korea University, Department of Computer Science and Engineering
Anam-dong, Seongbuk-ku, Seoul 136-701, Korea
E-mail: swlee@image.korea.ac.kr

Tomaso A. Poggio
Massachusetts Institute of Technology
Department of Brain and Cognitive Sciences, Artificial Intelligence Laboratory
45 Carleton Street, Cambridge, MA 02142, USA
E-mail: tp@ai.mit.edu

Cataloging-in-Publication Data applied for

A catalog record for this book is available from the Library of Congress.

Bibliographic information published by Die Deutsche Bibliothek
Die Deutsche Bibliothek lists this publication in the Deutsche Nationalbibliografie; detailed bibliographic data is available in the Internet at <http://dnb.ddb.de>.

CR Subject Classification (1998): I.4, F.2, F.1.1, I.3.5, I.5, J.2, J.3, I.2.9-10

ISSN 0302-9743
ISBN 3-540-00174-3 Springer-Verlag Berlin Heidelberg New York

Springer-Verlag Berlin Heidelberg New York
a member of BertelsmannSpringer Science+Business Media GmbH

http://www.springer.de

Printed in Germany

Typesetting: Camera-ready by author, data conversion by PTP Berlin, Stefan Sossna e.K.
Printed on acid-free paper SPIN: 10873120 06/3142 5 4 3 2 1 0

Preface

It was our great pleasure to organize and host the Second International Workshop on Biologically Motivated Computer Vision (BMCV 2002), which followed the highly successful BMCV 2000 in Seoul. We welcomed biologists, computer scientists, mathematicians, neuroscientists, physicists, and psychologists to share their views of how the brain solves the ill-posed problems of vision. Nature is the best existence proof that there is a solution of the most fundamental vision problems, and we hope to learn from nature the way to build artificial vision systems which can adapt to different environments and tasks as easily and reliably as we do. We enjoyed a lively discussion of vision topics spanning early vision, mid-level vision, attention, recognition, robotics and cognitive vision systems.

Even though the decision to host the workshop in Tübingen came very late (March 2002), and therefore the deadlines were rather tight, we received a total of 97 papers by the end of June. Each of the papers was thoroughly reviewed by at least two members of the program committee and in addition by the local organizing committee. In this context, we especially want to thank the program committee and additional referees for the time and effort that went into the reviews. In the end, 22 papers were accepted for oral presentation and 37 for poster presentation. The selected papers span the whole range of vision from neuronal models of vision to psychophysical investigations of human recognition performance. Correspondingly, the workshop was divided into seven sessions, proceeding (roughly) from topics concerning low-level early vision to high-level cognitive aspects of vision. In addition to these presentations we are very grateful that six distinguished scientists accepted our invitation to give an introduction to these topics and present their work at BMCV 2002.

BMCV 2002 was organized by the Max Planck Institute for Biological Cybernetics in Tübingen and took place in the main lecture hall building (Kupferbau) of the University of Tübingen. We are grateful to the Max Planck Society for financial support and to the Eberhard Karls Universität for local support and for hosting the conference registration webpage.

On behalf of the organizing and program committees we welcomed attendees to BMCV 2002 in Tübingen. We deliberately arranged for ample time outside the lecture hall to meet colleagues during the posters sessions and coffee breaks. The posters were situated right outside the lecture hall and all posters were on display for the whole conference.

Finally, we hope you found the BMCV 2002 workshop a rewarding and memorable experience, and that you had an enjoyable stay in the beautiful old town of Tübingen and other parts of Germany.

September 2002 Heinrich H. Bülthoff, Christian Wallraven

Organization

BMCV 2002 was organized by the Max Planck Institute for Biological Cybernetics (MPI).

Sponsoring Institutions

Max Planck Institute for Biological Cybernetics, Tübingen, Germany
University of Tübingen, Germany
Computer Koch, Tübingen, Germany

Executive Committee

Conference Chair:	Heinrich H. Bülthoff (MPI Tübingen, Germany)
Program Chair:	Christian Wallraven (MPI Tübingen, Germany)
Co-chair:	Seong-Whan Lee (Korea University, Korea)
Co-chair:	Tomaso Poggio (MIT, USA)

Program Committee

Andrew Blake	Microsoft Research, Cambridge, UK
Volker Blanz	University of Freiburg, Germany
Joachim Buhmann	University of Bonn, Germany
Hans Burkhardt	University of Freiburg, Germany
Henrik I. Christensen	Royal Institute of Technology, Sweden
Chan-Sup Chung	Yonsei University, Korea
Luciano da F. Costa	University of Sao Paulo, Brazil
James Crowley	INPG, France
Gustavo Deco	Siemens, Germany
Shimon Edelman	Cornell University, USA
Jan-Olof Eklundh	KTH, Sweden
Dario Floreano	EPFL, Switzerland
Pascal Fua	EPFL, Switzerland
Kunihiko Fukushima	University of Electro-Communications, Japan
Martin Giese	University Clinic Tübingen, Germany
Luc van Gool	ETH Zürich, Switzerland
Stefan Hahn	DaimlerChrysler Research, Germany
Katsushi Ikeuchi	University of Tokyo, Japan
Christof Koch	Caltech, USA

Michael Langer	McGill University, Canada
Choongkil Lee	Seoul National University, Korea
James Little	University of British Columbia, Canada
David Lowe	University of British Columbia, Canada
Hanspeter Mallot	University of Tübingen, Germany
Heiko Neumann	University of Ulm, Germany
Heinrich Niemann	University of Erlangen, Germany
Giulio Sandini	University of Genoa, Italy
Bernt Schiele	ETH Zürich, Switzerland
Bernhard Schölkopf	MPI Tübingen, Germany
Pawan Sinha	MIT, USA
Tienu Tan	Academy of Sciences, China
Shimon Ullman	Weizmann Institute of Science, Israel
Thomas Vetter	University of Freiburg, Germany
Rolf Würtz	Ruhr University of Bochum, Germany
Hezy Yeshurun	Tel-Aviv University, Israel
Steven W. Zucker	Yale University, USA

Additional Referees

P. Bayerl
L. Bergen
O. Bousquet
D. Cheng
J. Daugman
B. Haasdonk
T. Hansen
B. Heisele
W. Hu
P. Huggins
S. Ilic
R. Jüngling
M. Kagesawa
D. Katsoulas
C. Koch
J. Koenderink
M. Kouh
V. Kumar
M. Levine
G. Li
J. Lou
M. Molkaraie
L. Natale
M. Riesenhuber
O. Shahar
A. Shahrokni
M. Tang
D. Walther
Y. Wei
J. Weston
F. Wichmann
S. Zucker

Local Support Team

Martin Breidt
Douglas Cunningham
Walter Heinz
Matthias Kopp
Dagmar Maier
Michael Renner
Kerstin Stockmeier

Table of Contents

Neurons and Features

Invited Paper (1)

Posters (1)

Recognition – From Scenes to Neurons

Invited Paper (4)

Posters (2)

Attention

Invited Paper (5)

Posters (3)

Robotics

Cognitive Vision

Invited Paper (6)

Ultra-Rapid Scene Categorization with a Wave of Spikes

Simon Thorpe

Centre de Recherche Cerveau & Cognition,
133, route de Narbonne, 31062, Toulouse, France
&
SpikeNet Technology S.A.R.L.
Ave de Castelnaudary, 31250, Revel, France
(www.spikenet-technology.com)

Abstract. Recent experimental work has shown that the primate visual system can analyze complex natural scenes in only 100-150 ms. Such data, when combined with anatomical and physiological knowledge, seriously constrains current models of visual processing. In particular, it suggests that a lot of processing can be achieved using a single feed-forward pass through the visual system, and that each processing layer probably has no more than around 10 ms before the next stage has to respond. In this time, few neurons will have generated more than one spike, ruling out most conventional rate coding models. We have been exploring the possibility of using the fact that strongly activated neurons tend to fire early and that information can be encoded in the order in which a population of cells fire. These ideas have been tested using SpikeNet, a computer program that simulates the activity of very large networks of asynchronously firing neurons. The results have been extremely promising, and we have been able to develop artificial visual systems capable of processing complex natural scenes in real time using standard computer hardware (see http://www.spikenet-technology.com).

1 Introduction – Rapid Scene Processing in Biological Vision

Although there are areas where computer vision systems easily outperform human observers (quantitative measurements in particular), there are many others where human vision leaves current artificial vision systems looking distinctly pale in comparison. One of the most obvious concerns the general area of scene perception. Pioneering work by researchers such as Irving Biederman and Molly Potter in the 1970s showed how human observers can grasp the "gist" of a scene with just a brief glance. Potter, in particular, was responsible for introducing the technique of Rapid Sequential Visual Presentation using natural images. Together with her student Helene Intraub, she showed that humans can detect particular categories of objects (a boat or a baby, for example) in sequences of images presented at up to 10 frames per second without

H.H. Bülthoff et al. (Eds.): BMCV 2002, LNCS 2525, pp. 1–15, 2002.

difficulty [1, 2]. Of course, one could argue that in such a task, the visual system has been primed to look for a specific set of visual features. But remarkably, Potter and Intraub showed that subjects could even perform the task if the target category was just defined by a negative category – such as "an object that is not used indoors".

Note that showing that the human visual system can process images at up to 10 frames per second (100 ms per image) does not mean that the processing time is actually 100 ms. This should be obvious to anyone familiar with the pipeline processing architectures used in today's computers: the 20-stage pipeline used in a Pentium 4 CPU means that a new set of data can be processed at each time step, but the total processing time for each item can be much longer.

Fortunately, there are other ways of trying to measure the time taken by the visual system to process a complex natural scene. In a series of experiments that we started in 1996 we have been studying a phenomenon that we have termed "Ultra-Rapid Visual Categorisation (URVC)" [3]. In these experiments, a previously unseen natural image is flashed briefly (typically for 20 ms) and subjects have to respond if the image contains a target category such as an animal. Half the images were targets (mammals, birds, fish, insects and reptiles in their natural environments) whereas the remainder was composed of a wide range of distracters (nature scenes, flowers, fruit, buildings etc). Although the observers have no clue as to the type of animal to look for, its size, orientation or number, performance is remarkably good – typically around 95%, with a mean reaction times that can be often under 400 ms. We were also able to determine a "minimum reaction time", defined as the shortest reaction time value for which responses to targets significantly outnumber responses to distractors. In the case of the animal detection task, the value is around 250 ms. Remember that this value includes not just the time required for visual processing, but also the time needed to initiate and execute the motor response (release a mouse button). Furthermore, by recording the electrical activity of the brain, we were able to show that well before this time, there is a clear differential electrical response that distinguishes targets from distracters starting only 150 ms after stimulus onset.

In the past few years, we have learned a great deal more about this remarkable ability. First, it is not specific to biological categories because both accuracy and processing time is virtually identical when the target category is not "animal", but "means-of-transport"[4]. Since we clearly do not come into the world pre-wired to detect items such as helicopters and trains, it is clear that the categories have to be learnt in this case. Second, it does not seem to require information about color, because gray-scale images are processed almost exactly as efficiently as images in color [5]. Third; we have shown that processing speed with images that have never been seen before is just as fast as with images that are highly familiar, suggesting that the underlying processing mechanisms are so highly optimized that further improvements in speed are effectively impossible [6]. Fourth, it is clear that we do not need to be looking at the animal in order to detect it. In one experiment, we flashed images at random positions across the entire horizontal extent of the visual field and found that although accuracy dropped off linearly with eccentricity, performance was still way above chance even at the extreme limit of the visual field [7].

In some recent experiments, images were presented either to the left or right of the fixation point, again demonstrating that fixation is not required. However, in addition we directly compared performance when either one image was presented on its own, or when both the images on the left and right sides were presented simultaneously [8]. Remarkably, processing speed was found to be exactly the same in both cases, providing strong evidence that the two images could be processed in parallel with no penalty. This result argues forcibly that this sort of processing can be done without the need for directing visual attention. Other evidence that animal detection in natural scenes can be done without invoking focussed attention comes from another set of experiments by Li and coworkers who found that performing a second highly demanding task at the fovea did not interfere with the subjects ability to detect animals in scenes flashed in parafoveal vision [9].

We have recently completed another series of experiments in which we used a particularly brief presentations (6.25 ms) followed after a variable interval by an extremely powerful high contrast mask [10]. By interleaving trials with different values for the Stimulus Onset Asynchrony (S.O.A.) between the test image and the mask we showed that performance rose very rapidly as S.O.A. increased, reaching near optimal levels with only 40-60 ms available for processing. But even with an S.O.A. of under 20 ms, performance was way above chance. This form of masking experiment provides strong temporal constraints that provide information about the amount of time for processing at each stage in the visual pathway.

The work on URVC in humans already provides some major constraints on visual processing models, but even more striking constraints are imposed by the results of studies on rhesus monkeys. Not only can they perform the same sorts of tasks efficiently, but that they have reaction times that are substantially shorter than those seen in humans. As we just mentioned, minimum reaction times in humans are around 250 ms, but in monkeys, the entire processing sequence from photoreceptor to hand can be completed in as little as 160-180 ms [11]. These numbers are very significant, because in the primate visual system we already know a great deal about the anatomical organization of the visual pathways. In the next section we will discuss how such data can be used to constrain models of visual processing.

2 Temporal Constraints and Visual System Architecture

Visual information in the retina has to pass via a relay in the lateral geniculate nucleus of the thalamus before reaching striate cortex – area V1. After that, object recognition is known to involve the so-called ventral processing stream going through V2, V4 and both posterior and anterior parts of the inferotemporal cortex (PIT and AIT). As we go from stage to stage, response latencies increase, receptive field sizes become larger and the neurons become selective for more and more complex visual forms [12].

Much can be learned from analyzing the response properties of neurons at the top end of the visual system [13, 14]. It has been know for some time that neurons in IT can be highly selective to stimuli such as faces, and that such neurons can respond only 80-100 ms after stimulus onset. Importantly, it was shown some years ago that the very beginning of the neural response of face selective neurons can be fully selective, a result that argues in favor of a rapid feed-forward processing mode [15]. Even stronger evidence for feed-forward processing was provided by a recent study that examined the responses of neurons in IT to rapidly presented sequences of images [16]. By varying the presentation rate from around 4 to 72 images per second, the authors were able to show that even at 72 frames per second, IT neurons were able to emit a statistically significant "blip" of activation each time the neuron's preferred stimulus was presented. Such results imply that the visual system is indeed capable of performing a form of pipeline processing – with only 14 ms available per image, it would appear that as many as 7 different images were being processed simultaneously – with different images being processed at different levels of the visual system (retina, LGN, V1, V2, V4, PIT and AIT). Note also the strong overlap between these electrophysiological findings and the results of the masking experiment mentioned in the previous section where it was also demonstrated that information can be processed very rapidly at each stage in the visual system with usable information becoming available within the first 10-20 ms.

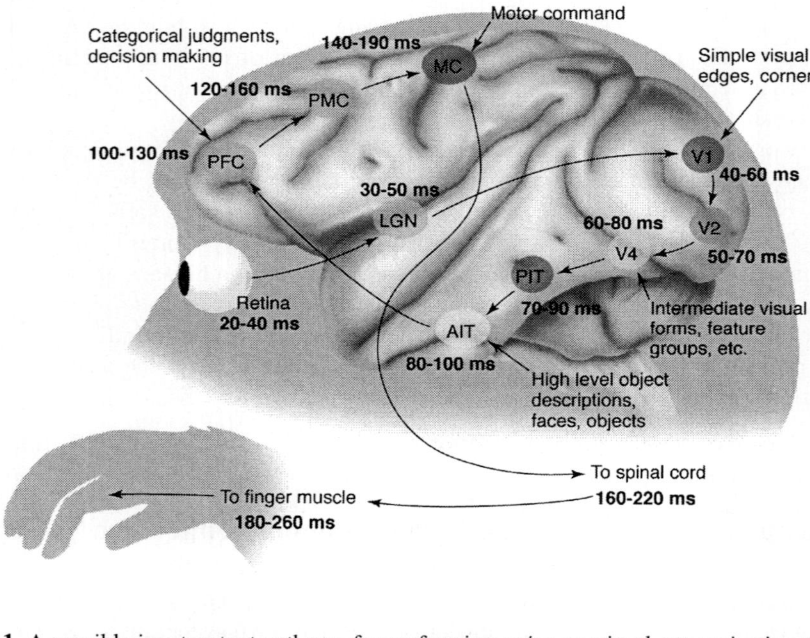

Fig. 1. A possible input-output pathway for performing go/no-go visual categorization tasks in monkeys. Information passes from retina to lateral geniculate nucleus (LGN) before arriving in cortical area V1. Further processing occurs in V2, V4 and in the posterior and anterior inferotemporal cortex (PIT and AIT) before being relayed to the prefrontal (PFC), premotor (PMC) and motor cortices (MC). Finally, motoneuron activation in the spinal cord triggers hand movement. For each area, the two numbers provide approximate latency values for (i) the earliest responses, and (ii) a typical average response (from Thorpe and Fabre-Thorpe, Science, 2001).

3 Implications for Computational Models

If the processing sequence illustrated in figure 1 is correct, we can start to put some specific numbers on the amount of time available for computation at each stage of the visual pathway. It seems clear that in order to get through the entire sequence in just 160-180 ms, the amount of time available at each stage may be as little as 10 or so milliseconds. In fact, this value fits well with the approximate shift in latency as one moves from stage to stage. Thus, neurons in V2 have latencies that are roughly 10 ms than those seen in V1, and V4 would appear to be roughly 10 ms later still [12]. However, it is very important to realize that not all the neurons in any particular structure will fire with the same latency, and there is in fact a very wide spread of onset latencies in every area. For example, in primate V1, the earliest responses start roughly 40 ms after stimulus onset, but 60 ms would be a more typical value. However, it is clear that some neurons will not fire at all until 100 ms or more after stimulus onset. This very wide range of onset latencies means that the start of firing in different processing areas will overlap considerably, leading some authors to argue that all areas will be active virtually simultaneously. However, if we consider the very fast processing that is involved in generating the earliest responses in our rapid visual categorization task, or the processing used to generate face-selective visual responses at latencies of 80-100 ms in IT, only the earliest responses in each area could be involved.

These results have important implications for our understanding of how the brain computes [17, 18]. It needs to be remembered that the overwhelming majority of theoretical approaches to neural computation make the assumption that the output of each neuron can be effectively summarized by a single analog value, corresponding to its firing rate. This assumption has permeated through virtually all the connectionist literature, as well as the vast majority of artificial neural networks. However, if computations really can be done using just 10 of so milliseconds of activity at each processing stage, the very notion of rate coding is called into question. The problem is that the firing rates seen in cortical neurons rarely go over about 100 spikes per second, which means that in 10 ms, one is very unlikely to see more than one spike. Normally, it is assumed that determining firing rate involves counting how many spikes are produced during a given time window, but clearly, with only 10 ms to monitor the output, the accuracy of such a code will be very limited. One could use the interval between two spikes to obtain an instantaneous measure of firing rate, but even this would be impossible for the vast majority of cells. It has recently been argued that the solution to this dilemma would be to calculate the rate of firing across a populations of cells [19]. While this is certainly an option, we have argued that the degree of compression required to transmit the entire contents of the retina to the brain using just a million or so axons would make this impracticable [20].

So, are there any alternatives to conventional rate coding schemes? We have been arguing for some years that one option is to consider neurons not so much as analog to frequency convertors (as is effectively the case when using a rate code scheme) but use of the fact that the time required for a typical integrate and fire neuron to reach threshold will depend on how strongly it is being stimulated – with stronger inputs, the neuron will typically depolarize and reach threshold more quickly [21]. It is strange that, even though all neurophysiologists would appear to agree that spike latency does indeed vary with stimulus strength, this basic fact does not seem to have been taken into account by models of information processing by the nervous system. In fact, once one realizes that the timing of the first response to a stimulus varies as a function of the stimulus, this opens up a whole range of interesting computational strategies [18]. One option would be to use the precise timing of each spike. However, determining the latency of the spike requires that we are able to determine the precise moment at which the stimulus was presented – something that would be virtually impossible within the nervous system. An alternative strategy, that is almost as powerful would be to simply look at the order in which cells fire. This is the basic idea behind the notion of Rank Order Coding, a proposition on which we have been working for the last few years [22, 23].

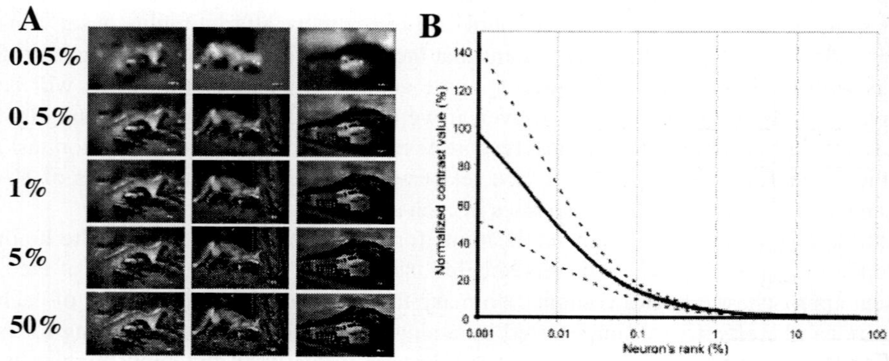

Fig. 2. **A** Progressive reconstruction of three natural images using the rank order coding scheme. Results are shown as a function of the percentage of retinal ganglion cells that have already fired one spike (adapted from VanRullen and Thorpe, 2001). **B** Mean contrast values as a function of the cell's rank (as a percentage of the total number of neurons) averaged over more than 3000 images.

4 Rank Order Coding

With Rank Order Coding, the important information is contained not in the precise firing rates of particular neurons, but rather in the order in which cells fire. In a recent paper, Rufin VanRullen and I compared the efficiency of conventional rate based coding with an order code for transmitting information between the retina and the brain [20]. We used a simple model of the retina, with ON- and OFF-center receptive fields at different spatial scales, and allowed the neurons to fire in sequence, starting with the points on the image where the local contrast was highest. Using just the order in which the cells fired, we were able to reconstruct the original image progressively as shown in figure 2a. To obtain the reconstructions, we plugged the receptive field of each neuron that fires at the appropriate location in the reconstructed image, but we used a weighting factor that depends on the rank of the cell – the earliest firing cells are given a high weighting, whereas those that fire later on are given less and less importance. Specifically, the weighting of each retinal spike was adjusted using the Look-Up Table shown in figure 2b. This Look-Up Table has a quite characteristic shape that we determined empirically by determining the average local contrast as a function of the neurons rank for a large set of natural images. It has a very steep slope, meaning that while the very first neurons to fire can be given a high weight, by the time 1% has fired, the typical contrast (and hence the weighting) had dropped to a few percent of the original value. This explains why the initial part of the propagation is so important, and why 1% propagation is often sufficient for recognition.

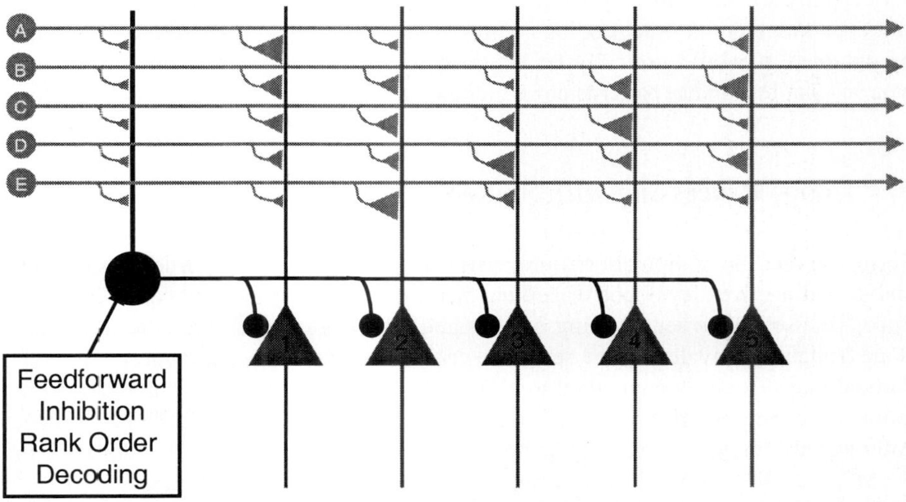

Fig. 3. A cortical circuit using feedforward shunting inhibition to produce rank order sensitivity. A-E are thalamic inputs making excitatory synapses with different weights onto cortical neurons 1-5. In addition they have fixed weight inputs to a feedforward inhibitory circuit that progressively decreases the sensitivity of all the cortical neurons as more an more inputs have fired. Suppose that the strengths of the synapses between units A-E and unit 1 are respectively 5, 4, 3, 2 and 1 and that each time one of the inputs fires, the sensitivity of all the post-synaptic units drops by 20%. If the inputs fire in the order A<B<C>D>E the total amount of excitation received by unit one will be (5*1.0)+(4*0.8)+(3*0.64)+(2*0.5)+(1*0.4) = roughly 11.5. This is the highest amount of activation that can be produced with one spike per input. By setting the threshold of output units to around 11, the units can be made to be selective to input order.

How might the visual system make use of the information contained in the order of firing of the retinal afferents? Clearly, the next stage in the visual system would need to have mechanisms that are order sensitive, but it might be that some relatively simple cortical circuits would provide just the sort of mechanism. Consider a neuron in visual cortex that receives direct excitatory inputs from several geniculate afferents with differing weights. Normally, the order in which those afferents fire will make relatively little difference – the total amount of excitation would be roughly the same. However, if we add in an additional inhibitory neuronal circuit such as the one illustrated in figure 3, we can arrange things so that the neuron will only fire when the inputs fire in a particular sequence. The trick is to use inhibitory units that receive strong equal strength inputs from all the afferents so that the amount of inhibition increases as a function of the number of inputs that have fired, rather than which particular ones are involved.

Using this strategy we can obtain neurons that are selective to a particular order of activation by setting the weights to high values for the earliest firing inputs and lower weights for those firing later. Note that, in principle, this sort of selectivity can be made arbitrarily high. With N inputs, there are N! different orders in which the inputs can fire. When N =5, this allows for 120 different patterns, but this value increases very rapidly so that with only 16 inputs, there are over 10^{13} different possible patterns. But even though rank order coding could in principle allow very selective responses to be obtained, it would typically be better to use a relatively small number of tuned neurons that respond to patterns close to the optimal order.

5 Image Processing with SpikeNet

To investigate the computational properties of this form of Rank Order based coding and decoding, we developed a spiking neuron simulation system called SpikeNet. SpikeNet uses the order of firing of ON- and OFF-center ganglion cells in the input stage (roughly equivalent to the retina) to drive orientation selective neurons in a set of cortical maps (roughly equivalent to V1). We then use the order in which these orientation selective units fire to drive feature and object selective units in the later stages. Although the input connectivity patterns between the retina and V1 cells is "hand-wired", we use a supervised learning procedure to specify the connection strengths between the V1 cells and the units in the recognition layer. In our early work with SpikeNet, aimed at face detection and identification, we obtained some very encouraging results [24] [25]. As a consequence, over the last 18 months the original SpikeNet code has been completely rewritten to make it more suitable for use in machine vision systems and the results have been very encouraging. The current system is able to take images from a variety of sources (images on disk, video files, webcams or cameras) and locate and identify objects within them. Figure 4 illustrates how the system is able to learn a wide range of targets and then correctly localize them in a montage. Despite the very wide range of forms that were used, accuracy is generally very high – in this case, all 51 targets were correctly localized with no misses and no false alarms. Note that no effort was made to choose particularly easy targets, we simply select a small region of each target as the image fragment to be learnt. The precise size of the region is not very critical. In this particular case, the image fragments were between roughly 20 and 30 pixels across, but the most important thing is that region has to contain some oriented structure.

Fig. 4. Example of a image montage labeled using SpikeNet. The montage contains 51 images taken from a wide variety of sources. They include paintings by Leonardo da Vinci, Van Gogh, Monet, Escher, Picasso and Dali, movie posters for E.T., Batman, The Shining and A Clockwork Orange, album covers for Fleetwood Mac and the Beatles, and photographs of Michael Jackson, Neil Armstrong and the World Trade Center Disaster. Training consisted of taking a small region from each image and using a one shot learning algorithm to specify the weights. The small circles indicate that the program correctly located one of the 51 items.

One of the most remarkable features of the algorithm used in SpikeNet is its speed. The time taken to process the 298*200 pixel image shown in Figure 4 and correctly localize all 51 targets was 241 ms using a 2 GHz Pentium 4 based machine. Because of the way in which the code has been written, the processing time scales roughly linearly with (i) the number of pixels in the image and (ii) the number of targets that are tested. Essentially, there is a fixed overhead associated with modeling the responses of neurons in the early parts of the visual system (up to the level of V1). In this particular case, this accounted for roughly 30 ms of the processing time. The remaining time was used to simulate the activity of 51 maps of neurons, each with the dimensions of the input image (there is effectively one unit dedicated for each target for each pixel in the image), with roughly 4 ms of processing time required for each additional target. In all, the simulation involves more than 3.5 million neurons and roughly 1.5 billion synaptic connections and yet the speed with which the computations are performed mean that even on a humble desktop machine, we are effectively modeling the activity of this very large network of neurons in close to biological time. In essence, the reason for this remarkable efficiency stems from the fact that we only allow a small percentage of neurons to fire. Since the simulation is "event-driven", computations are only performed when a neuron fires and so the computational overhead associated with very large numbers of inactive neurons is kept to a strict minimum.

Note that despite the very large size of the network being simulated, the memory requirements are actually quite low. This particular simulation runs quite happily with only 32 Mbytes of RAM. Note that by dividing the processing between more than one CPU it would be straightforward to achieve processing speeds faster than biological vision. Furthermore current progress in microprocessor technology means that we can assume that processing power will increase rapidly in the coming years. Currently shipping Pentium 4 processors operate at 2.8GHz but 4.7 GHz chips have already been tested so there is plenty of potential for improvements in the years to come.

The example illustrated in figure 4 is obviously not very realistic since the target forms in the test image were in fact identical to those used in training. Only the position of the target was unknown. It is worth noting that although we have achieved position invariance in this model, the cost in neurons is very high because we have effectively used one neuron for each pixel location. This is clearly not a strategy that could be used by the brain because the number of different targets that we can recognize is much higher than in this example. We can estimate that the typical human subject can probably identify at least 100 000 different objects, and the total might well exceed 1 million [17], ruling out such a scheme. The main justification for taking such an approach here is not biological realism, but rather that it demonstrates just how powerful a single wave of asynchronous spikes can be. Furthermore, by explicitly encoding the position of each object, we can produce an image processing system that can simultaneously solve both the "What" and the "Where" questions, something that almost certainly involves cooperative processing in both the dorsal and ventral cortical pathways in the human visual system.

Other major problems faced by the human visual system concerns the need for rotation and size invariance. How well does the sort of algorithm used in SpikeNet cope with such variations? Figure 5 shows another montage produced by taking an image of the Mona Lisa and progressively varying both orientation and zoom. A single training image was used (the one positioned at the center of the image), but despite using the same parameter settings used in the previous image, the system was able to correctly locate matching stimuli over a substantial range of variation. Note that the precise degree of tolerance can be adjusted by varying parameters such as the thresholds of the units in the output layers. Specifically, using higher thresholds results in units that require exactly the same orientation and scale as was used for training. In contrast, by lowering the thresholds, the units can be made to respond despite variations in orientation and zoom of roughly ±10° or ±10% respectively. The risk is that the units will start making false positive responses to non-targets, but in a sense, this is not so different to the way in which human observers behave in psychophysical detection tasks. The fact that the sort of recognition algorithm used in SpikeNet has some inbuilt tolerance to relatively small variations in orientation and scale means that one option would be simply to learn lots of different views of the same object. This is something that can indeed be done with SpikeNet, but as in the case of position invariance, the cost of such a brute force approach is very high in neurons. Having specialized units to recognize each of 20 or more different orientations (a separate mechanism for each

18° step) and at 10 or so different scales would require 200 different mechanisms for each object and at each location in the image. As we just noted, the brain could not afford to use so many neurons, so it seems very likely that a lot of extra computational tricks will be needed to cut down on the number of units that are used.

Fig. 5. A further example of a image montage labeled using SpikeNet. The montage contains 81 versions of the Mona Lisa at different orientations and scales. Each row contains rotated versions at –8°, -6°, -4°, -2°, 0°, +2°, +4°, +6° and 8°. Scale varies by 3% between each row, a total range of over 25%. Learning used just the image at the center of the montage. Despite this, the white circles indicate that the target was correctly detected for 69 of the 81 of the variants demonstrating substantial orientation and scale invariance.

Nevertheless, it should be stressed that in the architectures used here, the recognition layer is effectively immediately after the initial V1 representation. It is as if all we were trying to build all the face-selective neurons found in primate inferotemporal cortex using neurons in V2. This is clearly completely at odds with what we know about the visual system. However, the fact is that such an approach *can* be made to work, as demonstrated by the results of our simulations. Note also that this sort of relatively low level mechanism may actually be used in simpler visual systems in animals such as honey-bees [26] and pigeons [27] that are also capable of performing remarkably sophisticated visual recognition and categorization tasks and yet probably do not have the same type of sophisticated multi-layer architecture adopted by the primate visual system.

6 Conclusions

The remarkable speed with which the human and monkey visual system can process complex natural scenes poses a formidable challenge for our models of information processing. In just 150 ms, our visual systems can determine whether an image contains a target category such as an animal even when we have no prior knowledge of what type of animal to look for, what size it will be, where it will be positioned in the scene and what the lighting conditions are. In monkeys, it is likely that the same visual task can be performed even more rapidly, perhaps in as little as 100 ms. Since the is the latency at which neurons in the primate temporal lobe start to respond, it is difficult to escape the conclusion that the much of this processing can be achieved using a single feed-forward pass through the multiple layers of the visual system. Add to that recent results showing that categorization is possible even in the face of very severe backwards masking starting less than 20 ms after the presentation of the target and it is clear that at least some highly sophisticated computations can be done very rapidly.

In this chapter, we have argued that a key to understanding the extreme efficiency of natural vision system lies in the fact that the most strongly activated neurons at each stage of processing will tend to fire first. Thus, even when only 1% of the neurons in the retina have responded, there is enough information available to allow image reconstruction [20]. While this is certainly not really the aim of the visual system, it is a useful test case. However, more to the point, our work with SpikeNet has shown that if one just uses the first few percent of neurons to fire in V1 it is possible to develop neurons in the next processing stage that can respond selectively to most visual forms if they are sufficiently close to the original. There is still a long way to go, and there are a large number of obvious features of real biological visual systems that are not yet implemented. These include the use of horizontal connections within V1 that could well be important for contour integration [28] and feed-back connectivity from later processing stages [29, 30]. These feedback connections are extremely numerous in the visual system and they must clearly be important for some visual tasks. One particular task that may well be heavily dependent on feedback connections is scene segmentation. It is important to realize that the sorts of rapid image and object labeling that we have achieved with SpikeNet occurs without any form of explicit segmentation mechanism. This is a major difference when compared with the majority of conventional image processing approaches in which one first has to segment the scene into separate regions before the process of object identification can even begin. The relative failure of this approach in computer vision might well be directly attributable to the fact that it has proved impossible to devise a pure data driven approach to image segmentation that provides anything sensible as an output. In the approach outlined here, an extremely rapid feedforward pass is used to pinpoint interesting feature combinations such as those found around the eyes and mouth of a face or a wheel in the case of a car. In this sense the method we use is very reminiscent of that recently used by Shimon Ullman to categorize natural images [31]. Once those key trigger features have been located, this information can be used not only to generate useful behavioral responses (as in the case of our rapid categorization task) but also as a way of intelligently seeding the segmentation process occurring at earlier stages in the visual system. Once you have found an eye, there is a very high probability that there will also be the outline of a face not far away. Electrophysiological studies have recently provided evidence that this sort of segmentation linked processing starts with a delay of several tens of milliseconds, consistent with the idea that it involves feedback from later stages [32, 33].

There is clearly a very long way to go. Nevertheless, the results obtained so far with the spiking neural network simulation work are very encouraging. With smallish images and relatively small numbers of targets, the computational power of a desktop computer is already enough to allow real-time processing of natural scenes. With the rapid development of computer hardware that will no doubt continue in the years to come, there is good reason to believe that simulating many of the computations performed by the human visual system on standard computing devices will become feasible in the near future, without necessarily needing to switch to more exotic hardware approaches such as Analog VLSI or molecular computing. We believe that a major key to making this possibility a reality is the realization that biological neuronal networks use spikes for a good reason. Using spikes opens a whole range of computational strategies including the use of temporal coding schemes that are not available with more conventional computer vision strategies. Only time will tell whether an approach based on reverse engineering the visual system with large scale networks of spiking neurons will prove sufficient to allow us to develop efficient Biologically Inspired Computer Vision systems.

Acknowledgments. I would like to thank all the people that have contributed to the work described here. In particular, Jong-Mo Allegraud, Nadege Bacon, Dominique Couthier, Arnaud Delorme, Michèle Fabre-Thorpe, Denis Fize, Jacques Gautrais, Nicolas Guilbaud, Rudy Guyonneau, Marc Macé, Catherine Marlot, Ghislaine Richard, Rufin VanRullen and Guillaume Rousselet.

References

1. Potter, M.C., Meaning in visual search. Science, 187: (1975) 965-6.
2. Potter, M.C., Short-term conceptual memory for pictures. J Exp Psychol (Hum Learn), 2: (1976) 509-22.
3. Thorpe, S., Fize, D., Marlot, C., Speed of processing in the human visual system. Nature, 381: (1996) 520-2.
4. VanRullen, R., Thorpe, S.J., Is it a bird? Is it a plane? Ultra-rapid visual categorisation of natural and artifactual objects. Perception, 30: (2001) 655-68.
5. Delorme, A., Richard, G., Fabre-Thorpe, M., Ultra-rapid categorisation of natural scenes does not rely on colour cues: a study in monkeys and humans. Vision Res, 40: (2000) 2187-200.

6. Fabre-Thorpe, M., Delorme, A., Marlot, C., Thorpe, S., A limit to the speed of processing in ultra-rapid visual categorization of novel natural scenes. J Cogn Neurosci, 13: (2001) 171-80.
7. Thorpe, S.J., Gegenfurtner, K.R., Fabre-Thorpe, M., Bulthoff, H.H., Detection of animals in natural images using far peripheral vision. Eur J Neurosci, 14: (2001) 869-876.
8. Rousselet, G.A., Fabre-Thorpe, M., Thorpe, S.J., Parallel processing in high level categorisation of natural images. Nature Neuroscience, 5: (2002) 629-30.
9. Li, F.F., VanRullen, R., Koch, C., Perona, P., Rapid natural scene categorization in the near absence of attention. Proc Natl Acad Sci U S A, 99: (2002) 9596-601.
10. Thorpe, S.J., Bacon, N., Rousselet, G., Macé, M.J.-M., Fabre-Thorpe, M., Rapid categorisation of natural scenes: feed-forward vs. feedback contribution evaluated by backwards masking. Perception, 31 suppl: (2002) 150.
11. Fabre-Thorpe, M., Richard, G., Thorpe, S.J., Rapid categorization of natural images by rhesus monkeys. NeuroReport, 9: (1998) 303-308.
12. Nowak, L.G., Bullier, J., The timing of information transfer in the visual system, in J. Kaas, K. Rockland, and A. Peters, Editors. (eds) Extrastriate cortex in primates, Plenum: New York. (1997) 205-241.
13. Logothetis, N.K., Sheinberg, D.L., Visual object recognition. Annu Rev Neurosci, 19: (1996) 577-621.
14. Rolls, E.T., Deco, G., Computational Neuroscience of Vision. Oxford: Oxford University Press (2002)
15. Oram, M.W., Perrett, D.I., Time course of neural responses discriminating different views of the face and head. J Neurophysiol, 68: (1992) 70-84.
16. Keysers, C., Xiao, D.K., Foldiak, P., Perrett, D.I., The speed of sight. J Cogn Neurosci, 13: (2001) 90-101.
17. Thorpe, S.J., Imbert, M., Biological constraints on connectionist models., in R. Pfeifer, et al., Editors. (eds) Connectionism in Perspective., Elsevier: Amsterdam. (1989) 63-92.
18. Thorpe, S., Delorme, A., Van Rullen, R., Spike-based strategies for rapid processing. Neural Networks, 14: (2001) 715-25.
19. van Rossum, M.C., Turrigiano, G.G., Nelson, S.B., Fast propagation of firing rates through layered networks of noisy neurons. J Neurosci, 22: (2002) 1956-66.
20. VanRullen, R., Thorpe, S.J., Rate coding versus temporal order coding: what the retinal ganglion cells tell the visual cortex. Neural Comput, 13: (2001) 1255-83.
21. Thorpe, S.J., Spike arrival times: A highly efficient coding scheme for neural networks., in R. Eckmiller, G. Hartman, and G. Hauske, Editors. (eds) Parallel processing in neural systems, Elsevier: North-Holland. (1990) 91-94.
22. Gautrais, J., Thorpe, S., Rate coding versus temporal order coding: a theoretical approach. Biosystems, 48: (1998) 57-65.
23. Thorpe, S.J., Gautrais, J., Rank Order Coding, in J. Bower, Editor. (eds) Computational Neuroscience: Trends in Research 1998, Plenum Press: New York. (1998) 113-118.
24. VanRullen, R., Gautrais, J., Delorme, A., Thorpe, S., Face processing using one spike per neurone. Biosystems, 48: (1998) 229-39.
25. Delorme, A., Thorpe, S.J., Face identification using one spike per neuron: resistance to image degradations. Neural Networks, 14: (2001) 795-803.
26. Giurfa, M., Menzel, R., Insect visual perception: complex abilities of simple nervous systems. Curr Opin Neurobiol, 7: (1997) 505-13.
27. Troje, N.F., Huber, L., Loidolt, M., Aust, U., Fieder, M., Categorical learning in pigeons: the role of texture and shape in complex static stimuli. Vision Res, 39: (1999) 353-66.

28. VanRullen, R., Delorme, A., Thorpe, S.J., Feed-forward contour integration in primary visual cortex based on asynchronous spike propagation. Neurocomputing, 38-40: (2001) 1003-1009.
29. Bullier, J., Integrated model of visual processing. Brain Res Brain Res Rev, 36: (2001) 96-107.
30. Bullier, J., Hupe, J.M., James, A.C., Girard, P., The role of feedback connections in shaping the responses of visual cortical neurons. Prog Brain Res, 134: (2001) 193-204.
31. Ullman, S., Vidal-Naquet, M., Sali, E., Visual features of intermediate complexity and their use in classification. Nat Neurosci, 5: (2002) 682-7.
32. Lamme, V.A., Roelfsema, P.R., The distinct modes of vision offered by feedforward and recurrent processing. Trends Neurosci, 23: (2000) 571-9.
33. Roelfsema, P.R., Lamme, V.A., Spekreijse, H., Bosch, H., Figure-ground segregation in a recurrent network architecture. J Cogn Neurosci, 14: (2002) 525-37.

A Biologically Motivated Scheme for Robust Junction Detection

Thorsten Hansen and Heiko Neumann

Univ. Ulm, Dept. of Neural Information Processing, D-89069 Ulm, Germany
(hansen,hneumann)@neuro.informatik.uni-ulm.de

Abstract. Junctions provide important cues in various perceptual tasks, such as the determination of occlusion relationship for figure-ground separation, transparency perception, and object recognition, among others. In computer vision, junctions are used in a number of tasks like point matching for image tracking or correspondence analysis. We propose a biologically motivated approach to junction detection. The core component is a model of V1 based on biological mechanisms of colinear long-range integration and recurrent interaction. The model V1 interactions generate a robust, coherent representation of contours. Junctions are then implicitly characterized by high activity for multiple orientations within a cortical hypercolumn. A local measure of circular variance is used to extract junction points from this distributed representation. We show for a number of generic junction configurations and various artificial and natural images that junctions can be accurately and robustly detected. In a first set of simulations, we compare the detected junctions based on recurrent long-range responses to junction responses as obtained for a purely feedforward model of complex cells. We show that localization accuracy and positive correctness is improved by recurrent long-range interaction. In a second set of simulations, we compare the new scheme with two widely used junction detection schemes in computer vision, based on Gaussian curvature and the structure tensor. Receiver operator characteristic (ROC) analysis is used for a threshold-free evaluation of the different approaches. We show for both artificial and natural images that the new approach performs superior to the standard schemes. Overall we propose that nonlocal interactions as realized by long-range interactions within V1 play an important role for the detection of higher order features such as corners and junctions.

1 Introduction and Motivation

Corners and junctions are points in the image where two or more edges join or intersect. Whereas edges lead to variations of the image intensity along a single direction, corners and junctions are characterized by variations in at least two directions. Compared to regions of homogeneous intensity, edges are rare events. Likewise, compared to edges, corners and junctions are rare events of high information content. Moreover, corners and junctions are invariant under different viewing angles and viewing distances. Both the sparseness of the signal

H.H. Bülthoff et al. (Eds.): BMCV 2002, LNCS 2525, pp. 16–26, 2002.

and the invariance under affine transformations and scale variations establish corners and junctions as important image features.

Corners and junctions are useful for various higher level vision tasks such as the determination of occlusion relationships, matching of stereo images, object recognition and scene analysis. The importance of corner and junction points for human object recognition has been demonstrated in a number of psychophysical experiments (Attneave, 1954; Biederman, 1985). Junctions also seem to play an important role in the perception of brightness and transparency (Adelson, 2000; Metelli, 1974) and have been proposed to trigger modal and amodal surface completion (Rubin, 2001). In physiological studies in monkey visual cortex cells have been reported which selectively respond to corners and line-ends (Hubel and Wiesel, 1968) as well as curved patterns and angles (Pasupathy and Connor, 2001).

Recently (McDermott, 2001) studied the performance of human observers for the detection of junctions in natural images. He found that the ability to detect junctions is severely impaired if subjects could view the location of a possible junction only through a small aperture. Detection performance and observers' confidence ratings decreased with decreasing size of the aperture. The results suggest that a substantial number of junctions in natural images cannot be detected by local mechanisms.

In this paper we propose a new mechanism for corner and junction detection based on a distributed representation of contour responses within hypercolumns (Zucker et al., 1989). Unlike local approaches as proposed in computer vision (Harris, 1987; Mokhtarian and Suomela, 1998), the new scheme is based on a more global, recurrent long-range interaction for the coherent computation of contour responses. Such nonlocal interactions evaluate local responses within a more global context and generate a robust contour representation. A measure of circular variance is used to extract corner and junctions points at positions of large responses for more than one orientation.

The paper is organized as follows. In Sec. 2 we present the model of recurrent colinear long-range interactions and detail the new junction detection scheme. Simulation results for a number of artificial and natural images are presented in Sec. 3. Section 3 concludes the paper.

2 A Neural Model for Corner and Junction Detection

Corner and junction configurations can be characterized by high responses for two or more orientations at a particular point in the visual space. A cortical hypercolumn is the neural representation for orientated responses at a particular point. Corners and junctions are thus characterized by significant activity of multiple neurons within a hypercolumn.

Multiple oriented activities as measured by a simple feedforward mechanism are sensitive to noisy signal variations. In previous work we have proposed a model of recurrent colinear long-range interaction in the primary visual cortex for contour enhancement (Hansen and Neumann, 1999, 2001). During the recurrent long-range interactions, the initially noisy activities are evaluated within a larger context. In this recurrent process, only coherent orientations responses are preserved, i.e., responses which are supported by responses in the spatial neighborhood, while other responses are suppressed. Besides the enhancement of coherent contours, the proposed model also preserves multiple activities at corners and junctions. Corners and junctions are thus implicitely characterized by a distributed representation of high multiple activity within a hypercolumn.

Such a distributed representation may suffice for subsequent neural computations. However, at least for the purpose of visualization and comparison to other junction detection schemes an explicit representation is requested. Following the above considerations, corners and junctions can be marked if multiple orientations are active and high overall activity exists within a hypercolumn.

In the following we first present the proposed model of colinear recurrent long-range interactions in V1 (Sec. 2.1), and then detail a mechanism to explicitely mark corner and junction points (Sec. 2.2).

2.1 Coherent Contour Representation by a Model of Colinear Recurrent Long-Range Interaction in V1

The model of colinear long-range interactions in V1 is motivated by a number of biological mechanisms. The core mechanisms of the model include localized receptive fields for oriented contrast processing, interlaminar feedforward and feedback processing, cooperative horizontal long-range integration, and lateral competitive interactions. The key properties of the model are motivated by empirical findings, namely (i) horizontal long-range connections (Gilbert and Wiesel, 1983; Rockland and Lund, 1983) between cells with colinear aligned RFs (Bosking et al., 1997); (ii) inhibitory, orientation-unspecific short-range connections (Bosking et al., 1997);and (iii) modulating feedback which cannot drive a cell but modulates initial bottom-up activity (Hirsch and Gilbert, 1991, Hupé et al., 1998). The model architecture is defined by a sequence of preprocessing stages and a recurrent loop of long-range interaction, realizing a simplified architecture of V1 (Fig. 1).

Feedforward Preprocessing. In the feedforward path, the initial luminance distribution is processed by isotropic LGN-cells, followed by orientation-selective simple and complex cells. The interactions in the feedforward path are governed by basic linear equations to keep the processing in the feedforward path relatively simple and to focus on the contribution of the recurrent interaction. In our model, complex cell responses C_θ (as output of the feedforward path, cf. (Fig. 1) provide an initial local estimate of contour strength, position and orientation which is used as bottom-up input for the recurrent loop. A more detailed description of the computation in the feedforward path can be found in Hansen and Neumann (1999).

Recurrent Long-Range Interaction. The output of the feedforward preprocessing defines the input to the recurrent loop. The recurrent loop has two

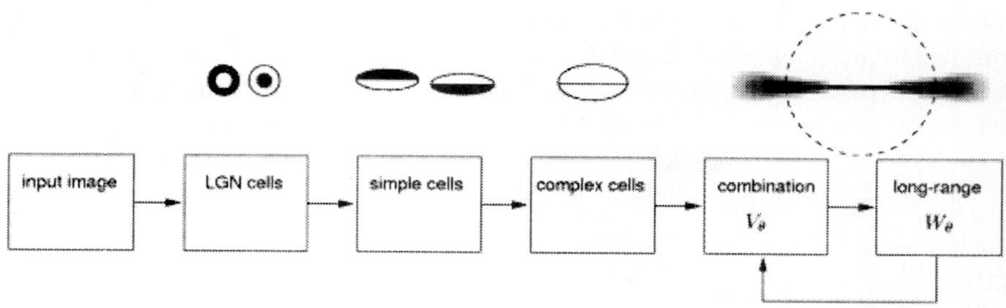

Fig. 1. Overview of model stages together with a sketch of the sample receptive fields of cells at each stage for 0° orientation. For the long-range stage, the spatial weighting function of the long-range filter is shown together with the spatial extend of the inhibitory short-range interactions *dashed circle.*

stages, namely a combination stage where bottom-up and top-down inputs are fused, and a stage of long-range interaction.

Combination Stage. At the combination stage, feedforward complex cell responses and feedback long-range responses are combined. Feedforward inputs C_θ and feedback inputs W_θ are added and subject to shunting inhibition

$$\partial_t V_\theta = -\alpha_V V_\theta + (\beta_V - V_\theta)\,\mathrm{net}_\theta \ , \qquad \text{where } \mathrm{net}_\theta = C_\theta + \delta_V W_\theta \ . \tag{1}$$

Solving the equation at equilibrium $\partial_t V_\theta = 0$ results in a normalization of activity

$$V_\theta = \beta_V \frac{\mathrm{net}_\theta}{\alpha_V + \mathrm{net}_\theta} \ . \tag{2}$$

The weighting parameter $\delta_V = 2$ is chosen so that dimensions of C_θ and W_θ are approximately equal, the decay parameter $\alpha_V = 0.2$ is chosen small compared to net_θ, and $\beta_V = 10$ scales the activity to be sufficiently large for the subsequent long-range interaction. For the first iteration step, feedback responses W_θ are set to C_θ.

Long-Range Interaction. At the long-range stage the contextual influences on cell responses are modeled. Orientation-specific, anisotropic long-range connections provide the excitatory input. The inhibitory input is given by isotropic interactions in both the spatial and orientational domain. Long-range connections are modeled by a filter whose spatial layout is similar to the bipole filter as first proposed by Grossberg and Mingolla (1985). The spatial weighting function of the long-range filter is narrowly tuned to the preferred orientation, reflecting the highly significant anisotropies of long-range fibers in visual cortex (Bosking et al., 1997). The size of the long-range filter is about four times the size of the RF of a complex cell, while the size of the short-range connections is about 2.5 times the size of the complex cell RF, as sketched in Fig. 1.

Essentially, excitatory input is provided by correlation of the feedforward input with the long-range filter B_θ. A cross-orientation inhibition prevents the integration of cells responses at positions where responses for the orthogonal orientation also exist. The excitatory input is governed by

$$\text{net}_\theta^+ = \left[V_\theta - V_{\theta\perp}\right]^+ \star B_\theta \ , \tag{3}$$

where $\star$ denotes spatial correlation and $[x]^+ = \max\{x, 0\}$ denotes half-wave rectification.

The profile of the long-range filter is defined by a directional term D_φ and a proximity term generated by a circle C_r of radius $r = 25$ which is blurred by an isotropic 2D Gaussian G_σ, $\sigma = 3$. The detailed equations read

$$B_{\theta,\alpha,r,\sigma}(x,y) = D_\varphi \cdot C_r \star G_\sigma \tag{4}$$

$$D_\varphi = \begin{cases} \cos(\frac{\pi/2}{\alpha}\varphi) & \text{if } |\varphi| < \alpha \\ 0 & \text{otherwise} \ , \end{cases} \tag{5}$$

where $\varphi = \varphi(\theta)$ is defined as atan2$\,(|y_\theta|, |x_\theta|)$ and $(x_\theta,\, y_\theta)^{\mathrm{T}}$ denotes the vector $(x, y)^{\mathrm{T}}$ rotated by θ. The operator $\cdot$ denotes the point-wise multiplication of two filter kernels or 2D matrices. The parameter $\alpha = 10°$ defines the opening angle of 2α of the long-range filter. The factor $\frac{\pi/2}{\alpha}$ maps the angle φ in the range $[-\alpha, \alpha]$ to the domain $[-\pi/2, \pi/2]$ of the cosine function with positive range. A plot of the long-range filter for a reference orientation of 0° is depicted in (Fig. 1) (top right inset).

Responses which are not salient in the sense that nearby cells of similar orientation preference also show strong activity should be diminished. Thus an inhibitory term is introduced which samples activity from both orientational $\widetilde{g}_{\sigma_o,\theta}$, $\sigma_o = 0.5$, and spatial neighborhood $G_{\sigma_{\text{sur}}}$, $\sigma_{\text{sur}} = 8$:

$$\text{net}_\theta^- = \text{net}_\theta^+ \circledast \widetilde{g}_{\sigma_o,\theta} \star G_{\sigma_{\text{sur}}} \ , \tag{6}$$

where $\circledast$ denotes correlation in the orientation domain. The orientational weighting function $\widetilde{g}_{\sigma_o,\theta}$ is implemented by a 1D Gaussian g_{σ_o}, discretized on a zero-centered grid of size $o_{\max}$, normalized, and circularly shifted so that the maximum value is at the position corresponding to θ. The spatially inhibitory interactions $G_{\sigma_{\text{sur}}}$ model the short-range connections.

Excitatory and inhibitory terms combine through shunting interaction

$$\partial_t W_\theta = -\alpha_W W_\theta + \beta_W V_\theta \left(1 + \eta^+ \,\text{net}_\theta^+\right) - \eta^- \,W_\theta \,\text{net}_\theta^- \ . \tag{7}$$

The equation is solved at equilibrium, resulting in a nonlinear, divisive interaction

$$W_\theta = \beta_W \frac{V_\theta \left(1 + \eta^+ \,\text{net}_\theta^+\right)}{\alpha_W + \eta^- \,\text{net}_\theta^-} \ . \tag{8}$$

where $\alpha_W = 0.2$ is the decay parameter and $\eta^+ = 5$, $\eta^- = 2$, and $\beta_W = 0.001$ are scale factors.

Activity W_θ from long-range integration is gated by the activity V_θ and thus implements a modulating rather than generating effect of lateral interaction on cell activities (Hirsch and Gilbert, 1991; Hué et al., 1998). The result of the long-range stage is fed back and combined with the feedforward complex cell responses, thus closing the recurrent loop. The shunting interactions governing both the long-range interactions and the combination of feedback and feedforward input ensure rapid equilibration of the dynamics after a few recurrent cycles resulting in graded responses within a bounded range of activations ("analog sensitivity", Grossberg et al., 1997).

The model is robust against parameter changes which is mainly caused by the compressive transformation equations employed. For the combination of responses (Eq. 2), however, it is crucial to have activities in both streams of a similar order of magnitude. Also the relative RF sizes must not be substantially altered.

2.2 Junction Detection by Read-Out of Distributed Information Using a Measure of Circular Variance

As stated above, corners and junction are characterized by points in the visual space where responses for multiple orientations are present and high overall activity exists within a hypercolumn. For the read-out of this distributed information a measure of circular variance is used to signal multiple orientation. The overall activity is given by the sum across all orientation within a hypercolumn. Thus, the junction map J for a distributed hypercolumnar representation such as the activity of the long-range stage W_θ (Eq. 8) is given by

$$J = \mathrm{circvar}(W)^2 \sum_\theta W_\theta \ , \quad \text{where } \mathrm{circvar}(W) = 1 - \left|\sum_\theta W_\theta \exp(2i\theta)\right| / \sum_\theta W_\theta \ . \tag{9}$$

The function "circvar" is a measure of the circular variance within a hypercolumn. The squaring operation enhances the response if the circular variance assumes high values. Circular variance takes values in the range $[0, 1]$. A circular variance of 0 denotes a single response, whereas a value of 1 occurs if all orientations have the same activity.

To precisely localize the junction points, the junction map J is first smoothed with a Gaussian G_σ, $\sigma = 3$. Junction points are then marked as local maxima whose strength must exceed a fraction $\kappa = 0.25$ of the maximum response in the smoothed junction map. Local maxima are computed within a 3×3 neighborhood.

3 Simulation and Evaluation

In this section we show the competencies of the proposed junction detection scheme for a variety of synthetic and natural images. In particular, the localization properties of the new scheme and the detection performance on natural images are evaluated. In the first part of this section, we compare the detected junctions based on recurrent long-range responses to junction responses as obtained for a purely feedforward model of complex cells to demonstrate the advantages of the recurrent long-range interaction. In the second part, we compare the new scheme with two junction detection schemes widely used in computer vision, based on Gaussian curvature and the structure tensor. Receiver operator characteristic (ROC) analysis (Green and Swets, 1974) is used for a threshold-free evaluation of the different approaches (Hansen, 2002). Model parameters as specified in Sec. 2 are used in all simulations, and 12 recurrent cycles were computed to generate the long-range responses.

3.1 Evaluation of Junction Detection Based on Feedforward vs. Recurrent Long-Range Processing

In order to focus on the relative merits of the recurrent long-range interactions for the task of corner and junction detection, the proposed scheme is evaluated using two different kinds of input, namely the activity W_θ of the long-range stage and the purely feedforward activity C_θ of the complex cell stage.

Localization of Generic Junction Configurations. From the outset of corner and junction detection in computer vision, the variety of junction types has been partitioned into distinct classes like T-, L-, and W-junctions, (Huffman, 1971), and more recently, Ψ-junctions (Adelson, 2000). In the first simulation we compare the localization accuracy of junction responses based on feedforward vs. recurrent long-range responses for L-, T-, Y-, W- and Ψ-junctions (Fig. 2). For all junction types, the localization is considerably better for the method based on the recurrent long-range interaction.

Processing of Images. We have also evaluated the junction detection performance on real world images, such as cubes within a laboratory environment (Fig. 3). At the complex cell stage, many false responses are detected due to noisy variations of the initial orientation measurement. These variations are reduced at the long-range stage by the recurrent interaction, such that only the positions of significant orientation variations remain. We have further employed ROC analysis for the threshold-free evaluation of the detection performance. The results show a better performance of the recurrent approach over the full range of thresholds (Fig. 3, right).

3.2 Evaluation of Detection Performance Compared to Other Junction Detection Schemes

In this section we compare the new scheme based on recurrent long-range interaction with two junction detection schemes proposed in computer vision that utilize only localized neighborhoods, namely the structure tensor (Förstner, 1986; Harris, 1987; Nitzberg and Shiota, 1992) and Gaussian curvature (Beaudet, 1978;

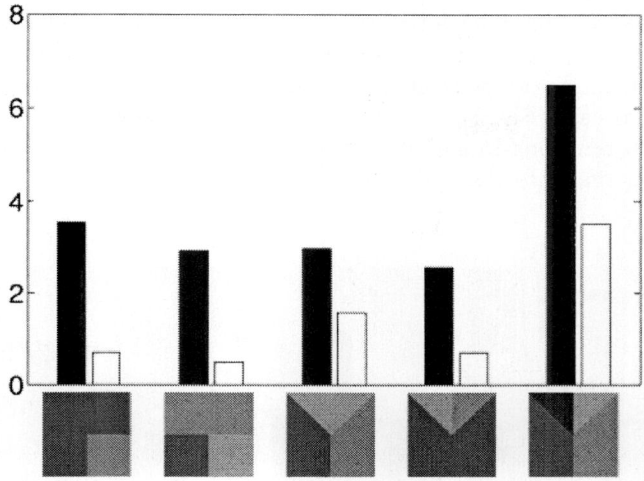

Fig. 2. Distance in pixels from ground-truth location *ordinate* for L-, T-, Y-, W- and Ψ-junctions *abscissa*. Deviation from ground-truth position is considerably smaller for the recurrent long-range interaction *open bars* compared to the complex cell responses *solid bars*.

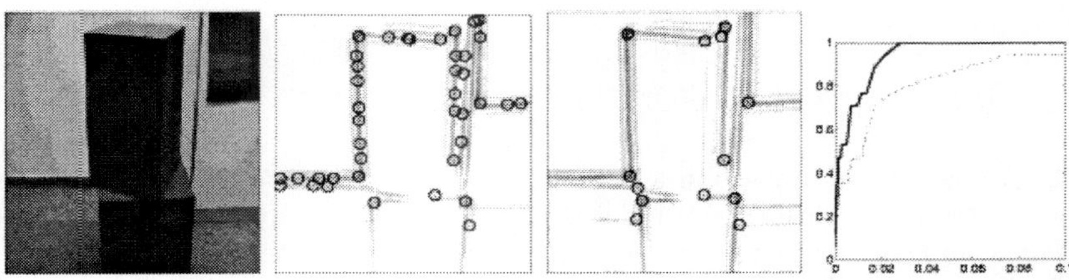

Fig. 3. Simulation of the junction detection scheme for cube images in a laboratory environment. The size of the images is 230×246 pixels. *Left to right:* Input image; detected corners and junctions based on the complex cell responses (CX); based on the long-range responses (LR); and the corresponding ROC curves (*solid lines* LR; *dashed lines* CX). For better visualization, a cut-out of the left part of the ROC curves is shown. The recurrent long-range interaction results in a decrease of circular variance along object contours and thus eliminates a number of false positive responses.

Zetzsche and Barth, 1990). Both schemes compute the first- or second-order derivatives of the image intensity values, respectively. For a fair comparison of methods one has to ensure that all junction detectors operate on (at least approximately) the same scale (Lindeberg, 1998). The derivatives used in the two standard methods are therefore approximated by Gaussian derivatives whose standard deviations are parameterized to fit the successive convolution of filter masks used to compute the complex cell responses. We show the results of the

ROC analysis when applied to a number of artificial and natural images, particularly a series of cube images within a laboratory environment (Fig. 3), and a second set of images containing an artificial corner test image from Smith and Brady (1997), a laboratory scene from Mokhtarian and Suomela (1998) and an image of a staircase (Fig. 5). For all images, the ROC curve for the new scheme based on recurrent long-range interactions is well above the ROC curves for the other schemes, indicating a higher accuracy of the new method.

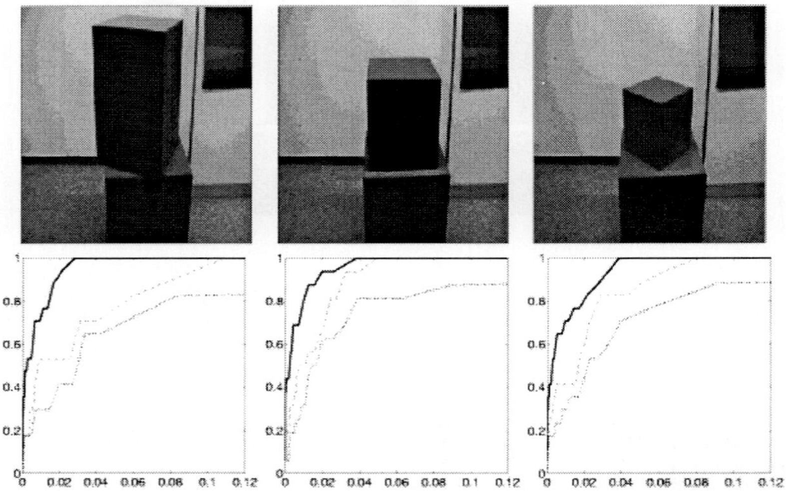

Fig. 4. *Top row:* Cube images in a laboratory environment. *Bottom:* ROC analysis of junction detection performance of the new scheme *solid* compared to other schemes based on Gaussian curvature *dashed*, and on the structure tensor *dotted*. For better visualization, a cut-out of the left part of the ROC curves is shown.

4 Conclusion

We have proposed a novel mechanism for corner and junction detection based on a distributed representation of orientation information within a cortical hypercolumn. The explicit representation of a number of orientations in a cortical hypercolumn is shown to constitute a powerful and flexible, multipurpose scheme which can be used to code intrinsically 1D signal variations like contours as well as 2D variations like corners and junctions. Orientation responses within a hypercolumn can be robustly and reliably computed by using contextual information. We have proposed a model of recurrent long-range interactions to compute coherent orientation responses. In the context of corner and junction detection we have demonstrated the benefits of using contextual information and recurrent interactions, leading to a considerable increase in localization accuracy and

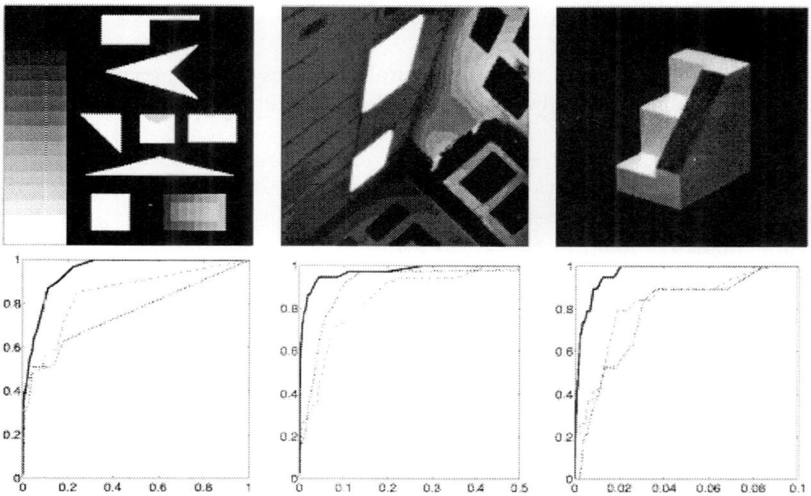

Fig. 5. *Top:* Input images. *Bottom:* ROC analysis of junction detection performance of the new scheme *solid* compared to other schemes based on Gaussian curvature *dashed*, and on the structure tensor *dotted. For better visualization, a cut-out of the left part of the ROC curves is shown.*

detection performance compared to a simple feedforward scheme and to local methods as proposed in computer vision. In the context of neural computation we have shown that junctions can be robustly and reliably represented by a suggested biological mechanism based on a distributed hypercolumnar representation and recurrent colinear long-range interactions.

References

Adelson, E. H. (200) Lightness perception and lightness illusions. In Gazzaniga, M. S., ed. *The New Cognitive Neurosciences*, pp. 339–351. MIT Press, Cambridge, MA, 2 edn.

Attneave, F. (1954) Some informational aspects of visual perception. *Psychol. Rev.*, 61(3):183–193.

Beaudet, P.R. (1978) Rotationally invariant image operators. In *4th Int. Joint Conf. on Pattern Recognition*, pp. 578–583, Kyoto, Japan.

Biederman, I. (1985) Human image understanding: recent research and a theory. *Computer Vision, Graphics, Image Proc.*, 32(1):29–73.

Bosking, W. H., Zhang, Y., Schofield, B., Fitzpatrick, D. (1997) Orientation selectivity and the arrangement of horizontal connections in tree shrew striate cortex. *J. Neurosci.*, 17(6):2112–2127.

Förstner, W. (1986) A feature based correspondence algorithm for image matching. In *Int. Arch. Photogramm. Remote Sensing*, volume 26, pp. 176–189.

Gilbert, C. D. and Wiesel, T. N. (1983) Clustered intrinsic connections in cat visual cortex. *J. Neurosci.*, 3:1116–1133.

Green, D. M. and Swets, J. A. (1974) *Signal Detection Theory and Psychophysics.* Krieger, Huntington, NY, 1974.

Grossberg, S. and Mingolla, E. (1985) Neural dynamics of form perception: boundary completion, illusory figures, and neon color spreading. *Psychol. Rev.*, 92:173–211, 1985.

Hansen, T. (2002) *A neural model of early vision: contrast, contours, corners and surfaces.* Doctoral dissertation, Univ. Ulm, Faculty of Computer Science, Dept. of Neural Information Processing. Submitted.

Hansen, T. and Neumann, H. (1999) A model of V1 visual contrast processing utilizing long-range connections and recurrent interactions. In *Proc. 9. Int. Conf. on Artificial Neural Networks (ICANN99)*, pp. 61–66, Edinburgh, UK.

Hansen, T. and Neumann, H. (2001) Neural mechanisms for representing surface and contour features. In Stefan Wermter, Jim Austin, and David Willshaw, editors, *Emergent Neural Computational Architectures Based on Neuroscience*, LNCS/LNAI 2036, pp. 139–153. Springer, Berlin Heidelberg.

Harris, C. J. (1987) Determination of ego-motion from matched points. In *Proc. Alvey Vision Conference*, pp. 189–192, Cambridge, UK.

Hirsch, J.A. and Gilbert, C.D. (1991) Synaptic physiology of horizontal connections in the cat's visual cortex. *J. Neurosci.*, 11(6):1800–1809.

Hubel,D. H. and Wiesel, T. N. (1968) Receptive fields and functional architecture of monkey striate cortex. *J. Physiol.*, 195:215–243.

Huffman, D. A. (1971) Impossible objects as nonsense sentences. In B. Meltzer and D. Michic, editors, *Machine Intelligence 6*, pp. 295–323. Edinburgh University Press, Edinburgh.

Hupé, J.M., James, A.C., Payne, B.R., Lomber, S.G., Girard, P. and Bullier, J.(1998) Cortical feedback improves discrimination between figure and background by V1, V2 and V3 neurons. *Nature*, 394:784–787.

Lindeberg, T. (1998) Feature detection with automatic scale selection. *Int. J. Comput. Vision*, 30(2):77–116.

McDermott, J.H. (2001) Some experiments on junctions in real images. Master's thesis, University Colledge London, 2001. Online available from `http://persci.mti.edu/~jmcderm`.

Metelli, F. (1974) The perception of transparency. *Sci. Am.*, 230(4):90–98.

Mokhtarian, F. and Suomela, R. (1998) Robust image corner detection through curvature scale space. *IEEE Trans. Pattern Anal. Mach. Intell.*, 20(12):1376–1381.

Nitzberg, M. and Shiota, T. (1992) Nonlinear image filtering with edge and corner enhancement. *IEEE Trans. Pattern Anal. Mach. Intell.*, 14:826–833.

Pasupathy, A. and Connor, C. E. (2001) Shape representation in area V4: position-specific tuning for boundary conformation. *J. Neurophysiol.*, 86(5):2505–2519.

Rockland, K. S. and Lund, J. S. (1983) Intrinsic laminar lattice connections in primate visual cortex. *J. Comp. Neurol.*, 216:303–318.

Rubin, N. (2001) The role of junctions in surface completion and contour matching. *Perception*, 30(3):339–366.

Smith, S. and Brady, J. (1997) SUSAN – a new approach to low level image processing. *Int. J. Comput. Vision*, 23(1):45–78.

Zetzsche, C. and Barth, E. (1990) Fundamental limits of linear filters in the visual processing of two-dimensional signals. *Vision Res.*, 30(7):1111–1117.

Zucker, S. W., Dobbins, A. and Iverson, L. A. (1989) Two stages of curve detection suggest two styles of visual computation. *Neural Comput.*, 1:68–81.

Iterative Tuning of Simple Cells for Contrast Invariant Edge Enhancement

Marina Kolesnik[1], Alexander Barlit, and Evgeny Zubkov

Fraunhofer Institute for Media Communication, Schloss Birlinghoven, D-53754 Sankt-Augustin, Germany

Abstract. This work describes a novel model for orientation tuning of simple cells in V1. The model has been inspired by a regular structure of simple cells in the visual primary cortex of mammals. Two new features distinguish the model: the iterative processing of visual inputs; and amplification of tuned responses of spatially close simple cells. Results show that after several iterations the processing converges to a stable solution while making edge enhancement largely contrast independent. The model suppresses weak edges in the vicinity of contrastive luminance changes but enhances isolated low-intensity changes. We demonstrate the capabilities of the model by processing synthetic as well as natural images.

1 Introduction

Forty years ago, Hubel and Wiesel ([1], 1962) discovered that *simple cells* in cat primary visual cortex (V1) are tuned for the orientation of light/dark borders. The inputs to V1 come from the lateral geniculate nucleus (LGN), whose cells are not significantly orientation selective [2]. LGN cells themselves get their input from the retinal ON and OFF *ganglion cells* with centre-surround receptive fields (RFs), first discovered by Kuffler ([3], 1953). The orientation selectivity of simple cells in V1, as proposed by Hubel and Wiesel ([1], Fig. 2, left), derives from an oriented arrangement of input from the LGN: ON-center LGN inputs have RF centres aligned over simple cell's ON subregions, and similarly for OFF-centre inputs. Because of this input arrangement, simple cells perform a linear spatial summation of light intensity in their fields and have an elongated shape of their RFs.

Area V1 is also known as the *striate cortex* because of the regular arrangement of cells with different properties in layers. Simple cells that respond more strongly to stimuli in one eye than in the other, and are said to show *ocular dominance*, are aligned into *ocular dominance stripes*. Moreover, when the orientation preference of cells in the ocular dominance stripes were related to their position, an astonishingly systematic organisation has emerged: the orientation preference changed linearly with position across V1 [4], [5].

The first major processing stage in the mammalian visual system consists of retinal

[1] To whom correspondence should be addressed: marina.kolesnik@imk.fraunhofer.de

H.H. Bülthoff et al. (Eds.): BMCV 2002, LNCS 2525, pp. 27–37, 2002.

ON and OFF ganglion cells. The RF profile of these cells is best modelled by a difference of Gaussians (DoG) filtering, first suggested by Enroth-Cudell and Robson in 1966 [6] and later confirmed experimentally by Croner and Kaplan [7]. Two types of ON and OFF cells give rise to two complementary ON and OFF pathways, which link retina to simple cells in V1 via respective ON and OFF LGN cells.

Several computational schemes have been proposed for the simulation of orientation selective responses. Most of them employ some type of interaction between the excitatory ON and inhibitory OFF pathways. In the classical proposal of Hubel and Wiesel [1], excitatory signals of ON ganglion cells drive the ON subfields of simple cells, whereas excitatory signals from OFF ganglion cells drive the OFF subfields. In an alternative scheme of opponent inhibition proposed by Fester [8], the ON subfield receives excitatory input from the ON pathway and inhibitory input from the OFF pathway. The reverse holds true for the OFF subfield of the simple cell. This scheme is employed in a computational model of brightness perception [9] and is investigated regarding its signal processing properties, in particular its scale-space behaviour [10] and robustness to noise [11].

All these schemes employ only forward connections for both ON and OFF pathways. But are the pathways between retina and the striate cortex areas one-way channels for the processing of visual information? There is convincing neurophysiological evidence that most, if not all, neural connections are matched by reciprocal "feedback" connections running in the opposite direction. Silito et al. [12] found that the feedback loop between V1 and the LGN operates in a positive fashion to increase the gain of cell responses, and to "lock the system on" to particular spatial patterns of light. A mechanism of dynamic formation of cell assemblies, in which responses of cells to an oriented bar are altered when a second bar is projected into nearby areas outside the receptive field is reported in [14]. It is likely that this kind of dynamic interaction is caused by long-range horizontal connections within the visual cortex, extending beyond the width of a receptive field and specifically linking cells with similar ocular dominance and orientation preference. It has been suggested that these horizontal connections provide a mechanism for perceptual grouping of co-oriented but fragmented line segments [15]. Completion of perceptual groupings over positions without contrastive visual inputs has been modelled via recurrent interaction of complex cells in V1 [16], as well as via feedback projections from V2 to V1 [13].

However, none of the above schemes has explicitly employed the impressive regularity in the spatial organisation of simple cells. For it is unlikely that this highly precise arrangement in orientation preferences has occurred in the course of evolutionary history by chance, it is logical to suggest that the spatial organisation of simple cells ought to have a distinguished role when processing local luminance changes. In this work we put forward a novel model in which responses of simple cells to visual input depend on current activation of neighbouring cells. Unlike previous approaches, the iterative orientation tuning occurs at an early stage of processing, namely in layer 4 of V1 (Section 2). Due to non-linear cross-channel interaction, the iterative tuning has a more pronounced facilitatory effect for low-contrast luminance changes than for high-contrast edges (Section 3). The iterative scheme performs robustly when processing noisy synthetic as well as real images (Section 4). We conclude that explicit incorporation of morphology of simple cells into the computational scheme leads to an efficient approach to contrast detection in images (Section 5).

2 The Model

We adopt the view that the brain has no internal representation of the outside world because it is continuously available "out there" for active perception and visual perception is a continuous process of interpretation of incoming visual data. While the eye is fixating a particular object, the low-level processing of a still visual input may be undergoing several iterative cycles. Every moment when light hits retina it would cause a different neural activity in the underlying visual circuitry, the activity which depends on a level of current neuronal excitation. Consequently, neural responses to the same visual input at different processing cycles would vary. This iterative approach to the low-level visual processing would account for the dynamic formation of cell assemblies reported in [14]. Furthermore, it is very likely that the impressive regular arrangement of simple cells in V1 has its particular role in the way this dynamic interaction takes place. In the model, we assume that activation of a simple cell is transmitted to proximate cells, thus tuning these neighbouring cells to a local orientation pattern. After several cycles of iterative tuning, the whole system reaches equilibrium and responses of simple cells to a constant visual input stabilise.

A model circuit for ON and OFF data streams is shown in Fig. 1. The two ON and OFF pathways interact via the mechanism of opponent inhibition. The model circuit consists of two major stages, namely, the retina-LGN stage, followed by a simple cell circuit in V1. Retinal ON and OFF ganglion cells are modelled as in [13] at each position *(i,j)* by the difference of input image I_{ij} and a convolution of I with a 2-dimensional Gaussian kernel:

$$X_{ij} = I_{ij} - G_\sigma * I_{ij},$$
$$u_{ij}^{+} = [X_{ij}]^{+}, \qquad u_{ij}^{-} = [-X_{ij}]^{+}$$

where S is the spatial convolution operator and G_σ is a centre Gaussian with standard deviation σ=3. The Gaussian is sampled within a 3σ interval, resulting in a filter mask of size 19x19 pixels. This modelling of retinal RFs produces sharper responses to luminance changes than the ones obtained by difference of two Gaussians (DoG) employed in [11].

Retinal ON and OFF ganglion cells synapse mainly onto respective ON and OFF LGN cells, which, in turn, project to V1 driving, among others, the orientation selective simple cells. In the model, signals from the ganglion cells do not change while passing the LGN.

Simple cells in V1 are modelled for twelve discrete orientations θ = 0°, 15°,..., 165°, and for two opposite contrast polarities *p=1, 2*. A sensitivity profile of the simple cell subfield is modelled by a difference of two elongated Gaussians (Fig. 2, right):

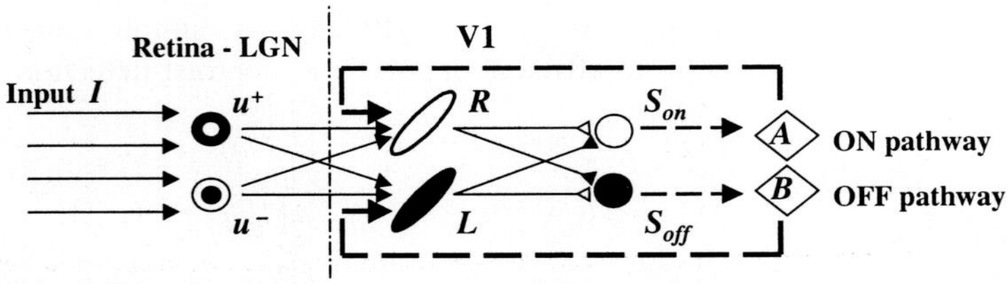

Fig. 1. Architecture of the neural circuitry in the iterative model for contrast detection. Axons of ON and OFF ganglion cells form the optic nerve which projects mainly to cells in the LGN. Responses of LGN cells drive simple cells in V1. The simple cells are engaged into the cross-channel interaction (triangles at the end of lines denote the excitatory input; filled-in-black triangles denote the inhibitory input) followed by interactive amplification of proximate cells in the 3-D structure of simple cells.

$$D_{\theta\sigma_M\sigma_m\boldsymbol{\tau}} = G_{\theta\sigma_M\sigma_m\boldsymbol{\tau}} - G_{\theta\sigma_M\sigma_m-\boldsymbol{\tau}} ,$$

$$G_{\theta\sigma_M\sigma_m\boldsymbol{\tau}} = \frac{1}{2\pi}\exp\left[-\frac{1}{2}\left((\mathbf{x}-\boldsymbol{\tau})^T\mathbf{R}^T\mathbf{C}\mathbf{R}(\mathbf{x}-\boldsymbol{\tau})\right)\right] ,$$

$$\mathbf{C} = \begin{pmatrix} 1/\sigma_m^2 & 0 \\ 0 & 1/\sigma_M^2 \end{pmatrix}, \qquad \mathbf{R} = \begin{pmatrix} \cos\theta & \sin\theta \\ -\sin\theta & \cos\theta \end{pmatrix},$$

where $\mathbf{x}^T = (i, j)$ denotes the (transposed) vector of position *(i,j)*, and $\boldsymbol{\tau}^T = (\cos\theta, \sin\theta)$ is the (transposed) vector of relative offset for two Gaussian lobes from their central position at *(i,j)*. Each filter, $D_{\theta\sigma_M\sigma_m\boldsymbol{\tau}}$, with the orientation θ and polarity *p=1* has its counterpart filter $-D_{\theta\sigma_M\sigma_m\boldsymbol{\tau}}$ with the opposite polarity *p=2*.

At each position, *(i,j)*, and for each orientation, *θ*, and polarity, *p*, the model has an even symmetric simple cell with two parallel elongated parts: an ON subfield, $R_{i,j,\theta,p}$, which receives excitation from LGN ON cells beneath it and is inhibited by LGN OFF cells at the same position; and an OFF subfield, $L_{i,j,\theta,p}$, for which the reverse relation to the LGN channels holds true. This physiology is embodied in the equation for the ON subfield by subtracting the half-wave rectified LGN OFF channel, u^-, from the rectified ON channel, u^+, and convolving the result with the positive lob of the oriented filter, $[D_{\theta\sigma_M\sigma_m\boldsymbol{\tau}}]^+$, [13]. The OFF subfield, $L_{i,j,\theta,p}$, is constructed similarly. In addition, each ON subfield, $R_{i,j,\theta,p}$, is amplified by the total excitatory input of all simple ON cells spatially close to position *(i,j)* in orientation preference columns, $A_{i,j,\theta,p}$. Similarly, the excitation of each OFF subfield, $L_{i,j,\theta,p}$, is amplified by total excitation, $B_{i,j,\theta,p}$, received from all spatially proximate OFF cells. This mutual amplification is a time varying function which is updated

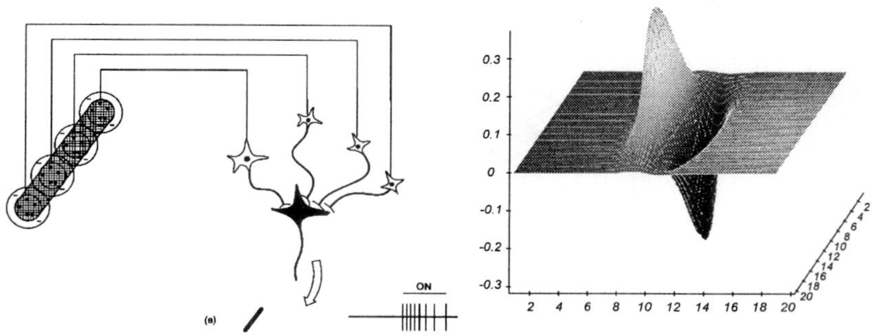

Fig. 2. A simple orientation selective cell and a spatial sensitivity profile for its modelling. Left: the simple cell behaves as it receives input from several centre-surround antagonistic cells of the LGN. Flashing a bar with an orientation as in *(a)*, which stimulates more of the excitatory centres, will stimulate the cell. (Redrawn from Hubel & Wiesel 1962, [5]). Right: the elongated profile for a simple cell subfield of orientation 0°. The oriented filter $D_{\theta\sigma_M\sigma_m\boldsymbol{\tau}}$ is sampled within a filter mask of size 19x19 pixels. The space constants $\sigma_m=1$ and $\sigma_M=4$ define the degree of filter's elongation. Relative offset has been set to $|\boldsymbol{\tau}|=1$.

iteratively. These considerations give the following expressions for $R^n_{i,j,\theta,p}$ and, $L^n_{i,j,\theta,p}$, at iteration *n:*

$$R^n_{i,j,\theta,p} = \left[\left(u^+_{ij} + A^n_{i,j,\theta,p} - u^-_{ij} - B^n_{i,j,\theta,p}\right) * \left[D^p_{\theta\sigma_M\sigma_m\boldsymbol{\tau}}\right]^+\right]^+$$

$$L^n_{i,j,\theta,p} = \left[\left(u^-_{ij} + B^n_{i,j,\theta,p} - u^+_{ij} - A^n_{i,j,\theta,p}\right) * \left[-D^p_{\theta\sigma_M\sigma_m\boldsymbol{\tau}}\right]^+\right]^+ \quad (1)$$

Here the amplification functions at initial iteration: *n=0*, are set to: $A_{\theta,p} = B_{\theta,p} = 0$, for all orientations and polarities. Note, that due to the offset of the positive and negative lobes of $D_{\theta\sigma_M\sigma_m\boldsymbol{\tau}}$, subfield responses are shifted from their central positions. To compensate, both subfields, $R_{i,j,\theta,p}$ and $L_{i,j,\theta,p}$, are shifted in the opposite directions, τ and $-\tau$, respectively.

The ON and OFF subfields undergo cross-channel interaction so that activation of the simple ON cell at iteration *n* is obtained as the steady-state solution of inhibitory shunting interaction [17]:

$$S^n_{on} = \left[(R^n - L^n)/(1 + R^n + L^n)\right]^+ \quad (2)$$

The corresponding equation for activation of the simple OFF cell is obtained by interchanging R^n and L^n. Here variables occur for all spatial positions, discrete orientations and polarities. The indexes *i, j, θ,* and *p* are omitted to simplify notations.

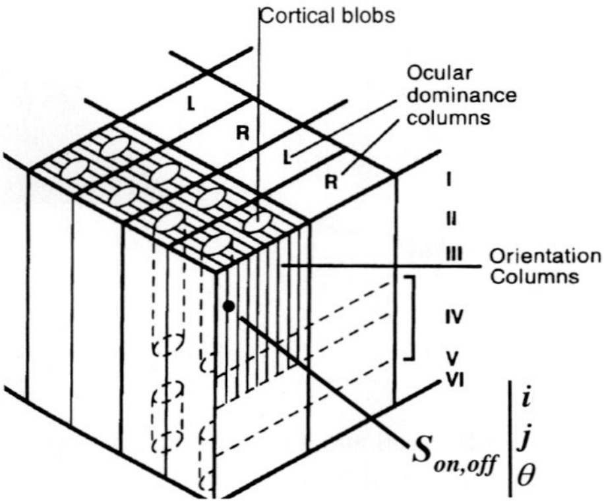

Fig. 3. A schematic diagram of the proposed spatial organisation of V1. The primary visual cortex is divided into modules containing two blobs and their intrablob region. The cortex is divided into ocular dominance columns; running perpendicular to these are orientation columns. Orientation preference within columns changes systematically so that each column represents directions from 0° to 180°. This spatial organisation of simple cells is modelled by the 3-D structure consisting of spatial layers and orientation columns so that each 3-D element of the structure, $(i,j,\theta,)$ has two spatial coordinates, i and j, for position within the layer and one orientation coordinate, θ, for position in the orientation column. It is assumed that each 3-D element of the structure contains a pair of ON and OFF cells, S_{on} and S_{off}. This array structure is repeated twice for both contrast polarities $p = 1,2$.

Each simple cell amplifies activity of neighbouring simple cells, so that S_{on} provides the excitatory input to simple ON cells in its neighbourhood and S_{off} sends excitation to proximate OFF cells. All simple cells are considered to be stacked into a 3-D structure (Fig. 3). It is assumed that each 3-D position, (i,j,θ) contains two opponent cells, the ON cell and the OFF cell. The amplification function $A^n_{i,j,\theta}$ at position (i,j,θ) and iteration n, is a weighted function of distance:

$$A^n_{i,j,\theta} = \lambda \sum_{l,m,\vartheta} \frac{S^n_{(on)l,m,\vartheta}}{D^2[(l,m,\vartheta),(i,j,\theta)]},$$
$$D^2[(l,m,k),(i,j,\theta)] = \omega\left((l-i)^2 + (m-j)^2\right) + (\theta-\vartheta)^2, \tag{3}$$

where λ - is a scaling factor set to: $\lambda = 0.14$, and ω - is a weighting factor set to $\omega = 16$, which effectively downscales the strength of amplification within spatial layer while scaling up the amplification of similarly oriented cells in orientation columns. Excitatory input B to the OFF-cell is obtained by interchanging S_{on} and S_{off}. Computation of A and B is repeated for both contrast polarities.

At this point the processing cycle turns to the next iteration: the amplification functions A and B are fed into (1) and the processing cycle is repeated. The cross-channel interaction (2) prevents arbitrary large growth of amplification functions. The iterative cycle is interrupted when the magnitudes of A and B after two subsequent iterations at all spatial locations (i,j,θ) do not rise by more than 4%.

3 Model Properties

In this section we discuss several important properties of the model, in particular: the effect of cross-channel interaction on the enhancement of responses to weak intensity changes; the strength of amplification of neighbouring cells, as well as stabilisation of responses after several iterative cycles. Input image values, I, to the model are normalized to the range [0,1]. The responses of ganglion cells, u^+ and u^-, have spatially juxtaposed adjacent profiles (Fig. 4, left). However, the profiles of ON and OFF subfields, R and L, are slightly overlapped. (Fig. 4, centre). Therefore, the cross-channel interaction (2) affects signals in the opponent pathways in two ways. First, subtraction of the opposite channels sharpens the activity profiles of simple cells (Fig. 4, right). Second, the non-linear normalisation embodied in the denominator of (2), tends to boost weaker responses over the stronger ones while normalising their overall magnitude to the range [0,1]. This leads to a key property of the model: after several iterations, responses to low-contrast luminance changes tend to grow faster than responses to contrastive luminance changes (Fig. 5). This property is supported by neurophysiological studies, which demonstrated the contrast invariance to orientation selectivity [18], [19].

Because the strength of amplification is an inverse function of squared distance, activation of proximate cells effectively decays within the distance of 3 units. Due to the weighting factor $\omega = 16$ in (3) the effect of amplification affects only one neighbouring cell in all 8 directions within the spatial layer, and about 6 neighbouring cells in the orientation column (3 orientations both up and down the column). Thus, the amplification of simple cells activates a process of selective orientation tuning, which enhances responses of those cells of "proper" orientations, and are situated at "right" spatial positions. As the iterative processing of visual input proceeds, the responses of these simple cells increase. It is however important that the model reaches equilibrium and the amplification of proximate cells stabilises. The corresponding balancing mechanism is provided by cross-channel interaction (2), which does not let responses of simple cells to grow indefinitely. Typically, it takes 4-5 iterations until the magnitudes of A and B slow their growth down to the level 1%-2%, although small changes below this level remain characteristic in the vicinity of contrastive edges.

4 Processing of Images

In this section we demonstrate the performance of the model for the processing of artificial and natural images. Model parameters are as given in Section 2 and remain

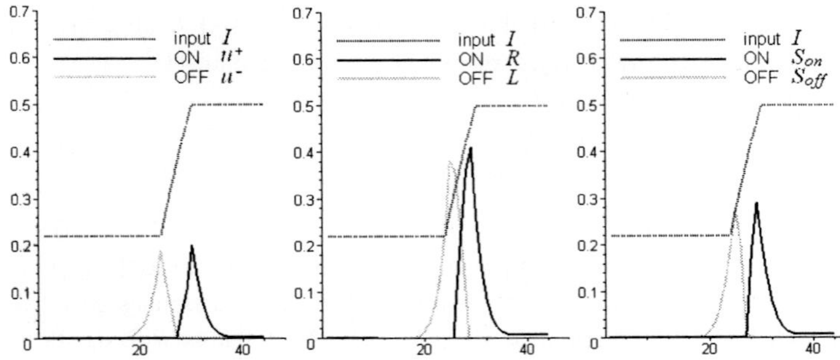

Fig. 4. The ramp profile processed by the ON and OFF pathways. Left: the complementary profiles of the ON and OFF ganglion cells. Centre: the responses of the ON and OFF subfields overlap in the range of about 3 pixels. Right: the responses of simple cells after cross-channel interaction are sharpened in the area where R and L overlap.

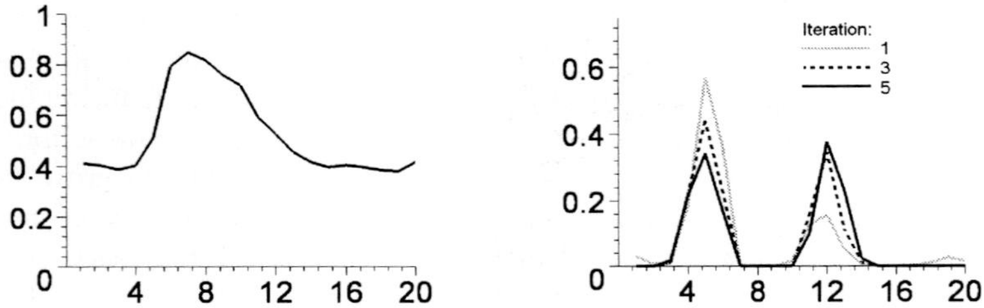

Fig. 5. Enhancement of the weak response at subsequent iterations. Left: input profile. Right: response S (Eq. 4) after 1st, 3rd, and 5th iteration. The initially stronger response on the left decreases over iterations whereas the weaker response on the right is advantageously enhanced. After five iterations the two become largely equalized.

constant for all processing trials. All result images are obtained by rectifying the sum of activities of ON and OFF subfields minus their difference and by pooling together the results of both contrast polarities for all twelve orientations:

$$S_{i,j} = \sum_{\theta,p} \left[R^N_{i,j,\theta,p} + L^N_{i,j,\theta,p} - \left| R^N_{i,j,\theta,p} - L^N_{i,j,\theta,p} \right| \right]^+ \tag{4}$$

where N is the last iteration number, and R and L are not shifted. In the images dark values indicate high cell responses.

In the first processing trial, we employ a synthetic image of a dark rectangle on a lighter background corrupted with 50% Gaussian noise. Fig. 6 shows the input image and the corresponding processing results after three different iterations. Responses to small contrast variations caused by noise are noticeably diminished after fifth iteration. Noise reduction is especially pronounced in the vicinity of sharp edges, where small responses are "cancelled out" by stronger responses that spread in the process of iterative tuning.

In the second experiment we employ a natural image as an input to the model. Fig. 7 shows the input image and the processing result after 5th iteration. To compare results after different iterations, we generate a binary image of edges by applying nonmaxima suppression to processing results, after 1st, 3rd, and 5th iteration. Fig. 8 clearly shows that new edges appear in the images as the model proceeds through iterative cycles. Weak spurious responses at the background vanish at later iterations, although this effect is not visible due to quality loss in the down-sized images.

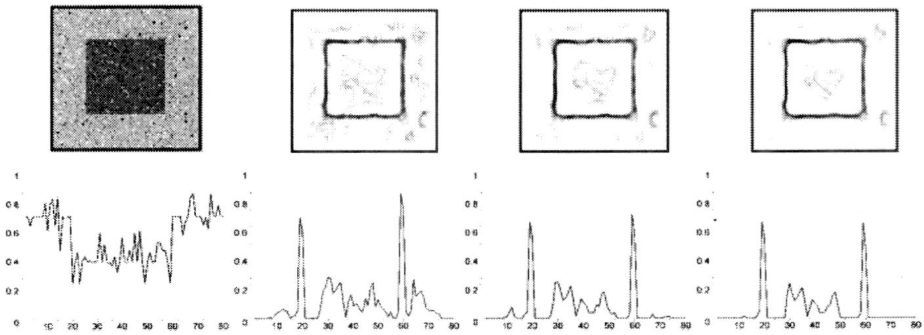

Fig. 6. Noisy input image and processing results after 1st, 3rd, and 5th iteration (top row) together with the corresponding cross sections taken at the centre of the images (bottom row). Responses to noise weaken noticeably as the model proceeds through iterative cycles.

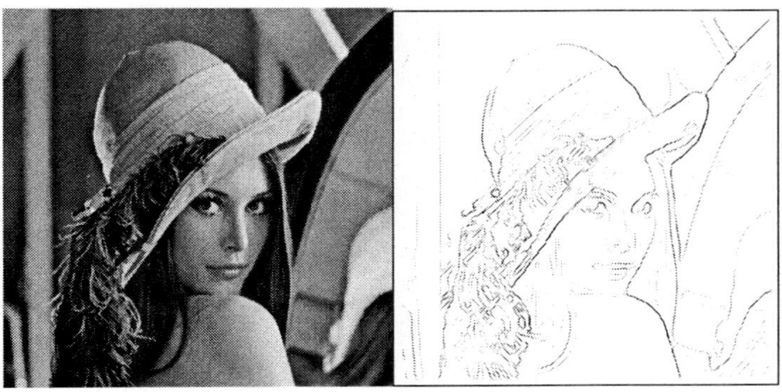

Fig. 7. Input image and processing result S (4) after 5th iteration.

5 Conclusions

We have proposed the model for iterative orientation tuning of simple cells that employs two novel propositions. First, the processing of visual input is iterative. Second, activation of simple cells is iteratively amplified via interaction of proximate cells and the strength of this amplification depends on the distance between cells within orientation preference columns. Further, the model employs the cross-channel inhibition of opponent pathways and depends on just a few parameters. The results show that the model is capable of detecting isolated low-intensity changes, while

Fig. 8. Binary edge images by iterative tuning after 1st, 3rd, and 5th iteration (left to right). The iterative processing closes gaps in pronounced edges and amplifies weak edges undetected at 1st iteration.

suppressing similar contrast variations when these are close to pronounced edges. A key feature of the model is that after several iterations, an enhancement of weak responses is more pronounced than the iterative enhancement of initially stronger responses. In a sense, simple cells become locally attuned to distinguished orientations in the visual pattern. This remarkable behaviour of the model results from the explicit involvement of the spatial organisation of orientation selective cells, or, in other words, the morphology of simple cells into the neural processing of visual signals.

A proposition that morphology should have an important role in cognitive processing and intelligent behaviour stems from a new direction in AI. (see [20] for a more elaborate discussion of this point). Several case studies on simulation of intelligent behaviour, which exploit or even evolve the morphology of an agent, have shown the efficiency of this idea [21]. Although the astonishingly regular structure of orientation selective cells has drawn much attention of researchers, little thinking of the role of this structure in detection of contours has been done. The iterative tuning of orientation selectivity, in which interaction of simple cells is explicitly related to their spatial organisation, illustrates one possible way of how this structure might be involved into the process of contrast detection. It should be noted that, although our processing scheme contains the feedback connections activated at iterations, these connections are quite different than feedback projections employed for recurrent interactions [16] and perceptual grouping [13]. The feedback here simulates the continuity of low-level visual processing in the striate cortex, as well as the fact that very same visual input may trigger different temporal responses of simple cells. Contrary to the attention and association grouping, the iterative amplification is a mechanism of subconscious enhancement of weak and isolated edges. Note, that same intensity edges will be effectively suppressed if these are close to stronger edges.

References

1. Hubel, D., H., Wiesel, T., N.: Receptive fields, binocular interaction and functional architecture in the cat's visual cortex. Journal of Psychology, 160:106-154, 1962.
2. Hubel, D., H., Wiesel, T., N.: Integrative action in the cat's lateral geniculate body. Journal of Psychology, 155:385-398, 1961.

3. Kuffler, S., W.: Discharge patterns and functional organization of mammalian retina. Journal of Neurophysiology, 16:37-68, 1953.
4. Hubel, D., H., Wiesel, T., N.: Sequence regularity and geometry of orientation columns in the monkey striate cortex. Journal of Comparative Neurology, 158:267-294, 1974.
5. Hubel, D., H., Wiesel, T., N.: Functional architecture of macaque monkey visual cortex. Proceedings of the Royal Cosiety of London, B, 198:1-59, 1977.
6. Enroth-Cugell, C., Robson, J., G.: The contrast sensitivity of retinal ganglion cells of the cat. Journal of Physiology, 187:517-552, 1965.
7. Croner, L., J., Kaplan, E.: Receptive fields of P and M ganglion cells across the primate retina. Vision research, 35:7-24, 1995.
8. Ferster, D.: The synaptic inputs to simple cells in the cat visual cortex. In: D. Lam and G. Gilbert (eds.): Neural mechanisms of visual perception, Ch. 3, Portfolio Publ. Co, The Woodlands, Texas:63-85, 1989.
9. Pessoa, L., Mingolla, E., Neumann, H.: A contrast- and luminance-driven multiscale network model of brightness perception. Vision Research, 35:2201-2223, 1995.
10. Neumann, H., Pessoa, L., Hansen, Th.: Interaction of ON and OFF pathways for visual contrast measurement. Biological Cybernetics, 81:515-532, 1999.
11. Hansen, Th., Baratoff, G., Neumann, H.: A simple cell model with dominating opponent inhibition for robust contrast detection. Kognitionswissenschaft, 9:93-100, 2000.
12. Silito, A., M., Jones, H., E., Gerstein, G., L., West, D., C.: Feature-linked synchronization of thalamic relay cell firing induced by feedback from the visual cortex. Nature, 369:479-482,1994.
13. Grossberg, S., Raizada, R., D., S.: Contrast-sensitive perceptual grouping and object-based attention in the laminar circuits of primary visual cortex. CAS/CNS TR-99-008, Boston University:1-35, 1999.
14. Gilbert, C., D., Wiesel, T., N.: The influence of contextual stimuli on the orientation selectivity of cells in primary visual cortex of the cat. Vision research, 30:1689-1701, 1990.
15. Grossberg, S., Mingolla, E., Ross, W., D. Visual brain and visual perception: how does the cortex do perceptual grouping? Trends in Neurosciences, 20:106-111, 1997.
16. Hansen, Th., Neumann, H. A model of V1 visual contrast processing utilizing long-range connections and recurrent interactions. In Proc. of the International Conference on Artificial Neural Networks, Edinburgh, UK, Sept. 7-10:61-66, 1999.
17. Borg-Graham, L. J., Monier, C., Fregnac, Y.: Visual input invokes transient and strong shunting inhibition in visual cortical neurons. Nature, 393, (1998) 369-373.
18. Sclar, G., Freeman, R.: Orientation selectivity in the cat's striate cortex is invariant with stimulus contrast. Experimental Brain research, 46, (1982) 457-461.
19. Skottun, B., Bradley, A., Sclar, G., Ohzawa, I., Freeman, R.: The effects of contrast on visual orientation and spatial frequency discrimination: a comparison of single cells and behavior. Journal of Neurophysiology, 57:773-786, 1987.
20. Pfeifer, R., and Scheier, C: Understanding intelligence. Cambridge, Mass.: MIT Press, 1999.
21. Pfeifer, R.: On the role of morphology and materials in adaptive behaviour. In: J.-A. Meyer, A. Berthoz, D. Floreano, H. Roitblat, and S.W. Wilson (eds.). From animals to animats 6. Proc. of the 6th Int. Conf. on Simulation of Adaptive Behaviour: 23-32, 2000.

How the Spatial Filters of Area V1 Can Be Used for a Nearly Ideal Edge Detection

Felice Andrea Pellegrino, Walter Vanzella, and Vincent Torre

INFM Unit and SISSA, Via Beirut 2-4 Trieste 34100 Italy
pellegri, vanzella, torre@sissa.it

Abstract. The present manuscript aims to address and possibly solve three classical problems of edge detection: i – the detection of all step edges from a fine to a coarse scale; ii – the detection of thin bars, i.e. of roof edges; iii – the detection of corners and trihedral junctions. The proposed solution of these problems combines an extensive spatial filtering, inspired by the receptive field properties of neurons in the visual area V1, with classical methods of Computer Vision (Morrone & Burr 1988; Lindeberg 1998; Kovesi 1999) and newly developed algorithms. Step edges are computed by extracting local maxima from the energy summed over a large bank of odd filters of different scale and direction. Thin roof edges are computed by considering maxima of the energy summed over narrow odd and even filters along the direction of maximal response. Junctions are precisely detected by an appropriate combination of the output of directional filters. Detected roof edges are cleaned by using a regularization procedure and are combined with step edges and junctions in a Mumford-Shah type functional with self adaptive parameters, providing a nearly ideal edge detection and segmentation.

1 Introduction

The detection and identification of important features in an image seem to require an extensive preprocessing of it. In fact, the detection of edges, corners and other important two dimensional (2D) features has been efficiently obtained by convolving the original image with directional filters with different orientation, size and shape (Freeman & Adelson 1991, Freeman 1992, Simoncelli & Farid 1996; Grossberg & Raizada 1999). When 2D features are detected by computing maxima of the local energy (Morrone & Burr 1988; Robbins & Owens 1997; Kovesi 1999) the image is first convolved with odd and even filters of different orientations. The need of analysing images at different scale, i.e. multi-scale analysis (Witkin 1983, Lindeberg 1998), is now widely recognized in Computer Vision and is a standard technique in image processing (Grossman 1988, Meyer 1993).

The visual system of higher vertebrates and mammals seems to have adopted a similar approach: the first stage of visual processing occurring in the cortex, i.e. in the visual area V1, consists in the convolution of the retinal image with filters with different orientation, size and shape (Hubel & Wiesel 1965). Neurons in this visual area have a rectangular receptive field, composed by excitatory and inhibitory regions, flanking their symmetry axis along a preferred direction, in an even or odd

H.H. Bülthoff et al. (Eds.): BMCV 2002, LNCS 2525, pp. 38–49, 2002.

configuration. These neurons act as directional filters having between 12 and 24 different orientations (Blakemore & Campbell 1969, Field & Tolhurst 1986) with a relative ratio between the two dimensions varying between 1 and 9 (Anderson & Burr 1991) and their size differing from 1 to 10 (Wilson et al. 1983, Anderson & Burr 1989). This set of different filters is certainly redundant from a mathematical point of view, but seems very useful, if not necessary for optimal performances of the visual system of higher vertebrates and mammals.

Both biological and artificial vision agree on the need of analysing images with a large battery of filters with different properties. The first cortical visual area V1 have been extensively characterized and can be described – in first approximation - as a large battery of filters used for an extensive preprocessing of images. Neurons of this area project into higher visual areas such as V2, V4 and inferotemporal (IT) areas. Receptive fields of neurons in V2 are more complex and some of them are selective for corners, junctions and other complex features (Hegde & Van Essen 2000). The receptive field of these neurons is presumably composed by appropriate projections from neurons of lowers visual areas, but very little is known of the neural mechanisms leading to the complex shape selectivity observed in visual areas V2, V4 and IT. Therefore we need to understand how to combine the output of elementary filters and which interactions are necessary and useful for obtaining the complex shape selectivity of biological and human vision.

The first and major aim of this paper is to use the rather large set of filters, present and implemented in the visual area V1, to obtain an almost ideal edge detection scheme, able to detect: i - step edges from a fine to a coarse scale; ii - thin bars or roof edges. The proposed scheme for edge detection combines several previously proposed approaches (Morrone & Burr 1988; Lindeberg 1998) with new algorithms. The information obtained by this extensive filtering is used for a final regularization of the original image using a modified version of the Mumford and Shah functional (Mumford & Shah 1989), providing a decomposition of it in a clean map of roof edges and in an image segmentation with precisely localized step edges and trihedral junctions. Technical details and a comparison with other methods and approaches will be presented elsewhere (Pellegrino, Vanzella & Torre 2003; Vanzella, Pellegrino & Torre 2003).

The present paper has a second aim, i.e. to investigate best ways to combine the output of V1-like filters for the detection of higher order features, such as corners and junctions, detected in the visual area V2 (Hegde & Van Essen 2000). These issues will be thoroughly presented and discussed in an other publication (Morrone, Pellegrino, Vanzella & Torre 2003).

2 The Proposed Approach to Edge Detection

Early approaches to edge detection (Torre & Poggio 1986; Canny 1986) primarily focused their analysis to the identification of the best differential operator, necessary to localize sharp changes of the intensity $g(x,y)$ at location (x,y). These approaches recognized the necessity of a previous filtering, identified as a regularizing stage, but did not explicitly realize the convenience of a full multi-scale analysis, useful for a reliable detection of both sharp and smooth edges (Deriche & Giraudon 1993).

Following some biological suggestions Morrone & Burr (1988) proposed to detect edges as maxima of the local energy $E_d(x,y)$ obtained as:

$$E_d(x,y) = \sqrt{{}_dO^2{}_{even}(x,y) + {}_dO^2{}_{odd}(x,y)} \ , \tag{1}$$

where ${}_dO_{even}(x,y)$ and ${}_dO_{odd}(x,y)$ are the convolution of the original image $g(x,y)$ with a quadrature pair of one-dimensional filters in the d direction. A quadrature pair of one-dimensional filters consists of one even and one odd-symmetric filters with zero mean, same norm and orthogonal with each other. These two filters are one the Hilbert transform of the other. Subsequent approaches (Kovesi 1999) suggested the local energy to be

$$E(x,y) = \sum_{s,d} E_{d,s}(x,y) \ , \tag{2}$$

i.e. the energy summed over different directions d and scales s. In these approaches edges are identified as local maxima of the energy of eq. (2). In one dimension maxima of local energy are also points of maximal phase congruency (Venkatesh & Owens 1990), i.e. points of particular interest in the image. Local maxima of the energy (2) correctly identify edges (Morrone & Burr 1988; Robbins & Owens 1997) when features to be detected are significantly larger than the size of used filters. This problem will inevitably occur with digital images of NxN pixels when bars with a width or length below 2 or 3 pixels have to be detected. The simplest way to overcome this problem is to oversample the image, but significantly increasing the computational burden of the analysis.

In this paper we adopt the view of detecting and localizing edges as local maxima of the energy (2), but we investigate how to combine the output of different V1-like filters with different scales, directions and parity for 'an almost ideal' detection of step edges, of thin roof edges and of thriedral junctions at fine and coarse scales. It will be shown that step edges are best detected by considering only the output of odd filters, summed over all directions and scales. On the contrary thin roof edges – of 1 or 2 pixels of width – are best localized by summing the energy from narrow even and odd filters only in the direction of maximal response. Trihedral junctions are localized by appropriately combining even and odd filters and their sides are precisely identified by the analysis of the polar plot (see Fig. 3), obtained by comparing the energy of the output of directional filters.

A rather different method to edge detection is obtained by considering variational approaches (Mumford & Shah 1989, Morel & Solimini, 1995). In these approaches, given an image $g(x,y)$ its set of edges k and a suitable approximation $u(x,y)$ of $g(x,y)$ are obtained by minimizing the functional

$$\Phi(u,k) = \gamma \int_{\Omega\backslash k} |\nabla u|^2 dx + \alpha H(k) + \int_{\Omega\backslash k} |u-g|^2 dx \ , \tag{3}$$

where $u(x,y)$ is a piece-wise smooth approximation of $g(x,y)$, $H(k)$ is the total length of the edges, ∇ is the gradient operator and α and γ are appropriate constants. Edges obtained by minimizing the functional (3) and by computing local maxima of eq (2) often coincide. Step edges at a given scale are usually well detected by minimizing the functional (3), but thin roof edges are not detected and are smeared out. In this paper the information obtained by the extensive filtering of the original image is used to make α and γ locally adapt to the local properties of the image. In this way step edges are detected at all scales. Thin roof edges obtained by considering local maxima of an appropriate energy function are usually noisy and are cleaned by minimizing an other functional, shown in eq (4). In this way, step and roof edges have the regularity and smoothness usually obtained from variational methods.

3 Combining V1-Like Filters

Local maxima of the energy (2) usually provide well localized edges, but not in the presence of thin bars. Let us consider a one dimensional intensity profile with a high grey value between pixel n and $n+m$ and a low value elsewhere. The energy (2) has three local maxima in n, $n+m$ and in $n+m/2$, with the first two maxima corresponding to step edges and the maximum at $n+m/2$ corresponding to a roof edge. When m becomes small the three local maxima coalesce and cannot be reliably identified. This problem is evident when considering the one dimensional intensity profile of Fig. 1a with a thin and a large bar. In this case step edges are properly localized at the feature boundaries. When odd and even filters are considered one maximum is obtained for the thin bar and two for the thicker bar (see Fig. 1b). Using only odd filters two energy maxima are correctly detected both for the thin and thicker bar (see Fig. 1c). In fact, edges obtained combining the output of odd and even filters (see Fig. 1e) are not as correctly localized as when only odd filters are considered (see Fig. 1f).

In order to detect step edges at fine and coarse scales it is necessary to use small and larger filters, with different frequency properties, but it is not obvious how to weight their relative contribution. The scale of odd filters in eq. (2) can be combined by using filters with the same energy (as those in Fig. 2a, continuous line) or with the same maximal response (as those in Fig. 2a, dashed line). When a fine and a coarse step edge - edges with a strong output at small and large scales - are present in the same region of the image (see Fig. 2b) and the output of fine and coarse filters superimpose spatially, their simultaneous detection may be difficult. Extensive experimentation has shown that small details, as those shown in Fig. 2b and 2d, are better detected by summing the output of filters at different scales with same maximal response, as when filters with same energy are used (see Fig. 2c,e and f). In this way it is possible to detect correctly high frequency details also near coarse step edges. Filters at different scales with same maximal response can cover the spectral content of an image in different ways: for instance the integral of their energy in the frequency domain may be almost flat (see continuous line in Fig. 2g) or with a broad central peak (see dotted line in Fig. 2g).

When the one dimensional intensity profile of Fig. 2h is considered the sum of the energy of the filters output shown in Fig. 2i is obtained: almost identical maxima are obtained with the two sets of filters covering the spectral content of the image as in Fig. 2g. This result suggests the exact frequency distribution of filters at different scales with the same maximal response is not highly critical for a precise and reliable edge detection.

It is not surprising that the detection of step edges is best obtained by using only odd filters, as they are the natural matched filters for these features (Canny 1988), which is not the case for thin roof edges or thin bars. The detection of thin bars of 1 or

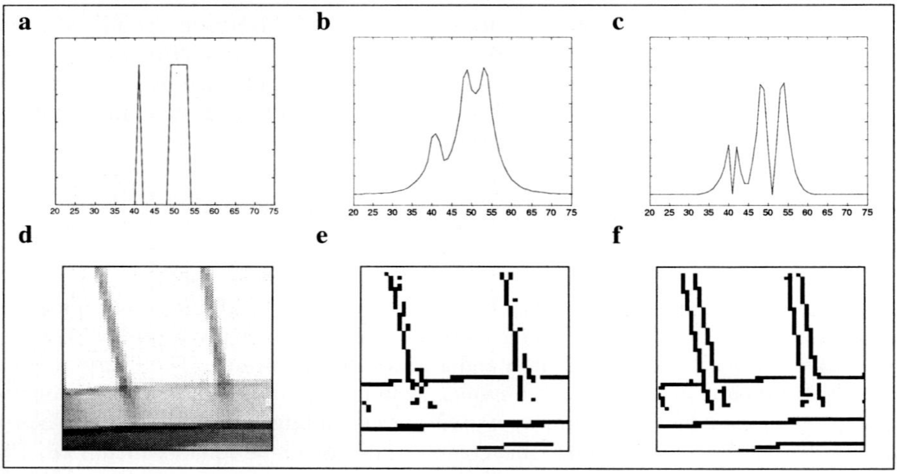

Fig. 1. Detection of step edges with odd and even filters. a): One dimensional intensity profile with a thin and a large bar. b): Energy profile using odd and even filters and c) using only odd filters. Odd and even filters are quadrature pairs, consisting of the first (for odd filters) and second derivative (for even filters) of a gaussian profile ($\exp(-x^2/\sigma_1^2)$) modulated by a gaussian profile ($\exp(-x^2/\sigma_2^2)$) in the orthogonal direction; eight orientations and nine scales, varying from 3 pixel/cycle to 18 pixel/cycle are used. The ratio of σ_1 to σ_2 was 1.2. d): A detail of an interior image. e): Step edges detected as local maxima using odd and even filters. f): Step edges detected using only odd filters

2 pixels of width (as those shown in Fig3a) is best obtained by using both small even and odd filters (see Fig. 3c), when the output of even filters dominate at the centre of the bar and the output of odd filters reduces and eliminates spurious maxima near the bar boundaries. If only even filters are used multiple maxima are detected, at the centre of the bar and at its boundaries, as shown in Fig. 3b. Therefore combining even and odd filters seems the best solution for the detection of thin bars, but it is not obvious whether it is convenient to sum the energy over a battery of even and odd filters with different orientations. The profile of the summed energy of the output of even and odd filters perpendicularly oriented to a thin bar (see Fig.3d) has one large central peak, correctly located at the center of the thin bar (see Fig. 3f). On the contrary, when even and odd filters are not perpendicular to the thin bar (see Fig. 3e) the profile of the energy has two smaller peaks (see Fig. 3f).

As a consequence summing over all directions is not advantageous for the detection of thin bars with a low contrast as those shown in Fig. 3g: the low contrast thin bar is better detected and localized when the energy only along the direction providing maximal response is considered (see Fig. 3i). When the energy is summed over all directions (see Fig. 3h) the low contrast thin bar is not well detected.

It is well known that edge detection based on the extraction of local maxima fails in the presence of trihedral junctions, such as those shown in Fig. 4a and edges are usually interrupted at junctions (see Fig. 4b). By appropriately combining the output

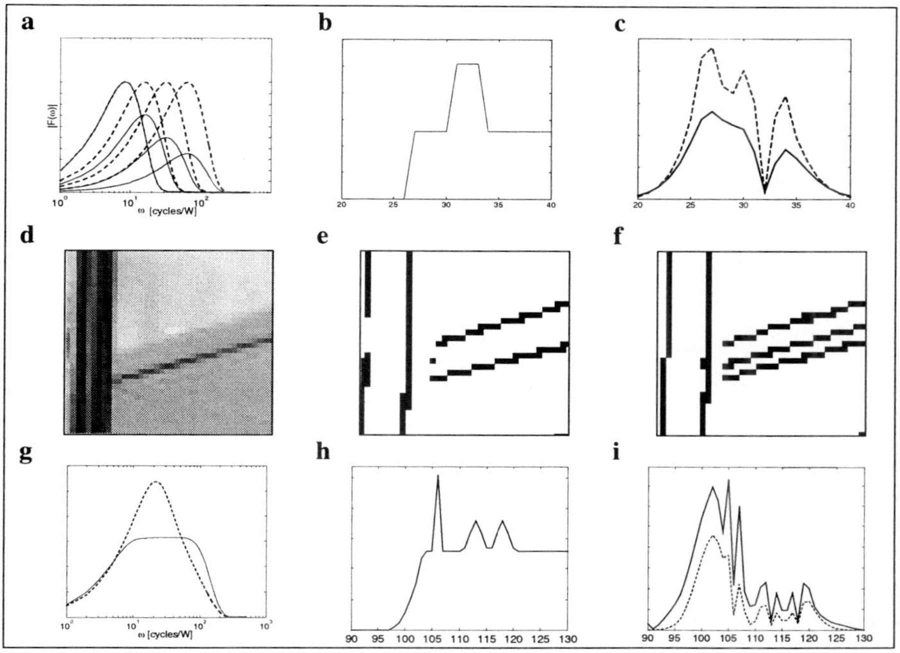

Fig. 2 Detection of step edge with filters at different scales. a): Fourier transform of filters at different scales normalized to the same energy (continuous lines) and to the same maximal response (dashed lines). b and c): one dimensional profile (b) and the corresponding summated energies (c) obtained for the two cases shown in a). d): a detail of an indoor image and the resulting edges summing the energy over filters with the same energy (e) and with same maximal response (f). g): Integral of the energy of filters at different scales providing an almost flat sampling of the image (continuous line) or with a broad central peak (dashed line). h and i): one dimensional energy profile (h) and the corresponding summated energy for the two cases shown in (g)

of V1-like filters it is possible to restore these important image features, which are inevitably lost using eq. (2). Trihedral junctions can be detected in several ways (Beaudet 1978, Dreschler & Nagel 1982; Kitchen & Rosenfeld 1982; Brunnstrom et al. 1992; Deriche e Giraudon 1993; Ruzon & Tomasi 2002), primarely by detecting regions of high curvature.

By using a modification of the method proposed by Kitchen & Rosenfeld (1982) high curvature regions are localized (Fig. 4c) where trihedral junctions are likely to be present: the output of even filters in the direction orthogonal to the local gradient is computed. End points of edge lines – in these regions – are detected (see Fig. 4d) and sides of trihedral junctions (see Fig. 4f) can be restored by analysing local polar plots (see Fig. 4e), obtained by comparing the energy of the output of suitable directional filters with a wedge like shape (Simoncelli & Farid 1996). This procedure is able to appropriately restore missing junctions (indicated by arrows in Fig. 4i) in the original edge map (see Fig. 4h) of a complex and noisy NMR image of a brain slice (see Fig. 4g).

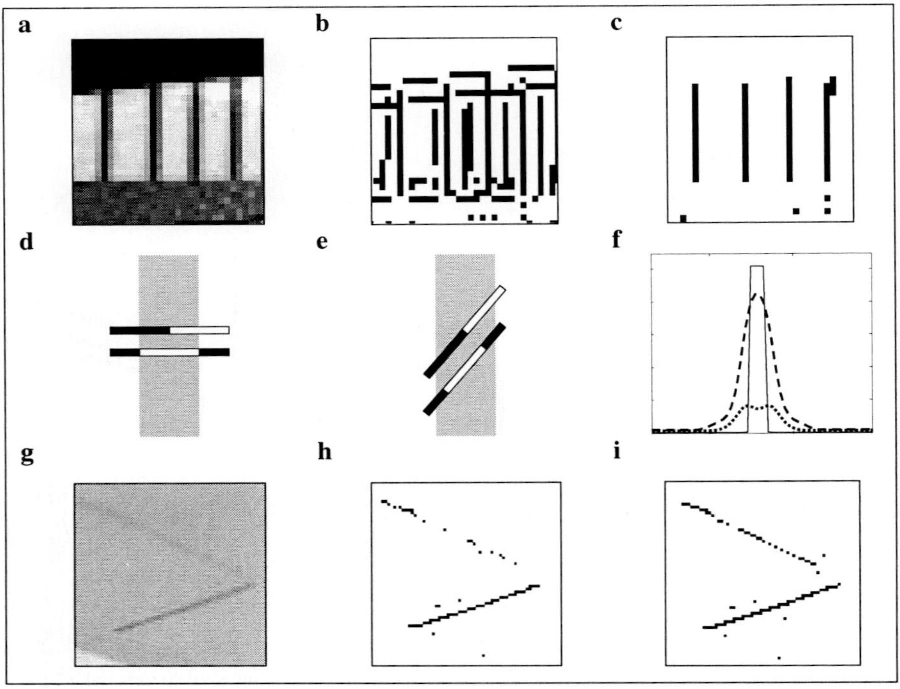

Fig. 3. Detection of thin roof edges. a): A detail of an interior image. b): Edges detected as local maxima using only four even filters. Filters have center wavelength in the frequency domain varying from 3 pixel/cycle to 8 pixel/cycle. c): Thin roof edges detected with even and odd filters with the same spectral properties. d and e): even and odd filters perpendicular (d) and oblique (e) to a thin bar. f): one dimensional energy profile (line) and the energy profile only along the direction providing maximal response (dashed line) and energy profile along an oblique direction. g): Another detail of the same image as in (a). h): Thin roof edges detected as local maxima of the energy summed over all directions. i): As in (h) but with the energy only along the direction providing maximal response

4 Regularization of Step and Roof Edges

Step and roof edges detected as described in the previous section are usually noisy and in order to be useful they have to be properly processed and cleaned. The simplest and most obvious way is to introduce a threshold on the local energy. This procedure is not satisfactory for the detection of low contrast edges in noisy images. Regularization procedures, based on the minimization of appropriate functionals, although computationally more complex and expensive, can provide a clean map of roof and step edges. First roof edges are cleaned by minimizing a newly proposed functional (see eq (4)) and secondly step edges and recovered trihedral junctions are cleaned by a modification of the classical Mumford and Shah functional (3).

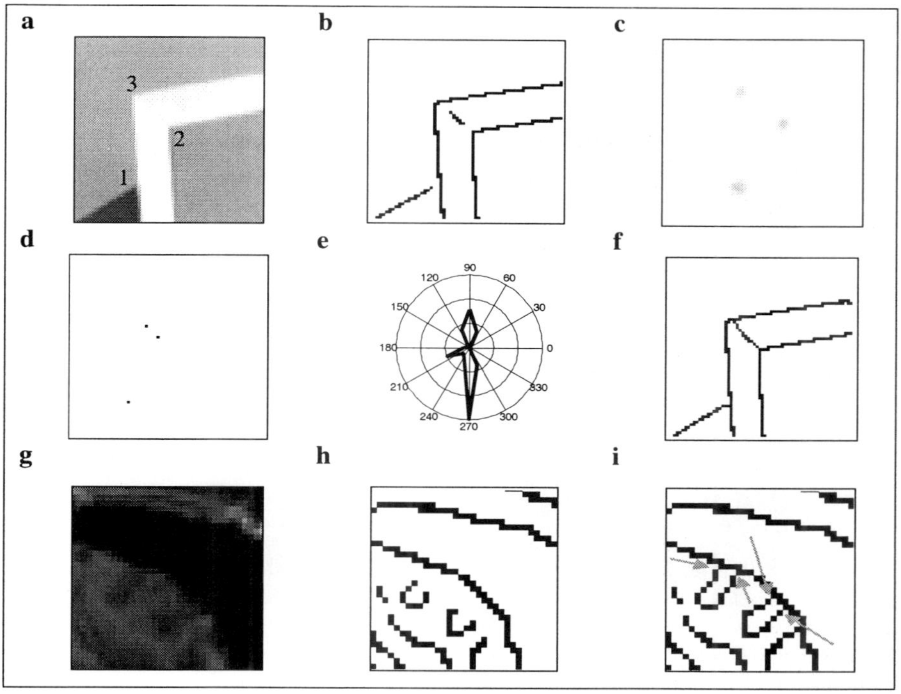

Fig. 4. Recovery of trihedral junctions. a): A detail of a cube. b): Detected edges. c): High curvature regions detected by combining the output of an odd filter with the output of an even filter in the orthogonal direction. d): End points of the edge map within the high curvature regions. e): Polar plot of the energy of the output odd filters at point 1. f): Restored sides of the trihedral junctions. g): NMR image of a brain slice. h): Detected edges. i): Restored junctions

The map of thin bars, detected as local maxima of the energy of the sum of even and odd filters in the direction of maximal output, as shown in Fig. 3i is usually noisy. Therefore, it needs to be cleaned and its broken segments must be restored.

This restoration can be obtained by the minimization of an appropriate functional (Vanzella, Pellegrino & Torre 2003). Let consider the collection R of connected roof edges previously detected, as illustrated in Fig. 3 and described in the text. A set of cleaned roof edges Γ formed by long continuous roofs can be obtained by minimizing the functional:

$$F(\Gamma, \bar{I}_{\Gamma(j)}) = \alpha \sum_{j} \left(\sum_{i \in \Gamma(j)} \left| I_i - \bar{I}_{\Gamma(j)} \right| \right) + \beta \sum_{j} HAMMING_{\Gamma(j)}(R, \Gamma) + \gamma Card(\Gamma) \qquad (4)$$

where j goes from 1 to $Card(\Gamma)$, i.e. the number of distinct continuous roofs of Γ, $\Gamma(j)$ is the set of pixel representing the j-th roof, I_i is the grey level of the i-pixel in the original image, $\bar{I}_{\Gamma(j)}$ is the mean grey value of the j-th roof, $HAMMING_{\Gamma(j)}(R,\Gamma)$ is the Hamming Distance between R and Γ and α, β, γ are appropriate constants.

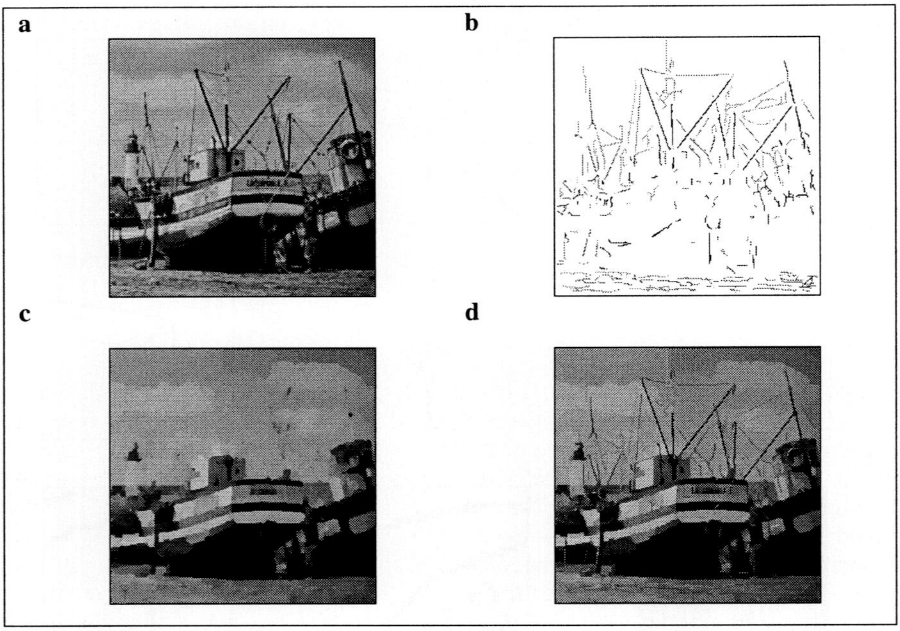

Fig. 5. Regularization of step and roof edges. a): The original image of 256 x 256 pixels. b): Regularized roof edges. c): The image segmentation obtained from the minimization of the functional (3) as described in the text. d): Regularized roof edges of panel b superimposed to the segmented image of panel c

The minimization of functional (4) is achieved by approximating the original set of roofs R, with a new set of roofs Γ, composed by a smaller number of continuous roofs (the term $\gamma\, Card(\Gamma)$), which is not too different from R (the term of the Hamming distance) and which have a constant grey value not too different from the original grey value (the first term in (4)). At the beginning $\Gamma = R$. The method of minimization proceeds in a greedy fashion trying to connect two roofs and/ or cancelling isolated week roofs. In this way isolated edges with a low contrast are eliminated and holes are filled obtaining continuous roofs. The regularization procedure assigns also to each continuous roof a mean grey value. Fig.5b illustrates regularized roof edges obtained from the image shown in Fig. 5a. These lines of roof edges usually have the correct location and grey level.

Similarly, the map of step edges detected as the local maxima of the energy of odd filters summed over all directions and scales is noisy and need to be cleaned. A set of clean and regular step edges can be obtained by combining the out put of directional odd filters into the regularization method of eq. (3). It is well known that the parameters α and γ in eq. (3) are related to the local scale as $\sqrt{\gamma}$ and to the local constrast as $\sqrt{2\alpha/\sqrt{\gamma}}$ (Mumford & Shah 1989, Morel & Solimini, 1995). Therefore by using the procedure proposed by Lindeberg (1998) it is possible to find the local scale and by analysing the output of directional filters at that scale the local contrast can be obtained. As a consequence the two parameters α and γ in eq. (3) can be tuned to the local scale and contrast. The local value of α and γ can be further modified so to cancel roof edges and preserve detected thriedral junctions and strong step edges (Vanzella et al 2003). The resulting regularized image is shown in Fig. 5c, where the image is segmented in extended and connected regions. The set of step edges k obtained by the minimization of the functional (3) represents an efficient way of cleaning step edges obtained as previously described and illustrated in Fig. 1 (Vanzella et al 2003). Regularized roof edges superimposed to the obtained image segmentation are shown in Fig. 5.

5 Discussion

In this paper three classical problems of edge detection are addressed: i – the detection of all step edges from a fine to a coarse scale; ii – the detection of thin bars, i.e. of roof edges; iii – the detection of corners and trihedral junctions. The solution of these problems is obtained by using an extensive spatial filtering, similar to that occurring in the visual area V1. The resulting map of step and roof edges is best cleaned and restored from noise by using regularization methods, based on the minimization of appropriate functionals, such as those in (3) and (4). The decomposition of the original image in a map of thin roof edges and in a segmentation of homogeneous regions, correctly preserving trihedral junctions represents in our view an almost ideal preprocessing and an adequate solution to edge detection, possible only by using the extensive filtering inspired by the receptive field properties of the first visual cortical area V1.

The proposed scheme uses a large variety of filters with different orientation, shape and size as already suggested by several previous works (Blakemore & Campbell 1969, Burr & Morrone 1992, Freeman & Adelson 1991-92, Kovesi 1999). However, it differs from previous approaches for two aspects. Firstly it combines the output of the extensive filtering in a regularization framework, provided by the Mumford-Shah functional (see eq.3) largely used in Computer Vision (see also Alvarez, Lions and Morel 1992; Nordstrom 1992). The regularization framework, based on the minimization of functional (eq. 3) with adaptive values of α and γ, provides a self adaptive threshold, necessary for a correct detection of edges with a strong and weak contrast over several scales. The local parameters α and γ depend on the outputs of V1-like filters, used for the detection of step and roof edges. Secondly, provides a distinct, but integrated, detection of roof and step edges. Roof edges are then cleaned and restored by the minimization of the novel functional (4).

The present paper also offers some suggestions how to combine the output of V1-like filters (Grossberg, Gove & Mingolla 1995, Grossberg & Raizada 1999, Hansen & Neumann 2001) for the best detection of step and roof edges and for higher order features, such as corners and junctions. Indeed step edges are best detected by combining odd filters with different orientations and sizes. On the contrary roof edges, i.e. of thin bars, are best detected by combining only narrow odd and even filters without mixing filters with different orientations. The combination of odd and even filters with different scales and orientations in a biological perspective will be discussed in more details elsewhere (Morrone, Pellegrino, Vanzella & Torre 2003).

Acknowledgments. We are indebted to Concetta Morrone and Gianni Dal Maso for many helpful discussions and useful suggestions.

References

Alvarez L., P.-L. Lions, Morel, "Image selective smoothing and edge detection by nonlinear diffusion", SIAM Journal on numerical analysis ", pp. 845-866, 1992

Anderson S.J. and Burr D.C., "Spatial summation properties of directionally selective mechanisms in human vision"J. Opt Soc Am A., Vol.8, No.8, pp.1330-9, 1991

Anderson S.J. and Burr D.C. "Receptive field properties of human motion detector units inferred from spatial frequency masking", Vision Res., Vol.29, No.10, pp.1343-58,1989

Beaudet P.R., "Rotational invariant image operators", in Int. Conference on Pattern Recognition, pp. 579-583,1978

Blakemore, C. and Campbell, F.W. "On the existence of neurones in the visual system selectively sensitive to the orientation and size of retinal images", J. Physiol. (London), No.225,pp.437-455, 1969

Brunnstrom K., Lindeberg T., Eklundh J.O., "Active detection and classification of junctions", Proc. of the Second European Conference on Computer Vision, Vol. LNCS 588, St. Margherita Ligure, Italy, pp. 701-709, 1992

Burr D. and Morrone M.C., "A nonlinear model of feature detection", in Nonlinear Vision, Determination of Receptive Field, Function and Networks, CRC Press, Boca Raton, Florida, 1992

Canny, J.F. "A Computational Approach to Edge Detection", IEEE Transanctions on Pattern Analysis and Machine Intelligence, No.8, pp.679-698,1986

Deriche R. and Giraudon G., "A Computational Approach to for Corner and Vertex Detection" International Journal on Computer Vision, Vol.10, No.2 pp. 102-124, 1993

Dreschler L., Nagel H.H., "On the selection of critical points and local curvature extrema of region boundaries for interframe matching", in Int. Conference on Pattern Recognition, pp. 542-544, 1982

Field D.J. and Tolhurst, D.J. "The structure and symmetry of simple-cell receptive field profiles in the cat's visual cortex", Proc. R. Soc. London B, No.228, 379-399, 1986

Freeman W.T. and Adelson E.H., "The design and use of steerable filters", IEEE Trans. on PAMI, Vol.13, No.9, pp.891-906, 1991

Freeman W.T., "Steereable Filters and Local Analysis of Image Structures", Ph.D. Thesis, MIT 1992

Grossberg S., Raizada R., "Contrast-Sensitive perceptual grouping and object-based attention in the laminar circuits of primary visual cortex", Tech. Rep. CAS/CNS TR 99-008, 1999

Grossberg S., Gove A., Mingolla E. "Brightness, perception, illusory contours an corticogeniculate feedback", Journal of Vision Neuroscience, 12 pp. 1027-1052, 1995

Grossman A. "Wavelet transforms and edge detection", in Albeverio S., Blanchard P., Hezewinkel M. and Streit L. (eds) Stochastic Processes in Physics and Engineering, pp.149-157, Reidel Publishing Company, 1988

Hansen T., Neumann H., "Neural Mechanisms for Representing Surface and Contour Features", Emergent Neural Computational Architectures, LNAI, pp. 139-153, 2001

Heeger D.J., "Normalization of cell responses in cat striate cortex", Visual Neuroscience, No.9, pp.181-197, 1992

Hegde, J. and Van Essen, D.C., "Selectivity for complex shapes in primate visual area V2", J. Neurosci. 20:RC, pp. 61-66., 2000

Hubel, D. H. and Wiesel, T. N. "Receptive fields and functional architecture in two nonstriate visual areas (18 and 19) of the cat", Journal of Neurophysiology, No.28, pp.229-289, 1965

Kitchen L. e Rosenfeld A., "Gray-level corner detection", Pattern Recognition Letters, Vol.1, No.2, pp.95-102, 1982

Kovesi P. "Image Features from Phase Congruency", Videre, Vol.1, No.3, pp.1-26, MIT Press, 1999

Lindeberg T., "Edge detection and ridge detection with automatic scale selection", International Journal of Computer Vision, Vol.30, No.2, 1998

Meyer Y., Wavelets - Algorithms and Applications, SIAM, 1993

Morel J.M. and Solimini S., Variational Methods in Image Segmentation, Birkhäuser, 1995

Morrone M.C. and Burr D., "Feature detection in human vision: a phase-dependent energy model", Proc. Royal Society London B, No.235, pp.221-245, 1988

Mumford D. and Shah J., 'Optimal aproximation of Piecewise Smooth Function and associated variational problems', Comm. in Pure and Appl. Math, No.42, pp.577-685, 1989

Nordstrom N.K.,"Variational edge detection", PhD Thesis, Univ. of California Berkeley,1992

Pellegrino F.A., Vanzella W. and Torre V. "Edge Detection Revisited:Filtering", 2003 in preparation

Robbins B. and Owens R., "2D feature detection via local energy", Image and Vision Computing, No.15, pp.353-368, 1997

Ruzon M.A. and Tomasi C., "Edge, Junction, and Corner Detection Using Color Distributions", IEEE Transactions on PAMI, Vol.23, No.11, pp.1281-1295, 2002

Simoncelli E. P. and Farid H., "Steerable wedge filters for local orientation analysis", IEEE Trans. Image Processing, Vol.5, No.9, pp.1377-1382, 1996.

Torre V. and Poggio T.A. "On edge detection", IEEE Trans. Pattern Anal. Mach. Intell., No.8, pp.148-163, 1986

Vanzella W., Pellegrino F.A. and Torre V., "Edge Detection Revisited: Regularization", 2003 in preparation

Venkatesh S. and Owens R.A., "On the classification of image features", Pattern Recognition Letters, No.11, pp.339-349, 1990

Wilson H.R., McFarlane D.R. and Phillips G.C., "Spatial frequency tuning of orientation selective units estimated by oblique masking", Vision Res., No.23, pp.873-882, 1983

Witkin, A.," Scale-space filtering", in Int. Joint Conf. on Artificial Intelligence, pp. 1019-1022, 1983

Improved Contour Detection by Non-classical Receptive Field Inhibition

Cosmin Grigorescu, Nicolai Petkov, and Michel A. Westenberg

Institute of Mathematics and Computing Science
University of Groningen,
P.O. Box 800, 9700 AV Groningen, The Netherlands.
{cosmin,petkov,michel}@cs.rug.nl

Abstract. We propose a biologically motivated computational step, called non-classical receptive field (non-CRF) inhibition, to improve the performance of contour detectors. We introduce a Gabor energy operator augmented with non-CRF inhibition, which we call the bar cell operator. We use natural images with associated ground truth edge maps to assess the performance of the proposed operator regarding the detection of object contours while suppressing texture edges. The bar cell operator consistently outperforms the Canny edge detector.

1 Introduction

In the early 1960s, an important finding in the neurophysiology of the visual system of monkeys and cats was that the majority of neurons in the primary visual cortex function as edge detectors. Such neurons react strongly to an edge or a line of a given orientation in a given position of the visual field [1]. The computational models of two types of orientation selective cell, called the simple cell and the complex cell, which were developed, gave the basis for biologically motivated edge detection algorithms in image processing. In particular, a family of two-dimensional Gabor functions was proposed as a model of the receptive fields of simple cells [2] and subsequently used widely in various image processing tasks, such as image coding and compression, face recognition, texture analysis, and edge detection.

The behaviour of orientation selective cells has turned out to be more complex than suggested by early measurements and models. In particular, the concept of a receptive field — the region of the visual field in which an optimal stimulus elicits response from a neuron — had to be reconsidered. This region is presently referred to as the classical receptive field (CRF). Detailed studies have shown that once a cell is activated by a stimulus in its CRF, another, simultaneously presented stimulus outside that field can have effect on the cell response (cf. Fig. 1(a)). This, mostly inhibitive effect is referred to as *non-classical receptive field inhibition*, and it is exhibited by 80% of the orientation selective cells [3]. In general, an orientation selective cell with non-CRF inhibition responds most strongly to a single bar, line, or edge in its receptive field, and shows reduced response when other such stimuli are present in the surrounding. In an extreme case, the cell responds only to an isolated bar or line. Such cells have been found by neurophysiologists: Schiller et al. [4] found many cells in area V1 which responded

H.H. Bülthoff et al. (Eds.): BMCV 2002, LNCS 2525, pp. 50–59, 2002.

strongly to single bars and edges but did not respond to sine-wave gratings. Similar cells were encountered by Peterhans and Von der Heydt [5]. This type of cell was called the *bar cell* and a computational model was proposed for it elsewhere [6].

The above mentioned neurophysiological behaviour of bar cells correlates well with the results of various psychophysical experiments, which have shown that the perception of an oriented stimulus, such as a line, can be influenced by the presence of other such stimuli (distractors) in its neighbourhood. This influence can, for instance, manifest itself in an overestimation of an acute angle between two lines [7], or in an orientation pop-out effect, Fig. 1(b), or in a decreased saliency of groups of parallel lines [8]. Figure 1(c) illustrates the latter effect, where the perception of a contour is suppressed by a grating.

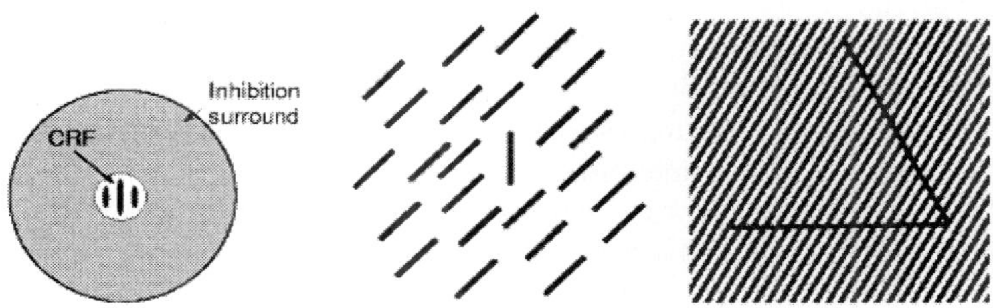

(a) (b) (c)

Fig. 1. (a) Non-CRF inhibition is caused by the surround of the CRF. (b) The pop-out effect of an oriented line segment on a background of other segments (distractors): the segment pops out only if its orientation is sufficiently different from that of the background. (c) The three legs of the triangle are not perceived in the same way: the leg which is parallel to the bars of the grating does not pop out as the other two legs.

In this paper, we examine the role of the non-CRF inhibition mechanism in the process of edge detection and its potential usefulness in image processing and computer vision. Our main hypothesis is that this mechanism suppresses edges which make part of texture, while it does not suppress edges that belong to the contours of objects. An edge detector which employs this inhibition mechanism will thus be more useful for contour-based object recognition tasks, such as shape comparison [9], than traditional edge detectors, which do not distinguish between contour and texture edges.

The paper is organized as follows. Section 2 describes the computational model. The simple cell and complex cell models and the related Gabor and Gabor energy filters are briefly discussed, and the bar cell operator is introduced. In Section 3, we evaluate the performance of the bar cell operator, and compare it to the Canny edge detector. Finally, we discuss possible extensions of the proposed model in Section 4.

2 Computational Model

2.1 Simple Cells and Gabor Filters

The spatial summation properties of simple cells can be modeled by a family of two-dimensional Gabor functions [2]. We use a modified parameterization to take into account restrictions found in experimental data [6]. A receptive field function of such a cell, in engineering terms the impulse response, $g_{\lambda,\sigma,\theta,\varphi}(x, y)$, $(x, y) \in \Omega \subset \mathbb{R}^2$, which is centered around the origin, is given by:

$$\begin{aligned} g_{\lambda,\sigma,\theta,\varphi}(x, y) &= e^{-\frac{\tilde{x}^2+\gamma^2\tilde{y}^2}{2\sigma^2}} \cos(2\pi\frac{\tilde{x}}{\lambda} + \varphi) \\ \tilde{x} = x\cos\theta + y\sin\theta, &\qquad \tilde{y} = -x\sin\theta + y\cos\theta, \end{aligned} \tag{1}$$

where $\gamma = 0.5$ is a constant, called the spatial aspect ratio, that determines the ellipticity of the receptive field. The standard deviation σ of the Gaussian factor determines the linear size of the receptive field. The parameter λ is the wavelength and $1/\lambda$ the spatial frequency of the cosine factor. The ratio σ/λ determines the spatial frequency bandwidth, and, therefore, the number of parallel excitatory and inhibitory stripe zones which can be observed in the receptive field. In this paper, we fix the value of the ratio σ/λ to $\sigma/\lambda = 0.56$, which corresponds to a half-response bandwidth of one octave. The angle parameter θ, $\theta \in [0, \pi)$, determines the preferred orientation. The parameter φ, $\varphi \in (-\pi, \pi]$, is a phase offset that determines the symmetry of $g_{\lambda,\sigma,\theta,\varphi}(x, y)$ with respect to the origin: for $\varphi = 0$ and $\varphi = \pi$ it is symmetric (or even), and for $\varphi = -\frac{\pi}{2}$ and $\varphi = \frac{\pi}{2}$ it is antisymmetric (or odd); all other cases are asymmetric mixtures.

The response $r_{\lambda,\sigma,\theta,\varphi}(x, y)$ of a simple cell at position (x, y) to an input image with luminance distribution $f(x, y)$ is computed by convolution:

$$\begin{aligned} r_{\lambda,\sigma,\theta,\varphi}(x, y) &= f(x, y) * g_{\lambda,\sigma,\theta,\varphi}(x, y) \\ &= \iint_{\Omega} f(u, v) g_{\lambda,\sigma,\theta,\varphi}(x - u, y - v) \, \mathrm{d}u\mathrm{d}v. \end{aligned} \tag{2}$$

The model used in [6] also involves thresholding and contrast normalization, but we do not need these aspects of the function of simple cells in the context of this paper. In image processing and computer vision, the filter defined by (2) is known as the Gabor filter.

2.2 Complex Cells and Gabor Energy Filters

The Gabor energy is related to a model of complex cells which combines the responses of a pair of simple cells with a phase difference of $\frac{\pi}{2}$. The results of a pair of symmetric and antisymmetric filters are combined, yielding the Gabor energy $E_{\lambda,\sigma,\theta}(x, y)$ as follows:

$$E_{\lambda,\sigma,\theta}(x, y) = \sqrt{r^2_{\lambda,\sigma,\theta,0}(x, y) + r^2_{\lambda,\sigma,\theta,-\frac{\pi}{2}}(x, y)}, \tag{3}$$

where $r_{\lambda,\sigma,\theta,0}(x, y)$ and $r_{\lambda,\sigma,\theta,-\frac{\pi}{2}}(x, y)$ are the outputs of a symmetric and an antisymmetric filter, respectively.

In the following, we will use Gabor energy images $E_{\lambda,\sigma,\theta_i}(x, y)$ for a number of N_θ different orientations, with θ_i given by

$$\theta_i = \frac{i\pi}{N_\theta}, \qquad i = 0, 1, \ldots, N_\theta - 1. \tag{4}$$

2.3 Non-CRF Inhibition

We now extend the Gabor energy operator presented above with an inhibition term to qualitatively reproduce the above mentioned non-CRF inhibition behaviour of most orientation selective cells. For a given point in the image, the inhibition term is computed in a ring-formed area surrounding the CRF centered at the concerned point, see Fig. 1(a). We use a normalized weighting function $w_\sigma(x,y)$ defined as follows:

$$w_\sigma(x,y) = \frac{1}{||H(G_{4\sigma} - G_\sigma)||} H(G_{4\sigma}(x,y) - G_\sigma(x,y))$$
$$H(z) = \begin{cases} 0 & z < 0 \\ z & z \geq 0 \end{cases} \tag{5}$$

where $G_\sigma(x,y)$ is a Gaussian defined by

$$G_\sigma(x,y) = \frac{1}{\sqrt{2\pi\sigma^2}} e^{-\frac{x^2+y^2}{2\sigma^2}}. \tag{6}$$

and $||H(G_{4\sigma} - G_\sigma)||$ is the L_1 norm of $G_{4\sigma}(x,y) - G_\sigma(x,y)$:

$$||H(G_{4\sigma} - G_\sigma)|| = \iint |H(G_{4\sigma}(x,y) - G_\sigma(x,y))| \, dx \, dy.$$

We model non-CRF inhibition by computing an inhibition term $t_{\lambda,\sigma,\theta_i}(x,y)$ for each orientation θ_i. This inhibition term is computed as a convolution of the Gabor energy $E_{\lambda,\sigma,\theta_i}(x,y)$ with the weighting function $w_\sigma(x,y)$:

$$t_{\lambda,\sigma,\theta_i}(x,y) = E_{\lambda,\sigma,\theta_i}(x,y) * w_\sigma(x,y) \tag{7}$$

We now introduce a new operator $\tilde{b}_{\lambda,\sigma,\theta_i}(x,y)$ which takes as its inputs the Gabor energy $E_{\lambda,\sigma,\theta_i}(x,y)$ and the inhibition term $t_{\lambda,\sigma,\theta_i}(x,y)$:

$$\tilde{b}_{\lambda,\sigma,\theta_i}(x,y) = H(E_{\lambda,\sigma,\theta_i}(x,y) - \alpha t_{\lambda,\sigma,\theta_i}(x,y)), \tag{8}$$

with $H(z)$ defined as in (5). The factor α controls the strength of the inhibition of the surround on the Gabor energy operator. If there is no texture in the surrounding of a given point, the response of this operator at that point will be equal to the response of the Gabor energy operator. An edge passing through that point will be detected by the introduced operator in the same way as it is detected by the Gabor energy operator (of appropriate orientation). However, if there are other edges in the surrounding, the inhibition term $t_{\lambda,\sigma,\theta_i}(x,y)$ may become so strong that it cancels completely the contribution of the Gabor energy operator, resulting in zero response of the operator introduced above. Notice that edges of the same orientation as the main stimulus will have stronger suppression effect than edges of different orientations. We refer to this type of suppression as *anisotropic* inhibition.

We now construct a new map $b_{\lambda,\sigma}(x,y)$ with values of maximum response of $\tilde{b}_{\lambda,\sigma,\theta_i}(x,y)$ over all orientations:

$$b_{\lambda,\sigma}(x,y) = \max\{\tilde{b}_{\lambda,\sigma,\theta_i}(x,y) \mid i = 0, 1, \ldots, N_\theta - 1\}, \tag{9}$$

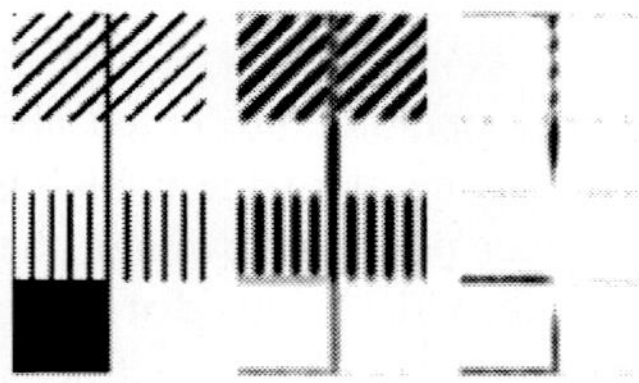

Fig. 2. (a) Synthetic input image. (b) The Gabor energy operator responds to lines and edges independently of the context, i.e., the surrounding in which these lines and edges are embedded. (c) The bar cell operator responds selectively to isolated lines and edges and lines that are surrounded by a grating of a different orientation. It does not respond to bars which make part of a grating.

and an orientation map $\Theta(x, y)$ with the orientation for which this maximum response is achieved:

$$\begin{aligned} \Theta(x, y) &= \theta_k, \\ k &= \operatorname{argmax}\{\tilde{b}_{\lambda,\sigma,\theta_i}(x, y) \mid i = 0, 1, \ldots, N_\theta - 1\}. \end{aligned} \tag{10}$$

The orientation map is needed in the binarization post-processing step, which involves nonmaxima suppression and hysteresis thresholding [10]. The operator defined by (9) will respond to isolated lines, edges, and bars, but it will not respond to groups of such stimuli that make part of texture grating having the same orientation as a bar of optimal orientation in the CRF, see Fig. 2(c). We will refer to this operator briefly as the 'bar cell operator', in analogy with the function of the type of visual neuron that exhibits a similar behaviour [6].

3 Performance Evaluation

Since the bar cell operator behaves as any traditional edge detector on isolated contours, bars, and edges, but behaves differently on contours in the presence of surrounding texture, we evaluate its performance on images representing objects on textured background. We selected a set of 20 images, and for each image, an associated ground truth binary edge map was specified by a subject.

3.1 Performance Measure

Let E_{GT} and B_{GT} be the set of edge pixels and background pixels of the ground truth edge image, respectively, and E_{D} and B_{D} be the set of edge pixels and background pixels of the operator-detected edge image, respectively. The set of correctly detected edge pixels is $E = E_{\mathrm{D}} \cap E_{\mathrm{GT}}$. False negatives, i.e. ground-truth edges missed by the edge detector, are given by the set $E_{\mathrm{FN}} = E_{\mathrm{GT}} \cap B_{\mathrm{D}}$, while false positives (spurious edges) are given by the set $E_{\mathrm{FP}} = E_{\mathrm{D}} \cap B_{\mathrm{GT}}$. We define the following measure of the *performance* of the edge detector as:

$$P = \frac{\mathrm{card}(E)}{\mathrm{card}(E) + \mathrm{card}(E_{\mathrm{FP}}) + \mathrm{card}(E_{\mathrm{FN}})}, \tag{11}$$

in which $\mathrm{card}(X)$ denotes the number of elements of set X. The performance measure P is a scalar taking values in the interval $[0, 1]$. If all true edge pixels are correctly detected and no background pixels are falsely detected as edge pixels, then $P = 1$. For all other cases, the performance measure takes values smaller than one, being closer to zero as more edge pixels are falsely detected and/or missed by the edge detector operator. Since edges cannot always be detected at exact integer image coordinates, we consider that an edge pixel is correctly detected if a corresponding ground truth edge pixel is present in a 5×5 square neighborhood centered at the respective pixel coordinates.

3.2 Experimental Results

We assess the performance of the bar cell contour detector, and compare it to the performance of the Canny edge detector [10]. This operator involves gradient magnitude computation followed by nonmaxima suppression and hysteresis thresholding [10]. We compute the gradient magnitude by convolution with the two directional derivatives of a Gaussian, as proposed in [11].

The Canny edge detection operator has three parameters: (1) σ, the standard deviation of a Gaussian smoothing kernel, (2) p, a percentage of candidate edge pixels which are retained in the final edge map, from which a corresponding threshold value t_h is computed, and (3) t, a fraction of t_h. The parameters p and t are used by hysteresis thresholding. The bar cell contour detector has an additional parameter α, which is the texture suppression factor.

For the Canny edge detector, we used eight scales, $\sigma \in \{1.0, 1.2, 1.4, 1.6, 1.8, 2.0, 2.2, 2.4\}$. For the bar cell contour detector, we used four scales covering the same domain, $\sigma \in \{1.2, 1.6, 2.0, 2.4\}$ and two texture suppression factors, $\alpha \in \{1.0, 1.2\}$. For both methods, we applied five values of p, $p = \{50\%, 40\%, 30\%, 20\%, 10\%\}$; t was fixed to $t = 0.5\ t_h$. This results in 40 parameter combinations for each of the methods. We used $N_\theta = 12$.

Figure 3 shows edge maps for some of our test images. The first and second column show the input image and the ground truth image, respectively, while the third, and fourth column show the results for the Canny edge detector and the bar cell contour detector, respectively. The result images shown in Figure 3 correspond to parameter values for which best results were obtained according to the performance measure introduced in (11). We also computed the percentage of false positives e_{fp} as the number of false positives divided by the number of correctly detected edge pixels ($e_{\mathrm{fp}} = \mathrm{card}(E_{\mathrm{FP}})/\mathrm{card}(E)$), and the percentage of false negatives e_{fn} as the number of false negatives divided by the number of ground truth edge pixels ($e_{\mathrm{fn}} = \mathrm{card}(E_{\mathrm{FN}})/\mathrm{card}(GT)$). The performance measures and percentages of false positives and false negatives are displayed below each image.

The results show that the bar cell contour detector indeed suppresses edges in the presence of surrounding texture. The second row (Goat 3) and third row (Gazelle) are very good examples of this behaviour. The example on the second row (Goat 3) shows also that the Canny edge map contains so many spurious edges that it is hard to distinguish

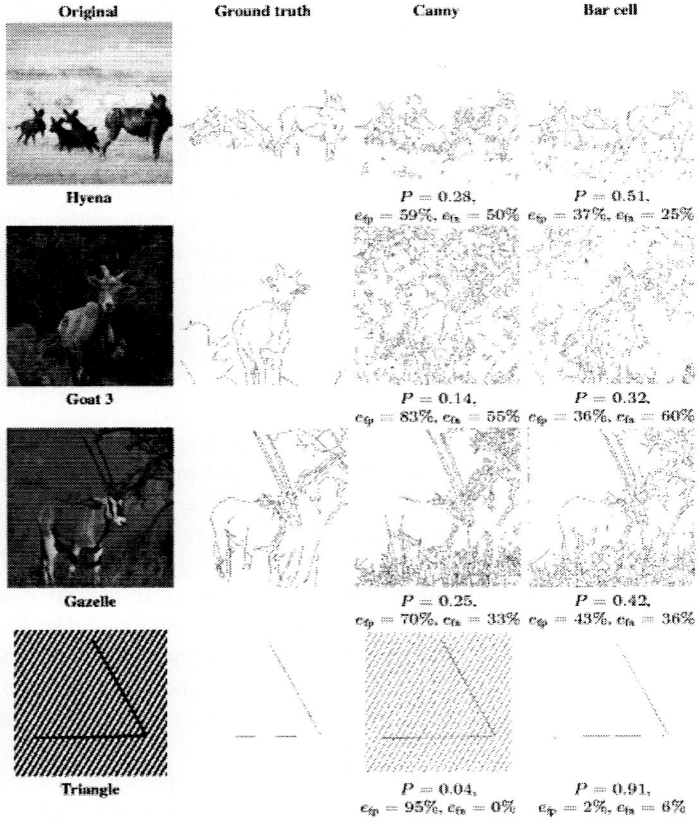

Fig. 3. Natural scenes with objects on textured background (first column), their corresponding ground truth edge maps (second column), edge maps obtained with the Canny edge detector (third column), and edge maps obtained with the bar cell contour detector (last column). Note that for a given image the best performance results (top end of the whisker) need not be obtained for the same combination of parameters of the two methods. The best performance result for the "Gazelle" image, for instance, is obtained at a finer scale (i.e. smaller value of σ) of Canny's algorithm than the scale of the bar cell operator.

the contours of the object. In contrast, distinguishing the object contours in the bar cell edge map can be done without difficulty. The performance measure is consistently higher for the bar cell contour detector (Fig. 4), and this is mostly due to a reduced percentage of false positives. This is in agreement with the proposed model of the bar cell: edges resulting from a texture background are suppressed, and object contours are retained. An interesting case is the synthetic image on the fourth row. The response of the bar cell operator agrees with our perceptual interpretation of the image: two lines superimposed on oriented texture.

4 Discussion

The non-CRF inhibition algorithm presented in this paper treats different classes of edges and lines in different ways: *single* contour lines and edges are not effected by the inhibition, since they are considered as non-texture features, while *groups* of lines and edges are suppressed, since they are viewed as texture features. The model of non-CRF inhibition we use in this study is simple and straightforward: the response of an orientation and scale specific operator in a given position is suppressed by the responses of the same operator in other positions outside the CRF. The model makes use of a single parameter α that is the coefficient with which the weighted summation inhibition term is taken into account. The value of this parameter can be determined in an optimization problem derived from a specific goal, e.g. maximization of the performance of the operator for a certain set of images. Actually, for almost all natural images used we obtained the best results with a value of α around 1. One can think of more intricate or general non-CRF inhibition models, such as the division normalization proposed in [12], where the inhibition weights of the responses of all orientation and scale channels and all positions are not fixed in advance but are determined such that mutual dependencies between the ultimate responses are minimized.

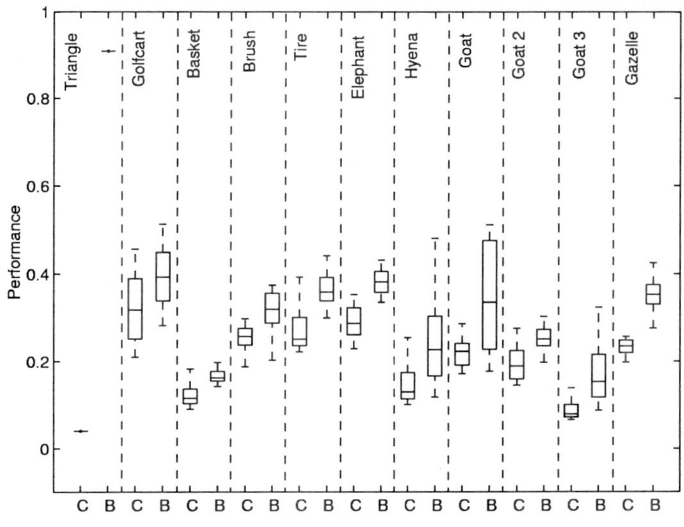

Fig. 4. Box-and-whisker plots of the performance of the Canny edge detector (denoted by C) and the bar cell contour detector with anisotropic inhibition (denoted by B) for some of the images used in our experiments.

Inhibition mechanisms have been applied previously to biologically motivated edge detectors in order to improve certain aspects of their function. A symmetric Gabor filter, will, for instance, respond not only along a line but also alongside the line at a certain distance from it. Similarly, the largest response of an antisymmetric Gabor filter to a line will be displaced from the line. In [13,14,15], various inhibition mechanisms have been proposed to remove these flanking responses. These works differ from the current work in two major aspects. First, the inhibition mechanisms act within the CRF. Second, the purpose of the inhibition is quite different: it deals with the removal of flanking responses, rather than with the suppression of texture edges.

In this paper we address an anisotropic inhibition mechanism only. However, there is physiological evidence that isotropic inhibition is equally important: approximately one third of the cells with non-CRF modulation exhibit anisotropic inhibition while another third are accounted for isotropic inhibition [16]. Elsewhere [17] we studied the effect of both mechanisms. For natural images like those shown in Figure 3 we obtain slightly better results using the isotropic inhibition, but perceptual effects like the ones illustrated by Figures 1(b) and (c) can only be adequately explained by anisotropic inhibition.

Applying inhibition on the Gabor energy may suggest that suppression takes place at the complex-cell level. The same inhibition mechanism can be applied to the Gabor filter output. This would correspond to suppression at the simple cell level.

The inhibitory term is computed by integrating in the surround of the response for a given preferred spatial frequency and orientation. This, however, does not mean that there will be inhibition only by gratings of that same frequency and orientation: within a certain frequency range gratings and textures of nearby orientations and frequencies will have an inhibitory effect as well. This range is determined by the band-pass characteristic of the Gabor filter [6].

Due to the limited space, various aspects could not be treated in this study. In this work we model only inhibitory modulations exhibited within the non-CRF. The physiological and psychophysical literature contains evidences for contextual facilitation as well [18]. Recent findings also show that the inhibition surround is not spatially symmetric, as suggested by our isotropic weighting function, but rather originates from particular sectors of the surround [19]. Other limitations of the current study are the fixed size of the inhibition surround and the limited range of the inhibition factor α. All these aspects are worth undertaking further investigations.

References

1. Hubel, D.H., Wiesel, T.N.: Receptive fields, binocular interaction, and functional architecture in the cat's visual cortex. J. Physiology (London) **160** (1962) 106–154
2. Daugman, J.G.: Uncertainty relations for resolution in space, spatial frequency, and orientation optimized by two-dimensional visual cortical filters. J. Optical Society of America A **2** (1985) 1160–1169
3. Knierim, J.J., van Essen, D.C.: Neuronal responses to static texture patterns in area V1 of the alert macaque monkey. J. Neurophysiology **67** (1992) 961–980
4. Schiller, P.H., Finlay, B.L., Volman, S.F.: Quantitative studies of single-cell properties in monkey striate cortex. III. spatial frequencies. J. Neurophysiology **39** (1976) 1334–1351
5. von der Heydt, R., Peterhans, E., Dürsteler, M.R.: Periodic-pattern-selective cells in monkey visual cortex. J. Neuroscience **12** (1992) 1416–1434
6. Petkov, N., Kruizinga, P.: Computational models of visual neurons specialised in the detection of periodic and aperiodic oriented visual stimuli: bar and grating cells. Biological Cybernetics **76** (1997) 83–96

7. Blakemore, C., Carpenter, R.H.S., Georgeson, M.A.: Lateral inhibition between orientation detectors in the human visual system. Nature **228** (1970) 37–39
8. Kanizsa, G.: Organization in Vision, Essays on Gestalt Perception. Praeger, New York (1979)
9. Belongie, S., Malik, J., Puzicha, J.: Shape matching and object recognition using shape contexts. IEEE Trans. Pattern Analysis and Machine Intelligence **24** (2002) 509–522
10. Canny, J.F.: A computational approach to edge detection. IEEE Trans. Pattern Analysis and Machine Intelligence **8** (1986) 679–698
11. Tagare, H., deFigueiredo, R.: On the localization performance measure and optimal edge detection. IEEE Trans. Pattern Analysis and Machine Intelligence **12** (1990) 1186–1190
12. Simoncelli, E.P., Schwartz, O.: Modeling surround suppression in V1 neurons with a statistically-derived normalization model. In Kearns, M.S., Solla, S.A., Cohn, D.A., eds.: Advances in Neural Information Processing Systems 11, Cambridge, MA, MIT Press (1999) 153–159
13. Heitger, F.: Feature detection using suppression and enhancement. Technical Report TR-163, Communication Technology Laboratory, Swiss Federal Institute of Technology (1995)
14. Petkov, N., Kruizinga, P., Lourens, T.: Lateral inhibition in cortical filters. In: Proc. Int. Conf. on Digital Signal Processing, Nicosia, Cyprus (1993) 122–129
15. Petkov, N., Lourens, T.: Interacting cortical filters for object recognition. In: Proc. of the Asian Conference on Computer Vision, Osaka, Japan (1993) 583–586
16. Nothdurft, H.C., Gallant, J., van Essen, D.: Response modulation by texture surround in primate area V1: Correlates of "popout" under unesthesia. Visual Neuroscience **16** (1999) 15–34
17. Grigorescu, C., Petkov, N., Westenberg, M.A.: Contour detection based on non-classical receptive field inhibition. submitted to IEEE Trans. Image Processing (2002)
18. Kapadia, M., Westheimer, G., Gilbert, C.: Spatial distribution of contextual interactions in primary cortex and in visual perception. Journal of Neurophysiology **84** (2000) 2048–2062
19. Walker, G., Ohzawa, I., Freeman, R.: Asymmetric suppression outside the classical receptive field of the visual cortex. Journal of Neuroscience **23** (1999) 10536–10553

Contour Detection by Synchronization of Integrate-and-Fire Neurons

Etienne Hugues, Florent Guilleux, and Olivier Rochel

LORIA, Université de Nancy 1, BP 239,
54506 Vandoeuvre-lès-Nancy, France
{hugues,rochel}@loria.fr

Abstract. We present a biologically inspired spiking neural network which is able to detect contours in grey level images by synchronization of neurons. This network is made of integrate-and-fire neurons, spaced on a triangular network, whose oriented receptive field is constructed by a wavelet which specifically detects edges. The neurons are excitatorily and locally connected between receptive fields that tend to detect the same contour. A contour, if its width is not too large, activates a chain of neurons, with some heterogeneity in the inputs. The capacity of a chain to synchronize with respect to such heterogeneity is studied. Synchronization on a contour is found to be possible for a sufficiently large width.

1 Introduction

Contour detection, or contour integration, is one of the perceptual grouping tasks our visual cortex carries out very efficiently. Psychophysical experiments for contour integration [1] have revealed that an association field governs how differently oriented contour elements could be grouped together to form a contour. The general problem of perceptual grouping poses the further problem of the underlying neuronal mechanism that supports it. It has been proposed that an efficient mechanism could exploit a temporal code such as neuronal synchronization [2,3]. This hypothesis has been supported by a series of experiments with cats [4,5], where synchronized neural groups were shown to be associated with a coherent stimulus. On the anatomical side, the primary visual cortex possesses cells (simple and complex cells [6]), which respond to an oriented stimulus. These cells are known to be laterally connected, which suggests that these connections may be the anatomical basis for contour detection/integration.

On the computational side, several attempts have been made to unravel the mechanisms by which orientation selective neurons could code for contours. Li [7] has studied, using a network of nonlinear non-spiking neurons, how the boundary between different regions induces a particular response of the neurons. Yen and co-workers [8,9] have demonstrated, using a biologically very realistic model, that synchronization occurs along a contour. Both studies have used specific connections, whose excitatory ones were mostly between neurons which tend to lay on a same contour. Choe [10] tried to understand how the connections of a

H.H. Bülthoff et al. (Eds.): BMCV 2002, LNCS 2525, pp. 60–69, 2002.

map of spiking neurons can self-organize to achieve synchronization in presence of a contour.

Though the model of Yen and co-workers shows that a contour can be coded by synchronized neurons, this mechanism was achieved using very complex neurons, which, from a practical point of view, precludes this model to be used for real images. From the theoretical point of view, this study raises the question of the existence of simpler models exhibiting similar properties, from which some insight could be gained on the synchronization properties of a given contour.

In this paper, we will try to define the simplest retinotopic network of locally connected and orientation selective spiking neurons which can achieve synchronization along contours. The above architecture is inspired by the layer $2-3$ of the cortical area $V1$. Our goal is to study the behaviour of the network relative to contour properties.

We will consider the kind of receptive fields of those simple cells which respond best to a single oriented edge, just as bar cells that respond best to a single oriented bar [11]. We will use the integrate-and-fire (IF) neuron model for its biological foundations, simplicity and capacity to synchronize. Similarly to the above mentioned studies, connectivity will be local between cells whose receptive fields tend to describe a same contour. What is far from biological knowledge is that only excitatory neurons will be considered, and that connectivity will be defined with this constraint.

In Section 2 we define a suitable edge detector and in Section 3 we study the conditions under which a chain of IF neurons with heterogeneous inputs synchronize. Then, in Section 4, we define the network and study its behaviour in the presence of a contour.

2 How to Dectect an Edge?

In general, contours in grey level images can be defined by a rapid variation of intensity occuring around some boundary. Extracting a contour consists in finding this boundary. As the contour will be detected locally, the only characteric of the boundary to consider, in the absence of corners, is its curvature, as any smooth boundary can be assimilated locally to its osculating circle. Furthermore, as receptive fields of neurons are small, at this scale, the boundary can be approximated by a straight line with a certain orientation.

Along the contour, the gradient of intensity is perpendicular to the boundary. For our analytical study, we need to define an idealized contour gradient, which can reasonably be given by a Gaussian integral. Around some point on the curve, if we define a local coordinate system (X, Y) whose Y axis is tangent to the boundary, one can write the local intensity profile l as

$$l(X) = l_0 + \frac{\Delta l}{\sqrt{2\pi}\sigma_c} \int_{-\infty}^{X} e^{-X'^2/2\sigma_c^2} dX' \qquad (1)$$

where l_0 is the value of intensity on one of the contour sides (the negative X side here), Δl is the jump across the contour and σ_c the characteristic width of the contour. When σ_c increases from a null value, the contour profile goes from a sharp step (Heaviside function shape) to smoother and smoother steps.

To extract such intensity profiles, one needs to localize the position and orientation of the step as well as possible, independent of intensity values on the sides of the contour, i.e. of l_0. One way to do this is to use an oriented wavelet ψ_σ where σ is the scale of the wavelet, whose integral cancels [12], making the result independent of l_0. The wavelet transform o of the contour is given by the convolution product of l and ψ_σ given by

$$o(x,y) = \int_{R^2} l(x-x', y-y')\psi_\sigma(x',y')\ dx'\ dy'. \tag{2}$$

The limit $\sigma_c = 0$ gives an indication for the choice of the wavelet: the derivative of the Dirac distribution along the direction perpendicular to the contour orientation is what we search. For a smooth contour, we will then take the derivative of a Gaussian in this direction. In a wavelet coordinate system whose y axis is along this orientation, this wavelet is

$$\psi_\sigma(x,y) = A\ x\ e^{-(x^2+(y/\gamma)^2)/2\sigma^2} \tag{3}$$

where A is a normalizing factor (see Appendix), σ and $\gamma\sigma$ ($\gamma > 1$) being the widths of the Gaussian in the x and y directions respectively.

Let's recall here that simple cells receptive fields are usually modeled by Gabor functions of the following form

$$g_{\sigma,k,\phi}(x,y) = B\ e^{-(x^2+(y/\gamma)^2)/2\sigma^2}\ cos(kx-\phi),$$

where, for $V1$ neurons, $1.7 \leq k\sigma \leq 6.9$ [13]. It is interesting to note that $g_{\sigma,1.7/\sigma,-\pi/2}$ is very close to ψ_σ, showing that the corresponding simple cells could serve as edge detectors.

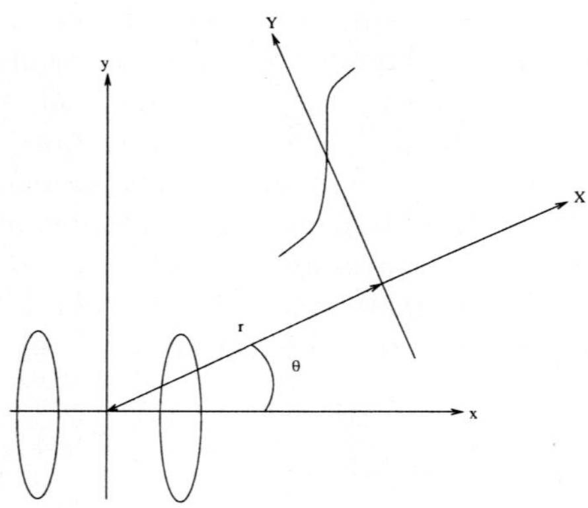

Fig. 1. The receptive field of a neuron and a contour passing by at the location (r, θ).

As neurons in the network will be activated by these output values o, it is important to predict them for any contour parameters. It can be shown (see Appendix) that for a contour passing at a distance r from the center of the receptive field of the neuron and making an angle θ with its preferred orientation (see Figure 1), the output o, defined by (2), is given by

$$o(r, \theta, \Delta l, \kappa) = \Delta l \frac{\cos\theta}{\sqrt{\chi(\theta, \kappa)}} e^{-r^2/2\chi(\theta,\kappa)\sigma^2} \tag{4}$$

where $\chi(\theta, \kappa) = 1+\kappa^2+(\gamma^2-1)\sin^2\theta$ and $\kappa = \sigma_c/\sigma$. The factor $(1+\kappa^2)$ appearing in (4), which is the minimum value of χ for a given contour, shows that the wavelet transform is wider than the contour profile, which is a general property of wavelet analysis. The output behaves radially as a Gaussian, decreases with θ and cancels for $\theta = 90$ degrees. For a given contour, the output is maximum when the position and the orientation of the latter and of the neuron receptive field coincide, and its value is

$$o_{c,max} = o(0, 0, \Delta l, \kappa) = \frac{\Delta l}{\sqrt{1+\kappa^2}}. \tag{5}$$

As the radial profile of the output widens and its maximum decreases with κ, the number of neurons activated in the direction perpendicular to the contour will increase: this indicates an upper limit of κ for the network to accurately localize the boundary (see figure 6).

3 Synchronization of a Chain of Integrate-and-Fire Neurons

We wish that neurons whose position and orientation lie on a contour synchronize. As the network discretizes space and orientation, these neurons, if connected, will form an heterogeneously activated chain. In this Section, after presenting the IF model, we will study the effect of this heterogeneity on the synchronization of a chain of IF neurons.

The IF model [14] is one of the simplest spiking models one can derive from biological neuron models, where only passive membrane properties are taken into account, a threshold mechanism being added for spike generation. The membrane potential v of the neuron obeys the equation

$$\frac{dv}{dt} = -v + i + \sum_{p=1}^{P} g_p \sum_k \delta(t - t_p^k) \tag{6}$$

where i is the applied current, and the last term is the total synaptic current, when the neuron is connected to P other neurons. Each synapse, characterized by a postsynaptic potential amplitude (or efficacy) g_p, transmits instantaneously the spikes emitted by a neuron p at times t_p^k, making the potential jump by an amount g_p. For excitatory connections, $g_p > 0$. The neuron will fire when its potential attains the threshold value $v_s = 1$, its potential being immediately reset to the reset potential $v_r = 0$. The neuron has a null refractory period so that the potential is insensitive to spikes arriving just after it fires. Between received spikes, the neuron simply integrates the current i. In the absence of synaptic currents, and if a constant current $i > 1$ is applied, the neuron fires regularly at the natural frequency $f = F(i) = -1/\log(1 - 1/i)$. When $i \leq 1$, the potential evolves monotonously towards a value under the firing threshold.

Networks of fully connected excitatory IF neurons are known to synchronize in the homogeneous input case [15]. In the heterogeneous case, and for more realistic synapses, synchronization has been found to be rapidly lost with increasing heterogeneity strength [16,17]. For local connectivity, the behaviour is less well known. In our case, heterogeneity can serve as a mechanism to form clusters of synchronized neurons when it is sufficiently low. The rules governing the formation of these clusters, or chains in our desired case, for nearest-neighbor coupling are not known. Only general results on phase-locked solutions have been obtained in the case of coupled oscillators in the phase approximation [18].

In our case, we will derive a sufficient condition for synchronization of a chain of IF neurons. Let's consider a chain of N neurons with nearest-neighbor coupling g, the neuron n having a natural frequency $f_n = F(i_n)$. In the chain, there are at least two neurons, say n_M and n_m of maximal frequency f_{n_M} and minimal frequency f_{n_m} respectively. Starting from some time t where all the neurons have emitted a spike synchronously, the next spike will be emitted by the neuron n_M at time $t + 1/f_{n_M}$. The propagation of this spike along the entire chain will instantaneously occur if the coupling g is sufficient to make their potential cross the threshold, that is, integrating (6), if

$$v_n(t + 1/f_{n_M}) = i_n(1 - e^{-1/f_{n_M}}) + g > 1$$

for every n. As F is a growing function, this condition is equivalent to one unique condition for the neuron n_m. If we define the dispersion in frequency as $(f_{n_M} - f_{n_m})/f_{n_M}$, it is found that, when $f_{n_M} > -1/\log g$, this dispersion has to be less than $\delta_f(f_{n_M}, g)$, where

$$\delta_f(f, g) = \left[1 - \frac{1}{f \log\left(\frac{1-ge^{1/f}}{1-g}\right)}\right]^{-1} . \tag{7}$$

If several neurons have maximal frequency, or if the chain is closed, this condition is only a sufficient condition. As shown in Figure 2, synchronization can be achieved for a reasonable frequency dispersion, especially at low frequency (see also [17]), or for large coupling.

4 Network Design and Behaviour

The network is made of a layer of IF neurons (cf. Eq. (6)) which are situated on a regular triangular grid whose dimensions match the image, this grid providing

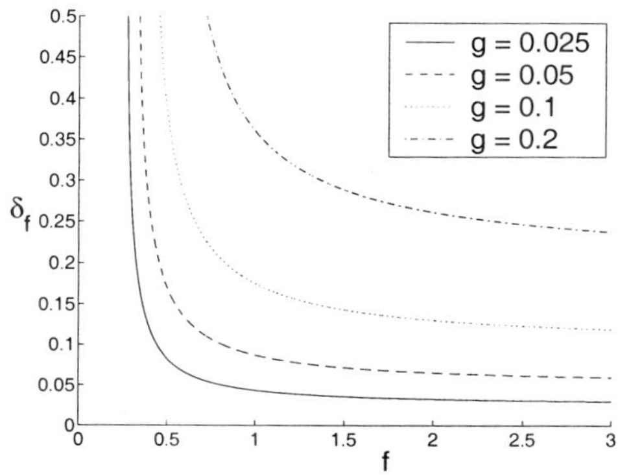

Fig. 2. Maximum dispersion in frequency $\delta_f(f, g)$ for automatic synchronization of a nearest-neighbor coupled chain as a function of frequency f, for different values of the coupling g.

the best symmetry properties. The triangle side length d is proportional to the scale σ of a receptive field. Six orientations, one every 30 degrees, are taken into account, half of them being parallel to the sides of the triangles. A neuron with a given orientation has excitatory and symmetric connections with only some of its nearest-neighbors whose orientation differ by less than 30 degrees, as shown in Figure 3. The choice of a short-range connectivity is due to the absence of inhibition in our present model: an increase in connectivity increases the size of the synchronized clusters.

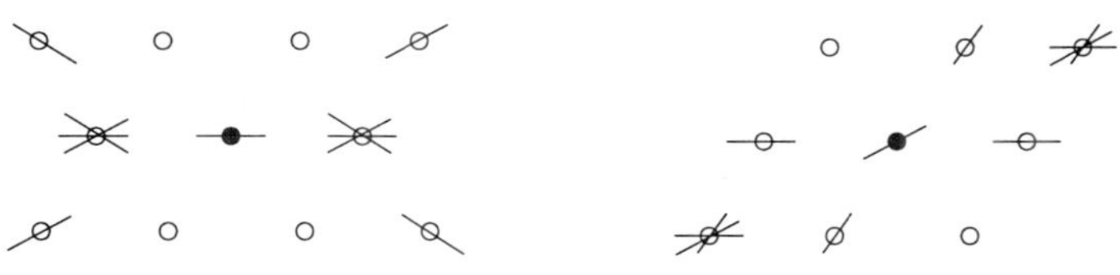

Fig. 3. Connectivity for an orientation along a triangle side (left) and otherwise (right). Neuron positions are indicated as circles and orientations as segments. A neuron (filled circle) with a given orientation is symmetrically connected to all its indicated neighbors.

For the preceding choices, and for $d < 2\ \sigma$, it can be shown that the chain made of the nearest neurons to a given contour will have a maximum output dispersion $(o_{c,max} - o_{c,min})/o_{c,max}$ less than $\delta_o(\kappa)$, where

$$\delta_o(\kappa) = 1 - \cos(15)\sqrt{\frac{\chi(0,\kappa)}{\chi(15,\kappa)}}e^{-\cos^2(15)d^2/8\chi(15,\kappa)\sigma^2}. \tag{8}$$

This value is obtained minimizing o in the domain of (r, θ) values characterizing the nearest neuron. As shown on Figure 4, δ_o is a decreasing function of κ.

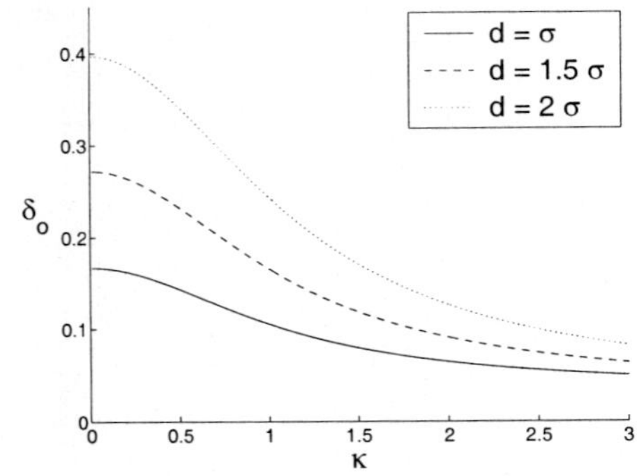

Fig. 4. Maximum dispersion of the output δ_o as a function of the contour width κ, for different values of the interneuronal distance d.

For simplicity, the natural frequency of a neuron is chosen to be a linear function of the absolute value of the output o, normalized in order to control the maximum natural frequency f_{max} and then the synchronization properties. More precisely, a neuron receives the following input current

$$i = F^{-1}(f_{max} o / o_{max}),$$

where o_{max} is the maximum output for the entire image. Due to the absence of inhibition, only one orientation by neuron position is activated, the one which receives the maximal output o. As the maximum frequency $f_c(\Delta l, \kappa)$ for a given contour scales with $o_{c,max} = \Delta l / \sqrt{1+\kappa^2}$, the maximum frequency dispersion δ_f increases with κ. The sufficient condition for the synchronization of a chain activated by a contour,

$$\delta_o(\kappa) < \delta_f(f_c(\Delta l, \kappa), g),$$

will then be, most of the time, fulfilled when κ is greater than some $\kappa_{min}(\Delta l, g)$.

The network behavior, with respect to κ, obeys the predictions: for small κ values, complete synchronization is not achieved, and for too large κ values, multiple synchronized chains appear, as it is the case in figure 6 *c)* and *d)*. The network can treat one (figure 5) or several contours at the same time (figure 6). From time to time, clusters made of chains with branches also appear, as in figure 6, due to the connectivity which excites more neurons than strictly necessary. It seems that independently of the connnectivity, such synchronized clusters will always exist, as they are very stimulus dependent.

5 Conclusion

The network defined in this paper appears to be able to detect contours accurately by synchronization of the associated neurons in a limited range of contour widths, defined relative to the width of the neuron receptive field. The complete

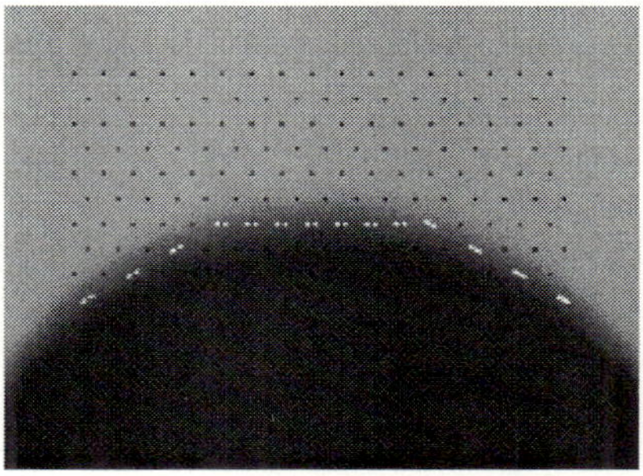

Fig. 5. Example of a synchronized chain of neurons along a contour, for $d = 1.5\ \sigma$, $\gamma = 1.5$, $g = 0.05$, $f_{max} = 0.5$ and for $\kappa = 1$. Points indicate the neuron locations and white segments represent the orientations of the synchronized neurons.

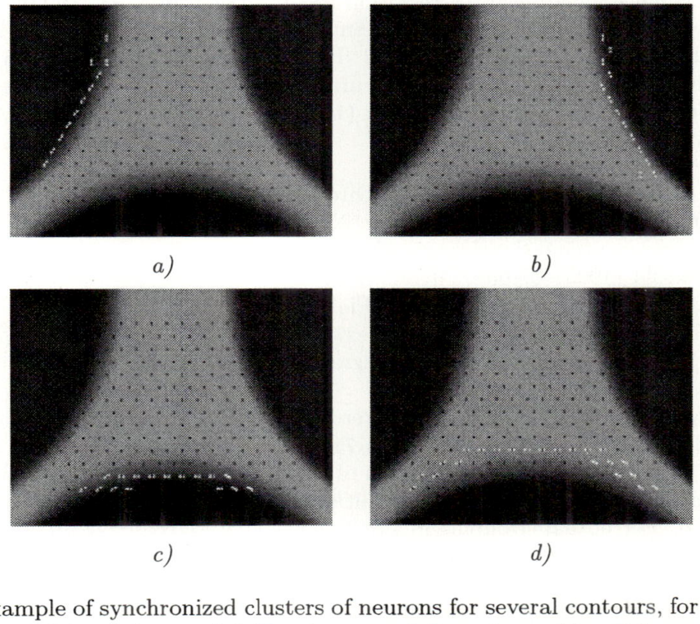

Fig. 6. Example of synchronized clusters of neurons for several contours, for $d = 1.5\ \sigma$, $\gamma = 1.5$, $g = 0.05$ and $f_{max} = 0.5$. For the upper left contour: $\Delta l = 100$, $\kappa = 1$. For the upper right contour: $\Delta l = 100$, $\kappa = 0.7$. And for the lower contour: $\Delta l = 150$, $\kappa = 1.5$. *c)* and *d)* show two different clusters for the lower contour.

width spectrum could then be covered by a superposition of such networks. An important property is that it can detects all contours at the same time. This study shows also that synchrony induced by a contour is a quite natural property of the network as long as connectivity obeys some precise rules. These conclusions are certainly more general as other receptive fields choices would have given similar results, and synchronization has been observed for other neuron models.

The synchronization properties of the network for the kind of contours considered here are due to the suitable choice of the wavelet/receptive field. Adding inhibition and redefining connectivity could make the synchronization on contours more precise and more reliable. In future work inhibition will be introduced both between different orientations at the same position and between similar orientations at locations along the perpendicular direction.

Acknowledgements. The authors would like to thank Alistair Bray and Dominique Martinez for numerous fruitful discussions, and the two anonymous reviewers for their comments.

References

1. Field, D.J., Hayes, A., Hess, R.F.: Contour Integration by the Human Visual System: Evidence for a Local "Association Field". Vision Res. **33** (1992) 173–193
2. von der Malsburg, C.: The Correlation Theory of Brain Function. MPI Biphysical Chemistry, Internal Report 81-2. Reprinted in: Domany, E., van Hemmen, J., Schulten, K. (eds): Models of Neural Networks, Vol. 2 of Physics of Neural Networks. Springer-Verlag, New York (1994) 95–120
3. von der Malsburg, C., Schneider, W.: A Neural Cocktail-Party Processor. Biol. Cybern., **54** (1986) 29–40
4. Engel, A.K., König, P., Singer, W.: Direct Physiological Evidence for Scene Segmentation by Temporal Coding. Proc. Natl. Acad. Sci. USA **88** (1991) 9136–9140
5. Singer, W.: Neuronal Synchrony: a Versatile Code for the Definition of Relations ? Neuron **24** (1999) 49–65
6. Hubel, D.H., Wiesel, T.N.: Receptive Fields, Binocular Interaction and Functionnal Architecture in the Cat's Visual Cortex. J. Physiol. (London) **160** (1962) 106–154
7. Li, Z.: A Neural Model of Contour Integration in the Primary Visual Cortex. Neural Comput. **10** (1998) 903–940
8. Yen, S.-C., Finkel, L.: Extraction of Perceptually Salient Contours by Striate Cortical Networks. Vision Res. **38** (1998) 719–741
9. Yen, S.-C., Finkel, L.H.: Identification of Salient Contours in Cluttered Images. In: Computer Vision and Pattern Recognition (1997) 273–279
10. Choe, Y.: Perceptual Grouping in a Self-Organizing Map of Spiking Neurons. PhD thesis, Department of Computer Sciences, University of Texas, Austin. TR A101-292 (2001)
11. Petkov, N., Kruizinga, P.: Computational Models of Visual Neurons Specialised in the Detection of Periodic and Aperiodic Oriented Visual Stimuli: Bar and Grating Cells. Biol. Cybern. **76** (1997) 83–96
12. Flandrin, P.: Temps-Fréquence. Hermes, Paris, 2nd ed. (1998)
13. Dayan P., Abbott L.F.: Theoretical Neuroscience : Computational and Mathematical Modeling of Neural Systems. MIT Press, Cambridge (2001)
14. Tuckwell, H.C.: Introduction to Theoretical Neurobiology. Cambridge University Press, Cambridge (1988)
15. Mirollo, R.E., Strogatz, S.H.: Synchronization of Pulse-Coupled Biological Oscillators. SIAM J. Appl. Math. **50** (1990) 1645–1662
16. Tsodyks, M., Mitkov, I., Sompolinsky, H.: Pattern of Synchrony in Inhomogeneous Networks of Oscillators with Pulse Interactions. Phys. Rev. Lett. **71** (1993) 1280–1283

17. Hansel, D., Neltner, L., Mato, G., Meunier, C.: Synchrony in Heterogeneous Networks of Spiking Neurons. Neural Comput. **12** (2000) 1607–1641
18. Ren, L., Ermentrout, G.B.: Monotonicity of Phaselocked Solutions in Chains and Arrays of Nearest-Neighbor Coupled Oscillators. SIAM J. Math. Anal. **29** (1998) 208–234

Appendix: Wavelet Transform of a Contour

We present here the derivation of Eq. (4). Let's consider the wavelet ψ_σ (see Eq. (3) and a contour defined by the intensity field $l(X)$ as in Eq. (1) whose position and orientation relative to the receptive field are r and θ (see Figure 1). In the wavelet coordinate system, the convolution product of l and ψ_σ can be written as

$$o(r, \theta, \Delta l, \sigma_c) = \int_{R^2} l(-r + \cos\theta x + \sin\theta y)\psi_\sigma(x, y)\ dx\ dy.$$

Integrating by parts in x, one gets the following Gaussian integral:

$$o(r, \theta, \Delta l, \sigma_c) = \frac{A}{\pi\sqrt{\gamma}} \frac{\Delta l}{\sigma_c} \cos\theta \int_{R^2} e^{-F(x,y)/2\sigma^2}\ dx\ dy \tag{9}$$

where, in matrix notation,

$$F(\mathbf{u}) = \tilde{\mathbf{u}} M(\theta)\mathbf{u} - 2\frac{r}{\kappa^2}\tilde{\mathbf{e}}(\theta)\mathbf{u} + \frac{r^2}{\kappa^2},$$

$\tilde{a}$ designating the matrix transpose of a, $\mathbf{u} = \begin{pmatrix} x \\ y \end{pmatrix}$, $\mathbf{e}(\theta) = \begin{pmatrix} \cos\theta \\ \sin\theta \end{pmatrix}$ and

$$M(\theta) = \begin{pmatrix} 1 + \frac{\cos^2\theta}{\kappa^2} & \frac{\cos\theta\sin\theta}{\kappa^2} \\ \frac{\cos\theta\sin\theta}{\kappa^2} & \frac{1}{\gamma^2} + \frac{\sin^2\theta}{\kappa^2} \end{pmatrix}.$$

M is symmetric, and can then be diagonalized by a rotation of the coordinate system. The rotation angle $\alpha(\theta)$ then verifies

$$\cot^2\alpha(\theta) = \frac{\cos 2\theta + \kappa^2(1 - \gamma^{-2})}{\sin 2\theta}. \tag{10}$$

In the new coordinate system, F no longer contains cross-terms, so the integral (9) can be split in two one dimensional Gaussian integrals. Finally, after some algebra, one obtains, for a suitable choice of A, the formula (4).

Reading Speed and Superiority of Right Visual Field on Foveated Vision

Yukio Ishihara and Satoru Morita

Faculty of Engineering, Yamaguchi University, 2557 Tokiwadai Ube 755-8611, JAPAN

Abstract. In this paper, we call the point on an object where human looks a subjective viewpoint and we call the point where the object and the straight line going through the center of pupil and the center of the fovea crosses an objective viewpoint. We realize eye movements in reading on the computer when an objective viewpoint is a subjective viewpoint and when an objective viewpoint is shifted to the right of a subjective viewpoint and we investigate the characteristics of eye movements. First, we realize a computer-simulation of human eye movements in reading. Secondly, the superiority of the right visual field appears in the foveated vision realized by shifting an objective viewpoint to the right of a subjective viewpoint. And we confirm that the gap between the subjective viewpoint and the objective viewpoint is important by comparing the characteristics of human eye movements to the characteristics of eye movements when an objective viewpoint is shifted to the right of a subjective viewpoint. Furthermore, we perform eye movements on the computer while shifting an objective viewpoint to the right of a subjective viewpoint and measure the speed at which an English sentence is read. We conclude that reading speed when the foveated vision has the superiority of the right visual field is faster than that when the foveated vision doesn't have it.

1 Introduction

Human eye movement in reading consists of fixations and saccades which are affected by the outer factors of letter size, letter shape, and letter color, and by the inner factors of the experience of reading and the difficulty of the sentence. Heller and Heinisch investigated the relation between saccade length and letter size, and the space between letters which were outer factors[1].Chung et al. and Nazir et al. investigated the relation between letter size and reading speed[2, 3]. Taylor investigated the relation between eye movements in reading and the experience of reading which was an inner factor. He reported that the longer the experience of reading, the more the number of fixations and the duration of a fixation per one hundred words was reduced and reading speed was fast[4]. It is difficult to investigate the relation between eye movements and the characteristics of the human eye which is an inner factor because we can't modify the eye's characteristics. We call the point on an object where human looks a subjective viewpoint and we call the point where the object and the straight line going

H.H. Bülthoff et al. (Eds.): BMCV 2002, LNCS 2525, pp. 70–79, 2002.

through the center of the pupil and crosser the center of the fovea an objective viewpoint. In this paper, We purpose to investigate the mechanism of the human eye. We realize human eye movements using a computer. We shift an objective viewpoint to the right of a subjective viewpoint and we investigate the effect of the gap between a subjective viewpoint and an objective viewpoint on eye movements during reading. A subjective viewpoint is usually the same position as an objective viewpoint. When human looks at a point on an object, the point is on the straight line going through the center of pupil and the center of the fovea and the point is projected to the center of the fovea. In the contrast, in the case that a subjective viewpoint is in a different position from an objective viewpoint, when human looks a point on object, the point is not on the straight line and the point is projected to the periphery of the fovea. In this paper, we perform eye movements in reading English on the computer in two cases that a subjective viewpoint is same position as an objective viewpoint and a subjective viewpoint is in a different position from an objective viewpoint. We investigate the characteristics of eye movements in these two cases.

At first, we realize human eye movements in reading English on the computer. McConkie, Kerr, Reddix and Zola reported the following two characteristics of human eye movements in reading English[5]. One was that the first fixation position in a word tended to be from the third letter to the fourth letter within the word[6,7,8]. The other was that if the fixation on a word was moved to left by 1 letter, the next fixation on a next word tended to be performed to left by 0.5 letter. The viewpoint used above shows a subjective viewpoint because the viewpoint monitored by Eyetracker used in their experiment is a subjective viewpoint. The viewpoint simply used below also shows a subjective viewpoint. Authors realized eye movements in reading English on a computer by using a foveated vision, the edge density of letters and the space between words[9]. The realized eye movements had the former characteristics. Furthermore, in this paper, we also incorporate the latter characteristics into eye movements in reading English.

Secondly, we simulate eye movements on the computer in two cases in which a subjective viewpoint is in the same position as an objective viewpoint and a subjective viewpoint is in a different position from an objective viewpoint. We indicate that the superiority of the right visual field regarding letter recognition[10, 11] appears in the foveated vision realized by shifting an objective viewpoint to the right of a subjective viewpoint. And we confirm that the gap between a subjective viewpoint and an objective viewpoint is important by comparing the reported characteristics of human eye movements with the characteristics of eye movements realized on the computer in the case that an objective viewpoint is shifted to the right of a subjective viewpoint. Furthermore, we simulate eye movements in reading on the computer while shifting an objective viewpoint to the right of a subjective viewpoint and measure the reading speed on English sentence. We conclude that reading speed in the case in which the foveated vision has the superiority of the right visual field is faster than that in the case in which the foveated vision does not have this superiority.

2 Simulating Eye Movements in Reading

In this paper, we use foveated vision based on following sampling model. We use the ratio of the number of sampled pixels to the number of pixels in an area as the resolution of the area. $Reso(x)$ is the resolution at a position being x pixels away from the center of the fovea and $Reso(x)$ is shown below using the sigmoid function,

$$Reso(x) = \frac{1 + \exp(-ab)}{1 + \exp(a(x - b))}(1.0 - 0.067) + 0.067. \quad (1)$$

Two parameters a, b depend on the decrease of resolution. $Reso(x)$ is 1.0 at the center of the fovea and reduces to 10000/150000≈0.067 on the periphery on account of the density of cones. The fovea image is generated by sampling every pixel in the original image according to the resolution at the pixel. The pixel where a resolution is 0.8 is sampled with 80%.

Eye movement in reading varies according to the outer factors of letter size, letter shape and letter color and with the inner factors of the experience of reading and the difficulty of the sentence. Even if human reads a sentence several times, eye movements always vary. But our eye movements in reading show similar behavior at all times. A viewpoint moves from the beginning of line to the end of it. When the viewpoint reaches the end of line, the viewpoint moves from the end of line to the beginning of the next line. Again, the viewpoint moves along the next line. Our eye movements repeat this processes. In this paper, we use following three processes to simulate this eye movements:

i Gazing at a word.
ii Finding the next word.
iii Finding the next line.

We explain the method simulateing these three processes using an attention region.

Process(i) is simulated by covering a word with the attention region. If the word in the attention region is recognized, Process(ii) is simulated. If the word is not recognized, a next fixation position is determined in the attention region. First, we rotate the attention region around a current fixation position to cover a word with the attention region and we calculate the number of edge pixels in the attention region rotated to every direction. The edge pixel is the that which determines an edge. We calculate the edge's value in every direction using the following equations, employing the number of edge pixels and the direction in which the attention region has moved.

We search the direction θ_1 where $V_1(\theta)$ is maximum and the direction θ_2 where $V_2(\theta)$ is maximum. We rotate the attention region to the direction θ_1 and θ_2. Then we calculate the number of edge pixels in a region while moving the region to the direction θ_1 and θ_2 in the field of view. The region has half the length of a letter and the height of a letter. We search the space between words where the number of edge pixels is 0 and we vary the attention region to cover a word.

Next, we recognize the word in the attention region. Nazir, O'Regan and Jacobs[13] calculated the probability of word recognition by multiplying that of every letter measured to the left and right of a viewpoint. In this paper, the probability of word recognition is also calculated by multiplying that of every letter in the word. In this paper, we regard the resolution of letter as the probability of letter recognition. The resolution of a letter is the ratio of the number of sampled pixels to the number of pixels in the region covering the letter. The word in the attention region is recognized according to the probability of the word recognition. If the word is recognized, Process(ii) is simulated. If the word is not recognized, a next fixation position is determined in the attention region. Determining the next fixation position is simulated by weighting edge pixels in the attention region and by selecting an edge pixel at random. In this paper, we regard the circle whose center is an edge pixel (i, j) and whose radius is 3 letters as the receptive field of $W(i, j)$. $W(i, j)$ is the weight of the edge pixel (i, j). The weight $W(i, j)$ is calculated by multiplying $W_1(i, j)$ by $W_2(i, j)$,

$$W(i,j) = W_1(i,j) \times W_2(i,j) \tag{2}$$

$$W_1(i,j) = \sum_{(i_1,j_1)\in M_1} (1 - Reso(r_1)) \tag{3}$$

$$W_2(i,j) = \sum_{(i_2,j_2)\in M_1 \cap M_2} \frac{1}{Reso(r_2)}. \tag{4}$$

M_1 is a set of sampled pixels in the receptive field of the weight $W(i, j)$. M_2 is a set of edge pixels in the attention region. r_1 is the distance between the center of the fovea and a position (i_1, j_1) and r_2 is the distance between the center of the fovea and position (i_2, j_2). $Reso(x)$ is the resolution at the position x pixels away from the center of the fovea and shown by equation(1).

In order to visually apprehend a word effectively, it is important to fix on the position where visual resolution is low and many edge pixels exist. We use two weights, $W_1(i, j)$ and $W_2(i, j)$: $W_1(i, j)$ is used to fixate the position where resolution is low. $W_2(i, j)$ is used to fixate the position where a lot of edge pixels exist.

Process(ii) is simulated by searching the space between words in the direction θ_1. We calculate the number of edge pixels in a region while moving the region to the direction θ_1 in the field of view. We determine the beginning and end position of the next word by searching the space between words. We then encompass the next word with the attention region and determine a next fixation position in the attention region. If the next word is not found, we judge that a viewpoint is at the end of a line and Process(iii) is then simulated. At this time, short term memory is used[14]. Short term memory stores the characteristics extracted from the fovea image at each fixation position when the viewpoint moves to the end of a line. An actual viewpoint on the sentence is at the end of a line while the viewpoint existing on the short term memory comes back to the beginning of a line.

Process(iii) is then simulated by searching the space between lines under a viewpoint. We calculate the number of edge pixels in a region while moving the region under the viewpoint by two lines. We find the next line by searching the space between lines.

Next, we confirm that the characteristics of human eye movements appears in the simulated eye movements. The parameters a and b stated in **2.1** are $a = 0.1$, and $b = 70$ respectively. The radius of the field of view is 200 pixels. We assume that a subjective viewpoint is same position as an objective viewpoint. First, we explain the characteristics of human eye movements. We then explain the characteristics of the eye movement simulated on the computer.

In the study performed by McConkie, Kerr, Reddix and Zola[5], subjects read an English sentence on a screen while their eyes movements were recorded. The researchers reported the following two characteristics of human eye movements based on over 40000 fixations. One was that the first fixation position in a word tended to be from the third letter to forth letter within the word. Figure 1(a) presents the proportion of first fixations at different letter positions within words of different lengths. The other was that if the fixation on a word was simulated to left by 1 letter, the next fixation on a next word tended to be simulated to the left by 0.5 letter.

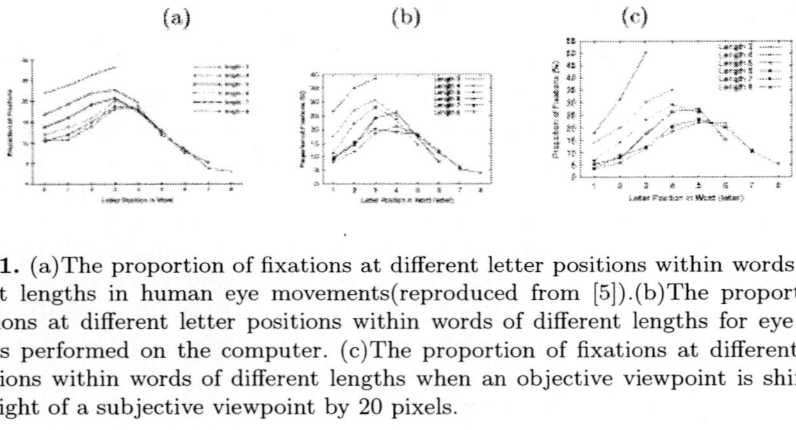

Fig. 1. (a)The proportion of fixations at different letter positions within words of different lengths in human eye movements(reproduced from [5]).(b)The proportion of fixations at different letter positions within words of different lengths for eye movements performed on the computer. (c)The proportion of fixations at different letter positions within words of different lengths when an objective viewpoint is shifted to the right of a subjective viewpoint by 20 pixels.

We simulated eye movements in reading English on the computer over 40000 times. The sentence used in experiment consists of letters having a length of 12 pixels and a height of 24 pixels. First, we explain the proportion of first fixations at different letter positions within words in the case of $W(i,j) = W_1(i,j), W(i,j) = W_2(i,j)$ and $W(i,j) = W_1(i,j) \times W_2(i,j)$ respectively. In the case of $W(i,j) = W_2(i,j)$, the proportion of first fixations was was high at the first and second letters of words having three or four letters, and was high at the fourth and fifth letters of words having from six to eight letters. The characteristics of human eye movements didn't appear in eye movements based on $W(i,j) = W_2(i,j)$. In the case of $W(i,j) = W_1(i,j)$ and $W(i,j) = W_1(i,j) \times W_2(i,j)$, the proportion of first fixations was high at the third and forth letter within words and the characteristics of human eye movements appeared in the simulated eye movements. Figure 1(2) presents the proportion of first fixations at different letter positions within words of different lengths in the case of $W(i,j) = W_1(i,j) \times W_2(i,j)$.

Next, we explain the relationship between the fixation position prior to saccade to a next word and the first fixation position in the next word in the case of $W(i,j) = W_1(i,j)$ and $W(i,j) = W_1(i,j) \times W_2(i,j)$ respectively. The slope of the regression line showing this relationship was from 0.75 to 1.14 with an average of 0.99 in the case of $W(i,j) = W_1(i,j)$. The slope of the regression line showing the relationship was from 0.51 to 0.81 and with an average of 0.63 in the case of $W(i,j) = W_1(i,j) \times W_2(i,j)$. The slope of the regression line showing the relationship approaches 0.49 by using $W(i,j) = W_1(i,j) \times W_2(i,j)$.

Therefore, it was confirmed that the two basic characteristics of human eye movements appeared in eye movements based on $W(i,j) = W_1(i,j) \times W_2(i,j)$.

3 Superiority of the Right Visual Field Due to the Gap between Subjective Viewpoint and Objective Viewpoint

The subjects were asked to look at a string consisting of 9 letters displayed on the screen for 20ms and to inform whether a prespecified letter was in the string by pressing a response key. Nazir, O'Regan, and Jacobs[13] investigated the relation between the frequency of recognition of the prespecified letter and the distance between a viewpoint and the letter. The more a letter was away from a viewpoint, the more the probability of the letter recognition decreased. They reported that the decrease of the probability of letter recognition to the left of a viewpoint was 1.8 times as large as the decrease of that to the right of a viewpoint.

The probability of letter recognition at different positions to a left and right of a viewpoint is measured when an objective viewpoint is shifted to the right of a subjective viewpoint by 12 pixels. A subjective viewpoint is at letter position 0. Because the resolution at an objective viewpoint is 1.0, if an objective viewpoint is shifted to the right of a subjective viewpoint, the resolution at the subjective viewpoint is lower than 1.0. The position where a resolution is 1.0 exists to the right of the subjective viewpoint. Therefore, the probability of letter recognition to the right of a subjective viewpoint is higher than that to left of a subjective viewpoint. And the superiority of the right visual field regarding letter recognition appears.

4 Optimal Viewing Position Effect and Change of Reading Speed by Superiority of the Right Visual Field

In this section, we simulate eye movements on the computer using foveated vision having the superiority of the right visual field. We also investigate an optimal viewing position.

Subjects were asked to look at a test word and a comparison word consisting of from 5 to 11 letters displayed on a screen in a way that the first fixation was on the test word, and then to inform whether the two words were the same by pressing a response key. O'Regan, Lévy-Schoen, Pynte, and Brugaillére measured the time spent for a viewpoint to move to the comparison word from the test word. They reported that the time depended on the first fixation position in the test word and that the optimal viewing position where the time was the shortest existed within words of different lengths[15]. This phenomenon is called the optimal viewing position effect[16,17,18,19]. Figure 2(1) presents the relation between the first fixation position in a test word and the time spent for a viewpoint to move to a comparison word. The horizontal axis shows the letter positions in a test word and the vertical axis shows the mean time spent for a viewpoint to move to a comparison word. As shown in Figure 2(1), the effect appears as a J-shaped curve, and the optimal viewing position is slightly to the left side within words. Nazir, O'Regan, and Jacobs reported that the factor determining that the optimal viewing position was slightly in the left side within words was that the probability of letter recognition to left of the viewpoint was lower than that to the right of the viewpoint[13].

We performed eye movements in reading English on the computer over 10000 times when a subjective viewpoint was at same position as an objective viewpoint and when an objective viewpoint was shifted to the right of a subjective viewpoint. And we examined the optimal viewing position effects. Figure 2(2) presents the optimal viewing position effect when a subjective viewpoint is in the same position as an objective viewpoint and when an objective viewpoint is shifted to the right of a subjective viewpoint by 12 pixels. In Figure 2(2)(a), the effect appears as a U-shaped curve and the optimal viewing position is at the center of words. In Figure 2(2)(b), the effect appears as a J-shaped curve and the optimal viewing position is slightly to the left within words.

The effect of the optimal viewing position appears as a J-shaped curve in Figure 2(1) and Figure 2(2)(b). The effect of the optimal viewing position on human eye movement is simulated on the computer, thus demonstrating that the gap between a subjective viewpoint and an objective viewpoint plays an important role in the effect of the optimal viewing position of human eye movement.

Next, we performed eye movements in reading on the computer over 10000 times while shifting an objective viewpoint to the right of a subjective viewpoint 2 by 2 pixels from -4 to 20 pixels, and measured reading speed. Figure 3 presents the change of reading speed by the distance between a subjective viewpoint and an objective viewpoint. The horizontal axis shows the distance between a subjective viewpoint and an objective viewpoint. The vertical axis shows the mean time in which a viewpoint stays on a word. As shown in Figure 3, the more an objective viewpoint is away from a subjective viewpoint, the faster reading speed.

We consider the phenomenon in which reading speed is increased by shifting an objective viewpoint to the right of a subjective viewpoint. Figure 2(3) presents the optimal viewing position effect in reading when a subjective viewpoint is in

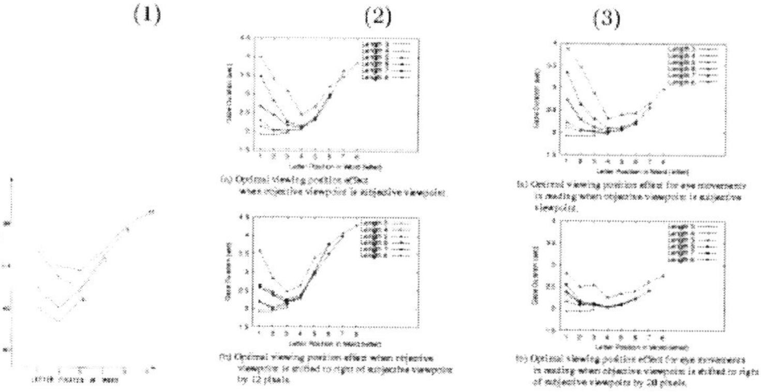

Fig. 2. (1)Optimal viewing position effect of human eye movements(reproduced from [15]).(2)Optimal viewing position effect. (a) A subjective viewpoint is in the same position as an objective viewpoint. (b) An objective viewpoint is shifted to the right of a subjective viewpoint by 12 pixels.(3)Optimal viewing position effect of eye movements in reading. (a) A subjective viewpoint is in the same position as an objective viewpoint. (b) An objective viewpoint is shifted to the right of a subjective viewpoint by 20 pixels.

the same position as an objective viewpoint and when an objective viewpoint is shifted to the right of a subjective viewpoint by 20 pixels. The optimal viewing position in reading tends to be on the right side within words because a next word is visible when a viewpoint stays on a word. A comparison of Figure 2(3)(a) with Figure 2(3)(b) shows that the time in which a viewpoint stays on a word shortens at the beginning of words by shifting an objective viewpoint to the right of a subjective viewpoint. This is because the probability of letter recognition to the right of a subjective viewpoint increases in relation that to the left of a subjective viewpoint by shifting an objective viewpoint to the right of a subjective viewpoint, and the position where the probability of word recognition is the highest moves to the beginning of words. Figure 1(2) and Figure 1(3) present the proportion of first fixations at different letter positions within words when a subjective viewpoint is in the same position as an objective viewpoint and when an objective viewpoint is shifted to the right of a subjective viewpoint by 20 pixels, respectively. We compare Figure 1(2) with Figure 1(3) demonstrates that the proportion of first fixations increases at the ends of words by shifting an objective viewpoint to the right of a subjective viewpoint. This is because the resolution at the right position of a subjective viewpoint increases and the weight $W(i,j)$ at it gets small by shifting an objective viewpoint, and the viewpoint doesn't move close to a current fixation position but moves to the end of a next word that is distant to the current fixation position. Therefore, the position where the proportion of first fixations is high moves to the end of words and the optimal viewing position moves to the beginning of words by shifting an objective viewpoint to the right of a subjective viewpoint. As a result, the time in which a viewpoint stays on a word decreased short at the position where the proportion of first fixations is high and reading speed increased.

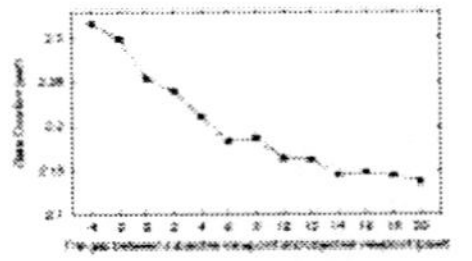

Fig. 3. The change of reading speed depending on the gap between a subjective viewpoint and an objective viewpoint.

5 Conclusion

In this paper, we simulated eye movements in reading English on the computer in order to investigate the characteristics of eye movement in the case that a subjective viewpoint was in the same position as an objective viewpoint and a subjective viewpoint was in a different position from an objective viewpoint. We first confirmed that two characteristics of human eye movements appeared in the simulated eye movements. One was that the first fixation position in a word tended to be from the third letter to the fourth letter within a word. The other was that if the fixation on a word was placed to the left by 1 letter, the next fixation on a next word tended to be placed to the left by 0.5 letter.

Secondly, we confirmed the superiority of the right visual field in letter recognition in foveated vision by shifting an objective viewpoint to the right of a subjective viewpoint. We then compared the optimal viewing position effect of eye movements in the case that an objective viewpoint was shifted to the right of a subjective viewpoint with that of human eye movements. We indicated that the gap between a subjective viewpoint and an objective viewpoint was important for the characteristics of human eye movements to appear. Furthermore, we measured reading speed while shifting an objective viewpoint to the right of a subjective viewpoint. We also indicated that reading speed in the case in which the foveated vision had the superiority of the right visual field was faster than reading speed in the case in which the foveated vision did not have this superiority.

References

1. Dieter Heller, Annelies Heinisch,Eye movement parameters in reading: effects of letter size and letter spacing, Eye Movements and Human Information Processing, pp. 173–182, 1985.
2. Chung, S. T. L., Mansfield, J. S., and Legge, G. E., Psychophysics of reading. XVIII. The effect of print size on reading speed in normal peripheral vision. Vision Research, 38, pp. 2949–2962, pp. 1998.

3. Nazir, T. A., Jacobs, A., and O'Regan, J. K., Letter legibility and visual word recognition. Memory and Cognition, 26, 810–821, 1998.
4. Taylor, S. E.Eye movements in reading: facts and fallacies, American Educational Research Journal, 2, pp. 187–202, 1965.
5. McConkie, G. W., Kerr, P. W., Reddix, M. D., and Zola, D., Eye movement control during reading: I. the location of initial eye fixations on words. Vision Research, 28(10), 1107–1118, 1988.
6. O'Regan K., Theconvenient viewing position hypothesis. In Eye Movements: Cognition and Visual Perception (Edited by Fisher D. F. Monty R. W.), pp. 289–298. Erlbaum, Hillsdale, NJ, 1981.
7. Rayner K., Eye guidance in reading: fixation locations with words. Perception 8, pp. 21–30 1979.
8. Zola D., Redundancy and word perception during reading. Percept. Psychophys. 36, pp. 277–284,1984.
9. Yukio Ishihara, Satoru Morita,Computation model of eye movement in reading using foveated vision, BMCV2000, pp. 108–117, 2000.
10. Bouma, H., Visual interference in the parafoveal recognition of initial and final letters of words. Vision Research, 13, pp. 767–782, 1973.
11. Bouma, H., and Legein, C. P., Foveal and parafoveal recognition of letters and words by dyslexics and by average readers. Neuropsychologia, 15, pp. 69–80, 1977.
12. M. H. Pirenne,Vision and the eye, 2nd ed., Chapman and Hall, London, 1967.
13. Nazir, T. A., O'Regan, J. k.,and Jacobs, A. M.On words and their letters, Bulletin of the Psychonomics Society, 29, pp. 171–174, 1991.
14. Satoru Morita, Simulating Eye Movement in Reading using Short-term Memory, proc. of Vision Interface 2002, pp. 206–212, 2002.
15. O'Regan, J. K., Lévy-Schoen, A., Pynte, J., and Brugaillére, B., Convenient fixation location within isolated words of different length and structure, Journal of Experimental Psychology : Human Perception and Performance, 10, pp. 250–257, 1984.
16. McConkie, G. W., Kerr, P. W., Reddix, M. D., Zola, D., and Jacobs, A. M., Eye movement control during reading: II. Frequency of refixating a word. Perception and Psychophysics, 46, pp. 245–253, 1989.
17. O'Regan, J. K., and Lévy-Schoen, A., Eye movement strategy and tactics in word recognition and reading. In M. Coltheart, Attention and performance XII: The psychology of reading (pp. 363–383). Hillsdale, NJ: Erlbaum, 1987.
18. O'Regan, J. K., and Jacobs, A. M., The optimal viewing position effect in word recognition: A challenge to current theory. Journal of Experimental Psychology: Human Perception and Performance, 18, pp. 185–197, 1992.
19. Vitu, F., O'Regan, J. K., and Mittau, M., Optimal landing position in reading isolated words and continuous text. Perception and Psychophysics, 47, pp. 583–600, 1990.

A Model of Contour Integration in Early Visual Cortex

T. Nathan Mundhenk and Laurent Itti

University of Southern California, Computer Science Department
Los Angles, California, 90089-2520, USA – `http://iLab.usc.edu`

Abstract. We have created an algorithm to integrate contour elements and find the salience value of them. The algorithm consists of basic long-range orientation specific neural connections as well as a novel group suppression gain control and a fast plasticity term to explain interaction beyond a neurons normal size range. Integration is executed as a series of convolutions on 12 orientation filtered images augmented by the nonlinear fast plasticity and group suppression terms. Testing done on a large number of artificially generated Gabor element contour images shows that the algorithm is effective at finding contour elements within parameters similar to that of human subjects. Testing of real world images yields reasonable results and shows that the algorithm has strong potential for use as an addition to our already existent vision saliency algorithm.

1 Introduction

We are developing a fully integrated model of early visual saliency, which attempts to analyze scenes and discover which items in that scene are most salient. The current model includes many visual features that have been found to influence visual salience in the primate brain, including luminance center-surround, color opponencies and orientation contrast (Itti & Koch, 2000). However, many more factors need to be included; one such factor is the gestalt phenomenon of contour integration. This is where several approximately collinear items, through their alignment, enhance their delectability. Figure 1 shows two examples where a circle is formed by roughly collinear Gabor elements. The current paper outlines our progress in building a computational model of contour integration using both currently accepted as well as novel techniques.

Over several years the topic of contour integration has yielded several known factors that should be used in shaping a model. The first is that analysis of an image for contour integration is not global, but seems to act in a global manner. That is, the overlap of neural connections in primary visual cortex (V1) rarely exceeds 1.5mm (Hubel and Weisel, 1974), which severely limits the spatial extent of any direct interaction. However, several studies have shown that contour saliency is optimal for contours with 8–12 elements, with a saturation at 12, which is longer than the spatial range of direct interaction, typically corresponding in these displays to the inter-element distance (Braun, 1999). In addition, if the contours are arranged in such a way that they form a closed shape such as a circle, saliency is significantly enhanced (Braun, 1999; Kovacs and Julesz, 1993). This suggests not only a non-local

H.H. Bülthoff et al. (Eds.): BMCV 2002, LNCS 2525, pp. 80–89, 2002.

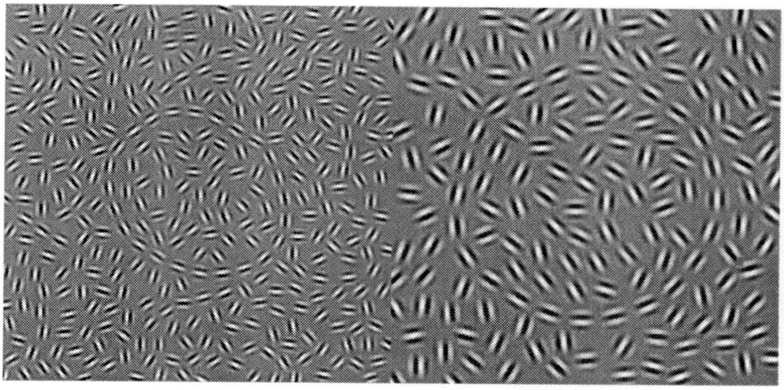

Fig. 1. Two examples of contours comprised of roughly collinear Gabor elements created by Make Snake(a Gabor element is the product of a 2D Gaussian and a sinusoidal grating).

interaction, but also a broader-range synergy between interacting neurons such that two neurons can affect each other without being directly connected.

Another noted factor playing a role in contour integration is the separation of elements usually measured in λ separation, which is the distance in units of the wavelength of the Gabor elements in the display. Studies by Polat and Sagi (1994) as well as Kapadia *et al.* (1995) indicate that an optimal separation exists for the enhancement of a central Gabor element by flanking elements. Polat and Sagi, using three Gabor elements (a test element and two flankers), found that a separation of approximately 2λ was optimal.

From these known factors several computational models have been proposed. Most start with a butterfly shape of neural connections. That is, elements are connected locally in such a way that the closer or more collinear another element is, the more the elements tend to stimulate each other (Braun, 1999). In addition many models add

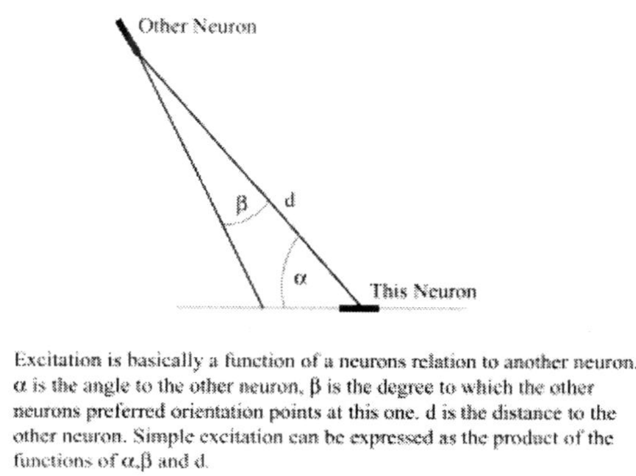

Fig. 2.A. The strength of interaction between two neurons is a product of α, β and d. The result is a set of 144 kernels (12 possible orientations, at each of two locations)

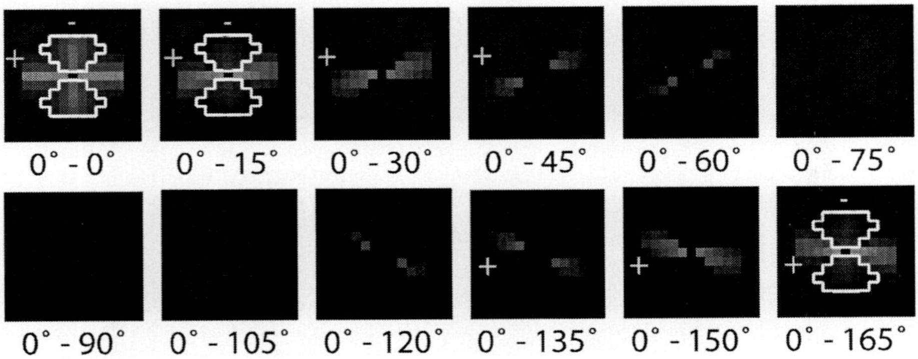

Fig. 2.B. 12 of the 144 kernels used by CINNIC are represented here. Each one in the figure show the weights of connections between a neuron with 0° preferred orientation and neurons with all other preferred orientations. The areas surrounded by a white boarder represent suppression while the other areas represent excitation. Lighter areas represent greater strength.

neural suppression whereby parallel elements suppress each other. This has the effect of allowing smaller contours to be suppressed more than larger contours. Figure 2a shows how these factors combine and 2b shows what the butterfly pattern looks like in our model.

In addition to simple local connections, several other behaviors have been used in models in an attempt to explain observed long range interactions. Such methods include temporal synchronization (Yen and Finkel, 1998) and cumulative propagation (Li, 1998). It has also been suggested by Braun (1999) that a form of fast plasticity (<250 ms) may enhance synaptic transmission along contours.

2 The Model

The current model which we have named CINNIC (Carefully Implemented Neural Network for Integrating Contours) starts with the basic butterfly local connections, but in addition to this, we have added the use of multiscale analysis, a local group suppression gain control and fast plasticity for long range effects. Figure 3 shows a schematic description of our model, which is also described by equations (1-5). The first step is analyzing the input image using Gabor filters turned for 12 different angles. This produces 12 images that represent elements from the original image at increments of 15 degrees. A noise factor of approx. 2% is introduced at this stage. These 12 images are then reduced into three different scales 64x64, 32x32 and 16x16 pixels in resolution, which are run separately and do not interact. A 4D convolution is run to simulate the interaction between the different orientation images. The convolution is done using a set of 144 kernels that represent all possible interactions between pairs of the 12 orientation images. These kernels specify the excitation and suppression that should occur between two elements in the images. The kernels take into account the colinearity of two elements as well as their separating distance. For simplicity, interaction strength decreases as a ramp function as two elements are further separated. The kernels are statically specified at the beginning of a program run by input parameters and do not interact.

Each scale is run separately from the other. Each element is convolved against every other element within its range in such a way that collinear elements tend to excite, while parallel elements tend to suppress each other (eq. 1). This is expressed as $x_{ij\alpha}$ being the source image pixel at location (i, j) and orientation α, and $x_{kl\beta}$ being the other image pixel at location (k,l) and orientation β then taking the product of these two by the kernel $k_{\alpha\beta(k-I)(l-j)}$ (12 of which are pictured in fig. 2.B). It should be noted that m and n equal the image scale for instance 64,32 or 16. Further, $(S_{ij})^t$ is a group suppression term for the current group (detailed below) with t being the current iteration. $(P_{ij\alpha})^t$ is a plasticity term (also detailed below). The resulting potential from a single iteration is sent to a saliency map $(V_{ij})^{t+1}$. Each pixel in the saliency map represents a column of pixels from each of the twelve orientation images summed. The saliency map itself is made up of leaky integrator neurons, which lose

$$(v_{ij\alpha})^{t+1} = (S_{ij})^t (P_{ij\alpha})^t (x_{ij\alpha}) \sum_{\substack{k\in[[0,m]] \\ l\in[[0,n]] \\ \beta\in[[0,11]]}} (x_{kl\beta})(k_{\alpha\beta(k-i)(l-j)}) \tag{1}$$

$$(V_{ij})^{t+1} = \sum_{\substack{k\in[[0,m]] \\ l\in[[0,n]] \\ \alpha\in[[0,11]]}} (v_{kl\alpha})^{t+1} - L \tag{2}$$

$$(S_{ij})^t = \upsilon[\sum_{(k,l)\in N_i \times N_j} ((V_{kl})^t - (V_{kl})^{t-1}] - T \tag{3}$$

with

$$N_i = [[i-(m/8);i+(m/8)]]$$
$$N_j = [[j-(m/8);j+(m/8)]]$$

$$(P_{ij\alpha})^t = (v_{ij\alpha})^t(C) \tag{4}$$

$$I_{ij} = \text{sig}((V_{ij})^t) \tag{5}$$

some constant potential L from one iteration to the next (eq. 2). To form a final saliency map for one of the three image resolutions, the potential from the leaky integrator neurons are fed through a sigmoidal function that simulates neural firing patterns (eq. 5) with I_{ij} being the final saliency map pixel for this scale.

Non-linearities are introduced in the form of the group suppression gain control (eq. 3) where T is the threshold constant and $(V_{kl})^t$ is the potential for a neuron in this group which are all summed for that group with υ as a constant multiplied by that

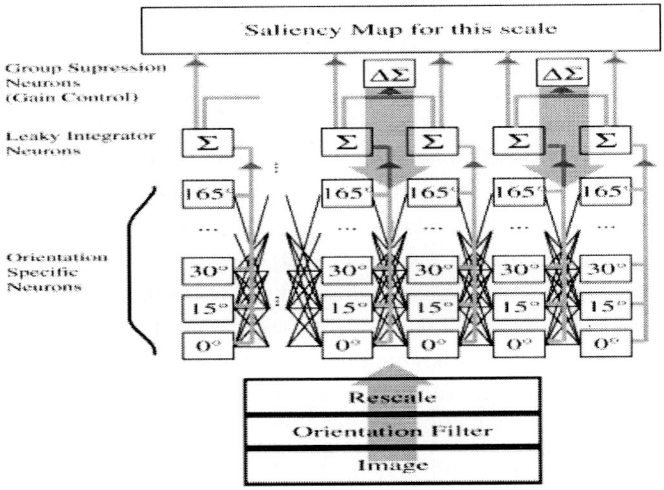

Fig. 3. This is a basic representation of the CINNIC algorithm. An input image is filtered, rescaled then interacted with images at other orientations including itself. The output goes to a saliency map of leaky integrator neurons. Group suppression is fed back from the change in group potential.

sum. m and n represent the image size at that scale The suppression is based upon the rate of the change of excitation. Fast plasticity (eq. 4) is introduced as $v_{ij\alpha}$ being the potential this neuron had multiplied by a constant C. The fast plasticity works by increasing all weights for a single simulated neuron, proportionally to the excitation it received in the previous iteration. That is, neurons that are stimulated more tend to stimulate collinear neighbors more as well as to suppress parallel neighbors more. This function is introduced to re-create non-local interactions that are observed in human subjects in an attempt to account for observed contour closure effect. The fast plasticity used here is bounded to 5 times the original connection strength for any given neuron.

IN our model the usage of fast plasticity was chosen for several reasons. The first was the suggestion by Braun (1999) that other methods that attempted to explain contour closure either occurred too fast such as cumulative propagation (Li, 1998), or were too slow such as temporal synchronization (Yen and Finkel, 1998) as to explain the time it takes for closure effect to happen which Braun measured at about 250 ms. Second we wished to test the idea of fast plasticity and find if it was a viable mechanism for explaining closure effect.

Another non-linearity introduced is a simple local gain control using group suppression. Neurons are grouped into local neighborhoods of size 1/8x1/8 pixels of the image size at the current scale (e.g. 8x8 pixels for a 64x64 pixel scale). If the total change in potential from a group surpasses a threshold then the neurons increase their suppression of parallel neighbors proportionally to the increase past threshold. The group includes all neurons in all orientation maps for a given visual location, which report to the same image location. There is no current cap on how much additional suppression can be added using this method.

The algorithm runs for eight iterations, which was a number chosen based upon its observed optimality. After the final iteration, the three scales are brought back together and combined using a fixed weighted average. This average is the total saliency map of contours for the input image. The entire process takes approximately 2 minutes using an Athlon 1400 MHz based PC running Linux. The time is mostly due to the enormous amount of computation needed to compute interactions between neurons from all possible pairs of the 12 images using 144 2D kernels.

3 Testing on Artificial Images

To tune our algorithm to human vision we are currently using a special program called Make Snake provided and created by J Braun (1999), to generate test images in which a salient contour is embedded among noise elements. Using these stimuli, we tested under which conditions our algorithm would detect the contour as being the most salient image element.

Make Snake creates images like the one presented in figure 1. The output is several Gabor patches aligned with randomized phase into a circular contour. The circle itself is carefully morphed by the program using energy to flex the joints of an "N-gon" to create a variety of circular contour shapes. The circles made up of foreground elements are controlled for the number of elements as well as the spacing in λ sinusoidal wavelengths. The elements can also be specified in terms of size and period. Background noise Gabors are added randomly. They are placed in such a way that they are moved like particles in liquid to a minimum spacing specified by the user. Gabors are added and floated until minimum spacing requirements are satisfied. The end result can also create accidental smaller contours among the noise background elements.

Test images were created using two different Gabor sizes, a small Gabor (70 pixels wide with a 20 pixel period) and a large Gabor (120 pixels wide with a 30 pixel period). The background elements were kept at a constant minimum spacing (48 for the smaller Gabors and 72 for the larger Gabors). Spacing for larger Gabors foreground elements was varied between 2 and 3.5 λ in steps of 0.1666. This was constrained since values above 3.5 made the circle larger then the images frame itself. The smaller Gabors had more levity and could be varied from 1.5 to 6 λ in steps of 0.5. For both Gabor sizes, the minimum size is set the way it is because below this, the foreground elements begin to overlap. It should be noted that the ratio of foreground separation to the minimum background separation was the same for both large and small Gabor patch conditions given the same λ.

For each condition, Gabor size and foreground spacing, 20 images were created. An output mask was also created representing where foreground elements were positioned. This was used for later statistical analysis. In all, 400 images were run.

Statistical analysis was done by taking the output salience map from CINNIC, which always ran with identical model parameter settings for all images, and comparing it to the mask; this was done by looking for the top most salient points in the salience image. When a salient point was found, the local region was flooded to prevent the same element area from being counted twice. Salient points were marked as first, second, third and so on depending on its value in the salience map. Analysis was done by finding the most salient point in an image, which was also found within the foreground element mask. The rank of the most salient point also within the mask was the rank given to the image. The number of images of each rank was summed to find out, for instance, how many images had their most salient point also lie within the mask (ranked as 1st).

As can be seen in figure 4, for the larger gabor images the most salient point falls on the foreground circle in 19 out of 20 images for separations from 2.33 to 2.833 λ, with the most salient point being found on all circles at a separation of 2.833λ. For smaller elements, in 19 out of the 20 images the most salient point was found in the foreground at a separation of 2.5λ. It should also be noted that the optimal results were obtained for the large Gabor size set with a ratio of 1.181 between the foreground element separation and background separation. The ratio for the smaller

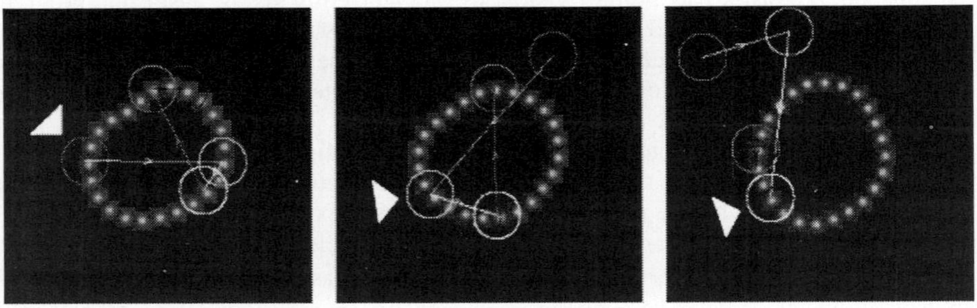

Fig. 4.A The top row of images shows contour image masks from make snake super imposed with what CINNIC found as the 5 most salient contour points. The arrow shows the most salient point CINNIC found that also lied on a contour circle. The first image is ranked as a 1st rank image since the most salient point in the image also lies on a contour. The second image is ranked as a 2nd rank image since the second most salient point is the first point to fall on a contour circle. Continuing this example the right most image is ranked as 3rd rank since the most salient point to be found on a contour circle is the third most salient point in the image.

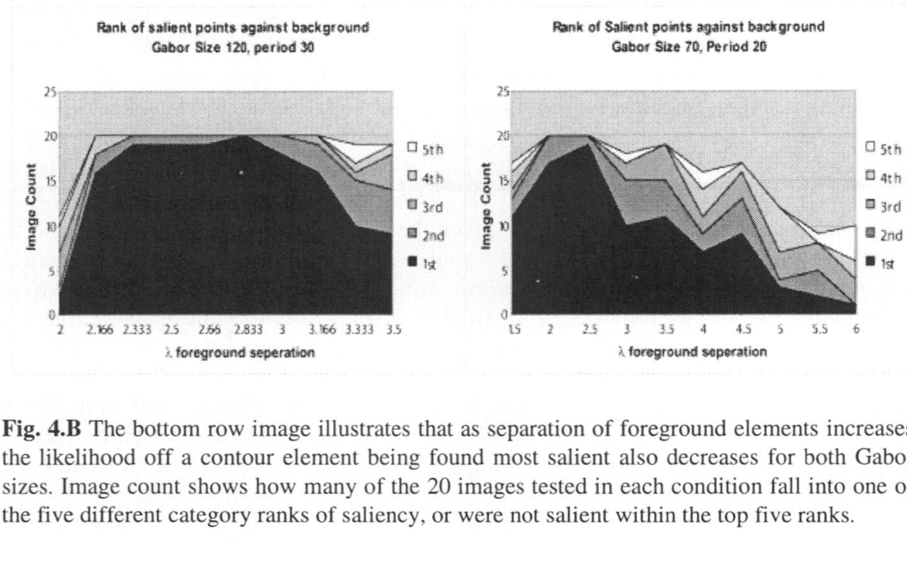

Fig. 4.B The bottom row image illustrates that as separation of foreground elements increases the likelihood off a contour element being found most salient also decreases for both Gabor sizes. Image count shows how many of the 20 images tested in each condition fall into one of the five different category ranks of saliency, or were not salient within the top five ranks.

elements was optimal at 1.041. This means that optimal results were obtained with a slightly greater distance between foreground contour elements than background elements. Bumps in figure 4 can probably be accounted for as an artifact of the discrete nature of the interactions between kernel and the image pixels.

A question raised by our results is that of why there seems to be an optimal separation distance in the data while an optimal distance is not explicitly defined in the neural connection weights (remember that weights decay linearly with distance). Further experimentation revealed that this was due to the group suppression gain control setting. We found that at a higher gain control threshold that salience in the smaller Gabor size images was reduced dramatically due to an increase in noise between irrelevant Gabors. Going in the opposite direction shows that the optimal distance for the larger Gabor size increases with a lowered threshold for the gain control. This is due to the closer elements over exciting past the lower threshold. These results are interesting in that they not only explain why we obtain optimal distances, but it allows our algorithm to agree with research by Polat and Sagi (1994) who also found an optimal distance between Gabor elements.

4 Testing on Real World Images

Part of the goal of our project has been to be able to incorporate the CINNIC algorithm to our more general bottom-up visual salience model. Thus, CINNIC must be able to analyze real world images much the same as the current saliency model does. At this point testing on real world images has been constrained to running the

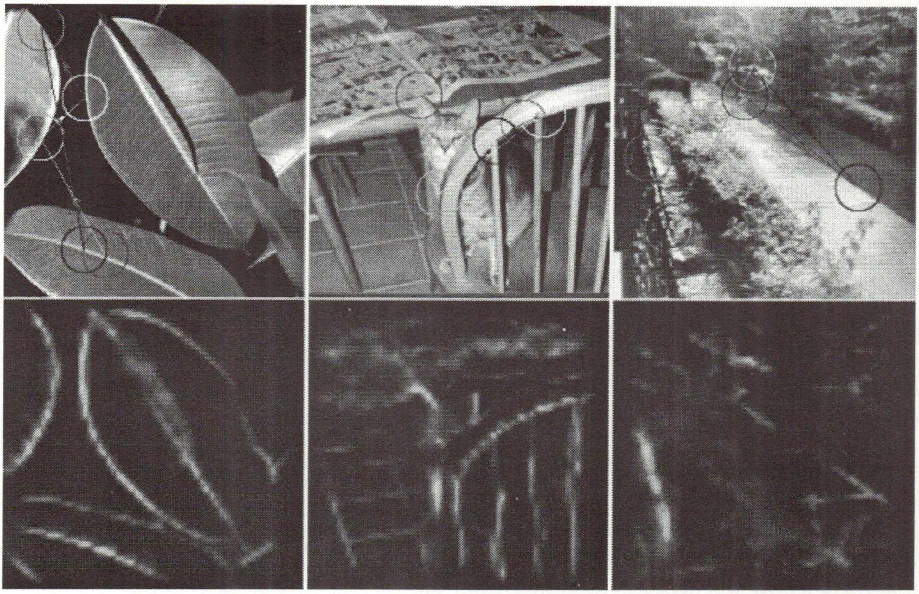

Fig. 5. The top row are real world images with the top 5 most salient points circled by the algorithm. The bottom row represents the raw saliency map for each image.

algorithm and inspecting the outputs to make sure that they seem reasonable. Although of a purely subjective and qualitative nature, such experimentations are particularly useful to estimate the applicability of our model to more general classes of stimuli. We found that in most cases, the algorithm behaves in a reasonable fashion when processing real world images. Noise is generally filtered out and the most salient points tend to lie on reasonable line elements and contours. Over 100 images were inspected in all; each image contained a different subject (e.g plants, city pictures, wilderness images). This was done by selecting one image at random from each image subject category on two image library CD's. Figure 5 shows some typical outputs on real world images. The top five most salient points are circled in the images.

From the three images presented, the most salient contours can be found in 5(a) on the edges and stem of the leafs, on the cats ear and the chair rim in 5(b) and in 5(c) the stone wall, sidewalk and street possess the most salient contours. This agrees with a common sense idea that the most salient contours are found on objects with long collinear continuity and is supported by data from Braun (1999) and Hess and Field (1999) which shows that longer contours with smoother continuity and more elements tend to be more salient then shorter more jagged ones.

5 Discussion

On artificially-generated contours CINNIC performs very well. Performance for identifying generated contours drops as foreground elements are separated relative to background elements. This is to be expected as the same thing is observed in human subjects (Braun, 1999). Not only does it perform well but it also has an optimal distancing between foreground Gabor elements, which agrees with Polat and Sagi (1994) and the performance of detection begins to drop at a foreground-to-background ratio of about 1.25, which is what is observed by Braun (1999). The fall-off for the model is complete at a spacing of about 6λ which is consistent with the spacing range proposed by Hess and Field (1999), which they estimate to be about 4 to 6 λ at maximum.

The model so far is also successful because all elements included in the model are biologically plausible. This is because the model is built upon basic long-range neural interactions (Gilbert et al., 2000). Our additions to this basic model include a previously untested neural plasticity and novel local gain control factors. It is our opinion that all of these factors are plausible and could help explain how contour integration occurs. It should also be noted that our use of fast plasticity may better explain long range interactions than previous models relying on synaptic transmission (Li, 1998; Pettet *et al* ,1998), temporal synchronization (Yen and Finkel, 1998), or NMDA-mediated plasticity (Braun *et al.*, 1994) since, as Braun states, the time required for their mechanisms do not closely match observed times needed for salience in contour integration under contour closure. (Braun, 1999). That is, synaptic transmission would cause contour closure far sooner then the approximately 250 ms observed by Braun, while temporal synchronization and NMDA-mediated plasticity take slightly too long.

It should also be noted that our novel usage of a group suppression was successful. As we found, it seemed to have an optimal value where by removing it, turning it up too high or in general adjusting it too high or too low yielded sub-optimal results. This suggests to us that it is useful in our approach.

Acknowledgements. We would like to acknowledge Jochen Braun, Christof Koch and Mike Olson for their help and suggestions. This research is supported by the National Imagery and Mapping Agency, the National Science Foundation, the National Eye Institute, the Zumberge Faculty Innovation Research Fund and the Charles Lee Powell Foundation.

References

Braun J, Niebur E. Schuster H G, Koch C, 1994, Perceptual contour completion: a model based on local anisotropic, fast-adapting interactions between oriented filters, *soc. Neurosci. Abstr.,* **20** 1665

Braun J , 1999, On the detection of salient contours, *Spatial Vision*, **12**(2):211-225

Gilbert C, Ito M, Kapadia M, Westheimer G, 2000, Interactions between attention, context and learning in primary visual cortex, *Vision Research*, **40**(10-12):1217-26

Hess R, Field D, 1999, Integration of contours: new insights, *Trends in Cognitive Science*, **3**(12):480-486

Hubel D H, Wiesel T N,1974, Uniformity of monkey striate cortex: a parallel relationship between field size, scatter and magnification factor, *Journal of Comparative Neurology*, **158**:295-306

Itti L, Koch C, 2000, A saliency-based search mechanism for overt and covert shifts of visual attention, *Vision Research,* **40**(10-12)1489-1506

Kapadia M K, Ito M, Gilbert C D, Westheimer G, 1995, Improvement in visual sensitivity by changes in local context: Parallel studies in human observers and in V1 of alert monkeys, *Neuron*, **15**:843-856

Kovacs I, Julesz B, 1993, A closed curve is much more than an incomplete one: Effect of closure in figure-ground segmentation, *Proceedings of the National Academy of Science USA*, **90**:7495-7497

Li Z, 1998, A neural model of contour integration, *Neural Computation*, **10**:903-940

Pettet M W, McKee S P, Grzywacz N M, 1998, Constraints on long-range interactions mediating contour integration, *Vision Research*, **38**:865-879

Polat U, Sagi D, 1994, The architecture of perceptual spatial interactions, *Vision Research*, **34**(1):73-78

Yen S, Finkel L H, 1998, Extraction of perceptually salient contours by striate cortical networks, *Vision Research*, **38**(5):719-741

Computational Cortical Cell Models for Continuity and Texture

Luís M. Santos and J.M. Hans du Buf

Vision Laboratory, University of Algarve
Campus de Gambelas – FCT, Faro, Portugal
{lmsantos,dubuf}@ualg.pt

Abstract. Area V1 and higher areas in the visual cortex contain many feature extraction engines that serve to build a symbolic image representation. In this paper we present models of cells that complement a multiscale line and edge extraction. After reviewing a frontend that comprises Gabor filters (simple cells), bar and grating cells, we introduce a bar cell grouping for completing occluded curvilinear structures (snakes), as well as a grating cell grouping for coding periodic textures with different complexities.

Keywords: Perceptual grouping, cortical cells, snakes, textures

1 Introduction

Many recent findings in neurophysiology show that feature extraction layers in V1 and higher areas in the visual cortex have correlates with visual effects that can be readily observed. For example, when looking at objects with different textures, we instantly separate them into different regions. When looking at an interrupted, e.g. partially occluded, line or edge, we perceive the parts as belonging to one and the same object. The processing involved must be rather simple, because all cells group activities of other cells (in other layers) in their dentritic fields, with local or more global horizontal connections for lateral excitation and inhibition processes.

A few cell models have already been developed. Heitger et al. [1] developed a model for cells that serve to detect vertices, so-called end-stopped operators, and then modelled cells that can complete illusory contours. Petkov and Kruizinga [2] developed a grating cell model. We improved this model and also provided a bar cell model [3] . Figure 1 gives an impression of the performance of our grating and bar cell models, i.e. for one tuning frequency/width but combining multiple orientations. It should be stressed that grating and bar cells are very nonlinear, because a bar cell does not respond to periodic bars in a grating and a grating cell does not respond to an isolated bar [4]. Grating and bar cells, as all other cells, provide input for higher-level cells in order to extract more advanced features. Here we go one step further: on the basis of bar and grating cell outputs, we developed grouping processes that address partially occluded

H.H. Bülthoff et al. (Eds.): BMCV 2002, LNCS 2525, pp. 90–98, 2002.

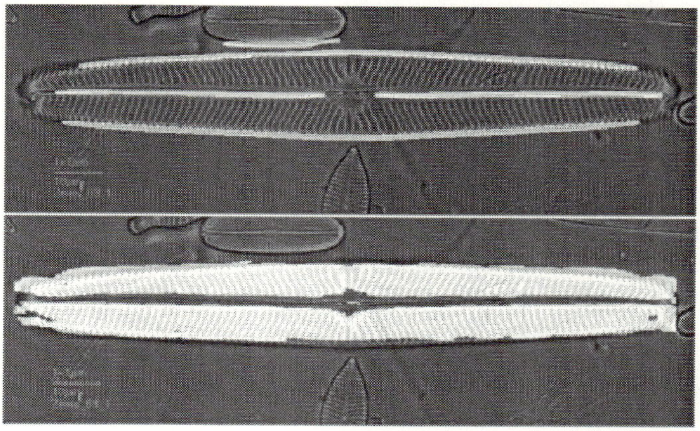

Fig. 1. Illustration of our cell models. The top image shows bar cell outputs superimposed on a darkened image of a *Navicula oblonga* diatom, whereas the bottom one shows grating cell outputs.

or interrupted structures in order to reconstruct continuity, and textures with different complexities in order to segregate them.

The results presented here are part of an effort directed towards developing more complete models of cortical processes, a processing hierarchy that is underpinned by findings in neurophysiology with respect to the behaviour of specific cells. This may serve to develop better models to explain higher cognitive effects. However, the models can also be applied to machine vision, now that normal PCs can attain a tremendous performance.

2 Grating and Bar Cell Models

These two models are based on a same frontend, but apply different grouping operators to detect either isolated bars or periodic bars in a grating. The first stage of these models consists of a contrast normalisation of the input image. This is obtained by two shunting centre-surround networks based on ON and OFF retinal ganglion cells, i.e. isotropic DOG filters [5]: on-centre with off-surround and off-centre with on-surround channels. This normalisation yields two signals, R^+ (ON) and R^- (OFF), both of which are either positive or zero. This processing assures a good response localisation, i.e. an ON response in the case of a bright bar against a dark background will not be wider than the bar itself. For further details please refer to [3,6].

The second stage consists of anisotropic filtering by Gabor functions that model simple cells. A Gabor kernel is defined by

$$G(x,y) = \exp\left[-\frac{1}{2s^2}\left(\frac{x^2}{\sigma_x^2}+\frac{y^2}{\sigma_y^2}\right)+\mathrm{i}\left(\frac{\omega x}{s}+\phi\right)\right], \quad (1)$$

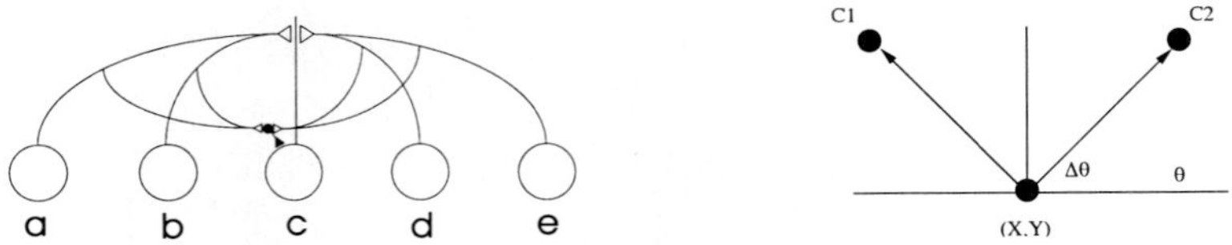

Fig. 2. Left: in the grouping model the centre cell can be excited by its four neighbouring cells through the open triangles, whereas the small solid triangle causes a smaller inhibition to prevent from oversaturation. Right: spatial cell relations used for snake grouping.

in which σ_x and σ_y define the size of the Gaussian envelope in x and y, ω is the spatial frequency and s is the scaling factor. The frequency ω was optimised experimentally to get a good compromise for different gratings (sine- and squarewave) and bar profiles. The value for $\gamma = \sigma_x/\sigma_y$, was set to 0.8 after [7]. Separate ON and OFF responses are obtained with $\phi = 0$ and $\phi = \pi$, respectively, and these responses are still positive or zero. In order to sharpen the results and to increase the robustness to noise, we apply a nonlinearity which amplifies responses that are above a local average activity level and which attenuates those that are below it. This leads to an edge sharpening of the ON and OFF responses, improving the selectivity of the final grouping operators.

2.1 Grating and Bar Groupings

The last stage consists of the grouping of the ON and OFF responses [8]. The grouping model shown in Fig. 2 (left) is done in two steps: (1) the detection of events along a line and (2) an amplitude-completion or filling-in process. The centre cell c has its own input (c_i) and its output equals

$$c_o = a_i + b_i + c_i + d_i + e_i - \max\{a_i, b_i, d_i, e_i\}. \tag{2}$$

This model implements a feedforward single-layer perceptron with an adaptive bias (the max term), defined by $\sum_{i=1}^{5} \omega_i x_i - \omega_0$. In this particular case, all weights ω_i are equal to 1, x_i correspond to the inputs $a_i \cdots e_i$, and ω_0 is the bias term obtained locally by the max function. The nonlinearity introduced by the max term prevents the cell c from becoming oversaturated.

The five cells receive input from equidistantly sampled ON and OFF responses. For a grating grouping, the $\{a, c, e\}$ cells should be located in another type of response than the $\{b, d\}$ cells, i.e. both ON,OFF,ON,OFF,ON and OFF,ON,OFF,ON,OFF are valid neighbourhoods, since a grating does not have a polarity. Some of the cells can be activated because they are positioned on a bar, whereas others cannot be because they lie in between two bars. If the c cell lies between two bars, it will be activated by some of its neighbours, i.e. the bars are nevertheless grouped together. This grouping only takes place between events, not beyond a region boundary. Bar cell grouping is obtained in a similar way, using OFF,ON,ON,ON,OFF for a bright bar against a dark background

Table 1. Priority (complexity) scheme of different events.

Event	Priority
Grating (symmetry order higher than 2)	*Higher priority* ↑
Simple grating	
Snake	
Bar	*Lower priority*

and ON,OFF,OFF,OFF,ON for a dark bar against a bright background; see [3, 6]. Both grating and bar cells are tuned to width (frequency) and orientation, and we assume a complete assembly of frequencies and orientations. Figure 1 presents results obtained with grating and bar cells.

When applying several event detectors in parallel, it is possible that a same position can be labelled differently, e.g. a bar cell can respond at a position where also a grating cell responds, simply because the periodicity of the grating is not constant. Hence, spurious responses could be suppressed by a priority system in order to distinguish concurrent events. An example is illustrated in Tab. 1: less complex events are given low priority (e.g. bars) and more complex ones (e.g. textures with high symmetry orders) have a higher priority. However, as will be shown below, the representations at the different detection layers could still be used at higher detection layers.

3 Snake Grouping

Often structures are partially occluded by other objects, but our visual system can detect or even reconstruct continuity [9]. Straight or curved, but interrupted line segments are called snakes. Kass, Witkin and Terzopoulos [10] have developed active contour models. However, these and other models [11,12] are not based on biological vision. A snake is defined as an energy-minimising spline—the snake's energy depends on its shape and location within the image. The energy is minimised by a weighted combination of internal and external forces. The internal forces are caused by the shape of the snake, whereas the external forces are based on the image contents and/or higher-level image understanding processes. Examples of active contours are shown in Figs 3 and 4.

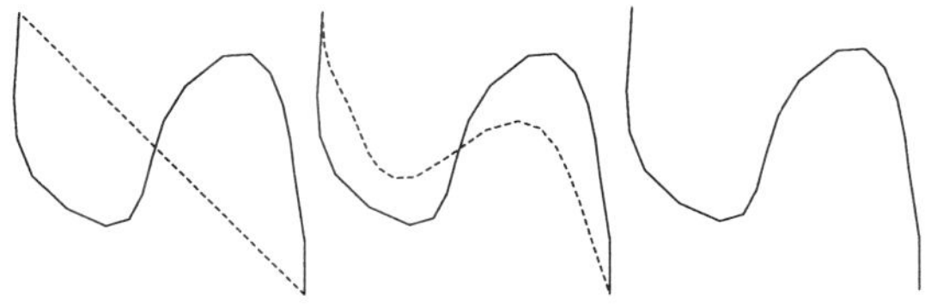

Fig. 3. Example of an active contour. Left: initial snake position (dotted) interactively defined near the true contour. Middle and right: iterations of energy minimisation—the snake is pulled towards the true contour.

Fig. 4. A snake attracted to edges and terminations. Left: contour illusion. Right: a snake attracted to the illusory contour. Example adapted from [10].

Here, in order to reconstruct continuity, we define several grouping hypotheses on the basis of bar cell outputs. Each hypothesis is tested by three cells. Assume that the centre cell is located at (x, y) (Fig. 2, right). The orientation of the group of three cells is defined by θ, which corresponds to the orientation of the centre cell (local bar orientation), and $\Delta\theta$ is the orientation of the lateral cells relative to the centre one, whereas ρ is the distance. The position of the first lateral cell is given by

$$x_1 = x + \rho\cos(\theta + \Delta\theta) \tag{3}$$

$$y_1 = y + \rho\sin(\theta + \Delta\theta) \tag{4}$$

and the position of the second by

$$x_2 = x + \rho\cos(\pi - \theta - \Delta\theta) = x - \rho\cos(\theta + \Delta\theta) \tag{5}$$

$$y_2 = y + \rho\sin(\pi - \theta - \Delta\theta) = y + \rho\sin(\theta + \Delta\theta) \tag{6}$$

In our tests we used 8 equidistant orientations on $[-\pi, \pi]$ for θ, which were also used for the Gabor filters and the bar cells, and three values for $\Delta\theta$: 0 and $\pm\pi/10$. Hence, at any position and for each orientation, the snake can be straight, completely curved (2 possibilities), or a combination between straight and curved (4 possibilities). Inflection points can be handled as well, but at the moment we use, at any position and for each of the 8 orientations, only 7 "snake cells." The outputs of these are OR-ed together by collector cells that only respond if the modulus of the local Gabor filter response (complex cell) is above a threshold. Figure 5 shows images with snakes composed of Gabor patches, one of them having a curved snake in randomly oriented patches. Note that our visual system instantly detects the snakes. The snake groupings obtained are quite accurate. An example of contour completion can be seen in Fig. 6.

4 Complex But Periodic Textures

Although often the Gabor filter responses are exploited for segmentation [13], advanced methods can be used to model the local power spectrum [14,15]. Here

Fig. 5. Left: two images with snakes consisting of real Gabor patches. Right: the results of the snake grouping using very few cell orientations.

Fig. 6. Top: zebra image without and with occlusion, a simulated tree. Bottom: outputs of grating cells (left) and snake cells that group bar cell outputs (right). Note that the grating cell outputs can be used to suppress spurious responses of bar cells (the hind leg) and that the illusory contrast contour (the back) has been completed.

we only address structured textures because we combine grating cell outputs, since these cells serve to detect periodic structures. Furthermore, we will focus on complexity by means of the symmetry order: linear textures (order 2), rectangular (order 4) and hexagonal (order 6) etc. Symmetry orders can be determined by combining grating cells adapted to different orientations. Some evidence has

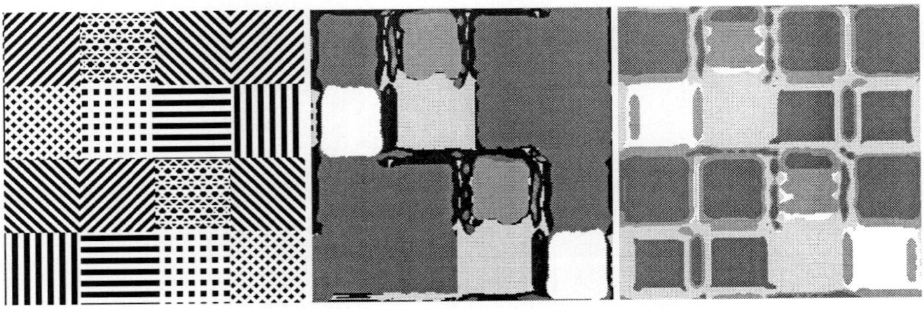

Fig. 7. Left: test image with patches of symmetry orders 2, 4 and 6. Middle: detected grating symmetry order, encoded in grayscale. Right: symmetry order obtained on the basis of the Gabor filter responses.

been found that there are "complexity cells" that serve to detect different local, but complex, image structures [16]. We show that such cells can play a role in texture segregation.

A processing scheme was proposed in [17] to detect symmetry orders, but this was based on summing Gabor responses according to specific orientation combinations. By applying this concept to grating cell outputs, we can obtain texture operators which are very selective and precise in terms of spatial localisation: a property of grating cells.

Let G_i be the binary outputs of grating cells with the same periodicity (this is not necessary because a rectangular texture can be composed of two gratings with different periodicities). Let us consider 12 orientations: $i = 1 \cdots 12$. In order to obtain rotation invariance we have to consider all possibilities and to select the most likely one. This must be done for all symmetry orders. The following notation will be used: $S^{l:m}$ is the l-th partial sum for symmetry order m. We obtain the following six partial sums for a 4-folded symmetry: $S^{1:4} = (G_1 + G_7)/2 \cdots S^{6:4} = (G_6 + G_{12})/2$. Likewise, for a 6-folded symmetry (hexagonal) we compute the four sums $S^{1:6} = (G_1 + G_5 + G_9)/3$ to $S^{4:6} = (G_4 + G_8 + G_{12})/3$, and so on for higher orders. Using $k = m/2$, the relations above can be formulated as

$$S^{l:m} = \frac{1}{k} \sum_{i=0}^{k-1} G_{(12i/k)+l+1}. \tag{7}$$

The last step consists of taking the maximum for each symmetry order: $M^N = \max S^{n:N}$, whereas $M^2 = \max G_i$ in the case of 2-folded symmetry; see Tab. 2.

Basically, this processing is based on summing in a cell's dentritic field, as applied in all cell models, but now with different weight factors, over grating cells with different orientations. For a 4-folded symmetry there are 6 summation cells, for a 6-folded symmetry there are 4 summation cells, etc. Maximum detection for any symmetry order is obtained by lateral excitation/inhibition (winner takes all), and the result codes both the symmetry order and the orientation, for example the orientation of the summation cell $S^{l:m}$ with the maximum response.

Fig. 8. Left: test image with 7 real textures. Right: Grating cell symmetries of order 4.

Table 2. Summation values obtained with different symmetry order detectors when applied to textures of different symmetry orders.

Model \ Order	2	4	6	8
M^2	**1**	1	1	1
M^4	1/2	**1**	1/2	1
M^6	1/3	1/3	**1**	1/3
M^8	1/4	1/2	1/4	**1**

Here, higher complexity order is given higher priority, i.e. on an octogonal texture both "octogonal cells" and "rectangular cells" will respond, even "linear cells," but the first will suppress the responses of the latter ones. In the same way, "hexagonal cells" and "rectangular cells" will suppress responses of cells with lower complexity. This is done in order to construct one and only one complexity map which may be part of a "segregation" system.

A complexity map, without any local orientations, is shown in Fig. 7 (middle) by different grey levels. This result is more stable than a symmetry order coding on the basis of Gabor filter responses (right). Real textures are used in Fig. 8, which consists of 7 different textures, most of them being rather unstructured. As expected, the 2 really periodic textures could be detected. Our method needs some relaxation in order to detect less periodic textures. Because the textures differ in scale, we selected grating cells tuned to these scales. As mentioned above, it is likely that area V1 or higher areas also contain complexity cells that combine outputs of grating cells that are tuned to different scales, rather than only single scales. All these cells could be combined by excitation/inhibition networks in order to detect the most likely hypothesis. But this is a speculation: at the moment we simply do not know whether, or how, the visual system uses complexity maps. The stacks of feature extraction engines provide already a very rich description. In the future we intend to do experiments with artificial networks and training on real data in order to see what can be achieved by different configurations.

Acknowledgements. This work was funded by the FCT (Fundação para a Ciência e a Tecnologia) contract SFRH/BD/1309/2000.

References

1. Heitger, F. et al.: Simulation of neural contour mechanisms: representing anomalous contours, Image and Vision Computing **16** (1998) 407–421.
2. Petkov, N., Kruizinga, P.: Computational models of visual neurons specialised in the detection of periodic and aperiodic oriented visual stimuli: bar and grating cells, Biol. Cybern. **76** (1997) 83–96.
3. Santos, L., du Buf, H.: Improved grating and bar cell models in diatom analysis, Image and Vision Computing (2001) (to appear).
4. von der Heydt, R., Peterhans, E., Dürsteler, M.: Periodic-pattern-selective cells in monkey visual cortex, J. of Neuroscience **12** (1997) 83–96.
5. Schiller, P.H., Sandell, J.H., Maunsell, J.H.R.: The functions of the ON and OFF channels of the visual system, Nature **32** (1986) 824–825.
6. Santos, L.M., du Buf, H.: Improved grating and bar cell models in diatom analysis, Proc. 7th Neural Computation and Psychology Workshop: Connectionist Models of Cognition and Perception, John A. Bullinaria & Will Lowe (eds), World Scientific, Singapore (2002).
7. Jones, J., Palmer, A.: An evaluation of the two-dimensional Gabor filter model of simple receptive fields in cat striate cortex, J. Neurophysiol. **58** (1987) 1233–1258.
8. Grossberg, S.: How does the cerebral cortex work? Learning, attention and grouping by the laminar circuits of visual cortex, Spatial Vision **12** (1999) 163–186.
9. Field, D.J., Hayes, A., Hess, R.F.: Contour integration by the human visual system: evidence for a local "association field," Vision Res., **33** (1993) 173–193.
10. Kass, M., Witkin, A., Terzopoulos, D.: Snakes – Active contour models. Int. Journal of Computer Vision, **1(4)** (1987) 321–331.
11. Xu, C., Prince, J.L.: Snakes, Shapes, and Gradient Vector Flow, IEEE Transactions on Image Processing, (1998) 359–369.
12. Sonka, M., Hlavac, V., Boyle, R.: Image Processing, Analysis, and Machine Vision, PWS, second edition (1998) Chapter 5.
13. Puzicha, J.: Multiscale annealing for grouping, segmentation and image quantization, PhD Thesis, Bonn (1999).
14. du Buf, J.M.H.: Abstract processes in texture discrimination, Spatial Vision, **6** (1992) 221–242.
15. du Buf, J.M.H., Bigün, J.: N-folded symmetries by complex moments in Gabor space and their application to unsupervised texture segmentation, IEEE Trans. Pat. Analysis and Machine Intel., **16:1** (1994) 80–87.
16. Gallant, J.L., Braun, J., Van Essen, D.C.: Selectivity for polar, hyperbolic, and Cartesian gratings in macaque visual cortex. Science, **259** (1993) 100–103.
17. du Buf, J.M.H., Heitger, F.: A neural network for detecting symmetry orders, Proc. 7th ICIAP, Bari (Italy): Progress in Image Analysis III, S. Impedovo (ed.) World Scientific, **72** (1994) 669–672.

A Neural Model of Human Texture Processing: Texture Segmentation vs. Visual Search

Axel Thielscher[1], Anna Schuboe[3], and Heiko Neumann[2]

[1] Department of Psychiatry,
[2] Department of Neural Information Processing,
University of Ulm, Germany,
{axel.thielscher@medizin, heiko.neumann@informatik}.uni-ulm.de
[3] Friedrich-Alexander-University, Erlangen-Nuremberg, Germany,
Schubo@rzmail.uni-erlangen.de

Abstract. Texture segmentation tasks are well-known paradigms to study human visual processing in the detection of salient stimulus items. In a recent EEG study, different event-related brain-potentials have been identified which reflect the underlying pre-attentive and attentive processes. We show that a neural model of texture boundary processing can account for the findings of the EEG study concerning the pre-attentive processes. The model identifies the functional role of these processes as well as their probable cortical origin. In addition, it is demonstrated that the proposed computational mechanisms can account for the differences between automatic segmentation and visual search.

Keywords. Event-related brain potentials, recurrent neural model, texture boundary processing, texture segmentation, visual search.

1 Introduction

Visual search tasks, in which test persons have to report the presence or absence of target elements embedded in a display of distractors, are well-established techniques to study human visual processing. The complexity of these tasks can be controlled by altering the number and spatial homogeneity of the distractors, ranging from displays containing only a few elements (resulting in classical visual search) to homogeneous arrays containing a popout element (resulting in effortless texture segmentation). In an EEG study by Schuboe and coworkes [15], the neural processes underlying texture segmentation were investigated by means of event-related brain potentials (ERPs). Potentials reflecting the underlying pre-attentive and attentive processes were identified. Furthermore, in a subsequent study [16] these potentials were contrasted with those elicited by visual search displays.

In this paper, we show that a previously developed neural model of human texture processing [18] enables us to trace back several main results of the ERP studies to the likely underlying neural mechanisms and visual cortical areas

H.H. Bülthoff et al. (Eds.): BMCV 2002, LNCS 2525, pp. 99–108, 2002.

involved. Pre-attentive cortical mechanisms are identified, which account for the difference between visual search and automatic texture segmentation.

In the ERP study by Schuboe [15] subjects had to judge target presence or absence in a texture array composed of oblique line elements. The target element was defined by a 90° orientation shift against the background. Event-related brain potentials were recorded and analyzed separately for target and non-target trials. Two components were found to be sensitive to the different texture stimuli, namely the posterior N2 (N2p) and a positive component in the P3 time interval. The N2p was observed about 300 ms after stimulus presentation at posterior electrode sites, where non-target trials elicited an enlarged N2 amplitude compared to target trials. This enlargement was also observed when target detection was made task irrelevant by instructing subjects to perform a different primary task. Therefore, the N2p modulation was interpreted as indicating an automatic, pre-attentive process in the processing of texture stimuli. Further, an increased positivity for target trials compared to non-target trials was found about 400 ms post stimulus. This increase, however, depended on the amount of available attentional capacity and was mainly observed when subjects had to respond to the texture stimuli. In the subsequent study [16], the number of line elements composing the stimulus was varied, resulting either in visual search arrays containing 5 or 25 elements or in a homogeneous texture array of 49 elements. While an increased positivity in the P3 time interval was again observed for all three set sizes, an increase in N2p amplitude was only observed with set size 49, indicating different processing in this condition.

2 Model of Human Texture Processing

2.1 Structure

We outline the structure of a model of pre-attentive segmentation of oriented textures that has been previously developed to explain cortical mechanisms of human texture processing. It builds upon two key assumptions, namely that (i) human texture processing is based on the detection of salient discontinuities signalling texture boundaries and that (ii) texture border detection is achieved by cells in higher visual areas having large receptive fields to integrate the pre-processed input from lower areas.

Segmentation based on feature contrast, such as orientation contrast between line elements, was psychophysically investigated in detail by Nothdurft [14]. He demonstrated that the ability to segregate between regions depends on the detection of salient local first-order feature dissimilarities at borders of texture regions. Results of single- and multi-unit recordings in visual area V1 of monkeys revealed an enhanced activity of orientation selective cells when their receptive fields lie at texture borders defined by an orientation contrast (e.g., [5]). Furthermore, a recent functional imaging study demonstrated a significant contribution of higher visual areas, including V4, in texture segmentation [8]. Likewise, lesion studies in monkeys showed that the detection of texture borders as well as the discrimination of shapes is impaired after ablation of V4 (e.g., [12]). Taken together, these observations render V4 a likely candidate area that is involved in texture border processing. Receptive field sizes increase monotonically within the hierarchy of cortical areas [17]. Consequently, V4 can pool information over wide areas in the retinal image in order to selectively identify the few meaningful orientation contrasts signalling a texture border.

We propose a hierarchical neural model of bi-directionally linked areas V1, V2 and V4 [4] each containing topographically organized maps of orientation selective cells (Fig. 1a). The cells are mutually interconnected single-compartment models representing groups of individual neurons of similar selectivity. The cells' receptive field sizes in different model areas have been parameterized in a ratio V1:V2:V4 = 1:2.5:8 [17]. Below, we describe the key elements and properties of the model neurons and their dynamics to provide a basic level description of the structure of our model. A more detailed specification can be found in [18].

2.2 Model Cells and Dynamics

The gradual activation level of a cell is determined by three successive computational stages (Fig. 1b). First, the bottom-up input is pooled within the cell's input weighting function to determine its initial activation, utilizing spatial convolution. Second, feedback activity delivered by descending cortical pathways multiplicatively enhances the initial activation. It is only effective at positions with non-zero initial activation, which prevents activity spreading in the topographic map. In other words, the feedback signals are gated by the bottom-up activities of feature responses. Feedback is selective to the spatial as well as to the orientation domain. Inhibitory feedback components pool activity in a wider spatial and orientational neighborhood. Third, the top-down modulated activity undergoes a stage of shunting ON-center/ OFF-surround competition between neighboring cells in the spatial as well as the orientation domain.

Feedback modulation and center-surround competition follow a common general scheme of gradual activation dynamics. With this competitive interaction, the initial top-down modulated activities are contrast enhanced and normalized. In combination, the three stages of computation realize a soft-gating mechanism: The initial activities, which match the context-sensitive feedback activity from higher levels, are further enhanced and, in turn, inhibit their neighborhood. Thus, salient texture arrangements will be enhanced while at the same time spurious and perceptually irrelevant activities are suppressed.

2.3 Model Areas, Spatial Weightings, and Simulations

The model consists of one subcortical area resembling LGN and three replica of cortical areas V1, V2 and V4 (Fig. 1a).

• *Model LGN and V1 simple cells* preprocess the initial luminance distribution to provide a realistic input to model V1 complex cells. Their activity is determined by pure feedforward processing. V1 simple cells have elongated subfields to pool the input delivered by appropriately aligned LGN cells. They respond to local

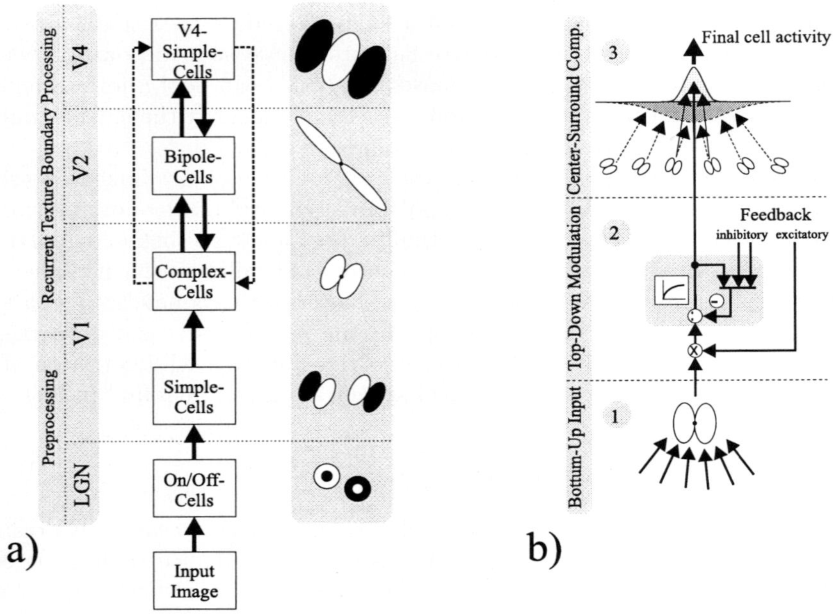

Fig. 1. a) Hierarchy of model areas and model cells. The spatial weights are sketched in the right column (excitatory (white)/inhibitory (black) subfields; sizes not drawn to scale). b) Model stages in each model area determining the activation of a cell. Bottom-up input is pooled by the cell's receptive field to constitute its initial activation (1); shunting feedback interaction from higher model areas modulates the initial activation (2), and subsequent shunting ON-center/OFF-surround competition in a spatial and orientational neighborhood (3).

luminance transitions along a given orientation preference and are selective to contrast polarity (dark-light and light-dark in 8 discrete orientations) [7].

• *Model V1 complex cells* form the lowest level of recurrent processing for texture boundary computation. Model complex cells pool the activity of two simple cells of opposite polarity at each position. Initial complex cell activation is now insensitive to direction of contrast. This activation is subsequently modulated by top-down interaction and center-surround competition following the three sequential computational stages described above.

• *Model V2 bipole cells* respond to luminance contrasts as well as to illusory contours [19]. Each cell has two prolated subfields which are aligned along the axis of the cell's orientation preference [13]. The cells only generate significant responses when both subfields are excited simultaneously. The initial responses are again modulated via top-down feedback and center-surround competition.

• *Model V4 cells* detect texture borders defined by activity transitions in the fields of oriented input responses generated by oriented model V1 and V2 cells. Activity discontinuities can occur in each input orientation field (depending on the orientation of the line elements) and can themselves have different orientations (depending on the orientation of the texture boundaries). Accordingly, model V4 cells of different orientation selectivities were defined each of which having one central excitatory and two lateral inhibitory subfields all selectively integrating from the same input orientation field (8 V4 cell orientations per input orientation result in a matrix of 8x8 = 64 V4 cells). All cells selective to the same input orientation undergo center-surround competition. The activities are subsequently pooled at each position for each separate input orientation and finally fed back to corresponding orientation channels in the preceding model areas.

Simulations were performed using the stimuli presented in Fig. 2&3 as input to the LGN cells. The model differential equations were solved at equilibrium. The input image was clamped and the activities of the model areas were sequentially updated until stable activation patterns were reached after a few iterative cycles. A comparison with results obtained by numerical integration of the model equations revealed that the use of equilibrium responses did not affect the reliability of the final solution. The final activation patterns of the different model areas were visualized by summing the model cell responses over all orientations at each location. The results were subsequently scaled with respect to the maximum activity of the summed responses in the particular model area.

2.4 Relation to Previous Models of Texture Segregation

Our neural model sketched above has certain parallels to previously developed models of texture segmentation, but also deviates and extends those earlier approaches. Many models start with an initial stage of orientation selective filtering, corresponding to V1 simple cells (e.g., [3,9]; see [1] for an overview). Some models utilize filters with different spatial frequency selectivity [2]. Responses are subsequently passed through a non-linear signal function, usually a half-wave rectification. The resulting activations are then processed by a second filtering stage. Approaches deviate here, several utilize a homologue of the first processing stage by using the same type of oriented filters but larger scale [2]. Other models apply filters that are oriented orthogonal to those of the initial processing stage [20]. Results from different orientation fields and scales are finally pooled in a possibly non-linear fashion.

Our model shares the computational stage of initial V1 filtering. Here, contrast sensitive responses were then pooled afterwards to mimic V1 complex cell computation. The activities then undergo a stage of shunting center-surround competition in space-orientation domain. This resembles the property of activity normalization that has been validated experimentally in primary visual cortex [6]. Our model proceeds with model areas V2 and V4. Perhaps the model most similar to our V1-V4 feedforward processing stream has been proposed in [10]. There, the rectified initial responses undergo a non-linear center-surround interaction computed over a neighborhood in the spatial and orientation domain, which is similar to our stage of shunting competition. In that model, these responses are then spatially blurred and gradients are measured in each orientation field separately. Finally, at each spatial location the maximum response is selected over all orientation channels. This cascade of processing stages is a simplified version of our model V4 computation. The output is processed separately for each orientation field by applying orientation selective filter that cover the full range of orientations. Thus, taking the gradient instead is a computational simplification of our neural model. Unlike the subsequent maximum selection, we again utilize a stage of center-surround competition and sub-sequent pooling of responses for each orientation field separately. This allows to compute gradual activity distributions for each orientation that are subsequently fed back to corresponding feature locations in the preceding areas. This computational strategy also substantially deviates from the neural model of V4 texture processing proposed in [20]. Here rectified output from oriented filters is processed by large-scale filters that were oriented orthogonally. These responses are summed over orientations and passed through a sigmoid non-linearity. In this model, gradual texture orientation gradients cannot be successfully detected, as in the case of our model and the one proposed in [10]. Our model extends previous approaches in a substantial way by including feedback connections such that results from later stages influence earlier results. This processing strategy highlights the importance of boundaries in texture processing for surface segmentation: Discontinuous arrangements in texture items lead to the detection of boundaries. The corresponding activities are fed back to enhance small-scale activations near those boundaries while responses to homogeneous arrangements are reduced or even suppressed through the competitive stages. This recurrent flow of activation creates more computational flexibility and circumvents simple all-or-none decisions necessary in feedforward models to generate localized results. For example, consider two juxtaposed line elements resulting in model V4 activations of equal strength after the first pass of feedforward processing. In this case, pure feedforward processing is not capable of signaling whether one of the two elements is more 'salient' compared to the other. Feedback modulation, however, will 'highlight' all potentially salient elements in the preceding model areas while suppressing cell activities due to unimportant image elements. This mechanism allows the model to focus processing on the important context information in the image. Even weak influences of essential context information resulting in a higher saliency of one of the two line elements can be detected and enhanced via the feedback loop, in turn leading to a more clear-cut decision.

Our model has been demonstrated to successfully explain human texture segmentation for texture flow patterns investigated by Nothdurft [14] and is also capable to successfully process real world texture images [18]. In the present study, we particularly investigate the predictive capabilities of the same model in texture segregation and visual search tasks when the density of textures composed of oriented items is varied. Although we believe that the major influences to texture segregation in these cases is contributed by feedforward processing, we claim that the action of feedback and the corresponding elaboration of network responses is also significantly related to the displayed ERP data. Gradual decision finding is achieved during the period of 150-200ms before N2p waves are generated.

3 Results

Computational experiments have been conducted with our full recurrent model depicted in Fig. 1. In this study, we particularly focussed on the processing of the texture stimuli used in Schuboe's ERP study [16].

• *Set Size 49.* The final activation patterns of model area V4 in response to the target and non-target stimuli of set size 49 are depicted in Fig. 2. Model V4 cells respond to the borders of the texture fields and in turn suppress via center-surround competition the responses to inner iso-oriented texture elements. In addition, they detect the orientation discontinuity caused by the perpendicular pop-out line element of the target stimulus. Consequently, the presence or absence of model V4 cell activity in the inner part of the map directly signals the presence or absence of a target line element in the stimulus. The activation patterns of model areas V1 and V2 in response to the target stimulus are depicted in Fig. 2 (left). Model V2 bipole cells bridge gaps between aligned line elements and form continuous smooth activation patterns. Model V2 cell responses to lines at the texture border as well as to the perpendicular target line are enhanced via modulatory feedback activity from model area V4. Increased model V2 activations in turn strengthen the model V4 responses at the corresponding topolographic positions, thus stabilizing the detection of salient line elements. Modulation of model V2 cell responses via V4 feedback leads to an indirect and weaker modulation of cells in model area V1. The strength of this modulation is about 15 % of the mean V1 cell responses to a line element. Unfortunately, this influence can hardly be seen in the gray scale pictures. Model areas V1 and V2 are not in the focus of the present study, as the main effects accounting for the results of the ERP-study turned out to be observable in model area V4. However, their activation patterns in response to the target stimulus have been presented to demonstrate how the complete model works (see details in [18]). In the following, the presentation of the results will focus on model area V4.

• *Set Size 5.* The final model V4 cell responses to the stimuli of set size 5 are given in Figure 3 (left). Each line element results in a separate V4 activity blob. The distance between the blobs and the inhomogeneity of their spatial arrangement prevent activity suppression via center-surround competition. In contrast to set size 49, no difference between V4 sum activity in response to non-target and target stimuli can be observed.

• *Set Size 25.* Figure 3 (right) depicts model V4 responses to stimuli of set size 25. These patterns exhibit some of the properties already observed for set size 49, namely the enhancement of model V4 responses to lines at stimulus boundaries and a marked reduction of responses to inner line elements by center-surround competition. However, due to the lower density and the inhomogeneity of the spatial arrangement, this suppression is far from being complete. Consequently, no single circumscribed activity blob caused by the perpendicular target line can be observed in the target trail. Nevertheless, model V4 activity at the position of the target line is clearly enhanced and its activation strength is comparable to V4 responses to elements at the stimulus border. These findings suggest that (i) similar pre-attentive ERP-patterns for target and non-target stimuli occur

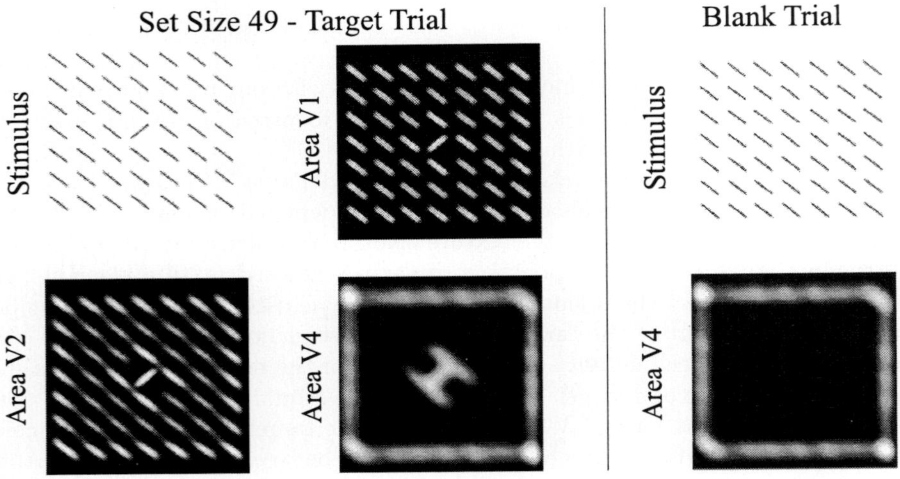

Fig. 2. Final cell responses summed over all orientations at each location for stimuli of set size 49. For the target stimulus, all model areas are shown. For the non-target stimulus, only model area V4 is depicted. Model V4 cells respond to the border of the texture regions and in turn the cell responses to the inner iso-oriented lines are completely suppressed via center-surround competition. In addtion, V4 cells detect the orientation discontinuity caused by the perpendicular target line. V2 cell responses are enhanced via feedback modulation by V4 activity at topographically corresponding positions.

for set size 25 (since quite similar model activation patterns were observed), but that (ii) the detection performance is higher for set size 25 compared to set size 5 (since target elements result in enhanced model V4 activity).

4 Discussion

In this paper, we investigated a neural model of texture boundary detection, which builds upon a large database of available anatomical and physiological data. In a previous study, we have demonstrated that this model can account for a large body of results from studies using single cell recordings as well as psychophysical paradigms [18]. Here, we used the unmodified model and exposed it to stimuli adapted from recently published texture segmentation and visual search studies [15,16]. We found that model V4 activation patterns in response to non-target and target trials exhibited an apparent difference only for set size 49. In contrast, the response patterns to stimuli of set sizes 5 and 25 differ either not at all or only slightly when target and non-target trials were compared. In the ERP study [16], significant differences in posterior N2 amplitude between non-target and target trials could only be observed for set size 49. Since N2p is thought to reflect pre-attentive processing, it is likely to assume that it is the

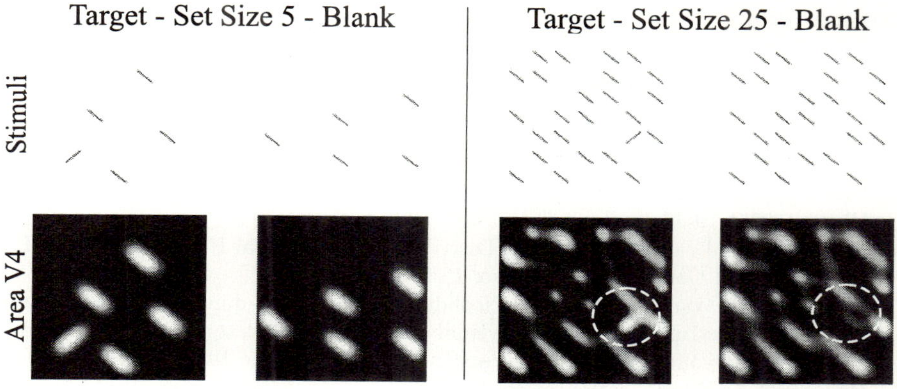

Fig. 3. Activation patterns of model area V4 in response to stimuli of set sizes 5 and 25. *Set Size 5:* Each line results in a separate V4 activity blob. No difference in mean cell response level betweeen target and non-target trials can be observed. *Set Size 25:* The V4 cell responses to inner iso-oriented line elements are markedly suppressed via center-surround competition and the responses to the perpendicular target line are enhanced. However, the suppression is not complete and the V4 activation patterns of target and non-target trials do not show the clear-cut differences observable for set size 49.

electrophysiological correlate of a segmentation process mediated by visual area V4, as proposed by the model.

Model V4 responses to target and non-target stimuli of set size 25 revealed no clear-cut differences. However, V4 activity at the position of the target line was markedly enhanced. We claim that this enhancement helps subsequent attentive processes to identify the target. More precisely, our results suggest that detection performance in visual search will decrease with increasing set size as long as model V4 center-surround competition is not effective due to the distance between elements. However, performance will start to increase again when the number of elements is further increased, allowing to suppress V4 activations to non-target line elements via center-surround competition. Indeed, a recent psychophysical study [11] demonstrated that detection performance follows exactly that behaviour.

According to the model, we propose that the same pre-attentive segmentation mechanisms are involved in texture segmentation as well as in visual search. This pre-processing is only effective when the spatial arrangement of the elements is sufficiently dense and homogeneous. The proposed computational mechanisms respond in a gradual fashion ranging from immediate target line identification (set size 49), over weakly enhanced target regions (set size 25) to complete absence (set size 5). The pre-processed display serves as input for subsequent attentive processing necessary to solve the detection task (reflected by the P3 component in the ERP study). This in turn results in visual search performance of gradual effectiveness.

References

1. Bergen, J.R.: Theories of visual texture perception. in: Spatial Vision. Editor: D. Regan. Vision and Visual Dysfunction, Vol. 10, MacMillan Press (1991) 114-134
2. Bergen, J.R., Adelson, E.H.: Early vision and texture perception. Nature **333** (1988) 363-364
3. Caelli, T.: Three processing characteristics of visual texture segmentation. Spatial Vis. **1** (1985) 19-30
4. Fellemann, D.J., van Essen, D.C.: Distributed Hierarchical Processing in the Primate Cerebral Cortex. Cereb Cortex **1** (1991) 1-47
5. Gallant, J.L., van Essen, D.C., Nothdurft, H.C.: Two-dimensional and three-dimensional texture processing in visual cortex of the Macaque monkey. in: Early Vision and Beyond. Editor: T.V. Papathomas (Cambridge 1995)
6. Heeger, D.J.: Normalization of cell responses in cat striate cortex. Vis. Neurosci. **9** (1992) 184-197
7. Hubel, D.H., Wiesel, T.N.: Receptive fields, binocular interaction and functional architecture in the cat's visual cortex. J Physiol. **160** (1962) 106-154
8. Kastner, S., de Weerd, P., Ungerleider, L.G.: Texture Segregation in the Human Visual Cortex: A Functional MRI Study. J Neurophysiol. **83** (2000) 2453-2457
9. Landy, M.S., Bergen, J.R.: Texture segregation and orientation gradient. Vis. Res. **31** (1991) 679-691
10. Malik, J., Perona, P.: Preattentive texture discrimination with early vision mechanisms. J. Opt. Soc. America A **7** (1990) 923-932
11. Meinecke, C., Donk, M.: Detection performance in pop-out tasks: nonmonotonic changes with display size and eccentricity. Perception **31** (2002) 591-602
12. Merigan, W.H.: Cortical area V4 is critical for certain texture discriminations, but this effect is not dependent on attention. Vis Neurosci. **17** (2000) 949-958
13. Neumann, H., Sepp, W.: Recurrent V1-V2 interaction in early visual boundary processing. Biol Cybern. **81** (1999) 425-444
14. Nothdurft, H.C.: Feature analysis and the role of similarity in preattentive vision. Percept Psychophys. **52** (1992) 355-375
15. Schuboe, A., Meinecke, C., Schroeger, E.: Automaticity and attention: investigating automatic processing in texture segmentation with event-related brain potentials. Cogn Brain Res. **11** (2001) 341-361
16. Schuboe, A.: Is preattentive processing in visual search similar to preattentive processing in texture segmentation? Proc. of 5th TWK (Tuebingen 2002)
17. Smith, A.T., Singh, K.D., Williams, A.L., Greenlee, M.W.: Estimating Receptive Field Size from fMRI Data in Human Striate and Extrastriate Visual Cortex. Cereb Cortex **11** (2001) 1182-1190
18. Thielscher, A., Neumann, H.: Neural Mechanisms of Cortico-cortical Interaction in Texture Boundary Detection. submitted
19. v.d. Heydt, R., Peterhans, E., Baumgartner, G.: Illusory contours and cortical neuron responses. Science **224** (1984) 1260-1262
20. Wilson, H.R.: Non-Fourier cortical processes in texture, form, and motion perception. in: Cerebral Cortex, Vol.13: Models of Cortical Circuits. Editors: P.S. Ulinski, E.G. Jones, A. Peters, Kluwer Academic/Plenum Publ. (1999) 445-477

Unsupervised Image Segmentation Using a Colony of Cooperating Ants

Salima Ouadfel[1,2] and Mohamed Batouche[2]

[1] Département Informatique, Université de Batna. Algérie
souadfel@wissal.dz
[2] Equipe Vision et Infographie, Laboratoire LIRE. Université de Constantine. Algérie
batouche@wissal.dz

Abstract. In this paper, we present a novel method for unsupervised image segmentation. Image segmentation is cast as a clustering problem, which aims to partition a given set of pixels into a number of homogenous clusters, based on a similarity criterion. The clustering problem is a difficult optimization problem for two main reasons: first the search space of the optimization is too large, second the clustering objective function is typically non convex and thus may exhibit a large number of local minima. Ant Colony Optimization is a recent multi-agent approach based on artificial ants for solving hard combinatorial optimization problems. We propose the use of the *Max-Min* Ant System (*MMAS)* to solve the clustering problem in the field of image segmentation. Each pixel within the image is mapped to its closest cluster taking into account its immediate neighborhood. The obtained results are encouraging and prove the feasibility of the proposed algorithm.

Keywords. Image, Segmentation, Clustering, Ant Colony Optimization, Max-Min Ant System.

1 Introduction

Image segmentation is a fundamental task in a vision system. Its purpose is to subdivide an image into meaningful non-overlapping regions. Image segmentation can be viewed as a clustering problem, which aims to partition the image into clusters such that the pixels within a cluster are as homogenous as possible whereas the clusters among each other are as heterogeneous as possible with respect to a similarity measure. Several clustering methods are provided; the simplest one is the standard K-means [1,9]. Starting from a set of K reference points chosen either randomly or using a priori knowledge and representing the centroids of K clusters, partitioning is done by assigning each pixel to the closest cluster, according to its distance to the cluster centroid. The new centroids for the obtained clusters are computed and the points are re-assigned again to their closest cluster until a termination criterion is reached. K-means has been widely used because of its simplicity and its rapid convergence. However, the K-means algorithm requires a free–noise image and a good starting partition (good initial centroids). Moreover, the K-means is a descend gradient method and so can be often trapped in a local minimum which may be far from the

H.H. Bülthoff et al. (Eds.): BMCV 2002, LNCS 2525, pp. 109–116, 2002.

global minimum. To treat this problem stochastic global optimization methods have been proposed like genetic algorithms [5] and simulated annealing [6].

Ant Colony Optimization (ACO) is a recent metaphor for the solution of combinatorial optimization problem. ACO has been inspired from the behavior of real ants, and in particular from their collective foraging behavior. Ants based algorithms make use of simple agents called artificial ants, which collaborate together in order to find the solution of NP hard problems. Each ant construct iteratively a solution guided by a simulate pheromone and a heuristic information which depend on the problem to be solved.

In this paper, we propose the use of an adapted version of *Max-Min* Ant System *MMAS* [7,8] to the clustering problem in the field of image segmentation. The underlying idea is to take advantage from the ACO meta-heuristic characteristics to develop a multi-agent approach to segment an image and find the optimal partition. The remainder of the paper is organized as follows. A brief description of ACO metaheuristic principle and a general *MMAS* algorithm are given in section 2. In section 3, we describe our approach for image segmentation. Experimental results are reported in section 4. Finally concluding remarks are drawn in section 5.

2 Ant Colony Optimization

ACO is a population-based approach inspired from the studies of the foraging behavior of real ants. Ethological research demonstrates that while walking from food sources to the nest, and, going back, real ants deposit on the ground along their path a chemical substance called pheromone. Ants can smell pheromone and therefore will probably follow the path marked by strongest pheromone concentrations, which permits the emergence of shortest paths. Inspired from this ant-based optimization, ACO algorithms are distributed algorithms based on a population of agents called artificial ants. Simple agents collaborate using an artificial pheromone to emerge a complex collective behavior and solve NP hard combinatorial optimization problems.

The first ant-based system was introduced by Marco Dorigo and was called Ant System (AS)[2]. In AS, an ant build a solution to a combinatorial optimization problem by exploiting the search history represented by the pheromone trails and a heuristic information that depend on the problem to solve. AS was applied to the traveling salesman problem (TSP)[2] and it has been evaluated as a viable approach. Some improvements have been performed afterwards to the basic AS algorithm, concerning the transition rules, the pheromone trail updating and the use of a local search, leading to more elaborate variants algorithms. A good review of applications of ant algorithms for benchmark problems can be found in [4].

Max-Min Ant System (*MMAS*) [7,8] has been proposed in order to improve the quality solution of AS and differs from it in essentially three points:

1. Pheromone trails are updated after each iteration, only by the ant which found the iteration-best solution;

2. Pheromone trails values are restricted to a given interval $[\tau_{min}, \tau_{max}]$ in order to avoid premature convergence;
3. Pheromone trails are initialized to the maximum trail value τ_{max} to encourage the exploration of a large set of solutions at the start of the algorithm.

In addition, the authors improved the results of the first version of *MMAS* with the introduction of the local search procedure and the use of the pseudo random rule defined in ACS [3] as a selection rule. We give in the following a general algorithm for *MMAS* [7]:

Procedure *Max-Min* ant system with local search
1. Initialize the pheromone trails and the parameters;
2. While (termination condition is not reached) do
   - For each ant do
     Construct a solution for the ant;
     End for
   - Select ants to improve their solution by a local search;
   - Apply local search to selected ants;
   - Update the pheromone trail, and maintain it in the interval selected;
3. Return the best solution found.

Fig. 1. General algorithm for *Max-Min* Ant System with local search procedure.

3 Image Segmentation Using MMAS

The clustering problem may be described in this manner. Given a set *S* of *n* pixels, each pixel $s \in S$ is defined by its location (i,j) and its grey value y_s, we seek to partition *S* into K clusters $\{c_1, c_2, c_3, \ldots c_k\}$. Each cluster c_k has n_k pixels and each pixel *s* is in one cluster that is $\sum_{i=1}^{k} n_i = n$. The mean grey level of the cluster c_k is given by: $\mu_k = \frac{1}{n_k} \sum_{s \in c_k} y_s$

The *MMAS* based clustering algorithm goal is to find the optimal partition in which each pixel is mapped to its closest cluster taking into account its immediate neighborhood. The clustering process can be presented as follow:

1. Initialize all entries of the matrix of the pheromone trails to τ_{max};
2. While (not convergence or the maximum number of iterations is not reached) do
   – For each ant k
     Build a possible partition using the transition rule;
     Evaluate the quality of the partition found;
   – End For
   – Update the amount of pheromone trails using the iteration best partition;

3. End Do;
4. Return the best partition.

We have to define:

- The transition rule and the pheromone updating formula;
- The clustering metric which measures the quality of a partition;
- The values of τ_{min} and τ_{max}.

The Transition Rule

An ant agent chooses to assign a pixel s to a candidate cluster c applying the following pseudo random rule:

$$c=\begin{cases}\operatorname{argmax} \tau(s,c)\cdot(\eta(s,c))^{\beta} & \text{if } q\leq q_0\\ C & \text{otherwise}\end{cases} \tag{1}$$

Where:

- $\tau(s,c)$ is the amount of pheromone trail deposit by the ant when the pixel s is mapped into the cluster c;
- $\eta(s,c)$ is the heuristic function;
- β is the weight of the importance of the pheromone trail and the heuristic function;
- q is a random value in [0,1];
- q_0 is a parameter that controls the exploitation of the history search represented by the pheromone trails versus the exploration of new solutions.

C is a random variable (a random cluster or label) selected according to the following probability distribution:

$$p(s,c)=\frac{\tau(s,c)\cdot(\eta(s,c))^{\beta}}{\sum_{u}\tau(s,u)\cdot(\eta(s,u))^{\beta}} \tag{2}$$

Where u is a possible label in the set of labels $\{c_1,c_2,c_3,\ldots c_k\}$ and $p(s,c)$ is the probability with which ant chooses to place a pixel s into a cluster c.

The probabilistic choice of a cluster c to a pixel s is biased by the pheromone trail $\tau(s,c)$ that represents the learned desirability of assigning the pixel s to the cluster c, and by the heuristic function η, which quantifies the attractiveness of an assignement, and maintains spatial regularity. According to a Markov assumption, the heuristic function η imposes that a pixel must belong to the closest cluster taking into account its immediate neighborhood. For this reason, η consists of two parts: the first part measures the Euclidian distance d_e between the grey level of the pixel and the mean grey level of the candidate cluster. The second part describes how compatible is the pixel with its neighborhood in terms of their labels with a contiguity measure d_c. The heuristic function η has the following formulation:

$$\eta(s,c) = d_e(s,c) + \alpha \cdot d_c(s,c) \quad (3)$$

Where:

$$d_e(s,c) = \left\| y_s - \mu_c \right\| \quad (4)$$
$$d_c(s,c) = \sum_{s \in V_s} \left(1 - \delta(c_s, c_{s'})\right)$$

Where c_s and $c_{s'}$ are respectively the label of the pixel *s* and of its neighbor s'. V_s is the set of 8-neighbors of the pixel *s* and α is a parameter within [0,1].

Pheromone Trail Updating

After all ants have built a possible partition, pheromone trails are updated, but only by the ant that found the iteration best quality solution. Pheromone trail values of the corresponding pairs (s,c) in this best partition is updated according to the following updating rule:

$$\tau(s,c) = \rho\tau(s,c) + 1/Q_{best} \quad (5)$$

Where ρ in] 0,1[is the persistence of the pheromone trail and (1-ρ) represents the factor of lowing the pheromone trail as in the behavior of the real ants. The lower ρ, the faster information gathered in previous iterations is forgotten. Q_{best} is the best quality partition found during an iteration of the algorithm.

Quality of a Partition

Many criteria have been developed for measuring the quality of a partition. The common goal is to find the partition that results in compact clusters, which are well separated taking into account that neighboring pixels must share the same cluster. For this purpose, we propose the use of a quality measure Q that balances the fitness to the data and the smoothness of the assignement map.

$$Q = \sum_{i=1}^{k} \sum_{s \in c_i} \frac{1}{n_i} \cdot \eta(s, c_i) \quad (6)$$

Where $\eta(s,c_i)$ is the heuristic function defined in equation 3.

Pheromone Trails Limits

In *MMAS*, pheromone trails are limited to an interval between maximum trail τ_{max} and minimum trail τ_{min}. This constraint prevents a premature convergence and reduces the differences of pheromone trails on pairs (s,c). The maximum and minimum trail limits are chosen in a problem-dependent way. For the maximum trail limit τ_{max} we use $\tau_{max} = 1/Q_{opt}$. Q_{opt} is the optimal quality partition produced during the run of the algorithm. The minimum pheromone trail τ_{min} is fixed to a value different from 0.

4 Experimental Results

To illustrate the performance of the method described in this paper, two examples are presented below with synthetic image and real world image. We compare our results with results obtained from the conventional K-means algorithm. In all experiments the numerical parameters are set to the following values: $\beta = -1$, $q_0 = 0.9$, $\rho = 0.9$, $\tau_{min} = 0.001$, and $\alpha = 0.9$. The number of ants used is set to 10.

4.1 Synthetic Image

Fig 3 shows results obtained by segmenting a synthetic noisy image shown in Fig 2, comparatively for the K-means algorithm and our method. As may be seen, results obtained by the K-means algorithm suffer from the noise, while our approach succeeds in finding correctly the homogenous regions.

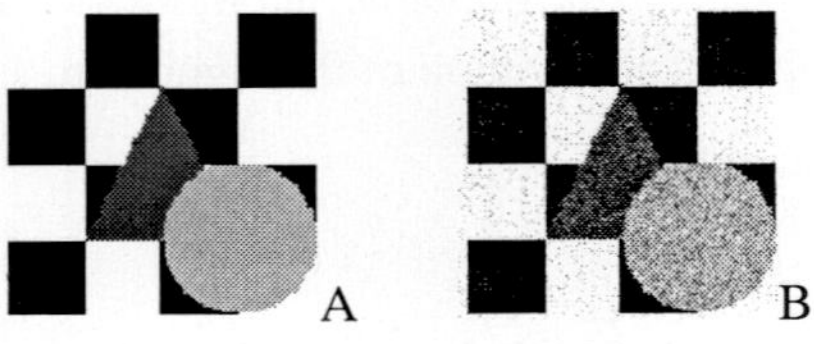

Fig. 2. A) Synthetic image with 4 classes, B) Synthetic noisy image with 10 db

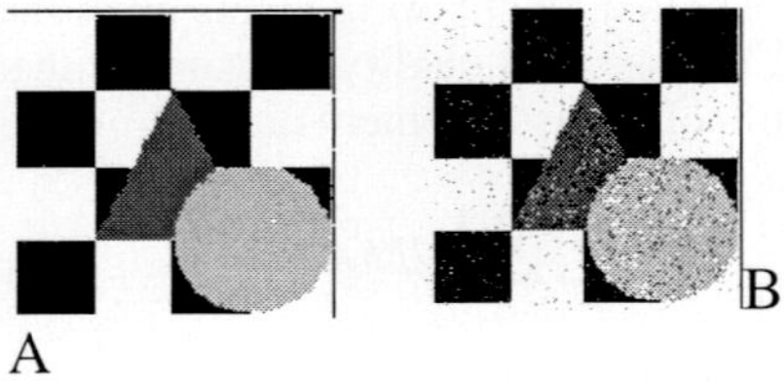

Fig. 3. Results obtained using the K-means algorithms and our approach. A) Our classification results. B) K-means classification results.

Results validation is done by comparing the segmentation results with the original image. For this we calculate for each class the following values:

TP: True Positives, pixels positively detected;
FP: False Positives, pixels wrongly detected;
FN: False Negatives, pixels missing.

Validation measure is based on the two coefficients: Building Detection Percentage (BDP) and Branching Factor (BF) where:

$$BDP=\frac{TP}{TP+FN} \qquad BF=\frac{FP}{TP} \tag{7}$$

BDP represents the fraction of the correctly classified pixels and BF provides a measure on the over-detection pixels. The optimum setting of these two measures for an algorithm is usually one in which BDP is near 1 and BF is near 0. Table 1 presents the results.

Table 1. BDP and BF Coefficients calculated from the segmentation results with the K-means algorithm and our segmentation approach.

		Classes			
		1	2	3	4
K-means	BDP	0.94	0.93	0.83	0.84
	BF	0.052	0.043	0.159	0.431
MMAS clustering algorithm	BDP	0.99	0.98	0.99	0.99
	BF	0.024	0.002	0.003	0.019

From the Table 1, we observe that our method performs well compared to K-means and is less sensitive to the presence of the noise.

4.2 Real World Images

Our algorithm has been applied to a muscle cell image. The results are presented in Fig 4 and show that our method produced more compact regions as a whole.

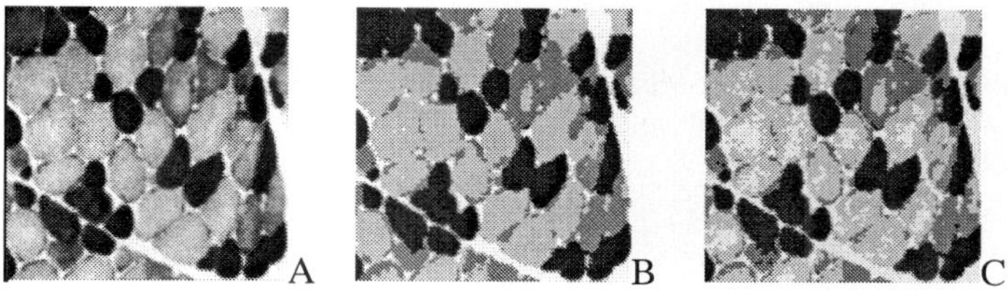

Fig. 4. Results of segmentation of a muscle cell image. A) a muscle cell image. B) Result of our method. C) Result of the K-means algorithm.

5 Conclusion

In this paper we have presented a new method for image segmentation, based on a novel metaphor for solving combinatorial optimization problems. The *MMAS* clustering algorithm goal is to find the optimal partition in which each pixel is mapped to its closest cluster taking into account its immediate neighborhood. Probabilistic clustering is biased by the pheromone trail, which represents the learned desirability of an assignment, and by the heuristic function, which maintains spatial regularity. The proposed clustering algorithm was numerically tested for its effectiveness and has shown that it outperforms the traditional K-means algorithm and provides encouraging results. We currently study the introduction of a local search into the clustering process for improving the performance of the algorithm, and the use of a suitable Multigrid architecture in order to speed up the total execution time of the algorithm that increases with the dimension of the image.

References

[1] A.k. Jain , M. Murty and P. Flynn. «Data Clustering, A Review». ACM Computing Survey. Vol. 31, N° 3 . 1999.

[2] M. Dorigo, V. Maniezzo. and A. Colorni. « The Ant System: Optimization by a Colony of Cooperating Agents ». IEEE Transactions on Systems, Man and Cybernetics-Part B, Vol. 26, N° 1, pp: 29-41. 1996.

[3] M. Dorigo, and L. Gambardella. «Ant Colony System: A Cooperative Learning Approach to the Traveling Salesman Problem. ». IEEE Transactions on Evolutionary Computation 1, pp: 53-66, 1997.

[4] M. Dorigo, G. Di Caro, and L. Gambardella. « Ant Algorithms for Discrete Optimization ». Artificial Life. Vol. 5, N°2, pp: 137-172. 1999.

[5] P. Andrey and P. Tarroux. « Unsupervised image segmentation using a distributed genetic algorithm». Patt. Recogn., Vol. 27, N°5, pp: 659-673, 1994.

[6] S. Laskshmanan and H. Derin. «Simultaneous segmentation pg Gibbs Random Field using Simulated Annealing. » IEEE Trans. On Pattern Analysis and Machine Intelligence. Vol. 11, N°8, pp: 799-813, 1989.

[7] T. Stutzle and H. Hoos. « Improvement on Ant System: Introducing the MAX-MIN Ant System». In the proceeding of the International Conference on Artificial Neural Networks and Genetic Algorithms, pp: 245-249. Springer-Verlag, Wien, 1997.

[8] T. Stutzle and H. Hoos. « MAX-MIN Ant System and Local Search for Combinatorial Optimization Problems. Towards Adaptive Tools for Combinatorial Global Optimization». 2nd Metaheuristics International Conference, Sophia-Antipolis, France.1997.

[9] Z. Selim and A. Ismail. « K-Means-Type Algorithm: Generalized convergence theorem and characterization of local optimality». IEEE. Trans. Anal. Mach. Intell. Vol. 6, pp: 81-87, 1984.

Image Reconstruction from Gabor Magnitudes*

Ingo J. Wundrich[1], Christoph von der Malsburg[1,2], and Rolf P. Würtz[1]

[1] Institut für Neuroinformatik, Ruhr-Universität Bochum
D-44780 Bochum, Germany

[2] Laboratory for Computational and Biological Vision
University of Southern California, Los Angeles, USA

Abstract. We present an analysis of the representation of images as the *magnitudes* of their transform with complex-valued Gabor wavelets. Such a representation is very useful for image understanding purposes and serves as a model for an early stage of human visual processing. We show that if the sampling of the wavelet transform is appropriate then the reconstruction from the magnitudes is unique up to the sign for almost all images. We also present an iterative reconstruction algorithm derived from the ideas of the proof, which yields very good reconstruction up to the sign and minor numerical errors in the very low frequencies.

Keywords. Gabor wavelets, reconstruction, feature extraction, phase retrieval, Gabor magnitudes, visual cortex.

1 Introduction

In the visual system of humans or monkeys an early stage is concerned with processing image information by convolution with some point spread function and ensuing non-linear operations that enhance edges and lead to some contrast normalization. A recognized problem [13] with edge-enhancing convolutions is their sensitivity to image shift, whereas one of the most important features of human vision is the positional invariance with which objects can be recognized. The two-dimensional power spectrum can represent images in a shift-invariant way, but it has the great drawback of being non-local, each component being influenced by all image pixels. On the other extreme, pixels as image features are maximally localized but achieve notoriously little in terms of analyzing image contents.

We focus here on Gabor functions as an adjustable compromise between pixel representation and Fourier components. They seem to be implemented in the first stages of processing in the visual cortex of higher vertebrates, as the receptive fields of the so-called *simple cells* can be described to some accuracy as Gabor functions [1,7]. There is also evidence that the *magnitudes* of the Gabor filter responses (short *Gabor magnitudes*) are calculated by another set of cells called *complex cells* [12].

* This work has been supported by grants from BMBF, ONR and ARO.

H.H. Bülthoff et al. (Eds.): BMCV 2002, LNCS 2525, pp. 117–126, 2002.

The simplest model for these findings is that simple cell responses are calculated from the image intensities by a feedforward neural net, and that complex cells build on their information by another feedforward net. The complex cells, in turn, can be combined to more complicated feature detectors such as corner detectors [21]. They have also proven useful for higher image understanding tasks such as texture classification [3], recognition of faces [9,20,2], vehicles [18], and hand gestures [14]. The deeper reason for this is that the magnitude operation introduces some local shift invariance in the sense that under small shifts in the image the Gabor magnitudes are more robust than the full complex valued responses, because they are much smoother. This robustness is crucial for recognition systems, which have to cope with small local deformations. As a practical consequence, similarity landscapes between local features are smoother if magnitudes are used, which makes matching faster and less prone to local maxima [9, 20,17].

If the Gabor functions are arranged into a wavelet transform and the sampling is dense enough then the original image can be recovered from the transform values with arbitrary quality (except for the DC-value). Given the useful properties of the magnitudes of the Gabor transform an important theoretical question is how much image information can be recovered from that.

There are many results on the reconstruction of images from localized phase [15], and they show convincingly that localized phase is more useful than global Fourier phase. There seems to be general agreement that reconstruction from phase is simpler than reconstruction from local magnitude.

In this paper we are concerned with the latter. It must be noted that the study of reconstruction is not the most important issue for an object recognition system, where most of the visual information must be *discarded*. Nevertheless, it is of importance to study as well as possible the course of information through the system in order to understand its mechanism. If images of different objects could be reconstructed from the data format used by a recognition algorithm, this algorithm would be rather limited in its value. Additionally, our results may be of importance to other applications of Gabor wavelets.

In the following we briefly outline the theory of wavelets and frames necessary to understand reconstruction from the linear transform, introduce the Gabor wavelet transform, and review some literature on phase retrieval from power spectra of images. We then outline the proof of a theorem stating that, given the right transform parameters and appropriate band-limitation, no image information is lost by applying Gabor magnitudes to an image except the DC-value of the image and a global sign. The proof uses techniques from [5] and applies to all images except a subset of measure zero.

Finally, we explore the quality of reconstruction by numerical experiments based on the ideas of the proof. The results are not perfect because much of the proof depends on transform values being exactly zero, which does not translate very well into numerical computation. However, for all images we tested, we were able to retrieve very good approximations of either the image itself or its negative.

2 Gabor Wavelets and Frames

For the analysis of signal properties at various scales the *wavelet transform* has been introduced in [4]. The signal is projected onto a family of wavelet functions $\psi_{x_0,a}(x)$ derived from a so-called *mother wavelet* $\psi(x)$ by applying translations by x_0 and dilations by a factor $a > 0$. For image processing, we follow the proposal by Murenzi [10] and choose the 2-dimensional Euclidean group $IG(2)$ with dilations for the construction of a wavelet family. This leads to daughter wavelets which are translated, rotated and scaled versions of the mother.

The transition to wavelets defined on $\mathbb{R}^2$ leads to a wavelet family parameterization by the translation vector $\boldsymbol{x}_0 \in \mathbb{R}^2$, scale factor $a > 0$ and the orientation angle $\vartheta \in [0, 2\pi[$. This extension of the affine linear group to two spatial dimensions preserves the idea of scaling the transformation kernel ψ. Analogous to the 1D case the 2D wavelet transform consists of projection of the image data $I(\boldsymbol{x})$ onto the wavelet family ($\mathrm{Q}(\vartheta)$ stands for the 2D rotation matrix by the angle ϑ):

$$\mathcal{I}(\boldsymbol{x}_0, a, \vartheta) = \langle I, \psi_{\boldsymbol{x}_0,a,\vartheta} \rangle, \tag{1}$$

$$\psi_{\boldsymbol{x}_0,a,\vartheta}(\boldsymbol{x}) = a^{-1}\psi[a^{-1}\mathrm{Q}(\vartheta)(\boldsymbol{x} - \boldsymbol{x}_0)] \tag{2}$$

The mother wavelet (and, consequently, all wavelets) must satisfy the *admissibility condition* [8]:

$$0 < C = 4\pi^2 \int_{\mathbb{R}^2} d^2\omega \, \frac{|\hat{\psi}(\boldsymbol{\omega})|^2}{\|\boldsymbol{\omega}\|^2} < \infty. \tag{3}$$

Consequently, the wavelets must have zero DC-value ($\hat{\psi}(\mathbf{0}) = 0$) and decay sufficiently quickly for increasing $\|\boldsymbol{\omega}\|$. This condition, together with implementing the translations of wavelets as convolutions means that wavelets are bandpass functions.

We now narrow our focus to the Gabor function as mother wavelet. As Gabor functions are not DC-free, an additional term must be introduced to ensure that wavelet property. Following Murenzi [10], we let:

$$\psi(\boldsymbol{x}) = \frac{1}{\sigma\tau} \exp\left(-\frac{1}{2}\|\mathrm{S}_{\sigma,\tau}\boldsymbol{x}\|^2\right)\left(\exp\left(j\boldsymbol{x}^T\boldsymbol{e}_1\right) - \exp\left(-\frac{\sigma^2}{2}\right)\right) \tag{4}$$

In these equations the diagonal matrix $\mathrm{S}_{\sigma,\tau} = Diag(1/\sigma, 1/\tau)$ controls the shape of the elliptical Gaussian relative to the wavelength. Different ways of removing the DC-value can be used, but the one above is the most elegant for analytical treatment.

Different Gabor functions are, in general, not orthogonal and the wavelet families are usually not linearly independent. That means that (1) yields an overcomplete representation of the image signal $I(\boldsymbol{x})$. To handle linear transforms of this nature the *frame* concept, which can be seen as a generalization of the basis in a linear space. We follow the description in [8].

For a Hilbert space $\mathcal{H}$ and a measure space $(\mathcal{M}, \mu)$ linear transforms H from $\mathcal{H}$ into $L^2(\mathcal{M}, \mu)$ are defined by the projection onto a family of functions $\mathcal{H}_\mathcal{M} = \{h_\xi \in \mathcal{H} : \xi \in \mathcal{M}\}$ via $\mathrm{H}f(\xi) = \langle h_\xi, f \rangle$, such that H is measurable for every $f \in \mathcal{H}$. This family is called a *frame* if there exist positive finite constants A and B such that for every $f \in \mathcal{H}$

$$A\|f\|^2_{\mathcal{H}} \leq \|\mathrm{H}f\|^2_{L^2(\mathcal{M},\mu)} \leq B\|f\|^2_{\mathcal{H}} \,. \tag{5}$$

Such constants are called *frame bounds.* If $A = B$ the frame is called *tight.* The freedom in the choice of μ can be put to different uses, e.g., the frame elements can be normalized or one of the frame bounds can be fixed at 1. Furthermore, it allows a coherent formulation of discrete and continuous wavelet transforms. In our concrete case, the measure space is $\mathcal{M} = \mathbb{R}^2 \times \mathbb{R}^+ \times \mathcal{U}$ for the two spatial dimensions, scale and orientation, and the accompanying measure is given by

$$d\mu = d^2x_0 \; a^{-3} da \; d\vartheta \,. \tag{6}$$

In the continuous case the so constructed inverse 2D wavelet transform becomes:

$$I(\boldsymbol{x}) = \frac{1}{C} \int\limits_{\mathbb{R}^+} \frac{da}{a^3} \int\limits_0^{2\pi} d\vartheta \int\limits_{\mathbb{R}^2} d^2x_0 \, \mathcal{I}(\boldsymbol{x}_0, a, \vartheta) \psi_{\boldsymbol{x}_0,a,\vartheta}(\boldsymbol{x}) \,, \tag{7}$$

with the C from (3).

For practical purposes, it is not desirable to expand the image representation from a function on $\mathbb{R}^2$ to one on $\mathbb{R}^4$, so *sampling* of translations, scales and orientations $\boldsymbol{x}_0 = \boldsymbol{n}_0 \Delta$, $a = a_{\min} a_0^m$, $\vartheta = 2\pi l / L$ with $\boldsymbol{n}_0 \in \mathbb{Z}^2$, $m \in \{0, 1, \ldots, M-1\}$, and $l \in \{0, 1, \ldots, L-1\}$, becomes inevitable.

We now switch from continuous functions to discretely sampled images of $N_1 \times N_2$ pixels. The underlying finite lattice will be called $\mathcal{S}_{\boldsymbol{N}}$. Now, the discrete Gabor wavelet transform can be computed in either domain by the inner product $\mathcal{I}(\boldsymbol{n}_0, m, l) = \langle I, \psi_{\boldsymbol{n}_0,m,l} \rangle$.

3 From Fourier to Gabor Magnitudes

In order to state theorems about the reconstructability of an image from its Gabor magnitudes $|\mathcal{I}(\boldsymbol{n}_0, m, l)|$ we choose a collection of theorems on Fourier magnitudes as a starting point.

In general the Fourier transform $\hat{I}(\boldsymbol{\omega})$ is a complex-valued function which can be described in terms of a magnitude and a phase. The fact that the inverse DFT applied to a modified transform with all magnitudes set to 1 and original phases preserves essential image properties [11] is frequently interpreted as saying that the Fourier magnitudes contain "less" image information than the phases. However, analytical results and existing phase retrieval algorithms provide hints that the situation is not as simple.

These theorems are based on the fact that the Fundamental Theorem of Algebra does not hold for polynomials in more than one variable. More precisely, the set of polynomials in more than one variable which can be factored in a nontrivial way are of measure zero in the vector space of all polynomials of the same degree [6]. A nontrivial factorization is very undesirable because the number of ambiguities caused by phase removal increases exponentially with the number of factors.

Hayes's theorem identifies the 2D z-Transform,

$$\check{I}(\boldsymbol{z}) = \frac{1}{2\pi} \sum_{\boldsymbol{n} \in \mathcal{S}_{\boldsymbol{N}}} I(\boldsymbol{n}) z_1^{-n_1} z_2^{-n_2}, \tag{8}$$

and the 2D discrete space Fourier transform (DSFT) on a compact support, with polynomials in two variables.

Theorem 1 (Hayes, [5]). *Let I_1, I_2 be 2D real sequences with support $\mathcal{S}_{\boldsymbol{N}} = \{0, \ldots, N_1 - 1\} \times \{0, \ldots, N_2 - 1\}$ and let Ω a set of $|\Omega|$ distinct points in $\mathcal{U}^2$ arranged on a lattice $\mathcal{L}(\Omega)$ with $|\Omega| \geq (2N_1 - 1)(2N_2 - 1)$. If $\check{I}_1(\boldsymbol{z})$ has at most one irreducible nonsymmetric factor and*

$$\left|\check{I}_1(\boldsymbol{\nu})\right| = \left|\check{I}_2(\boldsymbol{\nu})\right| \; \forall \boldsymbol{\nu} \in \mathcal{L}(\Omega) \tag{9}$$

then

$$\begin{aligned} I_1(\boldsymbol{n}) \in \{ & I_2(\boldsymbol{n}) \;\; I_2(\boldsymbol{N} - \boldsymbol{n} - \boldsymbol{1}), \\ & -I_2(\boldsymbol{n}), \; -I_2(\boldsymbol{N} - \boldsymbol{n} - \boldsymbol{1})\}\,. \end{aligned} \tag{10}$$

Theorem 1 states that DSFT magnitudes-only reconstruction yields either the original, or a negated, a point reflected, or a negated and point reflected version of the input signal. Together with the main statement from [6] that the set of all reducible polynomials $\check{I}(\boldsymbol{z})$ is of measure zero, the technicality about the irreducible nonsymmetric factors can be omitted, and we generalize Theorem 1 to complex-valued sequences as follows:

Theorem 2. *Let I_1, I_2 be complex sequences defined on the compact support $\mathcal{S}_{\boldsymbol{N}}$ and let $\check{I}_1(\boldsymbol{\nu})$ and $\check{I}_2(\boldsymbol{\nu})$ be only trivially reducible (i.e. have only factors of the form $z_1^{p_1} z_2^{p_2}$), and*

$$\left|\check{I}_1(\boldsymbol{\nu})\right| = \left|\check{I}_2(\boldsymbol{\nu})\right| \; \forall \boldsymbol{\nu} \in \mathcal{L}(\Omega) \tag{11}$$

with $\mathcal{L}(\Omega), |\Omega|$ as in Theorem 1 then

$$I_1(\boldsymbol{n}) \in \{\exp(j\eta)\, I_2(\boldsymbol{n}),\, \exp(j\eta)\, I_2^*(\boldsymbol{N} - \boldsymbol{n} - \boldsymbol{1}) \,|\, \eta \in [0, 2\pi[\}\,. \tag{12}$$

Transferring the modified Hayes theorem to the spatial magnitudes of the Gabor wavelet transform yields ambiguities which are reduced by inter- and intrasubband structures. More concretely, the Gabor magnitudes relate to the autocorrelation of the spectra of the subband images. However, due to the known localization of the Gabor responses in frequency space, the lost information can be recovered. This line of reasoning has allowed us to prove the following:

Theorem 3 (Gabor Magnitude Theorem). *Let $\mathcal{B}(N_1, N_2)$ be the space of all functions on the grid $\mathcal{S}_{\boldsymbol{N}}$ such that* $\mathrm{DFT}I(\boldsymbol{\rho}) = 0$ *for* $|\rho_1| \geq \frac{N_1}{4}, |\rho_2| \geq \frac{N_2}{4}$*, and let the wavelet family $\psi_{\boldsymbol{n}_0,m,l}$ constitute a frame in $\mathcal{B}(N_1, N_2)$. For all $I_1, I_2 \in \mathcal{B}(N_1, N_2)$ such that $\langle I_1, \psi_{\boldsymbol{n}_0,m,l}\rangle$ and $\langle I_2, \psi_{\boldsymbol{n}_0,m,l}\rangle$ are only trivially reducible polynomials and $|\langle I_1, \psi_{\boldsymbol{n}_0,m,l}\rangle| = |\langle I_2, \psi_{\boldsymbol{n}_0,m,l}\rangle|$ $\forall \boldsymbol{n}_0, m, l$ it follows that $I_1(\boldsymbol{n}) = \pm I_2(\boldsymbol{n})$.*

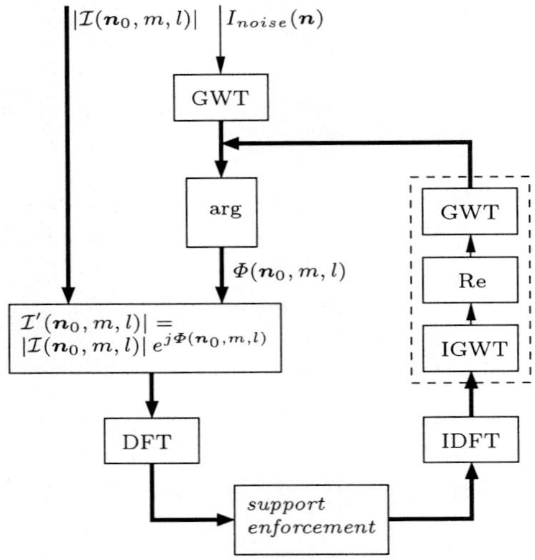

Fig. 1. Scheme for Gabor phase retrieval. Within one iteration loop each subband image is filtered according to its required signal energy concentration and boundary in frequency domain. In the next step the Gabor transform is computed which is nearest to the subspace of all Gabor-transformed real images. Last, the phases of the updated subband images are extracted and combined with the true magnitudes.

To complete the argument, Hayes' theorems can again be used to state that the Gabor transforms of almost all images are only trivially reducible. A detailed proof of the theorem can be found in [19]. Thus, we may conclude, that a low-pass filtered version of almost all images can be reconstructed from their Gabor transform magnitudes up to the sign.

The condition about the vanishing Fourier coefficients (band limitation) is not a restriction on the class of images to which the theorem applies, because each image of final resolution can be turned into a band-limited one by interpolation through zero-padding in the frequency domain. Put the other way around, from a Gabor wavelet transform of a certain spatial resolution, images of *half* that resolution can be reconstructed uniquely up to the sign.

4 Numerical Retrieval of Gabor Phases

In this section we construct a Gabor phase retrieval algorithm using one major idea from the proof of Theorem 3. In that proof, we have interchanged spatial

Fig. 2. The first row shows some original images, the second their reconstructions from their magnitudes of their Gabor wavelet transform after 1300 iterations. The reconstruction of the Lena image actually yielded its negative. The original images from which the magnitudes are taken are 128×128 images interpolated to 256×256. For display the grey value range has been normalized to [0,255].

and frequency domain for the application of Hayes's theorems, and the same can be done in the phase retrieval algorithm.

The given magnitudes for reconstruction are combined with the phases of an *arbitrary* Gabor-transformed image. Then, band limitation and subband localization are enforced by zeroing all frequencies above the boundary and outside the appropriate region of frequency concentration for a certain scale and orientation. That region is determined by applying a threshold of 0.1 to the Gabor kernel in frequency space. The result is transformed back into an image and transformed forward in order to project it onto the space of all Gabor wavelet transforms of real-valued images. Then the next cycle starts with the combination of the given magnitudes with the updated phases.The full course of the algorithm is shown in figure 1.

The main problem with the reconstruction from magnitudes is that the set of all transforms with given magnitudes but arbitrary phases is not convex, in contrast to the set of all transforms with given phases and variable magnitudes. Therefore, the iterative projection algorithm is not a POCS (projection onto convex sets) algorithm, and there is no straightforward convergence proof. This is in contrast to magnitude retrieval [15].

An alternative approach [16] uses a gradient descent algorithm to estimate an image minimizing an error functional. This minimization yields near to perfect results on bandpass filtered images.

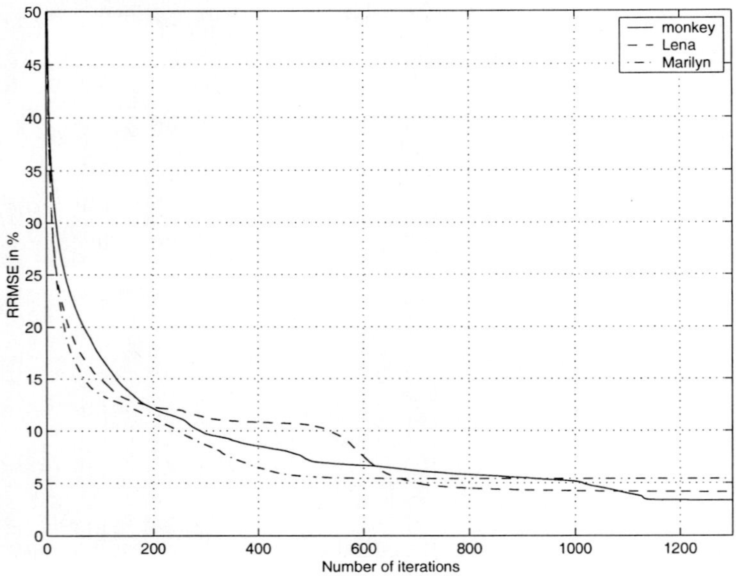

Fig. 3. The development of the error (RRMSE) for all three tested images

5 Reconstruction Experiments

We ran numerical reconstruction experiments on three different images with several hundred iterations. A real white noise "image" was chosen as initialization. The results of the reconstruction on some natural images are shown in figure 2. The transform parameters used to produce the images were $\sigma = 4$, $M = 8$, $L = 16$, $a_0 = \sqrt{2}$. With these parameters, reconstruction from the *linear* transform is perfect up to the DC-value. For display, all images are normalized to the gray value range [0,255], which dictates a DC-value.

In order to assess convergence we measured a relative RMSE defined as

$$\mathrm{RRMSE} = \sqrt{\frac{\sum_{m=0}^{M-1}\sum_{l=0}^{L-1}\sum_{\boldsymbol{n}_0\in\mathbb{S}_N} a_0^{-2m}\left[|\mathcal{I}(\boldsymbol{n}_0,m,l)| - |\mathcal{I}^{\mathrm{rec}}(\boldsymbol{n}_0,m,l)|\right]^2}{\sum_{m=0}^{M-1}\sum_{l=0}^{L-1}\sum_{\boldsymbol{n}_0\in\mathbb{S}_N} a_0^{-2m}|\mathcal{I}(\boldsymbol{n}_0,m,l)|^2}}\,. \tag{13}$$

As displayed in figure 3, the reconstruction does not converge to zero error. The remaining RRMSE corresponds to slight gray level deviations in uniform (low-frequency) image zones as can be seen comparing the reconstructions to the originals, (see figure 2). We interpret reconstruction errors as accumulated numerical errors from the SVD regularization of low frequencies in the IGWT, which is repeated in each iteration. However the reconstructed images retain local texture properties very well, which is crucial for image understanding based on representation by such features.

After a rapid improvement in some 10 iterations, which already yield a perfectly recognizable image, convergence becomes rather slow. There are local inversions of sign, which compete to dictate the global sign.

6 Discussion

We have shown that almost all images can be recovered from their Gabor magnitudes. As natural images, which are the only interesting ones for computer vision, constitute only a tiny subset of all functions with compact support, it is theoretically possible that many of them fall into the subset of images not represented uniquely by their Gabor magnitudes, which we will call *ambiguous*. Although possible, this appears highly unlikely, because slight modifications of natural images still yield natural images. However, neither the set of natural images nor the precise form of the set of ambiguous images is known. The latter can not be uncovered with the simple dimensionality argument used in this paper and definitely requires further research. Furthermore, it is unclear how much the different reconstructions of ambiguous Gabor magnitudes will differ. If there should be two images with definitely different contents but nevertheless identical Gabor magnitudes, this would make the method problematic for image understanding. We have shown that this is very unlikely, but still have no absolute proof that it cannot happen.

For further evidence, we have implemented a numerical algorithm for Gabor phase retrieval, which is based on the ideas of the proof. In the cases we tested, we could always recover a good approximation of the image up to the sign and numerical errors in the low frequency contents. Our theorem suggests that twice the sampling rate is needed in each dimension for reconstruction from magnitudes only than for reconstruction from the full transform. As a simple rule of thumb, this looks very plausible in neuronal terms, if one considers a single complex number to be represented by *four* positive real numbers (because cell activities cannot be negative). Thus, four simple cells, which code for the linear wavelet coefficient, must be replaced by four complex cells at slightly different positions in order to convey the same information.

References

1. John G. Daugman. Uncertainty relation for resolution in space, spatial frequency, and orientation optimized by two-dimensional visual cortical filters. *Journal of the Optical Society of America A*, 2(7):1362–1373, 1985.
2. Benoît Duc, Stefan Fischer, and Josef Bigün. Face authentication with gabor information on deformable graphs. *IEEE Transactions on Image Processing*, 8(4):504 – 516, 1999.
3. I. Fogel and Dov Sagi. Gabor filters as texture discriminator. *Biological Cybernetics*, 61:103–113, 1989.
4. A. Grossmann and J. Morlet. Decomposition of Hardy functions into square integrable wavelets of constant shape. *SIAM Journal of Mathematical Analysis*, 15(4):723 – 736, July 1984.

5. Monson H. Hayes. The Reconstruction of a Multidimensional Sequence from the Phase or Magnitude of Its Fourier Transform. *IEEE Transactions on Acoustics, Speech, and Signal Processing*, 30(2):140 – 154, April 1982.
6. Monson H. Hayes and James H. McClellan. Reducible Polynomials in More Than One Variable. *Proceedings of the IEEE*, 70(2):197 – 198, February 1982.
7. J.P. Jones and L.A. Palmer. An evaluation of the two-dimensional Gabor filter model of simple receptive fields in cat striate cortex. *Journal of Neurophysiology*, 58(6):1233–1258, 1987.
8. Gerald Kaiser. *A Friendly Guide to Wavelets*. Birkhäuser, 1994.
9. Martin Lades, Jan C. Vorbrüggen, Joachim Buhmann, Jörg Lange, Christoph von der Malsburg, Rolf P. Würtz, and Wolfgang Konen. Distortion invariant object recognition in the dynamic link architecture. *IEEE Transactions on Computers*, 42(3):300–311, 1993.
10. R. Murenzi. Wavelet Transforms Associated to the n-Dimensional Euclidean Group with Dilations: Signal in More Than One Dimension. In J. M. Combes, A. Grossmann, and P. Tchamitchian, editors, *Wavelets – Time-Frequency Methods and Phase Space*, pages 239 – 246. Springer, 1989.
11. Alan V. Oppenheim and Jae S. Lim. The Importance of Phase in Signals. *Proceedings of the IEEE*, 96(5):529 – 541, May 1981.
12. Daniel A. Pollen and Steven F. Ronner. Visual cortical neurons as localized spatial frequency filters. *IEEE Transactions on Systems, Man, and Cybernetics*, 13(5):907–916, 1983.
13. Eero P. Simoncelli, William T. Freeman, Edward H. Adelson, and David J. Heeger. Shiftable Multiscale Transforms. *IEEE Transactions on Information Theory*, 38(2):587 – 607, March 1992.
14. Jochen Triesch and Christoph von der Malsburg. Robust classification of hand postures against complex backgrounds. In *Proceedings of the Second International Conference on Automatic Face and Gesture Recognition*, pages 170–175. IEEE Computer Society Press, 1996.
15. Sharon Urieli, Moshe Porat, and Nir Cohen. Optimal reconstruction of images from localized phase. *IEEE Trans. Image Processing*, 7(6):838–853, 1998.
16. Christoph von der Malsburg and Ladan Shams. Role of complex cells in object recognition. *Nature Neuroscience*, 2001. Submitted.
17. Laurenz Wiskott, Jean-Marc Fellous, Norbert Krüger, and Christoph von der Malsburg. Face recognition by elastic bunch graph matching. *IEEE Transactions on Pattern Analysis and Machine Intelligence*, 19(7):775–779, 1997.
18. Xing Wu and Bir Bhanu. Gabor Wavelet Representation for 3-D Object Recognition. *IEEE Transactions on Image Processing*, 6(1):47 – 64, January 1997.
19. Ingo J. Wundrich, Christoph von der Malsburg, and Rolf P. Würtz. Image representation by the magnitude of the discrete Gabor wavelet transform. *IEEE Transactions on Image Processing*, 1999. In revision.
20. Rolf P. Würtz. Object recognition robust under translations, deformations and changes in background. *IEEE Transactions on Pattern Analysis and Machine Intelligence*, 19(7):769–775, 1997.
21. Rolf P. Würtz and Tino Lourens. Corner detection in color images through a multiscale combination of end-stopped cortical cells. *Image and Vision Computing*, 18(6-7):531–541, 2000.

A Binocular Stereo Algorithm for Log-Polar Foveated Systems

Alexandre Bernardino and José Santos-Victor

Instituto Superior Técnico
ISR – Torre Norte, Piso 7
Av. Rovisco Pais, 1049-001 Lisboa, Portugal
{alex,jasv}@isr.ist.utl.pt

Abstract. Foveation and stereopsis are important features on active vision systems. The former provides a wide field of view and high foveal resolution with low amounts of data, while the latter contributes to the acquisition of close range depth cues. The log-polar sampling has been proposed as an approximation to the foveated representation of the primate visual system. Although the huge amount of stereo algorithms proposed in the literature for conventional imaging geometries, very few are shown to work with foveated images sampled according to the log-polar transformation. In this paper we present a method to extract dense disparity maps in real-time from a pair of log-mapped images, with direct application to active vision systems.

1 Introduction

Stereoscopic vision is a fundamental perceptual capability both in animals and artificial systems. At close ranges, it allows reliable extraction of depth information, thus being suited for robotics tasks such as manipulation and navigation. In the last decades a great amount of research has been directed to the problem of extracting depth information from stereo imagery (see [25] for a recent review). However, the best performing techniques are still too slow to use on robotic systems which demand real-time operation. The straightforward way to reduce computation time is to work with coarse resolution images but this restricts the acquisition of detailed information all over the visual field. A better solution, inspired in biological systems, is the use of ocular movements together with foveated retinas. The visual system of primates has a space-variant nature where the resolution is high on the fovea (the center of the retina) and decreases gradually to the periphery of the visual field. This distribution of resolution is the evolutionary solution to reduce the amount of information traversing the optical nerve while maintaining high resolution in the fovea and a wide visual field. Moving the high resolution fovea we are able to acquire detailed representations of the surrounding environment. The excellent performance of biological visual systems led researchers to investigate the properties of foveated systems. Many active vision systems have adopted this strategy and since foveated images contain less information than conventional uniform resolution images, one obtains important reductions on the computation time.

H.H. Bülthoff et al. (Eds.): BMCV 2002, LNCS 2525, pp. 127–136, 2002.

We may distinguish between two main methods to emulate foveated systems, that we denote by *multi-scale uniform sampling* methods and *non-uniform sampling* methods. *Uniform* methods preserve the cartesian geometry of the representation by performing operations at different scales in multi-resolution pyramids (e.g. [17],[10],[13]). Sampling grids are uniform at each level but different levels have different spacing and receptive field size. Notwithstanding, image processing operations are still performed on piecewise uniform resolution domains. *Non-uniform* methods resample the image with non-linear transformations, where receptive field spacing and size are non-uniform along the image domain. The VR transform [2], the DIEM method [19], and several versions of the *logmap* [30], are examples of this kind of methods.

The choice of method is a matter of preference, application dependent requirements and computational resources. *Uniform methods* can be easier to work with, because many current computer vision algorithms can be directly applied to these representations. However, *non-uniform* methods can achieve more compact image representations with consequent benefits in computation time. In particular the *logmap* has been shown to have many additional properties like rotation and scale invariance [31], easy computation of time-to-contact [28], improved linear flow estimation [29], looming detection [23], increased stereo resolution on verging systems [14], fast anisotropic diffusion [11], improved vergence control and tracking [7,3,4].

Few approaches have been proposed to compute disparity maps for foveated active vision systems, and existing ones rely on the foveated pyramid representation [17,27,6]. In this paper we describe a stereo algorithm to compute dense disparity maps on *logmap* based systems. Dense representations are advantageous for object segmentation and region of interest selection. Our method uses directly the gray/color values of each pixel, without requiring any feature extraction, making this method particularly suited for non-cartesian geometries, where the scale of analysis depends greatly on the variable to estimate (disparity).

To our knowledge, the only work to date addressing the computation of stereo disparity in *logmap* images is [15]. In that work, disparity maps are obtained by matching laplacian features in the two views (zero crossing), which results in sparse disparity maps.

2 Real-Time Log-Polar Mapping

The log-polar transformation, or *logmap*, $\mathbf{l}(\mathbf{x})$, is defined as a conformal mapping from the *cartesian* plane $\mathbf{x} = (x, y)$ to the *log-polar* plane $\mathbf{z} = (\xi, \eta)$:

$$\mathbf{l}(\mathbf{x}) = \begin{bmatrix} \xi \\ \eta \end{bmatrix} = \begin{bmatrix} \log(\sqrt{x^2 + y^2}) \\ \arctan \frac{y}{x} \end{bmatrix} \tag{1}$$

Since the *logmap* is a good approximation to the retino–cortical mapping in the human visual system [26,12], the cartesian and log-polar coordinates are also called "retinal" and "cortical", respectively. In continuous coordinates, a cortical image I^{cort} is obtained from the corresponding retinal image I by the warping:

$$I^{cort}(\mathbf{z}) = I(\mathbf{l}^{-1}(\mathbf{x}))$$

A number of ways have been proposed to discretize space variant maps [5]. We have been using the *logmap* for some years in real-time active vision applications [3,4]. To allow real-time computation of *logmap* images we partition the retinal plane into *receptive fields*, whose size and position correspond to a uniform partition of the cortical plane into *super-pixels* (see Fig. 1). The value of a *super-pixel* is given by the average of all pixels in the corresponding receptive field.

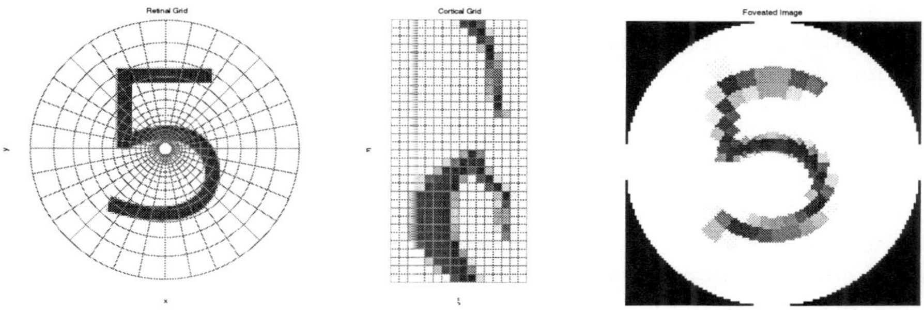

Fig. 1. The log-polar sampling scheme is implemented by averaging the pixels contained within each of the *receptive fields* shown in the left image. These space-variant receptive fields are angular sections of circular rings corresponding to uniform rectangular *super-pixels* in the cortical image (center). To reconstruct the retinal image, each receptive field gets the value of the corresponding *super-pixel* (right).

3 Disparity Map Computation

We start describing an intensity based method to find the likelihood of stereo matches in usual cartesian coordinates, $\mathbf{x} = (x, y)$. Then we show how the method can be extended to cope with *logmap* images. Finally we describe the remaining steps to obtain the disparity maps.

Let I and I' be the left and right images, respectively. For depth analysis, we are interested in computing the horizontal disparity map, but since we consider a general head vergence configuration, vertical disparities must also be accounted for. Therefore, disparity is a two valued function defined as $\mathbf{d}(\mathbf{x}) = (d_x, d_y)$. Taking the left image as the reference, the disparity at point $\mathbf{x}$ is given by $\mathbf{d}(\mathbf{x}) = \mathbf{x}' - \mathbf{x}$, where $\mathbf{x}$ and $\mathbf{x}'$ are the locations of matching points in the left and right images. If a pixel at location $\mathbf{x}$ in the reference image is not visible in the right image, we say the pixel is occluded and disparity is undefined ($\mathbf{d}(\mathbf{x}) = \varnothing$).

3.1 Bayesian Formulation

To obtain dense representations, we use an intensity based method similar to [32]. We formulate the problem in a discrete bayesian framework. Having a finite set of possible disparities, $D = \{\mathbf{d}_n\}, n = 1 \cdots N$, for each location $\mathbf{x}$ we define a set of hypothesis, $H = \{h_n(\mathbf{x})\}, n = 0 \cdots N$, where $h_0(\mathbf{x})$ represents the occlusion condition ($\mathbf{d}(\mathbf{x}) = \varnothing$), and the other h_n represent particular disparity values, $\mathbf{d}(\mathbf{x}) = \mathbf{d}_n$. Other working assumptions are the following:

1. Object appearance does not vary with view point (lambertian surfaces) and cameras have the same gain, bias and noise levels. This corresponds to the *Brightness Constancy Assumption* [16]. Considering the existence of additive noise, we get the following stereo correspondence model:

$$I(\mathbf{x}) = I'(\mathbf{x} + \mathbf{d}(\mathbf{x})) + \eta(\mathbf{x}) \tag{2}$$

2. Noise is modeled as being independent and identically distributed with a certain probability density function, f. In the unoccluded case, the probability of a certain gray value $I(\mathbf{x})$ is conditioned by the value of the true disparity $\mathbf{d}(\mathbf{x})$ and the value of I' at position $\mathbf{x} + \mathbf{d}(\mathbf{x})$:

$$Pr(I(\mathbf{x})|\mathbf{d}(\mathbf{x})) = f(I(\mathbf{x}) - I'(\mathbf{x} + \mathbf{d}(\mathbf{x})))$$

We assume zero-mean gaussian white noise, and have $f(t) = 1/\sqrt{2\pi\sigma^2}e^{-t^2/2\sigma^2}$ where σ^2 is the noise variance.

3. In the discrete case we define the *disparity likelihood* images as:

$$L_n(\mathbf{x}) = Pr(I(\mathbf{x})|h_n(\mathbf{x})) = f(I(\mathbf{x}) - I'_n(\mathbf{x})) \tag{3}$$

where $I'_n(\mathbf{x}) = I'(\mathbf{x} + \mathbf{d_n})$ are called *disparity warped images.*

4. The probability of a certain hypothesis given the image gray levels (posterior probability) is given by the Bayes' rule:

$$Pr(h_n|I) = \frac{Pr(I|h_n)Pr(h_n)}{\sum_{i=0}^{N} Pr(I|h_i)Pr(h_i)} \tag{4}$$

where we have dropped the argument $\mathbf{x}$ since all functions are computed at the same point.

5. If a pixel at location $\mathbf{x}$ is occluded in the right image, its gray level is unconstrained and can have any value in the set of M admissible gray values,

$$Pr(I|h_0(\mathbf{x})) = \frac{1}{M} \tag{5}$$

We define a prior probability of occlusion with a constant value for all sites:

$$Pr(h_0) = q \tag{6}$$

6. We do not favor any *a priori* particular value of disparity. A constant prior is considered and its value must satisfy $Pr(h_n) \cdot N + q = 1$, which results in:

$$Pr(h_n) = (1 - q)/N \tag{7}$$

7. Substituting the priors (5), (6), (7), and the likelihood (3) in (4), we get:

$$Pr(h_n|I) = \begin{cases} \frac{L_n(I)}{\sum_{i=1}^{N} L_i(I)+qN/(M-qM)} & \Leftarrow n \neq 0 \\ \frac{qN/(M-qM)}{\sum_{i=1}^{N} L_i(I)+qN/(M-qM)} & \Leftarrow n = 0 \end{cases} \tag{8}$$

The choice of the hypothesis that maximizes (8) leads us to the MAP (*maximum a posteriori*) estimate of disparity[1]. However, without any further assumptions, there may be many ambiguous solutions. It is known that in the general case, the stereo matching problem is under-constrained and ill-posed [25]. One way to overcome this fact is to assume that the scene is composed by piece-wise smooth surfaces and introduce spatial interactions between neighboring locations to favor smooth solutions. Later we will describe a cooperative spatial facilitation method to address this problem.

3.2 Cortical Likelihood Images

While in cartesian coordinates the *disparity warped images* can be obtained by shifting pixels by an amount independent of position, $\mathbf{x}' = \mathbf{x} + \mathbf{d}_n$, in cortical coordinates the disparity shifts are different for each pixel, as shown in Fig.2. Thus, for each cortical pixel and disparity value, we have to compute the corresponding pixel in the second image. Using the *logmap* definition (1), the cortical correspondences can be obtained by:

$$\mathbf{z}_n'(\mathbf{z}) = \mathbf{l}\left(\mathbf{l}^{-1}(\mathbf{z}) + \mathbf{d_n}\right) \tag{9}$$

This map can be computed off-line for all cortical locations and stored in a look-up table to speed-up on-line calculations. To minimize discretization errors, the weights for intensity interpolation can also be pre-computed and stored. A deeper explanation of this technique can be found in [22].

Using the pre-computed look up tables, the cortical *disparity warped images* can be efficiently computed on-line:

$$I_n^{cort'}(\mathbf{z}) = I^{cort'}(\mathbf{z}_n(\mathbf{z}))$$

From Eq. (3) we define $N+1$ *cortical likelihood images*, $L_n^{cort}(\mathbf{z})$, that express the likelihood of a particular hypothesis at cortical location $\mathbf{z}$:

$$L_n^{cort}(\mathbf{z}) = f(I^{cort}(\mathbf{z}) - I_n^{cort'}(\mathbf{z}))$$

Substituting this result in Eq. (8) we have the cortical posterior probabilities:

$$Pr^{cort}(h_n|I^{cort}) \propto \begin{cases} L_n^{cort}(I) & \Leftarrow n \neq 0 \\ qN/(M-qM) & \Leftarrow n = 0 \end{cases} \tag{10}$$

[1] The terms in the denominator are normalizing constants and do not need to be computed explicilty

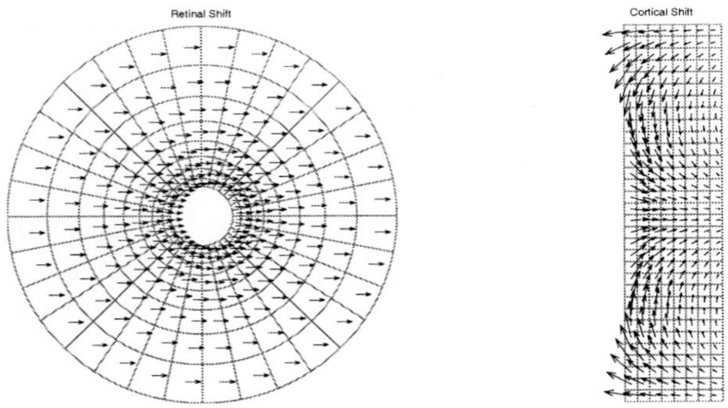

Fig. 2. A space invariant shift in retinal coordinates (left) corresponds to a space variant warping in the cortical array.

3.3 Cooperative Spatial Facilitation

The value of the likelihood images L_n^{cort} at each cortical location $\mathbf{z}$ can be interpreted as the response of disparity selective neurons, expressing the degree of match between corresponding locations in the right and left images. When many disparity hypothesis are likely to occur (e.g. textureless areas) several neurons tuned to different disparities may be simultaneously active. In a computational framework, this "aperture" problem is usually addressed by allowing neighborhood interactions between units, in order to spread information from and to non-ambiguous regions. A bayesian formulation of these interactions leads to Markov Random Fields techniques [33], whose existing solutions (annealing, graph optimization) are still computationally expensive. Neighborhood interactions are also very commonly found in biological literature and several cooperative schemes have been proposed, with different facilitation/inibhition strategies along the spatial and disparity coordinates [18,21,20]. For the sake of computational complexity we adopt a spatial-only facilitation scheme whose principle is to reinforce the output of units at locations whose coherent neighbors (tuned for the same disparity) are active. This scheme can be implemented very efficiently by convolving each of the *cortical likelihood images* with a low-pass type of filter, resulting on $N + 1$ *Facilitated Cortical Likelihood Images*, F_n^{cort}. We use a fast IIR isotropic separable first order filter, which only requires two multiplications and two additions per pixel. We prefer filters of large impulse response, which provide better smoothness properties and favor blob like objects, at the cost of missing small or thin structures in the image. Also, due to the space-variant nature of the cortical map, regions on the periphery of the visual field will have more "smoothing" than regions in the center.

At this point, it is worth noticing that since the 70's, biological studies show that neurons tuned to similar disparities are organized in clusters on visual cortex area V2 in primates [8], and more recently this organization has also been found on area MT [9]. Our architecture, composed by topographically organized maps of units tuned to the same disparity, agrees with these biological findings.

3.4 Computing the Solution

Replacing in (10) the *cortical likelihood images* L_n^{cort} by their filtered versions F_n^{cort} we obtain $N+1$ *cortical disparity activation images*:

$$D_n^{cort} = \begin{cases} F_n^{cort}(I) & \Leftarrow n \neq 0 \\ qN_f(M - qM) & \Leftarrow n = 0 \end{cases} \tag{11}$$

The disparity map is obtained by computing the hypothesis that maximizes the *cortical disparity activation* images for each location:

$$\hat{\mathbf{d}}(\mathbf{z}) = \arg\max_n (D_n^{cort}(\mathbf{z}))$$

In a neural networks perspective, this computation is analogous a winner-take-all competition between non-coherent units at the same spatial location, promoted by the existence of inhibitory connections between them [1].

4 Results

We have tested the proposed algorithm on a binocular active vision head in general vergence configurations, and on standard stereo test images. Results are shown on Figs. 3 and 4. Bright and dark regions correspond to near and far objects, respectively. The innermost and outermost rings present some noisy disparity values due to border effects than can be easily removed by simple post-processing operations.

Fig. 3. The image in the right shows the raw foveated disparity map computed from the pair of images shown in the left, taken from a stereo head verging on a point midway between the foreground and background objects.

Some intermediate results of the first experiment are presented in Fig. 5, showing the output of the cortical likelihood and the cortical activation for a particular disparity hypothesis. In the likelihood image notice the great amount of noisy points corresponding to false matches. The spatial facilitation scheme and the maximum computation over all disparities are essential to reject the false matches and avoid ambiguous solutions.

A point worth of notice is the blob like nature of the detected objects. As we have pointed out in section 3.3, this happens because of the isotropic nature

Fig. 4. The disparity map on the right was computed from the well known stereo test images from Tsukuba University. In the left we show the foveated images of the stereo pair. Notice that much of the detail in the periphery is lost due to the space variant sampling. Thus, this result can not be directly compared with others obtained from uniform resolution images.

and large support of the spatial facilitation filters. Also, the space variant image sampling, blurs image detail in the periphery of the visual field. This results in the loss of small and thin structures like the fingertips in the stereo head example and the lamp support in the Tsukuba images. However note that spatial facilitation do not blur depth discontinuities because filtering is not performed on the disparity map output, but on the likelihood maps before the maximum operation.

The lack of detail shown in the computed maps is not a major drawback for our applications, that include people tracking, obstacle avoidance and region of interest selection for further processing. As a matter of fact, it has been shown in a number of works that many robotics tasks can be performed with coarse sensory inputs if combined with fast control loops [24].

Fig. 5. Intermediate results for the experiment in Fig.3. This figure shows the cortical maps tuned to retinal disparity $d_i = 26$, for which there is a good match in the hand region. In the left group we show the likelihood images L_i^{cort} (left) and D_i^{cort} (right) corresponding to the cortical activation before and after the spatial facilitation step. In the right group, the same maps are represented in retinal coordinates, for better interpretation of results.

The parameters used in the tests are the following: log-polar mapping with 128 angular sections and 64 radial rings; retinal disparity range from -40 to 40 pixels (horizontal) and from -6 to 6 pixels (vertical), both in steps of 2; $q = 0.1$ (prior probability of occlusion); $M = 256$ (number of gray values); $\sigma = 3$ (white noise standard deviation); facilitation filtering with zero-phase forward/reverse filter $y(n) = 0.8y(n-1) + 0.2x(n)$.

The algorithms were implemented in C++ and take about three seconds to run in a PII 350MHz computer.

5 Conclusions

We have presented a real-time dense disparity estimation algorithm for foveated systems using the *logmap*. The algorithm uses an intensity based matching technique, which makes it easily extensible to other space variant sampling schemes. Some results were taken from an active stereo head and others obtained from standard test images. Many robots are currently equipped with foveated active vision systems and the availability of fast stereopsis will drastically improve their perceptual capabilities. Obstacle detection and tracking, region of interest selection and object manipulation are some possible applications.

Acknowledgements. This work was partially supported by EU project MIRROR: *Mirror Neurons based Robot Recognition, IST-2000-28159.*

References

1. S. Amari and M. Arbib. *Competition and Cooperation in Neural Nets*, pages 119–165. Systems Neuroscience. J. Metzler (ed), Academic Press, 1977.
2. A. Basu and K. Wiebe. Enhancing videoconferencing using spatially varying sensing. *IEEE Trans. on Systems, Man, and Cybernetics*, 38(2):137–148, Mar. 1998.
3. A. Bernardino and J. Santos-Victor. Binocular visual tracking : Integration of perception and control. *IEEE Trans. on Robotics and Automation*, 15(6):137–146, Dec. 1999.
4. A. Bernardino, J. Santos-Victor, and G. Sandini. Foveated active tracking with redundant 2d motion parameters. *Robotics and Autonomous Systems*, 39(3-4):205–221, June 2002.
5. M. Bolduc and M. Levine. A review of biologically motivated space-variant data reduction models for robotic vision *CVIU*, 69(2):170–184, Feb. 1998.
6. T. Boyling and J. Siebert. A fast foveated stereo matcher. In *Proc. Conf. on Imaging Science Systems and Technology*, pages 417 – 423, Las Vegas, USA, 2000.
7. C. Capurro, F. Panerai, and G. Sandini. Dynamic vergence using log-polar images. *IJCV*, 24(1):79–94, Aug. 1997.
8. T. Wiesel D. Hubel. Stereoscopic vision in macaque monkey. cells sensitive to binocular depth in area 18 of the macaque mokey cortex. *Nature*, 225:41–42, 1970.
9. G. DeAngelis and W. Newsome. Organization of disparity–selective neurons in macaque area mt. *The Journal of Neuroscience*, 19(4):1398–1415, 1999.
10. S. Mallat E. Chang and C. Yap. Wavelet foveation. *J. Applied and Computational Harmonic Analysis*, 9(3):312–335, Oct. 2000.
11. B. Fischl, M. Cohen, and E. Schwartz. Rapid anisotropic diffusion using space-variant vision. *IJCV*, 28(3):199–212, July/Aug. 1998.

12. G. Gambardella G. Sandini, C. Braccini and V. Tagliasco. A model of the early stages of the human visual system: Functional and topological transformation performed in the peripheral visual field. *Biological Cybernetics*, 44:47–58, 1982.
13. W. Geisler and J. Perry. A real-time foveated multi-resolution system for low-bandwidth video communication. In *Human Vision and Electronic Imaging, SPIE Proceedings 3299*, pages 294–305, Aug. 1998.
14. N. Griswald, J. Lee, and C. Weiman. Binocular fusion revisited utilizing a log-polar tessellation. *CVIP*, pages 421–457, 1992.
15. E. Grosso and M. Tistarelli. Log-polar stereo for anthropomorphic robots. In *Proc. 6th ECCV*, pages 299 – 313, Dublin, Ireland, June-July 2000.
16. B. Horn. *Robot Vision.* MIT Press, McGraw Hill, 1986.
17. W. Klarquist and A. Bovik. Fovea: A foveated vergent active stereo system for dynamic three-dimensional scene recovery. *IEEE Trans. on Robotics and Automation*, 14(5):755 – 770, Oct. 1998.
18. D. Marr and T. Poggio. Cooperative computation of stereo disparity. *Science*, 194:283–287, 1976.
19. M. Peters and A. Sowmya. A real-time variable sampling technique: Diem. In *Proc. ICPR*, pages 316–321, Brisbane, Australia, Aug. 1998.
20. S. Pollard, J. Mayhew, and J. Frisby. Pmf: A stereo correspondence algorithm using a disparity gradient limit. *Perception*, 14:449–470, 1985.
21. K. Prazdny. Detection of binocular disparities. *Biol. Cybern*, 52:93–99, 1985.
22. G. Metta R. Manzotti, A. Gasteratos and G. Sandini. Disparity estimation on log-polar images and vergence control. *CVIU*, 83:97–117, 2001.
23. G. Salgian and D. Ballard. Visual routines for vehicle control. In D. Kriegman, G. Hager, and S. Morse, editors, *The Confluence of Vision and Control.* Springer Verlag, 1998.
24. J. Santos-Victor and A. Bernardino. Vision-based navigation, environmental representations, and imaging geometries. In *Proc. 10th Int. Symp. of Robotics Research*, Victoria, Australia, Nov. 2001.
25. D. Scharstein and R. Szeliski. A taxonomy and evaluation of dense two-frame stereo correspondence algorithms. *IJCV*, 47(1):7–42, April-June 2002.
26. E. Schwartz. Spatial mapping in the primate sensory projection : Analytic structure and relevance to perception. *Biological Cybernetics*, 25:181–194, 1977.
27. J. Siebert and D. Wilson. Foveated vergence and stereo. In *Proc. of the 3rd Int. Conf. on Visual Search (TICVS)*, Nottingham, UK, Aug. 1992.
28. M. Tistarelli and G. Sandini. On the advantages of polar and log-polar mapping for direct estimation of the time-to-impact from optical flow. *IEEE Trans. on PAMI*, 15(8):401–411, April 1993.
29. H. Tunley and D. Young. First order optic flow from log-polar sampled images. In *Proc. ECCV*, pages A:132–137, 1994.
30. R. Wallace, P. Ong, B. Bederson, and E. Schwartz. Space variant image processing. *IJCV*, 13(1):71–90, Sep. 1995.
31. C. Weiman and G. Chaikin. Logarithmic spiral grids for image processing and display. *Comp Graphics and Image Proc*, 11:197–226, 1979.
32. R. Zabih Y. Boykov, O. Veksler. Disparity component matching for visual correspondence. In *Proc. CVPR*, pages 470–475, 1997.
33. R. Zabih Y. Boykov, O. Veksler. Markov random fields with efficient approximations. In *Proc. CVPR*, pages 648–655, 1998.

Rotation-Invariant Optical Flow by Gaze-Depended Retino-Cortical Mapping

Markus A. Dahlem and Florentin Wörgötter

Computational Neuroscience
Department of Psychology
University of Stirling
Stirling FK9 4LA
Scotland / UK
{mad1, faw1}@cn.stir.ac.uk
http://www.cn.stir.ac.uk/

Abstract. Computational vision models that attempt to account for perception of depth from motion usually compute the optical flow field first. From the optical flow the ego-motion parameter are then estimated, if they are not already known from a motor reference. Finally the depth can be determined. The better the ego-motion parameters are known by extra-retinal information to be restricted to certain values before the optical flow is estimated, the more reliable is a depth-from-motion algorithm. We show here, that optical flow induced by translational motion mixed with specific rotational components can be dynamically mapped onto a head-centric frame such that it is invariant under these rotations. As a result, the spatial optical flow dimension are reduced from two to one, like purely translational flow. An earlier introduced optical flow algorithm that operates in close approximation of existing brain functionality gains with this preprocessing a much wider range of applications in which the motion of the observer is not restricted to pure translations.

1 Introduction

One of the chief problems in computational vision is the three-dimensional reconstruction of a static scene from two-dimensional images [1]. Motion parallax is one of the depth cues that can be used to recover the three-dimensional structure of a viewed scene [2], [3]. Motion induces a velocity field on the retina called the optical flow [4]. In the most general motion case, i. e., object plus ego motion, the resulting curved optical flow field pattern cannot be resolved for depth analysis without additional assumptions [5] and even if simplifying assumptions are made, the problem of depth-from-motion remains rather complex.

The goal of this study is to generalize a neuronal algorithm one of us (FW) developed earlier [6]. So far this algorithm analysis radial optical flow fields, obtained by translational motion towards an object. The central advantage of this algorithm is that all computations remain local, which permits parallelization (see below). We now introduce a preprocessing step, that maps the visual data

H.H. Bülthoff et al. (Eds.): BMCV 2002, LNCS 2525, pp. 137–145, 2002.

such that the algorithm can still operate in parallel even when the flow fields are more complex. The preprocessing is actually a global operation in the sense that it effects the whole optical flow field, but it is strictly independent of any external information, such as the viewed scene, and can therefore be implemented separately. The main focus for our depth-from-motion algorithm is on a close approximation of existing brain functionality, i. e. (cortical) sensor maps, and local (neuronal) operations.

Radial flow fields are one of the simplest optical flow fields and are obtained when the observer is moving straight ahead with fixed gaze towards the direction of the translation. The optical flow has then a fixed point, called the focus of expansion (FOE). All optical flow trajectories move outwards from the FOE. It is readily seen that the motion in such a radial flow field (RFF) is one-dimensional in polar coordinates, along the radial coordinate. The possible reduction of the spatial dimensions of the optical flow field can be seen as the main reason why there is a simple relation between the flow velocity and the distance between objects and observer. However, RFF exits only for rather restricted motion, i. e., purely translational motion.

The flow velocity v_p at a certain point p of the RFF is reciprocally proportional to the Cartesian coordinate Z (depth).

$$Z \sim \frac{1}{v_p} \tag{1}$$

One of the Cartesian coordinates (X,Y,Z) of objects can therefore be recovered from the optical flow, except for a scaling constant. Two other coordinates are actually already implicitly known as the eccentricity θ and the azimuth ϕ of the retinal frame. These can be interpreted as the polar and azimuthal angles in three-dimensional spherical coordinates (ρ,θ,ϕ). The unknown radius ρ, that is, the only spherical coordinate that was lost by the central perspective projection, is given by $\rho = Z\theta/f$, where f is the focal length of the visual system. At last, the scaling constant in the Z coordinate (Eq. 1) can be eliminated, if the velocity of the ego-motion is known to the observer, for example by a motor reference. With these relations the three-dimensional world can be reconstructed.

The optical flow field and its relation to the distance between objects and observer is far more complicated, when there are rotational components in the ego-motion. When, for example, the direction of gaze changes while the body is moving straight, the directions of the optical flow field are not independent of the distance of objects. Therefore the direction of the optical flow field can not be known *a priori*. In this case, a two-dimensional correlation problem must be solved to obtain the optical flow direction and magnitude. Additionally, all ego-motion parameters must be known to re-construct a three-dimensional scene from the optical flow [7], [8]. Instead of analyzing the two-dimensional optical flow field, we suggest a dynamical mapping of the visual data such that the spatial dimensions of the resulting flow field are reduced to one and the same neuronal algorithm can be applied after this preprocessing as already used for purely translational motion.

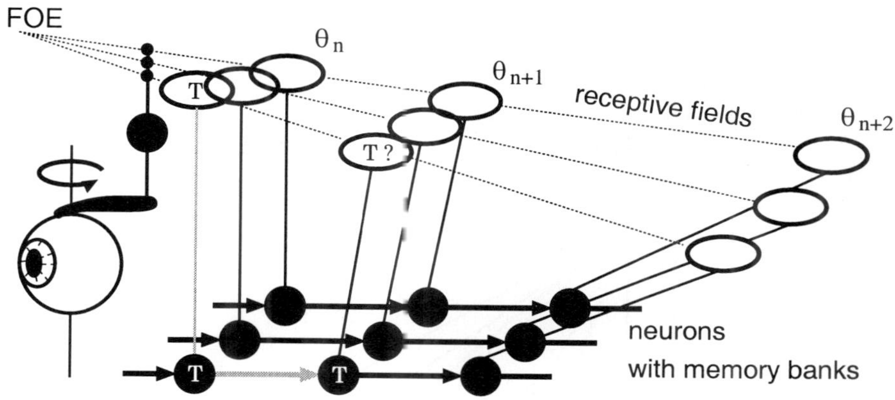

Fig. 1. Architecture of the two layer neuronal network. The input layer consists of receptive fields sampling the optical flow. Each receptive field projects to a neuron with a memory bank in the processing layer. A separate neuron represents a structure mapping eye-positions. A visual tokens (T) is passed from the receptive field along the exemplarily shown grey connections towards the memory bank of a consecutive neuron. A head-centric representation of visual input is achieved by dynamically mapping the receptive field positions according to the direction of gaze. To re-construct three-dimensional position of viewed objects, the processing layer needs only locally exchanged information in one spatial direction (from left to right).

2 The RFF-Algorithm

One of us (FW) introduced earlier an algorithm that efficiently analysis an RFF and reconstructs the viewed three-dimensional scene [6]. Details of the algorithm should be taken from that reference, but we will shortly describe its basics. Since the optical flow directions are fixed in an RFF, only the flow velocity is unknown. The velocity is measured by the time a specific visual token takes to pass successive points ("receptive fields") located on the retina at eccentricity θ_n and θ_{n+1} on a single radial line with azimuth ϕ. As the correspondence token changes in gray-level were chosen. When a significant change in gray-value is registered at a receptive field, this gray-level value is passed from θ_n, via a "neuron" n_n to a memory bank of a neuron n_{n+1} with the adjacent receptive field at θ_{n+1} (Fig. 1). The time taken to "see" this expected gray-level value on the receptive field θ_{n+1} is proportional to the depth of the object generating the gray-level token (Eq. 1). The RFF-algorithm was successfully tested on real images in real time, in other words it is sufficiently fast and noise robust. Head-centric maps [9], [10] are used now for the RFF-algorithm, and therefore straight head motion can be combined with eye-gaze movements. Any other algorithm, that is developed for one-dimensional RFFs, can as well profit from the dynamical mapping strategy introduced here. However, we would like to emphasize, that the main motivation of preprocessing the optical flow is that the remaining computations are strictly performed locally and thus can be done in parallel.

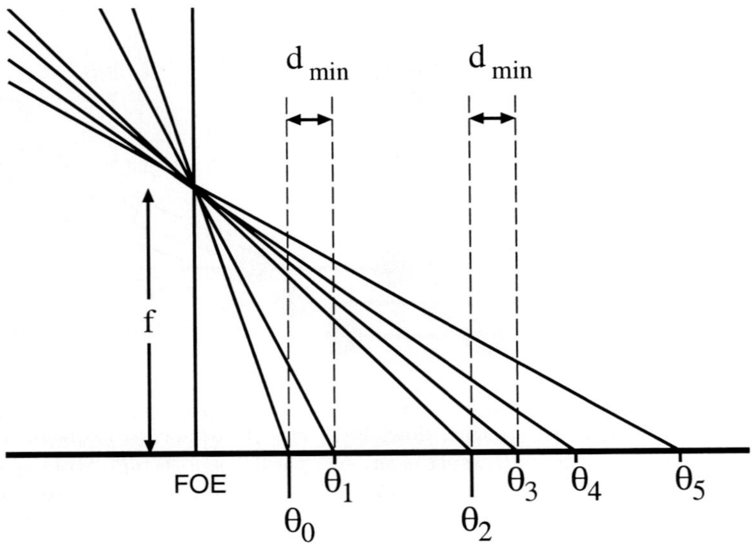

Fig. 2. Geometry of the layout of receptive fields along one radial component of the optical flow. The first receptive field θ_0 is set close to the focus of expansion (FOE) and defines the starting field of the first hyperbolic section. The second receptive field θ_1 is placed at the distance d_{min} from the first in the direction away from the FOE. In the example shown here, only one more receptive field θ_2 fits on this hyperbolic section before the distance of successive receptive field becomes too large. θ_2 is therefore the starting receptive field for the next hyperbolic section.

3 Dynamical Mapping

To map the retinal flow field to a head centric frame, the retina is initially sampled by point-like receptive fields (top layer in Fig. 1), such that the layout of the receptive fields matches the RFF. The receptive fields are placed on a polar grid defined by m radial axes expanding from the FOE. If the distance of successive receptive fields increases hyperbolically, the optical flow is sampled uniformly along one radius (Eq. 1). However, only few receptive fields would fit on a radial axis, when their positions increase hyperbolically. Therefore, the overall layout is composed of pice-wise hyperbolic sections. The design is arranged in the following way. The first receptive field of a hyperbolic section (θ_0) is set close to the FOE at position d. The second receptive field is placed at $\theta_1 = \theta_0 + d_{min}$, where d_{min} is the minimal allowed distance of receptive fields. All subsequent positions increase hyperbolically, until a maximal receptive field distance d_{max} between neighboring receptive field positions is reached. The next receptive field position is then set again the minimal distance d_{min} away from the former and a new hyperbolic section starts. This leads to:

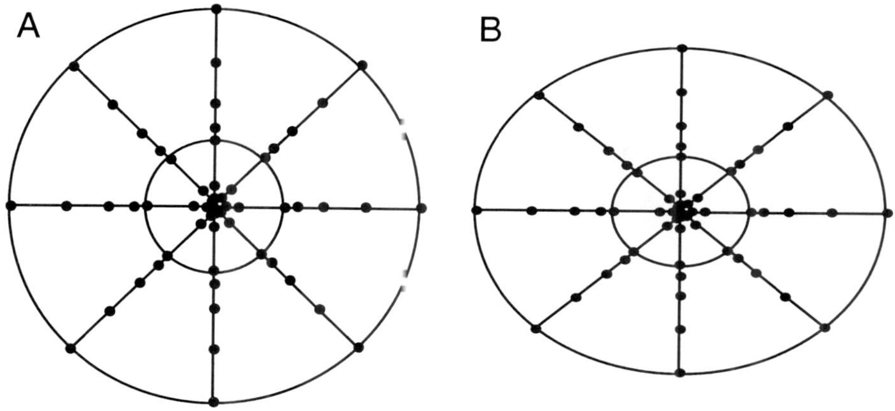

Fig. 3. Layout of receptive field grid with $m = 8$ radial axes. (A) If heading direction and direction of gaze coincide all radial axes of the receptive field grid are identical. (B) In the oblique case (α = constant $\neq 0$) the FOE is shifted and the receptive field grid has only a two-fold instead of a 8-fold cyclic symmetry for rotations about the FOE.

$$\theta_{n+1} = d\frac{d + d_{min}}{d - n\, d_{min}}, \tag{2}$$

where d denotes at each hyperbolic section the first receptive field position.

Receptive field positions, that are placed according to Eq. 2, optimally sample optical flow, only if the motion direction and direction of gaze coincide. When these directions differ by a constant angle α, these receptive field positions must be re-mapped to sample the flow equally well. Since in artificial visual systems the projection plane is usually flat, the transformation due to eye rotation about α must be lifted to a transformation of a flat plane. (Note that all equations concerning the projection plane, starting from Eq. 1, were derived for a flat retina, but these equations can be adapted to curved projection planes.) Two-dimensional Cartesian coordinates on the flat plane will be denoted with small letters (x,y). After a gaze shift α about the Y axis (angle of yaw) the optical flow is transformed according to lifted rotation:

$$x^{hc}(\alpha) = f\frac{x\cos\alpha - f\sin\alpha}{f\cos\alpha + x\sin\alpha} \quad \text{and} \quad y^{hc}(\alpha) = f\frac{y}{f\cos\alpha + x\sin\alpha} \tag{3}$$

To derive this equations see any book on projective geometry or computer graphics (e. g. [11]). It is a handy but not necessary feature of these mapping functions that straight lines are conserved: the optical flow is still along *straight* radial lines, thus justifying the term RFF also for α = constant $\neq 0$ (oblique case). The FOE is shifted by $f\tan(\alpha)$, but an oblique RFF has only a two-fold instead of a m-fold cyclic symmetry for rotations about the FOE, because the mapping is not conformal (Fig. 3).

The index hc in Equation 3) indicates that these coordinates are head-centric while without index they are retinotopic. On a head-centric map, the optical flow

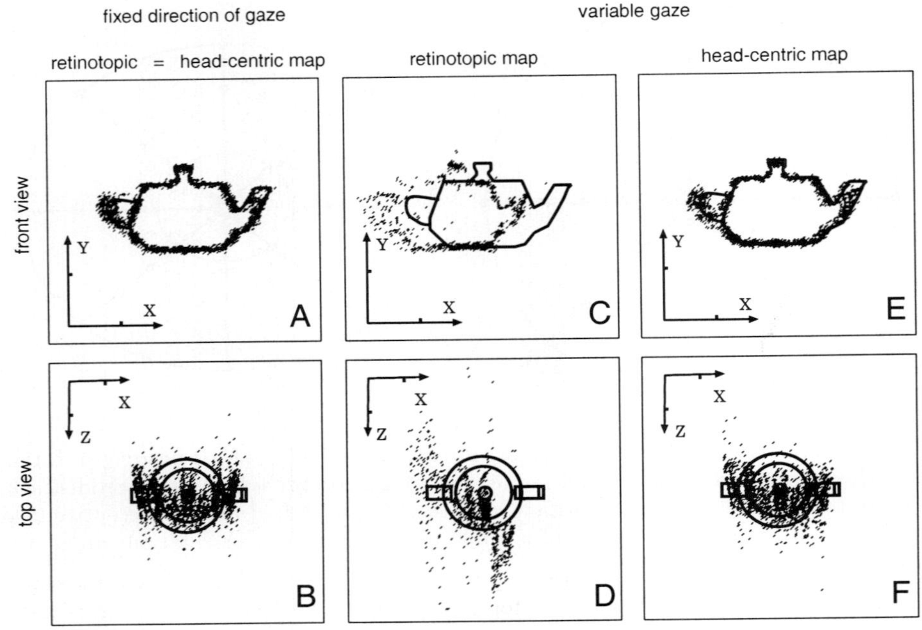

Fig. 4. A teapot viewed with stable and variable gaze. The position of the teapot in Cartesian coordinates (X,Y,Z) can be detected on a retinotopic map by the RFF-algorithm only when the gaze is pointing toward a fixed direction (A and B). The solid line is a reference to the actual position of the teapot, while the grey data points are the computed position of the visual tokens. If the direction of gaze varies while the observer is moving, the algorithm makes systematic errors (C and D). If the detected position of the teapot is to remain stable, this algorithm must operate on a head-centric map (E and F). See also text.

induced by translational motion combined with gaze shifts is congruent with an RFF. In other words, the RFF-algorithm is invariant under eye-gaze movements.

4 Results

An observer moving straight without changing the direction of gaze can adequately detect the three-dimensional position of the edges of objects in view by the RFF-algorithm [6]. For example, viewing a teapot and determining the optical flow field velocities in the corresponding RFF, produces the three-dimensional coordinates, shown in front view (Fig. 4 A) and top view (Fig. 4 B). These coordinate points outline the contour of a simulated three-dimensional teapot as seen and detected by the RFF-algorithm. Note that the depth coordinate Z, shown in the top view (Fig. 4 B), is the actual output of the RFF-algorithm. The position of the edges in the other two spatial coordinates, X and Y (the

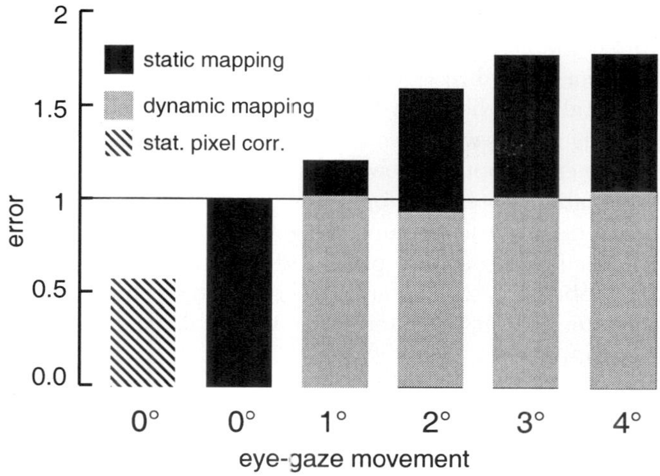

Fig. 5. Performance of the RFF-algorithm operating on a retinotopic map compared to a head-centric map obtained by dynamically mapping both with increasing eye-gaze movements. While on a head-centric map the performance is stable, on the retinotopic map is fastly deteriorates. On a retinotopic map one can take realizable receptive field positions positions into account improving the accuracy almost by a factor of two (left bar).

contour of the object in front view of Fig. 4 A) are projected onto the retina. Therefore they are already implicitly known, except for a scaling constant.

The detection of the teapot deteriorates when the straight body motion is combined with eye-gaze movements (front view Fig. 4 C, and top view D). There is even a shift of the projection of the teapot in the X-direction, that is, in the direction of one implicitly known coordinate (Fig. 4 C). This shift is inherently in the retinotopic map. Such a map can not statically store spatial locations, because the spatial registry between retina and external space changes every time the eyes move. To be precise, edges of the teapot that are located on the retina right (left) from the FOE are accelerated (slowed down) by the additional rotational flow component, when the gaze rotates clock-wise about the Y-axis. This change in the flow velocity is falsely interpreted by the RFF-algorithm as an edge too near (far), as shown by the tilt in Fig. 4 D. If the retinal coordinates are mapped on a head-centric map by continuously checking the eye position, thus taking the rotational shift into account, the RFF-algorithm can operate on the resulting head-centric optical flow field. On a head-centric map, the performance of the RFF-algorithm is invariant under gaze sifts. (Fig. 4 E and F).

To quantify the performance of the RFF-algorithm on both the retinal flow field and the head-centric flow field, we defined a standard detection task:
the three-dimensional reconstruction of a centric viewed square plane. For fixed direction of gaze this corresponds to a situation where edges move with hyperbolically increasing velocity along the receptive fields of an individual radial line.

The angles between the edge and the radius vary between 0° and 45°. The average error in the detected three-dimensional position of the square plane was normalized to 1 for fixed direction of gaze (Fig. 5). If the gaze direction rotates step wise by a total angle between 1° to 4° about the Y-axis, the error increases when the RFF-algorithm works on retinal optical flow fields, as expected (see Fig 5). On head-centric optical flow fields the performance of the standard detection task is stable. Note that for fixed direction of, gaze one can introduce correction terms taking into account the actual static location of the receptive fields, which must lie on a square pixel grid. Therfore a receptive field location can not exactly obey Eq. 2. The error decreases by almost a factor of 2, with these correction terms, but these terms are not straightforwardly obtained for a head-centric map.

5 Discussion

Purely translational ego-motion induces an RFF in the retina, that contains reliable and rather easily accessible information about the structure of the viewed three-dimensional scene. In polar coordinates the RFF is only along the radial dimension and therfore this flow field is essentially one-dimensional in any retinotopic map for a specific curve-linear coordinate system. For example, in the primary visual cortex radial flow is mapped along parallel alined neurons [12]. And indeed some animals, e.g. the housefly [13] or birds [14], seem to reduce the optical flow to a single, translational component. However there will often be additional rotational components in the optical flow, foremost in form of small saccades or smooth pursuit eye movements. As soon as a rotational component is mixed with translation motion, the optical flow is two-dimensional in any coordinate system of a retinotopic map. In this case, deducing depth from optical flow is far more complicated. We showed that with a dynamical mapping strategy of visual space, the effect of eye-gaze movements on the optical flow can be eliminated. The resulting flow field on a head-centric map is congruent to the one induced by pure translational motion. In other words, dynamical mapping induces an optical flow invariant under eye-gaze shifts.

Can other rotational components than eye-movements, e.g. head rotation that could be mapped into a stable body-centric frame, be accounted for in a similar way? In all cases in which rotational components come together with translational in the ego-motion the resulting optical flow is two-dimensional. The condition to reduce the spatial dimension of the flow field by dynamically mapping is that the axis of rotation must include the view point of the perspective projection. This is in good approximation true for eye-gaze movements and with less accuracy also for head rotations, or body rotation about the central body axis. Generally, the larger the distance between rotation axis and view point is, the farer away must objects be, to be accurately detected by the RFF-algorithm. If the heading direction changes slowly the center of rotation is far away from the view point but then the resulting trajectory can approximately split into linear parts in which the translation is again translational. Furthermore, if the rotation angle is too large, viewed object disappear on one side of the visual field and new objects come into existence on the other. Therefore the rotation must be small enough to have sufficient time to determine the distance of the object. Taken these facts together, eye-gaze movements are the most likely rotation that could be filtered from the optical flow by dynamical mapping.

References

1. Marr, D.: Vision. W.H. Freeman and Company, New York, 2000.
2. Nakayama, K., Loomis J.M.: Optical velocity patterns, velocity-sensitive neurons, and space perception: a hypothesis. Perception **3** (1974) 63–80.
3. . Longuet-Higgins H.C., Prazdny K.: The interpretation of a moving retinal image. Proc. R. Soc. Lond B Biol. Sci. **208** (1980) 385–397.
4. Gibson, J.J. The perception of the visual world. Houghton Mifflin, Boston, 1950.
5. Poggio G.F., Torre V., Koch C.: Computational vision and regularization theory. Nature, **317** (1985) 314–319.
6. Wörgötter, F., Cozzi, A., Gerdes V.: A parallel noise-robust algorithm to recover depth information from radial flow fields. Neural Comput. **11** (1999) 381–416.
7. Horn, B.K.P.: Robot Vision. The MIT Press, Boston, 1986.
8. Barron, J.L., Fleet, D.J., Beauchemin, S.S.: Performance of optical flow techniques. International Journal of Computer Vision, **12** (1994) 43–77.
9. Andersen R.A., Essick G.K., Siegel R.M.: Encoding of spatial location by posterior parietal neurons. Science. **230**(1985) 456–458.
10. Zipser D., Andersen R.A.: Related Articles A back-propagation programmed network that simulates response properties of a subset of posterior parietal neurons. Nature. **331** (1988) 679–684.
11. Marsh D.: Applied Geometry for Computer Graphics and CAD. Springer-Verlag, Berlin Heidelberg New York, 1999.
12. Schwartz, E.: Spatial mapping in the primate sensory projection: analytic structure and relevance to perception.: Biol. Cybern. **25** (1977) 181–194.
13. Wagner H.: Flight performance and visual control of flight of the free-flying housefly (*Musca domestica l.*). I. Organization of the flight motor. Phil. Trans. R. Soc. Lond., B**312** (186) 527–551.
14. Wallman J., Letelier J.-C.: Eye movments, head movments and gaze stabilization in birds. In Zeigler H.P., Bishop H.J. (Eds) Vision brain and behavior in birds. MIT Press. Cambridge, 1993.

An Analysis of the Motion Signal Distributions Emerging from Locomotion through a Natural Environment

Johannes M. Zanker [1,2] and Jochen Zeil [2]

[1] Department of Psychology, Royal Holloway, University of London, Egham, Surrey TW20 0EX, England, j.zanker@rhul.ac.uk
[2] Centre for Visual Sciences, RSBS, The Australian National University, Canberra, ACT 2601, Australia

Abstract. Some 50 years have passed since Gibson drew attention to the characteristic field of velocity vectors generated on the retina when an observer is moving through the three-dimensional world. Many theoretical, psychophysical, and physiological studies have demonstrated the use of such optic flowfields for a number of navigational tasks under laboratory conditions, but little is known about the actual flowfield structure under natural operating conditions. To study the motion information available to the visual system in the real world, we moved a panoramic imaging device outdoors on accurately defined paths and simulated a biologically inspired motion detector network to analyse the distribution of motion signals. We found that motion signals are sparsely distributed in space and that local directions can be ambiguous and noisy. Spatial or temporal integration would be required to retrieve reliable information on the local motion vectors. Nevertheless, a surprisingly simple algorithm can retrieve rather accurately the direction of heading from sparse and noisy motion signal maps without the need for such pooling. Our approach thus may help to assess the role of specific environmental and computational constraints in natural optic flow processing.

1 Background

Visual motion information is crucial for maintaining course, avoiding obstacles, estimating distance, and for segmenting complex scenes into discrete objects. Active locomotion generates large-scale retinal image motion that contains information both about observer movement – egomotion – and the three-dimensional layout of the world. The significance of optic flowfields has been recognised since Gibson (1950) illustrated the dynamic events in the image plane resulting from egomotion by sets of homogenously distributed velocity vectors. The actual structure of the two-dimensional motion signal distributions experienced by the visual system under natural operating conditions, however, is not only determined by the pattern of locomotion, but also by the specific three-dimensional layout of the local environment and by the motion detection mechanism employed. To understand the design of the neural processing mechanisms underlying flowfield analysis, and in particular the coding strategies of motion sensitive neurones, we thus need to know more about the actual motion signal distributions under real-life conditions.

H.H. Bülthoff et al. (Eds.): BMCV 2002, LNCS 2525, pp. 146–156, 2002.

An elaborate theoretical framework has been developed on how to extract egomotion parameters from flowfields (Longuet-Higgins and Prazdny, 1980; Heeger, 1987; Koenderink and Van Doorn, 1987; Dahmen et al., 1997). Most of these models assume implicitly that local motion signals are veridical, homogenously distributed, and carry true velocity information. Similarly, motion sensitive neurones in the visual systems of invertebrates and vertebrates that seem to be involved in flowfield processing (e.g., Hausen and Egelhaaf, 1989; Frost et al., 1990; Orban et al., 1992; Krapp and Hengstenberg, 1996) are usually investigated with coherently structured motion stimuli that densely cover large parts of the visual field. Franz & Krapp (2000) and Dahmen et al. (2001) recently used simulations to assess the number and the distribution of motion signals that are necessary to estimate egomotion parameters. Their studies suggest that surprisingly few local and low fidelity flow measurements are needed, provided these measurements are taken at widely distributed locations throughout the panoramic visual field. So far, however, we do not know what kind of motion signal distributions visual systems are confronted with in a normal ecological and behavioural context.

To address this issue, we reconstructed a "view from the cockpit" of flying insects, which have become model systems for optic flow analysis because of their extraordinary behavioural repertoire and because the neural machinery underlying optic flow processing is well understood (Hausen and Egelhaaf, 1989; Eckert and Zeil, 2001). We moved a panoramic imaging device along accurately defined paths in outdoor locations containing a mixture of close and distant vegetation. We then analysed the image sequences which we recorded during these movements with a two-dimensional motion detector model (2DMD) consisting of an array of correlation-type detector pairs for horizontal and vertical motion components (Zanker et al., 1997). The analysis of movie sequences recorded on comparatively simple flight paths is intended to help us evaluate the image processing requirements involved in extracting egomotion information under realistic conditions. In particular, we can assess the density and spatial distribution of local motion signals normally available and the amount of noise that the visual system has to cope with under natural operating conditions. Eventually such an analysis will enable us to identify the image processing strategies the visual system could in principle employ. In order to cope with various sources of unreliable signals, obvious candidates for such processing strategies are for instance local gain control, spatial or temporal averaging, or the selection or combination of adequately tuned spatiotemporal channels. The focus of the present account is on a simple procedure to estimate the quality of motion signal maps by assessing the recovery of direction of heading for purely translatory movements.

2 The Approach

A panoramic imaging device was mounted on a computer-controlled robotic gantry which allowed us to move it along accurately defined trajectories within a space of about 1 m^3. Servo-controlled DC motors moved the camera along the three orthogonal axes with an accuracy of 0.1 mm (system components by Isel, Germany). The gantry was mounted on a trolley to be positioned in a variety of outdoor locations. For the present analysis we chose a location with grass, shrubs and bushes amongst large

Eucalyptus trees, containing a mixture of close and distant objects, which would be representative of a typical habitat for flying insects.

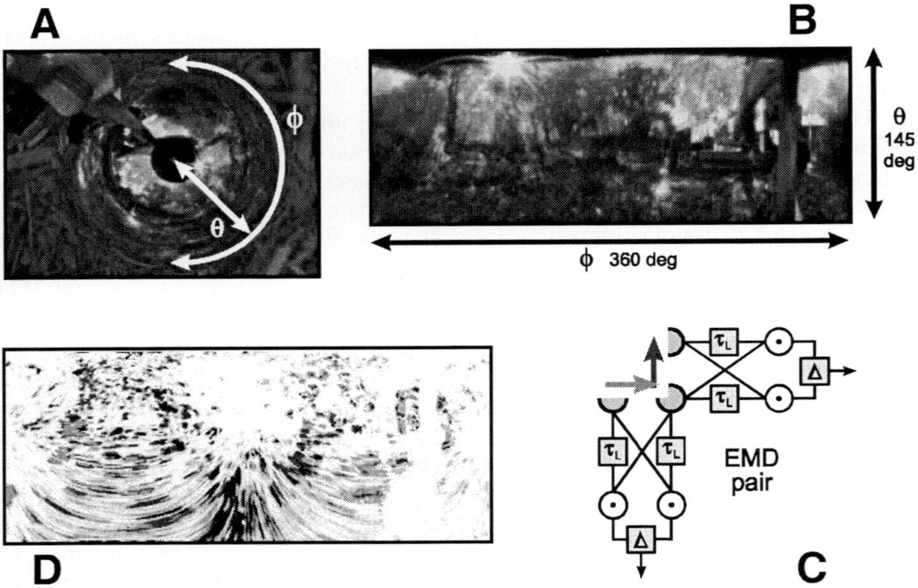

Fig. 1. A method to study flowfields in the real world. A video camera is used to capture panoramic images in polar coordinates (A) which are converted into cartesian coordinates (B; azimuth Φ, elevation θ). Image sequences were recorded while moving the camera through a natural scene and then used as input to a large array of motion detector pairs (one element sketched in C), to generate motion signal maps (D).

The panoramic imaging device consisted of a black and white video camera (Samsung BW-410CA) looking down onto a parabolic mirror which was optimised for constant spatial resolution (Chahl and Srinivasan, 1997). In the captured images the azimuth and elevation are represented in polar coordinates, as angular position and distance from the origin in the image centre, respectively (see figure 1A). Images were digitised with 8 bit greylevel resolution (Matrox Meteor framegrabber) and stored directly on a computer harddisk for off-line analysis. The image sequences were subsequently converted into cartesian coordinates, resulting in an image 450 pixels wide and 185 pixels high, which corresponds to a visual field size of 360° of azimuth, Φ, by 136° of elevation, θ, (figure 1B). In the default configuration, image sequences of 64 consecutive frames were taken at 25 frames/s during gantry speeds of 5 cm/s and 10 cm/s. The apparatus also allows to grab single images could at sequences of predefined positions, in order to generate more complex trajectories. Image sequences were analysed with a two-dimensional, correlation-type motion detector model (2DMD) which has been used previously to identify the processing requirements faced by fiddler crabs in detecting and recognising species-specific movement signals (Zeil and Zanker, 1997), to study the characteristic patterns of image motion produced by wasps during their learning flights (Zeil et al., 1998), and to simulate a wide range of psychophysical phenomena (e.g., Zanker et al., 1997; Patzwahl and Zanker, 2000; Zanker, 2001). The basic building block is tha elementary motion detector (EMD) of the correlation type which has been shown in many behavioural and physiological studies to be a very good candidate for the biological implementation of motion processing (for review, see Reichardt, 1987; Borst and Egelhaaf, 1989). This EMD model is a representative of a variety of luminance based operators (Adelson and Bergen, 1985; Van Santen and Sperling, 1985; Watson and Ahumada, 1985), and other models for local motion detection (e.g., Srinivasan, 1990; Johnston et al., 1999) could be used without affecting the main conclusions we draw from our results. Orthogonal pairs of local EMDs that detect horizontal and vertical motion components (sketched in figure 1C) are used to build a two-dimensional network of detectors, which constitutes the 2DMD model.

In a simple implementation (figure 1C), each EMD receives input from two points of the spatially filtered stimulus patterns. The signals interact in a nonlinear way after some temporal filtering, to provide a directionally selective signal. Difference of Gaussians (DOGs) with balanced excitatory centre and inhibitory surround are used as bandpass filters in the input lines to exclude DC components from the input. The sampling distance between the two inputs, which is the fundamental spatial model parameter, was set to 2 pixels (approximately 1.6°) for the present study. To prevent aliasing, the diameter of the receptive field was set to about twice the value of the sampling distance. The signal from one input line is multiplied with the temporally filtered signal from the other line, and two antisymmetric units of this kind are subtracted from each other with equal weights, leading to a fully opponent, and thus highly directionally selective EMD (Borst and Egelhaaf, 1989). The time constant of the first-order lowpass filter, which is the fundamental temporal model parameter, was set to 2 frame intervals (80 ms) for the present study. The time interval between successive image frames corresponded to 8 digital simulation steps; an increased temporal resolution was used in order to improve the accuracy in calculating the dynamic responses of the temporal filters.

Movie sequences were processed by two 2D-arrays of such EMDs (two sets of 450 x 185 correlators, one pair centred at each image pixel, oriented along the horizontal or along the vertical axis of the cartesian-coordinate images). The result is a two-dimensional motion signal distribution, the 2DMD response, with a horizontal and vertical signal component for each image point, which we call a *motion signal map* (see figure 1D). In some cases this raw 2DMD output was temporally averaged (over 8 to 64 frames) before further analysis. To be able to plot such signal maps at high spatial resolution, usually a two-dimensional colour code is used to represent the direction and the magnitude of local motion detector responses in terms of hue and saturation (Zeil and Zanker, 1997). For purposes of black and white reproduction, in the present study the horizontal and vertical motion components are plotted separately in grey-level maps. In the vertical components map a change from black through medium grey to white indicates a change from downwards motion through standstill to upwards motion (see figure 2A, D). Correspondingly, in the horizontal component map regions of motion to the left, no motion signal, and motion to the right correspond to black, medium grey and white regions, respectively (see figure 2B, E).

3 Analysing Motion Signal Maps

The 2DMD response for a simple forward translation is shown in figure 2, comparing the output for a single displacement step (A-C) to the average of 16 consecutive steps (D-F). The vertical components of the motion signal maps (figure 2A & D) are characterised by predominantly downwards directions in the lower half of the central image region, i.e. in the parts of the map that correspond to the field of view below the horizon looking forwards, and faint upwards signals in the upper half of the frontal region. The general direction is inverted for the image regions corresponding to the rear field of view, close to the left and right image borders. This pattern reflects the vertical expansion components from the expanding and contracting poles of the flowfield, which in the case of forward translation should be located in the centre and in the left/right border regions of the panoramic image. The horizontal components of the motion signal maps (figure 2B & E) are different in the left and the right half of the panoramic image, the former being dominated by dark spots that indicate leftward motion components, and the latter being dominated by bright spots that correspond to rightward motion. This distribution of local motion signals is typical for a forward translation of the camera which produces an expanding and contracting flowfield pole in the frontal and the rear field of view. Corresponding patterns of local motion signals, with different locations of the flowfield pole in the images, are found for translations in other directions (data not shown). Three peculiarities of the motion signal maps should be noted.

(a) The distribution of local motion signals is noisy and sparse. To emphasize the overall structure of the signal maps, a nonlinear grey-scale is used in figure 2 which saturates at about 10% of the local response maximum, thus leading to an underestimation of the sparseness of this map. To quantify the density and coherence of local motion signals, we focus on two typical regions extending approximately 15° by 15° (indicated by small frames in figure 2 A and B) just above and below the horizon in the left lateral field of view (-90° azimuth), where the flowfield should be characterised by strong, coherent motion in horizontal direction (+/- 180°). The actual sparseness of the motion map in these test regions is demonstrated by the fact that on average 93% of the signals are smaller than a tenth of the maximum motion signal present in the map, and 31% are smaller than a hundredth of the maximum signal. This result is not surprising because the density of the motion signal maps is determined by the strength of local motion detector responses, which depends on the abundance, contrast, and angular velocity of local contours. Far distant objects that only cause minute image displacements during translation, or a cloudless blue sky, for instance, do not elicit any significant motion detector response. Most importantly, the image region around the flowfield pole is characterised by a "hole", devoid of any clear motion signals. Furthermore, the directional noise level in the motion maps is reflected by the fact that the direction of no more than 17% of the motion signals in the test regions is found within a range of 30° (47% within a range of 90°) around the expected direction of +/- 180°. The fact that directions within small regions vary considerably can be attributed to fluctuations inherent to the EMD output (Reichardt and Egelhaaf, 1988) and to variations of local contour orientations which affect the direction of motion detected for these contours (Hildreth and Koch, 1987).

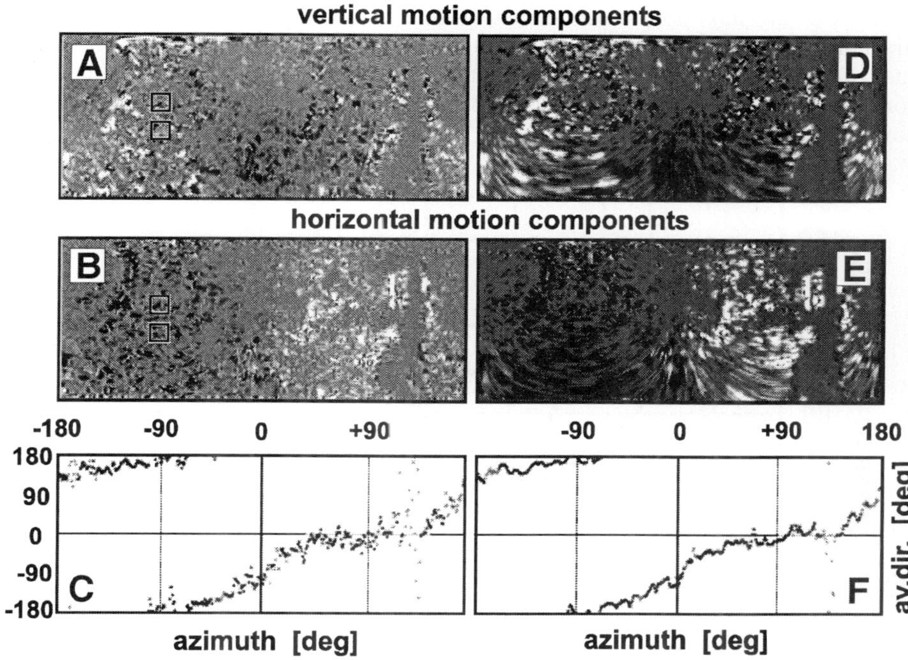

Fig. 2. 2DMD output. Motion signal maps (vertical motion response components A, D, up: white, no motion: medium grey, down: black; horizontal components B, E, right: white, no motion: medium grey, left: black) and average direction profiles (C, F) for a panoramic image sequence recorded during forward translation; A-C: response from a single displacement step; D-F: temporal average from 16 consecutive displacement steps.

(b) There is a general tendency that motion signals are denser and stronger in the lower than in the upper image regions, because the camera is moving close to the ground where nearby contours generate comparatively large image motion components. On the other hand, objects above the horizon are much further away and therefore generate much smaller image angular displacements during translation. To quantify this effect, we compared the distribution of motion signal strengths in two test regions shown in figure 2 A and B with each other. Whereas 17% of the motion signals in the test region below the horizon are smaller than a hundredth of the maximum signal, 31% of the motion signals in the test region above the horizon fall below this limit.

(c) In the temporal averages of several 2DMD response frames (figure 2D & E) motion signals are aligned along “motion streaks”, which reflect the trajectories of image contrast elements during the averaging interval. These small, oriented streaks, contain independent information about the structure of the motion signal map - the radial patterns in the front and the rear image regions provide a clear indication of the flowfield poles. Recent psychophysical experiments suggest that humans actually are able to use the orientation information of temporally blurred moving objects for motion processing (Geisler, 1999, Burr et al., ECVP 2002). It should be noted that such a combination of orientation and motion information goes beyond the interaction between collinear direction selective motion detectors along motion trajectories (Watamaniuk and McKee, 1998), which would correspond to the Gestalt law of "common fate". The motion signal maps presented here suggest that a combination of information across stimulus modalities could indeed be very powerful for the extraction of flowfield parameters.

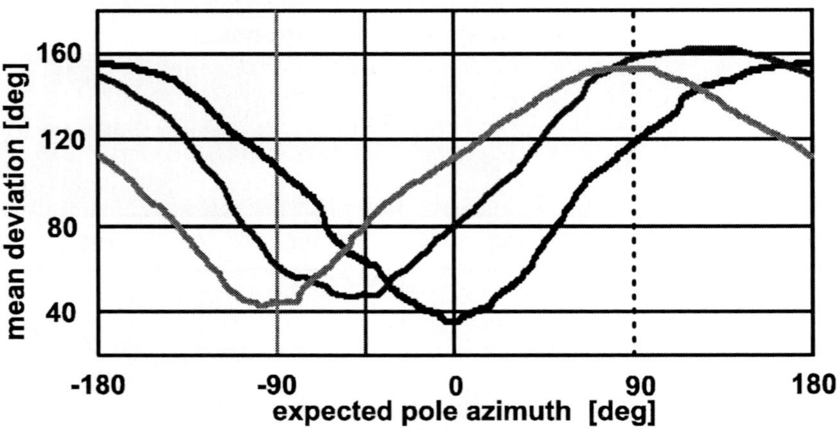

Fig. 3. Estimating the location of the flowfield pole. Average deviation between the expected direction profile function and the actual 2DMD output data plotted as function of the azimuth location of the expected flowfield pole for forward (black data points), sideways (light grey) and oblique (dark grey) translation. Minimum deviation indicate the best fit estimate of the flowfield pole, which are generally very close to the veridical values (indicated by vertical lines).

In a next step we condensed the motion signal maps to horizontal direction profiles by averaging EMD outputs along image columns, i.e. for a given horizontal position in the panoramic image. In these profiles, the direction of the average motion vector is plotted as a function of azimuth (figure 2C & F). The length of the average vector, i.e. motion signal strength which is determined by the average contrast and the inverse of the direction variance at a given azimuth, is represented by the greylevel of a given data point in the direction profiles (values above/below the overall average are plotted in black/grey). The response profiles capture some significant aspects of the motion signal maps, and in particular give a good indication of the location of the flowfield poles. In the lateral image regions the average motion direction is horizontal, close to +/- 180 deg on the left side (around -90 deg azimuth) and close to 0 deg on the right side, clearly reflecting the homogenous image flow in the field of view perpendicular to the direction of egomotion. In the frontal and rear image regions, the profiles are characterised by a transition between the two horizontal motion directions. The vertical average direction at the locations of the flowfield pole, downwards (about -90 deg) in the frontal region (around 0 deg azimuth) and upwards (about +90 deg) in the rear image region (around +/- 180 deg), confirm the earlier observation that the signal maps are dominated by the regions below the horizon (where expansion and contraction centred around the pole assumes these directions). The noise on the direction profiles is considerably reduced by temporal integration (compare figure 2C & F), and a similar effect is to be expected for spatial pooling. In summary, the directional profiles offer a fair account of the natural flowfield structure, as far as the location of poles is concerned, which indicate the direction of egomotion.

In order to analyse the direction profiles further, we fitted a simple mathematical function to the data which reflects the expectation of a basic directional profile. Because this technique intends to assess the quality of the information contained in the direction profiles and is not meant to suggest a particular mechanism dealing with optic flowfields, we made no attempt to specify anything like an optimal expectation function, similar to those used in matched filter approaches of estimating egomotion parameters (see, for instance, Franz and Krapp, 2000). Instead, we started from the idealised situation that in a homogenous flowfield generated by horizontal egomotion vertical velocity components would cancel each other, leading to a rectangular direction profile with horizontal motion to the left (+/- 180 deg) and to the right (0 deg) on the left and right side of the expansion pole, respectively. This simple expectation function was shifted relative to the direction profiles by variation of the azimuth location of the assumed flowfield pole ('expected pole'), and the root mean square of the deviation between expectation and data was calculated. The deviation should reach a minimum when the expected pole is closest to the direction of egomotion. The mean deviation between data and expectation function is plotted in figure 3 as function of expected pole azimuth for three individual 2DMD output frames from three different movie sequences. Forwards, leftwards, and oblique translation should lead to a minimum at 0, -45, and -90 deg of azimuth, respectively (indicated by vertical lines). It is obvious that the minima are very close to the respective veridical locations, with deviations of -0.8, 8.4, and 6.2 deg for the three cases tested. The mean deviation curves are virtually indistinguishable for different 2DMD output frames of an individual sequence, and no further improvement is found when motion signal maps are generated by averaging several frames (data not shown). This result suggests that the instantaneous information contained in the motion signals generated by a small camera displacement is comparable to the information that results from pooling signals over time while contours move along a trajectory, quite in contrast to the qualitative impression that averaged motion signal maps provide a much clearer flowfield structure (compare figure 2A-C with 2D-F). Elaborate mechanisms to estimate egomotion parameters (Perrone, 1992; Franz and Krapp, 2000) may thus not always be necessary, because under certain circumstances fast approximate procedures may be reliable and accurate enough (see also Dahmen et al. 1997).

4 Conclusions

The structure of optic flowfields that is influenced by the type of observer locomotion and by the structure of the environment, but also by neural processing strategies such as the basic motion detection mechanism or spatiotemporal pooling. The flowfield information available under realistic operating conditions was studied here by moving a panoramic imaging through natural environments and using the recorded image sequences as input to a biologically plausible motion detector network. The resulting motion signal maps have several interesting properties, which reflect specific environmental and computational constraints of optic flow processing. Firstly, motion signals are sparsely distributed across the visual field, even in densely contour-populated natural scenes. This property of motion signal maps would be predicted by motion detection theory, because the contrast dependence of the EMD response leads to irregular patterns of image regions at which the motion is clearly detectable. Secondly, local variation of motion direction is considerable, because the EMD output does not necessarily reflect the physical motion direction (Reichardt and Schlögl, 1988), a constraint which is well known in human psychophysics as the "aperture problem" (Adelson and Movshon, 1982; Nakayama and Silverman, 1988).

Nevertheless, panoramic motion signal maps contain sufficient information to estimate the direction of egomotion rather accurately, even with very simple estimation algorithms. This suggests that the inherent richness of flowfields in natural scenes might allow for fast, robust and simple mechanisms for sensing egomotion. We already know that under idealised conditions, the exact estimation of egomotion parameters requires only a small number of motion signals (Koenderink and Van Doorn, 1987; Dahmen et al., 2001), and we show here that this is also true for natural operating conditions. Future research will need to test whether this conclusion still holds for a wider range of movements, including mixtures of translation and rotation, and a variety of environments, including those with highly non-uniform distribution of objects. Conventional models of optic flow processing, which are able to separate translation and rotation components and control the direction of heading (Hildreth, 1984; Heeger, 1987; Perrone, 1992), usually rely on the assumption that dense and coherent motion signal maps are available. It will be essential to see how well such models deal with natural motion signal distributions and how the information content of natural flow fields is affected by the restricted field of view of many animals. In this context, it may become necessary to re-evaluate strategies to improve the spatial structure of the motion signal maps, such as local spatial pooling, temporal integration, or the extraction of true local velocity estimates (Verri et al., 1992) and to recognise the behavioural, sensory and neural adaptations animals are known to have evolved in response to the specific statistics of distance, contrast and contour orientation in their particular visual habitats (Nalbach and Nalbach, 1987; Nalbach, 1990; O'Carroll et al., 1997) (reviewed in Eckert and Zeil, 2001). It will be furthermore interesting to assess the value of additional information sources such as orientation cues provided by motion streaks.

To understand the evolution of behavioural and neural strategies of information processing and their adaptive quality, requires a more quantitative assessment of the natural operating conditions in which this evolution took and continues to take place. We hope to extend our preliminary study to a systematic and quantitative analysis of the motion signal distributions which are generated by different styles of locomotion in different environments.

Acknowledgements. We are grateful to M. Franz and W. Junger for their support during the design and testing of the gantry and the recording of some image sequences, and to J. Chahl, M. Hofmann, and M. V. Srinivasan for many discussions throughout the project. We acknowledge financial support from DSTO, HFSP and Wellcome Trust.

References

Adelson EH, Bergen JR. 1985. Spatiotemporal energy models for the perception of motion. Journal of the Optical Society of America A 2:284-299.

Adelson EH, Movshon JA. 1982. Phenomenal coherence of moving visual patterns. Nature 300:523-525.

Borst A, Egelhaaf M. 1989. Principles of visual motion detection. Trends in Neuroscience 12:297-306.

Chahl JS, Srinivasan MV. 1997. Reflective surfaces for panoramic imaging. Applied Optics 36:8275-8285.

Dahmen HJ, Franz MO, Krapp HG. 2001. Extracting egomotion from optic flow: limits of accuracy and neural matched filters. In: Zanker JM, Zeil J, Editors. Motion Vision - Computational, Neural, and Ecological Constraints. Berlin Heidelberg New York: Springer. p 143-168.

Dahmen HJ, Wüst RM, Zeil J. 1997. Extracting egomotion parameters from optic flow: principal limits for animals and machines. In: Srinivasan MV, Venkatesh S, Editors. From living eyes to seeing machines. Oxford: Oxford University Press. p 174-198.

Eckert MP, Zeil J. 2001. Towards an ecology of motion vision. In: Zanker JM, Zeil J, Editors. Motion Vision: Computational, neural and ecological constraints. Berlin Heidelberg New York: Springer Verlag. p 333-369.

Franz MO, Krapp HG. 2000. Wide-field, motion-sensitive neurons and matched filters for optic flow fields. Biological Cybernetics 83:185-197.

Frost BJ, Wylie DR, Wang Y-C. 1990. The processing of object and self-motion in the tectofugal and accesory optic pathways of birds. Vision Research 30:1677-1688.

Geisler WS. 1999. Motion streaks provide a spatial code for motion direction. Nature 400:65-69.

Gibson JJ. 1950. The perception of the visual world. Cambridge, MA: The Riverside Press.

Hausen K, Egelhaaf M. 1989. Neural Mechanisms of Visual Course Control in Insects. In: Stavenga DG, Hardie RC, Editors. Facets of Vision. Berlin Heidelberg: Springer Verlag. p 391-424.

Heeger DJ. 1987. Model for the extraction of image flow. Journal of the Optical Society of America A 4:1455-1471.

Hildreth E-C. 1984. The computation of the velocity field. Procedings of the Royal Society London B 221:189-220.

Hildreth E-C, Koch C. 1987. The analysis of visual motion: From computational theory to neuronal mechanisms. Annual Review of Neuroscience 10:477-533.

Johnston A, McOwan PW, Benton CP. 1999. Robust velocity computation from a biologically motivated model of motion perception. Procedings of the Royal Society London B 266:509-518.

Koenderink JJ, Van Doorn AJ. 1987. Facts on Optic Flow. Biological Cybernetics 56:247-254.

Krapp HG, Hengstenberg R. 1996. Estimation of self-motion by optic flow processing in single visual interneurons. Nature 384:463-466.

Longuet-Higgins HC, Prazdny K. 1980. The interpretation of a moving retinal image. Procedings of the Royal Society London B 208:385-397.

Nakayama K, Silverman GH. 1988. The aperture problem - II- Spatial integration of velocity information along contours. Vision Research 28:747-753.

Nalbach H-O. 1990. Multisensory control of eyestalk orientation in decapod crustaceans: an ecological approach. Journal of Crustacean Biology 10:382-399.

Nalbach H-O, Nalbach G. 1987. Distribution of optokinetic sensitivity over the eye of crabs: its relation to habitat and possible role in flow-field analysis. Journal of Comparative Physiology A 160:127-135.

O'Carroll D, Laughlin SB, Bidwell NJ, Harris SJ. 1997. Spatio-Temporal Properties of Motion Detectors Matched to Low Image Velocities in Hovering Insects. Vision Research 37:3427-3439.

Orban GA, Lagae L, Verri A, Raiguel S, Xiao D, Maes H, Torre V. 1992. First-order analysis of optical flow in monkey brain. Proceedings of the National Academy of Sciences USA 89:2595-2599.

Patzwahl DR, Zanker JM. 2000. Mechanisms for human motion perception: combining evidence from evoked potentials, behavioural performance and computational modelling. European Journal of Neuroscience 12:273-282.

Perrone JA. 1992. Model for the computation of self-motion in biological systems. Journal of the Optical Society of America A 9:177-194.

Reichardt W. 1987. Evaluation of optical motion information by movement detectors. Journal of Comparative Physiology A161:533-547.

Reichardt W, Egelhaaf M. 1988. Properties of Individual Movement Detectors as Derived from Behavioural Experiments on the Visual System of the Fly. Biological Cybernetics 58:287-294.

Reichardt W, Schlögl RW. 1988. A two dimensional field theory for motion computation. First order approximation; translatory motion of rigid patterns. Biological Cybernetics 60:23-35.

Srinivasan MV. 1990. Generalized Gradient Schemes for the Measurement of Two-Dimensional Image Motion. Biological Cybernetics 63:421-431.

Van Santen JPH, Sperling G. 1985. Elaborated Reichardt detectors. Journal of the Optical Society of America A 2:300-321.

Verri A, Straforini M, Torre V. 1992. Computational aspects of motion perception in natural and artificial vision systems. Philosophical Transactions of the Royal Society [Biology] 337:429-443.

Watamaniuk SNJ, McKee SP. 1998. Simltaneous encoding of direction at a local and global scale. Perception and Psychophysics 60:191-200.

Watson AB, Ahumada AJ. 1985. Model of human visual-motion sensing. Journal of the Optical Society of America A2:322-342.

Zanker JM. 2001. Combining Local Motion Signals: A Computational Study of Segmentation and Transparency. In: Zanker JM, Zeil J, Editors. Motion Vision: Computational, Neural and Ecological Constraints. Berlin Heidelberg New York: Springer.

Zanker JM, Hofmann MI, Zeil J. 1997. A two-dimensional motion detector model (2DMD) responding to artificial and natural image sequences. Investigative Ophthalmology and Visual Science 38:S 936.

Zeil J, Voss R, Zanker JM. 1998. A View from the Cockpit of a Learning Wasp. In: Elsner N, Wehner R, Editors. Gottingen Neurobiology Report 1998. Stuttgart: Georg Thieme Verlag. p 140.

Zeil J, Zanker JM. 1997. A Glimpse into Crabworld. Vision Research 37:3417-3426.

Prototypes of Biological Movements in Brains and Machines

Martin A. Giese

Laboratory for Action Representation and Learning
Dept. of Cognitive Neurology, University Clinic
Tübingen, Germany
martin.giese@tuebingen.mpg.de

Abstract. Biological movements and actions are important visual stimuli. Their recognition is a highly relevant problem for biological as well as for technical systems. In the domain of stationary object recognition the concept of a prototype-based representation of object shape has been quite inspiring for research in computer vision as well as in neuroscience. The paper presents an overview of some recent work aiming at a generalization of such concepts for the domain of complex movements. First, a technical method is presented that allows to represent classes of complex movements by linear combinations of learned example trajectories. Applications of this method in computer vision and computer graphics are briefly discussed. The relevance of prototype-based representations for the recognition of complex movements in the visual cortex is discussed in the second part of the paper. By devising a simple neurophysiologically plausible model it is demonstrated that many experimental findings on the visual recognition of "biological motion" can be accounted for by a neural representation of learned prototypical motion patterns.

1 Introduction

The processing of biological movements, like actions, gestures, or facial expressions is very important for many technical applications, for example people recognition, men machine interfaces or interactive robotics. The recognition of such patterns is also crucial for the survival of many biological species, e.g. for the recognition of predators and prey at large distances, or for mating behavior. Humans are highly sensitive for biological movement patterns. This is illustrated by a famous experiment by Johansson [14] who fixed small light bulbs on the joints of actors that were performing different actions. Just seeing the movements of the eleven moving lights subjects were able to recognize the executed actions very accurately. In subsequent experiments it was shown that such "point light walkers" are sufficient to extract even subtle details, like the gender or the identity of the walker [6].

The modeling and recognition of complex movements has been a major topic of research in computer vision over the last few years (see e.g. [8] for a review). Research in neuroscience has only started to investigate the neural and computational mechanisms that underlie movement recognition in the nervous system.

H.H. Bülthoff et al. (Eds.): BMCV 2002, LNCS 2525, pp. 157–170, 2002.

In the area of stationary object recognition approaches that represent classes of complex shapes based on a limited number of learned prototypical example patterns have been very successful for the development of new technical methods as well as theoretical model in neuroscience. Recently, attempts have been made to transfer such concepts to the domain of complex movement recognition. This paper reviews some of our recent work and discusses the relationships between technical and biologically plausible implementations of prototype-based representations of complex movements.

2 Prototype-Based Representations of Stationary Shape

In research on the recognition of non-moving stationary objects the idea of prototype-based representations of complex shape has been quite influential. Classes of similar shapes are assumed to be represented as elements of an abstract metric "shape space" that can be defined by learning example patterns. One example is the concept of a multi-dimensional "face space" [23] that has been helpful for the interpretation of experimental data on the recognition of faces and caricature effects. Another example are methods for the view-based representation of three-dimensional object shape (e.g. [22, 24, 7]). Multiple example views of the same object are stored as prototypes, and novel views are approximated by appropriate interpolation between these prototypes.

Because of the large dimensionality of the associated pattern spaces it is critically important how generalization between the prototypes is achieved [7]. An efficient representation by learning is however possible because similar shapes and different views of the same object are typically related by smooth transformations. One possibility to exploit this fact is to represent these smooth transformation functions with regularization networks (e.g. [20, 1]). Another possibility is to define interpolations by linear combinations of the prototypes. Ullman and Basri [22] have shown that, under appropriate conditions, the whole continuum of 2D images of a 3D object can be represented by linearly combining few 2D example views. Linear combination was defined by combining the 2D positions of corresponding features in different 2D pictures. This method was generalized by automatic computation of corresponding features using optic flow algorithms (e.g. [24, 15]). The result is a field of spatial correspondence shifts that are suitable for morphing one image into another. To define linear combinations that define parameterized classes of shapes that interpolate smoothly between the prototypes correspondence between the prototypes and a reference pattern is computed and the resulting correspondence shifts are linearly combined. Because new patterns are generated by morphing between the prototypes this technique has been called "morphable models" [15]. The advantage of such linear combination methods is that they map classes of complex shapes into a space with an Euclidean topology. This makes it possible to compute averages, and to introduce axes in this space that can be easily interpreted, like the "maleness" of "femaleness" of faces. Morphable models can be used for the analysis of images, e.g. face classification or pose estimation [1]. A very successful application domain is the synthesis of new photo-realistic images in computer graphics based on a number of learned example pictures (e.g. [2, 15]).

In neuroscience the idea of a representation of object shape in terms of learned two-dimensional example views has been supported by results from psychophysics and electrophysiology. For instance, certain "canonical" views of objects are recognized faster and more accurately than other views [18]. Also subjects could be trained to recognize new artificial complex shapes ("paperclips" and "amoebae") and, consistent with a view-based representation, recognition of views that are similar to the learned view is better than recognition of the same object in another view [5]. Support for such a prototype-based representation is also provided by electrophysiological results from area IT in the macaque. Some neurons in this area can be trained to respond to individual views of artificial shapes [17]. Recent modeling studies show that many psychophysical and neurophysiological results on the recognition and categorization of stationary objects can be quantitatively modeled using a hierarchical neural model that encodes object shape by view-tuned neurons that have learned example views of the same or different objects (e.g. [21]).

3 Spatio-Temporal Morphable Models

The technique of *spatio-temporal morphable models (STMM)* [11] generalizes morphable models for spatio-temporal patterns: Classes of similar movements are represented by linear combinations of previously learned prototypical example movement patterns.

3.1 Algorithm

In many cases complex biological movements can be represented by high-dimensional trajectories $\mathbf{x}(t)$ that specify e.g. the positions of the joints of a moving human or marker points on a moving face. For many classes of natural biological movements, like different gait patterns or the facial movements, the trajectories are related through smooth spatio-temporal transformations. This motivates modeling by spatio-temporal morphing between a set of learned prototypical patterns.

Movements can differ not only with respect to their spatial, but also with respect to their temporal characteristics: A movement might be accelerated or delayed without changing its trajectory in space. Such changes in timing can be described by a reparameterization of the time axis: The original time t is replaced by the new time $t' = t + \tau(t)$ with the smoothly changing temporal offset function $\tau(t)$. In addition, the two trajectories might differ by additional spatial shifts $\boldsymbol{\xi}(t)$. The exact mathematical relationship between two trajectories $\mathbf{x}_1$ and $\mathbf{x}_2$ is given by:

$$\mathbf{x}_2(t) = \mathbf{x}_1(t + \tau(t)) + \boldsymbol{\xi}(t) \tag{1}$$

We will refer to the function pair $(\boldsymbol{\xi}(t), \tau(t))$ as *correspondence field* between the two movement patterns $\mathbf{x}_1$ and $\mathbf{x}_2$. By determination of this function pair *spatio-temporal correspondence* is established between the two trajectories. [11].

It seems desirable to determine space-time correspondences that minimize the spatio-temporal shifts between the two patterns with respect to an appropriately chosen norm. The simplest possible norm is a weighted sum of the $\mathbf{L}_2$ norms of the spatial and temporal shifts. The correspondence field is determined by minimizing the error functional:

$$E[\boldsymbol{\xi}, \tau] = \int (|\boldsymbol{\xi}(t)|^2 + \lambda \tau(t)^2) \, \mathrm{d}t \tag{2}$$

This minimization has to be accomplished under the constraint that the new time axis $t' = t + \tau(t)$ is always monotonically increasing implying the constraint $\tau'(t) > -1$. The resulting constrained minimization problem is most efficiently solved by applying dynamic programming [4]. A precise description of the algorithm is given in [11].

For construction of parameterized models for spaces of similar trajectories the correspondence fields between each prototypical trajectory $\mathbf{x}_p(t)$, $1 \leq p \leq P$, and reference trajectory $\mathbf{x}_0(t)$ are computed. In practice, the reference trajectory is often an appropriately chosen average of the prototypes. Signifying the correspondence field between reference and prototype p by $(\boldsymbol{\xi}_p(t), \tau_p(t))$ one can, analogously to the case of morphable models for stationary patterns, linearly combine the correspondence fields of the different prototypes:

$$\begin{aligned} \boldsymbol{\xi}(t) &= \sum_{p=1}^{P} c_p \, \boldsymbol{\xi}_p(t) \\ \tau(t) &= \sum_{p=1}^{P} c_p \, \tau_p(t) \end{aligned} \tag{3}$$

The linearly combined correspondence field $(\boldsymbol{\xi}(t), \tau(t))$ is then used for spatio-temporal warping of the reference trajectory $\mathbf{x}_0(t)$ into the new linearly combined trajectory using equation (1). The linear weights α_p determine how much the individual prototypes contribute to the linear combination. Typically, convex linear combinations with coefficients α_p fulfilling $\sum_p \alpha_p = 1$ and $0 \leq \alpha \leq 1$ are chosen. By choosing $\alpha_p > 1$ spatio-temporal caricatures of movement patterns can be created [see *Giese, Knappmeyer & Bülthoff, this volume*].

3.2 Applications

An obvious application of STMMs is the synthesis of new movement patterns by motion morphing. For this purpose the linear weights α_p are pre-specified to obtained different "mixtures" different prototypical movements. Similar techniques have been used in computer graphics before to interpolate and edit trajectory data from motion capture systems (e.g. [4, 16]). STMMs provide a systematic approach for defining higher-dimensional pattern spaces with abstract style axes that can be easily interpreted. For instance, a continuum of styles from male to female walking can be generated by linearly combining the walks of a male and a female actor, or by averages from many males or females. Also different forms of locomotion can be linearly combined, often resulting in very naturally looking linear combinations [10]. We have also applied STMM to compute linear combinations of full-body movements for the simulation of different skill levels in martial arts, and have generated caricatures of facial movements[1] [see *Ilg & Giese and Giese, Knappmeyer & Bülthoff, this volume*].

The second application of STMMs is the analysis of complex movements. For this purpose new trajectories are approximated by linear combinations of learned prototypical trajectories. The linear weights α_p of the fitted models can then be used for classification and the estimation of continuous style and skill parameters. More specifically, first correspondence between the new trajectory and the reference trajectory is computed. The resulting correspondence field is approximated by a linear combination of the correspondence fields of the prototypes according to equation (3) using least squares fitting. Further details about the underlying algorithm are described in [11].

As one example we present here the identification of people from their walking trajectories. The trajectories were extracted by manual tracking from videos showing four different people walking orthogonally to the view directions of the camera. Five repetitions of the walk of each person were recorded. We used the 2D trajectories of 12 points on the joints of the walkers. Further details about data acquisition and preprocessing are described in [11]. Out of the five patterns of each actor one was used as prototype, and the others were used for testing. The weights were estimated by regularized least-squares estimation according to Eq. (3). A simple Bayesian classifier was used to map the weight vectors onto class assignments. The discriminant functions of the classifiers (assuming Gaussian distributions) are shown in Fig. 1. For the small tested data sets all actors were classified correctly showing that STMMs can be used for person recognition from trajectory data[2].

More interesting than classification is the possibility to map the linear weight vectors onto continuous parameters that characterize style parameters of movements [11]. As example we review here a result on the estimation of walking direction from 2D trajectory data. The linear weights are mapped onto the estimated walking direction using radial basis function networks that have been trained with only three directions (0, 22.5 and 45 deg). The estimates of two networks trained with walking and running were integrated using a gating scheme using the results from a classifier that detects the relevant locomotion pattern (walking or running). Tab. 1 shows a comparison of the accuracy (measured by the root mean-square errors of the estimated angles) of the estimates obtained with different algorithms for mapping the trajectories into a linear space: We

[1] Movies of these animations can be found on the Web site: `www.uni-tuebingen.de/uni/knv/arl/arl-demos.html`.

[2] We are presently testing the method on a larger data set.

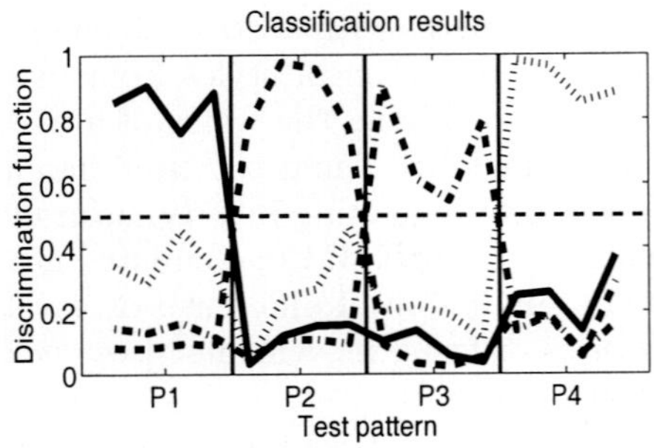

Fig. 1. Identification of people by their locomotion patterns. (Details see text.)

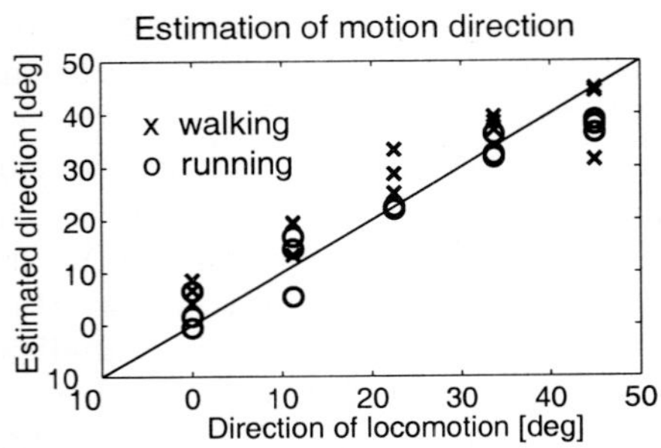

Fig. 2. Estimation of locomotion direction from trajectories. (See text.)

tested STMMs including time shifts, STMMs without time shifts[3], and a principal component analysis (PCA). The PCA was performed by concatenating all trajectory data (after normalization of gait cycle time) from a single pattern into a long vector, resulting in a large data matrix with P columns. As input signals for the basis function network the weights of the first four principle components were used. Including time shifts in the STMMs increases accuracy of the estimates. However, the estimates obtained by applying PCA on the trajectories are even more accurate for this data set. This indicates that, even though STMMs provide relatively accurate models of the individual trajectories, they not necessarily outperform simple standard algorithms in classification and estimation tasks.

A major limitation of the presented simple form of STMM is that they are applicable only to a sets of segmented simple movement elements, like one cycle of a gait, a single arm movement, or a technique from a sequence of movements in sports. This limitation can be overcome by decomposing longer trajectories automatically into movement elements that are matched with primarily learned templates [see *Ilg & Giese, this volume*].

Table 1. Root mean-square error of the estimates of locomotion direction from gait trajectories obtained with different methods

Method	RMS [deg]
STMM with time warping ($\lambda = 0.0001$)	5.1
STMM without time warping ($\lambda = 0.01$)	5.9
PCA (4 components)	4.2

[3] Time shifts were eliminated by setting the parameter λ to a large value.

4 Prototype-Based Representations of Movements in the Visual Cortex

The technical applications presented so far shows that prototype-based representations of movement patterns are useful for computer vision and computer graphics. This raises the question if such representations are also relevant for biological vision. We will address this question here from a computational point of view. Computational theory can help to clarify the following two specific questions: (1) Can a prototype-based representation account for the existing experimental data on biological movement recognition ? (2) Is it possible to implement a prototype-based representation with the neural mechanisms that are known to be present in the visual cortex ? We try to answer both questions by devising a biologically plausible model that neurally represents learned prototypes of complex movements. The tuning properties of the model neurons are matched, where possible, with the known properties of real cortical neurons. The model was tested with many stimuli that have been used in psychophysical, electrophysiological and fMRI experiments. Here only a small selection of the results can be presented. A more detailed description of the model and additional results in given in [9, 13, 12].

4.1 Neural Model

An overview of the model is shown in Fig. 3. It consists of two hierarchical neural pathways that process predominantly form and motion information, coarsely corresponding to the ventral and dorsal visual processing stream. Each pathway consists of a hierarchy of neural feature detectors that extract increasingly more complex features along the hierarchy. At the same time, the receptive field sizes and position and scale invariance of the detectors increases along the hierarchy. Invariance is achieved by pooling the responses of neural detectors from previous levels using a nonlinear maximum-like operation [21]. The two pathways are fused on the highest hierarchy level in *motion pattern neurons* that respond selectively to complex movement patterns, like walking, dancing or specific movements in sports. These neurons summate and temporally integrate the activity of neurons in the highest levels of the two pathways. Neurophysiological and fMRI experiments suggest that such neurons are present in the *superior temporal sulcus* (STS) in humans and monkeys (e.g. [19]). The model postulates that complex movements are encoded in two different ways. In the form pathway biological movements are encoded as sequences of body configurations. In the motion pathway the encoding is based on sequences of instantaneous optic flow fields. The detectors for these features are established by learning prototypical example movement patterns.

The form pathway achieves recognition of actions based on shape features. The first layer consists of Gabor filters that model simple cells in area V1. These neurons are selective for local oriented contours. The next hierarchy level models complex cells that have been found in areas V2 and V4 of macaques. Such neurons are selective for bars independent of their exact spatial phase and position.

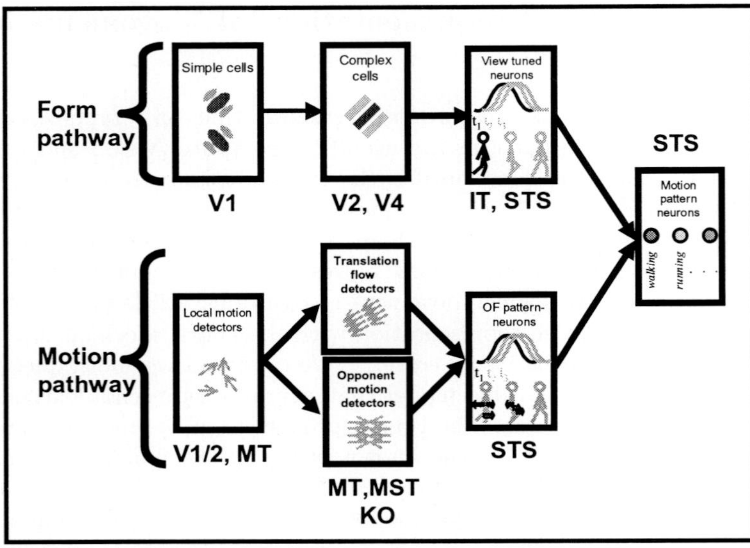

Fig. 3. Overview of the neural model for biological motion recognition

The next-higher level of the form pathway is formed by neurons that respond selectively to configurations of the human body. Each of these neurons responds to "snapshot" from the movement sequence. In fact there is evidence for the existence of such body configuration-selective neurons in human visual cortex and monkeys. These neurons are modeled by radial basis functions that are trained with example patterns (21 snapshots per training sequence). The centers of the basis functions are trained with the activity vectors from the complex cells that correspond to the individual "snapshots" from the training sequence.

In presence of a learned biological movement pattern the associated snapshot neurons are activated in sequence. If the frames of a biological movement are scrambled in time the impression of biological movements is disrupted. This implies that biological motion perception is selective for sequential order. Different plausible neural mechanisms can account for such sequence selectivity. A particularly simple mechanism is based on lateral couplings between the snapshot neurons. The activity dynamics of the neurons is modeled by the differential equation:

$$\tau\, \dot{u}_n(t) = -u_n(t) + \sum_k w(n-k)\theta(u_k(t)) + s_n(t) \tag{4}$$

The input signal of the neurons s_n are given by the outputs of the radial basis functions described before. The state variables $u_n(t)$ model the membrane potential of the snapshot neurons and $\theta(u)$ is a monotonically increasing threshold function (e.g. linear or sigmoidal threshold). The time constant τ was 150 ms. The non-symmetric function $w(k)$ describes the strength of the lateral interactions between the snapshot neurons. It can be shown that for asymmetric connections this network supports a stable localized solution with a large amplitude only if the stimulus movie is presented with the correct temporal order. For wrong or random order of the frames the stable solution breaks down and only very little activity is induced in the layer of the snapshot neurons [25]. Consistent with psychophysical and neurophysiological results the activity in the snapshot neurons raises very quickly so that biological motion stimuli as short as 200 ms are sufficient for recognition. We have tested that the required lateral connectivity can be learned with a simple biologically plausible time-dependent heeding learning rule.

The motion pathway contains detectors that analyze the optic flow field created by the movement stimuli. The neurons at the first level of the motion pathway extract *local motion energy*. Such neurons correspond to direction-selective cells in the primary visual cortex and potentially area MT. The second level of the motion pathway consists of two classes of neural detectors that analyze the local structure of the optic flow (OF) field. The first type of detectors is selective for *translational flow* in different directions and with different speeds. Lesion data in patients points to the fact that a substantial part of such detectors is located in area MT of humans. A second type of detectors is selective for *opponent motion*. Neurophysiological and fMRI results suggest that such detectors are present in area MT of monkeys and in the kinetic occipital area (KO) in humans. The highest level of the motion pathway is formed by *optic flow pattern neurons*. These neurons are equivalent to the snapshot neurons in the form pathway and are selective for complex instantaneous optic flow patterns that are characteristic for biological movements. These neurons are also modeled by radial basis functions that have been trained with the responses of neurons from the previous hierarchy level for individual frames of the training patterns. Like the snapshot neurons in the form pathway they have asymmetric lateral connections leading to sequence selectivity. The outputs of both, the snapshot neurons and the optic flow pattern neurons converge to the motion pattern neurons on the highest hierarchy level of the model.

4.2 Simulation Results and Predictions

Here only some examples of the simulations can be discussed. A detailed description of the results is given in [9, 13, 12]. The model was tested using trajectory data from real human actors. The trajectory data was used to animate a stick figure from which pixel maps and motion energy distributions were directly computed. (See [12] for further details.)

First, the selectivity of the model was tested. The model can easily distinguish more than 40 movement patterns, including different forms of locomotion, dancing and martial arts techniques [12]. Interestingly, this selectivity is also achieved with the information from either pathway (motion or form) alone. As further test of selectivity we tested whether the model is sensitive enough to recognize individuals by their gait, corresponding with the psychophysical literature [6]. Fig. 4 that shows the activities of motion pattern neurons that have

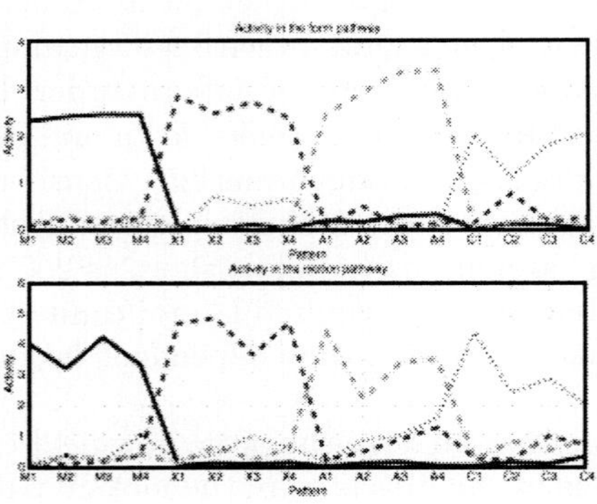

Fig. 4. Identification of people by their locomotion patterns using the form pathway (upper panel) and the motion pathway (lower panel). (Details see text.)

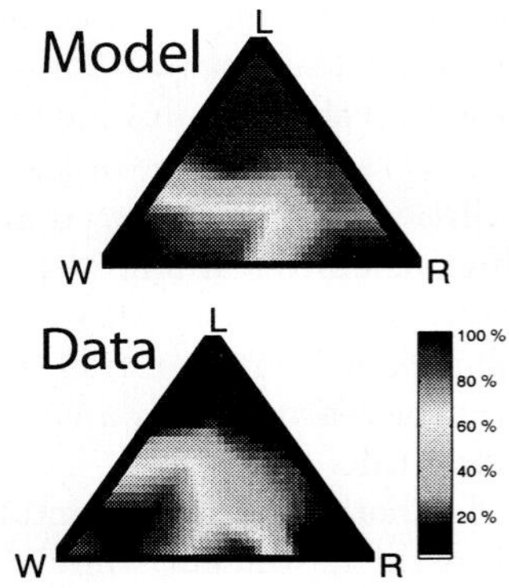

Fig. 5. Activation of motion pattern neuron encoding walking (upper panel) and correct classification rate of 7 subjects from different motion morphs (lower panel)

been trained with the gaits of four different individuals (indicated by the different line styles.) In order to test if the discrimination can be accomplished with information from each pathway alone we simulated two separate sets of motion pattern neurons that received input only from the form pathway (upper panel), or only from the motion pathway (lower panel). The figure shows that the motion pattern neurons trained with the movement pattern of a particular person (M, X, A, or C) respond selectively only for gait patterns of this person[4]. (Patterns are indicated on the horizontal axis the numbers signifying different trajectories from the same actor.) This result shows that form or optic flow information are computationally sufficient for people identification. In addition, this simulation shows that no complex computational mechanisms, such as internal kinematic models, are required to reproduce the psychophysically observed selectivity in movement recognition. Rather, very simple well-established neural mechanisms are sufficient.

Additional more systematic tests on the generalization properties of the model in comparison with human performance in psychophysical experiments have been performed. The model reproduces the regimes of position and speed invariance that have been observed in psychophysical experiments [12]. A test of generalization in motion pattern space is possible applying the motion morphing technique described in section 3. The model was trained with four locomotion patterns: walking, running, marching and limping. Then it was tested with different linear combinations of these patterns. In a psychophysical experiment [10] seven subjects were tested presenting the same stimuli as point light figures. Fig. 5 shows a comparison between the (normalized) neural activity of the motion

[4] None of the test patterns was identical with the training patterns.

pattern neuron in the model that was trained with "walking" (upper panel). The lower panel shows the color-coded frequency of correct classifications of walking. as color coded plots. The weights of the prototypes walking (W), running (R), and limping (L) are indicated by the positions of the pixels in the figure[5]. The figure shows a that the classification probability strongly covaries with the neural activity. The same is true for the motion pattern neurons that encode the other prototypes (see [12] for further results). A more detailed analysis shows that the model reproduces not only the approximate size of the generalization fields of the prototypical locomotion patterns in the pattern space defined by the morphs. It also predicts correctly (without special parameter fitting) that the generalization field of walking is larger than the ones of the other locomotion patterns. This illustrates that the generalization performance of the model is similar to the psychophysically measured behavior of humans.

Since the model is based on a view-based representation of snapshots of body configurations and instantaneous optic flow fields it reproduces the psychophysically and electrophysiologically measured view dependence of biological motion recognition. Fig. 6 shows the activity of a motion pattern neuron that was trained with walking orthogonal to the view direction. The response of the neuron decays gradually when the direction of the walker deviates from the learned walking direction, corresponding to a rotation of the walker in depth. This view dependence effect is quantitatively similar to the variation of the firing rate of a biological motion-sensitive neuron in area TPO in the *superior temporal sulcus* of a monkey [19]. The inset in the figure shows the firing rate of such a neuron for different walking directions (black) in comparison with the neural activation predicted by the model (after appropriate rescaling).

Another interesting property of the model that matches psychophysical performance is its robustness. In fact, the model after training with normal walker pattern can generalize to point light walker stimuli. This seems highly nontrivial, given the relatively simple architecture of the model. Interestingly, such generalization to point light walkers occurs only in the motion pathway, but not in the form pathway[6]. This is a prediction that can be tested, e.g. in fMRI experiments.

It is known that humans are very efficient in recognizing point light walkers even if they are embedded in moving noise dots. This is even true when each noise dot moves exactly like a dot of the walker, just with a different spatial offset ("scrambled walker noise"). To test the robustness of the model the model was trained with point light walkers walking either to the right or to the left side. Fig. 7 shows the activity of the neuron that has been trained with the walker walking rightwards for a rightwards (solid line) and a leftwards walking (dashed line) stimulus. A varying number of noise dots were added to the display. If the

---

5 The corners of the triangle correspond to presentation of the pure prototypes. The distance of the pixels from the corners of the triangle decreases with the weight of the corresponding prototype in the linear combination. Only the results for the linear combinations without contributions of "marching" are shown.

6 This is only true if the model has not been trained with point light displays.

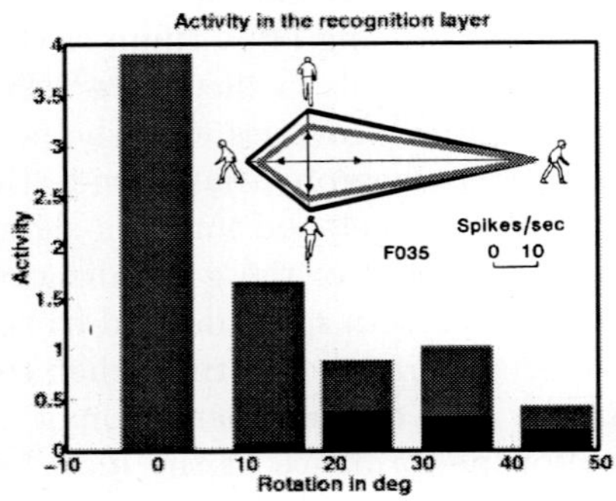

Fig. 6. View dependence: rotation of the walker in depth against the training view reduces the response. Inset shows electrophysiological data [19] (black) in comparison with the activity predicted by the model (gray)

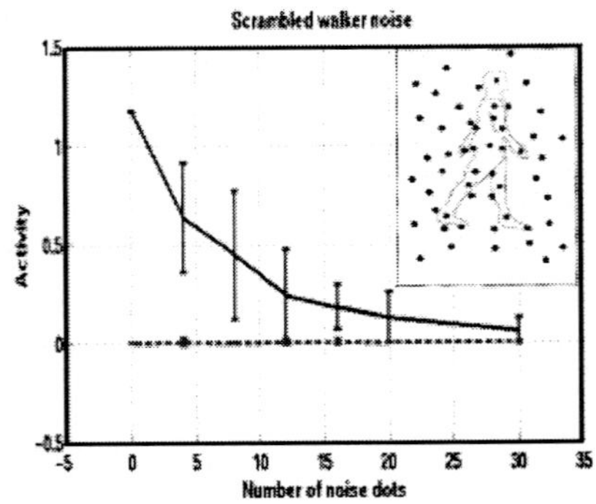

Fig. 7. Activity of a motion pattern neurons that detects walking right for a stimulus walker walking right (solid line) and left (dashed line) as function of the number of noise dots in the background

activity levels for the right and the left walking walker are significantly different the model can distinguish the two stimuli. The error bars were computed over 20 repeated simulations. The left-right discrimination is even possible even in presence of more then twenty noise dots. This is rather surprising, since the model has a predominantly feed-forward structure and contains no special mechanism that segments the walker out from the background noise. This implies that very simple biologically plausible neural mechanisms might be adequate to achieve a robust recognition of biological motion.

From the model a variety of other predictions can be derived, most of which can be tested experimentally. The model can predict contrasts in fMRI studies between different stimulus classes, or lesion deficits in neurological patients [13, 12]. One key prediction is that any sufficiently smooth movement pattern can be learned, independently of their biological plausibility. We have recently confirmed this prediction in a psychophysical experiment in which subjects had to learn unfamiliar complex movement patterns. Subjects were able to learn these patterns relatively quickly (in less than 30 trials), and the learned representation was view-dependent [*Giese, Jastorff & Kourtzi, ECVP 2002, in press*].

5 Conclusion

This paper has discussed approaches for the representation of complex biological movement patterns and actions by learned prototypical examples. Just like other groups in computer vision and computer graphics (e.g. [26, 3]) we have shown that representations based on learned prototypical example patterns can be very helpful for technical applications. The proposed method of spatio-temporal morphable models provides a systematic and relatively simple method to define metric spaces over classes of complex movement patterns. On one hand, this property is useful for synthesis, e.g. to simulate movements with specific style parameters, or to produce exaggerated and caricatured movements. On the other hand movement spaces are also useful for analysis of subtle details (style parameters, skill level, etc.) of complex movements. However, the exact modeling of the details of the movements might also sometimes hurt robustness. Simple classification or regression methods applied directly to the segmented trajectories might perform better in problems for which an exact modeling of the details of the motion is unimportant.

It seems that, like in the domain of stationary object recognition, prototype-based representations are also relevant for the recognition of complex movements in the brain. It seems that a large body of experimental data seems to be consistent with this idea. A variety of predictions arises from this hypothesis and the neural mechanisms proposed by the model that can be experimentally tested.

Even though prototypes of biological movements might be important in technical applications as well as in neuroscience it seems important to stress that the underlying implementations are very different. In my view it is rather unlikely that the brain explicitly represents something like space-time shifts in order to model classes of complex movements. However, the neural model shows that high selectivity and realistic generalization capability can be achieved with very simple well-established neural mechanisms that are biologically plausible. Representations based on learned prototypical movements seem therefore to be an interesting theoretical concept for the study of movement recognition in neuroscience.

Acknowledgements. This work was supported by the Deutsche Volkswagenstiftung. We thank H.H. Bülthoff and C. Wallraven for helpful comments and A. Casile and J. Jastorff for interesting discussions.

References

1. D Beymer and T Poggio. Image representations for visual learning. *Science*, 272:1905–1909, 1996.
2. V Blanz and T Vetter. Morphable model for the synthesis of 3d faces. In *Proceedings of SIGGRAPH 99*, Los Angeles, pages 187–194, 1999.
3. M Brand. Style machines. In *Proceedings of SIGGRAPH 2000, New Orleans, Lousiana*, USA, pages 23–28, 2000.
4. A Bruderlin and L Williams. Motion signal processing. In *Proceedings of SIGGRAPH 95, Los Angeles*, pages 97–104, 1995.
5. H H Bülthoff and S Edelman. Psychophysical support for a 2D-view interpolation theory of object recognition. *Proceedings of the National Academy of Sciences (USA)*, 89:60–64, 1992.
6. J E Cutting and L T Kozlowski. Recognising friends by their walk: Gait perception without familiarity cues. *Bulletin of the Psychonomic Society*, 9:353–356, 1977.

7. S Edelman. *Representation and Recognition in Vision.* MIT Press, Cambridge, USA, 1999.
8. D M Gavrila. The visual analysis of human movement: A survey. *Computer Vision and Image Understanding*, 73:82–98, 1999.
9. M A Giese. Dynamit neural model for the recognition of biological motion. In H Neumann and G Baratoff, editors, *Dynamische Perzeption 9*, pages 829–835. Infix, Sankt Augustin, 2000.
10. M A Giese and M Lappe. Measuring generalization fields of biological motion. *Vision Research*, 42:1847–1858, 2002.
11. M A Giese and T Poggio. Morphable models for the analysis and Synthesis of complex motion Pattern. *International Journal of Computer Vision*, 38:59–73, 2000.
12. M A Giese and T Poggio. Neural mechanisms for the recognition of biological movements and actions. *Nature Neuroscience*, (submitted), 2002.
13. M A Giese and L M Vaina. Pathways in the analysis of biological motion: computational model and fMRI results. *Perception*, 30 (Suppl.):ll6, 2001.
14. G Johansson. Visual perception of biological motion and a model for its analysis. *Perception and Psychophysics*, 14:201–211, 1973.
15. M J Jones and T Poggio. Multidimensional morphable models: A framework for representing and matching object classes. *International Journal of Computer Vision*, 29:107–131, 1998.
16. J Lee and S Y Shin. A hierarchical approach to interactive motion editing for human-like figures. In *Proceedings of SIGGRAPH 99, Los Angeles*, pages 39–48, 1999.
17. N K Logothetis, J Pauls, and T Poggio. Shape representation in the inferior temporal cortex of monkeys. *Current Biology*, 5:552–563, 1995.
18. S E Palmer. *Vision Science.* MIT Press, Cambridge, USA, 1999.
19. D I Perrett, P A J Smith, A J Mistlin, A J Chitty, A S Head, D D Potter, Broennimann R, A D Milner, and M A Jeeves. Visual analysis of body movements by neurons in the temporal cortex of the macaque monkey: a preliminary report. *Behavioral Brain Research*, 16:153–170, 1985.
20. T Poggio and S Edelman. A network that learns to recognize three-dimensional objects. *Nature*, 343:263–266, 1990.
21. M K Riesenhuber and T Poggio. A hierarchical model for visual object recognition. *Nature Neuroscience*, 11:1019–1025, 1999.
22. S Ullman and R Basri. Recognition by linear combination of models. *IEEE Transactions on Pattern Recognition and Machine Intelligence*, 13:992–1006, 1991.
23. T Valentine. A unified account of the effects of distinctiveness, inversion and rate in face recognition. *Quarterly Journal of Experimental Psychology*, 43A:161–204, 1991.
24. T Vetter and T Poggio. Linear object classes and image synthesis from a single example. *IEEE Transactions on Pattern Recognition and Machine Intelligence*, 19(7):733–742, 1997.
25. X Xie and M A Giese. Nonlinear dynamics of direction-selective recurrent neural media. *Phys Rev E Stat Nonlin Soft Matter Phys*, 65 (5 Pt 1):051904, 2002.
26. Y Yacoob and M J Black. Parameterized modeling and recognition of activities. *Computer Vision and Image Understanding*, (in press), 1999.

Insect-Inspired Estimation of Self-Motion

Matthias O. Franz[1] and Javaan S. Chahl[2]

[1] MPI für biologische Kybernetik, Spemannstr. 38, D-72076 Tübingen, Germany, mof@tuebingen.mpg.de

[2] Center of Visual Sciences, RSBS, Australian National University, Canberra, ACT, Australia, javaan@zappa.anu.edu.au

Abstract. The tangential neurons in the fly brain are sensitive to the typical optic flow patterns generated during self-motion. In this study, we examine whether a simplified linear model of these neurons can be used to estimate self-motion from the optic flow. We present a theory for the construction of an optimal linear estimator incorporating prior knowledge about the environment. The optimal estimator is tested on a gantry carrying an omnidirectional vision sensor. The experiments show that the proposed approach leads to accurate and robust estimates of rotation rates, whereas translation estimates turn out to be less reliable.

1 Introduction

A moving visual system generates a characteristic pattern of image motion on its sensors. The resulting optic flow field is an important source of information about the self-motion of the visual system [1]. In the fly brain, part of this information seems to be analyzed by a group of wide-field, motion-sensitive neurons, the tangential neurons in the lobula plate [2]. A detailed mapping of their local motion sensitivities and preferred motion directions [3] reveals a striking similarity to certain self-motion-induced flow fields (an example is shown in Fig. 1). This suggests a possible involvement of the tangential neurons in the self-motion estimation process which might be useful, for instance, for stabilizing the fly's head during flight manoeuvres.

A recent study [4] has shown that a simplified computational model of the tangential neurons as a weighted sum of flow measurements was able to reproduce the observed response fields. The weights were chosen according to an optimality principle which minimizes the output variance of the model caused by noise and distance variability between different scenes. The question on how the output of such processing units could be used for self-motion estimation was left open, however.

In this paper, we want to fill a part of this gap by presenting a classical linear estimation approach that extends a special case of the previous model to the complete self-motion problem. We again use linear combinations of local flow measurements, but – instead of prescribing a fixed motion axis and minimizing the output variance - we require that the quadratic error in the estimated self-motion parameters be as small as possible. From this optimization principle, we

H.H. Bülthoff et al. (Eds.): BMCV 2002, LNCS 2525, pp. 171–180, 2002.

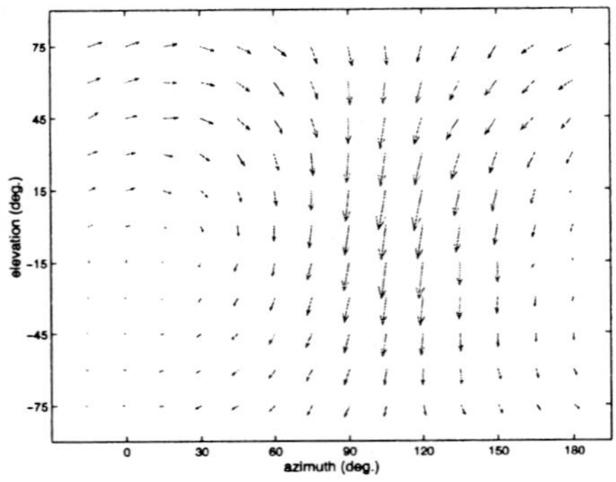

Fig. 1. Mercator map of the response field of the neuron VS7. The orientation of each arrow gives the local preferred direction (LPD), and its length denotes the relative local motion sensitivity (LMS).

derive weight sets that lead to motion sensitivities similar to those observed in tangential neurons (Sect. 2). In contrast to the previous model, this approach also yields the preferred motion directions and the motion axes to which the neural models are tuned. We subject the obtained linear estimator to a rigorous real-world test on a gantry carrying an omnidirectional vision sensor (Sect. 3). The experiments show that the proposed approach leads to accurate and robust estimates of rotation rates, whereas translation estimates turn out to be less reliable. We conclude from these results that the simple, computationally cheap neural estimator constitutes a viable alternative to the more elaborate schemes usually employed in computer vision, especially in tasks requiring fast and accurate rotation estimates such as, e.g., sensor stabilization (Sect. 4).

2 Modeling Fly Tangential Neurons as Optimal Linear Estimators for Self-Motion

2.1 Sensor and Neuron Model

In order to simplify the mathematical treatment, we assume that the N elementary motion detectors (EMDs) of our model eye are arranged on the unit sphere. The viewing direction of a particular EMD with index i is denoted by the radial unit vector $\mathbf{d}_i$. At each viewing direction, we define a local two-dimensional coordinate system on the sphere consisting of two orthogonal tangential unit vectors $\mathbf{u}_i$ and $\mathbf{v}_i$ (Fig. 2a). We assume that we measure the local flow component along both unit vectors subject to additive noise. Formally, this means that we obtain at each viewing direction two measurements x_i and y_i along $\mathbf{u}_i$ and $\mathbf{v}_i$, respectively, given by

$$x_i = \mathbf{p}_i \cdot \mathbf{u}_i + n_{x,i} \quad \text{and} \quad y_i = \mathbf{p}_i \cdot \mathbf{v}_i + n_{y,i}, \tag{1}$$

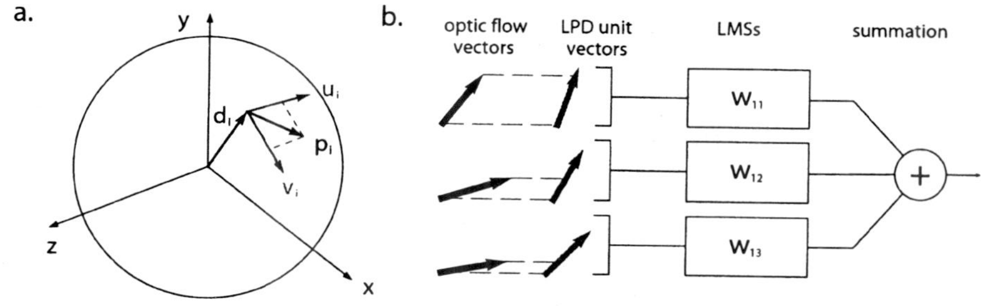

Fig. 2. *a.* Sensor model: At each viewing direction $\mathbf{d}_i$, there are two measurements x_i and y_i of the optic flow $\mathbf{p}_i$ along two directions $\mathbf{u}_i$ and $\mathbf{v}_i$ on the unit sphere. *b.* Simplified model of a tangential neuron: The optic flow and the local noise signal are projected onto a unit vector field. The weighted projections are linearly integrated to give the estimator output.

where $n_{x,i}$ and $n_{y,i}$ denote additive noise components and $\mathbf{p}_i$ the local optic flow vector[1]. The formulation as a scalar product between the flow and the unit vector implies a linear motion sensitivity profile of the EMD used to obtain the flow measurement. In the fly, this is only the case at low image velocities. At higher velocities, real EMDs show a saturation and a subsequent decrease in their response.

When the spherical sensor translates with $\mathbf{T}$ while rotating with $\mathbf{R}$ about an axis through the origin, the self-motion-induced image flow $\mathbf{p}_i$ at $\mathbf{d}_i$ is [5]

$$\mathbf{p}_i = -\mu_i(\mathbf{T} - (\mathbf{T} \cdot \mathbf{d}_i)\mathbf{d}_i) - \mathbf{R} \times \mathbf{d}_i. \tag{2}$$

μ_i is the inverse distance between the origin and the object seen in direction $\mathbf{d}_i$, the so-called "nearness". The entire collection of flow measurements x_i and y_i comprises the input to the simplified neural model of a tangential neuron which consists of a weighted sum of all local measurements (Fig. 2*b*)

$$\hat{\theta} = \sum_i^N w_{x,i} x_i + \sum_i^N w_{y,i} y_i \tag{3}$$

with local weights $w_{x,i}$ and $w_{y,i}$. As our basic hypothesis, we assume that the output of such model neurons is used to estimate the self-motion of the sensor. Since the output is a scalar, we need in the simplest case an ensemble of six neurons to encode all six rotational and translational degrees of freedom. The local weights of each neuron are chosen to yield an optimal linear estimator for the respective self-motion component.

---

1 This measurement model corresponds to the special case of the linear range model described in [4], Eq. (5).

2.2 Prior Knowledge and Optimized Neural Model

The estimator in Eq. (3) consists of a linear combination of flow measurements. Even if the self-motion remains exactly the same, the single flow measurements - and therefore the estimator output - will vary from scene to scene, depending on the current distance and noise characteristics. The best the estimator can do is to add up as many flow measurements as possible hoping that the individual distance deviations of the current scene from the average will cancel each other. Clearly, viewing directions with low distance variability and small noise content should receive a higher weight in this process. In this way, prior knowledge about the distance and noise statistics of the sensor and its environment can improve the reliability of the estimate.

If the current nearness at viewing direction $\mathbf{d}_i$ differs from the the average nearness $\bar{\mu}_i$ over all scenes by $\Delta\mu_i$, the measurement x_i can be written as (see Eqns. (1) and (2))

$$x_i = -(\bar{\mu}_i \mathbf{u}_i^\top, (\mathbf{u}_i \times \mathbf{d}_i)^\top) \begin{pmatrix} \mathbf{T} \\ \mathbf{R} \end{pmatrix} + n_{x,i} - \Delta\mu_i \mathbf{u}_i \mathbf{T}, \tag{4}$$

where the last two terms vary from scene to scene, even when the sensor undergoes exactly the same self-motion.

To simplify the notation, we stack all $2N$ measurements over the entire EMD array in the vector $\mathbf{x} = (x_1, y_1, x_2, y_2, ..., x_N, y_N)^\top$. Similarly, the self-motion components along the x-, y- and z-directions of the global coordinate systems are combined in the vector $\theta = (T_x, T_y, T_z, R_x, R_y, R_z)^\top$, the scene-dependent terms of Eq. (4) in the $2N$-vector $\mathbf{n} = (n_{x,1} - \Delta\mu_1 \mathbf{u}_1 \mathbf{T}, n_{y,1} - \Delta\mu_1 \mathbf{v}_1 \mathbf{T}, ...)^\top$ and the scene-independent terms in the 6xN-matrix $F = ((-\bar{\mu}_1 \mathbf{u}_1^\top, -(\mathbf{u}_1 \times \mathbf{d}_1)^\top), (-\bar{\mu}_1 \mathbf{v}_1^\top, -(\mathbf{v}_1 \times \mathbf{d}_1)^\top), ...)^\top$. The entire ensemble of measurements over the sensor can thus be written as

$$\mathbf{x} = F\theta + \mathbf{n}. \tag{5}$$

Assuming that $\mathbf{T}$, $n_{x,i}$, $n_{y,i}$ and μ_i are uncorrelated, the covariance matrix C of the scene-dependent measurement component $\mathbf{n}$ is given by

$$C_{ij} = C_{n,ij} + C_{\mu,ij} \mathbf{u}_i^\top C_T \mathbf{u}_j \tag{6}$$

with C_n being the covariance of n, C_μ of μ and C_T of $\mathbf{T}$. These three covariance matrices, together with the average nearness $\bar{\mu}_i$, constitute the prior knowledge required for deriving the optimal estimator.

Using the notation of Eq. (5), we write the linear estimator as

$$\hat{\theta} = W\mathbf{x}. \tag{7}$$

W denotes a $2N$x6 weight matrix where each of the six rows corresponds to one model neuron (see Eq. (3)) tuned to a different component of θ. The optimal weight matrix is chosen to minimize the mean square error of the estimator which results in the optimal weight set

$$W = \frac{1}{2} \Lambda F^\top C^{-1} \tag{8}$$

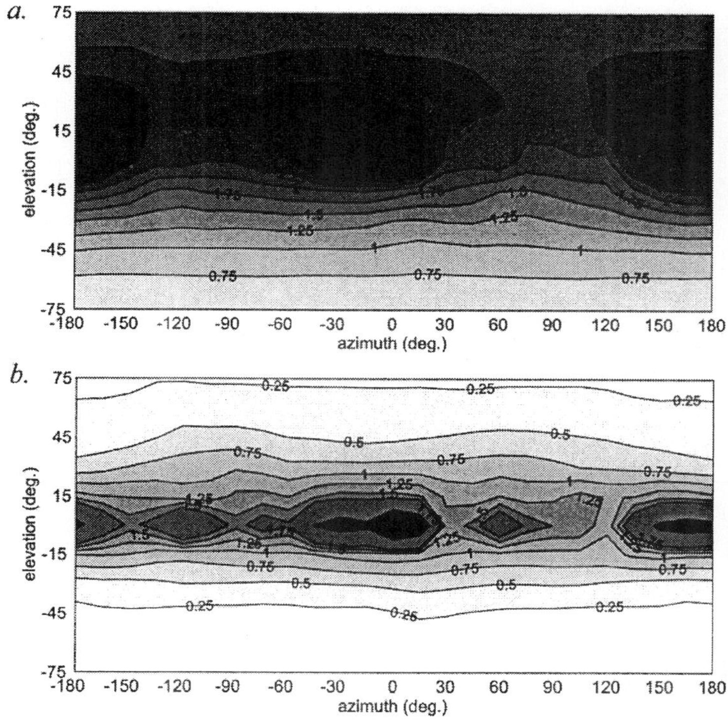

Fig. 3. Distance statistics of an indoor robot (0 azimuth corresponds to forward direction): *a*. Average distances from the origin in the visual field ($N = 26$). Darker areas represent larger distances. *b*. Distance standard deviation in the visual field ($N = 26$). Darker areas represent stronger deviations.

with $\Lambda = 2(F^\top C^{-1} F)^{-1}$. When computed for the typical inter-scene covariances of a flying animal, the resulting weight sets are able to reproduce the characteristics of the LMS and LPD distribution of the tangential neurons [4]. Having shown the good correspondence between model neurons and measurement, the question remains whether the output of such an ensemble of neurons can be used for some real-world task. This is by no means evident given the fact that - in contrast to most approaches in computer vision - the distance distribution of the current scene is completely ignored by the linear estimator.

3 Experiments

3.1 Distance Statistics

As our test scenario, we consider the situation of a mobile robot in an office environment. This scenario allows for measuring the typical motion patterns and

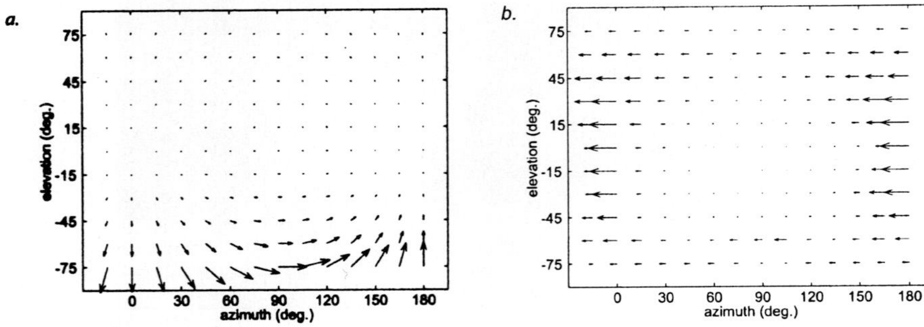

Fig. 4. Model neurons computed as part of the optimal estimator. Notation is identical to Fig. 1. The depicted region of the visual field extends from $-15°$ to $180°$ azimuth and from $-75°$ to $75°$ elevation. The model neurons are tuned to *a.* forward translation, and *b.* to rotations about the vertical axis.

the associated distance statistics which otherwise would be difficult to obtain for a flying agent.

The distance statistics were recorded using a rotating laser scanner. The 26 measurement points were chosen along typical trajectories of a mobile robot while wandering around and avoiding obstacles in an office environment. From these measurements, the average nearness $\bar{\mu}_i$ and its covariance C_μ were computed (Fig. 3, we used distance instead of nearness for easier interpretation).

The distance statistics show a pronounced anisotropy which can be attributed to three main causes: (1) Since the robot tries to turn away from the obstacles, the distance in front and behind the robot tends to be larger than on its sides (Fig. 3*a*). (2) The camera on the robot usually moves at a fixed height above ground on a flat surface. As a consequence, distance variation is particularly small at very low elevations (Fig. 3*b*). (3) The office environment also contains corridors. When the robot follows the corridor while avoiding obstacles, distance variations in the frontal region of the visual field are very large (Fig. 3*b*).

The estimation of the translation covariance C_T is straightforward since our robot can only translate in forward direction, i.e. along the z-axis. C_T is therefore 0 everywhere except the lower right diagonal entry which is the square of the average forward speed of the robot (here: 0.3 m/s). The EMD noise was assumed to be zero-mean, uncorrelated and uniform over the image, which results in a diagonal C_n with identical entries. The noise standard deviation of the used optic flow algorith was 0.34 deg./s. $\bar{\mu}$, C_μ, C_T and C_n constitute the prior knowledge necessary for computing the estimator (Eqns. (6) and (8)).

Examples of the optimal weight sets for the model neurons (corresponding to a row of W) are shown in Fig. 4. The resulting model neurons show very similar characteristics to those observed in real tangential neurons, however, with specific adaptations to the indoor robot scenario. All model neurons have

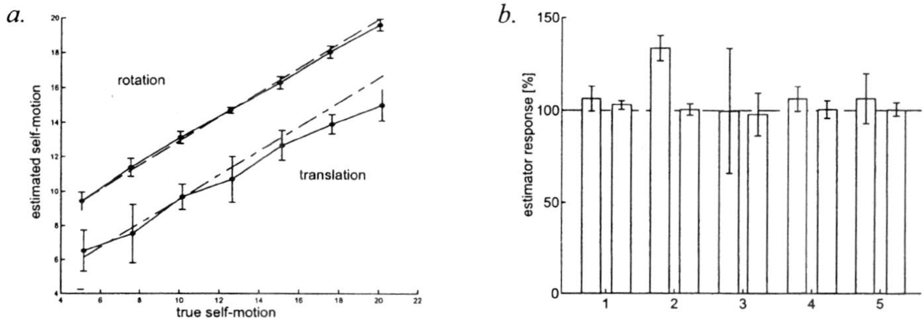

Fig. 5. Gantry experiments: Results are given in arbitrary units, true rotation values are denoted by a dashed line, translation by a dash-dot line. Grey bars denote translation estimates, white bars rotation estimates *a.* Estimated vs. real self-motion; *b.* Estimates of the same self-motion at different locations;

in common that image regions near the rotation or translation axis receive less weight. In these regions, the self-motion components to be estimated generate only small flow vectors which are easily corrupted by noise. Equation (8) predicts that the estimator will preferably sample in image regions with smaller distance variations. In our measurements, this is mainly the case at the ground around the robot (Fig. 3). The rotation-selective model neurons weight image regions with larger distances more highly, since distance variations at large distances have a smaller effect. In our example, distances are largest in front and behind the robot so that the rotation-selective neurons assign the highest weights to these regions (Fig. 3*b*).

3.2 Gantry Experiments

The self-motion estimates from the model neuron ensemble were tested on a gantry with three translational and one rotational (yaw) degree of freedom. Since the gantry had a position accuracy below 1mm, the programmed position values were taken as ground truth for evaluating the estimator's accuracy.

As vision sensor, we used a camera mounted above a mirror with a circularly symmetric hyperbolic profile. This setup allowed for a 360° horizontal field of view extending from 90° below to 45° above the horizon. Such a large field of view considerably improves the estimator's performance since the individual distance deviations in the scene are more likely to be averaged out. More details about the omnidirectional camera can be found in [6].

In each experiment, the camera was moved to 10 different start positions in the lab with largely varying distance distributions. The height above ground was always that of the sensor position on the real mobile robot used in Sec. 3.1. After recording an image of the scene at the start position, the gantry translated and rotated at various prescribed speeds and directions and took a second image.

The recorded image pairs (10 for each type of movement) were unwarped, low-pass-filtered and subsampled on a 9 x 152 grid with 5° angular spacing. For each image pair, we computed the optic flow using an image interpolation technique described in [7]. The resulting optic flow field was used as input to the model neuron ensemble from which the self-motion estimates were computed according to Eq. (7).

The average error of the rotation rate estimates over all trials (N=450) was 0.7°/s (5.7% rel. error, Fig. 5*a*), the error in the estimated translation speeds (N=420) was 8.5 mm/s (7.5% rel. error). The estimated rotation axis had an average error of magnitude 1.7°, the estimated translation direction 4.5°. The larger error of the translation estimates is mainly caused by the direct dependence of the translational flow on distance (see Eq. (2)) whereas the rotation estimates are only indirectly affected by distance errors via the current translational flow component which is largely filtered out by the LPD arrangement. The larger sensitivity of the translation estimates can be seen by moving the sensor at the same translation and rotation speeds in various locations. The rotation estimates remain consistent over all locations whereas the translation estimates show a higher variance and also a location-dependent bias, e.g., very close to laboratory walls (Fig. 5*b*). A second problem for translation estimation comes from the different properties of rotational and translational flow fields: Due to its distance dependence, the translational flow field shows a much wider range of values than a rotational flow field. The smaller translational flow vectors are often swamped by simultaneous rotation or noise, and the larger ones tend to be in the upper saturation range of the used optic flow algorithm. This can be seen by simultaneously translating and rotating the sensor (not shown here). Again, rotation estimates remain consistent while translation estimates are strongly affected by rotation.

4 Conclusion

Our experiments show that it is indeed possible to obtain useful self-motion estimates from an ensemble of linear model neurons. Although a linear approach necessarily has to ignore the distances of the currently perceived scene, an appropriate choice of local weights and a large field of view are capable of reducing the influence of noise and the particular scene distances on the estimates. In particular, rotation estimates were highly accurate - in a range comparable to gyroscopic estimates - and consistent across different scenes and different simultaneous translations. Translation estimates, however, turned out to be less accurate and less robust against changing scenes and simultaneous rotation. The first reason for this performance difference is the direct distance dependence of the translational flow which leads to a larger variance of the estimator output. This problem can only be overcome by also estimating the distances in the current scene (as, e.g., in the iterative scheme in [5]) which requires, however, significantly more complex computations. The second reason is the limited dynamic range of the flow algorithm used in the experiments, as discussed in the previous section. One way to overcome this problem would be the use of a flow algorithm that estimates image motion on different temporal or spatial scales which is, again, computationally more expensive.

Our results suggest a possible use of the linear estimator in tasks that require fast and accurate rotation estimates under general self-motion and without any knowledge of the object distances of the current scene. Examples for such tasks are image stabilization of a moving camera, or the removal of the rotational component from the currently measured optic flow. The latter considerably simplifies the estimation of distances from the optic flow and the detection of independently moving objects. In addition, the simple architecture of the estimator allows for an efficient implementation with a computational cost which is several orders of magnitude smaller than the cost of computing the optic flow input.

The components of the estimator are simplified model neurons which have been shown to reproduce the essential receptive field properties of the fly's tangential neurons [4]. Our study indicates that, at least in principle, the output of such neurons could be directly used for self-motion estimation by simply combining them linearly at a later integration stage. As our experiments have shown, the achievable accuracy would probably be more than enough to stabilize the fly's head during flight under closed loop conditions.

Finally, we have to point out a basic limitation of the proposed theory: It assumes linear EMDs as input to the neurons (see Eq. (1)). The output of fly EMDs, however, is only linear for very small image motions. It quickly saturates at a plateau value at higher image velocities. In this range, the tangential neuron can only indicate the presence and the sign of a particular self-motion component, not the current rotation or translation velocity. A linear combination of output signals, as in our model, is no more feasible but would require some form of population coding. In addition, a detailed comparison between the linear model and real neurons shows characteristic differences indicating that, under the conditions imposed by the experimental setup, tangential neurons seem to operate in the plateau range rather than in the linear range of the EMDs [4]. As a consequence, our study can only give a hint on what might happen at small image velocities. The case of higher image velocities has to await further research.

Acknowledgments. The authors wish to thank J. Hill, M. Hofmann and M. V. Srinivasan for their help. Financial support was provided by the Human Frontier Science Program and the Max-Planck-Gesellschaft.

References

[1] Gibson, J. J. (1950). The perception of the visual world. Houghton Mifflin, Boston.

[2] Hausen, K., Egelhaaf, M. (1989). Neural mechanisms of course control in insects. In: Stavenga, D. C., Hardie, R. C. (eds.), *Facets of vision*. Springer, Heidelberg, 391–424.

[3] Krapp, H. G., Hengstenberg, B., & Hengstenberg, R. (1998). Dendritic structure and receptive field organization of optic low processing interneurons in the fly. *J. of Neurophysiology*, **79**, 1902–1917.
[4] Franz, M. O. & Krapp, H C. (2000). Wide-field, motion-sensitive neurons and matched filters for optic flow fields. *Biol. Cybern.*, **83**, 185–197.
[5] Koenderink, J. J., & van Doorn, A. J. (1987). Facts on optic flow. *Biol. Cybern.*, **56**, 247–254.
[6] Chahl, J. S, & Srinivasan, M. V. (1997). Reflective surfaces for panoramic imaging. *Applied Optics*, **36**(31), 8275–8285.
[7] Srinivasan, M. V. (1994). An image-interpolation technique for the computation of optic flow and egomotion. *Biol. Cybern.*, **71**, 401–415.

Tracking through Optical Snow

Michael S. Langer[1] and Richard Mann[2]

[1] School of Computer Science, McGill University, Montreal, H3A2A7, Canada
langer@cs.mcgill.ca
http://www.cim.mcgill.ca/~langer

[2] School of Computer Science, University of Waterloo, Waterloo, Canada
mannr@uwaterloo.ca
http://www.cs.uwaterloo.ca/~mannr

Abstract. Optical snow is a natural type of image motion that results when the observer moves laterally relative to a cluttered 3D scene. An example is an observer moving past a bush or through a forest, or a stationary observer viewing falling snow. Optical snow motion is unlike standard motion models in computer vision, such as optical flow or layered motion since such models are based on spatial continuity assumptions. For optical snow, spatial continuity cannot be assumed because the motion is characterized by dense depth discontinuities. In previous work, we considered the special case of parallel optical snow. Here we generalize that model to allow for non-parallel optical snow. The new model describes a situation in which a laterally moving observer tracks an isolated moving object in an otherwise static 3D cluttered scene. We argue that despite the complexity of the motion, sufficient constraints remain that allow such an observer to navigate through the scene while tracking a moving object.

1 Introduction

Many computer vision methods have been developed for analyzing image motion. These methods have addressed a diverse set of natural motion categories including smooth optical flow, discontinuous optical flow across an occlusion boundary, and motion transparency. Recently we introduced a new natural motion category that is related to optical flow, occlusion and transparency but that had not been identified previously. We called the motion *optical snow*. Optical snow arises when an observer moves relative to a densely cluttered 3-D scene (see Fig. 1).

Optical snow produces dense motion parallax. A canonical example of optical snow is falling snow seen by a static observer. Although snowflakes fall vertically, the image speed of each snowflake depends inversely on its distance from the camera. Since any image region is likely to contain snowflakes at a range of depths, a range of speeds will be present. A similar example is the motion seen by an observer moving past a cluttered 3D object such as a bush. Any image region will contain leaves and branches at multiple depths. But because of parallax, multiple speeds will be present in the region.

H.H. Bülthoff et al. (Eds.): BMCV 2002, LNCS 2525, pp. 181–188, 2002.

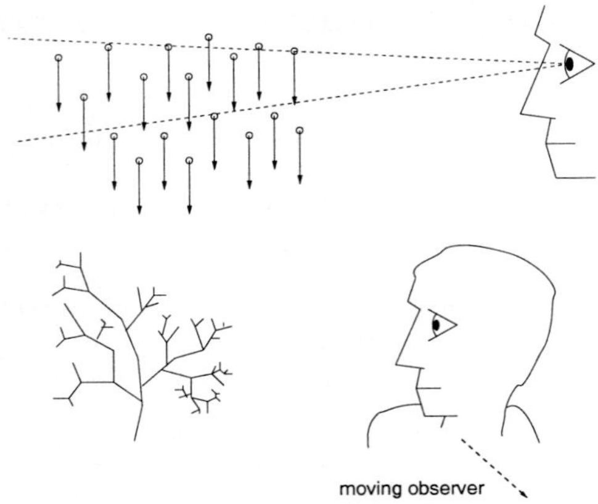

Fig. 1. Optical snow arises when a camera/observer moves relative to cluttered 3D scene.

Optical snow is a very common motion in nature which makes it especially relevant for computer vision models that are motivated by biological vision. Animals that are typically studied by visual neuroscientists include the rabbit, cat and monkey. These animals inhabit environments that are densely cluttered, for example, grasslands or forest. Since most of our knowledge of motion processing in the visual brain of mammals is obtained from experiments done on these animals, it is important to understand the computational problems of motion perception in the environments these animals inhabit, namely cluttered 3D environments.

In earlier papers on optical snow[1,2], we developed a mathematical model of the motion that extended the classical frequency domain analysis of Watson and Ahumada [3]. In the present paper, we generalize that model to the case of non-parallel optical snow, and we explicitly relate the model to classical equations of motion of a moving observer of Longuet-Higgins and Prazdny [4]. Implications for the problem of tracking are discussed.

2 Background

Previous research on image motion that uses the spatiotemporal frequency domain is based on the following motion plane property [3]: an image pattern that translates with a uniform image velocity produces a plane of energy in the frequency domain. The intuition behind the motion plane property is as follows. If an image sequence is created by a translating single image frame over time, say with velocity (v_x, v_y), then each of the 2D spatial frequency components of the single image frame will itself travel with that velocity. Each of these translating 2D sine waves will produce a unique spatiotemporal frequency component in the translating image sequence. The velocity vector (v_x, v_y) induces a specific relationship (see Eq. 2 below) between the temporal and spatial frequency of each translating component.

Formally, let $I(x, y, t)$ be a time varying image that is formed by pure translation, so that

$$I(x,\ y,\ t) \ = \ I(x + v_x dt,\ y + v_y dt,\ t + dt)\ . \tag{1}$$

Taking the Fourier transform, $\hat{I}(f_x, f_y, f_t)$, one can show [3,2] that

$$\hat{I}(f_x, f_y, f_t)\ (v_x\ f_x + v_y f_y + f_t) \ = \ 0\ .$$

Thus, any non-zero frequency component of the translating image satisfies

$$v_x\ f_x + v_y f_y + f_t \ = \ 0\ . \tag{2}$$

This is the motion plane property.

Several methods for measuring image motion have been based on this motion plane property. For example, frequency-based optical flow methods recover a unique velocity (v_x, v_y) in a local patch of the image by finding the motion plane that best fits the 3D power spectrum of that local patch [5,6,7,8]. The motion plane property has also been used by several methods that recover layered transparency. These methods assume linear superposition of two or more motion planes in the frequency domain and attempt to recover these planes for a given image sequence [9,10].

3 Optical Snow

The motion plane property was originally designed for pure translation, that is, for a unique image velocity (v_x, v_y). We observe that the property can be extended to motions in which there is a one-parameter family of velocities within an image region. Suppose that the velocity vectors in an image region are all of the form $(u_x + \alpha\ \tau_x, u_y + \alpha\ \tau_y)$ where $\{u_x, u_y, \tau_x, \tau_y\}$ are constants and the parameter α varies between points in the region. We do not make any spatial continuity assumptions about α since we are modelling densely cluttered 3D scenes.

From Eq. (2), this one parameter family of image velocities produces a one-parameter family of planes in the frequency domain,

$$(u_x + \alpha\ \tau_x)\ f_x \ + \ (u_y + \alpha\ \tau_y)\ f_y + f_t \ = \ 0 \tag{3}$$

where α is the free parameter. This claim must be qualified somewhat because of occlusion effects which are non-linear, but we have found that as long as most of the image points are visible over a sufficiently long duration, the multiple motion plane property above is a good approximation. See also [11,12] for discussion of how occlusions can affect a motion plane.

From the family of motion planes above, we observe the following:

Claim: *The one parameter family of motion planes in Eq. (3) intersect at a common line that passes through the origin in the frequency domain* (f_x, f_y, f_t). (see Fig. 2)

Proof: Each of motion planes in Eq. (3) defines a vector $(u_x + \alpha\, \tau_x, u_y + \alpha\, \tau_y,\ 1)$ that is normal to its motion plane. These normal vectors all lie on a line in the plane $f_t = 1$. Let us call this line l. The line l, together with the origin, span a plane π in the frequency domain. The vector perpendicular to π is, by definition, perpendicular to each of the normal vectors in l. Hence, the line from the origin in the direction of this perpendicular vector must lie in each of the motion planes. This proves the claim.

We say that the family of planes has a *bowtie pattern* and we say the line of intersection of the planes is the *axis of the bowtie.* The direction of the axis of the bowtie can be computed by taking the cross product of any two of the normal vectors in l. Taking the two normal vectors defined by $\alpha = \{0, 1\}$ yields that the axis of the bowtie is in direction $(-\tau_y,\ \tau_x,\ u_x \tau_y - \tau_x u_y)$.

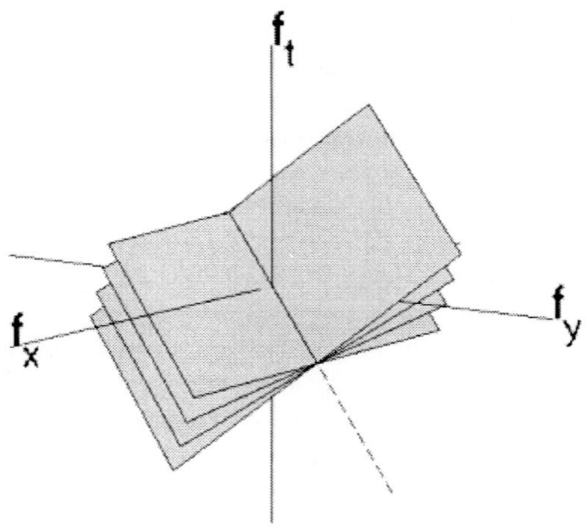

Fig. 2. Optical snow produces a bowtie pattern in frequency domain.

In our previous papers [1,2], we considered the case that the axis of the bowtie lies in the (f_x, f_y) plane, that is, (u_x, u_y) is parallel to (τ_x, τ_y). In this special case, there is a unique motion direction. We showed how a vision system could recover the parameters of optical snow, namely how to estimate the unique motion direction and the range of speeds α in the motion. In the present paper, we investigate the more general case that (u_x, u_y) is not parallel to (τ_x, τ_y). As we will see shortly, both the special case and the general case just mentioned have a natural interpretation in terms of tracking an object in the scene.

4 Lateral Motion

A canonical example of optical snow occurs when an observer moves laterally through a cluttered static scene. One can derive an expression for the resulting instantaneous image motion using the general equations of the motion field for an observer moving through a static scene which are presented in [4,13]. Let the observer's instantaneous translation vector be (T_x, T_y, T_z) and let the rotation vector be $(\omega_x, \omega_y, \omega_z)$. Lateral motion occurs when the following approximation holds:

$$|T_z| \ll \|(T_x, T_y)\|.$$

In this case, the focus of expansion is well away from the optical axis. Similar to [14], we also restrict the camera motion by assuming

$$\omega_z \approx 0 \, ,$$

that is, the camera may pan and tilt but may not roll (no cyclotorsion). These two constraints reduce the basic equations of the motion field to

$$(v_x, v_y) = (-\omega_y, \omega_x) + \frac{1}{Z}(T_x, T_y) \qquad (4)$$

where Z is the depth of the point visible at a given pixel. (We have assumed without loss of generality that the projection plane is at $z = 1$.) The model of Eq. (4) ignores terms that are second order in image coordinates x, y. These second order terms are relatively small for pixels that are say ± 20 degrees from the optical axis. Note that Eq. (4) is a particular case of optical snow defined in the previous section, with constants $(u_x, u_y) = (-\omega_y, \omega_x)$, $(\tau_x, \tau_y) = (T_x, T_y)$, and $1/Z$ being the free parameter α.

5 Tracking an Object

One common reason for camera rotation during observer motion is for the observer to track a surface patch in the scene, that is, to stabilize it in the image in order to better analyze its spatial properties. We assume first that the entire scene including the tracked surface patch is static and only the observer is moving. Tracking a surface patch at depth Z' stabilizes the projection of the patch on the retina by reducing its image velocity to zero. For this to happen, the camera rotation component of the image motion must exactly cancel the image translation component of that surface patch, that is, from Eq. (4),

$$(v_x, v_y) = (0, 0) \quad \text{if and only if} \quad (-\omega_y, \omega_x) = -\frac{1}{Z'}(T_x, T_y)$$

When the observer tracks a particular surface patch, scene points at other depths will still undergo image motion. From the previous equation and Eq. (4), the image velocity of a point at depth Z in the scene will be:

$$(v_x, v_y) = (\frac{1}{Z} - \frac{1}{Z'}) \, (T_x, T_y).$$

Two observations follow immediately. First, if the observer is tracking a particular point in the scene then Eq. (4) implies that all velocity vectors in the image will be in direction (T_x, T_y) and hence parallel.[1] We call this case of *parallel optical snow.* Notice that parallel optical snow also arises when $(-\omega_y, \omega_x) = (0, 0)$ which is the case of no camera rotation. In this case, the observer is tracking at point at infinity.

The second observation is that a point in front of the tracked point $(Z < Z')$ will have image motion in the opposite direction of a point behind the tracked point $(Z > Z')$. For example, consider walking past a tree while tracking a squirrel that is sitting in the tree. Leaves and branches that are nearer than the squirrel will move in the opposite direction in the image as those that are farther than the squirrel.

The above discussion assumed the observer was tracking a static surface patch in a *static* 3D scene. One natural way to relax this assumption is to allow the tracked surface patch (object) to move in the scene, with the scene remaining static otherwise, and to suppose the observer tracks this moving object while the observer also moves. A natural example is a predator tracking its moving prey [15]. In this scenario, the camera rotation needed to track the object may be in a different direction than the camera's translation component. For example, the predator may be moving along the ground plane and tracking its prey which is climbing a tree. In this case the translation component of motion (T_x, T_y) is horizontal and the rotation component of motion $(-\omega_y, \omega_x)$ is vertical.

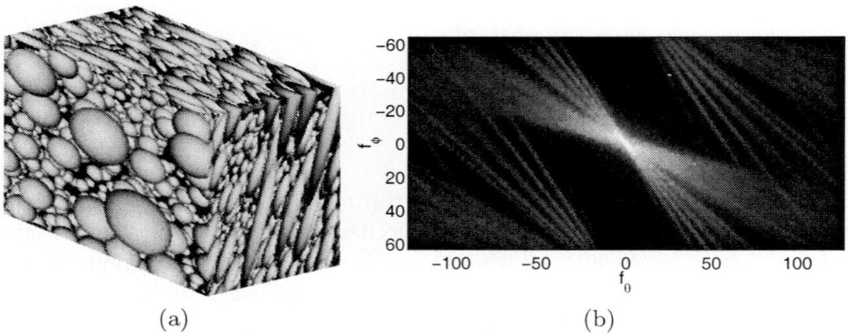

Fig. 3. (a) xyt cube of sphere sequence. (b) Projection of power spectrum in the direction of the axis of the bowtie. Aliasing effects (wraparound at boundaries of frequency domain) are due to the "jaggies" of OpenGL. Such effects are less severe in real image sequences because of optical blur [1,2].

A contrived example to illustrate non-parallel optical snow is shown in Figure 3. A synthetic image sequence was created using OpenGL. The scene was a set

[1] Recalling the approximation of Section 4, this result breaks down for wide field of views, since second order effects of the motion field become significant.

of spheres distributed randomly in a view volume. The camera translates in the y direction so that (T_x, T_y, T_z) is in direction $(0, 1, 0)$. As the camera translates, it rotates about the y axis so that $(\omega_x, \omega_y, \omega_z)$ is in direction $(0, 1, 0)$ and the rotation component of the image motion is in direction $(1, 0, 0)$. In terms of our tracking scenario, such a camera motion would track a point object moving on a helix

$$(X(t), Y(t), Z(t)) = (r \sin t, t, r \cos t)$$

where r is the radius of the helix and t is time.

For our sequence, the camera rotates 30 degrees (the width of the view volume) in 128 frames. Since the image size is 256×256 pixels, this yields $(u_x, u_y) = (2, 0)$ pixels/frame. Fig. 3(a) shows the xyt video cube [16] and Fig. 3(b) shows a summed projection of the 3D power spectrum onto a plane. The projection is in the bowtie axis direction $(1, 0, 1)$. The bowtie is clearly visible.

6 Future Work

One problem that is ripe for future work is to develop algorithms for estimating the bowtie that are more biologically plausible than the one we have considered which uses an explicit representation of the Fourier transform. To be consistent with motion processing in visual cortex, a biologically plausible algorithms would be based on the measurements of local space-time motion energy detectors [16]. Such algorithms could generalize current biological models for motion processing such as [5,7,8] which assume a pure translation motion. These current algorithms estimate the velocity of the pure translation motion in a space-time image patch by combining the responses of motion energy detectors, and estimating a single motion plane in the frequency domain.

Our idea for analyzing optical snow in this manner to estimate a bowtie pattern rather than a single motion plane. Since a motion plane is just a bowtie whose range of speeds collapses to a single speed, the problem of estimating a bowtie generalizes the previous problem of estimating a motion plane. The details remain to be worked out. However, biologically plausible models of layered motion transparency have been proposed already [17]. We expect similar algorithms could be designed for optical snow as well.

Acknowledgments. This research was supported by the Natural Sciences and Engineering Research Council of Canada (NSERC).

References

1. M. S. Langer and R. Mann. Dimensional analysis of image motion. In *IEEE International Conference on Computer Vision*, pages 155–162, 2001.
2. R. Mann and M. S. Langer. Optical snow and the aperture problem. In *International Conference on Pattern Recognition*, Quebec City, Canada, Aug. 2002.

3. A.B. Watson and A.J. Ahumada. Model of human visual-motion sensing. *Journal of the Optical Society of America A*, 2(2):322–342, 1985.
4. H.C. Longuet-Higgins and K. Prazdny. The interpretation of a moving retinal image. *Proceedings of the Royal Society of London B)*, B-208:385–397, 1980.
5. D.J. Heeger. Optical flow from spatiotemporal filters. In *First International Conference on Computer Vision*, pages 181–190, 1987.
6. D. J. Fleet. *Measurement of Image Velocity.* Kluwer Academic Press, Norwell, MA, 1992.
7. N.M. Grzywacz and A.L. Yuille. A model for the estimate of local image velocity by cells in the visual cortex. *Proceedings of the Royal Society of London. B*, 239:129–161, 1990.
8. E P Simoncelli and D J Heeger. A model of neural responses in visual area mt. *Vision Research*, 38(5):743–761, 1998.
9. M. Shizawa and K. Mase. A unified computational theory for motion transparency and motion boundaries based on eigenenergy analysis. In *IEEE Conference on Computer Vision and Pattern Recognition*, pages 289–295, 1991.
10. P. Milanfar. Projection-based, frequency-domain estimation of superimposed translational motions. *Journal of the Optical Society of America A*, 13(11):2151–2162, November 1996.
11. D. J. Fleet and K. Langley. Computational analysis of non-fourier motion. *Vision Research*, 34(22):3057–3079, 1994.
12. S.S. Beauchemin and J.L. Barron. The frequency structure of 1d occluding image signals. *IEEE Transactions on Pattern Analysis and Machine Intelligence*, 22(2):200–206, February 2000.
13. E. Trucco and A. Verri. *Introductory Techniques for 3-D Computer Vision.* Prentice-Hall, 1998.
14. M. Lappe and J. P. Rauschecker. A neural network for the processing of optical flow from egomotion in man and higher mammals. *Neural Computation*, 5:374–391, 1993.
15. S. W. Zucker and L. Iverson. From orientation selection to optical flow. *Computer Vision Graphics and Image Processing*, 37:196–220, 1987.
16. E.H. Adelson and J.R. Bergen. Spatiotemporal energy models for the perception of motion. *Journal of the Optical Society of America A*, 2(2):284–299, 1985.
17. R. S. Zemel and P. Dayan. Distributional population codes and multiple motion models. In D. A. Cohn M. S. Kearns, S. A. Solla, editor, *Advances in Neural Information Processing Systems 11*, pages 768–784, Cambridge, MA, 1999. MIT Press.

On Computing Visual Flows with Boundaries: The Case of Shading and Edges

Ohad Ben-Shahar, Patrick S. Huggins, and Steven W. Zucker

Department of Computer Science and Interdisciplinary Neuroscience Program,
Yale University,
New Haven, Connecticut 06520, USA
{ben-shahar,huggins,zucker}@cs.yale.edu

Abstract. Many visual tasks depend upon the interpretation of visual structures that are flow fields, such as optical flow, oriented texture, and shading. The computation of these visual flows involves a delicate trade-off: imaging imperfections lead to noisy and sparse initial flow measurements, necessitating further processing to infer dense coherent flows; this processing typically entails interpolation and smoothing, both of which are prone to destroy visual flow discontinuities. However, discontinuities in visual flows signal corresponding discontinuities in the physical world, thus it is critical to preserve them while processing the flow. In this paper we present a computational approach motivated by the architecture of primary visual cortex that directly incorporates boundary information into a flow relaxation network. The result is a robust computation of visual flows with the capacity to handle noisy or sparse data sets while providing stability along flow boundaries. We demonstrate the effectiveness of our approach by computing shading flows in images with intensity edges.

1 Introduction

Many visual structures, including optical flow [7], oriented texture [14], and shading [4], appear as flow fields in the image plane. Accurate knowledge of the geometry of these flows is a key step toward the interpretation of visual scenes, both two dimensional [13,14] and three dimensional [19,21].

Perceptually, visual flow fields are characterized by their dense, smoothly varying (almost everywhere) oriented structure. Formally a flow is an orientation function $\theta(x, y)$ over the image plane. Initial measurements of a flow field, made locally with imperfect sensors (like V1 receptive fields), are likely to suffer from noise and perhaps even fail altogether in some regions of the image. Hence, an effective computational process for the inference of coherent visual flow must be able to do so from a noisy, incomplete set of measurements. Furthermore, as we discuss below, it should localize singularities, reject non-flow structures, and behave appropriately along line discontinuities and boundaries. We have developed a computational model that addresses all these issues within a framework that is inspired by the columnar architecture of the primary visual cortex [2,1].

H.H. Bülthoff et al. (Eds.): BMCV 2002, LNCS 2525, pp. 189–198, 2002.

The requirement that flow discontinuities be preserved is particularly important since their presence typically indicates physical discontinuities in the world. However, there is a delicate trade-off between handling sparse and noisy data sets and achieving stability along boundaries. To solve this some nonlinear interaction between the flow and its boundaries needs to be made explicit. In this paper we describe a biologically motivated way of achieving that goal.

Of the different types of visual flows, one – the *shading flow field* [4] – has a special relationship to its corresponding visual boundaries. The relationship between the geometry of the shading and that of the bounding edge provides a basis for classifying edges [4], and can be used to resolve occlusion relationships [10]. Since shading flow boundaries (i.e., the curves along which the flow should be segmented into coherent parts) are defined as intensity edges, shading is a clear example of a visual flow for which both the flow field and its boundaries can be directly measured from the image. Thus in this paper we focus on the case of shading and edges.

2 The Differential Geometry of Coherent Visual Flows

Given that the initial measurements of a visual flow field may contain spurious or missing values, we would like to refine the flow field so as to counteract these effects. Interpolating and fitting [18], smoothing [17], and diffusing [20] the orientation function $\theta(x,y)$ corresponding to the flow are commonly used approaches to achieving this goal, but they also prone to affect the underlying geometry of the flow in undesirable ways. In particular, they can distort flow singularities that must be preserved to correctly interpret visual scenes [1,2]. To overcome this problem we process the visual flow by enforcing local coherence, that is, by ensuring that each local measurement of the flow field is consistent with its neighboring measurements. Toward this we first examine the differential geometry of visual flows.

A natural representation of a visual flow which highlights its intrinsic geometry is its *frame field* [15]. Here a local frame $\{E_T, E_N\}$ is attached to each point q of the flow, with E_T tangent and E_N normal to the flow. Small translations in direction V from the point q rotate the frame, a change which is characterized through the covariant derivatives $\nabla_V E_T$ and $\nabla_V E_N$ of the underlying pattern. Cartan's connection equation [15] expresses these covariant derivatives in terms of the frame field itself:

$$\begin{pmatrix} \nabla_V E_T \\ \nabla_V E_N \end{pmatrix} = \begin{bmatrix} 0 & w_{12}(V) \\ -w_{12}(V) & 0 \end{bmatrix} \begin{pmatrix} E_T \\ E_N \end{pmatrix} . \tag{1}$$

The connection form $w_{12}(V)$ is a linear function of the tangent vector V and can thus be represented by two scalars at each point. In the basis $\{E_T, E_N\}$ these scalars are defined as $\kappa_T \triangleq w_{12}(E_T)$ and $\kappa_N \triangleq w_{12}(E_N)$, which we call the *tangential curvature* and the *normal curvature* - they represent the rate of change of the flow's dominant orientation in the tangential and normal directions, respectively. In terms of $\theta(x,y)$ and its differential, these curvatures become:

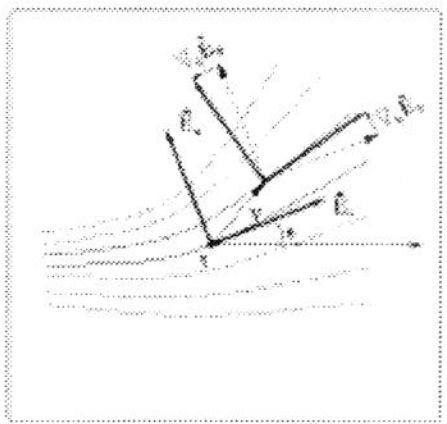

Fig. 1. The frame field representation of visual flows. The local behavior of the frame is described by its covariant derivatives $\nabla_V E_T$ and $\nabla_V E_N$ which are always normal to E_T and E_N, respectively. Since the connection form – the operator that describes the frame's rotation for any direction V – is linear, it is fully characterized by two numbers computed as projections on two independent directions. In the basis of the frame this yields the curvatures κ_T and κ_N.

$$\begin{aligned} \kappa_T &= d\theta(E_T) = \nabla\theta \cdot E_T = \nabla\theta \cdot (\cos\theta, \sin\theta) \\ \kappa_N &= d\theta(E_N) = \nabla\theta \cdot E_N = \nabla\theta \cdot (-\sin\theta, \cos\theta). \end{aligned} \tag{2}$$

Knowledge of E_T, E_N, κ_T, and κ_N at a point q enables us to construct a local approximation to the flow which has the same orientation and curvatures at q; we call such an approximation an *osculating flow field*. The osculating flow field is important in that it predicts flow values in the neighborhood of q. Comparing these predictions to the measured flow values indicates how consistent the measured values of the flow at q are with those at its neighbors and suggests how to update them to be consistent. An analogous technique to refine curve measurements using cocircularity was developed in [16].

There are an infinite number of possible osculating flow fields to choose from. However, there exist criteria for "good" osculating flow fields. One such criterion is the minimization of the harmonic energy $E[\theta] = \int\int \|\nabla\theta\|^2 dxdy$ associated with the orientation function of the flow, as is used in orientation diffusion [20]. Viewing the orientation function as a surface in $\mathbb{R}^2 \times \mathcal{S}^1$, however, suggests that the osculating flow field should minimize the surface area $A[\theta] = \int\int \sqrt{1 + \theta_x^2 + \theta_y^2} dxdy$. Finally, the duality of the curvatures κ_T and κ_N suggests that the osculating flow field should exhibit unbiased curvature covariation. Surprisingly, there is a unique osculating flow field which satisfies all of these criteria simultaneously [1,2]. In the space $\mathbb{R}^2 \times \mathcal{S}^1$ of orientations over the image plane it takes the form of a *right helicoid* (Fig. 2):

Proposition 1. *Assume (w.l.o.g) that a visual flow $\theta(x,y)$ satisfies $q = (0,0)$ and $\theta(q) = 0$, $\kappa_T(q) = K_T$, and $\kappa_N(q) = K_N$. Of all possible orientation functions $\theta(x,y)$ around q that satisfy these constraints, the only one that extremizes both $E[\theta]$ and $A[\theta]$, and has curvature functions that covary* identically *(i.e., $\frac{\kappa_T(x,y)}{\kappa_N(x,y)}$ =const= $\frac{K_T}{K_N}$) is the right helicoid $\theta(x,y) = \tan^{-1}(\frac{K_T x + K_N y}{1 + K_N x - K_T y})$.*

Armed with a model of the local structure of visual flow we are in a position to compute a globally coherent flow, the procedure for which is described in the next section.

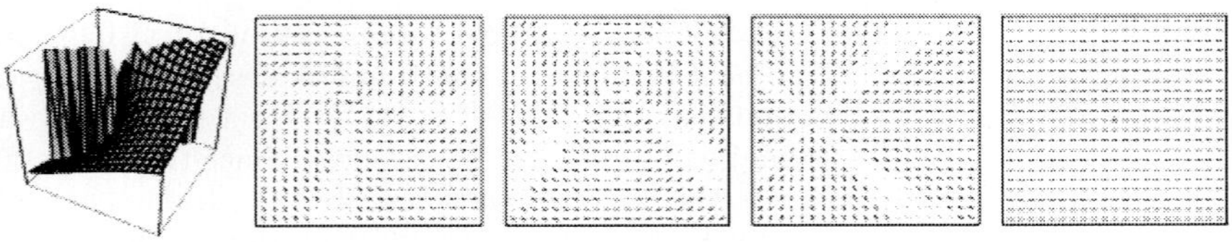

Fig. 2. Examples of right helicoidal visual flows, both in (x, y, θ) space (left) and the image plane. Note that tuning to different curvatures at the origin (point marked with a cross) produces qualitatively different coherent behaviors in its neighborhood.

3 Computing Coherent Visual Flows

The advantage of having a model for the local behavior of visual flow lies in the ability to assess the degree to which a particular measurement is consistent with the context in which it is embedded. This, in turn, can be used to refine noisy measurements, remove spurious ones, and fill in "holes" so that global structures become coherent. A framework in which one can pursue this task by iteratively maximizing the average local consistency over the domain of interest is *relaxation labeling* [11]. We have developed such a network for the organization of coherent visual flows [2]. The following is a short overview of that system.

A direct abstraction of the relaxation process for visual flow should involve an image-based 2D network of nodes $i = (x, y)$ (i.e., pixels) whose labels are drawn from the set $\Lambda = \{\text{no-flow}\} \cup \{(\theta, \kappa_T, \kappa_N) \mid \theta \in (-\frac{\pi}{2}, \frac{\pi}{2}]\ ,\ \kappa_T, \kappa_N \in [-K, K]\}$ after the appropriate quantization. To allow for the representation of either "no-flow" or multiple flows at a pixel, we replace this abstraction with a 5D network of nodes $i = (x, y, \theta, \kappa_T, \kappa_N)$ whose labels are either $TRUE$ (T) or $FALSE$ (F). For each node i, $p_i(T)$ denotes the confidence that a visual flow of orientation θ and curvatures κ_T, κ_N passes through pixel (x, y). Since $p_i(F) = 1 - p_i(T)$ we need to maintain and update the confidence of only one label at each node.

The geometrical compatibilities $r_{ij}(\lambda, \lambda')$ that drive our relaxation process are computed from the osculating flow field as defined by the right helicoid. Measurement quantization implies that every possible node i represents an equivalence class of measurements, each of which induces a field of compatible labels in the neighborhood of i. In the continuum, the union of all these fields forms a consistent 5D "volume" that after quantization results in a set of excitatory labels. See Fig. 3

With the network structure, labels, and compatibilities all designed, one can compute the support $s_i(\lambda)$ that label λ at node i gathers from its neighborhood. $s_i(\lambda)$ is typically the sum of the individual support of all labels j in the neighborhood of i

$$s_i(\lambda) = \sum_j \sum_{\lambda'} r_{ij}(\lambda, \lambda') p_j(\lambda') \ . \tag{3}$$

Having computed the support for a label, $s_i(\lambda)$ is then used to update the confidence $p_i(\lambda)$ by gradient ascent, followed by non-linear projection. Under the

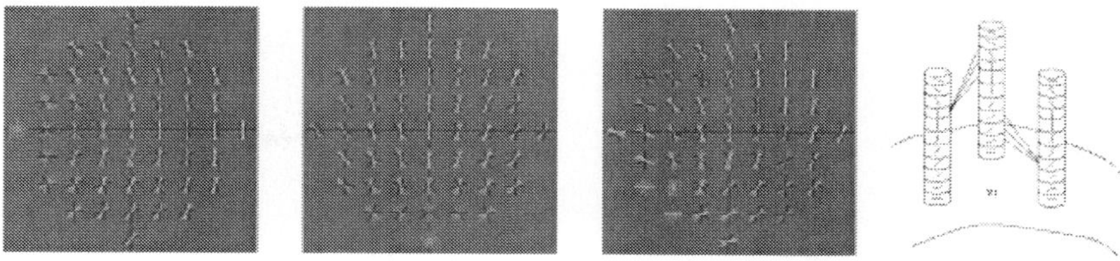

Fig. 3. Examples of compatibility structure (for different values of θ, κ_T and κ_N) projected onto the image plane (brightness represents degree of compatibility, black segments represent an inhibitory surround). As is illustrated on the right, these structures are closely related to long range horizontal connections between orientation columns in V1.

2-label paradigm and the appropriate weighing of negative (F) versus positive (T) evidence [2], the projection operator takes a particularly convenient form and the update rule reduces to

$$p_i(\lambda) \leftarrow \Pi_0^1 \left(p_i(\lambda) + \delta s_i(\lambda)\right) \tag{4}$$

where $\Pi_0^1(x)$ projects its operand to the nearest point on the interval $[0, 1]$ and δ is the step size of the gradient descent.

While the relaxation labeling network described is an abstraction based on the differential geometry of flow fields, it is motivated by the architecture of the primary visual cortex. The columnar structure of V1 clearly lends itself to the representation of orientation fields [9], and is capable of the necessary curvature computations [6]. Considerable speculation surrounds the functional significance of long-range horizontal connections [8] between orientation columns; we posit that they may play a role not unlike the compatibility structures of our network (Fig. 3, right panel).

3.1 Stability at Discontinuities

In computing coherent visual flows it is important to respect its discontinuities, as these often correspond to significant physical phenomena. The relaxation process described above does not destroy these structures because in the high dimensional space in which it operates the flow structures that meet along a line discontinuity, either in orientation or curvature, are separated and thus do not interact. However, without proper tuning, the relaxation process will quickly shrink or expand the flow in the neighborhood of boundaries. It is this behavior we seek to suppress.

To achieve stability we normalize the compatibility function, and thus the support function $s_i(\lambda)$, to account for reduced support in the neighborhood of a discontinuity. Given the compatibility volume V_i which corresponds to a particular node i, we compute the maximal support a node can receive, s_{max}, as the integral of the compatibility coefficients assuming a consistent flow traverses

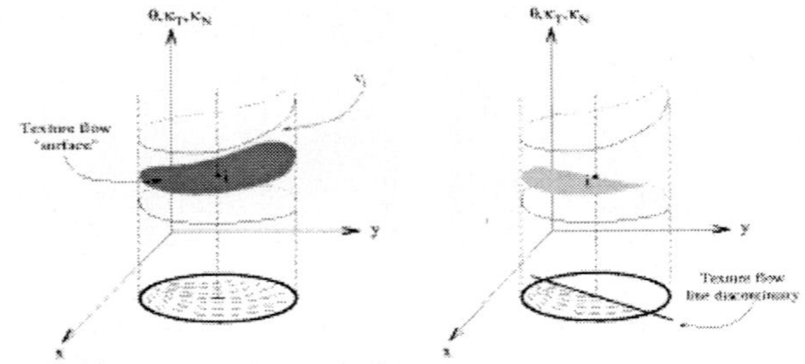

(a) Maximal expected support (b) Minimal acceptable support

Fig. 4. Practical stability of the relaxation labeling process at line discontinuities in the flow can be achieved through the normalization of the support function. (a) At each node i, s_{max} is determined by integrating the support gathered from a full confidence, compatible flow that traverses the entire compatibility volume V_i. (b) The minimal accepted support s_{min} of a flow of some minimally accepted confidence $\rho_{min} < 1$ (depicted here by the brighter surface intensity) that terminates along a line that intersects i.

V_i with all supporting nodes at full confidence (Fig. 4). It is clear that the closer i is to a flow discontinuity, the less context supports it. At the discontinuity, the flow should neither grow nor shrink, leading us to define the minimal level of support for which no change in confidence occurs, s_{min}. Observe that s_{min} depends on both the geometry of the discontinuity and the minimally accepted confidence of the supporting nodes. For simplicity we assume the discontinuity (locally) occurs along a straight line. The support from neighboring nodes of minimally accepted average confidence ρ_{min} (Fig. 4) can be approximated as $s_{min} = \frac{\rho_{min} s_{max}}{2}$. Normally ρ_{min} would be set to 0.5, which is the minimal confidence that cannot be disambiguated as the $TRUE$ label. In the context of the two-label relaxation labeling paradigm and the gradient ascent update rule (Eq. 4), a decrease in the confidence of a label occurs only if $s_i < 0$. Thus, it remains to normalize the support values by mapping the interval $[s_{min}, s_{max}]$ to the unit interval $[0, 1]$ via the transformation $s_i \leftarrow \frac{s_i - s_{min}}{s_{max} - s_{min}}$ before applying the update rule.

The result of the normalized relaxation process is usually very good (Fig. 5). Nevertheless, the fact that both the support function (Eq. 3) and the normalization are linear creates a delicate balance: while better noise resistance suggests smaller s_{min}, it also implies that at discontinuities the flow will eventually grow uncontrollably. Some solutions to this problem are discussed in [2]. However, in the case of shading flow fields, discontinuities are intensity edges and thus can be explicitly identified by edge detection. As we discuss below, this information can be directly embedded into the network to decouple the handling of discontinuities from the support normalization.

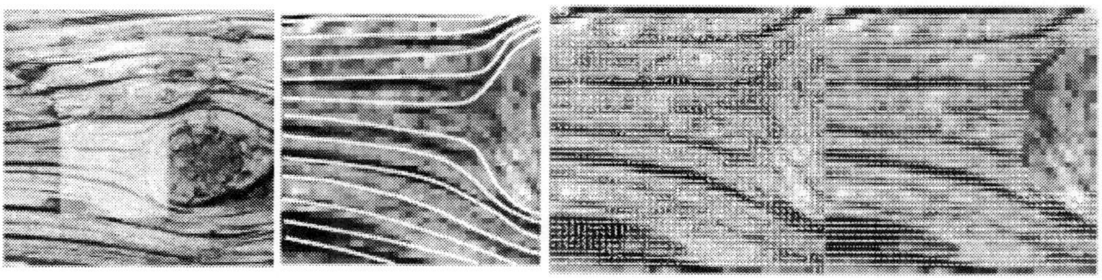

Fig. 5. Visual flow organization based on right helicoidal compatibilities. Shown (left to right) are: Tree bark image and a region of interest (ROI), perceptual structure (drawn manually), initial flow measurements (gradient based filter), and the relaxed visual flow after few iterations of relaxation labeling with the right helicoidal compatibilities. Compare the latter to the perceptual structure and note how the non-flow region was rejected altogether.

4 Edges as Shading Flow Boundaries

Edges in images are important because they signify physical changes in a scene; hence the numerous efforts to detect them. The physical nature of an edge is often discernible from the appearance of the edge in the image. In particular, the relationship between the edge and the shading flow field in the neighborhood of the edge can be used to identify the physical cause of the edge. The shading flow field is defined as the unit vector field aligned with the iso-brightness contours of the image [4]. For example, the shading flow field is continuous across an edge caused by an abrupt albedo change but discontinuous across an edge caused by a cast shadow [4].

Significantly, occlusion edges can be distinguished on the basis of the shading flow field as well. At an occlusion edge of a smooth object, the edge results from the object's surface curving away from the viewer; we call this type of edge a *fold.* At a fold, the shading flow field is generically tangent to the edge due to the projective geometry of the situation (Fig. 6). On the occluded side of the edge the shading flow has an arbitrary relationship to the edge and is generically non-tangent; we call this side of the edge a *cut* [10].

The ability to compute the flow field structure in the neighborhood of the edge is exactly what we are looking for to classify the edge. However, techniques that compute flow field structure without explicitly accounting for edges can destroy the relationship between the flow field and the edge and thus prevent the correct interpretation and classification of the edge. What we describe next is how we endow the connectivity structure of our relaxation labeling network with the ability to explicitly consider edge information and thus prevent the problem just mentioned. Naturally, this places some dependence on the edge detector used; however this is clearly preferable to completely ignoring the edge.

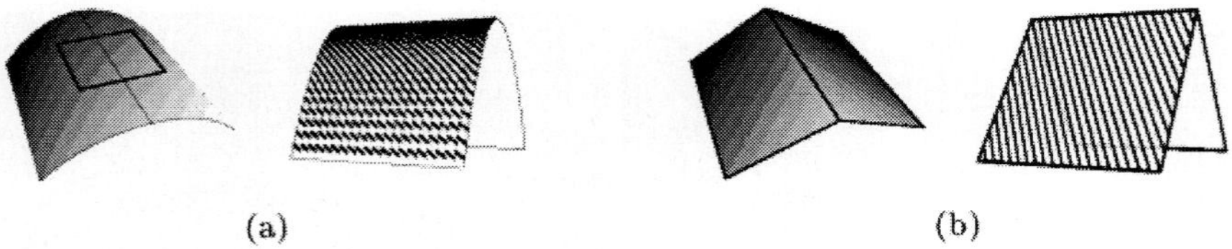

Fig. 6. Illustration of shading flow in the neighborhood of an edge. When a shaded surface is viewed such that an edge appears, the shading flow field takes on different appearances depending on the nature of the edge. A fold occurs (a) when the surface bends smoothly away from the viewer (the typical occlusion case), and the shading flow field appears tangent to the edge. At a cut (b), the surface is discontinuous (or occluded), and shading flow is generally non-tangent to the edge.

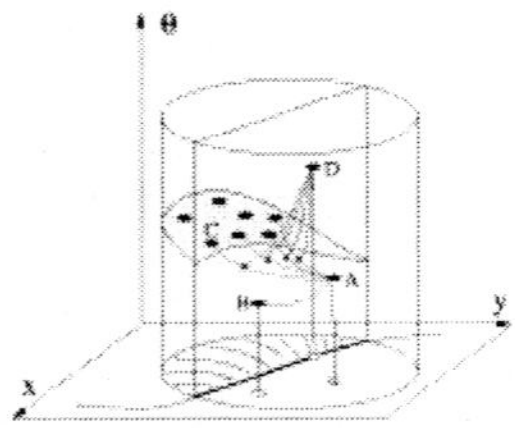

Fig. 7. Edge-flow interactions for boundary stability. Assume the flow structure in the image plane is bounded by the indicated edge. *Flow* cell A is connected to a set of other cells (B and C) which are a part of the same coherent flow. Although A is not active (there is no flow in its corresponding retinotopic position), its facilitory interaction with the cells on the other side of the edge may eventually raise its activity level. To prevent cell C from affecting A, an active *edge* cell D blocks the facilitory inputs from C, thus effectively limiting A's context to cell B only. Unless enough of these cells are also active, A will not reach its activation potential, and thus will not signal any flow.

5 Edges as Nonlinear Inhibition

Due to its physical nature, an edge can be thought of as dividing the shading flow field domain into distinct regions, implying that the computation of the shading flow on either side of the edge can and should be done separately. This is an intuitive but powerful argument: incorporating edges into the relaxation labeling network to regulate the growth of flow structure obviates the trade-off between high resistance to noise and strict stability along discontinuities we mentioned in Section 3.

To implement this idea in the framework of relaxation labeling, what is needed is a specialized set of interactions between edge nodes and nearby shading flow nodes. These interactions would block the flow input if it comes from across the edge. With this input blocked, and so long as s_{min} is positive, the flow on one side of the edge will not extend across the edge, because the total support contributed to the other side will never exceed zero. This frees the selection of s_{min} from stability considerations and allows us to determine it solely on

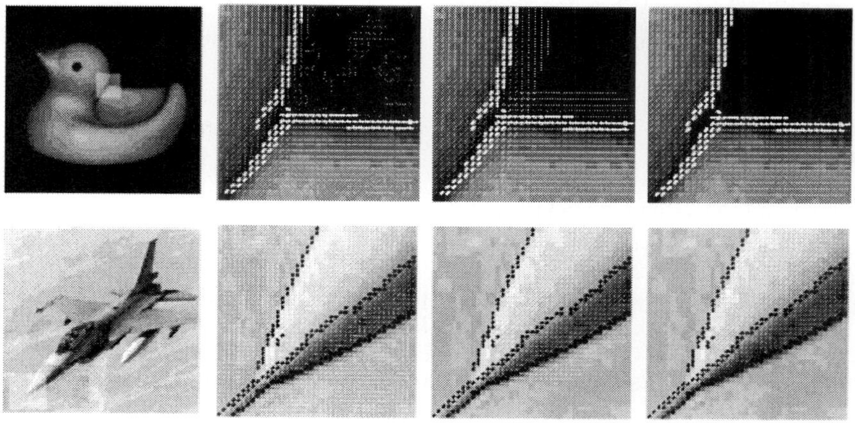

Fig. 8. Examples of shading flow field relaxation with edges as boundary conditions. Shown are (left to right) image and ROI, initial shading flow (thin segments) and edges (thick segments), relaxation without boundaries, and relaxation with boundaries. Note that while both relaxations compute correct flow structure, the one without boundaries extends the flow beyond the edge, making classification more difficult. On the other hand, edge classification and occlusion relationship is trivial based on the result using edges as boundary conditions.

the basis of noise resistance and structural criteria. A cartoon illustrating these interactions appears in Fig. 7. Interestingly, a nonlinear veto mechanism that is reminiscent of the one proposed here also exists in biological systems in the form of shunting inhibition [3].

We have tested this adaptive relaxation labeling network on a variety of synthetic and natural images, two of which are shown in Fig. 8. We used the Logical/Linear [12] and the Canny [5] edge detectors and the shading flow fields were measured using standard differential operators.

6 Conclusions

In this paper we have described a computational approach that integrates boundary and visual flow cues for the computation of coherent shading flow fields in images. It is important to capture this interaction between flows and boundaries accurately as it indicates the geometry of the scene underlying the image. Based on a geometrical analysis, our computation is carried out in a relaxation labeling network whose nodes are tuned to position, orientation, and two flow curvatures. Boundary information is used to adaptively alter the context which influences a given node, a mechanism which enables the network to handle noisy and sparse data sets without affecting the flow's discontinuities. Both the flow computation and the incorporation of edges as boundary conditions are motivated by the columnar architecture of the primary visual cortex and neurophysiological shunting inhibition. While here we applied our system to shading flow fields and edges, the same ideas can be used for other flow-like visual cues like motion, texture, and color.

References

1. O. Ben-Shahar and S. Zucker. On the perceptual organization of texture and shading flows: From a geometrical model to coherence computation. In *CVPR*, pages 1048–1055, 2001.
2. O. Ben-Shahar and S. Zucker. The perceptual organization of texture flow: A contextual inference approach. *IEEE PAMI.*, 2002. In press.
3. L. Borg-Graham, C. Monier, and Y. Fregnac. Visual input evokes transient and strong shunting inhibition in visual cortical neurons. *Nature*, 292:369–373, 1998.
4. P. Breton and S. Zucker. Shadows and shading flow fields. In *CVPR*, 1996.
5. J. Canny. A computational approach to edge detection. *IEEE PAMI*, 8(6):679–698, 1986.
6. A. Dobbins, S. Zucker, and M. Cynader. Endstopped neurons in the visual cortex as a substrate for calculating curvature. *Nature*, 329(6138):438–441, 1987.
7. J. Gibson. *The Perception of the Visual World.* The Riverside Press, 1950.
8. C. Gilbert. Horizontal integration and cortical dynamics. *Neuron*, 9:1–13, 1992.
9. D. Hubel and T. Wiesel. Functional architecture of macaque monkey visual cortex. In *Proc. R. Soc. London Ser. B*, volume 198, pages 1–59, 1977.
10. P. Huggins and S. Zucker. Folds and cuts: how shading flows into edges. In *ICCV*, 2001.
11. R. Hummel and S. Zucker. On the foundations of the relaxation labeling proceeses. *IEEE PAMI*, 5:267–287, 1983.
12. L. Iverson and S. Zucker. Logical/linear operators for image curves. *IEEE PAMI*, 17(10):982–996, 1995.
13. G. Kanizsa. *Organization in Vision: Essays on Gestalt Perception.* Praeger Publishers, 1979.
14. M. Kass and A. Witkin. Analyzing oriented patterns. *CVGIP*, 37:362–385, 1987.
15. B. O'Neill. *Elementary Differential Geometry.* Academic Press, 1966.
16. P. Parent and S. Zucker. Trace inference, curvature consistency, and curve detection. *IEEE PAMI*, 11(8):823–839, 1989.
17. P. Perona. Orientation diffusion. *IEEE Trans. Image Processing*, 7(3), 1998.
18. A. Rao and R. Jain. Computerized flow field analysis: Oriented texture fields. *IEEE PAMI*, 17(7):693–709, 1992.
19. K. Stevens. The line of curvature constraint and the interpretation of 3d shape from parallel surface contours. In *Proc. IJCAI*, pages 1057–1061, 1983.
20. B. Tang, G. Sapiro, and V. Caselles. Diffusion of general data on non-flat manifolds via harmonic maps theory: The direction diffusion case. *IJCV*, 36(2):149–161, 2000.
21. J. Todd and F. Reichel. Visual perception of smoothly curved surfaces from double-projected contour patterns. *J. Exp. Psych.: Human Perception and Performance*, 16(3):665–674, 1990.

Biological Motion of Speech

Gregor A. Kalberer[1], Pascal Müller[1], and Luc Van Gool[1,2]

[1] D-ITET/BIWI, ETH Zurich, Switzerland,
[2] ESAT/PSI/Visics, KULeuven, Belgium
{kalberer,mueller,vangool}@vision.ee.ethz.ch

Abstract. The paper discusses the detailed analysis of visual speech. As with other forms of biological motion, humans are known to be very sensitive to the realism in the ways the lips move. In order to determine the elements that come to play in the perceptual analysis of visual speech, it is important to have control over the data. The paper discusses the capture of detailed 3D deformations of faces when talking. The data are detailed in both a temporal and spatial sense. The 3D positions of thousands of points on the face are determined at the temporal resolution of video. Such data have been decomposed into their basic modes, using ICA. It is noteworthy that this yielded better results than a mere PCA analysis, which results in modes that individually represent facial changes that anatomically inconsistent. The ICs better capture the underlying, anatomical changes that the face undergoes. Different visemes are all based on the underlying, joint action of the facial muscles. The IC modes do not reflect single muscles, but nevertheless decompose the speech related deformations into anatomically convincing modes, coined 'pseudo-muscles'.

Introduction

Humans are all experts at judging the realism of facial animations. We easily spot inconsistencies between aural and visual speech, for instance. So far, it has been very difficult to perform detailed, psychophysical experiments on visual speech, because it has been difficult to generate groundtruth data that can also be systematically manipulated in three dimensions. Just as is the case with body motion, discrete points can give useful information on speech [12]. Nevertheless, the authors of that study concluded that '... point-light stimuli were never as effective as the analogous fully-illuminated moving face stimuli'.

In general two classes of 3D facial analysis and animation can be distinguished – physically based (PB) and terminal analog (TA) [8]. In contrast to the PB class, that involves the use of physical models of the structure and function of the human face, the TA class cares only about the net effect (a face surface) without resorting to physically based constructs.

In this paper, we follow the TA strategy, because this strategy has the advantage that correspondences between different faces and different movements stand by at any time. Furthermore, for animation the mere outer changes in the

H.H. Bülthoff et al. (Eds.): BMCV 2002, LNCS 2525, pp. 199–206, 2002.

polygonal face shapes can be carried out faster than muscle and tissue simulations. As human perception also only takes visible parts of the face into account, such a simplification seems justified.

We propose a system that measures in 3D the detailed facial deformations during speech. The data are quite detailed in that thousands of points are measured, at the temporal resolution of video. Several contributions in this direction have already been undertaken, but with a substantially smaller number of points (see e.g. Pighin *et al.* [10], Reveret *et al.* [11], Lin *et al.* [7] and Guenter *et al.* [1]). But as the aforementioned psychophysical experiments have demonstrated, it is important to have control over more detailed data when setting up experiments about the visual perception of speech.

The paper also analyses the extracted 3D dynamics. The data are decomposed into basic deformation modes. Principal Component Analysis yields modes that are anatomically inconsistent, but Independent Components are better able to split the deformations up into modes that make sense in their own right. This suggests that they are also better able to home in on the kind of actions facial muscles excerce on the face. They could be considered to each represent a 'pseudo-muscle', of which the actions can be linearly combined to yield realistic speech. Such animations have actually been tried, with good results. The animation aspects have been discussed elsewhere [4,5,6].

1 Extracting 3D Face Deformations

This section describes how groundtruth data were acquired by observing real, talking faces. People where asked to read sentences, with a sufficient variety of phonemes.

For the 3D shape extraction of the talking face, we have used a 3D acquisition system that uses structured light [3]. It projects a grid onto the face, and extracts the 3D shape and texture from a single image. By using a video camera, a quick succession of 3D snapshots can be gathered. The acquisition system yields the 3D coordinates of several thousand points for every frame. The output is a triangulated, textured surface. The problem is that the 3D points correspond to projected grid intersections, not corresponding, physical points of the face. Hence, the points for which 3D coordinates are given change from frame to frame. The next steps have to solve for the physical correspondences.

1.1 Mapping the Raw Data onto a Face Topology

Our approach assumes a specific topology for the face mesh. This is a triangulated surface with 2268 vertices for the skin, supplemented with separate meshes for the eyes, teeth, and tongue (another 8848, mainly for the teeth).

The first step in this fitting procedure deforms the generic head by a simple rotation, translation, and anisotropic scaling operation, to crudely align it with the neutral shape of the example face. In order to correct for individual physiognomies, a piecewise constant vertical stretch is applied. This transformation

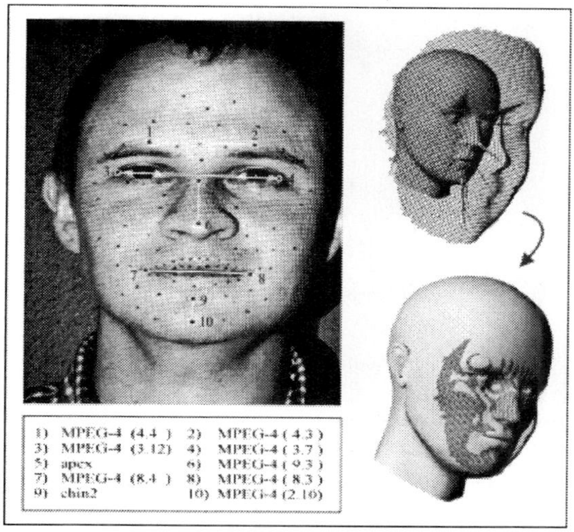

Fig. 1. A first step in the deformation of the generic head to make it fit a captured 3D face, is to globally align the two. This is done using 10 feature points indicated in dark grey in the left part of the figure. The right part shows the effect: patch and head model are brought into coarse correspondence.

minimizes the average distance between a number of special points on the example face and the model (10 points; they are indicated in black in figure 1). These have been indicated manually on the example faces, but could be extracted automatically [9]. A final adaptation of the model consists of the separation of the upper and lower lip, in order to allow the mouth to open. This first step fixes the overall shape of the head and is carried out only once (for the neutral example face). The result of such process is shown in the right column of figure 1.

The second step starts with the transformed model of the first step and performs a local morphing. This morphing maps the topology of the generic head model precisely onto the given shape. This process starts from the correspondences for a few salient points. This set includes the 10 points of the previous step, but also 106 additional points, all indicated in black in figure 2. Typically, the initial frame of the video sequence corresponds to the neutral expression. This makes a manual drag and drop operation for the 116 points rather easy. At that point all 116 points are in good correspondence. Further snapshots of the example face are no longer handled manually. From the initial frame the points are tracked automatically throughout the video, and only a limited manual interaction was necessary.

The 3D positions of the 116 points served as anchor points, to map all vertices of the generic model to the data. The result is a model with the shape and expression of the example face and with 2268 vertices at their correct positions. This mapping was achieved with the help of Radial Basis Functions.

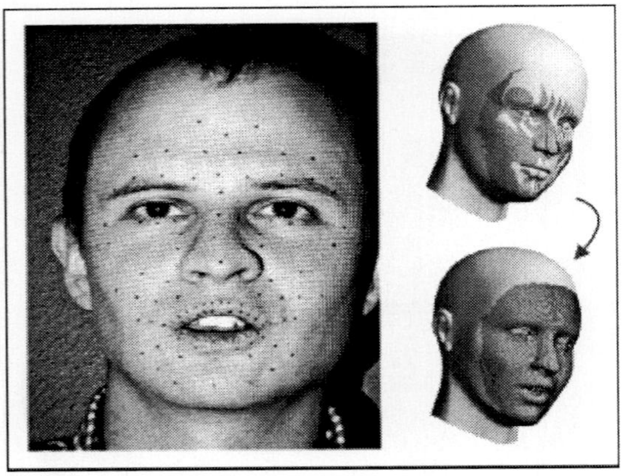

Fig. 2. To make the generic head model fit the captured face data precisely, a morphing step is applied using the 116 anchor points (black dots) and the corresponding Radial Basis Functions for guiding the remainder of the vertices. The right part of the figure shows a result.

Radial Basis Functions (RBFs) have become quite popular for face model fitting [10,9]. They offer an effective method to interpolate between a network of known correspondences. RBFs describe the influence that each of the 116 known (anchor) correspondences have on the nearby points in between in this interpolation process. Consider the following equations

$$\boldsymbol{y}_{\boldsymbol{i}_{new}} = \boldsymbol{y}_{\boldsymbol{i}} + \sum_{j=1}^{n} w_j \boldsymbol{d}_{\boldsymbol{j}} \tag{1}$$

which specify how the positions $\boldsymbol{y}_{\boldsymbol{i}}$ of the intermediate points are changed into $\boldsymbol{y}_{\boldsymbol{i}_{new}}$ under the influence of the n vertices $\boldsymbol{m}_{\boldsymbol{j}}$ of the known network (the 116 vertices in our case). The shift is determined by the weights w_j and the virtual displacements $\boldsymbol{d}_{\boldsymbol{j}}$ that are attributed to the vertices of the known network of correspondences. More about these displacements is to follow. The weights depend on the distance of the intermediate point to the known vertices:

$$w_j = h(s_j/r) \qquad s_j = \|\boldsymbol{y}_{\boldsymbol{i}} - \boldsymbol{m}_{\boldsymbol{j}}\| \tag{2}$$

for $s_j \leq r$, where r is a cut-off value for the distance beyond which h is put to zero, and where in the interval $[0, r]$ the function $h(x)$ is of one of two types:

$$h_1 = 1 - x^{log(b)/log(0.5)} \qquad b \approx 5 \tag{3}$$

$$h_2 = 2x^3 - 3x^2 + 1 \tag{4}$$

The exponential type is used at vertices with high curvature, limiting the spatial extent of their influence, whereas the hermite type is used for vertices in a region of low surface curvature, where the influence of the vertex should reach out quite far. The size of the region of influence is also determined by the scale r. Three such scales were used (for both RBF types). These scales and their spatial distribution over the face vary with the scale of the local facial structures.

A third step in the processing projects the interpolated points onto the extracted 3D surface. This is achieved via a cylindrical mapping. This mapping is not carried out for a small subset of points which lay in a cavity, however. The reason is that the acquisition system does not always produce good data in these cavities. The position of these points should be determined fully by the deformed head model, and not get degraded under the influence of the acquired data.

The interior of the mouth is part of the model, which e.g. contains the skin connecting the teeth and the interior parts of the lips. Typically, scarcely any 3D data will be captured for this region, and those that are captured tend to be of low quality. The upper row of teeth are fixed rigidly to the model and have already received their position through the first step (the global transformation of the model, possibly with a further adjustement by the user). The lower teeth follow the jaw motion, which is determined as a rotation about the midpoint between the points where the jaw is attached to the skull and a translation. The motion itself is quantified by observing the motion of a point on the chin, standardised as MPEG-4 point 2.10.

It has to be mentioned at this point that all the settings like type and size of RBF's, as well as whether vertices have to be cylindrically mapped or not, are defined only once in the generic model as attributes of its vertices.

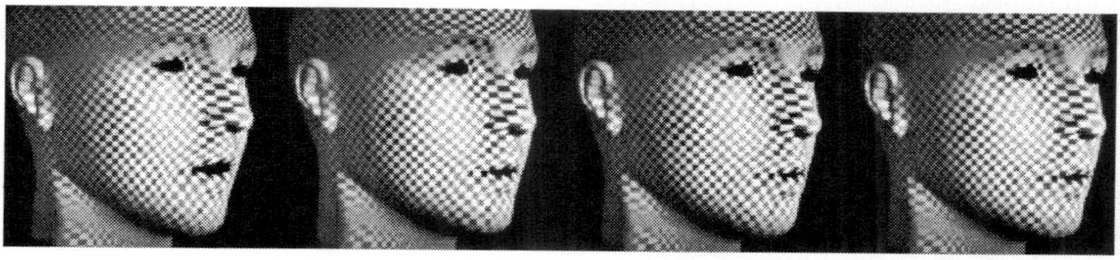

Fig. 3. Four of the sixteen Principal Components, in order of descending importance (eigenvalue).

1.2 Decomposing the Data into Their Modes

Principal Component Analysis probably is the most popular tool to analyse the relevant variability in data. A PCA analysis on the observed, 3D deformations has shown that 16 components cover 98.5% of the variation, which seems to suffice. When looking at the different Principal Components, several of them could not represent actual face deformations. Such components need to be combined with others to yield possible deformations. Unfortunately, this is difficult to illustrate with static images (Fig.3), as one would have to observe the relative motions of points. Indeed, one of the typical problems was that areas of the face would be stretched in all directions simultaneously to an extent never observed in real faces (e.g. in the cheek area).

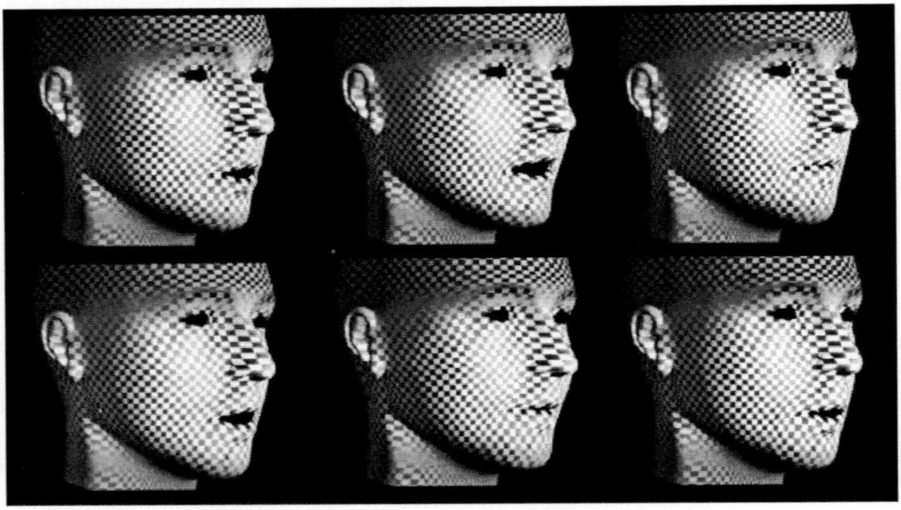

Fig. 4. Six of the sixteen Independent Components.

Independent Component Analysis (our implementation of ICA follows that propounded by Hyvärinen [2]), on the other hand, has yielded a set of modes that are each realistic in their own right. In fact, PCA is part of the ICA algorithm, and determines the degrees of freedom to be kept, in this case 16. ICA will look for modes (directions) in this PC space that correspond to linear combinations of the PCs that are maximally independent, and not only in the sense of being uncorrelated. ICA yields directions with minimal mutual information. This is mathematically related to finding combinations with distributions that are maximally non-Gaussian: as the central limit theorem makes clear, distributions of composed signals will tend to be more Gaussian than those of the underlying, original signals. The distributions of the extracted independent components came out to be quite non-Gaussian, which could clearly be observed from their χ^2 plots. This observation corroborated the usefulness of the ICA analysis from a mathematical point of view.

A face contains many muscles, and several will be active together to produce the different deformations. In as far as their joint effect can be modeled as a linear combination of their individual effects, ICA is *the* way to decouple the net effect again. Of course, this model is a bit naive, but nevertheless one would hope that ICA is able to yield a reasonable decomposition of face deformations into components that themselves are more strongly correlated with the facial anatomy than the principal components. This hope has proved not to be in vane. Fig.4 shows 6 of the 16 independent components. Each of the Independent Components would at least correspond to a facial deformation that is plausible, whereas this was not the case for the Principal Components.

Finally, on a more informal score, we found that only about one or two PCs could be easily described, e.g. 'opening the mouth'. In the case of ICs, 6 or so components could be described in simple terms. When it comes to a simple action like rounding the mouth, there was a single IC that corresponds to this effect, but in the case of PCs, this rounding is never found in isolation, but is combined with the opening of the mouth or other effects. Similar observations can be made for the other ICs and PCs.

2 Conclusions

In this paper, we have described an approach to extract groundtruth data of the biological motion corresponding to 3D facial dynamics of speech. Such data are a prerequisite for the detailed study of visual speech and its visemes. The paper also discussed the variability found in the deformation data, and it was argued that ICA seems to yield more natural and intuitive results than the more usual PCA.

Acknowledgments. This research has been supported by the ETH Research Council and the EC IST project MESH (www.meshproject.com) with the assistance of our partners Univ. Freiburg, DURAN, EPFL, EYETRONICS, and Univ. of Geneva.

References

1. Guenter B., Grimm C., Wood D., Malvar H. and Pighin F., "Making Faces", *SIGGRAPH'98 Conf. Proc.*,vol. 32, pp. 55–66, 1998.
2. Hyvärinen A., "Independent Component Analysis by minimizing of mutual information", *Technical Report A46, Helsinki University of Technology*, 1997.
3. http://www.eyetronics.com
4. Kalberer G. and Van Gool L., "Lip animation based on observed 3D speech dynamics", *SPIE Proc.*,vol. 4309, pp. 16–25, 2001.
5. Kalberer G. and Van Gool L., "Face Animation Based on Observed 3D Speech Dynamics" *Computer Animation 2001. Proc.*, pp. 20–27, 2001.
6. Kshirsagar S., Molet T. and Magnenat-Thalmann N., "Principal components of expressive speech animation", *Computer Graphics Int. Proc.*, pp. 38–44, 2001.
7. Lin I., Yeh J. and Ouhyoung M., "Realistic 3D Facial Animation Parameters from Mirror-reflected Multi-view Video", *Computer Animation 2001 Conf. Proc.*, pp. 2–11, 2001.
8. Massaro D. W., "Perceiving Talking Faces", *MIT. Press*, 1998.
9. Noh J. and Neumann U., "Expression Cloning", *SIGGRAPH'01 Conf. Proc.*, pp. 277–288, 2001.
10. Pighin F., Hecker J., Lischinski D., Szeliski R. and Salesin D., "Synthesizing Realistic Facial Expressions from Photographs", *SIGGRAPH'98 Conf. Proc.*, pp. 75–84, 1998.

11. Reveret L., Bailly G. and Badin P., "MOTHER, A new generation of talking heads providing a flexible articulatory control for videorealistic speech animation", *ICSL'00 Proc.*, 2000.
12. Rosenblum, L.D. and Saldaña, H.M, "Time-varying information for visual speech perception", In *Hearing by Eye*,vol. 2, pp. 61–81, ed. Campbell R., Dodd B. and Burnham D.,1998.

Object Perception: Generative Image Models and Bayesian Inference

Daniel Kersten

Psychology Department, University of Minnesota
75 East River Road,
Minneapolis, Minnesota, 55455
U.S.A.
kersten@umn.edu
http://kersten.org

Abstract. Humans perceive object properties such as shape and material quickly and reliably despite the complexity and objective ambiguities of natural images. The visual system does this by integrating prior object knowledge with critical image features appropriate for each of a discrete number of tasks. Bayesian decision theory provides a prescription for the optimal utilization of knowledge for a task that can guide the possibly sub-optimal models of human vision. However, formulating optimal theories for realistic vision problems is a non-trivial problem, and we can gain insight into visual inference by first characterizing the causal structure of image features–the generative model. I describe some experimental results that apply generative models and Bayesian decision theory to investigate human object perception.

1 Object Surface Interactions

Consider a collection of objects in a scene. Given an image of their surfaces, one can ask many questions: Do the surfaces belong to the same object? If part of the same object, how are they oriented with respect to each other? If separate, is one occluding the other? Are they in contact? How far apart? What kind of materials are they made of? What color? Answers to each of these questions requires the definition of a visual task. Task definition declares some variables more useful than others, and thus which need to be made explicit and accurately estimated. When the visual system answers these questions, it has solved a complex inference problem. We better understand the nature of visual ambiguity and its resolution by first considering how image features are generated through the combination and interaction of potentially useful scene variables (e.g. object shape) with other scene variables that may be less useful (e.g. illumination direction). Generative models help to identify the key information used by human visual perception, and thus provide a basis for modeling vision as Bayesian statistical inference [27,16,34].

Modeling the image formation or generative process makes explicit the causal structure of image features. Identifying causal influences on the image is typically

H.H. Bülthoff et al. (Eds.): BMCV 2002, LNCS 2525, pp. 207–218, 2002.

well-defined, and thus easier than the inverse problem of inference. A generative model helps to make clear where the ambiguities lie, and set the stage for psychophysical inquiry into what variables are important to human vision, as well as to identify and simplify the constraints needed to solve the computational inverse problem [27]. Generative models describe the probability of an image description I, as a function of key causal factors in the scene S. Both knowledge of image formation, $p(I|S)$, and prior knowledge $p(S)$ contribute to the generative model. Such a model can be either image-based or scene-based (cf. [35] and [13]). Image-based models seek concise statistical descriptions of an image ensemble (e.g. all images of apples). Examples include texture models [32] and 2D shape models in terms of deformable templates [10]. Scene-based models describe image ensembles in terms of scene constructions, using computer graphics [6]. In either case, a generative model identifies the factors that characterize image variability, making it possible to experimentally test which ones are important for a human visual task. We describe experimental results from several scene-based models in the examples below.

I will next provide an overview of vision as statistical inference, focusing on three classes of problems: invariance, cue integration, and perceptual "explaining away". Then I will illustrate each of these with psychophysical results on: 1) Perception of depth and color given illumination variation; 2) Perception of surface contact; and 3) Perceptual organization given occlusion. Finally, I address the question of whether the visual brain may recapitulate aspects of the generative model in order to test its own models of incoming visual measurements.

2 Invariance, Cue Integration, & "Explaining Away"

From a Bayesian perspective, knowledge is specified in terms of a joint probability distribution on all relevant variables, both image measurements and object variables. It is helpful to characterize object inference problems in terms of a graph that illustrates how image measurements are influenced by the object hypotheses [29,30]. Many object perception studies fall into one of three simple sub-cases which will here be referred to as invariance, cue integration, and "explaining away" (Figure 1). The generative model expressed by the graph can be interpreted as specifying how the joint probability is factored into the conditional probabilities[1].

[1] If I_i and S_j indicate the ith and j^{th} image and object variables respectively, then $p(..., I_i ..., S_j, ...)$ is the joint probability. Invariance, cue integration and the explaining away example have joints: $p(I_1, S_1, S_2)$, $p(I_1, I_2, S_1)$ and $P(I_1, I_2, S_1, S_2)$. The influence relations simplify the joint probability distributions:

$$p(I, S_1, S_2) = p(I|S_1, S_2)p(S_1)p(S_2)$$

$$p(I_1, I_2, S_1) = p(I_1, I_2|S_1)p(S_1) \; and$$
$$p(I_1, I_2, S_1, S_2) = p(I_2|S_2)p(I_1|S_1, S_2)p(S_1)p(S_2)$$

The task definition adds additional constraints to the estimation problem in specifying which nodes are fixed measurements (black), which are variables to be estimated (green), and which are confounding variables to be discounted (red; See Figure 1). Discounting can be formalized with a utility function (or its complement, a loss function). Visual ambiguity is often reduced by auxiliary measurements (yellow node) that may be available in a given image, or actively sought. These auxiliary measurements may provide diagnostic information regarding a confounding variable, and as a consequence help to explain away ambiguity in another image measurement that pertains more directly to the useful target variable of interest. "Explaining away" refers to the case when new or auxiliary evidence under-cuts an earlier explanation [26].

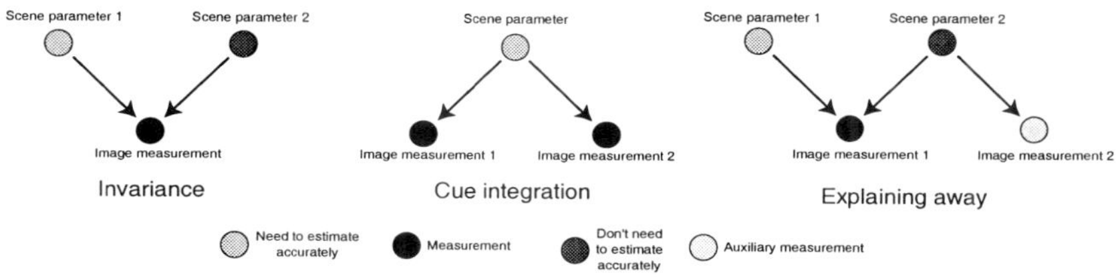

Fig. 1. Graphs for three classes of generative models. The nodes represent random variables that fall into four classes. The variables may be: 1) known (black); 2) unknown and need to be estimated accurately (green); 3) unknown, but do not need to be explicitly and accurately estimated (red); 4) not directly influenced by the object variable of interest, but may be useful for resolving ambiguity (yellow). The arrows indicate how scene or object properties influence image measurements or features. Left panel illustrates a causal structure that gives rise to the invariance problem. (See Section 2.1.) Middle panel illustrates cue integration (See Section 2.2). Right panel illustrates a case that can lead to "explaining away" (See Sections 2.3 and 3).

Bayesian decision theory combines probability with task requirements to derive quantitative, optimal theories of perceptual inference [15,8,3]. Human perception is often surprisingly close to optimal, thus such "ideal observer" theories provide a good starting point for models of human vision [8]. The basic concepts are illustrated with a simple example in Figure 2. A flat elliptical object in 3D projects an ellipse onto the image. One can measure the aspect ratio of the image of the ellipse. This information constrains, but does not uniquely determine the aspect ratio of the ellipse in the three-dimensional world. A unique estimate can be made that depends on combining prior knowledge and task utility assumptions. A special case assumes there is a uniform cost to all errors in the estimates of the confounding variable (the green bar in Figure 2 would span the whole space in one direction). This case corresponds to marginalizing or integrating out the confounding variable from the posterior probability $p(S_1, S_2|I_1)$. So for example, inference in the invariance case requires finding the value of *s*cene parameter 1 (S_1) that maximizes: $\int_{S_2} p(I_1|S_1, S_2)p(S_1)p(S_2)/p(I_1)dS_2$, where scene parameter 2 (S_2) is the confounding variable, and I_1 is the image feature.

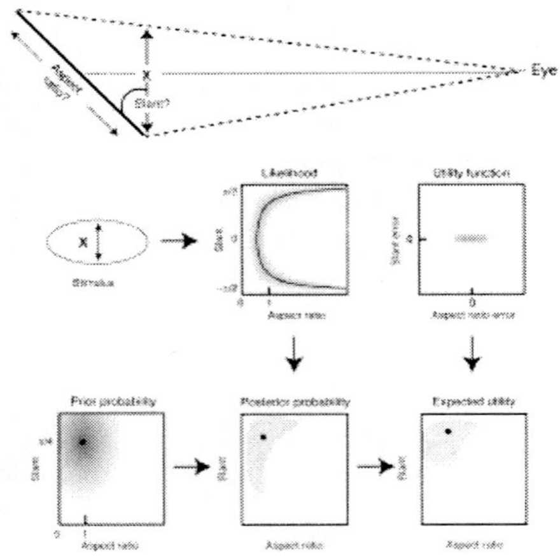

Fig. 2. Example of applying Bayesian theory to the problem of estimating the slant α and *aspect ratio d in 3D* of a flat ellipse, given x *the aspect ratio measured in the image*. The generative model $x = dsin(\alpha) + noise$ is well-defined and tells us how scene variables determine an image measurement x. Generative knowledge determines the likelihood function $p(x|\alpha, d)$. The Bayesian observer first computes the likelihood of stimulus x for each pair of scene values α, d. The solid black curves in the likelihood plot show the combinations of slant and aspect ratio that are exactly consistent with with the generative model if there were no noise. Non-zero likelihoods occur because of noise in the measurement of x. The Bayesian observer then multiplies the likelihood function by the prior probability distribution for each pair of scene values to obtain the posterior probability distribution, $p(\alpha, d|x)$. The prior probability distribution corresponds to the assumption that surface patches tend to be slanted away at the top and have aspect ratios closer to 1.0. Accuracy along some dimensions can be more important than along other dimensions depending on the task. For example, recognizing a a particular tea-cup could require accurate estimation of aspect ratio of the top, but not the slant with respect to the viewpoint. In this case slant is the confounding variable. On the other hand, stepping on to a flat stone requires accurate estimation of the slant, but not the aspect ratio. Thus, the 3D aspect ratio is the confounding variable. To take task-dependence into account, the posterior probability distribution is convolved with a utility function, representing the costs and benefits of degrees of accuracy, to obtain the expected utility associated with each interpretation. The Bayesian decision theory observer picks the interpretation that maximizes the expected utility, as indicated by the black dot in the lower right panel. (Black dots and curves indicate the maximum values in the plots.) The asymmetric utility function would correspond to the assumption that it is more important to have an accurate estimate of slant than aspect ratio. Figure reprinted with permission ?? from Nature Neuroscience.

2.1 Invariance: Discounting Confounding Variables

How does the visual system enable us to infer the same object despite considerable image variation due to viewpoint, illumination, occlusion, and background changes? This is the well-known problem of invariance, or object constancy. Here the target variable is constant, but the image measurements vary as a function of variations in the confounding variable (Left panel of Figure 1). Confounding variables play the role of "noise" in classical signal detection theory; however, the generative modeling is typically more complex (as illustrated by 3D computer graphics synthesis), and the formal inference problem can be complex involving high dimensions, non-Gaussian distributions, and non-linear estimators. Illumination variation is perhaps the most dominant source of variation for the tasks of vision. Let's look at illumination variation in the context of two tasks, depth and material perception.

Illumination variation. The vagaries of illumination generate enormous variations in the images of an object. Typically illumination results from an infinite number of point sources, both direct (luminous) and indirect (reflected). Illumination varies in dominant direction, level, spatio-temporal distribution, and spectral content. Further, it interacts with surface properties to produce complex effects of specular reflection. These are confounding variables for many of the tasks of object perception.

How far apart are two objects?. Cast shadows are an effective cue for relative depth [22], despite ambiguity between relative depth between the casting object and the background, and light source angle. At first one might guess that the visual system requires accurate knowledge of the lighting arrangement in order to estimate depth from shadows. However, if one assumes that there is uniform cost to errors in light source slant estimates, decision theory analysis can predict, based on the geometry alone that cast shadows should be most reliable when near the object, and that the"optimal" estimate of object location is that it is as far from the background as the shadow is from the object [14].

What is the material color of an object?. Color constancy has been studied for well over a century. Everyday variations in the spectral content, levels, and gradients of the illuminant have relatively little effect on our perception of surface color. One way of formalizing the problem is to understand how the objective surface invariant, surface reflectivity, can be estimated given variations in illumination [3]. Most such studies have been restricted to the perception of material color or lightness on flat surfaces with no illumination contributions from neighboring surfaces. Bloj, Kersten, and Hurlbert [1] showed that color perception is influenced by the 3D arrangement of a nearby surface. They constructed a chromatic version of the classic Mach Card (Figure 3). With it, they showed that a white surface appears white when its pinkish tinge can be explained in terms of a near facing red surface, but appears pigmented pink when the red surface appears to be facing away. The experimental results showed that the human visual system has intrinsic knowledge of mutual illumination or inter-reflections–i.e. how the color of light from near-by surfaces can confound image measurements. A Bayesian ideal observer that has generative knowledge of indirect lighting and that integrates out contributions from illumination direction predicted the central features of the psychophysical data and demonstrated that this shape-color contingency arises because the visual system "understands" the effects of mutual illumination [1,7] [2].

2.2 Cue Integration

Cue integration is a well-known problem in perceptual psychology. For example, one can identify over a dozen cues that the human visual system utilizes for depth perception. In computer vision and signal processing, cue integration is studied under the more general rubric of "sensor fusion" [2]. There has been recent interest in the degree to which the human visual system combines image measurements optimally. For example, given two conflicting cues to depth, the visual system might get by with a simple averaging of each estimate, even though inaccurate. Or it may determine that one measurement is an outlier, and should not be integrated with the other measurement [17,4]. The visual system could be more sophisticated and combine image measurements weighted according to their reliability [12,33]. These issues have their roots in classical questions of information integration for signal detectability, e.g. probability vs. information summation [9]. Even when we do not have a specific idea of what image information vision uses when integrating cues, we can sometimes investigate the information in terms of the scene variables that contribute. So while

---

[2] The Bayesian calculation goes as follows. The target variable of interest is the reflectivity ($S_1 = \rho$) (measured in units of chroma). The likelihood is determined by either a one-bounce (corner) or zero-bounce generative model (roof condition) of illumination. Assume that the shape is fixed by the stereo disparity, i.e. condition on shape (*roof or corner*). From the one-bounce model, the intensity equation for white pigmented side (surface 1) is:

$$I_1(\lambda, x, \rho, E, \alpha_1, \alpha_2) = E(\lambda)\rho_1 * (\lambda)[cos\alpha_1 + f_{21}\rho_2(\lambda)cos\alpha_2]$$

where the first term represents the direct illumination with respect to the surface and the second term represents indirect illumination due to light reflected from the red side (surface 2) [5]. $f_{21}(x)$ is the form factor describing the extent to which surface 2 reflects light onto surface 1 at distance x from the vertex [6]. The angles α_1 and α_2 denote the angle between the surface normal and the light source direction for surfaces 1 and 2 respectively. $E(\lambda)$ is the irradiance as a function of wavelength λ For the zero-bounce generative model (roof condition), the form factor $f_{21} = 0$, so that:

$$I_1(\lambda, x, \rho, E, \alpha) = E(\lambda)\rho_1 * (\lambda)cos\alpha_1$$

These generative models determine the likelihood functions. Observers do not directly measure I_1, but rather chroma C_{obs}, modeled by the capture of light by the retinal cones. When an observer is asked to match the surface color to the ith test patch, the optimal decision is based on $P(\rho_1^i|C_{obs})$, which is obtained by integrating out x and the confounding variable α from $p(C_{obs}|\rho^i, x, \alpha, E)$. To a first approximation, observers' matches were predicted well by an observer which is ideal apart from an internal matching variability. For more details see [1,31].

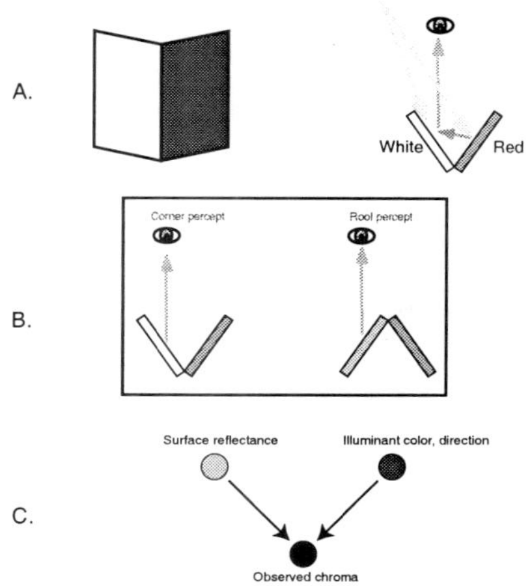

Fig. 3. A. The "colored Mach card" consists of a white and red half [1]. It is folded such that the sides face each other. The viewer's task is to determine the material color of the white side, given the viewing and illumination arrangement illustrated. B. If the card's shape is seen as it truly is (a concave "corner"), the white side is seen as a white card, tinted slightly pink from the reflected red light. However, if the shape of the card *appears* as though the sides face away from each other (convex or "roof" condition), the white card appears pink–i.e. more saturated towards the red. Note that there may be little or no difference in the image information for these two percepts. C. The black, green and red nodes represent an image measurement (e.g. pinkishness), a scene hypothesis (is the material's spectral reflectivity closer to that of white or pink pigmented paper?), and a confounding variable (illumination direction), respectively. See Section 2.1).

a quantitative description of the relevant image measurements may be lacking, this approach has the advantage of using realistic images. Further, even without an objective formulation of the problem and its ideal observer, psychophysics can provide insights into how well cues are integrated. This is illustrated in the following example.

Are two surfaces in contact?. Surface contact decisions are a special case of relative depth estimation, whose effects in the image are the result of surface and illumination interactions as discussed earlier in Section 2.1. Determining whether or not two surfaces are in contact is a common visual function, useful for deciding whether the surfaces belong to an object, or if an object is detachable or graspable. What is the visual information for the perception of surface contact? The interaction of light with surfaces in close proximity results in characteristic shadows as well as in surface inter-reflections. Inter-reflections and shadows can each potentially provide information about object contact (Figure 4). Psychophysical measurements of contact judgments show that human observers combine image information from shadows with inter-reflections to achieve higher sensitivity than when only shadows or inter-reflections are present [21].

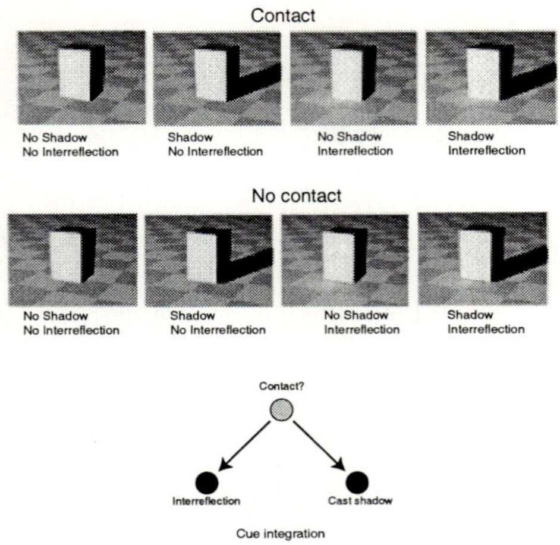

Fig. 4. A. Computer generated images of a box on an extended textured ground plane that was either in contact with the ground plane or slightly above it [21]. Images were rendered for four conditions: 1) no shadow plus no inter-reflection, 2) shadow only, 3) inter-reflection only, and 4) shadow plus inter-reflection. Observers were required to judge the degree of contact for each image. In the images with no shadow or inter-reflections, observers performed at chance. Inter-reflections, shadows, and a combination of inter-reflections and shadows all resulted in a high sensitivity for judging object contact. Information from shadows and inter-reflections was combined to result in near-perfect judgement of surface contact. B. The graphical structure for the cue integration problem. The green node represents an hypothesis of contact or not, and the black nodes image measurements or evidence (i.e. the image effects of a cast shadow and/or mutual illumination. Figure adapted with permission ?? from Perception & Psychophysics.

2.3 "Explaining Away"

Different scene variables can give rise to different kinds of image measurements. Conversely, different image measurements in the same, or subsequently acquired images (e.g. fixations), can be differentially diagnostic regarding their causes in terms of object properties. The generative model can provide insights into what information should, in principle, help to disambiguate hypotheses regarding the properties of a target object.

Object color, shape and mutual illumination revisited. We illustrate perceptual "explaining away" by revisiting the colored Mach card of Figure 3. Because of the ambiguity of perspective, a rigid folded card can appear as concave or convex from a fixed viewpoint. Stereo disparity can provide reliable information for one or the other shape interpretations. When this happens, the shape hypothesis changes with the surface material hypothesis in explaining the pinkish tinge of the observed white pigmented card face as shown in Figure 5. Examples of this type of inference occur more generally in the context of Bayes networks [29]. The relevant concepts are also related to the idea of "strong fusion" [2].

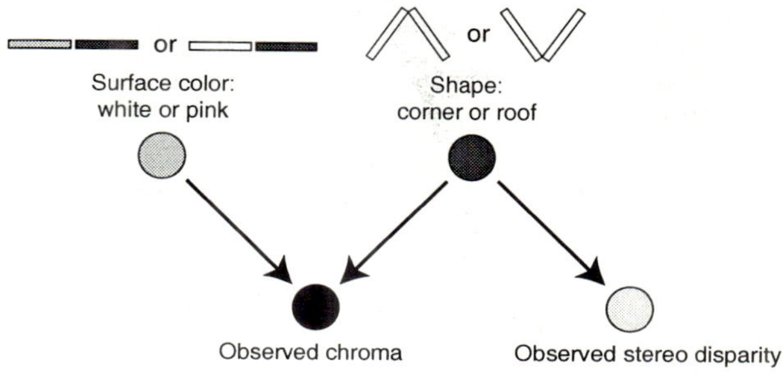

Fig. 5. Illustrates "explaining away" (Sections 2.3 and 3). One hypothesis (pink paint) may explain a "pinkish" image chroma measurement, but another hypothesis (nearby red surface) could also explain the pinkish chroma, but in terms of indirect reddish illumination. An auxiliary image measurement (yellow node, disparity indicating a concave relationship between a white and red surface) could tip the balance, and the joint hypothesis "concave white-red card" could explain both image measurements with high probability. The pink pigment hypothesis is no longer probable.

There are many examples where explaining away does not work in human perception, and we may ultimately gain more insight into the mechanisms of vision from these cases. Mamassian et al. (1998) describe an example where a pencil that casts a shadow over a folded card fails to disambiguate the shape of the card, resulting in physically inconsistent perceptions of the shadow and geometry [22].

3 Perceptual "Explaining Away" in the Brain?

The primate visual system is composed of a hierarchy of more than thirty visual areas, pairs of which communicate through both feedforward and feedback connections. A possible role for higher-level visual areas may be to represent hypotheses regarding object properties that could be used to resolve ambiguities in the incoming retinal image measurements. These hypotheses could predict incoming data through feedback and be tested by computing a difference signal or residual at the earlier level [24,28]. Thus, low activity at an early level would mean a "good fit" or explanation of the image measurements. One way of testing this idea is to use fMRI to compare the activity of early areas for good and bad fits given the same incoming retinal signal.

Consider the problem of perceiving a moving occluded diamond as shown in Figure 6A. The four moving line segments can appear to cohere as parts of a single horizontally translating diamond or can appear to have separate vertical motions [19]. In order to perceive a moving object as a whole, the brain must measure local image features (motion direction and speed), select those likely to belong to the same object, and integrate these measurements to resolve the local ambiguity in velocity [33]. The selection process involves choosing which of the four segments belong together, and this in turn is closely tied to the

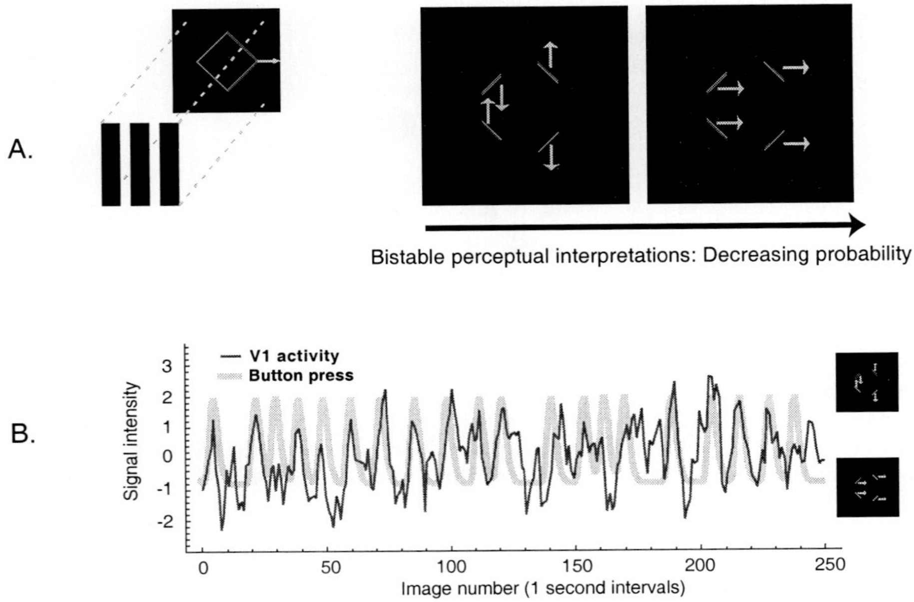

Fig. 6. A. Occluded view of a translating diamond generates ambiguous perceptual interpretations. The diamond's vertices are covered by black occluders so that an observer sees just four moving line segments [19,20]. The perception is bistable: the four segments appear to be moving in different vertical directions, or to cohere as part of a horizontally moving diamond. B. fMRI activity in human V1 (red) predicts an observer's reported perceptual state (thick gray lines). Further, fMRI activity *d*ecreases when the segments are perceived to be part of a single object. A similar pattern of results is found for other manipulations [25]. These findings are consistent with predictive coding models of vision in which the inferences of higher-level visual areas inhibit incoming sensory signals in earlier areas through cortical feedback.

visual system accounting for the missing vertices as due to occlusion. Neurons in primary visual area V1 have spatially localized receptive fields selective for edge orientation and motion direction. A good fit to incoming data would occur when all four contour segments are perceptually grouped as a diamond. This happens when the segments appear to move horizontally in synchrony for the horizontally moving diamond percept. However, when the line segments appear to move separately or have other multiple groupings, the apparent movement of the segments not grouped is poorly predicted, resulting in a poorer fit to the local measurements in V1.

Experiments showed that when observers viewed the bistable stimulus of Figure 6A, fMRI BOLD activity in V1 *decreased* when the segments were perceived to be part of a single object. Further, in other experiments, the BOLD response to visual elements that appeared either to be grouped into objects or incoherently arranged showed reductions of activity in V1 when elements formed coherent shapes (See Figure 6; [25]). One might further conjecture that activation in higher-level areas should show the opposite direction of activity change. The lateral occipital complex (LOC) is a higher level object processing area that has received considerable recent attention [18,11]. Measurements here showed increases in LOC activity were concurrent with reductions of activity in primary visual cortex (V1) when elements formed coherent shapes [25]. These results are consistent with the idea that activity in early visual areas may be reduced as a result of object hypotheses represented in higher areas.

In a general sense, feedback between visual areas may be the internal recapitulation of the external generative processes that give rise to the images received.

References

1. Bloj, M. G., Kersten, D., & Hurlbert, A. C. (1999). Perception of three-dimensional shape influences colour perception via mutual illumination. *Nature*, **402**, 877-879.
2. Clark, J. J., & Yuille, A. L. (1990). Data Fusion for Sensory Information Processing. Boston: Kluwer Academic Publishers.
3. Brainard, D. H., & Freeman, W. T. (1997). Bayesian color constancy. *J Opt Soc Am A*, **14**, (7), 1393-411.
4. Bülthoff, H. H., & Mallot, H. A. (1988). Integration of depth modules: stereo and shading. *Journal of the Optical Society of America, A*, **5**, (10), 1749-1758.
5. Drew, M., & Funt, B. (1990). Calculating surface reflectance using a single-bounce model of mutual reflection. *Proceedings of the 3rd International Conference on Computer Vision* Osaka: 393-399.
6. Foley, J., van Dam, A., Feiner, S., & Hughes, J. (1990). Computer Graphics Principles and Practice, (2nd ed.). Reading, Massachusetts: Addison-Wesley Publishing Company.
7. Gegenfurtner, K. R. (1999). Reflections on colour constancy. *Nature*, **402**, 855-856.
8. Geisler, W. S., & Kersten, D. (2002). Illusions, perception and Bayes. *Nat Neurosci*, **5**, (6), 508-10.
9. Green, D. M., & Swets, J. A. (1974). Signal Detection Theory and Psychophysics. Huntington, New York: Robert E. Krieger Publishing Company. 1974.
10. Grenander, U. (1996). Elements of Pattern theory. Baltimore: Johns Hopkins University Press.
11. Grill-Spector, K., Kourtzi, Z., & Kanwisher, N. (2001). The lateral occipital complex and its role in object recognition. *Vision Res*, **41**, (10-11), 1409-22.
12. Jacobs, R. A. (2002). "What determines visual cue reliability?" Trends Cogn Sci 6(8): 345-350.
13. Kersten, D. (1997). Inverse 3D Graphics: A Metaphor for Visual Perception. *Behavior Research Methods, Instruments, & Computers*, **29**, (1), 37-46.
14. Kersten, D. (1999). High-level vision as statistical inference. In Gazzaniga, M. S. (Ed.), *The New Cognitive Neurosciences – 2nd Edition*(pp. 353-363). Cambridge, MA: MIT Press.
15. Kersten, D., & Schrater, P. R. (2002). Pattern Inference Theory: A Probabilistic Approach to Vision. In Mausfeld, R.,& Heyer, D. (Ed.), *Perception and the Physical World* (pp. Chichester: John Wiley& Sons, Ltd.
16. Knill, D. C., & Richards, W. (1996). Perception as Bayesian Inference. Cambridge: Cambridge University Press.

17. Landy, M. S., Maloney, L. T., Johnston, E. B., & Young, M. J. (1995). Measurement and modeling of depth cue combination: In defense of weak fusion. *Vision Research*, **35**, 389-412.
18. Lerner, Y., Hendler, T., & Malach, R. (2002). Object-completion Effects in the Human Lateral Occipital Complex. *Cereb Cortex*, **12**, (2), 163-77.
19. Lorenceau, J., & Shiffrar, M. (1992). The influence of terminators on motion integration across space. *Vision Res*, **32**, (2), 263-73.
20. Lorenceau, J., & Alais, D. (2001). Form constraints in motion binding. *Nat Neurosci*, **4**, (7), 745-51.
21. Madison, C., Thompson, W., Kersten, D., Shirley, P., & Smits, B. (2001). Use of interreflection and shadow for surface contact. *Perception and Psychophysics*, **63**, (2), 187-194.
22. Mamassian, P., Knill, D. C., & Kersten, D. (1998). The Perception of Cast Shadows. *Trends in Cognitive Sciences*, **2**, (8), 288-295.
23. McDermott, J., Weiss, Y., & Adelson, E. H. (2001). Beyond junctions: nonlocal form constraints on motion interpretation. *Perception*, **30**, (8), 905-23.
24. Mumford, D. (1992). On the computational architecture of the neocortex. II. The role of cortico-cortical loops. *Biol Cybern*, **66**, (3), 241-51.
25. Murray, S. O., Kersten, D, Olshausen, B. A., Schrater P., & Woods, D.L. (Under review) Shape perception reduces activity in human primary visual cortex. Submitted to the *Proceedings of the National Academy of Sciences.*
26. Pearl, J. (1988). Probabilistic reasoning in intelligent systems : networks of plausible inference, (Rev. 2nd printing. ed.). San Mateo, Calif.: Morgan Kaufmann Publishers.
27. Poggio, T., Torre, V., & Koch, C. (1985). Computational vision and regularization theory. *Nature*, **317**, 314-319.
28. Rao, R. P., & Ballard, D. H. (1999). Predictive coding in the visual cortex: a functional interpretation of some extra-classical receptive-field effects [see comments]. *Nat Neurosci*, **2**, (1), 79-87.
29. Ripley, B. . Pattern Recognition and Neural Networks. Cambridge University Press. 1996.
30. Schrater, P. R., & Kersten, D. (2000). How optimal depth cue integration depends on the task. *International Journal of Computer Vision*, **40**, (1), 73-91.
31. Schrater, P., & Kersten, D. (2001). Vision, Psychophysics, and Bayes. In Rao, R. P. N., Olshausen, B. A., & Lewicki, M. S. (Ed.), *Probabilistic Models of the Brain: Perception and Neural Function*(pp. Cambridge, Massachusetts: MIT Press.
32. Simoncelli, E. P. (1997). Statistical Models for Images: Compression, Restoration and Synthesis. Pacific Grove, CA.: IEEE Signal Processing Society.
33. Weiss, Y., Simoncelli, E. P., & Adelson, E. H. (2002). Motion illusions as optimal percepts. *Nat Neurosci*, **5**, (6), 598-604.
34. Yuille, A. L., & Bülthoff, H. H. (1996). Bayesian decision theory and psychophysics. In D.C., K., & W., R. (Ed.), *Perception as Bayesian Inference*(pp. Cambridge, U.K.: Cambridge University Press.
35. Zhu, S.C., Wu, Y., and Mumford, D. (1997). "Minimax Entropy Principle and Its Application to Texture Modeling". Neural Computation. **9**(8).

The Role of Propagation and Medial Geometry in Human Vision

Benjamin Kimia and Amir Tamrakar

LEMS, Brown University, Providence RI 02912, USA
kimia@lems.brown.edu,
Amir_Tamrakar@brown.edu

Abstract. A key challenge underlying theories of vision is how the spatially restricted, retinotopically represented feature computations can be integrated to form abstract, coordinate-free object models. A resolution likely depends on the use of intermediate-level representations which can on the one hand be populated by local features and on the other hand be used as atomic units underlying the formation of, and interaction with, object hypotheses. The precise structure of this intermediate representation derives from the varied requirements of a range of visual tasks, which motivate a significant role for incorporating a *geometry of visual form*. The need to integrate input from features capturing surface properties such as texture, shading, motion, color, *etc.*, as well as from features capturing surface discontinuities such as silhouettes, T-junctions, *etc.*, implies a geometry which captures both regional and boundary aspects. Curves, as a geometric model of boundaries, have been extensively and explicitly used as an intermediate representation in computational, perceptual, and physiological studies. However, the *medial axis* which has been popular in computer vision as a geometric region-based model of the interior of closed boundaries, has not been explicitly used as an intermediate representation. We present a unified theory of perceptual grouping and object recognition where the intermediate representation is a *visual fragment* which itself is based on the medial axis. Through various sequences of transformations of the medial axis representation, visual fragments are grouped in various configurations to form object hypotheses, and are related to stored models. The mechanisms underlying both the computation and the transformation of the medial axis is a lateral *wave propagation* model. Recent psychophysical experiments depicting contrast sensitivity map peaks at the medial axes of stimuli, and experiments on perceptual filling-in, and brightness induction and modulation, are consistent with both the use of a medial axis representation and a propagation-based scheme. Also, recent neurophysiological recordings in V1 correlate with the medial axis hypothesis and a horizontal propagation scheme. This evidence supports a geometric computational paradigm for processing sensory data where both dynamic in-plane propagation and feedforward-feedback connections play an integral role.

1 Introduction

Despite the tremendous progress in computer vision in the last three decades, the fact is that the only working general purpose vision system is the biological one. Thus, it

H.H. Bülthoff et al. (Eds.): BMCV 2002, LNCS 2525, pp. 219–229, 2002.

would seem natural for the designers of a computer vision system to closely examine biological systems for guiding principles. Beyond the clear benefits underlying the use of a working system as a model, that the basic concepts used in computational vision paradigm, *e.g.*, texture and color, are thoroughly ingrained in our perceptual mechanisms, are based on our neural machinery, and are without direct physical correlates argues for an even stronger statement: designers of vision systems must ultimately be concerned with and address biological vision [1] On the other hand, it can also be equally argued that researchers in biological vision must explicitly take into account a computational paradigm in their interpretation of perceptual and neurophysiological data. To illustrate this, consider the task of mapping the functional role of an electronic component in a modern PC using only end-to-end behavior (perception), electrical recordings (neurophysiology), evident connections (neuroanatomy), *etc.* Without postulating an explicit computational paradigm involving notions of bits and bytes, words, pointers, and linked lists, an understanding gained through these means is incomplete [15]. A simultaneous effort involving both computational and biological paradigms is therefore required.

The simultaneous view we present here concerns the notions of **propagation** and the **medial axis**. First, from a computational perspective, we will argue that the need to integrate local features into global percepts, the need for bottom-up as well as top-down communication in visual processing, and the duality of contour-based and surface-based nature of early visual measurements motivate the use of an intermediate-level representation that encodes the **geometry** of objects in a visual scene and their spatial relationships. Further, the medial axis represents this geometry well and we will show that it can be used for figure-ground segregation, object recognition, categorization, navigation, *etc.* The medial axis can be computed by horizontal wave propagation [26] and can be transformed by propagation as well. Second, from a perceptual perspective, brightness filling-in [17], brightness induction [4] and brightness modulation [16] are consistent with the idea of propagation while bisection, point separation discrimination, and contrast sensitivity enhancement phenomena point to a medial representation. Third, from a neurophysiological perspective, the onset latency of intracellular recordings reveal a roughly linear relationship with distance, suggesting propagation [3]; optical imaging [8] as well as LFP recordings using multi-electrode arrays show spreading activity over large distances from the site of the stimulus. Recent neurophysiological recordings in V1 [14] show heightened responses at texture boundaries as well as at medial locations, thus, correlating with the medial axis hypothesis and a horizontal propagation scheme. Such a simultaneous view of three mutually constraining perspectives support the notion of propagation and the medial axis as basic elements of computation in the visual cortex.

2 Intermediate Representation: Medial Axis and Propagation

Theories of visual processing, whether focused on computational implementation, perception, or neurophysiology, face a grand challenge in bridging a large representation gap

[1] Note that this strong statement pertains to a general purpose vision system where the relevance of visual constructs is dictated by the human visual system. Clearly, special purpose vision systems, *e.g.*, for industrial inspection, can be considered as problems isolated from the human visual system.

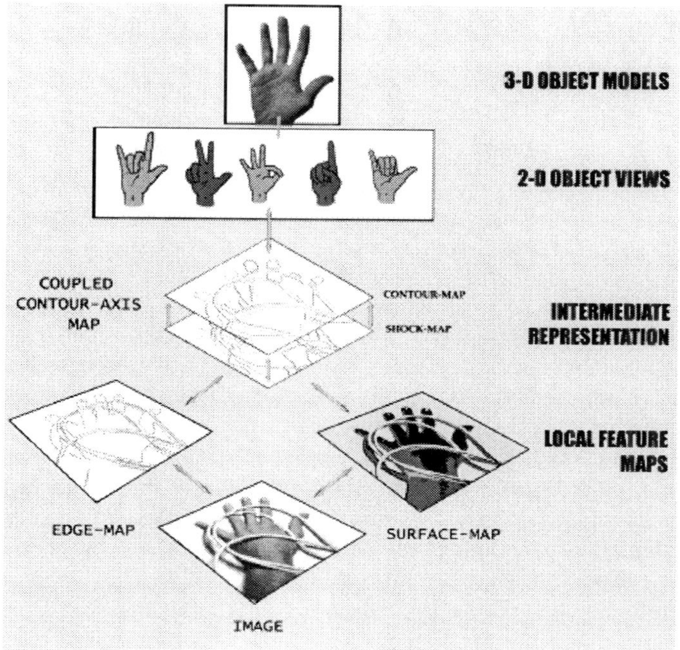

Fig. 1. The proposed representation and computational paradigm

between low-level, retinotopic feature maps bound to image coordinates, and high-level object-centered descriptions. Three decades of computer vision research has cast doubt on the feasibility of models that rely solely on bottom-up schemes (figure-ground segmentation followed by recognition) or solely on top-down schemes (matching projected object models directly) for general purpose vision. There is, in fact, ample evidence that figure-ground segregation does not necessarily precede object recognition [6,14]. Rather, a framework involving simultaneous figure-ground segregation and recognition is much more appropriate: the recognition of a partially segregated region of an object can identify potentially relevant models which then can in turn be verified by comparison to low-level features. The assertion that figure-ground segregation and recognition must necessarily be accomplished simultaneously requires an intense bottom-up *and* top-down flow of information between low-level retinal maps and high-level object models.

This argument not only motivates the need for an intermediate-level structure, but it also dictates an optimal form for it. Since the early visual features, either region-based or contour-based, are ambiguous and noisy, a common intermediate representation must be employed that can interact with *both* partially organized blobs of homogeneous areas and partially grouped contour segments of edge elements, Figure 1. The intermediate-level representation must, therefore, be capable of (i) working with properties of the interior of an object, *e.g.*, texture, shading, color, *etc.*, (ii) relating regional fragments of an object to the entire object, (iii) working with the properties of the bounding and

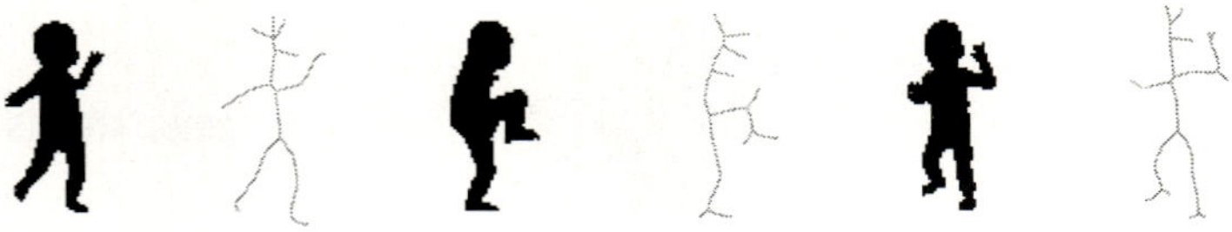

Fig. 2. These figure-sticks or skeletons are computed by the wave propagation and shock detection models. They can be also encode surface information when computed from gray scale or color images.

internal contours of a shape, and (iv) relating *contour fragments* of an object silhouette to the entire silhouette.

Curves have been used predominantly in computer vision as the intermediate structure, for both figure-ground segregation and object recognition. There is a tremendously large literature in computer vision on the extraction of this contour geometry, *e.g.*, in edge detection, edge linking, active contours or *snakes*. Computational methods for perceptual grouping have adopted a general bottom-up approach to *automatically* disambiguate edge maps by assigning an affinity measure to each pair of edges and then using a global saliency measure to extract salient curves [29]. The implicit intermediate structure therefore is a set of long, smooth curves. This dominant use of a set of curves as the intermediate-level representation, however, ignores both internal object properties, as well as the spatial interactions of contours and their arrangements. Other intermediate structures have used languages that are based on primitives, such as Geons [1], Superquadrics [28] and MDL methods [18] . These *primitive-based* languages for free-form shape description are frequently unstable with respect to small changes in shape.

Harry Blum in a significant and seminal series of papers, *e.g.* [2], introduced the *medial axis* (MA), the locus of maximal bitangent circles, or loosely referred to as the "skeleton" of a shape, Figure 2. This is essentially a joint representation of a pair of contours which encodes the spatial arrangement of contours. The advantages of using the medial axis over contours are many: the medial axis represents the spatial arrangement of curves, the interior of objects, makes explicit the symmetry of a region, captures the continuity of an object fragmented behind an occluder, is invariant to bending, stretching, and other deformations, among many others. We propose to make both the medial axis and the contours explicit in the representation by using a *coupled* pair of retinotopic maps, Figure 1, one a contour map and the other a medial-axis (shock) map, as an appropriate intermediate representation for mediating between low-level and high-level visual processes. The coupled map simultaneously makes explicit the information necessary to interact with both low-level edge-based and region based processes, on the one hand, and with object-centered description on the other.

The medial axis can be computed in a neurally viable model by a discrete, local wave propagation scheme [26] initiated from local orientation sensitive cell responses. Waves initiated from an edge map are carried from each orientation element to neighboring cells of like orientation (Eulerian propagation). When two such waves collide, the propagating fronts stop propagating and give rise to shocks. The shocks (medial axis points) are then explicitly represented and propagated along with the waves themselves (Lagrangian propagation), Figure 3. This wave propagation mechanism is a formalization of Blum's

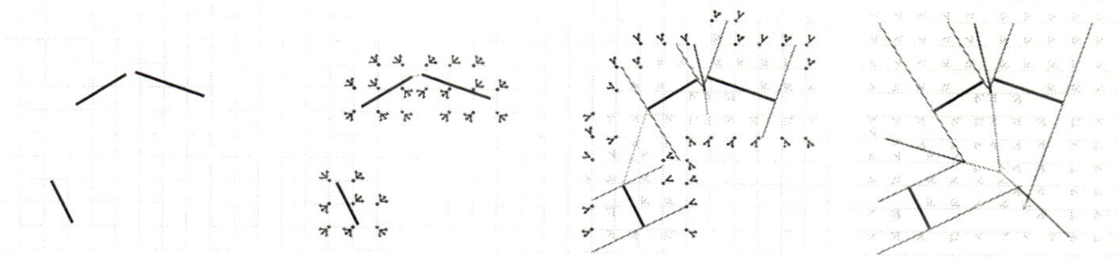

Fig. 3. The results of the Eulerian and the Langragian propagation are superimposed together with the initial edge map consisting of three edge elements. The red(darker) arrows represent the wavefronts emanating from the edge responses while the yellow/green (lighter) arrows indicate those wavefronts that have been quenched due to collision with other wavefronts. Shocks can be seen in these regions, themselves propagating with the wavefronts until all wavefronts are quenched or leave the grid.

grassfire. Tek and Kimia showed that this dynamic wave propagation scheme operating on a pair of locally connected retinotopic maps can recover the medial axis/shock graph reliably with a high degree of accuracy [26,27].

3 Perceptual Support for the Medial Axis and Propagation

We now review several psychophysics studies that support the relevance of the medial axis in the human visual system and the existence of propagation effects which are consistent with our computational paradigm. In a series of experiments, Paradiso and Nakayama [17] proposed that perceptual *filling-in mechanisms* which were observed in cases related to the blind spot, pathological scotoma, and stabilized images, are in fact a fundamental component of normal visual processing. Specifically, three sets of psychophysical experiments were performed based on two-stimulus masking experiments to show that (*i*) edge information largely determines the perception of brightness and color in homogeneous areas, and (*ii*) this relationship is not spontaneous, but rather involves a *dynamic spread of activation*. Figure 4 shows that the bright suppression resulting from the mask largely depends on the configuration of the embedded geometry (line, a shape, closed circle).

Paradiso and Hahn [16] investigated the dynamics of the effect of luminance modulation of a region on brightness modulation. They showed that when the luminance of a homogeneous spot of light is swept from high to low values at a certain range of rates, the perceived brightness of the spot does not uniformly and simultaneously follow. Rather, the darkening of the spot is *swept* inward so that the center of the spot is brighter than the periphery for the duration of the luminance modulation.

A similar phenomenon which supports the idea of brightness propagation is that of brightness induction. Devalois et al [4] showed that the brightness of a grey area surrounded by a larger area whose luminance is modulated sinusoidally undergoes a roughly anti-phase sinusoidal modulation. However, brightness induction occurs only for modulations with quite low temporal frequencies. Rossi and Padariso [20] quantified an upper-bound for the temporal frequency range leading to brightness induction as a function of the spatial frequency of the luminance, and measured the amplitude and the phase of the brightness induction, based on which, they proposed a filling-in mechanism for brightness induction. Since induction has a longer time course for larger induced areas, a propagation of brightness changes at an edge take longer to complete leading to a decrease in the induction cutoff frequency, as well as an increased phase lag.

Kovacs and Julesz showed that the detection of closed curves in an ambiguous scene is much easier than the detection of open curves [12]. Furthermore, they showed that this notion of closure is associated with an enhancement of feature detection inside the figure as opposed to outside the figure. The non-uniformity of this enhancement showed peaks at central loci of the figure, Figure 5, which they correlated very closely with the medial axis of the shape [11].

4 Neural Evidence for the Medial Axis and Propagation

Bringuier *et al* [3] note that while the Minimal Discharge Field (MDF) of foveal neurons in area 17 of cat typically average 2 degrees of visual angle in size, the neural firing rate can be modulated by stimulation in a surrounding region up to 10°. Intracellular recording in the primary cortex of the cat using two-dimensional impulse-like input, optimally oriented bars, and sinusoidal grating characterized the synaptic activation beyond the MDF in two interesting ways. First, the asymptotic integration field is typically much larger than the MDF, an average of four times. Second, and more significantly, the onset latency was strongly correlated with the eccentricity of the flashed stimulus relative to the MDF center depicting a roughly *linear relationship*. Bringuier *et al* explored the hypothesis that the intracortical horizontal connections [7,10] are principally responsible for these results. First, the linear nature of the latency is consistent with a constant propagation velocity of action potentials along intracortical axons: the speed of hypothetical cortical wave of activity, when derived from the latency slope estimates and converted to cortical distance from visual degrees, has a range of apparent speed of horizontal propagation which is consistent with the measurement from optical imaging technique (0.1-0.25m/s) [7,8]. Feedback projections from extra-striate cortical areas can explain the large synaptic integration field but does not necessarily explain the linear latency relationship. Thus, they conclude that the activation reaching the cell from periphery is propagating using intracortical horizontal axons.

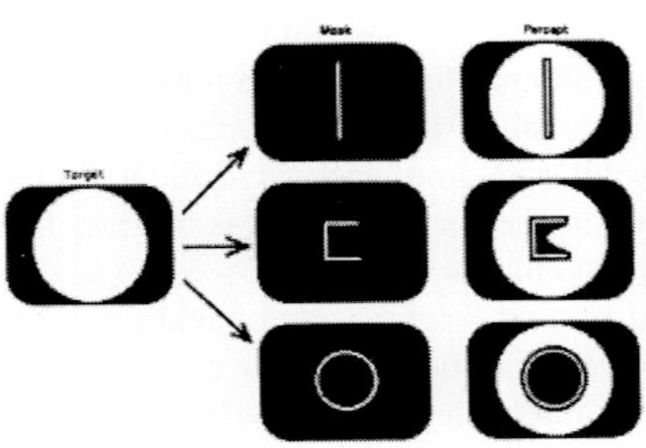

Fig. 4. From [17]. The target and masks used to study brightness suppression. The column on the right shows the percept formed

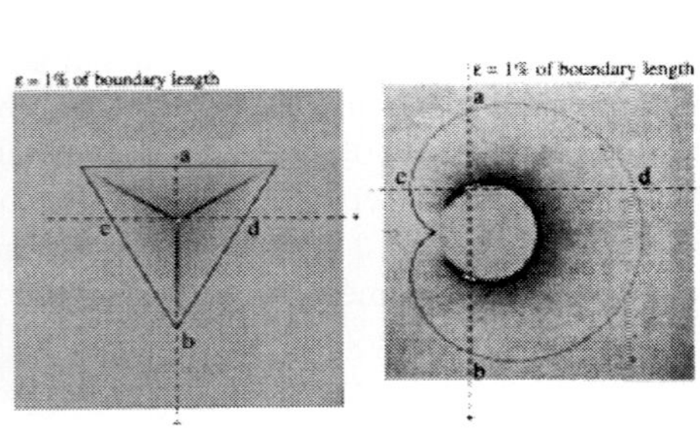

Fig. 5. From [11]. Differential contrast sensitivity map for a triangular shape and a cardioid depicts the medial axis structure.

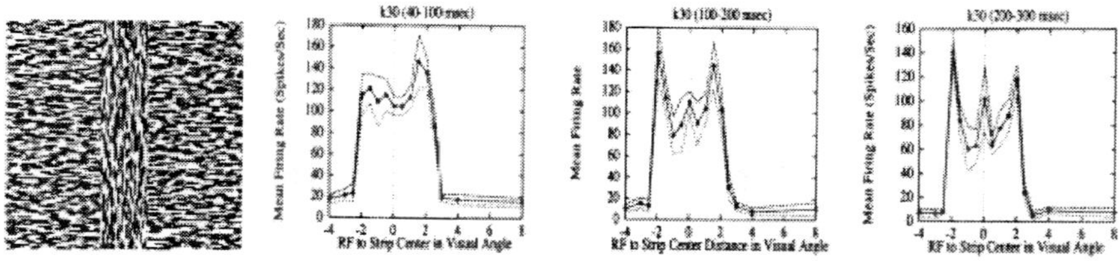

Fig. 6. From [14]. The time course of the spatial profile of response for a V1 neuron with a vertically preferred orientation; The cell initially responds to its preferred orientation. The later stages of response shows a reduction in homogeneous areas, with relative peaks emerging at the boundary and at the medial axis.

In another line of investigation, Lee *et al* [14] confirmed Lamme's empirical findings of an enhancement inside a figure indicated by texture or motion boundaries [13], and explored the spatial and dynamical aspects of such a response. They showed that the enhancement in response was not spatially uniform but rather showed distinct peaks at the boundary of the figure, and more interestingly, at its medial axis, Figure 6, if the preferred orientation of the cell was aligned with the boundary. If the preferred orientation of the cell was orthogonal to the boundary, the enhancement was fairly uniform. Second, the dynamics of the response enhancement indicated an initial stage (40-60ms) of filter-like local feature response and a later stage (80-200ms) dependent on contextual and high-order computations. Observing that V1 is the only cortical area

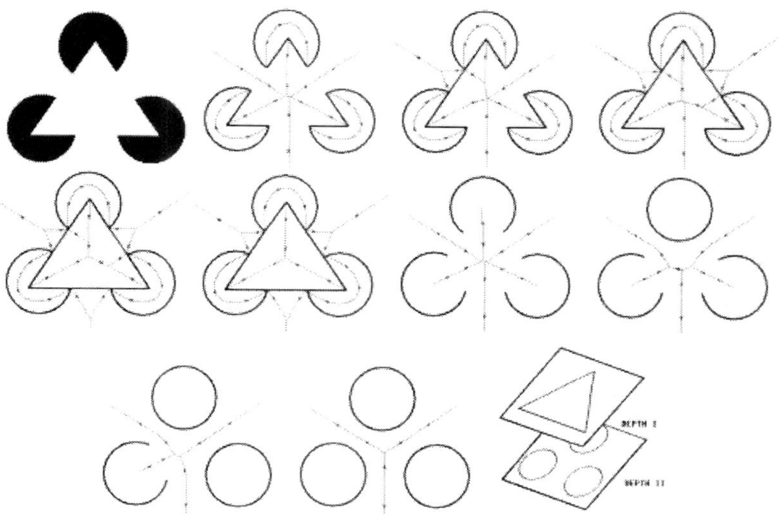

Fig. 7. The Kanizsa triangle. Its medial axis undergoes a sequence of transforms that recovers the illusory triangle at one depth and completes the "pacmen" at another. It is the recognition of the triangle as a possible occluding figure that allows the contours belonging to the triangle to be removed thus triggering the completion of the "pacmen" into circles.

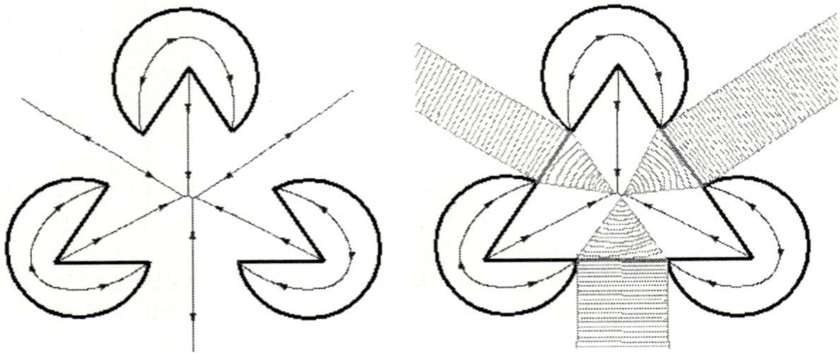

Fig. 8. A particular sequence of transformations removes the three branches representing the gaps. This is achieved by local wave propagation which bridges the gaps to form a new object hypothesis.

which provides topological maps of highest spatial precision and orientation resolution, they hypothesize a central role for V1 as a "unique high resolution buffer available to cortex for calculations...". Thus, the initial local edge contrast response which is noisy and poor is expected to improve with feedback from higher areas which have a more abstract and global view of the image. Their single unit recording of neurons in V1 in awake behaving Macaque monkeys [14] supports the involvement of V1 in higher order perceptual computations including the detection of surface boundaries, figure-ground segregation, and computation of the medial axis of shape.

5 Computational Role of the Medial Axis and Propagation

We now discuss how the coupled contour-axis can be used in various human visual processing tasks such as object recognition, perceptual grouping, categorization, *etc.* This coupled contour-axis map is used by the higher-level processes, in a hypothesis-driven mode of visual analysis where the intermediate-level representation is modified in various way under known laws of grouping. Specifically, a task of later processes is to examine the various sequences of transformations of visual data to either match against cognitively stored learnt models or to achieve "good form", an iterative examination which may best be described as "perceptual reasoning" [19]. To elaborate, in absence of any cognitive knowledge, the process is largely bottom-up and relies on regularities

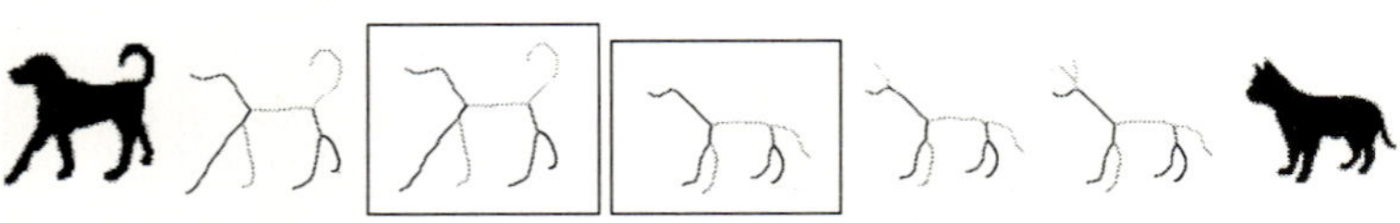

Fig. 9. Examples of the optimal deformation path between two shapes (a dog and a cat) represented each at the extremes of the sequence [22]. The sequence shows operations (symmetry transforms) applied to the medial axis and the resulting intermediate shock graphs. The boxed shock graphs which have the same topology, are where the deformation of the two shapes meet in a common simpler shape. These transforms can be achieved by selective local wave propagation on a retinotopic map.

such as the Gestalt notion of "good form". On the other hand, when a grouping of visual fragments is sufficiently organized to be recognized or to be related to cognitive knowledge, this exerts a top-down influence in the sequence of visual transforms which are applied to the coupled contour-axis map representing the image, Figure 7.

In computer vision, the medial axis has been used in object recognition tasks [30, 23]. In these approaches, shape similarity is measured by comparing an abstraction of the shape in the form of the medial axis hierarchy, which is represented as a tree/graph. The differences among various methods lie in the exact form of this abstraction and in the method for comparing the resulting graphs. Specifically, a significant distinction is whether in relating two shapes, a dynamic deformation path is explicitly generated. We have proposed that in measuring shape similarity, various deformation paths between the two shape be explicitly considered where the cost of the best path reflects shape dissimilarity, Figure 9.

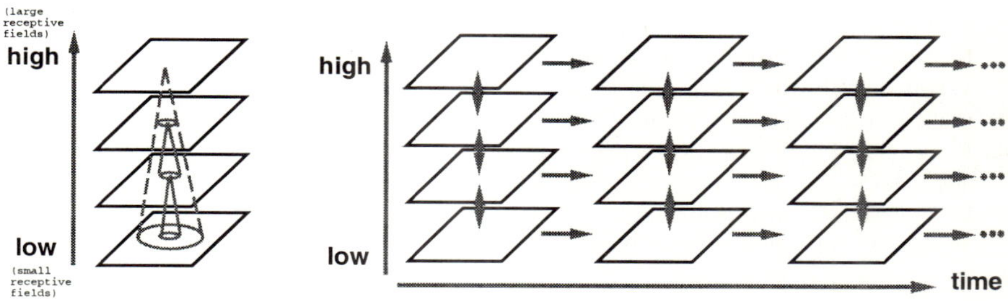

Fig. 10. The proposed paradigm takes advantage of time or horizontal propagation as an additional dimension of processing, folding space into time, in contrast to the traditional feedforward architectures with modulating feedback connections.

The medial axis has also been used for perceptual grouping [9] using the same mechanism used for recognition. While in object recognition all paths of deformation between two objects are explicitly considered, in perceptual grouping, only one (potential) object is available, and the missing second object is substituted with a measure of "good form". Thus, among all sequences deforming the initial edge map to various hypothetical figure-ground segregations, those that optimize this measure are considered. Considering that a visual system must allow for a learning component, it is critical that perceptual grouping and object recognition components be integrated in this fashion. Our recent work on object categorization [24] further illustrates the need for this connection.

6 Discussion and Conclusion

The simultaneous view of three disparate perspectives on object recognition and figure-ground segregation leads us to challenge the traditional computational architecture of primarily feedforward connections with modulating feedback connections. There is now ample evidence that in the classical anatomic connectivity [5] higher level areas respond before or at the same time as the lower areas [21]. The alternative view is one where higher areas are tightly time coupled with lower areas (e.g., V1 and V2) and where the time component of processing translates into lateral propagation instead of, or in addition to, vertical propagation, Figure 10. Thus, the ingenious solution which our visual system seems to have adopted to the dilemma of building global percepts from local features is not one of building yet larger receptive fields of increasingly more complex response, but lateral in-plane propagation to fold the spatial component into the temporal one. This lateral propagation forms connections among local features which can then be used for figure-ground segregation, mapping spatial layout of objects, object recognition, navigation, *etc.* This view is also consistent with data on "synchrony" [25] but developing this connection is beyond the scope of this paper.

References

1. I. Biederman. Recognition-by-components: A theory of human image understanding. *Psychological Review*, 94:115–147, 1987.
2. H. Blum. Biological shape and visual science. *J. Theor. Biol.*, 38:205–287, 1973.
3. V. Bringuier, F. Chavane, L. Glaeser, and Y. Fregnac. Horizontal propagation of visual activity in the synaptic integration field of area 17 neurons. *Science*, 283:695–699, January 1999.
4. R. Devalois, M. Webster, K. Devalois, and B. LingelBach. Temporal properties of brightness and color induction. *Vision Research*, 26:887–897, 1986.
5. D. V. Essen, C. Anderson, and D. Felleman. Information processing in the primate visual system: An integrated systems perspective. *Science*, 255(5043):419–423, 1992.
6. B. Gibson and M. Peterson. Does orientation-independent object recognition precede orientation-dependent recognition? Evidence from a cueing paradigm. *Journal of Experimental Psychology: Human Perception and Performance*, 20:299–316, 1994.
7. C. D. Gilbert and T. N. Wiesel. Clustered intrinsic connections in cat visual cortex. *Journal of Neuroscience*, 3:1116–1133, 1983.
8. A. Grinvald, E. Lieke, R. Frostig, and R. Hildesheim. Cortical point-spread function long-range lateral iteraction revealed by real-time optical imaging of macaque monkey primary visual cortex. *J. Neuroscience*, 14:2545–2568, 1994.
9. M. S. Johannes, T. B. Sebastian, H. Tek, and B. B. Kimia. Perceptual organization as object recognition divided by two. In *Workshop on Perceptual Organization in Computer Vision*, pages 41–46, 2001.
10. Z. Kisvarday and U. Eysel. Functional and structural topography of horizontal inhibitory connections in cat visual cortex. *European Journal of Neuroscience*, 5:1558–72, 1993.
11. I. Kovacs, A. Feher, and B. Julesz. Medial-point description of shape: a representation for action coding and its psychophysical correlates. *Vision Research*, 38:2323–2333, 1998.
12. I. Kovacs and B. Julesz. A closed curve is much more than an incomplete one: Effect of closure in figure-ground segmentation. *PNAS*, 90:7495–7497, August 1993.
13. V. Lamme. The neurophysiology of figure-ground segmentation. *J. Neurosci*, 15:1605–1615, 1995.
14. T. S. Lee, D. Mumford, R. Romero, and V. A. Lamme. The role of primary visual cortex in higher level vision. *Vision Research*, 38:2429–2454, 1998.
15. D. Marr. *Vision*. W.H. Freeman, San Fransisco, 1982.
16. M. Paradiso and S. Hahn. Filling-in percepts produced by luminance modulation. *Vision Research*, 36:2657–2663, 1996.
17. M. A. Paradiso and K. Nakayama. Brightness perception and filling in. *Vision Research*, 31:1221–36, 1991.

18. A. Pentland. Automatic extraction of deformable part models. *Intl. J. of Computer Vision*, 4(2):107–126, March 1990.
19. I. Rock. *An introduction to Perception*. MacMillan, 1975.
20. A. Rossi and M. Paradiso. Temporal limits of brightness induction and mechanisms of brightness perception. *Vision Research*, 36:1391–1398, 1996.
21. M. Schmolesky, Y. Wang, D. Hanes, K. Thompson, S. Leutgeb, J. Schall, and A. Leventhal. Signal timing across the macaque visual system. *Journal of Neurophysiology*, 79(6):3272–8, 1998.
22. T. Sebastian, P. Klein, and B. Kimia. Recognition of shapes by editing their shock graphs. *IEEE Trans. Pattern Analysis and Machine Intelligence*, page Submitted, 2001.
23. T. B. Sebastian, P. N. Klein, and B. B. Kimia. Recognition of shapes by editing shock graphs. In *Proceedings of the Eighth International Conference on Computer Vision*, pages 755–762, Vancouver, Canada, July 9-12 2001. IEEE Computer Society Press.
24. T. B. Sebastian, P. N. Klein, and B. B. Kimia. Shock-based indexing into large shape databases. In *Seventh European Conference on Computer Vision*, pages Part III:731 – 746, Copenhagen, Denmark, May 28-31 2002. Springer Verlag.
25. W. Singer and C. Gray. Visual feature integration and the temporal correlation hypothesis. *Annu. Rev. Neuro.*, 18:555–86, 1995.
26. H. Tek and B. B. Kimia. Symmetry maps of free-form curve segments via wave propagation. In *Proceedings of the Fifth International Conference on Computer Vision*, pages 362–369, KerKyra, Greece, September 20-25 1999. IEEE Computer Society Press.
27. H. Tek and B. B. Kimia. Symmetry maps of free-form curve segments via wave propagation. *Intl. J. of Computer Vision*, page Accepted to appear, 2002.
28. D. Terzopoulos and D. Metaxas. Dynamic 3D models with local and global deformations: Deformable superquadrics. *IEEE Trans. Pattern Analysis and Machine Intelligence*, 13(7):703–714, July 1991.
29. L. Williams and K. Thornber. A comparison of measures for detecting natural shapes in cluttered backgrounds. *IJCV*, 34(2-3):81–96, November 1999.
30. S. C. Zhu and A. L. Yuille. FORMS: A flexible object recognition and modeling system. *Intl. J. of Computer Vision*, 20(3):187–212, 1996.

Ecological Statistics of Contour Grouping

James H. Elder

Centre for Vision Research, York University, Toronto, Canada, M3J 1P3
jelder@yorku.ca http://elderlab.yorku.ca

Abstract. The Gestalt laws of perceptual organization were originally conceived as qualitative principles, intrinsic to the brain. In this paper, we develop quantitative models for these laws based upon the statistics of natural images. In particular, we study the laws of proximity, good continuation and similarity as they relate to the perceptual organization of contours. We measure the statistical power of each, and show how their approximate independence leads to a Bayesian factorial model for contour inference. We show how these local cues can be combined with global cues such as closure, simplicity and completeness, and with prior object knowledge, for the inference of global contours from natural images. Our model is generative, allowing contours to be synthesized for visualization and psychophysics.

1 Introduction

While many aspects of Gestalt perceptual theory have not survived the test of time, their original taxonomy of distinct principles or "laws" of perceptual organization continues to form the backbone for psychophysical and computational research on the subject [1]. This longevity suggests that their taxonomy is in some sense the natural one.

In this paper, we explore the link between these classical principles and the statistics of natural images. In particular, we study the laws of proximity, good continuation and similarity as they relate to the perceptual organization of contours, and ask whether their distinction as separate principles may reflect statistical independence in the natural world.

In order to measure the statistics of contour grouping cues in natural images, we use computer vision algorithms to detect and represent local contour tangents [2,3] (Fig. 1(middle)). To demonstrate the accuracy of this representation we have invented a method for inverting our edge representation to compute an estimate of the original image [4] (Fig. 1(right)).

Using this representation, we have developed software tools that allow human participants to rapidly trace the sequences of tangents they perceive as contours in natural images [5] (Fig. 1(left)). These are then used to estimate the relevant statistics [6].

In the next section we briefly develop the probabilistic framework for the paper. We then report results of a study of local principles for contour grouping, discuss implications, and demonstrate how these can be combined with global constraints for the inference of complete contours from natural images.

H.H. Bülthoff et al. (Eds.): BMCV 2002, LNCS 2525, pp. 230–238, 2002.

Fig. 1. *(Left)* Example contour traced by a human participant. *(Middle)* Edge map from which contours are defined. *(Right)* Reconstruction of image from edge representation.

2 A Probabilistic Model for Tangent Grouping

We let T represent the set $\{t_1, ...t_N\}$ of tangents in an image, and let S represent the set of possible sequences of these tangents. We assume there exists a correct organization of the image $C \subset S$. A visual system may use a number of observable properties D to decide on the correctness of a hypothesized contour:

$$p(s \in C|D) = \frac{p(D|s \in C)p(s \in C)}{p(D)}$$

We are interested in how properties $d_{\alpha_i \alpha_j} \in D$ defined on pairs of tangents $\{t_{\alpha_i}, t_{\alpha_{i+1}}\}$ may influence the probability that a contour $c = \{t_{\alpha_1}, ..., t_{\alpha_n}\}$ is correct. We model contours as Markov chains, i.e. we assume conditional and unconditional independence of these d_{ij}, and of the priors $\{t_{\alpha_i}, t_{\alpha_{i+1}}\} \in C$. Then

$$p(s \in C|D) = \prod_{i=1}^{n-1} p_{\alpha_i, \alpha_{i+1}}, \quad \text{where} \quad p_{\alpha_i, \alpha_{i+1}} = \frac{1}{1 + (L_{\alpha_i, \alpha_{i+1}} P_{\alpha_i, \alpha_{i+1}})^{-1}}$$

$$\text{and} \quad L_{ij} = \frac{p(d_{ij}|\{t_i, t_j\} \in C)}{p(d_{ij}|\{t_i, t_j\} \notin C)}, \quad P_{ij} = \frac{p(\{t_i, t_j\} \in C)}{p(\{t_i, t_j\} \notin C)}$$

The grouping of tangents t_i, t_j may be determined by multiple cues $d_{ij}^k \in d_{ij}$, where k indicates the type of grouping cue. These are assumed to be independent when conditioned upon $\{t_i, t_j\} \notin C$ or $\{t_i, t_j\} \notin C$.

In this paper, we are concerned with three local cues (Fig. 3(left)): proximity, good continuation and similarity (in intensity).

3 Statistical Results

3.1 Proximity

Fig. 2(left) shows a log-log plot of the contour likelihood distribution $p(r_{ij}|\{t_i, t_j\} \in C)$, where r_{ij} is the separation between tangents. For gaps greater than 2 pixels, the data follow a power law:

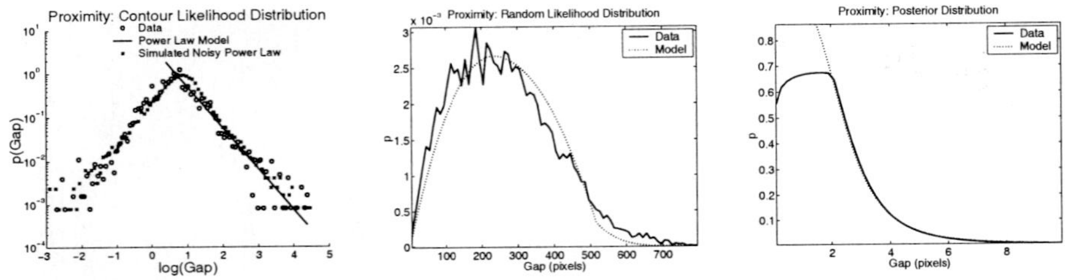

Fig. 2. *(Left)* Estimated likelihood distribution $p(r_{ij}|\{t_i, t_j\} \in C)$ for the proximity cue between two tangents known to be successive components of a common contour. *(Middle)* Estimated likelihood distribution $p(r_{ij}|\{t_i, t_j\} \notin C)$ for the proximity cue between two tangents selected randomly from the image. *(Right)* Practical (with estimation noise) and theoretical (without estimation noise) estimates of the posterior distribution $p(\{t_i, t_j\} \in C|r_{ij})$ for tangent grouping based on the proximity cue.

$$p(x) = ax^{-b}, \quad a = 3.67 \pm 0.09, \quad b = 2.92 \pm 0.02, \quad x_0 = 1.402 \pm 0.007 \quad \text{pixels}$$

Power laws generally suggest scale-invariance, which has been observed psychophysically for the action of proximity in the perceptual organization of dot lattice stimuli [7]. Oyama [8] modelled the perceptual organization of these stimuli using a power law, estimating exponents of $b = 2.88$ and $b = 2.89$ in two separate experiments. The striking agreement with our estimate ($b = 2.92$) suggests that the human perceptual organization system may be quantitatively tuned to the statistics of natural images.

We believe the falloff in probability for small gaps is due to the error of ± 1 pixel we observe in localization of tangent endpoints. Simulated data generated from the power law model and corrupted by this localization error appears very similar to the real data we observed (Fig. 2(left)).

The random likelihood distribution $p(r_{ij}|\{t_i, t_j\} \notin C)$ for the proximity cue is modelled by assuming a uniform distribution of tangents over the image (Fig. 2(middle)). Having models of the likelihood distributions for both contour and random conditions, we can compute the posterior probability $p(\{t_i, t_j\} \in C|r_{ij})$ (Fig. 2(right)).

3.2 Good Continuation

Using a first-order model of contour continuation (Fig. 3(left)), the grouping of two tangents generates two interpolation angles $\overrightarrow{\theta_{ij}}, \overleftarrow{\theta_{ji}}$ which are strongly anti-correlated in the contour condition (Fig. 3(middle)). Recoding the angles into sum $(\overleftarrow{\theta_{ji}} + \overrightarrow{\theta_{ij}})$ and difference $(\overleftarrow{\theta_{ji}} - \overrightarrow{\theta_{ij}})$ cues leads to a more independent and natural encoding (Fig. 3(right)) . The sum variable represents parallelism: the two tangents are parallel if and only if $\overleftarrow{\theta_{ji}} + \overrightarrow{\theta_{ij}} = 0$. The difference variable represents cocircularity: the two tangents are cocircular if and only if $\overleftarrow{\theta_{ji}} - \overrightarrow{\theta_{ij}} = 0$.

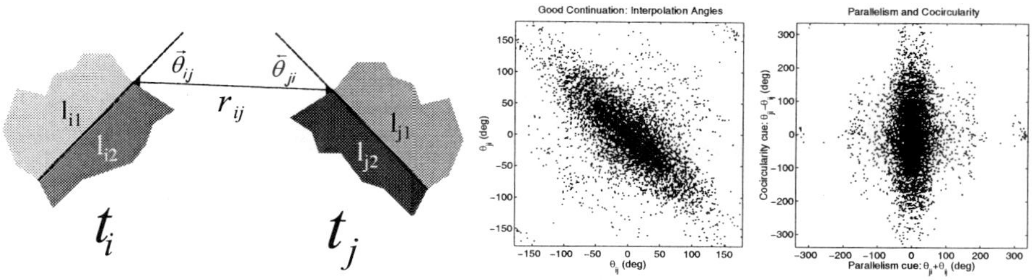

Fig. 3. *(Left)* Observable data relating two tangents. See text for details. *(Middle)* Scatterplot showing negative correlation of the two interpolation angles. *(Right)* Linear recoding into parallelism and cocircularity cues results in a more independent code. All data are drawn from the contour condition.

We employed a generalized Laplacian distribution [9] to model the likelihood distributions for the good continuation cue, (Fig. 4). The fit improves if we incorporate a model of the error in tangent orientation, estimated to have a standard deviation of 9.9 deg. The random likelihood distribution for the good continuation cues is modelled by assuming an isotropic tangent distribution.

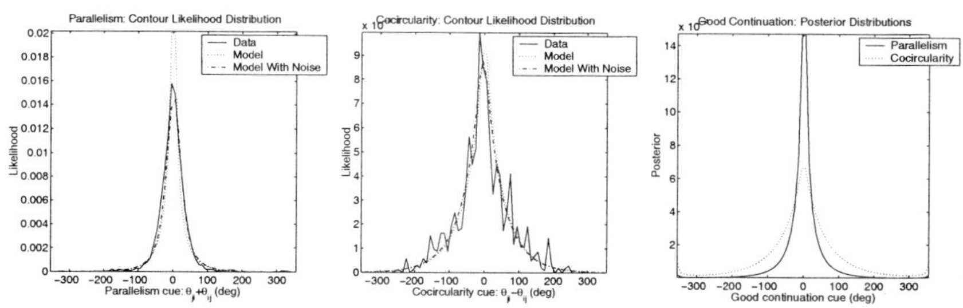

Fig. 4. Statistical distributions for the good continuation cues. *(Left)* Likelihood distribution for the parallelism cue in the contour condition. *(Middle)* Likelihood distribution for the cocircularity cue in the contour condition. *(Right)* Posterior distributions for the good continuation cues.

3.3 Similarity

In this paper we restrict our attention to contours that do not reverse contrast polarity. One obvious way of encoding intensity similarity is to consider the difference $l_{j1} - l_{i1}$ in the intensity of the light sides of the two tangents t_i, t_j as one cue, and the difference $l_{j2} - l_{i2}$ in the intensity of the dark sides of the two tangents as a second cue. However, the positive correlation between these two variables in the random condition (Fig. 5(left)) suggests an alternate encoding that forms a *brightness cue* $b_{ij} = \bar{l}_j - \bar{l}_i = (l_{j1} + l_{j2} - l_{i1} - l_{i2})/2$, measuring the difference between the two tangents t_i, t_j in the mean luminance of the underlying edge, and a *contrast cue* $c_{ij} = \Delta l_j - \Delta l_i = |l_{j1} - l_{j2}| - |l_{i1} - l_{i2}|$, measuring the difference in the amplitudes of the intensity steps at the two tangents (Fig. 5(middle)). For brevity we omit the likelihood distributions for the similarity cues: Fig. 5(right) shows the posterior distributions.

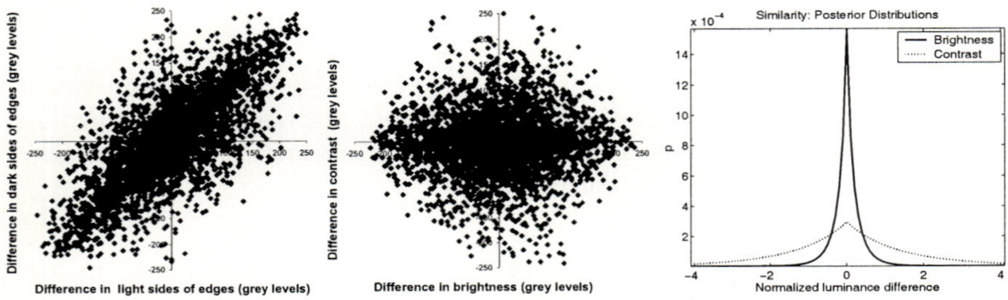

Fig. 5. *(Left)* Dark and light luminance cues between randomly selected tangents are strongly correlated. *(Middle)* Brightness and contrast cues for randomly selected tangents are approximately uncorrelated. *Right* Posterior distributions $p(\{t_i, t_j\} \in C|b_{ij})$ and $p(\{t_i, t_j\} \in C|c_{ij})$ for tangent grouping based on the brightness and contrast cues.

4 Discussion

4.1 Cue Independence

We have attempted to encode the Gestalt cues to maximize their independence, permitting a factorial model for perceptual organization. As a preliminary assessment of this idea, we compute the Pearson correlation coefficients between the absolute values of the cues in the contour condition. We find that correlations are relatively small (less than 0.1) except for the brightness/contrast correlation (0.54). However, the relatively weak statistical power of the contrast cue (see below) suggests it could be ignored without substantial loss in performance.

4.2 Statistical Power

We measure the statistical power of each Gestalt cue by the mutual information $I(G_{ij}, d_{ij})$ between the cue and the decision of whether to group two tangents, normalized by the prior entropy $H(G_{ij})$ in the grouping decision (Fig. 6(left)). The proximity cue is seen to be the most powerful, reducing the entropy in the grouping decision by 75%. The combined power of the good continuation cues appears to be roughly comparable to the power of the similarity cues. We can also see that the parallelism cue is substantially more powerful than the cocircularity cue, and the brightness cue is much more powerful than the contrast cue.

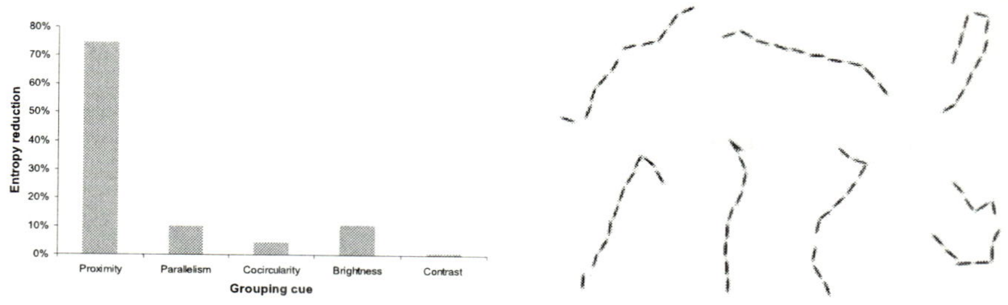

Fig. 6. *(Left)* Statistical power of contour grouping cues, as measured by the proportion of entropy in the grouping decision eliminated by knowledge of the cue. *(Right)* Sample contours generated from natural image statistics

4.3 On the General Shape of the Distributions

Contour likelihood distributions and posteriors for all cues were found to be kurtotic, with long tails. Thus extreme values for these cues occur as generic events. Fig. 6(right) shows sample contours generated using our factorial statistical model. While these contours are generally continuous and smooth, sudden gaps and corners occur fairly frequently.

Generated sample contours allow us to visually evaluate the statistical information captured in the model, and can be used in psychophysical experiments to assess the tuning of human vision to natural images statistics.

5 Global Constraints and Applications

5.1 Closure

In order to reliably infer global contours, the local cues we have been studying must be augmented with global cues and constraints. One global cue known to be very powerful psychophysically is closure [10] (Fig. 7).

Fig. 8 demonstrates how this global constraint can be powerfully combined with local cues to yield interesting results. In each example, the most probable contour passing through a tangent on the lower lip of the model is estimated. The inference on the left uses an iterative mutual satisfaction algorithm. The middle result is the most probable contour of a given length. The right result uses a shortest-path algorithm to compute the most probable closed contour passing through the tangent [3]. Only the closure constraint yields useful results.

5.2 Prior Models

While most work on perceptual organization is focused on bottom-up computation, the human visual system likely uses higher-level, task-specific knowledge when it is available. A good example is guided visual search: a mental model of the search target may accelerate grouping in a cluttered display.

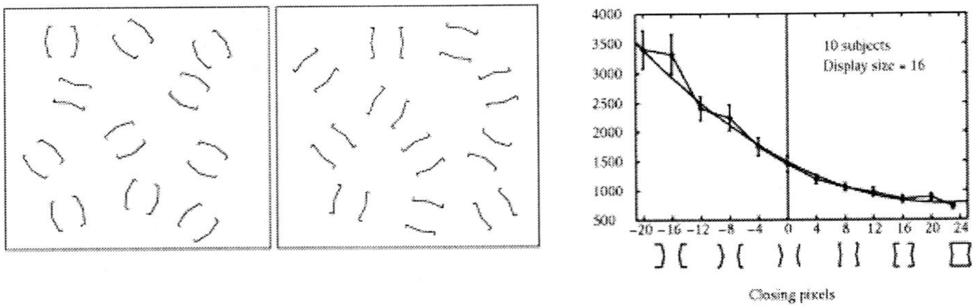

Fig. 7. Closure acts as a global psychophysical constraint for the grouping of contours into two-dimensional shapes. *(Left)* Visual search for a concave target shape in convex distractors depends strongly on the closure of the figures. *(Right)* Shape discrimination performance is a continuous function of the degree of closure of the figures.

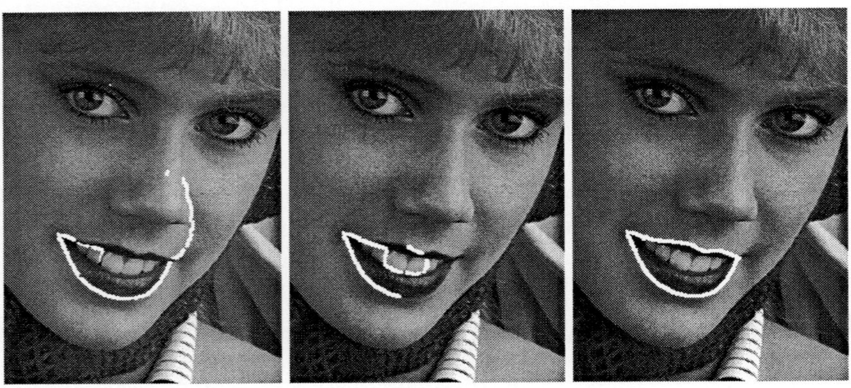

Fig. 8. The power of closure. *(Left)* Result of mutual satisfaction constraint. *(Middle)* Result of length constraint. *(Right)* Result of closure constraint.

In order to incorporate these ideas into algorithms, we need a rigorous way to combine probabilistic knowledge of the search target with more general probabilistic knowledge about grouping. We have recently demonstrated such a system in a geomatics application [11]. Given an approximate polygonal model of a lake boundary, and high-resolution IKONOS satellite data (Fig. 9(left)), we address the problem of computing a more detailed model of the lake boundary.

We wish to solve this problem in the contour domain, and thus infer the sequence of tangents that bounds the object. We use a number of object cues, such as the intensity on the dark side of the tangents (lakes in IKONOS imagery generally appear dark). In addition, we used global constraints of closure, simplicity (no self-intersections) and completeness (the model must account for the entire boundary). Neither the completeness nor the simplicity constraint can be

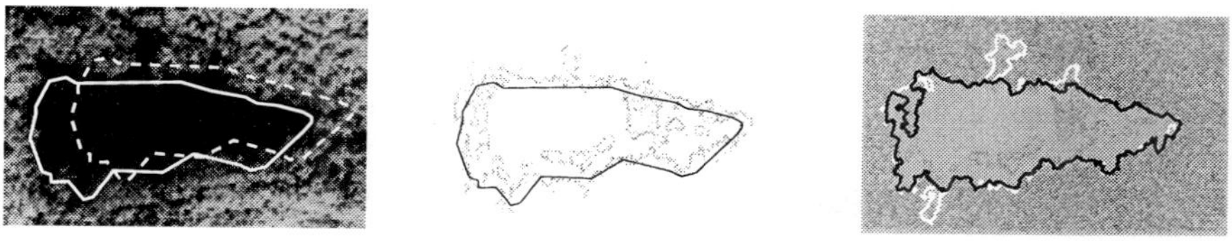

Fig. 9. *(Left)* Example test lake. Initial prior model (dashed) and prior model after registration (solid). *(Middle)* Map of posterior probability of object membership $p(t_{\alpha_i} \in T^o | d^o_{\alpha_i})$ for the 4 object cues combined. Tangent intensity is inversely proportional to the posterior probability. *(Right)* Results: *Dark Grey:* non-lake edges, *White:* human-traced boundary. *Black:* computer-estimated boundary. Where the human-traced boundary is not visible, it is coincident with the computer-traced boundary.

incorporated into a shortest-path computation; we employ a probabilistic search method for this application.

Fig. 9(middle) shows how the object knowledge has reduced the complexity of the problem. Fig. 9(right) shows an example result. We find that our algorithm improves the accuracy of the prior models by an average of 41%, and performs at the level of a human mapping expert [11].

6 Conclusion

We have related the classical Gestalt laws of proximity, good continuation and similarity to the statistics of the natural world, and have argued that the utility of the Gestalt taxonomy of perceptual organization laws is due in part to their approximate statistical independence. We have developed a generative, parametric model for perceptual organization based upon natural image statistics, and have shown how this model can be used in combination with powerful global constraints to yield useful results for specific applications.

References

1. M. Wertheimer, "Laws of organization in perceptual forms," in *A sourcebook of Gestalt Psychology*, W. D. Ellis, Ed., pp. 71–88. Routledge and Kegan Paul, London, 1938.
2. J. H. Elder and S. W. Zucker, "Local scale control for edge detection and blur estimation," *IEEE Transactions on Pattern Analysis and Machine Intelligence*, vol. 20, no. 7, pp. 699–716, July 1998.
3. J. H. Elder and S. W. Zucker, "Computing contour closure," in *Proceedings of the 4th European Conference on Computer Vision*, New York, 1996, pp. 399–412, Springer Verlag.
4. J. H. Elder, "Are edges incomplete?," *International Journal of Computer Vision*, vol. 34, no. 2, pp. 97–122, 1999.

5. J. H. Elder and R. M. Goldberg, "Image editing in the contour domain," *IEEE Transactions on Pattern Analysis and Machine Intelligence*, vol. 23, no. 3, pp. 291–296, 2001.
6. J. H. Elder and R. M. Goldberg, "Ecological statistics of Gestalt laws for the perceptual organization of contours," *Journal of Vision*, vol. 2, no. 4, pp. 324–353, 2002, http://journalofvision.org/2/4/5/, DOI 10.1167/2.4.5.
7. M. Kubovy and A. O. Holcombe, "On the lawfulness of grouping by proximity," *Cognitive Psychology*, vol. 35, pp. 71–98, 1998.
8. T. Oyama, "Perceptual grouping as a function of proximity," *Perceptual and Motor Skills*, vol. 13, pp. 305–306, 1961.
9. S. G. Mallat, "A theory for multiresolution signal decomposition: the wavelet representation," *IEEE Transactions on Pattern Recognition and Machine Intelligence*, vol. 11, no. 7, pp. 674–693, Jul 1989.
10. J. H. Elder and S. W. Zucker, "The effect of contour closure on the rapid discrimination of two-dimensional shapes," *Vision Research*, vol. 33, no. 7, pp. 981–991, 1993.
11. J. H. Elder and A. Krupnik, "Contour grouping with strong prior models," in *Proceedings of the IEEE Conference on Computer Vision and Pattern Recognition*, Kauai, Hawaii, December 2001, IEEE Computer Society, pp. 414–421, IEEE Computer Society Press.

Statistics of Second Order Multi-modal Feature Events and Their Exploitation in Biological and Artificial Visual Systems

Norbert Krüger and Florentin Wörgötter

University of Stirling, Scotland, {norbert,worgott}@cn.stir.ac.uk

Abstract. In this work we investigate the multi-modal statistics of natural image sequences looking at the modalities orientation, color, optic flow and contrast transition. It turns out that second order interdependencies of local line detectors can be related to the Gestalt law collinearity. Furthermore we can show that statistical interdependencies increase significantly when we look not at orientation only but also at other modalities.
The occurrence of illusionary contour processing (in which the Gestalt law 'collinearity' is tightly involved) at a late stage during the development of the human visual system (see, e.g., [3]) makes it plausible that mechanisms involved in the processing of Gestalt laws depend on visual experience about the underlying structures in visual data. This also suggests a formalization of Gestalt laws in artificial systems depending on statistical measurements. We discuss the usage of statistical interdependencies measured in this work within an artificial visual systems and show first results.

1 Introduction

A large amount of research has been focused on the usage of Gestalt laws in computer vision systems (overviews are given in [19,18]). The most often applied and also the most dominant Gestalt principle in natural images is collinearity [5,12]. Collinearity can be exploited to achieve more robust feature extraction in different domains, such as, edge detection (see, e.g., [9,10]) or stereo estimation [4,18]. In most applications in artificial visual systems, the relation between features, i.e., the applied Gestalt principle, has been defined heuristically based on semantic characteristics such as orientation or curvature. Mostly, explicit models of feature interaction have been applied, connected with the introduction of parameters to be estimated beforehand, a problem recognized as extremely awkward in computer vision.

In the human visual system beside local orientation also other modalities such as color and optic flow are computed (see, e.g. [7]). All these low level processes face the problem of an extremely high degree of vagueness and uncertainty [1]. However, the human visual systems acquires visual representations which allow for actions with high precision and certainty within the 3D world under rather

H.H. Bülthoff et al. (Eds.): BMCV 2002, LNCS 2525, pp. 239–248, 2002.

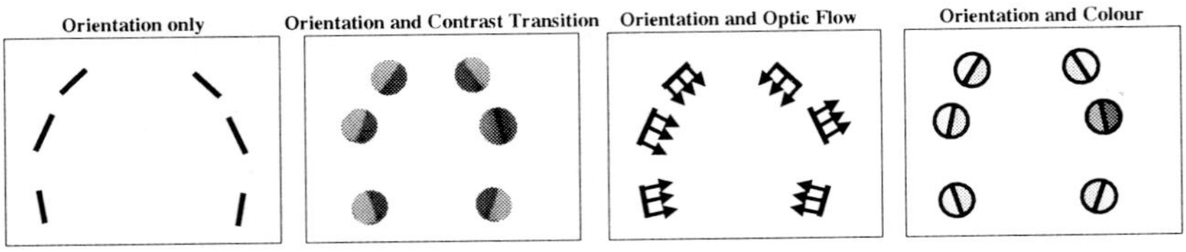

Fig. 1. Grouping of visual entities becomes intensified (left triple) or weakened (right triple) by using additional modalities: Since the visual entities are not only collinear but show also similarity in an additional modality their grouping becomes more likely.

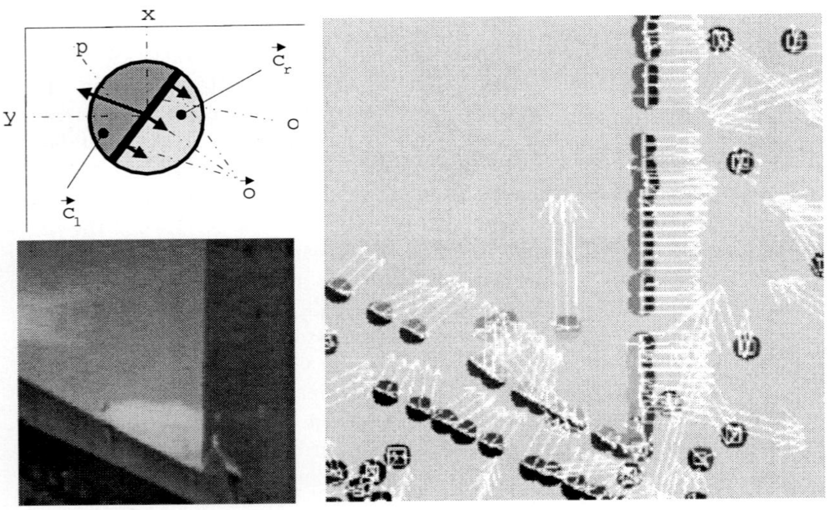

Fig. 2. Top left: Schematic representation of a basic feature vector. **Bottom left:** Frame in an image (the frame is part of the image sequence shown in figure 3 left). **Right:** Extracted Feature vectors.

uncontrolled conditions. The human visual system can achieve the necessary certainty and completeness by *integrating* visual information across modalities (see, e.g., [17,11]). This integration is manifested in the dense connectivity within brain areas in which the different visual modalities are processed as well as in the large number of feedback connections from higher to lower cortical areas (see, e.g., [7]).

Also Gestalt principles are affected by multiple modalities. For example, figure 1 shows how collinearity can be intensified by the different modalities contrast transition, optic flow and color. This paper addresses statistics of natural images in these modalities. As a main result we found that statistical interdependencies corresponding to the Gestalt law "collinearity" in visual scenes become significantly stronger when multiple modalities are taken into account (see section 3). Furthermore, we discuss how these measured interdependencies can be used within artificial visual systems (see section 4).

2 Feature Processing

In the work presented here we address the multi–modal statistics of natural images. We start from a feature space (see also figure 1 and 2) containing the following sub-modalities:

Orientation: We compute local orientation o (and local phase p) by the specific isotropic linear filter [6].

Contrast Transition: The contrast transition of the signal is coded in the phase p of the same filter.

Color: Color is processed by integrating over image patches in coincidence with their edge structure (i.e., integrating over the left and right side of the edge separately). Hence, we represent color by the two tuples $(c_r^l, c_g^l, c_b^l), (c_r^r, c_g^r, c_b^r)$ representing the color in RGB space on the left and right side of the edge.

Optic Flow: Local displacements (f_1, f_2) are computed by a well known optical flow technique ([15]).

All modalities are extracted from a local image patch[1]. The output is a local interpretation of the image patch by semantic properties (such as orientation and displacement) in analogy to the sparse output of a V1 column in visual cortex.

For our statistics we use 9 image sequences with a total of 42 images of size 512x512 (18 images) and 384x288 (24 images). Our data (see figure 3 (left) for examples) contains variations caused by object motion as well as camera motion. There is a total of 3900 feature vectors in the Data set (approximately 2600 from the outdoor images) and the statistic is based on 1555548 second order comparisons.

3 Statistical Interdependencies in Image Sequences

We measure statistical interdependencies between events by a mathematical term that we call 'Gestalt coefficient'. The Gestalt coefficient is defined by the ratio of the likelihood of an event e^1 given another event e^2 and the likelihood of the event e^1:

$$G(e^1, e^2) = \frac{P(e^1|e^2)}{P(e^1).} \tag{1}$$

For the modeling of feature interaction a high Gestalt coefficient is helpful since it indicates the modification of likelihood of the event e^1 depending on other events. A Gestalt coefficient of one says, that the event e^2 does not influence the likelihood of the occurrence of the event e^1. A value smaller than one indicates a negative dependency: the occurrence of the event e^2 reduces the likelihood that e^1 occurs. A value larger than one indicates a positive dependency: the occurrence of the event e^2 increases the likelihood that e^1 occurs. The Gestalt coefficient is illustrated in figure 3(right). Further details can be found in [14].

[1] In our statistical measurements we only use image patches corresponding to intrinsically one-dimensional signals (see [22]) since orientation is reasonably defined for these image patches only.

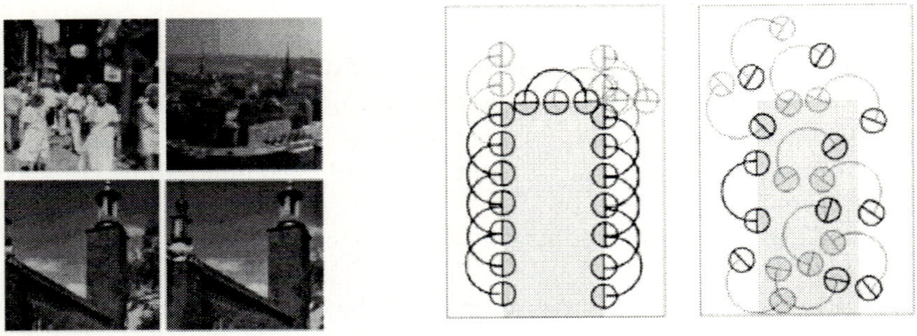

Fig. 3. Left: Images of the data set (top) and 2 images of a sequence (bottom). **Right:** Explanation of the Gestalt coefficient $G(e^1|e^2)$: We define e^2 as the occurrence of a line segment with a certain orientation (anywhere in the image). Let the second order event e^1 be: "occurrence of collinear line segments two units away from an existing line segment e^2". Left: Computation of $P(e^1|e^2)$. All possible occurrences of events e^1 in the image are shown. Bold arcs represent real occurrences of the specific second order relations e^1 whereas arcs in general represent possible occurrences of e^1. In this image we have 17 possible occurrences of collinear line segments two units away from an existing line segment e^2 and 11 real occurrences. Therefore we have $P(e^1|e^2) = 11/17 = 0.64$. Right: Approximation of the probability $P(e^1)$ by a Monte Carlo method. Entities e^2 (bold) are placed randomly in the image and the presence of the event 'occurrence of collinear line segments two units apart of e^2' is evaluated. (In our measurements we used more than a 500000 samples for the estimation of $P(e^1)$). Only in 1 of 11 possible cases this event takes place (bold arc). Therefore we have $P(e^1) = 1/11 = 0.09$ and the Gestalt coefficient for the second order relation is $G(e^1|e^2) = 0.64/0.09 = 7.1$.

3.1 Second Order Relations Statistics of Natural Images

A large amount of work has addressed the question of efficient coding of visual information and its relation to the statistics of images. Excellent overviews are given in [22,21]. While many publications were concerned with the statistics on the pixel level and the derivation of filters from natural images by coding principles (see, e.g. [16,2]), recently statistical investigation in the feature space of local line segments have been performed (see, e.g., [12,5,8]) and have addressed the representation of Gestalt principles in visual data.

Here we go one step further by investigating the second order relations of events in our *multi–modal feature space*

$$e = ((x, y), o, p, ((c^l_r, c^l_g, c^l_b)), ((c^r_r, c^r_g, c^r_b)), (f_1, f_2))$$

In our measurements we collect second order events in bins defined by small patches in the (x_1, x_2)–space and by regions in the modality–spaces defined by the metrics defined for each modality (for details see [14]). Figure 4 shows the Gestalt coefficient for equidistantly separated bins (one bin corresponds to a square of 10×10 pixels and an angle of $\frac{\pi}{8}$ rad). As already been shown in [12,8] collinearity can be detected as significant second order relation as a

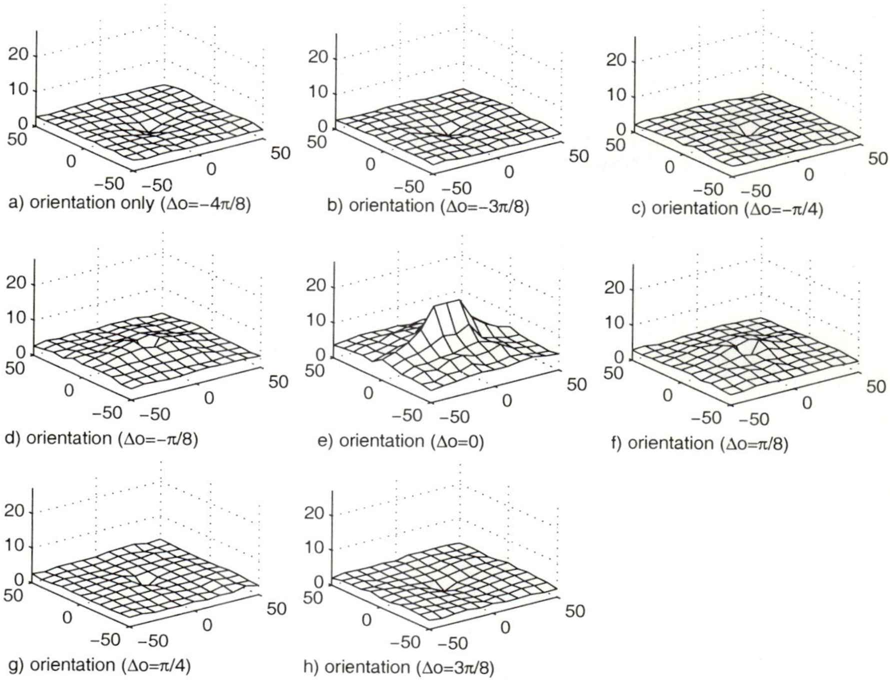

Fig. 4. The Gestalt coefficient for differences in position from -50 to 50 pixel in x– and y– direction when orientation only is regarded. In a) the differecne of orientation of the line segments is $\frac{\pi}{2}$ (the line segments are ortogonal) while in e) the difference of orientation is 0, i.e., the line segments have same orientation. The b), c), d) represent orientation difference between $\frac{\pi}{2}$ and 0. Note that the Gestalt coefficient for position (0,0) and $\Delta o = 0$ is set to the maximum of the surface for better display. The Gestalt coefficient is not interesting at this position, since e^1 and e^2 are identical.

ridge in the surface plot for $\Delta o = 0$ in figure 4e. Also parallelism is detectable as an offset of this surface. A Gestalt coefficient significantly above one can also be detected for small orientation differences (figure 4d,f, i.e., $\Delta o = -\frac{\pi}{8}$ and $\Delta o = \frac{\pi}{8}$) corresponding to the frequent occurrence of curved entities. The general shape of surfaces is similar in all following measurements concerned with additional modalities: *we find a ridge corresponding to collinearity and an offset corresponding to parallelism and a Gestalt coefficient close to one for all larger orientation differences.* Therefore, in the following we will only look at the surface plots for equal orientation $\Delta o = 0$. These result shows that Gestalt laws are reflected in the statistics of natural images: *Collinearity and parallelism are significant second order events of visual low level filters* (see also [12]).

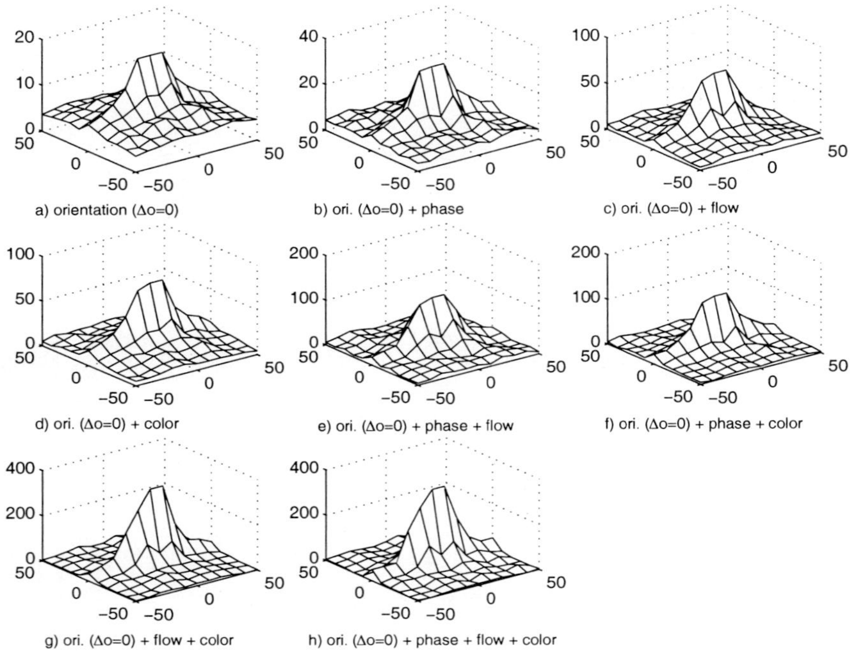

Fig. 5. The Gestalt coefficient for $\Delta o = 0$ and all possible combination of modalities.

3.2 Pronounced Interdependencies by Using Additional Modalities

Now we can look at the Gestalt coefficient when we also take into account the modalities contrast transition, optic flow and color.

Orientation and Contrast Transition: We say two events $((x_1, x_2), o)$ and $((x'_1, x'_2), o')$ have similar contrast transition (i.e., 'similar phase') when $d(p, p') < t^{p+}$. The metrics in the different modalities are precisely defined in [14]. t^{p+} is defined such that only 10% of the comparisons $d(p, p')$ in the data set are smaller than t^p. Figure 5b shows the Gestalt coefficient for the events 'similar orientation and similar contrast transition'. In figure 6 the Gestalt coefficient along the x-axes in the surface plot of figure 5 is shown. The Gestalt coefficient on the x-axes correspond to the 'collinearity ridge'. The first column represents the Gestalt coefficient when we look at similar orientation only, while the second columns represent the Gestalt coefficient when we look at similar orientation and similar phase. We see a significant increase of the Gestalt coefficient compared to the case when we look at orientation only for collinearity.

This result shows that assuming a line segment with a certain contrast transition does exist in an image it is not only that the likelihood for the existence of a collinear line segment increases but that it also becomes more likely that it has similar contrast transition.

Orientation and Optic Flow: The corresponding surface plot is shown in figure 5c and the slice corresponding to collinearity is shown in the third column

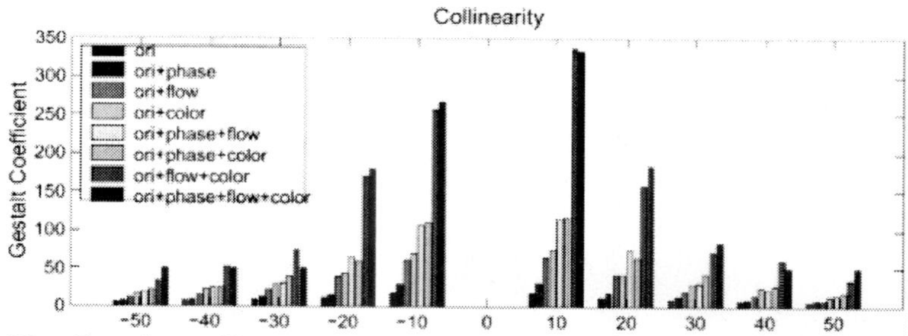

Fig. 6. The Gestalt coefficient for collinear feature vectors for all combinations of modalities. For (0,0) the Gestalt coefficient is not shown, since e^1 and e^2 would be identical.

in figure 6. An even more pronounced increase of inferential power for collinearity can be detected.

Orientation and Color: Analogously, we define that two events have 'similar color structure'. The corresponding surface plot is shown in figure 5d and the slice corresponding to collinearity is shown in the fourth column in figure 6.

Multiple additional Modalities: Figure 5 shows the surface for similar orientation, phase and optic flow (figure 5e); similar orientation, phase and color (figure 5f) and similar orientation, optic flow and color (figure 5g). The slices corresponding to collinearity are shown in the fifth to seventh columns in figure 6. We can see that the the Gestalt coefficient for collinear line segments increases significantly. Most distinctly for the combination optic flow and color (seventh column). Finally, we can look at the Gestalt coefficient when we take all three modalities into account. Figure 5h and the eighth column in figure 6 shows the results. Again an increase of the Gestalt coefficient compared to the case when we look at only two additional modalities can be achieved.

4 Summary and Examples of Possible Applications

In this paper we have addressed the statistics of local oriented line segments derived from natural scenes by adding information to the line segment concerning the modalities contrast transition, color, and optic flow. We could show that statistical interdependencies in the orientation–position domain correspond to the Gestalt laws collinearity and parallelism and that they become significantly stronger when multiple modalities are taken into account. Essentially it seems that visual information bears a high degree of intrinsic redundancy. This redundancy can be used to reduce the ambiguity of local feature processing.

The results presented here provide further evidence for the assumption that despite the vagueness of low level processes stability can be achieved by *integration of information across modalities*. In addition, the attempt to model the application of Gestalt laws based on statistical measurements, as suggested

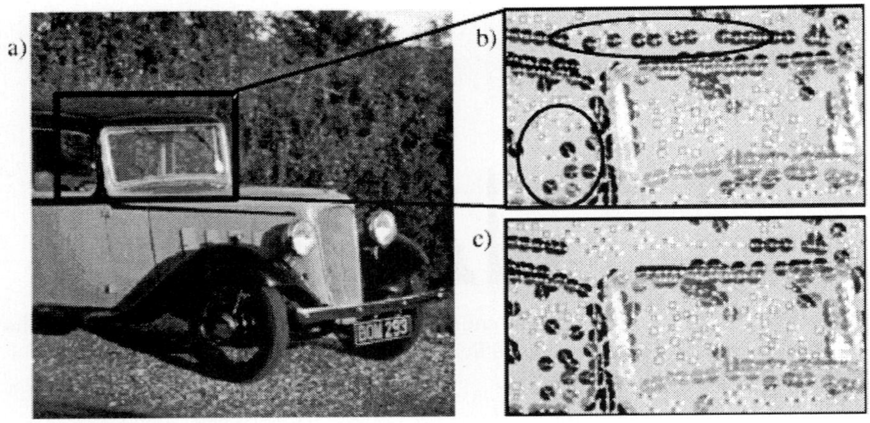

Fig. 7. Left: Image of a car. Right top: Extraction of features with grouping based on the Gestalt coefficient. Right bottom: Feature extraction without grouping.

recently by some researchers (see, [8,5,12,20]) gets further support. Most importantly, the results derived in this paper suggest to formulate the application of Gestalt principles in a multi-modal way.

Illusionary contour processing (in which the Gestalt law 'collinearity' is tightly involved) occurs at a late stage (after approximately 6 months) during the development of the human visual system (see [3] and [13]). This late development of the above mentioned mechanisms makes it likely that those mechanisms depend on visual experience of the underlying structures in visual data. This also suggests a formalization of Gestalt laws in artificial systems depending on statistical measurements.

Motivated by the measurable reflectance of Gestalt principles in the statistics of natural images (as shown in this paper) and the late development of abilities in which these Gestalt principles are involved, it is our aim to replace heuristic definition of Gestalt rules by interaction schemes based on statistical measurements. We want to describe two examples: A process of self–emergence of feature constellations and low–contrast edge detection. In both cases only a simple criterion based on the Gestalt coefficient is applied to realize the collinear relation.

Self–Emergence of Feature Constellations: The need of entities going beyond local oriented edges is widely accepted in computer vision systems across a wide range of different viewpoints. Their role is to extract from the complex distribution of pixels in an image patch (or an image patch sequence) a sparse and higher semantical representation which enables rich predictions across modalities, spatial distances and frames. Accordingly, they consist of groups of early visual features (such as local edges).

These higher feature constellations have been already applied in artificial systems but were needed to be defined heuristically. By using a link criterion based on the Gestalt coefficient (stating that there exist a link when the Gestalt coefficient is high) and the transitivity relation (if two pairs of entities are linked then all entities have to be linked) we are able to define a process in which groups of local entities do self emerge.

Detection of Low Contrast Edges: Once the groups have self–emerged they can be used to detect low contrast edges and reduce falsely detected edges caused by structural noise by combining local confidence and contextual confidence selected within the group an entity belongs to. In figure 7b and c all features above the very same threshold are displayed with a filled circle while features below this threshold are displayed without these circles. Note the detection of the low contrast edge (figure 7b, horizontal ellipse) when applying grouping based on the Gestalt coefficient and the reduction of non–meaningful features (vertical ellipse) without grouping.

The exact formalization of grouping and feature disambigution based on the statistical measurements explained here is part of our current research and will be described in a forthcoming paper.

References

[1] J. Aloimonos and D. Shulman. *Integration of Visual Modules – An extension of the Marr Paradigm.* Academic Press, London, 1989.

[2] A.J. Bell and T. Sejnowski. Edges are the 'independent components' of natural Scenes. *Advances in Neural Information Processing Systems*, 9:831–837, 1996.

[3] B.I. Bertenthal, J.J. Campos, and M.M. Haith. Development of visual organisation: The perception of subjective contours. *Child Development*, 51(4):1072–1080, 1980.

[4] R.C.K. Chung and R. Nevatia. Use of monucular groupings and occlusion analysis in a hierarchical stereo System. *Computer Vision and Image Understanding*, 62(3):245–268, 1995.

[5] H. Elder and R.M. Goldberg. Inferential reliability of contour grouping cues in natural images. *Perception Supplement*, 27, 1998.

[6] M. Felsberg and G. Sommer. The monogenic Signal. *IEEE Transactions on Signal Processing*, 41(12), 2001.

[7] M.S. Gazzaniga. *The Cognitive Neuroscience.* MIT Press, 1995.

[8] W.S. Geisler, J.S. Perry, B.J. Super, and D.P. Gallogly. Edge co-occurrence in natural images predicts contour grouping performance. *Vision Research*, 41:711–724, 2001.

[9] G. Guy and G. Medioni. Inferring global perceptual contours from local features. *International Journal of Computer Vision*, 20:113–133, 1996.

[10] F. Heitger, R. von der Heydt, E. Peterhans, L. Rosenthaler, and O. Kübler. Simulation of neural contour mechanisms: representing anomalous contours. *Image and Vision Computing*, 16:407–421, 1998.

[11] D.D. Hoffman, editor. *Visual Intelligence: How we create what we see.* W.W. Norton and Company, 1980.

[12] N. Krüger. Collinearity and parallelism are statistically significant second order relations of complex cell responses. *Neural Processing Letters*, 8(2):117–129, 1998.

[13] N. Krüger and F. Wörgötter. Different degree of genetical prestructuring in the ontogenesis of visual abilities based on deterministic and statistical regularities. *Proceedings of the Workshop On Growing up Artifacts that Live SAB 2002*, 2002.

[14] N. Krüger and F. Wörgötter. Multi modal estimation of collinearity and parallelism in natural image sequences. to appear in Network: *Computation in Neural Systems*, 2002.
[15] H.-H. Nagel. On the estimation of optic flow: Relations between different approaches and some new results. *Artificial Intelligence*, 33:299–324, 1987.
[16] B.A. Olshausen and D. Field. Emergence of simple-cell receptive field properties by learning a sparse code for natural images. *Nature*, 381:607–609, 1996.
[17] W.A. Phillips and W. Singer. In search of common foundations for cortical processing. *Behavioral and Brain Sciences*, 20(4):657–682, 1997.
[18] S. Posch. *Perzeptives Gruppieren und Bildanalyse.* Habilitationsschrift, Universität Bielefeld, Deutscher Universitäts Verlag, 1997.
[19] S. Sarkax and K.L. Boyer. *Computing Perceptual Organization in Computer Vision.* World Scientific, 1994.
[20] M. Sigman, G.A. Cecchi, C.D. Gilbert, and M.O. Magnasco. On a common circle: Natural Scenes and gestalt rules. *PNAS*, 98(4):1935–1949, 2001.
[21] E.P. Simoncelli and B.A. Ohlshausen. Natural image statistics and neural representations. *Anual Reviews of Neuroscience*, 24:1193–1216, 2001.
[22] C. Zetzsche and G. Krieger. Nonlinear mechanisms and higher-order statistics in biologial vision and electronie image processing: review and perspectives. *Journal of Electronic Imaging*, 10(1):56–99, 2001.

Qualitative Representations for Recognition

Pawan Sinha

Department of Brain and Cognitive Sciences
Massachusetts Institute of Technology
Cambridge, MA 02142
sinha@ai.mit.edu

Abstract. The success of any object recognition system, whether biological or artificial, lies in using appropriate representation schemes. The schemes should efficiently encode object concepts while being tolerant to appearance variations induced by changes in viewing geometry and illumination. Here, we present a biologically plausible representation scheme wherein objects are encoded as sets of qualitative image measurements. Our emphasis on the use of qualitative measurements renders the representations stable in the presence of sensor noise and significant changes in object appearance. We develop our ideas in the context of the task of face-detection under varying illumination. Our approach uses qualitative photometric measurements to construct a face signature ('ratio-template') that is largely invariant to illumination changes.

1 Introduction

The appearance of a 3D object can change dramatically with variations in illumination conditions and viewing position. The challenge a recognition system faces is to classify all these different instances as arising from the same underlying object. The system's success depends on the nature of the internal object representations, against which the observed images are matched. Here we describe a candidate representation scheme that possesses several desirable characteristics, including tolerance to photometric variations, computational simplicity, low memory requirements and biological plausibility.

We develop the scheme in the context of a specific recognition task – detecting human faces under variable lighting conditions. Two key sources of difficulty in constructing face detection systems are (a) the variability of illumination conditions, and (b) differences in view-points. Experimental evidence [Bruce, 1994; Cabeza et al., 1998] suggests that the prototypes the visual system uses for detecting faces may be view-point specific. In other words, it is likely that distinct prototypes are used to encode facial appearance corresponding to different view-points. This hypothesis leaves open the question of how to collapse the illumination induced appearance variations for a given view-point into a compact prototype. The representation scheme we propose provides a candidate solution to this problem. Of course, many schemes for face detection have already been proposed in the computer vision literature [Govindaraju et al., 1989; Yang & Huang, 1993, 1994; Hunke, 1994; Sung & Poggio, 1994; Rowley et al, 1995; Viola & Jones, 2001]. What distinguishes our proposal from past work is that it is motivated primarily by psychophysical and physiological studies

H.H. Bülthoff et al. (Eds.): BMCV 2002, LNCS 2525, pp. 249–262, 2002.

of the human visual system, as summarized in the next section. Our problem domain is shown in figure 1.

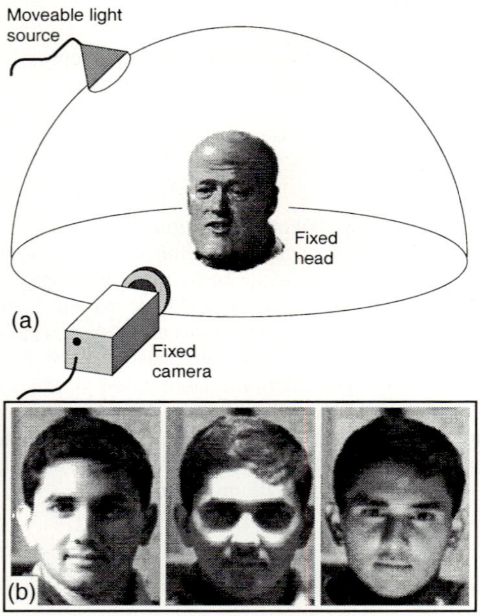

Fig. 1. Our problem domain. (a) Front facing upright heads being imaged under varying illumination conditions to yield images such as those shown in (b).

2 Face Detection by Human Observers

In order to investigate the roles of different image attributes in determining face detection performance by human observers, we conducted a series of psychophysical experiments, details of which can be found in [Torralba and Sinha, 2001]. Here we focus on two experiments that are most relevant to the design of our representation scheme. The first seeks to determine the level of image detail needed for reliable face-detection and the second investigates the encoding of contrast relationships across a face.

2.1 Experiment 1: Face Detection at Low-Resolution

What is the minimum resolution needed by human observers to reliably distinguish between face and non-face patterns? More generally, how does the accuracy of face classification by human observers change as a function of available image resolution? These are the questions our first experiment is designed to answer.

2.1.1 Methods

Subjects were presented with randomly interleaved face and non-face patterns and, in a 'yes-no' paradigm, were asked to classify them as such. The stimuli were grouped in blocks, each having the same set of patterns, but at different resolutions. The presentation order of the blocks proceeded from the lowest resolution to the highest. Ten subjects participated in the experiment. Presentations were self-timed. Our stimulus set comprised 200 monochrome patterns. Of these, 100 were faces of both genders under different lighting conditions (set 1), 75 were non-face patterns (set 2) derived from a well-known face-detection program (developed at the Carnegie Mellon University by Rowley et al [1995]) and the remaining 25 were patterns selected from natural images that have similar power-spectra as the face patterns (set 3). The patterns included in set 2 were false alarms (FAs) of Rowley et al's computational system, corresponding to the most conservative acceptance criterion yielding 95% hit rate. Sample non-face images are shown in figure 2. Reduction in resolution was accomplished via convolution with Gaussians of different sizes (with standard deviations set to yield 2, 3, 4, and 6 cycles per face; these correspond to 1.3, 2, 2.5 and 3.9 cycles within the eye-to-eye distance.

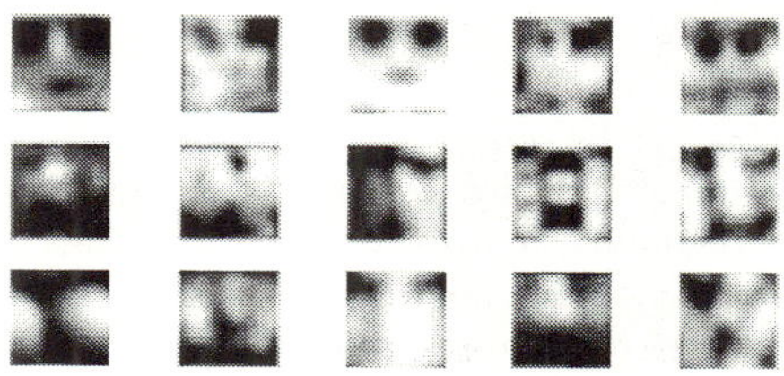

Fig. 2. A few of the non-face patterns used in our experiments. The patterns comprise false alarms of a computational face-detection system and images with similar spectra as face images.

From the pooled responses of all subjects at each blur level, we computed the mean hit-rate for the true face stimuli and false alarm rates for each set of distractor patterns. These data indicated how subjects' face-classification performance changed as a function of image resolution.

2.1.2 Results of Experiment 1

Figure 3 shows data averaged across 10 subjects. Subjects achieved a high hit rate (96%) and a low false-alarm rate (6% with Rowley et al's FPs and 0% with the other distractors) with images having only 3.9 cycles between the eyes. Performance remained robust (90% hit-rate and 19% false-alarm rate with the Rowley et al's FA distractor set) at even higher degrees of blur (2 cycles/ete).

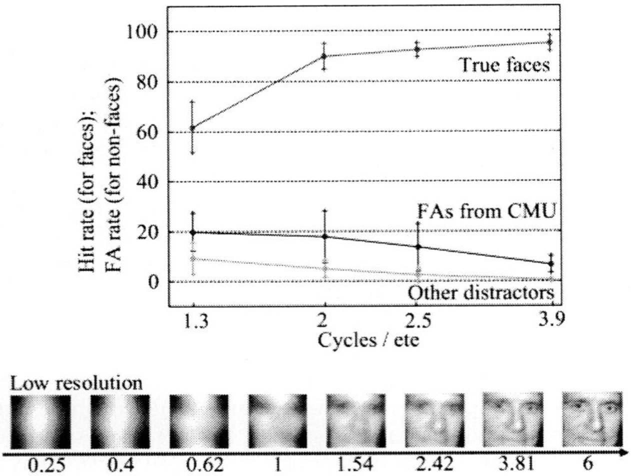

Fig. 3. Results from experiment 1.The units of resolution are the number of cycles eye to eye.

The data suggest that faces can be reliably distinguished from non-faces even at just 2 cycles eye-to-eye. Performance reaches an asymptote around 4 cycles/ete. Thus, even under highly degraded conditions, humans are correctly able to reject most non-face patterns that the artificial systems confuse for faces. To further underscore the differences in capabilities of current computational face detection systems and the HVS, it is instructive to consider the minimum image resolution needed by a few of the proposed machine-based systems: 19x19 pixels for Sung and Poggio [1994]; 20x20 for Rowley et al [1995]; 24x24 for Viola and Jones [2001] and 58x58 for Heisle et al. [2001]). Thus, computational systems not only require a much larger amount of facial detail for detecting faces in real scenes, but also yield false alarms that are correctly rejected by human observers even at resolutions much lower than what they were originally detected at.

2.2 Experiment 2: Role of Contrast Polarity in Face Detection

In studies of face identification, it has been found that contrast negation compromises performance [Galper, 1970; Bruce & Langton, 1994]. However, it is unknown how this affects the face-detection task. A priori, it is not clear whether this transformation should have any detrimental effects at all. For instance, it may well be the case that though it is difficult to identify people in photographic negatives, the ability to say whether a face is present may be unaffected since contrast negation preserves the basic geometry of a face. Experiment 2 is designed to test this issue. The basic experimental design follows from experiment 1. However the stimulus set of experiment 2 was augmented to include additional stimuli showing the faces and non-faces contrast negated.

2.2.1 Results of Experiment 2

Figure 4 shows that contrast negation causes significant decrements in face-detection performance. These results suggest that contrast reversal of face-patterns destroys the diagnostic information that allows their detection at low-resolution. Figure 5 also highlights the important role of contrast polarity in recognizing a pattern to be a face.

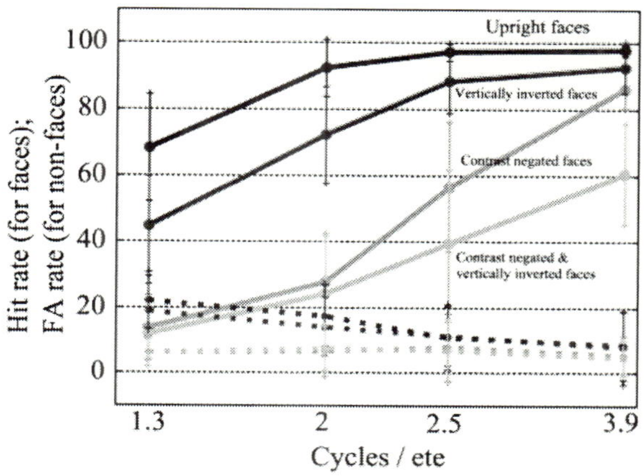

Fig. 4. Face detection performance following contrast negation.

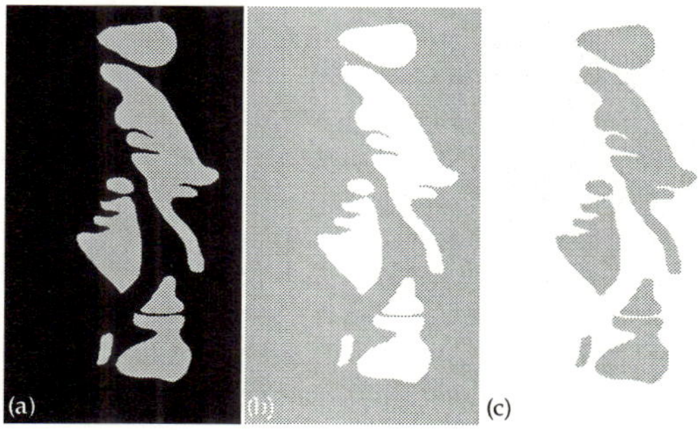

Fig. 5. Preserving absolute brightnesses of image regions is neither necessary nor sufficient for recognition. The patches in (a) and (b) have very different brightnesses and yet they are perceived as depicting the same object. The patches in (a) and (c), however, are perceived very differently even though they have identical absolute brightnesses. The direction of brightness contrast appears to have greater perceptual significance. (Mooney image courtesy: Patrick Cavanagh, Harvard University)

The significance of low-resolution image structure and contrast polarity rather than contrast magnitude per se is also reflected in the response properties of neurons in the early stages of the mammalian visual pathway. Beginning with the pioneering studies of Hubel and Wiesel, it has been established that many of these cells respond best to contrast edges. Many of these cells have large receptive fields and are, therefore, best suited to encoding coarse image structure. Additionally, studies exploring changes in response magnitude as a function of contrast strength have revealed that most neurons exhibit a rapidly saturating contrast response curve [DeAngelis et al, 1993]. In other words, the cell reaches its maximal response at very low levels of contrast so long as the contrast polarity is appropriate. For higher values of contrast, the cell-response does not change and is, therefore, uninformative regarding contrast magnitude. Such a cell thus serves as an ordinal comparator indicating whether the contrast polarity across the regions in its receptive field is correct and providing little quantitative information about contrast magnitude. The idealization of such a cell serves as the basic building block of our 'qualitative' image representation scheme.

3 'Ratio Templates': A Qualitative Scheme for Encoding Faces

The psychophysical results summarized above lead to two clear conclusions. First, human face detection performance is robust even at very low image resolutions and, second, it is sensitive to contrast polarity. The challenge is to devise a representation scheme that can take into account these results.

We propose a representation that is a collection of several pair-wise ordinal contrast relationships across facial regions. Consider figure 6. It shows several pairs of average brightness values over localized patches for each of the three images included in figure 1(b). Certain regularities are apparent. For instance, the average brightness of the left eye is always less than that of the forehead, irrespective of the lighting conditions. The relative magnitudes of the two brightness values may change, but the sign of the inequality does not. In other words, the *ordinal* relationship between the average brightnesses of the <left-eye, forehead> pair is invariant under lighting changes. Figure 6 also shows several other such pair-wise invariances. By putting all of these pair-wise invariances together, we obtain a larger composite invariant (figure 7). We call this invariant a *'ratio template'*, given that it is comprised of a set of binarized ratios of image brightnesses. It is worth noting that dispensing with precise measurements of image brightnesses not only leads to immunity to illumination variations, but also renders the ratio-template robust in the face of sensor noise. It also reconciles the design of the invariant with known perceptual limitations - the human visual system is far better at making relative brightness judgments than absolute ones. The 'ratio-template' is not a strict invariant, in that there exist special cases where it breaks. One such situation arises when the face is strongly illuminated from below. However, for almost all 'normal' lighting conditions (light sources at or above the level of the head), the ratio-template serves as a robust invariant.

3.1 The Match Metric

Having decided on the structure of the ratio-template (which, in essence, is our model for a face under different illumination setups), we now consider the problem of

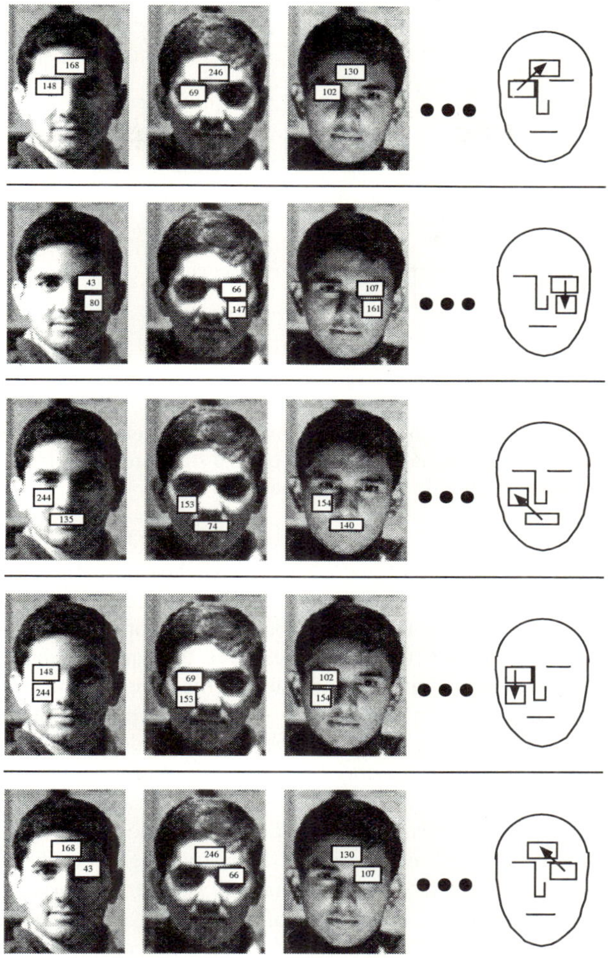

Fig. 6. The absolute brightnesses and even their relative magnitudes change under different lighting conditions but several pair-wise ordinal relationships are invariant.

matching it against a given image fragment to determine whether or not that part of the image contains a face. The first step involves averaging the image intensities over the regions laid down in the ratio-template's design and then determining the prescribed pair-wise ratios. The next step is to determine whether the ratios measured in the image match the corresponding ones in the ratio-template. An intuitive way to think of this problem is to view it as an instance of the general graph matching problem. The patches over which the image intensities are averaged constitute the nodes of the graph and the inter-patch ratios constitute the edges. A directed edge exists between two nodes if the ratio-template has been designed to include the

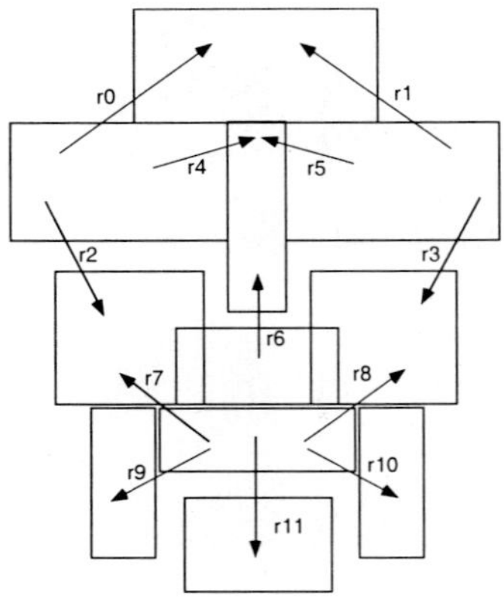

Fig. 7. By putting together several pair-wise invariants, we obtain what we call a 'ratio-template'. This is a representation of the invariant ordinal structure of the image brightness on a human face under widely varying illumination conditions.

brightness ratio between the corresponding image patches. The direction of the edge is such that it points from the node corresponding to the brighter region to the node corresponding to the darker one. Each corresponding pair of edges in the two graphs is examined to determine whether the two edges have the same direction. If they do, a predetermined positive contribution is made to the overall match metric, and a negative one otherwise. The magnitude of the contribution is proportional to the 'significance' of the ratio. A ratio's significance, in turn, is dependent on its robustness. For instance, the eye-forehead ratio may be considered more significant than the nose-tip-cheek ratio since the latter is more susceptible to being affected by such factors as facial hair and is therefore less robust. The contributions to be associated with different ratios can be learned automatically from training examples although in the current implementation, they have been set manually. After all corresponding pairs of edges have been examined, the magnitude of the overall match metric can be used under a simple threshold based scheme to declare whether or not the given image fragment contains a face. Alternatively, the vector indicating which graph edges match could be the input to a statistical classifier.

3.1.1 First Order Analysis

It may seem that by discarding the brightness ratio magnitude information, we run the risk of rendering the ratio-template too permissive in terms of the patterns that it will accept as faces; several false positives would be expected to result. In this section, we present a simple analysis showing that the probability of false positives is actually quite small. We proceed by computing how likely it is for an *arbitrary* distribution of image brightnesses to match a ratio-template. In the treatment below, we shall use the graph representation of the spatial distribution of brightnesses in the image and the template.

Let us suppose that the ratio-template is represented as a graph with n nodes, and e directed edges. Further suppose that if all the edges in this graph were to be replaced by undirected edges, it would have c simple cycles. We need to compute the cardinality of the set of all valid graphs defined on n nodes with e edges connecting the same pairs of nodes as in the template graph. A graph is 'valid' if it represents a physically possible spatial distribution of intensities. A directed graph with a cycle, for instance, is invalid since it violates the principle of transitivity of intensities. Each of the e edges connecting two nodes (say, A and B) can take on one of three directions:

1. if A has higher intensity value than B, the edge is directed from A to B, or
2. if B has higher intensity value than A, the edge is directed from B to A, or
3. if A and B have the same intensity values, the edge is undirected.

The total number of graphs on n nodes and e edges, therefore, is 3^e. This number, however, includes several invalid graphs. A set of m edges that constitute a simple cycle when undirected, introduce $2(2^m - 1)$ invalid graphs, as illustrated in figure 8. For c such sets, the total number of invalid graphs are

$$\sum_{i=1 \text{ to } c} 2(2^{m_i} - 1)$$

where m_i is the number of edges in the 'cycle set' i.

Therefore, the total number of valid graphs on n nodes, e edges and c cycles is

$$3^e - \sum_{i=1 \text{ to } c} 2(2^{m_i} - 1)$$

Of all these graphs, only one is acceptable as representing a human face. For most practical ratio-template parameters, the total number of valid graphs is quite large and the likelihood of an arbitrary distribution of image brightnesses accidentally being the same as that for a face is very small. For instance, for $e = 10$ and two cycle sets of sizes 6 and 3, the number of valid graphs is nearly 59,000. If all the corresponding intensity distributions are equally likely, the probability of a false positive is only $1.69 * 10^{-5}$.

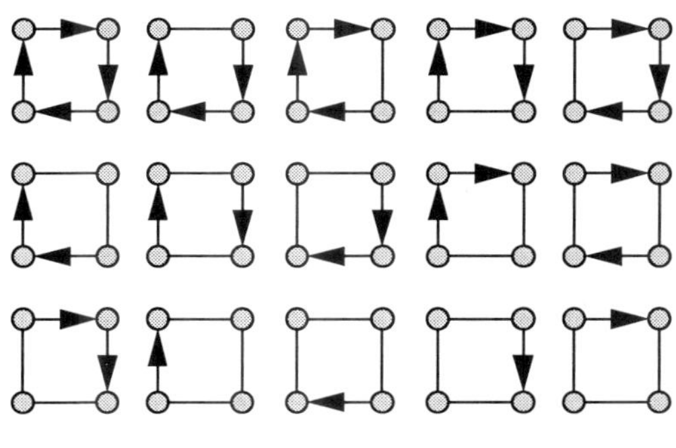

Fig. 8. A cycle set of m edges yields $2(2^m - 1)$ invalid graphs. A cycle set of 4 edges, for instance, yields 30 invalid graphs, 15 of which are shown above (the other 15 can be obtained by reversing the arrow directions). Each of these graphs leads to impossible relationships between intensity values (say, a and b) of the form a > b & b > a or a > b & a = b.

3.2 Implementation Issues

The face-invariant we have described above requires the computation of the average intensities over image regions of different sizes. An implementation that attempted to compute these averages over the image patches at each search location would be computationally wasteful of the results from previous search locations. A far more efficient implementation can be obtained by adopting a multi-resolution framework. In such a framework, the input image is repeatedly filtered and subsampled to create different levels of the image pyramid. The value of a single pixel in any of these images corresponds to the average intensity of an image patch in the original image if the filter used during the construction of the pyramid is a diffusing one (like a Gaussian). The deeper the pyramid level is, the larger the patch. Thus, a pyramid construction equips us with a collection of values that correspond to precomputed averages over patches of different sizes in the original image. The process of determining the average value for any image patch is thus reduced to picking out the appropriate pixel value from the bank of precomputed pyramid levels, leading to a tremendous saving in computation. The appropriate scale of operation for a given ratio-template depends on the chosen spatial parameters such as the patch sizes and the distances between them. By varying these parameters systematically, the face detection operation can be performed at multiple scales. Such a parameter variation is easily accomplished in the pyramid based implementation described above. By tapping different sets of the levels constituting the image pyramid, the presence of faces of different sizes can be determined. To have a denser sampling of the scale space, the inter-patch distances can be systematically varied while working with one set of levels of the pyramid. The natural tolerance of the approach to minor changes in scale takes care of handling the scales between the sample points. It is worth noting that the higher the pyramid levels, the lesser is the computational effort required to scan the whole image for faces. Therefore, the total amount of computational overhead involved in handling multiple scales is not excessive.

3.3 Tests

Figure 9 shows some of the results obtained on real images by using a ratio-template for face detection. Whenever it detects a face, the program pinpoints the location of the center of the head with a little white patch or a rectangle. The results are quite encouraging with a correct detection rate of about 80% and very few false positives. The 'errors' can likely be reduced even further by appropriately setting the threshold of acceptance. The results demonstrate the efficacy of the ratio-template as a face detector capable of handling changes in illumination, face identity, scale, facial expressions, skin tone and degradations in image resolution.

3.4 Learning the Signature

Our construction of the ratio-template in the preceding sections relied on a manual examination of several differently illuminated face images to determine whether there existed any regularities in their brightness distributions. A natural question to ask is whether we can design a learning system that can automatically extract a ratio-template from example streams. In principle, to accomplish this task, a learning system needs to determine which members of a potentially large set of image measurements are highly correlated with the presence of a face in the example images. We have tested this conceptually simple idea by extracting a ratio-template from a set of synthetic face images. Figure 10(a) shows some of the input images we used. These were generated using a program that embedded certain face-like invariances in variable random backgrounds. The task of the learning system was to recover these invariances from labeled (face/non-face) examples.

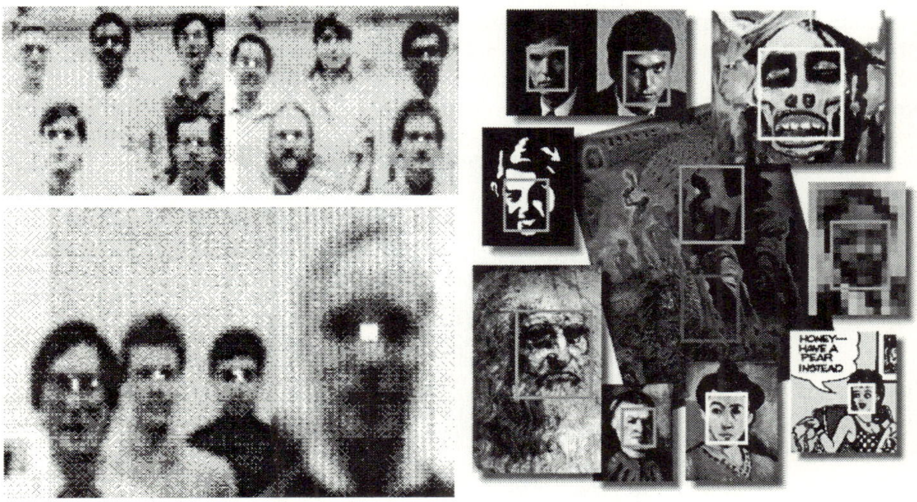

Fig. 9. Testing the face-detection scheme on real images. The program places a small white square at the center of, or a rectangle around, each face it detects. The results demonstrate the scheme's robustness to varying identity, facial hair, skin tone, eye-glasses and scale.

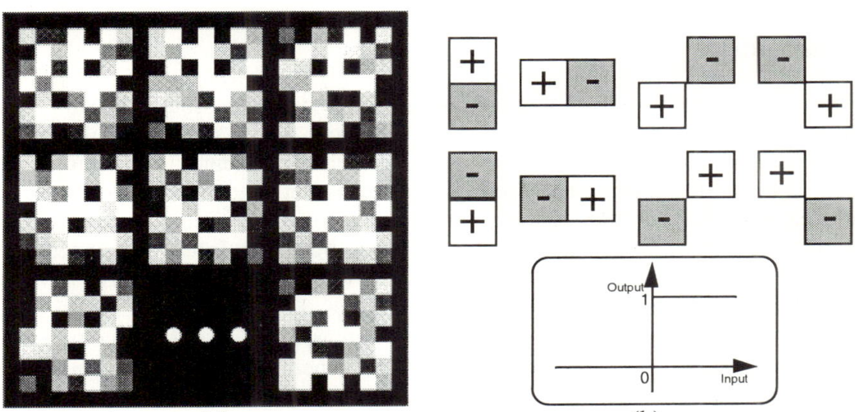

(a) (b)

Fig. 10. (a) These images are representative of the inputs to the learning system. The images are synthetic and are meant to represent differently illuminated faces on varying random backgrounds. (b) The receptive fields of the pre-processors and their output function.

The 'receptive fields' of the pre-processor units are shown in figure 10(b). These units can be thought of as detecting inequality relations between adjacent image patches. The learning system needs to estimate the correlation of each measurement with the presence of a face. As is to be expected, only the measurements that are part of the invariant survive through all the examples while others weaken. This is shown in figure 11. It is important to notice that by the end of the computation, we have not only constructed the object concept (the 'ratio-template' in this case) but have also implicitly learned to segment it from the background. This approach, therefore, simultaneously addresses two important issues in recognition: 1. What defines an object?, and 2. How can one segment a scene into different objects? In recent work (Thoresz and Sinha, 2002), we have successfully tested this learning approach on real images besides the synthetic ones shown here.

Fig. 11. Detecting relevant features via correlational learning over a set of examples. The output is the object concept. Segmentation is a side-effect.

4 Endnote

We have suggested the use of a qualitative face signature, that we call a ratio-template, as a candidate scheme for detecting faces under significant illumination variations. One can think of this specific scheme as an instance of a more general object recognition strategy that uses qualitative object signatures. Such a strategy would be attractive for the significant invariance to imaging conditions that it can potentially confer. However, it also has a potential drawback. Intuitively, it seems that the 'coarseness' of the measurements they use would render qualitative invariants quite useless at tasks requiring fine discriminations. How might one obtain *precise* model indexing using qualitative invariants that are, by definition, comprised of *imprecise* measurements? Depicting this problem schematically, figure 12(a) shows a collection of object models positioned in a space defined by three attribute axes. To precisely index into this model set, we can adopt one of two approaches: 1. we can either be absolutely right in measuring at least one attribute value (figure 12(b)), or 2. we can be 'approximately right' in measuring *all three* attributes (figure 12(e)). Being approximately right in just one or two attributes is not expected to yield unique indexing (figures 12(c) and (d)).

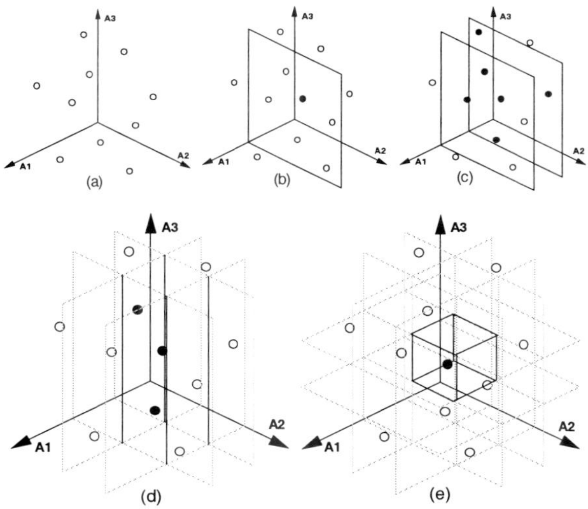

Fig. 12. (a) A schematic depiction of a collection of object models positioned in a space defined by three attribute axes. To precisely index into this model set, we can adopt one of two approaches: 1. we can either be absolutely right in measuring at least one attribute value (figure (b)), or 2. we can be 'approximately right' in measuring all three attributes (figure (e)). Being approximately right in just one or two attributes is not expected to yield unique indexing (figures (c) and (d)).

The qualitative invariant approach constructs unique signatures for objects using several approximate measurements. The ratio-template is a case in point. It achieves its fine discriminability between face and non-face images by compositing several very imprecise binary comparisons of image brightnesses. In several real world situations, there might in fact be no alternative to using approximate measurements. This could be either because precise invariants just might not exist or because of noise in the measurement process itself. The only recourse in these situations would be to exploit several attribute dimensions and be 'approximately good' in measuring all of them. This is what qualitative invariants are designed to do. The 'recognition by qualitative invariants' approach is eminently suited to a complex visual world such as ours. Most objects vary along several different attribute dimensions such as shape, color, texture, and motion, to name a few. The qualitative invariant approach can exploit this complexity by constructing unique object signatures from approximate measurements along all of these dimensions. Evidence for the generality of this approach is provided by some of our recent work. We have implemented recognition schemes based on qualitative templates (that use not only qualitative photometric measurements but also spatial ones) for robustly recognizing a diversity of objects and scenes including natural landscapes, graphic symbols and cars.

A related observation is that the ratio-template representation is a 'holistic' encoding of object structure. Since each ordinal relation by itself is too coarse to provide a good discriminant function to distinguish between members and non-members of an object-class, we need to consider many of the relations together (implicitly processing object structure holistically) to obtain the desired performance. At least in the context of face-detection, this holistic strategy appears to be supported by our recent studies of concept acquisition by children learning to see after treatment for congenital blindness [Sinha, 2002, in preparation].

Acknowledgements. The author wishes to thank Prof. Tomaso Poggio, Dr. Peter Burt, and Dr. Shmuel Peleg for several insightful discussions regarding this work.

References

Bruce, V. (1994) Stability from variation: the case of face recognition. *Quarterly Journal of Experimental Psychology*, 47A, 5–28.

Bruce, V. & Langton, S. (1994). The use of pigmentation and shading information in recognizing the sex and identities of faces. *Perception,* 23, 803–822.

Cabeza, R., Bruce, V., Kato, T. & Oda, M. (1998). The prototype effect in face recognition: Extension and limits. *Memory and Cognition.*

Galper, R. E. (1970). Recognition of faces in photographic negative. *Psychonomic Science*, 19, 207–208.

Gregory C. DeAngelis, Izumi Ohzawa, and Ralph D. Freeman (1993). Spatiotemporal organization of simple-cell receptive fields in the cat's striate cortex. I. General Characteristics and postnatal development. *J. Neurophysiol.* 69: 1091–1117.

Heisle, B., T. Serre, S. Mukherjee and T. Poggio. (2001) Feature Reduction and Hierarchy of Classifiers for Fast Object Detection in Video Images. In: *Proceedings of 2001 IEEE Computer Society Conference on Computer Vision and Pattern Recognition (CVPR 2001)*, IEEE Computer Society Press, Jauai, Hawaii, December 8–14, 2001.

Hunke, H. M. (1994) Locating and tracking of human faces with neural networks. Master's thesis, University of Karlsruhe.

Govindaraju, V., Sher, D. B., Srihari, R. K. and Srihari, S. N. (1989) Locating human faces in newspaper photographs. *Procs. of the Conf. on Comp.Vision and Pattern Recog.*, pp. 549–554.

Rowley, H. A., Baluja, S., Kanade, T. (1995) Human face detection in visual scenes, CMUtechnical-report,#CS-95-158R.

Sinha, P. (2002). Face detection following extended visual deprivation. (In preparation).

Sung, K. K., and Poggio, T. (1994) Example based learning for view-based human face detection, AI Laboratory memo # 1521, MIT.

Thoresz, K. and Sinha, P. (2002) Common representations for objects and scenes. *Proceedings of the Annual Meeting of the Vision Sciences Society,* Florida.

Torralba, A. and Sinha, P. (2001). Detecting faces in impoverished images. MIT AI Laboratory Memo, Cambridge, MA.

Viola, P. and Jones, M. (2001). Rapid object detection using a boosted cascade of simple features. In: *Proceedings of 2001 IEEE Computer Society Conference on Computer Vision and Pattern Recognition (CVPR 2001)*, IEEE Computer Society Press, Jauai, Hawaii, December 8–14, 2001.

Yang, G. and Huang, T. S. (1993) Human face detection in a scene. *Proceedings of the Conference on Computer Vision and Pattern Recognition*, 453–458.

Yang, G. and Huang, T. S. (1994) Human face-detection in a complex background. *Pattern Recognition*, 27(1) pp. 53–63.

Scene-Centered Description from Spatial Envelope Properties

Aude Oliva[1] and Antonio Torralba[2]

[1] Department of Psychology and Cognitive Science Program
Michigan State University
East Lansing, MI 48824, USA
aoliva@msu.edu
[2] Artificial Intelligence Laboratory, MIT
Cambridge, MA 02139, USA
torralba@ai.mit.edu

Abstract. In this paper, we propose a scene-centered representation able to provide a meaningful description of real world images at multiple levels of categorization (from superordinate to subordinate levels). The scene-centered representation is based upon the estimation of spatial envelope properties describing the shape of a scene (e.g. size, perspective, mean depth) and the nature of its content. The approach is holistic and free of segmentation phase, grouping mechanisms, 3D construction and object-centered analysis.

1 Introduction

Fig. 1 illustrates the difference between object and scene-centered approaches for image recognition. The former is *content*-focused: the description of a scene is built from a list of objects (e.g. sky, road, buildings, people, cars [1,4]). A scene-centered approach is *context*-focused: it refers to a collection of descriptors that apply to the whole image and not to a portion of it (the scene is man-made or natural, is an indoor or an outdoor place, etc.). Object and scene-centered approaches are clearly complementary.

Seminal models of scene recognition [2,8] have proposed that the highest level of visual recognition, the identity of a real world scene, is mediated by the reconstruction of the input image from local measurements, successively integrated into decision layers of increasing complexity. In this chain, the role of low-level and medium levels of representation is to make available to the high-level a useful and segmented representation of the scene image. Following this approach, current computer vision models propose to render the process of "recognizing" by extracting a set of image-based features (e.g. color, orientation, texture) that are combined to form higher-level representations such as regions [4], elementary forms (e.g. geons, [3]) and objects [1]. Scene identity level is then achieved by the recognition of a set of objects or regions delivered by the medium level of processing. For instance, the medium-level visual representation of a forest might be a "greenish and textured horizontal surface, connected to

H.H. Bülthoff et al. (Eds.): BMCV 2002, LNCS 2525, pp. 263–272, 2002.

several textured greenish blobs, and brownish, vertically oriented shapes" ([4]). High level processes might interpret these surfaces as a grass land, bushes and trees [1]).

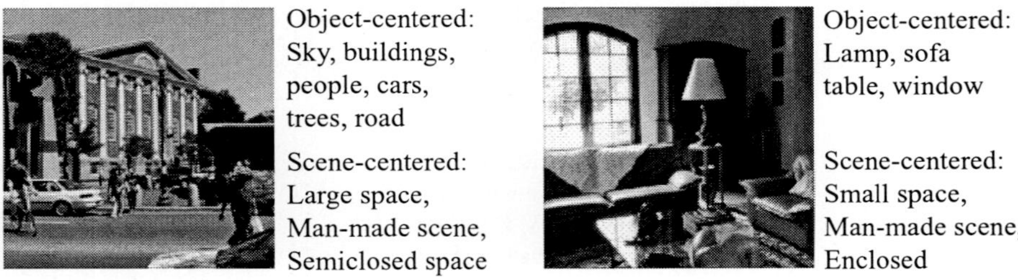

Fig. 1. Example of object-centered and space-centered descriptions.

On the other hand, some image understanding studies suggest that human observers can apprehend the meaning of a complex picture within a glance [11] without necessarily remembering important objects and their locations [7,13]. Human observers are also able to recover scene identity under image conditions that have degraded the objects so much that they become unrecognizable in isolation. Within a glance, observers can still identify the category of a scene picture with spatial frequency as low as 4 to 8-cycles/image [15,9]. Scene meaning may also be driven from the arrangement of simple volumetric forms, the "geons" [3]. In both cases (blobs or geons), detailed information about the local identity of the objects is not available in the image. All together, those studies suggest that the identity of a real world scene picture may also be recovered from scene-centered based features not related to object or region segmentation mechanisms.

In an effort to by-pass the segmentation step and object recognition mechanisms, a few studies in computer vision have proposed an alternative scene-centered representation, based on low-level features extraction [16,20], semantic axes [10,14] or space descriptors [10,18]. Common to these studies is the goal to find the basic-level category of the image (e.g. street, living room) directly from scene descriptors bypassing object recognition as a first step. As an illustration, a scene-centered representation based on space descriptors [10,18] could resemble the description provided in Figure 1: the picture of the street represents a man-made, urban environment, a busy and large space, with a semi-closed volume (because of the facades of the building). Such a scene-centered representation could be built upon space properties correlated with the scene's origin (natural, outdoor, indoor), its volume (its mean depth, its perspective, its size), the occupancy of the volume (complexity, roughness), etc. These spatial scene-centered characteristics happened to be meaningful descriptors highly correlated with the semantic category of the image [10,18].

This paper is dedicated to the description of a scene-centered representation, at the medium level of visual processing. Our goal is to generate a meaningful description of real world scene, based on the identification of simple spatial properties. In the following sections, we describe how to compute a set of volumetric properties of a scene image, as they would appear in the 3D world, based on computations made on 2D images. The resulting space-centered scheme is independent of the complexity of the scene image (e.g. number of objects and regions) and able to provide multiple level of scene description (from superordinate to subordinate levels).

2 Scene Space Descriptors

In order to identify the candidate descriptors of real world scenes, we ran a behavioral experiment similar to the procedures used by [12,6] for classifying textures. For example, the perceptual properties suitable for representing the texture of a forest may be its orientation, its roughness, and its homogeneity [12,6]. These properties are meaningful to an observer that may use them for comparing similarities between two texture images. As a scene is inherently a 3D environment, in [10], we asked observers to classify images of scenes according to spatial characteristics. Seventeen observers were asked to split 81 pictures into groups. They were told that scenes belonging to the same group should have similar global aspect, similar spatial structure or similar elements. They were explicitly told not to use a criteria related to the objects (e.g. cars vs. no cars, people vs. no people) or a scene semantic groups (e.g. street, beach). At the end of each step, subjects were asked to explain the criteria they used with few words (see [10] for a detailed explanation).

The initial list of space descriptors described in [10] is given below. In this paper, we propose to use these perceptual properties as the vocabulary used to build a scene-centered description. We split the descriptors used by the observers in two sets:

The descriptors that refer to the volume of the scene image are:

- *Depth Range* is related to the size of the space. It refers to the average distance between the observer and the boundaries of the scene [18].
- *Openness* refers to the sense of enclosure of the space. It opposes indoor scenes (enclosed spaces) to open landscapes. Openness characterizes places and it is not relevant for describing single objects or close-up views.
- *Expansion* represents the degree of perspective of the space. The degree of expansion of a view is a combination of the organization of forms in the scene and the point of view of the observer. It is relevant to man-made outdoors and large indoors.
- *Ruggedness* refers to the deviation of the ground with respect to the horizon. It describes natural scenes, opposing flat to mountainous landscapes.
- *Verticalness*: It refers to the orientation of the "walls" of the space, whenever applicable. It opposes scenes organized horizontally (e.g. highways, ocean views), to scenes with vertical structures (buildings, trees).

The descriptors that refer to the scene content are:

- *Naturalness* refers to the origin of the components used to build the scene (man-made or natural). It is a general property that applies to any picture.
- *Busyness* is mostly relevant for man-made scenes. Busyness represents the sense of cluttering of the space. It opposes empty to crowded scenes.
- *Roughness* refers to the size of the main components (for man-made scenes, from big to small) or the grain of the dominant texture (for natural scenes, from coarse to fine) in the image.

We proposed to refer to the *spatial envelope* of a real world scene and a scene image, as a combination of space descriptors, in reference to the architectural notion of "envelope" of urban, landscape and indoor environments. In the next section, we defined the image-based representation that allows extracting spatial envelope descriptors from raw image, in order to generate the scene-centered description (cf. Fig. 4 and 5).

3 Scene-Space Centered Representation

Opposed to object-centered image representation, we describe here an image representation [10,18] that encodes the distribution of textures and edges in the image and their coarse spatial arrangement without segmentation stage (see also [16,20]). The resulting "sketchy" representation, illustrated in fig. 2, is not adequate for representing regions or objects within an image, but it captures enough of the image structure to reliably estimate structural and textural attributes of the scene (see sections 5-7). The sketch is based on a low-resolution encoding of the output magnitude of multiscale oriented Gabor filters:

$$A_M^2(\mathbf{x}, k) = \left\{ |i(\mathbf{x}) * g_k(\mathbf{x})|^2 \downarrow M \right\} \tag{1}$$

$i(\mathbf{x})$ is the input image and $g_k(\mathbf{x})$ is the impulse response of a Gabor filter. The index k indexes filters tuned to different scales and orientations. The notation $\downarrow M$ represents the operation of downsampling in the spatial domain until the resulting representation $A_M(\mathbf{x}, k)$ has a spatial resolution of M^2 pixels. Therefore, $A_M(\mathbf{x}, k)$ has a dimensionality M^2K where K is the total number of filters used in the image decomposition. Fig. 2 illustrates the information preserved by this representation. It shows synthesized texture-like images that are constrained to have the same features $A_M(\mathbf{x}, k)$ ($M = 4$, $K = 20$) than the original image. This scene-centered representation contains a coarse description of the structures of the image and their spatial arrangement.

Each scene picture is represented by a features vector $\mathbf{v}$ with the set of measurements $A_M(\mathbf{x}, k)$ rearranged into a column vector. Note that the dimensionality of the vector is independent of the scene complexity (e.g. number of regions). Applying a PCA further reduces the dimensionality of $\mathbf{v}$ while preserving most of the information that accounts for the variability among pictures. The principal components PCs are the eigenvectors of the covariance matrix $\mathbf{C} = E[(\mathbf{v} - \mathbf{m})(\mathbf{v} - \mathbf{m})^T]$ where $\mathbf{v}$ is a column vector composed by the image

Fig. 2. Examples of sketch images obtained by coercing noise to have the same features than the original image. This scene-centered representation encodes the spatial arrangement of structures (here, at 2 cycles/image) without a previous step of segmentation. Each sketch has been reconstructed from 320 features (see [18]).

features, and $\mathbf{m} = E[\mathbf{v}]$. We will refer to the column vector $\mathbf{v}$ as the L dimensional vector obtained by projection of the image features onto the first L PCs with the largest eigenvalues.

4 From Image Features to Spatial Envelope Descriptors

The system described below is designed to learn the relationship between the sketch representation (image features $\mathbf{v}$) and the space descriptors. Each picture has two values associated to each space descriptor $\{R_j, \alpha_j\}$. The first parameter, R_j is the relevance of a specific space descriptor for a given picture, scaled between 0 and 1. To annotate the database (3,000 pictures), three observers selected, for each picture, the set of space descriptors that were appropriate. For example, a street image can be described in terms of its *mean depth*, its degree of *openness* and *expansion* and how cluttered it is. But for describing an object or an animal, *expansion* and *busyness* are not relevant descriptors. *Verticalness*, on the other hand, may apply specifically to some objects (e.g. a bottle), indoors (e.g. a stairs view) urban places (e.g. a skyscraper) and natural scenes (e.g. forest). *Naturalness* and *mean depth* are relevant descriptors of any image. The second parameter, α_j is the value of a specific space descriptor, normalized between 0 and 1. For instance, a city sky-line will have a large value of mean depth and openness; a perspective view of a street will have a high value of expansion and an intermediate value of depth and openness. To calibrate α_j, each picture was ranked among a set of pictures already organized from the lowest to the highest value of each descriptor (e.g., from the more open to the less open space). The position index for each picture corresponded to α_j.

The system learnt to predict the *relevance* and the *value* of each space descriptor, given a set of image features $\mathbf{v}$. Three parameters are estimated for each new picture:

- *Relevance.* Relevance of a space descriptor is the likelihood that an observer uses it for describing volumetric aspects of the scene. The Relevance may be approximated as: $P(R_j = 1|\mathbf{v})$.
- *Value.* Value of a space descriptor estimates which verbal label would best apply to a scene. It can be estimated from the image features as $\hat{\alpha_j} = E\,[\,\alpha_j\,|\,\mathbf{v}]$.

– *Confidence.* Confidence value gives how reliable is the estimation of each space descriptor provided the image features $\mathbf{v}$. It corresponds to $\sigma_j^2 = E[(\hat{\alpha_j} - \alpha_j)^2 | \mathbf{v}]$. The higher the variance σ_j^2 the less reliable is the estimation of the property α_j given the image features $\mathbf{v}$.

The *Relevance* is calculated as the likelihood:

$$P(R_j = 1|\mathbf{v}) = \frac{p(\mathbf{v}|R_j = 1)p(R_j = 1)}{p(\mathbf{v}|R_j = 0)P(R_j = 0) + p(\mathbf{v}|R_j = 1)P(R_j = 1)} \tag{2}$$

The PDFs $p(\mathbf{v}|R_j = 1)$ and $p(\mathbf{v}|R_j = 0)$ are modeled as mixture of gaussians: $p(\mathbf{v}|R_j = 1) = \sum_{i=1}^{N_c} g(\mathbf{v}, c_i)\, p(c_i)$. The parameters of the mixtures are then estimated with the EM algorithm [5]. The prior $P(R_j = 1)$ is approximated by the frequency of use of the attribute j within the training set.

Estimation of the value of each descriptor can be performed as the conditional expectation $\hat{\alpha_j} = E\,[\alpha_j \,|\, \mathbf{v}] = \int \alpha_j f(\alpha_j \,|\, \mathbf{v}) d\alpha_j$. The function can be evaluated by estimating the join distribution between that values of the attribute and the image features $f(\alpha_j, \mathbf{v})$. This function is modeled by a mixture of gaussians: $f(\alpha_j, \mathbf{v}) = \sum_{i=1}^{N_c} g(\alpha \,|\, \mathbf{v}, c_i)\, g(\mathbf{v} \,|\, c_i)\, p(c_i)$ with $g(\alpha \,|\, \mathbf{v}, c_i)$ being a gaussian with mean $a_i + \mathbf{v}^T \boldsymbol{b}_i$ and variance σ_i. The learning of the model parameters for each property is estimated with the EM algorithm and the training database [5,18]. Once the learning is completed, the conditional PDF of the attribute value α_j, given the image features, is:

$$f(\alpha_j \,|\, \mathbf{v}) = \frac{\sum_{i=1}^{N_c} g(\alpha_j \,|\, \mathbf{v}, c_i)\, g(\mathbf{v} \,|\, c_i)\, p(c_i)}{\sum_{i=1}^{N_c} g(\mathbf{v} \,|\, c_i)\, p(c_i)} \tag{3}$$

Therefore, given a new scene picture, the attribute value is estimated from the image features as a mixture of local linear regressions:

$$\hat{\alpha_j} = \frac{\sum_{i=1}^{N_c} (a_i + \mathbf{v}^T \boldsymbol{b}_i)\, g(\mathbf{v} \,|\, c_i)\, p(c_i)}{\sum_{i=1}^{N_c} g(\mathbf{v} \,|\, c_i)\, p(c_i)} \tag{4}$$

We can also estimate the scene attribute using the maximum likelihood: $\hat{\alpha_j} = \max_{\alpha_j} \{f(\alpha_j \,|\, \mathbf{v})\}$. The estimation of the PDF $f(\alpha_j|\mathbf{v}, S)$ provides a method to measure the confidence of the estimation provided by eq. (4) for each picture:

$$\sigma_j^2 = E[(\hat{\alpha_j} - \alpha_j)^2 | \mathbf{v}] = \frac{\sum_{i=1}^{N_c} \sigma_i^2\, g(\mathbf{v} \,|\, c_i)\, p(c_i)}{\sum_{i=1}^{N_c} g(\mathbf{v} \,|\, c_i)\, p(c_i)} \tag{5}$$

The confidence measure allows rejecting estimations that are not expected to be reliable. The bigger the value of the variance σ_j^2 the less reliable is the estimation $\hat{\alpha_j}$.

5 Performances of Classification

Each space property is a one-dimensional axis along which pictures are continuously organized [10]. Fig. 3.a shows correlation values between the ranking

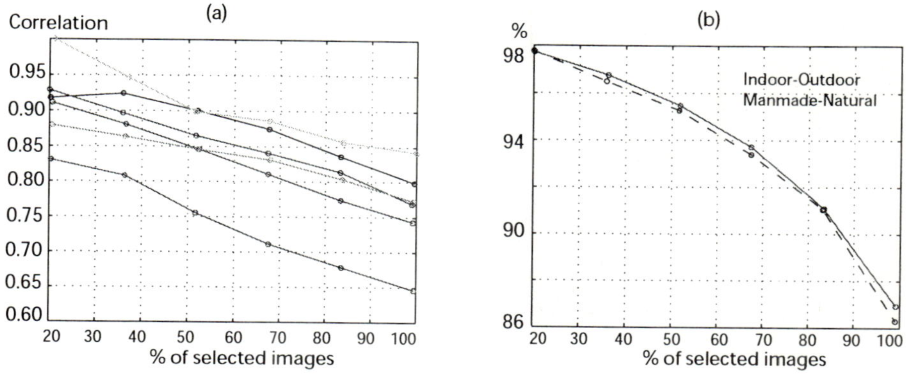

Fig. 3. a) correlation of picture ranking, for each space dimension, between observers and the model as a function of the percentage of images selected. The images are selected by putting a threshold to the confidence σ_j^2. From top to bottom: verticalness, openness, mean depth, ruggedness, expansion, busyness. b) Performance of correct classification in man-made vs. natural scenes and indoor vs. outdoor.

made by human observers and the ranking computed by the model (from eq. 4). We asked two observers to perform 10 orderings, of 20 images each (images not used in the training), for each of the spatial envelope properties. Orderings were compared by measuring the Spearman rank correlation:

$$Sr = 1 - 6\frac{\sum_{i=1}^{n}(rx_i - ry_i)^2}{n(n^2-1)} \tag{6}$$

with $n = 20$. rx_i and ry_i are respectively the rank positions of the image i given by the algorithm and by one subject. A complete agreement corresponds to $Sr = 1$. When both orderings are independent, $Sr = 0$. When considering the entire image database, correlation values go from 0.65 to 0.84 for the different attributes of the spatial envelope. When considering a percentage of images with the highest level of confidence (σ_j^2, Eq. 5), performances improve.

6 Generating Space-Centered Descriptions

The value α_j of a specific descriptor assigned to an image can be translated into a verbal description. Each space axis was split in a few subgroups (from 2 to 5). For example, the mean depth axis was separated in 4 groups: close-up view, small space, large space, and panoramic view. The openness descriptor was represented by 5 categories (open, semi-open, semi-closed, closed, and enclosed). All together, the verbal labels are expected to form a meaningful description of the scene (see Fig. 4). Whenever a property was not relevant for a type of image ($R_j < threshold$) or the level of confidence (σ_j^2) was not high enough, the system did not use the corresponding verbal label. Therefore, instead of being wrong, the model provides a less precise description.

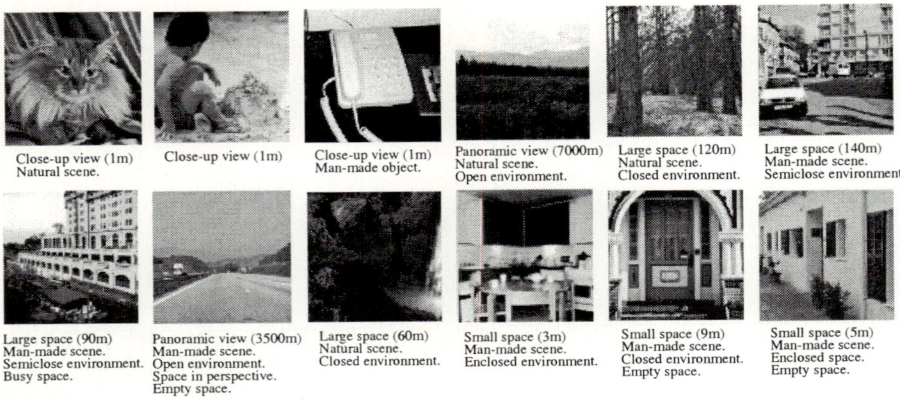

Fig. 4. Examples of space-centered descriptions automatically generated. For each image, the description contains only the space properties that are relevant and that provided high confidence estimates.

7 Computing Space-Centered Similarities

In [10], we provided *space-features* based image similarities: pictures with similar spatial envelope values were closed together in a multi-dimensional space formed by the set of space descriptors. Within this space, neighbor images look alike.

The spatial envelope representation is able to generate descriptions at different levels of categorization (fig. 5): the super-ordinate level of the space (e.g. large scaled views), a more basic-level (e.g. open and expanded urban space), and a subordinate-level (e.g. open and expanded urban space, crowded) where pictures are more likely to look similar. To which extend a specific space property is relevant for a subordinate or super-ordinate level of description in regard to human observers, still need to be determined, but the general principle illustrated in fig. 5 shows the potentiality of the spatial envelope description for categorizing very different pictures at multiple levels of categorization, as human observers do.

8 Conclusion

The scene-centered representation based on spatial envelope descriptors show that the highest level of recognition, the identity of a scene, may be built from of a set of volumetric properties available in the scene image. It defines a general recognition framework within which complex image categorization may be achieved free of segmentation stage, grouping mechanisms, 3D interpretation and object-centered analysis. The space-centered approach provides a meaningful description of scene images at multiple levels of description (from superordinate to subordinate levels) and independently of image complexity. The scene-centered scheme provides a novel approach to context modeling, and can be used to enhance object detection algorithms, by priming objects, their size and locations [17]).

Fig. 5. Scene categorization at different levels of description.

Acknowledgments. Many thanks to Whitman Richards, Bill Freeman, John Henderson, Fernanda Ferreira, Randy Birnkrant and two anonymous reviewers whose comments greatly helped improve the manuscript. Correspondence regarding this article may be sent to both authors.

References

1. Barnard, K., Forsyth, D.A.: Learning the semantics of words and pictures. Proceedings of the International Conference on Computer Vision, Vancouver, Canada (2001) 408–415

2. Barrow, H. G., Tannenbaum, J.M.: Recovering intrinsic scene characteristics from images. In: Hanson, A., Riseman, E. (eds.): Computer Vision Systems, New York, Academic press (1978) 3–26
3. Biederman, I.: Recognition-by-components: A theory of human image interpretation. Psychological Review. **94** (1987) 115–148
4. Carson, C., Belongie, S., Greenspan, H., Malik, J.: Blobworld: Image segmentation using Expectation-Maximization and its Application to Image Querying. IEEE Transactions on Pattern Analysis and Machine Intelligence. **24** (2002) 1026–1038
5. Gershnfeld, N.: The nature of mathematical modeling. Cambridge university press (1999)
6. Heaps, C., Handel, S.: Similarity and features of natural textures. Journal of Experimental Psychology: Human Perception and Performance. **25** (1999) 299–320
7. Henderson, J.M., Hollingworth, A.: High level scene perception. Annual Review of Psychology. **50** (1999) 243–271.
8. Marr, D.: Vision. San Francisco, CA. WH Freeman (1982)
9. Oliva, A., Schyns, P. G.: Diagnostic color blobs mediate scene recognition. Cognitive Psychology. **41** (2000) 176–210.
10. Oliva, A., Torralba, A.: Modeling the shape of the scene: a holistic representation of the Spatial Envelope. International Journal of Computer Vision. **42** (2001) 145–175
11. Potter, M. C.: Meaning in visual search. Science. **187** (1975) 965–966.
12. Rao, A.R., Lohse, G.L.: Identifying high level features of texture perception. Graphical Models and Image Processing. **55** (1993) 218–233
13. Rensink, R. A., O'Regan, J. K., Clark, J. J.: To see or not to see: the need for attention to perceive changes in scenes. Psychological Science. **8** (1997) 368–373
14. Rogowitz, B., Frese, T., Smith, J., Bouman, Kalin, E.: Perceptual image similarity experiments. Human Vision and Electronic Imaging, SPIE Vol 3299. (1998) 576–590
15. Schyns, P.G., Oliva, A.: From blobs to boundary edges: evidence for time- and spatial-scale dependent scene recognition. Psychological Science. **5** (1994) 195–200
16. Szummer, M., Picard, R. W.: Indoor-outdoor image classification. IEEE International Workshop on Content-based Access of Image and Video Databases, Bombay, India (1998)
17. Torralba, A.: Contextual Modulation of Target Saliency. In: Dietterich, T. G., Becker, S, Ghahramani, Z. (eds.): Advances in Neural Information Processing Systems, Vol. 14. MIT Press, Cambridge, MA (2002)
18. Torralba, A., Oliva, A.: Depth estimation from image structure. IEEE Transactions on Pattern Analysis and Machine Intelligence. **24** (2002)
19. Torralba, A., Sinha, P.: Statistical context priming for object detection: scale selection and focus of attention. Proceedings of the International Conference in Computer Vision, Vancouver, Canada (2001) 763–770.
20. Vailaya, A., Jain, A., Zhang, H. J.: On image classification: city images vs. landscapes. Pattern Recognition. **31** (1998) 1921–1935

Visual Categorization: How the Monkey Brain Does It

Ulf Knoblich[1], Maximilian Riesenhuber[1], David J. Freedman[2], Earl K. Miller[2], and Tomaso Poggio[1]

[1] Center for Biological and Computational Learning, McGovern Institute for Brain Research, Artificial Intelligence Lab and Department of Brain and Cognitive Sciences, Massachusetts Institute of Technology, Cambridge, MA, USA
`{knoblich,max,tp}@ai.mit.edu`,

[2] Picower Center for Learning and Memory, RIKEN-MIT Neuroscience Research Center and Department of Brain and Cognitive Sciences, Massachusetts Institute of Technology, Cambridge, MA, USA
`davidf@mit.edu,ekm@ai.mit.edu`

Abstract. Object categorization is a crucial cognitive ability. It has also received much attention in machine vision. However, the computational processes underlying object categorization in cortex are still poorly understood. In this paper we compare data recorded by Freedman *et al.* from monkeys to that of view-tuned units in our HMAX model of object recognition in cortex [1,2]. We find that the results support a model of object recognition in cortex [3] in which a population of shape-tuned neurons responding to individual exemplars provides a general basis for neurons tuned to different recognition tasks. Simulations further indicate that this strategy of first learning a general but object class-specific representation as input to a classifier simplifies the learning task. Indeed, the physiological data suggest that in the monkey brain, categorization is performed by PFC neurons performing a simple classification based on the thresholding of a linear sum of the inputs from examplar-tuned units. Such a strategy has various computational advantages, especially with respect to transfer across novel recognition tasks.

1 Introduction

The ability to group diverse items into meaningful categories (such as "predator" or "food") is perhaps the most fundamental cognitive ability of humans and higher primates. Likewise, object categorization has received much attention in machine vision. However, relatively little is known about the computational architecture underlying categorization in cortex.

In [3], Riesenhuber and Poggio proposed a model of object recognition in cortex, HMAX, in which a general representation of objects in inferotemporal cortex (IT, the highest area in the cortical ventral visual stream, which is believed to mediate object recognition), provides the basis for different recognition tasks — such as identification and categorization — with task-related units located further downstream, *e. g.*, in prefrontal cortex (PFC). Freedman and Miller recently

H.H. Bülthoff et al. (Eds.): BMCV 2002, LNCS 2525, pp. 273–281, 2002.

performed physiology experiments providing experimental population data for both PFC and IT of monkeys trained on a "cat/dog" categorization task ([4] and Freedman, Riesenhuber, Poggio, Miller, *Soc. Neurosci. Abs.*, 2001), allowing us to test this theory. In this paper, using the same stimuli as in the experiment, we analyze the properties of model IT units, trained without any explicit category information, and compare them to the tuning properties of experimental IT and PFC neurons. Compatible with the model prediction, we find that IT, but not PFC neurons show tuning properties that can be well explained by shape tuning alone. We then analyze the data to explore how a category signal in PFC could be obtained from shape-tuned neurons in IT, and what the computational advantages of such a scheme are.

2 Methods

2.1 The Model

We used the HMAX model of object recognition in cortex [1,2], shown schematically in Fig. 1. It consists of a hierarchy of layers with linear units performing template matching, and non-linear units performing a "MAX" operation. This MAX operation, selecting the maximum of a cell's inputs and using it to drive the cell, is key to achieving invariance to translation, by pooling over afferents tuned to different positions, and scale, by pooling over afferents tuned to different scales. The template matching operation, on the other hand, increases feature specifity. A cascade of these two operations leads to C2 units (roughly corresponding to V4/PIT neurons), which are tuned to complex features invariant to changes in position and scale. The outputs of these units provide the inputs to the view-tuned units (VTUs, corresponding to view-tuned neurons in IT [5, 2]). Importantly, the responses of a view-tuned model unit is completely determined by the shape of the unit's preferred stimulus, with no explicit influence of category information.

2.2 Stimulus Space

The stimulus space is spanned by six prototype objects, three "cats" and three "dogs" [4]. Our morphing software [7] allows us to generate 3D objects that are arbitrary combinations of the six prototypes. Each object is defined by a six-dimensional morph vector, with the value in each dimension corresponding to the relative proportion of one of the prototypes present in the object. The component sum of each object was constrained to be equal to one. An object was labeled a "cat" or "dog" depending on whether the sum over the "cat" prototypes in its morph vector was greater or smaller than those over the "dog" prototypes, resp. The class boundary was defined by the set of objects having morph vectors with equal cat and dog component sums.

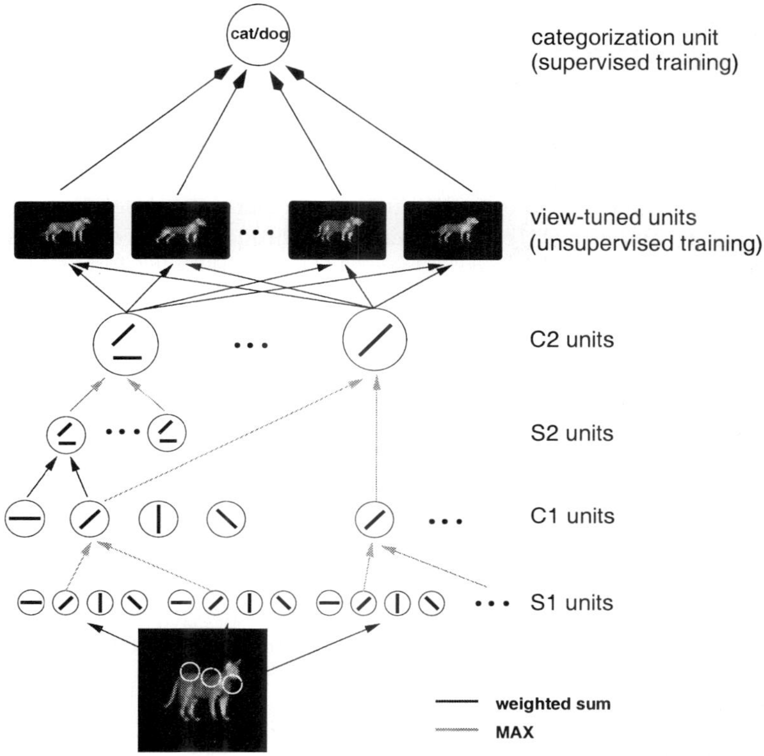

Fig. 1. Scheme of our model of object recognition in cortex [2]. The model consists of layers of linear units that perform a template match over their afferents ("S" layers, adopting the notation of Fukushima's Neocognitron [6]), and of non-linear units that perform a "MAX" operation over their inputs ("C" layers), where the output is determined by the strongest afferent (this novel transfer function is a key prediction of the model — for which there is now some experimental evidence in different areas of the ventral visual pathway (I. Lampl, M. Riesenhuber, T. Poggio, D. Ferster, *Soc. Neurosci. Abs.*, 2001; and T.J. Gawne and J.M. Martin, in press) — and a crucial difference to the aforementioned Neocognitron). While the former operation serves to increase feature complexity, the latter increases invariance by effectively scanning over afferents tuned to the same feature but at different positions (to increase translation invariance) or scale (to increase scale invariance, not shown).

2.3 Learning a Population of Cat/Dog-Tuned Units

We performed simulations using a population of 144 VTUs, each tuned to a different stimulus from the cat/dog morph space. The 144 morphed animal stimuli were a subset of the stimuli used to train the monkey, *i. e.*, chosen at random from the cat/dog morph space, excluding "cats" ("dogs") with a "dog" ("cat") component greater than 40%. This population of VTUs was used to model a general stimulus representation consisting of neurons tuned to various shapes, which might then provide input to recognition task-specific neurons (such as for cat/dog categorization) in higher areas [3]. Each VTU had a tuning width of $\sigma = 0.2$ and was connected to the 32 C2 afferents that were most strongly activated by its respective preferred stimulus [1], which produced neurons with realistic broadness of tuning (see [8] for details).

Test set. The testing set used to determine an experimental neuron's or model unit's category tuning consisted of the nine lines through morph space connecting one prototype of each class. Each morph line was subdivided into 10 intervals, with the exclusion of the stimuli at the mid-points (which would lie right on the class boundary, with an undefined label), yielding a total of 78 stimuli.

2.4 Training a "Categorization" Unit (CU)

The activity patterns over a subset of VTU or C2 units to each of the 144 stimuli were used as inputs to train a Gaussian RBF output unit (see Fig. 1), which performed a weighted sum over its inputs, with weights chosen to have the CU's output best match the stimulus' class label (we used +1 for cat and −1 for dog as desired outputs, for details, see [9]). The performance of the categorization unit was then tested with the test stimuli described above (which were not part of the training set), and a classification was counted as correct if the sign of the CU matched the sign of the class label.

2.5 Evaluating Category Tuning

We use three measures to characterize the category-related behavior of experimental neurons and model units: the between-within index (BWI), the class coverage index (CCI) and the receiver operating characteristics (ROC).

BWI. The *between-within index* (BWI) [4] is a measure for tuning at the class boundary relative to the class interior. Looking at the response of a unit to stimuli along one morph line, the response difference between two adjacent stimuli can be calculated. As there is no stimulus directly on the class boundary, we use 20% steps for calculating the response differences. Let btw be the mean response difference *between* the two categories (*i. e.*, between morph index 0.4 and 0.6) and wi the mean response difference *within* the categories. Then the between-within index is

$$\mathrm{BWI} = \frac{btw - wi}{btw + wi}. \tag{1}$$

Thus, the range of BWI values is −1 to +1. For a BWI of zero the unit shows on average no different behavior at the boundary compared to the class interiors. Positive BWI values indicate a significant response drop across the border (*e. g.*, for units differentiating between classes) whereas negative values are characteristic for units which show response variance within the classes but not across the boundary.

CCI. The *class coverage index* (CCI) is the proportion of stimuli in the unit's preferred category that evoke responses higher than the maximum response to stimuli from the other category. Possible values range from $\frac{1}{39}$, meaning out of the 39 stimuli in the class only the maximum itself evokes a higher response than the maximum in the other class, to 1 for full class coverage, *i. e.*, perfect separability. When comparing model units and experimental neurons, CCI values were calculated using the 42 stimuli used in the experiment (see section 3.1), so the minimum CCI value was $\frac{1}{21}$.

ROC. The *receiver operating characteristics* (ROC) curve [10] shows the categorization performance of a unit in terms of correctly categorized preferred-class stimuli (hits) *vs.* miscategorized stimuli from the other class (false alarms). The area under the ROC curve, A_{ROC}, is a measure of the quality of categorization. A value of 0.5 corresponds to chance performance, 1 means perfect separability, *i. e.*, perfect categorization performance.

3 Results

3.1 Comparison of Model and Experiment

We compared the tuning properties of model units to those of the IT and PFC neurons recorded from by Freedman [4] from two monkeys performing the cat/dog categorization task. In particular, the monkeys had to perform a delayed match-to-category task where the first stimulus was shown for 600ms, followed by a 1s delay and the second, test, stimulus. In the following, we restrict our analysis to the neurons that showed stimulus selectivity by an ANOVA ($p < 0.01$), over the 42 stimuli along the nine morph lines used in the experiment (in the experiment, stimuli were located at positions 0, 0.2, 0.4, 0.6, 0.8, and 1 along each morph line). Thus, we only analyzed those neurons that responded significantly differently to at least one of the stimuli.[1]

In particular, we analyzed a total of 116 stimulus-selective IT neurons during the "sample" period (100ms to 900ms after stimulus onset). Only a small number of IT neurons responded selectively during the delay period. For the PFC data, there were 67 stimulus-selective neurons during the sample period, and 32 stimulus-selective neurons during the immediately following "delay" period (300 to 1100 ms after stimulus offset).

Figs. 2 and 3 show the BWI, CCI, and A_{ROC} distributions for the IT neurons (during the sample period — IT neurons tended to show much less delay activity than the PFC neurons), and the PFC neurons (during the delay period — responses during the sample period tended to show very similar CCI and ROC values and slightly lower average BWI values (0.09 *vs.* 0.15).[2]

[1] Extending the analysis to include all *responsive* neurons (relative to baseline, $p < 0.01$) added mainly untuned neurons with CCIs close to 0, and A_{ROC} values close to 0.5.

[2] For comparison with the model, the indices and ROC curves were calculated using a neuron's averaged firing rate (over at least 10 stimulus presentations) to each stimulus.

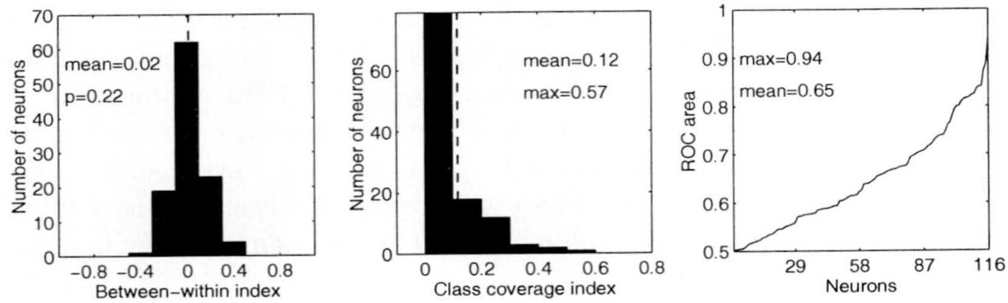

Fig. 2. Experimental IT data. The plots show the distribution of BWI (left), CCI (center) and ROC (right) area values.

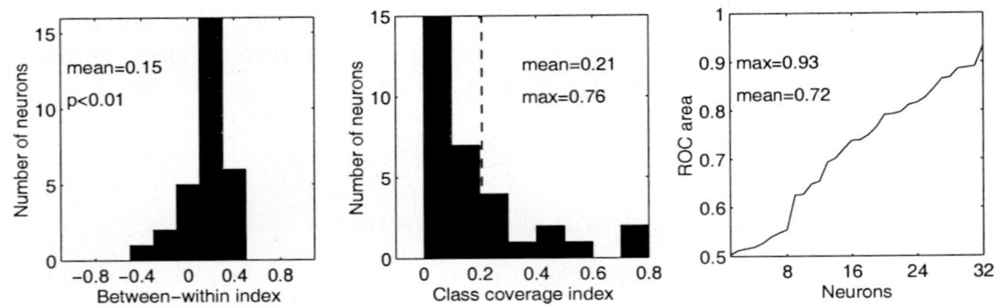

Fig. 3. Experimental PFC data (delay period). The plots show the distribution of BWI, CCI and ROC area.

We compare the tuning of experimental neurons to that of the 144 model VTUs. As model units — unlike real neurons — show deterministic responses that might lead to artificially high ROC and CCI values, we chose to add independent Gaussian noise to the model unit responses for a fairer comparison (not adding any noise produces units with significantly higher CCI values and slightly higher ROC values; for more details, see [8]). We observe a very good agreement of simulation and experiment (Fig. 4): BWI and A_{ROC} distributions are not statistically significantly different ($p \geq 0.2$, Wilcoxon rank sum test), and the CCI distribution is only marginally different ($p = 0.06$).

3.2 Comparison of Model Units *vs.* PFC neurons

Unlike the IT neurons, the PFC neurons show a BWI distribution with a positive mean significantly different from zero (sample period: 0.09, delay: 0.15), combined with higher average CCI values (sample: 0.21, delay: 0.21), with single neurons reaching values as high as 0.76 (sample and delay). This maximum value lies outside the range of CCI values of model units. A positive average BWI of the magnitude found in the PFC data could only be obtained in the model with a significant number of of border-tuned neurons, but such border-tuned units have very low CCI values (see [8]). CCI values of PFC neurons are higher than those of IT neurons, however. Thus, the tuning properties of PFC neurons *can-*

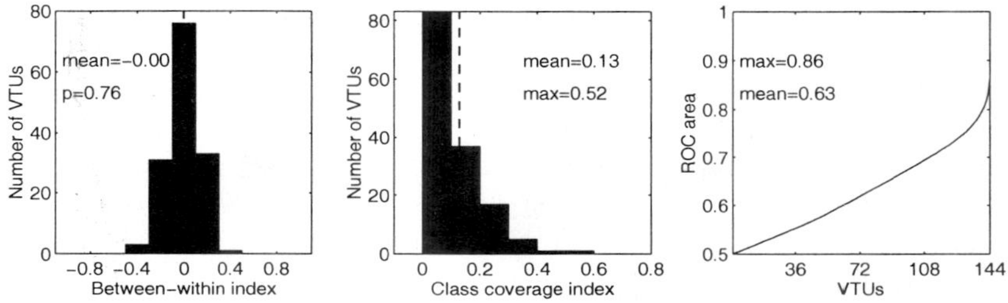

Fig. 4. Tuning of model VTUs with added independent Gaussian noise of amplitude $n = 0.1$. The plots show the distribution of BWI, CCI, and A_{ROC}. Values shown are the average over 100 trials.

not be explained in the model by mere shape tuning alone, but seem to require the influence of explicit category information during training.

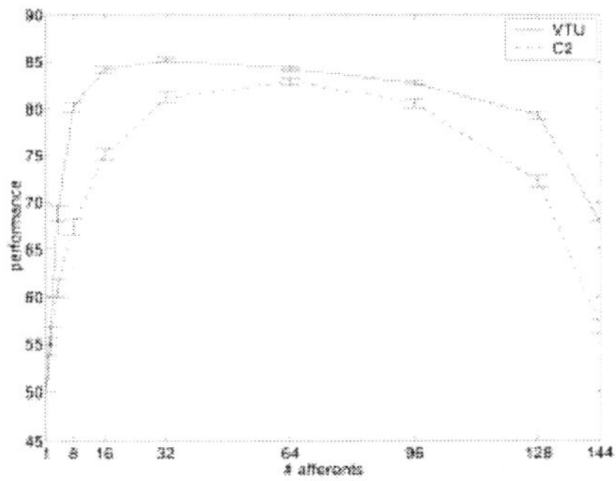

Fig. 5. Categorization performance of a "category neuron" trained on a stimulus space representation based on either different numbers of C2 units (selected at random from the 256 C2 units) or different numbers of cat/dog VTUs (chosen at random from the 144 cat/dog VTUs in the training set). Values shown are the average over 100 trials. Errorbars show the standard error of the mean. The decreasing performance for large numbers of units are due to overfitting.

3.3 Categorization Using C2 or VTU Inputs

Unlike the VTUs whose training was *unsupervised*, *i. e.*, without any category information, the categorization unit (CU) was trained in a *supervised* fashion to respond with a positive value to cats and with a negative value to dogs. Fig. 5 shows the averaged categorization performance of CUs trained with either a randomly selected subset of C2 units or a randomly selected subset of the 144 VTUs as input.

We see that performance is substantially better for the CU trained on the VTU representation. For the same number of inputs, performance based on the C2 input representation generally lies below that obtained with a VTU representation. Quantitatively, the performance in particular of the VTU CU is similar to that of the monkeys on the same stimuli (whose performance was around 90%, [4]).

The advantage of using a VTU *vs.* a C2 input representation is likely due to the fact that the VTU are tuned to the objects the categorization task is defined over. This endows the system with good categorization performance already with few inputs. C2 units, on the other hand, do not show a selectivity that is particularly suitable for the task. This necessitates the use of a greater number of inputs for a CU based on C2 inputs to obtain a comparable level of performance.

4 Discussion

The different response properties of neurons in the two brain areas, with IT neurons coding for stimulus shape and PFC neurons showing more task-related tuning, are compatible with our recent model of object recognition in cortex [3, 2] in which a general object representation based on view- and object-tuned cells provides a basis for neurons tuned to specific object recognition tasks, such as categorization. This theory is also supported by data from another experiment in which different monkeys were trained on an identification and a categorization task, respectively, using the same stimuli [11], and which found no differences in the stimulus representation by inferotemporal neurons of the monkeys trained on different tasks. On the other hand, a recent experiment [12] reported IT neuron tuning emphasizing category-relevant features over non-relevant features (but no explicit representation of the class boundary, unlike in [4]) in monkeys trained to perform a categorization task. Further studies comparing IT neuron tuning before and after training on a categorization task or even different tasks involving the same set of stimuli, and studies that investigate the possibility of top-down modulation from higher areas (*e. g.*, PFC) during task execution, will be needed to more fully understand the role of top-down task-specific information in shaping IT neuron tuning.

In any case, the data and simulations support a very simple classifier, in which task-specific PFC neurons linearly combine inputs from IT, and category membership can be determined by a simple thresholding operation. The observed increase in the average CCI value from IT to PFC is compatible with this idea.

A further advantage of using an exemplar-based representation for categorization lies in the transfer across tasks such a representation affords: after learning a class-specific but task-independent representation for one task, it would be expected that learning another recognition task on the same set of objects would take less time than if the latter task were to be learned without the benefit of the former (note that this is a difference to other exemplar-based models of categorization [13,14] where all categorization schemes have to be known at the time of learning, and all objects have to be represented in the same similarity space, making it difficult to represent situations where two objects can be judged as very similar under one categorization scheme but as rather different under another; as, for instance, a chili pepper and a candy apple in terms of color and taste, resp., see [9]). Such a behavior would be very attractive in human vision, where the same object usually belongs to a variety of categorization schemes (for instance, an apple can be categorized as "fruit", or as "food" etc.), not all known in advance. It will be interesting to test this hypothesis in future experiments.

References

1. M. Riesenhuber and T. Poggio. Are cortical models really bound by the "Binding Problem"? *Neuron*, 24:87–93, 1999.
2. M. Riesenhuber and T. Poggio. Hierarchical models of object recognition in cortex. *Nat. Neurosci.*, 2:1019–1025, 1999.
3. M. Riesenhuber and T. Poggio. Models of object recognition. *Nat. Neurosci. Supp.*, 3:1199–1204, 2000.
4. D.J. Freedman, M. Riesenhuber, T. Poggio, and E.K. Miller. Categorical representation of visual stimuli in the primate prefrontal cortex. *Science*, 291:312–316, 2001.
5. N.K. Logothetis, J. Pauls, and T. Poggio. Shape representation in the inferior temporal cortex of monkeys. *Curr. Biol.*, 5:552–563, 1995.
6. K. Fukushima. Neocognitron: A self-organizing neural network model for a mechanism of pattern recognition unaffected by shift in position. *Biol. Cyb.*, 36:193–202, 1980.
7. C. Shelton. Three-Dimensional Correspondence. Master's thesis, MIT, Cambridge, MA, 1996.
8. U. Knoblich, D.J. Freedman, and M. Riesenhuber. Categorization in IT and PFC: Model and Experiments. AI Memo 2002-007, CBCL Paper 216, MIT AI Lab and CBCL, Cambridge, MA, 2002.
9. M. Riesenhuber and T. Poggio. A note on object class representation and categorical perception. AI Memo 1679, CBCL Paper 183, MIT AI Lab and CBCL, Cambridge, MA, 1999.
10. N.A. Macmillan and C.D. Creelman. *Detection Theory: A User's Guide.* 1991.
11. H.O. de Beeck, J. Wagemans, and R. Vogels. Inferotemporal neurons represent low-dimensional configurations of parametrized shapes. *Nat. Neurosci.*, 4:1244–1252, 2001.
12. N. Sigala and N. Logothetis. Visual categorization shapes feature selectivity in the primate temporal cortex. *Nature*, 415:318–320, 2002.
13. N. Intrator and S. Edelman. Learning low dimensional representations via the usage of multiple class labels. *Network*, 8:283296, 1997.
14. S. Edelman. *Representation and Recognition in Vision.* MIT Press, Cambridge, MA, 1999.

A New Approach towards Vision Suggested by Biologically Realistic Neural Microcircuit Models[1]

Wolfgang Maass[1], Robert Legenstein[1], and Henry Markram[2]

[1] Institute for Theoretical Computer Science, Technische Universitaet Graz
Inffeldgasse 16b, A-8010 Graz, Austria
{maass, legi}@igi.tu-graz.ac.at
http://www.igi.tugraz.at/maass/;
http://www.igi.tugraz.at/legi/
[2] Brain Mind Institute, Ecole Polytechnique Federale de Lausanne, CE-Ecublens
CH- 1015 Lausanne
henry.markram@epfl.ch
http://www.weizmann.ac.il/neurobiology/labs/markram/markram.html

Abstract. We propose an alternative paradigm for processing time-varying visual inputs, in particular for tasks involving temporal and spatial integration, which is inspired by hypotheses about the computational role of cortical microcircuits. Since detailed knowledge about the precise structure of the microcircuit is not needed for that, it can in principle also be implemented with partially unknown or faulty analog hardware. In addition, this approach supports parallel real-time processing of time-varying visual inputs for diverse tasks, since different readouts can be trained to extract concurrently from the same microcircuit completely different information components.

Keywords. Cortical microcircuits, recurrent connections, spiking neurons, dynamic synapses, dynamical systems, movement prediction, direction of motion, novelty detection, parallel computing.

1 Introduction

Cortical neural circuits differ in several essential aspects from circuit models arising in the context of computer science or artificial neural networks. The computational units of cortical circuits (neurons and synapses) are quite heterogeneous, being endowed with a multitude of different dynamical processes on several time scales (see for example [Gupta et al., 2000] and [Markram et al., 1998]). Furthermore these units are highly recurrent ("loops within loops") but sparsely connected, with accidental features in the connectivity patterns. It appears to be virtually impossible to implement any previously suggested approach for real-time processing of dynamically changing visual inputs on such circuits.

---

[1] The work was partially supported by the Austrian Science Fond FWF, project # P15386.

H.H. Bülthoff et al. (Eds.): BMCV 2002, LNCS 2525, pp. 282–293, 2002.

We show that nevertheless biologically realistic neural microcircuit models can be used for analyzing complex time-varying visual inputs once they are viewed from a suitable organisational perspective. Instead of collecting information about preceding input frames in a suitable datastructure, and then applying time consuming algorithms in order to extract the desired information, we demonstrate through computer simulations that a quite different strategy is in principle feasible, and may in fact be biologically more realistic. One can inject continuously time-varying visual stimuli $u(\cdot)$ directly into a simulated generic neural microcircuit. Realistic models for cortical microcircuits are sparse but highly recurrently connected, and involve diverse dynamical components. Therefore the current spike output $x(t)$ of such circuit, which is an n-dimensional vector if the circuit consists of n neurons, contains information about the trajectory of preceding inputs $u(s)$ for $s < t$, although in a highly nonlinear encoding. Nevertheless simple algorithms for static pattern classification and regression can be applied to extract at any time t from the current circuit output $x(t)$ information about recent movements $u(\cdot)$. The decoding of this information from the current circuit output $x(t)$ presents a virtually unsolvable task for a human observer, or any explicit decoding algorithm, especially if this circuit output is high dimensional (for example about 10.000-dimensional in the case of a cortical column). But the nonlinearity and high dimensionality of the "code" $x(t)$ enhance the chances for being able to train simple linear readout devices to extract the desired information – without the danger of getting stuck in local minima of the error function. The reason is that the transformation of the time-varying inputs $u(\cdot)$ into a subsequent high dimensional circuit state $x(t)$ tends to act like a kernel for support vector machines that facilitates linear readout.

In order to demonstrate the possible contribution of generic cortical circuit structures for typical visual processing tasks, no attempt has been made in the simulations discussed in this article to endow the neural microcircuit model in addition with specialized feature detectors such as orientation- or direction selective neurons, or neurons with particular receptive fields, or a more specialized connectivity structure. These features are likely to enhance the performance of such microcircuit models for a range of visual tasks. In fact, the generic recurrent sparse connectivity and heterogeneity of our microcircuit model may provide the previously missing organisational scheme for combining the outputs of such specialized feature detectors for a wide variety of tasks that require real-time processing of rapidly varying visual information, even tasks that are not well-matched to the sizes of receptive fields or other details of specialized feature detectors. Thus the approach discussed in this article may provide new concepts and ideas for investigating the role of neural circuits in the visual cortex: by viewing them as wetware implementations of kernels that are particularly useful for processing time-varying visual inputs (analogously to the kernels discussed in [Schölkopf and Smola, 2002], which are particularly useful for other types of tasks).

Earlier neural circuit models for visual processing, such as for example those of [Abbott and Blum, 1996] and [Rao and Sejnowski, 2000], focused on neural circuits that had essentially "no hidden neurons". They consisted of arrays of neurons where each excitatory neuron in the network was directly targeted by exactly one "sensory" input, with excitatory or inhibitory (mediated by point-to-point interneurons) lateral connections between these directly input-driven neurons. Consequently these earlier articles focused on predictions of input movements of *pointwise* objects whose direction and speed was aligned with the specific pattern of connections and transmission delays of the lateral connections between the array of input-driven neurons. In contrast, we consider in this article generic randomly connected networks of integrate-and-fire neurons with (biologically realistic) very short synaptic delays, into which the input is mapped by random connections that favor a topographic map. We demonstrate that the computational advantage of this biologically more realistic architecture lies in its capability to support analyzes of a much larger diversity of shapes, directions and speeds of moving objects that could possibly be anticipated in the pattern of connections and transmission delays of an explicitly constructed circuit.

The idea to train just the neurons that read out information from a recurrent neural circuit had apparently first been proposed by [Buonomano and Merzenich, 1995]. The computational power of the resulting model has previously been analyzed in [Maass et al., 2001]. A related model for artificial neural networks was proposed in [Jaeger, 2001].

2 The Generic Neural Microcircuit Model

We employed circuit models that reflect empirical data from microcircuits in rat somatosensory cortex (see [Gupta et al., 2000] and [Markram et al., 1998]) with regard to the types of dynamic synapses and their relationship to the type of presynaptic and postsynaptic neuron (excitatory or inhibitory). The biological models for neurons and dynamic synapses that were used were rather realistic (in contrast to the neurons and synapses used in artificial neural network models). Connections between neurons were chosen randomly, but with a biologically realistic bias towards local connections. The resulting circuits, each consisting of 768 leaky integrate-and-fire neurons (of which 20 % were randomly chosen to be inhibitory), were sparsely but highly recurrently connected. We refer to [Maass et al., 2001] for details.

If one excites such complex and highly dynamic recurrent circuit with a continuous input stream $u(s)$, and looks at a later time $t > s$ at the current output $x(t)$ of the circuit, then $x(t)$ is likely to hold a substantial amount of information about recent inputs. We as human observers may not be able to understand the "code" by which this information about $u(s)$ is encoded in $x(t)$, but that is obviously not essential. Essential is whether a readout neuron that has to extract such information at time t for a specific task can accomplish this. But this amounts to a classical (static) pattern recognition or regression problem, since the temporal dynamics of the input stream $u(s)$ has been transformed by the recurrent circuit into a single high dimensional spatial pattern $x(t)$. This pattern classification or regression task tends to be relatively easy to learn, even by a memoryless readout, provided the desired information is present in the circuit output $x(t)$. We demonstrate that a single readout can be trained to accomplish this task for many different time points t.

If the recurrent neural circuit is sufficiently large, it may support this learning task by acting like a kernel for support vector machines (see [Vapnik, 1998]), which presents a large number of nonlinear combinations of components of the preceding input stream to the readout. Such nonlinear projection of the original input stream $u(\cdot)$ into a high dimensional space tends to facilitate the extraction of information about this input stream at later times t, since it boosts the power of linear readouts for classification and regression tasks. Linear readouts are not only better models for the readout capabilities of a biological neuron than for example multi-layer-perceptrons, but their training is much easier and robust because it cannot get stuck in local minima of the error function (see [Vapnik, 1998]). These considerations suggest new hypotheses regarding the computational function of generic neural circuits in the visual cortex: to serve as general-purpose temporal integrators, and simultaneously as kernels (i.e., nonlinear projections into a higher dimensional space) to facilitate subsequent linear readout of information whenever it is needed. Note that in all experiments described in this article only the readouts were trained for specific tasks, whereas always the same recurrent circuit (with a randomly chosen fixed setting of synaptic "weights" and other parameters) was used for generating $x(t)$.

Input to this recurrent circuit was provided by 64 simulated sensors that were arranged in an 8×8 2D array (see Figure 1). The receptive field of each sensor was modeled as a square of unit size. The sensor output (with range [0, 1]), sampled every 5 ms, reflected at any moment the fraction of the corresponding unit square that was currently covered by a simulated moving object. The outputs of the 64 sensors were projected as analog input to the circuit in a topographic manner.[2]

Neural readouts from this randomly connected recurrent circuit of leaky integrate-and-fire neurons were simulated as in [Maass et al., 2001] by pools of 50 neurons (without lateral connections) that received postsynaptic currents from all neurons in the recurrent circuit, caused by their firing. The synapses of the neurons in each readout pool were adapted according to the p-delta rule of [Auer et al., 2002]. But in contrast to [Maass et al., 2001], this learning rule was used here in an unsupervised mode, where target output values provided by a supervisor were replaced by the actual later activations of the sensors which they predicted (with prediction spans of 25 and 50 ms into the future). Other readouts were trained in the same unsupervised manner to predict whether a sensor on the perimeter was going to be activated by more than 50 % when the moving object finally left the sensor field. These neurons needed to predict farer into the future (100 – 150 ms, depending on the speed of the

[2] The $16 \times 16 \times 3$ neuronal sheet was divided into 64 $2 \times 2 \times 3$ *input regions*, and each sensor from the 8×8 sensor array projected to one such input region in a topographic manner, i.e., neighboring sensors projected onto neighboring input regions. Each sensor output was injected into a randomly chosen subset of the neurons in the corresponding input region (selection probability 0.6) in the form of additional input current (added to their background input current). One could just as well provide this input in the form of Poisson spike trains with a corresponding time-varying firing rate, with a slight loss in performance of the system.

moving object, since they were trained to produce their prediction while the object was still in the mid-area of the sensor field). The latter readouts only needed to predict a binary variable, and therefore the corresponding readout pools could be replaced by a single perceptron (or a single integrate-and-fire neuron), at a cost of about 5 % in prediction accuracy.

We wanted to demonstrate that the same microcircuit model can support a large number of different vision tasks. Hence in our simulations 102 readout pools received their input from the same recurrent circuit consisting of 768 leaky integrate-and-fire neurons. 36 of them were trained to predict subsequent sensor activation 25 ms later in the interior 6×6 subarray of the 8×8 sensor array, 36 other ones were trained for a 50 ms prediction of the same sensors (note that prediction for those sensors on the perimeter where the object enters the field is impossible, hence we have not tried to predict all 64 sensors). 28 readout pools were trained to predict which sensors on the perimeter of the 8×8 array were later going to be activated when the moving object left the sensor field. All these 100 readout pools were trained in an unsupervised manner by movements of two different objects, a ball and a bar, over the sensor field. In order to examine the claim that other readout pools could be trained simultaneously for completely different tasks, we trained one further readout pool in a supervised manner by the p-delta rule to classify the object that moved (ball or bar), and another readout pool to estimate the speed of the moving object.

3 Demonstration That This New Approach towards Visual Processing Is in Principle Feasible

The general setup of the prediction task is illustrated in Figure 1. Moving objects, a ball or a bar, are presented to an 8×8 array of sensors (panel a). The time course of activations of 8 randomly selected sensors, resulting from a typical movement of the ball, is shown in panel b. Corresponding functions of time, but for all 64 sensors, are projected as 64 dimensional input by a topographic map into a generic recurrent circuit of spiking neurons (see Section 2). The resulting firing activity of all 768 integrate-and-fire neurons in the recurrent circuit is shown in panel c. Panel d of Figure 1 shows the target output for 8 of the 102 readout pools. These 8 readout pools have the task to predict the output that the 8 sensors shown in panel b will produce 50 ms later. Hence their target output (dashed line) is formally the same function as shown in panel b, but shifted by 50 ms to the left. The solid lines in panel d show the actual output of the corresponding readout pools after unsupervised learning. Thus in each row of panel d the difference between the dashed and predicted line is the prediction error of the corresponding readout pool.

The diversity of object movements that are presented to the 64 sensors is indicated in Figure 2. Any straight line that crosses the marked horizontal or vertical line segments of length 4 in the middle of the 8x8 field may occur as trajectory for the center of an object. Training and test examples are drawn randomly from this – in

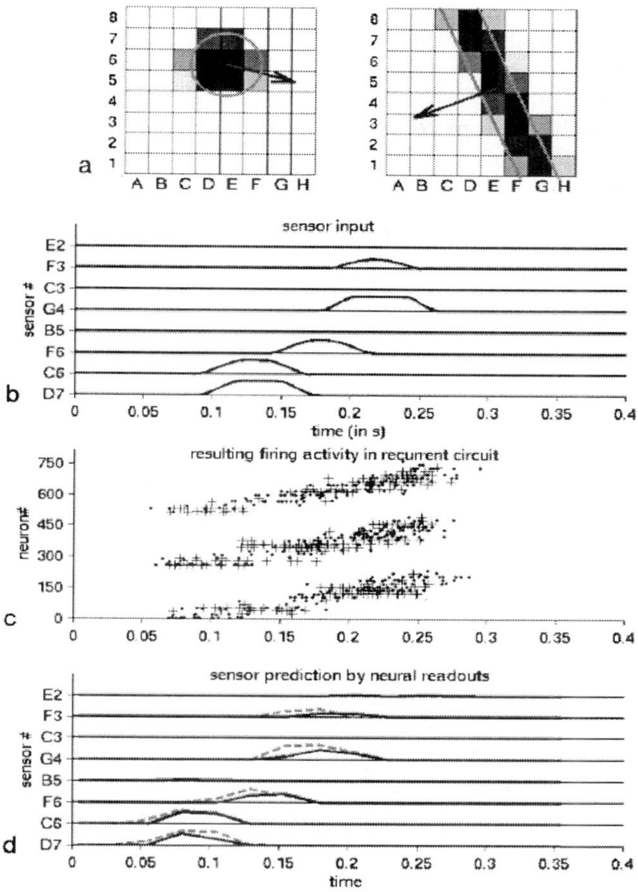

Fig. 1. The prediction task.

a) Typical movements of objects over a 8 x 8 sensor field.
b) Time course of activation of 8 randomly selected sensors caused by the movement of the ball indicated on the l.h.s. of panel a.
c) Resulting firing times of 768 integrate-and-fire neurons in the recurrent circuit of integrate-and-fire neurons (firing of inhibitory neurons marked by +). The neurons in the 16 x 16 x 3 array were numbered layer by layer. Hence the 3 clusters in the spike raster result from concurrent activity in the 3 layers of the circuit.
d) Prediction targets (dashed lines) and actual predictions (solid lines) for the 8 sensors from panel b. (Predictions were sampled every 25 ms, solid curves result from linear interpolation.)

principle infinite – set of trajectories, each with a movement speed that was drawn independently from a uniform distribution over the interval from 30 to 50 units per second (unit = side length of a unit square). Shown in Figure 2 are 20 trajectories that were randomly drawn from this distribution. Any such movement is carried out by an independently drawn object type (ball or bar), where bars were assumed to be oriented vertically to their direction of movement. Besides movements on straight lines one could train the same circuit just as well for predicting nonlinear movements, since nothing in the circuit was specialized for predicting linear movements.

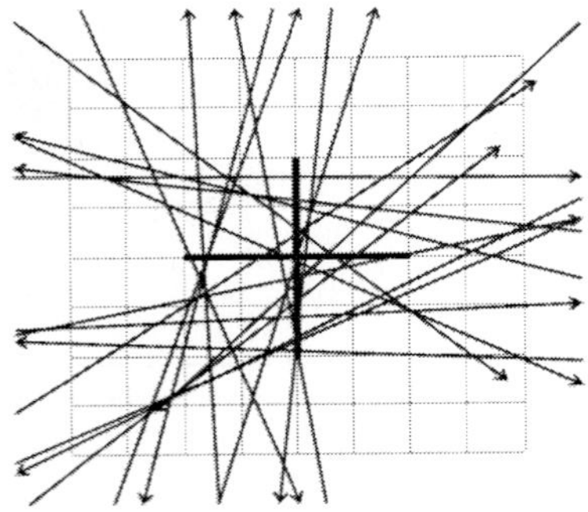

Fig. 2. 20 typical trajectories of movements of the center of an object (ball or bar).

36 readout pools were trained to predict for any such object movement the sensor activations of the 6 × 6 sensors in the interior of the 8 × 8 array 25 ms into the future. Further 36 readout pools were independently trained to predict their activation 50 ms into the future, showing that the prediction span can basically be chosen arbitrarily. At any time t (sampled every 25 ms from 0 to 400 ms) one uses for each of the 72 readout pools that predict sensory input ΔT into the future the actual activation of the corresponding sensor at time $t + \Delta T$ as target value ("correction") for the learning rule. The 72 readout pools for short-term movement prediction were trained by 1500 randomly drawn examples of object movements. More precisely, they were trained to predict future sensor activation at any time (sampled every 25 ms) during the 400 ms time interval while the object (ball or bar) moved over the sensory field, each with another trajectory and speed.

Among the predictions of the 72 different readout pools on 300 novel test inputs there were for the 25 ms prediction 8.5 % false alarms (sensory activity erroneously predicted) and 4.8 % missed predictions of subsequent sensor activity. For those cases where a readout pool correctly predicted that a sensor will become active, the mean of the time period of its activation was predicted with an average error of 10.1 ms. For the 50 ms prediction there were for 300 novel test inputs 16.5 % false alarms, 4.6 % missed predictions of sensory activations, and an average 14.5 ms error in the prediction of the mean of the time interval of sensory activity.

One should keep in mind that movement prediction is actually a computationally quite difficult task, especially for a moving ball, since it requires context-dependent integration of information from past inputs over time and space. This computational problem is often referred to as the "aperture problem": from the perspective of a single sensor (or a small group of sensors) that is currently partially activated because the moving ball is covering part of its associated unit square (i.e., its "receptive field") it is impossible to predict whether this sensor will become more or less activated at the next movement (see [Mallot, 2000]). In order to decide that question, one has to know whether the center of the ball is moving towards its receptive field, or is just passing it tangentially. To predict whether a sensor that is currently not even activated will be activated 25 or 50 ms later, poses an even more difficult problem that requires

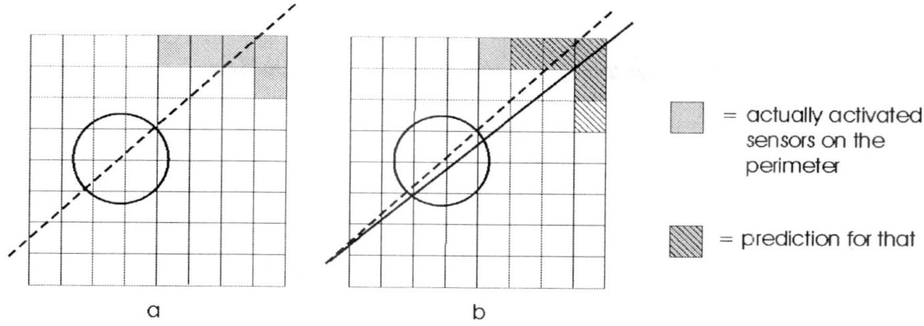

Fig. 3. Computation of movement direction. Dashed line is the trajectory of a moving ball. Sensors on the perimeter that will be activated by ≥ 50 % when the moving ball leaves the sensor field are marked in panel a. Sensors marked by stripes in panel b indicate a typical prediction of sensors on the perimeter that are going to be activated by ≥ 50 %, when the ball will leave the sensor field (time span into the future varies for this prediction between 100 and 150 ms, depending on the speed and angle of the object movement). Solid line in panel b represents the estimated direction of ball movement resulting from this prediction (its right end point is the average of sensors positions on the perimeter that are predicted to become ≥ 50 % activated). The angle between the dashed and solid line (average value 4.9° for test movements) is the error of this particular computation of movement direction by the simulated neural circuit.

not only information about the direction of the moving object, but also about its speed and shape. Since there exists in this experiment no preprocessor that extracts these features, which are vital for a successful prediction, each readout pool that carries out predictions for a particular sensor has to extract on its own these relevant pieces of information from the raw and unfiltered information about the recent history of sensor activities, which are still "reverberating" in the recurrent circuit.

28 further readout pools were trained in a similar unsupervised manner (with 1000 training examples) to predict *where* the moving object is going to leave the sensor field. More precisely, they predict which of the 28 sensors on the perimeter are going to be activated by more than 50 % when the moving object leaves the 8×8 sensor field. This requires a prediction for a context-dependent time span into the future that varies by 66 % between instances of the task, due to the varying speeds of moving objects. We arranged that this prediction had to be made while the object crossed the central region of the 8×8 field, hence at a time when the current position of the moving object provided hardly any information about the location where it will leave the field, since all movements go through the mid area of the field. Therefore the tasks of these 28 readout neurons require the computation of the direction of movement of the object, and hence a computationally difficult disambiguation of the current sensory input. We refer to the discussion of the disambiguation problem of sequence prediction in [Levy, 1996] and [Abbott and Blum, 1996]. The latter article discusses difficulties of disambiguation of movement prediction that arise already if one has just pointwise objects moving at a fixed speed, and just 2 of their possible trajectories

cross. Obviously the disambiguation problem is substantially more severe in our case, since a virtually unlimited number of trajectories (see Figure 2) of different extended objects, moving at different speeds, crosses in the mid area of the sensor field. The disambiguation is provided in our case simply through the "context" established inside the recurrent circuit through the traces (or "reverberations") left by preceding sensor activations. Figure 3 shows in panel a a typical current position of the moving ball, as well as the sensors on the perimeter that are going to be active by ≥ 50 % when the object will finally leave the sensory field. In panel b the predictions of the corresponding 28 readout neurons (at the time when the object crosses the mid-area of the sensory field) is also indicated (striped squares). The prediction performance of these 28 readout neurons was evaluated as follows. We considered for each movement the line from that point on the opposite part of the perimeter, where the center of the ball had entered the sensory field, to the midpoint of the group of those sensors on the perimeter that were activated when the ball left the sensory field (dashed line). We compared this line with the line that started at the same point, but went to the midpoint of those sensor positions which were predicted by the 28 readout neurons to be activated when the ball left the sensory field (solid line). The angle between these two lines had an average value of 4.9 degrees for 100 randomly drawn novel test movements of the ball (each with an independently drawn trajectory and speed).

Another readout pool was independently trained in a supervised manner to classify the moving object (ball or bar). It had an error of 0 % on 300 test examples of moving objects. The other readout pool that was trained in a supervised manner to estimate the speed of the moving bars and balls, which ranged from 30 to 50 units per second, made an average error of 1.48 units per second on 300 test examples. This shows that the same recurrent circuit that provides the input for the movement prediction can be used simultaneously by a basically unlimited number of other readouts, that are trained to extract completely different information about the visual input.

Finally, we show in Figure 4 what happens if from some arbitrarily chosen time point on (here $t = 125$ ms) the sensor input to the recurrent circuit is removed, and replaced by predictions of future inputs by the readout pools. More precisely, the time series of inputs (sampled every 5 ms) was replaced for each sensor after $t = 125$ ms by the preceding prediction of the corresponding readout pool (that had been trained for this prediction in an unsupervised manner as described before). Hence further predictions after time $t = 125$ ms are made based on an increasing portion of imagined rather than real inputs to the recurrent circuit. The resulting autonomously "imagined" continuation of the object movement is shown in panels b – d. It turned out that this imagined movement proceeded by 87.5 % faster than the initial "real" part of the movement. Panel e shows the firing activity of 100 neurons in the recurrent circuit for the case where the input arises from the "real" object movement, and panel f shows the firing activity of the same neurons when the "real" input is replaced after $t = 125$ ms by imagined (predicted) inputs.

4 Discussion

We have demonstrated through computer simulations that a radically different paradigm for processing dynamically changing visual input is in principle feasible. Instead of storing discrete frames in a suitably constructed datastructure, and then applying a time-consuming algorithm for extracting movement information from these frames, we have injected the time-varying (simulated) visual input continuously into a high dimensional dynamical system consisting of heterogeneous dynamic components. As dynamical system we took a generic cortical microcircuit model, with biologically realistic diverse dynamic components. Then we trained neural readouts to extract at any time t from the current output $x(t)$ of the dynamical system information about the continuous input stream that had recently entered the dynamical system, not in order to reconstruct that earlier input, but to output directly the computational targets which required that information. The theoretical potential of this general approach had previously been explored in [Maass et al., 2001] and [Haeusler et al., 2002].

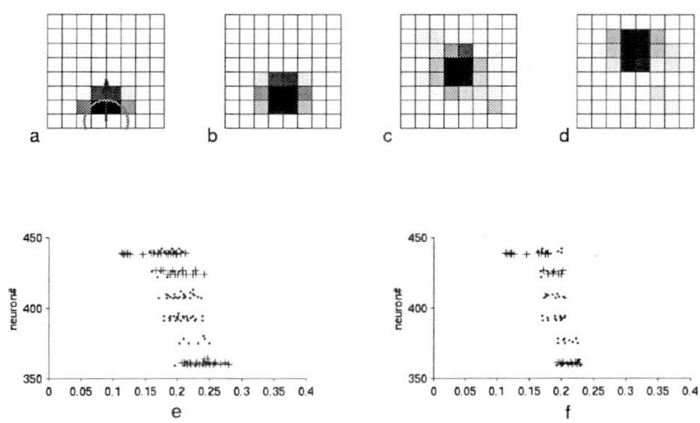

Fig. 4. Imagined movement generated by the neural circuit. Panels a-d show the predictions of object positions at times $t = 130$ ms, 155 ms, 180 ms, 205 ms. Only the first prediction, shown in panel a, is based on sensor input. The predictions in panels b-d are primarily based on preceding input predictions, that were fed back as input into the recurrent neural circuit. This imagined movement happens to proceed faster than the actual movement which it continues, demonstrating that it is not constrained to have the same speed. Panel f shows the firing activity of a subset of 100 neurons in the recurrent neural circuit during this "imagined movement". Compared with the firing pattern of these neurons during a continuation of sensory input from the actual object movement after $t = 125$ ms (if it would continue on the same trajectory, with the same speed as at the beginning), shown in panel e, the firing pattern is very similar, but contracted in time.

In this way we have shown that generic neural microcircuits are in principle capable of learning in an autonomous manner to augment and structure the complex visual input stream that they receive: They can learn to predict individual components of the subsequent frames of typical "input movies", thereby allowing the system to focus both on more abstract and on surprising aspects of the input. For example, they can autonomously learn to extract the direction of movement of an object, which requires integration of information from many sensors ("pixels") and many frames of the input movie. Because of the diversity of moving objects, movement speeds, movement angles, and spatial offsets that occurred, it appears to be very difficult to construct explicitly any circuit of the same size that could achieve the same performance. Furthermore the prediction errors of our approach can be reduced by simply employing a larger generic recurrent circuit. On the other hand, given the complexity of this prediction task (for two different objects and a large diversity in movement directions and movement speeds), the recurrent circuit consisting of 768 neurons that we employed – which had not been constructed for this type of task – was doing already quite well. Its performance provides an interesting comparison to the analog VLSI circuit for motion analysis on a 7×7 array of sensors discussed in [Stocker and Douglas, 1999].

Whereas a circuit that would have been constructed for this particular task is likely to be specialized to a particular range of moving objects and movement speeds, the circuit that we have employed in our simulations is a completely generic circuit, consisting of randomly connected integrate-and-fire neurons, that has not at all been specialized for this task. Hence the same circuit could be used by other readouts for predicting completely different movements, for example curved trajectories. We also have demonstrated that it can at the same time be used by other readout neurons for completely different tasks, such as for example object classification. Obviously this generic neural circuit that has been trained in an unsupervised manner to predict future inputs automatically supports novelty detection when being exposed to new types of input movements. Finally we have demonstrated that if from some time point on the circuit input is replaced by input predictions that are fed back from neural readouts, the emerging sequence of further predictions on the basis of preceding predictions may generate a fast imagined continuation of a movement, triggered by the initial sequence of inputs from the beginning of that movement.

The results of this article are quite stable, and they work for a large variety of recurrent neural circuits and learning algorithms. In particular they can be implemented with the most realistic computer models for neural microcircuits that are currently known. Hence one could view them as starting points for building biologically realistic models of parts of the visual system which are not just conceptually interesting or which produce orientation selective cells, but which can really carry out a multitude of complex visual processing tasks. In our current work this paradigm is applied to real-time processing of actual visual input and input from infrared sensors of a mobile robot.

Other current work focuses on the combination of top down processing of expectations with bottom up processing of visual information – which makes biologically vision systems so powerful. Obviously our circuit models are ideally suited for such investigations, because in contrast to virtually all other circuits that have been constructed for solving vision tasks, the circuits considered in this article have not been chosen with a bias towards any particular direction of processing.

References

[Abbott and Blum, 1996] Abbott, L. F., and Blum, K. I. (1996) Functional significance of long-term potentiation for sequence learning and prediction, *Cerebral Cortex*, vol. 6, 406–416.

[Auer et al., 2002] Auer, P., Burgsteiner, H., and Maass, W. (2002) Reducing communication for distributed learning in neural networks. In *Proc. ICANN'2002*, 2002. Springer-Verlag.

[Buonomano and Merzenich, 1995] Buonomano, D. V., and Merzenich, M. M. (1995) Temporal information transformed into a spatial code by a neural network with realistic properties, *Science*, vol. 267, Feb. 1995, 1028–1030.

[Gupta et al., 2000] Gupta, A., Wang, Y., and Markram, H. (2000) Organizing principles for a diversity of GABAergic interneurons and synapses in the neocortex, *Science* 287, 2000, 273–278.

[Haeusler et al., 2002] Haeusler, S., Markram, H., and Maass, W. (2002) Observations on low dimensional readouts from the complex high dimensional dynamics of neural microcircuits, submitted for publication. Online available as # 137 on http://www.igi.tugraz.at/maass/publications.html.

[Jaeger, 2001] Jaeger, H. (2001) The "echo state" approach to analyzing and training recurrent neural networks, submitted for publication.

[Levy, 1996] Levy, W. B. (1996) A sequence predicting CA3 is a flexible associator that learns and uses context to solve hippocampal-like tasks, *Hippocampus*, vol. 6, 579–590.

[Maass et al., 2001] Maass, W., Natschlaeger, T., and Markram, H. (2001) Real-time computing without stable states: A new framework for neural computation based on perturbations, *Neural Computation* (in press). Online available as # 130 on http://www.igi.tugraz.at/maass/publications.html.

[Mallot, 2000] Mallot, H. A. (2000) *Computational Vision*, MIT-Press (Cambridge, MA).

[Markram et al., 1998] Markram, H., Wang, Y., and Tsodyks, M. (1998) Differential signaling via the same axon of neocortical pyramidal neurons, *Proc. Natl. Acad. Sci.*, 95, 5323–5328.

[Rao and Sejnowski, 2000] Rao, R. P. N., and Sejnowski, T. J. (2000) Predictive sequence learning in recurrent neocortical circuits, *Advances in Neural Information Processing Systems* 12, (NIPS*99), 164–170, S. A. Solla, T. K. Leen, and K. R. Muller (Eds.), MIT Press.

[Schölkopf and Smola, 2002] Schölkopf, B., and Smola, A. J. (2002) *Learning with Kernels*, MIT-Press (Cambridge, MA).

[Stocker and Douglas, 1999] Stocker, A., and Douglas, R. (1999) Computation of smooth optical flow in a feedback connected analog network. *Advances in Neural Information Processing Systems* 11, (NIPS*98), 706–712.

[Tsodyks et al., 2000] Tsodyks, M., Uziel, A., and Markram, H. (2000) Synchrony generation in recurrent networks with frequency-dependent synapses, *J. Neuroscience*, Vol. 20, RC50.

[Vapnik, 1998] Vapnik, V. N. (1998) *Statistical Learning Theory*, John Wiley (New York).

Interpreting LOC Cell Responses

David S. Bolme and Bruce A. Draper

Computer Science Department
Colorado State University
Fort Collins, CO 80523 U.S.A.
bolme@cs.colostate.edu

Abstract. Kourtzi and Kanwisher identify regions in the lateral occipital cortex (LOC) with cells that respond to object type, regardless of whether the data is presented as a gray-scale image or a line drawing. They conclude from this data that these regions process or represent structural shape information. This paper suggests a slightly less restrictive explanation: they have identified regions in the LOC that are computationally down stream from complex cells in area V1.

1 Introduction

The lateral occipital complex (LOC) is an early part of the human ventral visual pathway. In [2], Kourtzi and Kanwisher present functional magnetic resonance imaging (fMRI) data for previously uninterpreted regions in the LOC. In particular, they identify regions that are not part of the early vision system and respond to both gray scale images and line drawings. Most importantly, they observe adaptation, in the identified regions, across the format type indicating that the identified regions respond to the type of object presented, and not to the presentation format (image or line drawing).

Kourtzi and Kanwisher interpret their data as identifying regions in the LOC that process and/or represent structural (shape) information [2]. This paper proposes a simpler explanation for their data: they have identified regions in the LOC that are computationally downstream from complex cell responses in V1. Our hypothesis is supported by a computer simulation that implements standard models of simple and complex cells. It shows that the complex cell responses to images and line drawings of the type used in [2] are indistinguishable.

These two interpretations are not incompatible. It may be that the LOC computes shape features based on complex cell responses. However, our explanation is less restrictive, since there are other properties that can be extracted from complex cell responses, including texture features and size features. At the same time, there are other regions of the brain that could provide input for format invariant shape descriptors. More experiments are therefore needed to distinguish between these hypotheses.

H.H. Bülthoff et al. (Eds.): BMCV 2002, LNCS 2525, pp. 294–300, 2002.

2 LOC Response DATA

Prior to [2], it was known that regions in the LOC respond better to intact images of objects than to scrambled images, and respond equally to familiar and unfamiliar objects. Kourtzi and Kanwisher hypothesized that some of these LOC regions might process shape information. To test this hypothesis, they generated images and line drawings of synthetic objects, similar to the ones shown in Figure 1, in both scrambled and intact forms.

They focused their attention on voxels in the LOC that are activated more strongly by intact than scrambled objects, but respond equally to images and line drawings. They then searched for cellular adaptation to probe what these regions might compute. In particular, they show that activation in these regions is suppressed on the second consecutive presentation of the same object, but not when two different objects are presented in succession. This suggests that different cells within the LOC are responding to each object type, and these cells are subject to adaptation. They then showed that the adaptation happens across format type (image or line drawing), suggesting that the same cells respond to an image of an object and its line drawing. Their hypothesis is that these cells must be processing structural or shape information.

Kourtzi and Kanwisher performed additional experiments that examined the region localized in this part of the study. Two more similar experiments were presented in [2]. The second experiment repeated the first, using familiar household objects rather than synthetic shapes. The other used partially occluded images and line drawings. In both cases, the same cells responded to object shape accross stimulus formats. Additional exploration of this region was presented in [3]. This study attempts to determine discern if the region in the LOC responds to percieved shape or simple contours.

3 Complex Cells in V1

Area V1 of the visual cortex receives input directly from the lateral geniculate nucleus (LGN), and is the starting point for higher cortical regions of the ventral visual pathway. We know from single cell recording studies dating back to Hubel and Wiesel [1] that there are at least three types of cells in V1: simple cells, complex cells, and hyper-complex cells. Of these, complex cells make up the majority (approximately 75%) of the cells in V1 [6].

It is now generally accepted that the early responses ($\sim$40 msec post stimulus presentation) of simple cells in V1 can be modeled as half-rectified Gabor filters, where the Gabor filters are parameterized by location, orientation, scale and phase (sometimes called parity) [7]. Depending on the phase, a Gabor filter can act like either a bar or edge detector at a particular location, orientation and scale.

It is also generally accepted that complex cells combine the responses of simple cells that differ in phase, but not orientation (except for $\pm$ 180 degrees) or scale. The complex cell response is the total energy at a given frequency, orientation, and location [7]. As a result, complex cell responses combine simple edge and bar responses.

Complex cells therefore respond similarly to gray scale images and line drawings of an object. More specifically, complex cells respond strongly to edges in gray-scale images, which are formed by the object's silhouette and by internal contours. Since they also respond to the lines (bars) in line drawings, they should respond similarly to both formats.

It should be noted that Zipser et al [8] observed contextual adaptation in V1 cells. While the initial responses of V1 cells can be modelled in terms of Gabor functions, later responses (80 msec or more post stimulus) are modified by contextual factors outside of the cell's classically defined receptive field. This contextual adaptation enhances or suppresses a cell's response to a bar or edge. These observations are confirmed by Lee, et al [5], who also observed a second wave of adaptation approximately 200 msec post stimulus.

4 A Computational Simulation

This paper depends on the hypothesis that complex cells in V1 respond indistinguishably to images and line drawings of an object. To verify this, we simulate the initial responses of complex cell to gray scale images and line drawings of objects. The simulation replicates the setup of Kourtzi and Kanwisher's experiments in terms of formats, and uses correlation to measure the similarity of complex cell responses.

4.1 Test Imagery

The test imagery is based on 256 randomly generated, three dimensional shapes. These stone-like shapes are composed of smooth faces and sharp contours. The objects were rendered using orthographic projection from a random viewing angle. Images and line drawings were rendered for each object. The gray scale images were generated using OpenGL, with realistic lighting techniques and smooth shading. Line drawings were created by rendering lines for the outline and internal contours of the three dimensional objects. The images were rendered at 300 X 300 pixels and rescaled to 150 X 150 pixels for use in the simulation. See Figure 1 for sample images.

4.2 Cell Models

The cell models are based on Gabor filters [7,4]. Simple cell responses (S) are computed for every pixel in the image using four different orientations and one frequency. The frequency was chosen to be in a range that responds well to sharp edges and thin lines. The Gabor kernels were generated using the following equation:

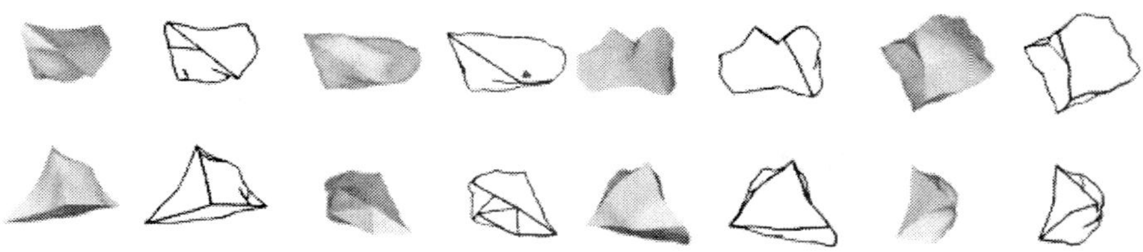

Fig. 1. Gray scale images and line drawings for eight sample objects.

$$S(x, y, \theta, \varphi) = e^{-\frac{(x'^2+\gamma^2 y'^2)}{2\sigma^2}} \cos(2\pi \tfrac{x'}{\lambda} + \varphi)$$
$$x' = x\cos\theta + y\sin\theta$$
$$y' = -x\sin\theta + y\cos\theta$$

where $\lambda = 4$, $\gamma = 0.5$, $\sigma = 0.56\lambda$, $\theta = 0, \frac{\pi}{4}, \frac{\pi}{2}, \frac{3\pi}{4}$, and $\varphi = 0, \frac{\pi}{2}$. (These parameters are consistent with biological models of simple cells, as discussed in [4].)

The complex cell response (C) at any point and orientation is based on the simple cells for that same location and orientation, and combines the symmetric (bar-like) and anti-symmetric (edge) filter responses. The model can be computed as [7]:

$$C(x, y, \theta) = \sqrt{S(x, y, \theta, 0)^2 + S(x, y, \theta, \tfrac{\pi}{2})^2}$$

Because Kourtzi and Kanwisher's first experiment [2] did not exploit texture boundaries, stereo disparity or color, the initial and adapted V1 cell responses to their images should be approximately the same. Hence the data gives no basis for distinguishing whether the LOC regions are responding to the initial or adapted responses. See Figure 2 for examples of complex cell responses.

4.3 Results

Example complex cell responses are shown in Figure 2. Qualitatively, the outline of the gray scale images is the dominant feature. The internal contours are present, however they exhibit a much lower response. For line drawings, the complex cells respond equally well to both the outline and internal contours. Dispite this difference the complex cell responses still show a remarkable qualitative similarity.

Standard linear correlation was used to measure the similarity of the complex cell responses. In particular, we correlated the complex cell responses to images and line drawings of the same object. As a baseline, we correlated the responses to images and line drawings of different objects. Histograms were produced to illustrate the distributions of these correlation scores (see Figure 3), and show that the complex cell responses to images and line drawings of the same object are virtually the same.

It is also neccesary to examine the relationship between the correlation values for different objects of the same format to the correlation values for different

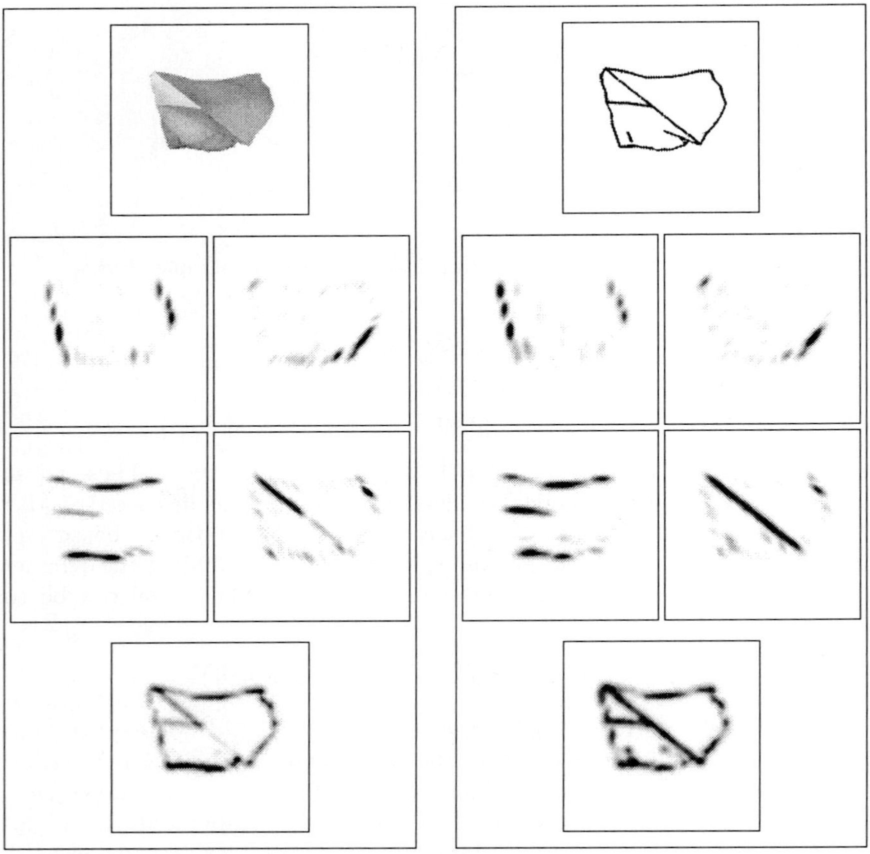

Fig. 2. Complex cell responses for one object. The top two images are the raw data. The middle images show the complex cell responses for each orientation. The bottom images show the sum of all four complex cell outputs.

formats. These results shown in Figure 4 illustrate that complex cell responses are virtually unchanged by format type.

5 Conclusions

Kourtzi and Kanwisher have identified regions in the LOC that respond to specific objects regardless of the format of the data. They conclude that these regions respond to the structure (shape) of the object. The simulations conducted in this paper show that complex cell responses are qualitatively and quantitatively similar for line drawings and gray scale images. Therefore, we believe that the simplest explanation is that Kourtzi and Kanwisher have identified regions of the LOC that rely indirectly on complex cell responses in V1. We believe that

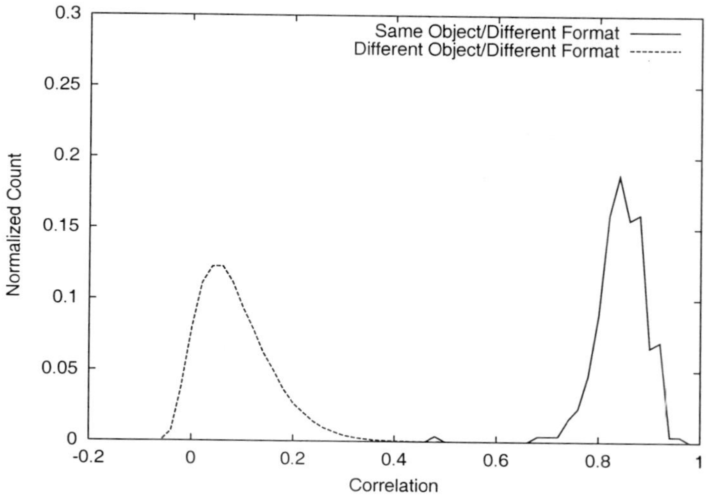

Fig. 3. Histograms of the (high) correlations between complex cell responses to images and line drawing of the same object, and the (low) correlations between responses to images and line drawings of different objects.

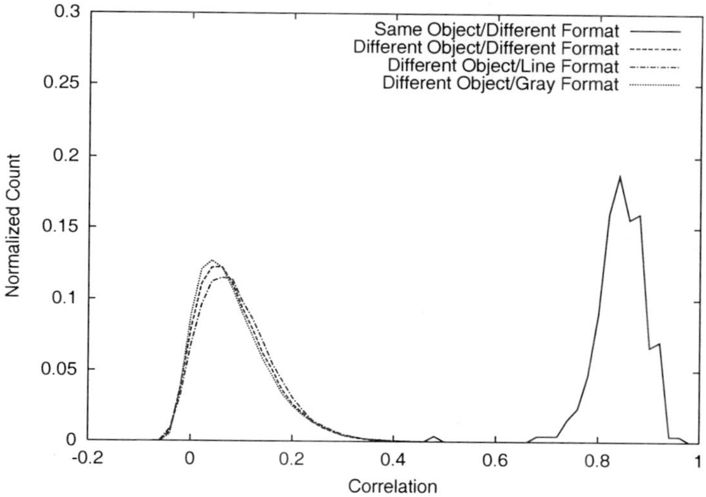

Fig. 4. Histograms comparing correlation scores between different objects presented as gray scale/gray scale, gray scale/line drawing, and line drawing/line drawing. This shows that complex cell responses do not depend on image format. The correlation histogram for the same objects/different format is also included in purple as a reference point.

this explanation fits the latter experiments in their paper as well. Unfortunately, we are unable to distinguish from the data whether these LOC regions rely on the initial or adapted V1 cell responses.

Kourtzi and Kanwisher note that of the regions in the LOC that respond to either type of stimulus, a majority of them responded to both types of stimuli. Since 75% of the cells in V1 are complex cells, it is highly plausible that many of the regions in the LOC would respond to the outputs of complex cells.

Acknowledgments. I would like to thank Zoe Kourtzi for providing initial data and for her words of encouragement. David Bolme was supported under grant DUE-0094514 from the National Science Foundation Computer Science, Engineering, and Mathematics Scholarship Program.

References

1. D. Hubel and T. Wiesel. "Receptive Fields of Single Neurons in the Cat's Striate Cortex," *Journal of Physiology (London),* 148:574–591.
2. Z. Kourtzi and N. Kanwisher. "Cortical Regions Involved in Perceiving Object Shape," *Neuroscience* 20(9):3310–3318, 2000.
3. Z. Kourtzi and N. Kanwisher. "Representation of Perceived Object Shape by the Human Lateral Ocipital Complex," *Science* 293:1506–1509, 2001.
4. P. Kruizinga, N. Petkov and S.E. Grigorescu. "Comparison of texture features based on Gabor filters," *International Conference on Image Analysis and Processing,* Venice, p.142–147, 1999.
5. T.S. Lee, D. Mumford, R. Romero and V.A.F. Lamme. "The Role of the Primary Visual Cortex in Higher Level Vision," *Vision Research,* 38:2429–2454, 1998.
6. S. Palmer. *Vision Science: Photons to Phenomenology,* MIT Press, Cambridge, MA, 1999.
7. D. Pollen, J. Gaska and L. Jacobson. "Physiological Constraints on Models of Visual Cortical Function," *Models of Brain Functions,* M. Rodney and J. Cotterill (eds.), Cambridge University Press, New York, 1989.
8. K. Zipser, V.A.F. Lamme, P.H. Schiller. "Contextual Modulation in Primary Visual Cortex," *Neuroscience,* 16(22):7376–7389, 1996.

Neural Mechanisms of Visual Flow Integration and Segregation – Insights from the Pinna-Brelstaff Illusion and Variations of It

Pierre Bayerl and Heiko Neumann

Department of Neural Information Processing, University of Ulm, Germany,
{pierre, hneumann}@neuro.informatik.uni-ulm.de

Abstract. The mechanisms involved in the cortical processing of large-field motion patterns still remain widely unclear. In particular, the integrative action of, e.g., cells and their receptive fields, their specificity, the topographic mapping of activity patterns, and the reciprocal inter-areal interaction needs to be investigated. We utilize a recently discovered relative motion illusion as a tool to gain insights into the neural mechanisms that underlie the integration and segregation of such motion fields occurring during navigation, steering and fixation control. We present a model of recurrent interaction of areas V1, MT, and MSTd along the dorsal cortical pathway utilizing a space-variant mapping of flow patterns. In accordance with psychophysical findings, our results provide evidence that recurrent gain control mechanisms together with the non-linear warping of the visual representation are essential to group or disambiguate motion responses. This provides further evidence for the importance of feedback interactions between cortical areas.

1 Introduction

The analysis of radial, rotational, and spiral large-field motion patterns plays an essential role during self-motion, e.g. for the detection of heading [1,2,3]. In order to gain insights in the neural mechanisms underlying the cortical processing of such motion patterns, we investigate a relative motion illusion presented by Pinna and Brelstaff [4]. The stimulus pattern consists of two concentric rings of circularly arranged tiles each bounded by light and dark lines (Fig. 1a, b). While fixating the center of the pattern a fore and backward moving human observer perceives a strong illusory motion of opposite clockwise or counter-clockwise rotation of both rings. The contrast arrangement along the boundary of individual tiles as well as between the tiles and the peripheral location of the items is important to generate the illusion. We claim that the relation between stimulus configuration and (illusory) percept reveals key principles of the neural processing of flow patterns in the dorsal pathway.

We present a model of recurrent interaction of areas V1, MT, and MSTd along the dorsal cortical pathway utilizing a space-variant mapping of flow patterns. Our results provide evidence for the mechanisms that underlie motion

H.H. Bülthoff et al. (Eds.): BMCV 2002, LNCS 2525, pp. 301–310, 2002.

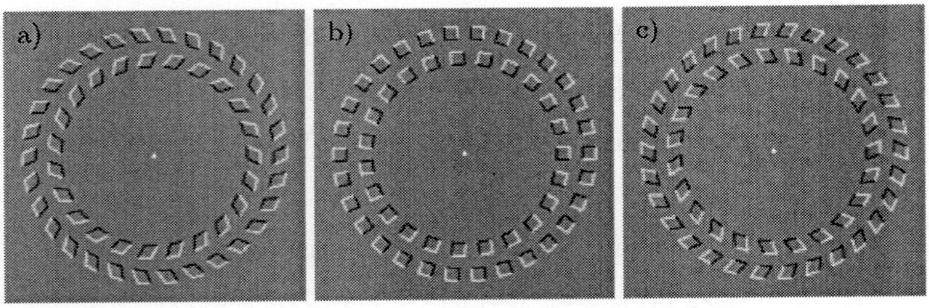

Fig. 1. Different contrast configurations of the original stimulus [4]: (a) and (b) induce illusory motion, (c) has no illusory effect.

integration and segregation as they are used for basic visual tasks such as navigation, steering or fixation control. Related models often focus on single visual areas [5] while others do not take into account the non-linear format of cortical mapping [6] or do not include feedback connections [3,7].

2 Empirical Data

Pinna and Brelstaff [4] found that in most cases where an illusory motion is perceived in patterns like those in Fig. 1 observers reported two rings rotating in opposite directions. Sometimes, however, one ring is perceived as static while the other is rotating. Peripheral viewing is important in order to get these illusory effects. The stength of the perceived motion seems to be proportional to the normal flow being projected on the vector perpendicular to the true radial motion vector resulting in a rotational illusory motion. Therefore the dominant contrast orientation of the elements plays an essential role. An analysis of the orientation distribution within the elements showed that patterns with a single dominant orientation in the inner and outer ring, respectively, gave a much stronger effect than patterns with multimodal distributions where no single orientation can be identified. Depending on the different dominant orientations the illusory effect can even be canceled out (see Fig. 1c). The illusion also depends on the radial distance of the two rings. The effect is weakened when the distance between the rings either becomes too small or too large. A single ring also induces a very weak illusory motion. Another observation was that subjects tend to see the two rings on different depth planes.

As suggested by Pinna and Brelstaff peripheral blurring is crucial to suppress (blur) image features like corners which would give perfect cues to extract the true radial motion. If the observer is too far away the stimulus pattern appears at foveal retina positions and no illusory motion is perceived. Peripheral blurring is a consequence of the non-linear cortical mapping described by Schwartz [8,9]: A complex logarithmic transformation represents a good fit to the true topographic structure for some mammalian cortices, with an increased degree of fit for peripheral vision. The main properties of this transformation are a compression of peripheral image regions and a mapping of rotational and radial patterns into linear oriented patterns. The increasing compression with growing eccentricity is consistent with the linearly increasing size of cells towards the periphery shown for MT cells [10]. This makes the retinal periphery appear more blurred than foveal regions. As a consequence we did not consider motion cues arising from high frequency patterns like line-endings.

We claim that non-illusory stimulus configurations like Fig. 1c can be explained in terms of motion transparency with directional suppression in V5/MT. Qian and Andersen [11] showed that the perception of motion transparency in patterns with two groups of random dots moving in opposite direction depends strongly on the arrangement of the dots: If the dots are arranged to create pairs with opposite directions no motion is perceived while for all dots being placed randomly two transparent layers of motion are seen. We conclude that opposite directions that were grouped together due to proximity inhibit each other. We will show that non-illusory stimuli (like Fig. 1c) induce initial contradicting rotational flow information within the rings (see Fig. 4c) while illusory stimuli yield two regions of relatively homogenous spiral motion directions. Spatial proximity and form cues lead to flow patterns grouped together within the rings. Therefore, contradicting rotational flow information in non-illusory input patterns represents motion properties of individual rings. Similar to motion transparency grouped opposite directions are canceled out due to mutual inhibition.

Pinna and Brelstaff [4] suggested that the illusory rotation is correlated with normal flow (the flow component parallel to local contrast orientation). In psychophysical experiments [12] we showed that the illusion cannot be explained by the aperture effect alone: for illusory patterns inducing almost radial directed normal flow the effect is much stronger than a simple normal flow model would predict. An additional mechanism is necessary to segregate the flow estimations that were integrated along the feedforward path and to enhance direction contrast within and between the rings. MSTd cells with their large receptive fields are sensitive to large-field motion patterns like those induced by the investigated stimuli. Their spatial resolution is not fine enough to explain the percept of two clearly separated rings. We conclude that salient patterns are detected with less spatial accuracy in higher areas, such as MSTd. In order to retain spatial accuracy the resulting activities have to be fed back to segregate information at higher spatial resolution provided in earlier areas MT and V1.

Graziano et al. [1] studied the properties of MSTd neurons. These cells mainly receive projections from MT neurons and have very large receptive fields. They are sensitive to radial, circular, spiral, and translation motion patterns. Cells have been found with preferred directional patterns distributed over the whole continuum of spiral motions ranging from circular to radial patterns. The size of the receptive fields of about 50° (Duffy and Wurtz [2]) manifests the global character of the responses. Increasing receptive field sizes along the visual pathway stress the importance of the ability to handle transparent information: at the level of MSTd or even MT integrated motion information is heavily blurred due to the size of receptive fields. Different flow directions of adjacent image regions, like those in the two rings of the investigated stimuli, cannot be spatially separated and therefore have to be represented as transparent layers. Recurrent feedback of transparent information is spatially separated in earlier visual areas and helps disambiguating initial unspecific cell activations.

We claim that the final percept emerges from the computations within and between the different visual areas. Recurrent gain control or attention may resolve ambiguous signals and reduce the effect of noise. Ill-formed artificial input signals like the Pinna illusion reveal the presence of such neural feedback mechanisms.

3 Neural Model

Motion information is processed primarily along cortical pathways involving areas V1, V2, MT, and MSTd, respectively. We focus on the primary stages of the dorsal pathway including areas V1, MT, and MSTd. Additional shape information from V2/V4 is supplied as auxiliary signal to increase model performance. An essential part of our model is the complex logarithmic transformation of the retinal input flow pattern to the V1 log-polar representation as proposed by Schwartz [9]. Motion information from two successive frames of a movement simulation are integrated along the V1-MT-MSTd feedforward pathway utilizing direction selective cells of increasing spatial kernel size (ratio 1:11:30).

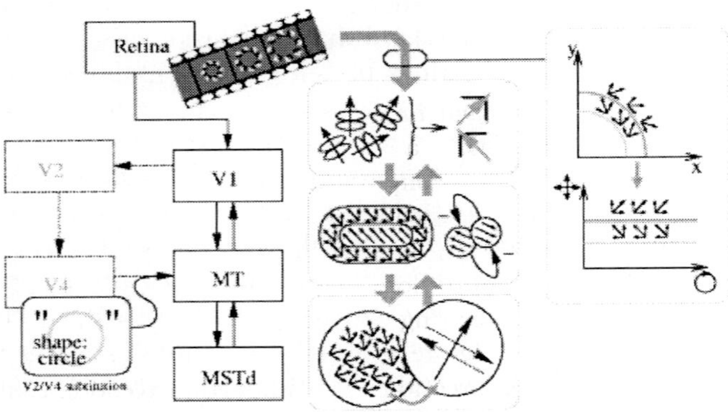

Fig. 2. Model overview. Modeled areas V1, MT, and MSTd and inter-areal connections. Iconic representations of the main model features: **Input/Retina→V1:** Complex logarithmic transformation of an image sequence. **V1:** Small scale motion analysis, normal flow detection. **MT:** Medium scale motion analysis, inhibition of opponent directions. **MSTd:** Large scale motion analysis, directional decomposition.

Fig. 2 displays the key stages of the proposed model. Each model visual area consists of a similar set of layers, which incorporate the following computing stages: First, an **integration stage** collects data from the input activity patterns. Second, a **feedback stage** from a higher cortical area modifies the signal using a gain control mechanism. Finally, a center-surround **competition stage** sharpens the signal and inhibits undesired activities achieving an activity normalization [13]. The general computational mechanisms were derived from a previously developed model of recurrent V1-V2 boundary processing and illusory contour formation [14].

$$
\begin{aligned}
\dot{v}^{(1)} &= -v^{(1)} + f_{\mathrm{FF}}(\mathrm{input}) \\
\dot{v}^{(2)} &= -A \cdot v^{(2)} + v^{(1)} \cdot (1 + C \cdot v_{\mathrm{FB}}) \\
&\quad - B \cdot v^{(2)} v_{\mathrm{FB}} * \Lambda^{-} * \Psi^{-} \\
\dot{v}^{(3)} &= -\alpha v^{(3)} + v^{(2)} - \beta v^{(2)} * \Lambda^{-} * \Psi^{-} \\
&\quad - \gamma v^{(3)} v^{(2)} * \Lambda^{-} * \Psi^{-}
\end{aligned}
$$

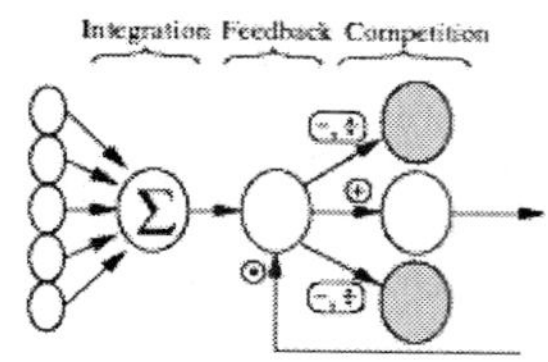

Fig. 3. Overview of different stages within modeled areas V1, MT, and MSTd: Feed-forward (FF) integration of the input signal ($v^{(1)}$), modulatory feedback (FB) from higher cortical areas ($v^{(2)}$), and lateral competition ($v^{(3)}$).

In **V1** the integration stage consists of motion sensitive cells based on spatial and temporal gradients. Due to relative small receptive fields these cells are strongly affected by the aperture problem: Only the part of the true optic flow parallel to the local gradient direction can be detected (normal flow). The cells directional tuning is set to 45° half-width and half-height.

On a small scale, as in foveal image regions, V1 cells will respond mainly to motion along fine contrasts. On a large scale, as in the retinal periphery, V1 cells will be sensitive to motion along coarse contrasts. Fig. 4 shows schematic illustrations of detected normal flow in cortical intensity representations for different stimuli with large blurring factors. In cases where illusory motions are perceived (Fig. 4a,b) two rings of flow vectors pointing in spiral directions are detected for the inner and outer ring, respectively. In cases that generate no or very weak illusory percepts (Fig. 4c) the flow vectors do not form two distinct rings of homogeneous motion directions. It is important to note, that processing in model V1 alone does not explain the percept. Motion activity patterns in V1 are unspecific and even contradicting in cases where no illusory pattern is perceived.

Area **MT** integrates activities over larger image areas and partly disambiguates unspecific directional information in V1 [5,15]. Further long-range interactions activated from V2/V4 generate groupings of input signals that belong to the same contours. V2/V4 were not modeled and included explicitly, but contour grouping information is artificially substituted. The competition stage includes strong inhibitory connections of spatially adjacent cells sensitive to opposite directions as proposed in psychophysical and modeling studies of Qian and Andersen [11,16].

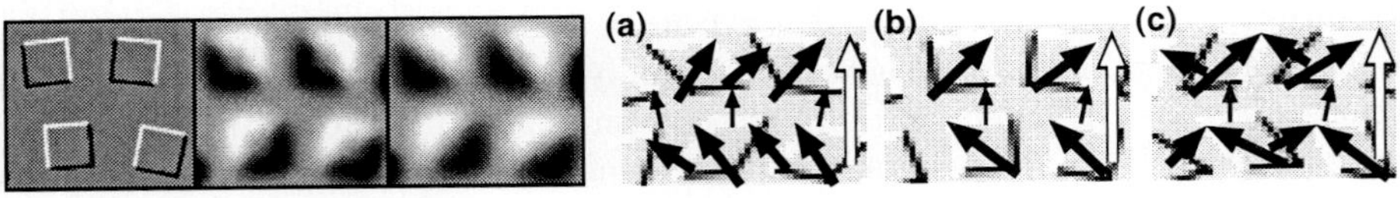

Fig. 4. Left: Different levels of blurring for one segment of the stimulus in Fig. 1b. **Right:** Schematic normal flow for illusory patterns (a) and (b) and a non-illusory pattern (c), corresponding to the stimuli in figure 1. Dark arrows denote the normal flow along contrast orientations within and between the patterns. White arrows indicate the direction of true radial motion. Note that normal flow induced by illusory patterns (a,b) is more homogeneous within both rings than for the non-illusory pattern (c). Within the rings of pattern (b) there is no flow information between adjacent tiles because the contrast orientation is perpendicular to the true flow direction. Within the rings of pattern (c) the rotational component of the normal flow (pointing leftwards and rightwards in the drawing) yield contradicting information in opposite directions.

In cases where V1 cell activations of opposite directions are integrated within receptive fields in MT (as in Fig. 4c) the corresponding MT neurons remain inactivated. At this point the original patterns described by Pinna and Brelstaff [4] with contrast configurations that do not lead to an illusory percept can be explained by the action of mutual inhibition of opposite directions, similar to motion transparency [11].

Neurons in the dorsal part of **MST (MSTd)** have receptive field sizes covering very large parts of the visual field. These cells detect the dominant direction of motion within their receptive fields [1,3]. They are particularly modeled to solve the aperture problem for large-field motion stimuli (induced by, e.g., self-motion of an observer). The dominant direction of motion signals coming from MT within the receptive fields of MSTd is computed using a least square optimization. With this information MSTd cells perform a directional decomposition: MSTd neurons that are selective for the detected dominant axis of motion and the axis orthogonal to it are weighted with the activities of corresponding MT neurons. A single peak within MSTd activities around the detected dominant direction indicates a uniform motion pattern at a specific location. Additional peaks within the large-scale receptive fields for different directions indicate an uncertainty due to a multimodal distribution of directions in MT. MSTd cell activations are fed back to MT to stabilize the dominant direction of motion and to disambiguate initially unspecific directional flow information. The directional decomposition of MT activities in MSTd leads to segregated directional cell activities in MSTd with coarse spatial resolution. Feedback processing combines the separated directional activities of MSTd cells with motion information of higher spatial accuracy represented by MT cells.

Since many receptive fields of MSTd cells cover both rings in the stimuli configurations discussed above (see Fig. 1) the dominant direction will be the true radial direction. The initial activations of spiral directions for illusory stimuli in MT are getting separated from the dominant radial direction in MSTd.

Model simulations showed that feedback processing leads to segregated opponent motions along circular directions when perceptual splitting occurs, while homogeneous and more coherent motion fields are detected when no splitting is observed.

None of the model visual areas above can explain the final percept on its own. Only recurrent gain control leads to final activations corresponding to the illusory percept. The feedback acts to bias competition on preceding visual areas to disambiguate cell activations and enforce the actual activity pattern. Multiplicative feedback helps to group similar flow patterns, while inhibitory connections within visual areas (via subtractive and divisive competition) and between visual areas (through shunting on-center/off-surround feedback) segregate different regions of homogenous motion.

4 Computational Results

In this section we present computational results from model simulations with different variations of the illusion described by Pinna and Brelstaff. We investigated three different contrast configurations, two of them induce an illusory percept while one of them fails (see Fig. 1). We also tested a neutral stimulus consisting of filled, black and white circles, which induces no illusory percept at all (see Fig. 6d).

Fig. 5 shows the temporal development of MT cell responses for the stimulus shown in Fig. 1b. For each time step, a grid of 5 x 16 activation patterns representing cortical cell activities from a region of the visual field is shown. Cells are characterized by a specific speed and directional selectivity. The transition from the initial spiral normal flow (feedforward) to the final percept of illusory circular motion is clearly visible.

Fig. 6 summarizes the results for four different stimuli. MT activities are plotted as lines scaled by the sum of cell activities at different locations and for different directions. The results match the corresponding percepts: For non-illusory patterns (Fig. 6c,d) only the true radial flow is computed while for illusory patterns (Fig. 6a,b) additional circular motion activity is generated.

5 Discussion and Conclusion

The experiments demonstrate that feedback connections, especially those from MSTd to MT, are essential to obtain psychophysically consistent results for the investigated stimuli. The model suggests that feedback from large-scale neurons is necessary to perform a grouping of similar flow patterns and to generate a splitting of dissimilar flow patterns. It is important to note that the illusion is not a result of processing in one specific area but rather evolves through the interaction between different cortical areas.

The proposed model is designed for the analysis of large-field motion patterns typically occurring during self-motion. Our computational model simulations are consistent with the psychophysical results of experiments with large-field

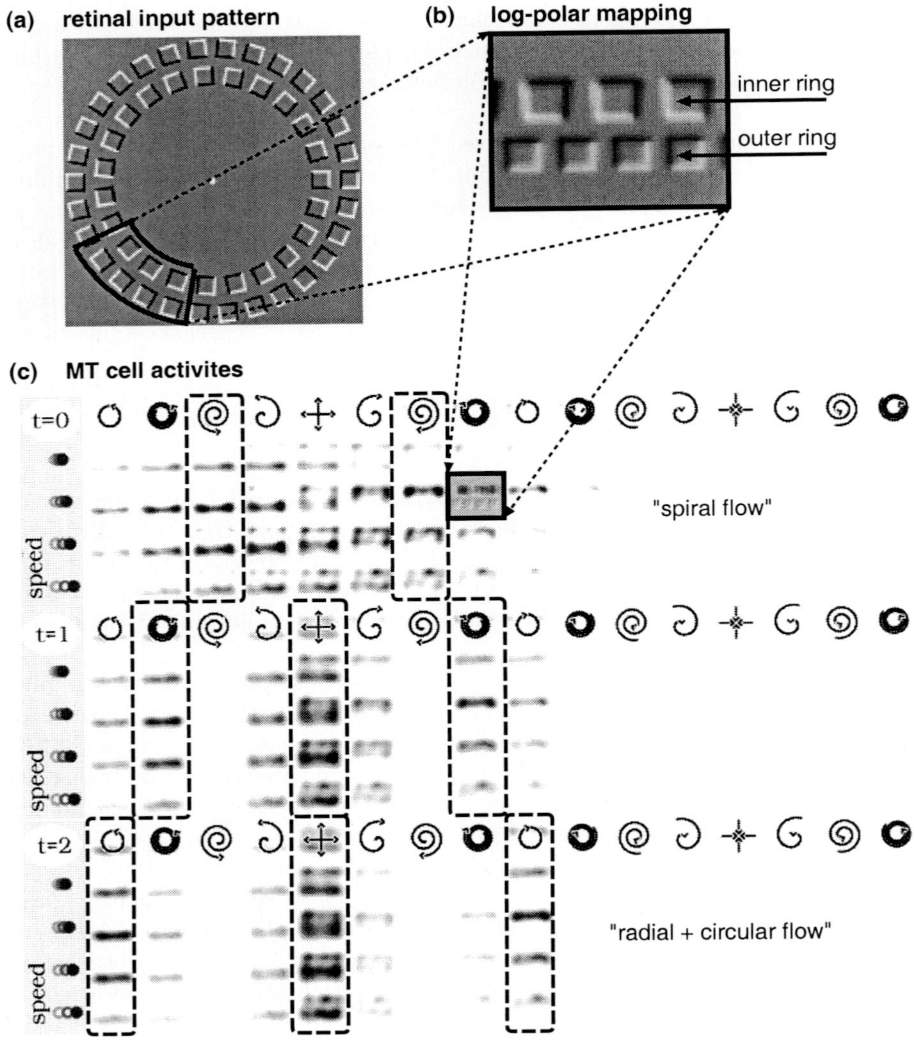

Fig. 5. **(a)** Looming retinal input pattern (simulates an observer approaching the stimulus). **(b)** *Cortical image*: subimage of a space variant representation of (a). **(c)** Temporal development of MT cell activities. Each time step (t=0,1,2) is visualized as a grid of activation maps for cells sensitive for a specific speed (rows) and direction (columns). Dark regions encode high activity, light regions low activity. Each activation-map represents locations in the cortical image. Directions corresponding to local maxima of MT-cell activities are highlighted with dashed borders. **t=0:** Unspecific activations for spiral directions. **t=1:** Activation maxima moving from spiral directions to more circular directions. **t=2:** Sharp peaks at radial (expansion) and circular (clockwise and counter-clockwise) directions.

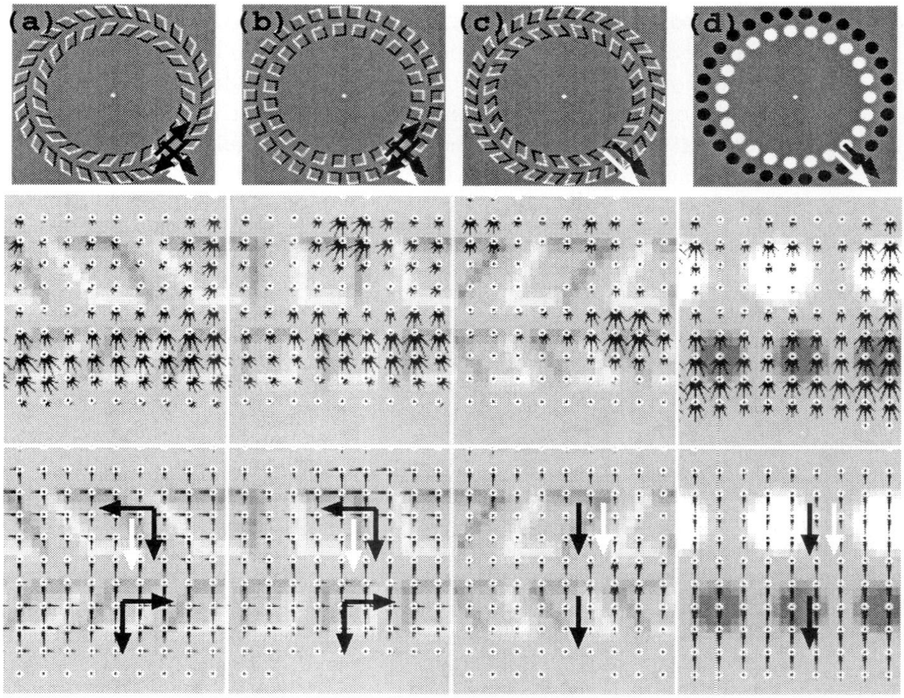

Fig. 6. MT representation of the perceived (model) flow: The dots and lines in the center and the bottom row encode activities of model MT cells sensitive to the indicated direction (lines) at the corresponding location (dots). The background represents a subimage of the log-polar mapped input stimulus (circular directions are plotted along the abscissa, radial directions along the ordinate). Dark arrows indicate the mean directions of detected motion components, light arrows the direction of true motion. (a)-(c) correspond to the results using the stimuli illustrated in Fig. 1, (d) shows the results using a non-illusory stimulus consisting of black and white discs. **Top row:** (looming) input stimuli. **Center row:** model results without feedback. **Bottom row:** model results after 8 iterations of feedback processing. Cell activations are already completely disambiguated. Illusory patterns (a,b) yield segregated motion fields with rotational components in opposite directions, while non-illusory patterns (c,d) induce true radial motion only.

motion patterns introduced by Pinna and Brelstaff [4]. The model incorporates basic principles such as center-surround competition, spatial integration utilizing kernels of increasing widths, interareal feedback, and topographic mapping of the visual input pattern.

As proposed by Pinna and Brelstaff [4], peripheral blurring is essential to explain why high frequency patterns (like corners or line-endings) are ignored which leads to their theory that is based on the aperture effect. Peripheral blurring is a side-effect of the biologically motivated log-polar transformation [9] which is essential to our model as well. However, some aspects of the original illusion and variations of it [12] cannot be assigned exclusively to the aperture effect: the amplification of circular motions for illusory stimuli and psychophysical results for certain pattern configurations both lead to perceptual effects which are not proportional to normal flow. The experimental results demonstrate that the recurrent interactions between model areas are essential for explaining the investigated phenomena. Furthermore, selectively lesioned feedback connections in our model lead to failure in disambiguating such motion patterns.

References

1. Graziano, M.S.A., Andersen, R.A., Snowden, R.J.: Tuning of MST neurons to spiral motions. The Journal of Neuroscience, **14** (1994) 54–67
2. Duffy, C.J., Wurtz, R.H.: Sensitivity of MST neurons to optic flow stimuli. I. A continuum of response selectivity to large-field stimuli. Journal of Neurophysiolgy, **65** (1991) 1329–1345
3. Grossberg, S., Mingolla, E., Pack, C.: A neural model of motion perception and visual navigation by cortical area MST. Cerebral Cortex, **9** (1999) 878–895
4. Pinna, B., Brelstaff, G.J.: A new visual illusion of relative motion. Vis. Res., **40** (2000) 2091–2096
5. Lappe, M.: A model of the combination of optic flow and extraretinal eye movement signals in primate extrastriate visual cortex Neural Networks, **11** (1998) 397–414
6. Grossberg, S., Mingolla, E., Viswanathan, L.: Neural dynamics of motion integration and segmentation within and across apertures. Vis. Res., **41** (2001) 2521–2553
7. Sabatini, S.P., Solari, F., Carmeli, R., Cavalleri, P., Bisio, G.: A physicalist approach to first-order analysis of optic flow fields in extrastriate cortical areas. Proc. ICANN (1999) 274–279
8. Schwartz, E.L.: Computational anatomy and functional architecture of striate cortex: a spatial mapping approach to perceptual coding, Vis. Res., **20** (1980) 645–669
9. Schwartz, E.L.: Computational studies of the spatial architecture of primate visual cortex. In A. Peters and K. Rocklund, editors, Cerebral Cortex, **10** (1994) 359–411
10. Albright, T.D., Desimone, R.: Local precision of visutopic organization in the middle temporal area (MT) of the macaque. Experimental Brain Research, **65** (1987) 582–592
11. Qian, N., Andersen, R.A., Adelson, E.H.: Transparent motion perception as detection of unbalanced motion signals. I. Psychophysics. The Journal of Neuroscience, **14** (1994) 7357–7366
12. Bayerl, P.A.J., Neumann, H.: Cortical mechanisms of processing visual flow – Insights from the Pinna-Brelstaff illusion. Workshop Dynamic Perception (2002) in print
13. Grossberg, S.: How Does a Brain Build a Cognitive Code? Psychological Review, **87** (1980) 1–51
14. Neumann, H., Sepp, W.: Recurrent V1-V2 interaction in early visual boundary processing Biological Cybernetics, **81** (1999) 425–444
15. Rodman, H.R., Albright, T.D.: Coding of the visual stimulus velocity in area MT of the macaque. Vis. Res., **27** (1987) 2035–2048
16. Qian, N., Andersen, R.A., Adelson, E.H.: Transparent motion perception as detection of unbalanced motion signals. III. Modeling. The Journal of Neuroscience, **14** (1994) 7381–7392

Reconstruction of Subjective Surfaces from Occlusion Cues

Naoki Kogo[1], Christoph Strecha[1], Rik Fransen[1], Geert Caenen[1], Johan Wagemans[2], and Luc Van Gool[1]

[1] Katholieke Universiteit Leuven, ESAT/PSI, B-3001 Leuven, Belgium
naoki.kogo@esat.kuleuven.ac.be
http://www.esat.kuleuven.ac.be/psi/visics
[2] Katholieke Universiteit Leuven, Department of Psychology B-3000 Leuven, Belgium

Abstract. In the Kanizsa figure, an illusory central area and its contours are perceived. Replacing the pacman inducers with other shapes can significantly influence this effect. Psychophysical studies indicate that the determination of depth is a task that our visual system constantly conducts. We hypothesized that the illusion is due to the modification of the image according to the higher level depth interpretation. This idea was implemented in a feedback model based on a surface completion scheme. The relative depths, with their signs reflecting the polarity of the image, were determined from junctions by convolution of Gaussian derivative based filters, while a diffusion equation reconstructed the surfaces. The feedback loop was established by converting this depth map to modify the lightness of the image. This model created a central surface and extended the contours from the inducers. Results on a variety of figures were consistent with psychophysical experiments.

1 Introduction

A well-known figure that provokes an illusory perception, known as the Kanizsa figure, has been a key instrument to investigate the perceptual organization of our brain (see [1] [2] [3] for review). In this paper, a model with biologically plausible architecture was built to reproduce these subjective properties. In the following subsections, some principles implemented in this model are explained.

1.1 Depth Recognition Task

Fig. 1 shows the Kanizsa square (1A) as well as its variations with modified inducers. Replacing the 'pacman' inducers by crosses as in 1B causes the disappearance of the illusory perceptions. Fig. 1C rather shows a weakening of the effect. The key question is what brain function in our visual system causes this context sensitive perception. We hypothesized that the constantly conducted

H.H. Bülthoff et al. (Eds.): BMCV 2002, LNCS 2525, pp. 311–321, 2002.

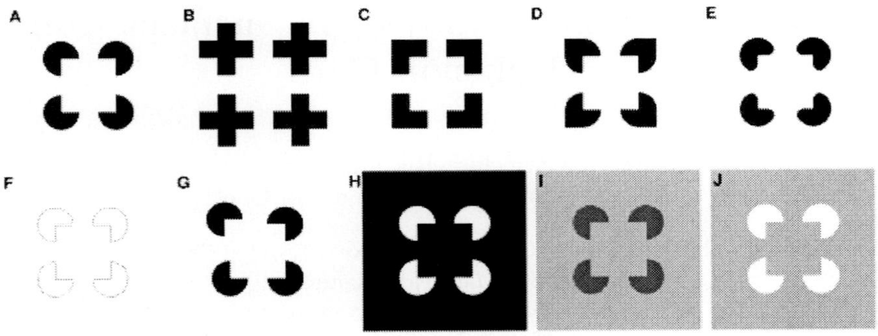

Fig. 1. Variations of Kanizsa image (A). The illusion disappears in B and F, and is weaker in C. The central square appears lighter in A and I, and darker in H and J.

task in our visual system, the determination of the depth order of objects, is responsible for this phenomenon. The key property of the Kanizsa image is that it is constructed such that the depth interpretation at the higher level vision is in conflict with the physical data of the input. A visual agnosia patient could not perceive this illusion unless it was presented with stereo disparity [4], presumably due to the lack of brain functions to detect non-stereoscopic pictorial depth cues. Also, when a Kanizsa image is created as an isoluminant figure, the illusion is not evoked [5]. De Weert [6] showed that our depth recognition mechanism is colour blind and its function is suppressed severely with isoluminant images. Finally, Mendola et.al. [7] reported on the active area of the brain when human subjects are seeing Kanizsa images. The results indicated that the area corresponded to the active area during depth recognition tasks. These results suggest that the depth recognition is playing the fundamental role in the Kanizsa illusion.

1.2 Usage of Differentiated Form of Signals

From the beginning of history of neural recording from the visual cortex, it has been known that the neurones respond to borders but not to the interior between them [8]. This neural behavior has been considered as somewhat puzzling since it is a fact that we perceive the interior region. One plausible explanation is that the neurones encode the differentiated signal and in this way the original image can always be reconstructed by integration. In other words, the interior information is indeed preserved in the differentiated form of the signal. To conduct depth recognition in a computer vision model, this provides a quite convenient approach. The model only needs to focus on the local properties of the image to determine the relative depth between the immediately neighbouring loci. After collecting the individual local information, the macroscopic features of the image can be reconstructed by integrating the differentiated signal.

1.3 Feedback System

From perceptual experiments, it is clear that higher level visual processing is involved in the illusion. Indeed, lesions (by artificial or accidental brain damage) in the higher level visual cortex resulted in the elimination of such illusions [4][9]. However, neural activities at the lower level already show responses to illusory contours [10]. This apparent paradox can be solved if a feedback connection from higher level to lower level is considered. Psychophysical studies have demonstrated feedback effects on lower level vision by biasing its response properties [11] [12]. Electrophysiologically, it has been shown that the feedback connections from the higher level visual cortex to V1 and V2 can modify the receptive field properties of the neurones [13] [14]. If indeed the feedback projection changes the lower level responses according to macroscopically detected features, it would create a mechanism of "biased" perception through the feedback loop. We assume that this biased control in the feedback system must be quite effective when the image is ambiguous, as is the case in illusory figures.

1.4 Depth Lightness Conversion

It is important to note that the illusion is a result of a modification of the physically defined input image measured in intensity of lightness. If depth perception plays a key role in the illusion, as we hypothesise, then, the modification of the image has to reflect the perceived depth. This is justified by the fact that there is a dependency of the perception of lightness on the perception of depth [15]. Once this conversion from depth to lightness is established, the image can be modified accordingly. Apparently, this is a necessary step for the feedback system described above to iteratively modify the image's lightness measurement. However, this modification has to be done with caution. As shown in Fig. 1H, and more prominently in 1J, when the figure has white inducers on black or gray background, the central area is perceived darker, i.e. opposite to the effect in Fig. 1.A and I. The decrementing configuration of the figure (black on white) creates "whiter than white" effect, while the incrementing one creates "blacker than black" effect in the central area. The modification of the image has to reflect not only the depth but also the polarity of the image.

1.5 Model Architecture and Comparison with Earlier Models

In summary, we developed a model that integrated the hypotheses discussed above: (1) the depth recognition task is involved in the creation of the illusion, (2) analysis of local properties gives relative depth information that is represented by the differentiated form of the signal, (3) global integration of the signal determines the perceived depth which, in turn, modifies the image by a top-down projection in the feedback loop, (4) this feedback modification is conducted through a mechanism that links between lightness perception and depth perception.

Several earlier models for the Kanizsa phenomenon have focused on edge completion driven by local cues (see [16], [17] for example). As a result, some models could not distinguish between modal subjective contours (the contours along the central square) and amodal contours (the missing part of the circular contours). It is also very likely that they can not differentiate between the cases in Figs 1A and 1B. Models that were constructed by a surface reconstruction scheme based on the judgment of occlusions, on the other hand, showed more robust properties reflecting the differences between the variations of the figure [18] [19]. Our model, which is based on the analysis of junction properties to construct a depth map, will be closer to the surface completion models. We, however, corroborate the rather intuitive point of departure of surface completion models by arguments obtained from perception research, as mentioned above. In addition, our model, differing from other surface completion models, is based on filter convolutions that are constructed from derivatives of Gaussian functions, which are known to be relevant to the biological system.

The rest of the paper is organized as follows: Section 2 describes the model in more detail, section 3 shows some results obtained with our model, and section 4 concludes the paper with a discussion.

2 The Model

2.1 Junction Properties

In our model, it is assumed that the only depth cue in the simplified image like the Kanizsa figure is provided by the property of junctions (or concavity in general) indicating the occurrence of occlusions. The model has to determine the depth relationship between areas s1 and s2 in Figure 2, for instance. In the model, it is assumed that the area (s1) on the side of the narrower angle (less than 180°) of the junction (j1) is the "occluding" area and the other one with the wider angle (more than 180°) being the "occluded" area (s2). In other words, such junction is taken as a cue that s1 is closer to the viewer than s2. There are two other junctions in the inducer (j2 and j3), which act as opposite cues. However, they contain curved borderlines in the Kanizsa figure, which will weaken the strengths of these cues. This is in contrast with cases B and C in Figure 1, where the junctions all consist of long straight lines. This difference is reflected in the amplitude of the junction signal simply because the elongated filters used in the model will give smaller responses to curved lines.

2.2 Filter Convolutions: Border Map and Junction Detection

In the first stage of the algorithm, we (1) detect the border of the image by a first convolution with elongated 2-D Gaussian derivative (GD) filters (section 2.2), (2) compute the location of junctions and create the "differentiated signal" to indicate the relative depth by a second convolution applied to the detected borderlines (section 2.3). Next, we integrate the "relative depth" information

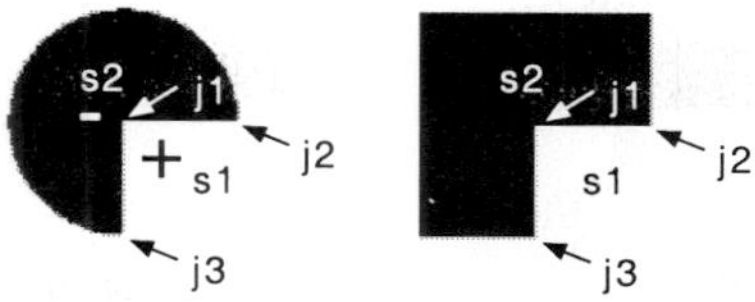

Fig. 2. "Occluding" (+) and "occluded" (-) areas near junctions of pacman inducer (left) in the Kanizsa figure and non-determined areas in L-shape corner (right) of the four corners figure (Fig. 1C).

to create a global depth map using an anisotropic diffusion equation (section 2.4). Finally, we modify the input to create a feedback system by linking depth information to lightness perception (section 2.4).
To detect the borders, the image is convolved with GDs of different orientations. The result is called the "signed first convolution", F_s. The border map, F_b, is defined as the absolute value taken from F_s (eq.1 and 2). For the junction detection, a "half" Gaussian derivative (hGD) is created to generate a sharp signal at a junction of known orientation so that it aids the creation of the relative depth map described below. This filter was created as follows. A first GD filter was elongated perpendicular to the direction of the differentiation. A second GD filter whose differentiation and elongation directions are the same as the elongation direction of the first GD filter, was created and rectified. The first GD filter was multiplied by this second "positive only" GD filter. Depending on the polarity of the first GD filter, "right-handed" and "left-handed" filters were created (Fig. 3). Two filters with opposite polarities and 90° angle differences (angle for left-handed filter being 90° incremented from the angle for right-handed filter[1]) are always used as a pair. After the convolutions with the borders detected above (F_b), only the positive portions of the results are taken. The results from the two filters are multiplied to signal the location of the junction. The amplitude of this response reflects the straightness of the two borderlines that belong to the junction as well as the contrast between two adjacent areas.

2.3 Polarized Relative Depth Map

Next, the relative depth map (RDM) is constructed using the values always on the side of the narrower angle of the junction, with their signs reflecting the polarity of the image (eq.1). First, a convolution ($*$) of Gaussian (G) to the junction map (J) is made to determine the territory of the junction. Here, territory means the area where the local analysis of the junction property can influence the result. The square of this value is multiplied with the "second convolution of

[1] The "angle" of filter indicates the direction of the filter from the origin toward the elongation. When its positive portion is on the right side of the direction, it is called right-handed and if it is on the left, left-handed. The angle is measured counter-clockwise from x direction. The angles of the filters used in this model are from 0° to 270° in 90° increments.

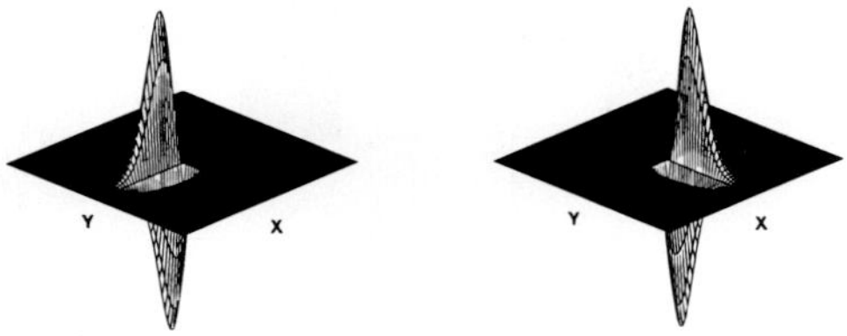

Fig. 3. Half Gaussian derivative (hGD). A: Right-handed (180°) B: Left-handed (270°)

border", S_b, obtained by convolving F_b with hGD filters. By rectifying the result (rect), it creates the relative depth value (R_d) along each border. However, to reflect the polarity of the image (i.e. incrementing and decrementing configuration of the image, see section 1.4), it has to create the polarized relative depth value (R_p), instead. This is achieved by multiplying R_d with the "signed second convolution", S_s, obtained by convolution of F_s with a hGD (eq.2). Adding this value from all angle combinations creates the polarized relative depth map (pRDM).

$$R_d = rect((G * J)^2 \times S_b) \quad S_b = hGD * F_b \tag{1}$$

$$R_p = R_d \times S_s \quad S_s = hGD * F_s \tag{2}$$

2.4 Integration: Surface Reconstruction and the Feedback Loop

In our model, the integration of the pRDM signal is done by using a modified anisotropic diffusion equation developed in our group [20] as shown in eq.3. With this method, the positive and negative values in the pRDM spread in 2-D space where they are restricted by the borders of the original image, F_b.

$$\frac{\partial f}{\partial t} = div(C_f \nabla f) - \lambda(1 - F_b)(f - pRDM) \quad C_f = e^{-\frac{F_b}{K_f}^2} \tag{3}$$

Here, f is the result of diffusion and λ and K_f are constants. This diffusion creates the depth map that also reflects polarity of the figure (polarized depth map, PDM) as shown in Fig. 4B. As discussed in section 1.4, the perceived depth can be used to modify the image to reproduce the perception of the figure. This was done by first obtaining the product of the PDM with a conversion factor from depth to lightness, α (eq.4), and then giving it an offset. Since the PDM has no values at the background area which corresponds to the fact that no subjective modifications of the image take place in this area, this offset value was determined to be 1 so that the value in the background area indicates no change, as shown in Fig. 4C. The so-called modification factor and is multiplied to the original image (I_0) to create the modified image (I, Fig. 4D). This modified image is then used to feed the next iteration of the feedback loop.

$$I = I_0 \times (1 + \alpha f) \tag{4}$$

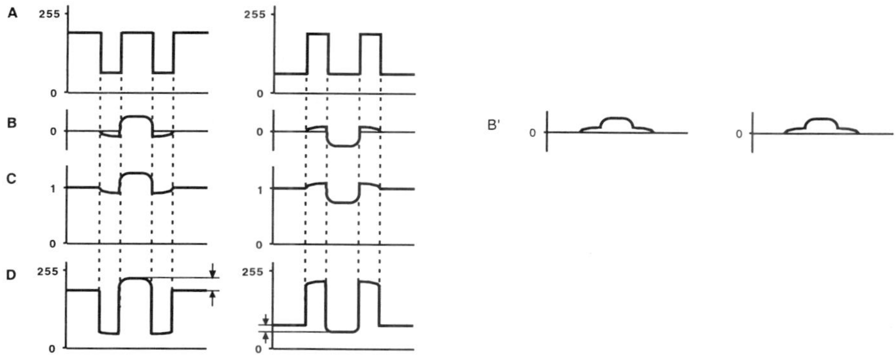

Fig. 4. Polarized depth map (PDM) and the computation of the modification factor explained in a 1-D plot. A: Original image plotted in gray scale. The left image indicates the decrementing configuration (white background and two black objects) while the right image indicates the opposite polarity of the figure. B: PDM, C: Modification factor, D: Modified image, B': Non-polarized depth map. Note that the change in the central ares is stronger in decrementing configuration as indicated by arrows.

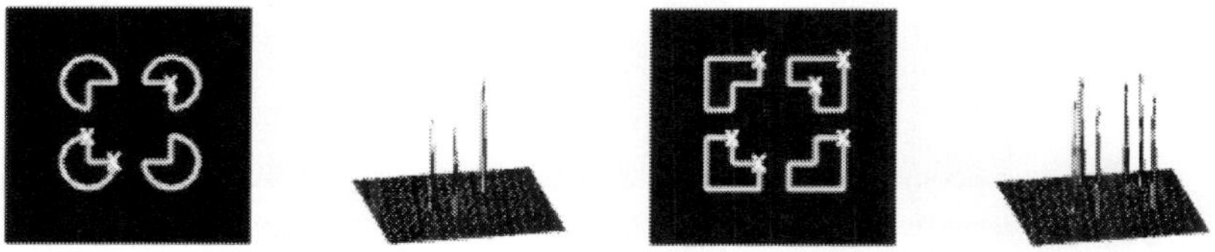

Fig. 5. Border and junction maps created by the two filters of 0 & 90°. The position of the detected junctions are shown in the border map (X). Left Kanizsa figure and right the four corners figure.

3 Results

The border and junction maps of the Kanizsa and the four corners figures (Fig. 5A and C) are shown in Fig. 5. Only the junctions of the same direction (pointing to 45°) detected by the right-handed 0° and left-haded 90° filter pair are shown. By repeating the procedure for different angle combinations, all the junctions present in these figures are detected correctly. Adding all together yields the pRDM (Fig. 6, top). In the Kanizsa figure, the signals near the middle junctions of the inducers are stronger than the ones in the four corners figure due to the fact that the competing information from middle and side junction cancel out each other in the four corners figure while in the Kanizsa figure, the information from the middle junction wins. The borderline-restricted diffusion of pRDM created the surface with different height (PDM, Fig. 7, bottom). The central square in Kanizsa was either lifted (D) or lowered (E) from the ground depending on the polarity of the image (note the reversal of signs in corresponding pRDM in Fig. 7A and B). The modification factor was created from the PDM and multiplied to the input image, resulting in the modified output image (Fig. 7 B, plotted as "reflectance map"). Fig. 8 shows the responses to variations of the Kanizsa figure (Fig. 1). Importantly, (1) the four crosses figure did not create contrast between the central area and the background, (2) the four corners figure created a lighter central area in lesser extent than the Kanizsa figure, (3) change in the skeltonized Kanizsa was negligible, (4) the response reflected the polarity of the image with lesser extent in the incrementing configuration. The result is fed into the first step of the border detection, and the whole procedure is repeated. The result is shown in Fig. 9. This clearly shows that the central square became more prominent after the iteration of the feedback loop. Through the iterations of the feedback loop, the extension of the edges from the inducers is observed (Fig. 10) due to the fact that the contrast now exists between the central square and the background generating responses in the convolution with GD filters.

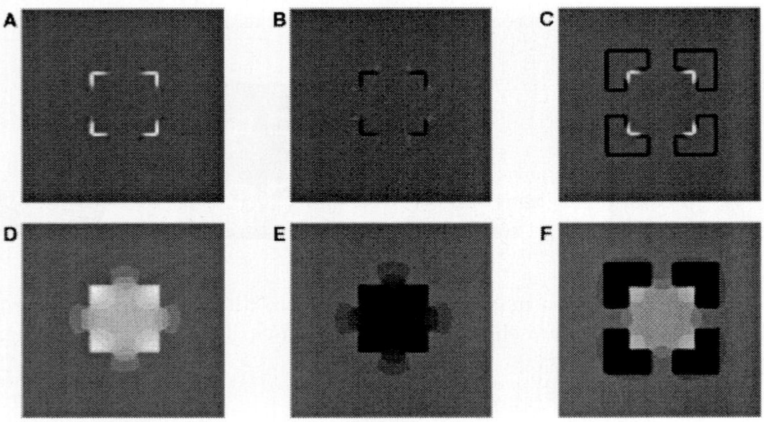

Fig. 6. A, B and C: Polarized relative depth map (pRDM) of Kanizsa with decrementing (A), and incrementing (B) configuration, and the four corners figure (C). D,E and F: The result of the integration (PDM) of pRDMs from above. Whiter color indicates positive, and blacker, negative value.

4 Discussion

Our model was designed to detect the relative depth of surfaces based on junction properties. It is somewhat related to earlier surface completion models [18]. Our model, however, is based on filter convolutions and therefore responds to the contrast of the image quantitatively. In addition, the model induces lightness effects (perceived reflectance) based on the measured depth. It also reflects the

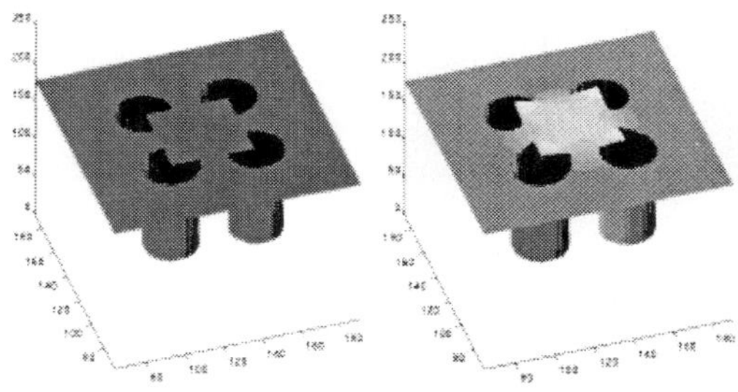

Fig. 7. The input (A) and the modified (B) image plotted as a lightness map.

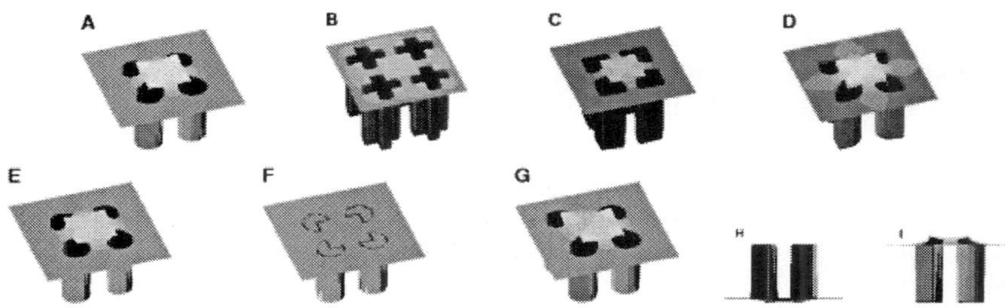

Fig. 8. Output of the model to variations of Kanizsa figures corresponding to the figures shown in Fig. 1, except H and I are responses to incrementing and decrementing Kanizsa (side view).

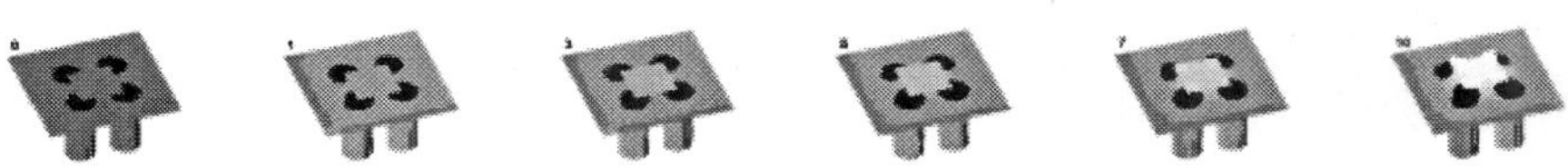

Fig. 9. Development of the central surface of Kanizsa figure through the feedback loop. From left, the original image and the results after iterations.

polarity of the figure, depending on whether black inducers are on a white background or vice versa. The model showed quite robust responses which strongly correlates to psychophysical data from the different types of Kanizsa figures. The model, for instance, enhanced the lightness in the central area in decrementing configuration (whiter than white effect) or reduced it (blacker than black effect) in incrementing configuration (see Fig. 7C and D). It also correctly responded to the skeltonized Kanizsa image (Fig. 1) by not producing the subjective modification due to the filter convolution only giving a small signal for this image constructed with thin lines. Finally, through the iteration of the feedback loop, the edges of the pacman inducers started to extend which mimics the contour completion effect surrounding the central square.

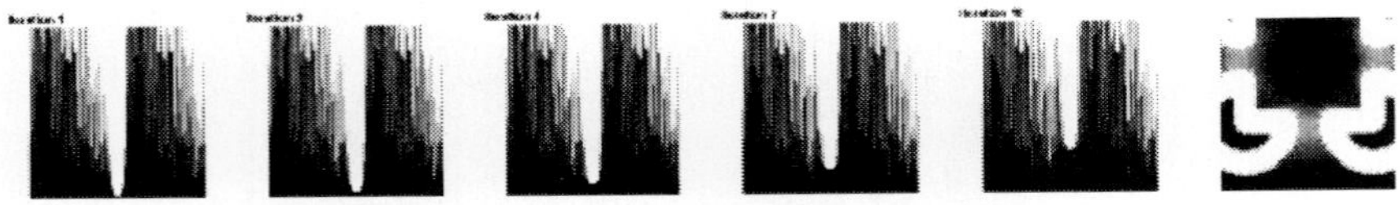

Fig. 10. Magnified of the border map (side view). In the gap between the pacman inducers, edge extensions are observed during the iteration of the feedback loop. The right most figure is a magnified top view from the 10th iteration.

To improve the robustness of our model, some additional studies are necessary. First, the enhanced responses to the end-stopped portion of the lines needs to be introduced by adding a surrounding "inhibitory field" (negative area) to the hGD filter. The responses of the model with this "end-stopped filter" to Kanizsa type images is being investigated along with its responses to T junctions. In this paper, only the junctions with 90° angle gap are detected. The new algorithm to detect junctions with various angle gaps and orientations is being developed. The quantitative aspects of the responses are being analysed in conjunction with some psychophysical experiments to achieve the plausible measure of α value and the gray scaling of the perceived lightness of the image. And finally, the feedback system which dynamically modifies the parameters of the convolution filters is being developed to further enhance the effects such as the extension of the edges from the inducers. In addition, the performances of this algorithm with real-life images and more complex illusory figures are being investigated.

References

[1] Kanizsa, G.: Subjective Contours. Sci. Am. 234 (1976) 48-52

[2] Lesher, G.W.: Illusory Contours: Toward a neurally based perceptual theory. Psych. Bull. Riview 2 (1995) 279-321

[3] Dresp, B.: On "illusory" Contours and Their Functional Significance. Cahiers Psy. Cog. 16 (1997) 489-518

[4] Stevens, K.A.: Evidence Relating Subjective Contours and Interpretations Involving Interposition. Perception 12 (1983) 491-500

[5] Brusell, E.M., Stober, S.R., Bodlinger, D.M.: Sensory Information and Subjective Contours. Am. J. Psychol. 90 (1977) 145-156

[6] de Weert, C.M.M.: Colour Contrast and Stereopsis. Vision Research 19 (1979) 555-564

[7] Mendola, J.D., Dale, A.M., Fischl, B., Liu, A.K., Tootell, R.B.H.: The Representation of Illusory and Real Contours in Human Cortical Visual Areas Revealed by Functional Magnetic Resonance Imaging. J. Nuerosci. 19 (1999) 8560-8572

[8] Hubel, D.H., Wiesel, T.N.: Ferrier lecture. Functional Architecture of Macaque Monkey Visual Cortex. Proc. R. Soc. Lond. B Biol. Sci. 198 (1977) 1-59

[9] Huxlin, K.R., Saunders, R.C., Marchionini, D., Pham, H., Merigan, W.H.: Perceptual Deficits after Lesions of Inferotemporal Cortex in Macaques. Cerebral Cortex 10 (2000) 671-683

[10] Peterhans, E, von der Heydt, R.: Mechanisms of Contour Perception in Monkey Visual Cortex. II. J. Neurosci. 9 (1989) 1749-1763

[11] Mecaluso, E., Frith, C.D., Driver, J.: Modulation of Human Visual Cortex by Crossmodal Spatial Attention. Science 289 (2000) 1206-1208

[12] Aleman, A., Rutten, G.M., Sitskoorn, M.M., Dautzenberg, G., Ramsey, N.F.: Activation of Striate Cortex in the Absence of Visual Stimulation:an FMRI Study of Synthesia Neuroreport 12 (2001) 2827-2830

[13] Hupé, J.M., James, A.C., Payne, B.R., Lomber, S.G., Girard, P., Bullier, J.: Cortical Feedback Improves Discrimination Between Figure and Background by V1, V2 and V3 Neurons. Nature 394 (1998) 784-787

[14] Wang, C., Waleszczyk, W.J., Burke, W., Dreher, B.: Modulatory Influence of Feedback Projections from Area 21a on Neuronal Activities in Striate Cortex of the Cat. Cerebral Cortex 10 (2000) 1217-1232

[15] Gilchrist, A.L.: Perceived Lightness Depends on Perceived Spatial Arrangement. Science 195 (1977) 185-187

[16] Heitger, F., Hyde, R.V.D., Peterhans, E., Rosenthaler, L., Kubler, O.: Simulation of Neural Contour Mechanisms: Representing Anomalous Contours. Image. Vis. Comput. 16 (1998) 407-421

[17] Grossberg, S., Mingolla, E., Ross, W.D.: Visual Brain and Visual Perception: How Does the Cortex Do Perceptual Grouping? Trends Neruosci. 20 (1997) 106-111

[18] Kumaran, K., Geiger, D., Gurvits, L.: Illusory Surface Perception and Visual Organization. Network-Comp. Neural. 7 (1996) 33-60

[19] Williams, L., Hanson, A.: Perceptual Completion of Occluded Surfaces. Comput. Vis. Image. Understand. 64 (1996) 1-20

[20] Proesmans, M., Van Gool, L.: Grouping Based on Coupled Diffusion Maps. Lect. Notes. Comput. Sc. 1681 (1999) 196-213

Extraction of Object Representations from Stereo Image Sequences Utilizing Statistical and Deterministic Regularities in Visual Data

Norbert Krüger[1]*, Thomas Jäger[2], and Christian Perwass[2]

[1] University of Stirling, Scotland, norbert@cn.stir.ac.uk
[2] University of Kiel, Germany, {chp,thj,gs}@ks.informatik.uni-kiel.de

Abstract. The human visual system is a highly interconnected machinery that acquires its stability through integration of information across modalities and time frames. This integration becomes possible by utilizing regularities in visual data, most importantly motion (especially rigid body motion) and statistical regularities reflected in Gestalt principles such as collinearity.
In this paper we describe an artificial vision system which extracts 3D–information from stereo sequences. This system uses deterministic and statistical regularities to aquire stable representations from unreliable sub-modalities such as stereo or edge detection. To make use of the above mentioned regularities we have to work within a complex machinery containing sub–modules such as stereo, pose estimation and an accumulation scheme. The interaction of these modules allows to use the statistical and deterministic regularities for feature disambiguation within a process of recurrent predictions.

1 Introduction

Vision, although widely accepted as the most powerful sensorial modality, faces the problem of an extremely high degree of vagueness and uncertainty in its low level processes such as edge detection, optic flow analysis and stereo estimation [1]. This arises from a number of factors. Some of them are associated with image acquisition and interpretation: owing to noise in the acquisition process along with the limited resolution of cameras, only rough estimates of semantic information (e.g., orientation) are possible. Furthermore, illumination variation heavily influences the measured grey level values and is hard to model analytically. Extracting information across image frames, e.g., in stereo and optic flow estimation, faces (in addition to the above mentioned problems) the correspondence and aperture problem which interfere in a fundamental and especially awkward way (see, e.g., [10]).

However, by integrating information across visual modalities (see, e.g., [7]), the human visual systems acquires visual representations which allows for actions with high precision and certainty within the 3D world even under rather

* This work has been performed to large extent at the University of Kiel

H.H. Bülthoff et al. (Eds.): BMCV 2002, LNCS 2525, pp. 322–330, 2002.

uncontrolled conditions. The power of modality fusion arises from the huge number of intrinsic relations given by deterministic and statistical regularities across visual modalities. The essential need for fusion of visual modalities, beside their improvement as isolated methods, has also been recognised by the computer vision community during the last 10 years (see, e.g., [1,2]).

Two important regularities in visual data with distinct properties are *motion* (most importantly rigid body motion, RBM, see, e.g., [4]) and *statistical interdependencies* between features such as collinearity and symmetry (see, e.g., [19]).[1] RBM reflects a geometric dependency in the time-space continuum. If the 3D motion between two frames is known then feature prediction can be postulated since the change of the position and the semantic properties of features can be computed (see, e.g., [12]). This can be done by having physical control over the object (as in [12]) or by *computing the RBM* as done in this paper.

However, computation of RBM is a non trivial problem. A huge amount of literature is concerned with its estimation from different kinds of feature correspondences (see, e.g., [17,18]). One fundamental problem of RBM-estimation is that methods are in general very sensitive to outliers. The RBM estimation algorithm we do apply [18] computes the rigid body motion presupposing a 3D model of the object and a number of correspondences of 3D–entities between the object model and their projections in the consecutive frame. In [18] a *manually designed* 3D model was used for RBM estimation. Here, we want to replace this model knowledge by substituting the manually created model by 3D information extracted from stereo. However, by using stereo we face the above mentioned problems of uncertainty and reliability of visual data as described above. Because of the sensitivity of pose estimation to outliers in the 3D–model we need to compensate these disturbances. We can sort out unreliable 3D–features by applying a grouping mechanism based on *statistical interdependencies* in visual data. Once the RBM across frames is known (and for the computation of RBM we need a quite sophisticated machinery) we can utilize and a scheme which uses the *deterministic regularity* RBM to disambiguate 3D entities over consecutive frames [12].

2 Visual Sub-modalities

Our system acquires stable representations from stereo image sequences by integrating the following visual sub–modalities: edge detection based on the monogenic signal [5], a new stereo algorithm which makes use of geometric and appearance based information [13], optic flow [16], pose estimation [18] and an accumulation scheme which extracts stable representations from disturbed data over consecutive frames [12]. An overview of the system is given in figure 1.

At this point, we want to stress the difference between two different sources of disturbances:

[1] There exists evidence that abilities based on rigid body motion are to a much higher degree hard coded in the human visual system than abilities based on statistical interdependencies (for a detailed discussion see [14]).

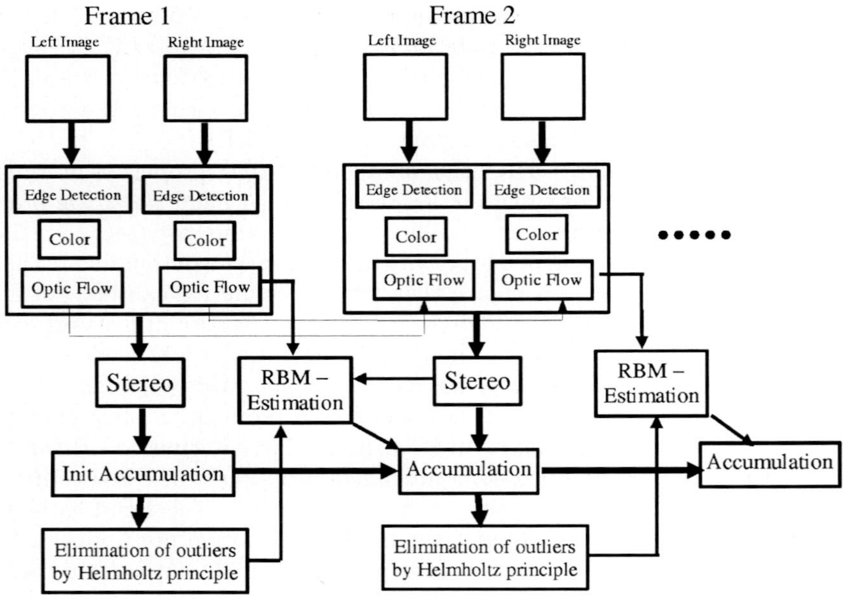

Fig. 1. Scheme of Interaction of visual sub–modalities

- Outliers: 3D entities caused by wrong stereo correspondences. They have an irregular non–Gaussian distribution (see figure 3 (top row))
- Feature inaccuracy: Deviation of parameters of estimated 3D entities (e.g., 3D orientation and 3D position) caused by unreliable position and orientation estimates in images. This kind of disturbance can be expected to have Gaussian like distribution with its mean close to the true value.

Both kinds of disturbances have distinct distribution and the visual modules have a different sensitivity to both errors: for example, while outliers can lead to a completely wrong estimation of pose, feature inaccuracy would not distort the results of pose estimation that seriously.

We will deal with these two kinds of disturbances in distinct ways: *Outliers* are sorted out by a filtering algorithm utilizing the statistical interdependency "collinearity" in 3D and by a process of recurrent predictions based on rigid body motion estimation. Both processes *modify confidences* associated to features. *Feature inaccuracy* becomes reduced by *merging* corresponding 3D line segments over consecutive frames. During the merging process semantic parameter (here 3D–position and 3D–orientation) are iteratively adapted.

In the following we briefly introduce the applied sub–modalities and their specific role within the whole system.

Feature extraction: Edge detection and orientation estimation is based on the isotropic linear filter [5] and on phase congruence over neighbouring frequency bands (see e.g., [11]). The applied filter [5] performs a *split of identity*: it orthogonally divides an intrinsically one-dimensional bandpass filtered signal in

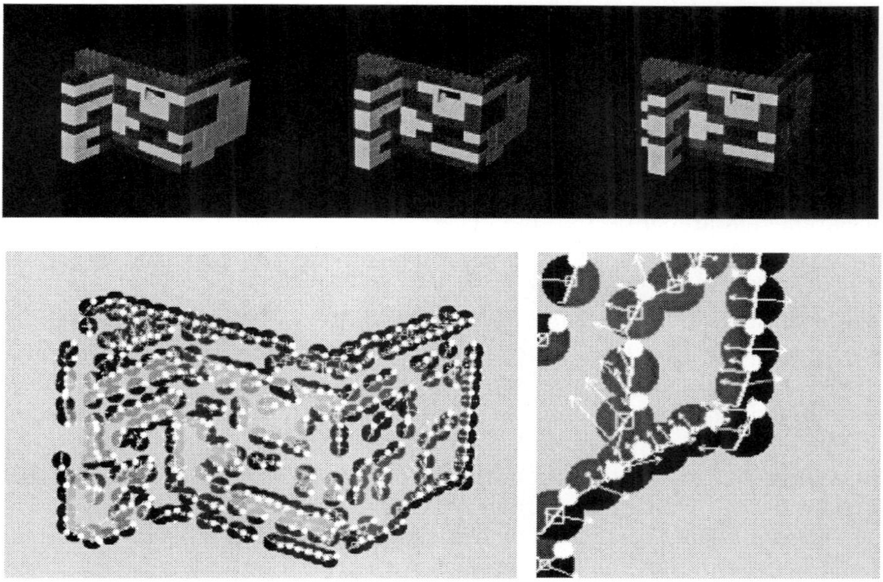

Fig. 2. Top: Three images of an image sequence. **Bottom:** Feature processing (left: complete image, right: Sub-area). Shown are the orientation (center line), phase (single arrow), color (half moon on the left and right side of the edge) and optic flow (three parallel arrows).

its energy information (indicating the likelihood of the presence of a structure), its geometric information (orientation) and its contrast transition expressed in the phase (called 'structure' in [5]). Furthermore, we use structural information in form of color averaged at the left and right side of the edge separately. Figure 2 shows the results of preprocessing.

Stereo: In stereo processing with calibrated cameras we can reconstruct 3D points from two corresponding 2D points by computing the point of intersection of the two projective lines generated by the corresponding image points and the optical centers of the camera. However, most meaningful image structure is intrinsically one-dimensional [20], i.e., is dominated by edges or lines. Orientation at intrinsically one-dimensional image structures can be estimated robustly and precisely by various methods (see, e.g., [9]). Therefore, it makes sense to use also 3D–orientation information for the representation of visual scenes: from two corresponding 2D points with associated orientation we can reconstruct a 3D point with associated 3D orientation (in the following called '3D–line segment'). A more detailed description can be found in [12].

To find stereo correspondences in the left and right image we can use geometrical as well as structural information in form of phase and color. In [13] we can show that both factors are important for stereo–matching and that the optimal result is achieved by *combining* both kinds of information.

The basic feature we extract from the stereo module is a 3D line segment coded by its mid–point (x_1, x_2, x_3) and its 3D orientation coded by two parameter (θ, ϕ). Furthermore a confidence c is associated to the parametric description of the 3D entity. We therefore can formalize a 3D–line segment by

$$\mathbf{l} = ((x_1, x_2, x_3), (\theta, \phi); c). \quad (1)$$

All parameters are subject to modifications by contextual information (as described below) utilizing the Gestalt law Collinearity and the regularity RBM across frames.

Pose estimation: To be able to predict 3D–features in consecutive frames, we want to track an object in a stereo image sequence. More precisely, we want to find the rigid body motion from one frame to the consecutive frame. To compute the rigid body motion we apply the pose estimation algorithm [6] which requires a 3D model of the object as well as correspondences of image entities (e.g., 2D line segments) with 3D object entities (e.g., 3D line segments)[2]. A 2D–3D line correspondence defines a constraint on the set of possible rigid body motions that (using a linear approximation of a rigid body motion [6]) can be expressed by two linear equations. In combination with other constraints we get a set of linear equations for which a good solution can be found iteratively [6] using a standard least square optimization algorithm.

Optic flow: The 3D model of the object is extracted by our stereo algorithm. Correspondences between 3D entities (more precisely by their 2D projections respectively) and 2D line segments in the consecutive frame are found by the optic flow. After some tests with different optic flow algorithms (see [8]) we have chosen the algorithm developed by Nagel [16] which showed good results especially at intrinsically 1D structures. Correspondences are established by simply moving a local line segment according to its associated optic flow vector.

Using collinearity in 3D to eliminate outliers: The pose estimation algorithm is sensitive to outliers since these outliers can dominate the over–all error in the objective function associated with the equations established by the geometric constraints. We therefore have to ensure that no outliers are used for the pose estimation.

According to the *Helmholtz Principle*, every large deviation from a "uniform noise" image should be perceivable, provided this large deviation corresponds to an *a priori* fixed list of geometric structures (see [3]). The *a priori* geometric structure we do apply to eliminate wrong 3D–correspondences are *collinear structures in 3D*: We assume that (according to the Helmholtz principle) a local 3D line segment that has many neighbouring collinear 3D line segments is very unlikely to be an outlier and we only use those line segments for which we find

[2] This pose estimation algorithm has the nice property that it can combine different kinds of correspondences (e.g., 3D point–3D point, 2D point–3D point, and 2D line–3D line correspondences) within one system of equations. This flexible use of correspondences makes it especially attractive for sophisticated vision systems which process multiple kinds of features such as 2D junctions, 2D line segments or 3D points.

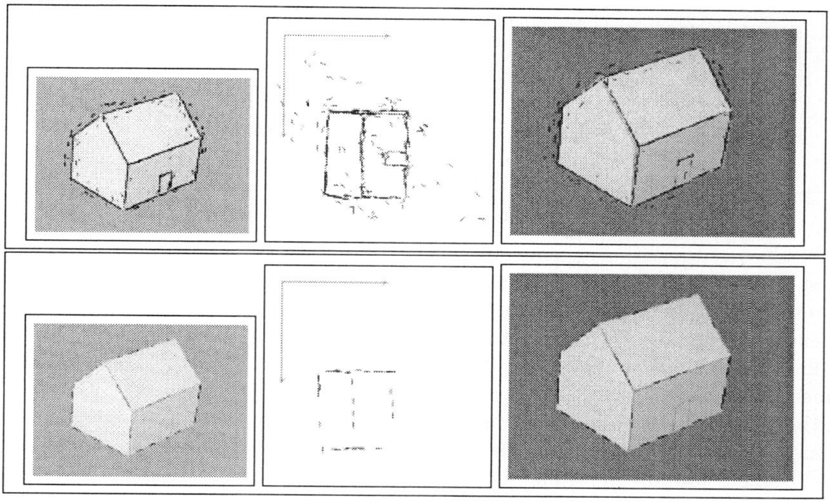

Fig. 3. Top: Using the stereo module without elimination procedure. Left: Projection onto the image. Middle: Projection onto the xz plane. Note the large number of outliers. Right: Pose estimation with this representation. Note the deviation of pose from the correct position. **Bottom:** The same after the elimination process. Note that all outliers could be eliminated by our collinearity criterion and that pose estimation does improve.

at least a couple of collinear neighbours. More precisely, we lower the confidence c in (1) for all line segments that have only few collinear neighbours. Figure 3 (middle) shows the results of the elimination process for a certain stereo image). We can show that the elimination process improves pose estimation (see figure 3right). For a more in depth discussion about applying Gestalt principles within our system see [15].

Acquisition of object representations across frames: Having extracted a 3D representation by the stereo module and having estimated the RBM between two frames we can apply an accumulation scheme (for details see [12]) which uses correspondences across frames to accumulate confidences for visual entities. Our accumulation scheme is of a rather general nature. Confidences associated to visual entities are increased when correspondences over consecutive frames are found and decreased if that is not the case. By this scheme, only entities which are validated over a larger number of frames (or for which predictions are often fulfilled) are considered as existent while outliers can be detected by low confidences (in Figure 4 a schematic representation of the algorithm for two iterations is shown). Since the change of features under an RBM can be computed explicitly (e.g., the transformation of the square to the rectangle from the first to the second frame), the rigid body motion can be used to compute the correspondences (see also [12]).

This accumulation scheme presupposes a metrical organisation of the feature space. If we want to compare visual entities derived from two frames even when we know the exact transformation corresponding to the rigid body motion, the corresponding entities cannot be expected to be exactly the same (the two

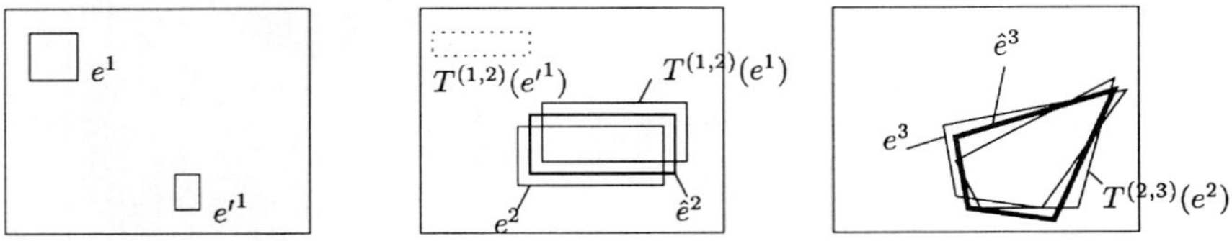

Fig. 4. The accumulation scheme. The entity e^1 (here represented as a square) is transformed to $T^{(1,2)}(e^1)$. Note that without this transformation it is barely possible to find a correspondence between the entities e^1 and e^2 because the entities show significant differences in appearance and position. Here a correspondence between $T^{(1,2)}(e^1)$ and e^2 is found because a similar square can be found close to $T^{(1,2)}(e^1)$ and both entities are merged to the entity $\hat{e}^2$. The confidence assigned to $\hat{e}^2$ is set to a higher value than the confidence assigned to e^1 indicated by the width of the lines of the square. In contrast, the confidence assigned to e'^1 is decreased because no correspondence in the second frame is found. The same procedure is then applied for the next frame for which again a correspondence for e^1 has been found while no correspondence for e'^1 could be found. The confidence assigned to e^1 is increased once again while the confidence assigned to e'^1 is once again decreased (the entity has disappeared). By this scheme information can be accumulated to achieve robust representations.

squares in figure 4 are only similar not equal) because of factors such as noise during the image acquisition, changing illumination, non–Lambertian surfaces or discretization errors. Therefore it is advantageous to formalize a measure for the likelihood of correspondence by using a metric (for details see [12]). Once a correspondence is established we apply an update rule on the confidence c as well as the semantic parameters (x_1, x_2, x_3) and (θ, ϕ). for the confidence and semantic properties of the line segment (for details see [12] and [8]). That means that by the accumulation scheme our 3D line segments are embedded in the time domain, they represent features in 3D-space and time.

Integration of visual sub-modalities: The recurrent process based on the sub-modalities described above is organised as shown in figure 1. For each frame we perform feature extraction (edge detection, optic flow) in the left and right image. Then we apply the stereo algorithm and the elimination process based on the Helmholtz principle. Using the improved accumulated model (i.e., after eliminating outliers), we apply the pose estimation module which uses the stereo as well as the optic flow information. Once the correct pose is computed, i.e., the RBM between the frames is known we transform the 3D entities extracted from one frame to the consecutive frame based on the known RBM (for details see [12]).Then we are able to perform one further iteration of the accumulation scheme.

We have applied our system to different image sequences, one of them is shown in figure 2. Figure 5 (left) shows the results. At the top the extracted stereo representation at the first frame is shown while at the bottom the accumulated representation after 6 frame is shown. We see that the number of outliers can be reduced significantly. In figure 5 (right) the mean difference of the semantic parameters (3D–position and 3D–orientation) from a ground truth (manually measured beforehand) is shown. We see that the difference between the extracted representation (consisting of line segments with high confidence) compared to the ground truth for position and orientation decreases during accumulation. Further simulations can be found in [8].

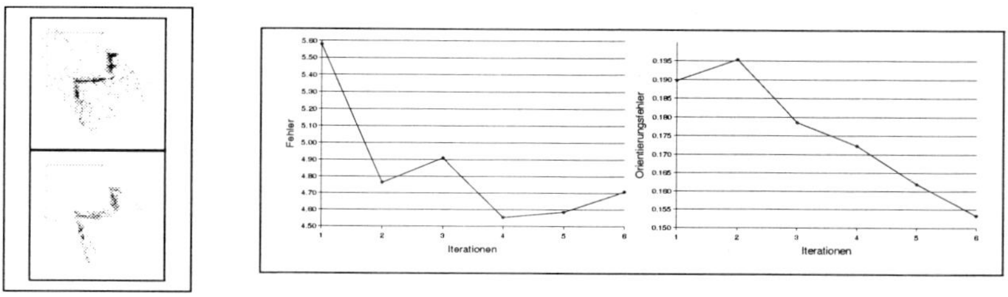

Fig. 5. Left: Projection of representations (extracted from the image sequence shown in figure 2) on xz-plane at the beginning of accumulation (top) and after 6 steps of accumulation (top). **Right:** Deviation of 3D position (left) and 3D orientation (right) from the ground truth during accumulation. Estimation of both semantic parameters improves during accumulation.

3 Summary and Discussion

We have shown that through integration of different visual modalities we are able to extract reliable object representation from disturbed low–level processes. Since we want to make use of the regularity RBM across frames we need a complex mechanism (which uses different sub–modules) that allows to compute the RBM. This mechanism also made use of statistical regularities to eliminate outliers for pose estimation. Our feature representation allows for a modification of features depending on contextual information. The confidence c codes the likelihood of the existence of the visual entity while semantic parameters describe properties of the entity. Both kind of descriptors are subject to modification by contextual information, i.e., by the statistical and deterministic regularities coded within the system.

There are some steps we intend to achieve in future research. First, our application of Gestalt principles is based on a *heuristic* formulation of collinearity. In our research we intend to replace these heuristics by statistical measurements (see [15]) . Secondly, we have applied our accumulation scheme to geometric 3D entities. However, this scheme is generic and we intend to apply our accumulation scheme to other visual domains (such as color, texture or other appearance based information).

Acknowledgment. We would like to thank Gerald Sommer and Florentin Wörgötter for fruitful discussions. Furthermore, we would like to express our thankfulness for the work of the students at the University of Kiel who have been involved in this project.

References

[1] J. Aloimonos and D. Shulman. *Integration of Visual Modules – An extension of the Marr Paradigm.* Academic Press, London, 1989.

[2] A. Cozzi and F. Wörgötter. Comvis: A communication framework for computer vision. *International Journal of Computer Vision*, 41:183–194, 2001.

[3] A. Desolneux, L. Moisan, and J.M. Morel. Edge detection by the Helmholtz principle. *JMIV*, 14(3):271–284, 2001.

[4] O.D. Faugeras. *Three–Dimensional Computer Vision.* MIT Press, 1993.

[5] M. Felsberg and G. Sommer. The monogenic signal. *IEEE Transactions on Signal Processing*, 41(12), 2001.

[6] O. Granert. Poseschaetzung kinematischer Ketten. *Diploma Thesis, Universität Kiel*, 2002.

[7] D.D. Hoffman, editor. *Visual Intelligence: How we create what we see.* W.W. Norton and Company, 1980.

[8] Thomas Jäger. Interaktion verschiedener visueller Modalitäten zur stabilen Extraktion von Objektrepräsentationen. *Diploma thesis (University of Kiel)*, 2002.

[9] B. Jähne. *Digital Image Processing – Concepts, Algorithms, and Scientific Applications.* Springer, 1997.

[10] R. Klette, K. Schlüns, and A. Koschan. *Computer Vision – Three-Dimensional Data from Images.* Springer, 1998.

[11] P. Kovesi. Image features from phase congruency. *Videre: Journal of Computer Vision Research*, 1(3):1–26, 1999.

[12] N. Krüger, M. Ackermann, and G. Sommer. Accumulation of object representations utilizing interaction of robot action and perception. *Knowledge Based Systems*, 13(2):111–118, 2002.

[13] N. Krüger, M. Felsberg, C. Gebken, and M. Pörksen. An explicit and compact coding of geometric and structural information applied to stereo processing. *Proceedings of the workshop 'Vision, Modeling and Visualization 2002'* 2002.

[14] N. Krüger and F. Wörgötter. Different degree of genetical prestructuring in the ontogenesis of visual abilities based on deterministic and statistical regularities. *Proceedings of the Workshop On Growing up Artifacts that Live SAB 2002*, 2002.

[15] N. Krüger and F. Wörgötter. Multi modal estimation of collinearity and parallelism in natural image sequences. *To appear in Network: Computation in Neural Systems*, 2002.

[16] H.-H. Nagel. On the estimation of optic flow: Relations between different approaches and some new results. *Artificial Intelligence*, 33:299–324, 1987.

[17] T.Q. Phong, R. Haraud, A. Yassine, and P.T. Tao. Object pose from 2-d to 3-d Point and line correspondences. International Journal of Computer Vision, 15:225-243, 1995.

[18] B. Rosenhahn, N. Krüger, T. Rabsch, and G. Sommer. Automatic tracking with a novel pose estimation algorithm. *Robot Vision 2001*, 2001.

[19] S. Sarkar and K.L. Boyer. *Computing Perceptual Organization in Computer Vision.* World Scientific, 1994.

[20] C. Zetzsche and E. Barth. Fundamental limits of linear filters in the visual processing of two dimensional signals. *Vision Research*, 30, 1990.

A Method of Extracting Objects of Interest with Possible Broad Application in Computer Vision

Kyungjoo Cheoi[1] and Yillbyung Lee[2]

[1]Information Technology Group Division R&D Center, LG CNS Co., Ltd.
Prime Tower, #10-1, Hoehyun-dong, 2-ga, Jung-gu, Seoul, 100-630, Korea
{choikj}@lgcns.com

[2]Dept. of Computer Science and Industrial Systems Engineering, Yonsei University
134, Sinchon-dong, Seodaemoon-gu, Seoul, 120-749, Korea
{yblee}@csai.yonsei.ac.kr

Abstract. An approach of using a biologically motivated attention system to extracting objects of interest from an image is presented with possible broad application in computer vision. Starting with an RGB image, four streams of biologically motivated features are extracted and reorganized in order to calculate a saliency map allowing the selection of the most interesting objects. The approach is tested on three different types of images showing reasonable results. In addition, in order to verify the results on real images, we performed human test and compared the measured behaviors of human subjects with the results of the system.

1 Introduction

It is well known that, in most biological vision systems, only a small fraction of the information registered at any given time reaches level of processing that directly influence behavior. This biological mechanism, what so called selective attention, is used by a wide variety of biological systems to optimize their limited parallel-processing resources by identifying relevant sub-regions of the sensory input space and processing them in a serial fashion, shifting spatially from one sub-region to the other. This mechanism act as a dynamic filter that allows the system to determine what information is relevant for the task at hand and to process it, while suppressing the irrelevant information that the system is not analyze simultaneously. It can be a very effective engineering tool for designing artificial systems that need to process in real-time sensory information and that have limited computational resource [1].

Biological selective attention mechanisms are believed to be modulated by bottom-up(stimulus-driven) and top-down(goal-driven) factors. Bottom-up selective attention appears to be a rapid task-independent mechanism, while top-down selective attention appears to act in a slower volition controlled manner. There has been extensive work in modeling attention and understanding the neurobiological mechanisms of generating the visual attention both from bottom-up and top-down approach, and several

H.H. Bülthoff et al. (Eds.): BMCV 2002, LNCS 2525, pp. 331–339, 2002.

computational models of selective attention have been proposed. In bottom-up approach, the system selects regions of interest by bottom-up cues obtained by extracting various elementary features of visual stimuli [4,5,6,7,10,12,14]. And in top-down approach, the system uses top-down cues obtained from a-priori knowledge about current visual task [9,15]. A hybrid approach combining both bottom-up and top-down cues has also been reported [2,3,11,13]. It may note that the previous systems, although they are useful to understand and explain human visual attention, are defined in terms closer to the language of cognitive science than computer vision. The method used in our research is very similar to the model of the stimulus driven form of selective attention [5], based on the saliency map concept, originally put forth by Koch and Ullman [4]. Saliency map based models of selective attention account for many of the observed behaviors in neurophysiological and psychophysical experiments [8] and have interesting computational properties that led to several software implements, applied to machine vision and robotic tasks [3,5,10,11,12,13]. Our system proposed here is designed to extend the capabilities of previous systems. And an effort to ensure a wide field of real applications for the system is made, while retaining compatibility with some major properties of the human visual system.

A diagram describing the main processing stage of the system is shown in Fig. 1. The system includes following three components : i) several feature maps known to influence human visual attention, which are computed directly from the input image in parallel, ii) importance maps, each of which has the measure of "perceptual importance" of pixels in each corresponding feature maps, and are computed by oriented center-surround operator, and iii) single saliency map, integrated across multiple importance maps based on a simple iterative non-linear mechanism which uses statistical information and local competition relation of pixels in each importance maps.

In following sections we describe the architecture of our system and present experimental results that demonstrate the expected functionality of the system and make conclusions.

2 The Architecture of the System

As can be seen in Fig.1, RGB color image is provided to the system and separated into four early-vision feature maps in parallel. Then, each map is reorganized in order to extract orientations and to enhance the regions of pixels whose values are largely different from their surroundings'. The resulting importance maps are then integrated into a single saliency map. The fundamental description of the system is presented in this section.

The system takes digitized images as input and this input is separated into four early-vision feature maps in parallel. As early-vision feature maps, two kinds of feature maps known to influence human visual attention are generated from the input image : two achromatic feature maps for intensity contrast(F^1, F^2) and two color feature maps for color contrast(F^3, F^4). As two achromatic feature maps, F^1 and F^2 are generated by ON and OFF intensity information of input image, respectively. As In

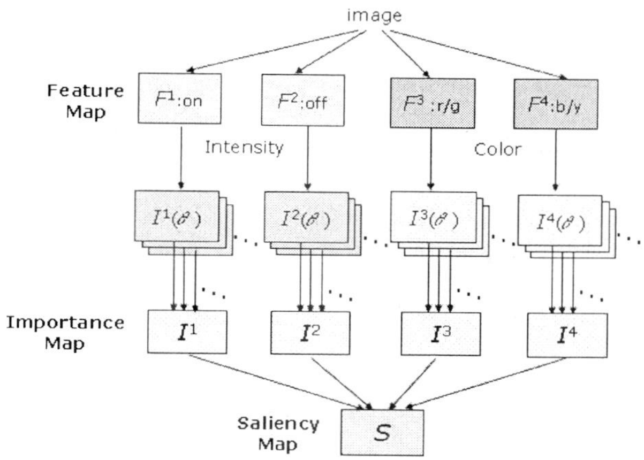

Fig. 1. Detailed view of the system proposed. An input raw image is separated into two kinds of four early-vision feature maps, F^1 and F^2 for intensity contrast, and F^3 and F^4 for color contrast. Then, these four early-vision feature maps are reorganized into importance map, $I^1 \sim I^4$, respectively. Each map has one more feature(i.e., orientation) than early-vision feature maps, and also has enhanced pixel values whose values are largely different from their surroundings'. These reorganized importance maps are integrated into one single saliency map S by statistical information and competitive relations of the pixels in each reorganized feature map. The most interesting objects are selected based on this saliency map.

the nature, as well as in human made environments, color can distinguish objects and signal(e.g., traffic signs or warning signs in industrial environments). So, two color feature maps, F^3 and F^4 are generated. F^3 and F^4 are modeled with the two types of color opponency exhibited by the cells with homogeneous type of receptive fields in visual cortex, which respond very strong to color contrast. F^3 is generated to account for 'red/green' color opponency and F^4 for 'blue/yellow' color opponency. These four generated feature maps are then normalized in the range of 0~1 in order to eliminate the differences due to dissimilar feature extraction mechanisms, and to simplify further processing of the feature maps.

At the second stage of the processing, each of the early-vision feature maps, F^k (k=1~4), is convolved with the oriented ON-center, OFF-surround operators($\theta \in \{0, \pi/8, 2\pi/8, \cdots, 7\pi/8\}$) by

$$I^k_{x,y} = \sum_{\theta}\left(\sum_{m,n} F^k_{m,n} \cdot \left|K_1 \cdot G_{x-m,y-n}(\sigma, r_1 \cdot \sigma, \theta) - K_2 \cdot G_{x-m,y-n}(r_2 \cdot \sigma, r_1 \cdot r_2 \cdot \sigma, \theta)\right|\right)^2 \quad (1)$$

where K_1, K_2 denote positive constants, r_1, denote the eccentricities of the two Gaussians, r_2, denote the ratio between the widths of the ON and OFF Gaussians, and $G_{x,y}(\cdot,\cdot,\cdot)$, 2-D oriented Gaussian functions. And the resulting maps are squared to enhance the contrast, and multiple oriented measures(θ) are integrated to provide a single measure of interest of each location. Through this process, reorganized importance map I^k extracts additional feature, orientation, and enhances the regions of pixels whose values are largely different from their surroundings'.

Although many features that influence visual attention have been identified, little quantitative data exist regarding the exact weighting of the different features and their relationship. Some features clearly have very high importance, but it is difficult to define exactly that how much the one feature is more important than another. A particular feature may be more important than another in one image, while in another image the opposite may be true. We integrated four importance maps which provide various measure of interest for each location into one single saliency map in order to provide global measure of interest by

$$S^k_{x,y} = \frac{SI^k_{x,y} - MinSI}{MaxSI - MinSI} \tag{2}$$

where

$$SI^k_{x,y} = I^k_{x,y} \times \left(MaxI^k - AveI^k\right)^2,$$

$$MaxI^k = \max(I^k_{x,y}),\ AveI^k = \frac{1}{N-1}\left[(\sum_{x,y} I^k_{x,y}) - MaxI^k\right] \tag{3}$$

$$MaxSI = \max\left(SI^1_{x,y}, SI^2_{x,y}, SI^3_{x,y}, SI^4_{x,y}\right),\ MinSI = \min\left(SI^1_{x,y}, SI^2_{x,y}, SI^3_{x,y}, SI^4_{x,y}\right)$$

In Ex. 3, N denotes the size of I^k map. In making SI^k map, we used the main idea proposed by Itti and Koch [5]. This processing enhances the values associated with strong peak activities in the map while suppressing uniform peak activities by the statistical information of the pixels in the map. Also, comparing the map with other maps enables to retain relative importance of a feature map with respect to other ones. And irrelevant information extracted from ineffective feature map would be singled out. So, we just sum four S^k maps to make saliency map.

3 Experimental Results

We tested our system with a set of three large classes of images.

The first are 313 simple computer generated images in which the 'targets' are differed in orientations, in colors, in sizes, in shapes, or in intensity contrast, with a set of 'distractors'. See Fig. 2 for example images and the results.

The second are 115 color images of natural environment, which were taken from different domains. Each of which contains the salient objects such as signboard, signal lamp, traffic sign, mailbox, placard, and so forth as well as distractors such as strong local variations in illumination, textures, or other non-targets. By the way, evaluating the performance of the results of our system with such complex real images is not easy, because there are no objective criteria to evaluate the system. Thus, it is difficult to determine what is the basic ideal output of the system. For these reasons we used a subjective evaluation, i.e., we compared between the output of the system and the

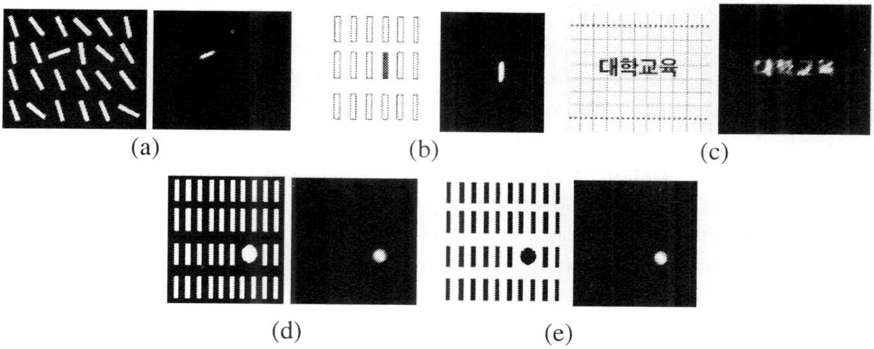

Fig. 2. Some examples of simple computer generated images used in the experiment and the results of them : (a) orientation pop-out (b) color pop-out (c) color and size pop-out (d)~(e) size and intensity pop-out. Test image in (d)'s background is black and its foreground is white, while the color of test image in (e)'d background and foreground is reverse to the input image shown in (d). The results with these two images((d) and (e)) indicate that our system does not always promotes high valued object as the most interesting object, and it guarantees that our system has the symmetry in choosing attended object as an interesting object.

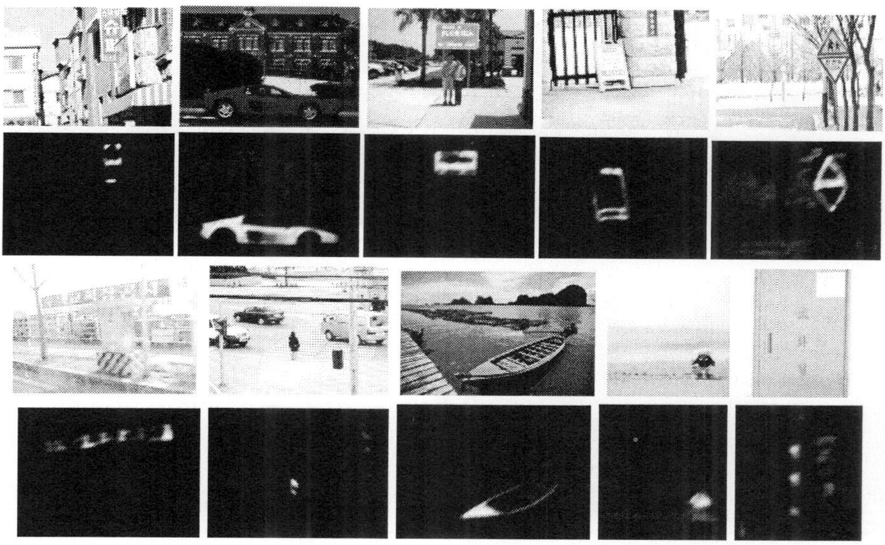

Fig. 3. Some examples of real images used in the experiment and the results of them : listed in order of complexity degree of the background(high→low).

Table 1. The results of the system on 115 complex real images compared to human test

Test Image: No.		Right Detection No.	Right Detection Rate
complexity degree of the background	high : 55	47.26	85.93%
	middle : 28	24.45	87.32%
	low : 32	27.75	86.71%

measured behaviors of normal human subjects. Forty human subjects(19 were girl and 21 were boy) aged 12 years, were participated in the experiment. Subjects were first presented with the same test images which were inputted to the system. We asked subjects to mark the most attended region or object as soon as they found it during each trial. According to the results of human experiment, when subjects were presented with the very left upside images of Fig. 3, most of human subjects marked a red sign board(35:red car, 5:blue striped ceiling), and the right detection rate of the system on this image compared to measured behaviors of human is 87.5%. Table. 1 shows the overall results of the system on 115 real images compared to human test.

Last, the third are 304 noisy images which were corrupted with heavy amounts of noise. The noise has some properties : its distribution is gaussian or uniform distribution, and has color information not only intensity information. See Fig. 4, Table. 2, and Fig. 5 for more detailed explanations of the experiments and the results on noisy images.

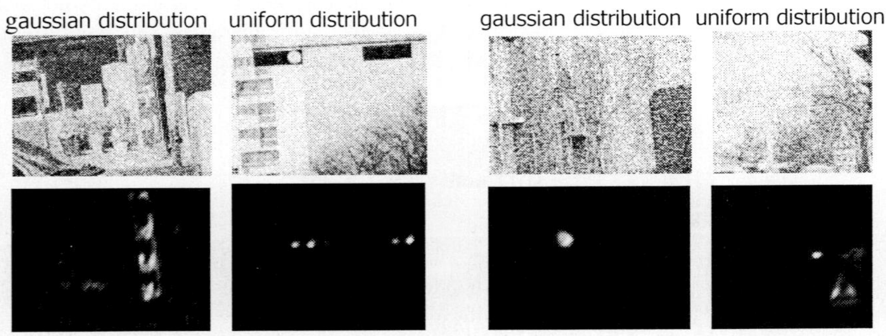

(a) color noise (b) intensity noise

Fig. 4. Some examples of 45% noised images used in the experiment and the results of them. In order to study whether our system is robust to various noisy images, we intentionally added 45% noise having 4 properties to 51 real images, resulting 204 images. Above figures show some results on them, and Table.2 shows overall results of the model using 204 45% noised image.

Table 2. The results of the model using 45% noised image

Noise Property		Right Detection No. / Total Image No.	Right Detection Rate (%)
color noise	gaussian distribution	32 / 51	62.74%
	uniform distribution	40 / 51	78.43%
intensity noise	gaussian distribution	51 / 51	100%
	uniform distribution	51 / 51	100%

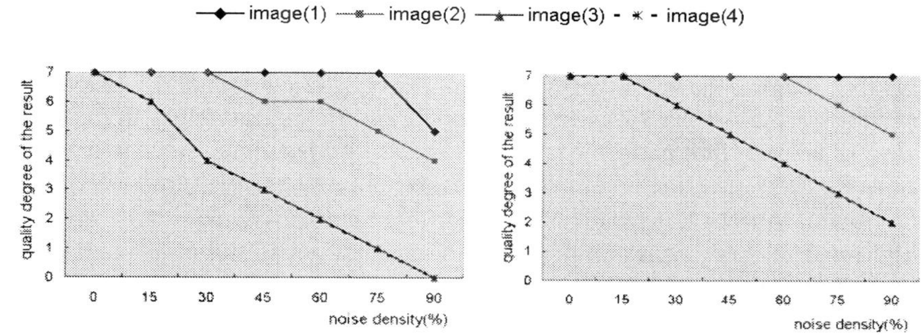

(a) color noise

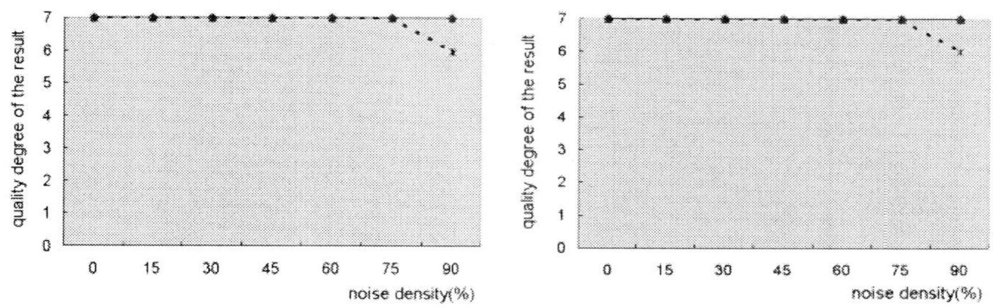

(b) intensity noise

Fig. 5. Some results on noisy images in which the density of the added noise is increased from 0% to 90%. We selected 4 real color images which were not corrupted with severe noise and which were already tested by the system. And we added noise by intention. Added noise has 4 properties(see text for more explanation) with noise density 0%, 15%, 30%, 45%, 60%, 75%, and 90% resulting 100 images. The results shown in (a) is the results on image whose added noise is color noise with gaussian distribution for left image, and with uniform distribution for right image. And in case (b), added noise is intensity noise with gaussian distribution for left image and with uniform distribution for right image. Horizontal axis indicates noise density(%) of the image and vertical axis indicates the quality degree of the result image(0 to 7). We assigned 7 if the quality of the result for detecting objects of interest is very good compared to the result when it was not corrupted with noise, and we assigned 0 if the target cannot be founded from the result image. The graph shown indicates that the system is very robust to intensity noise even if the density of the noise in image is very high, and also indicates that color noise disturbs the system in detecting salient objects as the density of the noise is increased more and more.

4 Conclusion

We presented in this paper a system of extracting objects of interest from an image with possible broad application in computer vision. Starting with an RGB image, four streams of features are extracted and reorganized to calculate a saliency map allowing the selection of the most interesting objects. As our system assumes that no a-priori knowledge might be available on target objects, this guarantees a general-purpose character which can be exploited by any computer vision system. And our system provides not only a set of interesting locations, but also gives the boundary of the surrounding regions. In this way regions containing complete objects can eventually be singled out. The system was tested on a variety of images taken from different domains. In addition, we performed human test and compared the measured behaviors of human subjects with the results of the system in order to verify the results of the system on real images are good or not. Experimental results using a large data set of 707 different types of images demonstrate the feasibility and the functionality of the system, and various complex test scenes prove for the robustness of the method.

Acknowledgement. This work was supported by the Brain Science and Engineering Research Program sponsored by the Korea Ministry of Science and Technology.

References

1. Burt, P.J.:Attention mechanisms for vision in a dynamic world. Proc. of Intl. Conf. on Pattern Recognition 2 (1998) 977–987
2. Cave, K., Wolfe, J.: Modeling the Role of Parallel Processing in Visual Search. Cognitive Psychology 22 (1990) 225–271
3. Exel, S., Pessoa, L.:Attentive visual recognition. Proc. of Intl. Conf. on Pattern Recognition 1 (1998) 690–692
4. Koch, C., Ullman, S.: Shifts in Selective Visual Attention : Towards the Underlying Neural Circuitry. Human Neurobiology 4 (1985) 219–227
5. Itti, L., Koch, C., Niebur, E.: Model of saliency-based visual attention for rapid scene analysis. IEEE Transactions on Pattern Analysis and Machine Intelligence (1998) 1254–1259
6. Itti, L., Koch, C.,: A saliency-based search mechanism for overt and covert shifts of visual attention. Vision Research 40 (2000) 1489–1506
7. Itti. L, Koch. C.: A comparison of feature combination strategies for saliency-based visual attention systems. In Proc. SPIE Human Vision and Electronic Imaging IV 3644 (2000) 1473–1506
8. Itti. L, Koch. C.: Computational modeling visual attention. Nature Neuroscience Review. 2 (2001) 194–204
9. Laar, P., Heskes, T., Gielen, S.:Task-Dependent Learning of Attention. Neural Networks 10, 6 (1997) 981–992
10. Milanese, R., Bost,J., Pun, Thierry.: A Bottom-up Attention system For Active Vision. Proc. of 10th European Conf. on Artificial Intelligence (1992)
11. Milanese, R., Wechsler, H., Gil, S., Bost, J.,Pun, T.: Integration of Bottom-up and Top-down Cues for Visual Attention Using Non-Linear Relaxation. Proc. of IEEE Conf. on Computer Vision and Pattern Recognition (1994) 781–785
12. Mozer, M.: The Perception of Multiple Objects : a Connectionist Approach. MIT Press, Cambridge, MA (1991)

13. Olivier, S., Yasuo, K., Gordon, C.:Development of a Biologically Inspired Real-Time Visual Attention System. In:Lee, S.-W.,Buelthoff, H.-H., Poggio, T.(eds.): BMCV 2000.Lecture Notes in Computer Science, Vol. 1811. Springer-Verlag, Berlin Heidelberg New York (2000) 150–159
14. Olshausen, B., Essen, D., Anderson, C.: A neurobiological model of visual attention and Invariant pattern recognition based on dynamic routing of information. NeuroScience 13 (1993) 4700-4719
15. Parasuraman. R.,:The attentive brain. MIT Press, Cambridge, MA, (1998)

Medical Ultrasound Image Similarity Measurement by Human Visual System (HVS) Modelling

Darryl de Cunha[1], Leila Eadie[2], Benjamin Adams[1], and David Hawkes[1]

[1]Division of Imaging, Guy's Hospital, King's College London, London Bridge, London, SE1 9RT, U.K.
{darryl.decunha,david.hawkes}@kcl.ac.uk
[2]Department of Surgery and Liver Transplantation, Royal Free Hospital, Pond Street, Hampstead, London, U.K.

Abstract. We applied a four stage model of human vision to the problem of similarity measurement of medical (liver) ultrasound images. The results showed that when comparing a given image to a set that contained images with similar features, the model was able to correctly identify the most similar image in the set. Additionally, the shape of the similarity function closely followed a subjective measure of visual similarity for images around the best match. Removing some computational steps to reduce processing time enabled the comparison method to run in near real-time (< 5 seconds), but with some acceptable loss of accuracy. These results could not be achieved using conventional similarity measurements based on image grey level statistics.

1 Introduction

Advances in the generation and display of multiple 2D ultrasound slices [1] give the possibility of ultrasound based surgical planning and interactive image guided surgery, requiring the simultaneous display of an interoperative pointer with the preoperative surgical plan. A simple solution to the problem of an effective pointer would be to use the ultrasound transducer that produced the original images, as the real time guide and link between the internal view of the patient and the surgical plan. This has the advantage that the ultrasound gain and other image controls can be kept constant, maintaining imaging characteristics between live and recorded views. The current real time view can then be matched to the closest individual slice in the preoperative plan, using image processing techniques. However, problems still remain in trying to match a live ultrasound image that may include tissue deformation and transducer displacement, relative to the previously recorded image set. In particular, changes in shadowing, speckle, feature shape and visibility are common in ultrasound images that are taken after repositioning of the transducer.

Conventional statistical measures of image similarity [2,3] are based upon point-to-point variations of grey level within the images. However, the typical variations found in ultrasound images lead to significant grey level differences, even though the

H.H. Bülthoff et al. (Eds.): BMCV 2002, LNCS 2525, pp. 340–347, 2002.

human visual system is able to easily and rapidly identify the similarity of features when the images are viewed side by side. Similar pre-attentive matching of image features within the human visual system to achieve stereopsis, is known to depend upon matching overlapping image spectral distributions [4] by Human Visual System (HVS) Modelling within certain bandpass ranges [5]. Computational models of human vision [6] have been based upon feature extraction using wavelet decomposition of images in filter-rectify-filter type models, typically using one-octave Gabor filter sets [7]. Gabor patterns resemble receptive fields of simple cells in the visual cortex and sensitivity of the visual system has been shown to be more efficient to Gabor patterns than to simple edge information [8]. Efficient information extraction using Gabor and wavelet analysis has been successfully applied to medical ultrasound images in determining texture boundaries [9], feature edges [10] and to produce lossy compression algorithms with minimum visual distortion [11]. Wavelet transforms have also been successfully applied to other medical imaging modalities, for example in the detection of microcalcifications [12] and shapes of masses [13] in X-ray mammograms.

Detection of features by the visual system and therefore judgments of similarity, depend on the context within which features are viewed [14]. The size and orientation [15], distance [16] and spatial frequency content [17] of surrounding or spatially overlapping features can either mask or facilitate feature detection. In addition to lateral interactions, relative disparities of features between image pairs in binocular matching can co-operate [18], to the extent that matching of ambiguous large scale patterns can be solved (disambiguated) across spatial scales by independent small scale patterns with unambiguous matching properties [19]. The exact neural mechanisms of similarity judgements are unknown, but are likely to involve higher level processes of complex pattern discrimination from recoded primary-level information [20]. Field et al [21] suggest the presence of an "associative field" that uses associated but non-aligned features to form global patterns. The detection of second order (non-Fourier) global patterns has been shown to be tied to first order texture scale [22]. This suggests pattern detection by first order orientation selective filtering, followed by second order filtering between eight and sixteen times lower in frequency than the first order [23]. In this study we sought a robust similarity measure that could be calculated in real-time, to identify the best match in a set of multiple 2D images to a comparison image. The measurement of image similarity by *Human Visual System* (HVS) modeling used known processes in human binocular matching to objectively measure feature pattern similarity between images.

2 Method

To investigate the use of HVS modeling in assessment of ultrasound image similarity, we implemented a four stage model based on distinct processing steps in human vision. The model was tested on two sets of ultrasound data and chosen comparison images. Ultrasound images of livers were used in this study because they exhibit poor image quality, lack of feature definition and non-rigid distortion. These characteristics are known to cause problems to conventional matching techniques [24]. One set of images were taken by a sweep of a human liver and the other from two separate sweeps of a phantom gelatin liver that exhibited the same ultrasound characteristics as a human liver scan. The two phantom image sweeps had a relative displacement of about 5mm on the phantom liver surface, for each corresponding image. To judge the effectiveness of the technique, we applied the standard image grey level statistical measures of cross-correlation and normalized mutual information to the data for comparison. To get a measure of the ideal visual similarity function, three observers judged the similarity of each image in a given set to the comparison image and assigned a value as a percentage. The results were averaged to get a subjective function measure. For application to the processing of live images that act as a pointer in image guided surgery, we increased speed by removing redundant and fine scale processing steps, although some accuracy was likely to be lost.

2.1 Initial Preprocessing Stage

For the first stage of processing, the images were given a non-linear grey scale to luminance transform of the form

$$\text{Luminance} = \text{Alut}^{2.2}\,. \tag{1}$$

where A is a calibration constant and lut = pixel grey level.
The resultant luminance images were then scaled to display the maximum luminance at the maximum grey level available, equivalent to visual adaptation to the stimulus. Each images' spectral distribution was then weighted according to the human contrast sensitivity function [25] (c.s.f.) given by equations (2) and (3).

$$\text{c.s.f.} = a\omega e^{-b\omega}(1+0.6e^{b\omega})^{1/2}\,. \tag{2}$$

$$a = \frac{540\left(1+0.7/L\right)^{-0.2}}{1+\left(\frac{12}{p}\right)\left(1+1/3\omega\right)^{-2}},\quad b = 0.3\left(1+100/L\right)^{0.15} \tag{3}$$

where ω is the angular spatial frequency in cycles/degree; L is the average display luminance in cd/m^2; and p is the total angular display size of the image. The images were then bandpass filtered into four separate octave bands with boundaries at 1.76 c/d, 3.6 c/d, 7.0 c/d and 14.0 c/d. The frequency band above 14.0 c/d was disregarded. The bandpassed spectrum was converted back to image space for Gabor analysis.

2.2 Gabor Analysis

In the second stage of analysis, the individual bandpassed images (representing visually independent features) were decomposed using Gabor wavelets of the form given in (4).

$$G(x, y) = 1.0 \cos[2\pi f(x\cos\theta - y\sin\theta)]\exp[-(x^2+y^2)/2\sigma^2]\,. \tag{4}$$

where f is the Gabor carrier frequency (taken to be the central frequency of the band being analyzed); θ is the orientation of the Gabor; and σ is the standard deviation (s.d.) of the Gaussian envelope. To limit the quantity of processing, a sub-set of six orientations were used at 0°, 18°, 36°, 54°, 72° and 90°. Further orientations to 180° were not implemented in this pilot study. The s.d. (σ) of the envelope was set to one third of the carrier frequency and the convolution kernel of the Gabor was truncated at $\pm 2\sigma$. The convolution summation was rectified and the final result was also scaled in intensity to display the result as a raster image for visual examination.

2.3 Cortical Hypercolumn Construction and Matching

The third analysis stage arranged the Gabor analyzed images into a quantized 3D matrix that resembled the layout of hypercolumns in the primary visual cortex [26]. One axis in the 3D configuration corresponded to Gabor orientation and the other two axes to x and y directions in image space. The image space was quantized in x and y into 32 x 32 elements, by summing values from the spatial Gabor analyzed image. Two hypercolumns were constructed with slightly different quantization boundaries; one with the quantization aligned with the image borders and one with a horizontal and vertical shift of half the quantization width, allocating slightly different features to each quantization element.

In a fourth processing stage of image feature matching, the corresponding hypercolumns of the compared images were correlated using a search space of ±3 elements, in all directions at the same orientation.

2.4 Comparison with Conventional Image Similarity Measurements

To compare the performance of the visual model with conventional statistical measures of similarity, Cross-Correlation CC and Normalized Mutual Information NMI measures (5) were applied to each experimental image set. H(A) and H(B) are the individual image entropies and H(A,B) is the joint entropy.

$$\mathrm{CC} = \frac{\sum (x-\bar{x})(y-\bar{y})}{\sqrt{\sum (x-\bar{x})^2}\sqrt{\sum (y-\bar{y})^2}}, \quad \mathrm{NMI} = \frac{H(A)+H(B)}{H(A,B)} . \tag{5}$$

3 Results

The results from the initial processing stage of luminance conversition, c.s.f. weighting (Fig. 1.) and octave bandpass filtering, showed that the main image features were significantly represented in the two lowest octave bands only. The bandpassed results from a typical human liver image (*Fig. 1, right*) can be seen in Fig. 2 for the lowest band (*top left*) and one octave higher (*bottom left*). We therefore applied the two lowest octave band to Gabor analysis and subsequent cortical hypercolumn construction (*Fig. 2. right*).

The similarity results for the real and phantom liver image sets are shown in Fig 3. In the real image set, image number 15 in a sweep of forty images was compared to the ten closest images on both sides in the same set (and including matching to itself). Comparing a given image to other images from the same sweep set represents the best possible alignment of a comparison ultrasound image to a previously recorded data set.

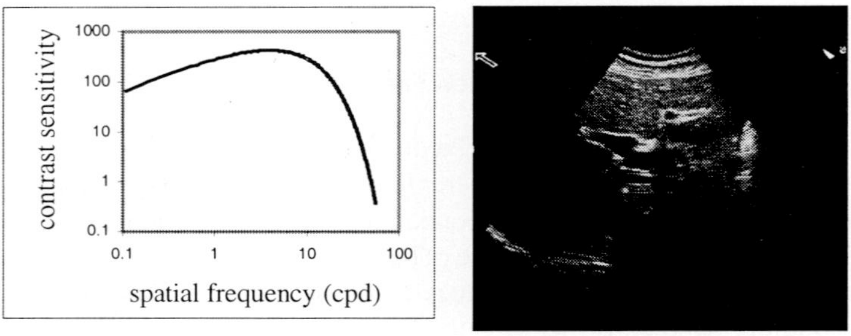

Fig. 1. Human Contrast Sensitivity Function (*left*) exhibiting low pass filter characteristics and ultrasound image of human liver (*right*) after preprocessing

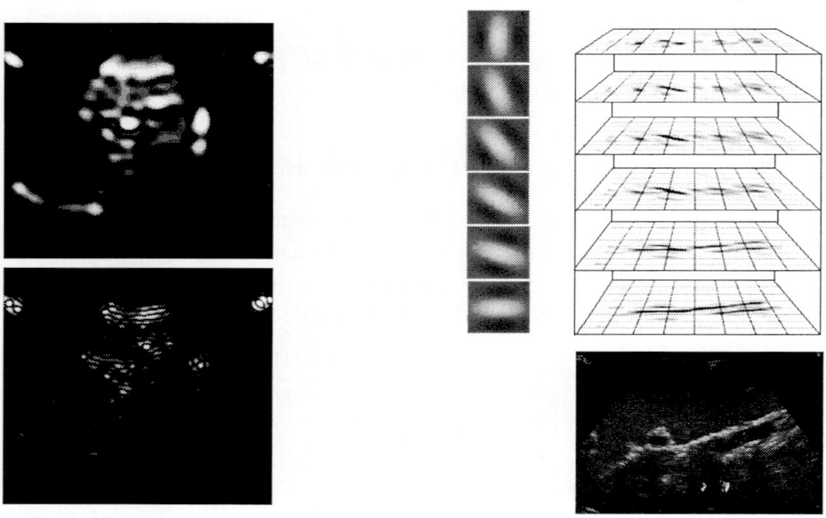

Fig. 2. Two lowest octave bandpassed images (left) of the liver image in Fig. 1. On the right is a representation of a constructed cortical hypercolumn of an ultrasound phantom image (*lower right*), with the corresponding Gabor orientations next to each layer

The results showed that the model was able to identify a best match of a real liver image with the comparison and although the CC and NMI were also able to correctly identify the best match, the visual model gave a closer match to the observers' subjective similarity function. For the phantom liver comparison, an image from the first sweep was compared to fourteen images in the second sweep, surrounding the position of visual best match (image number 4). This configuration closely matched the situation in surgical planning where the transducer had been replaced to a close but not identical position to a previously taken image sweep. The results show that the visual similarity model was able to correctly identify the most similar image and also closely followed the subjective similarity function, for images immediately adjacent to the closest match. The conventional similarity measures were unable to identify the best match in this case.

To increase the speed of the processing model, we reduced the processing steps by removing some components of the computational model. The hypercolumns were constructed using only the 0° orientation Gabor and the Gabor kernel was sub-sampled to only use one hundredth of the available points. This reduced the processing time from five minutes to less than five seconds. The reduced processing results were nearly identical to the full processing model in the case of the real liver, but showed an error of one image position in the phantom data.

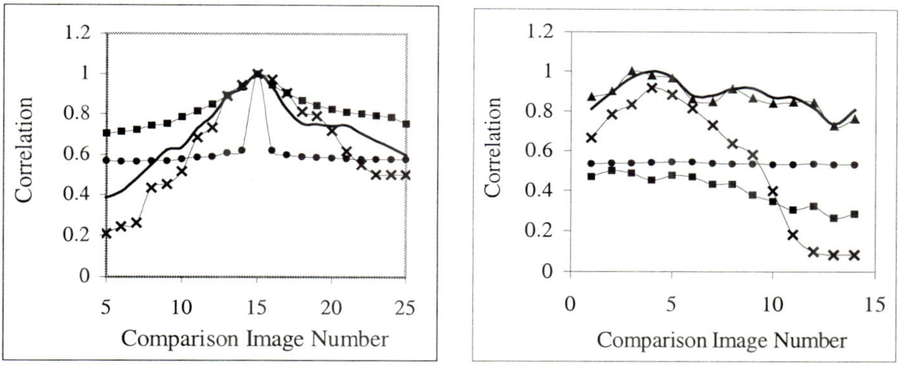

Fig. 3. The results for the real liver (*left*) and the phantom liver (*right*). The line with crosses shows the subjective measure of similarity; the thick line shows the calculated similarity function from the visual model. The line with squares is the CC results and the line with circles is NMI. The line with triangles is the reduced processing result (shown for the phantom only)

4 Discussion

The results of the computational model show accurate identification of the most similar images in both the real and phantom liver image sets, relative to a comparison image. For the real liver image calculations, the comparison image had been taken from a set obtained by a 'sweep' of a human liver and compared to surrounding images in the same sweep set. The subjective image similarity function showed how features in the images became increasingly different as the images in the sweep become more distant from the best match to the comparison image. For the real liver set, we would expect all similarity measures to correctly identify the best match (as this compared two identical images), but the point of interest was that the HVS computational model closely modeled the subjective similarity function across the range of comparison images.

In the phantom images where the two ultrasound sweeps were taken over two slightly different positions on the phantom liver surface, image features were displaced both laterally and in rotation between the image sweeps. However, the subjective measurement of similarity by observers showed that visually, corresponding features could be matched and used to estimate similarity between images in the two different sweeps. The computational measure of similarity closely matched the subjective measure in images adjacent to the comparison image. Away from the closest match where comparison images did not contain similar anatomical features, the results dropped to a background level.

Removing computational steps and sub-sampling the Gabor kernel significantly reduced computational time, but was also associated with loss of accuracy. It is still to be determined if this loss of accuracy is within the tolerance required for using the ultrasound probe as a pointer in a preoperative plan.

Refining the method will require validation on more extensive data sets and subsequent removal of redundant processing steps, in favor of enhancing visually important features used in matching. An objective measurement method of image similarity is also required to provide an accurate baseline for validation.

References

1. Candiani, F.: The Latest in Ultrasound: Three-Dimensional Imaging. Part 1. European Journal of Radiology. 27 (1998) S179–S182
2. Penney, G.P., Weese, J., Little, J.A., Desmedt, P., Hill, D.L.G., Hawkes, D.J.: A Comparison of Similarity Measures for Use in 2-D–3-D Medical Image Registration. IEEE Trans. Med. Imaging. 17(4) (1998) 586 – 595
3. Studholme, C., Hill, D.L.G., Hawkes, D.J.: An Overlap Invariant Entropy Measure of 3D Medical Image Alignment. Pattern Recognition. 32 (1999) 71–86
4. Mayhew, J.E.W., Frisby, J.P.: Rivalrous texture stereograms. Nature. 264 (4) (1976) 53–56
5. Julesz, B., Miller, J.E.: Independent Spatial-Frequency-Tuned Channels in Binocular Fusion and Rivalry. Perception. 4 (1975) 125–143
6. Marr D., Poggio, T.:A Computational Theory of Human Stereo Vision. Proc. R. Soc. Lond. B. 204 (1979) 301–328
7. Jin, J.S., Yeap, Y.K., Cox, B.G.: A Stereo Model Using LoG and Gabor Filtering. Spatial Vision. 10(1) (1996) 3–13
8. Westheimer, G.: Lines and Gabor Functions Compared as Spatial Visual Stimuli. Vision Research, 38(4) (1998) 487–491
9. Chen, C., Lu, H.H., Han, K.: A Textural Approach Based on Gabor Functions for Texture Edge Detection in Ultrasound Images. Ultrasound in Med. & Biol. 27(4) (2001) 515–534
10. Kaspersen, J.H., Langø, T., Lindseth, F.: Wavelet-Based Edge Detection in Ultrasound Images. Ultrasound in Med. & Biol. 27(1) (2001) 89–99

11. Chiu, E., Vaisey, J., Atkins, M.S.: Wavelet - Based Space - Frequency Compression of Ultrasound Images. IEEE Transactions on Information Technology in Biomedicine. 5(4) (2001) 300–310
12. Strickland, R.N., Hahn, H.I.: Wavelet Transforms for Detecting Microcalcifications in Mammograms. IEEE Trans. Med. Imaging. 15(2) (1996) 218–229
13. Bruce, L.M., Adhami, R.R.,: Classifying Mammographic Mass Shapes Using the Wavelet Transform Modulus-Maxima Method. IEEE Trans. Med. Imaging. 18(12) (1999) 1170–1177
14. Unzicker, A., Jüttner, M., Rentschler, I.: Similarity-Based Models of Human Visual Recognition. Vision Research. 38 (1998) 2289–2305
15. Foley, J.M.: Human Luminance Pattern-Vision Mechanisms: Masking Experiments Require a New Model. J. Opt. Soc. Am. A. 11(6) (1994) 1710–1719
16. Polat, U., Sagi, D.: Lateral Interactions Between Spatial Channels: Suppression and Facilitation Revealed by Lateral Masking Experiments. Vision Research. 33(7) (1993) 993–999
17. Glenn, W.E.: Digital Image Compression Based on Visual Perception. In: A.B. Watson, A.B. (Ed.): Digital Images and Human Vision. MIT press, Cambridge, Massachusetts, (1993) 63–71
18. Petrov, Y.: Disparity Capture by Flanking Stimuli: A Measure for the Cooperative Mechanism of Stereopsis. Vision Research. 42 (2002) 809 – 813
19. Smallman, H.S.: Fine-to-Course Scale Disambiguation in Stereopsis. Vision Research. 35(8) (1995) 1047–1060
20. Olzak, L.A., Thomas, J.P.: Neural Recoding in Human Pattern Vision: Model and Mechanisms. Vision Research. 39 (1999) 231–256
21. Field, D.J., Hayes, A., Hess, R.: Contour Integration by the Human Visual System: Evidence for a Local "Association Field. Vision Research. 33(2) (1993) 173–193
22. Kingdom, F.A.A., Keeble, D.R.T.: On the Mechanism for Scale Invariance in Orientation-Defined Textures. Vision Research. 39 (1999)1477–1489
23. Sutter, A., Sperling, G., Chubb, C.: Measuring the Spatial Frequency Selectivity of Second-Order Texture Mechanisms. Vision Research. 35(7) (1995) 915–924
24. Shekhar, R., Zagrodsky, V.: Mutual Information-Based Rigid and Nonrigid Registration of Ultrasound Volumes. IEEE Trans. Med. Imaging. 21(1) (2002) 9–22
25. MacDonald, L.W., Lui, M.R. (eds): Colour Imaging: Vision and technology. Wiley & Sons, Chichester, England (1999) 342–345
26. Sekuler, R., Blake, R.: Perception. McGraw-Hill, New York (1994) 125–127

Seeing People in the Dark: Face Recognition in Infrared Images

Gil Friedrich and Yehezkel Yeshurun

School of Computer Science , Tel-Aviv University, Israel

Abstract. An IR image of the human face presents its unique heat-signature and can be used for recognition. The characteristics of IR images maintain advantages over visible light images, and can be used to improve algorithms of human face recognition in several aspects. IR images are obviously invariant under extreme lighting conditions (including complete darkness). The main findings of this research are that IR face images are less effected by changes of pose or facial expression and enable a simple method for detection of facial features. In this paper we explore several aspects of face recognition in IR images. First, we compare the effect of varying environment conditions over IR and visible light images through a case study. Finally, we propose a method for automatic face recognition in IR images, through which we use a preprocessing algorithm for detecting facial elements, and show the applicability of commonly used face recognition methods in the visible light domain.

1 Introduction

State-of-the-art algorithms for face recognition in the visible light domain achieve a remarkable high level of recognition under controlled environmental conditions. However, these algorithms perform rather poorly under variable illumination, position and facial expression. On the other hand, all known computer algorithms developed for face recognition seem to significantly deteriorate in their performance even when minor alterations to basic conditions are imposed (Ref. [4]), in sharp contrast to the phenomenal ability of the human brain to correctly identify human faces (Ref. [3]) under many variations and even after long periods of time or when the face is partially disguised.

While most existing Computer Vision algorithms are naturally based on visible light, heat signature was not vastly examined (Ref. [9], [10]). We have thus set out to explore the potential benefits of using Infra Red (IR) data for object detection and recognition, and specifically for face detection and recognition. Our IR camera was sensitive to 8-14 nm, as in general body heat temperature is around 9.2 nm.

The main finding of this report is that IR based face recognition is more invariant than CCD based one under various conditions, specifically varying head 3D orientation and facial expressions.

H.H. Bülthoff et al. (Eds.): BMCV 2002, LNCS 2525, pp. 348–359, 2002.

Modifying both facial expressions and head orientation cause direct 3D structural changes, as well as changes of shadow contours in CCD images, which deteriorate the accuracy of any classification method. In an IR image this effect is greatly reduced.. In the following we demonstrate this finding through a case study of two faces, and then proceed to show the benefits for a full fledged face recognition algorithm for a set of 40 persons.

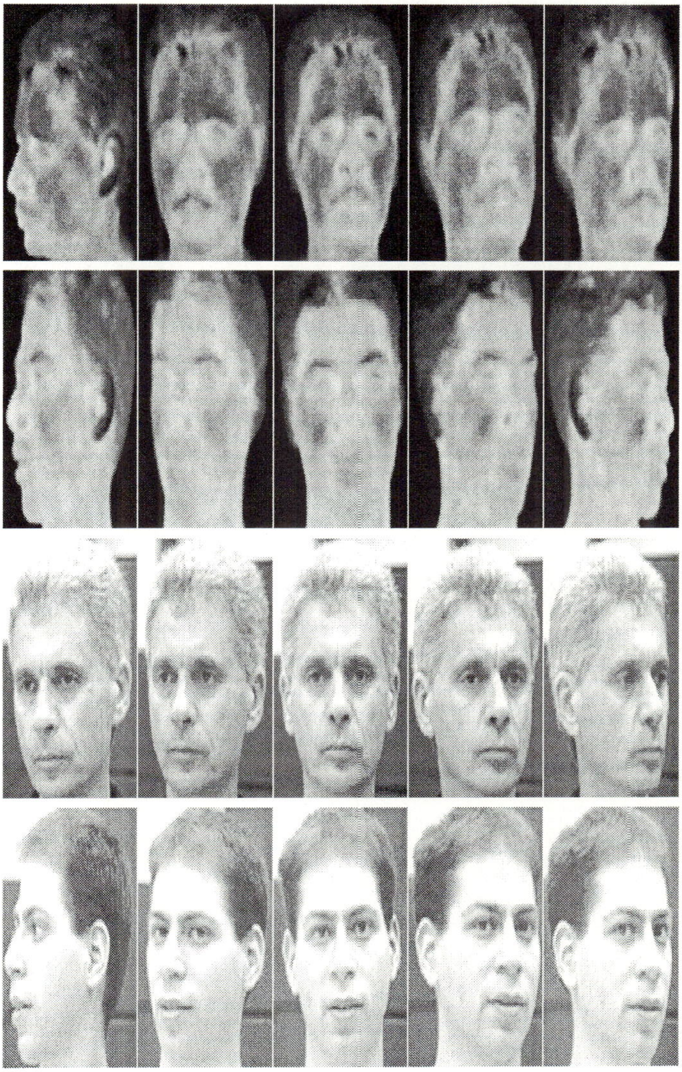

Fig. 1. Examples of IR (top) and CCD (bottom)images with head orientation variations

2 IR vs. CCD Image Invariance

2.1 Head Orientation

3D position variations naturally give rise to 2D image variations. The hypothesis we were making, based on the type of observation depicted in Fig. 1, is that the effect of 3D head rotation in IR images might be less prominent.
3D position variations naturally give rise to 2D image variations. The hypothesis we were making, based on the type of observation depicted in Fig. 1, is that the effect of 3D head rotation in IR images might be less prominent.
This section tests this hypothesis quantitatively over the presented test case. The comparison is done by comparing the ratio of Euclidean distances between images of the same class and the distances of images from the two different classes. First, we align all images using two manually selected interest points (later we present an automatic method to accomplish this task in IR images). Then the average face is found and subtracted from each image. Finally, the matrix of euclidean distances between every pair is calculated. In order to rule out the possibility that the mere difference between the IR and CCD images is the basic resolution, we have repeated the test with CCD images blurred to attain the same resolution of the IR images.

Let $\overline{d}_{In}$ and $\overline{d}_{Ext}$ be the averages of Euclidean distances within and between the classes respectively. Table 1 summarizes the ratio $\frac{\overline{d}_{In}}{\overline{d}_{Ext}}$.

Table1. Ratio of Euclidian distance within and between classes (Figure1 images)

	Face 1	**Face 2**
CCD	0.522	0.751
Blurred CCD	0.521	0.738
IR	0.384	0.532

This result clearly indicates that IR face images are less effected by face 3D orientation in comparison to CCD images. Blurring the CCD images indeed made a small difference, but clearly did not bring the CCD corresponding within/between ratio to what is achieved for IR images.

2.2 Facial Expression

As was the case for head orientation, based on observation similar to Fig.2, we have set out to examine the relative effect of varying facial expressions on their corresponding IR images.

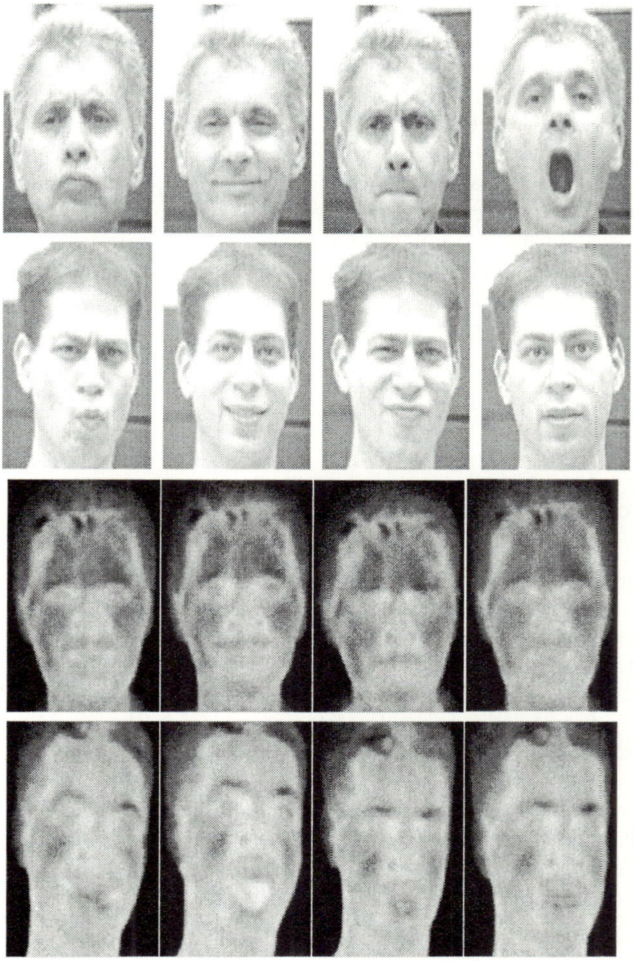

Fig. 2. Examples of CCD (top) images and IR (bottom) with facial expressions variations

Table 2. Ratio of Euclidian distance within and between classes (Figure2 images)

	Face 1	Face 2
CCD	0.817	0.518
Blurred CCD	0.763	0.511
IR	0.350	0.408

Table 2 summarizes the comparison results, which show that indeed facial expression variations are less prominent in IR images.

Several explanations to these results can be found by analyzing the type of information revealed in IR images with comparison to CCD images.

First, changing face parameters modifies the skin surface, thus creating additional image contours. By observing the CCD images, one can see that several parts of the human's face change their shadow pattern, as the expression is altered. Also important is the fact that in the IR image several elements on the face's skin, like pigmentation, are hidden, since they are exactly of the same temperature as the rest of the skin. As a result the skin in the IR image creates a more unified pattern. When the face's expression changes the rather unified pattern in the IR image creates only a slight change between two images, whereas the rich pattern in the CCD image increases the distinction between the two images, reducing the possibility of correct identification. The trivial explanation that IR based images have a better within/between ratio is just an artifact that reflects the fact that IR images "blur" images by definition (due to a more uniform heat distribution than visibly patterns distribution) is ruled out by using blurred CCD images.
In conclusion, face images taken in the IR range inherently contain characteristics that improve correct identification under varying conditions.

3 Detection and Recognition Algorithms

Having obtained the basic finding contributing to facial image invariance, we have implemented an algorithm for human face recognition of infrared images.
Forty face images were used in this study. Each face was captured in 10 different images. All faces were frontal, slightly varying in angle, face size (distance from camera's lens) and expression. The images of each face were divided into a training sample set (2-3 images per face) and the testing sample set. All the images were preprocessed to obtain automatic segmentation, alignment and normalization. Finally, the processed faces are used for an Eigenfaces (Ref. [1]) based classification. We emphasize that the main motivation behind the implementation is the relative lack of data regarding the characteristics of IR face images and the validation of our IR specific segmentation and detection approach, and thus we have chosen to use a common recognition methodology.

3.1 Segmenting Background Temperature

A crucial initial stage in any face processing system involves segmentation of target (faces) and background. Looking for IR specific characteristics, we have found out that the typical distribution of gray (heat) level associated with faces, is markedly different from the typical distribution of the background heat levels. This might be related to some of he human body heat distribution, as opposed to the relatively narrow range of temperature found at "room temperature", and was found to be quite consistent under various environmental circumstances.
This observation gives rise to the following background removal algorithm:

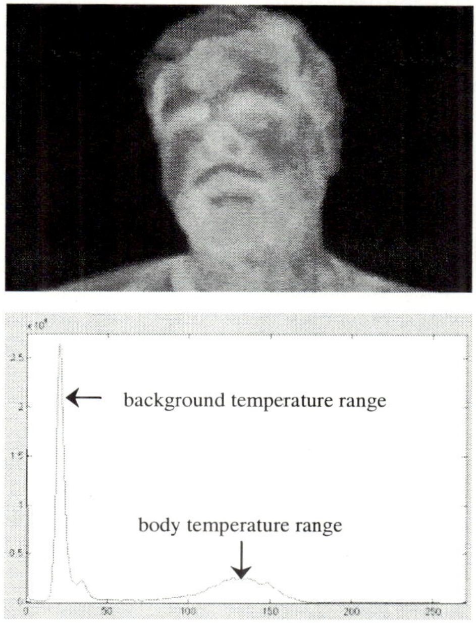

Fig. 3. Gray-level Histogram of IR face image

Let Nbody, Nback be the number of pixels and Maxbody, Maxback be the respective maximal value in the histogram, then,

$$\frac{N_{body}}{N_{back}} \approx \frac{1}{2} \quad \text{but} \quad \frac{Max_{body}}{Max_{back}} \approx \frac{1}{10}$$

(Although the background covers an area only 2 times larger than the rest of the image, its heat is presented in the histogram by a maximum 10 times larger then the maximum created by face heat). The heuristics works over the image histogram in the following way. Let

$$\{h_i\}_{i=0}^{255}$$

be the bin values in the gray-level histogram (256 possible values). Then,

$$Max, j_{\max} = Max\{h_i\}_{i=1}^{255} \tag{1}$$

and,

$$Med, j_{med} = Median(\{h_i > 0\}) \tag{2}$$

are the value and index of maximal and median respectively (for the median value we omit zero bins). Then we seek the first bin after jmax that has value smaller then median value,

$$k = \min_j\{j > j_{\max}, h_j < Med\} \tag{3}$$

Now, bins $\{0...k\text{-}1\}$ represent the background temperature gray-level values and are set to 0, thus completing the stage of background segmentation and removal. Notice that it is possible that objects other than faces will be left as well after the background removal, due to their heat distribution. This, however, is being taken care of in a subsequent stage.

3.2 Clustering

Background removal leaves areas possessing certain intensity distribution levels intact. These areas consist of faces and potentially other objects. Locating and clustering the image pixel corresponding to faces is the next stage of the algorithm. This goal, which is far from trivial with regular CCD images (Ref. [15], [18]), could be much simpler for IR images. We carry this out by using a narrowly tuned heat filtering (Ref. [17]), followed by removal of pixels with only a single 8-connected neighbor. Since sometimes facial elements are colder then the lower limit of the body temperature (brows, nose etc.), an additional flood-fill operation is performed. The algorithm takes a binary image I and starts 4-connected flooding from frame boundary pixels. At the end, flooded pixels J include all non-holes background pixels, therefore the new image Inew=(~J | I) is the original image with all the holes filled.

Figure 4 demonstrate the process.

A= original image

$$B_{ij} = \begin{cases} 1 & h_{low} < A_{ij} < h_{high} \\ 0 & elsewhere \end{cases}$$

J= FloodFill(B)
$C_{ij}=(\sim J_{ij} \mid B_{ij})$

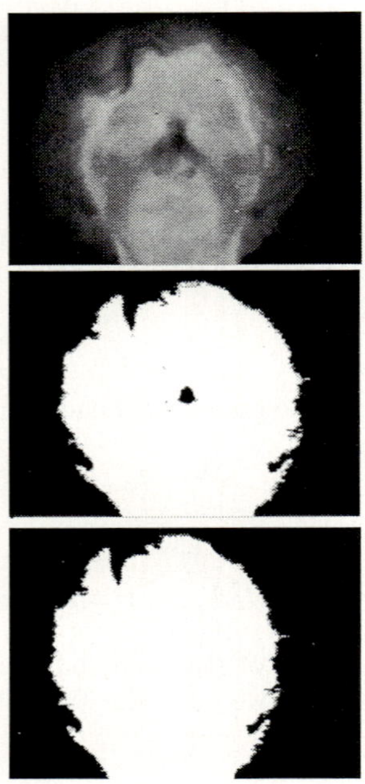

Fig. 4. Flood-filling holes in a cluster

We finalize the clustering stage by filtering out clusters that are not elliptical, using the following simple metric. Let ,

$$e = (A, B, C, D, E) \tag{1}$$

be the ellipse coefficients and

$$r = (X^2, Y^2, XY, X, Y) \tag{2}$$

is calculated from the set of edge-point coordinates $\{X\},\{Y\}$. Ellipse parameters e should satisfy:

$$\left\| e \cdot r' - \vec{1} \right\| \longrightarrow Min \tag{3}$$

It follows that

$$e = (\vec{1} \cdot r) \cdot (r' \cdot r)^{-1} \tag{4}$$

From which we derive the radii $\{r_x, r_y\}$ and rotation angle θ. On our sample data, we have found the following thresholds (5) to be most useful:

$$-30^\circ \leq \theta \leq 30^\circ \quad 1 \leq \frac{r_y}{r_x} \leq 5 \tag{5}$$

In summation, this stage serves for two purposes. First to horizontally align the image, which is a significant for next section. Secondly, it segments the head image from the full body image, by heat filtering (which removes anything that is not skin surface including clothing) and then by elliptic fitting that removes parts of neck and shoulders).

3.3 Finding Points of Reference

There are quite a number of approaches in the face recognition literature for detection reference points in images (e.g eyes). We were looking for specific IR face image features that are characteristic and could be used in general. From comparing a vast database of IR images it was possible to conclude the following:
Since the eyes are always hotter then their surroundings (even when the eyes are

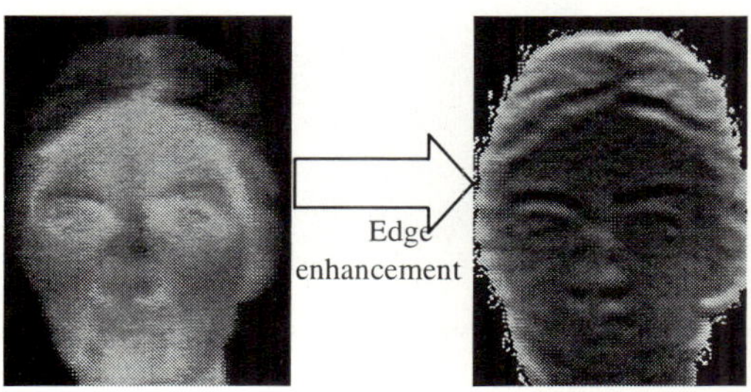

Fig. 5. Edge enhancement used for emphasizing the forehead-brows-eyes pattern

closed!) and the brows were significantly colder then their surroundings, it turned out the most prominent IR related feature that is robust over all the sample data we have used is the edge created by the difference between the eyes and the brows temperature. In order to utilize this property, we have applied edge enhancement (Fig 5), followed by thresholding (lower 1%) (Fig 6).

Fig. 6. Lowest 1% values leaves mainly the brows within the image

And using an horizontal histogram to detect the brows (Figure 7).

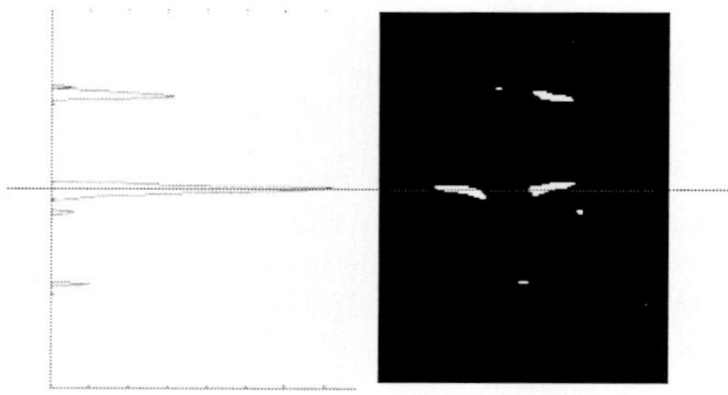

Fig. 7. Horizontal histogram on low-values image used to localize the brows

Finally, by finding the average point of each of the two clusters, we get the two center points of the image. This is illustrated over the original face in Figure 8.

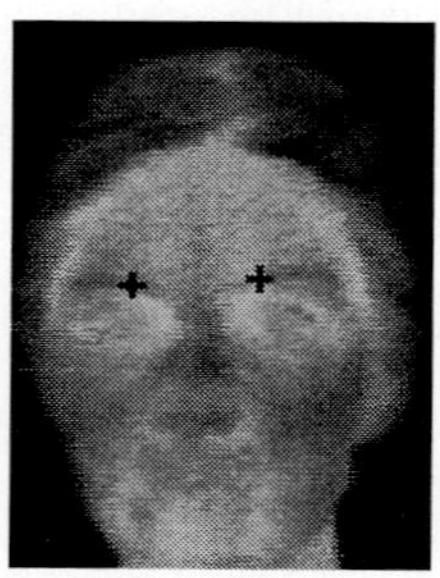

Fig. 8. Points of interest

This method had proved to work properly for all our sample data. We finally align the face image using bilinear interpolation.

3.4 Face Recognition

The previous sections had shown that IR face images are less effected by specific factors such as face orientation and expression, and suggested methods for face detection and normalization. Still, the ability to correctly classify IR face images over a large number of faces needs to be proved. The main point that should be looked for, is whether the invariance gained using IR images and any other potential IR specific features, like face-specific heat spatial distribution compensate for the loss of specific visual information, like visible edges, skin patterns and texture and so on.

We have addressed this issue by implementing an Eigenfaces based classification algorithm (See [1], [2], [4] and [9], [10]). By comparing its performance over IR images with typical CCD based algorithms, we expected to quantify the relative amount of face-specific information within IR images.

The database we have used consisted of 40 different faces, under various head positions and facial expressions (see Fig 1 and 2 for typical examples). For each face 2-4 images were included in the training sample set (total of 96) images, and 5-10 images were tested for recognition quality (total of 250 images). In order to select the most significant Eigenfaces, a threshold of 99% was selected. This threshold yielded a set of 78 Eigenfaces. Some of the Eigenfaces used are shown in Fig. 9.

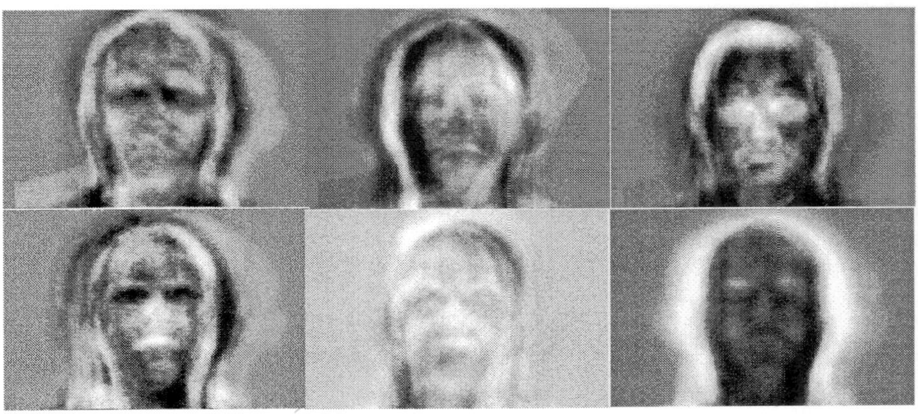

Fig. 9. Examples of IR eigenfaces

Failing to recognize an image consisted of one of the following:

1. **Non-Face.** (Threshold $t_1=1.0$). [1]
2. **Reject.** (Threshold $t_2=0.10$). [2]
3. **Misclassify.**

---

1 Let d_0 be the maximal distance of a training sample set image to the average image, and d be the distance of the tested image, then if $d>(1+t_1)d_0$ then the image is a non-face.

2 Let ε be the minimal distance of the tested image with any image from the training sample set. Then if $\varepsilon>t_2$ it is categorized as an unfamiliar face.

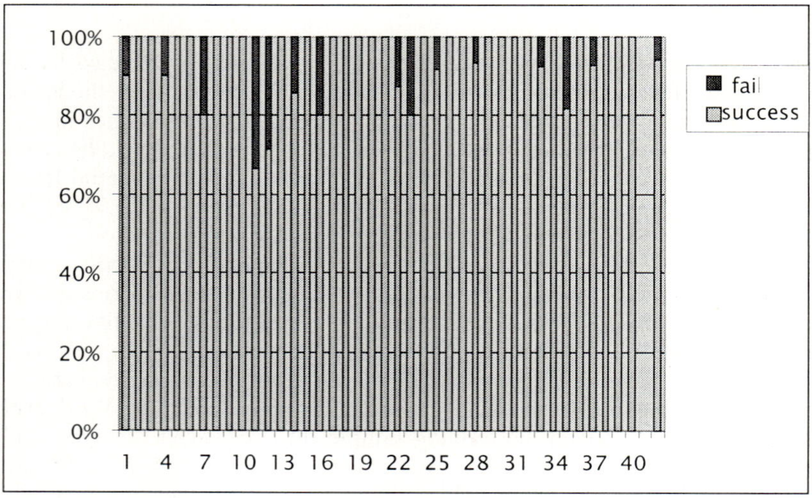

Fig. 10. Recognition results by face indexes

Figure 10 plots success rates for each of the 40 faces used, and the total success rate, which is 94%, in the last column. This rate is comparable to the typical recognition rate reported for CCD based systems (94%-98%), and is clearly superior to the typical recognition rate of CCD based systems where the sample, like in our case, consists of highly varying pose and facial expressions (around 80%). Out of the 40 faces tested, In 26 all face instances were correctly identified, in 10 faces one image classification failed, and in 4 faces two images classification failed. In all misclassification errors, the 2nd and 3rd candidates were the right ones, meaning that a more sophisticated classification algorithm (which is not the main goal of this paper) might improve the recognition results even further.

4 Conclusions

IR based face processing methods have recently gained more attention ([19], [20]) and tested with standard face recognition algorithms ([9], [10]). This field of research still calls for further analysis in order to make optimal use of IR specific features. Some of the advantages of using IR images for face recognition (like invariance under illuminating conditions) are self evident, and some others (automatic detection of faces based on heat signature) are less self evident but natural.
However, IR specific research will undoubtedly yield new features and methods that could immensely facilitate the task, comparing to CCD based methods. In this regard, the main finding of this research is that IR specific feature are significant in eliminating some pose and facial expression variance, thus increasing significantly the typical performance of face recognition algorithms over highly variable pose and expression face images. Future research along the same lines might involve similar analysis for time varying and aging effects, where IR images might prove useful.

References

1. M. Turk and A. Pentland (1991). Eigenfaces for recognition, *J. Cog. Neuroscience*, vol. 3, no. 1, pp. 71–86.
2. M. Kirby and L. Sirovich (1990). Application of the karhunen-loeve procedure for the characterization of human faces, *IEEE Pattern Analysis and Machine Intelligence*, vol. 12, no. 1, pp. 103–108.
3. R. Chellappa, C. Wilson, and S. Sirohev (1995). *Human and machine recognition of faces: A survey*, in Proceedings of IEEE, May 1995, vol. 83, pp. 705–740.
4. P. Phillips, H. Wechsler, J. Huang, and P. Rauss (1998). *The FERET database and evaluation procedure for face recognition algorithms,*Image and Vision Computing, vol. 16, no. 5, pp. 295–306.
5. L. Wiskott, J-M. Fellous, N. Kruger, and C. von der Malsburg (1997). *Face recognition by elastic bunch graph matching*, IEEE Pattern Analysis and Machine Intelligence, vol. 19, no. 7, pp. 775–779.
6. K. Etemad and R. Chellappa (1997). *Discriminant analysis for recognition of human face images*, Journal of the Optical Society of America, vol. 14, pp. 1724–1733.
7. B. Moghaddam and A. Pentland (1997). *Probabalistic visual recognition for object recognition,* IEEE Pattern Analysis and Machine Intelligence, vol. 19, no. 7, pp. 696–710.
8. M. Weiser (1991). *The computer for the 21st century,* Scientific American, vol. 265, no. 3, pp. 66–76.
9. R. Cutler (1996). *Face recognition using infrared images and eigenfaces.* http://research.microsoft.com/~rcutler/face/face.htm.
10. J. Wilder, P.J. Phillips, C. Jiang, and S. Wiener. *Comparison of Visible and Infra-Red Imagery for Face Recognition,* Proceedings of the 2nd International Conference on Automatic Face and Gesture Recognition, Killington, VT, pp.182–187, October 1996
11. F. Prokoski. *History, Current Status, and Future of Infrared Identification*, IEEE Workshop on Computer Vision behind the Visible Spectrum: Methods and Applications (CVBVS 2000), pp 5–14.
12. D. Reisfeld and Y. Yeshurun. *Preprocessing of Face Images: Detection of Features and Pose Normalization*, Computer Vision and Image Understanding, Vol. 71 No. 3 pp 413–430, Sep 1998.
13. M. Irani and P. Anandan. *Robust Multi-Sensor Image Alignment*, International Conference on Computer Vision , Mumbai, January *1998.*
14. N. Intrator, D. Reisfeld, Y. Yeshurun. *Face Recognition using a Hybrid Supervised/ Unsupervised Neural Network*, Pattern Recognition Letters 17:67–76, 1996.
15. Zhang, Y.J. *Evaluation and Comparison of Different Segmentation Algorithms*, PRL(18), No. 10, October 1997, pp. 963–974.
16. Zhou, Y.T, Venkateswar, V. and Chellappa R. *Edge Detection and Linear Feature Extraction Using a 2-D Random Field Model*, PAMI(11), No. 1, January 1989, pp. 84-95.
17. Harley, R.L., Wang, C.Y, Kitchen, L. and Rosenfeld, A. *Segmentation of FLIR Images: A Comparative Study*, SMC(12), No. 4, July/August 1982, pp. 553-566, or DARPA82 (323–341).
18. John F. Haddon and James. F. Boyce. *Image Segmentation by Unifying Region and Boundary Information*, IEEE Transactions on Pattern Analysis and Machine Intelligence, 12(10), pp. 929–948, October, 1990.
19. J. Dowdall, I. Pavlidis, and G. Bebis. *A Face Detetcion Method Based on Multi-Band Feature Extraction in Near IR Spectrum*, IEEE Workshop on Computer Vision Beyond the Visible Spectrum. Kauai, December 2001.
20. Socolinsky, D., Wolff, L., Neuheisel, J., and Eveland, C. *Illumination Invariant Face Recognition Using Thermal Infrared Imagery*, Computer Vision and Pattern Recognition, Kauai, December 2001.

Modeling Insect Compound Eyes: Space-Variant Spherical Vision

Titus R. Neumann

Max Planck Institute for Biological Cybernetics
Spemannstraße 38, 72076 Tübingen, Germany
titus.neumann@tuebingen.mpg.de

Abstract. Insect compound eyes are highly optimized for the visual acquisition of behaviorally relevant information from the environment. Typical sampling and filtering properties include a spherical field of view, a singular viewpoint, low image resolution, overlapping Gaussian-shaped receptive fields, and a space-variant receptor distribution. I present an accurate and efficient compound eye simulation model capable of reconstructing an insect's view of highly realistic virtual environments. The algorithm generates low resolution spherical images from multiple perspective views which can be produced at high frame rates by current computer graphics technology. The sensitivity distribution of each receptor unit is projected on the planar views to compensate for perspective distortions. Applications of this approach can be envisioned for both modeling visual information processing in insects and for the development of novel, biomimetic vision systems.

1 Introduction

The compound eyes of flying insects are the primary source of visual information for a variety of highly efficient orientation strategies and can be regarded as the initial processing stage in the insect visual system. Thus, an accurate and efficient eye model is a prerequisite for comprehensive computer simulations of insect vision and behavior. Furthermore, it facilitates the development of novel, insect-inspired computer vision systems specialized on tasks like visual flight control and navigation.

The fundamental sampling and filtering properties of insect compound eyes [1,2] include discrete receptor units (ommatidia) separated by an interommatidial angle $\Delta\varphi$ (Fig. 1) and distributed over a spherical field of view with a singular viewpoint (valid in the context of flight behavior). The image resolution is low and ranges from approximately 700 ommatidia in the fruitfly *Drosophila* to a maximum of >28000 in the dragonfly *Anax junius*. Spatial wavelengths shorter than $2\Delta\varphi$ cannot be resolved without artifacts, thus high spatial frequencies are suppressed by overlapping Gaussian-shaped receptive fields with acceptance angle $\Delta\rho$ (Fig. 1). Many compound eyes exhibit a space-variant receptor distribution resulting from ecological and behavioral specialization. Insects living in flat environments, such as desert ants or water striders, have an increased resolution around the horizon, whereas some dragonflies have dual 'acute zones' in the frontal and frontodorsal regions for prey detection and tracking.

A number of insect eye simulation models have been developed during the past decade. Early studies include a ray tracing-based simulation of a hoverfly compound

H.H. Bülthoff et al. (Eds.): BMCV 2002, LNCS 2525, pp. 360–367, 2002.

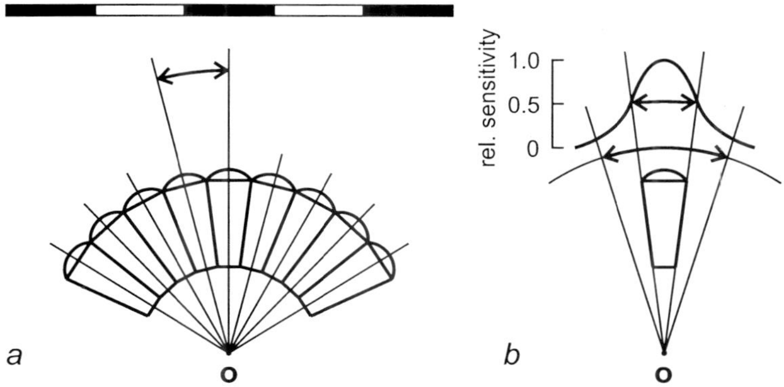

Fig. 1. Visual acuity of compound eyes (Götz, 1965; Land, 1997). *a*. The interommatidial angle $\Delta\varphi$ defines the spatial sampling frequency. *b*. For each receptor unit, the half-width of the Gaussian-shaped sensitivity distribution is defined by the acceptance angle $\Delta\rho$. In the simulation model presented here the receptive field size is restricted by an aperture angle $\Delta\alpha$.

eye looking at a simple black and white stripe pattern [3], and a demonstration of what static planar images might look like for a honeybee [4]. More recently, neural images present in an array of simulated fly visual interneurons have been reconstructed from an image sequence recorded in a simple virtual environment [5], and the visual input of *Drosophila* has been approximated by applying a regular sampling grid to a Mercator projection of the surrounding environment [6]. The common goal of these studies is the reconstruction of particular stimulus properties as seen through a specific insect eye.

Aspects of compound eye optics are also implemented in various insect-inspired computer vision systems. Examples are a one-dimensional, space-variant distribution of optical axes used for altitude control [7], a one-dimensional, panoramic receptor arrangement for view-based navigation [8], and a spherical arrangement of receptor clusters for 3D flight control [9]. Since most of these applications are based on ray tracing, both the eye model and the visual stimulus are strongly simplified to speed up processing.

All of these eye models suffer from one or more of the following restrictions: The field of view is limited and does not comprise the entire sphere [4,5,7,8,9], point sampling or insufficient filtering may lead to spatial aliasing [3,4,7], and regular sampling grids in the Mercator plane result in systematic errors due to polar singularities [6]. Furthermore, ray tracing is not supported by current computer graphics hardware and is therefore inefficient and slow for complex scenes and large numbers of samples.

In this work I present a novel compound eye simulation model that is both more accurate and more efficient than previous approaches.

2 Compound Eye Model

The compound eyes of flying insects map the surrounding environment onto a spherical retinal image. Thus, the involved filtering operations have to be defined on the sphere.

2.1 Space Variant Image Processing on the Sphere

Each viewing direction corresponds to a point on the sphere and can be described by a three-dimensional unit vector

$$\mathbf{d} \in U = \{\mathbf{u} \in \Re^3 \mid \mathbf{u} \cdot \mathbf{u} = 1\}\,. \tag{1}$$

Extending a notation for space-variant neural mapping [10] to the spherical domain, the set of all possible viewing directions originating from the current eye position is denoted as source area S, the set of all directions covered by the retinal image as target area T, with $S, T \subseteq U$. The current source and target images are defined by the functions $I_S(\mathbf{d}) : S \to \Re$ and $I_T(\mathbf{d}) : T \to \Re$, respectively, assigning a gray value to each local viewing direction on the sphere. An extension for color images is straightforward.

The compound eye model determines the retinal image from the surrounding environment using a space-variant linear operator

$$I_S(\mathbf{d}_S) \longmapsto I_T(\mathbf{d}_T) := \int_S I_S(\mathbf{d}_S)\, K(\mathbf{d}_S; \mathbf{d}_T)\; d\mathbf{d}_S \tag{2}$$

integrating over the two-dimensional, spherical source domain S. For each local viewing direction $\mathbf{d}_S \in S$ in the source area and each direction $\mathbf{d}_T \in T$ in the retinal target area the space-variant kernel

$$K(\mathbf{d}_S; \mathbf{d}_T) : S \times T \to \Re \tag{3}$$

specifies the weight by which the input stimulus influences the retinal image. A kernel closely approximating the spatial low pass filtering properties of compound eye optics is the Gaussian function [1].

2.2 Omnidirectional World Projections

The spherical input images required for the compound eye model described above cannot be generated directly since current raster graphics technology is optimized to produce planar, perspective images. However, the entire surrounding environment can be represented as a cube environment map composed of six square perspective views, one for each face of a cube centered around the viewpoint (Fig. 2 and 3*a*). A color value is determined by intersecting a viewing direction with the corresponding face of the environment map.

To avoid aliasing due to point sampling, Greene and Heckbert [11] proposed the elliptical weighted average filter, a Gaussian-shaped, concentric weight distribution around the intersection point in the image plane. As shown in Fig. 4, this approximation deviates from the correct spherical weight distribution which is defined as a function of the angular distance from the viewing direction (Fig. 3*b*). Since the error increases with the angular width of the filter mask, the elliptical weighted average filter is not suitable for the large ommatidial acceptance angles of compound eyes. In the following I describe the correct spherical filtering transformation.

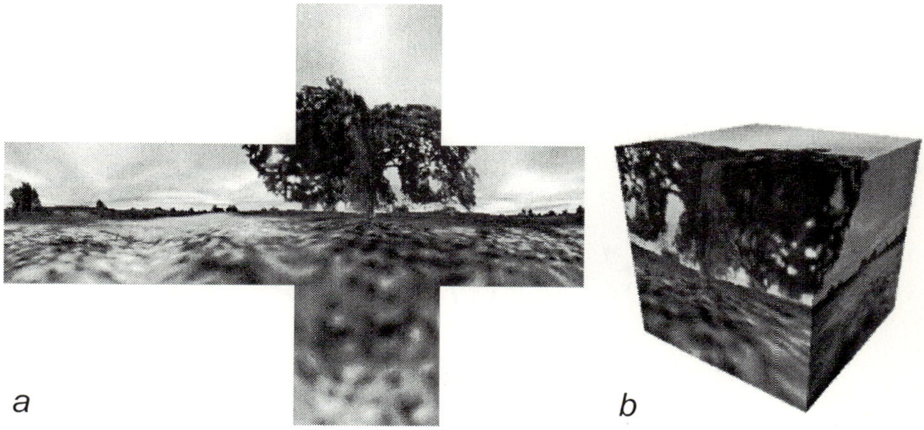

Fig. 2. Cube environment map composed of six square perspective images. *a*. Unfolded. *b*. On a cube surface.

2.3 Filtering Transformation for Discrete Pixels

Both the environment map and the compound eye retinal image are composed of discrete pixels, referred to as source pixels $p \in P_S = \{1, 2, \ldots, |P_S|\}$ and target pixels $q \in P_T = \{1, 2, \ldots, |P_T|\}$, respectively. The source image is represented by the one-dimensional vector $I_S \in \Re^{|P_S|}$ containing the entire environment map. Each source pixel p has a gray value $I_S[p]$. The target image $I_T \in \Re^{|P_T|}$ contains one gray value $I_T[q]$ for each receptor unit q.

The receptive field of receptor unit $q \in P_T$ is described by the weight vector

$$\mathbf{w}_q^{\mathrm{Rcpt}} = \left(w_{q,1}, \ldots, w_{q,p}, \ldots, w_{q,|P_S|}\right)^{\mathrm{T}} \tag{4}$$

indicating the contribution of each input pixel value $I_S[p]$ to the output value $I_T[q]$. The weight matrix $\mathbf{W}^{\mathrm{Rcpt}} \in \Re^{|P_T| \times |P_S|}$ is defined as

$$\mathbf{W}^{\mathrm{Rcpt}} = \left(\mathbf{w}_1^{\mathrm{Rcpt}}, \ldots, \mathbf{w}_q^{\mathrm{Rcpt}}, \ldots, \mathbf{w}_{|P_T|}^{\mathrm{Rcpt}}\right)^{\mathrm{T}} \tag{5}$$

and contains the receptive fields of all $|P_T|$ receptor units. The complete filtering transformation from the input image I_S to the vector I_T of receptor responses is

$$I_T = \mathbf{W}^{\mathrm{Rcpt}} \cdot I_S \,. \tag{6}$$

2.4 Receptive Field Projection

Each receptor unit q has a specific local viewing direction $\mathbf{d}_q \in U$. To prevent spatial aliasing due to point-sampling, the incoming light intensity is integrated over a conical receptive field around $\mathbf{d}_q$. Here, a Gaussian-shaped sensitivity distribution

$$G_q(\zeta) = \exp(-2\zeta^2/\Delta\rho_q^2) \tag{7}$$

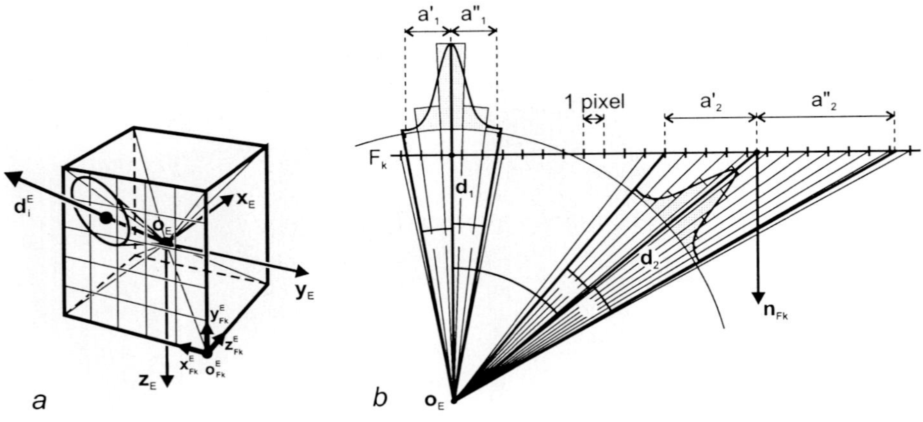

Fig. 3. Receptive field projection. *a*. Eye (E) and face (F_k) coordinate systems of a cube environment map. *b*. Projection and distortion of a Gaussian-shaped sensitivity distribution on a face of the environment map. Although the aperture angle $\Delta\alpha = 2\alpha$ remains constant, the receptive field diameter $\Delta \mathrm{a}_i = \mathrm{a}_i' + \mathrm{a}_i''$ varies for different viewing directions $\mathbf{d}_i$.

with space variant half-width angle $\Delta\rho_q$ (Fig. 1*b*) is used. It is defined as a function of the angular distance ζ from the optical axis. Thus, the relative sensitivity of the receptive field q in the direction $\mathbf{p}_p \in U$ of pixel p is

$$\widehat{w}_{q,p}^{\mathrm{Rcpt}} = \begin{cases} G_q\left(\arccos\left(\mathbf{d}_q \cdot \mathbf{p}_p\right)\right) \cdot A_p, & \arccos\left(\mathbf{d}_q \cdot \mathbf{p}_p\right) \leq \frac{1}{2}\Delta\alpha_q \\ 0, & \text{else} \end{cases} . \tag{8}$$

The solid angle A_p covered by pixel p depends on the position on the image plane (Fig. 3*b*) and is therefore required as a correction factor. The space-variant aperture angle $\Delta\alpha_q$ (Fig. 1*b*) truncates the Gaussian sensitivity distribution to a conical region around the optical axis. Thus, each receptive field (Eq. 4) needs to be normalized to yield a unit gain factor.

2.5 Lookup Table Implementation

Each weight vector $\mathbf{w}_q^{\mathrm{Rcpt}}$ has one entry for each pixel of the input image. This leads to a large but sparsely occupied weight matrix $\mathbf{W}^{\mathrm{Rcpt}}$, since each receptive field covers only a small solid angle containing only a small portion of the environment map. An efficient implementation of the weight matrix is achieved by storing only non-zero weights together with the corresponding pixel indices in a pre-computed lookup table. For each receptive field q the set $\widetilde{P}_q$ of source pixel indices with non-zero weights is determined by

$$\forall q \in P_T : \widetilde{P}_q = \{p \in P_S | w_{q,p}^{\mathrm{Rcpt}} \neq 0\} . \tag{9}$$

With an arbitrary bijective function $\widetilde{o}_q : \{1, \ldots, |\widetilde{P}_q|\} \to \widetilde{P}_q$ ordering the source pixel indices, and a weighting function $\widetilde{w}_q : \{1, \ldots, |\widetilde{P}_q|\} \to \Re$ defined as

$$\widetilde{w}_q(p) := w_{q,\widetilde{o}_q(p)}^{\mathrm{Rcpt}} \tag{10}$$

the filtering transformation can be efficiently computed by

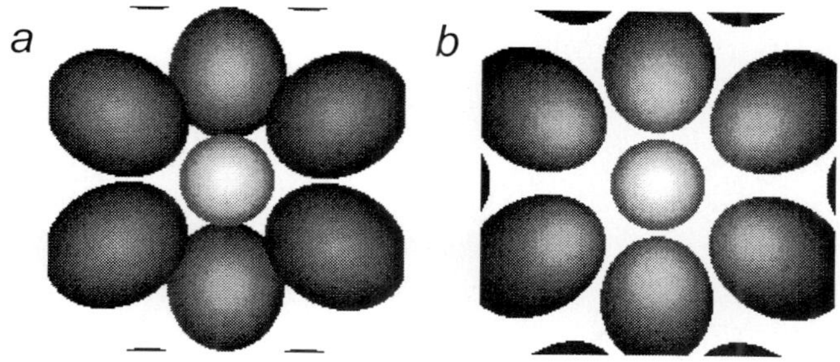

Fig. 4. Distorted receptive fields on a cube map face. *a*. The elliptical weighted average filter (Greene & Heckbert, 1986) shifts the receptive fields towards the image center. *b*. Correct distortion using the receptive field projection method presented here.

$$\forall q \in P_T : I_T[q] = \sum_{p=1}^{|\widetilde{P}_q|} \widetilde{w}_q(p) \cdot I_S[\widetilde{o}_q(p)] \,. \tag{11}$$

3 Results

The algorithm was implemented on a standard PC with Intel Pentium II 450 MHz CPU and Nvidia GeForce2 GTS graphics accelerator, and tested for an eye model with 2562 receptor units, an interommatidial angle of $\Delta\varphi = 4.3°$, an acceptance angle of $\Delta\rho = 5.0°$, and an aperture angle of $\Delta\alpha = 10.0°$. On a cube environment map with a face width of 72 pixels and a total number of 31104 pixels, this receptor configuration resulted in distorted receptive fields with a minimum, mean, and maximum size of 30, 58.9, and 126 pixels, respectively. The complete simulation included rendering the example scene (Fig. 2), copying the resulting images to CPU memory, as well as the filtering transformation, and was updated with 9.7 Hz. The isolated filtering transformation achieved 107.9 Hz.

For large aperture and acceptance angles the elliptical weighted average filter [11] leads to considerable deformations of the eye geometry since it shifts the receptive fields towards the image center (Fig. 4*a*). In contrast, the correct projection method presented here preserves the centroid directions of the receptive fields coincident with their optical axes (Fig. 4*b*).

Fig. 5 shows different spherical receptor distributions and the resulting omnidirectional images. The relative local receptor densities are modeled after biological examples [2].

4 Conclusion

The compound eye simulation model presented here is both accurate and efficient. It allows to specify arbitrary, space-variant receptor distributions in a spherical field of view, and is capable of reconstructing an insect's view in highly realistic virtual environments at high frame rates.

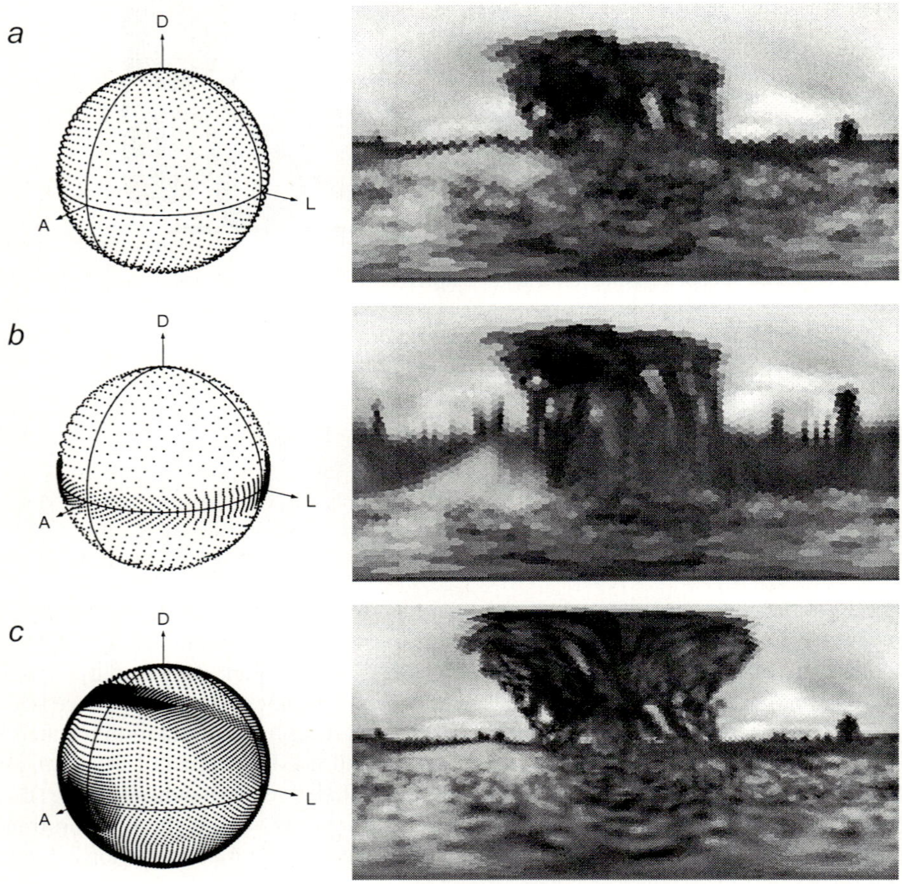

Fig. 5. Space-variant vision with different spherical eye models. Left column: receptor distributions on the sphere (A:anterior, L:lateral, D:dorsal). Right column: example scene (Fig. 2) as seen through each eye model, shown as distorted Mercator projections with full $360° \times 180°$ field of view. *a*. Homogeneous receptor distribution. *b*. Increased resolution along the horizon as in desert ants, water striders or empid flies. *c*. Overall increased resolution and double acute zones in the frontal and the frontodorsal regions as in dragonflies.

Applications of this approach can be envisioned for both modeling visual information processing in insects and for the development of biomimetic computer vision systems. In biological studies the compound eye simulation can be used to reconstruct the exact visual stimulus as it is perceived by an insect during an experiment. This allows to find correlations of the visual input with the recorded physiological or behavioral responses. If the resulting processing and control models are implemented as part of the simulation, they can be tested and evaluated in the same open- and closed-loop experiments as the animals, and the observed responses can be compared immediately.

A further application of the proposed eye model is the development of novel, insect-inspired computer vision systems for tasks like visual self-motion control and navigation [12]. These systems are expected to be simpler, more robust and more efficient than existing technical solutions which are easily outperformed by flying insects in spite of their low visual acuity and small brain size.

Acknowledgments. The author thanks Heinrich Bülthoff, Roland Hengstenberg and Karl Götz for support and discussions, and Björn Kreher for technical assistance.

References

1. Götz, K.G.: Die optischen Übertragungseigenschaften der Komplexaugen von *Drosophila*. Kybernetik **2** (1965) 215–221
2. Land, M.F.: Visual acuity in insects. Annual Review of Entomology **42** (1997) 147–177
3. Cliff, D.: The computational hoverfly: A study in computational neuroethology. In Meyer, J.A., Wilson, S.W., eds.: From Animals to Animats: Proceedings of the First International Conference on Simulation of Adaptive Behavior (SAB'90), Cambridge, MA, MIT Press Bradford Books (1991) 87–96
4. Giger, A.D.: B-EYE: The world through the eyes of a bee (http://cvs.anu.edu.au/andy/beye/beyehome.html). Centre for Visual Sciences, Australian National University (1995)
5. van Hateren, J.H.: Simulations of responses in the first neural layers during a flight (http://hlab.phys.rug.nl/demos/fly_eye_sim/index.html). Department of Neurobiophysics, University of Groningen (2001)
6. Tammero, L.F., Dickinson, M.H.: The influence of visual landscape on the free flight behavior of the fruit fly *Drosophila melanogaster*. Journal of Experimental Biology **205** (2002) 327–343
7. Mura, F., Franceschini, N.: Visual control of altitude and speed in a flying agent. In Cliff, D., Husbands, P., Meyer, J.A., Wilson, S.W., eds.: From Animals to Animats 3: Proceedings of the Third International Conference on Simulation of Adaptive Behavior (SAB'94), Cambridge, MA, MIT Press Bradford Books (1994) 91–99
8. Franz, M.O., Schölkopf, B., Mallot, H.A., Bülthoff, H.H.: Learning view graphs for robot navigation. Autonomous Robots **5** (1998) 111–125
9. Neumann, T.R., Bülthoff, H.H.: Insect inspired visual control of translatory flight. In Kelemen, J., Sosik, P., eds.: Advances in Artificial Life, Proceedings of ECAL 2001. Volume 2159 of LNCS/LNAI., Springer-Verlag, Berlin (2001) 627–636
10. Mallot, H.A., von Seelen, W., Giannakopoulos, F.: Neural mapping and space-variant image processing. Neural Networks **3** (1990) 245–263
11. Greene, N., Heckbert, P.S.: Creating raster Omnimax images from multiple perspective views using the elliptical weighted average filter. IEEE Computer Graphics and Applications **6** (1986) 21–27
12. Neumann, T.R., Bülthoff, H.H.: Behavior-oriented vision for biomimetic flight control. In: Proceedings of the International Workshop on Biologically-Inspired Robotics: The Legacy of W. Grey Walter. (2002) 196–203

Facial and Eye Gaze Detection

Kang Ryoung Park[1], Jeong Jun Lee[2], and Jaihie Kim[2]

[1] Digital Vision Group, Innovation Center, LG Electronics Institute of Technology, 16 Woomyeon-Dong, Seocho-Gu, Seoul, 137-724, Republic of Korea

[2] Computer Vision Laboratory, Department of Electrical and Electronic Engineering, Yonsei University, Seoul, 120-749, Republic of Korea

Abstract. Gaze detection is to locate the position on a monitor screen where a user is looking. In our work, we implement it with a computer vision system setting a IR-LED based single camera. To detect the gaze position, we locate facial features, which is effectively performed with IR-LED based camera and SVM(Support Vector Machine). When a user gazes at a position of monitor, we can compute the 3D positions of those features based on 3D rotation and translation estimation and affine transform. Finally, the gaze position by the facial movements is computed from the normal vector of the plane determined by those computed 3D positions of features. In addition, we use a trained neural network to detect the gaze position by eye's movement. As experimental results, we can obtain the facial and eye gaze position on a monitor and the gaze position accuracy between the computed positions and the real ones is about 4.8 cm of RMS error.

Keywords. Facial and Eye Gaze detection, IR-LED based camera

1 Introduction

Gaze detection is to locate the position where a user is looking. Previous studies were mostly focused on 2D/3D facial rotation/translation estimation[1][15][20][21], face gaze detection[2-8][16][17][19] and eye gaze detection[9-14][18]. However, the gaze detection considering face and eye movement simultaneously has been rarely researched. Ohmura and Ballard et al.[4][5]'s methods have the disadvantages that the depth between camera plane and feature points in the initial frame must be measured manually and it takes much time(over 1 minute) to compute the gaze direction vector. Gee et al.[6] and Heinzmann et al.[7]'s methods only compute gaze direction vector whose origin is located between the eyes in the face coordinate and do not obtain the gaze position on a monitor. In addition, if 3D rotations and translations of face happen simultaneously, they cannot estimate the accurate 3D motion due to the increase of complexity of least-square fitting algorithm, which requires much processing time. Rikert et al.[8]'s method has the constraints that the distance between a face and the monitor must be kept same for all training and testing procedures and it can be cumbersome to user. In the methods of [10][13][14][16][17], a pair of glasses having marking points is required to detect facial features, which can

H.H. Bülthoff et al. (Eds.): BMCV 2002, LNCS 2525, pp. 368–376, 2002.

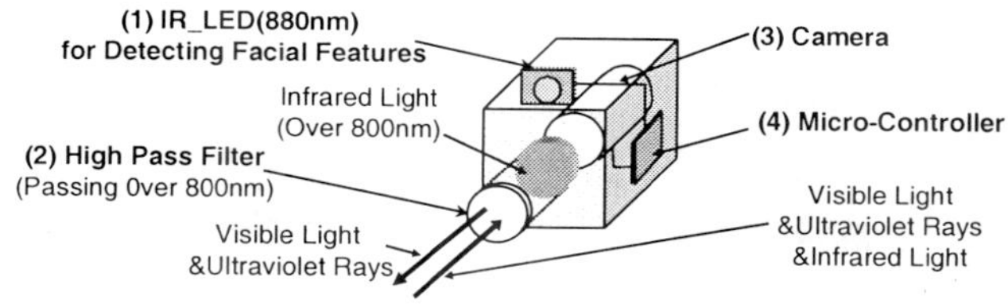

Fig. 1. The Gaze Detecting Camera

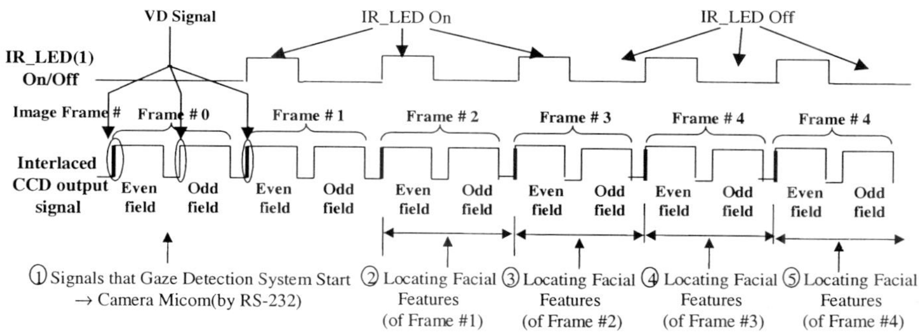

Fig. 2. The Gaze Detecting Camera

give inconvenience to a user. The methods of [2][3] shows the gaze detection by facial movements, but have the limits that the eye movements do not happen. To solve such problems of previous researches, this paper describes a new method for detecting the facial and eye gaze position on a monitor.

2 Locating Facial Feature Points

In order to detect gaze position on a monitor, we firstly locate facial features(both eye centers, eye corners, nostrils and lip corners) in an input image. We use the method of detecting specular reflection to detect eyes. It requires a camera system equipped with some hardware as shown in Fig. 1.

In details of Fig. 1, the IR-LED(1)(880nm) is used to make the specular reflections on eyes as shown in Fig. 3. The HPF(2)(High Pass Filter) in front of camera lens can only pass the infrared lights(over 800 nm) and the input images are only affected by the IR-LED(1) excluding external illuminations. We use a normal interlaced CCD camera(3) and a micro-controller(4) embedded in camera sensor which can detect the every VD(the starting signal of even or odd Field as shown in Fig. 2) from CCD output signal. From that we can control the Illuminator as shown in Fig. 2.

In details of Fig. 2, when a user starts our gaze detection system, then the starting signal is transferred into the micro-controller in camera by RS-232C.

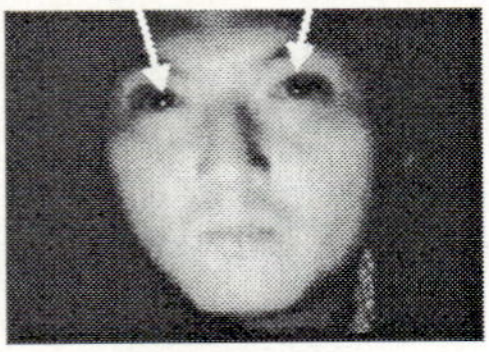

(a)

(b)

Fig. 3. The even and odd images of frame #1 (a)Even field image (b)Odd field image

Then, the micro-controller detects the next VD signals of Even Field and successively controls IR-LEDs as shown in Fig. 2. From the frame #1, we detect facial features in every frames. The Fig. 3 shows the Frame #1 of Fig. 2.

From that, we can get a difference image between the even and the odd image and the specular points of both eyes can be easily detected in both no glasses and glasses, because its gray level is higher than any other region. In some case, the gray level of eye specular reflection is similar to the reflection of the skin. In such a case, the eye position detection error may happens. In order to reduce such a error, we use the RED-EYE effect. It is that when the angle between camera(3) and light(1) is below 5 degree, that the light is passing into pupil and it is reflected in retina vein. In such a case, the user's eye is captured in extreme white in camera. From the information, we can easily detect the eye positions. When the specular points are detected, then we can restrict the eye region around the detected specular points. With the restricted eye searching region, we locate the accurate eye center. To detect eye center, we use the circular edge matching method. Because we search the restricted eye region, it does not take much time to detect the exact eye center(almost 5-10 ms in Pentium-II 550MHz). After locating the eye center, we detect the eye corner by using eye corner shape template. Because we use the HPF(2) as shown in Fig. 1 and the input image is only affected by the IR-LED(1) excluding external illumination, it is not necessary to normalize the illumination of the input image or the template. With the eye corner template, we use Support Vector Machine to detect the exact eye corner positions. SVMs perform pattern recognition between two point classes by finding a decision surface determined by certain points of the training set, termed Support Vectors (SV). When plenty of positive and negative data are not obtained and input data is very noisy, the Multi-Layered Perceptron(MLP) cannot show the reliable classification results. And, MLP requires many initial parameter settings determined by user's heuristic experience. The input eye corner image is size-normalized as 30×30 pixels and we use polynomial kernels of degree 5 in order to solve non-linearly separable problem, because the dimension of input data is big. In this case, the problem is defined as 2 class problem. The first class shows eye corner and the second one does none eye corner. It is reported that the other inner product as RBF, MLP, Splines, B-Splines

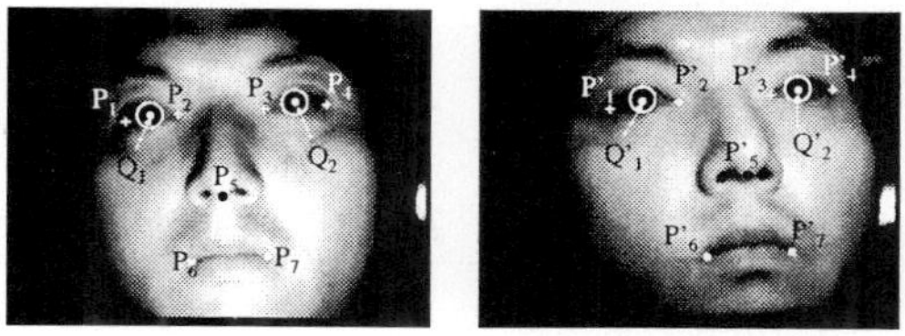

(a) (b)

Fig. 4. The feature points for estimating 3D facial and eye movements (a)Gazing at monitor center (b)Gazing at some other point on a monitor

do not affect the generated support vector and our experimental results comparing the polynomial kernel to MLP show the same results. The C factor affect the generalization of SVM and we use 10000 as C, which is selected by experimental results. We get 2000 successive image frames(100 frames $\times$ 20 persons who have various sitting positions) and from that, 8000 eye corner samples (4 eye corners $\times$ 2000 images) are obtained and another 1000 images are used for testing. As experimental results show the 798 positive support vectors and 4313 negative ones are selected. In general, support vectors are data which are difficult to be classified among training data. From that, we can guess the input data contains too much noise and our problems of data generalization is difficult. As experimental results show the generalization error from training data is 0.11% (9/8000) and that from testing data is 0.2%(8/4000). In our experimental results, MLP show error of 1.58% from training data and 3.1% from testing data. In addition, the classification time is so small as like 13 ms in Pentium-II 550MHz. After locating eye centers and eye corners, the positions of both nostrils and lip corners can be detected by anthropometric constraints in a face and SVM similar to eye corner detection. Experimental results show that RMS error between the detected feature positions and the real ones(manually detected positions) are 1 pixels (of both eye centers), 2 pixels (of both eye corners), 4 pixels (of both nostrils) and 3 pixels (of both lip corners) in 640$\times$480 image. Here, we tested 3000 successive image frames(2000 training images and 1000 testing images). From the detected feature positions, we select 7 feature points $(P_1, P_2, P_3, P_4, P_5, P_6, P_7)$ for estimating 3D facial rotation and translation as shown in Fig. 4. When the user gazes at other point on a monitor, the positions of 7 feature points are changed to $P_1', P_2', \sim P_7'$ as shown in (b) Fig. 4. Here, $Q_1, Q_2, P_1, P_2, P_3, P_4$, and $Q_1', Q_2', P_1', P_2', P_3', P_4'$ are used for computing gaze positions by eye movements.

3 Estimating the Initial 3D Positions of Feature Points

After feature detection, we take 4 steps in order to compute a gaze position on a monitor as shown in Fig. 5. In the first step, when a user gazes at 3 known positions on a monitor, the 3D positions of initial feature points are computed automatically. In the second and third step, when the user moves(rotates and

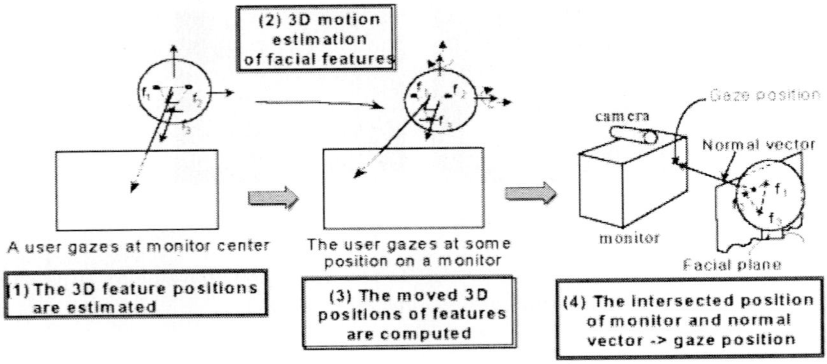

Fig. 5. 4 steps in order to compute a gaze position on a monitor

translates) his head in order to gaze at one position on a monitor, the moved 3D positions of those features can be computed from 3D motion estimation. In the 4th step, one facial plane is determined from the moved 3D positions of those features and the normal vector of the plane represents a gaze vector by facial movements. In addition, we use a trained neural network(multi-layered perceptron) to detect the gaze position by eye's movement. Then, the gaze position on a monitor is the intersection point between the monitor plane and the gaze vector. The detail methods about the first step of Fig. 5 can be referred to [2]. Experimental results show that the RMS error between the real 3D feature positions(measured by 3D position tracker sensor) and the estimated one is 1.15 cm(0.64cm in X axis, 0.5cm in Y axis, 0.81cm in Z axis) for 20 person data which were used for testing the feature detection performance[2].

4 Estimating the 3D Facial Rotation and Translation

This section explains the 2nd step of Fig. 5. Many 3D motion estimation algorithms have been investigated, for example, EKF(Extended Kalman Filter)[1], neural network[21] and affine projection method[6][7], etc. Fukuhara et al [21]'s method does not obtain the accurate 3D motions and only estimate the 3D rotations and translations in the limited range due to the classification complexity of neural network. The 3D estimation method using affine projection algorithm [6][7] has the constraint that the depth change of the object does not exceed 0.1 times of the distance between camera and object. In addition, if 3D rotations and translations of feature points happen simultaneously, it cannot estimate the accurate 3D motion due to the increase of complexity of least-square fitting algorithm. So, we use the EKF for 3D motion estimation algorithm and refer to the EKF which has been investigated in previous researches[1] for our 3D motion estimation. When a user moves(rotates and translates) his head in order to gaze at one position on a monitor like the 2nd step of Fig. 5, the moved 3D positions of those features can be estimated from 3D motion estimations by EKF like Eq(1) and affine transform. The EKF converts the measurements of 2D feature positions(detected while a user moves his face) into 3D estimates of the translation and orientation of the face using constant acceleration model[1]. In order to estimate the 3D motions by EKF, we define a state vector(18×1) of $x(t) = (p(t), q(t), v(t), w(t), a(t), b(t))^T$ per feature point. Here , $p(t) = (x(t), y(t), z(t))$:3D translation of face coordinate axis to monitor coordinate axis, $q(t) = (\theta_x(t), \theta_y(t), \theta_z(t))$: 3D rotation of feature positions in the face coordinate, $v(t) = (v_x(t), v_y(t), v_z(t))$, $w(t) = (w_x(t), w_y(t), w_z(t))$: the velocity of translation and rotation, $a(t) = (a_x(t), a_y(t), a_z(t))$, $b(t) = (\alpha_x(t), \alpha_y(t), \alpha_z(t))$: the acceleration of translation and rotation).

$$\widehat{x}(t) = \widehat{x}(t)^- + K(t)(y(t) - h(\widehat{x}(t)^-)) \tag{1}$$

where $K(t)$ is the Kalman gain matrix $K(t) = P(t-1)H(t)^T(H(t)P(t-1)H(t)^T + R(t))^{-1}$, $H(t) = \frac{\partial h}{\partial x(t)}\Big|_{\widehat{x}(t)^-}$ and $P(t)$ is the state prediction error covariance. EKF is distinguished from DKF(Discrete Kalman Filter) in terms of using nonlinear observation function(h). EKF predicts the current state vector ($\widehat{x}(t)^-$) from the previous updated state vector ($\widehat{x}(t-1)$) including 3D rotations and translations of feature points using the assumptions that the 3D motions conform to the constant acceleration model. Detail accounts can be referred to [1][20]. The estimation accuracy of EKF is compared with 3D position tracker sensor. Our experimental results show the RMS errors between EKF estimates and 3D position tracker sensor are about 1.4 cm and 2.98° in translation and rotation.

5 Detecting the Gaze Position on the Monitor

5.1 By Facial Motion

This section explains the 3rd and 4th step of Fig. 5. The initial 3D feature positions($P_1 \sim P_7$ in Fig. 4) computed in monitor coordinate in section III are converted into the 3D feature positions in face coordinate[2] and using these converted 3D feature positions(X_i, Y_i, Z_i), 3D rotation[R] and translation[T] matrices estimated by EKF and affine transform, we can obtain the moved 3D feature positions(X_i', Y_i', Z_i') in face and monitor coordinate when a user gazes at a monitor position[2]. From that, one facial plane is determined and the normal vector of the plane shows a gaze vector. The gaze position on a monitor is the intersection position between a monitor and the gaze vector.

5.2 By Eye Motion

In 5.1, the gaze position is determined by only facial movement. In most case, when a user gazes at a monitor position, both the face and eyes are moved.

So, we compute the eye movements from the detected features points(Q_1, Q_2 in Fig. 6). In general, the eye movements and shape are changed according to a user gaze position. The distance between the eyeball center and left or right eye corner is changed according to user's gaze positions. We use a neural network to train the relations between the eye movements and gaze positions like Fig. 6. From the neural network for detecting eye gaze position, we locate final gaze positions on a monitor by both face and eye movements as shown in Fig. 7. The gaze detection error of proposed method is compared to our previous methods[2][3][19] like table 1, 2. The test data are acquired when 10 users gaze at 23 gaze positions on a 19" monitor. Here, the gaze error is the RMS error between the real gaze position and the computed ones. Shown in table 1, the gaze error of the proposed method is the smallest. However, it is often the case that the facial and eye movements happen simultaneously, when a user gazes at. So, we tested the gaze error about test data including facial and eye movements like table 2.

Table 1. Gaze error about test data including only facial movements (cm)

Method	Linear interpolation[19]	Single neural net[19]	Two neural nets[19]	[2] method	[3] method	Proposed method
error	5.1	4.23	4.48	5.35	5.21	3.40

Table 2. Gaze error about test data including face and eye movements (cm)

Method	Linear interpolation[19]	Single neural net[19]	Two neural nets[19]	[2] method	[3] method	Proposed method
error	11.8	11.32	8.87	7.45	6.29	4.8

Shown in table 2, the gaze error of the proposed method is the smallest. In the second experiment, points of radius 5 pixels are spaced vertically and horizontally

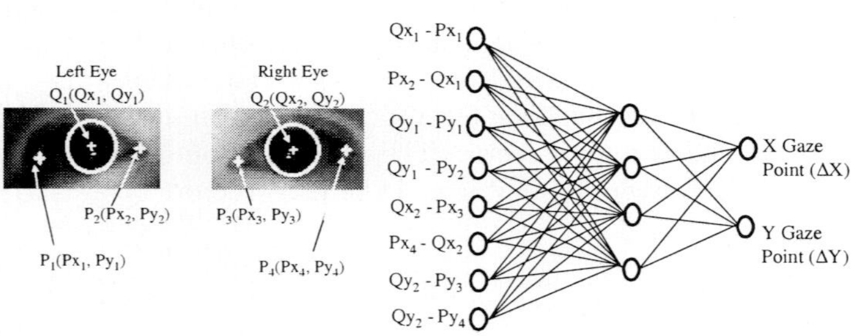

Fig. 6. The neural network for detecting gaze position by eye movements

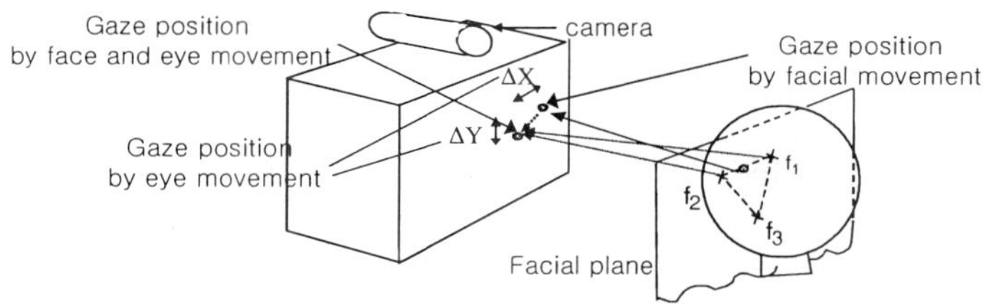

Fig. 7. Detecting gaze position on a monitor by face and eye movements

at 150 pixel intervals(2.8 cm) on a 19" monitor with 1280×1024 pixels. The test conditions are almost same as Rikert's research[8] and total 560 examples(10 persons×56 gaze positions) are used for computing gaze error. The RMS gaze error of between the real and calculated position is 4.85 cm and it is superior to Rikert's method(almost 5.08 cm). In addition, Rikert has the limits that Z distance between user and monitor must be kept same for training and testing, but we do not. We tested the gaze errors according to the Z distance(55, 60, 65cm). The RMS errors are like; 4.75cm in the distance of 55cm, 4.79cm in 60cm, 4.89cm in 65cm. It shows that our method does not have limits that Z-distance must be kept same. And Rikert's method takes much processing time(1 minute in alphastation 333MHz), compared to our method(about 1 sec in Pentium-II 550MHz).

6 Conclusions

This paper describes a new gaze detecting method. Shown in results, the gaze error is about 4.8 cm. In addition, more exact gaze position can be acquired by the additional moving(like mouse dragging) of the user's head.

References

1. A. Azarbayejani., 1993. Visually Controlled Graphics. IEEE Trans. PAMI, Vol. 15, No. 6, pp. 602–605
2. K. R. Park et al., Gaze Point Detection by Computing the 3D Positions and 3D Motions of Face, IEICE Trans. Inf.&Syst.,Vol. E.83-D, No.4, pp.884-894, Apr 2000 (http://search.ieice.org/2000/pdf/e83-d-4-884.pdf)
3. K. R. Park et al., Gaze Detection by Estimating the Depth and 3D Motions of Facial Features in Monocular Images, IEICE Trans. Fundamentals, Vol. E.82-A, No. 10, pp. 2274–2284, Oct 1999
4. K. OHMURA et al., 1989. Pointing Operation Using Detection of Face Direction from a Single View. IEICE Trans. Inf.&Syst., Vol. J72-D-II, No.9, pp. 1441–1447
5. P. Ballard et al., 1995. Controlling a Computer via Facial Aspect. IEEE Trans. on SMC, Vol. 25, No. 4, pp. 669–677
6. A. Gee et al., 1996. Fast visual tracking by temporal consensus, Image and Vision Computing. Vol. 14, pp. 105–114

7. J. Heinzmann et al., 1998. 3D Facial Pose and Gaze Point Estimation using a Robust Real-Time Tracking Paradigm. Proceedings of ICAFGR, pp. 142–147
8. T. Rikert et al., 1998. Gaze Estimation using Morphable Models. Proc. of ICAFGR, pp. 436-441
9. A.Ali-A-L et al., Man-machine interface through eyeball direction of gaze. Proc. of the Southeastern Symposium on System Theory 1997, pp. 478–82
10. A. TOMONO et al., 1994. Eye Tracking Method Using an Image Pickup Apparatus. European Patent Specification-94101635
11. Seika-Tenkai-Tokushuu-Go, ATR Journal, 1996
12. Eyemark Recorder Model EMR-NC, NAC Image Technology Cooperation
13. Porrill-J et al., Robust and optimal use of information in stereo vision. Nature. vol.397, no.6714, Jan. 1999, pp. 63–6
14. Varchmin-AC et al., image based recognition of gaze direction using adaptive methods. Gesture and Sign Language in Human-Computer Interaction. Int. Gesture Workshop Proc. Berlin, Germany, 1998, pp. 245–57.
15. J. Heinzmann et al., 1997. Robust real-time face tracking and gesture recognition. Proc. of the IJCAI, Vol. 2, pp. 1525–1530
16. Matsumoto-Y, et al., An algorithm for real-time stereo vision implementation of head pose and gaze direction measurement. Proc. the ICAFGR 2000. pp. 499–504
17. Newman-R et al., Real-time stereo tracking for head pose and gaze estimation. Proceedings the 4th ICAFGR 2000. pp. 122-8
18. Betke-M et al., Gaze detection via self-organizing gray-scale units. Proc. Int. Workshop on Recognition, Analysis, and Tracking of Faces and Gestures in Real-Time System 1999. pp. 70–6
19. K. R. Park et al., 2000. Intelligent Process Control via Gaze Detection Technology. EAAI, Vol. 13, No. 5, pp. 577–587
20. T. BROIDA et al., 1990. Recursive 3-D Motion Estimation from a Monocular Image Sequence. IEEE Trans. Aerospace and Electronic Systems, Vol. 26, No. 4, pp. 639–656
21. T. Fukuhara et al., 1993. 3D-motion estimation of human head for model-based image coding. IEE Proc., Vol. 140, No. 1, pp. 26–35

1-Click Learning of Object Models for Recognition

Hartmut S. Loos[1] and Christoph von der Malsburg[1,2]

[1] Institut für Neuroinformatik
Ruhr-Universität Bochum
D-44780 Bochum, Germany
{Hartmut.Loos,Malsburg}@neuroinformatik.ruhr-uni-bochum.de
http://www.neuroinformatik.ruhr-uni-bochum.de/VDM/people
[2] Computer Science Dept.
University of Southern California
Los Angeles, USA

Abstract. We present a method which continuously learns representations of arbitrary objects. These object representations can be stored with minimal user interaction (*1-Click Learning*). Appropriate training material has the form of image sequences containing the object of interest moving against a cluttered static background. Using basically the method of unsupervised growing neural gas modified to adapt to non-stationary distributions on binarized difference images, a model of the moving object is learned in real-time. Using the learned object representation the system can recognize the object or objects of the same class in single still images of different scenes. The new samples can be added to the learned object model to further improve it.

1 Introduction

The importance of understanding object recognition is readily illustrated if you look around the room that you are in now. Without doubt, most of what you see consists of objects. Each of these objects has a particular size, shape, color, and surface texture. Adults perceive objects immediately and effortlessly, even in complex and cluttered environments. Unlike adults, young infants do not appear to perceive object identity by analyzing the smoothness of object motion, by analyzing the constancy of objects' perceptible properties such as shape, color, and texture, or by recognizing objects as instances of familiar kinds.

But how do infants learn object representations which can be used to recognize the objects in different scenes?

Infants appear to perceive object identity in accord with the principle that objects exist continuously and move on paths that are connected over space and time. They seem to organize visual information into bodies that move cohesively, i.e. preserving their internal connectedness and their external boundaries [1,8, 13].

H.H. Bülthoff et al. (Eds.): BMCV 2002, LNCS 2525, pp. 377–386, 2002.

Any artificial system for scene analysis must have as a central ingredient the capability to robustly detect, classify and recognize objects. To be practical, the system must be capable to acquire new objects or object classes from sample images. This has to be possible without the need for further research, programming, or laborious manual intervention, with as few samples as possible, and in real-time. Due to these constraints, object identification must be based on examples picked up from images rather than on object characteristics which could be found only by specific theoretical analysis.

Most proposed solutions in computer vision, which learn an object representation, either need large databases of sample objects (see, e.g., [3,11,14]), require extensive training of specially designed neural network classifiers (see, e.g., [12]), use training images showing objects in front of a uniform background, or need the objects to be positioned in the same way throughout the training images (see, e.g., [2]).

To achieve the stated goal a fundamental difficulty has to be overcome: to identify object samples, an object model must be present, and to construct an object model, samples must first be found. To break this deadlock we use image sequences as initial sample material and pursue the strategy of *user-assistance*. First samples of a novel object are selected under human control. Such control is required anyway, as the definition of object classes is highly dependent on the goals of image analysis and thus must be furnished by humans.

However, segmenting an object from a scene is too awkward to be done by a human. Humans are unequaled vision experts, but it is a difficult task to get this valuable knowledge without overexerting them. Humans as computer user are very expensive resources, they tend to get tired and impatient. An important goal is to make efficient use of the user and to require no special qualification. All these prerequisites are fulfilled with the method we present in this article, which is an important part of a strategy we call *1-Click Learning.*

2 Method

In this context an *object model* is a sparse representation of one view of the real object at the moment of the user's decision. It is basically an image of the object covered with an undirected graph. The graph nodes are placed on object regions with high information (i.e. the rim or structured parts), the edges code the geometrical structure of the object.

So far, effort at object recognition had to rely to a considerable extent on rather laborious manual intervention at the stage of object model construction. Even if someone is willing to do this work it is not quite obvious where to place the nodes and edges of the object model G, an undirected graph, and how many of them. It is desirable to circumvent this effort during the acquisition of new types of objects. The algorithm 2.1 in figure 1 describes a method to achieve that goal. The role of the user is restricted, apart from selecting image material, to determine moments at which an object model is to be stored.

Algorithm 2.1: $G :=$ LEARNMOVINGOBJECT(S)

comment: Compute object model G of moving object in image sequence S

Sequence S of images $I_0, ..., I_n$
Undirected graph $G := (\mathcal{V}, \mathcal{U})$
Set of undirected edges is empty:
  $\mathcal{U} := \emptyset$
Initialize set of units $\mathcal{V}$ with two units c_1 and c_2
  $\mathcal{V} := (c_1, c_2)$
Set units to random positions in image:
  $\boldsymbol{p}_c :=$ (random), $\forall c \in \mathcal{V}$
Set of unit i's neighbors (all units with connections to i):
  $\mathcal{N}_i \subset \mathcal{V}$
Number of presented signals counter:
  $n := 0$
Constants:
  $\epsilon_b := 0.1,\ \epsilon_n := 0.01,\ \text{age}_{\text{max}} := 88,\ k := 3.0,\ \lambda := 300,\ \alpha := 0.5,$
  $\beta := 0.0005,\ u_{\text{max}} := 30,\ t_{\text{diff}} := 30$

while (**not** (End of sequence) **and** **not** (User-click))
  do
    $D :=$ BINARIZEDDIFFERENCEIMAGE(I_t, I_{t+1})   [see algorithm 2.2 in fig. 3]
    for each (select $\boldsymbol{\xi} \in D$ in random order)
      do $G :=$ ADAPTOBJECTMODEL($G, \boldsymbol{\xi}$)   [see algorithm 2.3 in fig. 5]
return (G)

Fig. 1. The algorithms used to learn a model of an moving object: the binarized difference of two consecutive images serves as input for the object adaptation algorithm.

Fig. 2. The binarized difference of two consecutive images: each black pixel is used as input for algorithm 2.3 in figure 5.

2.1 1-Click Learning: Acquisition of New Objects

Appropriate training material has the form of image sequences containing the object of interest moving against a static background, even if it is cluttered. The binarized difference of two consecutive images is computed (see figure 2 and algorithm 2.2 in figure 3).

Segmentation by binarized difference images has several advantageous features: no initial calibration is needed, smooth changes of contrast and lighting conditions during the learning process can be handled (in contrast to background subtraction), and it concentrates on regions along the object contours *and* on highly textured parts inside the object (in contrast to, e.g., active contours [4]). Furthermore, the computation is extremely fast and changing the camera position can be done without effort.

Each pixel position marked by the difference image is used as input for algorithm 2.3 in figure 5. Using basically the method of unsupervised *growing neural gas* [6] modified to adapt to non-stationary distributions [7], nodes are placed on the aspect of the moving object. The nodes are attracted by positions with image-to-image intensity difference, move continuously from image to image, and optimize their arrangement in terms of coverage and mutual distance. Object boundaries and their inner structure are fairly accurately located and covered by nodes, neighboring nodes are connected by links. The output is the object model G in form of an undirected graph (see figure 4).

The algorithm is highly adaptable and learns new objects within a few frames. Node positions are optimized to cover especially object boundaries and inner object regions with rich structure. The described method can process image resolutions of 320 x 240 pixels with 10 to 15 frames/s depending on the number of moved pixels and the used hardware (here: Intel Pentium III with 800 MHz and a standard USB webcam). In the absence of motion no adaptation takes place, the object model remains unchanged.

2.2 Recognition of Learned Objects in Still Images

After learning the object model G has adapted to the most interesting features of the object. It covers the object with high accuracy and can be directly used as basic structure for *elastic graph matching* [9]. Therefore, each node is labeled with a local Gabor feature vector called *jet* [5,16], which is extracted at the node position in the original sequence image. The labeled object model is called *model graph* (see figure 7). To minimize the influence of the background on the model graph, first the image outside the convex hull of all node positions is faded out

Algorithm 2.2: $D :=$ BINARIZEDDIFFERENCEIMAGE(I, J)

comment: Compute binarized difference of consecutive images

Compute difference image:
  $D_{x,y} = |I_{x,y} - J_{x,y}|$
Binarize difference image:
if $D_{x,y} > t_{\text{diff}}$
  then $D_{x,y} := 1$
  else $D_{x,y} := 0$
return (D)

Fig. 3. The algorithm for the binarized difference image generates the input for the object adaptation algorithm.

Fig. 4. The first two rows show different objects (pig, car, duck, face, hand, and human figure) moving in front of a camera at the moment of the user click, overlayed with the undirected graph G adapted to the moving object. In the last row the cropped learned objects are displayed after background suppression. The nodes of G are placed on object regions with high information (i.e. the rim or structured parts), the edges code the geometrical structure of the object. Object regions with no or poor structure are not covered with nodes.

before computing the Gabor transformation. This still leaves a small background region surrounding the object visible, but it avoids strong disturbing edges in the image, which would occur, if the background would be simply filled with a constant gray value (see figure 4).

The model graph can be used to recognize the learned object in different scenes with the help of elastic graph matching. Even minor occlusions or changes in appearance are tolerated, as long as the shape basically remains in the learned form (see figure 6). The whole recognition process based on the learned object model needs no user assistance and no object motion, it works automatically and with single still images.

2.3 Incremental Improvement of the Object Model

Samples found with the learned model graph can be used to incrementally improve the object recognition. The location of the object in the sample image can be found with elastic graph matching, i.e. the nodes of the model graph are

Algorithm 2.3: $G := \text{ADAPTOBJECTMODEL}(G, \boldsymbol{\xi})$

comment: Adapt units in G to input signal $\boldsymbol{\xi}$

$n := n + 1$

Find nearest unit s_1 and second nearest unit s_2 to input signal $\boldsymbol{\xi}$.

Add edge between winning units and set age:

$\mathcal{U} := \mathcal{U} \cup \{(s_1, s_2)\},\ \text{age}_{s1,s2} := 0$

Compute error:

$E_{s1} := E_{s1} + \|\boldsymbol{\xi} - \boldsymbol{p}_{s_1}\|^2$

Compute utility:

$U_{s1} := U_{s1} + \|\boldsymbol{\xi} - \boldsymbol{p}_{s_2}\|^2 - \|\boldsymbol{\xi} - \boldsymbol{p}_{s_1}\|^2$

Adapt positions:

$\boldsymbol{p}_{s1} := \boldsymbol{p}_{s1} + \epsilon_b(\boldsymbol{\xi} - \boldsymbol{p}_{s_1})$

$\boldsymbol{p}_i := \boldsymbol{p}_i + \epsilon_n(\boldsymbol{\xi} - \boldsymbol{p}_i), \forall i \in \mathcal{N}_{s1}$

Adapt age of edges:

$\text{age}_{s1,c} := \text{age}_{s1,c} + 1, \forall c \in \mathcal{N}_{s1}$

Remove too old edges:

if $\text{age}(e) > \text{age}_{\text{max}},\ \forall e \in \mathcal{U}$

then $\mathcal{U} := \mathcal{U} \setminus \{e\}$

Remove all units without edges:

if $\mathcal{N}_c = \emptyset,\ \forall c \in \mathcal{V}$

then $\mathcal{V} := \mathcal{V} \setminus \{c\}$

Determine unit q with maximum error and unit i with minimal utility:

$q := \max_{c \in \mathcal{V}} E_c,\ i := \min_{c \in \mathcal{V}} U_c$

Remove units with too low utility:

if $E_q/U_i > k$

then $\mathcal{V} := \mathcal{V} \setminus \{i\},\ \mathcal{U} := \mathcal{U} \setminus \{(i, c)\},\ \forall c \in \mathcal{N}_i$

Add new node if the number of presented signals is a multiple of λ, but stay below maximum size:

if (($n \bmod \lambda = 0$) **and** ($|\mathcal{V}| < u_{\text{max}}$))

then
- Add new unit r:
  $\mathcal{V} := \mathcal{V} \cup \{r\}$
- Determine unit with maximum error:
  $q := \max_{c \in \mathcal{V}} E_c$
- Determine neighbor unit with maximum error:
  $f := \max_{c \in \mathcal{N}_q} E_c$
- Position new unit between q and f :
  $\boldsymbol{p}_r := \frac{1}{2}(\boldsymbol{p}_q + \boldsymbol{p}_f)$
- Split edge between q and f and connect the loose ends with r :
  $\mathcal{U} := \mathcal{U} \cup \{(r, q), (r, f)\},\ \mathcal{U} := \mathcal{U} \setminus \{(q, f)\}$
- Adapt error of the involved units:
  $E_q := E_q - \alpha E_q,\ E_f := E_f - \alpha E_f,\ E_r := \frac{1}{2}(E_q + E_f)$

Reduce error and utility for all units:

$E_c := E_c - \beta E_c,\ U_c := U_c - \beta U_c,\ \forall c \in \mathcal{V}$

return (G)

Fig. 5. The algorithm used to adapt the object model is based on unsupervised growing neural gas modified to adapt to non-stationary distributions.

placed on the same local features of the new sample, thus allowing us to create another labeled model graph with the same structure as the learned model graph.

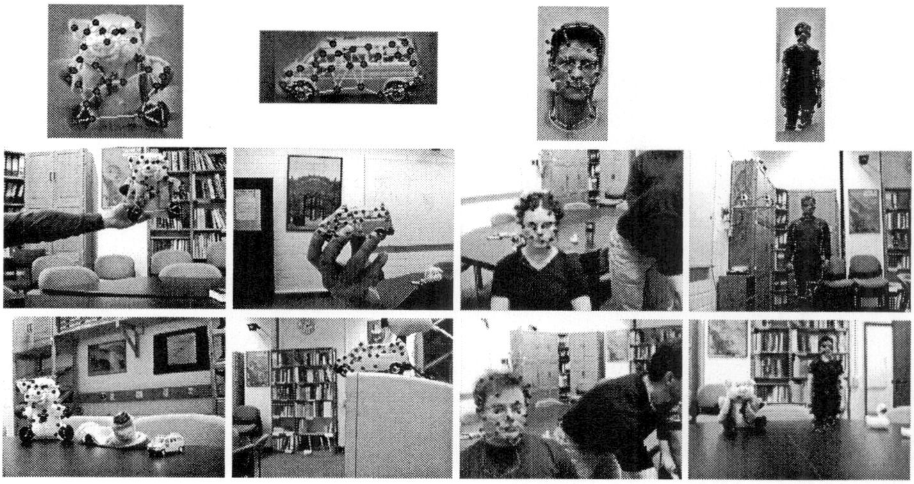

Fig. 6. Some examples where the learned object models displayed in figure 4 were used to recognize the learned objects (pig, car) or objects of the same class (face, human figure) in different scenes; minor occlusions or changes in appearance are tolerated. The recognition process works automatically and with single still images.

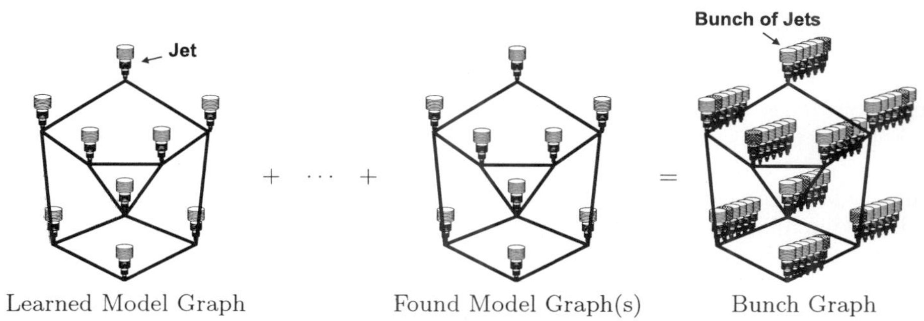

Fig. 7. A bunch graph is a stack–like structure composed of model graphs. During the matching process from each bunch any jet can be selected independently of the jets selected from the other bunches (gray shaded). That provides full combinatorial power of this representation and makes it so general even if constituted from few graphs only.

The individual model graphs are combined into a stack–like structure, the *object bunch graph*. Together with the extension of elastic graph matching, *elastic bunch graph matching* [16], the full combination of jets in the object bunch graph is available, covering a much larger range of possible object variation than represented in the individual model graphs (see figure 7).

The object bunch graph and elastic bunch graph matching can be used to acquire further object samples, which improve object recognition even more.

3 Discussion

Experiments by Arterberry et al. [1] suggest that infants perceive object boundaries by detecting the relative motion patterns of surfaces and edges. When a surface and its borders move as a unit relative to surrounding surfaces, infants perceive the surface as a bounded object. Such motions are normally produced when an object moves against a stationary background or when a stationary object stands in front of its background and is viewed by the baby with a moving head. The method presented in this paper also processes objects moving against a static background and generates object representations from this input.

In our experiments we have used a number of different object types, including toys (pig, car, duck, boat), human bodies, hands, and faces. It shows that all objects can be learned with the described algorithm without changing any parameters. The role of the user is restricted, apart from selecting image material, to determine the moments at which an object model is to be stored. This requires no special qualification and can be done with minimal user assistance (1-Click Learning). The object model can be used to acquire further object samples. Minor occlusions or changes in appearance of the object are tolerated, as long as the shape basically remains in the learned form. The acquired samples are added to the object model and improve the object recognition performance even more. After the 1-Click no user assistance is needed any more, the whole recognition process works automatically with single still images.

In order to get an impression of the quality of the learned object model, we used it to generate a face bunch graph consisting of 1, 7, 14, and 25 found example faces and compared it to a face bunch graph consisting of 14 hand-labeled examples. The learning process took only a few minutes. All face graphs were scaled to five different sizes (by factors of $\sqrt{2}$). Then they were tested on an image database compiled by *Kodak* [10] showing people of different age groups engaged in all kinds of activities (see figure 8). It must be noted that the database did not contain simple portraits as for example the often used FERET database. In fact, it contains faces in different sizes, partly occluded, and more than 50 degrees depth rotation. The example images of frontal faces used to create the face bunch graphs are completely unrelated to the database. The learned face bunch graphs performed very well on this gallery of very complex scenes using the system described in [15]. It found 85 % of the faces starting with only seven learned samples compared to 88 % of the hand-labeled bunch graph, both with the same parameter settings:

Kodak Image Database [10]	Hand-Labeled	Learned (1)	Learned (7)	Learned (14)	Learned (25)
Detected Faces	88 %	75 %	85 %	86 %	85 %
Faces Ranked Before Non-Faces	73 %	54 %	71 %	70 %	73 %
Equal-Error Rate	59 %	34 %	57 %	56 %	60 %
No-False-Detection Rate	59 %	22 %	50 %	50 %	50 %

The table shows the average detection rate in percent for the hand-labeled and learned face graphs. Moreover it shows the percentage of faces which were detected and were ranked higher in terms of overall similarity than any of the

Fig. 8. A few examples from the face finding process with the learned bunch graph consisting of 25 example faces. In all images the best facial hypotheses above a certain threshold with their relative ranking are displayed. The resolution of the images in the upper and lower part is 756 x 504 and 400 x 600 pixels respectively.

flawed hypotheses in the same picture. Although the employed similarity measure was initially only developed in order to rank the hypothesis regions according to their likelihood of containing a face, it was also tested whether a global threshold could be found, which allows to separate correct classifications from false positives. The table shows the equal-error rate, i.e. the rate of correct classification for the similarity threshold value, which yields as many false positives as undetected faces. It also shows the detection rate achievable without false positives.

Acknowledgments. This work has been partially funded by grants from KODAK, the German Federal Ministry for Education and Research (01 IB 001 D) and the European Union (RTN MUHCI). Our special thanks go to all developers of the FLAVOR libraries at the Institut für Neuroinformatik, Germany and the LCBV, USA for providing the basic software platform for this work, and Rolf Würtz for comments on the manuscript.

References

1. M. E. Arterberry, L. G. Craton, and A. Yonas. Infant's sensitivity to motion-carried information for depth and object properties. In C. E. Granrud, editor, *Visual perception and cognition in infancy*, Carnegie-Mellon Symposia on Cognition, 1993.
2. Marian Stewart Bartlett, Javier R. Movellan, and Terrence J. Sejnowski. Representations for Face Recognition by Independent Component Analysis. *to appear in: IEEE Transactions on Neural Networks*, 2002.
3. Peter N. Belhumeur, Joao Hespanha, and David J. Kriegman. Eigenfaces vs. Fisherfaces: Recognition Using Class Specific Linear Projection. In *ECCV (1)*, pages 45–58, 1996.
4. Vincent Caselles, Ron Kimmel, and Guillermo Sapiro. Geodesic Active Contours. In *ICCV*, pages 694–699, 1995.
5. John D. Daugman. Complete discrete 2-D Gabor transforms by neural networks for image analysis and compression. *IEEE Transactions on Acoustics, Speech, and Signal Processing*, 36:1169–1179, 1988.
6. Bernd Fritzke. A growing neural gas network learns topologies. In G. Tesauro, D. S. Touretzky, and T. K. Leen, editors, *Advances in Neural Information Processing Systems 7*, pages 625–632. MIT Press, Cambridge MA, 1995.
7. Bernd Fritzke. A self-organizing network that can follow non-stationary distributions. In *ICANN'97: International Conference on Artificial Neural Networks*, pages 613–618. Springer, 1997.
8. P. J. Kellman, E. S. Spelke, and K. R. Short. Infant perception of object unity from translatory motion in depth and vertical translation. *Child Development*, 57:72–86, 1986.
9. M. Lades, J. C. Vorbrüggen, J. Buhmann, J. Lange, C. von der Malsburg, R. P. Würtz, and W. Konen. Distortion Invariant Object Recognition in the Dynamic Link Architecture. *IEEE Transactions on Computers*, 42:300–311, 1993.
10. Alexander C. Loui, Charles N. Judice, and Sheng Liu. An image database for benchmarking of automatic face detection and recognition algorithms. In *Proceedings of the IEEE International Conference on Image Processing*, Chicago, Illinois, USA, October 4–7 1998.
11. Penio S. Penev and J. J. Atick. Local feature analysis: A general statistical theory for object representation. *Network: Comp. in Neural Systems*, 7(3):477–500, 1996.
12. H.A. Rowley, S. Baluja, and T. Kanade. Neural Network-Based Face Detection. *IEEE Transactions on PAMI*, 20(1):23–38, 1998.
13. E. S. Spelke, K. Breinlinger, K. Jacobson, and A. Phillips. Gestalt relations and object perception: A developmental study. *Perception*, 22(12):1483–1501, 1993.
14. M. Weber, M. Welling, and P. Perona. Towards automatic discovery of object categories. In *Proc. IEEE Conf. on Computer Vision and Pattern Recognition, Hilton Head Island, South Carolina*, 2000.
15. Jan Wieghardt and Hartmut S. Loos. Finding Faces in Cluttered Still Images with Few Examples. In *Artificial Neural Networks – ICANN 2001*, volume 2130, pages 1026–1033, Vienna, Austria, 2001.
16. Laurenz Wiskott, Jean-Marc Fellous, Norbert Krüger, and Christoph von der Malsburg. Face Recognition by Elastic Bunch Graph Matching. *IEEE Transactions on Pattern Analysis and Machine Intelligence*, 19(7):775–779, 1997.

On the Role of Object-Specific Features for Real World Object Recognition in Biological Vision

Thomas Serre, Maximilian Riesenhuber, Jennifer Louie, and Tomaso Poggio

Center for Biological and Computational Learning, Mc Govern Institute for Brain Research, Artificial Intelligence Lab, and Department of Brain and Cognitive Sciences, Massachusetts Institute of Technology, Cambridge, MA, USA
{serre, max, jenlouie, tp}@ai.mit.edu

Abstract. Models of object recognition in cortex have so far been mostly applied to tasks involving the recognition of isolated objects presented on blank backgrounds. However, ultimately models of the visual system have to prove themselves in real world object recognition tasks. Here we took a first step in this direction: We investigated the performance of the HMAX model of object recognition in cortex recently presented by Riesenhuber & Poggio [1,2] on the task of face detection using natural images. We found that the standard version of HMAX performs rather poorly on this task, due to the low specificity of the hardwired feature set of C2 units in the model (corresponding to neurons in intermediate visual area V4) that do not show any particular tuning for faces *vs.* background. We show how visual features of intermediate complexity can be learned in HMAX using a simple learning rule. Using this rule, HMAX outperforms a classical machine vision face detection system presented in the literature. This suggests an important role for the set of features in intermediate visual areas in object recognition.

1 Introduction

Object recognition in the macaque has mostly been explored using idealized displays consisting of individual (or at most two) objects on blank backgrounds, and various models of object recognition in cortex have been proposed to interpret the data from these studies (for a review, see [1]). However, ultimately models of the visual system have to prove themselves in real world object recognition settings, where scenes usually contain several objects, varying in illumination, viewpoint, position and scale, on a cluttered background. It is thus highly interesting to investigate how existing models of object recognition in cortex perform on real-world object recognition tasks.

A particularly well-studied example of such a task in the machine vision literature is face detection. We tested the HMAX model of object recognition in cortex [1] on a face detection task with a subset of a standard database previously used in [3]. We found that the standard HMAX model failed to generalize to cluttered faces and faces with untrained illuminations, leading to poor detection performance. We therefore extend the original model and propose an

H.H. Bülthoff et al. (Eds.): BMCV 2002, LNCS 2525, pp. 387–397, 2002.

algorithm, described in section 2, for learning object class-specific visual features of intermediate complexity. In section 3, we investigate the impact of the learned object-specific feature set on the model's performance for a face detection task. In particular, we trained and tested the same classifier (a Support Vector Machine) on the two sets of outputs collected with the different feature sets (*i. e.,* the standard HMAX features *vs.* the new learned object class-specific features). As a benchmark, we added performances of a classical machine vision face detection system similar to [4].

2 Methods

2.1 HMAX

The model is an hierarchical extension of the classical paradigm [5] of building complex cells from simple cells. The circuitry consists of a hierarchy of layers leading to greater specificity and greater invariance by using two different types of pooling mechanisms. "S" units perform a linear template match operation to build more complex features from simple ones, while "C" units perform a nonlinear MAX pooling operation over units tuned to the same feature but at different positions and scales to increase response invariance to translation and scaling while maintaining feature specificity [2]. Interestingly, the prediction that some neurons at different levels along the ventral stream perform a MAX operation has recently been supported at the level of complex cells in cat striate cortex (Lampl, I., Riesenhuber, M., Poggio, T., and Ferster, D., *Soc. Neurosci. Abs.*, 2001) and at the level of V4 neurons in the macaque [6].

Input patterns are first filtered through a continuous layer S1 of overlapping simple cell-like receptive fields (first derivative of gaussians) of different scales and orientations. Limited position and size invariance, for each orientation, is obtained in the subsequent C1 layer through a local non-linear MAX operation over neighboring (in both space and scale) S1 cells. Response of C1 cells to typical face and background stimuli are shown in Fig. 1. Features of intermediate complexity are obtained in the next level (S2) by combining the response of 2×2 arrangements of C1 cells (for all possible combinations, giving $4^4 = 256$ different features), followed by a MAX over the whole visual field in the next layer, C2, the final pooling layer in the standard version of HMAX [1]. An arbitrary object's shape is thus encoded by an activation pattern over the 256 C2 units.

2.2 Classification Stage

We wish to compare the impact of two different representations on HMAX's performance on a benchmark face detection task: (i) the representation given by hardwired features from the standard HMAX, and (ii) the representation given by the new learned object class-specific features. A standard technique in machine vision to compare feature spaces is to train and test a given classifier on the data sets produced by projecting the data into the different representation

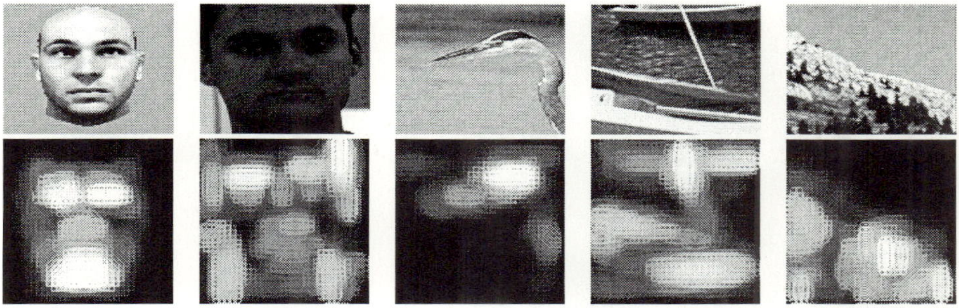

Fig. 1. Typical stimuli and associated responses of the C1 complex cells (4 orientations). The orientation of the ellipses matches the orientation of the cells and intensities encode response strength. For simplicity, only the response at one scale (std 2.75–3.75 pixels, 6×6 pooling range) is displayed. Note that an individual C1 cell is not particularly selective either to face or to non-face stimuli.

spaces. It is still unclear how categorization tasks are learned in cortex [7] (but see the accompanying BMCV paper by Knoblich *et al.*). We here use a Support Vector Machine [8] (SVM) classifier, a learning technique that has been used successfully in recent machine vision systems [4,3]. It is important to note that this classifier was not chosen for its biological plausibility, but rather as an established classification back-end that allows us to compare the quality of the different feature sets for the detection task independent of the classification technique.

2.3 Face Detection Task

Each system (*i. e.,* standard HMAX, HMAX with feature learning, and the "AI" system (see below)) was trained on a reduced data set similar to [3] consisting of 200 synthetic frontal face images generated from 3D head models [9] and 1,000 non-face image patterns randomly extracted from larger background images. After training, we tested each system on a test set of 1,300 face images (denoted "all faces" in the following) containing: (i) 900 "cluttered faces" and (ii) 400 "difficult faces". The "cluttered faces" were generated from 3D head models [9] that were different from training but were synthesized under similar illumination conditions. The "difficult faces" were real frontal faces presenting untrained extreme illumination conditions. The negative test set consisted of 1,845 difficult background images[1]. Examples for each set are given in Fig. 2.

[1] Both 400 difficult frontal faces and background images were extracted from the larger test set used in [3]. Background patterns were previously selected by a low-resolution classifier as most similar to faces.

Fig. 2. Typical stimuli used in our experiments. From left to right: Training faces and non-faces, "cluttered (test) faces", "difficult (test) faces" and test non-faces.

2.4 Feature Learning

The goal of the feature learning algorithm was to obtain a set of object class-specific features. Fig. 3 shows how new S2 features are created from C1 inputs in the feature learning version of HMAX: Given a certain *patch size* p, a feature corresponds to a $p \times p \times 4$ pattern of C1 activation $\mathbf{w}$, where the last 4 comes from the four different preferred orientations of C1 units used in our simulations. The precise learned features or prototypes $\mathbf{u}$ (the number of which was another parameter, n) were obtained by performing vector quantization (VQ, using the k-means algorithm) over randomly chosen patches of size $p \times p \times 4$ of C1 activation obtained from extraction at random position over 200 face images (also used in training the classifier). Choosing m patches per face image therefore leaded to $M = 200 \times m$ total patches for training. In all simulations, p varied between 2 and 20, n varied between 4 and 3,000, m varied between 1 and 750 and M varied between 200 and 150,000. S2 units behave like gaussian RBF-units and compute a function of the squared distance between an input pattern and the stored prototype: $f(x) = \alpha \exp - \frac{||x-\mathbf{u}||^2}{2\sigma^2}$, with α chosen to normalize the value of all features over the training set between 0 and 1.

2.5 The "AI" (Machine Vision) System

As a benchmark we added performances of a classical machine vision face detection system similar to [4]. Detection of a face was performed by scanning input images at different scales by use of a search window. At each scale and for each position of the window, gray values were extracted and pre-processed as in [4] to feed a second-degree polynomial SVM.[2] All systems (*i. e.*, standard HMAX, HMAX with feature learning, and the "AI" system) were trained and tested on the same data sets (see section 2.3).

[2] Using a linear SVM yielded comparable detection performance.

3 Results

3.1 Performance of Standard HMAX

As evident from Fig. 4, performance of the standard HMAX system on the face detection task is pretty much at chance: The system didn't generalize well to faces with similar illumination conditions but set into background ("cluttered faces") or to faces with less clutter (indoor scenes) and untrained illumination conditions ("difficult faces"). This indicates that the object class-unspecific dictionary of features in standard HMAX is insufficient to perform robust face detection. This is easily understood, as the 256 features cannot be expected to show any specificity for faces *vs.* background patterns. In particular, for a specific image containing a face on a background pattern, the activity of C2 model units (which pool over S2 units tuned to the same feature but having different receptive field locations) will for some C2 units be due to image patches belonging to the face. But, for other S2/C2 features, a part of the background might cause a stronger activation than any part of the face, thus interfering with the response that would have been caused by the face alone. This interference leads to poor generalization performances, as borne out in Fig. 4.

3.2 Feature Learning

As Fig. 5 makes clear, the challenge is to learn a set of features in the S2 layer that reliably permits the system to detect image patches belonging to a face and not be confused by non-face patterns, even though objects from the two classes can cause very similar activations on the C1 level (Fig. 1). In general, the learned features already show a high degree of specificity for faces and are not confused by simultaneously appearing backgrounds. They thus appear to offer a much more robust representation than the features in standard HMAX.

Using the learned face-specific features leads to a tremendously improved performance (Fig. 4), even outperforming the "AI" system. This demonstrates that the new features reliably respond to face components with high accuracy without being confused by non-face backgrounds.

3.3 Parameter Dependence

The results in Fig. 4 were obtained with a dictionary of $n = 480$, $m = 120$ and $p = 5$ features. This choice of parameters provided the best results. Fig. 6 (bottom) shows the dependence of the model's performance on patch size p and the percentage of face area covered by the features (the area taken up by one feature p^2 times the number of patches extracted per faces m divided by the area covered by one face). As the percentage of the face area covered by the features increases, the overlap between features should in principle increases. Features of intermediate sizes work best[3]: First, compared with large features, they probably

[3] 5×5 and 7×7 features for which performances are best correspond to cells' receptive field of about a third of a face.

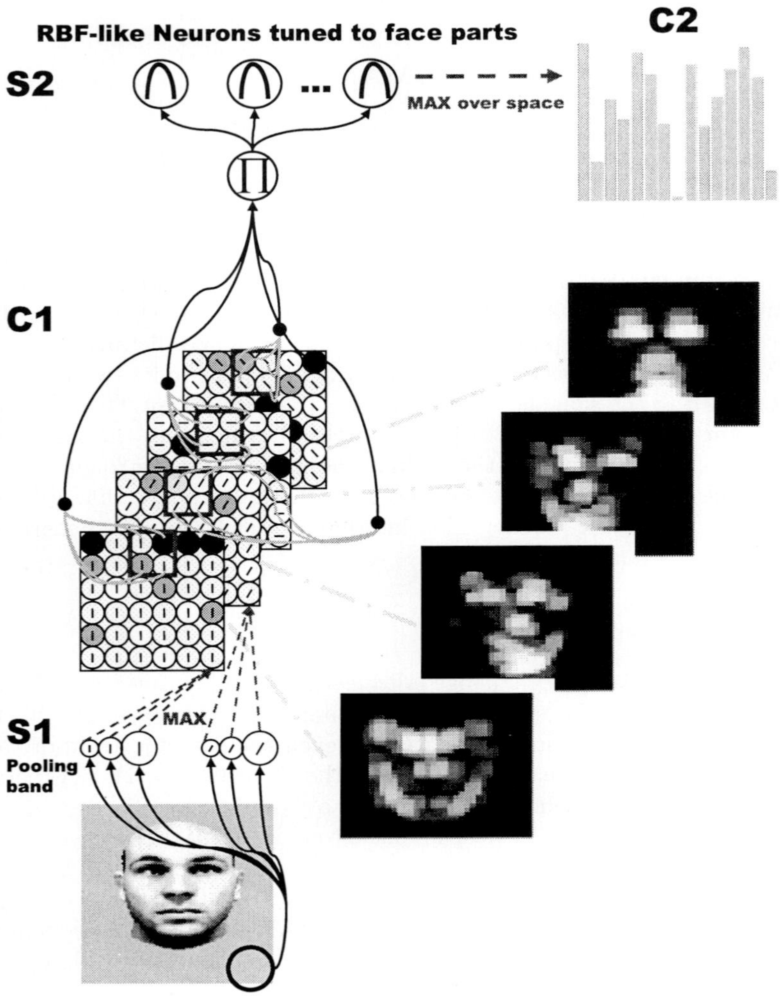

Fig. 3. Sketch of the HMAX model with feature learning: Patterns on the model "retina" are first filtered through a continuous layer S1 (simplified on the sketch) of overlapping simple cell-like receptive fields (first derivative of gaussians) at different scales and orientations. Neighboring S1 cells in turn are pooled by C1 cells through a MAX operation. The next S2 layer contains the RBF-like units that are tuned to object-parts and compute a function of the distance between the input units and the stored prototypes ($p = 4$ in the example). On top of the system, C2 cells perform a MAX operation over the whole visual field and provide the final encoding of the stimulus, constituting the input to the SVM classifier. The difference to standard HMAX lies in the connectivity from C1→S2 layer: While in standard HMAX, these connections are hardwired to produce 256 2×2 combinations of C1 inputs, they are now learned from the data.

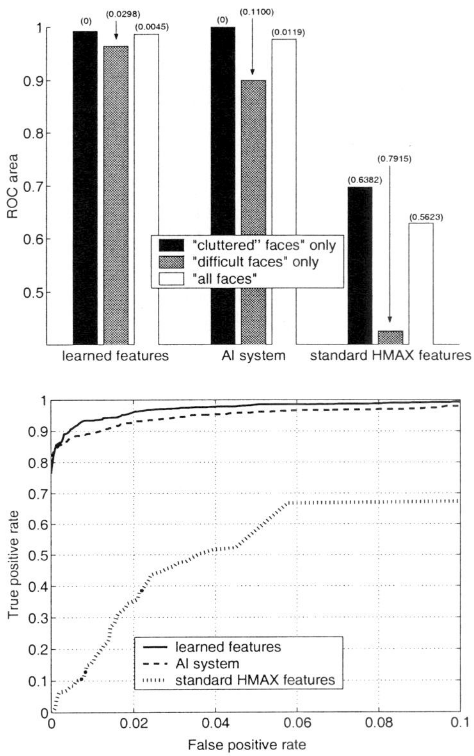

Fig. 4. Comparison between the new extended model using object-specific learned features ($p = 5$, $n = 480$, $m = 120$, corresponding to our best set of features), the "AI" face detection system and the standard HMAX. Top: Detailed performances (ROC area) on (i) "all faces", (ii) "cluttered faces" only and (iii) "difficult faces" only (background images remain unchanged in the ROC calculation). For information, the false positive rate at 90% true positive is given in parenthesis. The new model generalizes well on all sets and overall outperforms the "AI" system (especially on the "cluttered" set) as well as standard HMAX. Bottom: ROC curves for each system on the test set including "all faces".

have more flexibility in matching a greater number of faces. Second, compared to smaller features they are probably more selective to faces. Those results are in good agreement with [10] where gray-value features of intermediate sizes where shown to have higher mutual information. Similarly, performance as a function of the number of features n show first a rise with increasing numbers of features due to the increased discriminatory power of the feature dictionary. However, with large features, overfitting may occur. Fig. 6 (top) shows performances for $p = 2, 5, 7, 10, 15, 20$ and $n = 100$.

4 Discussion

In this paper, we have applied a model of object recognition in cortex to a real-world object recognition task, the detection of faces in natural images. While HMAX has been shown to capture the shape tuning and invariance properties from physiological experiments, we found that it performed very poorly on the face detection task. Because visual features of intermediate complexity in HMAX were initially hardwired, they failed to show any specificity for faces *vs.* background patterns. In particular, for an image containing a face on a background pattern, the activity of some (C2) top units could be due to image parts belonging to the

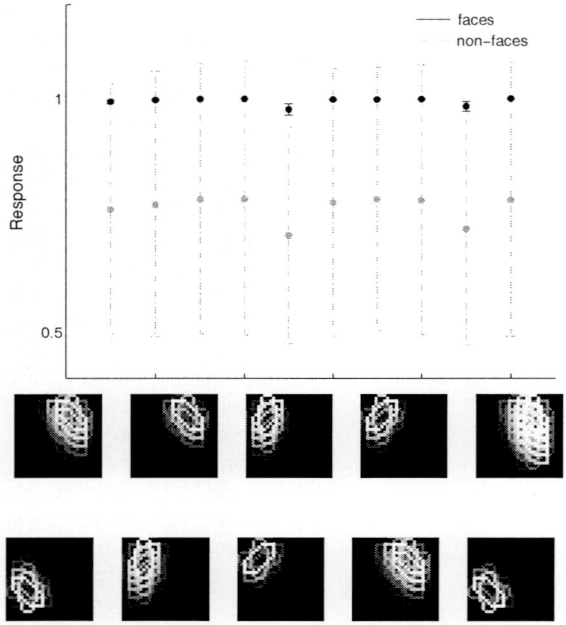

Fig. 5. Mean response over the training face and non-face stimuli, resp., for the top 10 learned features. The top ten features were obtained by ranking the learned features obtained with $p = 5$, $n = 480$, $m = 120$ according to their individual ROC value and by selecting the ten best. Individual features are already good linear separators between faces and non-faces. Bottom: Corresponding features. The orientation of the ellipses matches the orientation of the cells and intensities encode response strength.

face. For others, a part of the background could elicit a stronger activation than any part of the face thus interfering with the response that would have been caused by the face alone. This led to poor generalization performance.

Extending the original model, we proposed a biologically plausible feature learning algorithm and we showed that the new model was able to outperform standard HMAX as well as a benchmark classical face detection system similar to [4]. Learned features therefore appear to offer a much more robust representation than the non-specific features in standard HMAX and could thus play a crucial role in the representation of objects in cortex.

Interestingly, we showed that features that were chosen independently of any task (*i. e.,* independently of their ability to discriminate between face and non-face stimuli or between-class discrimination) produced a powerful encoding scheme. This is compatible with our recent theory of object recognition in cortex [2] in which a general, *i.e.,* task-independent object representation provides input to task-specific circuits. We would expect the same features to be useful for recognition tasks at different levels (*i.e.,* identification), possibly with different weights, and we intend to explore these questions further.

Our proposed mechanisms for learning object-specific features is partially supervised since features are only extracted from the target object class. However, preliminary results using unsupervised learning ($n = 200$ features, $p = 5$, learned from 10,000 face parts and 10,000 non-face parts) have produced encouraging results. As Fig. 7 makes clear, a system using the features learned with k-means over face and non-face stimuli performs slightly worse than the systems using

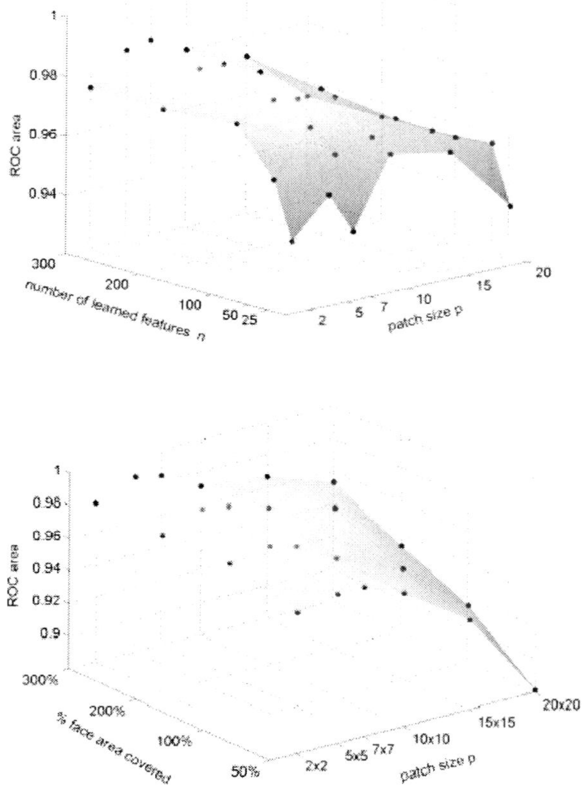

Fig. 6. Investigating prototypes tuning properties. Top: Performances (ROC area) with respect to the number of learned features n (fixed $p = 5$ and $m = 100$). Performances increase with the number of learned features to a certain level and larger patches start overfit. Bottom: features overlap (or equivalently % of the face area covered): overlapping intermediate features perform best. Best performances were obtained with $p = 5$, $n = 480$, $m = 120$.

features extracted from face parts only. However, weeding out non-selective features by keeping only the 100 most discriminant features (as given by their ROC value) is enough to bring the system at a higher level. It is worth emphasizing that selecting features based on their mutual information produced similar results. We are currently exploring how this feature selection can be done in a biologically plausible way.

Modelling the biological mechanisms by which neurons acquire tuning properties in cortical areas was not the scope of the present paper. Rather, we focused on the type of computation performed by cortical neurons. We proposed a 2-step learning stage where an object representation is first learned and then a strategy is selected. For simplicity, we chose the (non-biological) k-means algorithm to learn features that provide a suitable representation independently of any task. While it is unlikely that the cortex performs k-means clustering, there are more plausible models of cortical self-organization that perform very similar operations in a biologically more plausible architecture. It should be easy to replace with a more biologically plausible linear classifier the SVM classifier we

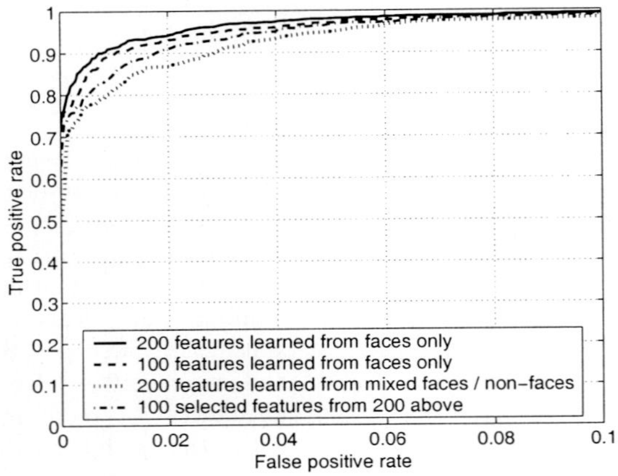

Fig. 7. Preliminary results on unsupervised feature learning: Comparison (ROC area) between features ($p = 5$) learned from face parts only ($n = 200$ and $n = 100$ features) and features learned from both face and non-face parts ($n = 200$, from an equal number of positive and negative examples). Performances on the "unsupervised" representation can be improved by selecting face-specific features for the detection task.

have used here, while accounting well for the sharp class boundary exhibited by some category-specific neurons in prefrontal cortex [7].

Acknowledgments. We thank T. Vetter for providing us with the 3D head models used to generate the synthetic faces.
This report describes research done at the Center for Biological & Computational Learning, which is affiliated with the Mc Govern Institute of Brain Research and with the Artificial Intelligence Laboratory, and which is in the Department of Brain & Cognitive Sciences at MIT.

This research was sponsored by grants from: Office of Naval Research (DARPA) Contract No. N00014-00-1-0907, National Science Foundation (ITR/IM) Contract No. IIS-0085836, National Science Foundation (ITR) Contract No. IIS-0112991, National Science Foundation (KDI) Contract No. DMS-9872936, and National Science Foundation Contract No. IIS-9800032.

Additional support was provided by: AT&T, Central Research Institute of Electric Power Industry, Center for e-Business (MIT), Daimler Chrysler AG, Compaq/Digital Equipment Corporation, Eastman Kodak Company, Honda R&D Co., Ltd., ITRI, Komatsu Ltd., Merrill-Lynch, Mitsubishi Corporation, NEC Fund, Nippon Telegraph & Telephone, Oxygen, Siemens Corporate Research, Inc., Sumitomo Metal Industries, Toyota Motor Corporation, WatchVision Co., Ltd., and The Whitaker Foundation.

References

1. M. Riesenhuber and T. Poggio. Hierarchical models of object recognition in cortex. *Nat. Neurosci.*, 2(11):1019–25, 1999.
2. M. Riesenhuber and T. Poggio. Models of object recognition. *Nature Neuroscience*, 3 supp.:1199–1204, 2000.

3. B. Heisele, T. Serre, M. Pontil, and T. Poggio. Component-based face detection. In *Proc. IEEE Conf. on Computer Vision and Pattern Recognition*, volume 1, pages 657–62, Hawaii, 2001.
4. K.-K. Sung. *Learning and Example Selection for Object and Pattern Recognition.* PhD thesis, MIT, Artificial Intelligence Laboratory and Center for Biological and Computational Learning, Cambridge, MA, 1996.
5. D. Hubel and T. Wiesel. Receptive fields, binocular interaction and functional architecture in the cat's visual cortex. *J. Phys.*, 160:106–54, 1962.
6. T.J. Gawne and J.M. Martin. Response of primate visual cortical V4 neurons to simultaneously presented stimuli. *To appear in J. Neurophysiol.*, 2002.
7. D.J. Freedman, M. Riesenhuber, T. Poggio, and E.K. Miller. Categorical representation of visual stimuli in the primate prefrontal cortex. *Science*, 291:312–16, 2001.
8. V. Vapnik. *The nature of statistical learning.* Springer Verlag, 1995.
9. T. Vetter. Synthesis of novel views from a single face. *International Journal of Computer Vision*, 28(2):103–116, 1998.
10. S. Ullman, M. Vidal-Naquet, and E. Sali. Visual features of intermediate complexity and their use in classification. *Nat. Neurosci.*, 5(7):682–87, 2002.

Object Detection in Natural Scenes by Feedback

Fred H. Hamker and James Worcester

California Institute of Technology, Division of Biology 139-74,
Pasadena, CA 91125, USA
fred@klab.caltech.edu
http://www.klab.caltech/~fred.html

Abstract. Current models of object recognition generally assume a bottom-up process within a hierarchy of stages. As an alternative, we present a top-down modulation of the processed stimulus information to allow a goal-directed detection of objects within natural scenes. Our procedure has its origin in current findings of research in attention which suggest that feedback enhances cells in a feature-specific manner. We show that feedback allows discrimination of a target object by allocation of attentional resources.

1 Introduction

The majority of biologically motivated object recognition models process the visual image in a feedforward manner. Specific filters are designed or learned to allow recognition of a subset of objects. In order to facilitate recognition, an attentional module was proposed to pre-select parts of the image for further analysis. This is typically done by applying a spotlight or window of attention that suppresses input from outside the window. Such an approach results in two major disadvantages: i) A spotlight selects a region but not object features. Even when the whole image is reduced to a region of interest, object recognition algorithms still have to cope with clutter, different backgrounds and with overlapping from other objects, which modify the filter responses. ii) Object recognition follows attentional selection. If a task requires the detection of a specific item such an approach calls for serially scanning the scene and sending the content of each selected location to a recognition module until the target is found. The use of simple target cues, like color, can reduce the search space, but the serial scan is unavoidable.

We suggest a top-down approach for a goal-directed search. Instead of specialized learned or designed features, we use a general set of features that filter the image and construct a population of active cells for each scene. The information about a target is sent top-down and guides the bottom-up processing in a parallel fashion. This top-down modulation is implemented such that the features of the object of interest are emphasized through a dynamic competetive/cooperative process. Related ideas have been suggested in the past [1] [2] [3] [4] but not further implemented for a model of vision in natural scenes.

H.H. Bülthoff et al. (Eds.): BMCV 2002, LNCS 2525, pp. 398–407, 2002.

We have been working out this concept with a computational neuroscience approach. The starting point was to understand the role of goal-directed visual attention [5] [6] [7]. Experimental findings support the concept of prioritized processing by a biased competition [8]. For example, an elevated baseline activity was observed in IT cells after a cue was presented [9]. This effect could be a priming in order to prepare the visual system for detecting the target in a scene. Further evidence for a feature-selective feedback signal is found in V4 [10] and in the motion system [11].

Although some scenes allow the detection of categories during very brief presentations even in the near absence of spatial attention [12], ambiguities in IT cell populations encoding features within the same receptive field limits recognition in natural images [13]. We use feedback to clean up the population activity in higher stages from all unimportant stimuli so that a full recognition can take place. In the following we describe how feedback modulates the feedforward process, which allows for a goal-directed detection of an object in a natural scene.

2 Model

We combine stimulus-driven saliency, which is primarily a bottom-up process, with goal-directed attention, which is under top-down control (Fig. 1). The fact that features that are unique in their environment 'pop-out' is to a first degree achieved by computing center-surround differences. In this regard, our saliency module mostly follows the approach of Itti, Koch and Niebur [14]. However, their purely salience-driven approach continues in combining the center-surround maps into conspicuity maps and then into a final saliency map. We suggest combining the feature value with its corresponding saliency into a population code which feeds V4 cells (Fig. 2). This approach allows us to create a parallel encoding of different variables and achieve the dynamic enhancement of relevant variables by feedback connections. The hierarchy of the model is motivated through a computational neuroscience study of attention [7]. Features of the target template are sent downwards in parallel and enhance features in the scene that match the template. Feedback from the premotor map enhances all features at a specific location. Such an approach unifies recognition and attention as interdependent aspects of one network.

2.1 Low Level Stimulus-Driven Salience

We largely follow the implementation of Itti et al. [14] to obtain feature and contrast maps from a color image (Fig. 2). We currently use color, intensity and orientation as basic features. Our approach differs from Itti et al. [14] in how saliency influences processing. Itti et al. suggest to compute saliency in the 'where' system, select the most salient part of the image and then preferably process this part in the 'what' pathway. We compute feature conspicuity maps within the 'what' pathway that directly modulate the features according to their saliency in parallel without any spatial focus. Thus, salient features do

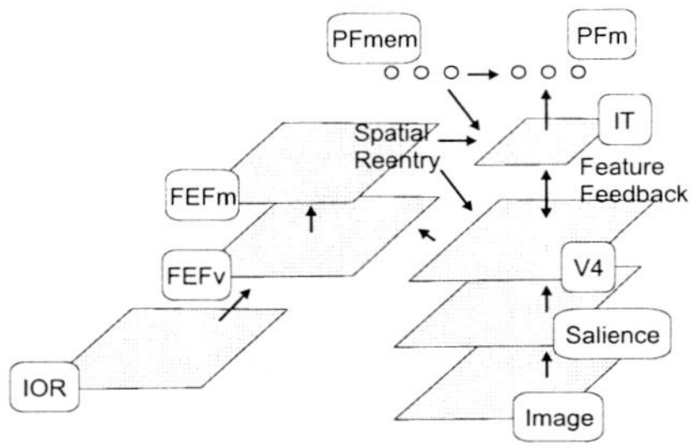

Fig. 1. Model for top-down guided detection of objects. First, information about the content and its low level stimulus-driven salience is extracted. This information is sent further upwards to V4 and to IT cells which are broadly tuned to location. The target template is encoded in PFmem. PFm cells indicate by comparison of PFmem with IT whether the target is actively encoded in IT. Feedback from PFmem to IT increases the strength of all features in IT matching the template. Feedback from IT to V4 sends the information about the target downwards to cells with a higher spatial tuning. FEFv combines the feature information across all dimensions and indicates salient or relevant locations in the scene. A winner-take-all process in FEFm (premotor) cells selects the strongest location. Even during this competition a reentry signal from this map to V4 and IT enhances all features at locations of activity in FEFm. The IOR map memorizes recently visited locations and inhibits the FEFv cells.

not have to be routed to higher areas by spatial attention. However, after 100ms spatial attention starts to implement a gain enhancement in order to prioritize processing at a certain location.

Feature maps: Starting from the color image, we extract orientation $O(\sigma, \theta)$ with varying resolution σ and orientation θ, intensity I, red-green $RG = R - G$ and blue-yellow $BY = B - Y$ information [14].

Contrast maps: Contrast maps determine the conspicuity of each feature and implement the known influence of lateral excitation and surround inhibition by center-surround operations '$\ominus$'. We construct orientation contrast $\mathcal{O}(c, s, \theta)$, intensity contrast $\mathcal{I}(c)$ as well as red-green $\mathcal{RG}(c)$ and blue-yellow $\mathcal{BY}(c)$ double opponency [14].

Feature conspicuity maps: For each variable or feature, we combine the feature information into an attribute $\mathbf{V}$ and its corresponding contrast value into a gain factor P of a population code. This dual coding principle is a very important characteristic. A feature is represented by the location of cell activity, and the conspicuity of this feature is represented by the strength of activity. At each location x_1, x_2 we construct a space, whose axes are defined by the represented features and by one additional conspicuity axis (Fig. 2). The population is then defined by a set of neurons $i \in N$ sampling the feature space, with each neuron tuned around its preferred value $\mathbf{u}_i$. For each neuron y_i we obtain an activity value:

$$y_i = P \cdot g(\mathbf{u}_i - \mathbf{V}) \tag{1}$$

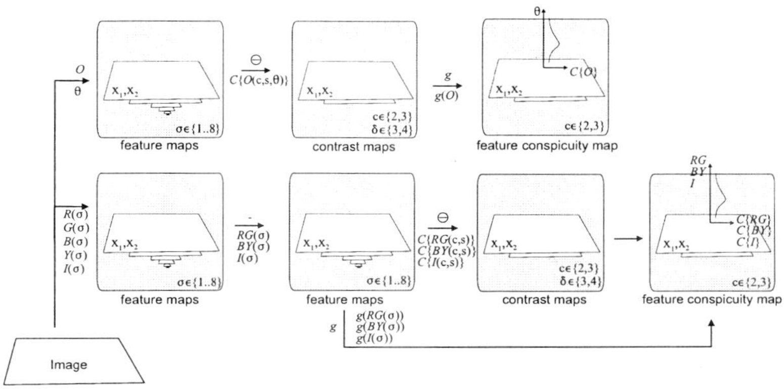

Fig. 2. Construction of a population indicating a feature and its stimulus-driven salience at each location in the image. Starting from a color image we construct broadly tuned color channels *R*ed, *G*reen, *B*lue and *Y*ellow, as well as an *I*ntensity channel. Each of these is represented by a Gaussian pyramid with the scale σ. The color channels are transferred into on opponency system RG and BY. By applying Gabor wavelets on the intensity image I with the scale σ and orientation θ we achieve for each orientation a pyramid that represents the match of the image with the filter. We use center-surround or contrast operations $\ominus$ for each of those feature maps to determine the location of conspicuous features. Both the feature maps and the contrast maps are then combined into feature conspicuty maps, which indicate the feature and its corresponding conspicuity value at each location x_1, x_2.

Specifically we use a Gaussian tuning curve with the selectivity parameter σ_g:

$$g(\mathbf{u}_i - \mathbf{V}) = \exp\left(-\frac{\|\mathbf{u}_i - \mathbf{V}\|^2}{\sigma_g^2}\right) \tag{2}$$

To apply the same range of selectivity parameters $\sigma_g^2 \in \{0.05 \ldots 0.2\}$ for all channels we normalize the feature values $\mathbf{V} \in \{I, RG, BY, \theta, \sigma\}$ of each channel between zero and one. The cell activity within the population should typically lie within the range of zero and one. Thus, we also normalize the contrast values to $\widetilde{\mathcal{I}}$, $\widetilde{\mathcal{RG}}$, $\widetilde{\mathcal{BY}}$, $\widetilde{\mathcal{O}}$. We finally receive the populations for each channel with scale c at each location $\mathbf{x}$:

$$\begin{aligned}
y_i^I(c, \mathbf{x}) &= \widetilde{\mathcal{I}}(c, \mathbf{x}) \cdot g(u_i - I(c, \mathbf{x})) \\
y_i^{RG}(c, \mathbf{x}) &= \widetilde{\mathcal{RG}}(c, \mathbf{x}) \cdot g(u_i - RG(c, \mathbf{x})) \\
y_i^{BY}(c, \mathbf{x}) &= \widetilde{\mathcal{BY}}(c, \mathbf{x}) \cdot g(u_i - BY(c, \mathbf{x})) \\
y_i^{\theta}(c, \mathbf{x}) &= \max_{\theta}\left(\widetilde{\mathcal{O}}(c, \theta, \mathbf{x}) \cdot g(u_i - \theta)\right) \\
y_i^{\sigma}(c, \mathbf{x}) &= \max_{\theta}\left(\widetilde{\mathcal{O}}(c, \theta, \mathbf{x}) \cdot g(u_i - \sigma)\right)
\end{aligned} \tag{3}$$

We now have $\#c$ maps, where $\#c$ is the number of center scales, with a population at each point $\mathbf{x}$ for a different center scale c. To combine these maps across space into one map with the lowest resolution (highest c) we use a maximum operation ($\max_{c,\mathbf{x}' \in RF(\mathbf{x})}$).

2.2 Goal-Directed Control

In order to compute the interdependence of object recognition and attention we need a continuous dynamic approach. Specifically, we use a population code simulated by differential equations. Each map in the model represents a functional area of the brain [7]. It contains at each location $\mathbf{x}$ a population of i cells encoding feature values (eq. 4), with the exception of the maps in the frontal eye field and IOR which only encode space ($i = 1$). In addition V4 and IT have separate maps for different dimensions d (RG, BY, etc.). The population of cells is driven by its input $y^{\uparrow}_{d,i,\mathbf{x}}$. Feedback implements an input gain control to enhance the representation of certain features and biases the competition [8] among active populations. Feature specific feedback (I^L) operates within the ventral pathway and enhances cell populations whose input matches the feedback signal. Spatial reentry (I^G) arrives from the frontal eye field and boosts features at a certain location, generally the target of the next saccade. $I^{f\,inh}$ induces competition among cells and I^{inh} causes a normalization and saturation. Both terms have a strong short range and weak long range inhibitory effect.

$$\tau \frac{d}{dt} y_{d,i,\mathbf{x}} = y^{\uparrow}_{d,i,\mathbf{x}} + I^L + I^G - y_{d,i,\mathbf{x}} \cdot I^{inh}_{d,\mathbf{x}} - I^{f\,inh}_{d,\mathbf{x}} \tag{4}$$

The following maps use implementations of the general equation quoted above (eq. 4).

V4: Each V4 layer receives input from a different dimension (d) in the feature conspicuity maps: $y^{\theta}_{i,\mathbf{x}}$ for orientation, $y^{I}_{i,\mathbf{x}}$ for intensity, $y^{RG}_{i,\mathbf{x}}$ for red-green opponency, $y^{BY}_{i,\mathbf{x}}$ for blue-yellow opponency and $y^{\sigma}_{i,\mathbf{x}}$ for spatial frequency. V4 cells receive feature specific feedback from IT cells ($I^L = I^L(y^{IT})$) and spatial reentry from the frontal eye field ($I^G = I^G(y^{FEFm})$).

IT: The populations from different locations in V4 project to IT, but only within the same dimension. We simulate a map containing 9 populations with overlapping receptive fields. We do not increase the complexity of features from V4 to IT. Thus, our model IT populations represent the same feature space as our model V4 populations. The receptive field size, however, increases in our model, so that several populations in V4 converge onto one population in IT: $y^{\uparrow}_{i,d,\mathbf{x}} = w^{\uparrow} \max_{\mathbf{x}' \in RF(\mathbf{x})} y^{\mathrm{V4}}_{i,d,\mathbf{x}'}$. IT receives feature specific feedback from the prefrontal memory ($I^L = I^L(y^{PFmem})$) and location specific feedback from the frontal eye field ($I^G = I^G(y^{FFEm})$).

FEFv: The perceptual map (FEFv) neurons receive convergent afferents from V4 and IT $y^{\uparrow a}_{\mathbf{x}} = w^{\mathrm{V4}} \sum_d \max_i y^{\mathrm{V4}}_{d,i,\mathbf{x}} + w^{\mathrm{IT}} \sum_d \max_{i,\mathbf{x}' \in RF(x)} y^{\mathrm{IT}}_{d,i,\mathbf{x}'}$. The information

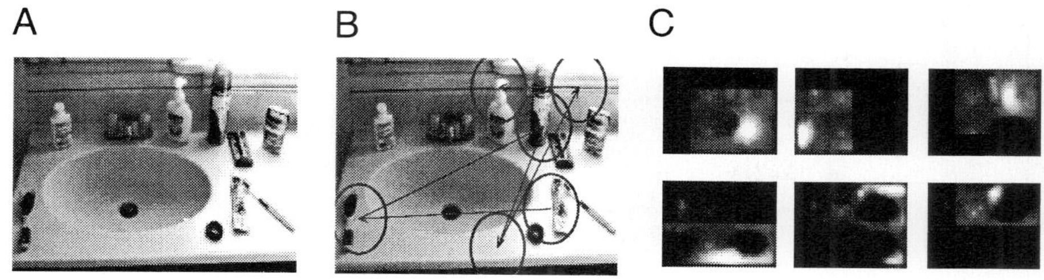

Fig. 3. Results of a free viewing task. (A) Natural scene. (B) Scanpath. It starts on the toothpaste, visits the hairbrush, the shaving cream, two salient edges and then the soap. (C) Activity of FEFv cells prior to the next scan. By definition they represent locations which are actively processed in the V4 and IT map and thus represent possible target locations. An IOR map inhibits FEFv cells at locations that were recently visited (causing the black circles).

from the target template additionally enhances the locations that result in a match between target and encoded feature $y_{\mathbf{x}}^{\uparrow b} = w^{\mathrm{PFmem}} \prod_{d} \max_{i} y_{d,i}^{\mathrm{PFmem}} \cdot y_{d,i,\mathbf{x}}^{\mathrm{V4}}$ at all locations simultaneously. This allows the biasing of specific locations by the joint probability that the searched features are encoded at a certain location. The firing rate of FEFv cells represent the saliency of locations, whereas the saliency of each feature is encoded in the ventral pathway.

FEFm: The effect of the perceptual map on the premotor cells (FEFm) is a slight surround inhibition: $y_{\mathbf{x}}^{\uparrow} = w^{\mathrm{FEFv}} y_{\mathbf{x}}^{\mathrm{FEFv}} - w_{inh}^{\mathrm{FEFv}} \sum_{\mathbf{x}} y_{\mathbf{x}}^{\mathrm{FEFv}}$. Thus, by increasing their activity slowly over time premotor cells compete for the selection of the strongest location.

IOR: There is currently no clear indication where cells that ensure an inhibition of return are located. We regard each location $\mathbf{x}$ as inspected, dependent on the selection of an eye movement at $y_{\mathbf{x}}^{\mathrm{FEFm}}(t_e) > \Gamma_o^{\mathrm{FEF}}$ or when a match in the PFm cells is lost. In this case the IOR cells are charged at the location of the strongest FEFm cell for a period of time T^{IOR}. This causes a suppression of the recently attended location in the FEFv map. IOR cells get slowly discharged by decay with a low weight w_{inh}.

$$\tau \frac{d}{dt} y_{\mathbf{x}}^{\mathrm{IOR}} = (1 - y_{\mathbf{x}}^{\mathrm{IOR}})(w^{\mathrm{FEFm}} I_{\mathbf{x}}^{\mathrm{FEFm}} - w_{inh} y_{\mathbf{x}}^{\mathrm{IOR}})$$

$$I_{\mathbf{x}}^{\mathrm{FEFm}} = \begin{cases} \exp(-\frac{(\mathbf{x}-\mathbf{x}_{\mathrm{m}})^2}{0.01}) & if \quad t < t_e + T^{\mathrm{IOR}} \\ 0 & else \end{cases} ;\; y_{\mathbf{x}_{\mathrm{m}}}^{\mathrm{FEFm}} = \max_{\mathbf{x}}(y_{\mathbf{x}}^{\mathrm{FEFm}}) \quad (5)$$

3 Results

We first show how the model operates in a free viewing task, which is only driven by the stimulus saliency (Fig. 3). The overall scanning behaviour is similar to

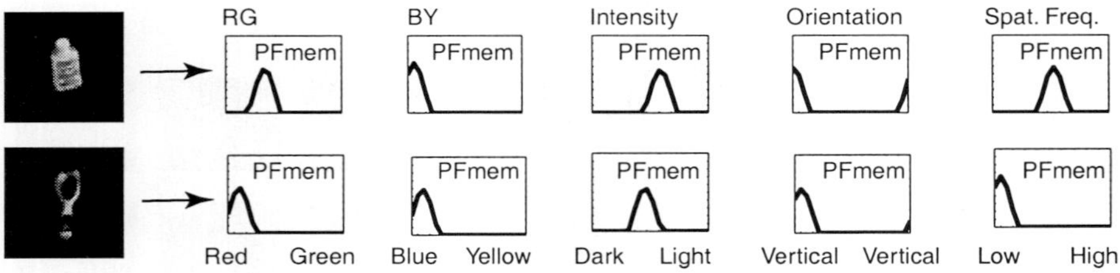

Fig. 4. We presented the asprin bottle and the hairbrush to the model and in each dimension the most salient feature was memorized in order to generate a target template. For the asprin bottle the stopper is most salient so that in the *RG*-dimension the memorized color is only slightly shifted to red. Altogether, we only use crude information about the object and do not generate a copy. Note, that the objects are placed on a black background whereas they appear in the image on a white background.

feedforward approaches (e.g. [14]). The major difference it that the saliency is actively constructed within the network as compared to a static saliency map (Fig. 3C). We could now generate prototypes of various objects and place them into the space spanned by the IT cells. By comparing the prototypes with IT activity during the scans we could then determine the selected object. However, this is not a very interesting strategy. Recognition fully relies on the stimulus-driven selection. According to our interpretation of findings in brain research, primates are able to perform a goal-directed search. The idea is that the brain might acquire knowledge about objects by learning templates. To mimic this strategy we present the model objects from which it generates very simple templates (Fig. 4).

If such an object is relevant for a certain task, the templates are loaded into the PFmem cells and IT cells get modulated by feature-specific feedback. When presenting the search scene, initially IT cells reflect salient features, but over time those features that match the target template get further enhanced (Fig. 5). Thus, the features of the object of interest are enhanced prior to any spatial focus of attention. The frontal eye field visual cells encode salient locations. Around 85-90ms all areas that contain objects are processed in parallel. Spatial attention then enhances all features at the selected location, in searching for the asprin bottle at around 110ms and for the hairbrush 130ms after scene onset. As a result the initial top-down guided information is extended towards all the features of the target object. For example, the very red color of the asprin bottle or the dark areas of the hairbrush are detected by spatial attention because those features were not part of the target template. This aspect is known as prioritized processing. In the beginning only the most salient and relevant features receive a high processing whereas later all features of a certain object are processed.

4 Discussion

We have presented a new approach to goal-directed vision based on feedback within the 'what'-pathway and spatial reentry from the 'where'-pathway. The

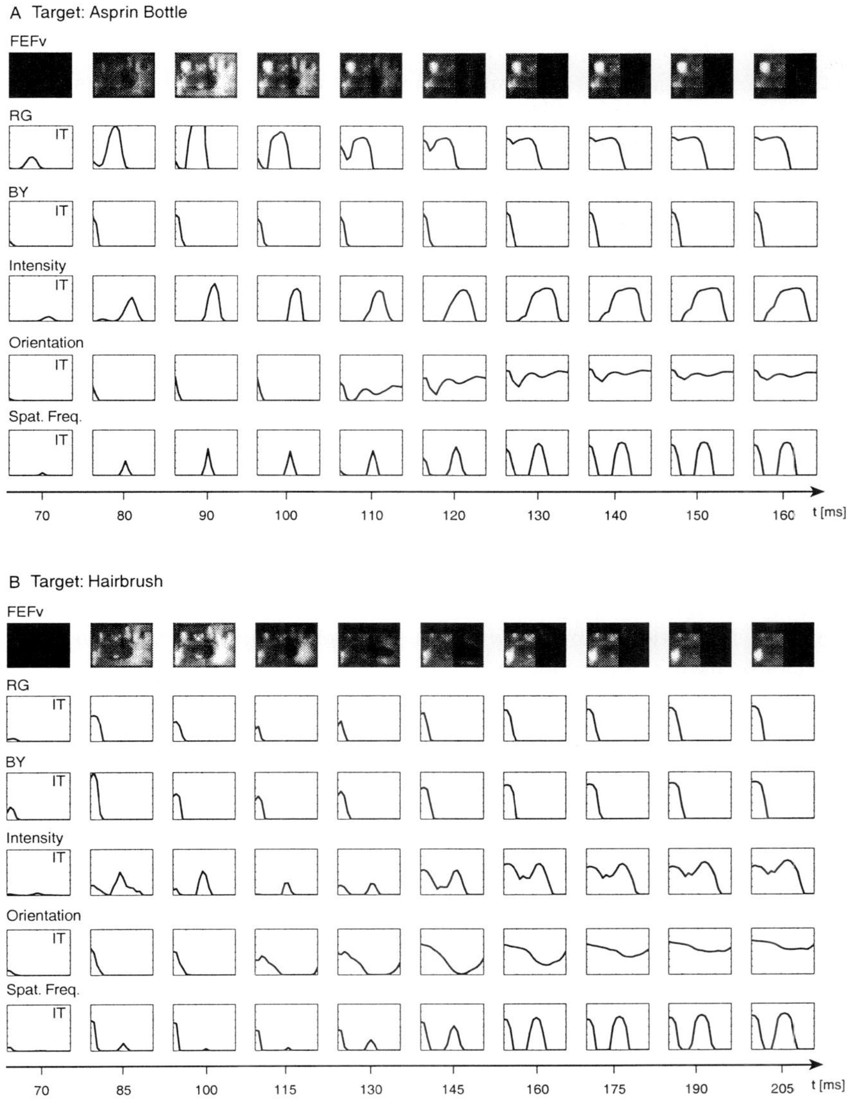

Fig. 5. The temporal process of a goal-directed object detection task in a natural scene. (A) Asprin bottle as target. (B) Hairbrush as target. The frontal eye field visual cells indicate preferred processing, which is not identical with a spatial focus of attention. At first they reflect salient locations whereas later they discriminate target from distractor locations. The activity of IT cell populations with a receptive field covering the target initially show activity that is inferred by the search template. Later activity also reflects other features of the object that were not searched for.

complex problem of scene understanding is here transformed into the generation of an appropriate target template. Once a template is generated, we show that a system can detect an object by an efficient parallel search as compared to pure saliency-driven models which rely on a sequential search strategy by rapidly selecting parts of the scene and analyzing these conspicuous locations in detail. Our model only uses a sequential strategy if the parallel is not efficient to guide the frontal eye field cells toward the correct location. Stimulus-driven saliency is suggested to prioritize the processing in a parallel fashion as compared to an early selection. Regarding the finding that categories can be detected even in the near absence of spatial attention [12], it is important to notice that in our model spatial attention is not a prerequisite of object detection. If the target sufficiently discriminates from the background, the match with the template in PFm can be used for report before any spatial reentry occurs. The simulation results also provide an explanation for Sheinbergs and Logothetis' [13] finding of early activation of IT cells if the target is foveated by the next fixation. Classical models of scene analysis would predict that the process of identifying objects begins after each fixation. In our model the match with the target template increases the firing rate of cells in the 'what'-pathway indicating the detection of the object. Such enhanced activity is picked-up by maps in the 'where'-pathway which locate the object for action preparation. Reentrant activity then enhances all features of the object in order to allow a more detailed analysis. Thus, object identification begins before the eyes actually fixate on the object.

Current simulations have shown that even very simple information about an object can be used in a parallel multi-cue approach to detect and focus an object. Future work should of course extend the model with more shape selective filters to perform object recognition tasks. We think that such an approach provides a serious alternative to present feedforward models of object recognition.

Acknowledgements. We thank Laurent Itti for sharing his source code, Rufin VanRullen for providing the test scene and Christof Koch for his support. This research was supported by DFG HA2630/2-1 and by the NSF (ERC-9402726).

References

1. Mumford D.: On the computational architecture of the neocortex. II. The role of cortico-cortical loops. Biol. Cybern. **66** (1992) 241–251.
2. Tononi, G., Sporns, O., Edelman, G.: Reentry and the problem of integrating multiple cortical areas: Simulation of dynamic integration in the visual system. Cereb. Cortex **2** (1992) 310–335.
3. Grossberg S. How does a brain build a cognitive code? Psychol Rev. **87** (1980) 1–51.
4. Ullman, S.: Sequence seeking and counter streams: A computational model for bidirectional flow in the visual cortex. Cerebral Cortex **5** (1995) 1–11.
5. Hamker, F.H.: The role of feedback connections in task-driven visual search. In: Connectionist Models in Cognitive Neuroscience. Springer Verlag, London (1999), 252–261.

6. Corchs, S., Deco, G.: Large-scale neural model for visual attention: integration of experimental single-cell and fMRI data. Cereb. Cortex **12** (2002) 339–348.
7. Hamker, F.H.: How does the ventral pathway contribute to spatial attention and the planning of eye movements? Proceedings of the 4th Workshop Dynamic Perception, 14-15 November 2002, Bochum, Germany, to appear.
8. Desimone, R., Duncan, J., Neural mechanisms of selective attention. Annu Rev Neurosci **18** (1995) 193–222.
9. Chelazzi, L., Duncan, J., Miller, E.K., Desimone, R.: Responses of neurons in inferior temporal cortex during memory-guided visual search. J. Neurophysiol. **80** (1998) 2918–2940.
10. Motter, B.C.: Neural correlates of attentive selection for color or luminance in extrastriate area V4. J. Neurosci. **14** (1994) 2178–2189.
11. Treue, S., Martínez Trujillo, J.C.: Feature-based attention influences motion processing gain in macaque visual cortex. Nature **399** (1999) 575–579.
12. Li, F.-F., VanRullen, R., Koch, C., Perona, P.: Rapid natural scene categorization in the near absence of attention. Proc Natl Acad Sci USA **99** (2002) 9596-9601.
13. Sheinberg, D.L., Logothetis, N.K.: Noticing familiar objects in real world scenes: the role of temporal cortical neurons in natural vision. J Neurosci. **21** (2001) 1340–1350.
14. Itti, L., Koch, C., Niebur, E.: A model of saliency-based visual attention for rapid scene analysis. IEEE Transactions on Pattern Analysis and Machine Intelligence (PAMI), **20** (1998), 1254–1259.

Appendix: Model Equations

Feature specific topological feedback from the origin ν:

$$I^L_{d,i,\mathbf{x}}(y^\nu) = \max_{\mathbf{x}' \in RF(\mathbf{x})} w^{\downarrow L} y_{i,d,\mathbf{x}'} \cdot y^\nu_{i,d} \tag{6}$$

Location specific topographic feedback from the origin ν:

$$I^G_{d,i,\mathbf{x}}(y^\nu) = y^\uparrow_{d,i,\mathbf{x}} \cdot \max_{\mathbf{x}' \in RF(\mathbf{x})} w^{\downarrow G} y_{i,d,\mathbf{x}'} \cdot y^\nu_{\mathbf{x}'} \tag{7}$$

Inhibition for normalization and saturation:

$$I^{inh}_{d,\mathbf{x}} = w_{inh} \sum_j y_{d,j,\mathbf{x}}(t) + w^{map}_{inh} z^{map}_d \tag{8}$$

Inhibition for competition among cells:

$$I^{f\,inh}_{d,\mathbf{x}} = w^{map}_{f\,inh} z^{map}_d(t) \tag{9}$$

using

$$\tau^{map}_{inh} \frac{d}{dt} z^{map}_d = \sum_{\mathbf{x}} \max_j (y_{j,d,\mathbf{x}}) - z^{map} \tag{10}$$

Stochastic Guided Search Model for Search Asymmetries in Visual Search Tasks

Takahiko Koike and Jun Saiki*

Department of Intelligence Science and Technology,
Graduate School of Informatics, Kyoto University,
Yoshida-honnmachi, Sakyo-ku, Kyoto, 606-8501 JAPAN
{koike, saiki}@cog.ist.i.kyoto-u.ac.jp
http://www.cog.ist.i.kyoto-u.ac.jp/

Abstract. We propose a stochastic guided search model for search asymmetries. Traditional saliency-based search model cannot account for the search asymmetry. Search asymmetry is likely to reflect changes in relative saliency between a target and distractors by the switch of target and distractor. However, the traditional models with a deterministic WTA always direct attention to the most salient location, regardless of relative saliency. Thus variation of the saliency does not lead to the variation of search efficiency in the saliency-based search models. We show that the introduction of a stochastic WTA enables the saliency-based search model to cause the variation of the relative saliency to change search efficiency, due to stochastic shifts of attention. The proposed model can simulate asymmetries in visual search.

1 Introduction

To understand the attentional mechanism in the human vision system, visual search tasks have been used in psychological studies. Many interesting phenomena have been observed in visual search tasks, for example, search asymmetry. Search asymmetry is a well-known phenomenon in which searching for stimulus A among a background of distractors B is more efficient than searching for B among A [8]. Many search asymmetry phenomena have been reported, and many researchers study what kind of stimulus sets cause search asymmetry. However, there is no clear explanation for why search asymmetries occur only by switching target and distractors.

Few model studies deal with search asymmetry explicitly [4] [10]. Li proposed a computational model of the primary visual cortex [4]. Li's model is constructed using horizontal intra-cortical connections among V1 cells with a similar orientation preference. Li argued that V1 neurons serve as a saliency map, a two

* This study was performed under the Project on Neuroinformatics Research in Vision through Special Coordination Funds for Promoting Science and Technology from the Ministry of Education, Culture, Sports, Science and Technology, the Japanese Government. And this work was also supported by Grants-in-Aid for Scientific Research from JMEXT (No. 13610084 and 14019053).

H.H. Bülthoff et al. (Eds.): BMCV 2002, LNCS 2525, pp. 408–417, 2002.

dimensional neuronal module whose activity represents saliency of the visual environment, by these intra-cortical connections. According to this model, saliency represented on V1 changes according to the stimulus set, and Li argued that this change in saliency is the reason for search asymmetry. Some electrophysiological studies have shown the existence of neuronal regions that encode the saliency of the stimulus [3]. However, there is no evidence that firing rates of V1 cells reflect the saliency of objects. Moreover, there are several psychological studies on search asymmetries involving with higher-level visual information, and Li's model appears to be insufficient to account for these findings.

However, the idea proposed in Li's model that search asymmetry is caused by a variation in the saliency map is interesting. Some psychological researchers have also proposed that a simple saliency-based model can simulate search asymmetries, using only a saliency map reflecting the similarity between target and distractors [5]. Also, Wolfe proposed a guided search model 2.0 [10] and he showed that similarity between target and distractors affects the search efficiency using the Signal Detection Theory. Although the guided search model well simulated the search asymmetry, the model did not show practical neuronal mechanism for search asymmetry.

Wolfe argued that our visual system consists of two stages of processing, preattentive parallel stage and attentive serial stage [9] [10]. This idea, human vision consists of two distinct processing stage, is generally accepted, and some neural network model has proposed, e.g. the saliency-based search model [2] The saliency-based search model [2] accounts for the shift of visual attention by a saliency map. To decide the location for shifting the focus of attention with a saliency map, the saliency-based search model introduced the deterministic Winner-Take-All (WTA) network, i.e., WTA based on a simple combination of lateral inhibition and self-excitation. This kind of WTA network detects the maximum value without failure. The saliency-based model can account for the characteristics of human vision in a simple visual search task, pop-out and conjunction search. So, the model seems able to incorporate the above-mentioned idea about search asymmetries.

The saliency-based search model implements the WTA mechanism to decide the next attended location using a saliency map. In general, the WTA mechanism has a common characteristic: the first attended location is always the most salient location, and next attended location is the second most salient. Owing to this characteristic, search efficiency depends on the ranking of the target's saliency.

Suppose the stimulus set whose target is defined by the absence of a feature, as in model A in Fig.1. In Fig.1, the target stimulus is *s2*. In this situation, the shape of the saliency map, computed by a simple summation of feature maps, is concavely curved, and the target stimulus has a minimum saliency. The saliency-based search model always shifts the attention to the target stimuli *s2* last, because the order of the search depends on the ranking of the target's saliency. Search efficiency on this variation of the saliency map is extremely bad. If we suppose the existence of a mechanism that detects the absence of features, "absence" becomes a kind of a feature, for example, as shown in model

B(Fig.1). In this case, variation of the saliency map may then be convexly curved. The target is always most salient, and attentional focus will always be directed to the target first, regardless of the saliency difference between the target and the distractors. As a result, according to the traditional model with a WTA network, changes in saliency never cause a change in efficiency in visual search asymmetries.

The reason why the traditional saliency-based search model cannot account for search asymmetries depends on the characteristics of a deterministic WTA network whose dynamics always make a winner of the location associated with maximum saliency. Thus we need a new WTA mechanism to account for the search asymmetries.

From this point of view, in this paper, we propose a *stochastic guided search model* introducing the *stochastic WTA*. In a stochastic WTA, saliency value represents the probability of attention being directed, so attentional focus *tends* to be directed to the most salient location, but *not always*. In this manner, if the saliency of distractors increases, the probability of directing attention to distractors increases. The number of false detections and search efficiency are affected by the saliency of the target relative to distractors.

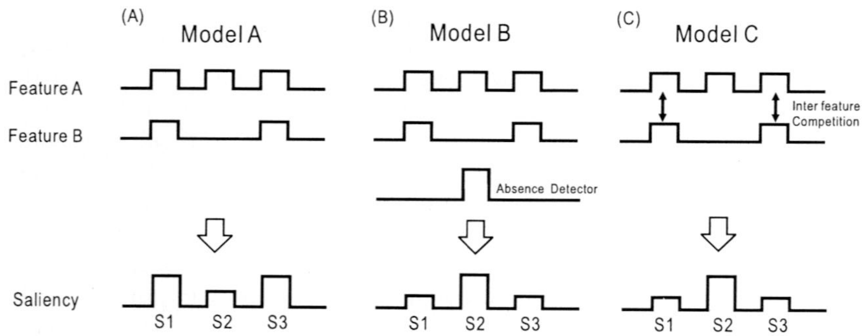

Fig. 1. Shape of the saliency map with three models. (A) Simple summation creates a concavely curved map. (B) The model which introduces a summation feature maps and absence detector creates the convexly curved saliency map. (C) The model with summation feature maps and inter feature competition creates the convexly curved saliency map.

2 Model

2.1 Saliency Map

A saliency map is assumed to encode the saliency of objects distributed in the visual environment. In this model, a construction of the saliency map is almost the same as that in Itti and Koch's model [2].

First, elementary visual features are extracted from an original visual image, and these early visual features are encoded topographically on neuronal modules, called "feature maps." It is assumed that there is interference among the stimuli with the same feature. For instance, a red stimulus interferes more with another red stimulus than with green stimuli. This interference within each feature map is realized by ON-center-OFF-surround filter. As a result of this intra-feature competition, for example, one red object has a high value of saliency, and many green objects have low saliency.

A general way to compute the saliency map consists of summation and lateral inhibition [2]. Using only these computational processes, it is impossible that the target, defined by the absence of a feature, becomes more salient than distractors (See Fig.1(A)). If the assumption that saliency affects search efficiency is right, then search for an absence of feature should be extremely difficult. However, it is clear that a singleton search is not a very hard task, therefore, the target appear to be more salient than distractors. In this study, we introduce the inter-feature competition between different feature maps, which works as an absence detector. If two or more features exist at the same location, these features compete at that location. Thus strength of the feature on that location decrease. If a single feature exists on the location, the feature has no competition, and strength of the feature on that location is not affected. Therefore, an object defined by single feature becomes more salient than an object defined by a combination of features. For example, suppose a red target coding one feature only, and an orange target coding for a summation of features, red and green. Under this supposition, orange distractors are affected by both intra-red-feature and inter-feature competition, though red targets are affected by only intra-red feature interference. As a result, by getting less competition from other objects, a red target defined by an absence of green becomes more salient than others. By introducing this inter-feature competition, an object defined by the absence of a feature is capable of being more salient than objects defined by the presence of features. Fig.2 shows a simple example for an influence of the inter-feature competition. Fig.2(A) is a saliency map computed without inter-feature competition. In this case, the target has minimum saliency among the objects. Fig.2(B) shows the saliency map computed with inter-feature competition, and the target has the most salient value.

After the intra-feature and inter-feature competition, these feature maps were linearly summed into conspicuity maps. Next, conspicuity maps were summed into the saliency map, with the maximum value of saliency normalized to 1, and minimum to 0. A large saliency value denotes high saliency of an object at that location, and a small value denotes low saliency. Neurons belonging to the saliency map generate spikes in the Poisson process whose rates are about 2-50Hz in proportion to the saliency.

2.2 Winner-Take-All Network

To find the most salient location, the saliency-based search model uses a WTA mechanism. In general, the combination of lateral inhibition and self-excitation is introduced in the model as a WTA mechanism, though different mechanisms have been used for the implementation of the WTA network [2]. However, these

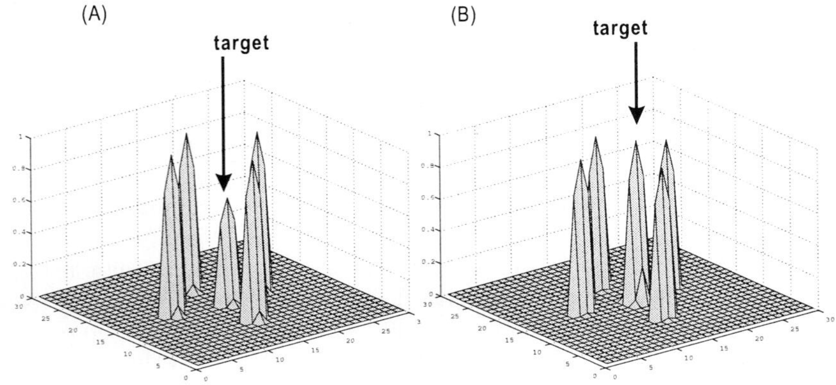

Fig. 2. Shape of the saliency map. (A) Without the inter-feature competition. (B) With the inter-feature competition.

WTA mechanisms have a common characteristic: the most salient location absolutely becomes the initial winner on the WTA network. Thus, the saliency-based search model using a traditional WTA network always shifts the attentional focus to the most salient location first. If the target does not exist at the attended location, some mechanism inhibits saliency of the location, and produces a new winner from other locations. In this manner, the order of attentional shift is absolutely decided by the saliency map, that is, the behavior of these models is *deterministic*.

In the present study, we assume that it is not necessarily the case that attentional focus is always directed to the most salient location first. The key property of our idea is that attentional shift only *tends* to be directed to the most salient location. To implement this idea in the model, we have to adopt a new mechanism that decides the location for directing attentional focus in a stochastic way. We introduced a *stochastic WTA*, that is, a mechanism which detects the synchronized firing on the saliency map.

Here, we show a simple example of the behavior of a deterministic WTA in Fig.3(A). A deterministic WTA consists of a group of neurons. Each neuron has an inhibitory connection with other neurons, and there is also an excitatory connection from neurons belonging to the saliency map. In the deterministic WTA, neurons on a WTA work as a pulse counter. If the number of pulses from the saliency map exceeds some threshold value, then the neurons generate a pulse frequently. These pulses are transmitted to other neurons via inhibitory connections, and transmitted to itself via self-excitatory connection. Thus, other neurons are strongly inhibited, and firing neuron is more excited. If the firing rate of the neuron exceeds sufficiently high threshold, the firing neuron becomes a winner on the WTA network. The number of received pulses is almost proportional to the value of saliency in the long term, thus the winner on WTA always

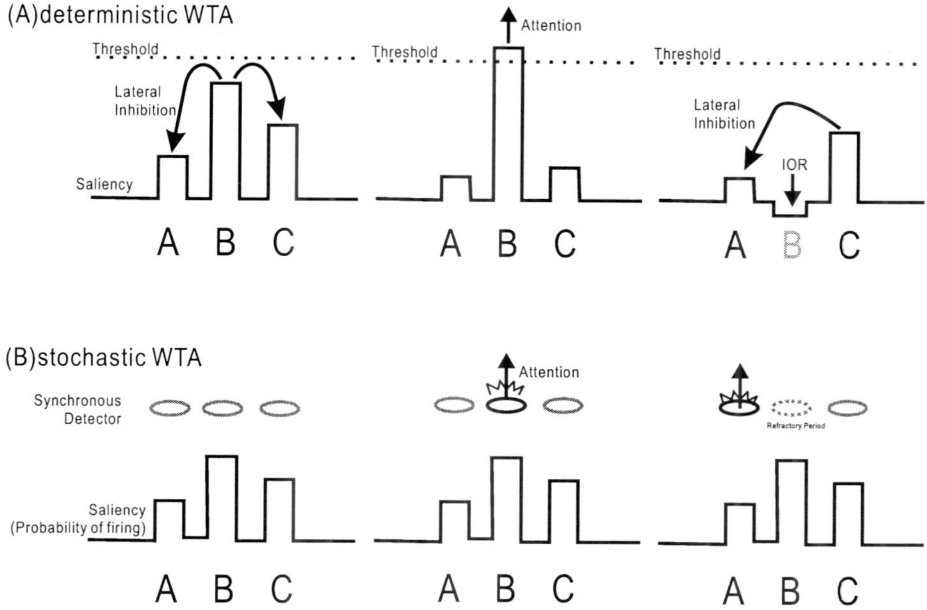

Fig. 3. Behavior of a deterministic WTA and a stochastic WTA. (A) According to the deterministic WTA, an order of attentional shift is determined by an order of a saliency. (B) According to the stochastic WTA, an attention tends to shift to the most salient location, but not always.

appears at the most salient location first, and the sequence of an attentional shift is determined by the sequence of the saliency.

Behavior of the stochastic WTA is shown in Fig.3 (B). The stochastic WTA also consists of a group of neurons, and the neurons are also connected with others by an inhibitory connection, and with the saliency map by an excitatory connection. But neurons on the stochastic WTA have a different role than neurons on the deterministic WTA. In the stochastic WTA, neurons work as a detector of synchronized pulses. If synchronized pulses occurred on the saliency map, a neuron on the stochastic WTA detects them and the neuron fires frequently. These firings are transmitted to other neurons via inhibitory connections, and the firing neuron, detecting the synchrony of pulses, becomes the winner. In this manner, because the neurons associated with the most salient location generate pulses frequently, the probability of a synchronized pulse is maximum at the most salient location. However, neurons in the most salient location do not necessarily generate synchronized pulses first, because each neuron on the saliency map fires only at random, i.e., the Poisson process. Thus, there is a probability that the focus of attention is directed first to an object that has less saliency.

3 Results

To compare the model with the human visual system, we conducted a simulation experiment.

3.1 Search Asymmetry

First, we tested our model on two visual input images which causes asymmetry of search efficiency [8]: (A) one orange target among red distractors with the same orientation; (B) one red target among orange distractors with the same orientation. We assumed that orange is represented by a combination of red and green. On this assumption, the target is defined by the existence of "green" in stimuli (A), and is defined by the absence of "green" in stimuli (B). [1]

We tested the model with a simple visual search task using these stimuli. We counted the number of false detections, i.e., the number of false shifts of attention before target detection, as a measure of the search efficiency. The results are presented in Fig.4.

Fig.4 show the behavior of the model in terms of relation between the number of distractors and false-detections. When the target is distinguished by the existence of feature "green", it is easy to find the target. On the other hand, when the target is distinguished by the lack of a feature "green", the number of false detections increased with the number of distractors, and the efficiency of the search decreased slightly.

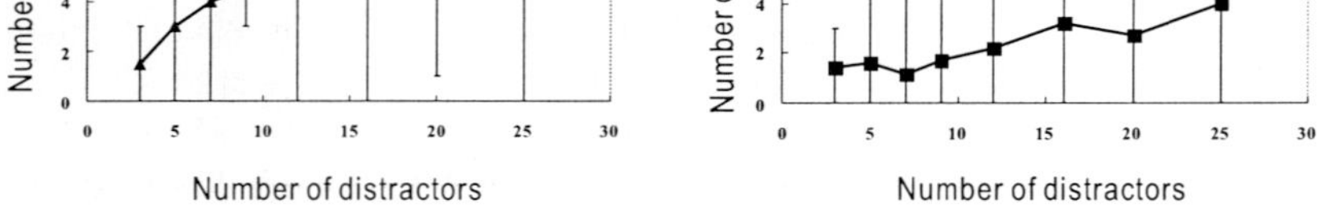

Fig. 4. Average number of false detection as a function of number of distractors. (A) In a search for an orange target among red distractors. (B) In a search for a red target among orange distractors.

[1] In general, it is thought that color information is coded on the Red-Green and Blue-Yellow channels, and orange is defined by combination of the red and yellow. In our model, for the computational simplicity, we assumed that information of the color is coded on the three feature maps, red, green, and blue. In this manner, orange is represented by a combination of the red and green.

3.2 Pop-out and Conjunction-Search

We also tested our model with other simple visual search tasks. We prepared two classes of stimulus sets to simulate the human characteristics in visual search tasks. (A) One red target among green distractors, and (B) one red target among green distractors and red distractors that had orthogonal orientation. All of the parameter is set to a same value treated in the previous section.

When the target was defined only by color, stimuli (A), there was no correlation between the number of distractors and the number of false detections. In this case, the search was efficient. On the other hand, when the target was different from distractors in a combination of features, the number of false detections increased with the number of distractors.

4 Discussion

In this study, we have demonstrated that the stochastic guided search model can simulate search asymmetry by using a combination of two mechanisms, saliency map and stochastic shift of attention. If the saliency of distractors is relatively small, it is less likely that attentional focus is directed first to a distractor, and attention is almost always directed to the target first. On the other hand, if the saliency of distractors is a relatively close to the saliency of the target, the attention tends to be directed to a distractor. Thus, the number of false detections increases, and the efficiency of the search decreases.

The traditional saliency-based search model [2], using the deterministic WTA to decide where to shift the attention, cannot simulate the asymmetries of search efficiency. According to the traditional model, if the target has the most salient value, attention is always directed to the target first regardless of the saliency of the distractors relative to the target. Thus, the search efficiency, defined by the number of false detections, never changes.

In the past model study [2] and our study, it is assumed that the mean time to shift the focus of attention is almost the same and search efficiency depends on the number of false shifts of attention. Under this assumption, the traditional saliency-based search model with deterministic WTA cannot account for search asymmetries. However, if we suppose another idea: search efficiency depends on the time until the winner appears on the WTA network, there is a possibility that the traditional deterministic model accounts for the search asymmetries. According to this idea, when the target and distractors have relatively close values of saliency, a long time is required until the appearance of the winner. Thus, the search efficiency decreased. On the contrary, if the saliency of the target is significantly higher than the saliency of the distractors, the winner on WTA appears quickly, and the search becomes more efficient. As a result, the deterministic model seems to be able to account for search asymmetry by introducing the idea that false shift of attention never occurs and efficiency of search depends on the time until the appearance of the winner.

However, if we introduce this idea, another serious problem occurs. Suppose that the saliency of the target and the distractors are very close. In this case, a long time is necessary to decide the location to attend first, because a long time is required for the winner on WTA to appear. Furthermore, in the conjunction search task, not all target is most salient. Thus, the model must repeat the search for a candidate of the target, again and again. Therefore, a great and unrealistic time must be spent to find the target. Although the traditional saliency-based search model accepting idea that search efficiency depends on the reaction time, can account for search asymmetries, the model appears to have difficulty in accounting for both search asymmetry and conjunction search simultaneously.

On the other hand, our stochastic guided search model can account for both search asymmetry and conjunction search tasks with same and identical parameter settings.

Some other model study mentioned about why asymmetry of search efficiency occurred.

Wolfe proposed a guided search model [9] and a revised version [10]. Wolfe claimed that the similarity between target and distractors affects search efficiency. There is some similarity between the Wolfe's guided search model and our proposed model. First, both models assumed that a mechanism for spatial attention consists of two stages, the saliency map (activation map in the original guided search) and serial attentional focus guided by processing in the saliency map. Second, both models argue that variation of the search efficiency is affected by variation of the saliency selecting a next attend location in stochastic way. Nevertheless, our model is different from Wolfe's original guided search model. In the original guided search model, a top-down control signal plays an essential role. According to the original model, a mechanism to decide the next attended location, a saliency map or an activation map, has two components, a special feature detector and normal feature integration mechanism. If a target has defined by an existence of special feature, a top-down signal emphasizes processing of a special feature detector, thus, searching for target becomes easy and efficient. If a target has defined by a lack of special feature, a top-down signal suppresses the special feature detector, and behavior of the search becomes practically at random and inefficient. Without a top-down control signal, original guided search model cannot explain the search asymmetry. On the other hand, our proposed model assumed no top-down signal.

We have pursued an argument on the assumption that a single focus of attention is driven by the saliency map. However, Deco and his colleagues proposed a neurodynamical mechanism of attention for visual search without assuming the explicit saliency map [1]. The model can account for the experimental modes of visual search, e.g. inefficient search and efficient search, and can reflect the similarity between the target and distractors to the search efficiency. Regarding on explicit single attentional focus, there is a difference between our model and Deco's model. Our model assumed that some neuronal mechanism serves as attentional focus. Deco and his colleagues claims that focus of attention does not exist in a visual system, and is only a result of a convergence of the dynamic behavior of the neural networks. We have to consider carefully about this issue, and further studies, both empirical and theoretical are necessary to resolve the issue.

In summary, the proposed model may account for the asymmetries of search efficiency using a stochastic WTA mechanism. To verify whether this model is appropriate, we have to test our model with many other situations.

References

1. Deco, G., Zihl, J.: Neurodynamical mechanism of binding and selective attention for visual search. *Neurocomputing*, **32-33**, (2000), 693-699
2. Itti, L., Koch, C.: A saliency-based search mechanism for overt and covert shifts of visual attention. *Vision Research*, **40**, (2000), 1489-1506
3. Kusunoki, M., Gottlieb, J., & Goldberg, M. E.: The lateral intraparietal area as a saliency map: the representation of abrupt onset, stimulus motion, and task relevance. *Vision Research*, **40**, (2000), 1459-1468
4. Li, Z.: A saliency map in primary visual cortex. *Trends in Cognitive Sciences*, **6**, (2002), 9-16
5. Rosenholtz, R.: Search asymmetries? What search asymmetries? *Perception & Psychophysics*, **63**(3), (2002), 476-489
6. Shen, J., Reingold, E. M.: Visual search asymmetry: The influence of stimulus familiarity and low-level features. *Perception & Psychophysics*, **63**(3), (2002), 464-475
7. Snyder, L. H., Batista, A. P., & Andersen, R. A.: Intention-related activity in the posterior parietal cortex: a review. *Vision Research*, **40**, (2000), 1433-1441
8. Treisman, A. M., Gormican, S.: Feature analysis in early vision: Evidence from search asymetries. *Psychological Review*, **95**, (1988), 15-48
9. Wolfe, J. M., Cave, K. R.: Guided Search: An alternative to the Feature Integration model for visual search. *Journal of Experimental Psychology -Human Perception and Performance*, **15**, (1989), 419-433
10. Wolfe, J. M.: Guided Search 2.0: A revised model of visual search. *Psychonomic Bulletin and Review*, **1**(2), (1994), 202-238

Biologically Inspired Saliency Map Model for Bottom-up Visual Attention

Sang-Jae Park[1], Jang-Kyoo Shin[2], and Minho Lee[2]

[1]Dept. of Sensor Engineering, [2]School of Electronic and Electrical Engineering
Kyungpook National University
1370 Sankyuk-Dong, Puk-Gu, Taegu 702-701 Korea
mholee@knu.ac.kr

Abstract. In this paper, we propose a new saliency map model to find a selective attention region in a static color image for human-like fast scene analysis. We consider the roles of cells in our visual receptor for edge detection and cone opponency, and also reflect the roles of the lateral geniculate nucleus to find a symmetrical property of an interesting object such as shape and pattern. Also, independent component analysis (ICA) is used to find a filter that can generate a salient region from feature maps constructed by edge, color opponency and symmetry information, which models the role of redundancy reduction in the visual cortex. Computer experimental results show that the proposed model successfully generates the plausible sequence of salient region.

1 Introduction

The human eye can focus on an attentive location in an input scene, and select an interesting object to process in the brain. Our eyes move to the selected objects very rapidly through the saccadic eye movement. These mechanisms are very effective in processing high dimensional data with great complexity. If we apply the human-like selective attention function to the active vision system, an efficient and intelligent active vision system can be developed.

Considering the human-like selective attention function, top-down or task dependent processing can affect how to determine the saliency map as well as bottom-up or task independent processing [1]. In top-down manner, the human visual system determines salient locations through a perceptive processing such as understanding and recognition. It is well known that the perception mechanism is one of the most complex activities in our brain. Moreover, top-down processing is so subjective that it is very difficult to model the processing mechanism in detail. On the other hand, with bottom-up processing, the human visual system determines salient locations obtained from features that are based on the basic information of an input image such as intensity, color and orientation, etc. [1]. Bottom-up processing can be considered as a function of primitive selective attention in human vision system since humans selectively attend to such a salient area according to various stimuli in input scene.

H.H. Bülthoff et al. (Eds.): BMCV 2002, LNCS 2525, pp. 418–426, 2002.

As a previous work, Yagi considered the non-uniform distribution of receptive field in human eye and generated a salient location based on the calculation of simple average in a specific region [2]. However, he did not consider the natural scene and also the selection mechanism is too heuristic. Also, Itti and Koch introduced more brain-like model to generate the saliency map. Based on the Treisman's result [3], they use three types of bases such as intensity, orientation and color information, to construct a saliency map in a natural scene [1]. However, the weight values of the feature maps for constructing the saliency map are determined artificially.

On the other hand, Barlow suggested that our visual cortical feature detectors might be the end result of a redundancy reduction process [4], in which the activation of each feature detectors is supposed to be as statistically independent from the other as possible. We suppose that the saliency map is one of the results of redundancy reduction of our brain. The scan path that is a sequence of salient locations may be the result of the roles of our brain for information maximization. In the Sejnowski's result by using the ICA, the redundancy reduction of a natural scene derives the edge filter [5]. Buchsbaum and Gottschalk found opponent coding to be most efficient way to encode human photoreceptor signals [6]. Wachtler and Lee used ICA for hyperspectral color image and got color opponent basis from analysis of trichromatic image patches [7].

It is well known that our retina has preprocessing such as cone opponent coding and edge detection [8], and the extracted information is delivered to the visual cortex through lateral geniculate nucleus (LGN). Symmetrical information is also important feature to determine the salient object, which is related with the function of LGN. In this paper, we propose a new saliency map that considers the preprocessing mechanism of cells in retina and the LGN with on-set and off-surround mechanism before the redundancy reduction in the visual cortex. Saliency map resulted by integration of the feature maps is finally constructed by applying the ICA that is the best way for redundancy reduction. Section 2 describes biological background of this paper. Proposed saliency map model and computer experimental results will be followed.

2 Biological Background

In the vertebrate retina, three types of cells are important processing elements for performing the edge extraction. Those are photoreceptors, horizontal and bipolar cells, respectively [9][10]. According to these well-known facts, the edge information is obtained by the role of cells in visual receptor, and it would be delivered to the visual cortex through the LGN and the ganglion cells. The horizontal cell spatially smoothes the transformed optical signal, while the bipolar cell yields the differential signal, which is the difference between optical signal and the smoothed signal. By the output signal of the bipolar cell, the edge signal is detected.

On the other hand, a neural circuit in the retina creates opponent cells from the signals generated by the three types of cone receptors [8]. R+G− cell receives inhibitory input from the M cone and excitatory input from the L cone. The opponent response of the R+G− cell occurs because of the opposing inputs from the M and L cones. The

B+Y- cell receives inhibitory input by adding the inputs from the M and L cones and excitatory input from the S cone. Those preprocessed signal transmitted to the LGN through the ganglion cell, and the on-set and off-surround mechanism of the LGN and the visual cortex intensifies the phenomena of opponency [8]. Moreover, the LGN plays a role of detecting a shape and pattern of an object [8]. In general, the shape or pattern of an object has symmetrical information, and resultantly the symmetrical information is one of important features for constructing a saliency map. Even though the role of visual cortex for finding a salient region is important, it is very difficult to model the detail function of the visual cortex. Owing to the Barlow's hypothesis, we simply consider the roles of the visual cortex as redundancy reduction.

3 Saliency Map Model Based on Color Information

Fig. 1 shows a proposed saliency map model. The photoreceptor transforms an optical signal into an electrical signal. The transformed signal for static image is divided into two preprocessing for edge and color opponent coding in the ganglion cell if we do not consider motion information [8]. The extracted visual information is transmitted to the visual cortex through the LGN in which the symmetrical information can be extracted by edge information. Those extracted information is used as a preprocessor of a model for the visual cortex to find a saliency region.

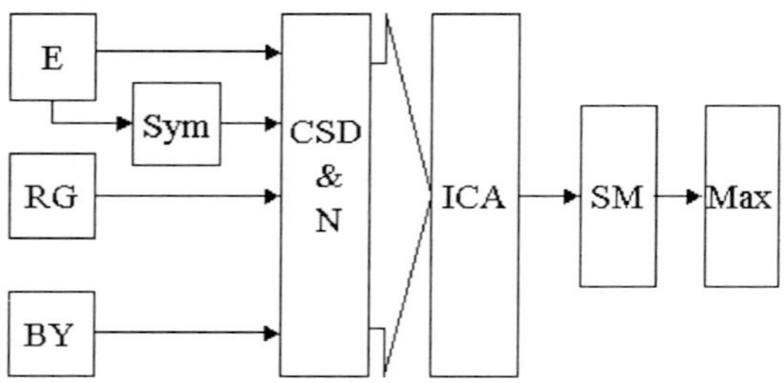

E : edge feature map, Sym : symmetry feature map, RG : red-green opponent coding feature map, BY : blue-yellow opponent coding feature map, CSD & N : center-surround difference and normalization, ICA : independent component analysis, SM : saliency map , Max : max operator

Fig. 1. The architecture of proposed saliency map model

In a course of preprocessing, we used Gaussian pyramid with different scales from 0 to n level, where each level is made by subsampling of 2^n for constructing four feature maps. It is to reflect the non-uniform distribution of retinotopic structure. Then, the center-surround is implemented in the model as the difference between fine and coarse scales of Gaussian pyramid images [1]. Consequently, the four feature maps are obtained by following equations.

$$E(c, s) = |E(c) - E(s)| \quad (1)$$

$$\boldsymbol{Sym(c,s)=|Sym(c) \ominus Sym(s)|} \tag{2}$$

$$\boldsymbol{RG(c,s)=|R(c)-G(c)| \ominus |G(s)-R(s)|} \tag{3}$$

$$\boldsymbol{BY(c,s)=|B(c)-Y(c)| \ominus |Y(s)-B(s)|} \tag{4}$$

where "⊖" represents interpolation to the finer scale and point-by-point subtraction. Totally, 24 feature maps are computed because the four feature maps have 6 different scales individually [1]. Feature maps are combined into four "conspicuity maps" as shown in Eq. (5) where $\overline{E}$, $\overline{Sym}$, $\overline{RG}$ and $\overline{BY}$ stand for edge, symmetry, RG opponency and BY opponency, respectively. They are obtained through across-scale addition "⊕" [1].

$$\overline{E} = \bigoplus_{c=2}^{4} \bigoplus_{s=c+3}^{c+4} N(E(c,s)),\ \overline{Sym} = \bigoplus_{c=2}^{4} \bigoplus_{s=c+3}^{c+4} N(S(c,s))$$

$$\overline{RG} = \bigoplus_{c=2}^{4} \bigoplus_{s=c+3}^{c+4} N(RG(c,s)),\ \overline{BY} = \bigoplus_{c=2}^{4} \bigoplus_{s=c+3}^{c+4} N(BY(c,s)) \tag{5}$$

Comparing with Itti and Koch's model, we use different bases such as edge feature map, symmetry feature map, and two color opponent coding feature maps instead of using the intensity, orientation and color feature maps. The proposed model reflects more biological visual pathways by considering of the roles of retina cells and the LGN. Moreover, the Itti and Koch's model does not sufficiently explain the integration method of the feature maps to make the saliency map. Considering only the bottom-up selective attention, it is very difficult to determine an optimal weight value of feature maps. In this paper, we use unsupervised learning to determine the relative importance of different bases to generate a suitable salient region.

Even though it is difficult to understand the mechanisms of our brain including the visual cortex to process the complex natural scene, Barlow's hypothesis might be reasonable to explain the roles of our brain simply. We suppose that eye movements according to the bottom-up processing are the result of our brain activity for maximizing visual information, and the eye sequence that we focus on an object can be modeled by redundancy reduction of the visual information. In order to model the saliency map, we use the ICA because the ICA algorithm is the best way to reduce the redundancy [5]. ICA algorithm is able to separate the original independent signals from the mixed signal by learning weights of neural network to maximize the entropy or log-likelihood of output signals, or to extract an important feature to minimize the redundancy or mutual information between output signals [12].

Fig. 2 shows the procedure of realizing the saliency map from feature maps. In Fig. 2, E_{ri} is obtained by the convolution between the r-th channel of feature maps(FM_r) and the i-th filters(ICs_{ri}) obtained by the ICA learning as shown in Eq. (6).

$$E_{ri} = FM_r * ICs_{ri} \qquad for \quad i = 1,\dots,N, \quad r = 1,..,4 \tag{6}$$

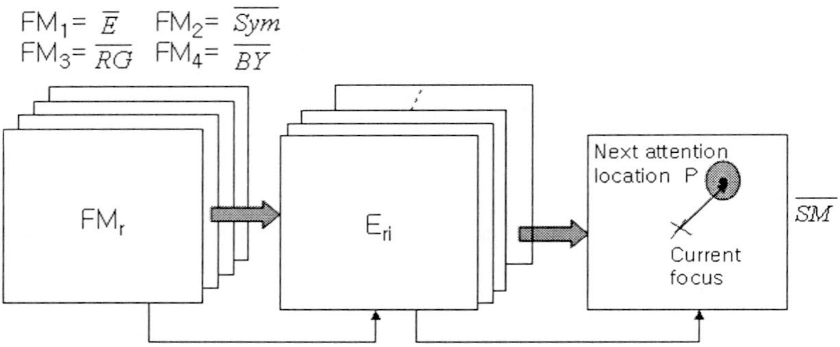

Fig. 2. Procedure of realizing the saliency map from feature maps

where N denotes the number of filters. The feature map, E_{ri} represents the influences of the four feature maps have on each independent component. A saliency map is obtained using Eq. (7).

$$S(x,y) = \sum E_{ri}(x,y) \quad for \ \ all \ \ i \tag{7}$$

The saliency map *S(x,y)* is computed by summation of all feature maps for every location (x, y) in an input image. Since we obtained the independent filters by ICA learning, the convolution result shown in Eq. (6) can be regarded as a measure for the independence of visual information. A salient location ***P*** is the maximum summation value in a specific window of a saliency map as shown in Eq. (8).

$$P = \{(x,y) : \max(\sum_{(u,v)\in W} (S(u,v)) \quad for \ \ all \ \ (x,y)\} \tag{8}$$

where (u,v) is a window with 20×20 size. The selected salient location ***P*** is the most salient location of an input image.

4 Computer Simulation and Results

In our simulation, to obtain filters, we used pre-processed four channel images of color natural scenes. Sobel operator with gray level was used to implement the edge extraction of our retina cell [11]. In order to implement the color opponent coding, four broadly-tuned color channels are created: R = r − (g + b)/2 for red, G = g − (r + b)/2 for green, B = b − (r + g)/2 for blue, and Y = (r + g)/2 − |r − g|/2 − b for yellow (negative values are set to zero) where r, b and g denote red, blue and green pixel values, respectively. RG and BY color opponent coding was obtained by considering the on-center and off-surround mechanism of the LGN as shown in Eq. (3) and (4). Also, we used the noise tolerant generalized symmetry transform (NTGST) algorithm to extract symmetrical information from edge information [13].

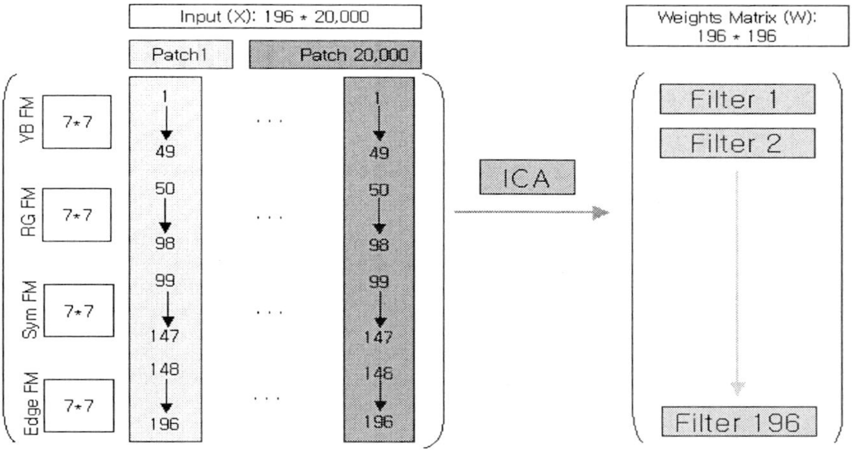

Fig. 3. Procedure of realizing the ICA filter

Using 8 levels Gaussian pyramid image, we could get the four conspicuity maps ($\overline{E}$, $\overline{Sym}$, $\overline{RG}$, and $\overline{BY}$) that is used for input patch of the ICA. Fig. 3 shows the procedure of realizing the ICA filter. We use randomly selected 20,000 patches of size 7×7×4 pixels from four feature maps. Each sample consists of a column in the input matrix of which the row and columns are 196 and 20,000, respectively. The basis functions **W** is learned using the extended infomax algorithm [7]. The learned **W** has a dimension of 196×196. Each row of **W** represents a filter and they are ordered in length of the filter vector. Figs. 4 (a), (b), (c) and (d) show resultant filters for edge, red-green, blue-yellow and symmetry channels, respectively.

We applied the ICA filters to the four channel images of color natural scenes to obtain a salient point. We compute the most salient point $\boldsymbol{P}$ as shown in Eq. (8). Then an appropriate focus area centered by the most salient location is masked off, and the next salient location in the input image is calculated using the salient map model. It means that previously selected salient location is not considered duplicate.

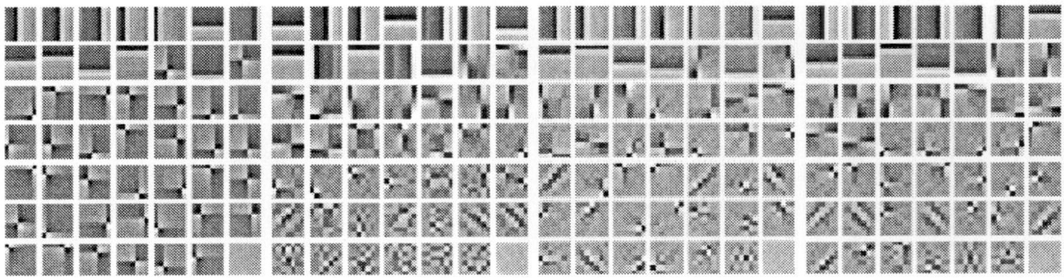

(a) Edge filters (b) Sym filters (c) RG filters (d) BY filters

Fig. 4. Resultant ICA filters for four-channel input

Fig. 5 shows the experimental results of the proposed saliency map model. In order to show the effectiveness of the proposed saliency map model, we used the simple images such as motorcycle and traffic signal images that can show a unique salient object. In Figs. 5 (b) and (d), the bright region in the saliency map ($\overline{SM}$) can be considered as the most salient region. As shown in these figures, the proposed method successfully generates plausible salient locations such as yellow motorcycle and red traffic signal in a natural scene.

(a) motorcycle (b) $\overline{SM}$ of motorcycle (c) traffic signal (d) $\overline{SM}$ of traffic signal

Fig. 5. Experimental results of saliency map model of simple natural images

Fig. 6 shows the experimental results of a complex natural image. Fig. 6 (a) shows a procedure to model the saliency map using feature maps. The preprocessed feature maps ($\overline{E}$, $\overline{Sym}$, $\overline{RG}$, $\overline{BY}$) from color image are convolved by the ICA filters to construct a saliency map ($\overline{SM}$). At first, we compute the most salient region by Eq. (8). Then an appropriate focus area centered by the most salient location is masked off, and the next salient location in the input image is calculated using the salient map model. It means that previously selected salient location is not considered duplicate. In Fig. 6 (b), the arrows represent the successive salient regions.

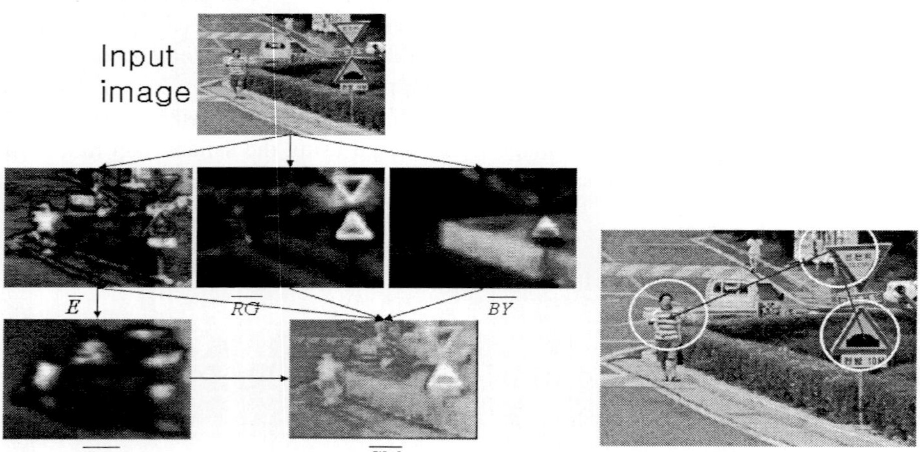

(a) Generated four feature maps and saliency map (b) Successive salient regions

Fig. 6. Experimental result of proposed saliency map model of a natural image

Fig. 7 shows the scan path examples generated by the proposed saliency map model of various natural images. Figs. 7 (a), (d) and (g) are the input images such as car, flower and street images. Figs. 7 (b), (e) and (h) show the saliency maps ($\overline{SM}$) of each input image, and Figs. 7 (c), (f) and (i) are the generated scan paths of each input image. As shown in Fig. 7, the proposed model successfully generates the human-like scan paths of complex natural images.

(a) Car image (b) $\overline{SM}$ of car image (c) Scan paths of car image

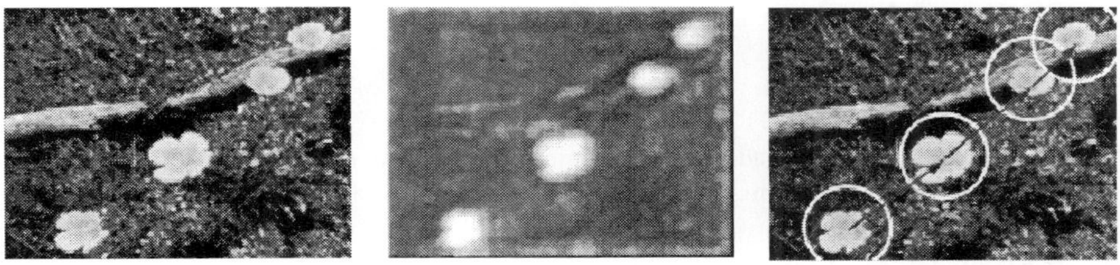

(d) Flower image (e) $\overline{SM}$ of flower image (f) Scan paths of flower image

(g) Street image (h) $\overline{SM}$ of street image (i) scan paths of street image

Fig. 7. Scan path examples generated by the proposed saliency map model for various images with complex background

5 Conclusion

We proposed a new saliency map model based on the four preprocessed feature maps of a static color natural scene. The function of retina and LGN to extract color opponent coding of RG and BY, symmetry and edge detection was modeled, and the result was used to the neural network for realizing the ICA filter which imitates the function of the visual cortex to reduce the redundancy. Computer simulation results showed that the proposed method gives a reasonable salient region and scan path.

Acknowledgement. This research is funded by the Brain Science & Engineering Research Program of Ministry of Korea Science and Technology and the Co-research program of Korea Research Foundation of Ministry of Korea Education & Human Resources Development.

References

1. Itti, L., Koch, C., Niebur, E.: A model of saliency-based visual attention for rapid scene analysis. IEEE Trans. Patt. Anal. Mach. Intell. 20(11) (1998) 1254–1259
2. Yagi, T., Asano, N., Makita, S., Uchikawa, Y.: Active vision inspired by mammalian fixation mechanism. Intelligent Robots and Systems (1995) 39–47
3. Treisman, Gelde, G., A.M.: A feature-intergation theory of attention. Cognitive Psychology 12(1) (1980) 97–136
4. Barlow, H. B., Tolhust, D. J.: Why do you have edge detectors? Optical society of America Technical Digest. 23 (1992) 172
5. Bell, A. J., Sejnowski, T.J. : The independent components of natural scenes are edge filters. Vision Research. 37 (1997) 3327–3338
6. Buchsbaum, G., Gottschalk, A.: Trichromacy, opponent colours coding and optimum colour information transmission in the retina. Proc. R. Soc. London Ser. B 220 (1983) 89–113
7. Wachtler, T., Lee, T. W., Sejnowski, T. J.: Chromatic structure of natural scenes. J. Opt. Soc. Am. A, Vol. 18 (2001) No. 1
8. Bruce Goldstein E.: Sensation and Perception. 4th edn. An international Thomson publishing company, USA (1995)
9. Majani, E., Erlanson, R., Abu-Mostafa, Y.: The Eye. Academic, New York (1984)
10. Kuffler, S. W., Nicholls, J. G., Martin, J. G.: From Neuron to Brain. Sinauer Associates, Sunderland, U.K (1984)
11. Gonzalez, R. G., Woods, R. E.: Digital Image Processing. Addison-Wesley Publishing Company, USA (1993)
12. Lee, T. W.: Independent Component Analysis-theory and application. Kluwer academic publisher, (1998)
13. Seo, K. S., Park, C.J., Cho, S.H., Choi, H. M.: Context-Free Marker-Controlled Watershed Transform for Efficient Multi-Object Detection and Segmentation. IEICE TRANS. Vol. E84-A. Jun. (2001) No. 6

Hierarchical Selectivity for Object-Based Visual Attention

Yaoru Sun and Robert Fisher

Division of Informatics, University of Edinburgh, Edinburgh, EH1 2QL, UK
{yaorus,rbf}@dai.ed.ac.uk

Abstract. This paper presents a novel "hierarchical selectivity" mechanism for object-based visual attention. This mechanism integrates visual salience from bottom-up groupings and the top-down attentional setting. Under its guidance, covert visual attention can shift not only from one grouping to another but also from a grouping to its sub-groupings at a single resolution or multiple varying resolutions. Both object-based and space-based selection is integrated to give a visual attention mechanism that has multiple and hierarchical selectivity.

1 Introduction

Machine vision research has recently had an increased interest in modelling visual attention and a number of computable models of attention have been developed [8,13,1]. However, these models are all space-based and do not account for the findings from recent research on object-based attention (see [2,12] for object-based attention views). These space-based attention models may fail to work in environments that are cluttered or where objects overlap or share some common properties. Three different requirements of attention are immediately identifiable: 1) attention may need to work in discontinuous spatial regions or locations at the same time; 2) attention may need to select an object composed of different visual features but from the same region of space; 3) attention may need to select objects, locations, and/or visual features as well as their groupings for some structured objects. For applying attention mechanisms in real and normal scenes, a computational approach inspired by the alternative theory of object-based attention is necessary. In contrast to the traditional theory of space-based attention, object-based attention suggests that visual attention can directly select discrete objects rather than only and always continuous spatial locations within the visual field [4,6,12]. A complete computable model of object-based attention is still an open research area. Moreover, as suggested in [12], "Attention may well be object-based in some contexts, location-based in others, or even both at the same time." Inspired by this idea, here we present a "hierarchical selectivity" mechanism which is a part of our computable model of object-based attention (not published in this paper). This mechanism guides (covert) attentional movements to deal with multiple selectivity in a complicated scene. The objects of selection can be spatial locations, objects, features,

H.H. Bülthoff et al. (Eds.): BMCV 2002, LNCS 2525, pp. 427–438, 2002.

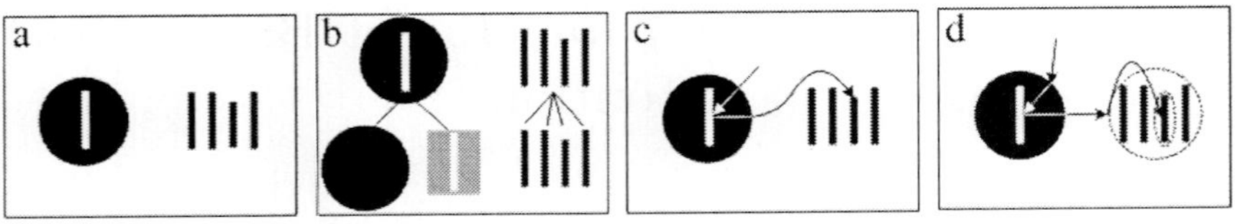

Fig. 1. An example of attention working on hierarchical grouping. a: the original display; b: Two hierarchical groupings obtained from the display c: Possible space-based attention movements; d: Possible object-based attention movements by hierarchical selectivity. Attention firstly selects the grouping consisting of the black circle and white bar and then shifts to the sub-grouping, i.e. white bar. The black bar belonging to another grouping including four black bars is attended after its parent is visited.

or their combinatorial groupings. Hierarchical selectivity works on the hierarchical structure of groupings competing for attention and navigates attention shifts between coarse groupings and fine groupings at single or multiple resolution scales. Stimulus-driven and top-down biasing are integrated together. Also, Winner-Take-All (WTA) and "inhibition of return" strategies are embedded within the mechanism.

In the following section, the background theory used to compute bottom-up salience is briefly introduced. Hierarchical selectivity is presented in Section 3 and experimental results are given in Section 4.

2 Background

The pivotal idea in our solution for object-based attention is the grouping-based salience computation and attention competition (see [14] for detailed implementation). The salience of a grouping measures how different this grouping contrasts with its surroundings and depends on various factors, such as feature properties, perceptual grouping, dissimilarity between the target and its neighbourhood [3, 10]. A grouping is a hierarchical structure of objects and space, which is also the common concept in the literature of perceptual grouping [11, p. 257-266]. A grouping may be a point, an object, a region, or a structured grouping. Figure 1 shows an example of attention working on hierarchical groupings. In this paper, we focus on presenting hierarchical selectivity and assume that the scene has already been segmented into groupings of similar colour, texture, intensity, etc. The input colour image is decomposed into 4 double-opponent colour (red R, green G, blue B, and yellow Y) pyramids, one intensity I pyramid and 4 or 8 orientation pyramids ($u(\theta)$ and $\theta = [0, \frac{\pi}{4}, \frac{\pi}{2}, \frac{3\pi}{4}]$ or $\theta = [0, \frac{\pi}{8}, \frac{\pi}{4}, \frac{3\pi}{8}, \frac{\pi}{2}, \frac{5\pi}{8}, \frac{3\pi}{4}, \frac{7\pi}{8}]$) to create feature maps using overcomplete steerable filters [7,8]. Then the salience of different groupings at different resolution scales is obtained from these feature maps by the computation of grouping salience. Finally, various groupings compete for visual attention based on the interaction between their bottom-up salience and top-down attentional setting through the hierarchical selectivity mechanism (see Section 3 for details). To save space, the following mathematical description of the grouping salience computation omits the expression of resolution scale. But note that the salience of all groupings is actually calculated at their current resolution and is dynamically varied with different scales and surroundings. Therefore the salience maps (including the salience maps for each grouping) are also multi-scale and dynamical. The discussion of recent psychophysical findings that support the salience computation approach (such as center-surround mechanisms used to encode the salience of visual objects, etc.) are omitted too to save space (see [9,14] for detailed and extensive discussion). Suppose $\Re$ is a grouping in an image at a given resolution, x, y are any two points in the image, (r, g, b) are the red, green, and blue colour components of the input image. Then the colour chromatic contrast ΔC and intensity contrast ΔI between x and y are calculated as:

$$\begin{aligned} \Delta C(x,y) &= \sqrt{\eta_{RG}^2 RG^2(x,y) + \eta_{BY}^2 BY^2(x,y)}; \\ \Delta I(x,y) &= |I_x - I_y|; \\ I_x &= \frac{(r_x + g_x + b_x)}{3}; \\ \eta_{BY} &= \frac{2\sqrt{B_x^2 + B_y^2 + Y_x^2 + Y_y^2}}{3 \times 255} \end{aligned} \tag{1}$$

$$\begin{aligned} \eta_{RG} &= \frac{R_x + R_y + G_x + G_y}{\sum\limits_{x,y} R_{x,y} + \sum\limits_{x,y} G_{x,y} + \sum\limits_{x,y} B_{x,y} + \sum\limits_{x,y} Y_{x,y}}; \\ RG(x,y) &= \frac{|(R_x - G_x) - (R_y - G_y)|}{2}; \\ BY(x,y) &= \frac{|(B_x - Y_x) - (B_y - Y_y)|}{2} \end{aligned} \tag{2}$$

$$\begin{aligned} R_x = r_x - (g_x + b_x)/2; \quad G_x = g_x - (r_x + b_x)/2; \\ B_x = b_x - (r_x + g_x)/2; \quad Y_x = (r_x + g_x)/2 - |r_x - g_x|/2 - b_x \end{aligned} \tag{3}$$

Let $S_{CI}(x, y)$ be the colour-intensity contrast and d_{gauss} be the Gaussian weighted distance between x and y, $\mathcal{NH}_{CI}$ be the neighbourhood surrounding x, $y_i \subset \mathcal{NH}_{CI}$ ($i = 1 \ldots n \times m - 1$, $n \times m$ is the input image size) be any neighbour. Then the colour-intensity salience $S_{CI}(x)$ of x is calculated by:

$$\begin{aligned} S_{CI}(x,y) &= \sqrt{\alpha \Delta C(x,y)^2 + \beta \Delta I(x,y)^2}; \; d_{gauss}(x,y) = \left(1 - \frac{\|x-y\|}{n-1}\right) e^{-\frac{1}{2\sigma^2}\|x-y\|^2}; \\ S_{CI}(x) &= \frac{\sum\limits_{i=1}^{n \times m - 1} S_{CI}(x, y_i) \cdot d_{gauss}(x, y_i)}{\sum\limits_{i=1}^{n \times m - 1} d_{gauss}(x, y_i)} \end{aligned} \tag{4}$$

where $||x - y||$ is the chessboard distance between x and y: $||x - y|| = MAX(|i - h|, |j - k|)$, (i, j), (h, k) are the coordinates of x, y in the current resolution image. The Gaussian scale σ is set to $\hat{n}/\rho$ and $\hat{n}$ is the largest of the width and length of the feature maps at the current resolution. ρ is a positive integer and generally $1/\rho$ may be set to a percentage of $\hat{n}$, such as 2%, 4%, 5%, or 20%, 25%, 50%, etc. α and β are weighting coefficients and we here set them to 1. Define the orientation contrast $C_O(x,y)$ between x and y as:

$$C_O(x,y) = d_{gauss}(x,y)\sin(\overline{\theta}_{x,y}); \qquad \overline{\theta}_{x,y} = \frac{\sum_{j=0}^{\zeta-1} j\varphi \sum_{i=0}^{\zeta-1} u_x(i\varphi)u_y((i\varphi + j\varphi) \mod \pi)}{\sum_{j=0}^{\zeta-1}\sum_{i=0}^{\zeta-1} u_x(i\varphi)u_y((i\varphi + j\varphi) \mod \pi)} \tag{5}$$

where *mod* is the standard modulus operator, ζ is the number of preferred orientations, $\varphi = \pi/\zeta$. When ζ is 4 or 8, φ is $\pi/4$ or $\pi/8$. Let $y_i, (i = 1 \ldots n_k)$ be a neighbour in the distance k neighbourhood $\mathcal{NH}_O(k)$ surrounding x (Distance k neighbourhood has $8k$ neighbours). The orientation contrast $\hat{C}_O(x, \mathcal{NH}_O(k))$ of x to its k-th neighbourhood is:

$$\hat{C}_O(x,\mathcal{NH}_O(k)) = \frac{\overline{C}_O(x,\mathcal{NH}_O(k))}{\xi + \omega_k} \qquad \overline{C}_O(x,\mathcal{NH}_O(k)) = \frac{1}{n_k}\sum_{y_i \in \mathcal{NH}_O(k)} C_O(x,y_i) \tag{6}$$

where $\omega_k = n_O - 1$ and n_O is the number of different directions within $\mathcal{NH}_O(k)$. ξ is a parameter used to prevent a zero denominator and usually set to 1.

Let m_r be the number of "rings" (one ring consists of the neighbours that have the same distance from their "center" x) in a neighbourhood and $d_{gauss}(k)$ be the Gaussian distance of the k-th neighbourhood to x, w_{ijk} be the value on k-th neighbour "ring" on θ_j orientation map of y_i, n_r be the number of "rings" in the whole neighbourhood of x. Then the orientation salience $S_O(x)$ of x to all of its neighbours is:

$$S_O(x) = \frac{\sum_k \hat{C}_O(x,\mathcal{NH}_O(k)) \cdot d_{gauss}(k)}{(\xi + \omega) \cdot m_r \cdot \sum_k d_{gauss}(k)}; \quad m_r = \sum_k 1 \text{ and } |\hat{C}_O(x,\mathcal{NH}_O(k))| > 0; \quad \omega = \sum_j \widehat{H}(\theta_j) \tag{7}$$

$$\widehat{H}(\theta) = \{\widehat{H}(\theta_j)\} = \left\{ \sum_k \frac{\left|H_k(\theta_j) - \overline{H}(\theta_j)\right|}{MAX\left\{H_k(\theta_j), \overline{H}(\theta_j)\right\}} \right\}; \tag{8}$$

$$\overline{H}(\theta) = \frac{1}{n_r}\sum_k H_k(\theta); \theta = [\theta_1 \ldots \theta_\zeta]; H_k(\theta) = \sum_{y_i \in \mathcal{NH}_O(k)} w_{ijk}(\theta_j, y_i)$$

Let x_i be an arbitrary component within a grouping $\Re$ (x_i may be either a point or a sub-grouping within $\Re$). Then visual salience S of a grouping $\Re$ is obtained from the following formula:

$$S(\Re) = \gamma_{CI}\sum_i S_{CI}(x_i) + \gamma_O \sum_i S_O(x_i) \tag{9}$$

where γ_{CI}, γ_O are the weighting coefficients for the colour-intensity, and orientation salience contributing to the grouping salience and i indicates all components in the grouping. More detailed mathematical descriptions for the computations of early feature extraction and grouping salience can be found in another paper [14].

3 Hierarchical Selectivity

Hierarchical selectivity operates on the interaction between bottom-up grouping salience and the top-down attentional setting. It is concerned with "where" attention is going next, i.e. the localization of the groupings to be attended, not "what" the identification of attended groupings are. Therefore, any top-down control related to recognizing objects or groupings is not considered here. The top-down attentional setting is used as a flag at each "decision point" (control whether to go to the next/finer level of a grouping or not) of each grouping in hierarchical selectivity, which is an intention request of whether to "view details" (i.e. view its sub-groupings at the current resolution scales or finer scales) of a current attended grouping. The competition for attention starts first between the groupings at the coarsest resolution. Temporary inhibition of the attended groupings can be used to implement inhibition of return for prohibiting attention from instantly returning to a previously attended winner. More elaborate implementations may introduce dynamic time control so that some previously-attended groupings can be visited again. But here we are only concerned that each winner is attended once. If continuing to check the current attended grouping, the competition for attention is triggered first among the sub-groupings that exist at the current resolution and then among the sub-groupings that exist at the next finer resolution. Sub-groupings at the finer resolution do not gain attention until their siblings at the coarser resolution are attended. If "no", attention will switch to the next potential winning competitor at the same or coarser scale level. By the force of WTA, the most salient sub-grouping wins visual attention. The priority order for generating the next potential winner is:

1. The most salient unattended grouping that is a sibling of the current attended grouping. The winning grouping has the same parent as the current attended grouping and both lie at the same resolution.
2. The most salient unattended grouping that is a sibling of the parent of the current attended grouping, if the above winner can not be obtained.
3. Backtracking continues if the above is not satisfied.

A more precise algorithmic description of hierarchical selectivity is given in Figure 2.

According to [4], [5], and [6], the competition for visual attention can occur at multiple processing levels from low-level feature detection and representation to high-level object recognition in multiple neural systems. Also, "attention is an emergent property of many neural mechanisms working to resolve competition for visual processing and control of behaviour" [4]. The above studies provide the direct support for the integrated competition for visual attention by binding object-selection, feature-selection and space-selection. The grouping-based saliency computation and hierarchical selectivity process proposed here, therefore, offer a possible mechanism for achieving this purpose.

Two goals can be achieved by taking advantage of hierarchical selectivity. One is that attention shifting from one grouping to another and from groupings/sub-groupings to sub-groupings/groupings can be easily carried out. Another is that

```
1. competition begins between the groupings at the coarsest resolution
2. if (no unattended grouping exists at the current resolution)    goto step 8;
3. unattended groupings at the current resolution are initialised to compete for attention based on
   their salience and top-down attentional setting;
4. attention is directed to the winner (the most salient grouping) by the WTA rule;
   set "inhibition of return" to the current attended winner;
5. if (the desired goal is reached)    goto step 10;
6. if ("view details" flag="no") (i.e. don't view details and shift the current attention)
     { set "inhibition" to all sub-groupings of the current attended winner; }
   if (the current attended winner has unattended brothers at the current resolution)
      { competition starts on these brothers; goto step 2 and replace the grouping(s) by these
        brothers; }    else goto step 9;
7. if ("view details" flag="yes") (i.e. continue to view the details of the current attended winner)
     if (the current attended winner has no sub-grouping at the current resolution)    goto step 8;
      else { competition starts on the winner's sub-groupings at the current resolution;
               goto step 2 and replace the grouping(s) by the winner's sub-groupings; }
8. if ((a finer resolution exists) and (unattended groupings/sub-groupings exist at that resolution))
     { competition starts on groupings/sub-groupings at the finer resolution;    goto step 2; }
9. if (the current resolution is not the coarsest resolution)
      { go back to the parent of the current attended winner and goto step 2; }
10. stop.
```

Fig. 2. The algorithmic description of hierarchical selectivity

the model may simulate the behaviour of humans observing something from far to near and from coarse to fine. Meanwhile, it also easily operates at a single resolution level. Support for this approach to hierarchical selectivity has been found in recent psychophysical research on object-based visual attention. It has been shown that features or parts of a single object or grouping can gain an object-based attention advantage in comparison with those from different objects or groupings. Also, visual attention can occur at different levels of a structured hierarchy of objects at multiple spatial scales. At each level all elements or features coded as properties of the same part or the whole of an object are facilitated in tandem (see [2] and [11, p. 547-549] for further discussion and detailed findings).

4 Experiments and Discussion

4.1 Grouping Effect and Hierarchical Selectivity on a Synthetic Display

Figure 3 shows a display in which the target is the only vertical red bar and no one of the bars has exactly the same colour as another bar. Three bars have the same exact orientation and others are separated by different oriented/colour surrounding bars. (Here we adopt the "orientation" of a bar following psychophysical experiments rather than the known concept in computer vision). If not using any grouping rule, each bar is a single grouping by itself. Then we obtain 36 single groupings. If segmenting the display by the bar's direction, the only structured grouping is formed by the 3 vertical bars (not including any black points in the background) which includes the target (forms one sub-grouping) and other two vertical green bars (forms another two-level sub-grouping). In this way, 34 groupings can be obtained in total: a structured three-level grouping and 33 single groupings formed by other bars respectively. The resulting salience maps

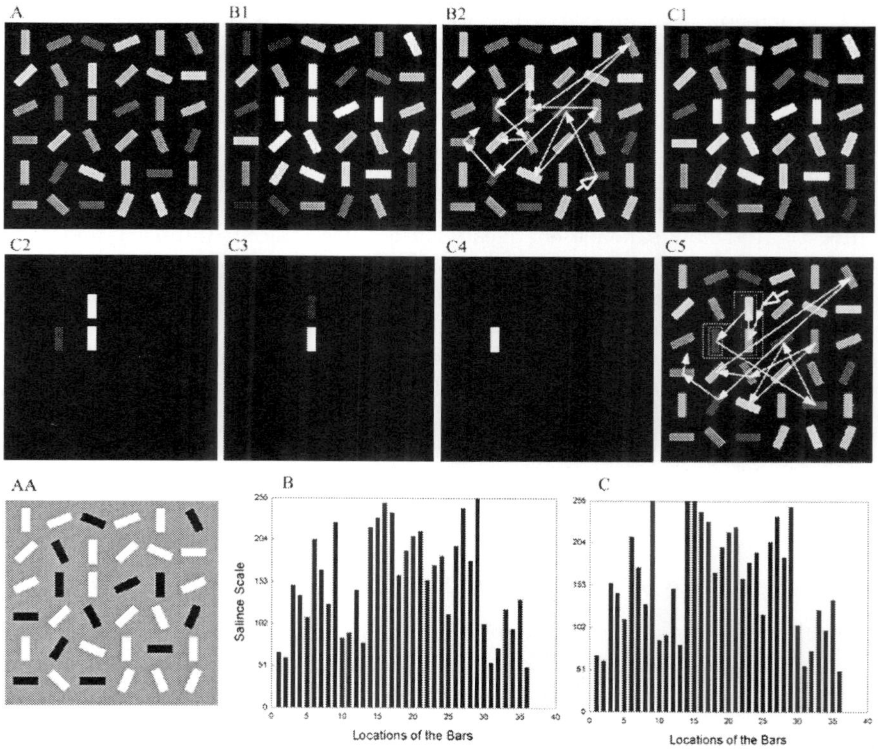

Fig. 3. An example for structured groups and hierarchical selection. In the display the target is the vertical bar at the third row and the second column. A: orignal colour display used in the experiment. AA: monochrome display for A to improve the visibility. All red, green bars are scaled to black, white bars respectively in the grey background. B1: salience map (in shades of grey) in the case of no grouping. B2: attention sequence of most salient bars for B1. C1: salience map in the case of grouping. C2, C3, C4: salience map of the grouped bars. C5: attention sequence of most salient bars for C1. B, C: histograms of B1, C1 respectively. The locations of the bars are simply encoded row column by number 1 to 36, such as the 6 bars in the first columns in B1 and C1 are identified 1 to 6 from left to right. Note the target (bar 9) is attended after 7 movements of attention in B2 but only 3 in C5.

of groupings and attention sequences for these two segmentations are given in Figure 3. The background (black pixels), colours, and orientations are all considered in the computation for salience. The top-down attentional setting is set to the free state, so this gives a pure bottom-up attention competition.

The results show different orders of paying attention to the targets. The target grouped with two green bars (see Figure 3 (C1), (C2), (C3), and (C4)) has an advantage in attracting attention much more quickly than the non-grouped target. When competition starts, the structured grouping of 3 vertical bars is the most salient and obtains attention firstly. Then the competition occurs within this grouping between the target and another sub-grouping formed by the two vertical but different colour bars. By competition, the target is attended after the two-level sub-grouping is attended. This grouping advantage for attentional competition has been confirmed by psychophysical research on object-based attention [2,12]. We have applied the model [14] to displays like Figure 3 where we investigated how salience changes with feature (colour, intensity and orientation) contrast, neighbourhood homogeneity and size, target distance, etc. The salience versus changed property curves are similar in shape to the comparable psychophysical results. Thus we claim the model has the desired heterarchical and hierarchical behaviours. More synthetic experiments for testing different behaviours of our model comparing results with those of human observers and other models can be seen elsewhere [14]. However, this research is not intended as a model of human attention, but instead aims at developing a machine vision attention system (inspired by recent psychophysical results) that has the high level of competence observed in humans.

4.2 Performance of Hierarchical Selectivity in a Natural Scene

Three colour images shown in Figure 4 are taken using different resolutions from far to near distance (64×64, 128×128, and 512×512) for the same outdoor scene. The scene is segmented (by hand) into 6 top groupings (identified by the black colour numbers: one object grouping 6 and five regions here) and 5 of them are hierarchically structured except grouping 4. In the coarsest image, only grouping 6 (one boat including two people) can be seen. In the finer image, sub-groupings 5-1 and 5-3 within top grouping 5 appear but they lose details at this resolution. The smallest boat (i.e. sub-grouping 5-2 of grouping 5) can only be seen at the finest resolution. The salience maps of groupings during attention competition are also briefly shown in Figure 4 where darker grey shades denote lower salience.

The competition first occurs among the top groupings at the coarsest scene. The most salient grouping 6 therefore gains attention. When giving a "yes" to the top-down attention setting ("view details" flag), attention will shift to the sub-groupings of 6. Two people and the boat then begin to compete for attention. If a "no" is given or after grouping 6 is attended, attention will shift to the next winner grouping 2. If a "yes" is given too to the "view details" flag of 2, attention will first select sub-grouping 2-1 and then shift to sub-grouping 2-2. After attending 2-2, if continuing to view the remainder of 2, attention will shift to the finer resolution to visit 2-3. When grouping 5 is attended, the lake (excluding grouping 6) is visited first and then attention shifts to the finer resolution scene where 5-1 and 5-3 start to compete for attention. In the case of giving a "yes" to the top-down flag of the winner 5-3, attention will shift to the finest resolution scene to check its details. Then attention goes back to the previous finer resolution scene and shifts to 5-1. After that, attention shifts again to the finest resolution scene. Thus the smallest boat 5-2 at the finest resolution is attended. Figure 4 shows the overall behaviour of attentional movements performed on the

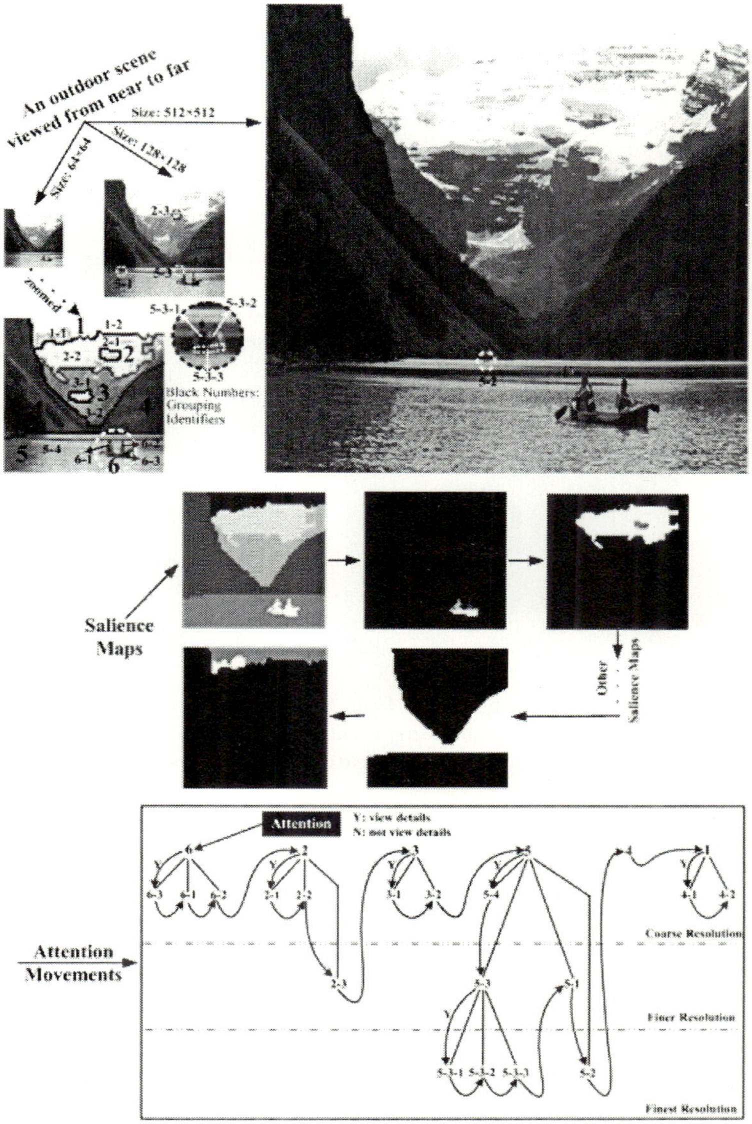

Fig. 4. An outdoor scene taken from different distances. The salience maps and identifiers (black numbers) of different groupings and their sub-groupings are also shown. The dotted circles are used to identify groupings but not their boundaries. The sequence of salience maps used for each selection of the next attended grouping is shown at the left bottom of the figure. Attention movements driven by hierarchical selectivity is shown at the right bottom using a tree-like structure.

scene. Using this same scene, when stronger and stronger noise was added above $\sigma = 17$ for Gaussian noise, the order of the attention movements changed. The above results clearly show hierarchical attention selectivity and appropriated believable performance in a complicated natural scene. In addition, although this model is aimed at computer vision applications, the results are very similar to what we might expect for human observers.

Fig. 5. An outdoor scene photographed from far and near distance respectively. The obtained images shown here are the same scene but different resolutions. The salience maps are shown too and the grey scales indicate the different salience of the groupings.

Hierarchical selectivity is a novel mechanism designed for shifting attention from one grouping to another or from a parent grouping to its sub-groupings as well as implementing attention focusing from far to near or from coarse to fine. It can work under both multiple (or variable) resolutions and single resolution environments. Here another outdoor scene (figure 5) is used to demonstrate the behaviour of hierarchical selectivity. In the scene, there are two groupings: a simple shack in the hill and a small boat including five people and a red box within this boat in a lake. The people, red box, and the boat itself constitute seven sub-groupings respectively for this structured grouping. The salience maps computed for these groupings are shown in Figure 5 and the sequence of attention deployments is shown in Figure 6. The attention visiting trajectory shown in Figure 6 reveals the reasonable movements of visual attention for this natural scene.

5 Conclusions and Future Research

Successful models of object-based attention require approaches different to the previous computable models of space-based attention (see [8] for a successful

Fig. 6. The attention movements implemented for the outdoor scene: solid arrows indicate attentional movements at fine resolution and hollow arrows denote attention shifts at coarse resolution.

computable model of space-based attention). The new mechanisms must consider the selections of objects and groupings, without losing the advantages of space-based attention, such as selectivity by spatial locations and by feature. A good solution should integrate object-based and space-based attention together in a combined framework so that the attention model can work in a dynamic and natural environment. In consequence, multiple (such as features, spatial locations, objects, and groupings) and hierarchical selectivity can be implemented to deal with the complex visual tasks. The presented mechanism of hierarchical selectivity in our object-based attention model shows performance similar to human behaviour and also explores details in a manner useful for machine vision systems. Further research will extend the scope of top-down attention setting, for example, to allow enhanced and suppressed top-down control as well as more elaborate designation of whether it is "valuable" or not to check sub-groupings according to the current visual task.

References

1. S. Baluja, and D. Pomerleau, "Dynamic relevance: Vision-based focus of attention using artificial neural networks," *Artificial Intelligence*, 97, pp. 381-395, 1997.
2. M. Behrmann, R. S. Zemel, and M. C. Mozer, "Occlusion, symmetry, and object-based attention: reply to Saiki (2000)," *Journal of Experimental Psychology: Human Perception and Performance*, 26(4), pp. 1497-1505, 2000.
3. C. Koch and S. Ullman, "Shifts in selective visual attention: towards the underlying neural circuity," *Human Neurobiology*, 4:481-484, 1985.
4. R. Desimone, and J. Duncan, "Neural mechanisms of selective visual attention," *Ann. Rev. Neurosci.*, 18, pp. 193-222, 1995.
5. R. Desimone, "Visual attention mediated by biased competition in extrastriate visual cortex," *Phil. Trans. R. Soc. Lond. B*, 353, pp. 1245-1255, 1998.
6. J. Duncan, "Converging levels of analysis in the cognitive neuroscience of visual attention," *Phil. Trans. R. Soc. Lond. B.*, 353, pp. 1307-1317, 1998.
7. H. Greenspan, S. Belongie, R. Goodman, P. Persona, S. Rakshit, and C. H. Anderson, "Overcomplete steerable pyramid filters and rotation invariance," In proc. IEEE Computer Vision and Pattern Recognition, pp. 222-228, Seattle, Washington, 1994.
8. L. Itti, C. Koch, and E. Niebur, "A model of saliency-based visual attention for rapid scene analysis," *IEEE Transactions on Pattern Analysis and Machine Intelligence*, 20(11), pp. 1254-1259, 1998.
9. L. Itti and C. Koch, "Salience-Based serach mechanism for overt and covert shifts of visual attention," 40(10-12):1489-1506, 2000.
10. S. Kastner and L. G. Ungerleider, "Mechanisms of visual attention in the human cortex," *Annu. Rev. Neurosci.*, 23:315-341, 2002.
11. S. E. Palmer, *Vision Science-Photons to Phenomenology*, Cambridge, MA: MIT Press, 1999.
12. B. J. Scholl, "Objects and attention: the state of the art," *Cognition,* 80, pp. 1-46, 2001.
13. J. K. Tsotsos, et al. "Modelling visual attention via selective tuning," *Artificial Intelligence*, 78, pp. 507-545, 1995.
14. Yaoru Sun and Robert Fisher, "Object-based visual attention for computer vision," submitted to *Artificial Intelligence.*

Attending to Motion: Localizing and Classifying Motion Patterns in Image Sequences

John K. Tsotsos[1], Marc Pomplun[2], Yueju Liu[1], Julio C. Martinez-Trujillo[1], and Evgueni Simine[1]

[1]Centre for Vision Research, York University, Toronto, Canada M3J 1P3
[2]Department of Computer Science, University of Massachusetts at Boston, Boston, MA 02125, USA

Abstract. The Selective Tuning Model is a proposal for modelling visual attention in primates and humans. Although supported by significant biological evidence, it is not without its weaknesses. The main one addressed by this paper is that the levels of representation on which it was previously demonstrated (spatial Gaussian pyramids) were not biologically plausible. The motion domain was chosen because enough is known about motion processing to enable a reasonable attempt at defining the feedforward pyramid. The effort is unique because it seems that no past model presents a motion hierarchy plus attention to motion. We propose a neurally-inspired model of the primate visual motion system attempting to explain how a hierarchical feedforward network consisting of layers representing cortical areas V1, MT, MST, and 7a detects and classifies different kinds of motion patterns. The STM model is then integrated into this hierarchy demonstrating that successfully attending to motion patterns, results in localization and labelling of those patterns.

1 Introduction

Attentive processing is a largely unexplored dimension in the computational motion field. No matter how sophisticated the methods become for extracting motion information from image sequences, it will not be possible to achieve the goal of human-like performance without integrating the optimization of processing that attention provides. Virtually all past surveys of computational models of motion processing completely ignore attention. However, the concept has crept into work over the years in a variety of ways.

One can survey the current computer vision literature and realize that attentive processing is not much of a concern. Many recent reviews of various aspects of motion understanding have not made any mention of attentive processing of any kind [1, 2, 3, 4, 5]. The review by Aggarwal and Cai [6] includes one example of work that uses motion cues to segment an object and to affix an attentional window on to it. This is a data-directed attentional tool. Gavrila's review [7] includes one example of where vision can provide an attentional cue for speech localization. Most of these cited papers make the claim that little or no work had been done on the topic of high level motion understanding previously (see [8] for a review that refutes this).

H.H. Bülthoff et al. (Eds.): BMCV 2002, LNCS 2525, pp. 439–452, 2002.

Many authors do not consider attention simply because of assumptions that eliminate the issue. An example of the kinds of assumptions that are typically made even in the best work follows [9]. The input to this system must satisfy the following: a) all frames in a given movie must contain the same number of figures; b) the figures in each frame must be placed in a one-to-one correspondence with figures in adjacent frames; and, c) the system must be given this correspondence as input. Others, such as in [10], assume that their algorithm starts off by being given the region of interest that corresponds to each object that may be moving. The processing that ensues is perhaps the best of its kind currently, but the algorithm critically depends on reasonable regions of interest and is not designed to find that region of interest either independently or concurrently as it processes the events in the scene. In a third example the values for the sensors are manually extracted by watching a video of the action and further, even determine the interval where every action and sub-action occurs [11]. The problem is not that any one effort makes these assumptions; the problem lies in the fact that it is now almost universal to assume the unreasonable. We are not trying to be critical of these authors; rather, the correct conclusion to draw from these comments is that we suggest a more balanced approach to the problem across the discipline, where at least some researchers study the attentive issues involved in a more general solution.

Attentive components have been included in systems not only through assumptions. At least three tools have appeared: the detection of salient tracking points/structures; search region predictions; and, Kalman filters and their extensions. Many examples have appeared [12, 13, 14, 15]. All are clearly strategies that help reduce search however, the overall result is an ad hoc collection of domain-specific methods.

A similar survey of computational neuroscience literature reveals many interesting motion models and better interest in motion attention. More discussion on these efforts appears later.

2 The Selective Tuning Model

Complexity analysis leads to the conclusion that attention must tune the visual processing architecture to permit task-directed processing [16]. In its original definition, [16], the Selective Tuning Model (STM), selection takes two forms: *spatial* selection is realized by inhibiting task-irrelevant locations in the neural network, and *feature* selection is realized by inhibiting the neurons that represent task-irrelevant features. When task constraints are available they are used to set priorities for selection; if not available, then there are default priorities (such as 'strongest response'). The two cornerstones of spatial and feature selection have since been experimentally supported [17, 18]. Only a brief summary is presented here since the model is detailed elsewhere [19].

The spatial role of attention in the image domain is to localize a subset of the input image and its path through the processing hierarchy such as to minimize any interfering or corrupting signals. The visual processing architecture is a pyramidal network composed of units receiving both feed-forward and feedback connections. When a stimulus is first applied to the input layer of the pyramid, it activates in a feed-forward manner all of the units within the pyramid to which it is connected. The result is the activation of an inverted sub-pyramid of units and we assume that the degree of unit activation reflects the goodness-of-match between the unit and the stimulus it represents.

Attentional selection relies on a hierarchy of winner-take-all (WTA) processes. WTA is a parallel algorithm for finding the maximum value in a set of variables, which was first proposed in this context by Koch and Ullman [20]. WTA can be steered to favor particular stimulus locations or features but in the absence of such guidance it operates independently. The processing of a visual input involves three main stages. During the first stage, a stimulus is applied to the input layer and activity propagates along feed-forward connections towards the output layer. The response of each unit depends on its particular selectivities, and perhaps also on a top-down bias for task-relevant qualities. During the second stage, a hierarchy of WTA processes is applied in a top-down, coarse-to-fine manner. The first WTA process operates in the top layer and covers the entire visual field at the top layer: it computes the unit or groups of contiguous units with the largest response in the output layer, that is, the *global winner*. In turn, the global winner activates a WTA amongst its input units in the layer immediately below. This localizes the largest response within the receptive field of the global winner. All of the connections of the visual pyramid that do not contribute to the winner are pruned (i.e., attenuated). This strategy of finding the winner within each receptive fields and then pruning away irrelevant connections, is applied recursively through the pyramid, layer by layer. Thus, the global winner in the output layer is eventually traced back to its perceptual origin in the input layer. The connections that remain (i.e., are not pruned) may be considered the *pass zone* of the attentional beam, while the pruned connections an *inhibitory zone* around that beam. A final feedforward pass then allows the selected stimulus to be processed by the network without signal interference from surrounding stimuli. This constitutes a single attentive processing cycle.

The processing exhibits serial search for displays with multiple objects using a simple inhibition of return mechanism, that is, the pass zone pathways are inhibited for one processing cycle so that in the next feedforward pass the second strongest responses form the global winner and the WTA hierarchy focuses in on the second strongest item in the display. The processing operates continuously in this manner

The selective tuning model was developed with the dual goals of computational utility and biological predictive power. The predictions (appearing mostly in [16, 19]) and supporting evidence are briefly described.

• An early prediction was that attention is necessary at any level of processing where a many-to-one mapping between neural processes is found. Further, attention occurs in all the areas in a coordinated manner. The prediction was made at a time when good evidence for attentional modulation was known for area V4 only [21]. Since then, attentional modulation has been found in many other areas both earlier and later in the visual processing stream, and that it occurs in these areas simultaneously [22]. Vanduffel et al. [23] have shown that attentional modulation appears as early as the LGN. The prediction that attention modulates all cortical and even subcortical levels of processing has been borne out by recent work from several groups [23, 24, 25].

• The notions of competition between stimuli and of attentional modulation of this competition were also early components of the model and these too have gained substantial support over the years [17, 22, 27].

• The model predicts an inhibitory surround that impairs perception around the focus of attention a prediction that seems to be gaining support, both psychophysically and neurophysiologically [23, 26, 28, 29, 30, 31].

• A final prediction is that latency of attentional modulations *decreases* from lower to higher visual areas. Although controversial, it seems that attentional effects do not appear until 150 ms after the onset of a stimulus in IT cortex [32] while in V1 they appear after 230 ms [33].

Additional predictions of the selective tuning model concern the form of spatial and temporal modulations of visual cortical responses around the focus of attention, and the existence of a WTA circuit connecting cortical columns of similar selectivity. The selective tuning model offers a principled solution to the fundamental problems of visual complexity, a detailed perceptual account of both the guidance and the consequences of visual attention, and a neurally plausible implementation as an integral part of the visual cortical hierarchy. Thus, the model "works" at three distinct levels – computational, perceptual, and neural – and offers a more concrete account, and far more specific predictions, than previous models limited to one of these levels.

Previous demonstrations of the Selective Tuning Model were not without their weaknesses. The main one addressed by this paper is that the levels of representation shown in [19] were not biologically plausible. Here, the motion domain is chosen in order to demonstrate that STM can indeed operate as desired with realistic representations because enough is known about motion processing to enable a reasonable attempt at defining the feedforward pyramid. In addition, the effort is unique because it seems that no past model presented a motion hierarchy plus attention to motion [34, 35, 36, 37, 38, 39, 40, 41, 42]. The remainder of this paper will focus on this issue.

3 The Feedforward Motion Pyramid

We propose a neurally-inspired model of the primate motion processing hierarchy. The model aims to explain how a hierarchical feed-forward network consisting of neurons in the cortical areas V1, MT, MST, and 7a of primates detects and classifies different kinds of motion patterns. At best, the motion model is a first-order one with much elaboration left for future work. Indeed, some of the previous motion models offer better sophistication at one or another level of processing; however, none cover all these levels and incorporate selective attentional processes. The primary goal is to demonstrate that the STM functions not only as previously demonstrated on Gaussian pyramids but also on a more biologically realistic representation.

Cells in *striate area V1* are selective for a particular local speed and direction of motion in at least three main speed ranges [43]. In the model, V1 neurons estimate local speed and direction in five-frame, 256x256 pixel image sequences using spatiotemporal filters (e.g., [44])[1]. Their direction selectivity is restricted to 12 distinct, Gaussian-shaped tuning curves. Each tuning curve has a standard deviation of 30º and represents the selectivity for one of 12 different directions spaced 30º apart (0º, 30º, …, 330º). V1 is represented by a 60x60 array of hypercolumns. The receptive

[1] The choices of parameters for sizes of representations, filters, etc. are mostly for convenience and variations in them has no effect on overall results intended by this demonstration.

fields (RFs) of V1 neurons are circular and homogeneously distributed across the visual field, with RFs of neighboring hypercolumns overlapping by 20%.

In *area MT* a high proportion of cells are tuned for a particular local speed and direction of movement, similar to direction and speed selective cells in V1 [45, 46]. A proportion of MT neurons are also selective for a particular angle between movement direction and spatial speed gradient [47]. Both types of neurons are represented in the MT layer of the model, which is a 30x30 array of hypercolumns. Each MT cell receives input from a 4x4 field of V1 neurons with the same direction and speed selectivity.

Neurons in *area MST* are tuned to complex motion patterns: expand or approach, contract or recede, rotation, with RFs covering most of the visual field [48, 49]. Two types of neurons are modeled: one type selective for translation (as in V1) and another type selective for spiral motion (clockwise and counterclockwise rotation, expansion, contraction and combinations). MST is simulated as a 5x5 array of hypercolumns. Each MST cell receives input from a large group (covering 60% of the visual field) of MT neurons that respond to a particular motion/gradient angle. Any coherent motion/gradient angle indicates a particular type of spiral motion.

Finally, *area 7a* seems to involve at least four different types of computations [50]. Here, neurons are selective for translation and spiral motion as in MST, but they have even larger RFs. They are also selective for rotation (regardless of direction) and radial motion (regardless of direction). In the simulation, area 7a is represented by a 4x4 array of hypercolumns. Each 7a cell receives input from a 4x4 field of MST neurons that have the relevant tuning. Rotation cells and radial motion cells only receive input from MST neurons that respond to spiral motion involving any rotation or any radial motion, respectively.

Fig. 1 shows the resulting set of neural selectivities that comprise the entire pyramidal hierarchy covering visual areas V1, MT, MST and 7a. It bears repeating that this should only be considered a first order model.

Fig. 2 shows the activation of neurons in the model as induced by a sample stimulus. Note that in the actual visualization different colors indicate the response to particular angles between motion and speed gradient in MT gradient neurons. In the present example, the gray levels indicate that the neurons selective for a 90° angle gave by far the strongest responses. A consistent 90° angle across all directions of motion signifies a pattern of clockwise rotation. Correspondingly, the maximum activation of the spiral neurons in areas MST and 7a corresponds to the clockwise rotation pattern (90° angle). Finally, area 7a also shows a substantial response to rotation in the medium-speed range, while there is no visible activation that would indicate radial motion.

Figures 3, 4, 5 and 6 provide additional detail required for explanation of Figures 1 and 2.

Fig. 1. The overall set of representations for the different types of neurons in areas V1, MT, MST, and 7a. Each rectangle represents a single type of selectivity applied over the full image at that level of the pyramid. Large grey arrows represent selectivity for direction. Coloured rectangels represent particular angles between motion and speed gradient. The three rectangles at each direction represent the three speed selectivity ranges in the model. In this way, each single 'sheet' may be considered an expanded view of the 'hypercolumns' in a visual area. In area V1, for example, direction and speed selectivities are represented by the single sheet of rectangles in the figure. In area MT, there are 13 sheets, the top one representing direction and speed selectivity while the remaining 12 represent the 12 directions of speed gradient for each combination of speed and direction ranges (Fig. 4 provides additional explanation of the speed gradient coding). MST units respond to patterns of motion – contract, recede, and rotate. This figure emphasizes the scale of the search problem faced by the visual system: to determine which responses within each of these representations belong to the same event.

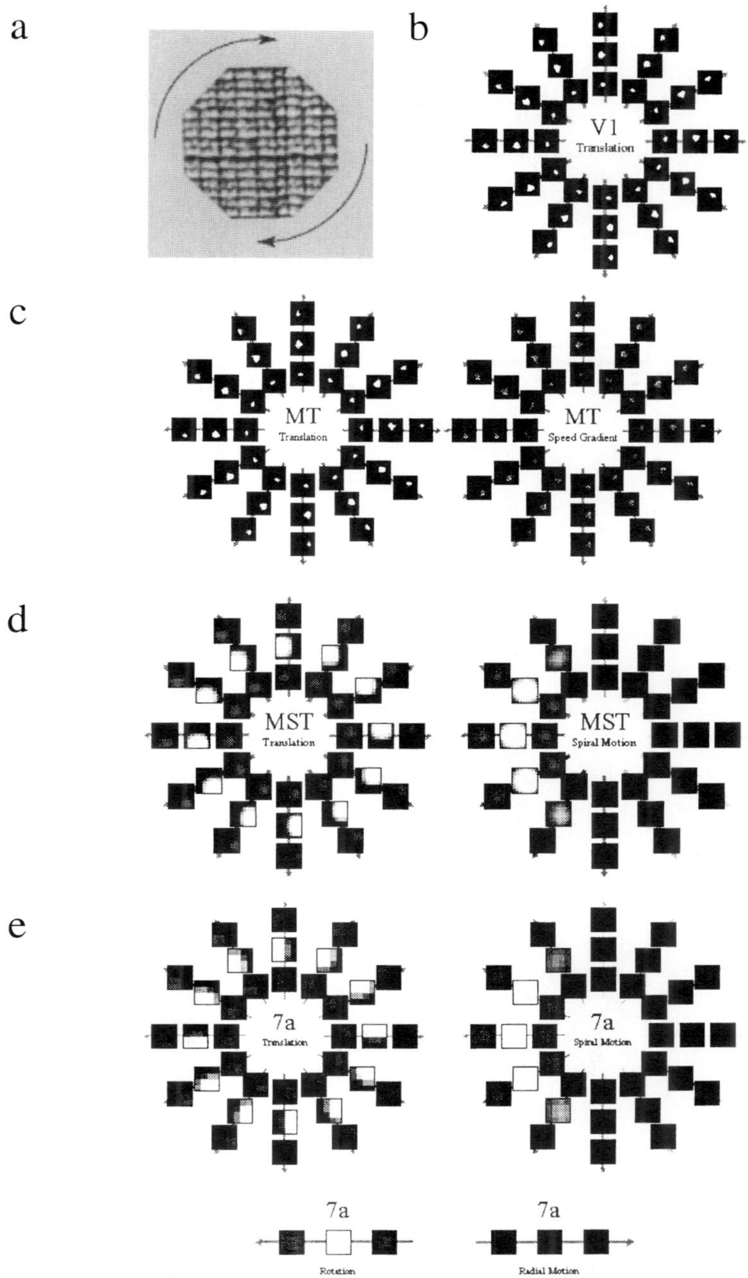

Fig. 2. The model's response to a clockwise rotating stimulus (a). Brightness indicates activation in areas V1, MT, MST, and 7a (b to e). Each of the figures represents the output of one representational sheet as depicted in Fig. 1. As is clear, even with a single object undergoing a single, simple motion, a large number of neurons respond.

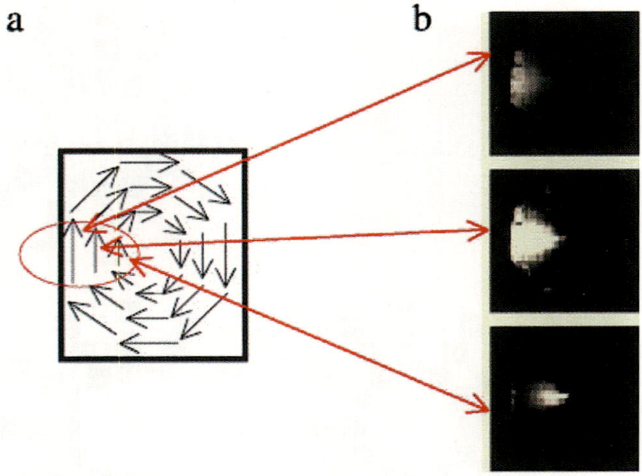

Fig. 3. Detail from area V1 in Fig. 2. (a) A depiction of the optic flow vectors resulting from the rotating motion. (b) The three speed selectivities for 'upwards' direction selectivity, the top being fast, the middle medium and the bottom low speed. The brightness shows responses across the sub-image due to the motion.

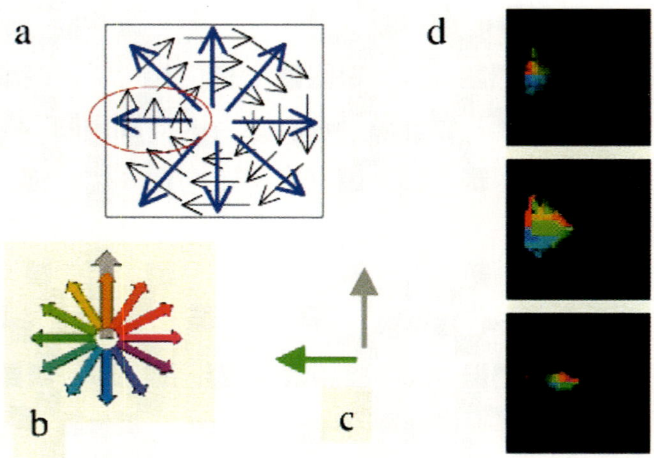

Fig. 4. Detail from area MT in Fig. 2. (a) The direction of the speed gradient for the rotating optic flow is shown with blue arrows. The red oval shows the only portion of the stimulus that activates the vertical motion selectivite neurons shown in (d), similarly to Fig. 3. (b) The colour coding used for the different directions of speed gradient relative to the direction of motion given by the gray arrow. (c) The particular 'ideal' speed gradient/direction tuning for the stimuli within the red oval. (d) Responses of the MT neurons with the tuning in (c) for three different speeds, the top being fast. The stimulus is the one shown in Fig. 2; responses are not perfectly clean (i.e., all light green in colour) due to the noise inherent in the processing stages.

Fig. 5. Detail from Fig. 2 for the neurons representing motion patterns in area MST. As is clear, the 'brightest' (strongest) responses occur in the representation of medium speed, clockwise rotation. There are many other responses some rather strong, through the sheet. It is the task of attentional selection to determine which responses are the correct ones to focus on in order to optimally localize the stimulus.

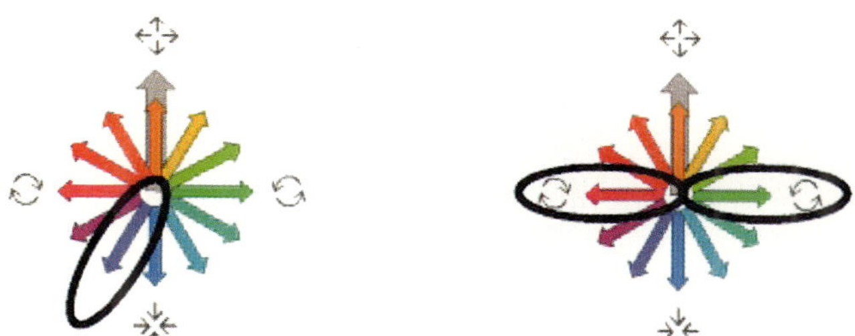

Fig. 6. Two examples of speed gradient coding. (a) If the stimulus object is both rotating clockwise and receding, the responses in area MT are coded blue. (b) If there are two objects in the image one rotating clockwise and the other counterclockwise, the responses in area MT will be coded light purple for the spatial extent of the former and light green for the spatial extent of the latter. Neurons in area MST spatially group common MT responses. The attention system then segments one from the other based on strength of response and motion type.

4 Using STM to Attend to and Localize Motion Patterns

Most of the computational models of primate motion perception that have been proposed concentrate on feedforward, classical types of processing and do not address attentional issues. However, there is strong evidence that the responses of neurons in areas MT and MST are modulated by attention [51]. As a result of the model's feedforward computations, the neural responses in the high- level areas (MST and 7a) roughly indicate the kind of motion patterns presented as an input but do not localize the spatial position of the patterns. The STM model was then applied to this feedforward pyramid, adding in the required feedback connections, hierarchical WTA processes, and gating networks as originally defined in [16, 19]. The result is that the model attends to object motion, whether it exhibits a single or concurrent motion, and serially focuses on each motion in the sequence in order of response strength.

The integration of the STM into this feedforward network requires one additional component not previously described. A *motion activity map* with the same size as a 7a layer is constructed after the feedforward processing. The value of a node in the activity map is a weighted sum of the activations of all 7a neurons at this position and it reflects the overall activation across all motion patterns. A location-based weighted sum is required in order to correctly detect single objects exhibiting simultaneous multiple motion types. This is not the same as the saliency map of [20] since it is not based on point locations and does not solely determine the attended region. Second, the hierarchical described earlier finds the globally most active region. Then for this region, two separate WTAs compete among all the translational motion patterns and spiral motion patterns respectively and thus result in a winning region is each representation. The remainder of processing proceeds as described in Section 2.0 for each of the winning patterns. Although not described here, the model also includes processes for tracking translating objects and for detecting onset and offset events (start and stop). Figures 7 and 8 present a 3D visualization of the model receiving an image sequence that contains an approaching object and a counterclockwise rotating object.

Fig. 7. The first image of the sequence used as demonstration in the next figure. The checkerboard is rotating while the box (in one of the authors' hands) is approaching the camera.

5 Discussion

Due to the incorporation of functionally diverse neurons in the motion hierarchy, the output of the present model encompasses a wide variety of selectivities at different resolutions. This enables the computer simulation of the model to detect and classify

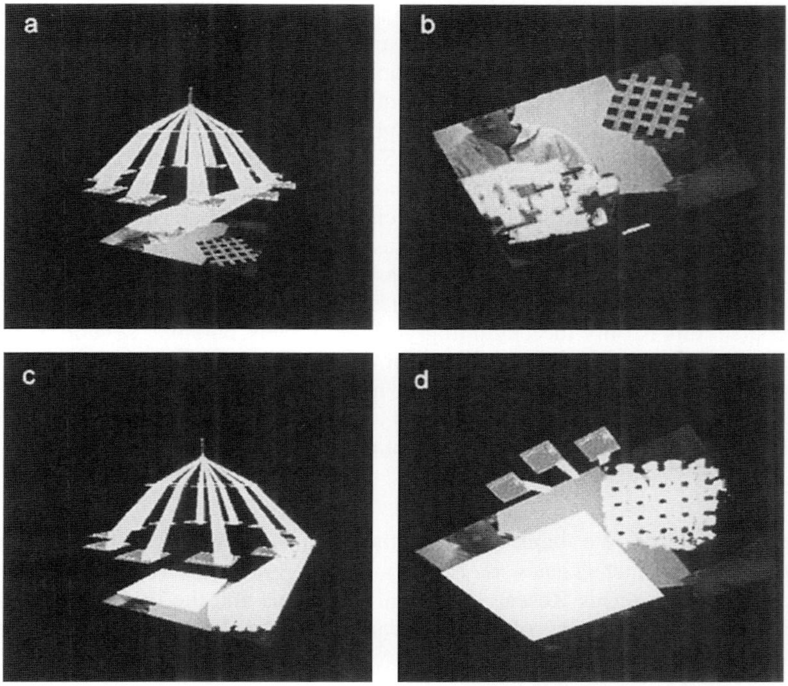

Fig. 8. Visualization of the attentional mechanism applied to an image sequence showing an approaching object and a counterclockwise rotating object at the same time. First, the model detects the approaching motion and attends to it (a); the localization of the approaching object can be seen most clearly from below the motion hierarchy (bright area in panel b). Then, the pass zone associated with it is inhibited, and the model attends to the rotating motion (c and d).

various motion patterns in artificial and natural image sequences showing one or more moving objects as well as single objects undergoing complex, multiple motions. Most other models of biological motion perception focus on a single cortical area. For instance, the models by Simoncelli and Heeger [34] and Beardsley and Vaina [35] are biologically relevant approaches that explain some specific functionality of MT and MST neurons, respectively, but do not include the embedding hierarchy in the motion pathway. On the other hand, there are hierarchical models for the detection of motion (e.g., [36, 37]), but unlike the present model they do not provide a biologically plausible version of the motion processing hierarchy.

Another strength of our model is its mechanism of visual attention. To our knowledge, there are only 2 other motion models employing attention for motion. The earlier one is due to Nowlan and Sejnowski [38]. There, processing that is much in the same spirit as ours but very different in form takes place. They compute motion energy with the goal of modelling MT neurons. This energy is part of a hierarchy of processes that include softmax for local velocity selection. They suggest that the selection permits processing to be focussed on the most reliable estimates of velocity. There is no top-down component nor full processing hierarchy. The relationship to attentional modulation that has been described after their model was presented of course is not developed; it does not appear to be within the scope of their model. The second one is from Grossberg, Mingolla, and Viswanathan [39], which is a motion integration and segmentation model for motion capture. Called the Formotion BCS model, their goal is to integrate motion information across the image and segment motion cues into a unified global percept. They employ models of translational processing in areas V1, V2, MT and MST and do not consider motion patterns. Competition determines local winners among neural responses and the MST cells encoding the winning direction have an excitatory influence on MT cells tuned to the same direction. A variety of motion illusions are illustrated but no real image sequences are attempted. Neither model has the breadth of processing in the motion domain or in attentional selection as the current work.

Of course, this is only the beginning and we actively pursuing several avenues of further work. The tuning characteristics of each of the neurons only coarsely model current knowledge of primate vision. The model includes no cooperative nor competitive processing among units within a layer. Experimental work examining the relationship of this particular structure to human vision is also on-going

Acknowledgements. We thank Albert Rothenstein for providing valuable comments on drafts of this paper. The work is supported by grants to JKT from the Natural Sciences and Engineering Research Council of Canada and the Institute for Robotics and Intelligent Systems, one of the Government of Canada Networks of Centres of Excellence.

References

1. Aggarwal, J.K., Cai, Q., Liao, W., Sabata, B. (1998). Nonrigid motion analysis: Articulated and elastic motion, *Computer Vision and Image Understanding 70(2)*, p142–156.
2. Shah, M., Jain, R. (1997). Visual recognition of activities, gestures, facial expressions and speech: an introduction and a perspective, in Motion-Based Recognition, ed. by M. Shah and R. Jain, Kluwer Academic Publishers.
3. Cedras, C., Shah, M. (1994). A survey of motion analysis from moving light displays, IEEE CVPR-94, Seattle, Washington, p214–221.
4. Cedras, C., Shah, M. (1995). Motion-based recognition: A survey, *Image and Vision Computing, 13(2)*, p129–155.
5. Hildreth, E. Royden, C. (1995). Motion Perception, in The Handbook of Brain Theory and Neural Networks, ed. by M. Arbib, MIT Press, p585–588.
6. Aggarwal, J.K., Cai, Q. (1999). Human motion analysis: A Review, *Computer Vision and Image Understanding 73(3)*, p428–440.
7. Gavrila, D.M. (1999). The visual analysis of human movement: A Survey, *Computer Vision and Image Understanding 73(1)*, p82–98.
8. Tsotsos, J.K., (2001). Motion Understanding: Task-Directed Attention and Representations that link Perception with Action, Int. J. of Computer Vision 45:3, 265–280.
9. Siskind, J. M. (1995). Grounding Language in Perception. *Artificial Intelligence Review 8*, p371–391.
10. Mann, R., Jepson, A., Siskind, J. (1997). The computational perception of scene dynamics, *Computer Vision and Image Understanding, 65(2)*, p113–128.

11. Pinhanez, C., Bobick, A. (1997). Human action detection using PNF propagation of temporal constraints, MIT Media Lab TR 423, April.
12. Tsotsos, J.K. (1980). A framework for visual motion understanding, Ph.D. Thesis, Dept. of Computer Science, University of Toronto, May.
13. Dickmanns, E.D., Wünsche, H.J. (1999). Dynamic vision for perception and control of motion, Handbook of Computer Vision and Applications Vol. 2, ed by B. Jahne, H. Haubeccker, P. Geibler, Academic Press.
14. Dreschler, L., Nagel, H.H. (1982). On the selection of critical points and local curvature extrema of region boundaries for interframe matching, Proc. Int. Conf. Pattern Recognition, Munich, p542–544.
15. Wachter, S., Nagel, H.H. (1999). Tracking persons in monocular image sequences, *Computer Vision and Image Understanding 74(3)*, p174–192.
16. Tsotsos, J.K. (1990). Analyzing vision at the complexity level, *Behavioral and Brain Sciences 13-3*, p423–445.
17. Desimone, R., Duncan, J., (1995). Neural Mechanisms of Selective Attention, *Annual Review of Neuroscience 18*, p193–222.
18. Treue, S., Martinez-Trujillo, J.C., (1999). Feature-based attention influences motion processing gain in macaque visual cortex, nayure, 399, 575–579.
19. Tsotsos, J.K., Culhane, S.M., Wai, W.Y.K., Lai, Y., Davis, N. & Nuflo, F. (1995). Modeling visual attention via selective tuning. Artificial Intelligence, 78, 507–545.
20. Koch, C., Ullman, S., (1985). Shifts in selective visual attention: Towards the underlying neural circuitry, *Hum. Neurobiology 4*, p219–227.
21. Moran, J., Desimone, R. (1985). Selective attention gates visual processing in the extrastriate cortex, *Science 229,* p782–784.
22. Kastner, S., De Weerd, P., Desimone, R., Ungerleider, L. (1998). Mechanisms of directed attention in the human extrastriate cortex as revealed by functional MRI, *Science 282*, p108–111.
23. Vanduffel, W., Tootell, R., Orban, G. (2000). Attention-dependent suppression of metabolic activity in the early stages of the macaque visual system, *Cerebral Cortex 10,* p109–126.
24. Brefczynski J.A., DeYoe E.A. (1999). A physiological correlate of the 'spotlight' of visual attention. *Nat Neurosci.* Apr;2(4), p370–374.
25. Gandhi S.P., Heeger D.J., Boynton G.M. (1999). Spatial attention affects brain activity in human primary visual cortex, *Proc Natl Acad Sci U S A*, Mar 16;96(6), p3314–9.
26. Smith, A., Singh, K., Greenlee, M. (2000). Attentional suppression of activity in the human visual cortex, *NeuroReport*, Vol 11 No 2 7, p271–277.
27. Reynolds, J., Chelazzi, L., Desimone, R. (1999). Competitive mechanisms subserve attention in macaque areas V2 and V4, *The Journal of Neuroscience, 19(5)*, p1736–1753.
28. Caputo, G., Guerra, S. (1998). Attentional selection by distractor suppression, *Vision Research 38(5)*, p669–689.
29. Bahcall, D., Kowler, E. (1999). Attentional interference at small spatial separations, *Vision Research 39(1)*, p71–86.
30. Tsotsos, J.K., Culhane, S., Cutzu, F. (2001). From theoretical foundations to a hierarchical circuit for selective attention, Visual Attention and Cortical Circuits, ed. by J. Braun, C. Koch and J. Davis, p285–306, MIT Press.
31. Cutzu, F., Tsotsos, J.K., The selective tuning model of visual attention: Testing the predictions arisiing from the inhibitory surround mechanism, Vision Research, (in press)
32. Chelazzi, L., Duncan, J., Miller, E., Desimone, R. (1998). Responses of neurons in inferior temporal cortex during memory-guided visual search, *J. Neurophysiology 80*, p2918–2940.
33. Roelfsema, P., Lamme, V., Spekreijse, H. (1998). Object-based attention in the primary visual cortex of the macaque monkey, *Nature 395*, p376–380.
34. Simoncelli, E.P. & Heeger, D.J. (1998). A model of neuronal responses in visual area MT. Vision Research, 38 (5), 743–761.

35. Beardsley, S.A. & Vaina, L.M. (1998). Computational modeling of optic flow selectivity in MSTd neurons. Network: Computation in Neural Systems, 9, 467–493.
36. Giese, M.A. (2000). Neural field model for the recognition of biological motion. Paper presented at the Second International ICSC Symposium on Neural Computation (NC 2000), Berlin, Germany.
37. Meese, T.S. & Anderson, S.J. (2002). Spiral mechanisms are required to account for summation of complex motion components. Vision Research, 42, 1073–1080.
38. Nowlan, S.J., Sejnowski, T.J., (1995). A Selection Model for Motion Processing in Area MT of Primates, The Journal of Neuroscience 15 (2), p 1195–1214.
39. Grossberg, S., Mingolla, E. & Viswanathan, L. (2001). Neural dynamics of motion integration and segmentation within and across apertures. Vision Research, 41, 2521–2553.
40. Zemel, R. S., Sejnowski, T.J., (1998). A Model for Encoding Multiple Object Motions and Self-Motion in area MST of Primate visual cortex, The Journal of Neuroscience, 18(1), 531–547.
41. Pack, C., Grossberg, S. Mingolla, E., (2001). A nerual model of smooth pursuit control and motion perception by cortical area MST, Journal of Cognitive Neuroscience, 13(1), 102–120.
42. Perrone, J.A. & Stone, L.S. (1998) Emulating the visual receptive field properties of MST neurons with a template model of heading estimation. *The Journal of Neuroscience*, 18, 5958–5975.
43. Orban, G.A., Kennedy, H. & Bullier, J. (1986). Velocity sensitivity and direction sensitivity of neurons in areas V1 and V2 of the monkey: Influence of eccentricity. Journal of Neurophysiology, 56 (2), 462–480.
44. Heeger, D.J. (1988). Optical flow using spatiotemporal filters. International Journal of Computer Vision, 1 (4), 279–302.
45. Lagae, L., Raiguel, S. & Orban, G.A. (1993). Speed and direction selectivity of Macaque middle temporal neurons. Journal of Neurophysiology, 69 (1), 19–39.
46. Felleman, D.J. & Kaas, J.H. (1984). Receptive field properties of neurons in middle temporal visual area (MT) of owl monkeys. Journal of Neurophysiology, 52, 488–513.
47. Treue, S. & Andersen, R.A. (1996). Neural responses to velocity gradients in macaque cortical area MT. Visual Neuroscience, 13, 797–804.
48. Graziano, M.S., Andersen, R.A. & Snowden, R.J. (1994). Tuning of MST neurons to spiral motions. Journal of Neuroscience, 14 (1), 54–67.
49. Duffy, C.J. & Wurtz, R.H. (1997). MST neurons respond to speed patterns in optic flow. Journal of Neuroscience, 17(8), 2839–2851.
50. Siegel, R.M. & Read, H.L. (1997). Analysis of optic flow in the monkey parietal area 7a. Cerebral Cortex, 7, 327–346
51. Treue, S. & Maunsell, J.H.R. (1996). Attentional modulation of visual motion processing in cortical areas MT and MST. Nature, 382, 539–541.

A Goal Oriented Attention Guidance Model

Vidhya Navalpakkam and Laurent Itti

Departments of Computer Science, Psychology and Neuroscience Graduate Program
University of Southern California – Los Angeles, CA 90089
{navalpak,itti}@usc.edu

Abstract. Previous experiments have shown that human attention is influenced by high level task demands. In this paper, we propose an architecture to estimate the task-relevance of attended locations in a scene. We maintain a task graph and compute relevance of fixations using an ontology that contains a description of real world entities and their relationships. Our model guides attention according to a topographic attention guidance map that encodes the bottom-up salience and task-relevance of all locations in the scene. We have demonstrated that our model detects entities that are salient and relevant to the task even on natural cluttered scenes and arbitrary tasks.

1 Introduction

The classic experiment of Yarbus illustrates how human attention varies with the nature of the task [17]. In the absence of task specification, visual attention seems to be guided to a large extent by bottom-up (or image-based) processes that determine the salience of objects in the scene [11,6]. Given a task specification, top-down (or volitional) processes set in and guide attention to the relevant objects in the scene [4,1]. In normal human vision, a combination of bottom-up and top-down influences attract our attention towards salient and relevant scene elements. While the bottom-up guidance of attention has been extensively studied and successfully modelled [13,16,14,8,5,6], little success has been met with understanding the complex top-down processing in biologically-plausible computational terms.

In this paper, our focus is to extract all objects in the scene that are relevant to a given task. To accomplish this, we attempt to solve partially the bigger and more general problem of modelling the influence of high-level task demands on the spatiotemporal deployment of focal visual attention in humans. Our starting point is our biological model of the saliency-based guidance of attention based on bottom-up cues [8,5,6]. At the core of this model is a two-dimensional topographic saliency map [9], which receives input from feature detectors tuned to color, orientation, intensity contrasts and explicitly encodes the visual salience of every location in the visual field. It biases attention towards focussing on the currently most salient location. We propose to extend the notion of saliency map by hypothesizing the existence of a topographic task-relevance map, which explicitly encodes the relevance of every visual location to the current task. In the proposed model, regions in the task-relevance map are activated top-down, corresponding to objects that have been attended to and recognized as being relevant. The final guidance of attention is derived from the activity in a further explicit topographic map, the attention guidance

H.H. Bülthoff et al. (Eds.): BMCV 2002, LNCS 2525, pp. 453–461, 2002.

map, which is the pointwise product of the saliency and task-relevance maps. Thus, at each instant, the model fixates on the most salient and relevant location in the attention guidance map.

Our model accepts a question such as "who is doing what to whom" and returns all entities in the scene that are relevant to the question. To focus our work, we have not for the moment attacked the problem of parsing natural-language questions. Rather, our model currently accepts task specification as a collection of object, subject and action keywords. Thus, our model can be seen as a question answering agent.

2 Related Work

Attention and identification have been extensively studied in the past. A unique behavioral approach to attention is found in [12] where the authors model perception and cognition as behavioral processes. They guide attention using internal models that store the sequence of eye movements and expected image features at each fixation. Their main thrust is towards object recognition and how attention is modulated in the process of object recognition. In contrast, we model human attention at a level higher than object recognition.

The Visual Translator (VITRA) [3] is a fine example of a real time system that interprets scenes and generates a natural language description of the scene. Their low level visual system recognises and tracks all visible objects and creates a geometric representation of the perceived scene. This intermediate representation is then analysed during high level scene analysis to evaluate spatial relations, recognise interesting motion events, and incrementally recognise plans and intentions. In contrast to VITRA, we track only those objects and events that we expect to be relevant to our task, thus saving enormously on computation complexity. The drawback of the VITRA project is its complexity that prevents it from being extended to a general attention model. Unlike humans that selectively perceive the relevant objects in the scene, VITRA attends to *all* objects and reports only relevant ones.

A good neural network model for covert visual attention has been proposed by Van der Laar [15]. Their model learns to focus attention on important features depending on the task. First, it extracts the feature maps from the sensory retinal input and creates a priority map with the help of an attentional network that gives the top down bias. Then, it performs a self terminating search of the saliency map in a manner similar to our salience model [6]. However, this system limits the nature of its tasks to pyschophysical search tasks that primarily involve bottom-up processes and are already fulfilled by our salience model successfully [7] (using databases of sample traffic signs, soda cans or emergency triangles, we have shown how batch training of the saliency model through adjustment of relative feature weights improves search times for those specific objects).

In [10], the authors propose a real time computer vision and machine learning system to model and recognize human behaviors. They combine top-down with bottom-up information in a closed feedback loop, using a statistical bayesian approach. However, this system focusses on detecting and classifying human interactions over an extended period of time and thus is limited in the nature of human behavior that it deals with. It

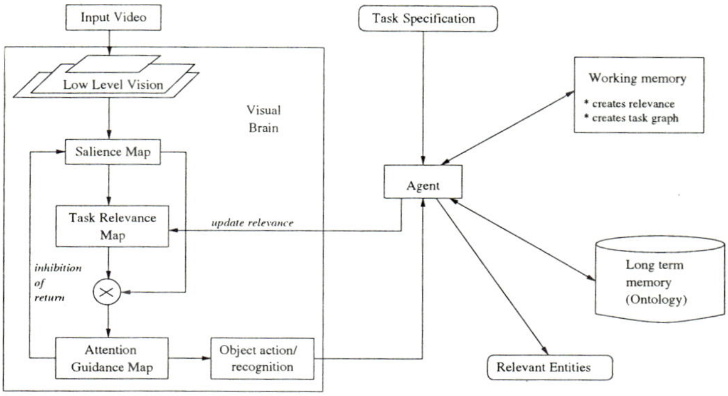

Fig. 1. An overview of our architecture

lacks the concept of a task/goal and hence does not attempt to model any goal oriented behavior.

3 Architecture

Our attention model consists of 4 main components: the visual brain, the working memory, the long term memory (LTM) and the agent. The visual brain maintains three maps, namely the salience map, task-relevance map and attention guidance map. The salience map (SM) is the input scene calibrated with salience at each point. Task-Relevance Map (TRM) is the input scene calibrated with the relevance at each point. Attention Guidance Map (AGM) is computed as the product of SM and TRM. The working memory (WM) creates and maintains the task graph that contains all entities that are expected to be relevant to the task. In order to compute relevance, the WM seeks the help of the long term memory that contains knowledge about the various real-world and abtract entities and their relationships. The role of the agent is to simply relay information between the visual brain and the WM; WM and the LTM. As such, its behavior is fairly prototyped, hence the agent should not be confused with a homunculus.

The schema of our model is as shown in figure 1. The visual brain receives the input video and extracts all low level features. To achieve bottom-up attention processing, we use the salience model previously mentioned, yielding the SM [8,5,6]. Then, the visual brain computes the AGM and chooses the most significant point as the current fixation. Each fixation is on a scene segment that is approximately the size of the attended object [2]. The object and action recognition module is invoked to determine the identity of the fixation. Currently, we do not yet have a generic object recognition module; it is done by a human operator. The agent, upon receiving the object identity from the visual brain, sends it to the WM. The WM in turn communicates with the LTM (via the agent) and determines the relevance of the current fixation. The estimated relevance of the current fixation is used to update the TRM . The current fixation is inhibited from returning in the SM. This is done to prevent the model from fixating on the same point continuously. The visual brain computes the new AGM and determines the next fixation. This process

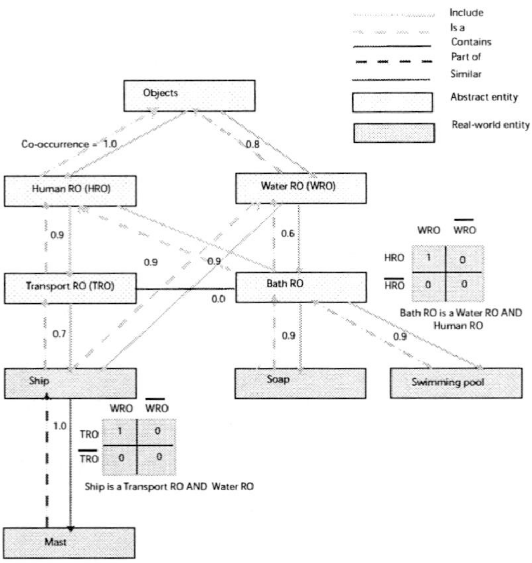

Fig. 2. A sample object ontology is shown. The relations include *is a*, *includes*, *part of*, *contains*, *similar*, *related*. While the first five relations appear as edges within a given ontology, the *related* relation appears as edges that connect the three different ontologies. The relations *contains* and *part of* are complementary to each other as in *Ship contains Mast*, *Mast is part of Ship*. Similarly, *is a* and *includes* are complementary. The co-occurrence measure is shown on each edge and the conjunctions, disjunctions are shown using the truth tables.

runs in a loop until the video is exhausted. Upon termination, the TRM is examined to find all the relevant entities in the scene.

The following subsections describe the important new components of our model in detail. The basic saliency mechanism has been described elsewhere [8,5,6].

3.1 LTM

The LTM acts as the knowledge base. It contains the entities and their relationships. Thus, for technical purposes, we refer to it as ontology from now on. As stated earlier, our model accepts task specification in the form of object, subject and action keywords. Accordingly, we have the object, subject and action ontology. In our current implementation, our ontology focusses primarily on human-related objects and actions. Each ontology is represented as a graph with entities as vertices and their relationships as edges. Our entities include real-world concepts as well as abstract ones. We maintain extra information on each edge, namely the granularity and the co-occurrence. Granularity of an edge ($g(u,v)$ where (u,v) is an edge) is a static quantity that is uniquely determined by the nature of the relation. The need for this information is illustrated with an example. While looking for the hand, fingers are considered more relevant than man because $g(hand, fingers) > g(hand, man)$. Co-occurrence of an edge ($c(u,v)$) refers to the probability of joint occurrence of the entities connected by the given edge. We illustrate the need for this information with another example. While looking for the hand, we consider pen to be more relevant than leaf because $c(hand, pen) > c(hand, leaf)$. Each entity in the ontology maintains a list of properties apart from the list of all its

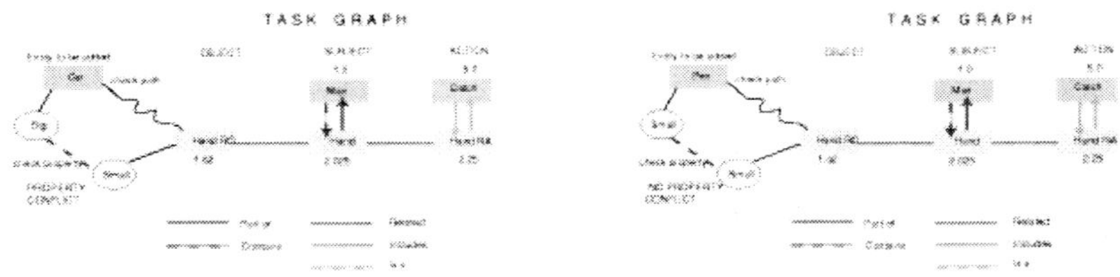

Fig. 3. To estimate the relevance of an entity, we check the existence of a path from entity to the task graph and check for property conflicts. While looking for a hand related object that is small and holdable, a big object like car is considered irrelevant; whereas a small object like pen is considered relevant.

neighbours. These properties may also serve as cues to the object recognition module. To represent conjunctions and disjunctions or other complicated relationships, we maintain truth tables that store probabilities of various combinations of parent entities. An example is shown in figure 3.

3.2 WM

The WM estimates the relevance of a fixation to the given task. This is done in two steps. The WM checks if there exists a path from the fixation entity to the entities in the task graph. If yes, the nature of the path tells us how the fixation is related to the current task graph. If no such path exists, we declare that the current fixation is irrelevant to the task. This relevance check can be implemented using a breadth first search algorithm. The simplicity of this approach serves the dual purpose of reducing computation complexity (order of number of edges in task graph) and still keeping the method effective. In the case of object task graph, we perform an extra check to ensure that the properties of the current fixation are consistent with the object task graph (see figure 3). This can be implemented using a simple depth first search and hence, the computation complexity is still in the order of the number of edges in task graph which is acceptable.

Once a fixation is determined to be relevant, its exact relevance needs to be computed. This is a function of the nature of relations that connect the fixation entity to the task graph. It is also a function of the relevance of neighbours of the fixation entity that are present in the task graph. More precisely, we are guided by the following rules: the mutual influence on relevance between any two entities u and v decreases as a function of their distance (modelled by a $decay\_factor$ that lies between 0 and 1). The influence depends directly on the nature of the edge (u, v) that is in turn determined by the granularity ($g(u, v)$) and co-occurrence measures ($c(u, v)$). Thus we arrive at the following formula for computing relevance (R).

$$R_v = \max_{u:\ (u,v)\ is\ an\ edge} (R_u * g(u, v) * c(u, v) * decay\_factor) \quad (1)$$

The relevance of a fixation depends on the entities present in the task graph. Hence, an important phase is the creation of the intial task graph. The initial task graph consists

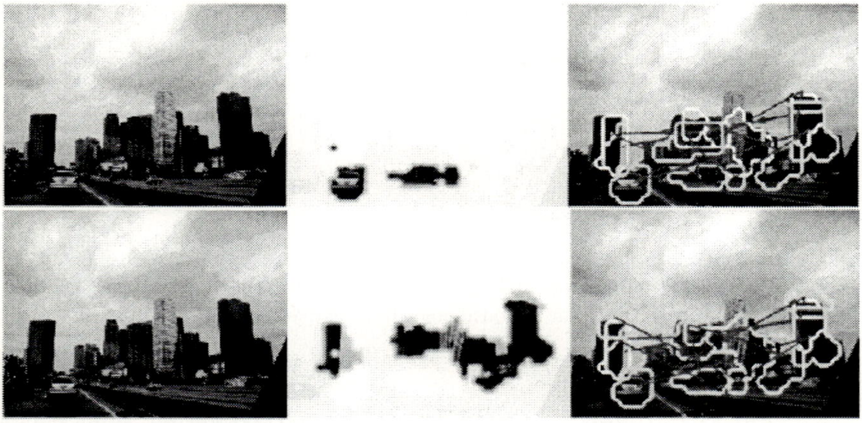

Fig. 4. In the figure, the first column shows the original scene, followed by the TRM (locations relevant to the task) and finally, the attentional trajectory. The shapes represent fixations where each fixation is on a scene segment that is approximately the size of the object. The human operator recognized fixations as car, building, road or sky. When asked to find the cars in the scene, the model displayed results as shown in the first row. When asked to find the buildings in the scene, the model's results were as shown in the second row.

of the task keywords. For instance, given a task specification such as "what is John catching"; we have "John" as the subject keyword and "catch" as the action keyword. After adding these keywords to the task graph, we further expand the task graph through the "is a " relations. Our new task graph contains "John is a man", "catch is a hand related action". As a general rule, upon addition of a new entity into the task graph, we expand it to related entities. Here, we expand the initial task graph to "hand related action is related to hand and hand related object". Thus even before the first fixation, we have an idea about what entities are expected to be relevant. Once the initial task graph is formed, the model fixates and the WM finds the relevance of the new fixation based on the techniques discussed above. Upon addition of every entity into the task graph, its relevance is propagated to its neighbours.

4 Results

We tested our model on arbitrary scenes including natural cluttered scenes. To verify the model, we ran it on several images asking different questions on the same image and the same question on different images. On the same scene, our model showed different entities to be relevant based on the task specification. Two such examples are illustrated here. On a city scene, we asked the model to find the cars. Without any prior knowledge of a city scene, our model picked the relevant portions of the scene. On the same scene, when the model was asked to find the buildings, it attended to all the salient features in the buildings and determined the roads and cars to be irrelevant (see figure 4). On a natural cluttered scene, we asked the model to determine the faces of people in the scene

Fig. 5. In the figure, the first column is the original image, followed by the TRM after five attentional shifts and the final TRM after twenty attentional shifts. When asked to find the faces of people in the scene, the model displayed results as shown in the first row. When asked to determine what the people were eating, the model's results were as shown in the second row. The human operator recognized fixations as some human body part (face, leg, hand etc) or objects such as bottle, chandelier, plate, window, shelf, wall, chair, table.

and find what they were eating. As expected, the model showed that the relevance of entities in the scene varied with the nature of the task. For the first task, the model looked for human faces and consequently, it marked human body parts as relevant and other objects as irrelevant. While in the second task, the model looked for hand related objects near the human faces and hands to determine what the people were eating (see figure 5). Thus, even in arbitrary cluttered scenes, our model picks up the entities relevant to the current task.

5 Discussion and Outlook

Our broader goal is to model how internal scene representations are influenced by current behavioral goals. As a first step, we estimate the task-relevance of attended locations. We maintain a task graph in working memory and compute relevance of fixations using an ontology that contains a description of worldly entities and their relationships. At each instant, our model guides attention based on the salience and relevance of entities in the scene. At this infant stage, most of the basic components of our proposed architecture are in place and our model can run on arbitray scenes and detect entities in the scene that are relevant to arbitrary tasks.

Our approach directly contrasts with previous models (see section 2) that scan the entire scene, track all objects and events and subsequently analyze the scene to finally determine the task-relevance of various objects. Our aim is to prune the search space, thereby performing as few object identifications and attentional shifts while trying to analyse the scene. Towards this end, our salience model serves as a first filtration phase where we filter out all non salient locations in the scene. As a second phase of filtration, we attempt to further prune the search space by determining which of these salient locations is relevant to the current task. Thus, our approach is to perform minimal attentional shifts and to incrementally build up knowledge of the scene in a progressive manner.

At this preliminary stage, the model has several limitations. It cannot yet make directed attentional shifts, nor does it support instantiation. In future, we plan to expand the ontology to include more real-world entities and model complex facts. We also plan to allow instantiation such as "John is an instance of a man"; where each instance is unique and may differ from each other. Including directed attentional shifts into our model would require that spatial relations also be included in our ontology (e.g., look up if searching for a face but found a foot) and would allow for more sophisticated top-down attentional control. Knowledge of such spatial relationships will also help us prune the search space by filtering out most irrelevant scene elements (e.g., while looking for John, if we see Mary's face, we can also mark Mary's hands, legs etc are irrelevant provided we know the spatial relationships). Several models already mentioned provide an excellent starting point for this extension of our model [12]. Finally, there is great opportunity within our new framework for the implementation of more sophisticated rules for determining the next shift of attention based on task and evidence accumulated so far. This in turn will allow us to compare the behavior of our model against human observers and to obtain a greater understanding of how task demands influence scene analysis in the human brain.

Acknowledgements. We would like to thank all ilab members for their help and suggestions. This research is supported by the Zumberge Faculty Innovation Research Fund.

References

1. M Corbetta, J M Kincade, J M Ollinger, M P McAvoy, and G L Shulman. Voluntary orienting is dissociated from target detection in human posterior parietal cortex [published erratum appears in nat neurosci 2000 may;3(5):521]. *Nature Neuroscience*, 3(3):292–297, Mar 2000.
2. D Walther, L Itti, M Reisenhuber, T Poggio, C Koch. Attentional Selection for Object Recognition - a Gentle Way. *BMCV2002*, in press.
3. Gerd Herzog and Peter Wazinski. VIsual TRAnslator: Linking perceptions and natural language descriptions. *Artificial Intelligence Review*, 8(2-3):175–187, 1994.
4. J B Hopfinger, M H Buonocore, and G R Mangun. The neural mechanisms of top-down attentional control. *Nature Neuroscience*, 3(3):284–291, Mar 2000.
5. L. Itti and C. Koch. A saliency-based search mechanism for overt and covert shifts of visual attention. *Vision Research*, 40(10-12):1489–1506, May 2000.
6. L. Itti and C. Koch. Computational modeling of visual attention. *Nature Reviews Neuroscience*, 2(3):194–203, Mar 2001.
7. L. Itti and C. Koch. Feature Combination Strategies for Saliency-Based Visual Attention Systems. *Journal of Electronic Imaging*, 10(1):161-169, Jan 2001.
8. L. Itti, C. Koch, and E. Niebur. A model of saliency-based visual attention for rapid scene analysis. *IEEE Transactions on Pattern Analysis and Machine Intelligence*, 20(11):1254–1259, Nov 1998.
9. C Koch and S Ullman. Shifts in selective visual attention: towards the underlying neural circuitry. *Human Neurobiology*, 4(4):219–27, 1985.

10. Nuria M. Oliver, Barbara Rosario, and Alex Pentland. A bayesian computer vision system for modeling human interactions. *IEEE Transactions on Pattern Analysis and Machine Intelligence*, 22(8):831–843, 2000.
11. D. Parkhurst, K. Law, and E. Niebur. Modeling the role of salience in the allocation of overt visual attention. *Vision Research*, 42(1):107–123, Jan 2002.
12. I. A. Rybak, V. I. Gusakova, A.V. Golovan, L. N. Podladchikova, and N. A. Shevtsova. A model of attention-guided visual perception and recognition. *Vision Research*, 38:2387–2400, 1998.
13. A M Treisman and G Gelade. A feature-integration theory of attention. *Cognitive Pyschology*, 12(1):97–136, Jan 1980.
14. J K Tsotsos. Computation, pet images, and attention. *Behavioral and Brain Sciences*, 18(2):372, 1995.
15. van de P. Laar, T. Heskes, and S. Gielen. Task-dependent learning of attention. *Neural Networks*, 10(6):981–992, 1997.
16. J M Wolfe. Visual search in continuous, naturalistic stimuli. *Vision Research*, 34(9):1187–95, May 1994.
17. A Yarbus. *Eye Movements and Vision.* Plenum Press, New York, 1967.

Visual Attention Using Game Theory

Ola Ramström and Henrik I. Christensen

Computational Vision and Active Perception
Numerical Analysis and Computer Science
Royal Institute of Technology
SE-100 44 Stockholm, Sweden
{olar,hic}@cvap.kth.se
http://www.bion.kth.se/

Abstract. A system using visual information to interact with its environment, e.g. a robot, needs to process an enormous amount of data. To ensure that the visual process has tractable complexity visual attention plays an important role.
A visual process will always have a number of implicit and explicit tasks that defines its purpose. The present document discusses attention mechanisms for selection of visual input to respond to the current set of tasks. To provide a truly distributed approach to attention it is suggested to model the control using game theory, in particular coalition games.

1 Introduction

The amount of visual information available to a system is enormous and in general it is computationally impossible to process all of this information bottom-up [10]. At the same time it is essential to note that a vision system is of limited interest when considered in isolation. A system will always have a set of tasks that defines the purpose of the visual process. To ensure that the process has tractable computational properties visual attention plays a crucial role in terms of selection of visual information. Visual attention is divided into two different components: *overt attention* – the control of the gaze direction and *covert attention* the selection of features, and internal control of processes. The present document only discusses covert attention.

The literature contains a number of different models for visual attention, a good overview of models can be found in [6]. An important goal of visual attention is to focus on the most important information given the systems current goals/tasks. To accommodate this the system must select the most relevant information for further processing. An obvious question is: how can the system choose the most important information without prior processing of all information to determine the utility of different cues. If attention is engaged early in the visual chain it is necessary to consider how models of objects, situations and tasks can be utilized to "predict" the value of different cues (property selection) and the approximate location of such cues (spatial selection). The literature contains at least three major theories of visual attention: i) The Spotlight

H.H. Bülthoff et al. (Eds.): BMCV 2002, LNCS 2525, pp. 462–471, 2002.

Metaphor [7] models selection as highlighting of a particular region while other regions are suppressed, i.e. a particular region or set of cues stand out. Once a region has been processed the spotlight can be moved to a new area through a disengage/move/engage process. This model has also been extensive studied computationally by [4] and [11]. ii) The Zoom Lens metaphor [2], where a zoom type mechanism is used for selection of the scale (the size of the field of processing), i.e. the "natural" scale is selected and one cannot attend to a leaf and the overall tree structure at the same time. iii) Object based approaches where selection is closely tied to the object/event of interest. While i) and ii) are directly related to selection of spatial regions iii) is tied to objects, parts, context, or relations. Object based approaches have been reported by [1], and evidence in association with tracking has been reported by [8]. For all three approaches it is essential to consider the mechanism for selection and its relation to cost, capacity and task/object information.

To accommodate intelligent spatial selection it is of interest to study methods that allow distributed processing of visual information to allow efficient control of the process with a minimum of centralised coordination. Centralised coordination would impose a challenge in terms of biological plausibility and it would at the same time introduce a potential bottleneck into a system. Distributed mechanisms for control are thus of interest, irrespective of the chosen attention model. One area that has considered distributed control extensively is game theory [3]. Both differential games and coalition games have interesting theoretical models that potentially could be used to study coordination/control mechanisms. This paper provides a discussion of the potential use of such a game theoretical model for visual attention.

1.1 Overview

The document is focused on a discussion of saliency measure using multiple cues and game theory concepts. As a precursor to this the set of feature maps used for the analysis are outlined in section 2. These feature maps are integrated using a scale space pyramid, the method is here similar to the attention mechanism described by Tsotsos in [11]. The integration of features and processing of the pyramid is outlined in section 3. The nodes of the pyramid are subject to trading on a market, the outcome of the trading represents the saliency. The basic dynamics of the market is outlined in section 4.1 and the implementation of the market in the pyramid is outlined in section 4.2. In section 5 we discuss the spotlight mechanism for finding the region of interest. Finally a set of experiments are described in section 6.

2 Feature Maps

The focus of the paper is on distributed selection of multiple cues for recognition with emphasis on selection and control. Consequently a relatively simple set of features has been selected to demonstrate the concept. The feature detectors operate on a color image of size 720*576 (see image 4 top left). For the experiments we chose to use the following 4 feature detectors:

1. Pseudo red (red): the red channel divided with the intensity (R/(R+G+B)).
2. Pseudo green (green): similar to the pseudo red.
3. Pseudo blue (blue): similar to the pseudo red.
4. Intensity (white): the intensity (R+G+B).

For more complex images it is obvious that more complex features/cues will be needed, but that is not the real issue here.

3 The Pyramid

We will use a pyramid for multi-scale attention processing. The pyramid is similar to the one presented by Tsotsos [11]. The responses from the feature maps are input to the pyramid. Each node in the pyramid will sum the values from a subset of the nodes in the layer below, see figure 1.

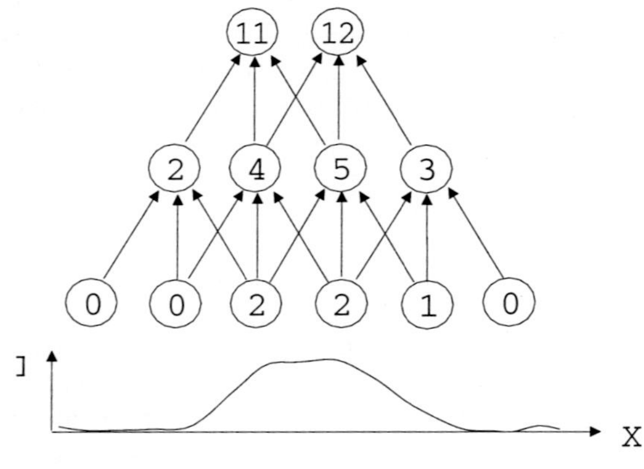

Fig. 1. One dimensional example of the integration across scales for one feature.

Since all layers in the pyramid have the same size, we can combine all feature maps and view each node as a vector of all features, see figure 2.

As we propagate the feature values up in the pyramid, a node in layer $l+1$ that is connected to the set A_l in layer l will get the value:

$$n_{x,y,l+1} = \sum_{x,y \in A_l} n_{x,y,l};$$

where $n \in \mathbf{R}^k$ and k is the number of features maps. A vector n corresponds to a feature dimension as discussed in [9].

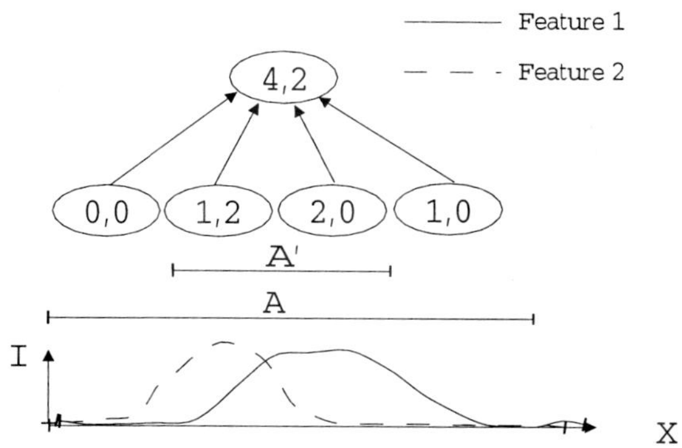

Fig. 2. One dimensional example of the integration across scales for two features.

Let us consider an example where we have one feature map for the red channel (R), one for the green channel (G), and one for the blue channel (B) then the node at position (x, y) in layer l has the value

$$n_{x,y,l} = (R_{x,y,l}, G_{x,y,l}, B_{x,y,l}).$$

A task for the attention system is described as a wanted feature vector (w), e.g.

$$w = (R, G, B).$$

Similarity is measured as:

$$\frac{w * n_{x,y,l}^T}{|w||n_{x,y,l}|}$$

Note that the absolute value of n and w is not interesting here. If we were interested in $|n| = \sqrt{R^2 + G^2 + B^2}$, i.e. brightness (I), we would add that feature to n and w:

$$n_{x,y,l} = (R_{x,y,l}, G_{x,y,l}, B_{x,y,l}, I_{x,y,l})$$

and

$$w = (R, G, B, I).$$

Let us define n_{A_l} as the sum

$$n_{A_l} = \sum_{x,y \in A_l} n_{x,y,l}.$$

Let A'_l be a subset of A_l, see figure 2. Then we can define a salient region A_l as

$$\frac{w * n_{A'_l}^T}{|w||n_{A'_l}|} > \frac{w * n_{A_l}^T}{|w||n_{A_l}|} \tag{1}$$

That is, a region that matches the wanted feature vector better than its surrounding. In section 4.2 we will discuss how we calculate and compare saliency.

The most salient node (at any scale) is selected. From that node we form a spotlight that points out the attention region in the image. In section 5 we will discuss how to that is done.

Finally, the selected region is inhibited and a new search can be carried out.

4 Saliency Computing

4.1 A Market

Competitive equilibrium of a market is commonly used in classical economy. A market is a place where actors can buy and sell goods. With a set of goods each actor can produce a value. The produced value is denoted utility, and the function that maps a set of goods to a utility value is concave. If the utility of the market can be shared among its members in arbitrary ways, e.g. if we use money exchange, we say that the market has a transferable payoff. In [5] it is shown that a market with transferable payoff will reach a competitive equilibrium. A competitive equilibrium is a state where all actors agrees on a price for each type of good and the actors will buy and sell until all have the same amount of all types of goods.

Let us consider a market with N actors and k number of available goods. Actor i has an allocation of goods $n_i \in \mathbf{R}^k$ and the utility $f(n_i) \in \mathbf{R}$. The utility function is concave and therefore most actors will gain on selling and buying goods on the market.

After trading actor i will have a new allocation of goods z_i, where $\sum_{i \in N} z_i = \sum_{i \in N} n_i$. Each agent will strive to get the z_i that solves

$$max_{z_i}(f(z_i) - p * (z_i - n_i)^T) \tag{2}$$

where $p \in \mathbf{R}^k$ a prize vector.

We denote the average allocation $\tilde{n} = \sum_{i \in N} n_i / N$. In [5] section 13.4 it is shown that the solution where $z_i = \tilde{n}$ for all $i \in N$ and the price vector $p = f'(\tilde{n})$ is a competitive equilibrium.

4.2 The Feature Market

Goods that are rare on a market and that increases the utility of the actors are expensive. If the inequality in equation (1) is large then the nodes in A' will sell at a high prize to the nodes outside A'. The wealth of the region A' depends on the value of its features and the need for them outside A'. We will define a wealthy region as a salient one.

In the proposed solution we use a market with transferable payoff (c.f. section 4.1) to define saliency.

In this market the goods are features and the actors are nodes. Let us define:

- k is the number of features.
- l is a layer in the pyramid.
- A_l is a set of nodes in layer l.
- A'_l is a subset of A_l.
- $A_l \backslash A'_l$ is the set of nodes A_l excluding A'_l.
- $n_i \in \mathbf{R}^k$ is the measured feature values at node $i \in A_l$.
- $n'_i \in \mathbf{R}^k$ is the measured feature values at node $i \in A'_l$.
- $\tilde{n} = \sum_{i \in A_l} n_i / |A_l|$.
- $z_i \in \mathbf{R}^k$ is the allocation of feature values after trading at node $i \in A_l$.
- $f(z_i) = w * z_i^T / |z_i|$ is the utility of node i, where $w \in \mathbf{R}^k$ is the wanted allocation given by the task.
- $p = f'(\tilde{n}) = \frac{w}{|\tilde{n}|} - \tilde{n} * \frac{w * \tilde{n}^T}{|\tilde{n}|^3}$ is a prize vector.

In section 4.1 we saw that $f(z_i)$ have to be concave. We observe that the $f(x)$ used in this solution is concave:

$$\frac{f(a)+f(b)}{2} = \frac{w}{2} * \left(\frac{a^T}{|a|} + \frac{b^T}{|b|}\right) \leq w * \frac{a^T + b^T}{|a+b|} = f\left(\frac{a+b}{2}\right)$$

In section 4.1 it is shown that the actors will trade goods on the market to get the allocation z_i that solves equation (2).

When the market has reached its competitive equilibrium all nodes will have the allocation $\tilde{n}$. The nodes that have sold more features than they have bought have a positive capital. From equation (2) we can derive that the capital C of actor i is

$$C_i = p * (n_i - \tilde{n}_i)^T = w * (I - \tilde{n}^T \tilde{n}) * (n_i - \tilde{n})^T;$$

$|\tilde{n}| = |n_i| = 1$.

The saliency of node $n_{l+1,x,y}$ which is connected to the set A_l is

$$S = p * (n'_i - \tilde{n}_i)^T = w * (I - \tilde{n}^T \tilde{n}) * (n'_i - \tilde{n})^T; \quad (3)$$

$|\tilde{n}| = |n'_i| = 1$.

Thus, the saliency of the node $n_{l+1,x,y}$ is the capital achieved by the connected nodes A'_l.

4.3 The Context Matrix

The saliency of node $n_{l+1,x,y}$ is defined in equation (3). We can rewrite that equation as:

$$S = w * A * b^T; \quad (4)$$

where $A = I - \tilde{n}^T \tilde{n}$, $b = n'_i - \tilde{n}$, and $|\tilde{n}| = |n'_i| = 1$

The vector b has the expected properties that the more the feature vector differ from the background the more salient it is. Matrix A adds some context properties to the vector b. Consider a matrix A built of a vector $\tilde{n} = (n_1, n_2, \cdots, n_N)$

$$A = \begin{pmatrix} 1 - n_1^2 & -n_1 n_2 & \cdots & -n_1 n_N \\ -n_2 n_1 & 1 - n_2^2 & \cdots & -n_2 n_N \\ \vdots & \vdots & \ddots & \vdots \\ -n_3 n_1 & -n_3 n_2 & \cdots & 1 - n_N^2 \end{pmatrix} \quad (5)$$

We can observe that if one element in $\tilde{n}$ is dominant, e.g. $n_1 = 1$, then:

$$A = \begin{pmatrix} 0 & 0 & \cdots & 0 \\ 0 & 1 & \cdots & 0 \\ \vdots & \vdots & \ddots & \vdots \\ 0 & 0 & \cdots & 1 \end{pmatrix} \tag{6}$$

If all elements are equal, $\tilde{n} = (\frac{1}{\sqrt{N}}, \frac{1}{\sqrt{N}}, \cdots, \frac{1}{\sqrt{N}})$, then:

$$A = \begin{pmatrix} 1-\frac{1}{N} & -\frac{1}{N} & \cdots & -\frac{1}{N} \\ -\frac{1}{N} & 1-\frac{1}{N} & \cdots & -\frac{1}{N} \\ \vdots & \vdots & \ddots & \vdots \\ -\frac{1}{N} & -\frac{1}{N} & \cdots & 1-\frac{1}{N} \end{pmatrix} \tag{7}$$

From equation (6) we can derive that b_1 will be uninteresting if $n_1 = 1$. From equation (7) we can derive that only $M << N$ elements in $\tilde{n}$ can be dominant if no element in $\tilde{n}$ is dominant.

In other words:

- If the background is e.g. red then a red foreground area cannot be salient.
- A large feature dimension ($N >> 1$), e.g. a texture dimension, can have strong responses on several textures at the same time at one area.
- A small feature dimension on the other hand, e.g. an intensity dimension, can only have strong response on one feature at one time and area (an area is dark or bright).

Hence, the matrix A adds some contextual properties to the vector b.

5 The Spotlight Mechanism

After having propagated the feature values up the pyramid, and calculated saliency values, each node has a saliency value $-1 \leq S \leq 1$. In the top layer we select the most salient node and form a spotlight. The spotlight is formed by selecting all nodes with a value greater than zero and that is connected to a selected node in the layer above, see image 3.

In the bottom layer a set of pixels will be selected, that is the region of interest. The receptive field of the top node is normally larger than the selected region of interest. All of the pixels in the receptive field are inhibited to prevent the system from returning attention to the same area.

6 Results

In the implementation for the experiments a pyramid with two layers is used. The input feature images have the size 720*576 pixels. The nodes in the bottom layer are connected to an area of 5*5 pixels in the feature images. The nodes are separated by 5 pixels, so there is no overlap. The top layer has one of two configurations:

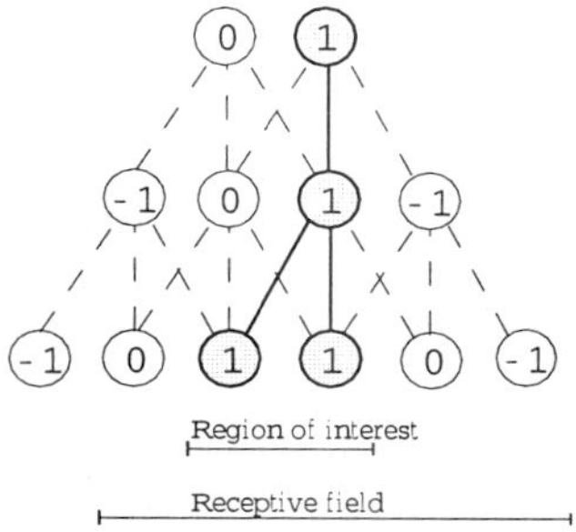

Fig. 3. The spotlight mechanism

1. The wide area scan: The top layer nodes are connected to an area of 60*60 nodes (a receptive field of 300*300 pixels, about 1/4 of the image size).
2. The narrow area scan: The top layer nodes are connected to an area of 30*15 nodes (a receptive field of 150*75 pixels, about the size of the items on the table).

For the experiments we used a picture of our colleague making a toast (figure 4 top left).

We want to verify how the solution integrates cues and handles scales, so we applied three different tasks:

1. We let all features have equal weight in a wide area scan. The left side of the white wall plus our colleagues right arm is much brighter than the surrounding, and thus captures the attention (see figure 4 top right).
2. We search for a wide white and blue area and found the white wall and the blue sofa. In the first run we found the left side and in the second we found the right side. The result is similar to the previous search (where no specific features was searched), exept that the sofa is included. In the market the background and the sofa will "sell" their features mainly to the red shirt and dark shadows (and green table in the 2.nd search) below the attention area. (see figure 4 middle left and right).
3. We searched for a narrow white and blue area and found the two plates in the top-left corner of the table. In the next run we found the plate in the lower-left corner of the table. We note that the white and blue plates will "sell" their features mainly to the dark surrounding to the left of the table and the green table. (see figure 4 bottom left and right).

7 Summary

A framework for visual attention has been discussed. The framework calculates saliency, with respect to a given task, using a multi-scale pyramid and multiple cues. The saliency computations is based on game theory concepts, or specifically a coalitional game. The most salient area is the region of interest.

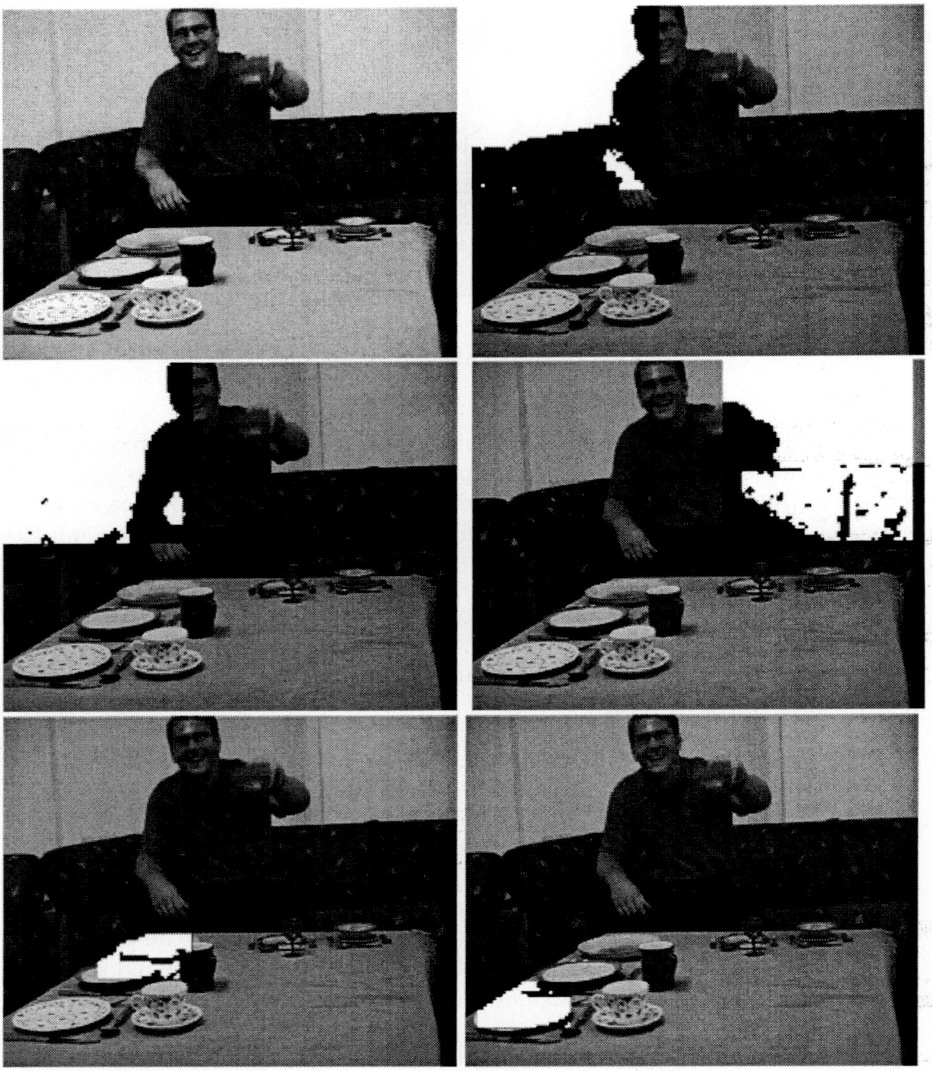

Fig. 4. (Top left) Input image. The background is white, the sofa is blue, our colleague has a red shirt, the table is green, and the plates to the left of the table are white and blue. (top right) Search for any salient wide area (middle) 1.st and 2.nd search for a wide white and blue area, (bottom) 1.st and 2.nd search for a narrow white and blue area.

The experiments basically reports expected results. However it should be noted that the task specification has been statically set by the authors from empirical study. Important improvements can be achieved by context aware tasks and the potential to improve tasks by learning.

Acknowledgement. This research has been sponsored by the EU through the project "Cognitive Vision Systems" – IST-2000-29375 Cogvis. This support is gratefully acknowledged.

References

1. J. Duncan. Selective attention and the organisation of visual information. *Journal of Experimental Psychology*, 113(4):501–517, 1984.
2. C. W. Eriksen and J. D. St. James. Visual attention within and around the field of focal attention: A zoom lens model. *Perception and Psychophysics*, 40(4):225–240, 1986.
3. Drew Fudenberg and Jean Tirole. *Game Theory.* MIT Press, Cambridge, MA, 6th edition, 1998.
4. C. Koch and S. Ullman *Shifts in selective visual attention: towards the underlying neural circuitry* Human Neurobiology, 4:219–227, 1985.
5. M.J. Osborne and A. Rubinstein. A course in game theory. 1999.
6. Stephen E. Palmer. *Vision Science: Photons to Phenomology.* MIT Press, 1999.
7. M. I. Posner. *Chronometric explanations of the mind.* Erlbaum, Hillsdale, NJ, 1978.
8. Z. W. Pylyshyn and R. W. Storm. Tracking multiple independent targets: evidence of parallel tracking mechanisms. *Spatial Vision*, 3(3):179–197, 1988.
9. A. Treisman and G. Gelade. A feature integration theory of attention. *Cognitive Psychology*, 12:97-136, 1980.
10. J.K. Tsotsos. Analyzing vision at the complexity level. *Behav. Brain Sci.*, 13(3):423–469, 1990.
11. J.K. Tsotsos, S. Culhane, W. Wai, Y. Lai, N. Davis, and F. Nuflo. Modeling visual attention via selective tuning. *Artificial Intelligence*, 78(1-2):507–547, 1995.

Attentional Selection for Object Recognition – A Gentle Way

Dirk Walther[1], Laurent Itti[2], Maximilian Riesenhuber[3], Tomaso Poggio[3], and Christof Koch[1]

[1] California Institute of Technology, Computation and Neural Systems Program
Mail Code 139-74, Pasadena, California 91125, USA
{Walther, Koch}@klab.caltech.edu, http://www.klab.caltech.edu
[2] University of Southern California, Computer Science Department
Los Angeles, California 90089, USA
itti@usc.edu, http://iLab.usc.edu
[3] Massachusetts Institute of Technology, Center for Biological and Computational Learning, Cambridge, Massachusetts 02139, USA
{max, tp}@ai.mit.edu, http://www.ai.mit.edu/projects/cbcl

Abstract. Attentional selection of an object for recognition is often modeled using all-or-nothing switching of neuronal connection pathways from the attended region of the retinal input to the recognition units. However, there is little physiological evidence for such all-or-none modulation in early areas. We present a combined model for spatial attention and object recognition in which the recognition system monitors the entire visual field, but attentional modulation by as little as 20% at a high level is sufficient to recognize multiple objects. To determine the size and shape of the region to be modulated, a rough segmentation is performed, based on pre-attentive features already computed to guide attention. Testing with synthetic and natural stimuli demonstrates that our new approach to attentional selection for recognition yields encouraging results in addition to being biologically plausible.

1 Introduction

When we look at a scene without any prior knowledge or task, our attention will be attracted to some locations mostly because of their saliency, defined by contrasts in color, intensity, orientation etc. [1,2]. Usually, attention is not attracted to a single location in the image, but rather to an extended region that is likely to constitute an object or a part of an object. We say "likely", because the bottom-up (image-based) guidance of attention appears to rely on low-level features which do not yet constitute well-defined objects [2]. It is only after the attention system has selected a region of the visual field that objects are identified by the recognition system in infero-temporal cortex. This makes object based attention a chicken and egg problem that is rather difficult to disentangle.

In previous work, we demonstrated that using a fast attention front-end to rapidly select candidate locations for recognition greatly speeds up the recognition of objects in cluttered scenes at little cost in terms of detection rate [3].

H.H. Bülthoff et al. (Eds.): BMCV 2002, LNCS 2525, pp. 472–479, 2002.

However, this approach, as others before, was based on a paradigm of selecting an "interesting" part of the image, cropping the image and routing the cropped section to the recognition unit via dynamical neural connections. Although it has been widely used in computational modeling [4,5], there is little physiological support for this paradigm. The main issue is the implementation of routing using all-or-nothing switching of neuronal connections, whereas physiological investigations usually only find moderate modulations of firing rates in early visual areas due to attentional effects [6].

We here investigate an alternative approach [7]. In a static architecture, we use the spatial information provided by the attention component of our model to modulate the activity of cells in the recognition part using a variable amount of modulation. We find that modulation by 20% suffices to successively recognize multiple objects in a scene.

In order to achieve this, however, the attention system needs to provide information not only about a location of interest, but also about the extent of the "interesting" region around this point, *i.e.*, we require a rough segmentation of the object of interest. We propose an approach that exploits the already-computed feature maps and thus comes at negligible extra computation cost for the segmentation.

2 Model

Bottom-Up Guidance of Attention. Attentional guidance is based on our earlier model for bottom-up saliency-based attention [1,2,8,9]. The model extracts feature maps for orientations, intensities and color, and builds up a saliency map using intermediary conspicuity maps. A winner-take-all network of integrate and fire neurons selects winning locations, and an inhibition-of-return mechanism allows the model to attend to many locations successively. For a more detailed description of the system see Fig. 1.

Recognition of Attended Objects. The recognition component is based on our previously published hierarchical model for object recognition HMAX [10,11] that considers recognition as a feedforward process in the spirit of Fukushima's Neocognitron [12]. HMAX builds up units tuned to views of objects from simple bar-like stimuli in a succession of layers, alternatingly employing a maximum pooling operation (for spatial pooling) and a sum pooling operation (for feature combination). For details see Fig. 1.

Riesenhuber and Poggio have demonstrated that the simultaneous recognition of multiple objects in an image is possible in HMAX if inputs to a view-tuned unit (VTU) are limited to the afferents strongly activated by the VTUs preferred object [11]. However, this comes at the cost of decreased shape specificity of VTUs due to the reduced number of features used to define its preferred object. In our present model we use HMAX with VTUs connected to all 256 C2 units, in order to demonstrate how attentional modulation provides a way to achieve recognition in clutter without sacrificing shape specificity.

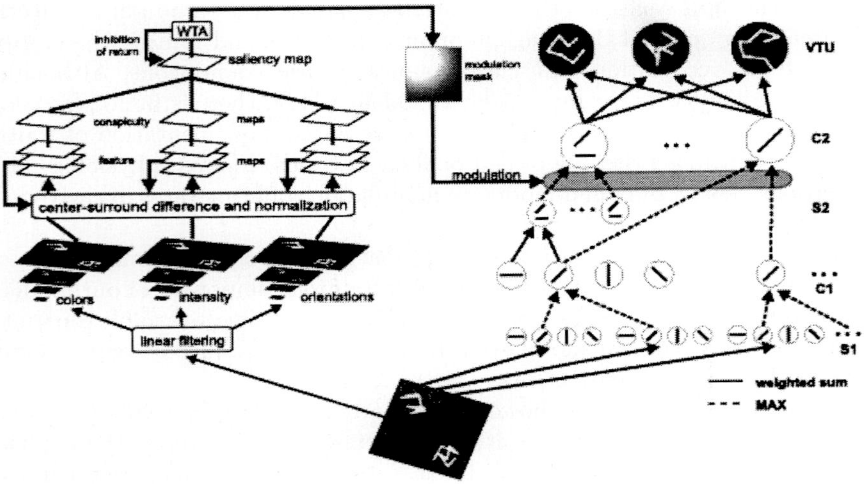

Fig. 1. Our model combines a saliency-based attention system [2,8,9] with a hierarchical recognition system [10,11]. For the attention system, the retinal image is filtered for colors (red-green and blue-yellow), intensities, and four orientations at four different scales, and six center-surround differences are computed for each feature. The resulting $7 \times 6 = 42$ feature maps are combined into three conspicuity maps (for color, intensity and orientations), from which one saliency map is computed. All locations within the saliency map compete in a winner-take-all (WTA) network of integrate and fire neurons, and the winning location is attended to. Subsequently, the saliency map is inhibited at the winning location (inhibition-of-return), allowing the competition to go on, so that other locations can be attended to. The hierarchical recognition system starts out from units tuned to bar-like stimuli with small receptive fields, similar to V1 simple cells. In a succession of layers, information is combined alternatingly by spatial pooling (using a maximum pooling function) and by feature combination (using a weighted sum operation). View-tuned units at the top of the hierarchy respond to a specific view of an object while showing tolerance to changes in scale and position [10]. The activity of units at level S2 is modulated by the attention system (Fig. 2).

Interactions Between Attention and Recognition. The goal of the attentional modulation is it to provide the recognition system with a first order approximation of the location and extent of "interesting" objects in the scene. For this, the feature maps and conspicuity maps can be re-used that have been created in the process of computing the saliency map. Fig. 2 details how information from the feature maps is used for object-based inhibition-of-return and for creating the modulation mask.

The advantage of going back to the most influential feature map for obtaining the mask instead of using the saliency map directly is the sparser representation in the feature map, which makes segmentation easier. This procedure comes at negligible additional computational cost, because the feature and conspicuity maps have already been computed during the processing for saliency.

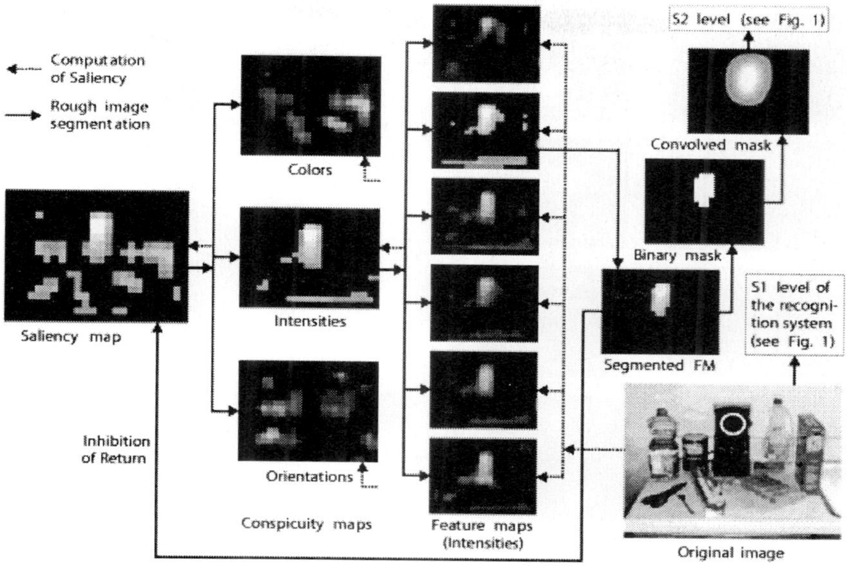

Fig. 2. To compute the modulation mask, the algorithm first determines which of the feature domains (colors, intensities, or orientations) contributed most to the saliency of the current focus of attention (FOA). In this figure, it is the intensity conspicuity map. In a second step, the feature map that contributed most to the winning conspicuity map at the FOA is found. Amongst the six feature maps for intensity, the second feature map from the top is the winner here. The winning feature map is segmented using a flooding algorithm with adaptive thresholding. The segmented feature map is used as a template for object-based inhibition-of-return of the saliency map. It is also processed into a binary mask and convolved with a Gaussian kernel to yield the modulation mask at image resolution. Finally, the modulation mask is multiplied to the activities of the S2 layer in the recognition system (see eq. 1).

The modulation mask modifies the activity of the S2 cells in the recognition system (Fig.1). With $0 \leq M(x, y) \leq 1$ being the value of the modulation mask at position (x, y) and $S(x, y)$ being the S2 activity, the modulated S2 activity $S'(x, y)$ is computed according to

$$S'(x, y) = [(1 - m) + m \cdot M(x, y)] \cdot S(x, y) \tag{1}$$

Where m is the modulation strength $(0 \leq m \leq 1)$.

Applying the modulation at the level of the S2 units makes sense for biological and computational reasons. The S2 layer corresponds in its function approximately to area V4 in the primate visual cortex. There have been a number of reports from electrophysiology [6,13,14,15,16] and psychophysics [17,18] that show attentional modulation of V4 activity. Hence, the S2 level is a natural choice for modulating recognition.

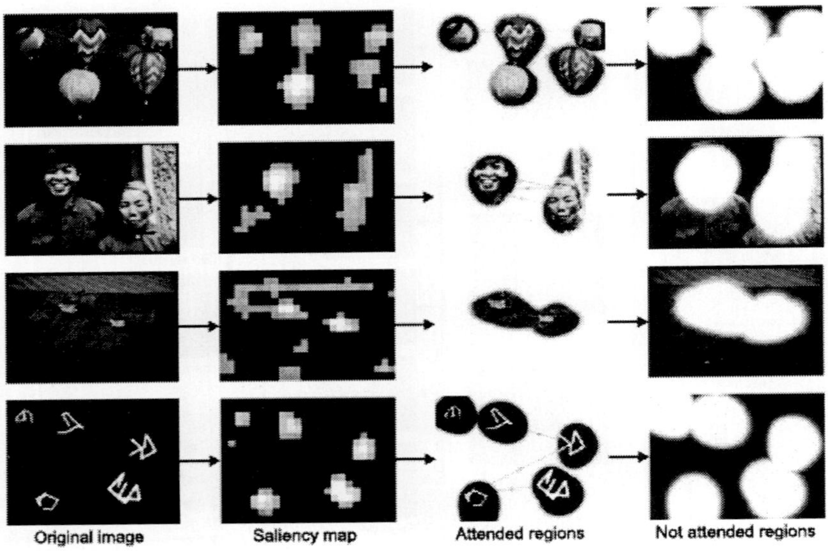

Fig. 3. Four examples for the extraction of modulation masks as described in Fig. 2. For each example, the following steps are shown (from left to right): the original image; the saliency map for the image; the original image contrast-modulated with the cumulative modulation mask, with the scan path overlayed; the inverse cumulative mask, covering all salient parts of the image. More examples are available in full color at `http://klab.caltech.edu/~walther/bmcv`

From a computational point of view, it is efficient to apply the modulation at a level as high up in the hierarchy as possible that still has some spatial resolution, *i.e.* S2. This way, the computation that is required to obtain the activations of the S2 units from the input image needs to be done only once for each image. When the system attends to the next location in the image, only the computation upwards from S2 needs to be repeated.

3 Results

Rapid Extraction of Attended Object Size. To qualitatively assess our rather simple approach to image segmentation using the feature maps, we tested the method on a number of natural images (e.g., Fig. 3). The method appears to work well for a range of images. In most cases, the areas found by the method indeed constitute objects or parts of objects. In general, the method has problems when objects are not uniform in their most salient feature, because those objects cannot be segmented in the respective feature map. At this point, we have no quantitative assessment of the performance of this method.

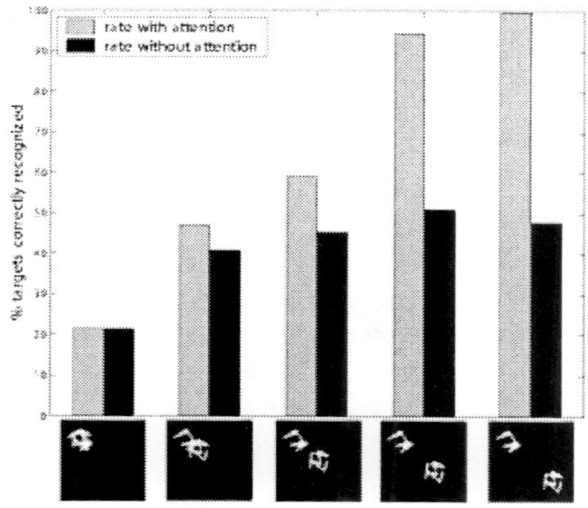

Fig. 4. Recognition performance of the model with (gray) and without (black) attentional modulation as a function of spatial separation between the two wire-frame objects. Improvement of recognition performance due to spatial attention is strongest for objects that are well separated, and absent when objects overlap. Recognition performance is defined as the ratio of the total number of clips that have been recognized successfully and the number of paperclips that the system was presented with. The modulation strength for the data with attention is 50% in this figure.

Improved Recognition Using Attention. It would be a big step to be able to recognize natural objects like the ones found by the segmentation procedure. The hardwired set of features currently used in HMAX, however, shows rather poor performance on natural scenes. We therefore applied the system to the artificial paperclip stimuli used in previous studies [10,11] and shown in Fig. 3.

The stimuli that we investigated consist of two twisted paperclips chosen from a set of 21 clips, yielding a total of $21^2 = 441$ different displays. In addition, the distance between the two paperclips was varied from total overlapping to clear separation of the paperclips as shown below the graph in Fig. 4.

In the simulations, the attention system first computed the most salient image location. Then, going back to the feature maps, the region of interest was found. The recognition system processed the image up to layer S2. The activity of the S2 cells was modulated according to eq. 1, and the C2 activity and the responses of the VTU were computed (Fig. 1). Inhibition-of-return was triggered, and the saliency map evolved further, until the next location was attended to, and so on. This procedure ran for 1000 ms simulated time of the integrate and fire winner-take-all network. A paperclip was counted as successfully recognized when the response of its VTU exceeded the threshold in at least one of the attended locations. The threshold was determined for each VTU separately by presenting it with 60 randomly chosen distracter paperclips that were not used for any other part of the simulation [10]. The maximum of the responses of the VTU to any of the distracter stimuli was set as the threshold for successful recognition.

Since we were using spatial attention to separate the two paperclip objects, we investigated the influence of the distance between the two objects in the displays. The results are shown in Fig. 4. There is no advantage to attending for overlapping paperclips, since this does not resolve the ambiguity between the two objects. As distance increases, the performance of the system with attention

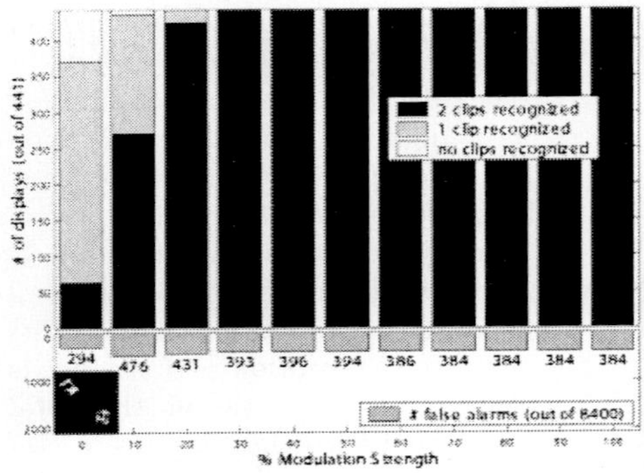

Fig. 5. For each stimulus, the recognition system can identify two, one or none of the two paperclip objects present. We show for how many stimuli each of the three cases occurs as a function of the attentional modulation. Zero modulation strength implies no attentional modulation at all. At 100% modulation, the S2 activation outside the FOA is entirely suppressed. As little as 20% attentional modulation is sufficient to boost the recognition performance significantly.

(gray) becomes more and more superior to the system without attentional modulation (black). For clearly separated objects, the performance with attention reaches almost 100%, while the system without attention only recognizes 50% of the paperclip objects.

Viewing the simulation results from another perspective, one can ask: In how many of the displays does the model recognize both, only one or none of the two objects present? This analysis is shown in Fig. 5 for varying modulation strength m; for an interpretation of m see eq. 1. Without attention ($m = 0$), both paperclips were only recognized in a few displays; indeed, in some fraction of the examples, neither of the two clips was recognized. With only 10% modulation strength, the model recognized both paperclips in more than half of the displays, and with 20% modulation, both paperclips were recognized in almost all displays. For all values of $m > 20\%$, both paperclips were recognized in all displays.

4 Conclusion

We introduced a simple method for image segmentation that makes use of precomputed features. Despite its simplicity, this method is robust for at least one class of images. We are currently evaluating its performance for natural scenes.

In our combined model of bottom-up spatial attention and object recognition we have shown that attentional modulation of the activity of units at the V4 level in the recognition system by as little as 20% is sufficient to successively recognize multiple objects in a scene. In our approach, there is no need for full dynamic routing of the contents of the attended image region to the recognition system.

Acknowledgments. This work was supported by NSF (ITR, ERC and KDI), NEI, NIMA, DARPA, the Zumberge Faculty Research and Innovation Fund (L.I.), the Charles Lee Powell Foundation, a McDonnell-Pew Award in Cognitive Neuroscience (M.R.), Eastman Kodak Company, Honda R&D Co., Ltd., ITRI,

Komatsu Ltd., Siemens Corporate Research, Inc., Toyota Motor Corporation and The Whitaker Foundation.

References

1. C. Koch and S. Ullman. Shifts in selectiv visual-attention – towards the underlying neural circuitry. *Hum. Neurobiol.* 4(4):219–227, 1985.
2. L. Itti and C. Koch. Computational modelling of visual attention. *Nat. Rev. Neurosci.* 2(3):194–203, 2001.
3. F. Miau and L. Itti. A neural model combining attentional orienting to object recognition: Preliminary explorations on the interplay between where and what. In *IEEE Engin. in Medicine and Biology Society (EMBS)*, Istanbul, Turkey, 2001.
4. B.A. Olshausen, C.H. Anderson, and D.C. Van Essen. A neurobiological model of visual-attention and invariant pattern-recognition based on dynamic routing of information. *J. Neurosci.* 13(11):4700–4719, 1993.
5. J.K. Tsotsos, S.M. Culhane, W.Y.K. Wai, Y.H. Lai, N. Davis, and F. Nuflo. Modeling visual-attention via selective tuning. *Artif. Intell.* 78:507–545, 1995.
6. J.H. Reynolds, T. Pasternak, and R. Desimone. Attention increases sensitivity of V4 neurons. *Neuron* 26(3):703–714, 2000.
7. D. Walther, M. Riesenhuber, T. Poggio, L. Itti, and C. Koch. Towards an integrated model of saliency-based attention and object recognition in the primate's visual system. *J. Cogn. Neurosci.* B14 Suppl.S: 46–47,2002.
8. L. Itti, C. Koch, and E. Niebur. A model of saliency-based visual attention for rapid scene analysis. *IEEE PAMI*, 20(11):1254–1259, 1998.
9. L. Itti and C. Koch. A saliency-based search mechanism for overt and covert shifts of visual attention. *Vision Res.* 40(10–12):1489–1506, 2000.
10. M. Riesenhuber and T. Poggio. Hierarchical models of object recognition in cortex. *Nat. Neurosci.* 2(11):1019–1025, 1999.
11. M. Riesenhuber and T. Poggio. Are cortical models really bound by the "binding problem"? *Neuron* 24(1):87–93, 111–25, 1999.
12. K. Fukushima. Neocognitron: A self-organizing neural network model for a mechan. of pattern recogn. unaffected by shifts in position. *Biol. Cybern.* 36:193–202, 1980.
13. S. Treue. Neural correlates of attention in primate visual cortex. *Trends Neurosci.* 24(5):295–300, 2001.
14. C.E. Connor, D.C. Preddie, J.L. Gallant, and D.C. Van Essen. Spatial attention effects in macaque area V4. *J. Neurosci.*17(9):3201–3214, 1997.
15. B.C. Motter. Neural correlates of attentive selection for color or luminance in extrastriate area V4. *J. Neurosci.* 14(4):2178–2189, 1994.
16. S.J. Luck, L. Chelazzi, S.A. Hillyard, and R. Desimone. Neural mechanisms of spatial selective attention in areas V1, V2, and V4 of macaque visual cortex. *J. Neurophysiol.* 77(1):24–42, 1997.
17. J. Intriligator and P. Cavanagh. The spatial resolution of visual attention. *Cogn. Psychol.* 43(3):171–216, 2001.
18. J. Braun. Visual-search among items of different salience – removal of visual- attention mimics a lesion in extrastriate area V4. *J. Neurosci.* 14(2):554–567, 1994.

Audio-Oculomotor Transformation

Robert Frans van der Willigen and Mark von Campenhausen

Institut für Biologie II, Lehrstuhl für Zoologie/Tierphysiologie,
RWTH Aachen Kopernikusstraße 16, D-52074 Aachen, Germany
willigen@bio2.rwth-aachen.de

Abstract. Sensorimotor transformation of signals stemming from the visual (eye position) and auditory (binaural information) peripheral organs into a common eye motor error signal was studied; as is observed in the deep layers of the colliculus superior that enables a head fixed monkey to direct its eyes towards an auditory target. By means of a computational model we explore how this transformation can be achieved by the responses of single neurons in the primate brainstem. Our audio-oculomotor model, a feed-forward four-layer artificial neural network, was trained with back-propagation of error to assign connectivity in an architecture consistent with known physiology of the primate brainstem at both the level of input, and the output layers. The derived mathematical formalism is consistent with known physiological responses of brainstem neurons and does not require a topographical organization according to their preferred parameter values.

1 Introduction

One of the most consistent responses to an unexpected sound is the orienting behavior in which the eyes (and head) are turned toward this auditory target [4]. This *auditory-evoked orienting* is a specific form of *sensorimotor transformation* – conversion of sensory stimuli into motor commands – that is vital to any biological organism or artificial system that possesses the ability to react to the environment. Auditory-evoked orienting, however, poses a computational problem for the brain because target location and eye position are initially encoded by different sensory reference or coordinate frames (craniocentric versus oculocentric) and in different formats (tonotopic versus retinotopic) [2].

Because of its role in the control of orienting movements of the eyes, head and pinnae towards sensory targets, the primate Superior Colliculus (**SC**) has been studied as a possible candidate of the site in the brain that enables sensorimotor transformation – directing the eyes toward an auditory source. Whereas the superficial layers of the SC receive exclusively visual input, the deep layers (**DLSC**) receive convergent visual, auditory and somatosensory input. Activation of DLSC neurons can produce a rapid shift of the eyes, ears and head to focus on the location in space that is represented at the stimulated site. For example, when a monkey moves its eyes but keeps its head and ears in their original position, the population of neurons responsive to an auditory

H.H. Bülthoff et al. (Eds.): BMCV 2002, LNCS 2525, pp. 480–490, 2002.

stimulus in a particular spatial location changes to a new collicular site in a compensatory fashion – a site representing the *new* eye motor error signal by means of *population coding* [10]. Thus auditory-evoked orienting (specifically, an eye movement) requires that auditory signals are translated into signals of eye motor error. Nonetheless, this transformation necessitates access to auditory space coding cells and an eye position signal. Mathematically, this can be achieved through vector subtraction (Fig. 1b). How the audio-oculomotor (Fig. 1a) system solves this problem at a computational level is matter of debate [2,3,8,10,11] and is investigated here by means of a neural network model (Fig. 1c).

2 Biological Plausibility and Model Implementation

Here we describe the biological basis and the implementation of our model. The flow of information in the primate audio-oculomotor system is channelled by two sensory and one sensorimotor pathway. One sensory pathway copes with the oculomotor information that carries the position of the eyes in orbit (*oculomotor information*; **3** in Fig. 1a) [7,11], the other copes with the auditory binaural information carrying sound position (*acoustic information*; **1** and **2** in Fig. 1a) [13]. Finally, the sensory information is converted into a common coordinate signal (*sensorimotor transformation*; **4** in Fig. 1a) [10].

2.1 Information Necessary to Compute Motor-Error

Oculomotor Information: To compute eye motor error (hereafter, *motor-error*) the brain requires information about eye position – visual information signaling the retinal coordinates of the eyes in their orbits. In the primate brainstem many sites are found which contain cells – *oculomotor neurons* – that relate to eye position [7]. The responses of pools of oculomotor neurons can be used to represent the signal required in the eye muscles to allow fixation [14].

Acoustic Information: Unlike the visual system, for which each eye has receptors focused on separate points in space, the auditory system, does not have a spatial representation of acoustic targets through an orderly projection of the receptor surface. Instead the receptor organ of the auditory system produces a one-dimensional map of frequency of sounds at the level of the CN. As a consequence of this *tonotopic* organization, localization of a sound must be based upon information from the monaural responses of both ears that determines its *azimuth* and *elevation* – position in the *horizontal* and *vertical* plane, respectively. This *binaural* information carries directional cues. In primates, the most important binaural cues in determining azimuth are the difference in the time of arrival of a sound source at the two ears **(ITD)** and the difference in intensity of a sound at the two ears **(IID)**. Because neurophysiological data shows that sensorimotor transformation involves parallel modules [8], and in

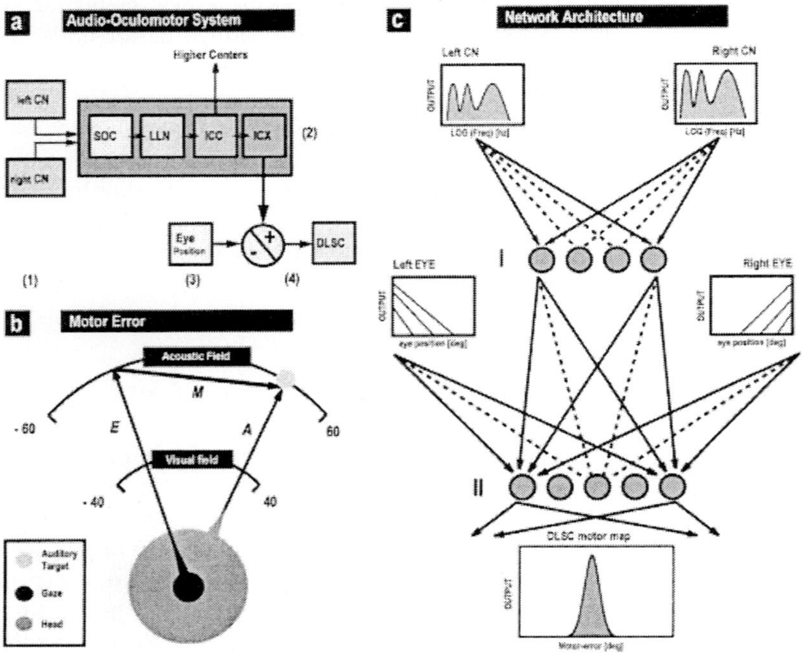

Fig. 1. **(a)** A highly schematic representation of the flow of signals in the audio-oculomotor system: cochlear nucleus (**CN**), medial and lateral superior olive of the superior olivary complex **(SOC)**, the lateral lemniscus nucleus (**LLN**) and the central and inferior nulei (**ICC** and **ICX**) of the inferior colliculus **(IC)**. **(b)** The vectorial relation between target and eye direction in the horizontal plane with respect to a fixed head. $\boldsymbol{A}$: direction of the target (or azimuth) in head centered coordinates; $\boldsymbol{E}$: horizontal direction of the eyes in orbit (or gaze); $\boldsymbol{M}$: motor error. Mathematically, eye motor error is computed by: $\boldsymbol{M} = \boldsymbol{A} - \boldsymbol{E}$. **(c)** Architecture of the model. Cochlear nucleus (**CN**) activity profiles are shown for a sound (three frequencies) at a rightward azimuth (Activity level left CN < right CN). Each CN projects to all binaural units **(I)**. The audiomotor units **(II)** combine oculomotor related activity of the left and right eye and the result of the binaural processing. Output of the network is a topographical representation of eye motor error in a population of DLSC cells.

view of the evidence that binaural cues are processed by two separate channels [1], the here implemented acoustic input carries only the IID cue.

Sensorimotor Transformation: At the DLSC, visual and auditory information merge (or have been merged) into a topographical organization – a common coordinate system that enables auditory-evoked eye movements (see Introduction). Thus, before or at the DLSC level a coordinate transformation of *place-coded* craniocentric auditory signals and the *rate-coded* retinocentric oculomotor signals has to occur to produce a place-coded motor-map representing all sounds relative to eye position. Note, however, the output map of our model – computing motor-error for sounds from the whole surrounding space – is unilateral whereas the primate DLSC map is bilateral (divided between the left and right side of the brain) were it processes the contralateral parts of space.

2.2 Input and Output Relationships of the Network

Acoustic input: (left/right CN Fig. 1b): The acoustic input is tonotopically organized and generates activity in two CN arrays (30 units each) where frequency is represented *logarithmically* along each array. In our model the index, i_o, of each cochlear unit is assumed to be monotonically related to the logarithm of the center frequency (CF) as:

$$i_o = \frac{log(CF) - log(F_{min})}{log(F_{max}) - log(F_{min})} \; (N_{coch} - 1) \; + \; 1 \tag{1}$$

where F_{min} equals 100 Hz and F_{max} equals 10000 Hz, and N_{coch} is the number of units that occupy one cochlear array. Each frequency component of the applied sound generated a Gaussian activity profile in both cochlear arrays according to:

$$R_{coch_i} = \begin{cases} Gain_{coch} \cdot I \cdot e^{-\frac{(i-i_o)^2}{2\sigma_c^2}} & \text{when} \quad R_i \leq I \\ I & \text{when} \quad R_i > I \end{cases} \tag{2}$$

where R_i is the firing rate of the ith cochlear unit (right or left) and i_o the index of that unit in the cochlear array which corresponds to the center frequency of that component in the CN layer (Eq. 1). The $Gain_{coch}$ factor is set to 1.0 and the bandwidth, σ_c, was set at 0.5 octave. The intensity, I, of a given sound frequency component at the left and right eardrum is assumed to be nonlinearly dependent on azimuth (lowest at the contralateral ear and highest at the ipsilateral ear) (Fig. 2).

Eye position input: (left/right EYE Fig. 1b): The eye position signals are coded in a recruitment/firing rate format as observed in oculomotor neurons [7]. The horizontal direction of the eyes was expressed by two pools, each containing 10 units, representing the leftward (neg. slope), and rightward (pos. slope) pulling directions, respectively:

$$RL_{pos_i} = \begin{cases} -\; Gain_{ocul} \cdot \dfrac{90 - E_{t_i}}{10} \; (e - E_{t_i}) & \text{when} \;\; e < E_{t_i} \\ 0 & \text{when} \;\; e \geq E_{t_i} \end{cases} \tag{3}$$

$$RR_{pos_i} = \begin{cases} +\; Gain_{ocul} \cdot \dfrac{90 + E_{t_i}}{10} \; (e - E_{t_i}) & \text{when} \;\; e > E_{t_i} \\ 0 & \text{when} \;\; e \leq E_{t_i} \end{cases} \tag{4}$$

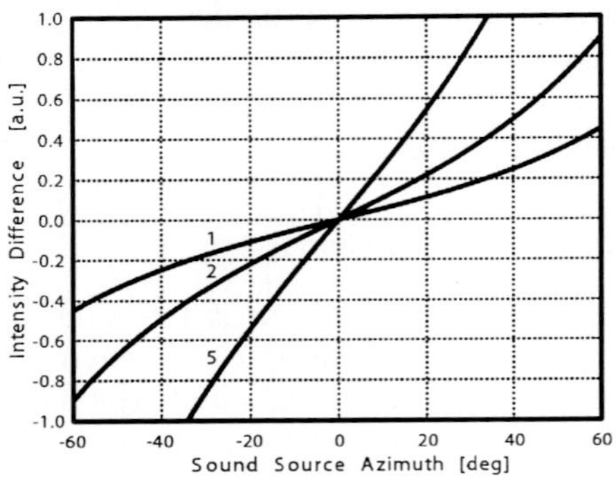

Fig. 2. Interaural intensity differences (total IID) as a function of azimuth. IID is here defined as the intensity of the sound on the right eardrum (I_R) minus intensity on the left eardrum (I_L). Thus when the function is positive then $I_R > I_L$. Numbers indicate the number of frequencies in the sound. Note that IID *per se* does not specify azimuth because sounds may contain more than one frequency.

where e is eye position $\in[-40^o, 40^o]$ and E_{t_i} is defined by $-50 + \frac{80(i-1)}{(N_{ocul}-1)}$ representing the threshold position of the ith unit; N_{ocul} denotes the number oculomotor units for a given eye muscle; the $Gain_{ocul}$ factor equaled 0.0025.

Hidden layers: The network contains two hidden layers (layers **I** and **II** of Fig. 1b). The first hidden layer contains 4 *binaural* units, which combines the auditory input from the left and right CN. In turn, the binaural hidden units and the eye position input units project to a second hidden layer of 10 units. These *audiomotor* units combine oculomotor signals and the result of binaural processing. Hidden unit activity, O_j, with input bias, θ_j, is determined by the connections w_{ji} and the activity from all N units i in the preceding layer (sigmoidal activation function):

$$O_j = \frac{1}{\left[1 + exp\left(-\sum_{i=1}^{N} w_{ji}o_i + \theta_j\right)\right]} \tag{5}$$

Output layer: (DLSC motor-map Fig. 1b): The audiomotor units are connected to an array of 20 units. The output of the network R_{dlsc_i} is compared to a topographical coded teacher signal representing motor-error through a Gaussian activation profile:

$$R_{teacher_i} = Gain_{teach}\ \mathrm{e}^{-\frac{(M_i - M)^2}{2\sigma_m^2}} \tag{6}$$

where $R_{teacher_i}$ is the desired firing rate of the ith unit of the output layer and the $Gain_{teach}$ factor equals 0.7. M represents the desired amplitude and constant σ_m, set at 10°, determines the bandwidth of the Gaussian activation profile. Amplitude, M_i, of the ith output unit in the DLSC map is linearly related to the index i by: $-M_{range} + \frac{2M_{range}(i-1)}{(N_{dlsc}-1)}$. Here M_{range} forced the M_i value in the $[-100^o, 100^o]$ range and N_{dlsc} equals the number of output units. The measure of a collicular unit's error $\delta_i^{(o)}$ was calculated by de difference between the desired activation and the actual output of the DLSC motor-map: $R_{teacher_i} - R_{dlsc_i}$.

2.3 Training Procedures and Performance Analysis

Between layers, every unit has feed-forward connections to each unit of the next layer. To assign connectivity the network was trained with back-propagation of error [6]. All connections between the subsequent layers used an initially random set of weights. During the training phase the input variables were all randomly selected (see Appendix). Global error E (Eq. 7) converged to 0.38 ± 0.2 deg after 50,000 training cycles. During simulations, when the network did not adjust its weights, the network performed the task with a mean global error of about 0.37 $\pm$ 0.2 deg calculated over 500 stimulus presentations.

$$E = \sum_{i=1}^{N_{dlsc}} (\delta_i^o)^2 \tag{7}$$

When summed over 500 stimulus presentations in relation to an average teacher output – the average desired activation of the output layer, computed over 10,000 randomly selected teacher activations – E equalled 0.64 which is approximately twice as high compared to a fully trained network.

3 Network Simulations and Tests of Generalization

The performed simulation operations were divided into two conditions: *i* all sensory input parameters were selected randomly or, *ii* some parameters were kept constant while others were set at random. Condition *i* simulations were used to determine the performance of the network, whereas condition *ii* simulations were used to analyze single unit activity.

3.1 Generalization to Noise

The biological validity of our model is an issue of concern because the learning mechanism used to find a solution – back-propagation of error [6] – is not likely to occur in the brain. Thus, when the model achieves a certain kind of optimality that also occurs in the brain, then it is likely that this solution emerged due to the biological plausibility of the input/output relationships and the internal architecture of the network connections [8,14]. To address this issue, the network was tested with an acoustic input simulating *white* noise. Because it is known that spectral properties of acoustic input hardly influence the response properties of DLSC cells, it was hypothesized that biological plausible behavior of single units necessarily requires the model to generalize across the frequency spectrum of the acoustic input.

Although the network was not trained with white noise (see Appendix) when tested with this broad band frequency stimulus, global error approximated 0.52 $\pm$ 0.2 deg; averaged over 500 stimulus representations. The latter deviates significantly from the performance value of a non-trained network [Wilcoxon rank-sum test, $p < 0.001$]. This generalization shows that the solution obtained by the network is not critically dependent on the frequency spectrum of the sound source.

4 Unit Response Properties Compared to Physiology

An important question in interpreting the solutions of the network obtained after back-propagation of error [6] is: *How closely does the model actually resemble audio-oculomotor data?* The main result is that the response properties (determined trough simulations) of the *neuron-like* units in the trained network closely resemble those of single neurons found in the primate brainstem. From this analysis it is concluded that the organization of the network is not a product of the spatial position of units within the neural arrays of the hidden-layers, but is contained in the pattern of weight projections of individual units. To exemplify this, we focus on the hidden layer units.

4.1 Binaural Units

Although binaural units in the first hidden layer (hereafter, *binaural layer*) of the network only receive tonotopically ordered acoustic information, analysis of their response properties showed that these units do no longer exhibit any specific frequency dependence. We also found that the response for a given unit was either dependent (Type **I**) or independent (Type **II**) of absolute sound source intensity. That is, weight strength analysis of connections to the binaural layer (Fig. 3) shows that these hidden units can be classified physiologically as binaural responsive cells.

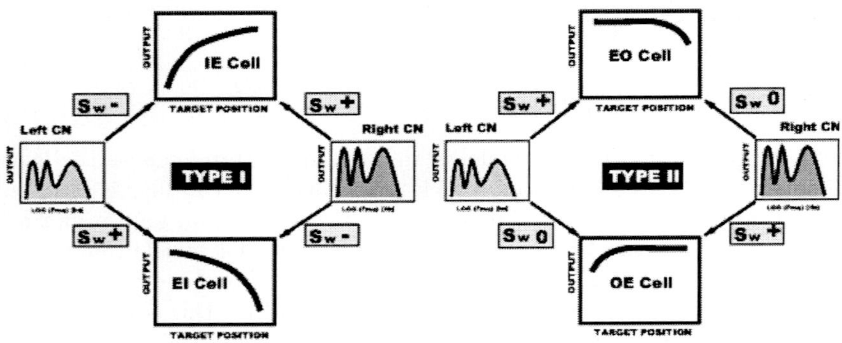

Fig. 3. Binaural layer analysis. The plots (**IE**, **EI**, **EO** and **OE**) show a physiological characterization of the binaural layer units according to their preferred parameter (x-axis) combined with the coinciding acoustic innervation. Coding of innervation: $\Sigma w+$: sum of all weights is positive (excitatory innervation); Σw-: sum of all weights is negative (inhibitory innervation); Σw**O**: no innervation.

Binaurally responsive cells can be divided into functional categories designated by two letters according to the sign of their predominant responses: excitatory response, **E**, inhibitory response, **I**, and no response, **O**. The first letter is the sign of the response produced by stimulation of the contralateral ear, and second is the sign produced by stimulation of the ipsilateral ear [13]. Accordingly, type **I** units functionally resemble **EI** or **IE** cells. Type **II** units functionally resemble **EO** or **OE** cells. Moreover, these neurons are thought to be involved in the coding of IIDs and are found already at the level of the SOC (Fig. 1a) [1].

Type **I** units appear to be sensitive to the total energy difference (Fig. 2) between the two ears. Type **II** units are monaural and appear to be sensitive to the total absolute energy input from one ear only. Intuitively, auditory binaural units should code sound source azimuth using IID, independent of eye position, but the computational mechanism that is responsible for this type of coding is by no means straightforward [3]. Nevertheless, our data indicate that azimuth – which the second hidden layer (hereafter, *audiomotor layer*) needs to extract – is coded by two different mechanisms which are both essential. First, by the total sound energy from one ear only (**EO/OE** units). Second, by the total sound energy difference between the sound energy levels as received by the two ears (**EI/IE** units). At the binaural layer, no topographic azimuth map has been formed. Thus, azimuth appears to be encoded in a distributed or rate-coded format by the two populations of binaural units.

4.2 Audiomotor Units

An important aspect of the response analysis of the second hidden layer is that only 40% of audiomotor units code motor-error (Fig. 4b). Thus eye position clearly affects the tuning of these so-called audiomotor units in much the same way as DLSC neurons, which are thought to be involved in auditory-evoked orienting [10,11]. However, our response profiles deviate from DLSC neurons since they do not show motor-error tuning, and exhibit activity for both ipsilateral and contralateral motor-error – no lateralization. Nevertheless, based on the here observed response properties we can separate the audiomotor units into two types: positive versus negative slope units (Fig. 4b). This suggest that the audiomotor layer codes motor-error in a *rate-coded* manner at the single unit level that occurs prior to the place-coded motor-error responses of the DLSC.

4.3 Solution of the Model to Perform Sensorimotor Transformation

From the finding that 40% of the audiomotor units code motor-error, it is clear that the aspect of connectivity – the projective fields that it receives from units of both the oculomotor and binaural layer – is of prime importance for interpreting the functional role of the audiomotor units.

It turned out that only 40% of the units in the second hidden layer received significant innervation. The remaining 60% were merely innervated and are therefore functionally redundant. As can be appreciated from Fig. 4 the solution adopted by the network for carrying out sensorimotor transformation is to encode both sound source azimuth and eye position in a distributed manner followed by a linearization of both signals through the projective fields of the oculomotor and auditory binaural units.

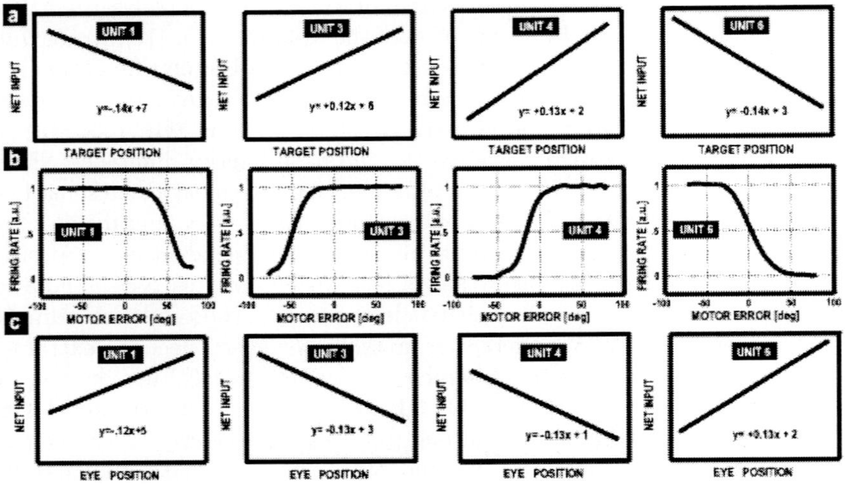

Fig. 4. Audiomotor layer analysis. Overview of acoustic **(a)** and oculomotor innervation **(c)** of four audiomotor units [1,3,4,6] out of a total of $N=10$. Equations are calculated by fitting activation data when the network was simulated at random. **(b)** Response properties of the same subset of units as in (a) and (c). Shown are fitted data: activity as a function of motor-error. Simulations occurred with random sound source intensity and random frequency spectrum of an auditory target, for three distinct eye positions.

Another important aspect of the connectivity to the audiomotor layer is the sign of the slopes of its innervation by both the oculomotor layer and the auditory binaural layer (Fig. 4a,c). Since motor-error can be obtained by subtracting eye position from the sound source azimuth, the network simply has to sum both the oculomotor and the acoustic innervation signals in order to compute motor-error.

5 Discussion and Further Work

Our approach to study sensorimotor transformation deviates from studies that are merely concerned to couple computer simulations of brain structures with the implementation in robotic systems (e.g., see [9]). Here we used neural network simulations as a tool to identify the function of response properties of *real* neurons [8,14]. The strength of our approach is that only a *very limited* but otherwise biologically plausible neural architecture, hierarchy and input/output relationship is modelled as it is thought to occur in the brain.

Although our neural network is by all means a highly simplified model of the audio-oculomotor system as it exist in the primate brain, the hidden unit's representation of *spatial* information is very similar to that observed in brainstem neurons. These neurons can thus play a similar role in primates – build up of an *intermediate* rate-coded computation of motor-error between input and output stages that are part of the audio-oculomotor transformation. Moreover, the fact that our model was limited to sound source azimuth – carrying only IID information –, eye position in the horizontal plane and the computation of motor-error suggests that the brain uses multiple modules for sensorimotor transformations. It would therefore be interesting to extend the model to stimuli that contain cues that code elevation. However, the input that primates require to code elevation reliably has to be modelled after the tonotopic representation of the stimulus spectrum in the auditory nerve. That is, this type of input has to consist out of a large set of transfer functions (so-called HRTFs) measured from free-field at a location near the eardrum [5]. A weaknesses of our model is that its output is unilateral whereas a realistic SC is bilateral. This has resulted in unrealistic tuning and response properties of the audiomotor units. It may therefore be useful to construct a bilateral DLSC.

In barn owls there are neurons in the IC that are not only sensitive to the position of sounds in space, but also to the direction of auditory motion. However, the computational strategy that underlies the localization of moving auditory targets is by no means straightforward (for a discussion see [12]). We therefore plan to extend our model to stimuli that simulate moving auditory targets. Hopefully we find interpretable single unit response properties that can be verified by electrophysiological recordings – made during sound localization experiments with behaving owls that are currently undertaken in our lab.

Acknowledgements. We gratefully acknowledge John van Opstal (Department of Biophysics, University of Nijmegen) who provided the original idea for the present study. The paper benefitted from discussions with Sebastian Möller.

References

1. Casseday, J.H. and Covey, E.: Central Auditory Pathways in Directional Hearing. Chapter 5. Yost, W.A. and Gourevitch, G. (Eds.) Directional Hearing. New York: Springer Verlag (1987) 108–145
2. Goossens, H.H. and Van Opstal, A.J.: Human eye-head coordination in two dimensions under different sensorimotor conditions. Exp Brain Res **114** (1997) 542–560
3. Groh, J.M., Trause, A.S., Underhill, A.M., Clark, K.R. and Inati, S.: Eye position influences auditory responses in primate IC. Neuron **29** (2001) 509–518
4. Heffner, H.E. and Heffner, R.S.: Visual Factors in Sound Localization in Mammals. The Journal of Comparative Neurology (1992) **317** 219–232
5. Hofman P.M. and van Opstal A.J.: Bayesian reconstruction of sound localization cues from responses to random spectra. Biological Cybernetics (2002) **86** 305–16.
6. Jones, W.P. and Hoskins, J.: Back-Propagation: a Generalized Delta Learning Rule. Byte **10** (1987) 155–162
7. Keller, E.L.: The brainstem. Chapter 9. Carpenter, R.H.S. (Ed.) Vision and Visual Dysfunction: Eye movements. **8** London: Macmillian Press (1991) 200–223
8. Pouget, A. and Snyder, L.H.: Computational approaches to sensorimotor transformations. Nature Neuroscience **3** (2000) 1192–1198

9. Rucci, M., Wray, J. and Edelman, G.M.: Robust localization of auditory and visual targets in a robotic barn owl. J Robotics and Autonomous Sys **30** (2000) 181–193
10. Sparks, D.L. and Groh, J.M.: The superior colliculus: A window for viewing issues in integrative neuroscience. Chapter 36. Gazzinga, M.S. (Ed) The cognitive neurosciences. Bradford book, Cambridge (1995) 565–584
11. Sparks, D.L.: Conceptual issues related to the role of the SC in the control of gaze. Current Opinion in Neurobiology (1999) **9** 689–707
12. Wagner, H., Kautz, D., Poganiatz, I.: Principles of acoustic motion detection in animals and man. Trends in Neuroscience (1997) **12** 583–593
13. Yin, T.C.T. and Kuwada, S.: Neural Mechanisms of Binaural Interaction. Chapter 9. Edelman G.M., Gall W.E. and Gowan W.M. (Eds.) Dynamic Aspects of Neocortical Function. New York: John Wiley and Sons (1984) 263–313
14. Zipser, D. and Andersen, R.A.: A back-propagation programmed network that simulates response properties of a subset of posterior parietal neurons. Nature (1988) **25** 679–84

Appendix: Parameter Settings and Stimulus Ranges

TRAINING PARAMETER SETTINGS

Layer Dimensions		**Stimulus Ranges**		**Learning parameters**
cochlear layers:	2x 30	eye position:	[-40,40] [deg]	learning rate: 0.5
eye position layers:	2x 10	azimuth:	[-60,60] [deg]	Initial weight values:[-0.5,0.5]
binaural layer:	4	motor error:	[-100,100] [deg]	Training cycles: 50000
audiomotor layer:	10	sound intensity:	[1.0,1.4] [a.u.]	networks trained: 100
motormap layer:	20	frequency spectrum: [100,10000][Hz]	number of freq. components: 1,2 or 5	

Gender Classification of Human Faces

Arnulf B.A. Graf and Felix A. Wichmann

Max Planck Institute for Biological Cybernetics
Spemannstrasse 38, 72076 Tübingen, Germany
{arnulf.graf, felix.wichmann}@tuebingen.mpg.de

Abstract. This paper addresses the issue of combining pre-processing methods—dimensionality reduction using Principal Component Analysis (PCA) and Locally Linear Embedding (LLE)—with Support Vector Machine (SVM) classification for a behaviorally important task in humans: gender classification. A processed version of the MPI head database is used as stimulus set. First, summary statistics of the head database are studied. Subsequently the optimal parameters for LLE and the SVM are sought heuristically. These values are then used to compare the original face database with its processed counterpart and to assess the behavior of a SVM with respect to changes in illumination and perspective of the face images. Overall, PCA was superior in classification performance and allowed linear separability.

Keywords. Dimensionality reduction, PCA, LLE, gender classification, SVM

1 Introduction

Gender classification is arguably one of the more important visual tasks for an extremely social animal like us humans—many social interactions critically depend on the correct gender perception of the parties involved. Arguably, visual information from human faces provides one of the more important sources of information for gender classification. Not surprisingly, thus, that a very large number of psychophysical studies has investigated gender classification from face perception in humans [1]. The aim of this study is to explore gender classification using learning algorithms. Previous work in machine learning focused on different types of classifiers for gender classification—e.g. SVM versus Radial Basis Function Classifiers or Nearest-Neighbor Classifiers—using only low resolution "thumbnail" images as inputs [2]. Here we investigate the influence of two popular dimensionality reduction methods on SVM classification performance using high-resolution images. Ultimately, the success and failure of certain pre-processors and classification algorithms might inform the cognitive science community about which operators may or may not be plausible candidates for those used by humans.

In sec. 2 the MPI human head image database is presented together with the "clean up" processing required to obtain what we refer to as the *processed*

H.H. Bülthoff et al. (Eds.): BMCV 2002, LNCS 2525, pp. 491–500, 2002.

database. The dimensionality of its elements is reduced in sec. 3 using PCA and LLE and we look at a number of common summary statistics to identify outliers and/or see how the choice of PCA versus LLE influences the homogeneity of the reduced "face space". In sec. 4 gender classification of the processed face database in its PCA and LLE representations is studied. The optimal parameters of the SVM (trade-off parameter and kernel function) and LLE (number of nearest neighbors) are determined heuristically by a parameter search. Furthermore, these parameters are used to compare the original to the processed database and to study the dependency of classification on illumination and perspective of the faces.

2 Original and Processed MPI Head Database

The original MPI human head image database as developed and described in [3] is composed of 100 male and 100 female three-dimensional heads. From these, 256x256 color images were extracted at seven different viewing angles (0, ± 9, ± 18 and $\pm 45°$) and three different illumination conditions (frontal, $\Theta = 0, \Phi = 0$; light from above and off center, $\Theta = 65, \Phi = 40$; light from underneath and off center, $\Theta = -70, \Phi = 35$; Θ is the elevation and Φ the azimuth in degrees). The following inhomogeneities in shape and texture can then be observed: on average the male faces are darker and larger than the females and the faces are not centered, with female faces, on average, slightly more offset to the left. In the processing of the database these cues are eliminated since they may be exploitable by an artificial classifier but are, for humans in a real environment, neither reliable nor scientifically interesting cues to gender: we do not normally have a bias to see people as female in the distance (small size), and neither do we have a tendency to see people in the shade (low luminance) as males. Thus the MPI head database was modified in the following way. First, we equalized the intensity of each face to the global mean intensity over all faces. Second, all faces were re-scaled to the mean face size. Finally all faces were centered in the image by aligning the center of mass to the center of the image. The set of faces obtained following the above scheme is referred to below as *processed* head database. Figure 1 shows 4 female and male exemplars of the original and the processed database for comparison. The above processing should be considered as a first step using *any* face database prior to machine classification or psychophysical investigation of gender classification.

3 Pre-processing Using PCA and LLE

Perhaps the first question to arise in machine categorization is the choice of data representation. Images, of faces or natural scenes, contain highly redundant information so a pixel-by-pixel representation appears not suitable. Thus adequate pre-processing in the context of gender classification of faces implies dimensionality reduction. First (truncated) PCA is considered as a benchmark

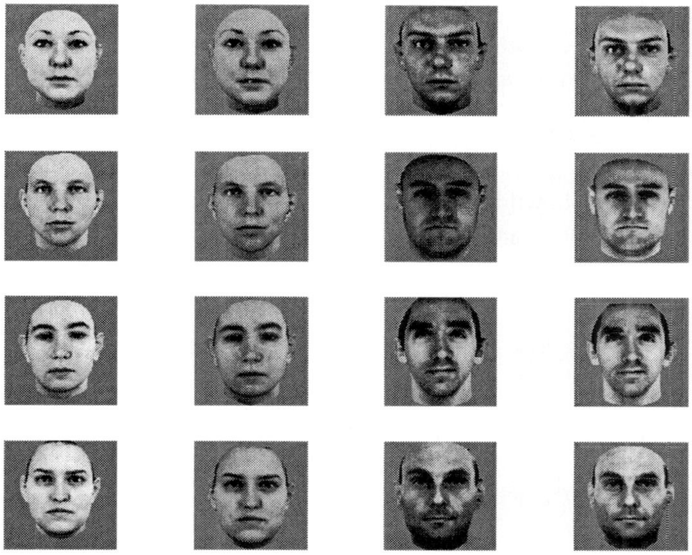

Fig. 1. Comparison between heads from the original database (1st and 3rd columns) and heads from the processed database (2nd and 4th columns).

because of its simplicity and wide domain of application [4]. Perhaps more importantly, PCA decomposition, with the eigenvectors with non-zero eigenvalues referred to as *eigenfaces*, has become a strong candidate as a *psychological* model of how humans process faces [5,6,7]. Second its nonlinear neighborhood-preserving extension, LLE, is considered [8,9]. The latter may be viewed as more biologically-plausible than PCA since it is invariant to rotations, re-scalings and translations: desirable properties for object representation in any biological or biologically-motivated vision system. Here we consider the nearest-neighbor version of LLE since the manifold underlying the face representation cannot be expected to be "smooth" or having a homogeneous sample density. Thus the construction of a local embedding from a fixed number of nearest neighbors appears more appropriate than from a fixed subspace, e.g all neighbors within a hypersphere of fixed radius. We limit the dimensionality of the reduced face space into which PCA or LLE are projecting to 128. In the case of LLE, we consider the 15 nearest neighbors out of a possible maximum of 99, this number being optimal for classification purpose as suggested by the experiments in the next section.

Looking at each of the 200 faces on-screen we find that in "psychological face space" (i.e our perception) no single face appears to be particularly "odd", i.e. the face database seems not to contain outliers. To explore the topography of the PCA- and LLE-induced face spaces the clustering of the elements of the face space is studied by examining the first four moments (mean, variance, skewness and kurtosis) of the distribution of distances between faces. In addition, by iteratively removing the faces corresponding to the tails of the distribution, i.e. the largest outliers, we see how homogeneous the distribution of faces in the respective face spaces is: large changes in the moments after removal of a small number of exemplars may indicate a sub-optimal pre-processing. In total we removed up to 15 faces for each gender.

The individual contributions—the faces—to the four moments of the processed database are shown in figure 2 for the whole database and with 5, respectively 15, outlying faces removed from it. From figure 2 it can be seen that for

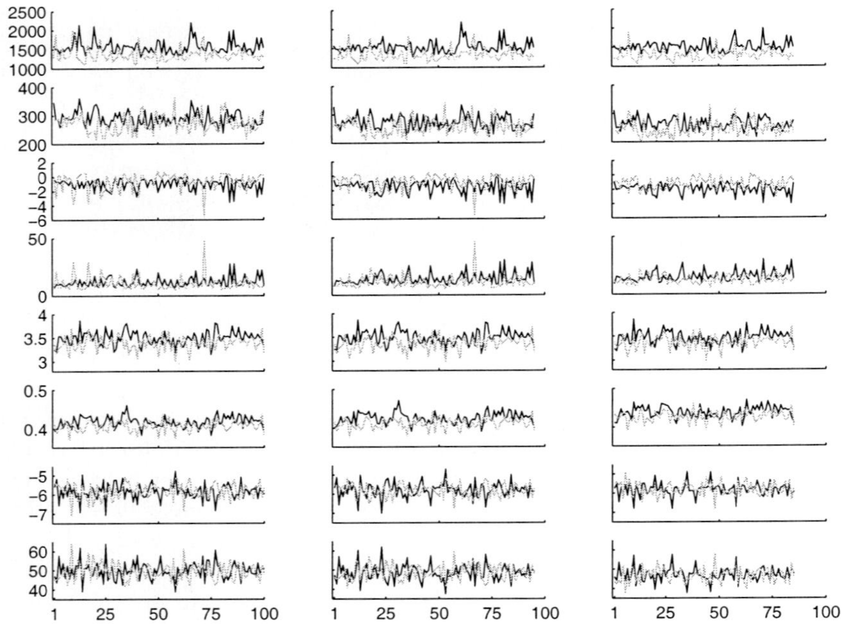

Fig. 2. Comparison of the first four moments (mean, variance, skewness and kurtosis) for each gender based upon PCA (4 first rows) and LLE (4 last rows) for the processed database with (respectively, from left to right) 0, 5, or 15 faces removed. The dark lines correspond to the males and the lighter ones to the females.

PCA one would have to remove 15% of the elements of the original database in order to eliminate the obvious peaks corresponding to outliers such as the one for skewness around female 70. For LLE, on the other hand, the statistics have clearly fewer peaks, even without removal of outliers, implying a better clustering of the data. This may be explained by recalling that LLE is based upon reconstruction of the data preserving local neighborhoods, and thus also the clusters which may be present in the database. If this analysis is correct, clustering algorithms such as one-class SVMs [10] should show superior clustering ability for LLE data representation than for PCA representation.

4 Classification Using SVMs

The purpose of this section is the study of gender classification in the reduced face space given by PCA or LLE using Support Vector Machines (SVMs, see [11]). The performance of SVMs is assessed though their classification error and the number of Support Vectors (SVs). The kernel functions are normalized and the offset of the optimal separating hyperplane is modified as introduced in [12]. The performance of the SVM is assessed using cross-validation experiments consisting of 100 repeats, each one using 60 random training and 40 random testing patterns for each gender. This 60/40% training/testing subdivision of the dataset was suggested by the study of the standard deviation of the classification error in a preliminary set of experiments.

4.1 Determination of Optimal Parameters

We are confronted with a three-parameter optimization problem: the trade-off parameter c of the SVM, its kernel function and the number of nearest neighbors of LLE. For reasons of computational feasibility, we shall proceed heuristically in the determination of these parameters using the processed database, all values being averaged across the 3 illumination conditions and the 7 perspectives. The first parameter, c, is determined separately for PCA and LLE as shown in figure 3 for a linear and a polynomial kernel of degree 2 respectively. These kernel functions were shown to be optimal during pre-run experiments.

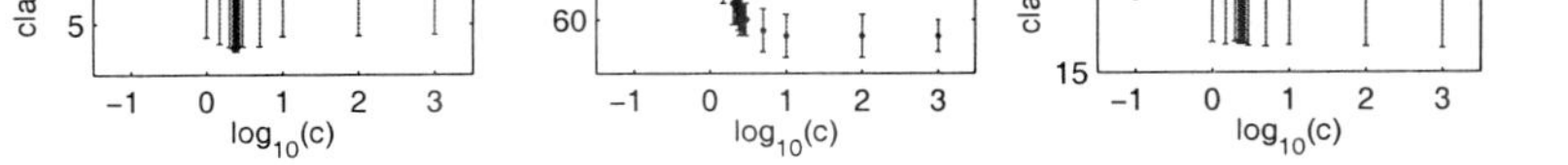

Fig. 3. Mean classification error and number of SVs as function of c using PCA with a linear kernel and LLE with a polynomial kernel of degree 2. In the last case, the number of SVs is found to be constant at a value of 120.

In the case of PCA, the value of c obtained for a minimum classification error differs from the one corresponding to a minimum number of SVs, but both values of c are at least of the same order of magnitude. Since in the context of classification a minimum classification error is more relevant than a reduced number of SVs[1], we shall consider $c_{opt} = 2.4$ as the optimal value of c for PCA in combination with a linear kernel. When doing the same for LLE in combination with a polynomial kernel of degree 2 the classification error curve does not exhibit a global minimum and the number of SVs is constant. We can thus choose c_{opt} as obtained for PCA to be the optimal value of c also in this case. Both classification error curves as function of c exhibits a flat behavior for $1 \leq c \leq 1000$. In this range, the value of c is not of practical importance. This fact combined with the generalization ability of SVMs allows us to extrapolate that the value obtained here for c_{opt} may nearly be also optimal for other kernel functions. However this cannot be guaranteed and this is the price to pay when proceeding heuristically in the three-parameter optimization since a full exploration of these parameters is, alas, computationally prohibitive. The determination of the optimal kernel function of the SVM for PCA and LLE is done by performing classification experiments at c_{opt} as shown in figure 4.

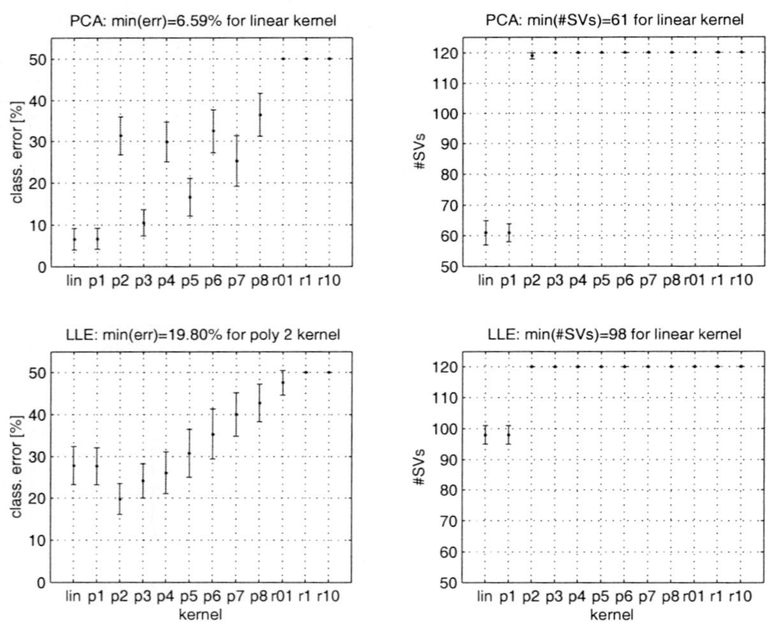

Fig. 4. Classification performance of PCA and LLE with 15 nearest neighbors as function of the kernels: *lin* 1 corresponding to a linear kernel $K(\boldsymbol{x}, \boldsymbol{y}) = \langle \boldsymbol{x}|\boldsymbol{y} \rangle$, *pd* to a polynomial kernel $K(\boldsymbol{x}, \boldsymbol{y}) = (1 + \langle \boldsymbol{x}|\boldsymbol{y} \rangle)^d$ with $d = 1, \ldots, 8$ and $r\gamma$ to a radial basis function $K(\boldsymbol{x}, \boldsymbol{y}) = \exp(-\gamma\|\boldsymbol{x} - \boldsymbol{y}\|^2)$ with $\gamma = 0.1, 1$ and 10 respectively.

[1] A reduced number of SVs may be of higher importance than the actual classification error in the context of minimal data representation or data compression.

From this figure we see that the best performance for PCA comes from using a linear kernel whereas for LLE a polynomial kernel of degree 2 gives the best results[2]. As far as the classification error is concerned, in the case of PCA, RBF kernels are at chance level and polynomial kernels of odd degree seem to be best. The error curve exhibits an instability for increasing degrees of the polynomial function. For LLE, on the other hand, the curve is smoother. Nonetheless, as data reduction method PCA clearly outperforms LLE in terms of classification error and data compression.

4.2 Original versus Processed Database

Here we evaluate classification performance for the processed and the original database for PCA and LLE using at the optimal settings from the previous section. Results are summarized in the following table, all values being averaged across illumination and perspective:

	PCA class. error	PCA $\sharp(SVs)$	LLE class. error	LLE $\sharp(SVs)$
original MPI	$5.16 \pm 2.18\%$	46 ± 4	$10.23 \pm 2.72\%$	120 ± 0
processed MPI	$6.59 \pm 2.60\%$	61 ± 4	$19.80 \pm 3.69\%$	120 ± 0

The superior classification performance for the original database confirms the need for the"clean up" processing applied to the MPI head database: the SVM used some of the obvious, but artifactual, cues for classification such as brightness and size. Note that in the case of LLE the number of SVs is constant for both databases but this is a ceiling effect: all the elements of the dataset are SVs, indicating that LLE may not be suited as a pre-processing algorithm for faces. LLE seems to be more sensitive to the "clean up" of the database suggesting that it may rely more strongly on obvious cues such as brightness or size. Again, the results of these simulations show that LLE performs poorly relative to PCA, both for classification and data compression. Since by definition LLE preserves local neighborhoods, the data is more difficult to be separated unless already *a priori* separable (what appears here not to be the case). PCA on the other hand finds the directions of main variance in the data therefore separating the data and doing an efficient preprocessing for classification. This may explain why LLE is less adapted for classification than PCA, at least for the face database under consideration.

4.3 Behavior with Respect to Illumination and Perspective

Here we assess the stability of the SVM with respect to changes in illumination (values averaged across perspectives) and perspective (values averaged along illuminations) of the processed database. The results are presented in figure 5 using the optimal parameter settings in each case. Classification performance

[2] We tried 5, 10 and 15 nearest neighbors for LLE using c_{opt} and found only very slight differences in performance for 10 and 15, 5 being clearly worse. In the following we always use the best, i.e. 15 nearest neighbors.

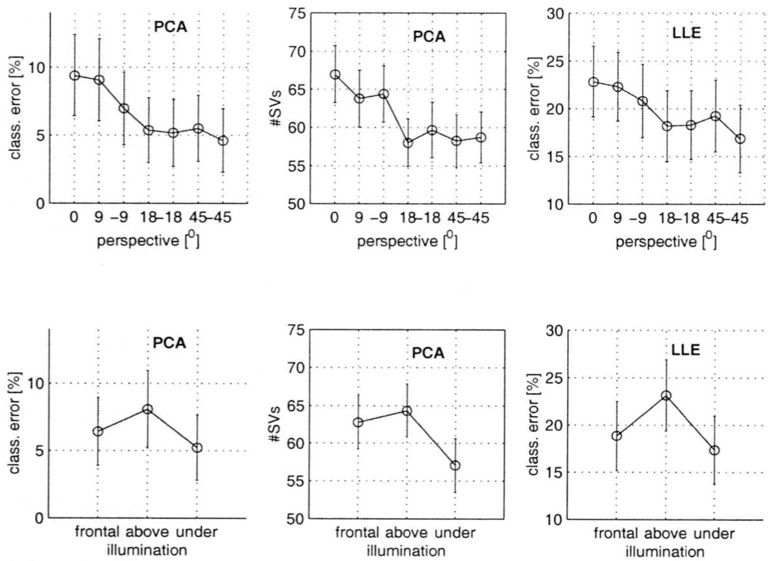

Fig. 5. Classification performance with respect to perspective and illumination for PCA and LLE (for LLE the number of SVs is not plotted since it is constant at 120).

as a function of orientation reveals a decrease of the classification error when moving away from a frontal perspective, i.e. classification is easier for non-frontal perspectives. This result holds for both PCA and LLE. Orientations of ± 18 and ± 45 seem largely equivalent. Note that this result indicates that some of the gender differences must be contained in the depth-profile of faces, for example, nose length or head curvature in depth, which are lost in a frontal projection. Furthermore, human subjects in psychophysical experiments exhibit a similar pattern of performance: they, too, show improved face recognition and gender classification for non-frontal presentation (the so called “3/4 view advantage” [13]).

Classification error and the number of SVs obtained as a function of illumination may show a pattern different from that of humans. Humans tend to perform best under natural illumination conditions, i.e light from above. Both for PCA and LLE performance is, however, worst for this illumination. Note that this effect is very small albeit consistent across PCA and LLE. A larger set of illumination conditions would be required to reach more definite conclusions on this issue.

5 Conclusions

The main results of the present study are, first, that PCA face space is clearly superior to that induced by LLE for classification tasks. Second, PCA face space is linearly separable with respect to gender. Having a linear output stage has recently become a topic of interest in the context of complex, dynamical systems ("echo state" recurrent neural networks [14] and "liquid state machines" [15]) as it allows learning in such systems. As suggested in [15], this may even be a generic working principle of the brain to attempt to transform the problem at hand such that it becomes linearly separable. LLE, on the other hand, seems to require a polynomial kernel of degree two, forfeiting linear separability. For the poor performance of LLE compared to PCA there is, as in the case of the orientation dependency of classification, yet again an interesting parallel to human vision. It has been claimed that human expertise in face recognition during development from children to adults is brought about at least in part by a change in processing strategy: children focus on details (e.g. eyes or nose) whereas adults look at the whole face (sometimes referred to as "holistic processing") [16]. Eigenfaces in PCA face space are certainly fairly global (or holistic). Despite the fact that LLE face space is more homogeneous, as shown in sec. 3, and despite the algorithm displaying some biologically interesting properties like translation and rotation invariance, our results suggest that it is not well suited for gender classification. Finally we showed that the MPI head database contains factors such as size and lightness which are correlated with the classification result (as shown in sec. 4.2) but which cannot necessarily be relied upon to be informative either in real life or in other test sets for which the machine might be applied. Hence the database needs to be "cleaned up" (size and brightness normalization, centering) before it is useful for machine learning. This is an important issue also for other databases. Future work will focus on including additional biologically-motivated pre-processing techniques such as non-negative matrix factorization [17].

References

1. A.J. O'Toole, K.A. Deffenbacher, D. Valentin, K. McKee, D. Huff and H. Abdi. The Perception of Face Gender: the Role of Stimulus Structure in Recognition and Classification. *Memory & Cognition*, 26(1), 1998.
2. B. Moghaddam and M.-H. Yang. Gender Classification with Support Vector Machines. *Proceedings of the International Conference on Automatic Face and Gesture Recognition* (FG), 2000.
3. V. Blanz and T. Vetter. A Morphable Model for the Synthesis of 3D Faces. *Proc. Siggraph99*, pp. 187–194. Los Angeles: ACM Press, 1999.
4. R. O. Duda and P.E. Hart and D.G. Stork. *Pattern Classification*. John Wiley & Sons, 2001.
5. L. Sirovich, and M. Kirby. Low-Dimensional Procedure for the Characterization of Human Faces. *Journal of the Optical Society of America A*, 4(3), 519–24, 1987.
6. M. Turk and A. Pentland. Eigenfaces for Recognition. *Journal of Cognitive Neuroscience*, 3(1), 71–86, 1991.
7. A.J. O'Toole, H. Abdi, K.A. Deffenbacher and D. Valentin. Low-Dimensional Representation of Faces in Higher Dimensions of the Face Space. *Journal of the Optical Society of America A*, 10(3), 405–11, 1993.
8. S. T. Roweis and L.K. Saul. Nonlinear Dimensionality Reduction by Locally Linear Embedding. *Science*, 290, 2000.

9. L.K. Saul and S. T. Roweis. An Introduction to Locally Linear Embedding. Report at AT&T Labs-Research, 2000.
10. B. Schölkopf, J. C. Platt, J. Shawe-Taylor, A. Smola and R.C. Williamson. Estimating the Support of a High-Dimensional Distribution. *Neural Computation*, 13(7), 2001.
11. V. N. Vapnik. *The Nature of Statistical Learning Theory.* Springer, 1995.
12. A. B. A. Graf and S. Borer. Normalization in Support Vector Machines. *Proceedings of the DAGM*, LNCS 2191, 2001.
13. V. Bruce, T. Valentine and A.D. Baddeley. The Basis of the 3/4 View Advantage in Face Recognition. *Applied Cognitive Psychology*, 1:109–120, 1987.
14. H. Jaeger, The "Echo State" Approach to Analysing and Training Recurrent Neural Networks. GMD Report 148, German National Research Center for Information Technology, 2001.
15. W. Maass, T. Natschläger, and H. Markram. Real-Time Computing without Stable States: A New Framework for Neural Computation Based on Perturbations. *Neural Computation*, 2002 (in press).
16. M. Baenninger. The Development of Face Recognition: Featural or Configurational Processing? *Journal of Experimental Child Psychology*, 57(3), 377–96, 1994.
17. D. D. Lee and H. S. Seung. Learning the Parts of Objects by Non-Negative Matrix Factorization. *Nature*, 401:788–791, 1999.

Face Reconstruction from Partial Information Based on a Morphable Face Model*

Bon-Woo Hwang[1] and Seong-Whan Lee[2]

[1] VirtualMedia, Inc., #1808 Seoul Venture Town,
Yoksam-Dong, Kangnam-Gu, Seoul 135-080, Korea
bwhwang@virtualmedia.co.kr

[2] Center for Artificial Vision Research, Korea University,
Anam-dong, Seongbuk-ku, Seoul 136-701, Korea
swlee@image.korea.ac.kr

Abstract. This paper proposes a method for reconstructing a whole face image from partial information based on a morphable face model. Faces are modeled by linear combinations of prototypes of shape and texture. With the shape and texture information of pixels in an given region, we can estimate optimal coefficients for linear combinations of prototypes of shape and texture. In such an over-determined condition, where the number of pixels in the given region is greater than the number of prototypes, we find an optimal solution using projection for least square minimization(LSM). Our experimental results show that reconstructed faces are very natural and plausible like real photos. We interpret the encouraging performance of our proposed method as evidence in support of the hypothesis that the human visual system may reconstruct an whole information from partial information using prototypical examples.

1 Introduction

In studies from past to present, modeling the properties of noise, which contrast with those of an image, has been used for removing noise[7][12]. However, those methods cannot remove the noise that is distributed in a wide region, because they use only local properties. In addition, the region in the image which has similar properties with noise gets degraded in the process of removing noise.

In contrast to such approaches, top-down, object-class-specific and model-based approaches are highly tolerant to sensor noise, incompleteness of input images and occlusion due to other objects[5]. Hence, the top-down approach to interpretation of images of variable objects are now attracting considerable interest in many studies[4][5][6][10]. The power of their algorithm derives from high-level knowledge learned from the set of prototypical components.

Turk and Pentland proposed a method for reconstructing missing parts of a partially occluded face using eigenfaces based on Principal Component

* This research was supported by Creative Research Initiatives of the Ministry of Science and Technology, Korea.

H.H. Bülthoff et al. (Eds.): BMCV 2002, LNCS 2525, pp. 501–510, 2002.

Analysis(PCA)[10]. Especially their method showed good results only when applied to an unknown face of a person of whom different images are in the training set or a face that was itself part of the initial training set.

Jones and Poggio proposed a method for recovering missing parts in an input face in addition to establishing correspondence of the input face with iteration of stochastic gradient procedure based on a morphable model[6]. Their algorithm is slow due to iterative procedure at each pyramid level and deterioration of convergence speed by exclusion of the fixed number of points regardless of the percentage of occlusion. However, their method has the advantage that it is not required to know which region of the face is damaged and establish correspondence on undamaged regions.

Hwang et al. proposed a method for reconstructing the face using a small set of feature points by least square minimization(LSM) method based on pseudoinverse without iteration procedure[4]. They assume that the number of feature points is much smaller than that of bases of PCA. As a result, the accuracy of reconstruction is restricted. Also, obtaining pseudoinverse by singular value decomposition needs heavy computation power in order to solve LSM.

2 2D Morphable Face Model

Our algorithm is based on the morphable face model introduced by Poggio et al.[1][2][8] and developed further by Vetter et al.[3][11]. Assuming that the pixelwise correspondence on the facial image has already been established[3], the 2D shape of a face is coded as the displacement field from a reference image that serves as the origin of our space. So the shape of a face image is represented by a vector $S = (d_1^x, d_1^y, \cdots, d_N^x, d_N^y)^T \epsilon\ \Re^{2N}$. Where (d_k^x, d_k^y) is the x, y displacement of a point that corresponds to a point x_k in the reference face and can be rewritten $S(x_k)$. The texture is coded as the intensity map of the image which results from mapping the face onto the reference face. Thus, the shape normalized texture is represented as a vector $T = (i_1, \cdots, i_N)^T \epsilon\ \Re^N$. Where i_k is the intensity of a point that corresponds to a point x_k among N pixels in the reference face and can be rewritten $T(x_k)$. By Principal Component Analysis, a basis transformation is performed to an orthogonal coordinate system formed by eigenvectors s_i and t_i of the covariance matrices C_S and C_T on the set of m faces. C_S and C_T are computed over the differences of the shape and the texture, $\tilde{S} = S - \bar{S}$ and $\tilde{T} = T - \bar{T}$. Where $\bar{S}$ and $\bar{T}$ represent the mean of shape and that of texture, respectively.

$$S = \bar{S} + \sum_{i=1}^{m-1} \alpha_i s_i, \quad T = \bar{T} + \sum_{i=1}^{m-1} \beta_i t_i, \tag{1}$$

where $\boldsymbol{\alpha}, \ \boldsymbol{\beta}\ \epsilon\ \Re^{m-1}$.

3 Face Reconstruction

3.1 Overview

We explain prior conditions and keywords and give an overview of the procedure for obtaining a reconstructed facial image from partial information.

Prior conditions:

- Positions of pixels in a damaged region by virtual objects on an input face are known.
- Displacement among pixels in an input face which correspond to those in the reference face except pixels in damaged region, is known.

We can satisfy two prior conditions by using the graphical user interface to segment damaged region and to outline the facial main component or by applying a semi-automatic algorithm in practical application.

Before explaining reconstruction procedure, we define two types of warping processes, forward and backward warping. Forward warping warps a texture onto each face with a shape. This process results in a facial image. Backward warping warps an input face onto the reference face with a shape. This process results in a texture. The mathematical definition and more details about the forward and backward warping can be found in [11].

The reconstruction procedure from a damaged face is as follows:

Step 1. Obtain the texture of a damaged face by backward warping.

Step 2. Reconstruct a full shape from the given incomplete shape which excludes damaged regions.

Step 3. Reconstruct a full texture from the obtained texture damaged by virtual objects.

Step 4. Synthesize a facial image by forward warping the reconstructed texture with the reconstructed shape.

Step 5. Replace the pixels in the damaged regions by the reconstructed ones and combine the original and the reconstructed image in the border regions outside of the damaged region using a weight mask according to the distance from the border.

Step 1 and 4 are explained about morphable face models in many studies[5][6][11]. Therefore, we mainly describe Step 2 and 3 for reconstructing occluded shape and texture.

3.2 Problem Definition for Reconstruction

Since there are shape and texture elements only for an unoccluded region, we can obtain an approximation to the deformation required for the unoccluded region by using coefficients of bases. Our goal is to find an optimal solution in such an over-determined condition. In other words, we want to find α which will satisfy Equation 2.

$$\tilde{S}(x_j) = \sum_{i=1}^{m-1} \alpha_i s_i(x_j), \ (j = 1, \cdots, n), \tag{2}$$

where $x_1, \cdots, x_n$ are pixels in an undamaged region. n, the number of pixels in the undamaged region is about ten times as great as $m-1$, the number of bases. We can imagine that the number n of observations is larger than the number $m-1$ of unknowns. Probably there will not exist a choice of α that perfectly fits the $\tilde{S}$. So, the problem is to choose α^* so as to minimize the error. We define an error function, $E(\alpha)$(Equation 4), as the sum of square of errors which are the difference between the known displacements of pixels in the undamaged region and its reconstructed ones. The problem(Equation 3) is to find α which minimizes the error function, $E(\alpha)$, which is given as:

$$\alpha^* = arg \min_{\alpha} E(\alpha), \tag{3}$$

with the error function,

$$E(\alpha) = \sum_{j=1}^{n} (\tilde{S}(x_j) - \sum_{i=1}^{m-1} \alpha_i s_i(x_j))^2. \tag{4}$$

where $x_1, \cdots, x_n$ are pixels in the undamaged region.

3.3 Solution by Least Square Minimization

According to Equation 3∼4, we can solve this problem using a least square solution. Equation 2 is equivalent to the following:

$$\begin{pmatrix} s_1(x_1) & \cdots & s_{m-1}(x_1) \\ \vdots & \ddots & \vdots \\ s_1(x_n) & \cdots & s_{m-1}(x_n) \end{pmatrix} \begin{pmatrix} \alpha_1 \\ \vdots \\ \alpha_{m-1} \end{pmatrix} = \begin{pmatrix} \tilde{S}(x_1) \\ \vdots \\ \tilde{S}(x_n) \end{pmatrix}. \tag{5}$$

We rewrite Equation 5 as:

$$\mathbf{S}\ \alpha = \tilde{\mathbf{S}}, \tag{6}$$

where

$$\mathbf{S} = \begin{pmatrix} s_1(x_1) & \cdots & s_{m-1}(x_1) \\ \vdots & \ddots & \vdots \\ s_1(x_n) & \cdots & s_{m-1}(x_n) \end{pmatrix},$$

$$\alpha = (\alpha_1, \cdots, \alpha_{\mathbf{m-1}})^T,\ \tilde{\mathbf{S}} = (\tilde{\mathbf{S}}(\mathbf{x_1}), \cdots, \tilde{\mathbf{S}}(\mathbf{x_n}))^{\mathbf{T}}. \tag{7}$$

The least square solution to an inconsistent $\mathbf{S}\alpha = \tilde{\mathbf{S}}$ of n equation in $m-1$ unknowns satisfies $\mathbf{S}^T\mathbf{S}\alpha^* = \mathbf{S}^T\tilde{\mathbf{S}}$. If the columns of $\mathbf{S}$ are linearly independent, then $\mathbf{S}^T\mathbf{S}$ has an inverse and

$$\alpha^* = (\mathbf{S}^T\mathbf{S})^{-1}\mathbf{S}^T\tilde{\mathbf{S}}. \tag{8}$$

The projection of $\tilde{\mathbf{S}}$ onto the column space is therefore $\hat{\mathbf{S}} = \mathbf{S}\alpha^*$. By using Equation 1 and 8, we obtain

$$S(x_j) = \bar{S}(x_j) + \sum_{i=1}^{m-1} \alpha_i^* s_i(x_j), \ (j = 1, \ldots, k), \tag{9}$$

where $x_1, \cdots, x_k$ are pixels in the whole facial region and k is the number of pixels in the whole facial region.

By using Equation 9, we can get the correspondence of all pixels. Similarly, we can reconstruct full texture T. We previously made the assumption that the columns of $\mathbf{S}$ are linearly independent in Equation 6. Otherwise, Equation 8 may not be satisfied. If $\mathbf{S}$ has dependent columns, the solution α^* will not be unique. The optimal solution in this case can be solved by pseudoinverse of $\mathbf{S}$[9]. But, for our purpose of effectively reconstructing a facial image from a damaged one, this is unlikely to happen.

4 Experimental Results and Analyses

4.1 Face Database

For testing the proposed method, we used 200 two dimensional images of Caucasian faces that were rendered from a database of three-dimensional head models recorded with a laser scanner($Cyberware^{TM}$)[3][11]. The resolution of the images was 256 by 256 pixels and the color images were converted to 8-bit gray level images. PCA was performed on a random subset of 100 facial images. The other 100 images were used for testing our algorithm. Specifically, test data is a set of facial images, which have components such as a left eye, a right eye, both eyes, a nose and a mouth occluded by virtual objects. The shape and size of the virtual objects are identical to every face, but each position of those is dependent on that of components for every face. The position of components is extracted automatically from correspondence to the reference face.

In our face database, we use a hierarchical, gradient-based optical flow algorithm to obtain a pixelwise correspondence[11]. The correspondence is defined between a reference facial image and a individual image in the database and is estimated by the local translation between corresponding gray-level intensity patches. In addition, the algorithm is applied in a hierarchical coarse-to-fine approach in order to efficiently handle the optical flow correspondences across multiple pixel displacements. For these reasons, the obtained correspondence of the neighbor pixels in a facial image has similar pattern and the correspondence of the facial components may be estimated by that of the skin region near the facial components even if the correspondence of the facial components is removed. Therefore, in order to prevent the unexpected information from preserving, we exclude not only the shape and texture of pixels in the damaged region of the test data set but also that in the skin region. In our experiments, the white region in Fig. 1 (b) is masked.

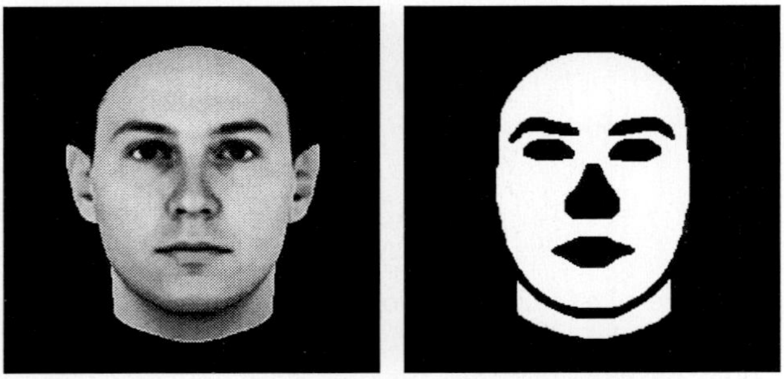

(a) (b)

Fig. 1. (a) Reference face. (b) mask of skin region in the reference image

4.2 Reconstruction of Shape and Texture

As mentioned before, 2D-shape and texture of facial images are treated separately. Therefore, a facial image is synthesized by combining the shape and texture after reconstructing both.

Fig. 2 shows the examples of the facial image reconstructed from the shape and texture damaged by virtual objects. The images on the top row are the occluded facial images by virtual objects and those on the middle row are the facial images reconstructed by the proposed method. Those on the bottom row are the original facial images. Fig. 2 (a) -(d) represents that a left eye, a nose, a mouth and all components of the face are occluded by the virtual objects, respectively. Not only the shape information of each component, but also the texture information of that is very naturally reconstructed. Although we don't apply heuristic algorithms like symmetry in Fig. 2 (a), the occluded eye is reconstructed similarly to the undamaged opposite eye. In case that all components of face are occluded in Fig. 2 (d), the shape and texture of only faceline can be used for reconstructing facial images. The reconstructed facial images are plausible, but are not much similar to the original ones.

Fig. 3 show the mean reconstruction errors for shapes, textures and synthesized images. Horizontal axes of Fig. 3 (a) and (b) represent the occluded components by virtual objects. Vertical axes of them represent the mean displacement error per pixel and the mean intensity error per pixel(for an image using 256 gray level), respectively. Standard deviations of errors are represented with mean errors, too. Err_S_x and Err_S_y in Fig. 3 (a) imply the x-directional mean displacement error and the y-directional one for shape, respectively. And Err_T and Err_I in Fig. 3 (b) imply the mean intensity error for texture and that for image, respectively. Notice that the mean errors of texture and image in the case that both eyes are occluded are greater than those in the case that all components are occluded. We guess that flat gray values in a nose and a mouth reduce the mean intensity errors per pixel for texture and image in the case that all components are occluded.

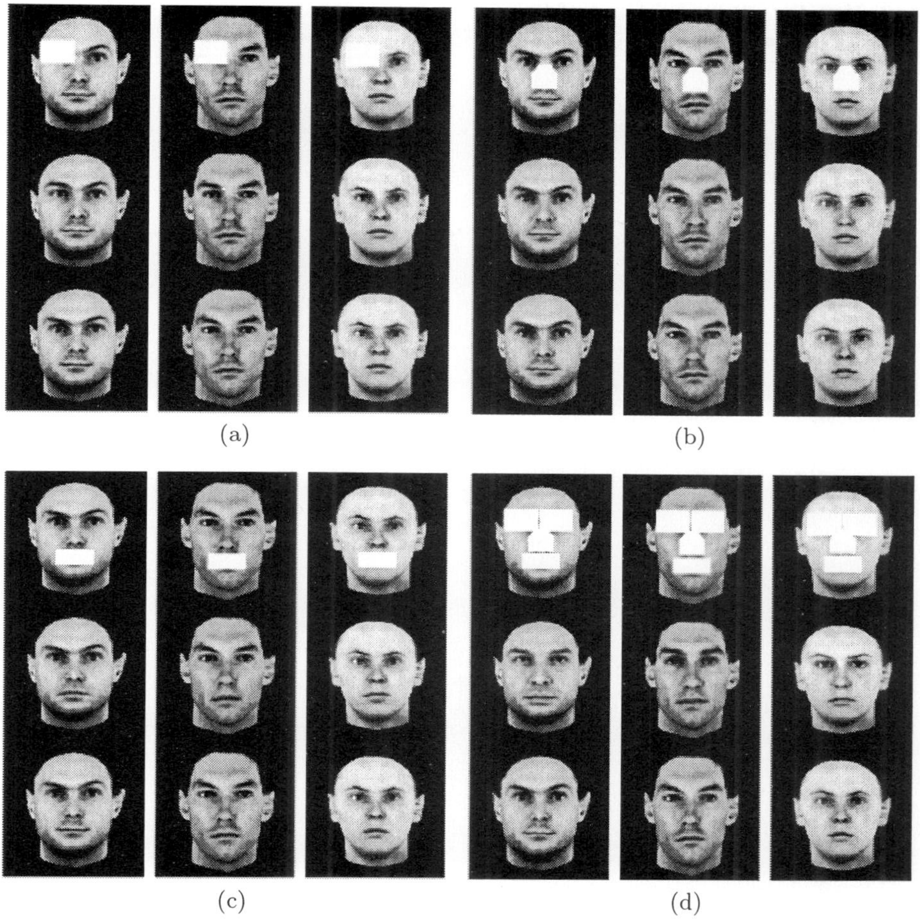

Fig. 2. Examples of reconstructed face

The quality of the reconstructed face was tested with increasing occlusion. An occluding square is randomly placed over the input face to occlude some percentage of the face contrary to the previous experiment, in which the virtual objects are inserted to main facial components. The percentages tested are 5% through 50% at steps of 5%. In Fig. 4, the horizontal axes and vertical axes of a graph represent the ratio of occluded area to face area and the mean $L2$-Norm error for 100 synthesized images, respectively. Fig. 4 shows that the error increases gradually with increasing occlusion.

Finally, we perform a reconstruction experiment with non-artificial data, faces damaged by real object under uncontrolled illumination condition. The images are normalized according to the distance between eyes of the reference face and are aligned to a common position at the tip of a nose. Fig. 5 represents

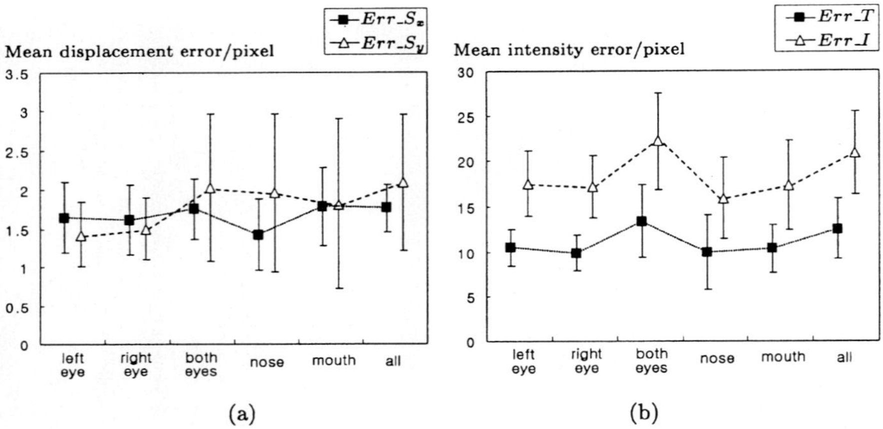

Fig. 3. Mean reconstruction errors

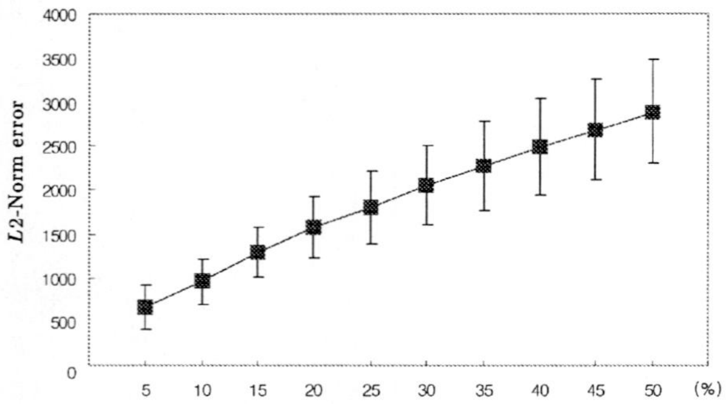

Fig. 4. The mean $L2$-Norm error for reconstructed images

the result of male and female faces damaged by real objects such as sunglasses and a pile of stones under various illumination conditions. Although the quality of reconstructed faces is lower than those of results of Fig. 2 performed on the carefully controlled database, we can confirm that the facial images are naturally reconstructed under uncontrolled environments except for the wrinkles and shadows on faces.

5 Conclusions and Further Research

In this paper, we have proposed an efficient face reconstruction method based on a 2D morphable face model. The proposed method uses a strategy: computing linear coefficients minimizing the error, difference between the given shape/texture and the linear combination of the shape/texture prototypes in the undamaged region. And applying the obtained coefficients to the shape and

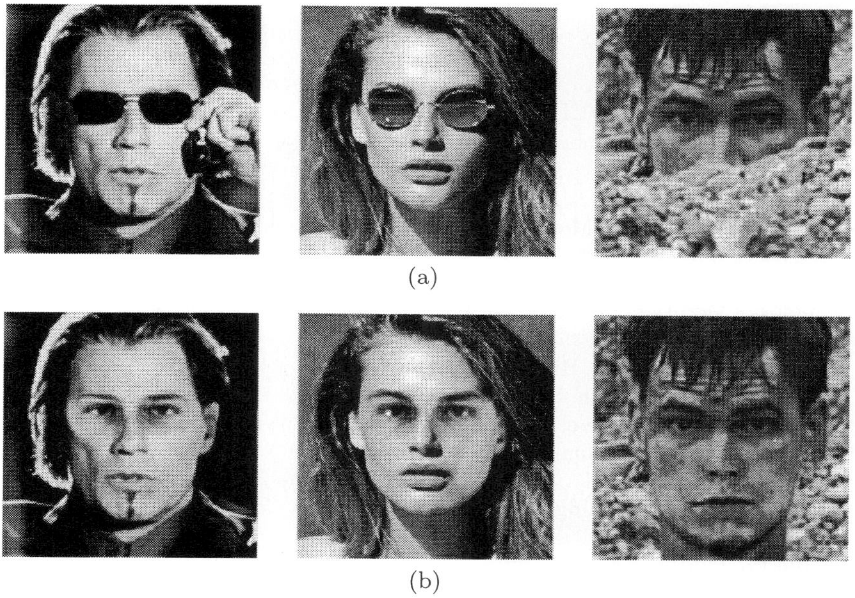

Fig. 5. (a) Facial images damaged by sunglasses or a pile of stones (b) facial images reconstructed by the proposed method.

texture prototypes in the damaged region, respectively. We interpret the encouraging performance of our proposed method as evidence in support of the hypothesis that the human visual system may reconstruct an whole information from partial information using prototypical examples.

In contrary to previous studies, this method does not require iterative processes, as well as is suitable for obtaining an optimal reconstruction image from partial information by simple projection for LSM. The experiment results, which are similar to the original ones or not, are very natural and plausible like real photos. However, the proposed method requires two prior conditions. First, positions of the pixels in the damaged regions on an input face are known. Second, displacement among the pixels in an input face which correspond to those in the reference face except pixels in the damaged region, is known. It is a challenge for researchers to obtain the correspondence between the reference face and a given face image being damaged or not. Our future work is to develop an automatic algorithm to overcome restrictions of these prior conditions.

Acknowledgement. We would like to thank Dr. Volker Blanz and Dr. Thomas Vetter for helpful discussions and advice. In addition, we thank the Max-Planck-Institute for providing the MPI Face Database.

References

1. Beymer, D., Shashua, A. and Poggio, T.: Example-based image analysis and synthesis. AI Memo 1431/CBCL Paper 80, Massachusetts Institute of Technology, Cambridge, MA, November (1993)
2. Beymer, D., Poggio, T.: Image representation for visual learning. Science **272** (1996) 1905–1909
3. Blanz, V., Vetter, T.: Morphable model for the synthesis of 3D faces. Proc. of SIGGRAPH'99, Los Angeles, (1999) 187–194
4. Hwang, B.-W., Blanz, V., Vetter, T., Lee, S.-W.: Face reconstruction from a small number of feature points. Proc. of Int. Conf. on Pattern Recognition **2**, Barcelona, September (2000) 842–845
   Jones, M. J., Poggio, T.: Hierarchical morphable models. Proc. of Computer Vision and Pattern Recognition, Santa Barbara (1998) 820–826
5. Jones, M. J., Sinha, P., Vetter, T., Poggio, T.: Top-down learning of low-level vision tasks[brief communication]. Current Biology **7** (1997) 991–994
6. Jones, M. J., Poggio, T.: Multidimensional morphable models: a framework for representing and matching object classes. Jornal of Computer Vision **29** 2 (1998) 107–131
7. Narendra, P. M.: A Separable median filter for image noise smoothing. IEEE Trans. on Pattern Analysis and Machine Intelligence **3** 1 (1981) 20–29
8. Poggio, T., Vetter, T.: Recognition and structure from one 2D model view: observations on prototypes, object classes and symmetries. AI Memo 1347/CBIP Paper 69, Massachusetts Institute of Technology, Cambridge, MA, February (1992)
9. Strang, G.: Linear algebra and its applications. Harcourt Brace Jovanovich College publishers, Orlando, FL, (1988) 442–451
10. Turk M., Pentland, A.: Eigenfaces for recognition. Journal of Cognitive Neuroscience **3** 1 (1991) 71–86
11. Vetter T., Troje, N. E.: Separation of texture and shape in images of faces for image coding and synthesis. Journal of the Optical Society of America A **14** 9 (1997) 2152–2161
12. Windyga, P. S.: Fast impulsive noise removal. IEEE Trans. on Image Processing **10** 1 (2001) 173–178

Dynamics of Face Categorization

Jeounghoon Kim

School of Humanities and Social Sciences, KAIST,
373-1 Kusong-dong, Yusong-gu, Taejon 305-701, Korea
miru@kaist.ac.kr

Abstract. A new class of synthetic face stimuli has been recently introduced for studying visual face processing. Using the synthetic faces, the aspects of visual process for face categorization were investigated. In a good agreement with previous studies using an entirely different set of stimuli, it was found that there is a hysteresis in face categorization. This dynamic property of face processing could be readily explained by a simple modification of current neural model incorporating recurrent inhibitory interactions among neural units.

1 Introduction

Several anatomical and physiological studies have revealed that there are two visual processing streams: "ventral pathway" for form and color processing, $V1 \rightarrow V2 \rightarrow V4 \rightarrow IT$ and "dorsal pathway" for motion processing, $V1 \rightarrow V2 \rightarrow MT \rightarrow MST$ [1,2]. It has been suggested that the aspects of the information processing at the early stages of ventral processing stream, so referred to as "what pathway", can be explained by linear operations through a bank of local orientation and spatial frequency filters. At the other end of this stream, electrophysiological study using single unit recording has also shown that neurons at the highest level in IT respond specifically to highly complex pattern such as faces. The characteristics of visual form processing from the early to late stages up to date could be summarized as shown in figure 1. In this processing stream, however, not much has been known about the transformations which occur in $V4$ between these two levels.

To investigate the characteristics of high level form information processing at this intermediate stage, we can exploit the observation that the optimal stimuli for many neurons in $V4$ area are smoothly curved shapes. A new class of synthetic face stimuli thus has been recently introduced for studying visual face processing [3,4]. A key idea is to use radial frequency components for creating a synthetic face. Different combinations of radial frequency components, defined as the sinusoidal modulation of the radius of a circle in polar coordinates, can result in all kinds of contour shapes. Here are brief descriptions for constructing a synthetic face proposed by Wilson and colleagues. They used a radial fourth derivative of a Gaussian as the base circular pattern, which is deformed then by applying a radial sinusoidal modulation to the radius. The equation for a radial fourth derivative of a Gaussian is as follows. In the equation 1, r_0 is the mean

H.H. Bülthoff et al. (Eds.): BMCV 2002, LNCS 2525, pp. 511–518, 2002.

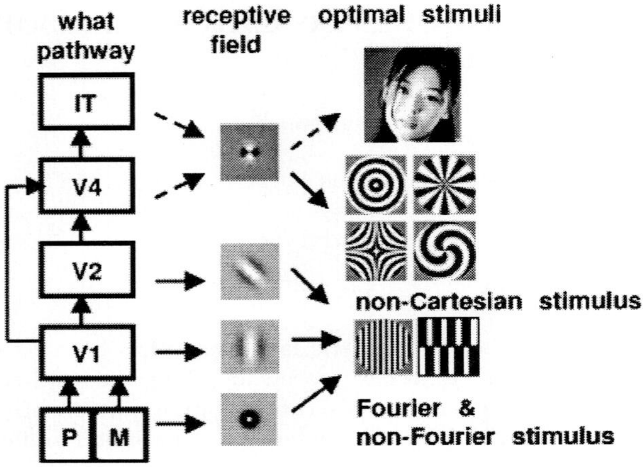

Fig. 1. Anatomical pathway, receptive fields and optimal stimuli for visual form processing from the early to late stages ($\rightarrow$ known; $\dashrightarrow$ unknown)

radius, C is the pattern contrast and σ determines the peak spatial frequency. The base circles are deformed by a sinusoidal modulation of the radius of a circle as described in equation 2, where A is the radial modulation amplitude, ω is the radial frequency and ϕ is the phase of the pattern (see [4] for the details).

$$D4(r) = C\left(1 - 4\left(\frac{r - r_0}{\sigma}\right)^2 + \frac{4}{3}\frac{r - r_0}{\sigma}\right)^4 \exp\left(-\left(\frac{r - r_0}{\sigma}\right)^2\right) \quad (1)$$

$$r(\theta) = r_0(1 + A\sin(\omega\theta + \phi)) \quad (2)$$

An illustration for combination of radial frequency components is shown in figure 2, where the shape resulting from adding components 3 and 10 is markedly different from the origins.

Fig. 2. The contour shape resulting from adding 3 and 10 radial frequency components

Synthetic faces are extracted from digital photographs of individual faces and bandpass filtered after converting into radial frequencies for the head shape as shown in figure 3. Thirty seven measurements including head shape (14 coefficients), hair line (9 coefficients), location of the eyes, mouth, height of the brows above the eyes, and nose (14 points) are represented by the dots superimposed on the photograph. Psychophysical experiments have shown that the synthetic faces are sufficiently complex to capture a significant portion of the geometric information that individuates faces [3,4]. The synthetic faces have another advantage in studying the face recognition processing without confounding cues such as hair type, skin texture, color, etc.

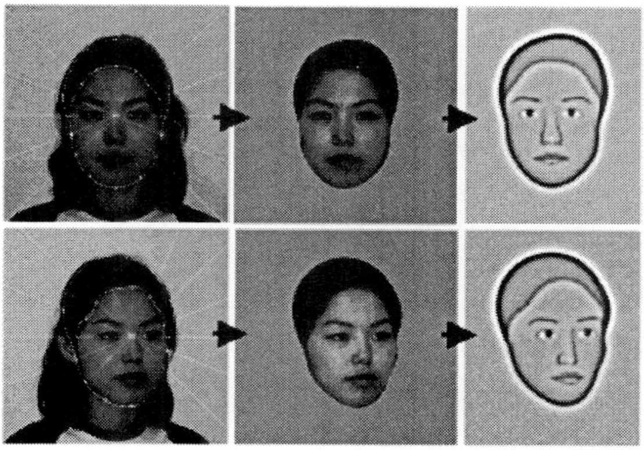

Fig. 3. Construction of a synthetic face. Head shape and hairline are digitized in polar coordinates at 16 and 9 positions. The locations of eyes, height of eyebrows, length and width of nose, location of mouse and thickness of lips are also digitized resulting total 37 numbers.

Wilson and colleagues [4] further devised hyper cubes, in which one face served as the origin of a local coordinate system, while four other served to define axes that were mutually orthogonal and normalized to the same total amount of geometric variation as shown in figure 4. Using the 4D hyper cubes, they measured the increment discrimination thresholds for familiar and unfamiliar faces and found that discrimination thresholds for unfamiliar faces are 1.45 times larger than for familiar faces. This result has been replicated using different race faces [5].

The hyper cubes with synthetic faces could give us a quantitative insight into the visual processing of categorization. Categorization is one of the oldest issues in visual perception. However, research on this issue up to date has been mainly qualitative in nature. The objects in this research are to explore the perceptual aspects of face categorization and design a neural model for the perceptual categorizing effect.

Fig. 4. Construction of a synthetic face cube. The faces served as origin are in the leftmost column. The rightmost column shows the five different faces normalized to 16% total variation from the origin. Each face was mutually orthogonal and normalized to the same total amount of geometric variation The faces between them are created at equally spaced in 37 dimensions.

2 Experiment

2.1 Background

Kelso and colleagues [6] suggested that categorical perception is a dynamical process. As a demonstration of multi-stability of the perceptual dynamics, they examined the transition of perceptual stability using Glass patterns. In their experiments, Glass patterns were sequentially presented from random to order or vice versa, where the dot positions were changed systematically at each frame. They found that there is a hysteresis in most, 72%, of trials and argued that perceptual persistence based on previous experience is a compelling evidence for nonlinearity and multi-stability in categorical perception. Hysteresis was also demonstrated in apparent motion and speech categorization, despite parameter changes that favor an alternative. Keep in line with this idea, an experiment is designed to explore the perceptual dynamics of face categorization. Instead of line-drawing type of faces used before, however, synthetic faces which are quantitatively well-defined in the perceptual metrics are used in this study.

2.2 Method

Forty individual synthetic faces for each gender were constructed by the method described above. Front or 20 degree side view faces were constructed. In each session of the experiment, two different male or female synthetic faces in front or 20 degree side view were chosen at random from the face database. One face was served as origin and a different face averaged 20% distance in 37 dimensions between two chosen faces was created. This difference is more than three times the discrimination thresholds [4, 5]. These two faces were served as anchors (1 and 17 in figure 5).

1

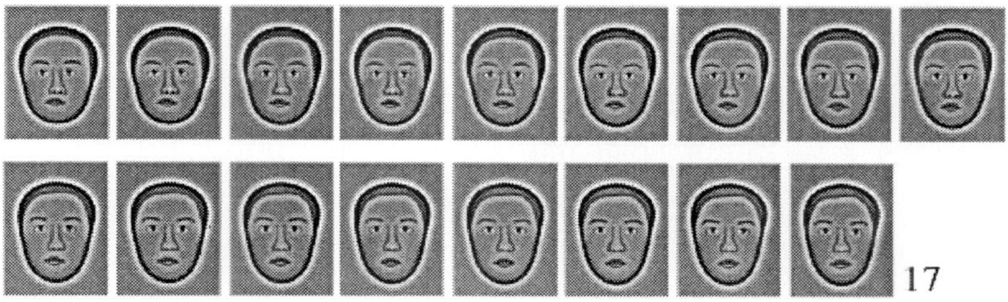

17

Fig. 5. Stimuli used in the experiment. Seventeen faces are equally spaced in 37 dimensions.

Fifteen faces equally spaced in 37 dimensions between the anchors were then created as shown in figure 5. Different sessions were run with different genders and with different views. Subjects were first trained to discriminate two anchors by showing them repeatedly in turn. When they were convinced to discriminate two faces, they were told that several modified faces between them would be displayed. Synthetic faces ranked from 1 to 17 were then sequentially presented on a computer screen for half a second and subjects indicated by clicking a mouse when the face on the screen is different from the previously displayed (starting anchor). The order of presentation (starting from face 1 or 17) is reversed randomly at different sessions. The number of total session for one subject was 8 (4 sessions for each presentation order) and average rank at each order to discriminate two categorical faces was calculated. Seven subjects participated in the experiment.

2.3 Results and Discussion

As seven subjects showed similar response trends at each gender and view stimuli, data for all subjects and conditions were collapsed. The result summarized in figure 6 clearly showed that there is a hysteresis in categorizing two faces. Wherever subjects started to see the faces, they perceived two different faces, but discriminated at a different point depending on the starting face. The average switching thresholds at ascending and descending order were 11.3% and 7.3% (about 13th and 8th ranks), respectively. It is worth to note that these points are beyond the increment discrimination threshold (average around 6%) reported previously [4,5].

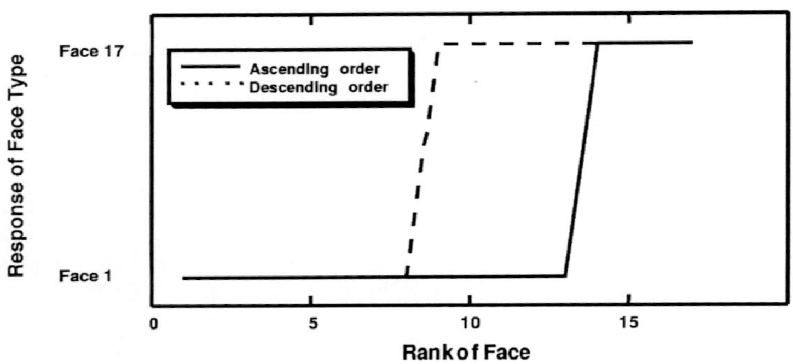

Fig. 6. The average switching points in which subjects categorized two synthetic faces.

This result indicates a strong effect of previous experience on the perceptual categorization. Although the experiment confirms the nonlinearity and multi-stability of face categorization, however, it does not reveal which perceptual property of face does affect the dynamics of face recognition (for example, head shape, the width of eyes etc.). Note that the face cube used in this experiment was based on the norm of all 37 dimensions. Thus, critical factors determining hysteresis remain to be further investigated.

3 A Neural Model for the Categorical Effect

For a simulation of categorical effect, Kelso proposed a theoretical model incorporating nonlinear dynamics. It was based on mapping stable categories onto attractors [6]. However, a transition between two percepts could be readily explained by a currently available neural model. Wilson and I have proposed a neural model incorporating recurrent inhibitory interactions among direction-specific motion units for a transition between coherent and transparent motion [7]. As a modification of a model for multi-stability of face categorization, inclusion of appropriate lateral interactions between units with response specificity for face processing can explain the present experimental result. As differential equations have been widely used to describe the dynamic properties of the neural system, a neural network could be described by the following first-order nonlinear differential equations:

$$\tau \frac{dF_\psi}{dt} = -F_\psi + S(C_\omega - \sum_{i=\psi_1}^{\psi_2} \alpha_i F_i) \qquad (3)$$

where

$$S(x) = \begin{cases} 0 & \text{for } x \leq 0 \\ x & \text{for } x > 0. \end{cases}$$

$S(x)$ is a threshold function that produces no response negative argument and α is the inhibitory coefficients. Although it has not been identified yet for the stimulus dimension of the face unit (F in the equation), it has been suggested that the combinations of radial frequency components (C in the equation) for head shape might be the ones [5,8,9]. The behavior of neural network then will be determined by a winning face unit response. Further, a simple neural network can be easily designed to make a face discrimination decision on the basis of the face unit responses as suggested for motion coherence and transparency decision previously [7].

4 Summary and Discussion

There is significant evidence that synthetic faces recently introduced by Wilson and colleagues capture a significant portion of the geometric face information and could provide a valuable tool to investigate the aspects of the visual face information processing in the "what pathway." Using synthetic faces, the present study showed the dynamics of face recognition. As reported previously with different set of stimuli, there is a hysteresis in face categorization. This dynamic property of face processing could be readily explained by a current neural model. However, the underlying neural process for the perceptual dynamics (eg. hysteresis) has not yet been fully explored. So, to investigate the pattern-forming and decision process in the brain, a fMRI study is currently in progress.

Acknowledgments. This work was supported by the BrainTech program sponsored by the Korea Ministry of Science and Technology

References

1. van Essen, D., Anderson, C., Felleman, D.: Information processing in the primate visual processing: an integrated systems prospective. Science **255** (1992) 419–423
2. Ungerleider, L. G., Mishkin, M.: Two Cortical Visual Systems. In: Ingle, D. J., Goodale, M. J., Mansfield, R. J. W. (eds.): Analysis of Visual Behaviour Cambridge, MA: MIT Press (1982) 549-586

3. Wilson, H. R., Loffler, G., Wilkinson, F.: Masking of Synthetic Faces: a New Approach to High Level Form Vision. IOVS **42** (2001) 732
4. Wilson, H. R., Loffler, G., Wilkinson, F.: Synthetic Faces, Face Cubes, and the Geometry of Face Space. Vision Research (2002) submitted
5. Kim, J., Wilson, H. R., Wilkinson, F.: Discrimination of Familiar and Unfamiliar Synthetic Faces by North Americans and Koreans. ECVP (2002) submitted
6. Kelso, J. A. S.: Dynamic Patterns (1995) MA:MIT Press
7. Wilson, H. R., Kim, J.: A Model for Motion Coherence and Transparency. Visual Neuroscience **11** (1994) 1205-1220
8. Wilkinson, F., Wilson, H. R., Habak, C.: Detection and Recognition of Radial Frequency Patterns. Vision Research **38** (1998) 3555-3568
9. Wilkinson, F., James, T. W., Wilson, H. R., Gati, J. S., Menson, R. S., Goodale, M. A.: An fMRI Study of the Selective Activation of Human Extrastriate Form Vision Areas by Radial and Concentric Gratings. Current Biology **10** (2000) 1455-1458

Recognizing Expressions by Direct Estimation of the Parameters of a Pixel Morphable Model

Vinay P. Kumar and Tomaso Poggio

Center for Biological and Computational Learning
Massachusetts Institute of Technology
Cambridge, MA 02142
{vkumar,tp}@ai.mit.edu
http://www.ai.mit.edu/projects/cbcl/

Abstract. This paper describes a method for estimating the parameters of a linear morphable model (LMM) that models mouth images. The method uses a supervised learning approach based on support vector machines (SVM) to estimate the LMM parameters directly from pixel-based representations of images of the object class (in this case mouths). This method can be used to bypass or speed up current computationally intensive methods that implement analysis by synthesis, for matching objects to morphable models. We show that the principal component axes of the flow space of the LMM correspond to easily discernible expressions such as openness, smile and pout. Therefore our method can be used to estimate the degrees of these expressions in a supervised learning framework without the need for manual annotation of a training set. We apply this to drive a cartoon character from the video of a persons face.

1 Introduction – Motivation

Systems that analyze human faces for expressions will play a crucial role in intelligent man-machine interfaces and in other domains such as video conferencing and virtual actor. Since faces are highly dynamic patterns which undergo non-rigid transformations, this is a challenging problem. Previous approaches for analyzing faces have relied on different kinds of *a priori* models such as - facial geometry and musculature [1,2] and parametrizable contours [3,4]) – or on motion estimation [5,6]. In [7] a supervised learning-based approach was used to design a real-time system for the analysis of mouth shapes. It was shown that a regression function can be learnt from a Haar wavelet based input representation of mouths to hand labeled parameters denoting openness and smile with good generalization properties. A drawback of this approach is that it relies on manual annotation of a training set. In this paper, we describe a system that retains the strengths of the approach in [7] while mitigating the problem of manual annotation.

From the perspective of cognitive science, this is a problem of inserting top-down knowledge into a bottom-up system that converts sensory data into higher level perceptual categories. The topic of top-down constraints on perceptual

H.H. Bülthoff et al. (Eds.): BMCV 2002, LNCS 2525, pp. 519–527, 2002.

tasks [8,9,10]) is one of great significance. However, we shall not address this issue since it lies beyond the scope of this paper. In the case of facial analysis the substantive question is of representing and modeling the class of mouth shapes and learning the relationship between such representations and pixel images. Amongst the many model-based approaches to modeling object classes, the Linear Morphable Model (LMM) is an important one. The antecedents of LMMs can be found in [11] which describes the modeling of multiple views of a single object by linear combination of prototypical views, and in [12,13] which describes the modeling of different objects of the same object class using a linear combination of prototypes.

LMMs have been used to model object classes such as faces, cars and digits [14,15,16], and visual speech [17]. But so far, it has mainly been a tool for image synthesis and its use for image analysis has been limited. Such analysis has been approached through a computationally intensive analysis by synthesis method only. In [14] and [16], the matching parameters are computed by minimizing the squared error between the novel image and the model image using a stochastic gradient descent (SGD) algorithm. This technique is computationally intensive (taking minutes to match even a single image). A technique that could compute the matching parameters with considerably less computations and using only view-based representations would make these models useful in real-time applications.

In this paper, we explore the possibility of learning to estimate the matching parameters of a LMM directly from pixel-based representations of an input image. We construct pixel LMMs (a LMM where the prototypes are pixel images) to model various mouth shapes and expressions. Following [14], the LMM is constructed from examples of mouths. Principal Component Analysis (PCA) on the example textures and flows allows us to reduce the set of parameters. We then use SVM regression [18] to learn a non-linear regression function from a sparse subset of Haar wavelet coefficients to the matching parameters of this LMM directly. The training set (in particular the y of the (x, y) pairs) for this learning problem is generated by estimating the true matching parameters using the SGD algorithm described in [14].

In [16] an approach to speed up the process of analysis by synthesis for computing the matching parameters of morphable models (which is called active appearance model) is described. The speed-up is achieved by learning several multivariate linear regressions from the error image (difference between the novel and the model images) and the appropriate perturbation of the model parameters (the known displacements of the model parameters), thus avoiding the computation of gradients. This method is akin to learning the tangent plane to the manifold in pixel space formed by the morphable model. Our approach is different in the sense that we learn the non-linear transformations that locate our data point directly in the manifold's co-ordinate system. We present some results on the speed-up achieved by initializing an SGD algorithm with the directly estimated LMM parameters.

As an application of this approach, we demonstrate a new system that can estimate degrees of facial expressions. The system works by estimating the parameters of a pixel LMM of the mouth shapes of a single person using SVM regression. While this allows us to track mouth movements, we also show that the principal components of the flow space of the mouth LMM correspond to distinct facial expressions. Therefore estimating LMM parameters allows us to estimate degrees of facial expressions. In contrast to all earlier systems tracking facial expressions [3,1,19,2,4,5,6,16,7] our system is able to directly estimate the relevant (LMM) parameters from pixel-based representations, and thus avoids manual annotation.

This paper is organized as follows: In the next section we give a brief overview of a (pixel) LMM that models mouth shapes. In section 3, we describe an algorithm for estimating the parameters of an LMM directly from images. In section 4, we present results of this approach and discuss synthesis and speed-up. In section 5, we apply this method to the problem of recognizing facial expressions. Finally we conclude with a discussion on unanswered questions and future work.

2 Linear Morphable Model for Modeling Mouths

In this section we provide a brief overview of LMMs and their application to modeling mouths.

2.1 Overview of LMMs

A linear morphable model is based on linear combinations of a specific representation of example images (or prototypes). The representation involves establishing a correspondence between each example image and a reference image. Thus it associates with every image a shape (or flow) vector and a texture vector. The flow vector consists of the displacements of each pixel in the reference image relative to its position in the prototype. The texture vector consists of the prototype *backward warped* to the reference image. A linear combination of images in the LMM framework involves linearly combining the prototype textures using coefficients $\mathbf{b}$ to yield a model texture, and the prototype flows using coefficients $\mathbf{c}$ to yield a model flow and warping the model texture along the model flow to obtain the model image (see [14] for more details).

2.2 Constructing an LMM for Modeling Mouths

In order to construct a single person mouth LMM we collected about 2066 images of mouths from one person. 93 of these images were manually chosen as the prototype images. The reference image can be chosen such that it corresponds to the average (in the vector space defined by the LMM) of the example images. A boot-strapping technique is used to improve the correspondence between the reference and other prototype images.

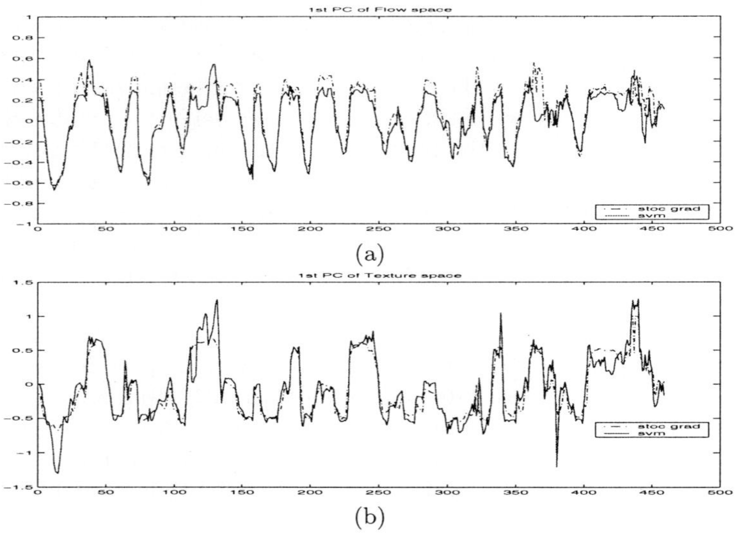

Fig. 1. Estimates for the first (a) flow and (b) texture principal component of a single person LMM using the SGD algorithm and SVM regression on a test sequence of 459 images.

Once the reference image is found and correspondence between the reference and prototypes established, we get a 93 dimensional LMM. The dimensionality of pixel space being 2688 (42×64), the LMM constitutes a lower dimensional representation of the space (or manifold) of mouth images. However since many of the example images are alike there is likely to be a great deal of redundancy even in this representation. In order to remove this redundancy, we perform PCA on the example texture and shape vectors and retain only those principal components with the highest eigenvalues. As a result we obtain an LMM where a novel texture is a linear combination of the principal component textures (which do not resemble any of the example textures) and similarly a novel flow is a linear combination of the principal component flows.

3 Learning to Estimate the LMM Parameters Directly from Images

The problem of estimating the matching LMM parameters directly from the image is modeled as learning a regression function from an appropriate input representation of the image to the set of LMM parameters. The input representation is chosen to be a sparse set of Haar wavelet coefficients while we use support vector regression as the learning algorithm.

3.1 Generating the Training Set

The training set was generated as follows.

- Each of the 2066 images is matched to the LMM using the SGD algorithm (for details of the SGD algorithm see [20]). The two main parameters that need to be fixed at this step is the number of principal components of texture and flow space to retain and the number of iterations of the SGD algorithm. We found that retaining the top three principal components of the texture and flow space and allowing 250 iterations of SGD was sufficient to give us a good match and achieve minimum pixel error on average. Each image is thus represented as a six dimensional vector, which form the outputs for the learning problem.
- Each of the 2066 images is subject to the Haar wavelet transform and feature selection involving selection of those Haar coefficients with the highest variance over the training images. We select 12 coefficients with the highest variance which form the inputs for the learning problem.

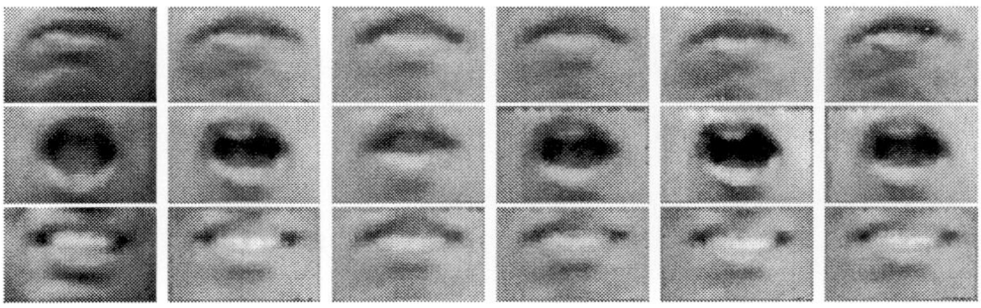

(a) (b) (c) (d) (e) (f)

Fig. 2. Comparison of reconstruction from LMM parameters estimated through SVM regression and through Stochastic Gradient Descent (SGD) for a single person mouth LMM. (a) Novel Image, (b) SVM Parameter Estimation followed by SGD for 10 iterations, (c) SGD for 10 iterations, (d) SGD for 50 iterations, (e) SVM Parameter Estimation alone and (f) the procedure which generates the training data i.e. SGD parameter estimation for 250 iterations.

4 Direct Estimation of LMM Parameters: Results

Quantitative measures of the accuracy of the estimate are 1) The closeness of the parameter estimate from SVM regression to the one obtained from applying Stochastic Gradient Descent or 2) The error in the reconstructed image. The two are clearly related and yet one cannot be subsumed in the other. The phenomenological likeness of image reconstruction is a qualitative measure and is extremely important for image synthesis. Since we are not directly concerned with image synthesis this measure has less significance for us.

In our experiments, we estimated six LMM coefficients corresponding to the top three principal components of the texture space and the flow space respectively. For each LMM coefficient a separate regression function was learnt. Preliminary experiments indicated that Gaussian kernels were distinctly superior to estimating the LMM parameters in terms of number of support vectors and training error compared to polynomial kernels. As a result we next confined ourselves to experimenting with Gaussian kernels only. The free parameters in this problem, namely, the insensitivity factor ϵ, a weight on the cost for breaking the error bound C and the normalization factor σ were estimated independently for each of the LMM parameters using cross-validation. The regression function was used to estimate the LMM parameters of a test sequence of 459 images. In Figure 1 we display the results of tracking the first principal component of the flow and texture space respectively, where we compare the performance of support vector regression with stochastic gradient descent. It shows the high degree of fidelity that one can get in estimating the LMM parameters directly from the image.

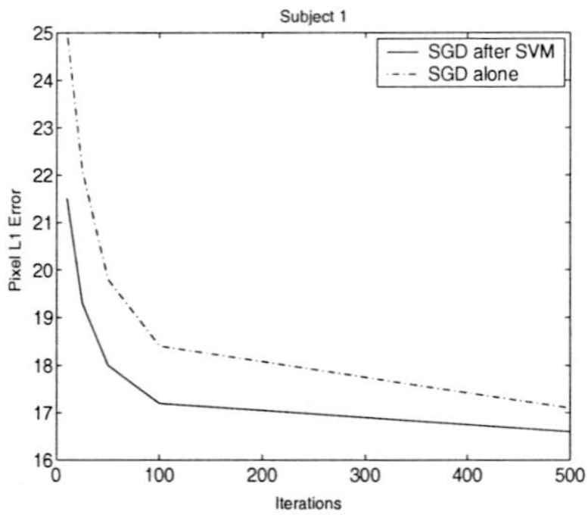

Fig. 3. Plot of pixel error vs the iterations of the SGD algorithm. Comparing the case of initialization with the SVM regression estimate and with that of no initialization.

Examples of matches using the two methods shown in Figure 2 reveals the speed advantage that one obtains by estimating the LMM parameters directly is quite clear. In only 10 iterations a SGD algorithm initialized with the estimate of an SVM regression is capable of achieving the same quality (and sometimes even better) than a SGD algorithm running solely for 50 iterations. In Figure 3 we also present the speed up results in the form of average error over test set for a given number of iterations of the SGD algorithm in the two cases when initialized with the SVM regression estimate and when not.

5 Recognizing Facial Expressions

So far, we have shown that the parameters of a pixel LMM can be directly estimated from mouth images using supervised learning. But this does not necessarily imply expression recognition. Can a generative structure such as an LMM represent facial expressions in a natural way? We answer this question in the affirmative and as a consequence we propose the design of an expression recognition system that is capable of mitigating, at least in part, the problem of manual annotation.

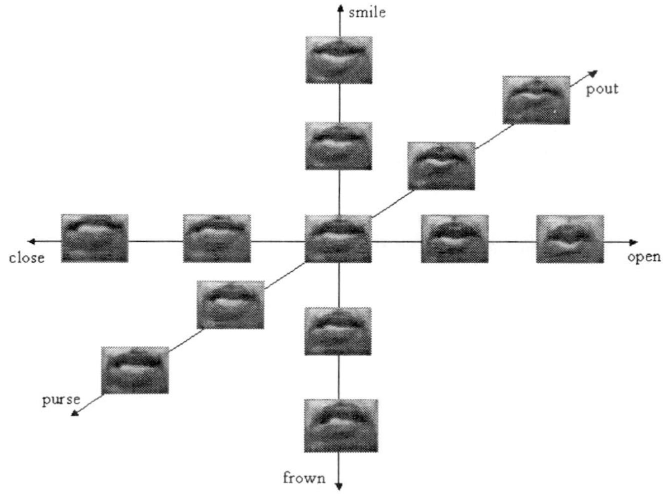

Fig. 4. The Expression Axes showing the result of morphing the average mouth image along the first three flow principal components.

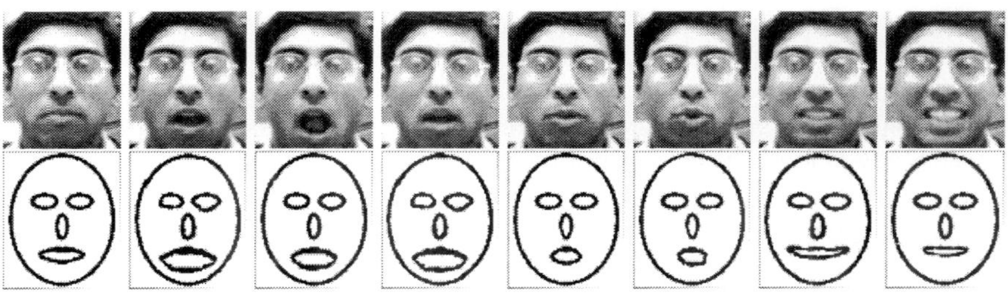

Fig. 5. Mapping the estimated expression axes parameters onto a line drawing LMM.

5.1 Expression Axes

The key idea behind the new expression recognition system is that of the *expression axes*. Do the principal components of the flow and texture space represent something meaningful about mouth shapes? To answer this question, we morph the average mouth image along the three main flow principal components. The results are shown in Fig. 4. The interesting outcome of this exercise is that morphing along the first three principal components of flow space leads to recognizable mouth deformations such as open-close, smile-frown and pout-purse. These axes which we can call the expression axes can be used to ascertain the degree of expression of each kind in a novel mouth image.

5.2 Experimental Details

A corpus of 468 mouth images of a single person with varying degrees of expressions is used to learn a map from a sparse wavelet-based representation to the expression axes The resultant map was tested using a test set of 430 mouth images collected under a different circumstance (different day, time and lighting conditions) than the training set. The estimated expression parameters were mapped onto a cartoon character which is capable of displaying the expressions of openness, smile and pout (Figure 5). Since the SVM regression training returns a small number of support vectors and therefore we can expect that real-time implementation will be easy.

6 Conclusions

With the growing application of morphable models in image analysis and synthesis, methods to estimate their parameters from images will become increasingly important. In this context, the learning-based approach to estimating the parameters of a LMM is natural as well as computationally feasible. In this paper, we have shown that a single person mouth morphable model is not only good at modeling mouths, it is also amenable to direct estimation by learning, showing significant speed-up compared to the SGD algorithm. Future work needs to work on building multiple person morphable models and use other models with better synthesis performance [17,16].

The results for expression recognition are also quite encouraging. They show the feasibility of extracting meaningful expressions from data without any significant human expert knowledge. In principle, this method could be extended to more complex mouth shapes and also to other facial regions such as eyes. Future work here needs to explore the possibility of learning maps between expressions encoded in a pixel morphable model described in this paper, and those that are represented by artists in line drawing morphable models.

References

1. Demetri Terzopoulos and Keith Waters. Analysis and synthesis of facial image sequences using physical and anatomical models. *IEEE Transactions on Pattern Analysis and Machine Intelligence*, 15(6):569–579, 1993.
2. Irfan A. Essa and Alex Pentland. A vision system for observing and extracting facial action parameters. In *Proceedings IEEE Conf. on Computer Vision and Pattern Recognition*, pages 76–83, Seattle, WA, 1994.
3. P. Hallinan A. Yuille and D. Cohen. Feature extraction from faces using deformable templates. *International Journal of Computer Vision*, 8(2):99–111, 1992.
4. M. Isard and A. Blake. Contour-tracking by stochastic propagation of conditional density. In *Proceedings of European Conference on Computer Vision*, pages 343–356, 1996.
5. M.J. Black and Y. Yacoob. Recognizing facial expressions in image sequences using local parameterized models of image motion. *International Journal of Computer Vision*, 1996. Revised preprint.

6. Tony Ezzat. Example-based analysis and synthesis for images of human faces. Master's thesis, Massachusetts Institute of Technology, 1996.
7. V. Kumar and T. Poggio. Learning-Based Approach to Real Time Tracking and Analysis of Faces. In *Proceedings of the Fourth International Conference on Automatic Face and Gesture Recognition*, pages 96–101, Grenoble, France, 2000.
8. P. Cavanagh. What's up in top-down processing. In *Representations of Vision*. Cambridge Univ. Press, 1991.
9. D. Mumford. Pattern theory: a unifying perspective. In *Perception as Bayesian Inference*. Cambridge Univ. Press, 1996.
10. T. Vetter M.J. Jones, P. Sinha and T. Poggio. Top-down learning of low-level vision tasks. *Current Biology*, 7(11):991–994, 1997.
11. S. Ullman and R. Basri. Recognition by linear combination of models. *IEEE Trans. on Pattern Analysis and Machine Intelligence*, 13:992–1006, 1991.
12. D. Beymer and T. Poggio. Image representations for visual learning. *Science*, 272(5270):1905–1909, June 1996.
13. T. Vetter and T. Poggio. Linear object classes and image synthesis from a single example image. *IEEE Transactions on Pattern Analysis and Machine Intelligence*, 19:7:733–742, 1997.
14. M. Jones and T. Poggio. Multidimensional morphable models: A framework for representing and matching object classes. In *Proceedings of the International Conference on Computer Vision*, Bombay, India, 1998.
15. V. Blanz. *Automated Reconstruction of Three-Dimensional Shape of Faces from a Single Image*. Ph.D. Thesis (in German), University of Tuebingen, 2000.
16. T. F. Cootes, G. J. Edwards, and C. J. Taylor. Active appearance models. In *Proceedings of the European Conference on Computer Vision*, Freiburg, Germany, 1998.
17. T. Ezzat and T. Poggio. Visual Speech Synthesis by Morphing Visemes. *MIT AI Memo No. 1658/CBCL Memo No. 173*, 1999.
18. V. N. Vapnik. *Statistical Learning Theory*. Wiley, New York, 1998.
19. D. Beymer, A. Shashua, and T. Poggio. Example based image analysis and synthesis. A.I. Memo No. 1431, Artificial Intelligence Laboratory, Massachusetts Institute of Technology, 1993.
20. M. Jones and T. Poggio. Model-based matching by linear combinations of prototypes. A.i. memo, MIT Artificial Intelligence Lab., Cambridge, MA, 1996.

Modeling of Movement Sequences Based on Hierarchical Spatial-Temporal Correspondence of Movement Primitives

Winfried Ilg and Martin Giese

Laboratory for Action, Representation and Learning
Department for Cognitive Neurology, University Clinic Tübingen, Germany
{wilg,giese}@tuebingen.mpg.de

Abstract. In this paper we present an approach for the modeling complex movement sequences. Based on the method of Spatio-Temporal Morphable Models (STMMs) [11] we derive a new hierarchical algorithm that, in a first step, identifies movement elements in the complex movement sequence based on characteristic events, and in a second step quantifies these movement primitives by approximation through linear combinations of learned example movement trajectories. The proposed algorithm is used to segment and to morph sequences of karate movements of different people and different styles.

1 Introduction

The analysis of complex movements is an important problem for many technical applications such as computer vision, computer graphics, sports and medicine. For several applications it is crucial to model movements with different styles. One method that seems to be very suitable to synthesize movements with different styles is the linear combination of movement examples. Such linear combinations can be defined efficiently on the basis of spatio-temporal correspondence. The technique of Spatio-Temporal Morphable Models (STMMs) defines linear combinations by weighted summation of spatial and temporal displacement fields that morph the combined prototypical movement into a reference pattern. This method has been successfully applied for the generation of complex movements in computer graphics (motion morphing [3]) as well as for the recognition of movements and movement styles from trajectories in computer vision [11]. The same techniques is interesting for psychophysical experiments since it allows to generate parameterized pattern classes of complex movements. By variations of the linear weights the perceptual similarity of such motion stimuli can be very gradually modified. In addition, subtle individual style parameters of the movement can be gradually varied, e.g. "male" vs. "female" walking [9].

So far, many application (see reviews in [7] and [17]) have focused on cyclic movements like walking or well-defined and segmented movements like ballet poses (exceptions can be found for example in [5][16][1]).

H.H. Bülthoff et al. (Eds.): BMCV 2002, LNCS 2525, pp. 528–537, 2002.

To generalize the method of linear combination for complex acyclic movements we extend the basic STMM algorithm by introducing a second hierarchy level that represents motion primitives. Such primitives correspond to parts of the approximated trajectories, e.g. individual facial expressions or techniques in a sequence of karate movements. These movement primitives are then modeled using STMMs by linearly combining example movements. This makes it possible to learn generative models for sequences of movements with different styles. The extraction of movement primitives is based on simple invariant features that are used to detect key events that mark the transitions between different primitives. Sequences of such key events are then detected by matching them to a learned example sequence. This matching is based on standard sequence alignment methods that are based on dynamic programming [13]. We apply this hierarchical algorithm to model and synthesizes complex karate movements. In particular, we show that movement primitives from different actors and with different styles can be generated and recombined to longer naturally-looking movement sequences.

2 Algorithm

2.1 Morphable Models as Movement Primitives

The technique of *spatio-temporal morphable models* [10,11] is based on linearly combining the movement trajectories of prototypical motion patterns in space-time. Linear combinations of movement patterns are defined on the basis of spatio-temporal correspondences that are computed by dynamic programming [3]. Complex movement patterns can be characterized by trajectories of feature points. The trajectories of the prototypical movement pattern n can be characterized by the time-dependent vector $\boldsymbol{\zeta}_n(t)$. The correspondence field between two trajectories $\boldsymbol{\zeta}_1$ and $\boldsymbol{\zeta}_2$ is defined by the spatial shifts $\boldsymbol{\xi}(t)$ and the temporal shifts $\tau(t)$ that transform the first trajectory into the second. The transformation is specified mathematically by the equation:

$$\boldsymbol{\zeta}_2(t) = \boldsymbol{\zeta}_1(t + \tau(t)) + \boldsymbol{\xi}(t) \tag{1}$$

By linear combination of spatial and temporal shifts the spatio-temporal morphable model allows to interpolate smoothly between motion patterns with significantly different spatial structure, but also between patterns that differ with respect to their timing.

The correspondence shifts $\boldsymbol{\xi}(t)$ and $\tau(t)$ are calculated by solving an optimization problem that minimizes the spatial and temporal shifts under the constraint that the temporal shifts define a new time variable that is always monotonically increasing. For further details about the underlying algorithm we refer to [10, 11].

Figure 1 shows schematically the proceeding for generating linear combinations of spatio-temporal patterns for complex movement sequences. First the movement sequence is segmented by extraction of movement primitives. For the individual movement primitives the correspondence between each individual prototypical patterns and a reference pattern is established. Signifying the spatial

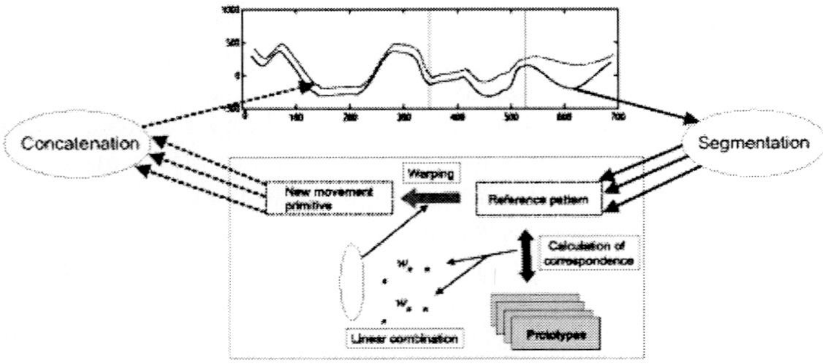

Fig. 1. Schematic description of the algorithm to analyze and synthesize complex movement sequences. In the first step the sequence is decomposed into movement primitives. These movement primitives can be analyzed and changed in style defining linear combinations of prototypes with different linear weight combinations. Afterward the individual movement primitives are concatenated again into one movement sequence. With this technique we are able to generate sequences containing different styles.

and temporal shifts between prototype n and the reference pattern by $\boldsymbol{\xi}_n(t)$ and $\tau_n(t)$, linearly combined spatial and temporal shifts can be defined by the two equations:

$$\boldsymbol{\xi}(t) = \sum_{n=1}^{N} w_n \, \boldsymbol{\xi}_n(t) \qquad \tau(t) = \sum_{n=1}^{N} w_n \, \tau_n(t) \tag{2}$$

The weights w_p define the contributions of the individual prototypes to the linear combination. We always assume convex combinations with $0 \leq w_n \leq 1$ and $\sum_p w_p = 1$. After linearly combining the spatial and temporal shifts the trajectories of the morphed pattern can be recovered by morphing the reference pattern in space time using the spatial and temporal shifts $\boldsymbol{\xi}(t)$ and $\tau(t)$. The space-time morph is defined by equation (1) where $\boldsymbol{\zeta}_1$ is the reference pattern and $\boldsymbol{\zeta}_2$ has to be identified with trajectory of the linearly combined pattern.

For the identification of a set of movement primitives within a complex movement sequence, we need prototypes of these movement primitives. These prototypes are generated from an average movement, that is computed by setting all weights w_n in eq. (2) to $w_n = 1/N$. These prototypical movement primitives are used as templates for the automatic segmentation of new trajectories.

2.2 Representation of Key Features for Movement Primitives

For the identification of movement primitives within a complex movement sequences it is necessary to identify characteristic features that are suitable for a robust and fast segmentation. Different elementary spatio-temporal and kinematic features like angle velocity [6][18] or curvature and torsion of the 3D trajectories [4] have been proposed in the literature. The key features of our algorithm are based on zeros of the velocity in few "characteristic coordinates" of the trajectory $\zeta(t)$. These features provide a coarse description of the spatio-temporal characteristics of trajectory segments that can be matched efficiently in order to establish correspondence between the learned movement primitives and new trajectories. For the matching process that is based on dynamic programming (see section 2.3) we represent the features by discrete events. Let m be the number of the motion primitive and r the number of characteristic coordinates of the trajectory. Let $\boldsymbol{\kappa}(t)$ be the "reduced trajectory" of the characteristic coordinates that has the values $\boldsymbol{\kappa}_i^m$ at the velocity zeros[1]. The movement primitive is then characterized by the vector differences $\Delta\boldsymbol{\kappa}_i^m = \boldsymbol{\kappa}_i^m - \boldsymbol{\kappa}_{i-1}^m$ of subsequent velocity zeros (see figure 2).

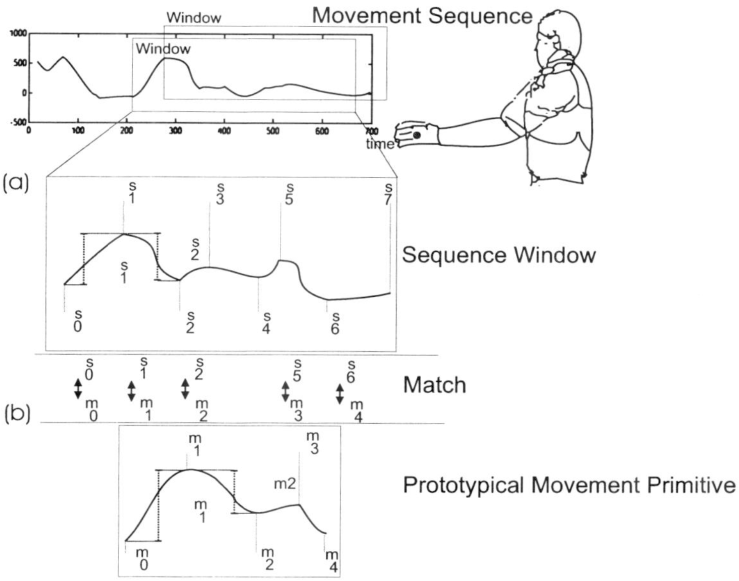

Fig. 2. Illustration of the method for the automatic identification of movement primitives: (a) In a first step all key features $\boldsymbol{\kappa}_i^s$ are determined. (b) Sequences of key features from the sequences (s) are matched with sequences of key features from the prototypical movement primitives (m) using dynamic programming. A search window is moved over the sequence. The length of the window is two times the number of key features of the learned motor primitive. The best matching trajectory segment is defined by the sequence of feature vectors that minimizes $\sum_j ||\Delta\kappa_i^s - \Delta\kappa_j^m||$ over all matched key features. With this method a spatio-temporal correspondence at a coarse level can be established.

[1] Zero-velocity is defined by a a zero of the velocity in at least one coordinate of the reduced trajectory.

2.3 Identification of Movement Primitives

A robust identification of movement primitives in noisy data with additional or missing zero-velocity points κ_i^s can be achieved with dynamic programming.

Purpose of the dynamic programming is an optimal sequence alignment between the key features of the prototypical movement primitive $\kappa_0^m \ldots \kappa_q^m$ and the key features of the search window $\kappa_0^s \ldots \kappa_p^s$ (see figure 2b). This is accomplished by minimizing a cost function that is given by the sum of $||\Delta\kappa_i^s - \Delta\kappa_j^m||$ over all matched key features. The above requirement to handle additional and missing key features is taken into account by appropriately constraining the set of admissible transitions for the dynamic programming as follows:

For the match of two successive key features κ_i^m and κ_{i+1}^m it is possible to skip up to two key features κ_{i+1}^s and κ_{i+2}^s in the sequence. In this case, i.e. the match $\kappa_i^s \rightarrow \kappa_j^m$ and $\kappa_{i+3}^s \rightarrow \kappa_{j+1}^m$ would be realized. Furthermore, it is possible to skip one key feature κ_j^m in the movement primitive. This implies that the match $\kappa_i^s \rightarrow \kappa_{j-1}^m$ and $\kappa_{i+1}^s \rightarrow \kappa_{j+1}^m$ is valid. The cost function that is minimized in order to find an optimal match between $\kappa_0^s \ldots \kappa_i^s$ and $\kappa_0^m \ldots \kappa_j^m$ under the given constraints can be written recursively:

$$\begin{aligned} D(i,j) = min(&D(i-1,j-1) + ||\Delta\kappa_i^s - \Delta\kappa_j^m||, \\ &D(i-2,j-1) + ||\Delta\kappa_{[i-1,i]}^s - \Delta\kappa_j^m||, \\ &D(i-3,j-1) + ||\Delta\kappa_{[i-2,i]}^s - \Delta\kappa_j^m||, \\ &D(i-1,j-2) + ||\Delta\kappa_i^s - \Delta\kappa_{[j-1,j]}^m||, \\ &D(i-2,j-2) + ||\Delta\kappa_{[i-1,i]}^s - \Delta\kappa_{[j-1,j]}^m||, \\ &D(i-3,j-2) + ||\Delta\kappa_{[i-2,i]}^s - \Delta\kappa_{[j-1,j]}^m||) \end{aligned} \tag{3}$$

where i and j denote the indices for the key feature κ_i^s respectively κ_j^m. The starting value $D(1,1)$ is given by

$$D(1,1) = ||\Delta\kappa_1^s - \Delta\kappa_1^m|| \tag{4}$$

where $\Delta\kappa_1^s$ is the first difference vector of the sequence window and $\Delta\kappa_1^m$ is the first difference vector of the movement primitive m. If one or more key features are skipped for the match, the difference vector $\Delta\kappa_i^s$ between successive key features must be adapted. An example is described in eq. (5) for the case that two key features κ_{i-2}^s and κ_{i-1}^s are skipped. The resulting difference vector between the two successive key features κ_{i-3}^s and κ_i^s is determined by

$$\Delta\kappa_{[i-2,i]}^s = \Delta\kappa_{i-2}^s + \Delta\kappa_{i-1}^s + \Delta\kappa_i^s \tag{5}$$

Let be p the number of key features in window ω and q the number of key features in the moment primitive m. To determine the best match between movement primitive m and the sequence window ω one has to find the key feature κ_k^s, $0 \leq k \leq p$, for which the cost function for matching the sequences $\kappa_0^s \ldots \kappa_k^s$ and $\kappa_0^m \ldots \kappa_q^m$ is minimal. The minimal costs δ of movement primitive m for window ω can be found by computing

$$\delta(m_\omega) = \min_k(D(k,q)) \tag{6}$$

3 Experiments

We demonstrate the function of the algorithm by modeling movement sequences from material arts. Using a commercial motion capture system (VICON) with 6 cameras and a sampling frequency of 120 Hz we have captured several movement sequences representing a "Kata" from karate from two actors. The first actor was a third degree black belt in Jujitsu, the second actor had the 1. Kyu degree in karate (Shotokan).

Both actors executed the same movement sequence but due to differences of the techniques between different schools of martial arts with different styles. In addition both actors also tried to simulate different skill levels, e.g. by mimicking a yellow belt. Three sequences of actor 1 have been segmented manually resulting in six movement primitives, which served as prototypes to define the morphable models of the first actor (see figure 3). Based on the 6 morphable models prototypical representations with key features for the automatic identification of the movement primitives were generated in the way described in section 2.1. The "reduced trajectories" $\boldsymbol{\kappa}(t)$ consist of the coordinates of the markers on both hands.[2]

3.1 Automatic Identification of Movement Primitives

Figure 4 shows the results for the identification procedure for one sequence of actor 2. Table 1 describes the segmentation results for all 6 movement primitives in comparison with the manual segmentation. The automatic segmentation was successful on for all 16 sequences recorded from both actors. Figure 3 shows a morph that was created based on the automatically identified primitives.

Table 1. Results of the automatic segmentation for a new sequence of different style of actor 1 (A1) and a sequence of actor 2 (A2). Shown is the beginning (b.) and the end (e.) of each movement primitive for the manual and automatic segmentation (measured in frames). The manual segmentation is done by visual guidance of the animated movements and has a tolerance of about ± 10 frames.

		A1	1.	2.	3.	4.	5.	6.	A2	1.	2.	3.	4.	5.	6.
man.	b.		1	221	361	601	701	881		1	116	161	273	345	418
	e.		220	360	600	700	880	1240		115	160	273	345	418	670
auto.	b.		9	233	420	580	718	871		1	112	179	267	341	410
	e.		183	380	569	673	860	1195		100	179	281	341	407	663

[2] The hand trajectories are computed relative to the shoulder markers. All marker trajectories were filtered using a Savitzky-Golay polynomial least-squares filter.

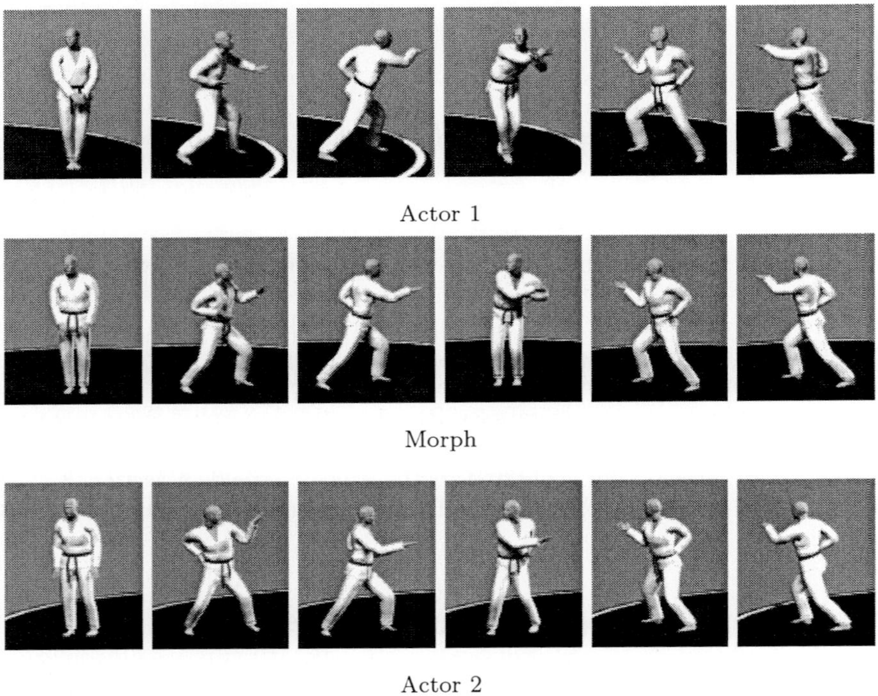

Fig. 3. Snapshots from a sequence of karate movements executed by two actors and a motion morph. The pictures show the initial posture at the beginning and the end postures of the movement primitives 1-5. The end posture is similar to the initial posture. The morphed sequence looks natural and there are no artifacts at the transitions between the 6 movement primitives. Especially interesting is the comparison between the different karate styles of the actors that becomes obvious in the third movement primitive (4th column). Actor 1 is doing a small side step with the left foot for turning. Instead of this, actor 2 turns without sidestep. The morph executes a realistic movement that interpolates the two actors.

3.2 Morphing between Different Actors

Based on the movement primitives identified by automatic segmentation morphs between movements of the two actors were realized. The individual movement primitives were morphed and afterward concatenated into a longer sequence. The details of this procedure are described in [8]. Figure 3 shows snapshots from a morphed motion sequence, which corresponds to the "average" of the two original sequences ($w_1 = w_2 = 0.5$ in eq. 2). This sequence looks very natural and shows no artifacts at the margins between the individual movement primitives. In cases, where the styles of both actors are different, the morph generates a realistic movement that interpolates between the styles of the two

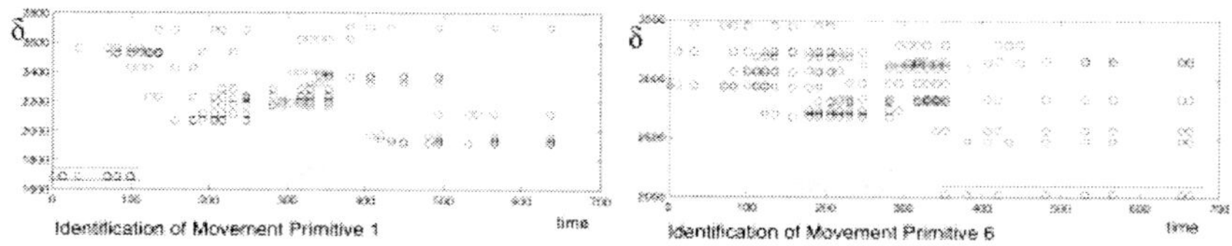

Fig. 4. Results of the automatic segmentation of one movement sequence of actor 2 based on the prototypical movement primitives of actor 1. As an example, the identification of the primitives 1 and 6 is shown. The diagrams show the distance measure δ (eq. 6) for different matches of the corresponding movement primitive over the whole sequence. The circles mark the time of the matched key feature κ_i^m in the sequence. Each match of a whole movement primitive is illustrated by a row of circles with the same δ. The number of circles corresponds to the number of key features of the movement primitive (in both diagrams two examples are indicated). Both movement primitives are correctly identified by a minimum in the δ-function.

actors original movements. Our technique is thus suitable to generate morphs that cover a continuous spectrum of styles between the actors[3].

4 Discussion

For the karate data our algorithm successfully morphs between the movements of the same, and of different actors without visible artifacts. In particular the transitions between the individual segments are invisible. The method allows the synthesis of the same Kata with different constant styles, or styles that vary over the movement sequence. We were also able to create exaggerations of the individual styles [8].

Interestingly, the algorithm even in the present very elementary form does not lead to the artifact that the feet are slide on the ground plane. This seems to be understandable because correct correspondence between the prototypical movements automatically implies that these constraints are fulfilled by the morphs. However, we expect that morphing between very dissimilar movements in uneven terrains might require to introduce a special handling of such constraints as done in [12][15].

Several other approaches rely on statistical methods like hidden markov models to perform a segmentation of movement trajectories [16] [1] [6] [2] [19]. The reason why we prefer dynamic programming, is that our algorithm is also designed for the quantitative analysis of patients with rare movement disorders. This requires algorithms, that contrary to most HHM-based methods work efficiently with very small amounts of data. Our method is particularly suited

[3] Movies of the karate animations are provided on the web site http://www.uni-tuebingen.de/uni/knv/arl/arl-demos.html

for medical applications because the parameter axes can be used to quantify the deviations of the movements of patients from the movements of healthy subjects. The method yields a description of such deviations in a higher-dimensional parameter space. This allows to identify specific types of deformations of the movements that might be indicative for different sub-classes of pathological degenerations, e.g. different causes of Parkinson's disease. As current project we examine the classification of walking and turning movements for Parkinson and cerebellar patients. This problem is particularly interesting for our method because there exists a continuous range of superpositioned Parkinson and cerebellar symptoms [14]. Based on automatically segmented movements we can one hand quantify the degree of Parkinson and cerebellar symptoms. On the other hand the linear model allows to synthesize typical gaits from Parkinson and cerebellar patients for illustration and training purposes.

Furthermore our method has also been applied successfully to face movements [8]. We think that the method is interesting for a number of applications. Beyond obvious applications in computer graphics and the quantification of movements in sports, we plan to apply the proposed method for the generation of stimuli for psychophysical experiments in order to test the recognition of movement sequences in humans.

Acknowledgments. This work is supported from the Deutsche Volkswagenstiftung. We thank H.P. Thier, H.H. Bülthoff and the Max Planck Institute for Biological Cybernetics for additional support.

References

1. M. Brand. Style machines. In *SIGGRAPH*, 2000.
2. C. Bregler. Learning and recognizing human dynamics in video sequences. In *Proceedings of the IEEE Conference on Computer Vision and Pattern Recognition*, 1997.
3. A. Bruderlin and L. Williams. Motion signal processing. In *SIGGRAPH*, pages 97–104, 1995.
4. T. Caelli, A. McCabe, and G. Binsted. On learning the shape of complex actions. In *International Workshop on Visual Form*, pages 24–39, 2001.
5. D.E. DiFranco, T.-J. Cham, and J. M. Rehg. Reconstruction of 3-d figure motion from 2-d correspondence. In *Proceedings of the IEEE Conference on Computer Vision and Pattern Recognition*, 2001.
6. A. Galata, N. Johnson, and D. Hogg. Learning variable lenth markov models of behavior. *Journal of Computer Vision and Image Understanding*, 81:398–413, 2001.
7. D.M. Gavrila. The visual analysis of human movement: a survey. *Journal of Computer Vision and Image Understanding*, 73:82–98, 1999.
8. M.A. Giese, B. Knappmeyer, and H.H. Bülthoff. Automatic synthesis of sequences of human movements by linear combination of learned example patterns. In *Workshop on Biologically Motivated Computer Vision*, 2002. accepted.
9. M.A. Giese and M. Lappe. Measurement of generalization fields for the recognition of biological motion. *Vision Research*, 42:1847–1856, 2002.

10. M.A. Giese and T. Poggio. Synthesis and recognition of biological motion pattern based on linear superposition of prototypical motion sequences. In *Proceedings of IEEE MVIEW 99 Symposium at CVPR, Fort Collins*, pages 73–80, 1999.
11. M.A. Giese and T. Poggio. Morphable models for the analysis and synthesis of complex motion patterns. *International Journal of Computer Vision*, 38(1):59–73, 2000.
12. M. Gleicher. Comparing constraint-based motion editing methods. *Graphical Models*, 63:107–134, 2001.
13. D. Gusfield. *Algorithms on Strings, Trees, and Sequences.* Cambridge University Press, 2000.
14. W. Ilg, M.A. Giese, H. Golla, and H.P. Thier. Quantitative movement analysis based on hierarchical spatial temporal correspondence of movement primitives. In *11th Annual Meeting of the European Society for Movement Analysis in Adults and Children*, 2002.
15. L. Kovar, M. Gleicher, and J. Schreiner. Footskate cleanup for motion capture editing. In *SIGGRAPH*, 2002.
16. J. Lee, J. Chai, P.S. Reitsma, J. K. Hodgins, and N. S. Pollard. Interactive control of avatars animated with human motion data. In *SIGGRAPH*, 2002.
17. T.B. Moeslund. A survey of computer vision-based human motion capture. *Journal of Computer Vision and Image Understanding*, 81:231–268, 2001.
18. T. Mori and K. Uehara. Extraction of primitive motion and discovery of association rules from motion data. In *Proceedings of the IEEE International Workshop on Robot and Human Interactive Communication*, pages 200–206, 2001.
19. T. Zhao, T. Wang, and H-Y. Shum. Learning a highly structured motion model for 3d human tracking. In *Proceedings of the 5th Asian Conference on Computer Vision*, 2002.

Automatic Synthesis of Sequences of Human Movements by Linear Combination of Learned Example Patterns

Martin A. Giese[1], Barbara Knappmeyer[2], and Heinrich H. Bülthoff[2]

[1] Lab. for Action Representation and Learning
Dept. for Cognitive Neurology, University Clinic
Tübingen, Germany
[2] Max Planck Institute for Biological Cybernetics
Tübingen, Germany
{giese,babsy,hhb}@tuebingen.mpg.de

Abstract. We present a method for the synthesis of sequences of realistically looking human movements from learned example patterns. We apply this technique for the synthesis of dynamic facial expressions. Sequences of facial movements are decomposed into individual movement elements which are modeled by linear combinations of learned examples. The weights of the linear combinations define an abstract pattern space that permits a simple modification and parameterization of the style of the individual movement elements. The elements are defined in a way that is suitable for a simple automatic resynthesis of longer sequences from movement elements with different styles. We demonstrate the efficiency of this technique for the animation of a 3D head model and discuss how it can be used to generate spatio-temporally exaggerated sequences of facial expressions for psychophysical experiments on caricature effects.

The synthesis of sequences realistic of human movements is a fundamental problem in computer animation and robotics. A central difficulty in this area is the parameterization and modification of the styles of such movements. One class of approaches for the generation of movements with different styles searches data bases with a sufficiently large number of movement styles exploiting statistical methods in order to make the search process computationally tractable (e.g. [11, 13]). Another approach is to use statistical generative models and to learn different movement styles by appropriate selection of the training data (e.g. [3,12]). The disadvantage of these methods is that a certain minimum amount of training data must be available, which is not the case for all applications. Less data is required for methods that generate new realistically looking movements by interpolation between few example movements (e.g. [15,4,14]). It has been shown before that, based on spatio-temporal correspondence, linear vector spaces of complex movements can be defined. For this purpose multiple example movements with different styles are linearly combined [7]. Such linear vector spaces allow a simple and intuitive parameterization of classes of similar movements and are useful for the generation and recognition of movements with different

H.H. Bülthoff et al. (Eds.): BMCV 2002, LNCS 2525, pp. 538–547, 2002.

style parameters. We present an extension of this technique that permits the automatic generation of movement sequences that consist of multiple movement elements with different styles. We apply this method to complex facial movements and show how it can be used to generate spatio-temporal exaggerations of sequences of facial movements. Such stimuli are particularly interesting for psychophysical studies of caricature effects in moving faces.

In the paper, we review first the method of spatio-temporal morphable models and present an extension for the generation of longer sequences that consist of multiple movement elements with different styles. We then discuss an application of the method for the generation of sequences of facial movements and demonstrate how the method can be used to create spatio-temporal exaggerations of facial expressions. Finally, we present a psychophysical experiment that applies our method for studying spatio-temporal caricature effects with moving faces.

1 Linear Combination of Individual Movements

The movement of an animated human or a face can be characterized by a high-dimensional trajectory vector $\mathbf{x}(t)$. The components of this vector can be the joint positions of the human or points on the face, but also joint angles or relative coordinates of individual parts of the skeleton. Assume that P such trajectories $\mathbf{x}_p(t)$, $1 \leq p \leq P$, are given as prototypical examples. Each of them is associated with a characteristic style, e.g. executed by a particular actor, or with a specific emotional affect. Spatio-temporal morphable models STMMs define linear combinations of these prototypes by establishing correspondence between each prototypical and a reference trajectory $\mathbf{x}_0(t)$ (that can be identical with one of the prototypes). Between each prototype and the reference pattern spatio-temporal correspondence is computed according to the relationship:

$$\mathbf{x}_p(t) = \mathbf{x}_0(t + \tau_p(t)) + \boldsymbol{\xi}_p(t) \tag{1}$$

The functions $\tau_p(t)$ and $\boldsymbol{\xi}_p(t)$ define for each point in time temporal and spatial shifts that map trajectory p onto the reference trajectory. The spatial and temporal shifts can be computed by minimizing the equation error of (1) under the constraint that the temporal shifts τ_p must define a rewarped new time axis that is monotonically related to the original time t. The underlying constrained optimization problem can be solved by dynamic programming [4,7]. Linear combinations of the prototypical trajectories are defined by linearly combining the spatial and the temporal shift functions using the linear weights α_p resulting in the linearly combined spatial and temporal shifts:

$$\boldsymbol{\xi}(t) = \sum_{p=1}^{P} c_p \, \boldsymbol{\xi}_p(t) \tag{2}$$

$$\tau(t) = \sum_{p=1}^{P} c_p \, \tau_p(t)$$

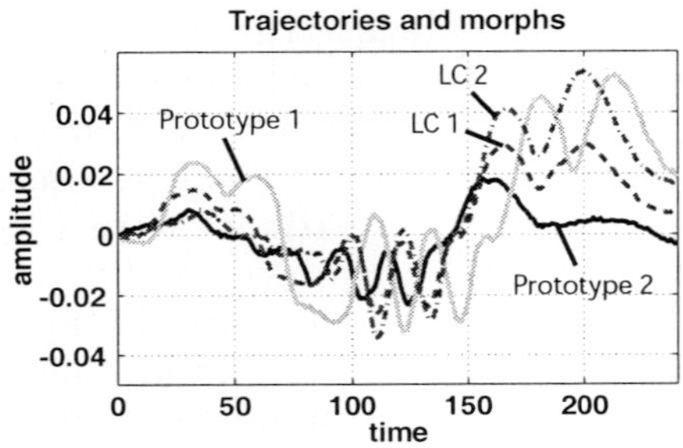

Fig. 1. Protypical trajectories and linear combination. (See text.)

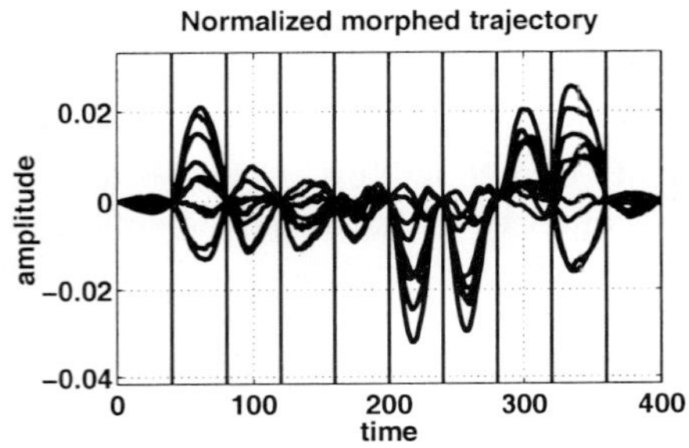

Fig. 2. Normalized linearly combined trajectory. (See text.)

The reference trajectory is then rewarped in space and time using these spatio-temporal shifts to obtain the trajectory of the linearly combined motion pattern. In general the coefficients α_p are chosen to fulfill $\sum_p \alpha_p = 1$ and $0 \leq \alpha \leq 1$.

2 Linear Combination of Movement Trajectories with Multiple Movement Elements

In many applications movement sequences must be generated that consist of multiple movement elements with individual styles. Such elements can be individual facial expressions or individual moves in a sequence of movements in sports. Fig. 1 shows a single coordinate of two prototypical trajectories (black and gray solid line) and two linear combinations generated with the method presented in this paper. One linear combination (LC 1) is obtained by combining the two prototypes with constant weights 0.5. The second linear combination (LC 2) combines movement elements with different styles. The first 5 movement elements follow the style of the second prototype, corresponding to a weight vector $\boldsymbol{\alpha} = [0, 1]$. The second 5 elements follow the first prototype with weight vector $\boldsymbol{\alpha} = [1, 0]$. To synthesize such composite sequences automatically we use an algorithm with the following four steps:

1. **Decomposition of the trajectories in movement elements:** Movement elements are defined, e.g. by individual facial expressions, or individual techniques in a sequence of karate moves. It is possible to segment such elements automatically from trajectory data as shown in [10]. This algorithm matches sparse sub-sequences of previously learned key events with parts of new movement sequences using sequence alignment by dynamic programming. Other methods have been described in the literature (e.g. [5]). The result of the segmentation step are L starting points $T^s_{p,l}$, and end points $T^e_{p,l}$ of the individual movement elements with $1 \leq l \leq L$.
2. **Normalization of the movement elements:** After separation into trajectory segments $\mathbf{x}_{p,l}(t)$ with boundaries that are given by the start and end

times $T^{s,e}_{p,l}$ each segment is resampled with a fixed number of time steps in an interval $[0, T_{\text{seg}}]$. In addition, a linear function in time is subtracted from the original trajectory segments resulting in a modified trajectory that is always zero at the transition points between subsequent movement elements. This makes it possible to concatenate the segments with different styles without inducing discontinuities in the trajectories. With the start and endpoints $\mathbf{x}^{\text{s}}_{p,l} = \mathbf{x}_{p,l}(T^{\text{s}}_{p,l})$ and $\mathbf{x}^{\text{e}}_{p,l} = \mathbf{x}_{p,l}(T^{\text{e}}_{p,l})$ the normalized trajectory segments can be written after resampling:

$$\tilde{\mathbf{x}}_{p,l}(t) = \mathbf{x}_{p,l}(t) - \mathbf{x}^{\text{s}}_{p,l} - (t/T_{\text{seg}})(\mathbf{x}^{\text{e}}_{p,l} - \mathbf{x}^{\text{s}}_{p,l}) \tag{3}$$

3. **Linear combination of the elements:** For each trajectory segment the movements are linearly combined separately. The normalized trajectory segments $\tilde{\mathbf{x}}_{p,l}(t)$ are combined using STMMs in the way described in section 1 using the linear weights $\alpha_{p,l}$. The result are the linearly combined normalized trajectory segments $\tilde{\mathbf{x}}_l(t)$. The start and end points are also linearly combined, as well as the total durations of the individual trajectory segments, which are given by $D_{p,l} = T^{\text{e}}_{p,l} - T^{\text{s}}_{p,l}$:

$$\mathbf{x}^{\text{s,e}}_l = \sum_{p=1}^{P} c_p\, \mathbf{x}^{\text{s,e}}_{p,l} \tag{4}$$

$$D_l = \sum_{p=1}^{P} c_p\, D_{p,l} \tag{5}$$

4. **Rewarping and concatenation of the movement elements:** The linearly combined trajectories $\tilde{\mathbf{x}}_l(t)$ of the movement elements are un-normalized and concatenated to obtain the final composite sequence. Un-normalization is achieved by applying equation (3) to obtain the trajectory segments $\mathbf{x}_l(t)$. If the linear weight vectors of subsequent trajectory segments are different the condition $\mathbf{x}^{\text{e}}_l = \mathbf{x}^{\text{s}}_{l+1}$ that ensures the continuity of the trajectories after concatenation might be violated. To ensure continuity, start and endpoint pairs that violate these conditions are replaced by the average $(\mathbf{x}^{\text{e}}_l + \mathbf{x}^{\text{s}}_{l+1})/2$ before un-normalization. Fig. 2 illustrates the normalized linearly combined trajectory segments. Ten coordinates of the normalized trajectory after concatenation of the movement elements are shown. The black vertical lines illustrate the boundaries between the movement elements.

3 Motion Data and Animation

The proposed method was tested with different data sets of complex human movements. One set of data of facial movements was created by recording the facial expressions from 10 non-professional actors using a commercial system (*Famous Faces, FAMOUS Technologies*). The actors executed a fixed sequence of facial expressions within a certain time interval (10 s): neutral, smile, frown, surprise, chew (3x), disgust, smile, neutral. Seventeen blue and green foam markers were placed on eyebrows, forehead, furrow, mouth, chin, nose and cheeks. The actors were filmed in a studio set-up using a Sony digital video camera. Actors were able to watch their faces in a monitor while performing the facial actions. The motion of the markers was tracked from the video clips with 25 f/s using vTracker by *FAMOUS Technologies*. The marker on the nose was used as a reference point to remove head translations in the image plane. These marker movements were defined relative to the neutral facial expression for each individual actor. The resulting trajectories served as data for the linear combination method. Another data set was generated by recording sequences of techniques from karate using a commercial motion capture system (VICON, Oxford). These results are described in [10].

A 3D head model was then animated with the morphed trajectories using commercial software (*FAMOUS Technologies*). Each morphed marker trajectory specified the movement of a certain "region of influence" of the face model. These regions were manually defined and optimized for a maximum quality of the animation. The animations were presented on an "average head". This head was computed by averaging the shapes and the textures of 200 laser-scanned heads from the Max Planck head data base by aligning their 3D geometry using a morphable 3D head model [2]. The advantage of presenting the movements on an average head is that the influence of facial movements can be studied without confounding effects from the form of individual faces [8]. The animated heads were finally rendered into AVI format.

4 Experiments

We conducted two experiments using naive subjects with normal or corrected-to-normal vision. The purpose of the first experiment was to evaluate the quality of the animations using the trajectories obtained by linear combination of the recorded trajectories in comparison with animations using original motion capture data. The second experiment investigated the perception of spatio-temporal caricatures.

For investigating the quality of the animations we used 7 naive subjects. They had to rate 33 animations on a scale ranging from "unnatural" to "natural". The animations were presented using the average head. 11 stimuli were generated using the original trajectories from 11 actors executing the facial movement sequence that was described in section 3. These movement sequences were also used as prototypes for the linear combinations. 11 further stimuli were created by approximating the original trajectories optimally by linear combinations. These stimuli served to test the quality of the approximations of the trajectories by the linear combination model. Finally, we presented 11 two-pattern morphs that were generated by linearly combining randomly chosen pairs out of the 11 prototypes using equal weights 0.5. All stimuli were presented in random order without limitation of presentation time.

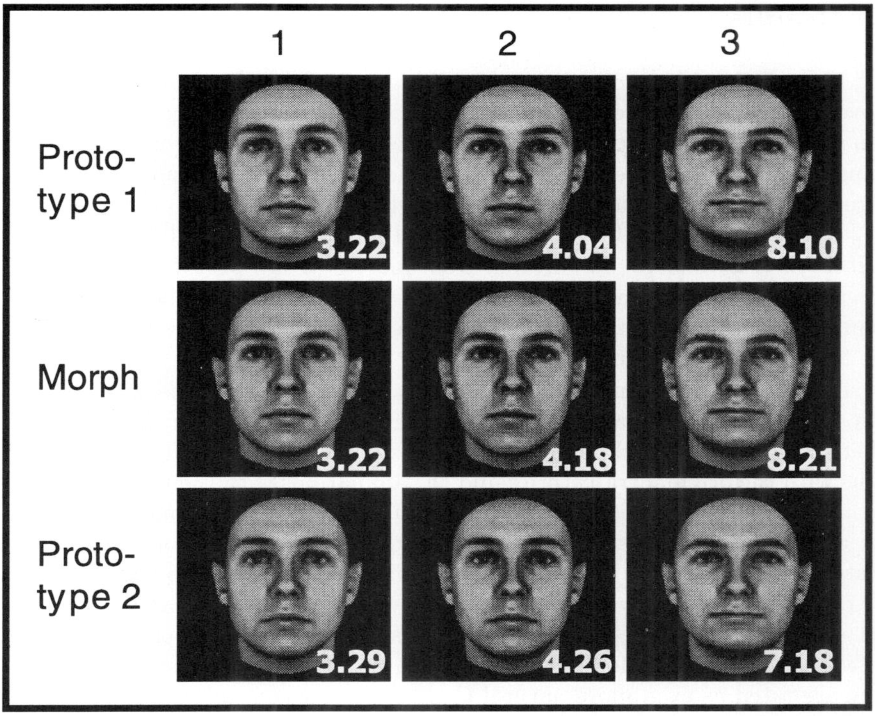

Fig. 3. Key frames from prototypes and linear combination. (Numbers: time in *s*.)

For the second experiment that tested spatio-temporal caricature effects we used 14 subjects. The experiment consisted of two blocks, a training block and a test block. During training subjects saw two different heads (A and B) animated with the movements of two different actors. These two heads had different shapes, but the same "average texture". The average texture was derived by averaging the texture of all heads in the MPI data basis after normalizing them to an average shape [2]. Subjects had to fill in a questionnaire asking for different "personality traits" of the two animated faces. No explicit discrimination task was given during training.

During test subjects saw the same two facial movement sequences as during training, but with three different caricature levels (1, 1.25, and 1.5). The movements were presented on an "average head" with average texture and average shape computed by averaging the shapes and the textures of the heads in the MPI data basis. During test subjects had to classify the face movements as corresponding to "face A" or "face B" from training. The stimuli were presented without limitation of viewing time.

5 Results

For both data sets our linear combination method generates naturally looking movements from the prototypes when the weights are in the regime $[0, 1]$. This was also the case when the movements were derived from different actors. In the transition regions between the different movement elements no discontinuities were visible. For the karate data set the linear combination of the durations $D_{l,p}$ of the movement elements was critical for simulation of different technical skill levels. Fig. 3 shows key frames from movies of two prototypical sequences, executed by two different people, and their linear combination with weights 0.5. Remark that the different movement sequences differ not only with respect to the form of the faces, but also with respect to their timing[1].

The quality of the linear combinations was tested more systematically in our first experiment. The naturalness ratings from 7 observers are shown in Fig. 4. There is no significant difference between the naturalness ratings of the animations with the original trajectories and the animations with their approximations by linear combinations ($t(6) = 2.42$, $p > 0.05$). This shows that the quality of the animations is not significantly reduced when the trajectories are approximated using the linear combination model. However, the two-pattern morphs are rated as significantly more natural than the approximated (and original) trajectories ($t(6) = 4.57$, $p < 0.01$). This shows that the tested linear combinations of two patterns are not looking less natural than the prototypes. The result that they are rated as even more natural than the prototypes might be based on the fact that the linear combinations tend to average out extreme facial movements. Subjects might have a tendency to rate extreme facial movements as unnatural.

Dynamically exaggerated facial movements can be generated by assigning coefficients larger than one to one prototype, maintaining the constraint $\sum_p \alpha_{p,l} = 1$. Key frames from such stimuli in comparison with the unexaggerated prototype are shown in Fig. 6. The first panel shows the neutral expression that was used as reference for defining the trajectories on the 3D head model (cf. section 3) For extreme exaggerations (weights $\alpha_{p,l} > 2$) artifacts can arise because of errors in the texture interpolation, and anomalies in the form of the faces resulting from the strong spatial displacements specified by the extrapolated marker trajectories[2].

Dynamically exaggerated stimuli can be used for psychophysical experiments that investigate "caricature effects" in the perception of moving faces. Caricature effects in static pictures of faces are experimentally well-established: Enhancement of the geometrical characteristics that are specific for individual faces improves the categorization performance in face recognition (e.g. [1]). It has been

[1] The dynamically presented facial expresions appear much more distinct than it appears from the static pictures shown in Fig. 3. Movies of the face animations are provided on the Web site:`www.uni-tuebingen.de/uni/knv/arl/arl-demos.html`.

[2] For exaggeration of facial movements we obtained better results if we did not morph the durations of individual movement elements. Instead, the durations were set to the average duration of the motion elements of the prototypes.

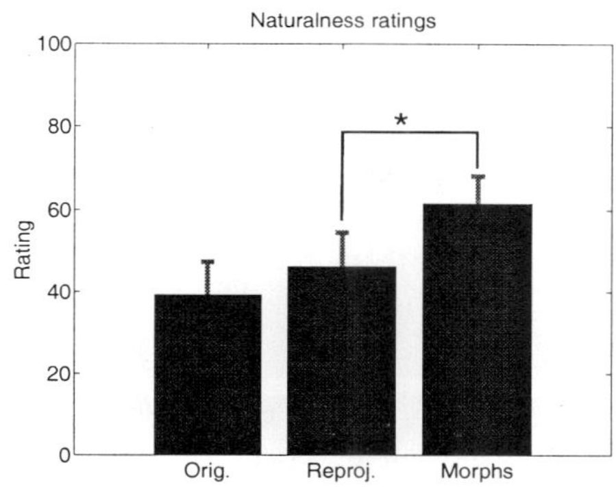

Fig. 4. Naturalness ratings for animations with original and approximated trajectories, and of two-pattern morphs.)

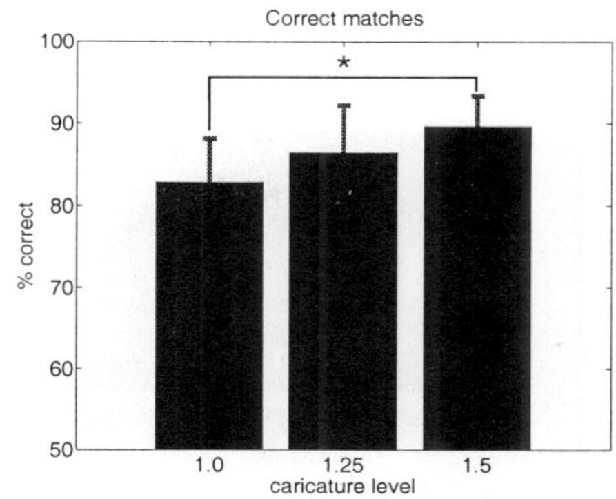

Fig. 5. Correct classifications of exaggerated sequences of facial movements.

shown recently that also temporal exaggeration can improve the recognition individuals from arm movements [9]. With the exaggeration stimuli described before we can study the effect of spatio-temporal exaggerations of movement elements in sequences of facial movements.

Fig. 5 show the results from the test block of the caricature experiment. The fractions of correctly classified facial movement sequences increases with the caricature level. For the tested caricature levels we found no significant main effect in a one-factor repeated measures ANOVA for the factor caricature level ($F(1, 24) = 3.0$, $p > 0.05$). However, the difference between the caricature levels 1 and 1.5 is significant ($t(13) = 2.5$, $p < 0.05$). In addition, using a contingency table analysis we find for these caricature levels a significant interaction between the type of the movement (motion pattern A or B) and caricature level ($\chi^2(1) = 5.4$, $p < 0.05$). Similar interactions between pattern type and caricature level have been found in experiments with stationary caricatures of faces (e.g. [6]).

It is remarkable that we found this caricature effect even though the test movements were presented using the average head model that has a different shape then the two heads used during training. In addition, the facial movements were learned "incidentally", i.e. without explicitly instructing subjects to learn the movements during training.

6 Conclusion

We have presented a method for the automatic generation of realistically looking human movements consisting of movement elements that vary in style. By linear combination of prototypes in space-time our method defines abstract linear pattern spaces that are suitable for a simple specification and quantification of the

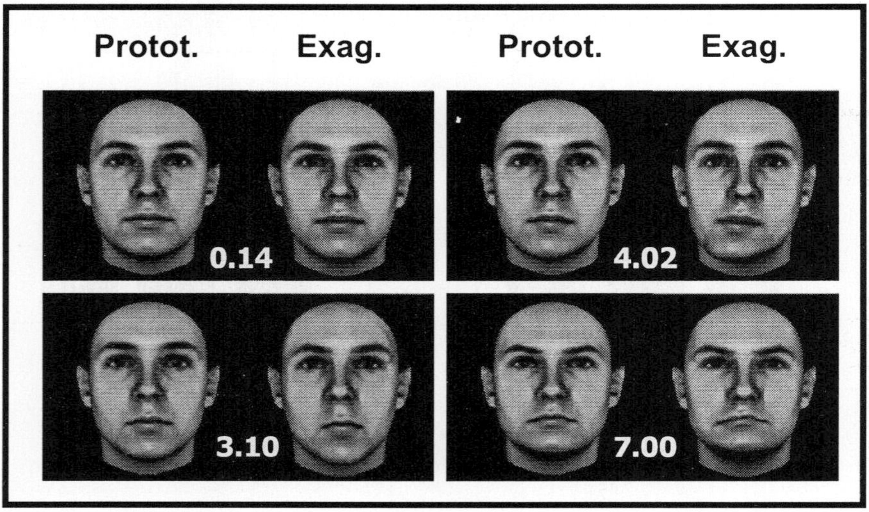

Fig. 6. Prototypes and exaggerations. (Numbers indicate time in *s*.)

styles of individual movement elements. We presented experimental data showing that convex linear combinations of sequences of face movements generated with our method are perceived a very natural. At the same time our method allows to model longer sequences with multiple movement elements without requiring editing or blending of the transition regions between these elements. Since the movement elements can be determined automatically [10] the method is suitable for learning generative models for long movement sequences with style parameters that vary over time.

We also demonstrated how this method can be applied to generate spatio-temporal exaggerations of complex movement sequences. Using such exaggerations of facial movement sequences we found a significant *spatio-temporal caricature effect*: facial identity can be extracted more easily from facial movements if the movements are exaggerated in space-time.

The quality of our animations could be substantially improved. We are presently recording 3D data with a much larger marker set using a commercial motion capture system. In this way we can model the facial movements in much finer detail, and artifacts resulting from the projection of the 2D tracking data onto the 3D head model, and the spatial interpolation between the individual markers will be reduced.

An interesting straight-forward extension of our approach is to use the obtained generative model for quantification of style parameters. We have shown elsewhere [7] that by approximation with spatio-temporal morphable models continuous style parameters of complex movements can be estimated. Compared with statistical approaches for the estimation of generative models from trajectory data (e.g. [3]) our method has the advantage that only a very small amount of data (prototypical trajectories) is required. We are presently exploiting this advantage for the analysis of data from patients with rare movement disorders.

Acknowledgements. This work was supported by the Deutsche Volkswagenstiftung. We thank C. Wallraven for helpful comments.

References

1. P Benson and D Perrett. Perception and recognition of photographic quality facial caricatures: Implications for the recognition of natural images. *Journal of Cognitive Psychology*, 3(1):105–135, 1991.
2. V Blanz and T Vetter. Morphable model for the synthesis of 3d faces. In *Proceedings of SIGGRAPH 99, Los Angeles*, pages 187–194, 1999.
3. M Brand. Style machines. In *Proceedings of SIGGRAPH 2000, New Orleans, Lousiana, USA*, pages 23–28, 2000.
4. A Bruderlin and L Williams. Motion signal processing. In *Proceedings of SIGGRAPH 95, Los Angeles*, pages 97–104, 1995.
5. T Caelli, A McCabe, and G Binsted. Learning the shape of complex actions. In C Arcelli, L Cordella, and G Sanniti, editors, *Proceedings of the International Workshop on Visual Form: IWVF2001*, pages 24–39;. Springen, Berlin, 2001.
6. A J Calder, D Rowland, A W Young, I Nimmo-Smith, J Keane, and D I Perrett. Caricaturing facial expressions. *Cognition*, 76:105–146, 2000.
7. M A Giese and T Poggio. Morphable models for the analysis and synthesis of complex motion pattern,. *International Journal of Computer Vision*, 38:59–73, 2000.
8. H Hill and A Johnston. Categorizing sex and identity from the biological motion of faces. *Current Biology*, 11:880–885, 2001.
9. H Hill and F E Pollick. Exaggerating temporal differences enhances recognition of individuals from point light displays. *Psychological Science*, 11:223–228, 2000.
10. W Ilg and M A Giese. Modeling of movement sequences based on hierarchical hierarchical spatio-temporal correspondence between movement primitives. In *Workshop on Biologically Motivated Computer Vision 2002*. Springer, Berlin, this volume.
11. A Lamouret and M van de Panne. Motion synthesis by example. In *Proceedings of 7th CAS '96 Eurographics Workshop on Animation and Simulation*, pages 199–212, 1996.
12. J Lee, J Chai, P S Reitsma, J K Hodgkins, and N S Pollard. Interactive control of avatars animated with human motion data. In *Proceedings of SIGGRAPH 2002, San Antonio, Texas, USA*, page (in press), 2002.
13. H Sidenbladh, M J Black, and L Sigal. Implicit probabilistic models of human motion for synthesis and tracking. In *Proceedings of the European Conference on Computer Vision (ECCV), Copenhagen, Danmark*, pages 784–800, 2002.
14. D J Wiley and J Hahn. Interpolation synthesis of articulated figure motion. *IEEE Transactions on Computer Graphics and Applications*, 11:39–45, 1997.
15. A Witkin and Z Popović. Motion warping. In *Proceedings of SIGGRAPH 95, Los Angeles*, pages 105–108, 1995.

An Adaptive Hierarchical Model of the Ventral Visual Pathway Implemented on a Mobile Robot

Alistair Bray

CORTEX Group, LORIA-INRIA, Nancy, France
bray@loria.fr
http://www.loria.fr/equipes/cortex/

Abstract. The implementation of an adaptive visual system founded on the detection of spatio-temporal invariances is described. It is a layered system inspired by the hierarchical processing in the mammalian ventral visual pathway, and models retinal, early cortical and infero-temporal components. A representation of scenes in terms of slowly varying spatio-temporal signatures is discovered through maximising a measure of temporal predictability. This supports categorisation of the environment by a set of view cells (view-trained units or VTUs [1]) that demonstrate substantial invariance to transformations of viewpoint and scale.

The notion of maximising an objective function based upon temporal predictability of output has been progressively applied in modelling the development of invariances in the visual system. Földiák introduced it indirectly via a Hebbian trace rule for modelling complex cell development [2] (closely related to other models [3,4]); this rule has been used to maximise invariance as one component of a hierarchical system for object and face recognition [5]. On the other hand, a function has been maximised directly in networks for extracting linear [6], and non-linear [7,8,9] invariances. Direct maximisation of related objective functions have been used to model complex cells [10,11], and as an alternative to maximising sparseness/independence in modelling simple cells [12]. This generality prompts the question whether temporal predictability can be applied as an objective function in the later stages of a hierarchical vision system which progressively extracts more complex and invariant features from image sequences. This might provide both a simple model of the ventral visual pathway and a practical system for object recognition. We explore this possibility through a practical implementation on a mobile robot.

The approach is useful since, although many theoretical models describe the adaptive visual processing from retina to higher cortical levels (these vary considerably in their degree of abstraction), and much progress has also been made in understanding spatial memory and navigation by exploiting the adaptive computational model, little has been done to exploit the theoretical implications to achieve practical results (see [13]). Practical applications of the adaptive biological theory of the visual system seem currently to exist only for simple models of face recognition (e.g. [5]), despite the prevalent use of mobile robots for testing biological theories of memory and navigation (e.g. [14])

H.H. Bülthoff et al. (Eds.): BMCV 2002, LNCS 2525, pp. 548–557, 2002.

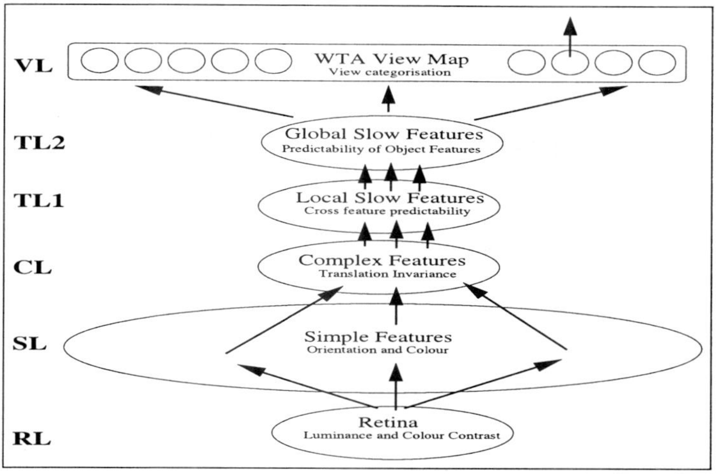

Fig. 1. Hierarchical feed-forward architecture. The architecture is a fine-to-coarse hierarchy of layers. The hard-wired retina **RL** processes contrast in luminance and colour. Simple layer **SL** learns a sparse coding of this information, with features based on orientation and colour. The complex layer **CL** learns translation invariance through maximising temporal predictability within simple features over space, and the temporal layers **TL** integrate this information across both features and space by maximising predictability. A competitive network **VL** categorises views using these predictable global parameters using Hebbian adaptation.

1 A Hierarchical Architecture

This section outlines the hierarchical architecture that includes a non-adaptive pre-cortical layer, a layer learning a sparse-coding of the image in terms of spatial statistics, and further layers learning progressively complex features through maximising a measure of temporal predictability. This is illustrated in Figure 1.

1.1 Colour and Contrast

The retinal layer **RL** mimics pre-cortical processing. It simultaneously rotates the colour space and performs a spatial Difference of Gaussian contrast operation, accentuating colour and luminance contrast. This mapping for three channels is defined in terms of red(r), green(g), blue(b), yellow(y) and grey as:

$$s_1.(d_1.C(r-g) - S.(r-g)) \mapsto CH_1$$

$$s_2.(d_2.C(b-y) - S.(b-y)) \mapsto CH_2$$

$$s_3.(d_3.C(grey) - S.(grey)) \mapsto CH_3$$

where the functions C and S are local Gaussian averaging functions with standard deviation ratio σ_S:σ_C=3:1 similar to that of retinal centre surround cells. The

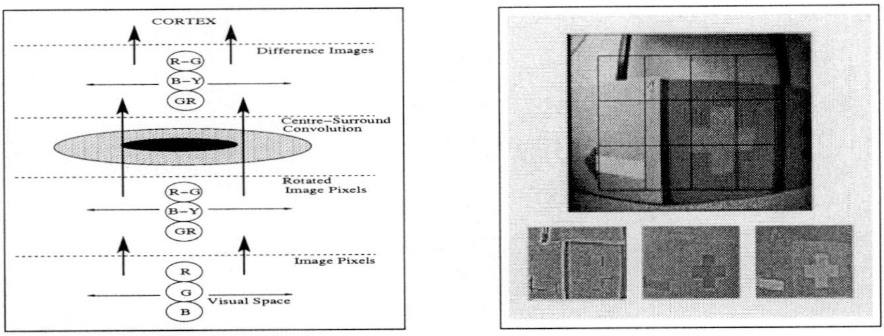

Fig. 2. Colour and contrast. **Left: colour sampling.** Pixels are coded by red, green, blue which are rotated to red-green, blue-yellow, grey (broadband). These new pixels are convolved with a DoG filter to simulate pre-cortical centre-surround processing. **Right: output.** Above, the image is shown with a grid defining the visual field. Below is the output of the three channels within this field: $d = \{1.1, 1.1, 1.0\}$ and $s = \{3, 3, 5\}$.

values $\{d_1, d_2, d_3\}$ determine the weighting of centre to surround and $\{s_1, s_2, s_3\}$ determine the contribution of each channel. The colour rotation is performed before the difference operation, whereas retinal ganglion cells perform both operations simultaneously. This modifies the function slightly, but allows the amount of boundary information transmitted and hence the degree of spatial contrast (colour and luminance) to be easily controlled via $\{d_1, d_2, d_3\}$. The result emphasises boundaries, efficiently reducing processing in regions of uniform colour; this may be a role of the lateral inhibition in the LGN. This is illustrated in Figure 2.

1.2 Sparse-Coding Features

Layer **SL** mimics simple cells in V1. The basic unit is a micro-circuit of columns, each column containing 25 cells. Each cell connects via weights w to 120 afferent inputs x sampled randomly from the three retinal channels, distributed around the same point in retinal space. The micro-circuit is illustrated in Figure 3(left). The circuit is replicated across the visual field to provide layer output, but all columns share weights. Initial cell output is defined $y = w.x$, but soft competition between all cells within the circuit (enforced by subtractive normalisation on $|y|$) ensures that only S=15% of response activity is retained. This results in a sparse coding y' such that $|y'| \propto \max(|y| - K, 0)$, where K (> 0) is a function of S and $\Sigma|y'| = 1$. Weights start with random values modulated by a Gaussian envelope in retinal space, and adapt using the Hebbian rule $\Delta w = \alpha.x.y'$ where α is the learning rate, whilst remaining subject to $\Sigma w^2 = 1$.

Two factors should be noted. First, a column in the microcircuit does not correspond to a cortical orientation column since its contains different competing units rather than similar enhancing ones; rather, it corresponds to a hypercolumn modelling a complete set of features. Second, the circuit is defined as

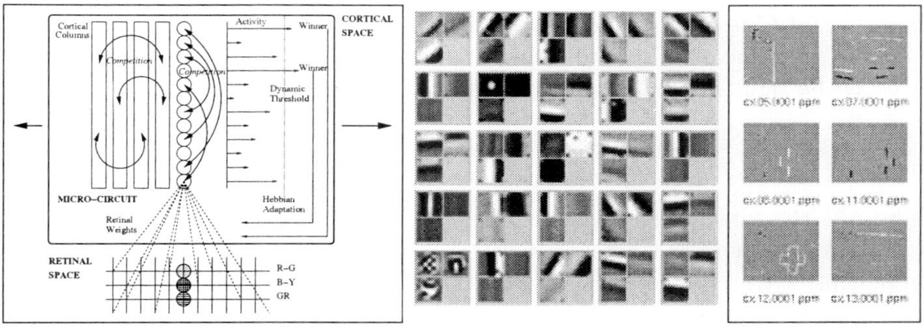

Fig. 3. Sparse phase-invariant filtering. **Left:** The micro-circuit. **Centre**: Each filter is shown in terms of its weights connecting to the three retinal channels (top-left is broadband, top right is red-green and bottom-left is blue-yellow). **Right:** Layer output for cells 5,7,8,11,12 & 13.

having multiple columns even though columns share weights. This is because each circuit column receives slightly different retinal inputs and there is competition between (as well as within) columns. This results in the column learning a set of phase-invariant features, which leads to greater resolution in the orientation and colour dimensions.

1.3 Slow Features

In computing the slow varying features in the image there is a variety of possible objective functions to maximise, each with its own algorithm. Földiák initially used a trace rule [2] combined with local competition (as does [5]). Wiskott recently detailed SFA that minimises the temporal derivative in a non-linear feature space subject to the diagonal covariance matrix constraint [8]; however, this suffers from the curse of dimensionality when computing features. We use an earlier measure based on the ratio of variances proposed by Stone [6,7] which in the linear case can be maximised using an efficient closed-form algorithm providing multiple parameters [15]; it can also be extended to the nonlinear domain using kernels [16,11].

The Objective Function

The function is defined

$$F = \frac{V}{S} = \frac{\sum_t \overline{y_t}^2}{\sum_t \widetilde{y_t}^2}$$

where $\overline{y}_t$ and $\widetilde{y}_t$ represent the output at t centered using long- and short-term means. It can be rewritten as

$$F = \frac{\mathbf{w}^T \overline{\mathbf{C}} \mathbf{w}}{\mathbf{w}^T \widetilde{\mathbf{C}} \mathbf{w}} \quad \textit{where} \quad \overline{\mathbf{C}} = \frac{1}{l} \sum_t \overline{\mathbf{x}}_t \overline{\mathbf{x}}_t^T \;\; \textit{and} \;\; \widetilde{\mathbf{C}} = \frac{1}{l} \sum_t \widetilde{\mathbf{x}}_t \widetilde{\mathbf{x}}_t^T$$

where $\overline{\mathbf{C}}$ and $\widetilde{\mathbf{C}}$ are covariance matrices estimated from the l inputs $\mathbf{x}$ centred using the same means. In maximising F (see [15] for details) the problem to be solved is the right-handed generalized symmetric eigenproblem:

$$\overline{C}\mathbf{w} = \lambda \widetilde{C}\mathbf{w}$$

where λ is the largest eigenvalue and $\mathbf{w}$ the corresponding eigenvector. In this case, the component extracted $y = \mathbf{w}^T\mathbf{x}$ corresponds to the most predictable component with F=λ. Most importantly, more than one component can be extracted by considering successive eigenvalues and eigenvectors which are orthogonal in the metrics $\overline{C}$ and $\widetilde{C}$, i.e. $\mathbf{w}_t^T\overline{\mathbf{C}}\mathbf{w}_j = 0$ and $\mathbf{w}_t^T\widetilde{\mathbf{C}}\mathbf{w}_j = 0$ for $i \neq j$.

Complex to Infero-temporal layers

In layer **CL** the visual field is divided into 12 regions receiving equivalent processing by 25 units. These are notionally replicated at each grid position to provide outputs for the whole visual field. Each unit connects to the output of just one simple cell type in **SL**. Its output is the most predictable function as defined by the largest eigenvalue maximising F (other components are discarded). Units learn to give a large smooth response when features (in terms of appropriate colour and orientation) pass across their receptive field; since each unit connects to a different filter, they are constrained to learn different functions. Such connectivity is consistent with models learning translation invariance via selective connections to specific simple cells, e.g. [2].

In layer **TLa** information is integrated within regions, across complex cell type. The most predictable functions are computed from the output of **CL**, and those with $\lambda > 1$ are passed forward. In our case all 25 components are used; note these components are not orthogonal and the layer is therefore not information preserving.

In layer **TLb** information is integrated across all 12 regions. The most predictable global functions are computed from the output of **TLa**. The input vector therefore has dimension 300. Visual interpretation of the features learnt in either of these two layers is not informative.

1.4 View Cell Categorisation

The layer **VL** uses the 138 outputs of **TLb** having eigenvalues $\lambda = V/U > 2$ as input to a winner-take-all competitive network with 100 units (VTUs). Weights commence random and the network uses standard non-temporal Hebbian learning for the single winner. Since strong temporal correlations already exist in the inputs there is no reason to use a temporal trace learning rule at this point. In consequence, although the system requires temporally correlated inputs for learning, images can be quickly categorised at the highest level instantaneously, without temporal integration.

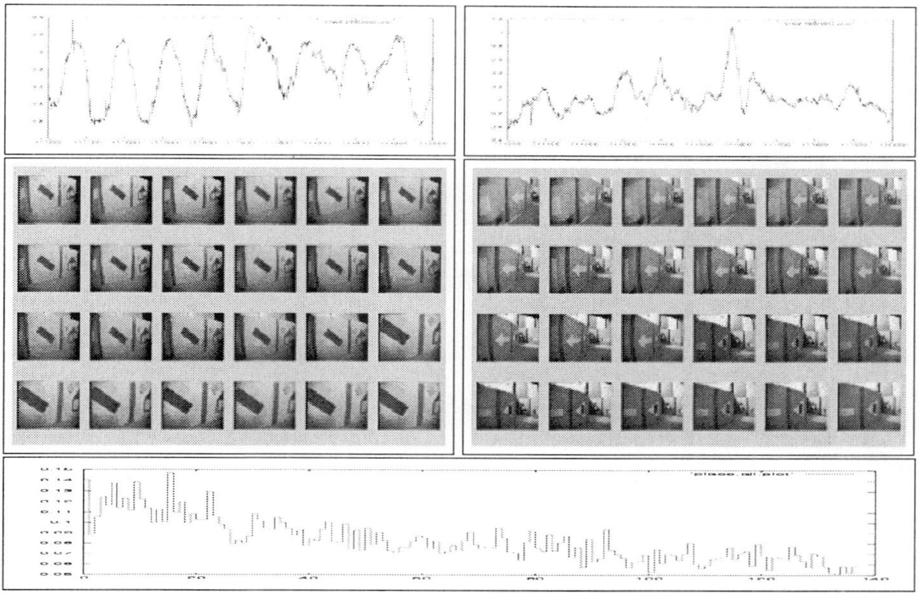

Fig. 4. System output. **Above:** The output of the two most predictable units in **TLb** learnt in the walled maze. The first shows a regular oscillation that has a temporal frequency equal to the camera tilt parameter, suggesting correlation with the amount of carpet texture in the visual field. **Middle:** views activating two different VTUs. A selection of quite different images activate the same view cells in **VL**. **Bottom:** The average absolute value of VTU weights. The strongest connections are to the most predictable units in **TLb**.

2 Performance Evaluation

The system is implemented in **C++** for a Koala robot with onboard video and a cordless connection to a 1000 MHz Pentium III; without graphics, this processes on average 2.2 frames per second[1], using approximately 4 Mbytes of RAM. The system has been evaluated in two different environments: the first is a walled maze environment rich in colour and orientation (providing the results presented so far); the second is the local office corridor at LORIA, which is larger, limited in colour, and abundant in vertical orientations (see Figure 5). The robot moves around its environment avoiding objects using infrared sensors and with camera tilt and pan oscillating smoothly. The robot speed and camera motion is determined so as to provide sufficient temporal correlations in visual input for layer **CL**. For practical reasons involving use of the Koala robot, the learning process used a sequence of 3200 images captured in this manner which is presented repetitively during adaptation, but with the visual field being randomly reposi-

[1] Although this is a function of the visual information in each image so 'uninteresting regions' of the environment are processed much faster.

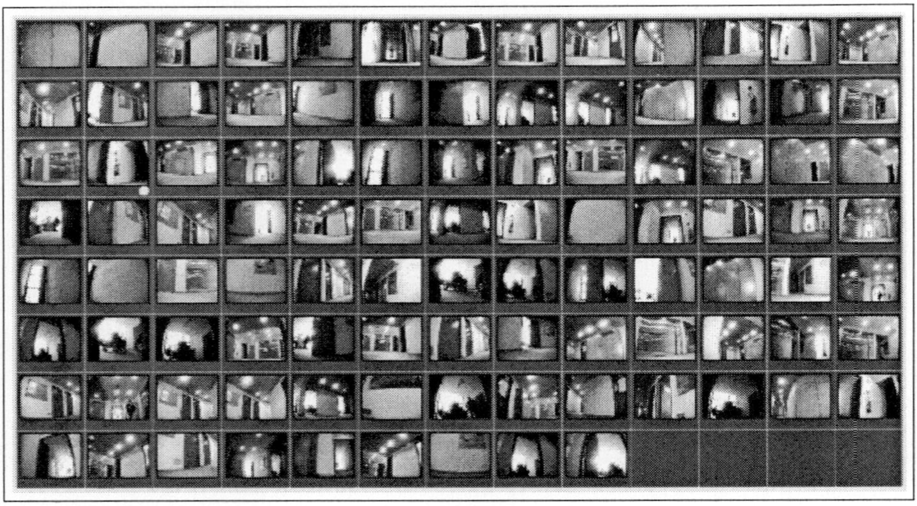

Fig. 5. View map of the corridor. The images in the corridor sequence that elicit the maximal response from each VTU (note that the visual field is only 66% of each image). The current image is categorised, correctly or otherwise, under one of these.

tioned in the image at the start of each repetition. Since the visual field (120x90) represents only 66% of the camera image (150x110 after precortical processing), there are 600 possible positions and therefore 1.92 million possible input images. Layers in the hierarchy are learnt progressively, each layer commencing adaptation when the one below it has stable parameters; this involves processing only around 0.5 million input images. The system learns a set of 'characteristic views' or VTUs, such that images within a view are similar enough to be categorised as the same and different from those within another view. Figure 4 shows a variety of images to which certain view cells responded in the walled maze environment. It can be seen that categorisation withstands a significant degree of transformation in terms of viewpoint, scale and translation; however, there can be misclassifications.

To quantify the classification error, we performed a statistical evaluation of correct categorisation on the training sequence for each environment, using a 'view map'. This view map is constructed after learning, when the system is run on the training sequence to find the particular image that provides maximal output for each VTU; such a view map for the corridor environment is shown in Figure 5. Using this map, we subsequently evaluated categorisation performance by hand on images from the training sequence. To do this we judged for each image whether it was well categorised by the image in the view map[2]. In this

[2] The criterion was simply whether the images were indeed of neighbouring parts of the environment (ignoring whether there was another VTU that seemed even closer to the image); in the maze this judgement was very easily made, so providing reliable statistics; in the corridor it was harder in unfeatured regions of blank wall.

process the visual field was randomly positioned in the camera image at **every** time step, so that input images were sampled uniformly over the 1.92 million possible and not just from those used for adaptation. Using this method, we found that after 6400 time steps the categorisation statistics had stabilised, with correct classification of the image **94%** of the time in the walled maze, but only **85%** in the corridor environment. This difference is mainly explained by the maze being both small and unambiguously featured: in the corridor VTUs were sometimes multi-modal, responding to images from different parts of the environment. Occasionally such images were quite different (presumably coded on different features in **TLb**), suggesting a need for more VTUs; more often they were similar, highlighting that a 'view cell' is not a 'place cell' (making classification hard), and suggesting a need for a further layer categorising views by places. Both problems relate to the simple approach adopted in **VL**.

We also tested the classification of the system online in the two different physical environments. We concluded for both that as long as the camera view corresponded well with the views categorised by the training sequence then the categorisation seemed of similar accuracy to that above. However, this highlighted a practical problem: the training sequences did **not** comprehensively cover all views of the environment. Once the view deviated outside those in the training sequence, performance degraded substantially. We have not quantified this error since we consider it a practical fault to be overcome through more extensive online training of the system which may then demand either an increase in the number of VTUs or a reduction of the degrees of freedom via, for example, freezing the camera tilt.

Finally, examination of the VTUs' weights after training in the walled maze revealed a distributed representation, with the trend for the strongest connections to be to the most predictable inputs (see Figure 4). This suggests that the clusters discovered by the network that define each view are not uniform across input dimension. These clusters may develop in a coarse-to-fine manner in terms of predictability, and spatial structure, as initially the clusters evolve around the most predictable features, but use less predictable features for finer discrimination; this has yet to be confirmed.

3 Conclusions

This work is an attempt at the practical application of recent theory of invariances. The system performs well in categorising two quite different environments, correctly classifying a high percentage of images that are generated in the same manner as those for training (94% for the smaller, unambiguous environment). In each environment it learns different features that are spatio-temporal functions of that environment at different spatial resolutions, the highest level learning global features that are used for classification by VTUs.

The major advantage of the system is that each layer learns features adapted to the appropriate spatio-temporal statistics, and also that layers must therefore only be retrained when these statistics change (most usually for high layers). Its major constraints are currently resource-based. First, its spatial resolution is poor, and it can therefore be deceived by differences on a small scale; this highlights the problem that distinctive features can be the improbable ones. Second, it must thoroughly sample all views of the environment during training for the categorisation to be satisfactory, which involves many images. We emphasise however that this categorisation layer is only used here to evaluate performance, since its WTA representation does not conform to the highly distributed representations reported in infero-temporal cortex ([17], chapter 5). More interesting will be the evaluation of the representation of slowly varying features in **TLa, TLb** for tasks involving navigation and spatial memory, which is yet to be done; further work therefore needs to evaluate performance via interactive behaviour.

Further work is also progressing in implementing more sophisticated methods for extracting temporal invariances that are currently evolving in this fast-developing field. The biggest theoretical challenge for our approach is in defining correct objective functions, and methods for maximising them through **non-linear** functions. One method avoids this, combining nonlinear competition with a linear learning rule [5]; another is subject to problems of dimensionality [8]. In our work we have used a linear method which is computationally efficient; however we recognise that this linearity is neither biologically proven at higher stages, nor necessarily optimal [13]. The question regarding appropriate objective functions, and whether they are conceptually similar at different stages is an open one. Recently temporal continuity has also been used to account for the development of simple linear cells [12], previously best described using sparseness/independence [18,19]; this suggests that temporal coherence may provide a generally useful objective function. However, we do not propose that the precise measure we use is optimal: for example, maximising a function of the long term variance of the output may be less appropriate than ensuring temporal continuity subject to a non-zero variance constraint. In this respect, our current work has concentrated particularly on an efficient modularisation of the system which now allows complete flexibility in constructing the hierarchy of layers, and plugging different 'microfunctions' into each layer to compute different spatio-temporal statistics. This has led to promising experiments that combine a recent linear algorithm [12] in the lowest layer with a non-linear algorithm [11] in higher ones.

Beyond these issues, we recognise that our approach ignores significant aspects of biological visual processing. Since we do not consider feedback within or between layers, phenomena such as perceptual grouping (that might arise from temporal synchronisation in a spiking representation) are not possible. Neither do we consider information provided by active saccadic control, or modelling the parietal "where" pathway; as such, our system can recognise but not locate.

Acknowledgements. I would like to thank members of the CORTEX Group at LORIA for supporting this work in all respects, and INRIA for funding the research.

References

1. M Reisenhuber and T Poggio. Hierarchical models of object recognition in cortex. *Nature Neuroscience*, 11(2):1019–1025, 1999.
2. P. Földiák. Learning invariance from transformation sequences. *Neural Computation*, 3(2):194–200, 1991.
3. H. G. Barrow and A. J. Bray. A model of adaptive development of complex cortical cells. In I. Aleksander and J. Taylor, editors, *Artificial Neural Networks II: Proceedings of the International Conference on Artificial Neural Networks*. Elsevier Publishers, 1992.
4. M. Stewart Bartlett and T.J. Sejnowski. Learning viewpoint invariant face representations from visual experience in an attractor network. *Network: Computation in Neural Systems*, 9(3):399–417, 1998.
5. E. T. Rolls and T. Milward. A model of invariant object recognition in the visual system: Learning rules, activation functions, lateral inhibition, and information-based performance measures. *Neural Computation*, 12:2547–2572, 2000.
6. J. V. Stone and A. J. Bray. A learning rule for extracting spatio-temporal invariances. *Network: Computation in Neural Systems*, 6(3):429–436, 1995.
7. J. V. Stone. Learning perceptually salient visual parameters using spatiotemporal smoothness constraints. *Neural Computation*, 8(7):1463–1492, October 1996.
8. L. Wiskott and T.J. Sejnowski. Slow feature analysis: Unsupervised learning of invariances. *Neural Computation*, 14(4), 2002.
9. D. Martinez and A. Bray. Nonlinear blind source separation using kernels. *IEEE: Neural Networks*, Accepted, September 2002.
10. K. Kayser, W. Einhäuser, O. Dümmer, P. König, and K. Körding. Extracting slow subspaces from natural videos leads to complex cells. In *ICANN 2001, LNCS 2130*, pages 1075–1080. Springer-Verlag Berlin Heidelberg 2001, 2001.
11. A.J. Bray and D. Martinez. Kernel-based extraction of slow features: Complex cells learn disparity and translation invariance from natural images. *Neural Information Processing Systems, NIPS*, Submitted, 2002.
12. J. Hurri and A. Hyvarinen. Simple-cell-like receptive fields maximise temporal coherence in natural video. *Submitted, http://www.cis.hut.fi/˜jarmo/publications*, 2002.
13. M. Reisenhuber and T. Poggio. Models of object recognition. *Nature Neuroscience*, 3:1199–1204, November 2000.
14. A Arleo and W. Gerstner. Spatial cognition and neuro-mimetic navigation: A model of hippocampal place cell activity. *Biological Cybernetics*, 83:287–299, 2000.
15. James V. Stone. Blind source separation using temporal predictability. *Neural Computation*, (13):1559–1574, 2001.
16. D. Martinez and A.J. Bray. Kernel temporal component analysis (KTCA): non-linear maximisation of temporal predictability. *ESANN: European Symposium on Artificial Neural Networks*, 2002.
17. E.T. Rolls and G. Deco. *Computational Neuroscience of Vision*. Oxford University Press, 2002.
18. B.A. Olhausen and D.J. Field. Emergence of simple-cell receptive field properties by learning a sparse code for natural images. *Nature*, 381:607–609, 1996.
19. A. J. Bell and T. J. Sejnowski. The independent components of natural scenes are edge filters. *Vision Research*, 37:3327–3338, 1997.

A New Robotics Platform for Neuromorphic Vision: Beobots

Daesu Chung[1], Reid Hirata[1], T. Nathan Mundhenk[1], Jen Ng[1], Rob J. Peters[2], Eric Pichon[1], April Tsui[3], Tong Ventrice[1], Dirk Walther[2], Philip Williams[1], and Laurent Itti[1]

[1] University of Southern California, Computer Science Department
Los Angeles, California, 90089-2520, USA – `http://iLab.usc.edu`
[2] California Institute of Technology, Computation and Neural Systems program
Mail Code 139-74 – Pasadena, California 91125, USA – `http://klab.caltech.edu`
[3] Art Center College of Design, Graduate Industrial Design Program
1700 Lida St. – Pasadena, California, 91103-1999, USA – `http://www.artcenter.edu`

Abstract. This paper is a technical description of a new mobile robotics platform specifically designed for the implementation and testing of neuromorphic vision algorithms in unconstrained outdoors environments. The platform is being developed by a team of undergraduate students with graduate supervision and help. Its distinctive features include significant computational power (four 1.1GHz CPUs with gigabit interconnect), high-speed four-wheel-drive chassis, standard Linux operating system, and a comprehensive toolkit of C++ vision classes. The robot is designed with two major goals in mind: real-time operation of sophisticated neuromorphic vision algorithms, and off-the-shelf components to ensure rapid technological evolvability. A preliminary embedded neuromorphic vision architecture that includes attentional, gist/layout, object recognition, and high-level decision subsystems is finally described.

1 Introduction

Animals demonstrate unparalleled abilities to interact with their natural visual environment, a task which remains embarrassingly problematic to machines. Obviously, vision is computationally expensive, with a million distinct nerve fibers composing each optic nerve, and approximately half of the mammalian brain dedicated more or less closely to vision [6]. Thus, for long, the poor real-time performance of machine vision systems could be attributed to limitations in computer processing power. With the recent availability of low-cost supercomputers, such as so-called "Beowulf" clusters of standard interconnected personal computers, however, this excuse is rapidly losing credibility. What could then be the reason for the dramatic discrepancy between animal and machine vision? Too often computer vision algorithms are designed with a specific goal and setting in mind, e.g., detecting traffic signs by matching geometric and colorimetric models of specific signs to image features [3]. Consequently, dedicated tuning or algorithmic alterations are typically required to accommodate for novel environments,

H.H. Bülthoff et al. (Eds.): BMCV 2002, LNCS 2525, pp. 558–566, 2002.

targets or tasks. For example, an algorithm to detect traffic signs from images acquired by a vehicle-mounted camera will typically not be trivially applicable to the detection of military vehicles in overhead imagery.

Much progress has been made in the field of visual neuroscience, using techniques such as single neuron electrophysiology, psychophysics and functional neuroimaging. Together, these experimental advances have set the basis for a deeper understanding of biological vision. Computational modeling has also seen recent advances, and fairly accurate software models of specific parts or properties of the primate visual system are now available, which show great promise of unparalleled robustness, versatility and adaptability. A common shortcoming of computational neuroscience models, however, is that they are not readily applicable to real images [6]. *Neuromorphic engineering* proposes to address this problem by establishing a bridge between computational neuroscience and machine vision. An example of neuromorphic algorithm developed in our laboratory is our model of bottom-up, saliency-based visual attention [8,6], which has demonstrated strong ability at quickly locating not only traffic signs in 512x384 video frames from a vehicle-mounted camera [7], but also — without any modification or parameter tuning — artificial targets in psychophysical visual search arrays [5], soda cans, emergency triangles [7], faces and people [10], military vehicles in 6144x4096 overhead imagery [4], and many other types of targets.

The new robotics platform described here is a test-bed aimed at demonstrating how neuromorphic algorithms may yield a fresh perspective upon traditionally hard engineering problems, including computer vision, navigation, sensorimotor coordination, and decision making under time pressure. This contrasts with the motivation behind biorobots [14,11], which aim at physically and mechanically resembling animal systems. To exploit real-time video streams and effectively base control on computationally-demanding neuromorphic vision algorithms, our new robots combine a small Beowulf cluster to a low-cost but agile four-wheel-drive robotics platform, together forming a "Beowulf-robot" or Beobot.

What will Beobots be capable of that existing robots cannot already achieve? Most robots have under-emphasized the vision component that is our main focus, and rely instead on dedicated sensors including laser range finders and sonars. Much progress has been made in developing very impressive *physically capable* robots (e.g., Honda humanoid). In addition, very sophisticated and powerful algorithms are now available that make robots *intelligent* [15]. However, we believe that some improvement still is possible in making robots more *visually capable*, as current systems often rely on simplified, low-computation visual tricks which greatly limit their autonomy.

Below we describe the basic hardware and software components of the Beobots, as implemented in a working prototype. We further describe a preliminary software system that builds upon these components, and implements a neuromorphic vision architecture that includes visual attention (modeled after processing in the dorsal visual stream of the primate brain), localized object recognition (modeled after processing in the primate ventral stream), rapid computation of the gist/layout of the scene, and high-level decision for basic navigation.

At the stage of development described, which is the successful creation of a working Beobot prototype, the present paper is limited to a fairly technical description of the various elementary hardware and software system. We hope, however, that the overall approach described here may trigger some useful discussion with respect to the feasibility of embedding neuromorphic vision algorithms onto a robotics platform. For further insight on the type of new algorithms that may become realizable with the availability of the Beobot platform, we refer the reader to the article by Navalpakkam and Itti in this volume.

2 The Robotics Platform

In this section we briefly describe the hardware components of the Beobots, as implemented in the prototype shown in Fig. 1. The development of a new robotics platform is justified by the current unavailability of any reasonably-priced commercial platform with processing power suitable for real-time neuromorphic vision. Guidelines for our design included:

- High-speed, agile chassis, at the cost of precision and ease of control;
- Standard off-the-shelf components that can easily be replaced or upgraded;
- Compatibility with open-source software and familiar development tools;
- Low cost of individual parts and of the complete assembly;
- Small size for ease of use and maneuverability.

It is important to note a few key differences between Beobots and existing, similarly-looking robots. A primary goal for Beobots, which may or may not turn out to be achievable, is *autonomous operation in unconstrained environments.* This directly contrasts with remotely-operated robots where computation is performed on a central server communicating with the robot via a radio link (e.g., Clodbuster robots [2]), with semi-autonomous robots which require overall guidance from a human operator but can shape this guidance according to environmental conditions (e.g., [9]), and with robots operating in constrained environments such as an artificial soccer field. The extent to which fully autonomous operation will be achievable will most probably depend on task difficulty (e.g., going to the library to pick up books is more difficult than the first test task described below, running around a track). However, it is our goal for Beobots to avoid developing algorithms that are task-specific, and rather develop a number of biologically-inspired computational modules. As mentioned in introduction, the existing bottom-up attention module is an example of such component that has been sccessfully applied to a very wide, unconstrained range of inputs.

2.1 Embedded Beowulf Cluster

The Beowulf in our Beobot prototype is a standard double dual-CPU embedded Linux system with Gigabit Ethernet link between both dual-CPU boards. We

Fig. 1. Anatomy of a Beobot. The machine uses standard off-the-shelf components and includes a Linux 4-CPU Beowulf cluster with Gigabit Ethernet transport and a FireWire color camera on a rugged 4-wheel-drive chassis. It is normally powered by camcorder batteries (not shown) and protected by a vacuum-formed shell (not shown).

use 1.1 GHz Pentium-III (PIII) CPUs, which may be upgraded to faster models as available. The motherboards rest on a custom-built 3-layer mounting platform, composed of a 5mm-thick laser-cut base plate made of bulletproof Lexan material, a 5mm-thick laser-cut rubber layer for firm yet shock-insulated resting of the motherboards, and a 1mm-thick laser-cut acrylic protective cover. Any motherboard with the standard PICMG form factor can be installed onto the CPU platform. We used two ROCKY-3742EVFG motherboards, as these integrate all of the peripherals required for our application, including: Support for dual Pentium-III CPUs, connector for solid-state (256MB CompactFlash) hard-disks, on-board sound for voice recognition and synthesis, on-board FireWire port for video capture, on-board Gigabit Ethernet for interconnection between both boards, and on-board 10/100 Ethernet for connection to host computers during software development.

The Beowulf cluster drains a maximum of 30A at 5V and 2A at 12V, which are provided by eight standard R/C battery packs (for an autonomy of approximately one hour) or eight high-capacity Lithium-Ion battery packs (for an autonomy of approximately two hours).

2.2 Mobile Platform

We have chosen to use a radio-controlled (R/C) vehicle as basis for the Beobots (Fig. 1), although these have overall poor reputation in the robotics community: indeed, they are optimized for speed and light weight, at the expense of accuracy in control. Yet in many respects they resemble full-size vehicles, which humans are able to control at high speed, without requiring laser range finders, wheel encoders and other typical robotics artifacts.

The Traxxas E-Maxx platform (www.traxxas.com) was well suited as the basis for Beobots. With dual high-torque electric motors, it can handle the additional weight of the CPUs and batteries. With a top speed of 25 MPH and an autonomy of 20 minutes on standard R/C NiMH battery packs, it is ideal for fast, ballistic operation and control, similar to the control we exert while driving real automobiles. The radio control is equipped with a high/low gear shift switch, which we have used to instead switch between autonomous and human radio-controlled modes (ideal for online learning). Thus, while the robot usually operates autonomously, it is possible for a human operator to easily override this behavior (e.g., in case of an imminent accident). A serial to pulse-width-modulation module is used to control the servos (steering, speed control with brakes, and 2-speed gearbox) from the on-board computers (see, e.g., www.seetron.com/ssc.htm). A speed sensor linked to the drive train is being developed to obtain speed estimates based on the mechanisms found in standard computer mice. The shocks have been stiffened and the tires filled with firm foam such as not to collapse under the payload.

For ease of connection to a host computer and to various equipment, the keyboard, mouse, video, USB, and Ethernet ports have all been deported to a single connection panel at the back of the Beobot. This panel also includes an external 15V/12A power connector, and a switch to select between external and battery power. Software has been developed to connect a small LCD screen to one of the serial ports of the robot, which will be mounted on the final protective shell over the motherboards. The cluster can accept a variety of accessory equipment, including GPS (connected to a serial port), wireless networking (through a USB port), additional hard-disk drives (through the IDE ports), and virtually any other standard PC peripheral that is supported by the Linux operating system.

3 The C++ Neuromorphic Vision Toolkit

The cluster runs a standard Linux distribution, which is simply installed from CD-ROM onto the 256MB CompactFlash solid-state disk of each motherboard. For our prototype, we used the Mandrake 8.2 distribution, which automatically detected and configured all on-board peripherals, except that an alternate Gigabit Ethernet driver was necessary for proper operation. To allow rapid development and testing of new neuromorphic vision algorithms, we are developing a comprehensive toolkit of C++ classes.

The toolkit provides a number of core facilities, which include:

- Reference-counted, copy-on-write memory allocation for large objects such as images (so that various copies of an image share the same physical memory until one of the copies attempts to modify that memory, at which point a copy of the memory is first made);
- Template-based classes, so that objects such as images or image pyramids can be instantiated with arbitrary pixel types (e.g., scalar byte or float pixels, color double pixels, integrate-and-fire neuron pixels, etc);
- Automatic type promotion, so that operations among template classes automatically avoid all overflows (e.g., multiplying an image of bytes by a float coefficient results in an image of floats);
- Automatic range checking and clamping during demotion of types (e.g., assigning an image of floats to an image of bytes transparently converts and clamps all pixel values to the 0..255 range);
- Smart reference-counted pointers, so that when the last pointer to an object is destroyed, memory allocated for the pointee is automatically freed;
- A convenient logging facility to report debugging and other messages to standard output, LCD screen or system logs.

Building on these core elements and concepts, the basic facilities provided by a set of generic C++ classes in the toolkit include:

- Low-level graphic elements such as 2D point, RGB pixel, rectangle, etc;
- A template Image class that defines a copy-on-write 2D array (of data type chosen through the C++ template mechanism) and provides numerous low-level image processing functions, such as convolution, rescaling, arithmetic operations, decimation & interpolation, various normalizations, drawing primitives, miscellaneous functions such as speckle noise, 3D warping, flooding, edge detection, 3/4 chamfer distance transforms, and finally neuromorphic operations including center-surround and retinal filtering;
- A template Image Pyramid class which implements dyadic pyramids of various data types (defined as template argument) and for various pyramid schemes [1], including Gaussian, Laplacian, Gabor, and Template Matching;
- Classes for storage, retrieval and display of Images in various file formats;
- Several classes specific to our model of bottom-up, saliency-based visual attention, including a Visual Cortex class (contains a run-time-selectable collection of pyramids, including for color, intensity, orientation and flicker information), a Saliency Map class (2D array of leaky integrate & fire neurons), a Winner-Take-All class (distributed neuronal maximum detector), an InferoTemporal class (with run-time selectable object recognition scheme, including backpropagation and HMAX [13]), a Brain class (contains a retina, visual cortex, saliency map, winner-take-all and a few other objects);
- Several classes specific to our model of contour integration in the primate brain, which simulates intricate patterns of connections between neurons visually responsive to various visual locations;
- A Jet class (vector of responses from neurons with various tuning properties but at a same location in the visual field), used by our ImageSpring model that rapidly segments a rough layout from an incoming scene;

- Classes to capture video frames through PCI, USB and FireWire interfaces, and to capture audio (including decoded radio-control signals);
- Classes to read/write configuration files and to manage internal program options (from configuration files or command-line arguments);
- A set of fast multi-threaded interprocess communication classes which allow quick transfer of images and other data from one CPU to another, using either TCP/IP or shared memory. These include a Beowulf class that automatically sets up interconnections between different computers on a network, and transparently handles sending and receiving of messages;
- Several accessory and Beobot-specific classes, such as Timer, XML parser, interface to LCD screen, and interface to servomechanisms.

Building on these core facilities, a number of additional classes and executable programs have been developed, to process movie sequences over a Beowulf cluster, to control the Beobots, and to implement various models of attention, contour integration, object recognition, scene layout computation, high-level scene interpretation, etc.

4 Results

A preliminary application is being developed for testing of the Beobots with a simple task: drive as fast as possible along the USC Olympic running track, avoiding obstacles such as joggers. The architecture used for this purpose shares some similarity to Rensink's triadic architecture of human vision [12], relying on: a rapid computation of scene layout, to localize the track; low-level visual processing that guides visual attention bottom-up, to locate obstacles; localized object recognition to identify obstacles and other salient scene elements being attended to; high-level decision based on a working memory of recent percepts and actions; and interfacing with the robot's electromechanical actuators (Fig. 2).

The application is being developed and refined with encouraging results. While layout and saliency are robustly computed in most situations, object recognition often is more problematic, especially when background clutter is present. Nevertheless, this simple application is a working example of how distributed neuromorphic architectures may be developed on Beobots using our C++ vision toolkit, for real-time outdoors operation.

5 Discussion and Outlook

With the successful development of a prototype Beobot for a total cost below \$5,000, we have shown how standard off-the-shelf PC and R/C components could be assembled to yield a robotics platform suitable to the real-time operation of neuromorphic vision algorithms. While evolvability typically is a major issue in robotics design, Beobots can be upgraded in minutes to faster CPUs, faster or better PICMG motherboards, new USB, FireWire, serial, IDE or other

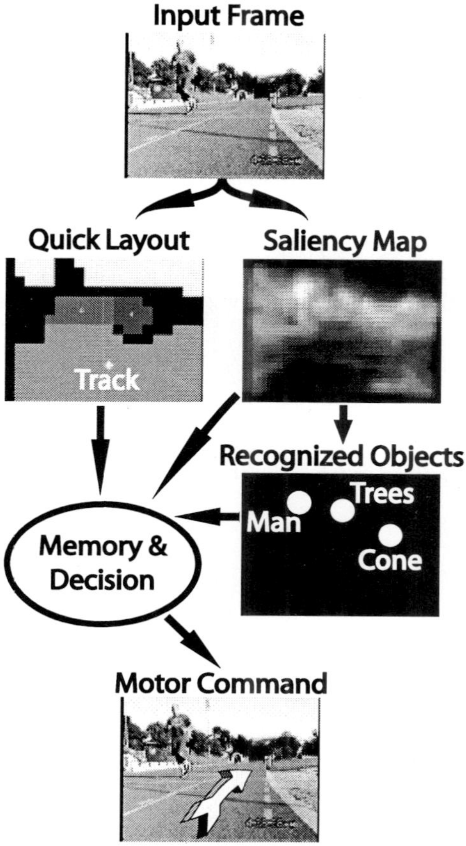

Fig. 2. A prototype distributed neuromorphic vision application developed for the Beobots. A very rough layout of each incoming frame is computed, and the road is located as the largest region in the lower half of the image. In parallel, low-level computation of early visual features (color opponencies, intensity contrast, oriented edges, and motion transients) is distributed over the four CPUs of the Beobot. A non-linear combination of the resulting feature maps yields the topographic saliency map (brighter regions indicate more salient locations). The saliency map guides focal visual attention, which selects objects from the image in order of decreasing saliency. Each selected object is passed to an object recognition module which attempts identification, with variable success depending on background clutter. Based on the current and past layouts, saliency maps, sets of recognized objects, and on the goal assigned to the robot, a rule-based agent determines the next action. This action is finally communicated to the motor components of the robots, after some smoothing and possible radio-control override.

peripherals, any faster or more powerful R/C chassis that uses standard R/C servomechanisms, new Linux distributions, and new application software.

Blueprints for the custom-designed components of the Beobots (CPU mounting platform, protective shell, and battery power conversion module) are being made available through our web site at `http://iLab.usc.edu/beobots/`. The source code for the C++ toolkit is already available through CVS access and at `http://iLab.usc.edu/toolkit/`. A discussion forum around this project and other neuromorphic models is also available through this web page.

A number of enhancements are being studied, including alternate models of localized objet recognition, voice recognition and synthesis, and algorithms for high-level scene understanding, navigation and planning. Although all software components currently are synchronized by the video rate of 30 frames/s, a smarter scheduler is also being studied to balance the computational load across the four CPUs, and allow subsystems running at different time scales to continuously exploit all computing resources. This would, for instance, allow the robot to perform object recognition asynchronously from the computation of salience and other low-level visual processing.

In summary, our approach directly follows the recent revolution brought to the high-performance computing community by Beowulf clusters, replacing costly and slowly-evolving custom CPUs and bus architectures by low-cost assemblies of mass-produced, rapidly-updated PC components. Based on our first prototype, we believe that the Beobot approach has potential for making the implementation of sophisticated neuromorphic algorithms onto robots a reality. The challenge which lies ahead will now be to adapt more general neuromorphic vision algorithms (such as, e.g., Navalpakkam and Itti, this volume) for real-time operation on the Beobots.

Acknowledgments. This work is supported the National Science Foundation, the National Eye Institute, the National Imagery and Mapping Agency, the Zumberge Research and Innovation Fund and the Charles Lee Powell Foundation.

References

1. P J Burt and E H Adelson. *IEEE Trans on Communications*, 31:532–540, 1983.
2. A Das, R Fierro, V Kumar, J Southall, J Spletzer and C Taylor, In *Proc IEEE Int. Conf. on Robotics and Automation,* Seoul, Korea, pp. 1714-1719, 2001.
3. A de la Escalera, L E Moreno, M A Salichs, and J M Armingol. *IEEE Trans Ind Elec*, 44(6):848–859, 1997.
4. L. Itti, C. Gold, and C. Koch. *Optical Engineering*, 40(9):1784–1793, Sep 2001.
5. L. Itti and C. Koch. *Vision Research*, 40(10-12):1489–1506, May 2000.
6. L. Itti and C. Koch. *Nature Reviews Neuroscience*, 2(3):194–203, Mar 2001.
7. L. Itti and C. Koch. *Journal of Electronic Imaging*, 10(1):161–169, Jan 2001.
8. L. Itti, C. Koch, and E. Niebur. *IEEE Transactions on Pattern Analysis and Machine Intelligence*, 20(11):1254–1259, Nov 1998.
9. L Matthies, Y Xiong, R Hogg, D Zhu, A Rankin, B Kennedy, M Hebert, R Maclachlan, C Won, T Frost, G Sukhatme, M McHenry and S Goldberg. In *Proc. of the 6th International Conference on Intelligent Autonomous Systems,* Venice, Italy, Jul 2000.
10. F. Miau and L. Itti. In *Proc. IEEE Engineering in Medicine and Biology Society (EMBS), Istanbul, Turkey*, Oct 2001.
11. G. M. Nelson and R. D. Quinn. In *Proceedings - IEEE International Conference on Robotics and Automation*, volume 1, pages 157–162, 1998.
12. R. A. Rensink. *Vision Res*, 40(10-12):1469–1487, 2000.
13. M Riesenhuber and T Poggio. *Nat Neurosci*, 2(11):1019–1025, Nov 1999.
14. B. Webb. *Behavioral and Brain Sciences*, 24(6), 2001.
15. B Werger and M J Mataric. *Annals of Mathematics and Artificial Intelligence*, 31(1-4):173–198, 2001.

Learning to Act on Objects

Lorenzo Natale, Sajit Rao, and Giulio Sandini

LIRA Lab, DIST. Univ of Genova, Italy Viale Francesco Causa, 13
Genova 16145, Italy
{sajit, nat, sandini}@dist.unige.it

Abstract. In biological systems vision is always in the context of a particular body and tightly coupled to action. Therefore it is natural to consider visuo-motor methods (rather than vision alone) for learning about objects in the world. Indeed, initially it may be necessary to act on something to learn that it is an object! Learning to act involves not only learning the visual consequences of performing a motor action, but also the other direction, i.e. using the learned association to determine which motor action will bring about a desired visual condition.
In this paper we show how a humanoid robot uses its arm to try some simple pushing actions on an object, while using vision and proprioception to learn the effects of its actions. We show how the robot learns a mapping between the initial position of its arm and the direction the object moves in when pushed, and then how this learned mapping is used to successfully position the arm to push/pull the target object in a desired direction.

1 Introduction

All biological systems are embodied systems, and an important way they have for recognizing and differentiating between objects in the environment is by simply acting on them. Only repeated interactions (play!) with objects can reveal how they move when pushed (e.g. sliding vs rolling), how the size of the object correlates with how much force is required to move it, etc. In a discovery mode, the visual system learns about the consequences of motor acts in terms of such features, and in planning mode the mapping may be inverted to select the motor act that causes a particular change. These two modes of learning; the consequences of a motor act, and selecting a motor act to achieve a certain result, are obviously intertwined, and together are what we mean by "learning to act".

Learning to act is important not only to guide motor behavior but may also be a necessary step for event-interpretation in general, even if the motor system is not involved in any way. For instance, by the age of 6 months children can predict that in a collision with a stationery object, the size of a moving object is related to how far the stationary object moves [1]. This is just one of several things that children appear to learn from experience about their physical environment [2] [3]. What is the source of this knowledge? and how can we build systems that learn to interpret events in the physical world? Computer vision approaches to "event-interpretation" have naturally tried to solve this problem in the domain of vision alone. However given that vision does not exist independently of other modalities in biological systems, and knowledge about

H.H. Bülthoff et al. (Eds.): BMCV 2002, LNCS 2525, pp. 567–575, 2002.

the world is acquired incrementaly in a developmental process we are taking a somewhat different approach. We assume that *it may be necessary to learn to act on objects first before we can learn to visually interpret more complicated events involving object-object interactions*. One source of evidence in support for this approach comes from the body of work about mirror neurons [4]. These are neurons in motor area F5 of the rhesus monkey that fire when the monkey performs a particular goal-directed action, but which also fire if it just sees another agent perform a similar action. While the mechanisms of this mapping are far from clear, the fact that the events are mapped to the monkey's existing motor repertoire gives a strong hint that the ability to visually interpret the motor-goal or behavioral/purpose of the action may be helped by the monkey's ability to perform that action (and achieve a similar motor goal) itself.

The focus of this paper, therefore is on *learning to act on objects*, not only because in itself it's a vital skill to understand the consequences of actions, and plan future actions, but also because it could be a necessary precursor to event-interpretation of other object-object interactions.

2 Learning the Effect of Pushing/Pulling Actions

We show how a humanoid robot [5] that has already learned to saccade, and reach towards points in space with its arm, now pushes/pulls an object around in front of it, and learns the effect of its actions on the object, and thereafter uses this knowledge to drive motor-planning.

It is important to note that by "effect" we mean not only the effect on the object, but also the effect on the robot - the force felt by the robot, or the amount it had to move its head to continue tracking, for example. In this initial experiment we consider only one effect: the direction that the object moves in, as a result of the action. There are naturally many other effects that one could also pay attention to: how far the object moves, how long the object continued moving after the initial touch, e.t.c. However, in the experiment described here the robot attends only to the instantaneous direction of motion of the target just after it has been pushed/pulled by the robot. The goal of the experiment is to learn the instantaneous direction of motion of the target object for each of several different approach motions of the hand from different directions. This learned knowledge is then later used by the robot to select the appropriate motor action to move an object in a desired direction.

3 Description of the Experiment

Figure 1 A Shows the experimental setup. The humanoid robot "Babybot" has a 5 DOF head, and a 6 DOF arm, and 2 cameras whose Cartesian images are mapped to a log-polar format [6]. The robot also has a force sensitive wrist, and a metal stub for a hand. The target is placed directly in front of the robot on the play-table. The robot starts from any of four different initial positions (shown in the figure) at the beginning of a trial run.

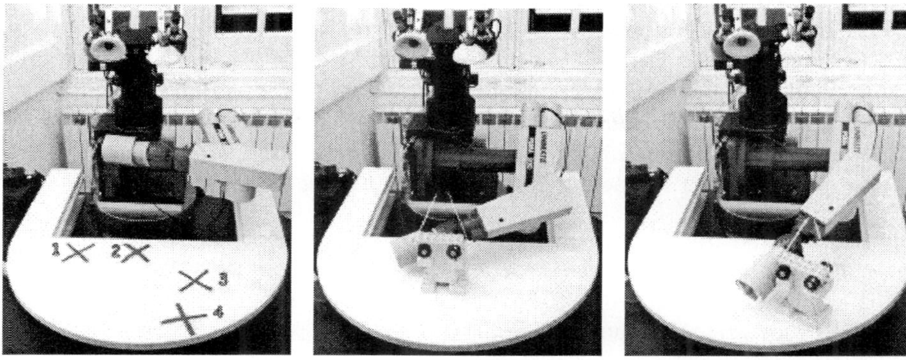

(a) initial arm-positions for target approach

(b) At the beginning of a pushing movement

(c) At the end of the movement

Fig. 1. The experimental setup

3.1 A Single Trial

In a typical trial run the robot continuously tracks the target while reaching for it. The target (even if it is moving) is thus ideally always centered on the fovea, while the moving hand is tracked in peripheral vision. Figure 1 (B) shows the arm at one of its initial positions and (C) shows the end of the trial with the target having been pushed to one side.

The moment of impact - when the hand first touches the object is an important event and its localization in time is critical. A sharp increase in the magnitude of retinal target position (caused by the instantaneous error in tracking) is used to localize this instant[1]. The direction of the *retinal* displacement of the target is extracted. Note that the target displacement is always in *retinal coordinates*, because associating the joint position of the arm with the retinal error is sufficient for this experiment without the need for a transformation to body-centered coordinates.

After the initial impact the system continues to try to reach for the centroid of the target and therefore ends up smoothly pushing the target in a particular direction. This continues until it either loses track of the target, which may fall off the table for example, or go outside the workspace. During each such trial run, the time evolution of several state variables are continuously monitored:

1. Vision: Position of the hand in Retinal coordinates - extracted from color segmentation of the hand.

[1] Another source of information that also carries information about the moment of impact are the force values - a sharp discontinuity in the force profiles marks the moment of impact. This information is not used at the moment but could be used to make the localization more robust, when the target is being obscured by the hand for instance.

2. Vision: Position of the target object in Retinal coordinates - extracted from color segmentation of the object.
3. Proprioception: 3 Joint coordinates of the arm (we fix the wrist for this experiment..thus eliminating 3 other degrees of freedom)
4. Proprioception: 5 Joint coordinates of the head
5. Proprioception: 3 Force components $[F_x F_y F_z]$ at the wrist.
6. Proprioception: 3 Torque components $[T_x T_y T_z]$ at the wrist

For the purpose of this experiment however we extract only two instantaneous values from this wealth of available data: one is the initial joint position of the arm (only the initial position, not the entire trajectory!), and the other is the instantaneous direction of target displacement at the moment of impact.

3.2 Visual Processes

Tracking: The first step of visual processing is conversion to a log-polar image format, similar to the topological transformation that happens between the LGN and the primary visual cortex (area V1) in primate brains. The main advantage of the log-polar representation is the increased resolution at the fovea, and therefore of the object being fixated. Thereafter, color-segmentation in HSV space is applied to both the left and right images to extract the retinal target position. Another process simultaneously finds the retinal displacement that best verges the left and right images. Tracking is implemented by a closed-loop controller that uses a linear combination of the retinal target error, and vergence shift to generate head and eye-movement commands.

Reaching with the hand is implemented by mapping head-position and retinal position to lookup a previously learned table of motor-commands to select the appropriate motor command to bring the hand to the current point of foveation. When the reaching behavior is run concurrently with tracking, it has the effect of the robot pushing or pulling an object as it continuously tries to reach for its centroid.

In this experiment the target object is always tracked and fixated upon, whereas the moving hand, and stationary toy (desired position of the target) are also tracked but not fixated on. The most important visual quantities are the displacement vector between the target and the stationary toy, and the instantaneous direction of motion of the target at the moment of impact as shown in Figure 2. The instantaneous retinal error in tracking (when the target moves away because of the impact) approximates this well in most cases.

3.3 The Target for Learning

The goal of this experiment is to learn the effect of a set of simple pushing/pulling actions from different directions on a toy object. As we mentioned earlier in section 1 there are many effects, both on the object and the robot, that could be attended to. But here we focus on only one effect, namely the direction of motion of the target. This is an effect to learn because, as we show, it can be used in motor-planning to move an object in a goal-directed mode. The target for learning (given a fixed target position directly in front of the robot) is a mapping from the initial position of the hand to the direction of

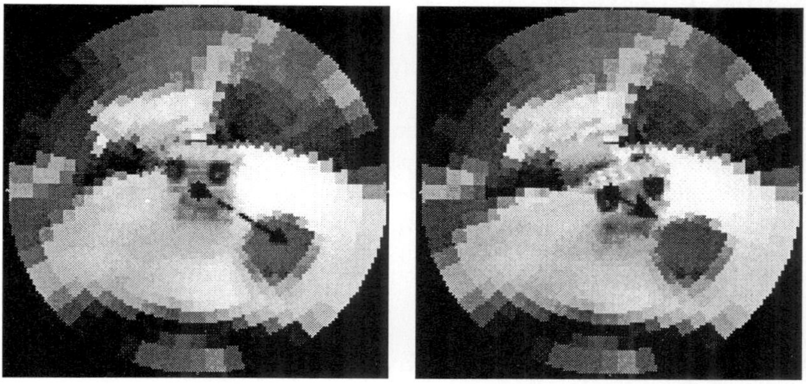

(a) Before impact: vector shows the desired target direction

(b) At moment of impact, target is moving: vector shows instantaneous target displacement

Fig. 2. Important visual features: The images are from the robot's point of view. The fall-off of resolution from the fovea to the periphery is due to the log-polar mapping.

target motion. Note that the initial hand-position uniquely determines the trajectory to the target. This trajectory could be different in different parts of the workspace, and is dependent on the kind of control used, (e.g. equilibrium point control) to generate the dynamics. However, because it is unique given the initial position of the hand and the (fixed) end position of the target, there is no need to remember the entire trajectory - the initial hand-position is sufficient.

The target for learning therefore is a mapping from initial hand position to direction of target movement. So, associated with each initial hand position is a direction map (a circular histogram) that summarizes the directions that the target moved in when approached from that position. After each trial the appropriate direction map is updated with the target motion for that particular trial.

Why map initial arm-position to target motion direction rather than say angle of approach of the hand at the moment of impact? The angle of approach of the hand would certainly correlate well with the direction of motion of the target. The reason we prefer the arm position instead is that the association lets us easily look up the answer to the inverse problem of motor planning, namely given a desired direction of motion of the target we can just lookup the position(s) where the arm should be initially positioned.

The testing of the learned maps is done by presenting a stationary toy as a new desired target position. The robot's goal is to use the learned maps to correctly pre-position the hand and start pushing the target so that it moves towards the toy.

4 Results of Learning

Approximately 70 trials, distributed evenly across the four initial starting positions, were conducted. Figure 3 shows the four direction maps learned, one for each initial arm position considered. The maps plot the frequency with which the target moved in a particular direction at the moment of impact. Therefore longer radial lines in the plot point towards the most common direction of movement. As we can see, the maps are sharply tuned towards a dominant direction.

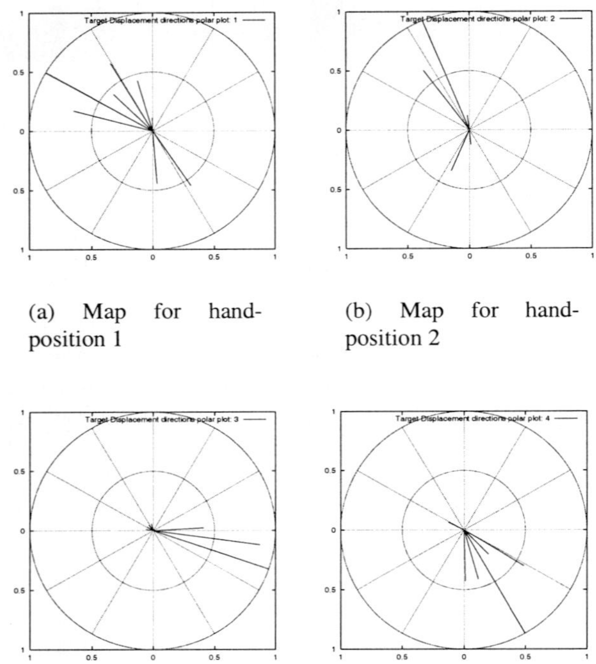

(a) Map for hand-position 1 (b) Map for hand-position 2

(c) Map for hand-position 3 (d) Map for hand-position 4

Fig. 3. The learned target-motion direction maps, one for each initial hand-position

5 Testing the Learned Maps

The learned maps are used to drive motor planning in a straightforward manner as shown in Figure 4.

1. The system is presented with the usual target as before, but this time also with another toy nearby (Figure 4 a). The goal is to push the target towards the new toy. The system first foveates on the target, while also locating the new toy in its peripheral vision. The retinal displacement of the toy is used as the desired position r_d,
2. The direction of this displacement vector Θ, is taken to be the direction of desired motion of the target and is used to find the direction map M_Θ with the closest matching dominant direction.
3. The robot first moves its hand to the hand-position associated with map M_Θ and then begins its motion towards the target (Figure 4b,c). The dynamics takes care of the rest, resulting in the motion of the target towards the desired direction.

Figure 4 shows one example of the learned maps being used to drive goal-directed action. The round toy is the new desired position towards which the target must be pushed. Note that initially in (a) the arm is in an inconvenient position to achieve the goal of pushing the target in the desired direction, but the prior learning selects a better starting position (b), leading to a successful action (c).

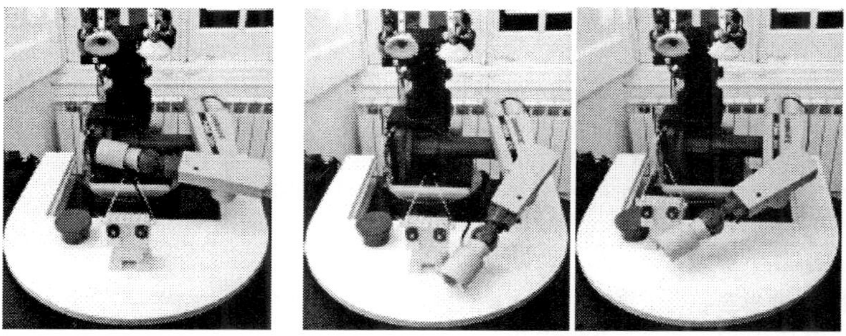

(a) The round toy is the new desired target position

(b) The learned maps are used to re-position the arm in preparation for the pushing movement

(c) At the end of the movement

Fig. 4. The learned direction maps are used to drive goal-directed action

5.1 Comparison of Performance before and after Learning

A quantitative measure of error is to look at the angle between the desired direction of motion (of the target towards the goal) and the actual direction that the target moved in when pushed, i.e. the angle between the two vectors shown in Figure 2.

First, as a control case (baseline) 54 trials were run with the goal position (round toy) being varied randomly and the initial hand-position being chosen randomly among

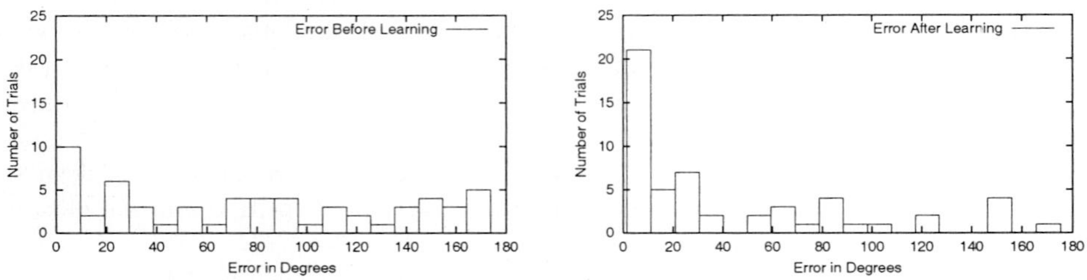

(a) Error distribution before learning (b) Error distribution after learning

Fig. 5. Improvement in performance: Plots of the distribution of the angle between the desired direction and actual direction, before and after learning. Zero degrees indicates no error, while 180 degrees indicates maximum error.

the four positions (i.e learned maps are not used to pick the appropriate hand position). Figure 5(a) shows the error plot. The distribution of errors is not completely flat as one would expect because the initial hand-positions are not uniformly distributed around the circle. Nevertheless, the histogram is not far from uniform. Doing the same experiment, but using the learned map to position the hand, yields the error plot shown in 5(b). As we can see the histogram is significantly skewed towards an error of 0, as a result of picking the correct initial-hand position from the learned map.

Why are there a few errors close to 180 degrees even after learning? This is in fact not an error in behavior, but an error in measurement. In other words, the target actually physically moved in the correct direction towards the goal position, but in a few cases was "perceived" to be moving exactly in the opposite direction. This happened because sometimes the head was moving while the retinal target displacement was being measured, resulting in an "apparent backward motion" of the target. The solution is to integrate the head movement signals to extract the "true" motion of the target, however we have not implemented this as yet.

The error would be even lower if more than four starting hand-positions were considered, as would be the case if we were running the experiment in continuous mode where we would uniformly sample the space of all hand-positions.

6 Discussion

The experiment discussed here is a first but important step towards "learning to act". While conventionally, the effect of a robot's action on an object is implicitly assumed in the planning, we choose to learn the effect through play/exploration and then use the knowledge to drive planning. The experiment makes some simplifying assumptions to test this basic idea. The main directions for improvement are:

- *Moving to a continuous space of hand-positions:* We have considered only four initial hand-positions in this experiment. To cover the whole space of initial hand positions however, a more natural approach is to pick hand-positions randomly during trials while building up a table with the hand-positions actually visited..and learning a target motion map for each of those hand-positions. Another approach is of course to train a neural network with the target motion directions as inputs and the hand-positions as outputs.

- *Interleaving the learning with the planning:* At present for simplicity we first have the learning/discovery phase and then the motor planning phase. But in principle there is no need for this separation and we intend to move to a more continuous mode where both learning and planning are happening continuously.
- *Increasing the number of event variables monitored:* In this particular experiment the same target and hand speed were used throughout and the only variable varied was initial-hand position. However the speed of the hand and the type of target could be varied too in future experiments. This would require paying attention to a much larger set of event features: the size of the target, the distance moved, the force profile on the hand, for instance to discover useful regularity.

7 Conclusion

We have shown a system that "learns to act" on a target object. In a play/discovery phase it pushes/pulls the target from several different directions while learning about the effect of the action. In another goal-directed play phase it uses its learned maps to select the initial arm position that will enable it to push a target toy towards another toy.

The work described here makes a novel contribution towards the area of "event-interpretation" because the constraints imposed by the combined modalities of vision, motor, and proprioception may make it easier to interpret certain self-generated events than with vision alone. Furthermore, interpreting self-generated events may be a necessary first step to interpret more complex object-object events.

References

1. Kovotsky, L., Baillargeon, R.: The development of calibration-based reasoning about collision events in young infants. Cognition, Vol 67 (1998), 311–351. Elsevier
2. Spelke, E.S.: Initial Knowledge: six suggestions. Cognition, Vol 50 (1994), 431–445. Elsevier
3. Spelke, E.S., Breinlinger, K., Macomber, J., Jacobsen, K.: Origins of Knowledge. Psychological Review, Vol 99 (1992), 605–632.
4. Rizzolatti, G., Fadiga, L., Gallese, V., Fogassi, L.: Premotor cortex and the recognition of motor actions. Cognitive Brain Research, Vol 3 (1996), 131–141. Elsevier
5. Metta, Panerai, Manzotti, Sandini: Babybot: an artificial developing robotic agent. From Animals to Animats: The sixth International Conference on the simulation of Adaptive Behavior. (2000)
6. Sandini, G., Tagliasco, V.: An Anthropomorphic Retina-like Structure for Scene Analysis. Computer Vision, Graphics and Image Processing, Vol 14(3) (1980), 365-372

Egocentric Direction and the Visual Guidance of Robot Locomotion Background, Theory and Implementation

Simon K. Rushton[1,2], Jia Wen[3], and Robert S. Allison[1,3]

[1]Centre for Vision Research, [2]Department of Psychology, [3]Department of Computer Science, York University,
4700 Keele Street, North York, ON, M3J 1P3, Canada.
rushton@hpl.cvr.yorku.ca; allison@cs.yorku.ca;
http://www.cs.yorku.ca/~percept/robot.html

Abstract and Overview. In this paper we describe the motivation, design and implementation of a system to visually guide a locomoting robot towards a target and around obstacles. The work was inspired by a recent suggestion that walking humans rely on perceived egocentric direction rather than optic flow to guide locomotion to a target. We briefly summarise the human experimental work and then illustrate how direction based heuristics can be used in the visual guidance of locomotion. We also identify perceptual variables that could be used in the detection of obstacles and a control law for the regulation of obstacle avoidance. We describe simulations that demonstrate the utility of the approach and the implementation of these control laws on a Nomad mobile robot. We conclude that our simple biologically inspired solution produces robust behaviour and proves a very promising approach.

1 Theoretical Background: Human Locomotion and Egocentric Direction

For the past 50 years it has been assumed that humans rely on optic flow for the visual guidance of locomotion. This assumption has underpinned psychophysical studies, neurophysiology, imaging and computational modelling (see [1] for a review). Recently this assumption has been challenged.

Rushton et al [2] reported an experimental result seemingly at odds with the use of optic flow. Rushton et al proposed instead a simple heuristic that better described the behaviour they observed. The proposal is that visual guidance of locomotion is achieved by keeping a target at a fixed direction, or *eccentricity,* relative to the body, rather than regulating behaviour so as to maintain a certain pattern of flow on the retina (the optic flow solution). In short, if the current direction of a target object is known, and the observer walks so as to keep the direction constant then they will reach the target. If the target is kept straight-ahead then a straight-line course to the target will result. If the target is maintained at some other direction then the path will be an equi-angular spiral.

The finding of Rushton et al has now been replicated by many others [3-7], and a concise summary of the original study is provided below. In a later section we

H.H. Bülthoff et al. (Eds.): BMCV 2002, LNCS 2525, pp. 576–591, 2002.

illustrate how this simple heuristic can be extended into a general model of the visual guidance of locomotion. We then describe a control law to avoid obstacles.

1.1 The Prism Study, Rushton et al. (1998)

The Rushton *et al.* [2] study involved observers wearing prism glasses. Observers were asked to walk briskly towards a target held out by an experimenter positioned about 10m to 15m away. The glasses contained either paired base-left or base-right wedge prisms. Prisms deflect the image and so shifted the perceived location of objects (relative to the body) approximately 15° to the right or left. Wearing prism glasses had a dramatic effect on the trajectory taken by observers when asked to walk towards the target. Observers veered whilst attempting to walk 'straight towards' the target. A typical veering trajectory is shown in the left panel of Figure 1.

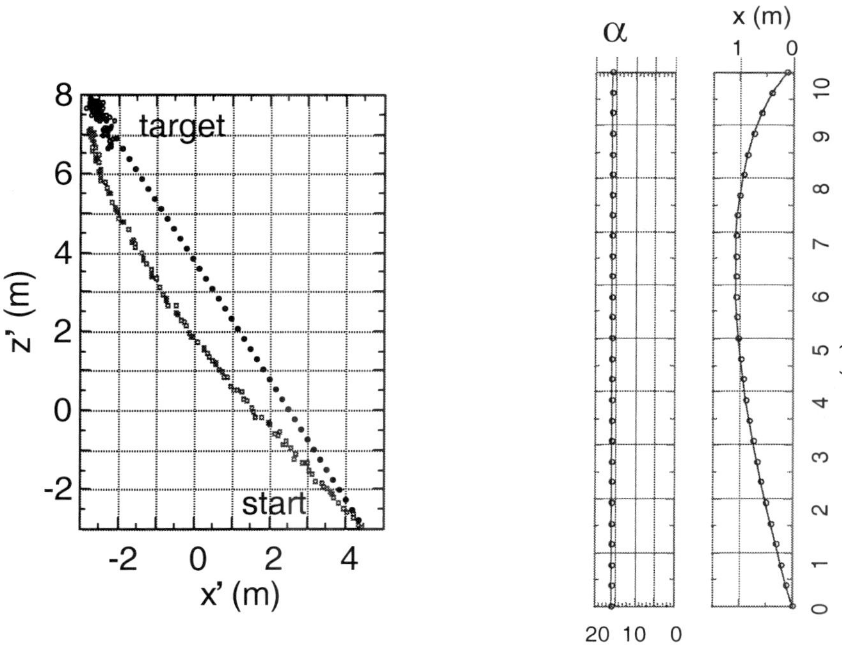

Fig. 1. *Left panel:* A representative trajectory of an observer, wearing a pair of wedge prisms that deflect right, approaching a target. The plot shows raw digitised data with axes x' and z' showing distances in world co-ordinates. *Right panel:* Simulated trajectory and direction error when wearing prisms by a model using target direction. *Right* Plan view of the predicted trajectory of a prism-wearing participant walking in the perceived direction of the target (which is offset from actual position by the simulated 16° angular deflection of the prisms). x and z are distances parallel and perpendicular, respectively, to the starting position of the participant (facing along the z-axis). *left* angle, α, between the instantaneous direction of the target and the direction of locomotion (tangent to the curve), which remains constant.

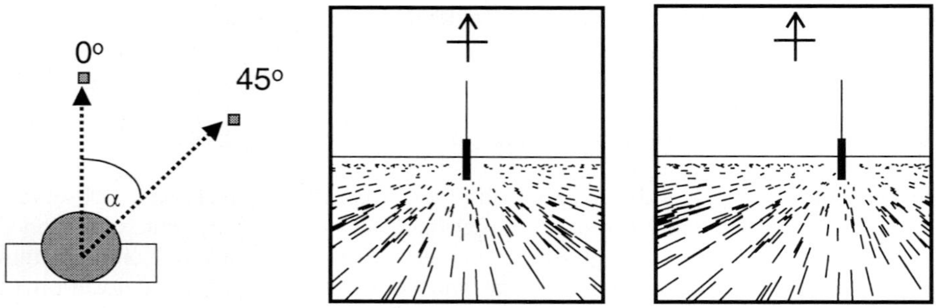

Fig. 2. *Left panel:* Egocentric directions, 'eccentricity', α, measured angle in cardinal plane. *Right panel:* Flow-field during forward translation (magnitude indicates image speed) toward target tower (solid black rectangle) at 16m. Thin vertical line indicates direction of travel. Arrow indicates egocentric straight ahead. *Left:* normal view, the 'focus of expansion' (FoE) is coincident with the tower, which indicates the observer is travelling directly towards tower. Arrow above tower indicates the perceived 'straight-ahead' direction, note it coincides with the tower. *Right:* displacement of whole image by prism. Note FoE is still directly over tower, thus flow indicates the observer is travelling directly towards tower. However, the perceived straight-ahead (denoted by the arrow above) no longer coincides with the tower.

1.1.1 A Flow Explanation?

Can use of optic flow account for such a trajectory? Flow based strategies rely on keeping the flow specified direction of heading (DoH) and the target coincident. More generally, they are concerned with relative positions or patterns within the flow-field. As can be seen from figure 2, although prisms displace the scene and change the perceived location of objects, the critical relations in the flow field are not perturbed. Specifically, the relative positions of the DoH and the target remain unchanged. Therefore, perception of direction of locomotion should remain unchanged and veridical if flow is used, and observers should end up on a straight trajectory towards to the target. The left panel of Figure 1 shows a markedly curved trajectory indicating that the observer did not use a DoH-target strategy. A model based on using the flow field specified DoH is therefore incompatible with the experimental results.

1.1.2 Egocentric Direction Account

A simple model, the *perceived direction* model [2], is compatible with the data. The model predicts that observers take a curved path because they attempt to keep the target perceptually straight-ahead of them. They veer because prisms change the perceived target direction. When wearing prisms, the perceived position of the whole scene, relative to the observer's body, is changed by the angular deflection of the prism – so if the prisms shifts the scene by 15° to the left, an object at 0° relative to the trunk will be seen at approximately 15° to the left. Thus, keeping the target *perceptually* straight-ahead requires the observer to keep the target at a fixed eccentricity (relative to the body) of approximately 15° to the right of the trunk mid-line. If this strategy is used then it should lead to a veering trajectory to the target. The trajectories walked by observers were very similar to those predicted by this simple *perceived-direction* model (compare the left and right panels of figure 1).

1.1.3 Recent Results

The direction of an object relative to the body trunk can be determined from a variety of sources of information. Classically it is assumed that trunk-centric direction is determined by combining non-visual information about the orientation of the eye and head (derived from 'extra-retinal information' – sensors that measure orientation, or copies of motor commands) with retinal target location. However it can be demonstrated theoretically that the eye orientation or head-centric target direction could be determined directly from the binocular disparity field. Visual motion, or slip, of a target as a result of a gaze or body movement could also be used in the determination of trunk-centric direction. Recent findings [3-7] on the visual guidance of locomotion can be interpreted as supporting this less simplistic model of the human perception of egocentric directions (see TICS note [8]). The use of disparity and motion information in refining or calibrating estimation of egocentric direction might usefully be revisited should it be desirable to implement the following algorithms on a robot with a mobile gaze system or stereoscopic vision.

2 The Test Rig

During the next section we complement theoretical predictions with empirical results so we first describe some details of our test rig.

The testing and development proceeded in two parallel stages. In the first stage, locomotion control algorithms were developed through simulations (using Matlab 6). During this stage, evaluation was done by both informal case-based testing and objective measures (derived by analysing the results of batches of simulations). In the second stage, simple image processing and motor output modules were added as front and backends to the locomotion module and experiments were performed on the actual robot. Unfortunately space constraints limited the complexity and length of the robot trajectories.

2.1 Robot

A Nomad Super Scout (Nomadic Technologies Inc.) robot was used for testing. Although the Nomad had a Pentium class CPU, the robot was tele-operated for convenience. A wireless network link was used to send motor commands to the robot. We used only two commands to drive the robot: `rotate()` and `move()`. Therefore, the solutions involved discrete steps. Simulations show that substituting radius of curvature and speed should produce approximately the same trajectories but represent a slightly more elegant solution.

An NTSC resolution camera was connected, via a cable to the image capture card of a Sun Blade 100 workstation. Images were captured on demand, at a resolution of 640x480 pixels. The horizontal field of view of the camera was approximately 60°, and the camera was pitched downwards by approximately 20°.

2.2 Visual Scene

Because the focus of this work was on visual guidance of locomotion and control laws we simplified the image processing requirements. Targets and obstacles were colour-coded, the former being coloured red, the latter blue.

3 From a Single Case to a General Account

The experiments described in section 1 are concerned with a single task, visually guiding locomotion to a static target. Rushton & Harris [9] explored the theoretical sufficiency of the egocentric direction proposal by attempting to extend it to a broader range of locomotion actions. Their ideas are the basis for the algorithms and implementation.

3.1 A List of Fundamental Locomotor Actions

Several authors have attempted to enumerate a list of fundamental locomotor behaviours [10-12]. The most important of these can be summarised as follows: 1) intercepting static and moving targets, 2) following a path, and 3) avoiding obstacles. Below we examine how the first two behaviours could be implemented within an egocentric direction framework. In section 4 we describe in detail our approach to obstacle avoidance.

3.2 Intercepting Static and Moving Targets

Interception of a target is achieved if during locomotion the target is (i) kept at a fixed direction relative to the robot, and (ii) the target gets closer on each step. The direction at which the target is kept will determine the exact trajectory taken. The resultant trajectories are low angle equi-angular spirals. The top left panel of figure 3 illustrates a family of trajectories that intercept a static target. If the target is moving then the same constant direction strategy works. The top middle panel demonstrates a family of constant direction trajectories that intercept a target moving with a constant velocity. The top right panel shows interception with an accelerating target. The lower panels show three constant angle trajectories taken by our robot to a static target.

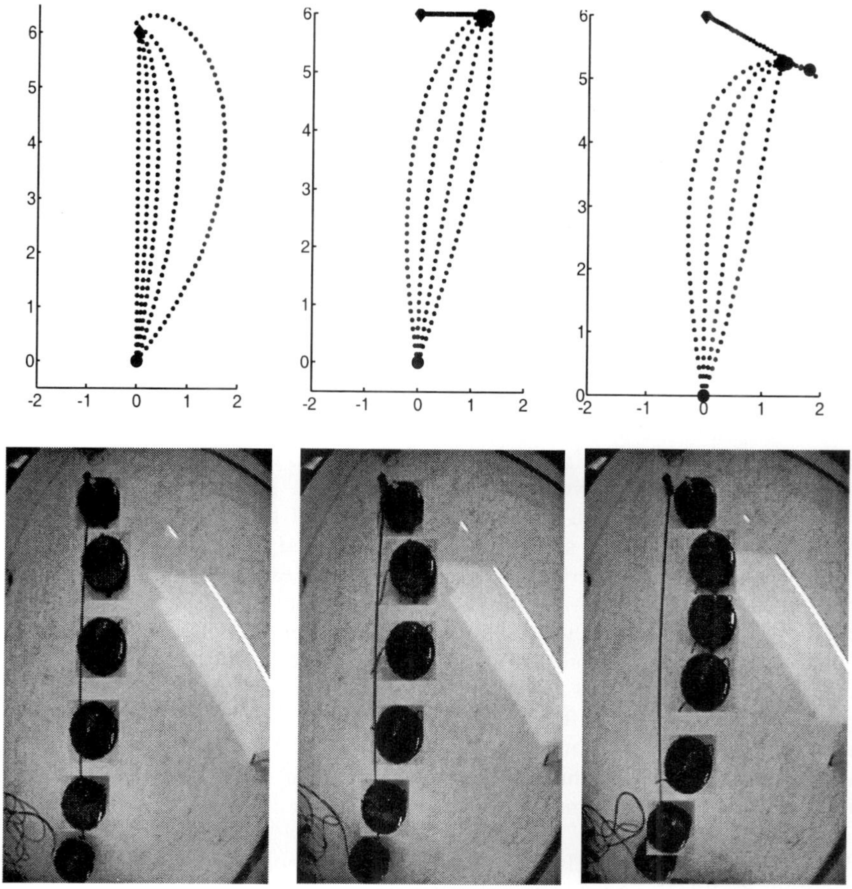

Fig. 3. *Upper Panels:* All panels display a plan view, with the robot starting at (0,0). *Left:* plan view of trajectories that would result from holding a target at a fixed eccentricity, α, of 0°, 5°, 10°, 20° and 40° (from left to right). Robot starts at (0,0), target is at (0, 6). Holding the target 'straight ahead', i.e. at 0° would produce a straight trajectory leading directly to the target. Any other trajectory based upon holding the target at an eccentricity other than zero results in the robot 'veering' to one side before finally reaching the target. *Middle:* Intercepting a moving target. Target starts at (0, 6), and moves rightwards, robot starts at (0,0). Four fixed eccentricity trajectories shown, -10°, 0°, 10°, 20°. *Right:* Intercepting an accelerating target. Target starts at (0, 40), and moves rightwards and downwards with increasing speed (constant acceleration), robot starts at (0,0). Fixed eccentricity trajectories shown are -10°, 0°, 10°, 20°. *Lower Panels:* Fixed eccentricity approaches to a target. Plan view of robot, travelling from bottom to top of the image. *Left*: eccentricity of 6°. *Middle*: eccentricity of 12°. *Right*: eccentricity of 18°.

3.3 Calibration of Straight-Ahead (0°) through Target Drift, or Visually Guiding Uncalibrated Systems

The algorithm described so far relies on a calibrated system. If straight-ahead (0°) is not known, or has drifted then an observer or robot could not take a straight-line course to a target if they wished to. How might the system be calibrated? Held [13] proposed that the focus of expansion of the optic flow field sampled by an observer could be used for calibration (humans normally walk either straight, or on a curving trajectory, seldom do they walk diagonally, therefore if the position of the focus of expansion was averaged over several minutes of locomotion it would provide a good estimate of straight-ahead or 0°). A faster, on-line alternative, more in keeping with the proposal outlined so far would be to use target drift.

Llewellyn [14] proposed a heuristic for visual guidance of locomotion that is related to the constant eccentricity heuristic described above. Llewellyn suggested that an observer could reach a target by simply cancelling target drift, that is the visual movement of the target. So if a target drifts 1° to the left after one step then if the observer rotates left by 1° (so returning the target to its original eccentricity) and takes another step they will eventually reach their target. It should be obvious that the course will be the same equi-angular spirals produced by the constant eccentricity strategy. The use of a motion signal instead of a direction signal has one disadvantage and one related advantage. First off it is not possible to explicitly choose a trajectory. A sharply curving 50° equi-angular trajectory cannot be selected in advance or distinguished from a 0° trajectory. However the problem of selecting a 0° trajectory can be avoided. During a non-zero approach, the target will drift on each step. By "overcompensating" for this drift the trajectory can be straightened into a 0° trajectory. So if the target drifts 1° left on a given step, if instead of rotating 1° left to compensate (100% compensation) the observer rotates 2° left (200% compensation) then they will end up reducing the eccentricity of their trajectory, and thus straightening the trajectory, until it reaches zero. This is illustrated in the left panel of figure 4 below.

The right and middle panels of figure 4 illustrate robot trajectories. It can be seen that in the set up here, the system calibrates rapidly. If target drift is to be used for calibration then once the target drift has settled below a preset limit, straight-ahead can be taken from the windowed average of target image position.

3.4 Path Following

Many models have been proposed to account for steering a car round a bend. Land & Lee [15] proposed that the curvature of a bend can be determined using a function of the direction of the 'tangent' (or 'reversal') point and its distance. The curvature can then be used to set the steering angle. Murray et al [16] proposed a similar rule for determining curvature and demonstrated that it could be used to guide a robot around a track.

Here we propose a simpler (but related) solution. Rather than estimate the curvature of the bend it is sufficient simply to keep a portion of the road a fixed distance ahead (and distance can be determined simply from either relative or absolute height in the visual field), or the tangent point, at a constant direction.

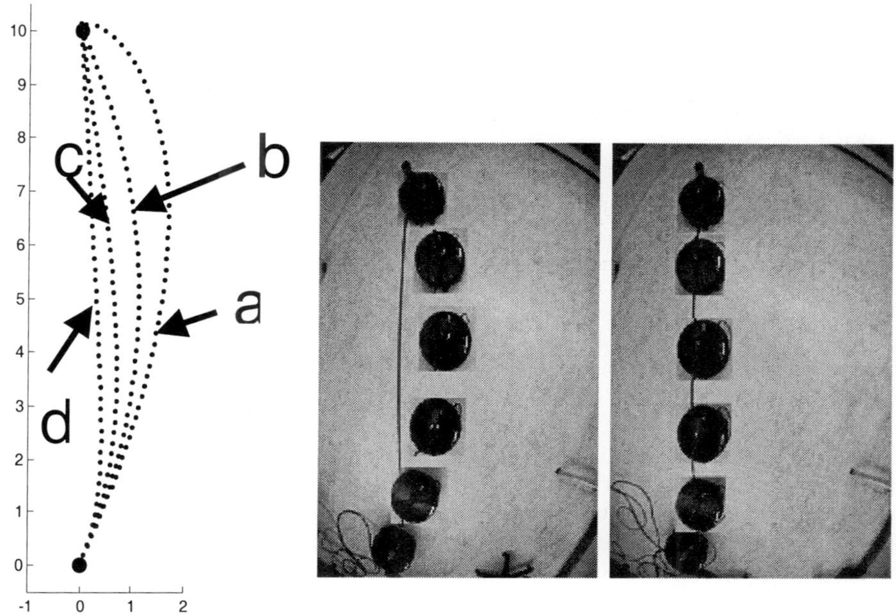

Fig. 4. *Left Panel:* Robot heads towards the target (0, 10). Initial target-heading direction, or eccentricity, is 25°. Trajectory **a** shows the course taken by cancelling target drift on each step (100% compensation) resulting in a constant direction trajectory. Trajectory **b** shows the course taken when the observer "over-compensates" for the target drift by a factor of 2 (200% compensation). Trajectory **c** "over-compensation" is 400%, trajectory **d** is 800%. *Middle and Right Panels:* Overhead view of robot travels from right to left. Initial heading angle is approximately 18 °. *Middle Panel:* Compensation of 200%. *Right Panel:* Compensation of 600%

In figure 5, in the panel A, the inside edge of the road a fixed distance ahead is kept at a constant direction. In panel B the outside edge is used. Logically if there was a centre line then this could be used instead. One disadvantage of using a fixed distance ahead strategy is that it only works if the observer does not use a portion of the road too far ahead. The maximum distance ahead is proportional to the radius of curvature of the bend. A strategy that automatically compensates for the curvature of the bend is to use the tangent point. The result of such a strategy is shown in fig. 5C.

An intuitive solution would be to scale the distance of the road edge that is used to control steering (control point) as a function of speed – to look a fixed time ahead. The distance of the control point could then be bound by the distance of the tangent point. If the control point would lie beyond the tangent point the observer could either use the tangent point (and so look less time ahead making visual control more difficult), or slow down so as to bring the control point back to the tangent point and the look-ahead distance back to an optimal value.

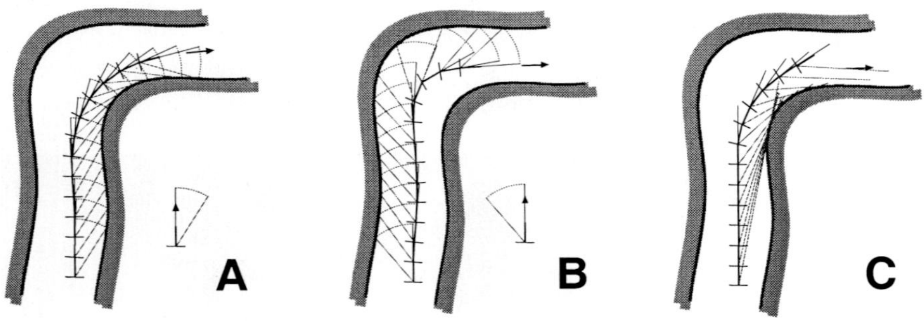

Fig. 5. A. Fixed distance, fixed direction inside of bend. **B**. Fixed distance, fixed direction outside of bend. **C**. Tangent point, fixed direction (30° threshold)

The maintain-eccentricity solution described above is unlikely to be used in isolation. If we consider a classic model of steering by Donges [17] we note that it relies on two control variables, a far point and lateral lane position. The lateral position is monitored to ensure that the car has not drifted. It is likely that walking observers would, and moving robots should, also respond to changes in lateral position. However it might be sufficient to monitor lateral position only intermittently and to correct any drift with an approximate ballistic/open-loop change in lateral position. Land [18] and Wann & Land [19] provide useful reviews of behavioural data and models and provide some alternative perceptual control solutions.

4 Detecting and Avoiding Obstacles

4.1 Detecting Obstacles

If during approach an object remains at a constant direction as you move then you are on a collision course. If the obstacles and the robot had zero horizontal extent then this would be sufficient for obstacle avoidance.

An observer could search for any imminent collisions, and if a collision is detected, change the eccentricity of their approach to the target. So they might go from a 0° eccentricity (straight) trajectory to a 10° trajectory. Note, this does not require that the observer change their immediate goal and navigate around an obstacle, but rather that they simply change the parameters of their current target approach trajectory. So even if an observer ended up changing direction by a large angle (eg 40°) to avoid a target they would still be on a course to their target. However, both the observer or robot, and obstacle have some non-zero horizontal extent, so identifying only objects that remain at a constant direction as obstacles is not sufficient.

So how might an obstacle be detected? It would be possible to use a ratio of the x (lateral) and z (depth) distances of an obstacle to generate a change of trajectory response.

Another solution would be to use other variables to which the human visual system is sensitive. One such variable is crossing distance [20-21]. Crossing distance is the lateral distance measured in the Cyclopean plane that passes through the eyes, at which a projectile will pass. It was first proposed by Bootsma [20], who showed that:

$$\frac{XDIST}{2R} = \frac{\dot{\alpha}}{\dot{\theta}} \tag{1}$$

where *XDIST* is the crossing distance, *R* the object radius, $\dot{\alpha}$ is the rate of changing direction, and $\dot{\theta}$ is the rate of changing size.

4.1.1 Calculation of XDIST

A variant of equation 1 based upon changing binocular disparity instead of changing size is:

$$\frac{XDIST}{I} = \frac{\dot{\alpha}}{\dot{\phi}} \tag{2}$$

where I is the inter-camera separation, and $\dot{\phi}$ is changing disparity [22].

We use neither of these variants, the problem with the first being that it returns *XDIST* as a multiple of obstacle width and therefore requires prior knowledge of obstacle dimensions. The second returns a more useful measure, *XDIST,* as a multiple of inter-ocular or inter-camera distance. However, use of this formulation would require a binocular viewing system and associated stereo matching algorithms.

Instead while acknowledging the utility of these sources of *XDIST* information, we elected to keep our implementation (hardware and software) as simple as possible and instead take advantage of one of the constraints in our setup. The robot always moves over a flat ground plane, and obstacles rest on the ground plane. Therefore we can modify the second *XDIST* equation and use change in height-in-the-image, $\dot{\rho}$, in place of change of disparity. We elected to use the changing direction of the inside or closest edge, $\dot{\beta}$:

$$\frac{XDIST}{H} = \frac{\dot{\beta}}{\dot{\rho}} \tag{3}$$

where H is the known height of the camera. In our system the camera is pitched downwards so we must multiply $\dot{\rho}$ by sec(pitch).

The inside edge of the obstacle is the edge that is closest to the straight-ahead direction of the camera, or the edge that is moving most slowly. The use of the nearest edge simplifies the algorithm as it avoids the need to explicitly calculate and take into account object width. Use of object edge also fits well with a recent suggestion that the human perceptuo-motor system works on the position of object edges rather than the object's centroid and width [23].

4.1.2 Detecting Collision

We can define a safe crossing distance, SAFEDIST, which is 'body-scaled' [24] to the robot. If the lateral distance at which an obstacle will pass the robot, XDIST is less than a minimum distance (SAFEDIST) then it is on a collision course. Therefore an observer or robot can continuously examine the obstacles in the scene and look for any on a collision course.

4.1.3 Knowing How Quickly to Turn

Once an obstacle is detected, how quickly does a change in trajectory need to occur? We can define "temporal distance" as the amount of time remaining before we will collide with the robot. The temporal distance can then be used to assess how urgent a change of course is.

4.1.4 Calculation of Temporal Distance

TTC (time to contact), the time remaining before an obstacle collides with the eye or camera can be determined (to a first order approximation) indirectly by the ratio of the obstacle distance to the obstacle's closing speed. It can be determined "directly" [25] from $\theta/\dot{\theta}$ where θ is the size of the image of the obstacle at the eye or camera. It is also given by $\phi/\dot{\phi}$ where ϕ is the binocular subtense of the obstacle viewed from eyes or a stereo-head. Rushton & Wann [26] recently proposed a computational solution that combines both these estimates and demonstrates robust behaviour in the case of cue-drop out, cue-conflict and optimal weighting of information from size and disparity as a function of object size.

$$TTC = (\theta + \phi)/(\dot{\theta} + \dot{\phi}) \tag{4}$$

Our implementation involved only a single camera so eq 4. cannot be used, however, the principle behind it can be used to optimise estimation of TTC from the monocular information:

$$TTC = (\theta_h + \theta_v)/(\dot{\theta}_h + \dot{\theta}_v) \tag{5}$$

where θ_h is the horizontal extent of the image of the obstacle, θ_v is the vertical extent.

The above equation will lead to the expansion of horizontal image size having the most influence with a short and wide obstacle, and vertical extent with a thin and tall obstacle. Therefore, it makes optimal use of the information available without the additional computational cost or the difficulty of determining priors or variance on the fly associated with Bayesian approaches.

4.2 Change of Path Equation

Our first constraint in deriving an obstacle avoidance algorithm is that we shouldn't lose track of our target, therefore any avoidance behaviour taken will simply change the parameters of the approach to the target rather than spawn an obstacle avoidance sub-goal. Therefore we only change the *eccentricity* parameter in our target approach algorithm.

If we set a safe crossing distance, SAFEDIST, then when XDIST < SAFEDIST, we can calculate a change in eccentricity or a turnrate, ϖ , to avoid the obstacle while proceeding to the target:

$$\varpi = k.\frac{(SAFEDIST - XDIST)}{TTC} \tag{6}$$

This equation is of the same form as that proposed by Peper et al [27] to describe projectile interception by human observers. Recent work indicates that human catching behaviour may be better described by models that include a prediction of lateral position [28], however work on human locomotion suggests that prediction is not used [2]. Therefore for now, we do not include a predictive term for future XDIST.

We change the eccentricity of the approach to the target as follows:

$$\alpha_{t+1} = \alpha_t + \varpi \tag{7}$$

Where α_t is the eccentricity of approach to the target at time t. Equation 6 leads to a response to obstacles as shown in figure 6.

On the basis of our interpretation of behavioural data [29] we only modify the eccentricity of approach on the basis of the closest obstacle. This decision contrasts with decisions made by others to include other obstacles too [30-31]. Closest obstacle could be decided on the basis of distance, TTC (time before collision with the observation point) or TTP (time before the obstacle will pass the robot). Distance is less useful when the environment is not static, therefore we used TTC.

4.3 Left vs. Right Decision Rules

Consider a robot approaching an obstacle. The robot could change the eccentricity of its target approach so as to pass to the left or the right of the obstacle. How should it decide?

- Our first rule says that it should take the route that requires the smallest change in eccentricity of approach.
- Our second rule says it should take the route that reduces the eccentricity of the current approach (gets it closest to zero or straight-ahead).

When the change in eccentricity associated with turning left vs. right is approximately the same we defer to the second rule. By varying the definition of "approximately the same" we can trade off the two rules.

5 Absolute Performance

We performed extensive testing through simulation. The system demonstrated robust performance in a range of environments (size, shape, number of obstacles, moving or stationary). It is difficult to capture the absolute performance of a system in a few

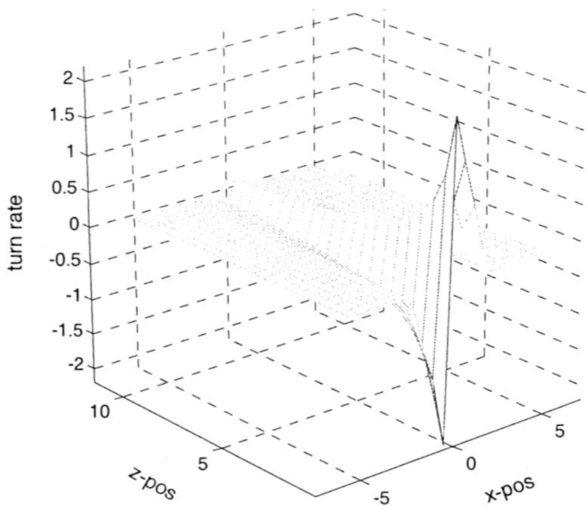

Fig. 6. Graphical representation of equation 6. X is lateral position, Z is distance in depth. Turn rate as a function of (x, z) position of an obstacle relative to the observer/robot.

statistics, as it is necessary to qualify results with an extensive description of the testing conditions, and to rigorously document any implementation specific functions, defaults or assumptions. We intend to report such details and results elsewhere.

5.1 Limitations of the Algorithm

The algorithm was designed to steer around obstacles, thus it does not deal with situations such as dead-ends or obstacles placed too close at beginning. We envisage that other processes would recognise and deal with these situations.

One implementation specific cause of failure was an inability to correctly segment obstacles when they overlapped in the projective view. This is not due to a shortcoming of our approach, but rather simply results from implementation decisions made (all obstacles were rendered flat-shaded in pure blue), and would not normally be a problem when features such as distance, texture, colour and so on could be used in the segmentation process.

One solution to this problem is to add predictive object tracking. Such an addition proves very useful as it removes other errors associated with mistaking object identity (and thus incorrectly calculating TTC etc). Every different implementation will bring its own specific problems, but it appears that predictive object tracking might be solve a whole raft of implementation specific problems and so it might be judicious to include an object tracking system by default.

A general problem that applies to any implementation of the algorithms described in this paper or any others is the problem of spatial scale. Our system can deal well with obstacles of varying width, but would run into problems when obstacles become so tall that the top of the obstacle falls out of the field of view. It is instructive consider what a human might do under such circumstances. They would be likely to switch to determining TTC, XDIST etc from local texture patches. In other words they use a different spatial scale. Trying to reformulate algorithms so that they are spatial scale invariant is an important and interesting problem.

6 Relative Performance

Although we have not done any formal testing of relative performance we can make the following comparisons to alternative approaches. Compared to potential field [31] and dynamical system [30] approaches, we have the following advantages: (i) simplicity; (ii) ability to deal with obstacles of varying size and shape (unlike the current formulation of the dynamical model [30]); (iii) based upon human perceptual variables.

Duchon et al [32] review the literature on the use of optic flow for obstacle avoidance and describe their own approach. From our understanding, the solution we propose is markedly simpler than the optic flow solutions, not least because we do not need to do optic flow processing over the visual field.

7 Some Examples

The following figures show some sample trajectories from our current model.

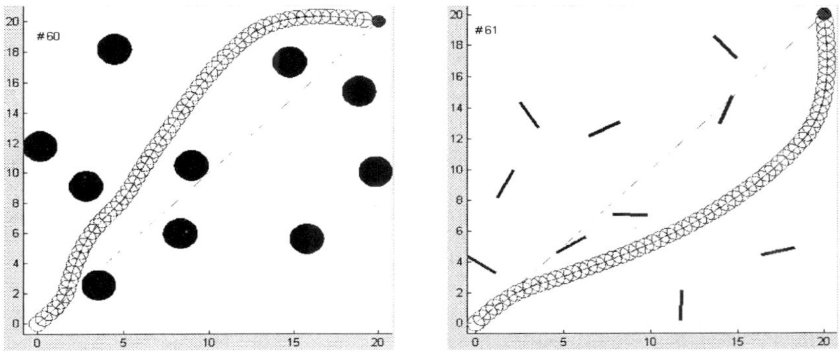

Fig. 7. Two example simulations of robot proceeding to target and avoiding obstacles along the way. Plan view with robot travelling from (0,0) to (20,20).

8 Summary and Conclusion

We have implemented a robot guidance system built on the regulation of object direction. This solution avoids the complexities associated with optic flow (computational cost, and the problems of a non-static environments). Our solution is inspired by research that suggests that humans navigate through the use of regulation of object direction. Fajen, et al [30] have recently modelled the locomotion of humans around obstacles and towards targets using a system of attractors (target) and repellors (obstacles). The work of Fajen et al is similar to the artificial potential field method and related methods of robot navigation [30-32]. These methods have the disadvantage of being computationally demanding. The work was constrained to only use simple visual variables to which humans have a documented sensitivity. Our approach leads to a system that is very simple, produces robust behaviour and utilises a biologically plausible strategy.

Acknowledgements. This research was supported in part by funds from Nissan Technical Center North America Inc, and the National Science and Engineering Research Council of Canada.

References

1. Lappe, M. Bremmer, F.; & van den Berg, A.V.: Perception of self-motion from visual flow *Trends in Cognitive Sciences* 3 (1999) 329–336.
2. Rushton, S.K., Harris, J.M., Lloyd, M.L. & Wann, J.P.: Guidance of locomotion on foot uses perceived target location rather than optic flow. *Current Biology* 8 (1998) 1191-1194
3. Rogers, B.J. & Allison, R.S.: When do we use optic flow and when do we use perceived direction to control locomotion? *Perception* 28 (1999) S2
4. Wood, R.M et al.: Weighting to go with the flow *Current Biology* 10 (2000) 545–546
5. Harris, M.G. & Carré, G.: Is optic flow used to guide walking while wearing a displacing prism? *Perception* 30 (2001) 811–818
6. Harris, J.M. & Bonas W.: Optic flow and scene structure do not always contribute to the control of human walking. *Vision Research* 42 (2002), 1619–1626
7. Warren, W.H. et al: Optic flow is used to control human walking. *Nature Neuroscience* 4 (2001) 213–216
8. Rushton, S.K. & Salvucci, D.D.: An egocentric account of the visual guidance of locomotion. *Trends in Cognitive Science* 5 (2001) 6–7
9. Rushton, S.K. & Harris, J.M.: The utility of not changing direction and the visual guidance of locomotion (submitted).
10. Gibson J.J.: Visually controlled locomotion and visual orientation in animals. *British Journal of Psychology* 19 (1958) 182–194
11. Loomis, J. M. & Beall, A. C.: Visually controlled locomotion: Its dependence on optic flow, three - dimensional space perception, and cognition. *Ecological Psychology* 10 (1998) 271–286
12. Lee, D. N. Guiding movement by coupling taus. *Ecological Psychology* 10 (1998) 221–250
13. Held, R., & Bossom, J.: Neonatal deprivation and adult rearrangement: complementary techniques for analyzing plastic sensory–motor coordinations. *J. Comp. Physiol. Psychol.* (1961) 33–37
14. Llewellyn KR.: Visual guidance of locomotion. *Journal of Experimental Psychology* 91 (1971) 245–261.
15. Land, M.F. & Lee, D.N.: Where we look when we steer. *Nature* 369 (1994) 742–744.
16. Murray, D.W., Reid, I.D. & Davison, A.J.: Steering without representation with the use of active fixation *Perception* 26 (1997) 1519–1528

17. Donges, E. A two-level model of driver steering behavior *Human Factors* 20 (1978) 691–707.
18. Land, M.F..: The visual control of steering IN Harris, L.R. & Jenkin M. (eds): *Vision and Action.* Cambridge University Press.
19. Wann, J.P. & Land, M.F.: Steering with or without the flow: is the retrieval of heading necessary? *Trends in Cognitive Science* 4 (2000) 319–324
20. Bootsma, R.J.: Predictive information and the control of action: what you see is what you get. *International Journal of Sports Psychology* 22 (1991) 271–278
21. Regan, D. & Kaushall, S.: Monocular judgements of the direction of motion in depth. *Vision. Research* 34 (1994) 163–177
22. Laurent, M., Montagne G. & Durey A.: Binocular invariants in interceptive tasks: a directed perception approach. *Perception* 25 (1996) 1437–1450
23. Smeets, J.B.J. & Brenner, E.: A new view on grasping. *Motor Control* 3 (1999) 237–271
24. Warren WH & Whang S.: Visual guidance of walking through apertures: body-scaled information for affordances. *Journal Experimental Psychology Human Perception and Performance* 13 (1987) 371–83
25. Lee, D.N.: A theory of visual control of braking based on information about time-to-collision. *Perception* 5 (1976) 437–459.
26. Rushton, S.K. & Wann, J.P.: Weighted combination of size and disparity: a computational model for timing a ball catch. *Nature Neuroscience* 2 (1999) 186–190
27. Peper, L., Bootsma, R,J,, Mestre, D.R. & Bakker, F.C.: Catching Balls - How To Get The Hand To The Right Place At The Right Time. *Journal Of Experimental Psychology-Human Perception And Performance* 20 (1994) 591–612
28. Girshick, A. R., Rushton, S.K., and Bradshaw, M.F.: The use of predictive visual information in projectile interception. *Investigative Ophthalmology and Visual Science*, 42 (2001) S 3335
29. Duchon, A.P. & Warren,W.H.: Path Planning vs. on-line control in visually guided locomotion. *Investigate Ophthalmology & Vision Science* 38 (1997) s 384.
30. Fajen, B.R., Warren, W.H., Temizer, S & Kaelbling, L.P.: A dynamical model of visually-guided steering, obstacle avoidance, and route selection (in press) *International Journal of Computer Vision*
31. Khatib, O.: Real-time obstacle avoidance for manipulators and mobile robots. *International Journal of Robotics Research* 5 (1986) 90–99.
32. Duchon, A.P, Warren, W.H. & Kaelbling, L.P.: Ecological Robots. *Adaptive Behavior* 6 (1998) 473–507

Evolving Vision-Based Flying Robots

Jean-Christophe Zufferey, Dario Floreano,
Matthijs van Leeuwen, and Tancredi Merenda

Autonomous Systems Laboratory (asl.epfl.ch), Institute of Systems Engineering,
Swiss Federal Institute of Technology (EPFL), CH-1015, Lausanne, Switzerland

Abstract. We describe a new experimental approach whereby an indoor flying robot evolves the ability to navigate in a textured room using only visual information and neuromorphic control. The architecture of a spiking neural circuit, which is connected to the vision system and to the motors, is genetically encoded and evolved on the physical robot without human intervention. The flying robot consists of a small wireless airship equipped with a linear camera and a set of sensors used to measure its performance. Evolved spiking circuits can manage to fly the robot around the room by exploiting a combination of visual features, robot morphology, and interaction dynamics.

1 Bio-Inspired Vision for Flying Robots

Our goal is to develop vision-based navigation systems for autonomous miniature (below 80 cm, 50 g) flying robots [1]. Some research teams are working on even smaller dimensions [2,3,4], but their efforts are essentially concentrated on mechatronics issues. A major challenge for miniature flying robots is the ability to navigate autonomously in complex environments. Conventional distance sensors (laser, ultrasonic) cannot be used for these systems because of their weight. Vision is an interesting sensor modality because it can be lightweight and low-power. However, the mainstream approach to computer vision, based on segmentation, object extraction, and pattern recognition, is not always suitable for small behavioural systems that are unable to carry powerful processors and related energy sources.

An alternative consists in taking inspiration from simple circuits and adaptive mechanisms used by living organisms [5]. A pioneering work in this direction was achieved by Franceschini et al. [6], who developed a wheeled robot with a vision system inspired upon the visual system of the fly. The 10 kg synchro-drive robot featured an artificial compound eye with 100 discrete photoreceptors and was able to freely navigate at about 50 cm/s toward a light source while avoiding randomly arranged obstacles. Other successful realisations followed (for review, see [7]), but unlike the robot by Franceschini et al., where computation was executed onboard by analog electronics, those machines demanded more computing power and were therefore linked to offboard computers for image processing. More recent work uses bio-inspired visual algorithms in flying agents,

H.H. Bülthoff et al. (Eds.): BMCV 2002, LNCS 2525, pp. 592–600, 2002.

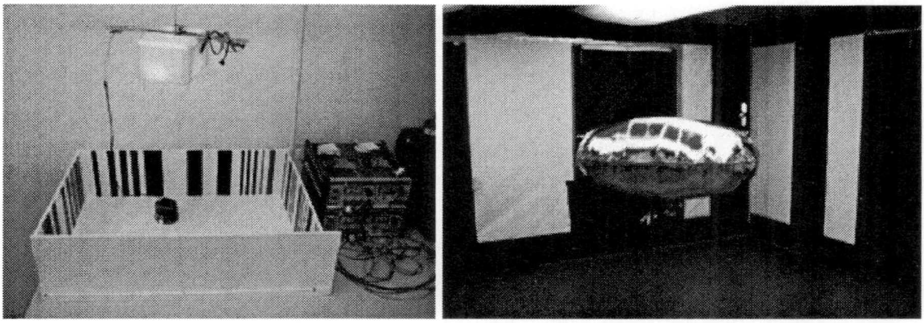

Fig. 1. Evolutionary vision-based robots. *Left*: The Khepera robot equipped with a linear camera (16 pixels, 36° FOV) was positioned in an arena with randomly sized black and white stripes. Random size was used to prevent development of trivial solutions whereby the control system would use the size of the stripes to measure distance from walls and self-motion. The robot was connected to a workstation through rotating contacts that provided serial data transmission and power supply. *Right*: The blimp-like flying robot, provided with a similar linear camera (16 pixels, 150° FOV), is closed in a 5x5x3 m room with randomly sized black and white stripes on the walls. The serial data transmission is handled by a Bluetooth^{TM} wireless connection and power supply by an onboard battery.

but these developments have been limited to tethered aircraft [8] and simulated flight [9].

The control systems of the robots mentioned above were 'hand-designed'. Some authors proposed to evolve vision-based navigation capabilities [10,11]. For example, Huber applied genetic algorithms to simulated 2D agents [12]. Those agents were equipped with only four photoreceptors making up two elementary motion detectors (EMD), symmetrically placed on each side of the agent. The parameters of those EMDs as well as the position and field of view (FOV) of the photoreceptors were evolved. The best individuals could successfully navigate in a simulated corridor with textured walls and obstacles. The simulation was rather simple though, especially because inertial forces were not taken into consideration.

In previous work [13], we evolved the architecture of spiking neural networks capable of steering a vision-based, wheeled robot. A Khepera robot with a linear camera was asked to navigate in a rectangular arena with textured walls (figure 1, left). The best individuals were capable of moving forward and avoiding walls very reliably. However, the complexity of the dynamics of this terrestrial robot is much simpler than that of flying agents.

In this paper, we extend that approach to a flying robot (figure 1, right) that is expected to navigate within a room using only visual information. Genetic algorithms [14] are used to evolve the architecture of a spiking circuit, which connects low resolution visual input to the motors of a small indoor airship. Notice that other teams are using blimps for studying insect-like vision-based navigation [15,16], but none of them are applying the concepts of evolutionary robotics [17].

In the following section, we describe the main challenges of running evolution with real flying systems and give an overview of the experimental setup. Section 3 summarizes the evolutionary and neural dynamics. The results are presented in section 4. Finally, a discussion and future work description are given in section 5.

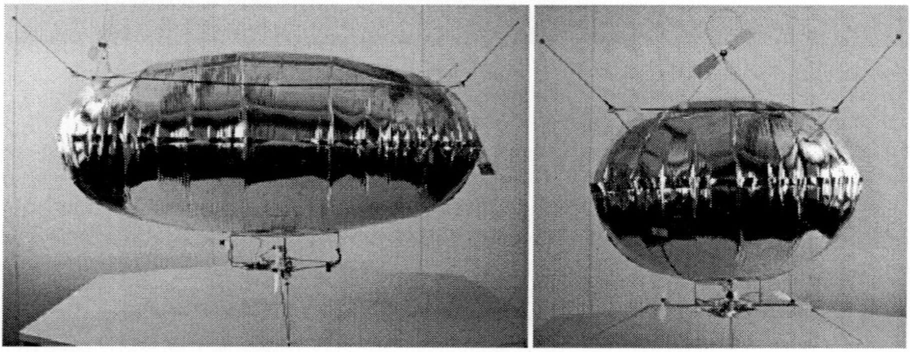

Fig. 2. The blimp features an ellipsoid envelope (100x60x45 cm) filled with helium for a lift capacity of approximately 250 g. On top and below the envelope are attached frames made of carbon fibre rods that support six bumpers (4 on top and 2 below) for collision detection. It is equipped with three engines (miniature DC motor, gear, propeller): two for horizontal movement (forward, backward and rotation around yaw axis) and one for vertical movement. In order to measure the relative forward airspeed, an anemometer (free rotating balsa-wood propeller with a mouse optical encoder) has been mounted on top of the envelope. The system is able to qualitatively measure airspeeds above 5 cm/s. A distance sensor has been mounted below the gondola and oriented toward the floor for altitude control in the preliminary experiments.

2 Experimental Setup

Evolving aerial robots brings a new set of challenges. The major issues of developing (evolving, learning) a control system for an airship, with respect to a wheeled robot, are (1) the extension to three dimensions[1], (2) the impossibility to communicate to a computer via cables, (3) the difficulty of defining and measuring performance, and (4) the more complex dynamics. For example, while the Khepera is controlled in speed, the blimp is controlled in thrust (speed derivative) and can slip sideways. Moreover, inertial and aerodynamic forces play a major role. Artificial evolution is a promising method to automatically develop

[1] Although the first experiments described hereafter are limited to 2D by the use of a pre-designed altitude regulator.

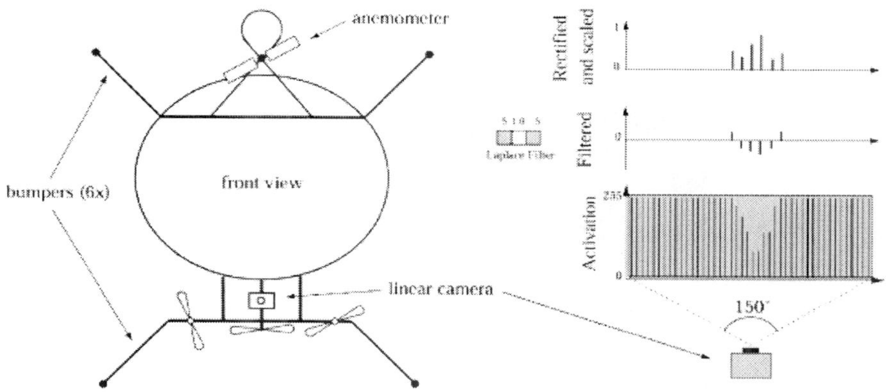

Fig. 3. *Left:* The blimp and its main components: the anemometer on top of the envelope, the linear camera pointing forward with 150° FOV giving a horizontal image of the vertical stripes, the bumpers and propellers. *Right:* Contrast detection is performed by selecting 16 equally spaced photoreceptors and filtering them through a Laplace filter spanning three photoreceptors. Filtered values are then rectified by taking the absolute value and scaling them in the range [0,1]. These values represent the probability of emitting a spike for each corresponding neuron. A linear camera fixed on the gondola is the only source of information for the evolutionary spiking network.

control systems for complex robots [17], but it requires machines that are capable of moving for long periods of time without human intervention and withstand shocks.

Those requirements led us to the development of the blimp shown in figure 2. All onboard electronic components are connected to a Microchip PIC™ microcontroller with a wireless connection to a desktop computer. The bidirectional digital communication with the computer is handled by a Bluetooth™ radio module, allowing more than 15 m range. The energy is provided by a Lithium-Ion battery, which lasts more than 3 hours under normal operation, during evolutionary runs. For purpose of analysis, the evolutionary algorithm and spiking circuits are implemented on the desktop computer which exchanges sensory data and motor commands with the blimp every 100 ms.[2]

In these experiments, a simple linear camera is attached in front of the gondola (figure 3), pointing forward. The fish-eye-view lens gives a horizontal 150° FOV mapped onto 16 photoreceptors (subsampled from about 50 active pixels) whose activations are convolved with a Laplace filter. The Laplace filter detects contrast over three adjacent photoreceptors.

[2] An adapted form of the evolutionary algorithm and spiking circuit could be run on the onboard microcontroller [18], but data analysis would be limited.

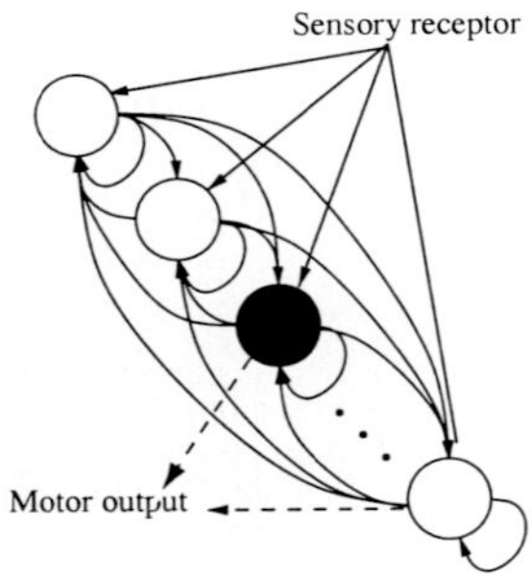

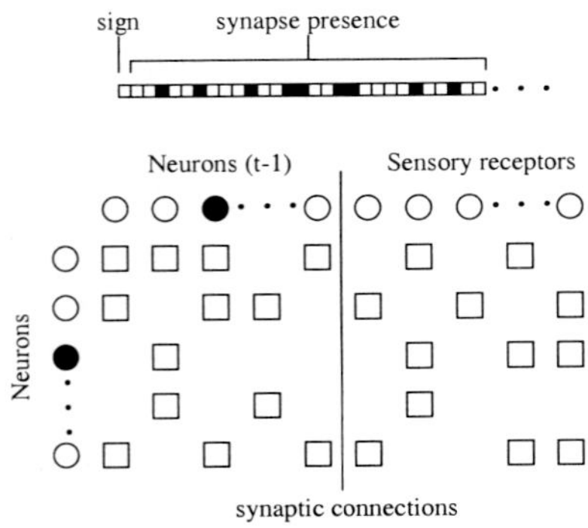

Fig. 4. Network architecture (only a few neurons and connections are shown) and genetic representation of one neuron. *Left*: A conventional representation showing the network architecture. Four neurons, two for each side, are used to set the speeds of the two horizontal propellers in a push-pull mode. *Right*: The same network unfolded in time (neurons as circles, synaptic connections as squares). The neurons on the column receive signals from connected neurons and photoreceptors shown on the top row. The first part of the row includes the same neurons at the previous time step to show the connections among neurons. Sensory neurons do not have interconnections. The signs of the neurons (white = excitatory, black = inhibitory) and their connectivity pattern is encoded in the genetic string and evolved.

3 Evolving Spiking Circuits

The evolutionary method and the spiking controller are very similar to what is described in [13]. The connectivity pattern and neuron signs of a network of 10 spiking neurons connected to 16 spiking visual receptors is genetically encoded and evolved using a standard genetic algorithm [14] with a population of 60 individuals sequentially evaluated on the same physical robot. The architecture is genetically represented by a binary string composed of a series of blocks, each block corresponding to a neuron. The first bit of a block encodes the sign of the corresponding neuron (1, -1) and the remaining 26 bits encode the presence/absence (1, 0) of a connection from the 10 neurons and from the 16 visual receptors (figure 4). The synaptic strengths of all existing connections are set to 1. The spiking neuron model includes the response profile of synaptic and neuron membranes to incoming spikes, time delays to account for axon length, and membrane recovery profile of the refractory period [19]. The parameter values for the equations are predefined and fixed for all networks (no tuning has been done on these parameter values).

The population of 60 individuals is evolved using rank-based truncated selection, one-point crossover, bit mutation, and elitism [17]. The genetic strings of the first generation are initialised randomly. After ranking the individuals according to their measured fitness values, the top 15 individuals produce 4 copies each to create a new population of the same size and are randomly paired for crossover. One-point crossover is applied to each pair with probability 0.1 and each individual is then mutated by switching the value of a bit with probability 0.05 per bit. Finally, a randomly selected individual is substituted by the original copy of the best individual of the previous generation (elitism).

Each individual of the population is tested on the robot two times for 40 seconds each (400 sensory-motor steps). The behaviour of an individual is evaluated by mean of the anemometer, which rotation speed is approximately proportional to the forward motion. The fitness function is thus the amount of estimated forward motion $\hat{v}$ at every time step t (100 ms) averaged over all T time steps available (T=800):

$$\Phi = \frac{1}{T}\sum_{t}^{T} \hat{v}^t \tag{1}$$

After each 40 s test, a preprogrammed random movement of 5 seconds is executed to create a randomised initial situation for the next test.

4 Results

We performed five evolutionary runs, each starting with a different random initialisation (figure 5, top left). All best evolved individuals of the five runs developed efficient strategies in less than 20 generations (2-3 days) to navigate around the room in the forward direction. Interestingly, walls are actively used by the robot to stabilise the trajectory. The fitness function (section 3) does not ask individuals to avoid walls, but only to maximise forward motion. The anemometer rotates only if the forward component of the speed vector is not null.

The trajectory of a typical best individual is shown on the top right plot of figure 5. It starts with a rotational movement due to the previous random movement (a) and keeps rotating until it hits a wall, which stabilises its course (b). It then moves straight forward until a wall is hit frontally (c), the motors are turned off, and the robot bumps backward. When the robot is free from the wall, the motors are turned on to move forward. Once again, a wall is used to stabilise the course and the same strategy is repeated over and over again.

The evolved spiking circuit clearly reacts when it hits the wall by turning off the motors, although the only input to the neural network is vision data. This behaviour can be seen also in the pattern of motor activity shown in the bottom graphs of figure 5, which indicates a strong correlation between a collision event[3] and change of motor speeds. It is quite remarkable that such a simple evolved spiking circuit is able to detect collisions with so poor visual information about the environment, using only 16 photoreceptors as input.

[3] Note that with the current setup, it is not possible to know which of the six bumpers is in contact with the walls. As a consequence, we cannot distinguish between a frontal and a side collision.

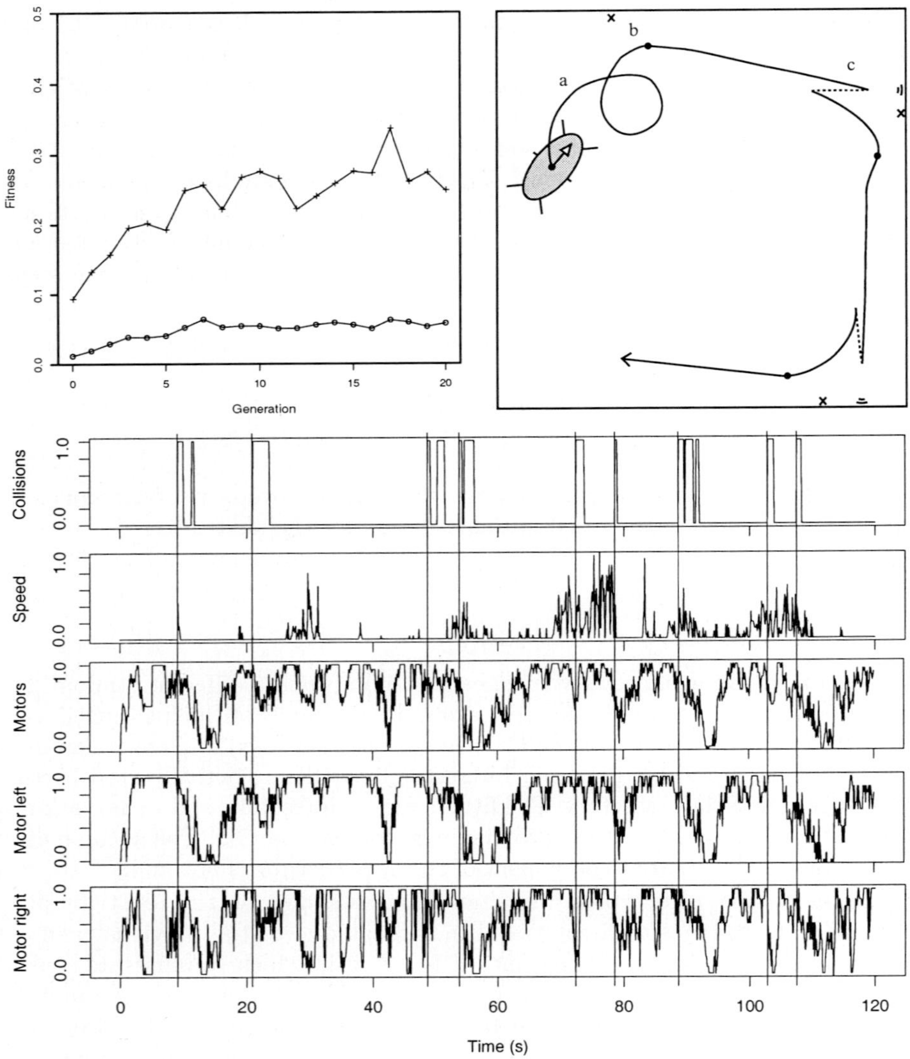

Fig. 5. *Top left*: Average fitness values of five evolutionary runs (best fitness = crosses, average fitness = circles). Each data point is the average of five evolutionary runs starting with different random initialisation of the chromosomes. *Top right*: Hand-drawn estimation of the typical path of the selected best individual (solid line = forward movement; dashed line = backward movement; small curves = front collision; cross and circle = place of collision with left back bumper). *Bottom*: Performance of the best selected individual during two minutes. The upper graph shows collisions, as detected by the bumpers. The second graph shows an approximation of the forward speed, as measured with the anemometer. The motor graphs show the forward thrust of the propellers, which is given by the neural network output ('Motors' is the average of both motors). Each vertical line indicates the start of a collision. Multiple collisions on the topgraph are generated by the switches of the bumpers as the robot touches the walls.

5 Conclusion

These initial explorations with simple neuromorphic vision controllers for flying robots indicate that artificial evolution can discover efficient (and unexpected) solutions that capitalize on a combination of visual information and interaction dynamics between the physical system and its environment. These evolved solutions can not only encompass visual mechanisms already discovered in insects (such as forms of elementary motion detection), but also incorporate new "tricks" that may, or may not, be used by biological flying organisms.

In current work, we are investigating the behavioural effects of different types of imaging devices (such as aVLSI retina) and preprocessing filters (temporal, spatial, spatio-temporal, EMDs, etc.). A 3D flight simulator under development will help us to speed up evolutionary runs, let the sensor morphology evolve along with the controller, but will require proper handling of the issues related to the differences between simulation and real world. This last point will probably be approached by evolving hebbian-like synaptic plasticity, which we have shown to support fast self-adaptation to changing environments [20]. Eventually, our goal is to apply this approach to indoor slow flyers with wings [1], instead of airships.

Acknowledgements. This work was supported by the Swiss NSF grant No. 620-58049. The authors are grateful to Jean-Daniel Nicoud (www.didel.com) for providing parts and support for building the blimp, and to Cyril Halter for the wind tunnel tests. Portescap (www.portescap.com) provided the motors equipping the blimp and Sensile (www.sensile.ch) the force gauges for the wind tunnel setup.

References

1. Nicoud, J.D., Zufferey, J.C.: Toward Indoor Flying Robots. To appear in proceedings of IEEE/RSJ International Conference on Intelligent Robots and Systems (2002)
2. Fearing, R.S., Chiang, K.H., Dickinson, M.H., Pick, D.L., Sitti, M., and Yan, J.: Wing Transmission for a Micromechanical Flying Insect. IEEE Int. Conf. Robotics and Automation (2000)
3. Pornsin-Sirirak, T.R., Lee, S.W., Nassef, H., Grasmeyer J., Tai, Y.C., Ho, C.M., Keennon, M.: MEMS Wing Technology for A Battery-Powered Ornithopter. The 13th IEEE International Conference on Micro Electro Mechanical Systems (MEMS'00), Miyazaki, Japan, pp. 799–804 (2000)
4. Kroo, I. et al.: The Mesicopter: A Meso-Scale Flight Vehicle. http://aero.stanford.edu/mesicopter/
5. Pfeifer, R., Lambrinos, D.: Cheap Vision – Exploiting Ecological Niche and Morphology. Theory and practice of informatics: SOFSEM 2000, 27th Conference on Current Trends in Theory and Practice of Informatics, pp. 202–226 (2000)
6. Franceschini, N., Pichon, J.M., Blanes, C.: From insect vision to robot vision. Phil. Trans. R. Soc. Lond. B, 337, pp. 283–294 (1992)

7. Weber, K., Venkatesh, S., Srinivasan, M.V.: Insect Inspired Behaviours for the Autonomous Control of Mobile Robots. From Living Eyes to Seeing Machines, pp. 226–248 (1997)
8. Netter, T., Franceschini, N.: A Robotic Aircraft that Follows Terrain Using a Neuromorphic Eye. To appear in Proceedings of IEEE/RSJ International Conference on Intelligent Robots and Systems (2002)
9. Neumann, T.R., Bülthoff, H.H.: Insect Inspired Visual Control of Translatory Flight. ECAL (2001)
10. Harvey, I., Husbands, P., Cliff, D.: Seeing the Light: Artificial Evolution, Real Vision. In From Animals to Animats III, MIT Press, pp. 392–401 (1994)
11. Dale, K., Collett, T.S. Using artificial evolution and selection to model insect navigation. Current Biology, 11:1305-1316 (2001)
12. Huber, S.A., Mallot, H.A., Bülthoff, H.H: Evolution of the sensorimotor control in an autonomous agent. In Proceedings of the Fourth International Conference on Simulation of Adaptive behaviour, MIT Press, pp. 449–457 (1996)
13. Floreano, D., Mattiussi, C.: Evolution of Spiking Neural Controllers for Autonomous Vision-Based Robots. In Gomi, T., ed., Evolutionary Robotics. From Intelligent Robotics to Artificial Life. Tokyo: Springer Verlag (2001)
14. Goldberg, D.E.: Genetic Algorithms in Search, Optimization and Machine Learning. Reading, MA: Addison-Wesley (1989)
15. Iida, F.: Goal-Directed Navigation of an Autonomous Flying Robot Using Biologically Inspired Cheap Vision. In Proceedings of the 32nd International Symposium on Robotics (2001)
16. Planta, C., Conradt, J., Jencik, A., Verschure, P.: A Neural Model of the Fly Visual System Applied to Navigational Tasks. In Proceedings of the International Conference on Artificial Neural Networks, ICANN (2002)
17. Nolfi, S., Floreano, D.: Evolutionary Robotics: Biology, Intelligence, and Technology of Self-Organizing Machines. Cambridge, MA: MIT Press. 2nd print (2001)
18. Floreano, D., Schoeni, N., Caprari, G., Blynel, J.: Evolutionary Bits'n'Spikes. Technical report (2002)
19. Gerstner, W.: Associative memory in a network of biological neurons. In Lippmann, R.P.; Moody, J.E.; and Touretzky, D.S., eds., Advances in Neural Information processing Systems 3. San Mateo,CA: Morgan Kaufmann. 84-90 (1991)
20. Urzelai, J., Floreano, D.: Evolutionary Robotics: Coping with Environmental Change. In Proceedings of the Genetic and Evolutionary Computation Conference (2000)

Object Detection and Classification for Outdoor Walking Guidance System*

Seonghoon Kang and Seong-Whan Lee

Center for Artificial Vision Research, Korea University,
Anam-dong, Seongbuk-ku, Seoul 136-701, Korea
{shkang, swlee}@image.korea.ac.kr

Abstract. In this paper, we present an object detection and classification method for OpenEyes-II. OpenEyes-II is a walking guidance system that helps the visually impaired to respond naturally to various situations that can occur in unrestricted natural outdoor environments during walking and reaching the destination. Object detection and classification is requisite for implementing obstacle and face detection which are major parts of a walking guidance system. It can discriminate pedestrian from obstacles, and extract candidate regions for face detection and recognition. We have used stereo-based segmentation and SVM (Support Vector Machines), which has superior classification performance in binary classification case such like object detection. The experiments on a large number of street scenes demonstrate the effectiveness of the proposed method.

1 Introduction

Object detection and classification is essential for the walking guidance for the visually impaired and the driver assistance system, etc. It is very difficult to detect object in varying outdoor scenes. There are two steps for detecting and classifying objects. The first is to separate foreground objects from the background. The second is to distinguish meaningful objects from other meaningless objects. The first procedure is object detection and the second one is object recognition. In this paper, we have used stereo-based segmentation for the object detection procedure and the SVM classification for object recognition.

This proposed method is the main part of an outdoor walking guidance system for the visually impaired, OpenEyes-II which is being developed in the Center for Artificial Vision Research at Korea University. OpenEyes-II enables the visually impaired to respond naturally to various situations that can happen in unrestricted natural outdoor environments while walking and finally reaching their destination. To achieve this goal, foreground objects(pedestrian, obstacles, etc.) are detected in real-time by using foreground-background segmentation based on stereo vision. Then, each object is classified as meaningful objects or

* This research was supported by Creative Research Initiatives of the Ministry of Science and Technology, Korea.

H.H. Bülthoff et al. (Eds.): BMCV 2002, LNCS 2525, pp. 601–610, 2002.

obstacles by an SVM classifier. These two main elements make the object detection and classification system robust and in real-time.

2 Related Works

Most human detection and tracking systems employs a simple segmentation procedure such as background subtraction or temporal differenciation in order to detect pedestrians. A people tracking system is an integrated system for the detecting and tracking of humans from image sequences. These systems have many various properties from input camera types to detailed methods for detection of body parts. Haritaoglu *et al.* introduced the W4 system [5] and the Hydra system [6] for detecting and tracking multiple people or the parts of their bodies. While the W4 system is an integrated tracking system that uses a monocular, monochrome, and static camera as an input device, Hydra is a sub-module, which allows W4 to analyze people moving in a group. Hydra segments a group of multiple people into each individual person by head detection and distance transformation. The Pfinder system [7] used a multi-class statistical model of a person and the background for person tracking and gesture recognition. This model utilizes stochastic, region-based features, such as blob and 2D contour. Although it performs novel model-based tracking, it is unable to track multiple people simultaneously. Darrell *et al.* [8] used disparity and color information for individual person tracking and segmentation. Their system uses stereo cameras, and computes the range from the camera to each person with the disparity. The depth estimation allows the elimination of the background noises, and disparity is fairly insensitive to illumination effects. Mohan, Papageorgious and Poggio [9] present a more robust pedestrian detection system based on the SVM technique. However, the system has to search the whole image at multiple-scales to detect many components of human for pedestrian detection. This would be an extremely computationally expensive procedure, and it may cause multiple responses from a single detection. To increase reliability, some systems integrate multiple cues such as stereo, skin color, face, shape to detect pedestrians [8,5]. These systems prove that stereo and shape are more reliable and helpful cues than color and face detection in general situations.

3 What Is OpenEyes?

3.1 OpenEyes-I

The basic goal of the OpenEyes is becoming a walking guidance system that enables the visually impaired to respond naturally to various situations that can happen in unrestricted natural outdoor environments while walking and finally reaching the destination. But it is not possible to apply in a natural environment with the current computer vision technology and limited computing power. Therefore, we have developed a prototype system, OpenEyes-I(Figure 1) that can guide the visually impaired in a building, a restricted environment[1].

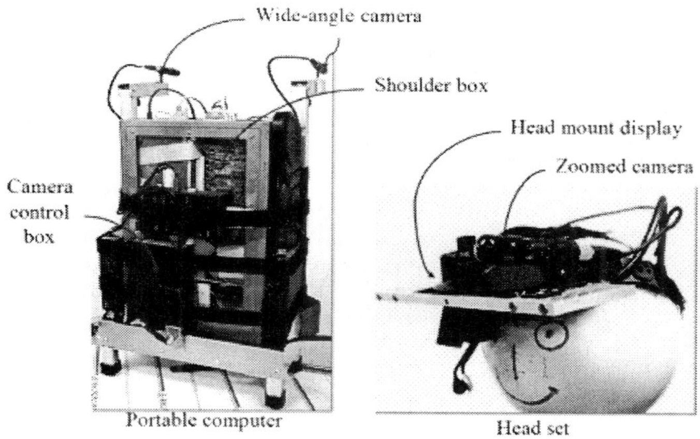

Fig. 1. OpeneEyes-I

It has several basic functions for walking guidance; passageway guidance, obstacle avoidance, face and facial recognition, character extraction and recognition, etc. But these functions can operate properly at indoor environments and this prototype system is too heavy for the visually impaired to carry.

3.2 OpenEyes-II

Currently, we have been developing an advanced system which is small and can operate in outdoor environments. Also, since the computer vision can only process local information that is in a field of view, it is not acceptable in processing global information, which is requisite for decision making on walking path to the destination and current location of the visually impaired. We will solve this problem with technical developments such as GPS(Global Positioning System), electrical map for walking and MapMatching.

Hardware and software configuration of OpeneEyes-II is as follows, according to the above requirements(Figure 2, 3).

OpenEyes-II consists of major two parts: portable computer which can be wear at belt, handset which can be carried by hand easily. A handset consists of several parts: stereo IEEE1394 cameras for image input, infra-red or ultrasonic sensors for distance measuring and some control buttons for handling whole system. A portable computer will be less than 1.5kg and include DGPS(Differential GPS) module for global position recognition. For interaction between system and user, we will use voice generation and recognition. Specially, for the output device, we select bone conduction headphone, which do not entirely cover the user's ears, and therefore do not impede hearing or understanding environment sounds. It is very important not to degrade the user's external auditory sense.

Software of OpenEyes has following functions. First, input natural video is analyzed in real-time for detecting and classifying the objects which means to

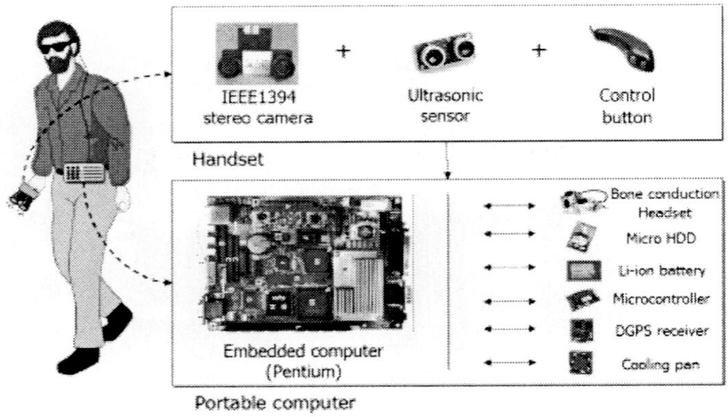

Fig. 2. Hardware configuration of OpenEyes-II

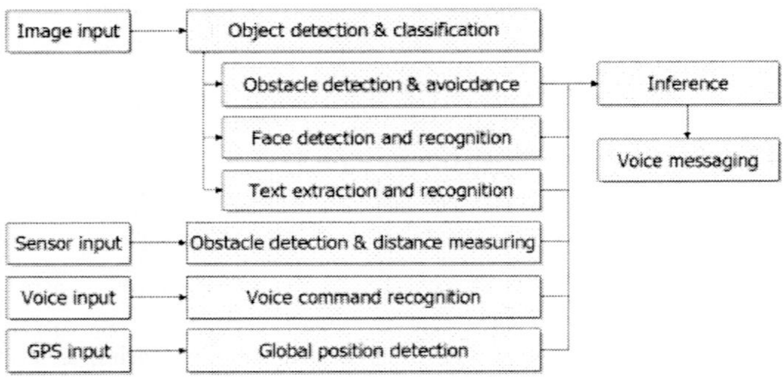

Fig. 3. Software configuration of OpenEyes-II

be important for the visually impaired. According to classes of detected objects, following operations are performed: obstacle analysis and avoidance, face detection and recognition and text extraction and recognition. Also, for furnishing global position information to the visually impaired, position recognition and walking path guidance are performed using DGPS with mapmatching. Finally, OpenEyes-II can generate voice messages for walking guidance by inferring all detected and measured information.

4 Object Detection and Classification

Until now, we looked closely at the OpenEyes system. From this section, we will describe object detection and classification method for OpeneEyes-II in detail. It is very important part of whole system. Especially, we have considered only pedestrian as target object to detect in this paper. Pedestrian detection is much more important than any other objects. In case of the driver assistance system, the pedestrian is an obstacle, which the driver should avoid. But, in case of the walking guidance system for the visually impaired, the pedestrian is an meaningful object to interact. So, pedestrian detection should be performed in real-time before the operator encounters other pedestrians. After a pedestrian is detected, we can extract and recognize a face effectively by reducing the candidate region to search faces.

The pedestrian detection system consists of a training module and detection module as shown in figure 4. First of all, the pedestrian detector model, which consists of SVM have been trained by training module. After the detector model is constructed, a pedestrian can be detected from the input of natural scenes by using the constructed detector model. Because most well-known pattern matching and model-based methods cannot be applied to varying natural scenes, we used the SVM algorithm for the main part of the classification. SVM is well-known as it can use statistical properties of various images by training, classifying and recognizing effectively in a huge data space by using a small number of training data. Because pedestrians have so many different colors and textures, it is difficult to use color or texture features for classifying pedestrians. So, we have used vertical edges, which can be extracted from arms, legs, and the body of pedestrians, as features for training and detection.

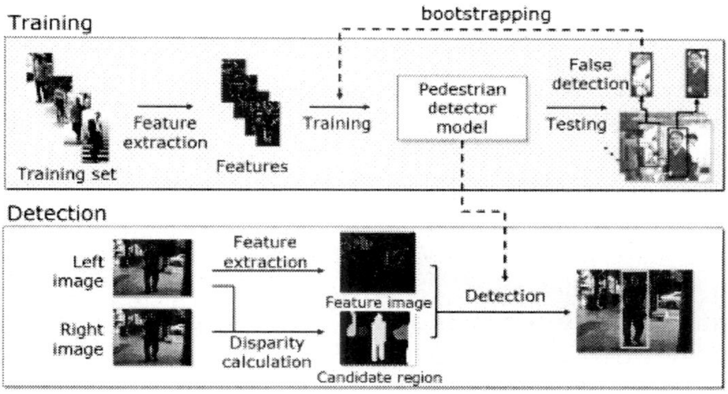

Fig. 4. Block diagram of pedestrian detection and classification

4.1 Detector Model Training

The pedestrian model target detection determines if a person exists 4-5m ahead. For model training, we have used a 32x64 size[1] of training images (manually collected pedestrian images for positive set and randomly collected background and other object images for negative set).

[1] It has been calibrated in half scale of input image (160x120 size) for fast and accurate detection.

For good detector model construction, we have used 'bootstrapping' training[2]. The combined set of positive and negative examples form the initial training database for the detector model. In the early stage, the detector model was trained by a 100 data set. After initial training, we run the system over many images that have various backgrounds. Any detections clearly identified as false positives are added to the training database of negative examples. These iterations of the bootstraping procedure allow the classifier to construct an incremental refinement of the non-pedestrian class until satisfactory performance is achieved.

4.2 Pedestrian Detection

In the pedestrian detection of a walking guidance system for the visually impaired, real-time issue is most important. If this system cannot operate in real-time, it is useless for real-world application. But, the SVM algorithm which is the main part of this system is too complicated to operate in real-time. So, it is very difficult to satisfy both detection accuracy and speed.

In order to overcome these problems, we have used a stereo vision technique which is frequently used in robot vision area. Stereo vision technique can provide range information for object segmentation. Using stereo vision to guide pedestrian detection carries with its some distinct advantages over conventional techniques. First, it allows explicit occlusion analysis and is robust to illumination changes. Second, the real size of an object derived from the disparity map provides a more accurate classification metric than the image size of the object. Third, using stereo cameras can detect both stationary and moving objects. Fourth, computation time is significantly reduced by performing classification where objects are detected; it is less likely to detect the background area as pedestrians since detection is biased toward areas where objects are detected[3].

Firstly, we have employed a video-rate stereo system[4] to provide range information for object detection. This system have used area correlation mothod for generating disparity image as shown in figure 5. By means of feature for correlation, LOG transform were chosen, because it gives good quality results. Figure 5(c) shows a typical disparity image. Higher disparities(closer objects) are indicated by brighter white.

Disparity image has range information. so we can separate the object region from background by using some filtering. In this paper, we have processed disparity image in three levels such like near distance, middle distance, far distance. We have been interested in only middle distance, because most objects to detect are in the middle distance. The areas in the far distance are regarded as background. So, the disparity image has been binarized and thresholded with some threshold values correspond to the middle distance, in order to extract the candidate region of the object as shown in Figure 6(c).

By extracting the candidate region of the object, we can reduce much more time to search the image, in order to detect pedestrians. For example as shown in Figure 7, the SVM classification must be performed 165 times without reducing the candidate region of the object using stereo vision, but only 2 times of

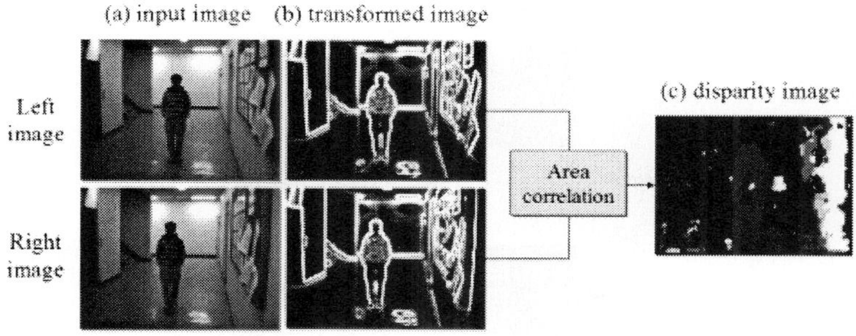

Fig. 5. Examples of disparity image based on area correlation

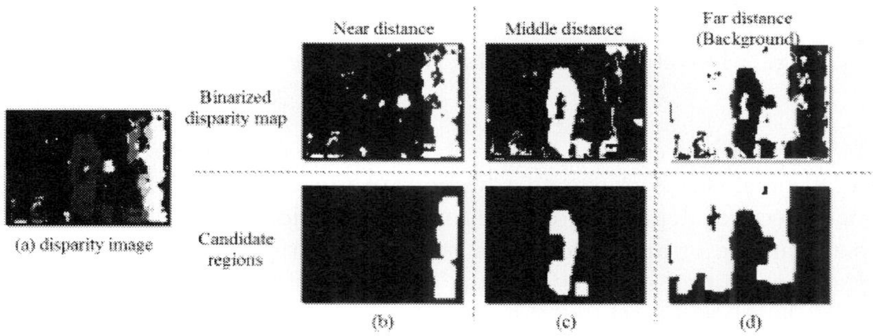

Fig. 6. Candidate regions of detected objects by distance

the SVM classification are needed while reducing the candidate region. When we assume that calculation time of disparity images is negligible, the proposed detection method with stereo vision is about 80 times faster than the detection method without stereo vision.

5 Experimental Result and Analysis

The experimental system has been implemented on a Pentium III 800 MHz system under Windows XP with a MEGA-D Megapixel Digital Stereo Head[11]. This stereo head has 12cm of base-line. Typically, it seems to be too small to obtain accurate range information. But in our application, we does not aim to obtain accurate range information, but aim to obtain object region information which exists in near distance. Also, we aim to miniaturize the size of handset. So, this stereo head, which has small base-line, is good for our system.

The pedestrian detector model is trained finally as followings. The training data set is consist of 140 positive data and 378 negative data. 3rd order polynomial have been used as the kernel function. By training, we have 252 support vectors. It has been tested extensively on large amounts of outdoor natural scene images including pedestrians. Over 900 instances of pedestrian and other

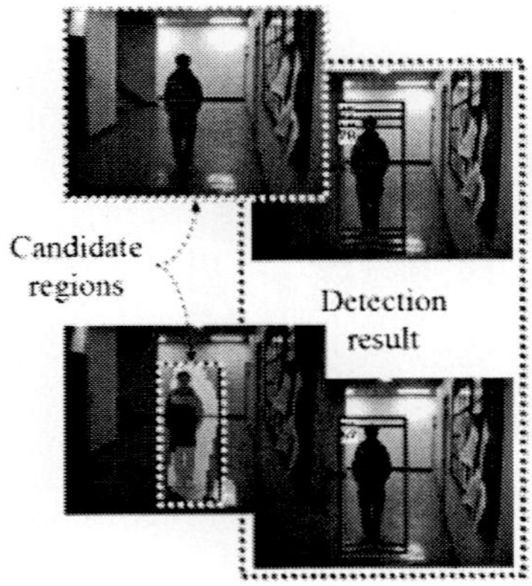

Fig. 7. Detection with reducing candidate regions vs. without one

objects have been presented. The system can detect and classify objects over a 320x240 pixel stereo image at a frame rate ranging from 5 frames/second to 10 frames/second, depending on the number of objects presented in the image. The performance of any detection system has a tradeoff between the positive detection rate and false detection rate. To capture this tradeoff, we vary the sensitivity of the system by thresholding the output and evaluate the ROC(Receiver Operating Characteristic) curve[10]. As shown in Figure 8, ROC curves comparing different representations, such like grey images and vertical edge images, for pedestrian detection. The detection rate is plotted against the false detection rate, measured on a logarithmic scale. The trained detection system has been run over test images containing 834 images of pedestrians to obtain the positive detection rate. The false detection rate has been obtained by running the system over 2000 images, which do not contain pedestrian. Experiments have been performed by four kinds of features. 64x128 size of gray and vertical edge images and 32x64 size of gray and vertical edge images are used. As shown in ROC curves, 32x64 size of vertical edge images superior than other features. It is more fast and accurate.

Figure 9 shows the results of our pedestrian detection system on some typical urban street scenes. This figure shows that our system can detect pedestrians in different size, pose, gait, clothing and occlusion status. However, there are some cases of failure. Most failures are occur when a pedestrian is almost similar in color to the background, or two pedestrians are too close to be separable.

6 Conclusion and Future Works

This system is part of the outdoor walking guidance system for the visually impaired, OpenEyes-II that aims to enable the visually impaired to respond naturally to various situations that can happen in unrestricted natural outdoor environments while walking and finally reaching the destination. To achieve this

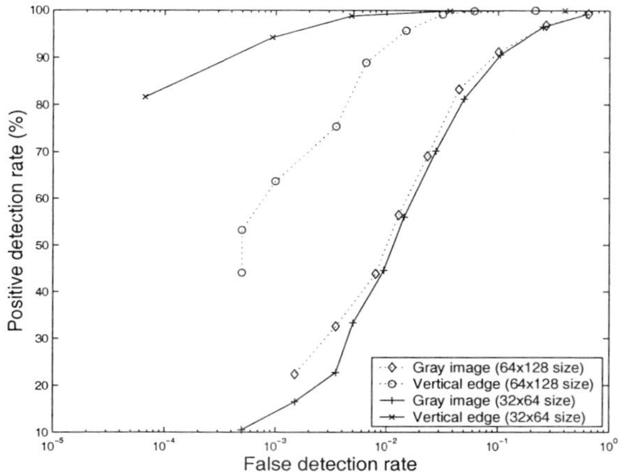

Fig. 8. ROC curves of pedestrian detector using SVMs

Fig. 9. Detection results

goal, foreground objects, such like pedestrian and obstacles, etc., are detected in real-time by using foreground-background segmentation based on stereo vision. Then, each object is classified as pedestrian or obstacle by the SVM classifier. These two main elements make the pedestrian detection system robust and real-time. But, this system has the problem that it becomes slower in case that there are many objects to classify in the field of view, because the complexity of the SVM algorithm. So, as future works, it is necessary to make the SVM algorithm faster through research about feature vector reduction and hardware implementation, etc. Also, multi-object discrimination and detection properties should be included for good application in real life.

References

1. Kang, S., Lee, S.-W.: Hand-held Computer Vision System for the Visually Impaired. Proceedings of the 3rd International Workshop on Human-friendly Welfare Robotic Systems, Daejeon, Korea, January (2002) 43–48
2. Sung, K.-K., Poggio, T.: Example-Based Learning for View-Based Human Face Detection. A.I. Memo 1521, AI Laboratory, MIT (1994)
3. Zhao, L., Thorpe, C.: Stereo- and Neural-Based Pedestrian Detection. Proc. of Internationl IEEE Conference on Intellegent Transprtation Systems, Tokyo, Japan, October. (1999) 5–10
4. Konolige, K: Small Vision Systems: Hardware and Implementation. Proceedings of 8th International Symposium on Robotics Research, Hayama, October (1997)
5. Haritaoglu, I., Harwood, D., Davis, L.S.: W4: Who? When? Where? What? A Real Time System for Detecting and Tracking People. Proceedings of International Conference on Face and Gesture Recognition, Nara, Japan, April (1998) 222–227
6. Haritaoglu, I., Harwood, D., Davis, L.S.: Hydra: Multiple People Detection and Tracking Using Silhouettes. Proceedings of 2nd IEEE Workshop on Visual Surveillance, Fort Collins, Colorado, June (1999) 6–13
7. Wren, C., Azarbayejani, A., Darrell, T., Pentland, A.: Pfinder: Real-Time Tracking of the Human Body. IEEE Transactions on Pattern Analysis and Machine Intelligence **19** 7 (1997) 780–785
8. Darrell, T., Gordon, G., Harville, M., Woodfill, J.: Integrated Person Tracking Using Stereo, Color, and Pattern Detection. Proceedings of IEEE Computer Society Conference on Computer Vision and Pattern Recognition, Santa Barbara, California (1998) 601–608
9. Mohan, A., Papageorgiou, C., Poggio, T.: Example-based Object Detection in Images by Components. IEEE Transactions on Pattern Recognition and Machine Intelligence **23** 4 (2001) 349–361
10. Oren, M., Papageorgiou, C., Sinha, P., Osuna, E., Poggio, T.: Pedestrian Detection Using Wavelet Templates. Proceedings of IEEE Computer Society Conference on Computer Vision and Pattern Recognition, San Juan, Puerto Rico (1997) 193–199
11. http://www.videredesign.com

Understanding Human Behaviors Based on Eye-Head-Hand Coordination

Chen Yu and Dana H. Ballard

Department of Computer Science
University of Rochester
Rochester, NY 14627,USA
{yu,dana}@cs.rochester.edu

Abstract. Action recognition has traditionally focused on processing fixed camera observations while ignoring non-visual information. In this paper, we explore the dynamic properties of the movements of different body parts in natural tasks: eye, head and hand movements are quite tightly coupled with the ongoing task. In light of this, our method takes an agent-centered view and incorporates an extensive description of eye-head-hand coordination. With the ability to track the course of gaze and head movements, our approach uses gaze and head cues to detect agent-centered attention switches that can then be utilized to segment an action sequence into action units. Based on recognizing those action primitives, parallel hidden Markov models are applied to model and integrate the probabilistic sequences of the action units of different body parts. An experimental system is built for recognizing human behaviors in three natural tasks: "unscrewing a jar", "stapling a letter" and "pouring water", which demonstrates the effectiveness of the approach.

1 Introduction

Humans perceive an action sequence as several action units [1]. This gives rise to the idea that action recognition is to interpret continuous human behaviors as a sequence of action primitives. However, we notice that a sequence of action primitives is not the final outcome of visual perception. Humans have the ability to group those units into high-level abstract representations that correspond to tasks or subtasks. For example, in our experiments, one subject performed some natural tasks while the other subject was asked to describe the actions of the performer. The verbal descriptions of the speaker mostly correspond to subtasks but not action units. For instance, the speaker would say "he is unscrewing a jar", but would not describe activities in such details as "his hand is approaching a jar", "then he is grasping it" and "he is holding the jar while unscrewing it". Thus, the speaker conceptualizes the sensory input into the abstract level corresponding to tasks or subtasks, then verbalizes the perceptual results to yield utterances. Based on this observation, we argue that to mimic human capabilities, such as describing visual events verbally, the goal of action recognition is to recognize not only action primitives but also tasks and subtasks. In light of this, this work concentrates on recognizing tasks instead of action primitives.

H.H. Bülthoff et al. (Eds.): BMCV 2002, LNCS 2525, pp. 611–619, 2002.

Recent results in visual psychophysics [2,3,4] indicate that in natural circumstances, the eye, the head, and hands are in continual motion in the context of ongoing behavior. This requires the coordination of these movements in both time and space. Land et al. [2] found that during the performance of a well-learn task(making tea), the eyes closely monitor every step of the process although the actions proceed with little conscious involvement. Hayhoe [3] has shown that eye and head movements are closely related to the requirements of motor tasks and almost every action in an action sequence is guided and checked by vision, with eye and head movements usually preceding motor actions. Moreover, their studies suggested that the eyes always look directly at the objects being manipulated. In our experiments, we confirm the conclusions by Hayhoe and Land. For example, in the action of "picking up a cup", the subject first moves the eyes and rotates the head to look towards the cup while keeping the eye gaze at the center of view. The hand then begins to move toward the cup. Driven by the upper body movement, the head also moves toward the location while the hand is moving. When the arm reaches the target place, the eyes are fixating it to guide the action of grasping.

Despite the recent discoveries of the coordination of eye, head and hand movements in cognitive studies, little work has been done in utilizing these results for machine understanding of human behavior. In this paper, our hypothesis is that eye and head movements, as an integral part of the motor program of humans, provide important information for action recognition in human activities. We test this hypothesis by developing a method that segments action sequences based on the dynamic properties of eye gaze and head direction, and applies Parallel Hidden Markov Models(PaHMMs) to integrate eye gaze and hand movements for task recognition.

2 Related Work

Early approaches [1] to action understanding emphasized on reconstruction followed by analysis. More recently, Brand [5] proposes to visually detect causal events by reasoning about the motions and collisions of surfaces using high-level causal constraints. Mann and Siskind [6] present a system based on an analysis of the Newtonian mechanics of a simplified scene model. Interpretations of image sequences are expressed in terms of assertions about the kinematic and dynamic properties of the scene. Presently, Hidden Markov Models(HMMs) have been applied within the computer vision community to address action recognition problems in which time variation is significant. Starner and Pentland [7] have developed a real-time HMM-based system for recognizing sentence-level American Sign Language(ASL) without explicitly modeling the fingers. Wilson and Bobick [8] have proposed an approach for gesture analysis that incorporates multiple representations into the HMM framework. Our work differs from theirs in that we take an agent-centered view and incorporate an extensive description of the agent's gaze, head and hand movements.

3 Attention-Based Action Segmentation

The segmentation of a continuous action stream into action primitives is the first step towards understanding human behaviors. With the ability to track the course of gaze and head movements, our approach uses gaze and head cues to detect agent-centered attention switches that can then be utilized to segment human action sequences.

In our experiments, we notice that actions can occur in two situations: during eye fixations and during head fixations. For example, in a "picking up" action, the performer focuses on the object first then the motor system moves the hand to approach it. During the procedure of approaching and grasping, the head moves towards the object as the result of the upper body movements, but eye gaze remains stationary on the target object. The second case includes such actions as "pouring water" in which the head fixates on the object involved in the action. During the head fixation, eye-movement recordings show that there can be a number of eye fixations. For example, when the performer is pouring water, he spends 5 fixations on the different parts of the cup and 1 look-ahead fixation to the location where he will place the water pot after pouring. In this situation, the head fixation is a better cue than eye fixations to segment the actions.

Based on the above analysis, we develop an algorithm for action segmentation, which consists of the following three steps:

1. **Head fixation finding** is based on the orientations of the head. We use 3D orientations to calculate the speed profile of the head, as shown in the first two rows of Figure 1.
2. **Eye fixation finding** is accomplished by a velocity-threshold-based algorithm. A sample of the results of eye data analysis is shown in the third and fourth rows of Figure 1.
3. **Action Segmentation** is achieved by analyzing head and eye fixations, and partitioning the sequence of hand positions into the action segments(shown in the bottom row of Figure 1) based on the following three cases:
   - Within the head fixation, it may contain one or multiple eye fixations. This corresponds to actions, such as "unscrewing". "Action 3" in the bottom row of Figure 1 represents this kind of action.
   - During the head movement, the performer fixates on the specific object. This situation corresponds to actions, such as "picking up". "Action 1" and "Action 2" in the bottom row of Figure 1 represent this class of actions.
   - During the head movement, eyes are also moving. It is most probable that the performer is switching attention after the completion of the current action.

4 Task Recognition through Parallel HMMs (PaHMMs)

Based on action segmentation, the courses of both eye and hand movements are partitioned separately into short segments that correspond to action units. Our method of task recognition is based on recognizing the action units and modeling the probabilistic sequences of those action primitives in tasks. Parallel HMMs consisting of two sets of HMMs are implemented to model the movements of different body parts in parallel. One set is to model eye movements in natural tasks, which is described in subsection 4.1. The other presented in subsection 4.2 uses hand movements as input. At the end point of a task, the probability estimates of two models are combined for recognizing tasks.

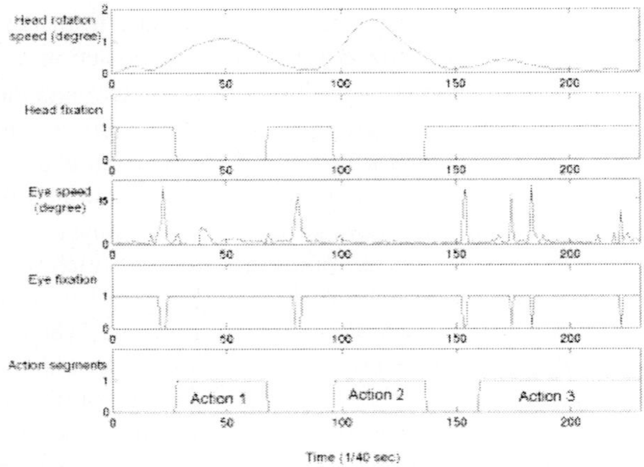

Fig. 1. Segmenting actions based on head and eye fixations. **The first two Rows:** point-to-point speeds of head data and the corresponding fixation groups(1–fixating, 0–moving).**The third and fourth rows:** eye movement speeds and the eye fixation groups(1–fixating, 0–moving) after removing saccade points. **The bottom row:** the results of action segmentation by integrating eye and head fixations.

4.1 Object Sequence Model Based on Gaze Fixations

Although there are several different modes of eye movements, the two most important for directing cognitive tasks are saccade and fixation. Saccades are rapid eye movements that allow the fovea to view a different portion of the display. Often a saccade is followed by one or multiple fixations when the objects in a scene are viewed. In the context of performing natural tasks, cognitive studies [2,3] show that the eyes always look directly at the objects being manipulated. Also, in the computer vision field, the usefulness of object context to perform action recognition is appreciated by the work of Moore et al.[9]. Based on these results, we argue that the sequence of the fixated objects in a natural task implicitly represents the agent's attention in time and provides helpful information for understanding human behaviors.

We develop discrete 6-state HMMs that model the sequences of the fixated objects. The observations of HMMs are obtained by the following steps:

1. **Eye fixation finding** is accomplished by a velocity-threshold-based algorithm. For each action unit obtained from segmentation, there can be a number of eye fixations ranging from 1 to 6.
2. **Object spotting** is implemented by analyzing snapshots with eye gaze positions during eye fixations. Figure 2 shows that the object of agent interest is spotted by using the eye position as a seed for region growing algorithm[10]. Then a color histogram and multidimensional receptive field histogram are calculated from the segmented image and combined to form a feature vector for object recognition. Further information can be obtained from [11].
3. **Observations of HMMs** are obtained by symbolizing the objects involved in tasks. In practice, we notice that there might be multiple eye fixations during an action. Distinct symbols are used to represent the possible combinations of fixated objects.

In this way, the discrete observations of HMMs consist of all the objects and their possible combinations in our experiments(described in Section 5), which include "cup", "water pot", "cup+water pot", "stapler", "paper", "stapler+paper", "jar", "lid", "jar+lid" and "nothing".

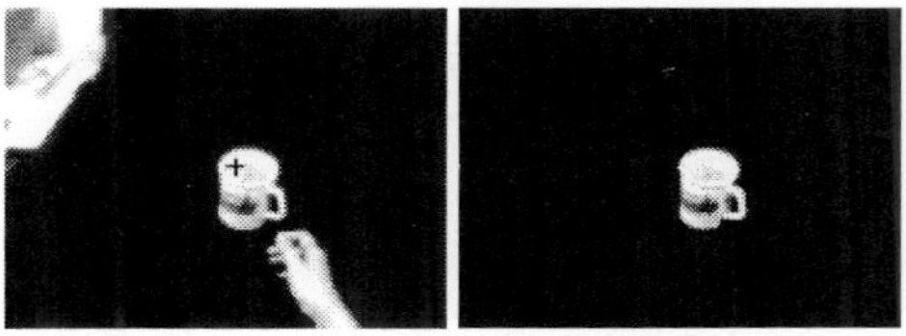

Fig. 2. Left: a snapshot with eye position(black cross) in the action of "picking up". **Right:** the object extracted from the left image.

4.2 Hand Movement Model

Figure 3 illustrates the hierarchical HMMs that are utilized to model hand movements. Firstly, a sequence of feature vectors extracted from the hand positions of each action segment is sent to low-level Hidden Markov Models(HMMs) to recognize the motion type. Then, motion types are used as observations of high-level discrete HMMs whose output will be merged with the models of other HMMs running in parallel.

We now give a brief description of the method for motion type recognition. Further information can be obtained from [11]. The six actions we sought to recognize in our experiments were: "picking up", "placing", "holding", "lining up", "stapling" and "unscrewing". We model each action as a forward-chaining continuous HMM plus a HMM for any other motions. Each HMM consists of 6 states, each of which can jump to itself and the next two forward-chaining states. Given a sequence of feature vectors extracted from hand positions, we determine which HMM most likely generates those observations by calculating the log-probability of each HMM and picking the maximum.

High-level HMMs model the probabilistic sequences of motion types in different tasks. The outputs of low-level HMMs, motion types, are used as the observation sequences of high-level HMMs, each of which is composed of 5 hidden states. The states and transition probabilities are determined by the Baum-Welch algorithm during the HMM training process.

4.3 Integration of Eye and Hand Movements Using PaHMMs

Regular HMMs are capable of modeling only one process(the movement of one body part) evolving over time. To model several processes(the movements of multiple body parts) in parallel, a simple approach is to model these parallel processes with a single HMM with multidimensional observations. This is unsatisfactory because it requires the processes evolving in lockstep. Recently, several methods of extending the basic Markov models have been proposed. Ghahraman and Jordan[12] have developed factorial Hidden

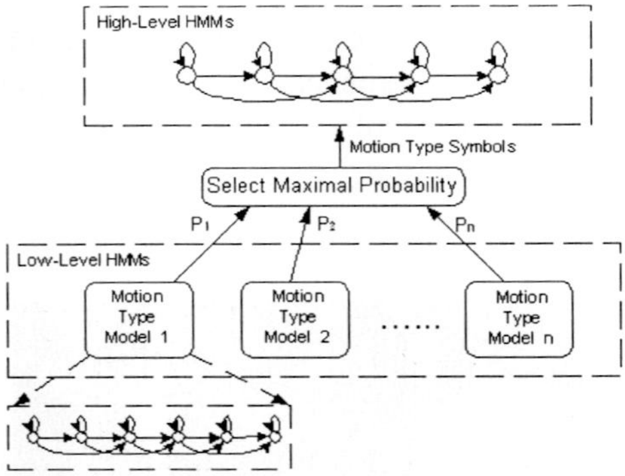

Fig. 3. The hierarchical HMM for action recognition consists of the low-level HMMs for motion types and the high-level HMMs for modeling the sequences of motion types in tasks.

Markov Models(FHMMs) that model the C processes in C separate HMMs and combine the output of the C HMMs in a single output signal. Brand, Oliver and Pentland[13] have proposed Coupled Hidden Markov Models(CHMMs) that model the C processes in C HMMs and couple the processes by introducing table conditional probabilities between their state variables. That is, the transition from state S_t^i for process i at time t to state S_{t+1}^i for process i at time $t+1$ depends on not only the state S_t^i but also the states in all other processes at time t.

In our approach, PaHMMs are applied to model and integrate the movements of different body parts. PaHMMs were first suggested by Bourlard and Dupont[14] in subband-based speech recognition. They divided the speech signals into subbands that were modeled independently. The outputs of subbands were then merged to eliminate unreliable parts of the speech signal. Vogler and Metaxas[15] first introduced PaHMMs in the computer vision field. They developed PaHMMs to model two hand movements for American Sign Language Recognition.

PaHMMs model C processes using C independent HMMs with separate output. The HMMs for the separate processes are trained independently to determine the parameters of each HMM. In the recognition phase, it is necessary to integrate information from the HMMs representing different processes. Using the likelihood-based criterion, we want to pick the model M^k maximizing:

$$\max_k \ logP(O_1, ..., O_C|M_1^k, ..., M_C^k) \tag{1}$$

where the kth PaHMM consists of $M_1^k, ..., M_C^k$, each of which is a HMM. $O_1, ..., O_C$ are observation sequences. Since each process is supposed to be independent to others, we can represent equation 1 as

$$\max_k \sum_{i=1}^{C} log(P(O_i|M_i^k)) \tag{2}$$

Figure 4 shows the approach to integrate eye and hand movements. In the merging state, the probabilities of individual HMMs are combined to yield global scores. When

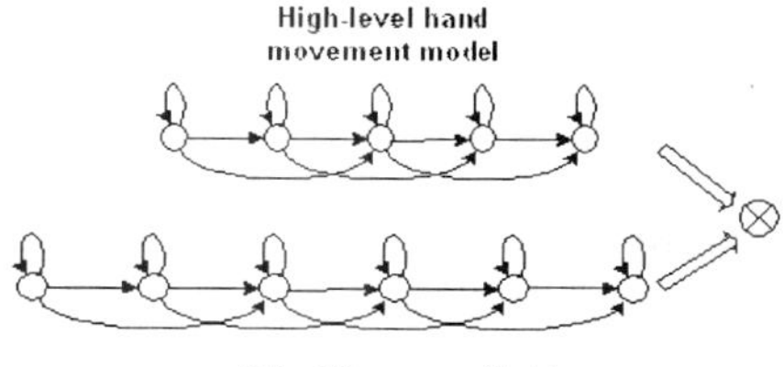

Fig. 4. Parallel HMMs. The streams of body movements are processed in parallel and integrated to yield global scores and a global recognition decision.

outputs are linearly combined, the expected error will decrease, both in theory and in practice. Therefore, the combination strategy used here is the linear weighted average:

$$\sum_{i=1}^{C} w_i log(P(O_i|M_i^k)) \quad (3)$$

where $w_i \in [0, 1]$ is a fixed weight for each stream. w_i reflects the extent to which the stream contains features that are useful for recognition. The weighting factors are computed by using maximum likelihood from the training data.

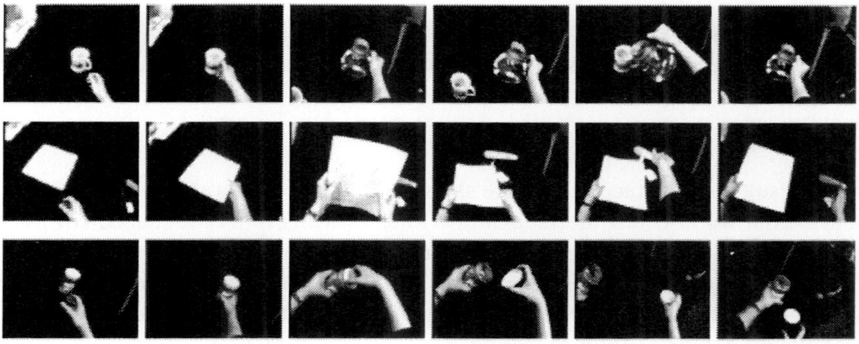

Fig. 5. The snapshots of three continuous action sequences in our experiments. **Top row:** pouring water. **Middle row:** stapling a letter. **Bottom row:** unscrewing a jar.

5 Experiments

A Polhemus 3D tracker was utilized to acquire 6-DOF hand and head positions at $40Hz$. The performer wore a head-mounted eye tracker from Applied Science Laboratories(ASL). The headband of the ASL holds a miniature "scene-camera" to the left of the performer's head that provides the video of the scene from a first-person perspective. The video signals are sampled at the resolution of 320 columns by 240 rows of pixels at the frequency of $15Hz$. The gaze positions on the image plane are reported at the frequency of $60Hz$. Before computing feature vectors for HMMs, all position signals pass through a 6th order Butterworth filter with cut-off frequency of $5Hz$.

In this study, we limited the possible tasks to those on a table. The three tasks we sought to detect were: "stapling a letter", "pouring water" and "unscrewing a jar". Figure 5 shows snapshots captured from the head-mounted camera when a subject performed three tasks. We collected 108 action sequences, 36 for each task. The first 18 sequences of each task are used for training and the rest for testing.

	Accuracy
PaHMMs	96.3%
Object Sequence HMMs	90.7%
Hand HMMs	78.5%

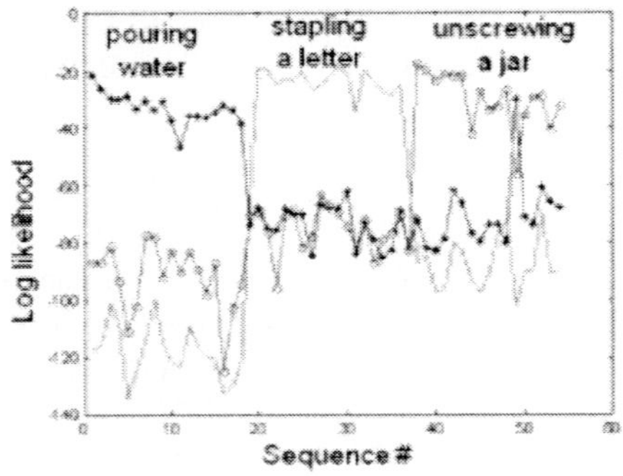

Fig. 6. Left table: the results of task recognition. **Right plot:** per-task sequence log likelihood. The sequences are sorted for ease of comparison. The left third represent the task of "pouring water", the middle third represent the task of "stapling a letter", and the right third represent the task of "unscrewing a jar".

The results of task recognition are shown in Figure 6. To evaluate the performance of PaHMMs, we also test the recognition rates of using object sequence HMMs and hand HMMs individually. PaHMMs provide a clear advantage compared with other approaches. We also note that object sequence HMMs outperform hand movement HMMs. This demonstrates that temporal object sequences implicitly indicate the performer's focus of attention during action execution and provide important information for machine understanding of human behavior.

6 Conclusion

This paper describes a novel method to recognize human behaviors in natural tasks. The approach is unique in that the coordination of eye, head and hand movements is utilized for task recognition. The integration of multistream body movements is achieved by PaHMMs, in which different streams of body movements are processed in parallel and integrated at the end point of a task. The advantages of this method are twofold. Firstly, the movement sequences of different body parts are not restricted to the same sampling rate and the underlying HMMs associated with individual sequences do not necessarily have the same topology. Secondly, merging different sources of body movements can improve the recognition rate in the way that possibly occurring noise in one stream does not degrade the performance so much since other uncorrupted streams yield sufficient information for recognition.

We are interested in learning more complicated actions in natural tasks. For future work, we will build a library of additional action units, like phonemes in speech recognition. As a result, when a performer works on different kinds of tasks over extended durations(e.g., over the course of an hour), the system could learn to recognize newly encountered actions and tasks without human involvement.

Acknowledgments. The authors wish to express their thanks to Mary Hayhoe for fruitful discussions. Brian Sullivan was a great help in building the experimental system.

References

1. Kuniyoshi, Y., Inoue, H.: Qualitative recognition of ongoing human action sequences. In: Proc. IJCAI93. (1993) 1600–1609
2. Land, M., Mennie, N., Rusted, J.: The roles of vision and eye movements in the control of activities of daily livng. Perception **28** (1999) 1311–1328
3. Hayhoe, M.: Vision visual routines: A functional account of vision. Visual Cognition **7** (2000) 43–64
4. Land, M.F., Hayhoe, M.: In what ways do eye movements contribute to everyday activities? Vision Research **41** (2001) 3559–3565
5. Brand, M.: The inverse hollywood problem: From video to scripts and storyboards via causal analysis. In: AAAI. (1997) 132–137
6. Mann, R., Jepson, A., Siskind, J.M.: The computational perception of scene dynamics. Computer Vision and Image Understanding: CVIU **65** (1997) 113–128
7. Starner, T., Pentland, A.: Real-time american sign language recognition from video using hidden markov models. In: ISCV'95. (1996)
8. Wilson, A., Bobick, A.: Learning visual behavior for gesture analysis. In: Proceedings of the IEEE Symposium on Computer Vision, Florida, USA (1995)
9. Moore, D., Essa, I., Hayes, M.: Exploiting human actions and object context for recognition tasks. In: In Proceedings of IEEE International Conference on Computer Vision 1999 (ICCV 99), Corfu, Greece (1999)
10. Adams, R., Bischof, L.: Seeded region growing. IEEE Transaction on Pattern Analysis and Machine Intelligence 16 (1994)
11. Yu, C., Ballard, D.H.: Learning to recognize human action sequences. In: Proceedings of the 2nd International Conference on Development and Learning, Boston, U.S. (2002) 28–34
12. Ghahramani, Z., Jordan, M.I.: Factorial hidden markov models. In Touretzky, D.S., Mozer, M.C., Hasselmo, M.E., eds.: Advances in Neural Information Processing Systems. Volume 8., The MIT Press (1996) 472–478
13. Brand, M., Oliver, N., Pentland, A.: Coupled hidden markov models for complex action recognition. In: IEEE CVPR97. (1997)
14. Bourlard, H., Dupont, S.: Subband-based speech recognition. In: Proc. ICASSP'97, Munich, Germany (1997) 1251–1254
15. Vogler, C., Metaxas, D.N.: Parallel hidden markov models for american sign language recognition. In: ICCV (1). (1999) 116–122

Vision-Based Homing with a Panoramic Stereo Sensor

Wolfgang Stürzl and Hanspeter A. Mallot

Universität Tübingen, Zoologisches Institut, Kognitive Neurowissenschaften, 72076 Tübingen, Germany
wolfgang.stuerzl@uni-tuebingen.de
http://www.uni-tuebingen.de/cog/

Abstract. A panoramic stereo sensor is presented which enables a Khepera robot to extract geometric landmark information ("disparity signatures") of its surroundings. By comparing the current panoramic disparity signature to memorized signatures the robot is able to return to already visited places ("homing"). Evaluating a database of panoramic stereo images recorded by the robot we compare homing performance of the proposed disparity-based approach with a solely image-based method considering the size of catchment areas. Although the image-based technique yields larger catchment areas, disparity-based homing achieves a much higher degree of invariance with respect to illumination changes. To increase homing performance, we suggest an extended homing scheme integrating both landmark types.

1 Introduction

There is strong evidence that rodents, see e.g. [1], [2], and also humans, e.g. [3], use memorized geometric cues to return to already visited places. Various mechanisms for visually estimating distances to surrounding objects are known, e.g. motion parallax, stereopsis, shape from shading (see [4] for an overview). It has been claimed that geometric landmark information has certain advantages compared to pure image or texture information because of its higher invariance regarding illumination changes or seasonal variations. In robotics, localization is usually based on distance measurements acquired with active sensors like ultrasonic or laser range finder. In this paper we investigate the use of geometric landmark information for recognizing known places and finding back to them ("homing navigation") using a small Khepera robot with a passive panoramic stereo sensor (see Fig. 1 a).

2 Panoramic Stereo Sensor

Panoramic visual information has been shown to be advantageous for various navigation tasks in insects, e.g. [5], [6], and in robotics, e.g. [7],[8]. In order to acquire geometric information of the robot's current place we have built a

H.H. Bülthoff et al. (Eds.): BMCV 2002, LNCS 2525, pp. 620–628, 2002.

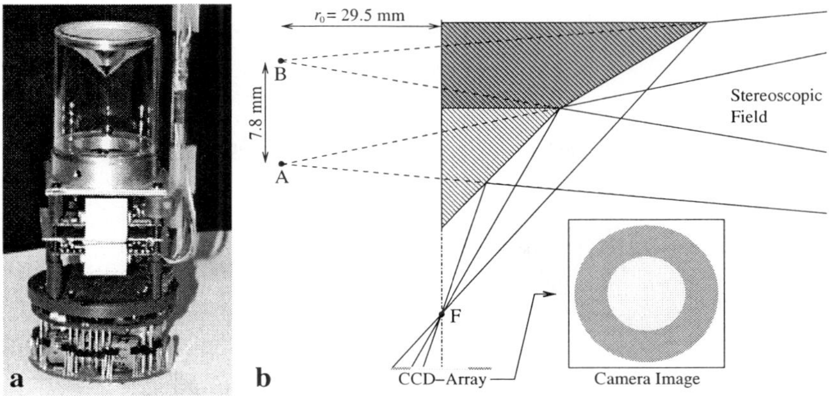

Fig. 1. a: Khepera with panoramic stereo camera on top (diameter ≈ 5 cm, height ≈ 13 cm). **b:** Schematic diagram of the bipartite mirror for an axial plane (not to scale). The imaging can be considered as "looking" through two vertically separated points (A, B) which are mirror images of the nodal point of the camera (F). The inset shows the resulting panoramic stereo image: The inner filled circle (light grey) depicts the part imaged through the lower cone; the outer part (dark grey) is imaged through the upper cone.

panoramic stereo sensor. A similar, but much larger omnidirectional stereo system with two cameras and parabolic mirrors has been presented in [9]. A single camera system is described e.g. in [10] where stereo panoramas are created from a video stream captured by a rotating video camera. However, to the authors' knowledge, none of these panoramic stereo imaging systems were used for navigation purposes on a robot.

Mounted on top of the Khepera, a CCD-camera is directed vertically towards a bipartite conic mirror (see Fig. 1 a). It consists of two conical parts with slightly different slopes (48.5° and 54.5° respectively) yielding an effective vertical stereo base line of ≈ 8 mm (Fig. 1 b).

3 Disparity Signatures of Places

As depicted in Fig. 2 a, raw stereo images, taken by the panoramic stereo sensor, are divided into $N = 72$ sectors (representing a 5° range horizontally). Each sector is subdivided into radial elements resulting in an array of 100 grey-scale pixels $I(x)$, $x = 0, 1, \ldots, 99$ (Fig. 2 b).

We have implemented a simple correlation based stereo algorithm to estimate the mean shift d (disparity) of the two image parts by minimization of the matching error (see Fig. 2 b,c),

$$d_{\min} := \arg\min_{d} E_{\mathrm{m}}(d) \tag{1}$$

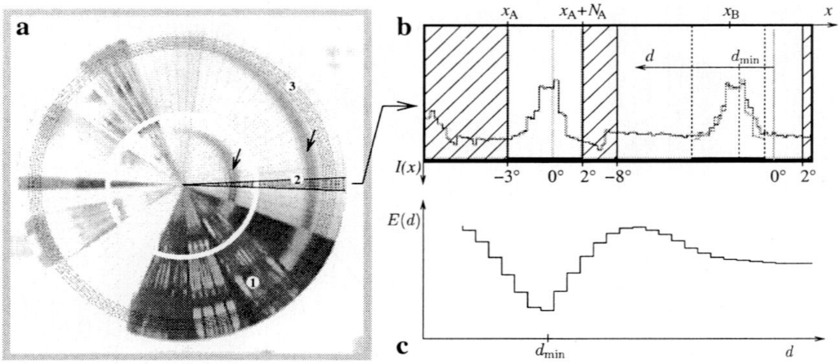

Fig. 2. a: Raw stereo image. Images of the toy houses can be seen in the lower right part (1). In the marked sector element (2), a horizontal line on the arena wall is imaged twice (arrows). The marked pixels on the 5 circles (3) are used to compute the image signature for image-based homing as described in Sect. 5. **b:** Grey values corresponding to the sector element in **a**. Linear search for maximum correlation (error function plotted in **c**) between the inner and outer part yields the disparity. The hatched parts are excluded because of low horizontal resolution in the image center (left) and because of imaging distortions at the transition area of the two different slopes of the mirror (middle).

$$E_{\mathrm{m}}(d) := \sum_{x=0}^{N_{\mathrm{A}}-1} \left(I(x_{\mathrm{A}}+x) - I(x_{\mathrm{B}}-d+x)\right)^2 , \qquad (2)$$

where $N_A = 20$ is the width of a window taken from the inner image, x_{B} is the outer image which has zero disparity with respect to x_{A} (start of inner image). Due to the set-up of the imaging mirrors only a one dimensional correspondence search is needed yielding a disparity range of $N_d = 30$ pixels, i.e. $d \in [0, 29]$. For each estimated disparity $d_{\mathrm{min},i}$, $i = 0, 1, \ldots, N-1$, we compute a quality value $q \in [0, 1]$ depending on uniqueness and reliability of the found match.

After the stereo computation, the current place can be represented in memory by $N = 72$ disparities and their corresponding quality values[1], $(\mathbf{d}, \mathbf{q}) = \{(d_i, q_i), i = 0, 1, \ldots, N-1\}$, which we call a "disparity signature" of the considered location. Due to occlusion caused by the cable for video transmission to the host computer (as can be seen in Fig. 1 a), no disparity calculation is possible in a range of 15° and the corresponding three quality values are set to zero.

Using elementary trigonometry, distances r to surrounding objects can be computed according to

$$r(d) \approx \alpha/d - r_0 , \quad \alpha \approx 2100\,\mathrm{mm} \times \mathrm{pixel} , \qquad (3)$$

[1] To simplify notation we omit the index 'min' in the following.

where $r_0 = 29.5\,\mathrm{mm}$ is the distance between the virtual nodal points (A,B) and the robot axis (see Fig. 1 b). The corresponding error,

$$\Delta r(d) = \left|\frac{\partial r(d)}{\partial d}\right| \Delta d \approx \alpha/d^2\, \Delta d \approx r(d)^2/\alpha\, \Delta d \ , \tag{4}$$

increases approximately with the square of distance.

4 Homing Algorithm

By comparing the current signature with a stored one, it should be possible to return to the place where the signature has been memorized within a certain neighborhood. To investigate this we have extended the homing algorithm described in [7] for the use of disparities:

Using the current disparity signature $(\mathbf{d}, \mathbf{q})$, we compute for several possible movements of the robot (turns by angle φ followed by a straight move of length l) predicted signatures $\{(\mathbf{d}^{\mathrm{c}}(\varphi_i, l_i), \mathbf{q}^{\mathrm{c}}(\varphi_i, l_i)), i = 0, 1, \ldots N_{\mathrm{c}} - 1\}$ using (3) and trigonometric calculus. Occlusions are dealt with by setting the corresponding quality values to zero. To avoid wrong disparity predictions due to uncertain disparities (low quality value) we have excluded disparities with $q < 0.7$. The similarities of the predicted signatures to the stored signature at the home position, $(\mathbf{d}^{\mathrm{h}}, \mathbf{q}^{\mathrm{h}})$, are estimated according to[2]

$$E_{\mathrm{h}}^{\mathrm{d}}(\varphi_i, l_i) := \min_s \sum_{k=0}^{N-1} q_k^{\mathrm{h}}\, q_{k_s}^{\mathrm{c}}(\varphi_i, l_i) \left(d_k^{\mathrm{h}} - d_{k_s}^{\mathrm{c}}(\varphi_i, l_i)\right)^2 \Big/ \sum_{k=0}^{N-1} q_k^{\mathrm{h}}\, q_{k_s}^{\mathrm{c}}(\varphi_i, l_i) \ , \tag{5}$$

where $k_s := (k + s) \bmod N$, $s = 0, 1, \ldots N - 1$[3]. In the current implementation the considered positions ($N_{\mathrm{c}} = 132$), lie on a hexagonal grid within a radius of approximately 10 cm. Subsequently the robot moves to the position $(\varphi_{\mathrm{opt}}, l_{\mathrm{opt}})$, which minimizes (5). We will call $(\varphi_{\mathrm{opt}}, l_{\mathrm{opt}})$ the "homing vector". To reduce influence of single wrong decisions, the covered distance is limited to $l < 5\,\mathrm{cm}$. These steps are repeated until the position of highest similarity deviates only marginally from the current position, i.e. $l_{\mathrm{opt}} < l_{\mathrm{thresh}} = 5\,\mathrm{mm}$.

5 Results

In order to test the panoramic stereo sensor and the proposed homing algorithm systematically, a database consisting of 1250 panoramic stereo images was automatically recorded by the Khepera robot inside a toy house arena with an approximate size of 140 cm × 120 cm, see Fig. 3 a. Recording positions were approximately on a rectangular 44 × 36 grid with cell size $2.5 \times 2.5\,\mathrm{cm}^2$. Minimum

[2] Since, as can be seen from (4) and Fig. 3, large distances are prone to errors, we compare disparities directly.

[3] If additional information, e.g. from odometry, about the robot's position or orientation relative to the landmark is available the range of φ, l and s can be restricted.

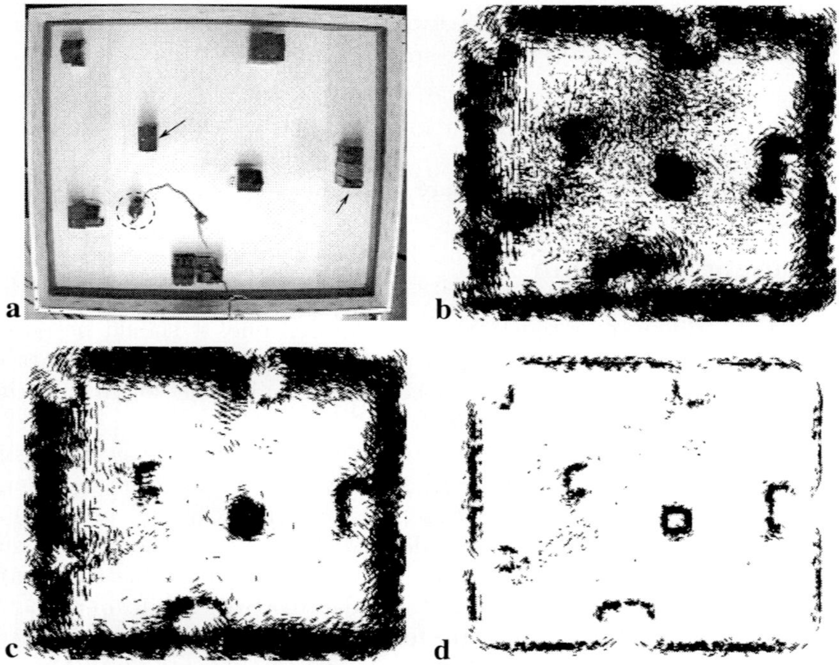

Fig. 3. a: The toy-house arena (approximate size of 140 cm × 120 cm) seen from the tracking camera at the ceiling. Arrows indicate non-textured walls of toy-houses; the Khepera robot is marked by the circle. **b-d:** Superposition of object positions measured from all robot positions of the database using (3). **b:** Distances $r(d_k)$ up to 40 cm are shown. **c:** Restricting the plotting to distances, where the quality values of corresponding disparities $q_k > 0.9$, reduces the number of false distance estimations. **d:** Additional restriction to distances $r(d_k) \leq 20$ cm decreases the scattering caused by low distance resolution for larger distances, Eq. (4).

distance of recording positions to walls were ≈ 15 cm, minimum distances to houses were ≈ 5 cm. The accuracy of the tracking system used for the estimation of the robot's pose is ≈ 2 mm (position) and 1.5° (orientation).

5.1 Geometry from Panoramic Stereo

A superposition of object positions calculated from disparity signatures using (3) is shown in Fig. 3 b-d. Increasing the quality threshold significantly reduces the number of wrong distance estimates (Fig. 3 c), although the low resolution for large distances is still obvious[4]. Since the basic geometry of the environment is revealed, the panoramic stereo sensor could be used for map building e.g. based on an occupancy grid.

[4] We have made no attempt to achieve sub-pixel accuracy from the stereo matching since it is unnecessary for the proposed homing algorithm.

5.2 Catchment Area Size and Homing Accuracy

We have simulated homing runs for all stereo images in the database, starting from every recording position.

Each time the simulated agent has traveled the homing vector, as described in Sect. 4, the distance to the nearest neighboring node in the data base is considered. If the distance exceeds 2 cm, the homing run is stopped ("run into obstacle"), otherwise the agent is placed at the position of the nearest node. If a single homing movement has not brought the agent to a different node the homing run is also stopped ("homing finished"). Hence small homing vectors in the correct direction, which – if occurring repeatedly – could have led the robot closer to the correct position in the real arena, go unnoticed.

We define the *catchment area*, which is usually a coherent region, as the set of all starting nodes, for which the home was reached up to a residual error of 10 cm or less, and their surrounding grid cells.

Comparison with imaged-based homing: In order to investigate homing performance for different signatures, we have also implemented a pure image-based homing scheme, similar to that introduced in [7]: 1D-images consisting of $N = 72$ pixels, each of them representing a $5°$ region (vertically) around the horizon, were extracted from panoramic stereo images (see Fig.2 a) and normalized using histogram equalization. The three grey values in the range occluded by the video cable were estimated using linear interpolation between the neighboring grey values. To calculate homing movements, (5) was replaced by the sum of squared (grey value) distances (I^{h} denotes image at home position),

$$E_{\mathrm{h}}^{\mathrm{i}}(\varphi_i, l_i) := \min_s \sum_{k=0}^{N-1} \left(I_k^{\mathrm{h}} - I_{k_s}^{\mathrm{c}}(\varphi_i, l_i)\right)^2 . \tag{6}$$

Predicted images I^{c} were computed using the assumption that all surrounding objects are located at the same distance D (D was set to 15 cm).

In Tab. 1 homing performance with respect to catchment area size are compared [5]. Two different illumination conditions are considered: Same illumination during recording and homing ("constant illum.") and strongly different illumination ("changed illum.") caused by a position change of the light source from above the arena to the "north".

As can be seen from Tab. 1, without illumination changes mean catchment area size of solely image-based homing is larger but breaks down under strong illumination changes whereas the disparity-based approach stays approximately at the same performance level. Examples of catchment areas and homing vectors for both illumination conditions are shown in Fig. 4.

[5] Values for homing runs of the Khepera are in a comparable range.

Table 1. Comparison of disparity and image-based homing at different illumination conditions (simulated homing runs with stereo images recorded by the Khepera): Large catchment areas are desirable. Mean values and standard deviation are given. For the illumination changes also the number of nodes without catchment area is listed (which did not occur for constant illumination).

		disparity-based	image-based	combination
constant illum.	catchment area size (number of grid cells)	198 ± 71	242 ± 59	223 ± 68
changed illum.	catchment area size (number of grid cells)	198 ± 64	23 ± 45	195 ± 68
	number of nodes (out of 1250) without catchment area	0	580	0

Combining image and disparity-based homing: In order to exploit the advantages of both signature types we combine both homing strategies:

$$(\varphi_{\mathrm{opt}}, l_{\mathrm{opt}}) := \arg\max_{(\varphi_i, l_i)} \Pi\Big(\frac{E_{\mathrm{h}}^{\mathrm{d}}(\varphi_i, l_i)}{\sigma_{\mathrm{h}}^{\mathrm{d}}}\Big)\, \Pi\Big(\frac{E_{\mathrm{h}}^{\mathrm{i}}(\varphi_i, l_i)}{\sigma_{\mathrm{h}}^{\mathrm{i}}}\Big) \tag{7}$$

$$\Pi(x) := (1-\epsilon)\frac{1}{1+x^2} + \epsilon \ . \tag{8}$$

For the results listed in Tab. 1 we have used the parameter values $\sigma_{\mathrm{h}}^{\mathrm{i}} = 10^4$, $\sigma_{\mathrm{h}}^{\mathrm{d}} = 1$ and $\epsilon = 0.01$.

6 Concluding Remarks and Future Work

Seeking for invariance properties of landmark information is essential for an efficient spatial representation of an environment. We have shown that robustness regarding illumination changes can be achieved using disparity signatures acquired by a panoramic stereo sensor. Since its effective stereo base line is only $\approx 8\,\mathrm{mm}$, the panoramic stereo sensor is limited to environments where distances are comparatively small ($< 1\,\mathrm{m}$). For navigation tasks in office environments we have built another single camera stereo sensor consisting of two separate mirrors with an effective stereo base line of $\approx 36\,\mathrm{mm}$.

Although we have shown that stereoscopic panoramic vision can be used as a rather minimalistic approach for acquiring useful spatial representations, stereo vision in animals is usually restricted to a small field of view. Dealing with a limited field of view for image and disparity based homing will be an integral part of future work. In addition, since many animals have no or only limited stereoscopic vision we will consider the use of optical flow for acquiring geometric landmark information. In both cases, strategies based on limited fields of view rather than on panoramic signatures will become necessary. Future work

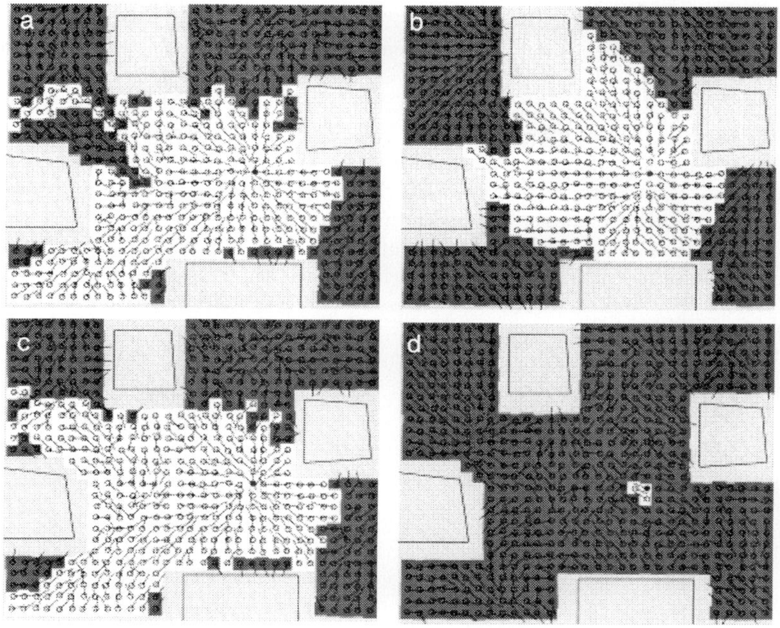

Fig. 4. Comparison of catchment areas (white regions) for a home node (black dot) in the lower left part of the arena: Same illumination during recoding and homing: **a:** disparity-based, **b:** image-based. Different illumination during recoding and homing: **c:** disparity-based, **d:** image-based (catchment area consists of only 3 grid cells). Houses are marked by polygons, small circles mark recording positions of images in the data base. Orientation and length (limited to 3 cm) of the homing vector is depicted as a line starting from the center of each node.

will therefore use a view based approach to spatial memory, as was introduced by [11].

References

1. Cheng, K.: A purely geometric module in the rat's spatial representation. Cognition **23** (1986) 149–178
2. Collett, T.S., Cartwright, B.A., Smith, B.A.: Landmark learning and visuo-spatial memories in gerbils. J. Comp. Physiol. A **158** (1986) 835–851
3. Hermer, L., Spelke, E.S.: A geometric process for spatial reorientation in young children. Nature **370** (1994) 57–59
4. Mallot, H.: Computational Vision. Information Processing in Perception and Visual Behavior. MIT Press, Cambridge, MA (2000)
5. Cartwright, B.A., Collett, T.S.: Landmark learning in bees. J. Comp. Physiol. A **151** (1983) 521–543
6. Dahmen, H., Wüst, R.W., Zeil, J.: Extracting egomotion parameters from optic flow: principal limits for animals and machines. In Srinivasan, M.V., Venkatesh, S., eds.: From living eyes to seeing machines. Oxford University Press (1997) 174–198

7. Franz, M.O., Schölkopf, B., Mallot, H.A., Bülthoff, H.H.: Where did I take that snapshot? Scene-based homing by image matching. Biol. Cybern. **79** (1998) 191–202
8. Adorni, G., Cagnoni, S., Enderle, S., Kraetzschmar, G.K., Mordonini, M., Plagge, M., Ritter, M., Sablatnög, S., Zell, A.: Vision-based localization for mobile robots. Robotics and Autonomous Systems **36** (2001) 103–119
9. Gluckman, J., Nayar, S., Thorek, K.: Real-time omnidirectional and panoramic stereo. In: DARPA Image Understanding Workshop. (1998) 299–303
10. Peleg, S., Ben-Ezra, M.: Stereo panorama with a single camera. In: IEEE Conference on Computer Vision and Pattern Recognition. (1999) 395–401
11. Schölkopf, B., Mallot, H.A.: View-based cognitive mapping and path planning. Adaptive Behavior **3** (1995) 311–348

Unsupervised Learning of Visual Structure

Shimon Edelman[1], Nathan Intrator[2,3], and Judah S. Jacobson[4]

[1] Department of Psychology
Cornell University, Ithaca, NY 14853, USA
[2] Institute for Brain and Neural Systems
Brown University, Providence, RI 02912, USA
[3] School of Computer Science
Tel-Aviv University, Tel Aviv 69978, Israel
[4] Department of Mathematics
Harvard University, Cambridge, MA 02138, USA

Abstract. To learn a visual code in an unsupervised manner, one may attempt to capture those features of the stimulus set that would contribute significantly to a statistically efficient representation (as dictated, e.g., by the Minimum Description Length principle). Paradoxically, all the candidate features in this approach need to be known before statistics over them can be computed. This paradox may be circumvented by confining the repertoire of candidate features to actual scene fragments, which resemble the "what+where" receptive fields found in the ventral visual stream in primates. We describe a single-layer network that learns such fragments from unsegmented raw images of structured objects. The learning method combines fast imprinting in the feedforward stream with lateral interactions to achieve single-epoch unsupervised acquisition of spatially localized features that can support systematic treatment of structured objects [1].

1 A Paradox and Some Ways of Resolving It

It is logically impossible to form a principled structural description of a visual scene without prior knowledge of related scenes. Adapting an observation made by R. A. Fisher, such knowledge must, in the first instance, be statistical. Several recent studies indeed showed that subjects are capable of unsupervised acquisition of statistical regularities (e.g., conditional probabilities of constituents) that can support structural interpretation of novel scenes composed of a few simple objects [2,3]. Theoretical understanding of unsupervised statistical learning is, however, hindered by a paradox perceived as "monstrous and unmeaning" already in the Socratic epistemology: statistics can only be computed over a set of candidate primitive descriptors if these are identified in advance, yet the identification of the candidates requires prior statistical data (cf. [4]).

The sense of paradox is well captured by the following passage from Plato's *Theaetetus* (360BC), in which Socrates points out the circularity in treating syllables as combinations of letters, if the latter are to be defined merely as parts of syllables:

H.H. Bülthoff et al. (Eds.): BMCV 2002, LNCS 2525, pp. 629–642, 2002.

Soc. ... there is one point in what has been said which does not quite satisfy me.

The. What was it?

Soc. What might seem to be the most ingenious notion of all: – that the elements or letters are unknown, but the combination or syllables known [...] can he be ignorant of either singly and yet know both together?

The. Such a supposition, Socrates, is monstrous and unmeaning.

Soc. But if he cannot know both without knowing each, then if he is ever to know the syllable, he must know the letters first; and thus the fine theory [that there can be no knowledge apart from definition and true opinion] has again taken wings and departed.

The. Yes, with wonderful celerity.

Figure 1 illustrates the paradox at hand in the context of scene interpretation. To decide whether the image on the left is better seen as containing horses (and riders) rather than centaurs requires tracking the representational utility of `horse` over a sequence of images. But for that one must have already acquired the notion of `horse` — an undertaking that we aimed to alleviate in the first place, by running statistics over multiple stimuli. In what follows, we describe a way of breaking out of this vicious circle, suggested by computational and neurobiological considerations.

Fig. 1. An intuitive illustration of the fundamental problem of unsupervised discovery of the structural units best suited for describing a visual scene (cf. *Left*). Is the being in the forefront of this picture integral or composite? The visual system of the Native Americans, who in their first encounter reportedly perceived mounted Spaniards as centaur-like creatures (cf. [5], p.127), presumably acted on a principle that prescribes an integral interpretation, in the absence of evidence to the contrary. A sophisticated visual system should perceive such evidence in the appearance of certain candidate units in multiple contexts (cf. *Middle*, where the conquistadors are seen dismounted). Units should not have to appear in isolation (*Right*) to be seen as independent.

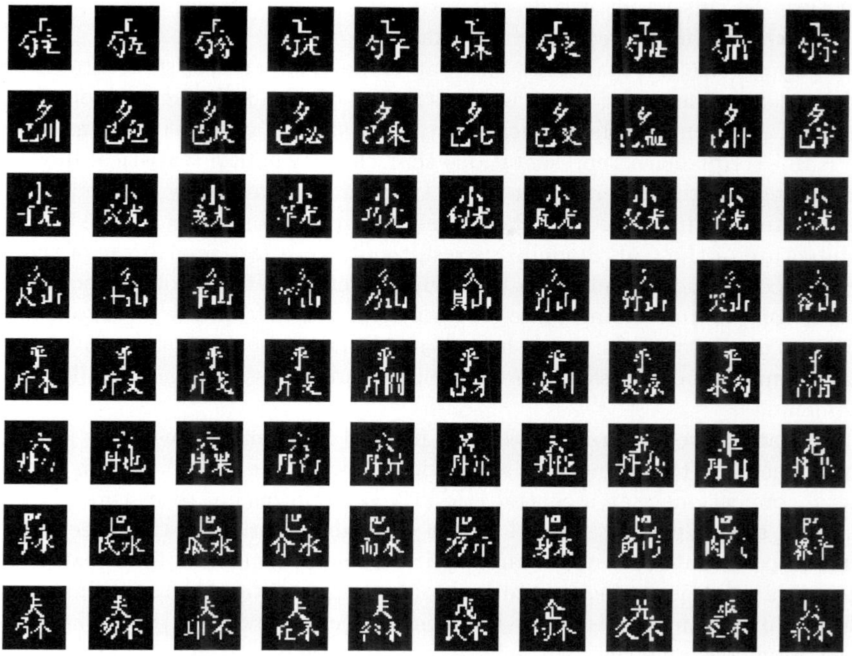

Fig. 2. The challenge of unsupervised learning of shape fragments that could be useful for representing structured objects is exemplified by this set of 80 images, showing triplets of Kanji characters. A recent psychophysical study [3] showed that observers unfamiliar with the Kanji script learn representations that capture the pair-wise conditional probability between the characters over this set, tending to treat frequently co-occurring characters as wholes. This learning takes place after a single exposure to the images in a randomly ordered sequence.

1.1 Computational Considerations

The choice of primitives or features in terms of which composite objects and their structure are to be described is the central issue at the intersection of high-level vision and computational learning theory. Studies of unsupervised feature extraction (see e.g. [6] for a review) typically concentrate on the need for supporting recognition, that is, telling objects apart. Here, we are concerned with the complementary need — seeking to capture commonalities between objects — which stems from the coupled constraints of making explicit object structure, as per the principle of systematicity [1], and maintaining representational economy, as per the Minimum Description Length (MDL) principle [7].

One biologically relevant representational framework that aims for systematicity while observing parsimony is the Chorus of Fragments (CoF [8,1]). In the CoF model, the graded responses of "what+where" cells [9,10] coarsely tuned both to shape and to location form a distributed representation of stimulus structure. In this paper, we describe a method for unsupervised acquisition of "what+where" receptive fields from examples.

To appreciate the challenges inherent in the unsupervised structural learning task, consider the set of 80 images of triplets of Kanji characters appearing in Figure 2. A recent psychophysical study showed that observers unfamiliar with the Kanji script learn representations that capture subtle statistical dependencies among the characters, after being exposed to a randomly ordered sequence of these images just once [3]. When translated into a constraint on the functional architecture of the CoF model, this result calls for a fast *imprinting* of the feed-forward connections leading to the "what+where" cells. Another requirement, that of *competition* among same-location cells, arises from the need to achieve a sufficient diversity of the local shape basis. Finally, *cooperation* among far-apart cells, seems to be necessary to detect co-occurrences among spatially distinct fragments.

The latter two requirements can be fulfilled by lateral connections [11] whose sign depends on the retinotopic separation between the cells they link. Although lateral connections play a central role in many approaches to feature extraction [6], their role is usually limited to the orthogonalization of the selectivities of different cells that receive the same input. In one version of our model, such short-range inhibition is supplemented by longer-range excitation, a combination that is found in certain models of low-level vision (see the review in [11]). These lateral connections are relevant, we believe, to the understanding of neural response properties and plasticity higher up in the ventral processing stream, in areas V4 and TEO/TE.

1.2 Biological Motivation

We now briefly survey the biological support for the functional model proposed above.

- *Joint coding of shape and location information.* Cells with "what+where" receptive fields, originally found in the prefrontal cortex [9], are also very common in the inferotemporal areas [10].
- *Lateral interactions.* The anatomical substrate for the lateral interactions proposed here exists in the form of "intrinsic" connections at all levels of the visual cortical hierarchy [12]. Physiologically, the "inverted Mexican hat" spatial pattern of lateral inputs converging on a given cell, of the kind used in our first model (described in section 2.1) is consistent with the reports of selective connections linking V1 cells with like response properties (see, e.g., the chapter by Polat et al. in [11]). The specific role of neighborhood (lateral) competition in shaping the response profiles of TE neurons is supported by findings such as that of selective augmentation of neuron responses by locally blocking GABA, a neurotransmitter that mediates inhibition [18].
- *Fast learning.* Fast synaptic modification following various versions of the Hebb rule [13], which we used in one of the models described below, has been reported in the visual cortex [14] and elsewhere in the brain [15]. Evidence

in support of the biological relevance of the other learning rule we tested, BCM [16] is also available [17].

2 Learning "What+Where" Receptive Fields

Intuitively, spatial ("where") selectivity of the "what+where" cell can be provided by properly weighting its feedforward connections, so as to create a window corresponding to a fragment of the input image; shape ("what") selectivity can then be obtained by fast learning (ultimately from a single example) that would create, within that window, a template for the stimulus fragment. The networks we experimented with consisted of nine groups of such cells, arranged on a loose grid (Figure 3, left). In the experiments described here the networks contained either 3 or 8 cells per location. Each cell saw the entire input image through a window corresponding to the cell's location; for reasons of biological plausibility, the windows were graded (Gaussian; see Figure 4, left). Results obtained with the two learning rules we studied, of the Hebbian and BCM varieties, are described in sections 2.1 and 2.2, respectively.

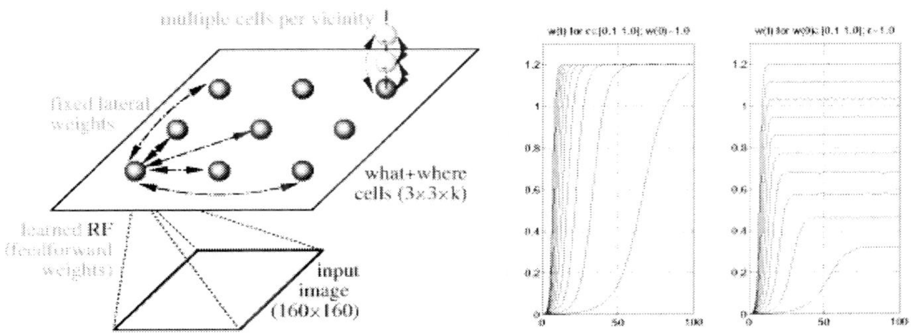

Fig. 3. *Left:* The Hebbian network consisted of groups of "what+where" cells arranged retinotopically, on a 3×3 loose grid, over the input image. Each cell received the 160×160 "retinal" input, initially weighted by a Gaussian window (Figure 4, left). In addition, the cells were fully interconnected by lateral links, weighted by a difference of Gaussians, so that weights between nearby cells were inhibitory, and between far-apart cells excitatory (Figure 4, right). *Right:* A numerical solution for the feedforward connection weight $w(t)$ given a constant input $x = 1$, with the learning rate ϵ (left pane) and $w(0)$ (right pane) varying in 10 steps between 0.1 and 1 (see eqns. 1 and 2).

2.1 Hebbian Learning

For use with the Hebbian rule, the "what+where" cells were fully interconnected by lateral links with weights following the inverted Mexican hat profile (Figure 4, right). Given an input image $\mathbf{x}$, the output of cell i was computed as:

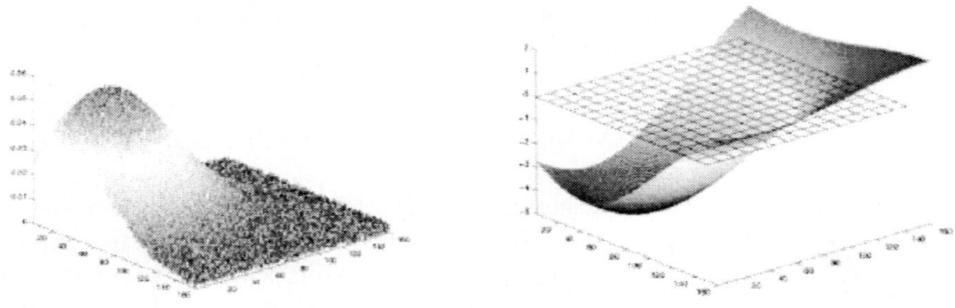

Fig. 4. *Left:* The initial (pre-exposure) feedforward weights constituting the receptive field (RF) of the cell in the lower left corner of the 3×3 grid (cf. Figure 3). The initial RF had the shape of a Gaussian whose standard deviation was 40 pixels (equal to the retinal separation of adjacent cells on the grid). The centers of the RFs were randomly shifted by up to ±10 pixels in each retinal coordinate according to a uniform distribution. The Gaussian was superimposed on random noise with amplitude uniformly distributed between 0 and 0.01. *Right:* The lateral weights in the Hebbian network, converging on the cell whose initial RF is shown on the left, plotted as a function of the retinotopic location of the source cell.

$$\begin{aligned} y_i &= \tanh(c_+) \\ c_+ &= c\ \mathrm{sign}(c) \\ c &= (\mathbf{x}.\mathbf{w}_i + \textstyle\sum_{j \neq i} v_{ij} y_j) - \theta \\ \theta(t) &= 0.5(\max\{c(t-h), \ldots, c(t-1)\} - \min\{c(t-h), \ldots, c(t-1)\}) \end{aligned} \tag{1}$$

where $\mathbf{w}_i$ is the synaptic weight vector, $\theta(t)$ is a history-dependent threshold (set to the mean of the last h values of c), $v_{ij} = G(d_{ij}, 1.6\sigma) - G(d_{ij}, \sigma)$ is the strength of the lateral connection between cells i and j; $G(x, \sigma)$ is the value at x of a Gaussian of width σ centered at 0 (the dependence of v on d is illustrated in Figure 4, right).

The training consisted of showing the images to the network in a random order, in a single pass (epoch), as in the psychophysical study [3]. Each input was held for a small number of "dwell cycles" (2-5), to allow the lateral interactions to take effect. In each such cycle, the feedforward weights w_{mn} for pixels x_{mn} were modified according to this rule:

$$w_{mn}(t+1) = w_{mn}(t) + \eta(y x_{mn}(t) w_{mn}(0) - y^2 w_{mn}(t)) \tag{2}$$

In this rule, the initial (Gaussian) weight matrix, $\mathbf{w}(0)$, determines the effective synaptic modification rate throughout the learning process. To visualize the dynamics of this process, we integrated eq. 2 numerically; the results, plotted in Figure 3, right, support the intuition just stated. Note that eq. 2 resembles Oja's self-regulating version of the Hebbian rule, and is local to each synapse, hence particularly appealing from the standpoint of biological modeling. Note also that the dynamic nature of the threshold $\theta(t)$ and the presence of a nonlinearity in eq. 1 resemble the BCM rule of [19].

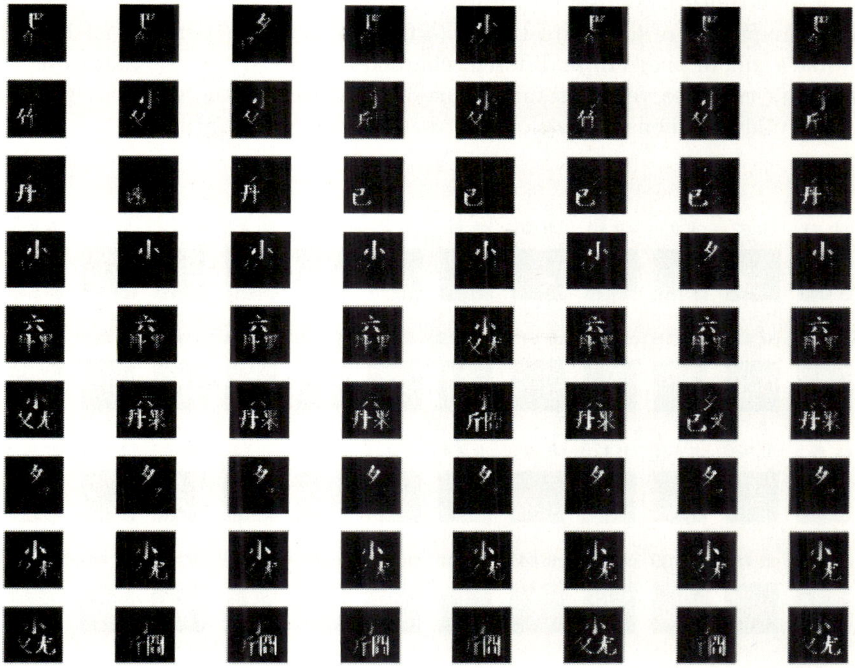

Fig. 5. The receptive fields of a 72-cell Hebbian network (8 cells per location) that has been exposed to the images of Figure 2. Each row shows the RFs formed for one of the image locations.

The receptive fields (RFs) of the "what+where" cells acquired in a typical run through a single exposure of the Hebbian network to a randomly ordered sequence of the 80 images of Figure 2, are shown in Figure 5. Characters more frequent in the training set (such as the ones appearing in the top locations in Figure 2) were generally the first to be learned. Importantly, the learned RFs are relatively "crisp," with the template for one (or two) of the characters from the training data standing out clearly from the background. Pixels from other characters are attenuated (and can probably be discarded by thresholding). A parametric exploration determined that (1) the learning rate η in eq. 2 had to be close to 1.0 for meaningful fragments to be learned; (2) the results were only slightly affected by varying the number of dwell cycles between 2 and 20; (3) the formation of distinct RFs for the same location depended on the competitive influence of the lateral connections.

To visualize concisely the outcome of 20 learning runs of the network (equivalent to running an ensemble of 20 networks in parallel), we submitted the resulting 1440 RFs (each of dimensionality $160 \times 160 = 25600$) to a k-means routine, set to extract 72 clusters. Among the RFs thus identified (Figure 6), one finds templates for single-character shapes (e.g., #1, 14), for character pairs with a high mutual conditional probability in the data set (e.g., #7), an occasional "snapshot" of an entire triplet (#52), as well as a minority of RFs that look like a mix of pixels from different characters (#50, 51). Note that even these latter RFs could serve as useful features for projecting the data on, given the extremely high dimensionality of the raw data space (25600).

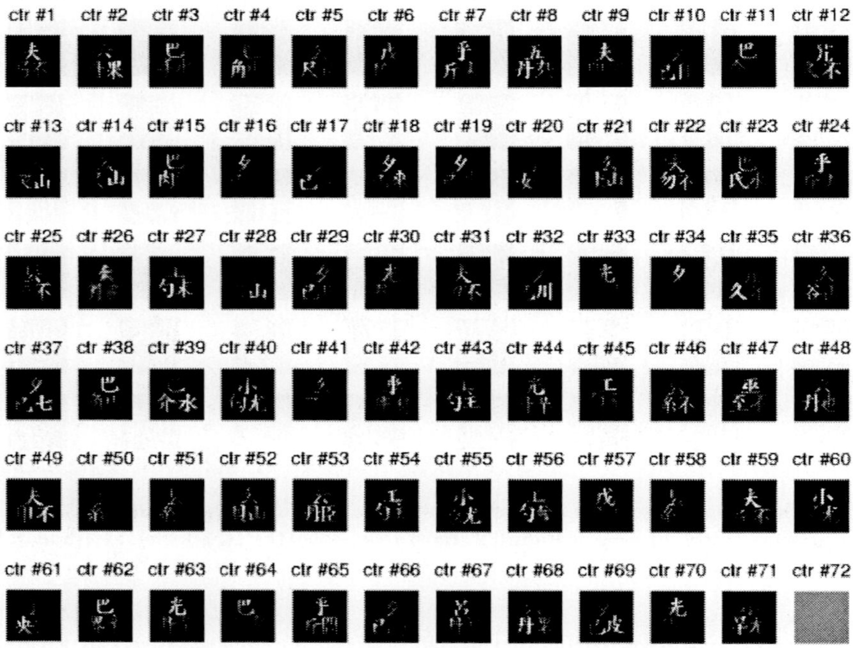

Fig. 6. The 72 RFs that are the cluster centroids identified by a k-means procedure in a set of 1440 RFs (generated by 20 runs of a $3 \times 3 \times 8$ Hebbian network, exposed to the images of Figure 2. See text for discussion.

The MDL and related principles [20,7] suggest that features that tend to co-occur frequently should be coded together. To assess the sensitivity of our RF learning method to the statistical structure of the stimulus set, we calculated the number of RFs acquired in the 20 learning runs, for each of the four kinds of input patterns whose occurrences in Figure 2 were controlled (for the purposes of an earlier psychophysical study [3]). The patterns could be of "fragment" or "composite" kind (consisting of one or two characters, respectively), and could belong to a pair that appeared together always (conditional probability of 1) or in half of the instances ($CP = 0.5$). The RF numbers reflected these probabilities, indicating that the algorithm was indeed sensitive to the statistics of the data set.

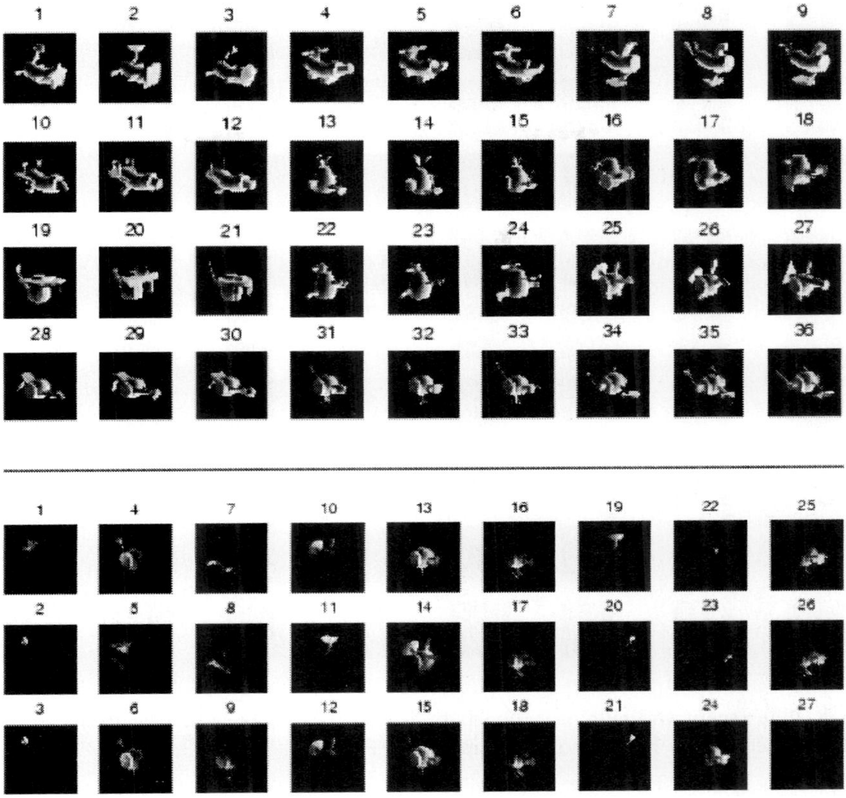

Fig. 7. Fribbles. *Top:* 36 images of "fribbles" (composite objects available for download from http://www.cog.brown.edu/~tarr/stimuli.html. *Bottom:* fragments extracted from these images by a $3 \times 3 \times 3$ Hebbian network of "what+where" cells.

To demonstrate that the learning method developed here can be used with gray-level images of 3D objects (and not only with binary character images), we ran a 27-unit network (3 cells per location) on the 36 images of composite shapes shown in Figure 7, top. As with the character images, the network proved capable of extracting fragments corresponding to meaningful parts (Figure 7, bottom; e.g., #1, 19) or to combination of such parts (e.g., #4, 13).

2.2 BCM Learning

The second version of the model learned its RFs by optimizing a BCM objective function [16] using simple batch-mode gradient descent with momentum. The total gradient was computed as a weighted sum of the gradient contributions from the feedforward BCM learning rule, a lateral inhibition term, and the

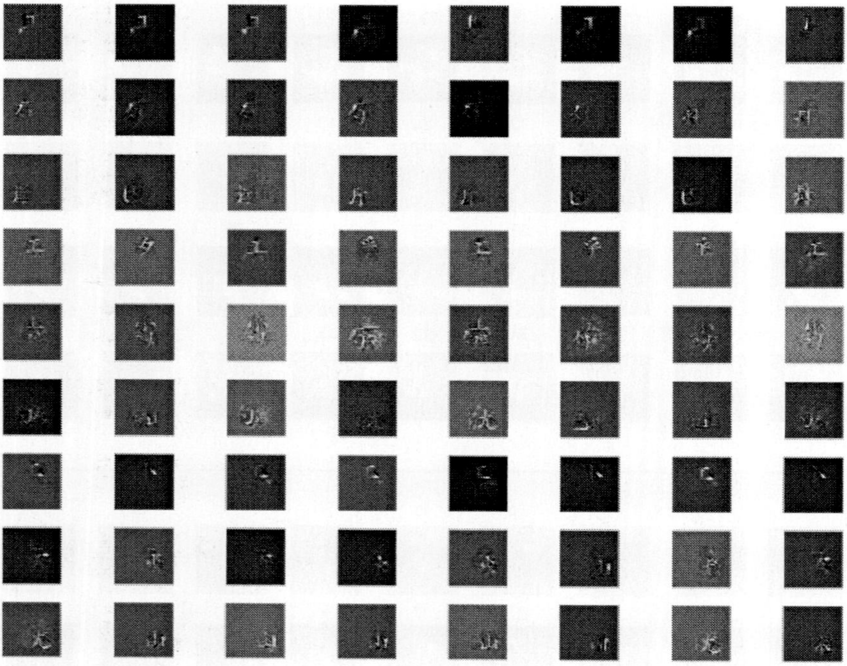

Fig. 8. The receptive fields of a 72-cell BCM network (8 cells per location) that has been exposed to the Kanji character images of Figure 2.

norm of the weights. The lateral inhibition pattern was uniform: activations were inhibited by a constant sum of the activations of the other neurons. A sigmoidal transfer function (tanh) was then applied to this modified activation in order to prevent individual activations from growing too high. The limiting value of this nonlinearity controls the minimal probability of the event to which a neuron becomes selectively tuned [16]. By limiting the activation to about 10, events with probability of about 1/10 could be found (without this step, each neuron would eventually converge to one of the individual inputs).

The activity of neuron k in the BCM network is $c_k = \mathbf{x}.\mathbf{w}_k$, where $\mathbf{w}_k$ is its synaptic weight vector. The inhibited activity of the k'th neuron and its threshold are:

$$\tilde{c}_k = c_k - \eta \sum_{j \neq k} c_j \qquad \tilde{\Theta}_M^k = E[\tilde{c}_k^2] \tag{3}$$

where $E[\cdot]$ denotes expectation. When the nonlinearity of the neuron is included, the inhibited activity is given by: $\tilde{c}_k = \tanh(c_k - \eta \sum_{j \neq k} c_j)$, and the learning rule becomes:

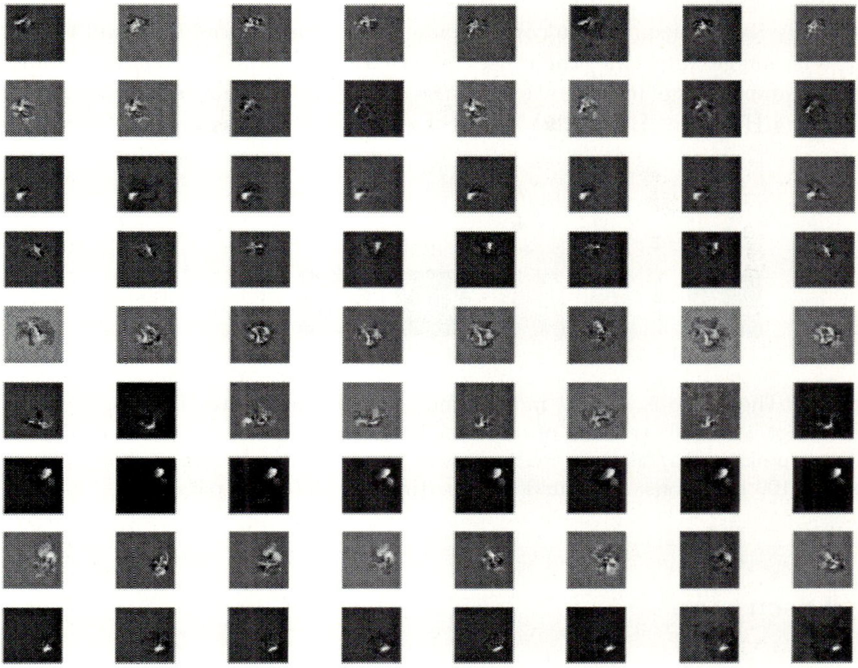

Fig. 9. The receptive fields of a 72-cell BCM network (8 cells per location) that has been exposed to the fribble images of Figure 7.

$$\dot{\mathbf{w}}_k = \mu \left(E\left[\phi(\tilde{c}_k, \tilde{\Theta}^k_M)\sigma'(\tilde{c}_k)x\right] - \eta \sum_{j \neq k} E\left[\phi(\tilde{c}_j, \tilde{\Theta}^j_m)\sigma'(\tilde{c}_j)x\right] \right) - \lambda \|\mathbf{w}_k\| \quad (4)$$

where σ' is the derivative of tanh, $\phi(c, \theta) \doteq c(c - \theta)$ [16]; μ and η are learning rates, the last term is the weight decay, and λ is a small regularization parameter determined empirically. Note that the lateral inhibition network performs a search of k-dimensional projections jointly; thus may find a richer structure, which a stepwise approach might miss [21].

The RFs learned by a 72-cell ($3 \times 3 \times 8$) BCM network are shown in Figures 8 and 9. As with the Hebbian network, individual characters and fribble fragments were picked up and imprinted onto the RFs of the neurons.

To compare the performance of the two biologically motivated statistical learning methods to a well-known benchmark, we carried out an independent component analysis (ICA) on the fribble image set, asking for 27 components. Although it is not clear a priori that the existing ICA algorithms are suitable for our extremely high-dimensional learning problem, pixels belonging to distinct parts of the fribble objects *are* statistically independent and should be amenable to detection by ICA. The first 9 of the components extracted by a publicly available implementation of ICA are shown in Figure 10. By and large, these are not nearly as localized as the components learned by the Hebbian and the BCM methods, suggesting that their use as structural primitives would be limited. A full, quantitative investigation of the utility of distributed representations employing Hebbian, BCM and ICA features is beyond the scope of the present study.

Fig. 10. The first 9 of 27 independent components extracted from the fribbles image set (36 vectors of dimensionality 25600) by FastICA (http://www.cis.hut.fi/projects/ica/fastica/, courtesy of A. Hyvärinen); we used symmetrical decorrelation, 100 iterations, and the default settings for the other parameters.

3 Discussion

The unsupervised acquisition of meaningful shape fragments from raw, unsegmented image sequences exhibited by our networks is made possible by two of their properties: (1) fast feedforward learning, and (2) lateral interactions. In the Hebbian case, these characteristics are crucial: learning must be fast (it occurs within a single epoch, or, if the learning constant is too low, not at all), and the lateral interactions must combine local competition (to keep the representation sparse) with global cooperation (to capture sufficiently large chunks of objects). A parallel can be drawn between our space-variable lateral/Hebb rule and the use of lateral inhibition for feature decorrelation in unsupervised learning in general (e.g., [22,19,16]). The "lateral" interactions in algorithms such as the extended BCM [16] are not normally described in spatial terms. Interestingly, experience with our BCM implementation indeed suggests that lateral interactions incorporated into it need not be spatially variant to ensure useful behavior. An inquiry into the role of these parameters in learning spatial structure across multiple scales is currently under way in our lab.

Our models learn to find structure in raw images residing in a very high-dimensional space, which makes the problem extremely difficult [19]; yet, presenting the images in register with each other obviates the need to tolerate translation, making the task much easier. In a more realistic setting, the learning would occur over base representations that are both more stable under stimulus transformations such as translation, and have lower dimensionality than the raw images. A biologically plausible modification to our models along these lines would involve feeding them the output of a simulated primary visual cortex, including simple, complex and hypercomplex cells, and employing space-variant resolution. Other challenges for the future include deriving our Hebbian learning rule from an objective function formulated from first principles such as MDL, and making its lateral interactions more realistic, e.g., by letting the network learn the strength of the lateral connections, perhaps using the same Hebbian mechanism as in the feedforward pathway. In the meanwhile, our results show that the paradox of unsupervised statistical learning can be circumvented: meaningful fragments of visual structure can be picked up from raw input by a joint application of computational and biological principles.

References

1. Edelman, S., Intrator, N.: Towards structural systematicity in distributed, statically bound visual representations. – (2001) – under review.
2. Fiser, J., Aslin, R.N.: Unsupervised statistical learning of higher-order spatial structures from visual scenes. Psychological Science **6** (2001) 499–504
3. Edelman, S., Hiles, B.P., Yang, H., Intrator, N.: Probabilistic principles in unsupervised learning of visual structure: human data and a model. In Dietterich, T.G., Becker, S., Ghahramani, Z., eds.: Advances in Neural Information Processing Systems 14, Cambridge, MA, MIT Press (2002)
4. Gardner-Medwin, A.R., Barlow, H.B.: The limits of counting accuracy in distributed neural representations. Neural Computation **13** (2001) 477–504
5. Eco, U.: Kant and the Platypus. Secker & Warburg, London (1999)
6. Becker, S., Plumbley, M.: Unsupervised neural network learning procedures for feature extraction and classification. Applied Intelligence **6** (1996) 185–203
7. Bienenstock, E., Geman, S., Potter, D.: Compositionality, MDL priors, and object recognition. In Mozer, M.C., Jordan, M.I., Petsche, T., eds.: Neural Information Processing Systems. Volume 9. MIT Press (1997)
8. Edelman, S., Intrator, N.: (Coarse Coding of Shape Fragments) + (Retinotopy) $\approx$ Representation of Structure. Spatial Vision **13** (2000) 255–264
9. Rao, S.C., Rainer, G., Miller, E.K.: Integration of what and where in the primate prefrontal cortex. Science **276** (1997) 821–824
10. Op de Beeck, H., Vogels, R.: Spatial sensitivity of Macaque inferior temporal neurons. J. Comparative Neurology **426** (2000) 505–518
11. Sirosh, J., Miikkulainen, R., Choe, Y., eds.: Lateral Interactions in the Cortex: Structure and Function. electronic book (1995) http://www.cs.utexas.edu/users/nn/lateral_interactions_book/cover.html.
12. Lund, J.S., Yoshita, S., Levitt, J.B.: Comparison of intrinsic connections in different areas of macaque cerebral cortex. Cerebral Cortex **3** (1993) 148–162
13. Brown, T.H., Kairiss, E.W., Keenan, C.L.: Hebbian synapses: biophysical mechanisms and algorithms. Ann. Rev. Neurosci. **13** (1990) 475–511
14. Fregnac, Y., Schulz, D., Thorpe, S., Bienenstock, E.: A cellular analogue of visual cortical plasticity. Nature **333** (1988) 367–370
15. Gluck, M.A., Granger, R.: Computational models of the neural bases of learning and memory. Ann. Rev. Neurosci. **16** (1993) 667–706
16. Intrator, N., Cooper, L.N.: Objective function formulation of the BCM theory of visual cortical plasticity: Statistical connections, stability conditions. Neural Networks **5** (1992) 3–17
17. Bear, M.F., Malenka, R.C.: Synaptic plasticity: LTP and LTD. Curr. Opin. Neurobiol. **4** (1994) 389–399

18. Wang, Y., Fujita, I., Murayama, Y.: Neuronal mechanisms of selectivity for object features revealed by blocking inhibition in inferotemporal cortex. Nature Neuroscience **3** (2000) 807–813
19. Intrator, N.: Feature extraction using an unsupervised neural network. Neural Computation **4** (1992) 98–107
20. Barlow, H.B.: Unsupervised learning. Neural Computation **1** (1989) 295–311
21. Huber, P.J.: Projection pursuit (with discussion). The Annals of Statistics **13** (1985) 435–475
22. Földiák, P.: Learning invariance from transformation sequences. Neural Computation **3** (1991) 194–200

Role of Featural and Configural Information in Familiar and Unfamiliar Face Recognition

Adrian Schwaninger[1,2*], Janek S. Lobmaier[2], and Stephan M. Collishaw[3]

[1] Max Planck Institute for Biological Cybernetics, Tübingen, Germany
[2] Department of Psychology, University of Zürich, Switzerland
[3] School of Cognitive and Computing Sciences, University of Sussex, UK

Abstract. Using psychophysics we investigated to what extent human face recognition relies on local information in parts (featural information) and on their spatial relations (configural information). This is particularly relevant for biologically motivated computer vision since recent approaches have started considering such featural information. In Experiment 1 we showed that previously learnt faces could be recognized by human subjects when they were scrambled into constituent parts. This result clearly indicates a role of featural information. Then we determined the blur level that made the scrambled part versions impossible to recognize. This blur level was applied to whole faces in order to create configural versions that by definition do not contain featural information. We showed that configural versions of previously learnt faces could be recognized reliably. In Experiment 2 we replicated these results for familiar face recognition. Both Experiments provide evidence in favor of the view that recognition of familiar and unfamiliar faces relies on featural and configural information. Furthermore, the balance between the two does not differ for familiar and unfamiliar faces. We propose an integrative model of familiar and unfamiliar face recognition and discuss implications for biologically motivated computer vision algorithms for face recognition.

1 Introduction

Different object classes can often be distinguished using relatively distinctive features like color, texture or global shape. In contrast, face recognition entails discriminating different exemplars from a quite homogeneous and complex stimulus category. Several authors have suggested that such expert face processing is holistic, i.e. faces are meant to be encoded and recognized as whole templates without representing parts explicitly [4,5,6]. In computer vision many face recognition algorithms process the whole face without explicitly processing facial parts. Some of these algorithms have been thought of being particularly useful to understand human face recognition and were cited in studies that claimed faces to be the example for exclusive holistic processing (e.g. [7,8] cited in [9], or the computation models cited in [6], p. 496).

In contrast to holistic algorithms like principal components analysis or vector quantization, recent computer vision approaches have started using local part-based or

* AS was supported by a grant from the European Commission (IST Programme).

H.H. Bülthoff et al. (Eds.): BMCV 2002, LNCS 2525, pp. 643–650, 2002.

fragment-based information in faces [1,2,3]. Since human observers can readily tell the parts of a face such algorithms bear a certain intuitive appeal. Moreover, potential advantages of such approaches are greater robustness against partial occlusion and less susceptibility to viewpoint changes.

In the present study we used psychophysics to investigate whether human observers only process faces holistically, or whether they encode and store the local information in facial parts (featural information) as well as their spatial relationship (configural information). In contrast to previous studies, we employed a method that did not alter configural or featural information, but eliminated either the one or the other. Previous studies have often attempted to directly alter the facial features or their spatial positions. However, the effects of such manipulations are not always perfectly selective. For example altering featural information by replacing the eyes and mouth with the ones from another face could also change their spatial relations (configural information) as mentioned in [10]. Rakover has pointed out that altering configuration by increasing the inter-eye distance could also induce a part-change, because the bridge of the nose might appears wider [11]. Such problems were avoided in our study by using scrambling and blurring procedures that allowed investigating the role of featural and configural information separately. The current study extends previous research using these manipulations (e.g. [12,13,14]) by ensuring that each procedure does effectively eliminate configural or featural processing.

2 Experiment 1: Unfamiliar Face Recognition

The first experiment investigated whether human observers store featural information *independent* of configural information. In the first condition configural information was eliminated by cutting the faces into their constituent parts and scrambling them. If the local information in parts (featural information) is encoded and stored, it should be possible to recognize faces above chance even if they are scrambled. In condition 2 the role of configural information was investigated. Previously learnt faces had to be recognized when they were shown as grayscale low-pass filtered versions. These image manipulations destroyed featural information while leaving the configural information intact. In a control condition we confirmed that performance is reduced to chance when faces are low-pass filtered and scrambled, thus showing that our image manipulations eliminate featural and configural information respectively and effectively.

2.1 Participants, Materials, and Procedure

Thirty-six participants, ranging in age from 20 to 35 years voluntarily took part in this experiment. All were undergraduate students of psychology at Zurich University and all reported normal or corrected-to-normal vision.

The stimuli were presented on a 17" screen. The viewing distance of 1 m was maintained by a head rest so that the faces covered approximately 6° of the visual angle. Stimuli were created from color photographs of 10 male and 10 female undergraduate students from the University of Zurich who had agreed to be photographed and to have their pictures used in psychology experiments. All faces were processed with Adobe Photoshop, proportionally scaled to the same face width of 300 pixels and placed on a black background. These intact faces were used in the learning phase (Figure 1a).

The scrambled faces were created by cutting the intact faces into 10 parts, using the polygonal lasso tool with a 2 pixel feather. The number of parts was defined by a preliminary free listing experiment, in which 41 participants listed all parts of a face. The following parts were named by more than 80% of the participants and were used in this study: eyes, eyebrows, nose, forehead, cheeks, mouth, chin. Four different scrambling versions, which appeared randomly, were used. Each version was arranged so that no part was situated either in its natural position or in its natural relation to its neighboring part. The parts were distributed as close to each other as possible, in order to keep the image area approximately the same size as the whole faces (Figure 1b).

The control stimuli were created in three steps. First, all color information was discarded in the intact faces. Second, the faces were blurred using a Gaussian filter with a sigma of 0.035 of image width in frequency space, which was determined in pilot studies. The formula used to construct the filter in frequency space was $\exp(\frac{-f^2}{2\sigma^2})$. In the third step these blurred faces were cut and scrambled as described above. Figure 1c shows an example of the control faces.

The blurred stimuli were created by applying the low-pass filter determined in the control condition to greyscale versions of the intact faces (Figure 1d).

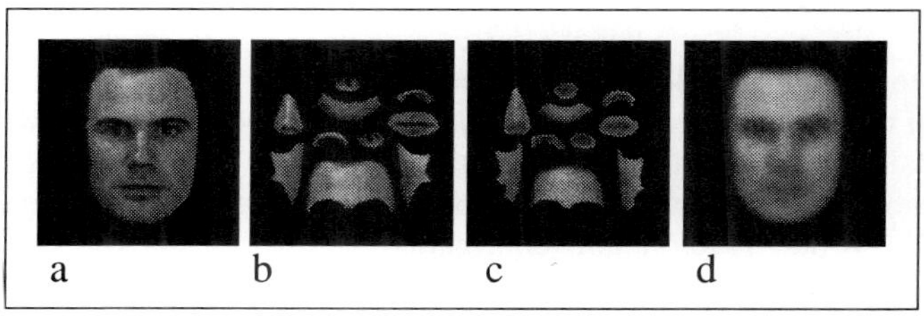

Fig. 1. Sample Stimuli. a) intact face, b) scrambled, c) scrambled-blurred, d) blurred face.

Participants were randomly assigned to one of three groups. Each group was tested in one experimental condition, either scrambled, scrambled-blurred, or blurred. Ten randomly selected faces served as target faces and the other 10 faces were used as distractors. In the learning phase the target faces were presented for ten seconds each. After each presented face the screen went blank for 1000 ms. Then the same faces were again presented 10 seconds each in the same order. The faces were presented in a pseudo-random order so that across participants no face appeared at the same position more than twice.

In the experimental phase, 20 scrambled faces were presented (10 targets and 10 distractors). Six random orders were created using the following constraints: within each random order no more than three target or distractor faces occurred on consecutive trials and between random orders no face appeared more than once on each position. The same random orders were used for all conditions.

Each trial started with a 1000 ms blank followed by a face. The participants were required to respond as fast and as accurately as possible whether the presented face was new (distractor) or whether it had been presented in the learning phase (target) by pressing one of two buttons on a response box. The assignment of buttons to responses was counterbalanced across participants.

2.2 Results and Discussion

Recognition performance was calculated using signal detection theory [15]. Face recognition performance was measured by calculating d' using an old-new recognition task [16]. This measure is calculated by the formula d' = z(H) – z(FA), whereas H denotes the proportion of hits and FA the proportion of false alarms. A hit was scored when the target button was pressed for a previously learned face (target) and a false alarm was scored when the target button was pressed for a new face (distractor). In the formula z denotes the z-transformation, i.e. H and FA are converted into z-scores (standard-deviation units). d' was calculated for each participant and averaged across each group (Figure 2, black bars).

One sample t-tests (one-tailed) were carried out in order to test the group means *M* against chance performance (i.e. d' = 0). Faces were recognized above chance, even when they were cut into their parts, $M = 1.19$, $SD = 0.58$, $t(11) = 7.07$, $p < .001$. This result suggests that local part-based information has been encoded in the learning phase, which provided a useful representation for recognizing the scrambled versions in the testing phase. These findings are contradictory to the view that faces are only processed holistically [4,5,6,9]. The recognition of blurred faces was also above chance, $M = 1.67$, $SD = 0.82$, $t(11) = 7.044$, $p < .001$. The blur filter used did indeed eliminate all featural information since recognition was at chance when faces were blurred and scrambled, $M = -0.22$, $SD = 1.01$, $t(11) = -.75$, $p = .235$.

Taken together, these results provide clear evidence for the view that featural and configural information are both important sources of information in face recognition. Furthermore, the two processes do not appear to be arranged hierarchically, as the results show that featural and configural information can be encoded and stored independently of one another[1].

3 Experiment 2: Comparison of Unfamiliar and Familiar Face Recognition

The results of Experiment 1 challenge the hypothesis that faces are only processed holistically. At the same time our results suggest that for unfamiliar face recognition in humans separate representations exist for featural information and configural information. The aim of Experiment 2 was to investigate whether the same is true for *familiar* face recognition. Moreover, by comparing recognition performance from Experiment 1 and Experiment 2 we addressed the question whether there is a shift in processing strategy from unfamiliar to familiar face recognition. Neuropsychological evidence suggests a dissociation between familiar face recognition and unfamiliar

---

[1] It is worth noting, however, that just because featural and configural processing *can* be recognized independently of one another, does not prove that the two don't interact when both are available (e.g. [5])

face matching [17,18], and experimental evidence suggests that familiar face recognition relies more heavily on the processing of inner areas of the face than does unfamiliar face recognition [19]. However, previous studies have found no evidence for a change in the balance between featural and configural processing as faces become more familiar [20,12]. Our study aimed to clarify this issue using a design that carefully controls the available featural and configural cues in the input image. Furthermore, in contrast to previous studies our study used the same faces in both experiments to eliminate other potential confounds with familiarity.

3.1 Participants, Materials, and Procedure

Thirty-six participants ranging in age from 20 to 35 years took part in this experiment for course credits. All were undergraduate students of psychology at Zurich University and were familiar with the target faces. All reported normal or corrected-to-normal vision. The materials and procedure were the same as in Experiment 1. The stimuli were also the same, but all the targets were faces of fellow students and thus familiar to the participants. All distractor faces were unfamiliar to the participants.

3.2 Results and Discussion

The same analyses were carried out as in Experiment 1. Again, one-sample t-tests (one-tailed) revealed a significant difference from chance (i.e. d' > 0) for recognizing scrambled faces, $M = 2.19$, $t(11) = 4.55$, $p < .001$, and blurred faces, $M = 2.92$, $t(11) = 9.81$, $p < .001$. As in Experiment 1, scrambling blurred grayscale versions provided a control condition for testing whether the blur filter used did indeed eliminate all local part-based information. This was the case – faces could no longer be recognized when they were blurred and scrambled, $M = 0.19$, $t(11) = 0.94$, $p = .184$.

In short, the results of Experiment 2 replicated the clear effects from Experiment 1 and suggest an important role of local part-based and configural information in both unfamiliar and familiar face recognition. By comparing recognition performance from both experiments (Figure 2) we addressed the question to what extent familiar and unfamiliar face recognition differ quantitatively (e.g. generally a better performance when faces are familiar) or qualitatively (e.g. better performance for familiar faces using more accurate configural processing). To this end, a two-way analysis of variance (ANOVA) was carried out with the data from the scrambled and blurred conditions of Experiments 1 and 2 with familiarity (familiar vs. unfamiliar) and condition (scrambled vs. blurred) as between-subjects factors. There was a main effect of familiarity, $F(1,42) = 12.80$, $MSE = 13.48$, $p < .01$, suggesting that familiar faces are more reliably recognized than unfamiliar faces (quantitative difference). There was also a main effect of condition, $F\ (1,42) = 6.7$, $MSE = 7.05$, $p < .05$, indicating that blurred faces were better recognized than scrambled faces. The relative impact of blurring and scrambling did not differ between the two experiments, since there was no interaction between condition and familiarity, $F(1,42) = 1.02$, $MSE = 1.08$, $p = 0.32$. This results suggests that there are no qualitative differences between familiar and unfamiliar face recognition on the basis of configural and featural information. In both cases both types of information are of similar importance.

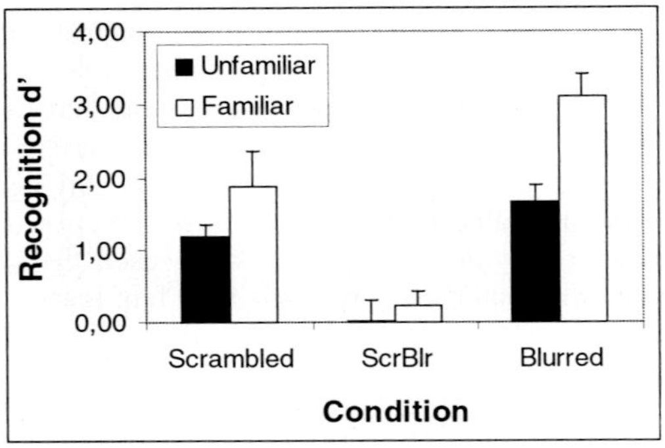

Fig. 2. Recognition performance in unfamiliar and familiar face recognition across the three different conditions at test. ScrBlr: scrambled and blurred faces. Error bars indicate standard errors of the mean.

4 General Discussion

In the present paper we investigated the role of local part-based information and their spatial interrelationship (configural information) using psychophysics. We found that human observers process familiar and unfamiliar faces by encoding and storing configural information as well as the local information contained in facial parts. These results challenge the assumption that faces are processed only holistically and suggest a greater biological plausibility for recent machine vision approaches in which local features and parts play a pivotal role (e.g. [1,2,3]).

Neurophysiological evidence supports part-based as well as configural and holisitic processing assumptions. In general, it has been found that cells responsive to facial identity are found in inferior temporal cortex while selectivity to facial expressions, viewing angle and gaze direction can be found in the superior temporal sulcus [21, 22]. For some neurons, selectivity for particular features of the head and face, e.g. the eyes and mouth, has been revealed [22,23,24]. Other groups of cells need the simultaneous presentation of multiple parts of a face and are therefore consistent with a more holistic type of processing [25,26]. Finally, Yamane et al. [27] have discovered neurons that detect combinations of distances between facial parts, such as the eyes, mouth, eyebrows, and hair, which suggest sensitivity for the spatial relations between facial parts (configural information).

In order to integrate the above mentioned findings from psychophysics, neurophysiology and computer vision we propose the framework depicted in Figure 3. Faces are first represented by a metric representation in primary visual areas corresponding to the perception of the pictorial aspects of a face. Further processing entails extracting local part-based information and spatial relations between them in order to activate featural and configural representations in higher visual areas of the

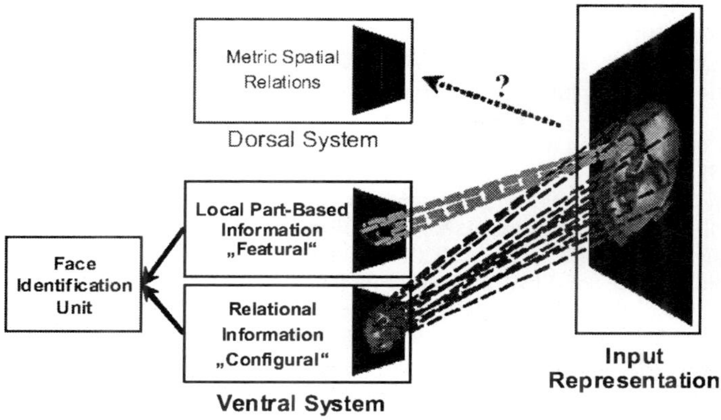

Fig. 3. Integrative model for unfamiliar and familiar face recognition.

ventral stream, i.e. face selective areas in temporal cortex[2]. In a recent study, repetition priming was used in order to investigate whether the outputs of featural and configural representations converge to the same face identification units [28]. Since priming was found from scrambled to blurred faces and vice versa we propose that the outputs of featural and configural representations converge to the same face identification units.

References

1. Heisele, B., Serre, T., Pontil, M., Vetter, T., and Poggio, T. (2001). Categorization by learning and combining object parts. NIPS proceedings.
2. Lee, D.D., & Seung, S. (1999). Learning the parts of objects by non-negative matrix factorization. Nature, 401, 788–791.
3. Ullman, S., & Sali, E. (2000). Object Classification Using a Fragment-Based Representation. BMCV 2000. Lecture Notes in Computer Science, 1811, pp. 73–87. Berlin: Springer.
4. Tanaka J. W. & Farah, M. J. (1991). Second-order relational properties and the inversion-effect: Testing a theory of face perception. Perception & Psychophysics, 50, 367-372.
5. Tanaka, J. W. & Farah, M. J. (1993). Parts and wholes in face recognition. Quarterly Journal of Experimental Psychology, 79, 471–491.
6. Farah, M. J., Tanaka, J. W., & Drain, H. M. (1995). What causes the face inversion effect? Journal of Experimental Psychology: Human Perception and Performance, 21, (3), 628–634.
7. Lades, M., Vorbrüggen, J.C., Buhmann, J., Lange, J., Malsburg, v.d., C., Würtz, R.P., & Konen, W. (1993). Distortion invariant object recognition in the dynamic link architecture. IEEE Transactions on Computers, 42, 300–311.

[2] Although a role of the dorsal system in encoding of metric spatial relations has been proposed for object recognition it remains to be investigated, whether it does play a role for the processing of configural information in faces.

8. Wiskott, L., Fellous, J.M., Krüger, N., & von der Malsburg, C. (1997). Face Recognition by Elastic Bunch Graph Matching. IEEE Transactions on Pattern Analysis and Machine Intelligence, 19(7), 775–779.
9. Biedermann, I., & Kalocsai, P. (1997). Neurocomputational bases of object and face recognition. Philosophical Transactions of the Royal Society of London, B, 352, 1203–1219.
10. Rhodes, G., Brake, S., & Atkinson, A.P. (1993). What's lost in inverted faces? Cognition, 47, 25–57.
11. Rakover, S. S. (2002). Featural vs. configurational information in faces: A conceptual and empirical analysis. British Journal of Psychology, 93, 1–30.
12. Collishaw, S.M., Hole G.J. (2000). Featural and configurational processes in the recognition of faces of different familiarity. Perception, 29, 893–910.
13. Davidoff, J., & Donnelly, N. (1990). Object superiority: a comparison of complete and part probes, Acta Psychologica, 73 1990 225–243.
14. Sergent J. (1985). Influence of task and input factors on hemispheric involvement in face processing. Journal of Experimental Psychology: Human Perception and Performance, 11(6), 846–61.
15. Green, D.M., & Swets, J.A. (1966). Signal detection theory and psychophysics. New York: Wiley.
16. McMillan, N.A., & Creelman, C.D. (1992). Detection theory: A user's guide. New York: Cambridge University Press.
17. Benton AL, 1980. The neuropsychology of facial recognition. American Psychologist, 35, 176–186.
18. Malone D.R., Morris H.H., Kay M.C., Levin, H.S., 1982. Prosopagnosia: a double dissociation between the recognition of familiar and unfamiliar faces. Journal of Neurology, Neurosurgery, and Psychiatry, 45, 820–822.
19. Ellis, H.D., Shepherd, J.W., Davies G.M., 1979. Identification of familiar and unfamiliar faces from internal and external features: some implications for theories of face recognition. Perception, 8, 431–439
20. Yarmey, A.D., 1971. Recognition memory for familiar "public" faces: Effects of orientation and delay. Psychonomic Science, 24, 286–288.
21. Hasselmo, M.E., Rolls, E.T., & Baylis, C.G. (1989). The role of expression and identity in the face-selective responses of neurons in the temporal visual cortex of the monkey. Experimental Brain Research, 32, 203–218.
22. Perret, D.I., Hietanen, J.K., Oram, M.W., & Benson, P.J. (1992). Organization and functions of cells in the macaque temporal cortex. Philosophical Transactions of the Royal Society of London, B, 335, 23–50.
23. Perret, D.I., Rolls, E.T., & Caan, W. (1982). Visual neurones responsive to faces in the monkey temporal cortex. Experimental Brain Research, 47, 329–342.
24. Perret, D.I., Mistlin, A.J., & Chitty, A.J. (1987). Visual neurones responsive to faces. Trends in Neuroscience, 10, 358–364.
25. Perret, D.I., & Oram, M.W. (1993). Image Vis. Comput., 11, 317–333.
26. Wachsmuth, E., Oram, M.W., & Perret, D.I. (1994). Recognition of objects and their component parts: responses of single units in the temporal cortex of the macaque. Cerebral Cortex, 4, 509–522.
27. Yamane, S., Kaji, S., & Kawano, K. (1988). What facial features activate face neurons in the inferotemporal cortex of the monkey? Experimental Brain Research, 73, 209–214.
28. Schwaninger, Lobmaier, & Collishaw (2002). Role and interaction of featural and configural processing in face recognition. Vision Sciences Society, 2nd annual meeting, Sarasota, Florida, May 10–15, 2002.

View-Based Recognition of Faces in Man and Machine: Re-visiting Inter-extra-Ortho

Christian Wallraven[1,*], Adrian Schwaninger[1,2,*], Sandra Schuhmacher[2], and Heinrich H. Bülthoff[1]

[1] Max Planck Institute for Biological Cybernetics, Tübingen, Germany
[2] Department of Psychology, University of Zürich, Switzerland

Abstract. For humans, faces are highly overlearned stimuli, which are encountered in everyday life in all kinds of poses and views. Using psychophysics we investigated the effects of viewpoint on human face recognition. The experimental paradigm is modeled after the inter-extra-ortho experiment using unfamiliar objects by Bülthoff and Edelman [5]. Our results show a strong viewpoint effect for face recognition, which replicates the earlier findings and provides important insights into the biological plausibility of view-based recognition approaches (alignment of a 3D model, linear combination of 2D views and view-interpolation). We then compared human recognition performance to a novel computational view-based approach [29] and discuss improvements of view-based algorithms using local part-based information.

1 Introduction

According to Marr [16] human object recognition can be best understood by algorithms that hierarchically decompose objects into their parts and relations in order to access an object-centered 3D model. Based on the concept of nonaccidental properties [14], Biederman proposed in his recognition by components (RBC) theory [1], that the human visual system derives a line-drawing-like representation from the visual input, which is parsed into basic primitives (geons) that are orientation-invariant. Object recognition would be achieved by matching the geons and their spatial relations to a geon structural description in memory. This theory has been implemented in a connectionist network that is capable of reliably recognizing line drawings of objects made of two geons [11].

In object recognition, view-based models have often been cited as the opposite theoretical position to the approaches by Marr and Biederman[1]. Motivated by the still unsolved (and perhaps not solvable) problem of extracting a perfect line drawing from

---

* Christian Wallraven and Adrian Schwaninger were supported by a grant from the European Community (CogVis).

[1] However, it is interesting that Biederman and Kalocsai [3] point out that face recognition – as opposed to object recognition – cannot be understood by RBC theory mainly because recognizing faces entails processing holistic surface based information.

H.H. Bülthoff et al. (Eds.): BMCV 2002, LNCS 2525, pp. 651–660, 2002.

natural images different view-based approaches have been proposed. In this paper we consider three main approaches: Recognition by alignment to a 3D representation [15], recognition by the linear combination of 2D views [25], and recognition by view interpolation (e.g., using RBF networks [19]). What these approaches have in common is that they match viewpoint *dependent* information as opposed to viewpoint *invariant* geons.

The biological plausibility of these models has been investigated by comparing them to human performance for recognizing paper clip and amoeboid like objects [5,7]. In contrast to those stimuli, faces are highly overlearned and seen in a vast variety of different views and poses. Therefore, we were interested whether a) human face recognition shows similar effects of viewpoint and b) by which of these view-based approaches face recognition can be best understood. We then compared human recognition performance to another view-based framework, namely the feature matching approach based on the framework introduced in [29]. Based on the results we discuss the role of parts and their interrelationship from a view-based perspective in contrast to the models proposed in [1,11].

2 Psychophysical Experiment on View-Based Recognition of Faces

2.1 Participants, Method, and Procedure

Ten right-handed undergraduates (five females, five males) from the University of Zürich volunteered in this study. The face stimuli were presented on a 17" CRT screen. The viewing distance of 1 m was maintained by a head rest so that the faces covered approximately 6° of the visual angle. Twenty male faces from the MPI face database [4] served as stimuli.

The experiment consisted of a learning and a testing phase. Ten faces were randomly selected as distractors and the other 10 faces were selected as targets. During learning, the target faces were shown oscillating horizontally ±5° around the 0° and the 60° extra view (see Figure 1). The views of the motion sequence were separated by 1° and were shown 67 ms per frame. The oscillations around 0° started and ended always with the +5° view, the oscillations around 60° started and ended always with the +55° view. Both motion sequences lasted 6 sec, i.e. 4 full back-and forth cycles. For half the faces the 0° sequence was shown first, for the other half of the faces the 60° sequence was shown first. The order of the ten faces was counterbalanced across the ten participants. After a short break of 15 min the learning block was repeated and for each face the order of the two motion sequences was reversed.

In the testing phase, the subjects were presented with static views of the 10 target and the 10 distractor faces. The faces were shown in blocks of 20 trials in which each face was presented once in a random order. The test phase contained 300 trials and each face was presented once in each of the 15 angles depicted in Figure 1. Each trial started with a 1000 ms fixation cross followed by the presentation of a face. Participants were instructed to respond as fast and accurately as possible whether the presented face had been shown in the learning face (i.e. it was a target) or whether it was a distractor by pressing the left or right mouse button. On each trial, the faces were presented until the button press occurred. The assignment of buttons to responses was counterbalanced across participants.

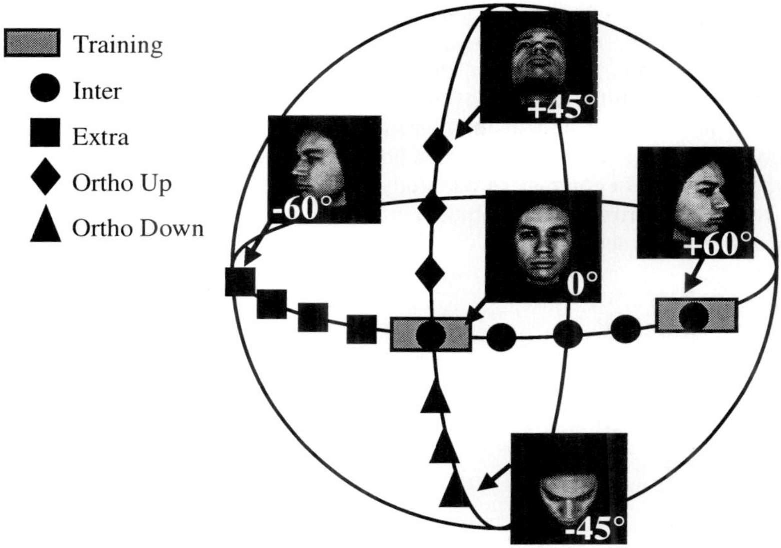

Fig. 1. Training occurred at 0° ±5° (frontal view) and 60° ±5° (side view). Testing was performed for 15 views separated by 15°. The four testing conditions are labeled (inter, extra, ortho up, ortho down).

2.2 Results and Discussion

Signal detection theory was used to measure recognition performance. The relevant measure is d' = z(H) – z(FA), whereas H equals the hit rate, i.e. the proportion of correctly identified targets, and FA the false alarm rate, i.e. the proportion of incorrectly reporting that a face had been learned in the learning phase. H and FA are converted into z-scores, i.e. to standard deviation units. Individually calculated d' values were subjected to a two-factor analysis of variance (ANOVA) with condition (extra, inter, orthoUp, orthoDown) and amount of rotation (0, 15, 30, 45) as within subjects factors. Mean values are shown in Figure 2.

Recognition d' was dependent on the condition as indicated by the main effect of this factor, $F(3, 27) = 23.1$, $MSE = .354$, $p < .001$. There was also a main effect of amount of rotation, $F(3, 27) = 10.93$, $MSE = 1.500$, $p < .001$. The effect of rotation was different across conditions as indicated by the interaction between amount of rotation and condition, $F(9,81) = 3.30$, $MSE = .462$, $p < .01$. The four conditions were compared to each other using Bonferroni corrected pairwise comparisons. Recognition in the inter condition was better than in the extra condition ($p < .05$). Recognition in inter and extra conditions was better than in both ortho conditions ($p < .01$). Finally, recognition performance did not differ in the two ortho conditions ($p = .41$). These results are difficult to explain by approaches using alignment of a 3D representation [15] because such a differential effect of rotation direction would not be expected. Moreover, human performance questions the biological plausibility of the linear combination approach for face recognition [25], because it cannot explain why performance in the inter condition was better than in the extra condition. The results can for example be understood by a linear interpolation within an RBF network [19] – in the next section, we present another view-based framework, which can model the results [29]. Both of these models predict inter > extra > ortho, which was shown clearly in the psychophysical data. Interestingly, the results of the present study lead to the same conclusions as the study in [5], who used paper clips and amoeboid objects in order to investigate how humans encode, represent and recognize *unfamiliar* objects. In contrast, in our study perhaps the most familiar object class was used. Thus, familiarity with the object class does not necessarily predict qualitatively different viewpoint dependence.

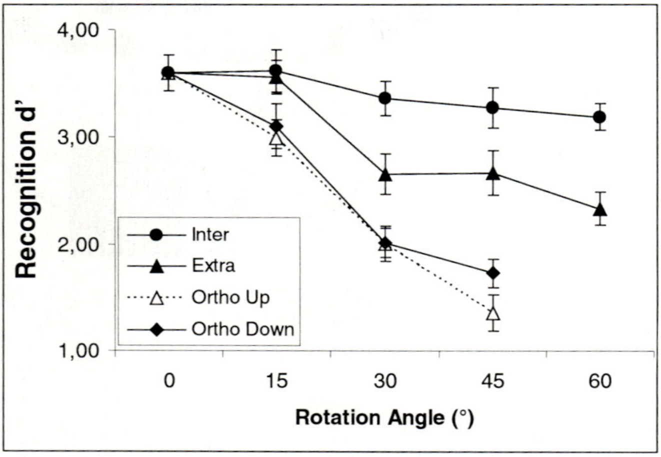

Fig. 2. Human recognition performance in the four rotation conditions (inter, extra, ortho up, ortho down) across viewpoint (0° is the frontal view).

3 Computational Modeling

3.1 Description of the System

The original inter-extra-ortho experiment was analyzed using radial basis function (RBF) networks, which were able to capture the performance of subjects in the various tasks (see also [18] for a study on face recognition using RBF networks). In this paper, we apply another kind of view-based computational model to the psychophysical data, which is based on a framework proposed in [29]. The motivation for the proposed framework came from several lines of research in psychophysics: First of all, evidence for a view-based object representation – as already stated above – has been found in numerous studies (also from physiological research). In addition, recent results from psychophysical studies showed that the temporal properties of the visual input play an important role for both learning and representing objects [28]. Finally, results from psychophysics (see e.g., [13,21,22]) support the view that human face recognition relies on encoding and storing local information contained in facial parts (featural information) as well as the spatial relations of these features (configural information).

A model, which can incorporate elements of these findings, was proposed in [29]. The framework is able to learn extensible view-based object representations from dynamic visual input on-line. In the following, we shortly describe the basic elements of the framework as used in this study. Each image is processed on multiple scales to *automatically* find interest points (in our case, corners). A set of visual features is constructed by taking the positions of the corners together with their surrounding pixel patches (see Figure 4a). In order to match two sets of visual features, we consider an algorithm based on [20]. It constructs a pair-wise similarity matrix **A** where each entry A_{ij} consists of two terms:

$$A_{ij} = \exp(-\frac{1}{\sigma_{dist}^2}\mathrm{dist}^2(i,j)) \cdot \exp(-\frac{1}{\sigma_{sim}^2}\mathrm{sim}^2(i,j)) \qquad (1)$$

where $\mathrm{dist}^2(i,j)) = ((x_i - x_j)^2 + (y_i - y_j)^2)$ measures the distance between a feature pair and *sim(i,j)* measures the pixel similarity of the pixel patches (in our case, using Normalized Cross Correlation). The parameters $\sigma_{dist}, \sigma_{sim}$ can be used to weight distance and pixel similarity. Basen on the SVD of this matrix $\mathbf{A=UVW^T}$ we then construct a re-scaled matrix $\mathbf{A'=UW^T}$, which is then used to find a feature mapping between the two sets [20,29]. The goodness of the match is characterized by the *percentage of matches* between the two feature sets. This feature matching algorithm ensures that both global layout and local feature similarity are taken into account. It is important to note that there is neither a restriction to a global spatial measure in pixel space nor to a local measure of pixel similarity. Any kind of view-based feature measure can be introduced in a similar manner as an additional term in equation 1.

One of the advantages of this framework, which a purely view-based holistic representation lacks, is its *explicit* representation of local features. This enables the system amongst other things to be more robust under changes in illumination and occlusion [29,30]. Since the input consists of image sequences the visual features can also be augmented with *temporal information* such as trajectories of features. Temporal information is given in our case by the learning trials in which a small *horizontal* rotation is presented. We thus modified the distance term in equation 1 such that it penalizes deviations from the horizontal direction for feature matches by an increased weighting of the vertical distance between features *i* and *j*:

$$\mathrm{dist}^2(i,j)) = ((x_i - x_j)^2 + \alpha(y_i - y_j)^2) \quad \text{with } \alpha \geq 1 \qquad (2) \cdot$$

Figure 3 shows matching features[2] between two images for two settings of α=1 and α=3: α=1 (Figure 3a) yields a matching score of 30 percent, whereas α=3 (Figure 3b) yields a matching score of 37 percent. The rationale behind using the penalty term not only comes from the dynamic information present in the learning phase, but is also motivated by the psychophysical results in [5,7], where humans showed a general tendency towards views lying on the horizontal axis.

---

[2] Some matches between features are not exactly horizontal due to localization inaccuracies inherent in the corner extraction method.

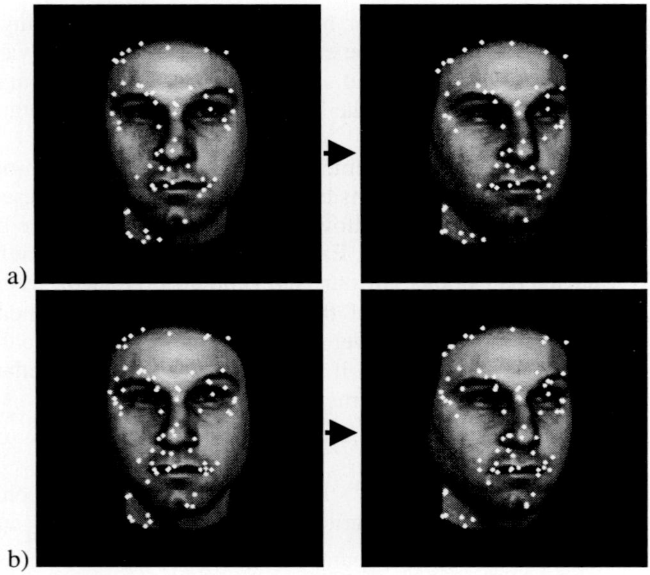

Fig. 3. Matching features between two views of a face a) without vertical penalty term b) with vertical penalty term.

3.2 Computational Recognition Results

In the following, we present recognition results, which were obtained using the same stimuli as for the human subjects. Again, the system was trained with two small image sequences around 0° and 60° and tested on the same views as humans. The final learned representation of the system consisted of the 0° and 60° view, each containing around 200 local visual features. Each testing view was matched against all learned views using the matching algorithm outlined above. To find matches, a winner-takes-all strategy was employed using the *combined matching score* of the two learned views for each face. The results in Figure 4b show that our computational model exhibits the *same* qualitative behavior in performance as human subjects replicating the drop in performance, i.e. inter>extra>ortho[3]. Inter performance was best due to support from two learned views as opposed to support only from the frontal view for the extra conditions. Recognition of ortho views was worst due to three factors: first, inter conditions had support from two views, second, the learned penalty term biased towards horizontal feature matches and third, the change in feature information for the same angular distance for faces is higher for vertical than for horizontal rotations.

[3] The difference between the conditions was confirmed to be statistically significant by repeating the test 10 times with different sets of faces from the database.

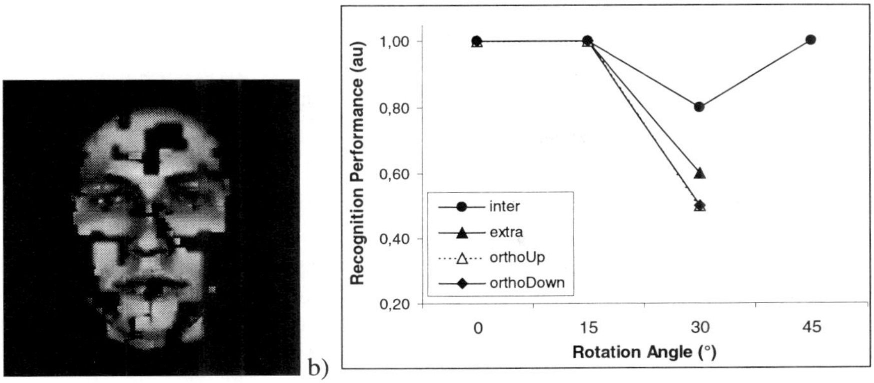

a) b)

Fig. 4. a) Feature representation as used by the computational framework – note that features focus on areas of interest (eyes, mouth, nose), b) machine recognition performance (arbitr. units) in the four rotation conditions (inter, extra, ortho up, ortho down) across viewpoint.

In Figure 4b, inter and extra conditions are plotted only for view-changes up to 30°. For larger view changes a global correspondence cannot be established anymore since the available feature sets are too different. This observation agrees with findings from a study in [27]. In order to address the issue of generalization over larger view changes, we propose the following extension to the framework, which consists of a two-step matching process.

First, in order to determine head position the image is matched on a coarse scale against different views from a database of faces. This is possible since the global facial feature layout guarantees a good pose recovery even for novel faces [30]. The second step then consists of using more detailed part layout information to match parts consisting of groups of features to the image in the corresponding pose. Parts (which would correspond in the ideal case to facial parts such as eyes, mouth, nose, etc.) can again be matched using the same algorithm as outlined above under the constraint of the global part layout information. Such a constraint can easily be built into the matching process as a prior on the allowed feature deformations. Again, this proposed framework is consistent with evidence from psychophysical studies (e.g., [13,21,22], see also [18] for a holistic two-stage model with alignment and view-interpolation).

In computational vision[4] the question how (facial) parts can be extracted from images and how a perceptually reasonable clustering of features can be created has recently begun to be addressed. A purely bottom-up way of extracting parts was suggested in [12], whereas [26,31] approach the issue from the perspective of categorization: extracting salient features, which maximize within-class similarity while minimizing between-class similarity. In [8], a 'Chorus of Fragments' was introduced, which is modeled after what/where receptive fields and also takes into account parts and their relations. One advantage of the framework proposed here, is its explicit use of features and their properties (such as pixel neighborhood, trajectory information, etc.), which provides the system with a rich representation and can be

[4] There is evidence from developmental studies that the basic schema of faces is innate [9,17], which could help newborn infants to learn encoding the parts of a face.

exploited for feature grouping. As shown in Figure 4a, the visual features already tend to cluster around facial parts and in addition also capture small texture features of the skin (such as birthmarks and blemishes), which were hypothesized [27] to be important features for less view-dependent face recognition.

4 General Discussion

Several previous studies have investigated face processing under varying pose (for a short review and further results see [24]). In order to further understand the viewpoint dependent nature of face recognition we investigated whether qualitatively similar effects of viewpoint apply to face recognition as found in studies using unfamiliar objects like wire-frames and amoeboid objects [5,7]. Indeed, this was the case, we found the same qualitative effects of viewpoint, which were consistent with a view interpolation model of object recognition [5,18,19]. In addition, a computational model based on local features and their relations [29] showed the same qualitative behavior as humans. The breakdown of this model for large view-changes motivates an extension of the framework to explicitly model parts. At the same time, this framework should provide greater robustness against partial occlusion and less susceptibility to viewpoint changes due to the use of parts [10,27].

The concept of representing objects by their parts and spatial relations has been proposed many years ago by structural description theories (e.g., [1,16]). There are, however, several important differences between these approaches and the framework we propose here. First of all, in contrast to the traditional approaches by Marr and Biederman, we are not convinced that it is biologically plausible and computationally possible to extract good edge-based representations as the input for recognition. Moreover, the parts we propose are completely different both conceptually and computationally from the geons used in the approaches in [1,11]. Geons are defined by using Lowe's nonaccidental properties [14] and are meant to be viewpoint-independent (or at least for a certain range of views, see [2]). In contrast to [3], we propose that face–recognition relies on processing local part-based and configural information (which could also apply to many cases of object recognition). In contrast to geons, the parts we propose are defined by grouping view-dependent image features. According to the type of features used, such parts are more or less viewpoint-dependent. We are currently running experiments, in which we explore to what extent *part-based* representations in human face recognition are viewpoint dependent. RBC theory assumes that a small set of geons suffices to explain the relevant aspects of human object recognition. In our view, in many cases of everyday object recognition, defining the features is a matter of perceptual learning [23], and we believe that the number of parts represented by the human brain for recognition exceeds a 24 or 36 geon set by far and in addition might be heavily task-dependent.

[5] There is evidence from developmental studies that the basic schema of faces is innate [9,17], which could help newborn infants to learn encoding the parts of a face.

References

1. Biederman, I. (1987). Recognition-by-components: A theory of human image understanding. Psychological Review, 94(2), 115–147.
2. Biederman, I., Gerhardstein, P.C. (1993). Recognizing depth-rotated objects: evidence and conditions for three-dimensional viewpoint invariance. Journal of Experimental Psychology: Human Perception and Performance, 19, 6, 1162–1182.
3. Biederman, I., Kalocsai, P. (1997). Neurocomputational bases of object and face recognition. Philosophical Transactions of the Royal Society London, B, 352, 1203-1219.
4. Blanz, V. , Vetter, T. (1999). A Morphable Model for the Synthesis of 3D Faces. In Proc. Siggraph99, pp. 187–194.
5. Bülthoff, H.H., Edelman, S. (1992). Psychophysical support for a two-dimensional view interpolation theory of object recognition. PNAS USA, 89, 60–64.
6. Collishaw, S.M., Hole G.J. (2000). Featural and configurational processes in the recognition of faces of different familiarity. Perception, 29, 893–910.
7. Edelman, S., Bülthoff, H, H. (1992). Orientation dependence in the recognition of familiar and novel views of three-dimensional objects. Vision Research, 32(12), 2385-4000.
8. Edelman, S. Intrator, N. (2000). A productive, systematic framework for the representation of visual structure. In Proc. NIPS 2000, 10–16.
9. Goren, C., Sarty, M., Wu, P. (1975). Visual following and pattern discrimination of face-like stimuli by newborn infants. Pediatrics, 56, 544–549.
10. Heisele, B., Serre, T., Pontil, M., Vetter, T., and Poggio, T. (2001). Categorization by learning and combining object parts. In Proc. NIPS 2001.
11. Hummel, J.E., Biederman, I. (1992). Dynamic binding in a neural network for shape recognition. Psychological Review, 99(3), 480–517.
12. Lee, D., Seung S. (1999). Learning the parts of objects by non-negative matrix factorization. Nature, 401:788–791.
13. Leder, H., Candrian, G., Huber, O., Bruce, V. (2001). Configural features in the context of upright and inverted faces. Perception, 30, 73–83.
14. Lowe, D.G. (1985). Perceptual organization and visual recognition. Boston: Kluwer Academic Publishing.
15. Lowe, D.G. (1987). Three-dimensional object recognition from single two-dimensional images. Artificial Intelligence, 31, 355–395.
16. Marr, D. (1982). Vision. San Francisco: Freeman.
17. Morton, J., Johnson, M.H. (1991). CONSPEC and CONLERN: A two-process theory of infant face recognition. Psychological Review, 98, 164–181.
18. O'Toole, A. J., Edelman, S., Bülthoff H.H. (1998). Stimulus-specific effects in face recognition over changes in viewpoint. Vision Research, 38 , 2351–2363.
19. Poggio T, Edelman S. (1990) A network that learns to recognize three-dimensional objects. Nature, 18, 343(6255), 263–266.
20. Pilu, M. (1997). A direct method for stereo correspondence based on singular value decomposition, In Proc. CVPR'97, 261–266.
21. Schwaninger, A., Mast, F. (1999). Why is face recognition so orientation-sensitive? Psychophysical evidence for an integrative model. Perception, 28 (Suppl.), 116.
22. Sergent J. (1985). Influence of task and input factors on hemispheric involvement in face processing. Journal of Experimental Psychology: Human Perception and Performance, 11(6), 846–61.
23. Schyns, P. G., Rodet, L. (1997) Categorization creates functional features. Journal of Experimental Psychology: Learning, Memory and Cognition, 23, 681–696.
24. Troje, N. F., Bülthoff, H.H. (1996). Face recognition under varying pose: the role of texture and shape. Vision Research, 36, 1761–1771.
25. Ullman, S., Basri, R. (1991). Recognition by linear combinations of models. IEEE Transactions on Pattern Analysis and Machine Intelligence, 13(10), 992–1006.

26. Ullman, S., Sali, E. (2000). Object Classification Using a Fragment-Based Representation. In Proc. BMCV'00, 73–87.
27. Valentin, D., Abdi, H., Edelman, B. (1999). From rotation to disfiguration: Testing a dual-strategy model for recognition of faces across view angles. Perception, 28, 817–824.
28. Wallis, G. M. , Bülthoff, H.H. (2001). Effect of temporal association on recognition memory. PNAS USA, 98, 4800–4804.
29. Wallraven, C., Bülthoff, H.H. (2001). Automatic acquisition of exemplar-based representations for recognition from image sequences. CVPR 2001 – Workshop on Models vs. Exemplars.
30. Wallraven, C., Bülthoff, H.H. (2001). View-based recognition under illumination changes using local features. CVPR 2001 - Workshop on Identifying Objects Across Variations in Lighting: Psychophysics and Computation.
31. Weber M., Welling M. and Perona P. (2000). Unsupervised Learning of Models for Recognition. In Proc. ECCV2000.

Author Index

Lecture Notes in Computer Science

For information about Vols. 1–2439

please contact your bookseller or Springer-Verlag

Vol. 2440: J.M. Haake, J.A. Pino (Eds.), Groupware: Design, Implementation and Use. Proceedings, 2002. XII, 285 pages. 2002.

Vol. 2441: Z. Hu, M. Rodríguez-Artalejo (Eds.), Functional and Logic Programming. Proceedings, 2002. X, 305 pages. 2002.

Vol. 2442: M. Yung (Ed.), Advances in Cryptology – CRYPTO 2002. Proceedings, 2002. XIV, 627 pages. 2002.

Vol. 2443: D. Scott (Ed.), Artificial Intelligence: Methodology, Systems, and Applications. Proceedings, 2002. X, 279 pages. 2002. (Subseries LNAI).

Vol. 2444: A. Buchmann, F. Casati, L. Fiege, M.-C. Hsu, M.-C. Shan (Eds.), Technologies for E-Services. Proceedings, 2002. X, 171 pages. 2002.

Vol. 2445: C. Anagnostopoulou, M. Ferrand, A. Smaill (Eds.), Music and Artificial Intelligence. Proceedings, 2002. VIII, 207 pages. 2002. (Subseries LNAI).

Vol. 2446: M. Klusch, S. Ossowski, O. Shehory (Eds.), Cooperative Information Agents VI. Proceedings, 2002. XI, 321 pages. 2002. (Subseries LNAI).

Vol. 2447: D.J. Hand, N.M. Adams, R.J. Bolton (Eds.), Pattern Detection and Discovery. Proceedings, 2002. XII, 227 pages. 2002. (Subseries LNAI).

Vol. 2448: P. Sojka, I. Kopecÿek, K. Pala (Eds.), Text, Speech and Dialogue. Proceedings, 2002. XII, 481 pages. 2002. (Subseries LNAI).

Vol. 2449: L. Van Gool (Ed.), Pattern Recognotion. Proceedings, 2002. XVI, 628 pages. 2002.

Vol. 2451: B. Hochet, A.J. Acosta, M.J. Bellido (Eds.), Integrated Circuit Design. Proceedings, 2002. XVI, 496 pages. 2002.

Vol. 2452: R. Guigó, D. Gusfield (Eds.), Algorithms in Bioinformatics. Proceedings, 2002. X, 554 pages. 2002.

Vol. 2453: A. Hameurlain, R. Cicchetti, R. Traunmüller (Eds.), Database and Expert Systems Applications. Proceedings, 2002. XVIII, 951 pages. 2002.

Vol. 2454: Y. Kambayashi, W. Winiwarter, M. Arikawa (Eds.), Data Warehousing and Knowledge Discovery. Proceedings, 2002. XIII, 339 pages. 2002.

Vol. 2455: K. Bauknecht, A M. Tjoa, G. Quirchmayr (Eds.), E-Commerce and Web Technologies. Proceedings, 2002. XIV, 414 pages. 2002.

Vol. 2456: R. Traunmüller, K. Lenk (Eds.), Electronic Government. Proceedings, 2002. XIII, 486 pages. 2002.

Vol. 2457: T. Yakhno (Ed.), Advances in Information Systems. Proceedings, 2002. XII, 436 pages. 2002.

Vol. 2458: M. Agosti, C. Thanos (Eds.), Research and Advanced Technology for Digital Libraries. Proceedings, 2002. XVI, 664 pages. 2002.

Vol. 2459: M.C. Calzarossa, S. Tucci (Eds.), Performance Evaluation of Complex Systems: Techniques and Tools. Proceedings, 2002. VIII, 501 pages. 2002.

Vol. 2460: J.-M. Jézéquel, H. Hussmann, S. Cook (Eds.), ÇUMLÈ 2002 – The Unified Modeling Language. Proceedings, 2002. XII, 449 pages. 2002.

Vol. 2461: R. Möhring, R. Raman (Eds.), Algorithms – ESA 2002. Proceedings, 2002. XIV, 917 pages. 2002.

Vol. 2462: K. Jansen, S. Leonardi, V. Vazirani (Eds.), Approximation Algorithms for Combinatorial Optimization. Proceedings, 2002. VIII, 271 pages. 2002.

Vol. 2463: M. Dorigo, G. Di Caro, M. Sampels (Eds.), Ant Algorithms. Proceedings, 2002. XIII, 305 pages. 2002.

Vol. 2464: M. O'Neill, R.F.E. Sutcliffe, C. Ryan, M. Eaton, N. Griffith (Eds.), Artificial Intelligence and Cognitive Science. Proceedings, 2002. XI, 247 pages. 2002. (Subseries LNAI).

Vol. 2465: H. Arisawa, Y. Kambayashi, V. Kumar, H.C. Mayr, I. Hunt (Eds.), Conceptual Modeling for New Information Systems Technologies. Proceedings, 2001. XVII, 500 pages. 2002.

Vol. 2466: M. Beetz, J. Hertzberg, M. Ghallab, M.E. Pollack (Eds.), Advances in Plan-Based Control of Robotic Agents. Proceedings, 2001. VIII, 291 pages. 2002. (Subseries LNAI).

Vol. 2467: B. Christianson, B. Crispo, J.A. Malcolm, M. Roe (Eds.), Security Protocols. Proceedings, 2001. IX, 241 pages. 2002.

Vol. 2469: W. Damm, E.-R. Olderog (Eds.), Formal Techniques in Real-Time and Fault-Tolerant Systems. Proceedings, 2002. X, 455 pages. 2002.

Vol. 2470: P. Van Hentenryck (Ed.), Principles and Practice of Constraint Programming – CP 2002. Proceedings, 2002. XVI, 794 pages. 2002.

Vol. 2471: J. Bradfield (Ed.), Computer Science Logic. Proceedings, 2002. XII, 613 pages. 2002.

Vol. 2473: A. Gomez-Perez, V.R. Benjamins, Knowledge Engineering and Knowledge Management. Proceedings, 2002. XI, 402 pages. 2002. (Subseries LNAI).

Vol. 2474: D. Kranzlmüller, P. Kacsuk, J. Dongarra, J. Volkert (Eds.), Recent Advances in Parallel Virtual Machine and Message Passing Interface. Proceedings, 2002. XVI, 462 pages. 2002.

Vol. 2475: J.J. Alpigini, J.F. Peters, A. Skowron, N. Zhong (Eds.), Rough Sets and Current Trends in Computing. Proceedings, 2002. XV, 640 pages. 2002. (Subseries LNAI).

Vol. 2476: A.H.F. Laender, A.L. Oliveira (Eds.), String Processing and Information Retrieval. Proceedings, 2002. XI, 337 pages. 2002.

Vol. 2477: M.V. Hermenegildo, G. Puebla (Eds.), Static Analysis. Proceedings, 2002. XI, 527 pages. 2002.

Vol. 2478: M.J. Egenhofer, D.M. Mark (Eds.), Geographic Information Science. Proceedings, 2002. X, 363 pages. 2002.

Vol. 2478: M.J. Egenhofer, D.M. Mark (Eds.), Geographic Information Science. Proceedings, 2002. X, 363 pages. 2002.

Vol. 2479: M. Jarke, J. Koehler, G. Lakemeyer (Eds.), KI 2002: Advances in Artificial Intelligence. Proceedings, 2002. XIII, 327 pages. (Subseries LNAI).

Vol. 2480: Y. Han, S. Tai, D. Wikarski (Eds.), Engineering and Deployment of Cooperative Information Systems. Proceedings, 2002. XIII, 564 pages. 2002.

Vol. 2483: J.D.P. Rolim, S. Vadhan (Eds.), Randomization and Approximation Techniques in Computer Science. Proceedings, 2002. VIII, 275 pages. 2002.

Vol. 2484: P. Adriaans, H. Fernau, M. van Zaanen (Eds.), Grammatical Inference: Algorithms and Applications. Proceedings, 2002. IX, 315 pages. 2002. (Subseries LNAI).

Vol. 2485: A. Bondavalli, P. Thevenod-Fosse (Eds.), Dependable Computing EDCC-4. Proceedings, 2002. XIII, 283 pages. 2002.

Vol. 2486: M. Marinaro, R. Tagliaferri (Eds.), Neural Nets. Proceedings, 2002. IX, 253 pages. 2002.

Vol. 2487: D. Batory, C. Consel, W. Taha (Eds.), Generative Programming and Component Engineering. Proceedings, 2002. VIII, 335 pages. 2002.

Vol. 2488: T. Dohi, R. Kikinis (Eds), Medical Image Computing and Computer-Assisted Intervention – MICCAI 2002. Proceedings, Part I. XXIX, 807 pages. 2002.

Vol. 2489: T. Dohi, R. Kikinis (Eds), Medical Image Computing and Computer-Assisted Intervention – MICCAI 2002. Proceedings, Part II. XXIX, 693 pages. 2002.

Vol. 2490: A.B. Chaudhri, R. Unland, C. Djeraba, W. Lindner (Eds.), XML-Based Data Management and Multimedia Engineering – EDBT 2002. Proceedings, 2002. XII, 652 pages. 2002.

Vol. 2491: A. Sangiovanni-Vincentelli, J. Sifakis (Eds.), Embedded Software. Proceedings, 2002. IX, 423 pages. 2002.

Vol. 2492: F.J. Perales, E.R. Hancock (Eds.), Articulated Motion and Deformable Objects. Proceedings, 2002. X, 257 pages. 2002.

Vol. 2493: S. Bandini, B. Chopard, M. Tomassini (Eds.), Cellular Automata. Proceedings, 2002. XI, 369 pages. 2002.

Vol. 2495: C. George, H. Miao (Eds.), Formal Methods and Software Engineering. Proceedings, 2002. XI, 626 pages. 2002.

Vol. 2496: K.C. Almeroth, M. Hasan (Eds.), Management of Multimedia in the Internet. Proceedings, 2002. XI, 355 pages. 2002.

Vol. 2498: G. Borriello, L.E. Holmquist (Eds.), UbiComp 2002: Ubiquitous Computing. Proceedings, 2002. XV, 380 pages. 2002.

Vol. 2499: S.D. Richardson (Ed.), Machine Translation: From Research to Real Users. Proceedings, 2002. XXI, 254 pages. 2002. (Subseries LNAI).

Vol. 2501: D. Zheng (Ed.), Advances in Cryptology – ASIACRYPT 2002. Proceedings, 2002. XIII, 578 pages. 2002.

Vol. 2502: D. Gollmann, G. Karjoth, M. Waidner (Eds.), Computer Security – ESORICS 2002. Proceedings, 2002. X, 281 pages. 2002.

Vol. 2503: S. Spaccapietra, S.T. March, Y. Kambayashi (Eds.), Conceptual Modeling – ER 2002. Proceedings, 2002. XX, 480 pages. 2002.

Vol. 2504: M.T. Escrig, F. Toledo, E. Golobardes (Eds.), Topics in Artificial Intelligence. Proceedings 2002. XI, 432 pages. 2002. (Subseries LNAI).

Vol. 2506: M. Feridun, P. Kropf, G. Babin (Eds.), Management Technologies for E-Commerce and E-Business Applications. Proceedings, 2002. IX, 209 pages. 2002.

Vol. 2507: G. Bittencourt, G.L. Ramalho (Eds.), Advances in Artificial Intelligence. Proceedings, 2002. XIII, 418 pages. 2002. (Subseries LNAI).

Vol. 2508: D. Malkhi (Ed.), Distributed Computing. Proceedings, 2002. X, 371 pages. 2002.

Vol. 2509: C.S. Calude, M.J. Dinneen, F. Peper (Eds.), Unconventional Models in Computation. Proceedings, 2002. VIII, 331 pages. 2002.

Vol. 2510: H. Shafazand, A Min Tjoa (Eds.), EurAsia-ICT 2002: Information and Communication Technology. Proceedings, 2002. XXIII, 1020 pages. 2002.

Vol. 2511: B. Stiller, M. Smirnow, M. Karsten, P. Reichl (Eds.), From QoS Provisioning to QoS Charging. Proceedings, 2002. XIV, 348 pages. 2002.

Vol. 2513: R. Deng, S. Qing, F. Bao, J. Zhou (Eds.), Information and Communications Security. Proceedings, 2002. XII, 496 pages. 2002.

Vol. 2514: M. Baaz, A. Voronkov (Eds.), Logic for Programming, Artificial Intelligence, and Reasoning. Proceedings 2002. XIII, 465 pages. 2002. (Subseries LNAI).

Vol. 2516: A. Wespi, G. Vigna, L. Deri (Eds.), Recent Advances in Intrusion Detection. Proceedings, 2002. X, 327 pages. 2002.

Vol. 2517: M.D. Aagaard, J.W. O'Leary (Eds.), Formal Methods in Computer-Aided Design. Proceedings, 2002. XI, 399 pages. 2002.

Vol. 2519: R. Meersman, Z. Tari, et al. (Eds.), On the Move to Meaningful Internet Systems 2002: CoopIS, DOA, and ODBASE. Proceedings, 2002. XXIII, 1367 pages. 2002.

Vol. 2521: A. Karmouch, T. Magedanz, J. Delgado (Eds.), Mobile Agents for Telecommunication Applications. Proceedings 2002. XII, 317 pages. 2002.

Vol. 2522: T. Andreasen, A. Motro, H. Christiansen, H. Legind Larsen (Eds.), Flexible Query Answering. Proceedings 2002. XI, 386 pages. 2002. (Subseries LNAI).

Vol. 2525: H.H. Bülthoff, S.-Whan Lee, T.A. Poggio, C. Wallraven (Eds.), Biologically Motivated Computer Vision. Proceedings 2002. XIV, 662 pages. 2002.

Vol. 2526: A. Colosimo, A. Giuliani, P. Sirabella (Eds.), Medical Data Analysis. Proceedings 2002. IX, 222 pages. 2002.

Vol. 2527: F.J. Garijo, J.C. Riquelme, M. Toro (Eds.), Advances in Artificial Intelligence – IBERAMIA 2002. Proceedings 2002. XVIII, 955 pages. 2002. (Subseries LNAI).

Vol. 2529: D.A. Peled, M.Y. Vardi (Eds.), Formal Techniques for Networked and Distributed Sytems – FORTE 2002. Proceedings 2002. XI, 371 pages. 2002.

Vol. 2534: S. Lange, K. Satoh, C.H. Smith (Ed.), Discovery Science. Proceedings 2002. XIII, 464 pages. 2002.

Vol. 2535: N. Suri (Ed.), Mobile Agents. Proceedings 2002. X, 203 pages. 2002.

Vol. 2536: M. Parashar (Ed.), Grid Computing – GRID 2002. Proceedings 2002. XI, 318 pages. 2002.

Vol. 2540: W.I. Grosky, F. Plášil (Eds.), SOFSEM 2002: Theory and Practice of Informatics. Proceedings 2002. X, 289 pages. 2002.